Theoretical Models
and Processes *of*
Reading
Third Edition

Editors

Harry Singer
University of California at Riverside

Robert B. Ruddell
University of California at Berkeley

 International Reading Association
800 Barksdale Road   Newark, Delaware 19714

Copyright 1985 by the
International Reading Association, Inc.

Library of Congress Cataloging in Publication Data
Main entry under title:

Theoretical models and processes of reading, third edition

   Includes bibliographies and indexes.
   1. Reading—Addresses, essays, lectures.   I. Singer, Harry.
II. Ruddell, Robert B.
LB1050.T48   1985   428.4   85-11858
ISBN 0-87207-437-4

Codistributed by the International Reading Association and Lawrence Erlbaum Associates.

Contents

Developmental Model

Information Processing Model

Interaction Model

Inferential Model

Transactional-Psycholinguistic Model

Affective Model

Section Four   TEACHING AND RESEARCH ISSUES

Teaching Issues

Research Issues

Foreword

The International Reading Association has, since its formation, had as one of its purposes the encouragement and stimulation of research, and has acted as a clearinghouse for information related to reading research. In this role it has published many research articles, books, and a journal devoted specifically to research, the *Reading Research Quarterly*. It is significant that both editors of this volume of research have, throughout their professional careers, held responsible positions in the Association. Their contributions over the years have done much to bring research to the teacher.

The practitioner often finds it difficult to keep up with the latest developments in research. Without encouragement and information about useful research findings, the practices that teachers experienced in their own school days can be easily followed as the course of least resistance. These practices may be of vintage age, may come into conflict with current knowledge, and can be a disservice to students.

Studies constantly provide updated information for teachers, so it is necessary for a collection such as is contained in this volume to be revised periodically. In this third edition, much new information and several new theories, models, and processes of reading are described, and controversies are aired.

It is significant that, in the complex area of reading, no single best method can be espoused, by the thoughtful teacher, for all individuals and class groups. Instead, differing situations, diverse students, and varied available materials enter into the decisions which must be made every day in the classroom. This volume is important to the practitioner for, without an understanding of the theoretical bases for reading, teaching can become tedious and diffuse, waste much student and teacher energy, and discourage the spirit of learning and enjoyment which should be the ultimate purpose of reading.

The primary reason for IRA's involvement in this book is to make available, out of the enormous accumulation of scientific reading research, those studies which will help current and future practitioners and research workers become acquainted with the most useful and important studies in the field. This continued fostering of research for improved practice in reading instruction is in the best interests of future generations of students who will continue, no matter what other means of communication are used, to depend upon reading and writing the printed word.

Ralph C. Staiger
October 1985

Foreword

The National Institute of Child Health and Human Development (NICHD) is one of the eight institutes, four bureaus, and four separate divisions that make up the National Institute of Health. The NICHD conducts and supports research and research training on biological and behavioral aspects of human development. In addition to its intramural program (research conducted in its own laboratories and clinics) the NICHD provides research support to investigators in this country and around the world through three extramural units: the Epidemiology and Biometry Research Program (EBRP), the Center for Population Research (CPR), and the Center for Research for Mothers and Children (CRMC).

Since it was established more than twenty years ago, the NICHD has supported research on the reading process, how it is acquired, and those factors which may interfere with the normal acquisition and development of this important skill. In the foreword to the first edition of *Theoretical Models and Processes of Reading*, there is a discussion of the national interest in the health problems of children which sets the stage for the establishment of the NICHD. The foreword to that edition also points out that in 1965 the first National Advisory Child Health and Human Development Council called special attention to the area of reading and urged the Institute's staff to stimulate and support basic research in reading. These senior scientific and lay advisors to the Institute expressed deep concern for the large number of apparently normal children who are unable to participate fully in our society because of inadequate reading ability. The Council was convinced, and the Institute's staff concurred, that in addition to a direct attack on the etiology of reading disability, an understanding of the reading failure could be achieved through study of the reading process and how this skill is acquired.

As reported in the forewords to the first and second editions of this book, since the earliest days of the NICHD a variety of activities have been undertaken by Institute staff to stimulate and encourage research related to reading. For example, a conference series entitled "Communicating by Language" was inaugurated in April 1964. This series reflected the Institute's conceptual framework for the study of reading and its disorders. That is, the reading process is an integral part of the human communication process, including speech, language, learning, and cognition. The titles of the published proceedings emanating from the NICHD conference series illustrate some points within that conceptual frame but do not set its boundaries. These titles are listed below.

The foreword to the second edition of *Theoretical Models and Processes of Reading* reports that the NICHD was providing more than US$15 million in sup-

vii

port of projects related to reading. Almost ten years later, as a result of the continuing efforts of Institute staff, the NICHD currently provides almost US$27 million in support of reading related research projects.

The Center for Research for Mothers and Children, and especially the Human Learning and Behavior Branch of the Center, will continue to offer support for research designed to help us to understand more fully the reading process, how children acquire this important skill, why some children fail or have difficulty learning to read, and point to appropriate ways to prevent or ameliorate this condition before reading failures occur.

James F. Kavanagh
October 1985

NICHD CONFERENCE SERVICE PUBLICATIONS

Frank Smith and George A. Miller. *The Genesis of Language: A Psycholinguistic Approach*. Cambridge, MA: MIT Press, 1966.

Arthur S. House (Ed.). *The Speech Process*. Washington, D.C.: Government Printing,1967.

James F. Kavanagh (Ed.). *The Reading Process*. Washington, D.C.: Government Printing Office, 1968. (0-324-414)

James F. Kavanagh and Ignatius G. Mattingly (Eds.). *Language by Ear and by Eye: The Relationships between Speech and Reading*. Cambridge, MA: MIT Press, 1972.

James F. Kavanagh and James E. Cutting (Eds.). *The Role of Speech in Language*. Cambridge, MA: MIT Press, 1975.

James F. Kavanagh and Winifred Strange (Eds.). *Speech and Language in the Laboratory, School, and Clinic*. Cambridge, MA: MIT Press, 1978.

James F. Kavanagh and Richard L. Venezky (Eds.). *Orthography, Reading, and Dyslexia*. Baltimore, MD: University Park Press, 1980.

Grace H. Yeni-Komshian, James F. Kavanagh, and Charles A. Ferguson (Eds.). *Child Phonology*. Volume I: Production. Volume II: Perception. New York: Academic Press, 1980.

David B. Gray and James F. Kavanagh (Eds.).*Behavioral Measures of Dyslexia*. Baltimore, MD: York Press. (Anticipated date of publication, 1985)

Preface

The first edition of *Theoretical Models and Processes of Reading* was dedicated to Jack Alroy Holmes (1911-1967). The second edition was dedicated to pioneers in research on reading and in theories about reading. Although new pioneers are still making progress on the frontiers, we have decided to dedicate the third edition to all the professors, researchers, and graduate students who are formulating theories of reading and testing hypotheses derived from them, constructing new models, conducting research on processes of reading, testing hypotheses on reading instruction, and generating new knowledge. If we were to name them, the list would be a sizeable part of the names referenced in this volume. They come from a multitude of institutions. Graduate reading programs exist in over 300 institutions in the United States and Canada alone (Blomenberg, 1981); participation in the International Reading Association's World Congress on Reading and researchers listed in such texts as *Comparative Reading* (Downing, 1973) are an indication of the professors and graduate students in other countries who are contributing to the knowledge based on the psychology and pedagogy of reading. Many of these countries also have their own research conference.

The theories, models, and research generated over the past ten years are reflected in the changes we have made in this third edition. Seventy percent of the materials in this volume are new. These materials appear in each of the four sections of this book: historical changes in reading, processes of reading, models of reading, and teaching and research issues. The materials we have retained, such as Constance McCullough's list of pioneers in reading from Javal in 1879 to Holmes in 1960, John Carroll's explanation of reading processes, Ray McDermott's anthropological view of how poor readers are taught to fail, Philip Gough's model of "One Second of Reading," and Irene Athey's warning about making invalid inferences from developmental processes to reading processes continue to be significiant contributions to our knowledge of reading. Several selections have been updated, such as Irene Athey's articles on language development and the affective domain and S. Jay Samuel's selection on word recognition.

New theories, models, and processes of reading can be found in the second and third sections. Ann Brown's selection on metacognition adds an entirely new dimension to our knowledge of reading. Schema interaction theory was only a reference in the last edition; a large number of the selections on comprehension are devoted to it in this edition. Robert Ruddell and Richard Speaker have formulated a new theory and model to explain knowledge utilization and control processes in reading. Walter Kintsch and Teun van Dijk's inferential model is new to this edition. Harry Singer has summarized substrata factor theory, its statistically constructed models, and research conducted on it to date. Grover Mathewson has constructed a revised model on the affective domain. Kenneth Goodman's recent formulation of his explanation and his implicit model of reading reveal the changes that have occurred in his view of reading since the last edition. John Bransford's schema acquisition theory is just beginning to have an impact on the field of reading. It appears in this edition as part of a critical discussion of Richard Anderson's schema activation theory. We anticipate that theory and research on schema acquisition will gain in prominence over the next decade.

Our last section is on teaching and research issues. We include in this section articles by P. David Pearson and Robert C. Tierney on teaching implications of schema activation theory and Ernst Z. Rothkopf's model and strategies for teaching students to learn from text. After presenting Irene Athey's analysis of invalid inferences made from developmental processes to reading processes, we conclude this edition with Harry Singer's article on "Hypotheses on Reading Comprehension in Search of Classroom Validation." Included in this article are principles and pitfalls on conducting research on comprehension.

Although this volume is a testimony to the progress made toward an understanding of what Huey (1908) called this "most remarkable specific performance that civilization has learned in all its history," the challenge remains to continue toward the goal "to completely analyze what we do when we read."

We conclude this introduction with the history behind this edition and acknowledgment of the people who helped produce it. We wrote the first edition primarily as a *Festschrift* to Jack Holmes. When we found it was being widely used as a textbook, we attempted to make the second edition serve this purpose better: we expanded the range of content to make it comprehensive and representative of viewpoints on theories, processes, and models of reading; we added introductory material and prepared questions for each part of the book; and we provided research exemplars for the chapters on processes of reading. The enthusiastic reception of the second edition led us to retain the same range of content, organization, and format for this edition.

We want to thank all those who have contributed to this edition and to its production. We are grateful to all our authors, those who have written original articles for this edition and those authors and their publishers who have given us permission to reproduce their articles. We thank the multitude of professors and graduate students who provided us with comments on the earlier editions. We also recognize the contributions of those who were instrumental in publishing this edition. Jennifer Stevenson, IRA Director of Publications, shepherded this volume through the entire publication process. Lawrence Erlbaum and Jack Burton arranged to produce and distribute this edition in hardback form. Finally,

Ralph Staiger, past Executive Director, and Ronald Mitchell, current Executive Director, and the IRA Board of Directors took all the necessary actions and made the decision to produce this third edition.

Harry Singer
Robert B. Ruddell

REFERENCES

Blomenberg, Paula (Ed.). *Graduate Programs and Faculty in Reading*, fourth edition. Newark, Delaware: International Reading Association, 1981.
Downing, John. *Comparative Reading*. New York: Macmillan, 1973.
Huey, Edmund B. *The Psychology and Pedagogy of Reading*. Cambridge, Massachusetts: MIT Press, 1968. First published by Macmillan in 1908.

The preparation of this book was supported in part by the National Institute of Child Health and Human Development, NIH, and includes a foreword by James F. Kavanagh, Associate Director, Center for Research for Mothers and Children, National Institute of Child Health and Human Development, NIH, Bethesda, Maryland.

Section One

HISTORICAL CHANGES IN READING

Introduction to Historical Changes in Reading

There are two papers in this section. In the first, Constance McCullough pays tribute to the pioneers of research in reading from Emile Javal in 1878 to Jack Holmes in 1960, and points out their major contributions to knowledge on the psychology and pedagogy of reading. She then stresses the impact that theories and research can have upon reading instruction, and the impact that interactions with teachers and classrooms can have upon researchers. She challenges teachers to experiment with insights gleaned from knowledge of theories, and researchers to conduct theory based research, gain insights for research from successful instructional practices, and focus research on new frontiers in reading. In the second, Harry Singer cites landmark theories, research, and instructional strategies in reading over the past century, and their impact on instruction, particularly at the secondary level.

The focal questions for this section are:

1. What contributions have the pioneers in reading research made to our knowledge of reading?

2. What current research instructional practices can be traced back to these pioneers and to landmark research studies in reading?

3. What component skills are necessary for a child to have or to learn in order to become a reader?

4. How has the definition of reading changed over the past 100 years? What research is associated with the change? How has the change in definition affected instruction? Research?

5. What else would you like to know about reading processes, theories, models of reading, and implications that this knowledge has for teaching and further research in reading?

The remaining sections of this book address these questions.

RELATED REFERENCES

Smith, Nila Banton. *American Reading Instruction,* Second Edition. Newark, DE: International Reading Association, 1965. A history of instruction from earliest colonial days to about 1965.

Singer, Harry. "Teaching the Acquisition Phase of Reading Development: An Historical Perspective," in O.J.L. Tzeng and H. Singer (Eds.), *Perception of Print: Reading Research in Experimental Psychology.* Hillsdale, NJ: Erlbaum, 1981. A summary of Smith's history with an emphasis on teaching and an update for the period between 1965 and 1980.

Venezky, Richard L. "The History of Reading Research," in P.D. Pearson (Ed.), *Handbook of Reading Research.* New York: Longman, 1984. The development of research on reading processes and reading instruction from the 1870s to about 1970.

Pioneers of Research in Reading

CONSTANCE M. MCCULLOUGH
Professor Emeritus, Education
San Francisco State University

The first edition of *Theoretical Models and Processes of Reading,* which appeared in 1970, was dedicated to Jack Alroy Holmes (1911-1967), Professor of Education and Research Psychologist in the Institute of Human Development at the University of California at Berkeley. The dedication described him as "a theorist, researcher, and teacher."

One of his distinguished contributions to the psychology of reading was his Substrata Factor Theory (1953), which made headlines throughout the United States when he reported it at the St. Louis Convention of IRA in 1961. One of its effects was to spur research scholars to generate additional research-based theories of the components of reading and the process of engaging in it.

That first edition of the present book filled a need. In many institutions it became the major textbook for a new course of the same title. Stocks of the volume were quickly depleted. In the United States, a relatively affluent society, there still were children and adults who were unsuccessful in learning how to read; yet there were elaborate curriculum guides and an abundance of books to read and instructional materials from which to choose. All of the attractiveness which money could buy beckoned the reader. Researchers were in abundance and more studies of reading instruction and reading materials appeared every year. But something was missing.

Existing concepts of reading, upon which materials and choices of aspects to be researched were based, were inheritances from established practices from many cultures. (According to the latest archeological evidence, the first invention of notation and the consequent need to transmit its meaning to another generation could have occurred at least 300,000 years ago.) Many conflicting opinions existed on reading, but the theoretical basis for many practices lacked the support of a body of sound research evidence. There was not even a good inventory of existing theories with research which could be thought to corroborate each one.

Reprinted from *Theoretical Models and Processes of Reading,* Second Edition, 1976.

If the field of reading was ever to make firm progress in perfecting the transmission of literacy, it would have to proceed from theories backed by substantial evidence and tailored to the code and the society. This implies that researchers must turn from random choices of areas of investigation toward participation in research ventures converging on the validation of a given theory. The relationships of one theory to another must also be determined, for one theory is not enough to account for "the most remarkable specific performance that civilization has learned in all its history."[1]

The Second Edition

In the long history of literate man, there were many pioneer teachers and philosophers. G. D. Sharma, our Indian correspondent in Mauritius and a Sanskrit scholar, quotes Manu, the Code Giver, as having written in his *Manusmriti,* Chapter 12, Verse 103: "Literates are better than illiterates, retainers [who can recollect] are better than literates, thinkers [who understand, interpret, and judge] are better than the retainers, and those who use [the learning] are better than the thinkers—and decidedly best of all."

Sharma writes: "This defines reading so well that it seems to be almost corresponding to Dr. Russell's formula."[2] Manu lived before 5,000 B.C., and thus about 7,000 years before modern research could assess this wisdom.

The second edition of *Theoretical Models and Processes of Reading* is dedicated to pioneers in research on reading and in theories about reading, upon whose shoulders current researchers (and their teachers' teachers' teachers) stand. Throughout this book, reference is made to a few of their many studies. It is an embarrassment to this writer to write so little after the name of each of these giants, but this is only an introduction, not an encyclopaedia. The names are listed here roughly in order of the dates of the studies cited:

Emile Javal, whose study of the saccadic movements of the reading eye was published in 1878.

James McKeen Cattell, whose discovery (1885) that it takes longer to read letters than to read words gave status to the whole-word approach.

Edmund B. Huey, who observed (1908) that "we read by phrases, words, or letters as may serve our purpose best. But . . . the reader's acquirement of ease and power in reading comes through increasing ability to read in larger units" (p. 116).

Edward L. Thorndike, whose zest in exploding clichés (practice makes perfect) influenced learning theory, whose vocabulary studies

(1944) were landmarks, and whose observations and insights into readers' comprehension errors (1917) are receiving renewed appreciation.

Guy T. Buswell, who studied the eye-voice span in reading (1920) and discovered that difficulties in the recognition of meaning are reflected in the character of eye movements.

Charles H. Judd, who, with Buswell (1922), studied various types of silent reading and found that readers change their patterns of eye movement behavior according to their purposes and the demands of the task, that numerous irregular eye movements indicate that the reader is having trouble in mentally parsing the sentence. (If linguistic science had reached a helpful stage at that time, Judd, Buswell, and Gray could have advanced the field by fifty years.)

James M. McCallister, whose study of content area reading in the secondary schools (1930) led to the publication of the first book on reading at that level (*Remedial and Corrective Instruction in Reading*. New York: Appleton, 1936).

Miles A. Tinker, author of more than one hundred laboratory studies of reading eye movements under various conditions, whose summary of research (1958) contained the conclusion that training readers to be more rhythmical in their eye movements did not lead to increased reading efficiency and/or comprehension.

Ernest Horn, whose valuable insights[3] include the following statement: "[The author] does not really convey ideas to the reader; he merely stimulates him to construct them out of his own experience. If the concept is . . . new to the reader, its construction more nearly approaches problem solving than simple association."

Ruth M. Strang, whose many trail-blazing contributions in reading interests, diagnosis, and evaluation included interview techniques as a mode of investigation, and whose *Explorations in Reading Patterns* (1942) was a clinical equivalent to substrata theory.

William S. Gray, who did research in such areas as readability (with B. Leary, 1935), vocabulary (with E. Holmes, 1938), and adult reading patterns (with B. Rogers, 1956) and who crowned decades of reporting and evaluating research studies related to reading with a theory and model on process.

Arthur I. Gates, whose numerous research studies in reading, spelling, and evaluation set a standard of quality in behavioral science research in design, execution, and interpretation.

Luther C. Gilbert, whose many studies of the eye movements of readers of all ages produced theories which influenced research and instruction such as the meaning of saccadic movements (1959), the persistence of characteristic eye movements in a given individual (longitudinal study), and the effect of listening to oral reading while looking at the page (1940).

David H. Russell, whose research studies in spelling (with A. I. Gates, 1937), vocabulary (1954), and children's thinking (1956) were among many original contributions.

Nila Banton Smith, whose classic *American Reading Instruction* (now published by IRA) follows the effects of theories in the classroom and who also conducted pioneer research in reading in the content areas.

Jack A. Holmes, whose teaching and substrata factor theory (1953) generated renewed and broad interest in the development and testing of theories of reading.

The above comments on each of these pioneers are meager tokens of their astounding productivity over lifetimes of dedication and ingenuity. Awesome is the word for their perception of the groundwork which had to be laid by someone before the field could function with any confidence in the wisdom of its choices. Very versatile people, they could and did make contributions to fields other than reading. It is fortunate for the world that they were so generous to this field in practice, in theory, and in the transmission of their skills, insights, and zeal to future researchers. But for them, this volume would not now exist.

The Reader

This book is a growing experience for readers, teachers of reading, researchers, writers, diagnosticians, and those who plan or administer reading programs. Every act, every thought which we employ in dealing with human beings as readers—teaching them, diagnosing them, prescribing for them, evaluating them, choosing for them or letting them choose for themselves—is expressive of a theory about what reading is, of what it is composed, what supports its being, how it can be engaged in successfully, and how its cultivation can be fostered. Some of us think that theory is one thing and practice is another. Not so. Every practice is would have been reason to experiment and explore with his students rather than to follow customary patterns? What if the producer of materials begins to see the wisdom in altering practices which previously have appeared to be right and fixed for all time? What if the researcher sees the importance of joining others to converge on critical truths about reading behavior, given certain linguistic constraints?

The power of this book to release and direct the power of the readers it attracts (or snares in courses) may well eject us out of the slow spiral of repeated returns to old solutions of old problems into a more direct course of progress. Researchers may consult teachers and teachers may consult researchers.[4] The more the teachers understand the frontier thinking, the more creative and helpful they can be in exploring practical solutions to problems. The more the researchers talk directly with teachers and study their classroom situations, the more they will understand about the realities of learning and teaching reading and the more they will learn to make themselves understood. Teachers will not find themselves ten to a hundred years behind the times for want of communication. Researchers will not expend their precious energies on overworked areas.

Some of the research cited in the articles shows differences between the behaviors of children and those of adults in reading. The thoughtful reader will be given to wonder whether there is a relationship between how and what we have taught the child and what he is unable to do. Undoubtedly, some of these differences are created by adult imposed emphases and adult inspired misconceptions of the reading task.

Certainly, no thoughtful reader can leave this book without wondering how a child can learn to read as a skillful reader reads, when instruction focuses on letter-sound correspondences, word form, word meaning, and questions on the meaning of what was read. If the child is led to believe that sounds and meanings of words are all that is needed to produce comprehension of natural reading material, he does not realize what else he must do, and what he must do instead of stringing words together. The successful teacher has been doing something which has failed to occur to most of us. The presentation in this book of a hundred years of research pointing to neglected features in the reading process is suggestive of reforms long overdue.

Editors Harry Singer and Robert Ruddell are to be commended for a masterful job in selecting articles for this volume. The early pioneers would approve.

A Century of Landmarks in Reading Research

HARRY SINGER
University of California at Riverside

A century has elapsed since Javal (1879) initiated the scientific study of reading. During this time a multitude of scholars, researchers, and teachers have created a great body of theory, research, and pedagogical strategies in reading. This accomplishment calls for a celebration to honor these people's work and to recognize that reading is "the most remarkable specific performance that civilization has learned in all its history" (Huey, 1908).

As a contribution to this centennial celebration, I have selected what I think are landmarks in theories, research, and instructional strategies for reading and learning from text at the secondary level. Applied to reading, landmarks are those events or developments that explained some aspect of reading and learning from text, confirmed a hypothesis essential to a theory, or represented an instructional strategy that resulted in a widespread innovation or change in educational practice, or should have done so.

I added the last category, "should have changed educational practice," because I realize a gap exists between the development of knowledge and its application. Indeed, some research has made a difference (Russell, 1961); other research should have made a difference, but didn't (Singer, 1970); some recent research should make a difference (Singer, 1978); and some research which made a difference, shouldn't have (Singer, 1970).

Almost all of the landmarks up to about the 1970s that I shall review fit into the categories of "made a difference" or "should have made a difference." I think the more recent contributions to reading and learning from text should make a difference in educational practice.

In evaluating these recent contributions, I hedge a bit because it usually takes some time before consequences become manifest. Diffusion of ideas in education is slow; we shall have to wait longer than 5 or 10 years before confidently judging whether these relatively recent contributions qualify as landmarks. Here, I only categorize them as events or developments that I think should make a difference.

With these qualifications in mind, we can look at the landmarks in reading and learning from text over the past 100 years. After a brief comment on each

Reprinted from *Journal of Reading*, 26 (January 1983), 332-342.

landmark, I shall interpret it, stressing its impact or potential effect upon educational practice. Included are some reviews of other research that supplements the landmark studies. The research can be divided into three major sections: psychological processes (including a progression from perception to cognition), theories of reading that integrate previous research, and instructional strategies.

Psychological Processes

Perception. Javal (1879) showed that in reading, the eyes move across the printed page in jumps, which he called saccades. These are very rapid, ballistic-like movements that last about 20 milliseconds and bring the print into the visual area of greatest discriminating power, the fovea centralis. The eyes then fixate on the print for 240 milliseconds. At the end of each line a sweep movement, lasting about 40 milliseconds, returns the eye to the next line. In each second of reading, with about four fixations per second, the high school student's eye is in motion only 6 percent of the time; the rest of the time is devoted to fixation pauses.

The implication for speeding up reading is not to get the eyes to move faster (because eye movement time is a negligible part of total reading time), but instead to try to reduce the amount of fixation time. Hence those devices and programs that promote faster eye movement, such as reading rate controllers, are focusing on an aspect of reading which is not only minor but at the high school level may be at its physiological limit. Gilbert (1953) found that functional oculomotor control of the eyes reaches maturity around grade nine. He also pointed out that development of oculomotor control best comes about indirectly from instruction and practice in reading.

Only when the eye is fixated can readers perceive print. However, only about 30 milliseconds of the fixation pause are necessary for seeing print; the rest of the fixation pause is devoted to stabilization and processing time (Gilbert, 1959). Consequently, speed of reading is determined more by processing time, getting information from the retina into long term memory.

As we shall see, processing time involves an interaction between the reader's knowledge and data in the text. Consequently, improvement in these components and in the efficiency of their interaction is likely to increase speed of reading significantly.

However, a component related to speed of reading is the size of the unit of perception. Cattell (1886) demonstrated that adult readers could perceive a whole word faster than its individual letters. This research was conducted at a time when synthetic phonics was prominent in instruction for beginning readers. Opponents of this method were quick to take Cattell's finding based on adults and overgeneralize it to children; they used it to justify whole word instruction. So, Cattell's research is a landmark that made a difference, but shouldn't have. Later, Buswell (1922) demonstrated that while beginning readers take two fixations to perceive each word, as they mature in reading, the number and duration of their fixations and regressions decrease. Their span of perception increases and their reading becomes more rapid and rhythmical. Adults, however, can perceive whole words (Adams and Collins, 1977) because they have formed associations among the letters in a word and developed schemata or expectations that enable them to fill in missing letters. For example, given "th-t," adults fill in the slot for the missing "a" rapidly and perhaps unconsciously.

However, this process works only for familiar words whose structure and interletter associations are well known from experience and instruction. Unfortunately, high school students do not yet have schemata for technical words being introduced in content area texts. Such schemata have to be built up by emphasis on pronunciation, spelling, and knowledge of the referents and properties of technical terms.

Cognition. Huey (1908) showed that as readers mature they shift to even longer units of perception. More recently Bransford and Franks (1974) demonstrated that readers perceive verbal relationships across sentences, referred to as "chunking." Although syntactic structures may be necessary for loading meaning into memory, these structures are then mostly lost to memory. It is integrated meaning that remains in long term memory. Consequently, instruction should include not only syntactic analysis but integration of meaning across sentences.

These reasoning processes are among those that Thorndike (1917) identified when he defined reading as reasoning. Analyzing errors made by mature readers in trying to comprehend a paragraph, he concluded that comprehending a passage is analogous to solving a problem in mathematics. Readers have to recognize that passages may fit into a formula, such as a problem-solution or question-answer device; they have to detect which ideas in a passage fit into the formula. Hence, teachers should instruct students in the rhetorical devices used in their textbooks to help them see the relationship between ideas. Students could then guide their own reading by noting a problem-solution type of text, and ask and answer their own questions as they read, such as, "What is the problem?" and "What is the solution?" If they have had some instruction in critical reading, they might also ask, "Is the solution correct?" "Can I find a solution I like better?"

Components of reading. Comprehension is one component; speed of reading is another. They are related but separate functions (Gates, 1921). Reading specialists should therefore measure both speed and power of reading, and instructional programs should note that speed of reading plays a role in comprehension. For example, LaBerge and Samuels (1976) theorized that a speed of processing print at a rate where readers can identify words automatically enables them to comprehend better because they can then give almost all of their attention to comprehension.

Readers who have not yet learned to read relatively easy material rapidly or process print automatically can take a shortcut to this stage for a particular passage. This shortcut is "repeated reading." In this method, students read the same passage repeatedly under teacher guidance, first identifying the words, then their meanings, and finally comprehending the entire passage. Samuels (1979) advocated this method for remedial readers, but all readers could probably profit from it in any content area in which they have to plow laboriously through a passage containing a high density of technical terms and complex ideas.

Patterns of abilities. Although a reader may be fast and powerful on a survey test, Judd and Buswell (1922) showed that readers vary their silent reading processes according to their purposes and the kind and difficulty of the material. This study supported a shift in teaching from oral to silent reading. Further, it established that the goal of instruction is to have a variety of reading processes, implying the need to use a variety of reading materials while stressing flexibility in shifting from one reading process to another. This goal of variation and flexibility differs from that of some speed reading courses which imply that readers should read everything at a fast rate.

The discovery of different types and processes of reading, plus multiplicity of skills and abilities involved in each type, gave Gates (1927) the basis for diagnostic tests. These tests led to the establishment of reading clinics, the forerunners of today's reading labs and centers.

Monroe (1932) formulated the hypothesis that general reading ability consists of a multiplicity of factors; success or failure in reading depends on whether a student's strengths in these factors outweigh his or her weaknesses. Holmes (1953, 1965) was the first to test this hypothesis statistically. He found that two students could be equally successful in reading by using different combinations of abilities. Consequently, it is not necessary for readers to develop equal mastery of each ability in speed and power of reading.

But reading ability and interest, contrary to popular opinion, are not completely developed in elementary school. Four investigators set the state for developmental reading instruction, that is, continuity in instruction from elementary grades all the way through high school. Strang (1938, 1942) was foremost in this movement. Others provided evidence that a student's level of reading comprehension is not uniform in all content areas (Bond, 1938) and that the processing of prose and nonprose depends on different abilities (Hall and Robinson, 1945; Robinson and Hall, 1941). Oddly, Gans (1940) demonstrated that little development occurred in reference reading during grades four to college.

The implication of these studies was that secondary students have a profile of reading abilities that reflects their previous reading experience, aptitudes, interests, and the school subjects they have studied. Consequently it is necessary to test students' reading ability in each content area, to have entry tests for each course, and to develop students' abilities in each content area. This insight led to the slogan that every teacher is a teacher of reading. As we shall find, high school teachers did not accept this slogan.

Theories of Reading

Substrata factor theory. Through the 1940s, research in reading in the U.S. was mostly atheoretical. In a landmark contribution, Holmes (1953) formulated his substrata factor theory that stated: Underlying each of reading's two components, speed and power, are a multiplicity of skills and processes; the reader organizes them into momentary working systems according to his or her purposes and the demands of the task.

This view of reading explains why different methods of reading instruction work. Each emphasizes one or more subsystems necessary for reading. As readers progress through school, their individual differences decrease in perceptual components of reading and increase in cognitive and linguistic subsystems (Singer, 1962, 1965). At the high school level, all readers still must draw upon at least a minimum of perceptual components, such as word identification. Thus it is still necessary in high school to teach word identification, especially for technical terms (Holmes and Singer, 1961, 1966).

Comprehension as interaction. Conceptually similar to Holmes's theoretical formulation (Singer, 1983) is Rumelhart's formulation (1976) of the interaction concept of reading. The comprehensibility of the concept has been aided by Adams and Collins's lucid explanation (1977) that comprehension is the result of an interaction between reader resources and text data.

Readers' resources. Readers allocate attention among their knowledge resources, and go back and forth from their knowledge to the data base of the text. One resource that a reader must bring to a text is world knowledge. Writers usually assume the reader already knows whatever is common knowledge (Winograd, 1972). For example, "The cigarette caused the forest fire" is readily comprehensible to most people, since they can supply the missing links in the causal chain by using their world knowledge of how cigarettes can cause forest fires.

A particular type of world knowledge that readers bring to text is the sequence of events in everyday situations, such as procedures in a restaurant or supermarket. Schank and Abelson (1977) call this type of knowledge "scripts." Pichert and Anderson (1977) and Anderson and Pichert (1977) demonstrated that the same story could be interpreted as "house buyers" or as "burglars." They concluded that a reader mobilizes a script or set of schemata for assimilating and recalling information. Their conclusion agrees with Bartlett's (1932). He used a story about an Indian ceremony to show that readers employ their schemata to interpret story events coherently. For recall, they draw upon their schemata again to reconstruct the text's meaning from memory (Anderson, Spiro, Montague, 1977; Bartlett, 1932).

However, we know that readers vary in how their knowledge is structured and in their perspectives for interpreting stories. To apply the interaction theory of reading, we have to take reader variation into account when we assess comprehension. We may still use a set of propositions (Kintsch, 1974; Meyer, 1975) to represent a text, but we should allow for a wide band of acceptable responses or propositions from readers (Tierney and LaZansky, 1980; Tierney and Spiro, 1979).

Most of the research in cognition has been on assimilation, little on accommodation or schema acquisition. We still need to know how readers acquire new information. However, we have a beginning in this research direction. Hayes (1979) demonstrated that analogies embedded in text help students extend their knowledge structures so that they can use them to comprehend new information.

The implications for instruction from the interaction concept of reading comprehension are clear: (1) Teach students the necessary knowledge structures, scripts, and cognitive frameworks for comprehending texts in the content areas; (2) consider that different cultural backgrounds and perspectives are likely to result in a range of acceptable variations in interpreting texts and events, and be prepared to accept as accurate a whole band of interpretations; and (3) teach students to activate prior knowledge and integrate it with new knowledge.

Text data. Although readers interact with texts to attain comprehension, texts have objective properties. Gray and Leary (1935) were the first to find that word frequency and sentence length are determinants of text difficulty. Almost all readability formulas use these two criteria. Hence, to make texts easier to comprehend, use higher frequency words and shorter sentences. However, sometimes complex sentences are easier to understand because the causal relationships among their clauses are explicit (Pearson, 1976).

Indeed, Stein and Bransford (1979) showed that texts with precise elaborations made readers aware of the significance or relevance of facts that enhanced memory. They therefore cautioned against simplification that results in an "arbitrary text," one that does not provide causal explanations for facts.

Content area texts also vary in their organizational features (Smith, 1964a, 1964b, 1965). Although Robinson (1975) provided numerous examples, Rumelhart (1975, 1977) was the first to specify a formal grammar for stories. This grammar can be induced in one narrative and transferred to facilitate comprehension in another narrative (Thorndyke, 1975, 1977).

A more general way of representing text is through propositional analysis. Kintsch (1974), Meyer (1975), and Frederiksen (1975) all argued that text information is stored in memory in the form of propositions. Van Dijk and Kintsch (1977) stated that texts could be organized into macro and microstructures, loosely defined as topic sentences and supporting details, respectively. When text was logically organized with its macro and microstructures arrayed in proper order, then readers processed it more rapidly. When it was presented in disarrayed order, readers were slower to process it, but apparently could reorganize the disarrayed text, since they recalled it in its proper array. Frase (1969a) also verified that retention is better when a passage presents a concept grouped with its attributes rather than separated.

Other features of text are (1) cohesion, a means of tying sentences together, for example, through the use of pronouns; (2) staging, a way of featuring information in text; and (3) content analyses, separation of content into events (participants and episodes) and nonevents (setting, background, collateral information, and evaluation) (Grimes, 1975). Information which is staged or made prominent in a text tends to be remembered better (Clements, 1975).

The implications are (1) select texts that are well organized and precisely elaborated with causal explanations, (2) use devices such as analogies for bridging prior and new knowledge, and (3) teach students to recognize and use the text's organizational features and content categories in processing and recalling information.

Instructional strategies

SQ3R. In the latter 1960s and the 1970s, theories and research in comprehension and instructional strategies became paramount. One strategy, SQ3R (Survey, Question, Read, Recite, Review), had been created earlier, but lacked evidence on its efficacy. Robinson (1961) nevertheless claimed that his SQ3R was based on concepts in learning theory, each with strong empirical support.

Advance organizers. Another instructional strategy was devised by Ausubel (1960). He showed that a rather abstract introductory passage, which he called an advance organizer, enabled readers to assimilate less abstract information from a passage. Subsequently, Barron (1969), who depicted advance organizers graphically, and Earle and Barron (1973) argued that technical vocabulary revealed the logical structure of its subject matter and could be used as an advance organizer.

However, only half the studies on using advance organizers showed positive effects (Barron and Cooper, 1973). What made a good advance organizer? Royer and Cable (1975) showed that better results came from using concrete information that leads up to organizers. Even so, advance organizers are likely to have greater effect for poor than for good readers (Smith and Hesse, 1969).

Hierarchical organization. Similar findings were reported for the hierarchical reading guides proposed by Herber in 1970 (Estes, 1973). Taba's (1965) questioning strategies, designed for group discussions, also take students through a hierarchical process. Thelen (1982) suggested that teachers elicit and graphically organize students' preexisting information on a topic into a hierarchical structure; the teacher can then depict where new knowledge fits into this graphic organizer as the lesson progresses. A general finding is that instructional hierarchies are especially helpful for highly interpretive and abstract material (Berget, 1973).

These results imply that good readers can assimilate information from print without using aids, such as reading guides and question strategies, until the text becomes relatively difficult for them (Tutolo, 1977). In short, the usefulness of the guides and the questioning process is a function of the difficulty of the materials relative to the abilities and backgrounds of readers (Koran and Koran, 1975).

Directed reading activity. Individual differences in abilities and background can be provided for through the directed reading activity (DRA). This six step method, long used in basal readers, teaches new vocabulary, provides background information, arouses curiosity, guides initial reading, has students complete the story silently under the direction of preposed questions and review the material to find answers to questions, sometimes skimming the story to check answers.

Stauffer (1969) added another component—directing the students to think about something specific while reading and checking conclusions against initiating purposes. He called this strategy a directed reading-thinking activity (DRTA). In high school, this method is useful for introducing students to text in any content area; it essentially models for students how a content teacher reads and thinks about a passage.

Questioning strategies. However, the location of questions can affect comprehension. Frase (1967, 1968a) found that preposed questions tend to reduce the amount of information stored in memory, while postposed questions stimulate a review of the entire passage that results in more retention. Later, Frase and Schwartz (1975) reported that pairing students for formulating and asking each other questions resulted in more comprehension than studying alone.

Anderson and Biddle (1975), who reviewed the research on teacher questioning, explained that questions had the function of transferring information from short to long term memory. However, teacher-posed questions are only the beginning in an instructional sequence, serving as a model of the kind of questions to pose. As students learn the types of questions to ask in a particular subject area and as they acquire background information and framework for comprehending that content (Anderson, Spiro, and Montague, 1977; Miyake and Norman, 1979), they can ask their own content-relevant questions. Consequently teacher's questions can phase out and student's questions phase in (Singer and Donlan, 1980).

We know that students can learn to ask appropriate questions (Rosenthal, Zimmerman, and Durnig, 1970). Used as a study technique, their questions have resulted in superior comprehension (Frase and Schwartz, 1975). Furthermore, students can learn to generate their own questions to relate abstract story grammar structures—such as problem, quest, and goal—to more concrete aspects of complex short stories, and in so doing formulate text-specific questions that enhance their comprehension (Singer and Donlan, 1982).

Mathemagenic behavior. Similar aids to learning from text were investigated by Rothkopf (1966, 1976, 1982), Rothkopf and Bisbicos (1967), and Rothkopf and Bloom (1970). Coining the term "mathemagenic behavior" for learning processes, Rothkopf found that learning is stimulated by such adjunct aids as directions given to the reader, questions embedded in texts, purposes and goals established for the reader, the means for achieving goals provided in the form of text information, and assessment of goal achievement based upon this information. The teacher affects each phase.

Thus, Rothkopf integrated knowledge from four areas: the concept of reading as an interaction between reader and text, learning theory and principles, criterion referenced measurement, and the role of adjunct aids or instruction. This integrated model has moved the field closer to a theory of learning from text that incorporates a broad range of components (Singer, 1982).

Summarization of text. Indeed, whatever gets students active in reading is likely to enhance their comprehension. For example, having students summarize paragraphs as they read them enhances their comprehension (Wittrock, Marks, and Doctorow, 1975).

Brown (1981) demonstrated that teaching students summarization strategies, such as deleting nonessential information, listing items under a main concept, and identifying or constructing topic sentences, enhanced elementary children's recall of important information. Her series of studies has effectively united study strategies and comprehension or learning from text strategies.

All the strategies for learning from text can be arrayed in a sequence that progresses from single to multiple text. Teachers can use this sequence to meet the wide range of individual differences in reading achievement. This range increases in grade equivalents from 8 years at grade 6 to 12 years at grade 12 (Singer and Donlan, 1980).

Although considerable knowledge on the psychology of reading and on strategies for teaching comprehension has accumulated over the past century, teachers still need to know more about teaching comprehension. Fortunately, we have a multitude of hypotheses available, but they need to be validated at the classroom level (Singer, 1981). When that occurs, they can join the repertoire of strategies available to teachers.

Teacher attitudes. Whether any of the strategies for teaching students to read and learn from texts becomes a part of classroom instruction depends upon teachers' attitudes. We often hear that secondary teachers will not adopt these strategies because they identify "reading" as an instructional process for the primary grades. Secondary teachers are more willing to accept the term "learning from text" as appropriate to their instruction. They recognize that students have to learn how to learn from texts in each content area and that it is their job to teach them how to do so. Therefore, a more appropriate slogan for high school instruction is "Every secondary teacher teaches students to learn from text" (Singer, 1979b).

REFERENCES

Adams, Marilyn J., and Allen Collins. *A Schema-Theoretic View of Reading.* Boston: Bolt, Beranek, and Newman, 1977.
Anderson, Richard C., and W. Barry Biddle. "On Asking People Questions about What They Are Reading," in *The Psychology of Learning and Motivation*, edited by Gordon H. Bower. New York: Academic Press, 1975.

Anderson, Richard C., and James W. Pichert. *Recall of Previously Unrecallable Information Following a Shift of Perspective*. Technical Report No. 41. Urbana, Ill.: Center for the Study of Reading, University of Illinois, April 1977.

Anderson, Richard C., Rand J. Spiro, and William E. Montague (Eds.). *Schooling and the Acquisition of Knowledge*. Hillsdale, N.J.: Erlbaum, 1977.

Ausubel, David. "The Use of Advance Organizers in the Learning and Retention of Meaningful Verbal Material," *Journal of Educational Psychology*, 51 (October 1960), 267-272.

Barron, Richard F. "The Use of Vocabulary as an Advance Organizer." In *Research in Reading in the Content Areas: First Year Report*, edited by Harold L. Herber and Peter L. Sanders. Syracuse, N.Y.: Syracuse University Reading and Language Arts Center, 1969.

Barron, Richard F., and Rose Cooper. "Effects of Advance Organizers and Grade Level upon Information Acquisition from an Instructional Level General Science Passage." In *Twenty-Second Yearbook of the National Reading Conference*, edited by Philip L. Nacke. Boone, N.C.: National Reading Conference, 1973.

Bartlett, Frederic C. *Remembering*. Cambridge, England: Cambridge University Press, 1932.

Berget, Ellsworth. "Two Methods of Guiding the Learning of a Short Story." In *Research in Reading in the Content Areas: Second Year Report*, edited by Harold L. Herber and Richard F. Barron, Syracuse, N.Y.: Syracuse University Reading and Language Arts Center.

Bond, Eva. *Reading and Ninth Grade Achievement*. New York: Bureau of Publications, Teachers College, Columbia University, 1938.

Bransford, John D., and Jeffrey J. Franks. "Memory for Syntactic Form as a Function of Semantic Context," *Journal of Experimental Psychology*, 103 (October 1974), 1037-1039.

Brown, Ann. "Writing and Reading and Metacognition." In *Directions in Reading: Research and Instruction*, edited by Michael Kamil. Thirtieth Yearbook of the National Reading Conference. Washington, D.C.: National Reading Conference, 1981.

Buswell, Guy T. *Fundamental Reading Habits: A Study of Their Development*, Supplementary Educational Monographs No. 21. Chicago: University of Chicago Press, 1922.

Cattell, James M. "The Time It Takes to See and Name Objects," *Mind*, 11 (January 1886), 63-65.

Clements, Paul. "The Effects of Staging on Recall from Prose," doctoral dissertation, Cornell University, 1975.

Earle, Richard, and Richard F. Barron. "An Approach for Teaching Vocabulary in Content Subjects." In *Research in Reading in the Content Areas: Second Year Report*, edited by Harold L. Herber and Richard F. Barron. Syracuse, N.Y.: Syracuse University Reading and Language Arts Center, 1973.

Estes, Thomas H. "Guiding Reading in Social Studies." In *Research in Reading in the Content Areas: Second Year Report*, edited by Harold L. Herber and Richard F. Barron. Syracuse, N.Y.: Syracuse University Reading and Language Arts Center, 1973.

Frase, Lawrence T. "Effect of Question Location, Pacing, and Mode on Retention of Prose Material," *Journal of Educational Psychology*, 59 (August 1968a), 244-249.

Frase, Lawrence T. "Learning from Prose Material: Length of Passage, Knowledge of Results, and Position of Questions," *Journal of Educational Psychology*, 58 (October 1967), 266-272.

Frase, Lawrence T. "Paragraph Organization of Written Materials: The Influence of Conceptual Clustering upon the Level and Organization of Recall," *Journal of Educational Psychology*, 60 (October 1969a), 394-401.

Frase, Lawrence T., and Barry J. Schwartz. "Effect of Question Production and Answering on Prose Recall," *Journal of Educational Psychology*, 67 (October 1975), 628-635.

Frederiksen, Carl H. "Representing Logical and Semantic Structure of Knowledge Acquired from Discourse," *Cognitive Psychology*, 7 (July 1975), 371-458.

Gans, Roma. "A Study of Critical Reading Comprehension in the Intermediate Grades." *Teachers College Contributions to Education, No. 811*. New York: Teachers College, Columbia University, 1940.

Gates, Arthur I. "An Experimental and Statistical Study of Reading and Reading Tests." *Journal of Educationl Psychology*, 12 (September 1921), 303-314.

Gates, Arthur I. *The Improvement of Reading*. New York: Macmillan, 1927.

Gilbert, Luther C. "Functional Motor Efficiency of the Eyes and Its Relation to Reading," *University of California Publications in Education*, 2 (March 1953), 159-232.

Gilbert, Luther C. "Speed of Processing Visual Stimuli and Its Relation to Reading," *Journal of Educational Psychology*, 50 (February 1959), 8-14.

Gray, William S., and Bernice Leary. *What Makes a Book Readable*. Chicago: University of Chicago Press, 1935.

Grimes, Joseph E. *The Thread of Discourse*. The Hague, The Netherlands: Mouton, 1975.

Hall, William E., and Francis P. Robinson. "An Analytical Approach to the Study of Reading Skills," *Journal of Educational Psychology*, 36 (October 1945). 429-442.

Hayes, David A. "The Effect of Text-Embedded Analogy upon Comprehension and Learning," unpublished doctoral dissertation, University of Arizona, 1979.

Herber, Harold L. *Teaching Reading in Content Areas*. Englewood Cliffs, N.J.: Prentice-Hall, 1970.

Holmes, Jack A. "Basic Assumptions Underlying the Substrata Factor Theory of Reading," *Reading Research Quarterly*, 1 (Fall 1965), 5-28.

Holmes, Jack A. *The Substrata-Factor Theory of Reading*. Berkeley, Calif.: California Book Co., 1953.

Holmes, Jack A., and Harry Singer. *Speed and Power of Reading in High School*. U.S. Office of Education, Cooperative Research Monograph No. 14. Washington, D.C.: U.S. Government Printing Office, 1966.

Holmes, Jack A., and Harry Singer. "The Substrata-Factor Theory: Substrata-Factor Difference Underlying Reading Ability in Known Groups, Final Report No. 538. Washington, D.C.: U.S. Office of Education, 1961.

Huey, Edmund B. *The Psychology and Pedagogy of Reading*. New York: Macmillan, 1908.

Javal, L. Emile. "Essai sur la Physiologie de Lecture," *Annales d'Oculistique*, 82 (1879), 243-253.

Judd, Charles H., and Guy T. Buswell. *Silent Reading: A Study of the Various Types*, Supplementary Educational Monographs, No. 23. Chicago: University of Chicago Press, 1922.

Kintsch, Walter. *The Representation of Meaning in Memory*. Hillsdale, N.J.: Erlbaum-Wiley, 1974.

Koran, Mary Lou, and John J. Koran, Jr. "Interaction of Learner Aptitudes with Question Pacing in Learning from Prose," *Journal of Educational Psychology*, 67 (February 1975), 76-82.

LaBerge, David, and S. Jay Samuels. "Toward a Theory of Automatic Information Processing in Reading." In *Theoretical Models and Processes of Reading*, edited by Harry Singer and Robert B. Ruddell. Newark, Del.: International Reading Association, 1976.

Meyer, Bonnie. *The Organization of Prose and its Effect upon Memory*. Amsterdam, The Netherlands: North Holland, 1975.

Miyake, Naomi, and Donald A. Norman. "To Ask a Question, One Must Know Enough to Know What Is Not Known," *Journal of Verbal Learning and Verbal Behavior*, 18 (June 1979), 357-364.

Monroe, Marion. *Children Who Cannot Read*. Chicago: University of Chicago Press, 1932.

Pearson, P. David. "The Effects of Grammatical Complexity on Children's Comprehension, Recall, and Conception of Certain Semantic Relations." In *Theoretical Models and Processes of Reading*, edited by Harry Singer and Robert B. Ruddell, Newark, Del.: International Reading Association, 1976.

Pichert, James W., and Richard C. Anderson. "Taking Different Perspectives on a Story," *Journal of Educational Psychology*, 69 (August 1977), 309-315.

Robinson, Francis P. "Study Skills for Superior Students in Secondary School," *The Reading Teacher*, 15 (September 1961), 29-33.

Robinson, Francis P., and Prudence Hall. "Studies of Higher Level Reading Abilities," *Journal of Educational Psychology*, 32 (September 1941), 445-451.

Robinson, H. Alan. *Teaching Reading and Study Strategies: The Content Areas*. Boston: Allyn and Bacon, 1975.

Rosenthal, Ted L., Barry J. Zimmerman, and Kathleen Durning. "Observationally Induced Changes in Children's Interrogative Classes," *Journal of Personality and Social Psychology*, 16 (December 1970), 681-688.

Rothkopf, Ernst Z. "Adjunct Aids and the Control of Mathemagenic Activities During Purposeful Reading." In *Reading Expository Material*, edited by Wayne Otto and Sandra White. New York: Academic Press, 1982.

Rothkopf, Ernst Z. "Learning from Written Instructive Materials: An Exploration of the Control of Inspection Behavior by Test-Like Events," *American Educational Research Journal*, 3 (November 1966), 241-249.

Rothkopf, Ernst Z. "Writing to Teach and Reading to Learn: A Perspective on the Psychology of Written Instruction." In *The Psychology of Teaching Methods*, edited by Nathan L. Gage. Seventy-Fifth Yearbook of the National Society for the Study of Education, Part I. Chicago: University of Chicago Press, 1976.

Rothkopf, Ernst Z., and Ethel E. Bisbicos. "Selective Facilitative Effects of Interspersed Questions on Learning from Written Materials," *Journal of Educational Psychology*, 58 (February 1957), 56-61.

Rothkopf, Ernst Z., and Richard D. Bloom. "Effects of Interpersonal Interaction on the Instructional Value of Adjunct Questions in Learning from Written Material," *Journal of Educational Psychology*, 61 (December 1970), 417-422.

Royer, James M., and Glenn W. Cable. "Facilitated Learning in Connected Discourse," *Journal of Educational Psychology*, 67 (February 1975), 116-123.

Rumelhart, David E. "Notes on a Schema for Stories." In *Representation and Understanding Studies in Cognitive Science*, edited by Daniel Bobrow and Allan Collins. New York: Academic Press, 1975.

Rumelhart, David E. *Toward an Interactive Model of Reading*, Technical Report No. 56. San Diego, Calif.: Center for Human Information Processing, University of California, 1976.

Rumelhart, David E. "Understanding and Summarizing Brief Stories." In *Basic Processes in Reading: Perception and Comprehension*, edited by David LaBerge and S. Jay Samuels, Hillsdale, N.J.: Erlbaum, 1977.

Russell, David H. "Reading Research that Makes a Difference," *Elementary English*, 38 (February 1961), 74-78.

Samuels, S. Jay. "The Method of Repeated Reading," *The Reading Teacher*, 32 (January 1979), 403-408.

Schank, Roger C., and Robert P. Abelson. *Scripts, Plans, Goals, and Understandings*. Hillsdale, N.J.: Erlbaum, 1977.

Singer, Harry. "Hypotheses on Reading Comprehension in Search of Classroom Validation." In *Directions in Reading: Research and Instruction*, edited by Michael Kamil. Thirtieth Yearbook of The National Reading Conference. Washington, D.C.: National Reading Conference, 1981.

Singer, Harry. "Research that Should Have Made a Difference," *Elementary English*, 42 (January 1970), 27-34.

Singer, Harry. "Research in Reading that Should Make a Difference in Classroom Instruction." In *What Research Has to Say about Reading Instruction*, edited by S. Jay Samuels. Newark, Del.: International Reading Association, 1978.

Singer, Harry. "Slogans and Attitudes." *Journal of Reading*, 22 (May 1979b), 756-757.

Singer, Harry. *Substrata-Factor Reorganization Accompanying Development of General Reading Ability at the Elementary School Level*, Final Report. Washington, D.C.: U.S. Office of Education, 1965.

Singer, Harry. "The Substrata-Factor Theory of Reading: Its History and Conceptual Relationship to Interaction Theory." In *Reading Research Revisited*, edited by Lawrence Gentile, Michael Kamil, and Jay Blanchard. Columbus, Ohio: Merrill, 1983.

Singer, Harry. "Substrata-Factor Theory of Reading: Theoretical Design for Teaching Reading." In *Challenge and Experiment in Reading*, edited by J. Allan Figurel. New York: Scholastic Magazines, 1962.

Singer, Harry. "Toward an Instructional Theory for Learning from Text: A Discussion of Ernst Rothkopf's 'Adjunct Aids and the Control of Mathemagenic Activities During Reading.'" In *Reading Expository Material*, edited by Wayne Otto and Sandra White. New York: Academic Press, 1982.

Singer, Harry, and Dan Donlan. "Active Comprehension: Problem-Solving Schema with Question Generation for Comprehension of Complex Short Stories," *Reading Research Quarterly,* 7 (February 1982), 166-186.

Singer, Harry, and Dan Donlan. *Reading and Learning from Text.* Boston: Little, Brown, 1980.

Smith, Nila B. "Patterns of Writing in Different Subject Areas, Part I," *Journal of Reading,* 8 (October 1964a), 31-37.

Smith, Nila B. "Patterns of Writing in Different Subject Areas, Part II." *Journal of Reading,* 8 (November 1964b), 97-102.

Smith, Nila B. "Reading in Subject Matter Fields," *Educational Leadership,* 22 (March 1965), 382-385.

Smith, Richard J., and Karl D. Hesse. "The Effects of Prereading Assistance on the Comprehension of Good and Poor Readers," *Research in the Teaching of English,* 3 (Fall 1969), 166-177.

Stauffer, Russell G. *Directing Reading Maturity as a Cognitive Process.* New York: Harper and Row, 1969.

Stein, Barry S., and John D. Bransford. "Constraints on Effective Elaboration: Effects of Precision and Subject Generation," *Journal of Verbal Learning and Verbal Behavior,* 18 (December 1979), 769-777.

Strang, Ruth. *Exploration in Reading Patterns,* Chicago: University of Chicago Press, 1942.

Strang, Ruth. *Problems in the Improvement of Reading in High School and College.* Ephrata, Pa.: Science Press, 1938.

Taba, Hilda. "The Teaching of Thinking," *Elementary English,* 42 (May 1965), 534-542.

Thelen, Judie. "Preparing Students for Content Reading Assignments," *Journal of Reading,* 25 (March 1982), 544-549.

Thorndike, Edward. "Reading as Reasoning: A Study of Mistakes in Paragraph Reading," *Journal of Educational Psychology,* 8 (January 1917), 323-332.

Thorndyke, Perry W. "Cognitive Structures in Comprehension and Memory of Narrative Discourse," *Cognitive Psychology,* 8 (January 1977), 77-110.

Thorndyke, Perry W. "Cognitive Structure in Human Story Comprehension and Memory," doctoral dissertation, Stanford University, 1975.

Tierney, Rob J., and Jill La Zansky. "The Rights and Responsibilities of Readers and Writers: A Contractural Agreement," *Language Arts,* 57 (September 1980), 606-613.

Tierney, Rob. J., and Rand J. Spiro. "Some Basic Notions about Reading Comprehension: Implications for Teachers." In *New Perspectives on Comprehension,* Monograph No. 3 in Language and Reading Series, edited by Jerome Harste and Robert F. Carey. Bloomington, Ind.: Indiana University, 1979.

Tutolo, Daniel J. "The Study Guide—Types, Purposes, and Value." *Journal of Reading,* 20 (March 1977), 503-507.

van Dijk, Teun, and Walter Kintsch. "Cognitive Psychology and Discourse Recalling and Summarizing Stories." In *Current Trends in Textlinguistics,* edited by Wolfgang U. Dressler. Berlin, N.Y.: DeGruyter, 1977.

Winograd, Terry. "Understanding Natural Language," *Cognitive Psychology,* 3 (January 1972), 1-191.

Wittrock, Merl C., Carolyn Marks, and Marleen Doctorow. "Reading as a Generative Process." *Journal of Educational Psychology,* 67 (August 1975), 484-489.

NOTES

[1] Edmund Burke Huey. *The Psychology and Pedagogy of Reading.* Cambridge, Massachusetts: M.I.T. Press, 1968. First published by Macmillan in 1908.

[2] David H. Russell. *Children Learn to Read.* Boston: Ginn, 1961.

[3] Ernest Horn. *Methods of Instruction in the Social Studies.* New York: Scribners, 1937, 154.

[4] Jeanne Chall. Keynote Speech: Reading and Development. Twentieth Annual Convention, International Reading Association, New York City, 1975.

Section Two

PROCESSES OF READING

Introduction to Processes of Reading

This section on processes of reading includes research reviews and research studies in seven interrelated areas: language, visual perception, word recognition, comprehension, metacognition, affect, and culture. We have selected studies which present significant research findings and demonstrate ways of investigating the processes reviewed in this section of the book. Two objectives guided our selection and organization of the content of the processing section. First, to provide a collection of work in the field of reading research extending from classical studies to current research. These selections range from the investigation of perception and comprehension to the most recent research on text structure and schema theory. This work provides the foundation for the construction of reading theory and offers suggestions for needed research. Second, to provide full length research studies that make significant contributions to reading research and provide the reader opportunity to examine rationale, design, findings, and conclusions. Eighty percent of the selections in this section of the third edition are new.

The interrelated nature of text and language processing is immediately evident in the initial selections on language. The next two sets of articles highlight the importance of visual perception and the development of higher order perceptual units in word recognition. Attention is also given to automaticity and schema activation in word recognition. The comprehension research selections account for factors in text processing, ranging from prior knowledge and text structure to vocabulary and instantiation of meaning. The role of metacognition, a recent and highly significant development in text processing, is explained in the next series of articles. The last two sets of papers consider the importance of affect and culture in the developing reader.

We suggest that the reader attempt to synthesize the information contained in these articles. The reader, however, should probe each selection for areas of the reading process which are not adequately explained and identify areas for further research. The reader is encouraged to actively participate in the formulation of new research hypotheses leading to an increased understanding of the nature of reading.

We have designed the following questions to assist the reader in research synthesis and hypothesis generation:

Language
1. What linguistic variables are involved in language and reading acquisition? Which are common to both areas, and which are different? Why?

2. What are the main theories of language development and what insight do they provide in understanding reading acquisition?

3. How does the lexicon develop and how is it related to reading achievement?

4. How does situation context influence the acquisition of meaning?

5. How does text context influence decoding and the construction of meaning?

6. What metalinguistic abilities affect reading acquisition? How do metalinguistic and linguistic abilities of teachers and learners interact to facilitate reading acquisition?

Visual Perception

1. How is visual perception related to reading development?

2. Under what conditions do early readers learn to perceive print?

3. How are syntactic and semantic variables related to visual processing of words and text?

4. What is the relationship between eye movement patterns of readers and density of text ideas being processed?

5. How does context influence visual processing of information?

Word Recognition

1. What is a perceptual unit? What perceptual units are used in word recognition? How do these units change developmentally?

2. What role do conceptualization and meaning play in word recognition?

3. How does "set for diversity" aid in the transfer of decoding knowledge?

4. How does conceptual flexability assist in the development of word recognition?

5. What role does sentence and intersentence context play in word recognition? What is the nature of the interaction between context and word recognition?

Comprehension

1. What is the relationship between text structure and reading comprehension? How does this relationship change developmentally?

2. How does the reader use text structure in comprehending text?

3. What is the role of prior knowledge in comprehending text?

4. How do the concepts of scripts and schemata explain text comprehension?

5. Why is vocabulary knowledge the most important predictor of reading comprehension?

6. How does a schema-theoretic model of reading explain text processing?

7. What effect do readers' self-generated questions have on the processing and recall of text?

Metacognition

1. How do metacognitive strategies affect the way a reader processes text?

24

2. Does metacognitive ability change as students progress through the grades? If so why?

3. Can metacognitive ability be affected by instruction? If so how?

4. How are metacognitive and cognitive abilities related?

5. What has metacognitive research contributed to our understanding of the reading process?

Affect

1. How are affective factors related to reading performance?

2. What is the relationship between affective and metacognitive abilities?

3. How does affect influence other reading processes while the reader is interacting with text?

4. What contribution has affective research made to our understanding of the reading process?

Culture

1. How is the culture of the classroom related to the acquisition of reading skills?

2. How do schools teach students to achieve failure? To achieve success?

3. How does the "culture" of a low achieving reading group differ from the "culture" of a high achieving reading group?

4. Under what conditions does the culture of the classroom conflict with the culture of the home? How does this conflict affect reading development?

Language

The Nature of the Reading Process

JOHN B. CARROLL
University of North Carolina at Chapel Hill

As you silently read this very paragraph, what are you doing? If you are a skilled reader and are attending carefully to what this paragraph is trying to say, you will notice the following. First, what are your eyes doing? Moving together in a swift and well-coordinated way, your eyes are making a series of fixations, jumping from place to place on the page of print. The jumps are exceedingly rapid; you see little while your eyes are jumping. What is important are the fixations, when your eyes come to rest. Most of these fixations are actually on or close to the line of print, but unless you are reading quite slowly you cannot easily predict or control where your eyes will fixate. The fixations are usually quite short in duration; each one will last about one-quarter of a second on the average.

Usually the fixations progress from left to right along the first line of print, then back to the beginning of the next line and again from left to right across the line, and so on. For the average adult reader there will be about two fixations per inch of ordinary type like this. Some of these fixations may be very brief, amounting to minor adjustments in order to bring the print better into view. During most of the fixations, you receive an impression of a certain amount of printed material; that is, you instantaneously perceive and recognize one or more words, perhaps up to four or five in some cases. You are more likely to recognize the words that are in the immediate area of fixation; words outside this immediate area may be less well recognized, but some of them have been recognized in a previous fixation, and others may be more clearly recognized in a future fixation. Some of the words may never be clearly recognized, but you apprehend enough of the stimulus to fill them in from the general drift of what you are reading.

Let us just think about this process of instantaneous word recognition. Most of the words you see are words you have seen many times before; even though in actuality they may be relatively rare, they are familiar enough to you to permit "instantaneous" recognition. Of course recognition is not really instantaneous; it takes a certain amount of time.

Reprinted from *Theoretical Models and Processes of Reading*, Second Edition, 1976.

Experiments in which words are exposed very briefly show that common words can be recognized quite accurately in less than 1/10 of a second; even words that are quite rare can be recognized with at least 50 percent accuracy in exposures of about 1/5 of a second. During the average fixation lasting 1/4 of a second it is often possible to take in several words. The point is that most words are recognized extremely rapidly. If you are a skilled reader you do not have to stop to figure out the pronunciation of a familiar word from its spelling; you are hardly conscious of the spelling at all. Still less do you attend to the particular phonetic values of the letters; in reading the word *women* it would scarcely occur to you to note that the "o" in the first syllable stands for a sound that rhymes with /i/ in *whim*. The printed word *women* is a gestalt-like total stimulus that immediately calls to mind the spoken word that corresponds to it—or if not the spoken word itself, some underlying response which is also made when the word is spoken. As a skilled reader, you can consider yourself lucky to have a large "sight" vocabulary.

The actual process by which we recognize words is not well understood, simply because the whole process of "pattern perception," as it is called, is one of the most mysterious problems in psychology. How, for example, do we recognize a table, a goblet, or a flagpole for what it is, regardless of the angle of regard? Nevertheless, it is a simple fact that we *can* learn to recognize words even though the words may be printed in different typefaces or written in different cursive styles, and in different sizes. Now even though word recognition is rapid, it obviously depends to a large extent on cues from the letters composing the word. There is little confusion among such highly similar items as *cob, rob, mob,* and *nob* even in fast single exposures. We do know that in recognizing longer words, the letters standing at the beginning and end are more critical than letters in the middle, for in fast exposures these middle letters can sometimes be altered or replaced without this being noticed by the reader. In ordinary reading we frequently fail to notice words that contain printer's errors. But there is little evidence to support the idea that a mature reader recognizes words merely by their outlines or general shape. It is unlikely that if you see the shape ⌐⌐ you will recognize the word *dog*; you might just as well think it to be *day* or *dug*. Beginning readers sometimes use mere shape cues in trying to recognize words, but they will be overwhelmed with confusion if they depend solely on such cues apart from the recognition of the letters themselves. In the mature reader the process of rapid word recognition seems to depend upon his ability to integrate the information provided by the separate letters composing the word, some letters being more critical as cues than others. Because the recognizability of a word is apparently correlated rather highly with its frequency of use, word perception seems to be a skill that depends upon large amounts of practice and exposure.

Suppose, however, that the skilled reader comes to a word that he has never seen before, like *dossal, cunctation,* or *latescent,* or an unfamiliar proper name like *Vukmanovich* or *Sbarra.* Though the skilled reader can hardly be said to "recognize" a word he has never seen before, he nevertheless recognizes elements of it—letters and patterns of letters that give him reasonably good cues as to how the word should be pronounced. *Dossal* may be recognized as similar to *fossil* and pronounced to rhyme with it, the first letter cuing the /f/ sound. *Cunctation* may give a little more difficulty but be recognized as somewhat similar to *punctuation* and at the same time to *mutation*; by following the total pattern of cues the reader may be able to infer the correct pronunciation. *Latescent* will probably be recognized not as a compound of *late* and *scent,* but as a member of a family of words like *quiescent, fluorescent,* etc. Somewhat the same principles apply to the reading of foreign proper names; even if he is not familiar with the foreign language involved, the skilled reader will be sensitive to the possible values of the letters and letter-combinations in the name, and come up with a reasonable pronunciation.

It should be noted that thus far we have been speaking of the recognition of words as particular combinations of letters. Actually, in English there are numerous instances of homographs—words that are pronounced in different ways depending on their use. The word "read" is an interesting example: in the context *to read* it rhymes with *bead,* but in the context *to have read,* it rhymes with *bed.* The skilled reader instantaneously interprets the word in its proper "reading" or pronunciation depending upon the context—i.e., the surrounding words and their meanings.

This takes us, in fact, to the next stage of our analysis of the reading process. As you take in material recognized in the succession of rapid fixations that is characteristic of skilled reading, it somehow merges together in such a way as to build up in your mind an impression of a meaningful message—a message that is in many ways analogous to the message you would apprehend if someone read the paragraph aloud to you, with all its proper inflections and accents. Some people report that as they read they can "hear" (in the form of internal auditory images) the message as it might be spoken; at least they report that they "hear" snatches of such a message. Other readers feel that they apprehend a meaning from the printed message directly—that is, without the intervention of any auditory images. In slow readers, or even in skilled readers reading very difficult material, one may notice slight articulatory movements that suggest that the reader is trying to pronounce the words subvocally.

The process of scanning a paragraph for a meaningful message does not, of course, always run smoothly. As one reads, there may be momentary lapses of attention (which can be due to lack of interest, distractions, or even stimulation from the content itself), or of comprehension (which can be due to the difficulty of the material, poor writing, or other conditions). The process of comprehension seems to have some influence on the movements of the eyes: when the reader fails to attend or comprehend, his eyes may "regress," moving back to fixate on a portion of the material already scanned. Difficulties in recognizing particular words may cause the eyes to dwell on or around a particular point in the text longer than the usual amount of time. There are large differences among individuals in all the reading processes we have mentioned. Some readers can read with markedly fewer fixations per line; some read with an abnormally high number of fixations per line and exhibit many more regressions than normal. Few individuals have the same pattern of eye movements, even when they read at approximately the same speed. Obviously, there are wide individual differences in rate and accuracy of comprehension.

The *essential* skill in reading is getting meaning from a printed or written message. In many ways this is similar to getting meaning from a *spoken* message, but there are differences, because the cues are different. Spoken messages contain cues that are not evident in printed messages, and conversely. In either case, understanding language is itself a tremendous feat, when one thinks about it. When you get the meaning of a verbal message, you have not only recognized the words themselves; you have interpreted the words in their particular grammatical functions, and you have somehow apprehended the general grammatical patterning of each sentence. You have unconsciously recognized what words or phrases constitute the subjects and predicates of the sentence, what words or phrases modify those subjects or predicates, and so on. In addition, you have given a "semantic" interpretation of the sentence, assigning meanings to the key words in the sentence. For example, in reading the sentence "He understood that he was coming tonight" you would know to whom each "he" refers, and you would interpret the word *understood* as meaning "had been caused to believe" rather than "comprehended." Somehow you put all these things together in order to understand the "plain sense" of what the message says.

Even beyond getting the simple meaning of the material you are reading, you are probably reacting to it in numerous ways. You may be trying to evaluate it for its truth, validity, significance, or importance. You may be checking it against your own experience or knowledge. You may find that it is reminding you of previous thoughts or experiences, or you may be starting to think about its implications for your future actions. You may be making inferences or drawing conclusions from what you read that go far beyond what is explicitly stated in the text. In doing any or all of these things, you are "reasoning" or "thinking." Nobody can tell you exactly what to think; much of your thinking will be dependent upon your particular background and experience. At the same time, some thinking is logical and justified by the facts and ideas one reads, while other kinds of thinking are illogical and not adequately justified by the facts and ideas one reads. One aspect of a mature reader's skill consists in his being able to think about what he reads in a logical and well-informed way. This aspect of reading skill sometimes takes years to attain.

We have described the process of reading in the skilled reader—a process that is obviously very complex. How is this process learned or attained?

As in the case of any skill, reading skill is not learned all at once. It takes a considerable amount of time. Furthermore, the process of learning to read is *not* simply a slow motion imitation of the mature reading process. It has numerous components, and each component has to be learned and practiced.

There are probably a great many ways to attain reading skill, depending upon the order in which the various components are learned and mastered. It may be the case that some ways are always better than others. On the other hand, children differ in their aptitudes, talents, and inclinations so much that it may also be the case that a particular way of learning is better for one child while another way is better for another child. It all depends upon which components of reading skill a given child finds easier to learn at a given stage of his development. In referring to different orders in which component skills would be learned, we do not mean to imply a lock-step procedure in which the child first learns and masters one skill, then goes on to learn and master another skill, and so on. Actually, a child can be learning a number of skills simultaneously, but will reach mastery of them at different periods in his development. From the standpoint of the teacher, this means that different skills may need to be emphasized at different periods, depending upon the characteristics of the individual child. This is particularly true in the case of the child who is having difficulty in learning to read.

Let us try to specify the components of reading skill. Some of these components come out of our analysis of the mature reading process; others out of a further analysis of *those* components.

1. *The child must know the language that he is going to learn to read.* Normally, this means that the child can speak and understand the language at least to a certain level of skill before he starts to learn to read, because the purpose of reading is to help him get messages from print that are similar to the messages he can already understand if they are spoken. But language learning is a lifelong process, and normally there are many aspects of language that the individual learns solely or mainly through reading. And speaking and understanding the language is not an absolute prerequisite for beginning to learn to read; there are cases on record of

children who learn to read before they can speak, and of course many deaf children learn the language only through learning to read. Foreign-born children sometimes learn English mainly through reading. Children who, before they begin to read, do not know the language, or who only understand but do not speak, will very likely require a mode of instruction specially adapted to them.

2. *The child must learn to dissect spoken words into component sounds.* In order to be able to use the alphabetic principle by which English words are spelled, he must be able to recognize the separate sounds composing a word and the temporal order in which they are spoken—the consonants and vowels that compose spoken words. This does not mean that he must acquire a precise knowledge of phonetics, but it does mean that he must recognize those aspects of speech sound that are likely to be represented in spelling. For example, in hearing the word *straight,* the child must be able to decompose the sounds into the sequence /s, t, r, ey, t/.

3. *The child must learn to recognize and discriminate the letters of the alphabet in their various forms (capitals, lower case letters, printed, and cursive).* (He should also know the names and alphabetic ordering of the letters.) This skill is required if the child is to make progress in finding correspondences between letters and sounds.

4. *The child must learn the left-to-right principle by which words are spelled and put in order in continuous text.* This is, as we have noted, a very general principle, although there are certain aspects of letter-sound correspon-dences that violate the principle—e.g., the reverse order of *wh* in repre-senting the sound cluster /hw/.

5. *The child must learn that there are patterns of highly probable correspon-dence between letters and sounds, and he must learn those patterns of correspon-dence that will help him recognize words that he already knows in his spoken language or that will help him determine the pronunciation of unfamiliar words.* There are few if any letters in English orthography that always have the same sound values; nevertheless, spellings tend to give good clues to the pronunciation of words. Often a letter will have highly predictable sound values if it is considered in conjunction with surrounding letters. Partly through direct instruction and partly through a little-understood process of inference, the normal child can fairly readily acquire the ability to respond to these complex patterns of letter-sound correspondences.

6. *The child must learn to recognize printed words from whatever cues he can use—their total configuration, the letters composing them, the sounds represented by those letters, and/or the meanings suggested by the context.* By "recognition" we mean not only becoming aware that he has seen the word before, but also knowing the pronunciation of the word. This skill is one of the most essential in the reading process, because it yields for the reader the equivalent of a speech signal.

7. *The child must learn that printed words are signals for spoken words and that they have meanings analogous to those of spoken words. While decoding a printed message into its spoken equivalent, the child must be able to apprehend the meaning of the total message in the same way that he would apprehend the meaning of the corresponding spoken message.* As in the case of adult reading, the spoken equivalent may be apprehended solely internally, although it is usual, in early reading efforts, to expect the child to be able to read aloud, at first with much hesitation, but later with fluency and expression.

8. *The child must learn to reason and think about what he reads, within the limits of his talent and experience.*

It will be noticed that each of these eight components of learning to read is somehow involved in the adult reading process—knowing the language, dissecting spoken words into component sounds, and so forth. Adult reading is skilled only because all the eight components are so highly practiced that they merge together, as it were, into one unified performance. The well-coordinated, swift eye movements of the adult reader are a result, not a cause, of good reading; the child does not have to be *taught* eye movements and therefore we have not listed eye-coordination as a component skill. Rather, skilled eye movements represent the highest form of the skill we have listed as 4—the learning of the left-to-right principle. The instantaneous word recognition ability of the mature reader is the highest form of the skill we have listed as 6—recognition of printed words from whatever cues are available, and usually this skill in turn depends upon the mastery of some of the other skills, in particular 5—learning patterns of correspondence between letters and sounds. The ability of the adult reader to apprehend meaning quickly is an advanced form of skill 7, and his ability to think about what he reads is an advanced form of skill 8.

The "great debate" about how reading should be taught is really a debate about the *order* in which the child should be started on the road toward learning each of the skills. Few will question that mature reading involves all eight skills; the only question is which skills should be introduced and mastered first. Many points of view are possible. On the one hand there are those who believe that the skills should be *introduced* in approximately the order in which they have been listed; this is the view of those who believe that there should be an early emphasis on the decoding of print into sound via letter-sound relations. On the other hand, there are those who believe that the skills should be introduced approximately in the following order:

1.   The child should learn the language he is going to read.
6.   The child should learn to recognize printed words from whatever cues he can use, but initially only from total configurations.

7. The child should learn that printed words are signals for spoken words, and that meanings can be apprehended from these printed words.

8. The child must learn to reason and think about what he reads.

4. The child should learn the left-to-right principle, but initially only as it applies to complete words in continuous text.

3. The child should learn to recognize and discriminate the letters of the alphabet.

2. The child should learn to dissect spoken words into component sounds.

5. The child should learn patterns of correspondence between letters and sounds, to help him in the advanced phases of skill 6.

This latter view is held by those who argue that there should be an early emphasis on getting the meaning from print, and that the child should advance as quickly as possible toward the word-recognition and meaning-apprehension capacities of the mature reader. Skills 2, 3, and 5 are introduced only after the child has achieved considerable progress towards mastery of skills 4, 6, 7, and 8.

These are the two main views about the process of teaching reading. If each one is taken quite strictly and seriously, there can be very clear differences in the kinds of instructional materials and procedures that are used. It is beyond our scope to discuss whether the two methods differ in effectiveness. We would emphasize, rather, that methods may differ in effectiveness from child to child. Furthermore, it is possible to construct other reasonable orders in which the various components of reading skill can be introduced to the child. There is currently a tendency to interlace the approaches distinguished above in such a way that the child can attain rapid sight recognition of words at the same time that he is learning letter-sound correspondences that will help him "attack" words that he does not already know.

For the child who is having difficulty in learning to read, it may be necessary to determine exactly which skills are causing most difficulty. The dyslexic child may be hung up on the acquisition of just one or two skills. For example, he may be having particular trouble with skill 3—the recognition and discrimination of the letters of the alphabet, or with skill 2—the dissection of spoken words into component sounds. On determining what skills pose obstacles for a particular child, it is usually necessary to give special attention to those skills while capitalizing on those skills which are easier for the child to master.

Uncertainties and Research Problems

The above description of the nature of the reading process is based on the findings of nearly three-quarters of a century of research. A good deal is known about reading behavior, yet there are many questions that have not been answered with precision and certainty. We shall list the most important of these.

Questions about the Mature Reading Process

1. How does the individual's ability to recognize words instantaneously develop? What cues for word recognition are most important? How and when does awareness of spelling clues and inner speech representation recede, if at all? What is the extent of the sight vocabulary of the mature reader? (It should be noted that most studies of word recognition processes have been conducted with adults; there is need for developmental studies in which word recognition processes would be investigated over different chronological age levels.)

2. How do skilled readers process unfamiliar words? To what extent, and how, do they use patterns of letter-sound correspondences?

3. How do skilled readers find the proper readings of homographs and other types of ambiguous words?

4. What are the detailed psychological processes by which skilled readers comprehend the simple meaning of what they read? In what way do lexico-semantic, syntactical, and typographical factors interact to yield this comprehension?

5. How are eye movements controlled by comprehension processes, and how does the individual develop skill in scanning print?

6. How does the mature reader acquire skill in reasoning and inferential processes?

7. What are the major sources of individual differences in rate and accuracy of comprehension in mature readers?

Questions about Certain Components of Reading Skill
as They Affect Learning

1. In what way does knowledge of the spoken language interact with learning to read? What kinds and amounts of competence are desirable before the child undertakes any given task in learning to read?

2. What is the nature of the ability to discriminate sounds in the spoken language and to dissect words in terms of these sounds? How does it develop, and what role does it play in the beginning reader's learning of letter-sound correspondences? How can this ability be taught?

3. How do children learn to recognize and discriminate alphabetic letters in their various forms? When children have difficulty with letter recognition, how can these difficulties be overcome?

4. How do children learn the left-to-right principle in orthography, both as applied to individual words and to the order of words in continuous text? Are there children with special difficulties in learning this component of reading skill?

5. Exactly what are the most useful and functional patterns of letter-sound correspondence in English orthography, and in what order should they be learned? How, indeed, *are* they learned? Is it better to give direct instruction in them, or is it better to rely upon the child's capacity to infer these patterns from the experience he acquires as he learns to read? Should the characteristics of particular children be taken into account in deciding this?

6. When a child has acquired the ability to recognize words and read them in order, yet does not appear to comprehend the message as he would if it were spoken to him, what is the nature of the difficulty?

Questions about the Ordering of the Components of
Reading Skill in the Teaching Process

1. In what way are the various skills prerequisite for each other? What aspects of each skill are necessary to facilitate progress in another skill?

2. Is there one best order in which to introduce the components of reading skill in the learning process, or are there different orders depending upon characteristics of individual children or groups of children? If so, how can these individual or group characteristics be determined?

3. On the assumption that there is an optimal ordering of skills for any given child, how much mastery of a given skill is desirable before another skill is introduced?

Language Models and Reading

IRENE ATHEY
Rutgers University

Fifteen years have elapsed since the U.S. Office of Education, as part of the Right to Read effort, first commissioned the Literature Search in an attempt to identify existing models or partial models of reading. Additional objectives included a determination of the extent to which each of these models had been submitted to empirical validation, and an assessment of the implications of both the models and the research emanating from them for research and instruction in reading. The project was based on the assumption that having such information available would accelerate progress toward the national goal of attaining functional reading competence for all learners and would provide the basis for a more systematic and efficient method of developing instructional systems than had existed in the past (Penney, Hjelm, and Gephart, 1970).

Sufficient time has now passed for us to have gained some perspective on the feasability and success of the original mission, on the fate that has befallen the models in the interim, and on the emergence of new models and lines of research. This chapter will not repeat the detailed exposition of the various models that appeared in the earlier document (Athey, 1971). It will instead be devoted to an evaluation of new research generated by these models, to an assessment of the status of these models in the light of this new research, and to an account of models that have appeared on the scene since the last report. Similarly, Hayes' (1970) tripartite classification employed in the earlier document has been replaced by a categorization of models pertaining to the acquisition of grammar as opposed to the acquisition of meaning. While fewer models have been included, the spectrum of prototypes is broader, ranging from models that deal with a restricted segment of language to those that view language in the broader context of communication. Finally, since the relationship between language and thought has an obvious bearing on reading comprehension, models that might be considered as belonging to the cognitive sphere but that have clear implications for language and reading, also will be included in this discussion.

Theoretical Models: A Basic Dichotomy

Since the time of Plato, philosophy has been divided into two major schools of thought revolving around a single basic issue: the nature of the human mind

35

and, specifically, how human beings acquire knowledge. The empiricist adopts an atomistic approach, maintaining that, starting with a "blank slate" (Locke's *tabula rasa*), or a few primitive reactions to stimuli (Watson's reflex responses), experience is built up slowly and cumulatively as these and successive responses are rewarded (e.g. Skinner's account of operant conditioning). Theoretically, this means that there is no predetermined limit to the amount of learning that may take place, except the limits imposed by experience. However, throughout this learning the person is essentially a passive recipient of experience. Field theorists (as those who espouse an organismic view are frequently called) believe, to the contrary, that the human mind is endowed at birth with certain predefining dispositions that result in experience being structurally organized in specific ways, but that these structures come about largely through the autonomous activity of the human organism (hence the appellation "organismic"). Over the centuries, each school of thought has responded to the often ferocious attacks of its opponents by elaborating its theory in an attempt to answer their criticisms. Indeed, the debate continues (Kamil, 1984, p. 42). It should be emphasized that, although the dichotomy described here (in admittedly simple form) pertains to schools of philosophical thought, the same divisive issues also pervade psychology and linguistics, and have influenced the thinking behind the language models described in this chapter. This issue has not been used as the basis for categorizing the models, but its influence on the models reviewed is readily apparent.

Empiricism (frequently denounced as "sterile," "dustbowl," etc., by its critics) enjoyed supremacy in America in the form of behaviorism for the first half of the 20th century. The great names that dominated psychology in its early days as an independent science (such as Woodworth, Thorndike, Watson), and those who carried on this tradition (such as Osgood, Hull, Spence, and Skinner), were all behaviorists who built their systems on a foundation of empiricist principles. The key concepts of generalization, discrimination, reinforcement, extinction, imitation, and mediation are capable (they claimed) of explaining all learning, including the acquisition of language. The advent of the "Chomskyan revolution" around 1960 ushered in a new era of psycholinguistic theory and research placing the earlier work in historical perspective. The language models we shall consider in this chapter clearly reflect this age-old dichotomy.

Phonology, syntax, and semantics are generally perceived as the three major components of that system of knowledge ("everywhere complex and at times abstract") we call a grammar (McNeill, 1970, p. 1061). Although phonology is a major concern of linguists and an explicit theory has long existed (Jakobson, 1941, 1968), little can be said about the acquisition of this "most visible part" of language (p. 1130), and probably even less about its import for reading. Hence, little attention will be given to phonological models in this chapter.

The Acquisition of Syntax

The study of children's syntactic structures goes back to Rousseau, and traces of modern theories of generative grammar may be found in the works of Preyer and Stern (Blumenthal, 1970, pp. 81-85).

To explain the acquisition of grammar, behaviorists have traditionally adopted a probabilistic model ("Markov process") in which each word in a sentence is determined by those immediately preceding it. Each word in the sentence becomes the stimulus for the next word in accordance with the associative laws (e.g. frequency, contiguity, reinforcement) of the particular version of behaviorism the theorist espouses. Reinforcement is especially important to most behaviorist theories of language, the prototype of all of them being Skinner's theory of operant conditioning.

Skinner. The basic principle is contained in Skinner's "three-term-contingency" model, s-r-s, in which the stimulus (sight of food) elicits the response (putting food in mouth) and the reinforcing stimulus (taste of food). Food is a primary reinforcer because it fulfills a biological need, but much of human behavior depends on secondary reinforcers which have been associated with primary reinforcers in the past. Language learning is explained in terms of the reinforcement of imitative behavior. For example, babbling gives way to infant speech because sounds that approximate adult speech become reinforcing in their own right as a result of being reinforced by the parents (Jenkins and Palermo, 1964; Mowrer, 1948). As the child grows older, language behavior is "shaped" — successive approximations to adult pronunciation and grammar are rewarded. Later, the child's speech is rewarded in other ways—when the hearer complies with a request, answers a question, responds to a comment. Verbal behavior is shaped by the reinforcement contingencies of the verbal community in which a person lives. Reinforcement and imitation play a fundamental role in operant-conditioning theories of language. In 1969, Skinner elaborated on the "contingencies" of reinforcement, without special reference to language.

Probabilistic models rely heavily on the concept of stimulus and response generalization whereby a range of stimuli may evoke the same response, or a range of responses may be attached to the same stimulus. The concept of generalization is basic to all behaviorist theories, but may occur in somewhat different form.

Braine. Braine (1963), for example, posits a "contextual-generalization" hypothesis emerging from his distinction between pivot and open classes. Pivot words (my, more, all gone, etc.) are relatively few in number, emerge slowly, and have a fixed position in the child's sentences. The open class contains many nouns, adjectives, etc., which fill the remaining slots in two and three word utterances, resulting in such phrases as "my big truck," "all gone milk," etc. Contextual generalization is the process whereby the child, having established the meaning of a pivot word, is able to expand the repertory of intelligible utterances considerably. It is not essentially different from stimulus or response generalization except that it takes place across temporal positions. This process explains the child's linguistic productivity.

Jenkins and Palermo. Jenkins and Palermo (1964) proposed a theory to explain the learning of grammar, which they view as a basic problem in language acquisition. From repeated hearings of sentences of the same form (e.g. subject-verb-object), the child abstracts the sequence enabling new sentences to be generated. Although the explanation is not carried beyond this level, more complicated structures presumably are acquired through the same process of generalization. In 1968, Jenkins modified this view, in recognition of the linguists' distinction between deep and surface structure. Psychologists tend to confine their investigations to the surface structure, hence their findings are necessarily restricted to this aspect of language. Jenkins believes that further study of deep structures will lead to an improved understanding of the relevant aspects of the surface structures of language behavior.

Chomsky. Chomsky's (1965) theory of syntax is based on the proposed existence of universals in the human mind. In language these univerals are manifested in the grammatical forms of sentences. They represent an underlying, biologically based structure that is shared by all members of the species.

Chomsky's basic model postulates a tripartite structure that includes deep structure, transformational rules, and surface structure. The deep structure defines, through transformational rules, the meaning and interpretation of language. It is abstract, and not represented in speech. "The rules that determine deep and surface structure and their interrelation in particular cases must themselves be highly abstract. They are surely remote from consciousness and cannot be brought to consciousness" (1968, p. 283). Although linguists are unable to describe the deep structure completely, it can be said that kernel sentences are an important feature representing the various acceptable strings to which the transformational rules stored in memory are applied.

Whereas traditional grammars and probabilistic models of language assume that meaning is dependent on grammar, in Chomsky's model what is grammatical is independent of what is meaningful. Of course, sentences can be ranked on a scale of grammaticality, just as they can be ranked on a scale of meaningfulness; there is no necessary relationship between the two.

The theory of syntax is also a theory of language acquisition. Chomsky (1965, pp. 30-31) describes the basic requisites a child must have to acquire a language:

1. a technique for representing input signals,
2. a way of representing structural information about these signals,
3. some initial delimitation of a class of possible hypotheses about a language structure,
4. a method for determining what each hypothesis implies with respect to each sentence, and
5. a method for selecting one of the (presumably infinite number of) hypotheses allowed by requisite 3, and compatible with the given primary linguistic data.

Chomsky (1968) has described language acquisition as "a kind of theory construction" in which "the child discovers the theory of his language with only small amounts of data from that language" (p. 284). This "theory of language" is predictive; that is, the child responds to the linguistic data received by forming generalizations that are then reflected in speech. Chomsky emphasizes that the process is much more than pure imitation (a key explanatory concept in behaviorist theories), as may be seen from the child's production of novel sentences. The child's activity is dependent on innate restrictions on the form of grammar. "The restriction on the form of grammar is a precondition for linguistic experience and it is surely the critical factor in determining the course and result of language learning" (1968, p. 284).

The fact that children can communicate meaning, the most abstract part of language, before they have acquired the grammar seems to call for some explanation. Chomsky (1957, 1965) introduces the concept of a language acquisition device (LAD), which takes the body of speech utterances to which the child is exposed and somehow constructs from it a grammatical theory. Thus the child uses the language universals present from birth to construct an internal picture of syntactic structures, gradually building a theory that approximates the ideal. The precise nature of this interaction between the child and the linguistic environment is unclear, as is the degree of activity, mental or otherwise, necessary for this achievement. "We must also bear in mind that the child constructs this ideal theory without specific instructions, that he acquires this knowledge at a time when he is not capable of complex intellectual achievement in many other domains, and that this achievement is relatively independent of intelligence, or the particular course of experience (1968, p. 284).

McNeill. McNeill (1966, 1968, 1970) adopts a nativistic thesis in an attempt to deal with the "fundamental problem...that language acquisition occurs in a surprisingly short time....Thus a basis for the rich and intricate competence of adult grammar must emerge in the short span of 24 months" (1966, p. 15). To explain this phenomenon, McNeill borrows from Chomsky (1961, 1965) and Katz (1966) the concept of a language acquisition device (LAD) which has the randomly received corpus of speech around it as input and grammatical competence as output. The internal structure of LAD is determined by the linguistic universals, which are of two types: 1) formal (e.g. grammatical rules), and 2) substantive (e.g. a hierarchy of categories). Equipped with these universals, "LAD operates something like a scientist constructing a theory," formulating, testing, and discarding hypotheses. "Thus the universals guide and limit acquisition" (1966, p. 39); they enable the child to progress step by step toward adult grammatical classes, starting with the simple dichotomy of open versus pivot classes and proceeding to later grammatical distinctions "in an order determined by the hierarchical arrangement of categories." McNeill distinguishes two components of LAD, one that analyzes and transforms the incoming speech data, the other comprising a body of linguistic information (e.g. that there are sentences, that sentences include noun and verb phrases), information which is universally applicable to any language.

Slobin. Slobin (1966a, p. 87), while sympathetic to the model set forth by

McNeill, finds the proposal of a significant innate component in language acquisition to pose a problem: namely, "how to determine just what sorts of things should be considered 'preprogramed'." McNeill views the child as being born with the entire set of linguistic universals which are used as a grid through which to filter language input.

> McNeill takes a "content approach" to LAD, while I would favor a "process approach." It seems to me that the child is born not with a set of linguistic categories but with some sort of process mechanism—a set of procedures and inference rules if you will—that he uses to process linguistic data....The linguistic universals, then, are the result of an innate cognitive competence rather than the content of such a competence (pp. 87-88).

Thus, language acquisition is subsumed under the more general rubric of cognitive development; that is to say, the development of language is controlled by the development of cognitive abilities such as memory storage, and information processing, which increase with age. In fact, the "preprograming" may consist simply of the ability to learn certain conceptual and semantic categories and to understand that these are the basis for grammatical structures. These learnings are not explicit, but are manifested in behavior. "To qualify as a native speaker...one must learn...rules....This is to say, of course, that one must learn to behave as though one knew the rules" (Ervin-Tripp as quoted in Slobin, 1971b, p. 55). Thus, Slobin favors a cognitive learning approach, which retains the innate species-specific factor as a system of broad intellectual potentialities and places the substantive aspects of language clearly in the domain of learning. Like other cognitive theorists, he sees the organism as an active participant in this learning, but maintains that "as yet, we have a very limited understanding of the psychological and physiological mechanisms underlying these achievements" (1971b, p. 66).

Research Literature on Syntactic Models

Behaviorist theory has been generally successful in stimulating research to validate or clarify the key concepts of reinforcement, generalization, discrimination, extinction, imitation, and mediation in many areas of inquiry, including language.

Reinforcement. Operant conditioning techniques have been used to teach language in a variety of situations. Bereiter and Engelmann (1966) and Osborn (1968) have used these methods to teach pronunciation and syntax to disadvantaged preschoolers. Hart and Risley (1968) used snacks, teacher approval, and access to play equipment as reinforcers to increase disadvantaged preschoolers' use of descriptive adjectives in spontaneous speech. Gray and Fygentakis (1968) employed the same principles to teach "linguistically divergent" children, but by varying the stimulus situation, they also worked for response generalization from the "is" paradigm, which was taught, to the the "is-ing" paradigm, which was not.

Sapon (1966) has attempted, with some success, to teach speech to Mongoloid children using operant-conditioning principles, although the children's speech after training is still far from normal. Similarly, Weiss and Born (1967 found that speech paradigms could be taught to a nonspeaking seven year old boy, as long as the original paradigms were followed.

Research following Chomsky and the other models that are an offshoot of his theory may be considered in the following three categories relating to:

1. the psychological reality of the model (usually referred to as "the correspondence hypothesis"),
2. the competence performance factor in the grammars of children, and
3. the patterns in children's grammars and the sequence in which their grammars are acquired.

The correspondence hypothesis. An early question stemming from the theory of generative grammar centered around the psychological reality of such grammatical features as transformations and phrase markers. According to the correspondence hypothesis, the relative difficulty a subject experiences in understanding a sentence (i.e. translating it into deep structure) should be correlated with the number of grammatical rules necessary for derivation. Early experiments seemed to provide impressive evidence of a direct relationship between the complexity of the transformation and the intricacies of the psychological processes involved. However, interest in the correspondence hypothesis seems to have declined in recent years. Bever (1970) views adult perception of language as contingent on the use of strategies such as isolating and relating the lexical sequences, relating clauses according to semantic construction, and identifying the actor-action-object in the sentences, rather than on the performance of transformations. Perhaps the issue is best summarized by Fodor (1969):

> Grammatical rules are themselves not a part of the recognition procedure....The mental operations which underlie the behavior of the speaker/hearer are not identical to, and probably do not include, the grammatical operations involved in generating sentences (p. 198).

Moreover, Slobin (1971b) believes that "we cannot hope for simple metrics of the difficulty involved in processing sentences on the basis of their syntax....They are used as syntactic and semantic and pragmatic entities "as well" (p. 37).

Competence vs. performance. Contemporary linguists deny that a theory of competence can ever be constructed from studies of linguistic productions (Chomsky, 1964). Distributional analyses describe children's grammatical classes and give some hints as to the rules they are using. A theory such as Chomsky's enables the experimenter to go far beyond this. For example, if adult grammar is the end point of linguistic developement, it may be used as a standard against which to judge the children's productions. The competence performance distinction may give rise to differing interpretations of the productions; for example, the absence of auxiliary verbs from a child's speech may signify their absence from the grammar, or may indicate the constraints of a limited memory span. Such issues can only be resolved by testing for comprehension.

The sequence of acquisition. The literature on the development of various grammatical categories is quite extensive and has been reviewed elsewhere (McNeill, 1970; Slobin, 1971a).

Critique of Syntactic Models

The major strengths of behaviorist theories lie in their parsimony and objectivity. Mentalistic concepts that are difficult to verify experimentally are exorcised, while those retained in the system are operationally defined in behavioral terms. There is a parsimony and coherence of relationships among the basic concepts, giving the entire theoretical system an air of elegance and scientific rigor. Moreover, it is held to be comprehensive in that its principles have explanatory power for all aspects of human and animal behavior. Critics of behaviorist theories maintain that this appearance of objectivity and rigor is illusory, and that parsimony of concepts is obtained at the expense of explanatory value.

Probabilistic models have come under some attack from psychologists as well as linguists. Lashley (1951) pointed out that there is no intrinsic order to words that could account for either comprehension or production of speech through association. He concludes that there must be an underlying level at which longer units than those momentarily being produced are being formulated. Moreover, there is a clearer intrinsic relationship among certain parts of a sentence. In a sentence such as "The boy hit the ball," "the ball" is a unit, whereas "hit the" is not. Chomsky (1957) further demonstrated that the model is incapable of differentiating between sentences that are grammatical and those that are not. The sentence "Colorless green ideas sleep furiously" is grammatical, but the probability of its occurrence (except in books on psycholinguistics) is virtually nonexistent. The model is equally incapable of accounting for the different structures underlying the two meanings of an ambiguous sentence ("They are cooking apples") and for the insertion of phrases between stimulus and response words that occurs in embedded sentences ("The man I met last week is here"). In brief, it appears that "our knowledge of language involves properties of a much more abstract nature, not indicated directly in the surface structure" (Chomsky, 1968, p. 32).

Several of the key concepts of operant theory have come under attack, notably imitation and generalization.

Imitation. With respect to imitation, it may be noted that: (1) children's ability to reproduce sentences they hear is limited to what they can produce in spontaneous conversation (Ervin, 1964); (2) the order in which inflections appear in children's speech is weakly correlated with the frequency of these forms in the speech of adults they hear (Bellugi, 1964); (3) when children fail to comprehend a sentence they are asked to imitate, the imitation either expresses a different meaning or no meaning at all (Slobin and Welsh, 1967); (4) since children reconstruct adult models to make their own grammars, imitation plays no role in the acquisition of new transformations (McNeill, 1970); (5) children often produce regular forms of irregular verbs (e.g. digged) even though they have never heard these forms in adult speech (Ervin, 1964); (6) children omit certain aspects of the model's utterance, e.g. gruffness of voice; and (7) a child can pick up a second language from other children who are not precise or accurate in their speech (Chomsky, 1959).

McNeill makes a distinction between two uses of the term *imitation*. The first is a general use, for example, writing prose in the style of Faulkner or driving on the righthand side of the road. In this broad sense, children acquire language through imitation. The second is a narrower, more technical use which involves copying the behavior of a model, e.g. making plural inflections on English nouns. McNeill maintains that this technical use is inappropriate for language acquisition.

Generalization. The concept of generalization also has been the object of some criticism. One difficulty appears to be that children classify words into the pivot or open class in ways consistent with more subtle differentiations that they will make in the future. McNeill (1970) cites the case of a child whose pivot class contained members of several adult grammatical classes (demonstratives, adjectives, possessives), although none of these were a part of the child's grammar at the time. Braine's contextual generalization has given rise to considerable dispute. While it is true that positional learning, extended through contextual generalization, can lead to grammatically correct complex sentences, a difficulty arises when the surface structure of sentences is not necessarily the same as the underlying structure (Bever, Fodor, and Weksel, 1965). Braine's (1965) solution of changing the syntactic analysis of sentences by construing them all as having the same surface and underlying structures is viewed by McNeill (1968) as avoiding the problem of language acquisition altogether. The theory also fails to explain the child's restriction on the use of pivot words (McNeill, 1970). Slobin (1971b) refers to two crosscultural studies (Blount, 1969; Kernan, 1969) which argue for the insufficiency of pivot analysis, and points out that for some children a distinct pivot stage may not occur.

Chomsky (1959), who led the attack in his critical review of Skinner's *Verbal Behavior* (1957), has pointed out that the terms stimulus, response, reinforcement, extinction, generalization, and discrimination are used in imprecise ways.

In summary, Chomsky's criticisms were:

1. The goal of the book is to provide a way to predict and control verbal behavior by observing and manipulating the physical environment, which is manifestly impossible. The only hope of predicting the behavior of a complex organism is through an indirect program of research that begins by studying the behavior and the particular capacities of the organism.

2. Skinner takes experimental results and, by making analogic guesses, creates the illusion of a theory having scientific rigor and broad scope whereas, in fact, the descriptions of real life and of behavior in the laboratory are only vaguely similar.

3. The concepts of stimulus, response, reinforcement, drive reduction, and probability of response are vague cover terms which are entirely inappropriate to describe verbal behavior. As McNeill (1970) points out, "It is the phenomenon of abstraction, which all children face and overcome, that eliminates stimulus-response theory as a possible explanation of language acquisition" (p. 1086).

Carroll (1964a) has also expressed some dissatisfaction with the Skinnerian model. He summarizes the major difficulties as follows:

1. The theory on the whole relies heavily on the concept of reinforcement, but not everyone is willing to accept the proposition that reinforcement is the crucial factor in learning.

2. The theory cannot account for the fact that a language response learned in one way is immediately available for use in other ways.

3. If we look more closely at the paradigms postulated by Skinner, we notice that in all cases there must be covert perceptual responses to the rewards (in case of mands) or to the discriminative stimuli (in case of tacts). In the process of operant conditioning, then, classical conditioning, or something very much like it, must be going on in parallel.

Ten years elapsed before the behaviorist school attempted to counteract the negative reactions to Skinner's book. By way of rebuttal, MacCorquodale (1969, p. 831) viewed these reactions as being brought about by the "uncritical acceptance of (Chomsky's) misconceptions concerning *Verbal Behavior's* content." The Skinnerian account is best conceived as a hypothesis that speech is within the domain of behaviors which can be accounted for by existing functional laws, based upon the assumption that it is orderly, lawful, and determined...." Like all hypotheses, Skinner's "asserts more than the author has yet demonstrated experimentally, and it sounds dogmatic. We expect and tolerate this in hypotheses" (p. 832). Skinner probably avoided the word "hypotheses" because it suggests some fictional element, but a strong argument for his theory is that "it contains no reference to fictional causal entities" (1970, p. 85). In fact, it is Chomsky who is being unparsimonious in supposing that nature maintains two sets of laws—one for the laboratory, another for real life.

All in all, MacCorquodale finds Chomsky's criticisms "irrelevant" (indeed, many of them are more applicable to non-Skinnerian theory), and concludes that "we do not yet know if verbal behavior is within the domain of Skinner's system" (p. 86).

Linguistic universals. Psycholinguistic models have not escaped entirely unscathed. In particular, the nature of linguistic universals has been the subject of considerable debate. It may be remembered that McNeill viewed the remarkable rapidity of language acquisition as evidence for the existence of innate linguistic properties. Fraser (1966) has retorted that the "astonishing speed" of language acquisition commented on frequently by linguists is less astonishing if we consider that the child is working constantly on acquiring language from birth to the age of six and beyond. The "mere exposure," which McNeill discounts as the medium for learning, actually exposes the child to the relational communication that occurs between adults and children. Fraser also suggests that instead of arguing about the nature of innate capacities, we should get on with the job of discovering what language behavior the innate capacities and mechanisms are supposed to be explaining. Slobin (1966b) rejects McNeill's adoption of "strong" universals (those based on uniquely linguistic capacities as opposed to "weak" universals which are dependent on universal cognitive abilities), and, indeed, one may argue that such adoption ignores the role of learning, especially learning through feedback. Granted that language is a unique phenomenon, there is no reason to suppose that the general laws of learning fail to apply. The fact that they cannot explain all of the phenomena of language does not imply that the rules of grammar are necessarily preprogramed.

Part of the problem is that the mechanism by which LAD performs the functions assigned to it is not entirely clear. To quote Slobin (1966b):

> McNeill...does not seem to speak to the question of why ontogenetic change in language performance is gradual; why it is that some grammatical categories are late to emerge. One reason could be—at least with regard to the substantive categories—that if the distinctions are semantic, they require varying amounts of experience to be learned. Another explanation could be that the child comes equipped with a set of hypotheses or inference rules that vary in their saliency and simplicity and that the child begins by trying out the more salient or simpler hypotheses (p. 90).

As yet, the field of psycholinguistics is unable to determine which among these, or other alternatives is the preferred choice.

Fodor (1966) also believes that the determination of the child's "intrinsic" structure can be made only by studying the linguistic input:

> In short, a comparison of the child's data with a formulation of the linguistic information necessary to speak the language the child learns permits us to estimate the nature and complexity of the child's intrinsic structure. If the information in the child's data closely approximates the linguistic information he must master, we may assume that the role of instrinsic structure is relatively insignificant. Conversely, if the linguistic information at which the child arrives is only indirectly and abstractly related to the data provided by the child's exposure to adult speech, we shall have to suppose that the child's intrinsic structure is correspondingly complex. We have already seen that the two limiting theories can be dismissed with some confidence. On the other hand, it seems that the data cannot contribute all the relevant information, for this would be logically incompatible with the fact that the child eventually learns to deal with utterances of sentences he has not previously encountered. It appears that the theory we want must lie somewhere between the two (p. 107).

The adult speech that the child hears is not random; it exhibits formal relationships among the utterances (e.g. answers to questions) and usually corresponds to certain nonlinguistic events. Fodor's suggestion is that the child brings to language learning a set of rules that lead to inferences from these formal relations about the possible range of underlying syntactic structures.

Deep structure. Among the linguistic universals that have been the object of criticism is the distinction between deep and surface structure. Olson (1970) points out that Chomsky's formulation of the relation between syntax and semantics led him to assume that grammar was "autonomous and independent of meaning and also primary, in that meaning could not be assigned until the sentence had been grammatically structured. Olson finds existing theories of the relation between words and their referents inadequate, and advances a theory of reference in terms of a cognitive theory of semantics. A semantic decision, such as the choice of a word, is made in terms of the information the speaker believes the hearer needs to distinguish an intended referent from some perceived or inferred set of alternatives. From this point of view, the postulation of deep structure becomes unnecessary:

> If the functions usually attributed to the deep structure, such as the semantic component and the effects of syntactic selection restrictions, can be accounted for without implicating the deep linguistic structure, there remains little virtue in postulating such a level (Olson, 1970, p. 171).

McCawley (1968), on the other hand, has argued that deep structure is not enough, that there is no justification for assuming an autonomous level of deep structure, and that semantics must be generative, not simply interpretive.

Chomsky's model has not only generated a great deal of research on related issues, but has enabled linguists to place the atheoretical studies that abounded prior to 1960 in theoretical perspective. In addition, it has provoked elaboration and counter proposals like those of McNeill and Slobin. Taken together, these facts indicate in some measure the revolution that has taken place in psycholinguistics.

The Acquisition of Meaning

McNeill (1970, p. 119) characterizes semantics as the most pervasive and least understood aspect of language acquisition—pervasive because it has repercussions in wide areas of cognition, little understood because linguistic theory has given few guidelines for exploration.

Staats and Staats. Staats and Staats (1962, 1963) and Staats (1968) developed a complex account of language behavior in the Skinnerian tradition using— in addition to reinforcement, imitation, successive approximation, generalization, and discrimination—the concept of mediation. A word is said to have meaning when part of the covert response to the object is transferred to the word by conditioning. This implicit response is a mediating response. Mediating responses include names, labels, or other linguistic responses that mediate between stimuli and behavior (Jensen, 1966). Mediation is derived from simple s-r associations in which one stimulus elicits several responses, or several stimuli elicit the same response, or a response in one situation is a stimulus in another situation. Mediation is thus held to account for much complex linguistic and cognitive behavior (Staats, 1968).

Mowrer. Mowrer (1948) relies heavily on the concept of mediation. Words are combined in sentences to produce new meanings (mediating responses), which cannot be produced by the individual words alone. Some of the responses to individual words are transferred to other words by virtue of their pairing in sentences. In this way, a person learns new associations through language, without experiencing objects and events directly.

Osgood. Osgood's (1969) theory of how words acquire their meaning is similar to Mowrer's. Words become signs for things because they produce some fraction of the actual behavior toward these things. This is accomplished through a representational mediation process in which the signs (words) are associated with the stimulus objects. Later, when the signs occur without the presence of the objects, "they tend to elicit some reduced portion of the total behavior elicited by the stimulus object" (p. 9). Those responses that require the most energy are the least likely to survive the reduction process. Therefore, although these responses may be overt, they are more likely to be covert, and are probably cortical in most instances. Osgood distinguishes between representational mediation theory, as exemplified by himself and Mowrer, and nonrepresentational theory, as exemplified by Skinner, Bousfield, Jenkins and, in a more complex fashion, Braine. In nonrepresentational mediation theory, the mediating response to the sign is a replica of the response to the stimulus object, while representational mediation theory holds that this response is a "nonobservable proper part (but not replica)" of the total response to the stimulus object (Osgood, 1968).

Representational mediation can be divided into two processes, decoding and encoding. Decoding involves the association of signs with their mediating responses, or meaning. These reactions automatically produce internal stimulation. Decoding corresponds to the transition from surface to deep structure which appears in the linguists' accounts of language. Encoding is the reverse process in which the internal stimulation produced by the mediating responses evokes overt acts such as speaking, gesturing, or obeying commands. Since these two processes can occur independently of one another, a child usually learns the meaning of words before learning how to speak them (Osgood, 1957). Osgood further suggests that semantic and syntactic features of language are not basically different, but fall on a continuum.

Osgood, Suci, and Tannenbaum (1969) see the mediating response as being compound rather than simple. They have developed a method for measuring this response called the semantic-differential technique. Subjects rate words in terms of a pair of polar terms, such as hot-cold. These judgments are then correlated and used in various ways. It is assumed that these pairs of polar terms correspond to the components of the mediating response. The particular pair of terms indicates which response is being measured, while the extremity of the judgment reflects the intensity of the response. Each component response is seen as a pair of "reciprocally antagonistic" reactions like the polar terms.

Goodman. Goodman (1968, 1976) is particularly concerned with the application of psycholinguistics to the reading process. Without going into the specifics of reading, we can extract the pertinent points that Goodman makes about children and language.

Words exist only within the flow of language. Neither words nor morphemes can be defined, pronounced, or classified outside of this language stream of varying intonation, pitch, stress, and juncture. Goodman's (1965) study showed that primary school children may be unable to decode words in isolation, but are able to read the same words successfully in a running context. When given a list of words to learn, children were "calling names," a procedure more difficult than reading. Syntactic context is essential in both language learning and reading. Recognition of individual words only contributes to comprehension of meaning, whereas total comprehension involves reactions to several signal cores such as: order of words (syntax pattern), intonation, inflection, and certain key functions that words play (pattern markers).

Children already know these systems, which operate in the perceptual process of knowing language, by the time they begin to read. Their knowledge of the structural system of the sound and grammar they use in speech sets up certain expectations that strongly influence perception. When this basic knowledge is recognized by instructors, it will be seen as forming the linguistic basis of perception in reading. Thus, Goodman views the reading process as a "psycholinguistic guessing game" in which thought and language interact. According to his model, the reader fixes at a point and begins a selection process, picking up graphic cues based on prior choices, language knowledge, cognitive styles, and learned strategies. From what is seen and what is expected, the reader forms a perceptual image, then searches memory for matching syntactic, semantic, and phonological cues. Then more graphic cues may be selected or the perceptual image may be reformed. Here the reader makes a guess or tentative choice, stores the extracted meaning in short term memory, and continues reading. If a guess is not possible, the recalled input is checked and another attempt is made. Thus, the reader can make a choice based on decoding or, if this is still not acceptable semantically or syntactically, can regress until an acceptable choice is forthcoming, at which point reading continues. Basically, proficient readers decode directly from the graphic stimuli and then encode from the deep structure. Improvement in reading skill, according to Goodman, is not due to greater precision, but to better sampling techniques, firmer control over language structure, broadened experience, and increased conceptual development, which make possible more accurate first guesses.

Although Goodman's model is based upon adult readers, it does have implications for the teaching of reading. Goodman's work on the oral reading of beginners indicates that it is wrong to emphasize exact recitation of the graphic stimulus, since this does not really indicate that the child understands what is being read. Moreover, correct meaning can be extracted without voicing the precise morphemes or phonemes.

Ruddell. Ruddell (1976) has proposed a systems of communication model, including use of language, perception, and reading. It is based on his division of language into the following three levels: 1) the "surface" level, including morphemic and syntactic components; 2) the "interpretation" level, including structural and semantic components; and 3) the "deep structure," including integration and storage. Ruddell's model assumes the reality of surface structure, language processing through structural and semantic readings, deep structure, short and long term memory, feedback mechanisms, and the importance of affective mobilizers and cognitive strategies. According to this model, reading is

> complex psycholinguistic behavior which consists of decoding written language units, processing the resulting language counterparts through structural and semantic dimensions, and interpreting the deep structure data relative to an individual's established objectives (1976, p. 452).

Ruddell points out two important aspects of a child's language development. First, he states that a childs ability to comprehend oral or written language seems to be a function of the ability to see relationships among the elements in a sentence. He cites Strickland's (1962) evidence that children who use movables and subordination in oral language are better at reading these features. Second, Ruddell's (1965) study of fourth graders' oral reading language patterns compared to written patterns in their reading texts, reveals that the children's reading comprehension scores were significantly higher for passages reflecting their oral patterns of speech than for those passages that differed from these oral patterns.

This model is interactive in the sense that Ruddell is interested in the mutual effects that reader and text have upon each other in the process of reading. Print activates both linguistic and cognitive (perhaps neutral) patterns in the mind of the reader. What these patterns are in turn influences the understanding of the text. As children develop cognitive strategies and more sophisticated language patterns, the two-way influence becomes stronger. For example, readers may use higher order clues at the morphophonemic-morphographemic level, or use feedback from the deep structure of the sentence to derive meaning. An important implication of Ruddell's work is that the child's linguistic development must be carefully appraised and, if necessary, specifically improved before effective communication through speaking and reading can be achieved.

Brown. E. Brown (1970) proposes a model of the reading process related to recent work in psycholinguistics. He contends that research into the acquisition of reading which emphasizes learning principles is misconceived. Learning, in its classical sense as a configuration of dynamic variables underlying a more or less unitary process, may not be the central factor in reading. Instead, he postulates that reading is far more intimately related to a necessary substratum of normal oral language development, having to do more with biological maturation than learning (cf. Lenneberg, 1964, 1967). His model is an elaboration of Chomsky and Halle's (1968) outline of the process of reading aloud with certain analysis by synthesis modifications. The text is scanned with syntactic and semantic expectancy; words and short phrases are recognized through a word filter device and stored in short term memory in the form of abstract articulatory features. The abstract set of symbols is checked for punctuation to determine where to segment the text. If the input is not compatible with the most recently generated surface, a heuristic analyzer searches the contents in short term memory for clues to the various deep structure strings that will generate the sequence. It identifies the logical subject and main verb paying special attention to the analysis of verbs, and attempts to recover the deep structure phrase marker configurations. The most probable hypothesis is first projected, but if blocking occurs, an error message signals the generation of another deep structure hypothesis. At this point, the reader determines whether the utterance is comprehensible, and may decide to recycle through the entire procedure.

Canale and Swain. A model of communicative competence has been advanced by Canale and Swain (1980) based on Halliday's work of the early 1970s on the functions of language. The "communicative competence" approach in foreign language teaching has assumed the force of a movement, superseding the overplayed audiolingual approach that enjoyed considerable popularity ten or fifteen years ago, but it has not had the same impact on the teaching of reading, even though conceptually there is no reason why it should not. There is fairly broad agreement that the model consists of four strands: grammatical competence, sociolinguistic competence, discourse competence, and strategic competence (Maley, 1984).

Grammatical competence involves mastery of the language code and focuses directly on the knowledge and skill required to understand and express accurately the literal meaning of utterances. This form of competence is well understood by teachers, and forms the larger part of communication instruction in many classrooms.

Sociolinguistic competence involves the ability to produce and understand utterances that are appropriate to the context in which they are uttered, and calls for sensitivity to such factors as status, role, social conventions, and degree of formality expected.

Discourse competence concerns the ability to combine grammatical forms and meanings expressed in different genres either in spoken or written language. A lack of such competence would be exhibited in a statement that, while linguistically sound, does not fit the discourse pattern. Both cohesion of form and coherence of meaning are necessary conditions for text unity, so a response may be grammatically and sociolinguistically correct, but appropriate in that it does not fit well with what has gone before. The features that distinguish rules of grammar from rules of discourse are still a matter of debate (Morgan, 1981).

Strategic competence refers to the verbal and nonverbal strategies used to compensate for breakdowns in communication or to enhance the effect of communication. In conversation, these might take the form of fillers such as "you know," and in print they might take the form of connecting sentences, recall devices such as "In our earlier discussion," or they might take the form of paraphrase in both spoken and written communication. Such features have recently been discussed in works by Fassman (1984) and Cusper (1984).

This fourfold classification has proved useful in terms of describing the dimensions of communicative competence, but it could also serve as a model for reading comprehension. Beyond comprehension of the literal message, comprehension becomes dependent on an appreciation of the nuances the writer's message has conveyed through the choice of words, the emphasis given to certain points, and the colorful use of prose. This appreciation is part of the prior knowledge a person brings to reading. Moreover, reading, like other forms of language learning, takes place in the social context of the classroom. Littlewood's (1981) description of the antecedents of children's confusions about the meaning of oral communication in terms of the four competencies could prove useful for reading diagnostic purposes.

A consideration of language acquisition models and their implications for reading soon leads to the problem of the relationship between cognition and language. The process of extracting meaning from print clearly involves not only a knowledge of the syntactic and semantic patterns of language, but also a shared background of concepts and ideas with the author of the text. McNeill (1970) believes that, unlike s-r theories, theories of cognitive development may be quite appropriate to the task of explaining language. The problem, as he sees it, is an empirical one. It consists of determining whether the known facts of linguistic development can be understood in terms of the theory. This enterprise, which he calls the problem of "cognition and language," must be distinguished from the opposite question of language influencing cognition, which historically has been called the problem of "language and cognition."

McNeill goes on to say that the problem of cognition and language has not been widely recognized, since the most comprehensive theories of cognitive development (Piaget, Bruner, Vygotsky) take the general form of language for granted. They have either concentrated on the problem of language and cognition, or the expression of thought in language — which again is a different problem. Moreover, McNeill expresses some doubt as to whether existing cognitive theories could be manipulated or extended to account for the known facts of linguistic development. Certainly it is difficult to take a global theory and make it fit a specific body of factual knowledge, though in principle it should be possible if the theory is as comprehensive as it claims to be.

Piaget. Piaget's (1970) theory is interdisciplinary and "involves, in addition to psychological elements, components belonging to biology, sociology, linguistics, logic, and epistemology" (p. 729). It begins by postulating a biologically based human need for activity and learning. The tendency toward equilibration is an internal regulatory force which is manifested in all life, but particularly in the development and activity of intelligence (Furth, 1969). Activity brings the child into situations that set up a tension. Through the complementary processes of assimilation and accommodation, the tension is resolved and the child moves to a new level of equilibrium. However, the developmental status of the child determines the kind of stimuli that will evoke a state of tension at any given time. During the sensorimotor period, for example, the child is learning about the environment by interacting with people and objects. The primary task at this age is to discover permanence and regularity in the objective phenomena that make up the child's world. Toward the end of this period, the child can hold these objects in memory by means of images and labels.

With regard to the relationship of his theory to linguistics, Piaget (1970) states that

> the contemporary work of Chomsky and his group on transformational grammars is not very far from our own operational perspectives and psychogenetic constructivism. But Chomsky believes in the hereditary basis of his linguistic structures, whereas it will probably be possible to show that the necessary and sufficient conditions for the construction of the basic units on which are founded the linguistic structures are satisfied by the development of sensorimotor schemata (p. 729).

The period of language acquisition falls almost entirely in the later sensorimotor and the preoperational stages of intellectual development, when the sounds of language come to have particular salience for the child. During this period (2 to 6 years) the semiotic function begins to operate. "[It] detaches thought from action and is the source of representation. Language plays an important part in this formative process" (Piaget and Inhelder, 1969, p. 85). The sensorimotor child's thought structures are limited to the here and now, and must progress step by step. By contrast, the preoperational child can represent all the elements of an organized thought simultaneously, can use a variety of symbols, and can range over space and time in the course of thinking. Use of symbols does not necessarily imply that the child knows the structures underlying the concepts expressed. Piaget and others have conducted a large number of studies showing the gradual metamorphosis in the content and structure of such concepts as space, time, right, left, brother, democracy, Protestant, justice. On the other hand, Piaget's theory implies that the prelingual child acquires a wealth of understanding about the continuity and regularity of the physical and social world without benefit of language. Language is structured by logic rather than the reverse. It is a highly sophisticated tool to be used in understanding the environment, but it cannot in itself bring about that understanding unless the symbol system is grounded in concrete experience.

Piaget draws a distinction between egocentric speech (which characterizes the first years of language usage and is largely an expression of the child's needs, impulses, and emotions) and sociocentric speech (which serves the purpose of relaying information). Egocentrism is an all-pervasive characteristic of the young child's thought; it represents an inability to view physical or mental phenomena from a perspective other than the one the child is currently taking. Speech is egocentric in the sense that it is not adapted to the listener. Manifestations of egocentric speech are found in monologues (individual and collective), repetitions, gestures, mimicry, and movements. Piaget's well-known example is the child's retelling of a story to a naive listener. The narrator omits significant detail and uses pronouns that are ambiguous in reference, etc. The result is a garbled and incomprehensible version of the original. It is also noticeable that, in making reference to themselves, children rarely use the personal pronoun, as though the implied subject were automatically understood by the listener.

In the preoperational stage, egocentric speech constitutes almost half of the child's utterances, but gradually it falls out of the language system to be replaced by socialized speech. The child is freed from dependence on immediate concrete experience by the use of symbols, but the symbols are still mobile and personal. However, the use of symbols is the first step in the development of representative thought. As the need to defend actions and thoughts is discovered, the child adapts and organizes thought to this end. Through repeated attempts to establish new levels of equilibrium, the child moves toward more sophisticated levels of logical, analytical thought characterized by the use of signs which, unlike the earlier symbol, have relatively fixed, interpersonal meaning. For Piaget, language is the vehicle which, through its interplay with the earliest forms of thought, enables the child to conceptualize the surrounding world, thus arriving at higher forms of representative thought.

The notion of schema plays a prominent role in Piaget's account of cognitive development. Schemata are the cognitive structures by which individuals intellectually adapt to and organize the environment (Wadsworth, 1971, p. 10). In infancy, schemata tend to be sequences of behavior such as sucking and grasping, but as the child's thought becomes operational, they will include informational items such as class membership as well as behavioral tendencies. Cognitive development is a process whereby schemata become elaborated and differentiated as well as coordinated with other schemata. Language plays an important role in this process.

Bruner. Bruner and his colleagues at the Harvard Center for Cognitive Studies have attempted to incorporate transformational grammar into a cognitive theory which in many respects resembles that of Piaget. Cognitive growth is "...the means by which growing human beings represent their experience to the world and...organize for future use what they have encountered" (Bruner, Goodnow, and Austin, 1956, p. 1).

Three major factors influence and guide cognitive growth: 1) the development of representation, 2) the impact of culture, and 3) the relationship of mankind's growth to evolutionary history. In western culture, language permeates all three factors. Language acquisition is included in the broader development of representation, cultural transmission is effected largely through the medium of language, so, through evolutionary history, language has become one of our most important and valued tools.

Development of representation follows three stages: the enactive (birth to 1 year), the iconic (1 to 4 years), and the symbolic representation period (4 and above). During the enactive period the child learns about the world through action, while in the iconic stage techniques of representation are acquired through imagery. Early in the iconic period the child's imagery is closely related to manipulation of objects, but by the end of this period the world can be represented "by an image, or spatial schema that is relatively independent of action" (Bruner, Olver, and Greenfield, 1966, p. 21). Like visual perception, the child's imagery is diffusely organized, concrete, marked by unsteadiness of attention, and organized around a minimal number of cues, but these characteristics are modified with the development of symbolic representation.

Symbolic activity stems from some primitive or protosymbolic system that is species-specific to humans (Bruner, Olver, and Greenfeld, 1966, p. 44) and is manifested in language, tool using, skilled forms of serial behavior, and the organization of experience. The first use of language involves the learning of arbitrary markers or names for the objects in the environment. Naming is accompanied by a primitive enactive form of categorization (e.g. the child places a pan in the kitchen cupboard showing that, in some sense, a class of "things that belong in the kitchen" has been developed). Meanings are gradually refined from early holophrastic speech (i.e. the use of single words to express complete sentences) enabling the child to organize thought by means of superordinate groupings. Hence, the emergence of language is dependent on prior experience, but once language is established, it serves as an instrument to advance thought to higher levels. This is possible because "surplus meaning" may be read into experience in accordance with the built-in implications of the rules of language. Language enables a child to think about thoughts, and to note contradictions between perceptions and linguistic representation of events. For example, in Piaget's well-known conservation experiment, a child may say: "This one looks bigger, but they are really the same," and can use this contradiction to grasp the concept of conservation.

The impact of the culture is seen in its predominant mode of representation. For an aborigine, the major mode is enactive as expressed in the work of farming and rituals of the dance. Bruner, Olver, and Greenfield (1966) point to differences in cognitive style between Mexican urban and rural children, and between Eskimo and suburban Boston children. The difference is "most compactly" described as a difference between abstractness and concreteness:

> We believe that the difference between the city child and the rural child derives from a differential exposure to problem solving and communication in situations that are not supported by context as is the case with, for example, most reading and writing (p. 315).

A technological society values abstracting abilities, and schools its children in their attainment. This achievement is possible only through the medium of language. Cognitive activity is a kind of information processing, and education is the learning of "technologies" that aid and direct cognition. Hence, the course of cognitive growth comes about not so much as a result of the individual's striving for equilibrium as in Piaget's theory, but rather through "the process of education."

Brown. For Roger Brown (1958), the major processes in acquiring a first language are: 1) the perception of linguistic categories, 2) the development of motor skills involved in pronunciation, 3) the formation of a generative grammar, and 4) the learning of referent categories. The central function of language is to make reference between linguistic and nonlinguistic forms. The nonlinguistic referents are classes or categories, not particular instances (e.g. "book" refers to a class of objects). Hence, in learning to apply names correctly, the child must learn to notice the distinctive characteristics of the members of a class, and to disregard the nonsignificant aspects. Much of this learning is prelinguistic. Even before the children speak or understand language, they are learning about the environment by handling objects and observing their surroundings. Thus, they form concepts of such universals as space, time, and physical objects. The child, and later the adult, learns to use knowledge of the environment to form the categories that correspond to names. Unlike the prelanguage universal concepts, later referent categories are of necessity culture bound, since words in different languages have different ranges of reference.

Brown cites evidence that, up to adolescence, children use classification strategies which are different from those of adults. Their notion of the relationship of subclasses to larger classes is imprecise. Being unable to subordinate a subclass to a larger grouping, they relate subclasses to one another. They classify in terms of "chain complexes" (i.e. to two objects which have a common characteristic is added a third object having a different characteristic in common with one of the first pair), rather than on the adult basis of a common denominator. Hence, although the formation of new reference categories goes on throughout the lifetime of the individual, it proceeds differently in childhood. For Brown, then, the model of language development is intimately bound up with the process of concept acquisition.

Schema theory. The notion of schema goes back to the gestalt psychologists and was postulated by Bartlett (1932) in his famous study on memory. Schema is also a key concept in Piaget's theory, as previously noted. However, the concept has recently been adopted by information processing theorists (Rumelhart, 1980; Schank and Abelson, 1977) and extended to explanations of basic processes of reading (Anderson and Pearson, 1984). Specifically, schema theory has raised a number of interesting related issues such as how information is stored in schemata (e.g. Collins and Quillian's cognitive economy hypothesis), how the choice of one schema from among many occurs in a given context, how the "slots" in a schema are "instantiated" (e.g. when the reader decides that Queen Elizabeth fits the slot for celebrity in the schema of "ship christening"), the allocation of attentional resources among various elements of a text, and the kinds of inference that must be postulated in a schematic-theoretic account of cognitive processing, especially as it takes place in reading (Anderson and Pearson, 1984).

Research on Semantic and Cognitive Models

Mediation. A wealth of literature on human mediation is available, primarily in the United States (reviewed by Spiker, 1963), and in the Soviet Union (reviewed by Slobin, 1966). It has been suggested that very young children do not make mediating responses (the "mediation-deficiency hypothesis," Reese, 1962), but that in older children such responses become unconscious and automatic (Jensen, 1966) as well as highly facilitating in problem-solving tasks, since they enable the subject to hold the solution in memory (Boat and Clifton, 1968; Potts, 1968). Of course, the mediating response may occasionally produce an incorrect solution, as when perceptual memory is distorted by the application of a label (Carmichael, Hogan and Walter, 1932), but this confirms rather than weakens the concept of mediation.

Hence, there is considerable experimental evidence to support the contention that the basic concepts of behaviorism correspond to psychological processes occurring within the organism.

Piaget's theory has generated a vast body of research, most of it related to the validation of his stages of intellectual development as manifested through the appearance of such concepts as conservation of mass, weight; and volume; number; class; moral rules. The study of language in the context of this theory and the nature of the relationship between the linguistic and cognitive aspects of development have received less attention.

Egocentrism. As noted earlier, a central concept in Piaget's theory is the egocentrism of the child. To study the egocentric nature of early speech, Glucksberg, Krauss, and Weisberg (1966) devised a task requiring young children to develop verbal referents for communicating about novel forms. The results showed that pairs of nursery school children were unable to converge upon a shared nomenclature for the novel form, though they performed better using phrases formulated by adults.

Egocentric speech, according to Piaget, falls out of the child's language system and is replaced by socialized speech. Vygotsky (1962) has hypothesized that egocentric speech becomes subvocal, but remains as a cognitive planning device. Kohlberg, Yaeger, and Hjertholm (1968) report that private speech is common among children four to six years of age, declines regularly thereafter, and is virtually absent in older children. The incidence of egocentric speech appears to reflect primarily the child's level of cognitive development, but also reflects the functional demands of the situation.

Elkind (1970) has pointed out another aspect of egocentrism which has direct application to reading. According to Piaget, the preoperational child's perception and thought are "centered"—the child can focus on only one aspect of a situation at a time. A young child whose perception is not yet decentered will have problems with figure-ground effects, in this case with the discrimination of printed symbols. Elkind has designed a series of games to train perceptual skills, and has discovered that innercity children's reading improves as a result of such training (Elkind and Deblinger, 1969). Centration also means that the child has difficulty dealing with two elements at the same time. According to Elkind (1970), this may mean that the child is having difficulty dealing simultaneously with the shape and sound of the letter, the phoneme-grapheme relationship that

Gibson and her colleagues (1975) have indicated as being an important feature in learning to read.

Research stemming from schema theory has accumulated rapidly and is too voluminous to be summarized here. However, the interested reader will find several reviews, the most recent being the previously cited chapter by Anderson and Pearson (1984).

Critique of Semantic and Cognitive Theories

Mediation. Fodor (1965) has objected to the analysis of meaning in terms of mediational responses, pointing out that not all words refer directly to things, and that even those that do may have several referents; words refer to categories, not things (Brown, 1958). The mediating responses often seem to be images (Mowrer, 1960; Staats and Staats, 1963), but image theories of meaning present many problems (Brown, 1958).

Basically, the linguists' position is that behaviorist models are simply incapable of accounting for the known facts of language development. Behaviorists in turn dismiss this contention, maintaining that "integrated learning theory is fully capable of indicating in a credible and useful manner how language behaviors mediate such cognitive behaviors as reasoning, problem solving, intelligence, perception, and so on" (Staats, 1968, p. 158). Likewise, MacCorquodale (1969, 1970) has dismissed Chomsky's review as irrelevant to Skinner's account of verbal behavior. In spite of these disclaimers, satisfactory response to the powerful arguments enumerated are no more forthcoming today than they were ten years ago.

Goodman's model is important because it emphasizes the element of meaning that is often lost sight of in perceptual or component skills models. Extracting meaning from the printed page is the essence of reading, but even the fluent reader sometimes fails to grasp what is being read if attention is diverted elsewhere, even though all the words have been correctly decoded. The material has been perused, recognized as grammatical and meaningful, but in some way has failed to be assimilated into the deep structure. We need to understand more fully the nature of this assimilation process. Schema theory may provide a partial answer, but much work remains to be done.

Ruddell's is one of the most comprehensive models, encompassing as it does considerations of grapheme-phoneme correspondence, short and long term memory, linguistic and nonlinguistic meanings, transformational and rewrite rules, feedback mechanisms, affective mobilizers, and cognitive strategies. However, the relationships among these components require further clarification. The research literature Ruddell cites in support of his model is rather loosely related to the model and cannot be considered as constituting a test of the model.

Perhaps the greatest criticism of cognitive models is that they fail to account specifically for the facts of language development. It is not so much that linguistic facts are incompatible with the models as that they seem irrelevant to them.

Yet the cognitive and language functions are interdependent, and their developmental paths are intertwined. It is difficult to see how a theory in either area can be considered adequate if it fails to take account of existing theories and facts in the other. Piaget's theory is one of the most comprehensive and interdisciplinary of the cognitive models and, as previously noted, he and Sinclair-de-Zwart have attempted to incorporate linguistic data into the general framework of the theory.

Schema theoretic models have had an enormous influence on reading research and, to a lesser extent, on reading instruction. Kamil (1984) suggests that one reason for this burst of activity and for the change in research style that he sees as another outcome is that "schema theoretic models are at the same time more powerful and less constrained than their predecessors. They explain flexible behaviors in reading well. They also explain other behaviors, however, including logically inconsistent ones" (p. 40). Schema theory provides a cognitive account of the ways in which individuals process and store information which is later retrieved and brought to the task of comprehending text. As such, it deals with the propositional content of the stored schema. One task that remains, however, is to determine how the linguistic content of schemata develops, especially if the theory is to be equal to the task of explaining reading acquisition (cf. Kamil, 1984, p. 43). Perhaps Piaget's extensive work on the development of his version of schemata would be germane to this effort.

Future Model Building

The pursuit of research stemming from the various models described has done much to improve our understanding of the reading process. However, there is no model, psychological or linguistic, that is adequate to explain reading. Even less could it truthfully be asserted that the goal of integrating the existing models (which was the aim of the Literature Search Project) is any closer today than it was fifteen years ago. In fact, doubt has been expressed in some quarters (Gibson and Levin, 1975) as to the value of models, and this may account for a decreased reliance on models as a basis for research (Kamil, 1984). On the other hand, it may be that some model building has been premature. It is the complexity of the reading process rather than the inadequacy of models that is responsible for their limited usefulness. However, it does not follow that the search for models should be abandoned. They have served a useful purpose, not only in stimulating research, but in provoking counterproposals. The process whereby models are formulated, tested, criticized, elaborated, modified, and finally discarded in favor of more acceptable explanations is the process of science itself. All of the models reviewed here have implications for reading, and hence, for reading instruction. How they should be brought together is not entirely clear. What is clear is that the work of developing, integrating, and assessing the implications of the models must go on.

REFERENCES

Anderson, R.C., and P.D. Pearson, "A Schema-Theoretic View of Basic Processes in Reading." In P.D. Pearson, R. Barr, M.L. Kamil, and P. Mosenthal (Eds.), *Handbook of Reading Research.* New York: Longman, 1984, 255-291.

Athey, I. "Language Models and Reading," *Reading Research Quarterly,* 1971, 7, 16-110.

Bartlett, F.C. *Remembering.* Cambridge: Cambridge University Press, 1932.

Bellugi, U. "The Emergence of Inflections and Negation Systems in the Speech of Two Children," paper presented at the meeting of the New England Psychological Association, Boston, 1964.

Bereiter, C., and S. Engelmann, *Teaching Disadvantaged Children in the Preschool.* Englewood Cliffs, N.J.: Prentice-Hall, 1966.

Bever, T.G. "The Cognitive Basis for Linguistic Structures." In J.R. Hayes (Ed.), *Cognition and the Development of Language.* New York: Wiley, 1970.

Bever, T.G., J.A. Fodor, and W. Weksel. "On the Acquisition of Syntax: A Critique of 'Contextual Generalization'." *Psychological Review,* 72 (1965), 467-482.

Blount, B.G. "Acquisition of Language by Luo Children," unpublished doctoral dissertation, University of California at Berkeley, 1969.

Blumenthal, A.L. *Language and Psychology: Historical Aspects of Psycholinguistics.* New York: Wiley, 1970.

Boat, B.H., and C. Clifton, Jr. "Verbal Mediation in Four Year Old Children," *Child Development,* 39 (1968), 505-514.

Braine, M.D.S. "The Ontogeny of English Phrase Structure: The First Phase," *Language,* 39 (1963), 1-13.

Braine, M.D.S. "On the Basis of Phrase Structure: A Reply to Bever, Fodor, and Weksel." *Psychological Review,* 72 (1965), 483-492.

Brown, E.R. "Bases of Reading Acquisition," *Reading Research Quarterly,* 6 (1970), 49-74.

Brown, R.W. *Words and Things.* Glencoe, Ill.: Free Press, 1958.

Bruner, J.S., J.J. Goodnow, and G.A. Austin. *A Study of Thinking.* New York: Wiley, 1956.

Bruner, J.S., R.R. Olver, and P.M. Greenfield. *Studies in Cognitive Growth.* New York: Wiley, 1966.

Canale, M., and N. Swain. "Theoretical Bases of Communicative Approaches to Second Language Teaching and Testing," *Applied Linguistics,* 1 (1980), 1-47.

Carmichael, L., H.P. Hogan, and A.A. Walter. "An Experimental Study of the Effect of Language on the Representation of Visually Perceived Form," *Journal of Experimental Psychology,* 15 (1932), 73-86.

Carroll, J.B. *Language and Thought.* Englewood Cliffs, N.J.: Prentice-Hall, 1964(a).

Chomsky, N.A. *Syntactic Structures.* The Hague: Mouton, 1957.

Chomsky, N.A. "Review of B.F. Skinner," *Verbal Behavior. Language,* 35 (1959), 26-58.

Chomsky, N.A. "Some Methodological Remarks on Generative Grammar," *Word,* 17 (1961), 219-239.

Chomsky, N.A. *Current Issues in Linguistic Theory.* The Hague: Mouton, 1964.

Chomsky, N.A. *Aspects of a Theory of Syntax.* Cambridge, Mass.: MIT Press, 1965.

Chomsky, N.A. "Language and Mind." *Psychology Today,* 2 (1968), 280-286.

Chomsky, N.A., and M. Halle. *The Sound Pattern of English.* New York: Harper and Row, 1968.

Cusper, L. *It's Up to You: Language Skills and Strategies for Getting a Job.* New York: Longman, 1984.

Elkind, D. "Reading, Logic, and Perception: An Approach to Reading Instruction." In D. Elkind, *Children and Adolescents: Interpretive Essays on Jean Piaget.* New York: Oxford University Press, 1970.

Elkind, D., and J. Deblinger. "Perceptual Training and Reading Achievement in Disadvantaged Children," *Child Development,* 40 (1969), 11-19.

Ervin, S.M. "Imitation and Structural Change in Children's Language." In E.H. Lenneberg (Ed.), *New Directions in the Study of Language.* Cambridge, Mass.: MIT Press, 1964.

Fassman, P. *Listening and Communication Practices for Low/Intermediate Students.* New York: Longman, 1984.

Fodor, J.A. "How to Learn to Talk: Some Simple Ways." In F. Smith and G.A. Miller (Eds.), *The Genesis of Language: A Psycholinguistic Approach.* Cambridge, Mass.: MIT Press, 1966.

Fodor, J.A. "Current Approaches to Syntax Recognition," *Perception of Language*, a symposium of the Learning Research and Development Center, University of Pittsburgh, 1969.

Fodor, J.A., and T.G. Bever. "The Psychological Reality of Linguistic Segments," *Journal of Verbal Learning and Verbal Behavior*, 4 (1965), 4-20.

Fraser, C.C. "Comments in Response to McNeil's 'The Creation of Language by Children'." In J. Lyons and R. Wales (Eds.), *Psycholinguistics Papers*. Edinburgh: University of Edinburg Press, 1966.

Furth, H. *Piaget and Knowledge*. Englewood Cliffs, N.J.: Prentice-Hall, 1969.

Gibson, E.J., and H. Levin. *The Psychology of Reading*. Cambridge: MIT Press, 1975.

Glucksberg, S., R. Krauss, and R. Weisberg. "Referential Communication in Nursery-School Children: Method and Some Preliminary Findings." *Journal of Experimental Child Psychology*, 3 (1966), 333-342.

Goodman, K.S. "A Linguistic Study of Cues and Miscues in Reading," *Elementary English*, 42 (1965), 639-643.

Goodman, K.S. (Ed.). *The Psycholinguistic Nature of the Reading Process*. Detroit: Wayne State University Press, 1968, 15-26.

Goodman, K.S. "Behind the Eye: What Happens in Reading." In H. Singer and R.B. Ruddell (Eds.), *Theoretical Models and Processes of Reading*, second edition. Newark, Del.: International Reading Association, 1976, 259-272.

Gray, B.B., and L. Fygentakis. "The Development of Language as a Function of Programmed Conditioning," *Behavioral Research and Therapy*, 6 (1968), 455-460.

Hart, B.M., and T.R. Risley. "Use of Descriptive Adjectives in the Speech of Preschool Children, *Journal of Applied Behavior Analysis*, 1 (1968), 109-120.

Hayes, J.R. (Ed.). *Cognition and the Development of Language*. New York: Wiley, 1970.

Jakobson, R. *Kindersprache, Aphasie, and Allgemeine Lautgesetze*. Uppsala: Almquist and Weksell, 1941.

Jakobson, R. *Child Language, Aphasia, and General Sound Laws* (translated by A. Keller). The Hague: Mouton, 1968.

Jenkins, J.J., and D.S. Palermo. "Mediation Processes and the Acquisition of Linguistic Structure. *Monographs of the Society for Research in Child Development*, 29 (1964), 141-169.

Jensen, A.R. "Conceptions and Misconceptions about Verbal Mediation." *Proceedings, Claremont Reading Conference,*1966, 134-141.

Kamil, M.L. "Current Traditions in Reading Research." In P.D. Pearson, R. Barr, M.L. Kamil, and P. Mosenthal (Eds.), *Handbook of Reading Research*. New York: Longman, 1984, 39-62.

Katz, J. *The Philosophy of Language*. New York: Harper and Row, 1966.

Kernan, K.T. "The Acquisition of Language by Samoan children," unpublished doctoral dissertation. University of California at Berkeley, 1969.

Kohlberg, L., J. Yaeger, and E. Hjertholm. "Private Speech: Four Studies and a Review of Theories," *Child Development*, 39 (1968), 671-690.

Lashley, K.S. "The Problem of Serial Order in Behavior." In L.A. Jeffress (Ed.), *Cerebral Mechanisms in Behavior*. New York: Wiley, 1951, 112-136.

Lenneberg, E.H. "Biological Perspectives of Language." In E.H. Lenneberg (Ed.), *New Directions in the Study of Language*. Cambridge, Mass.: MIT Press, 1964.

Lenneberg, E.H. *Biological Foundations of Language*. New York: Wiley, 1967.

Littlewood, W.T. "Situational Variation in English." *English Language Journal*, 35 (1981), 97-100.

MacCorquodale, K. "B.F. Skinner's *Verbal Behavior:* A Retrospective Appreciation," *Journal of Experimental Analysis of Behavior*, 12 (1969), 831-841.

MacCorquodale, K. "On Chomsky's Review of Skinner's *Verbal Behavior*," *Journal of Experimental Analysis of Behavior*, 13 (1970) 83-99.

Maley, A. "On Chalk and Cheese," Keynote address, TESOL Conference, Houston, 1984.

McCawley, J.D. "The Role of Semantics in a Grammar." In E. Bach and R.T. Harms (Eds.), *Universals in Linguistic Theory*. New York: Holt, Rinehart, and Winston, 1968, 125-170.

McNeill, D. "Developmental Psycholinguistics." In F. Smith and G.A. Miller (Eds.), *The Genesis of Language: A Psycholinguistic Approach*. Cambridge, Mass.: MIT Press, 1966, 15-84.

McNeill, D. "On Theories of Language Acquisition." In T.R. Dixon and D.L. Horton (Eds.), *Verbal Behavior and General Behavior Theory*. Englewood Cliffs, N.J.: Prentice-Hall, 1968.

McNeill, D. "The Development of Language." In P.H. Mussen (Ed.), *Carmichael's Manual of Child Psychology*, third edition. New York: Wiley, 1970, 1061-1161.

Morgan, J. *Discourse Grammar and Linguistic Theory*. Georgetown University Round Table, March 1981.

Mowrer, O.H. "Hearing and Speaking: An Analysis of Language Learning." *Journal of Speech and Learning Disorders,* 23 (1948), 143-152.

Mowrer, O.H. The Psychologist Looks at Language," *American Psychologist,* 9 (1984), 660-694.

Mowrer, O.H. *Learning Theory and the Symbolic Process.* New York: Wiley, 1960.

Olson, D.R. "Language and Thought: Aspects of a Cognitive Theory of Semantics," *Psychological Review,* 77 (1970), 257-273.

Osborn, J. "Teaching a Teaching Language to Disadvantaged Children." In M.C. Templin (Ed.), *Monographs of the Society of Research in Child Development.* Chicago: University of Chicago Press, 1968.

Osgood, C.E. "Motivational Dynamics of Language Behavior." In M.R. Jones (Ed.), *Nebraska Symposium on Motivation.* Lincoln: University of Nebraska Press, 1957.

Osgood, C.E. "Toward a Wedding of Insufficiencies." In T.R. Dixon and D.L. Horton (Eds.), *Verbal Behavior and General Behavior Theory.* Englewood Cliffs, N.J.: Prentice-Hall, 1968.

Osgood, C.E. "The Nature and Measurement of Meaning." In J.S. Snider and C.E. Osgood (Eds.), *Semantic Differential Techniques.* Englewood Cliffs, N.J.: Prentice-Hall, 1969, 406-420.

Osgood, C.E., G.J. Suci, and P.H. Tannenbaum. "The Measurement of Meaning." In J.S. Snider and C.E. Osgood (Eds.), *Semantic Differential Techniques.* Englewood Cliffs, N.J.: Prentice-Hall, 1969.

Penney, M., H.F. Hjelm, and W.J. Gephart. "The Targeted Research and Development Program on Reading," *American Educational Research Journal,* 7 (1970), 425-448.

Piaget, J. "Piaget's Theory." In P.H. Mussen (Ed.), *Carmichael's Manual of Child Psychology,* third edition. New York: Wiley, 1970, 703-732(a).

Piaget, J., and B. Inhelder. *The Psychology of the Child.* New York: Basic Books, 1969.

Potts, M. "The Effect of a Morphological Cue and of Distinctive Verbal Labels on the Transposition Responses of Three, Four and Five Year Olds," *Journal of Experimental Child Psychology,* 6 (1968), 75-86.

Reese, H.W. "Verbal Mediation as a Function of Age Level," *Psychological Bulletin,* 59 (1962), 502-509.

Ruddell, R.B. "The Effect of the Similarity of Oral and Written Patterns of Language Structure on Written Comprehension," *Elementary English,* 42 (1965), 403-410.

Ruddell, R.B. "Psycholinguistic Implications for a Systems of Communication Model." In H. Singer and R.B. Ruddell (Eds.), *Theoretical Models and Processes of Reading,* second edition. Newark, Del.: International Reading Association, 1976, 452-469.

Rumelhart, D.E. "Schemata: The Building Blocks of Cognition." In R.J. Spiro, B.C. Bruce, and W.F. Brewer (Eds.), *Theoretical Issues in Reading Comprehension.* Hillsdale, N.J.: Erlbaum, 1980.

Sapon, S.M. "Shaping Productive Verbal Behavior in a Nonspeaking Child: A Case Report," *Georgetown University Monograph Series,* No.19, 1966.

Schank, R.C., and R. Abelson. *Plans, Scripts, Goals, and Understanding.* Hillsdale, N.J.: Erlbaum, 1977.

Skinner, B.F. *Contingencies of Reinforcement: A Theoretical Analysis.* New York: Appleton-Century-Crofts, 1969.

Slobin, D.I. "Comments on Developmental Linguistics: A Discussion of McNeill's Presentation." In F. Smith and G.A. Miller (Eds.), *The Genesis of Language.* Cambridge, Mass.: MIT Press, 1966(a).

Slobin, D.I. "Grammatical Transformations and Sentence Comprehension in Childhood and Adulthood," *Journal of Verbal Learning and Verbal Behavior,* 5 (1966b), 219-227(b).

Slobin, D.I. *The Ontogenesis of Grammar: Facts and Theories.* New York: Academic Press, 1971(a).

Slobin, D.I. *Psycholinguistics.* Glenview, Ill.: Scott, Foresman, 1971(b).

Slobin, D.I., and C.A. Welsh, "Elicited Imitation as a Research Tool in Developmental Psycholinguistics," unpublished paper, Department of Psychology, University of California at Berkeley, 1967.

Spiker, C.C. "Verbal Factors in the Discrimination Learning of Children," *Monographs of the Society for Research in Child Development,* 28 (1963), 53-68.

Staats, A.W. *Learning Language and Cognition.* New York: Holt, Rinehart, and Winston, 1968.

Staats, A.W., and C.K. Staats. "A Comparision of the Development of Speech and Reading Behaviors with Implications for Research." *Child Development,* 33 (1962), 831-346.

Staats, A.W., and C.K. Staats. *Complex Human Behavior.* New York: Holt, Rinehart, and Winston, 1963.

Strickland, R.G. "The Language of Elementary School Children: Its Relationship to the Language of
    Reading Textbooks and the Quality of Reading of Selected Children," *Bulletin No. 38.*
    Bloomington, Ind: School of Education, Indiana University, 1962.
Vygotsky, L. *Thought and Language.* Cambridge, Mass.: MIT Press, 1962.
Wadsworth, B.J. *Piaget's Theory of Cognitive Development.* New York: McKay, 1971.
Weiss, H.H., and B. Born. "Speech Training or Language Acquisition," *American Journal of Ortho-
    psychiatry,* 37 (1967), 49-55.

Oral and Written Language Acquisition and the Reading Process

ROBERT B. RUDDELL
University of California at Berkeley

MARTHA RAPP HAGGARD
Sonoma State University

Language acquisition is indeed a complex process. Upon entry into first grade, children have become skilled users of their native language. Their demonstrated ability ranges from recognition and production of novel sentences to comprehension of sentences possessing an identical surface structure but a different semantic base; e.g., "Ms. Jones is easy to please." versus "Ms. Jones is eager to please." They can effectively comprehend stories, and possess the ability to retell stories using features of a specific genre; e.g., "once upon a time...." Skilled though they are, however, children acquire substantial language maturity as they progress through elementary school. The purpose of this paper is to examine continued language acquisition in the early school years and explore its relationship to the reading process.

A major theme emerging from recent literature in language development is the notion that children are theory builders and hypothesis testers. Clark and Clark (1977) and DeStefano (1978) suggest that throughout the process of acquiring oral language, children actively construct "rules" about how the language works based upon adult models and responses. Hypotheses, subsequently generated according to operating principles (Slobin, 1973), are then tested to achieve a fit between the language of their environment and the language they produce. Parallel views are held in the areas of written language development (Ferriero, 1978a; Clay, 1980; Harste, Burke and Woodward, 1982), spelling (Read, 1975; C. Chomsky, 1975), and reading (Clay, 1969; 1979). Central to this view is the importance of meaning as a driving force in all language growth (Halliday, 1975). Children are constantly searching to make sense of their world through hypothesis generation and testing, and at various stages, change or adjust these hypotheses when they notice a sufficient number of conflicting exemplars (Clay, 1983). Support for the hypothesis building perspective can be found in the consistency with which children advance through stages of oral and written language development, and the observed tendency for children to overregularize oral and written language forms within these stages (Clark and Clark, 1977). The following discussion will address the acquisition and control of the structure and functions of oral language, the acquisition of written language structure and forms, and the relationship between language production and the reading process.

Oral Language Acquisition

Phonological and morphological development. Various studies have consistently shown that by the time children enter first grade they have a high degree of control over the phonological system (McCarthy, 1954; Templin, 1957). In fact, by the age of four or five, children have mastered the great majority of English sounds (Ervin and Miller, 1963). Exceptions generally occur as a result of developmental differences (Menyuk, 1971) or in the acquisition of strident clusters (Menyuk, 1984). Whorf (1956) and Gibson and Levin (1975) suggest that by age four, children have developed a phonological rule system. Messer (1967) found that when preschool children were asked to judge which of a possible and impossible cluster sounded more like a word, e.g., klec vs dlek, they chose words conforming to English phonology. Menyuk (1968) and Morehead (1971) examined the ability of children and adults to imitate pronunciation of possible and impossible clusters. At all ages, subjects imitated English-like words more correctly than impossible clusters, and demonstrated a higher percentage of correctness the closer the pseudowords resembled English.

Morphological development, as with phonological development, is well along upon entrance to school (Berko, 1958; Ruddell and Graves, 1967). Age differences do exist, however, in acquisition and control of various morphemes (Berko, 1958; Newfield and Schlanger, 1968; Anisfeld and Tucker, 1967), with acquisition extending well into primary grades. Nevertheless, the order of acquisition appears to be highly consistent (R. Brown, 1973; De Villiers and De Villiers, 1973); children go through four developmental stages consisting of 1) little or no use, 2) sporadic use, 3) overregularization, and 4) adult like use, in gaining control of each morpheme (Cazden, 1968).

Syntactical development. The control of syntactical patterning by preschool and primary grade children has been demonstrated in various studies including those by Fraser, Bellugi, and Brown (1963); Brown and Fraser (1964); Strickland (1962); Loban (1963, 1976); Ruddell and Graves (1967); O'Donnell, Griffin, and Norris (1967); Chomsky (1969); and Athey (1977). These studies indicate that kindergarten and first grade children are able to comprehend sentences and produce expanded and elaborated sentences through the use of movables (words, phrases, or clauses with no fixed position in the sentence) and transformed subordinating elements. Menyuk (1984) suggests further that children first acquire the ability to comprehend and produce structures; second, to judge the correctness of structures; and finally, to make corrections.

The research evidence also suggests that development in syntactical control extends well into and perhaps through the elementary grades. Menyuk (1963) and Chomsky (1969) have identified sequential components in children's syntax extending from nursery school into the early grades. Menyuk noted that even in the first grade some patterns such as "if" and "so" clauses, perfects, and nominalizations were still in the process of development. DeStefano (1978) indicates that throughout the elementary years children's production of sentences moves from multiply conjoined ("I have a cat and he's black and he likes hot milk."), to embedded ("My black cat likes hot milk."). Lenneberg (1964) has discussed the difficulty presented by transformations in the passive voice for mentally retarded children. Strickland's work (1962) shows a definite relationship between oral production of complex sentences and grade level. Loban's research (1963) reveals a developmental sequence of sentence production complexity as children progress through the elementary grades.

The work of O'Donnell, Griffin, and Norris (1967) at kindergarten and grades one, two, three, four, and seven also lends support to the general notion of a developmental sequence of syntax acquisition in the elementary grades. These researchers have observed that some transformations, e.g., relative clause ("The man who was wearing a coat...") were used much more frequently in kindergarten than in later grades while other items, e.g., noun modification by a participle ("The man wearing a coat...") were more frequent in later grades. The researchers observed that such a developmental sequence would appear to be a logical one from the standpoint of subordination and sentence complexity in that many of the later constructions are derived from more complex deletion rules. Written language acquisition appears to follow a similar developmental pattern; it will be discussed in a later section.

Lexical development. Children's conceptual and lexical development make rapid progress during the preschool years; they recognize and possess control over many hundreds of words by the first year of school (Smith, 1926; Smith, 1941; Anderson and Freebody, 1981). During this time a variety of concepts are formulated as youngsters associate common properties of an object with the object label. As Vygotsky (1962) has pointed out, preschoolers call a cow a cow because it has horns, and a calf a calf because its horns are still small, while a dog is called a dog because it is small and has no horns. Eventually children come to conceptualize the arbitrary nature of language itself as they understand that word labels are assigned to concepts and that a particular label may represent several concepts, depending upon its contextual use.

Piagetian theorists (Piaget, 1967; Sinclair-deZwart, 1969) view language as stemming from thought that originates in sensorimotor experience; as children move through the cognitive stages of sensorimotor, preoperational thought, concrete operations, and formal operations, conceptual development precedes vocabulary acquisition. Lenneberg (1967) also believes that concept formation must occur prior to lexical development.

There is ample evidence to support the view that concepts develop along a continuum from concrete, through the semiconcrete or functional, to the abstract levels as illustrated in the research of Feifel and Lorge (1962). The work of Russell and Saadeh (1962) is also illustrative of research supporting such a continuum. These researchers contrasted student conceptual responses at grades three, six, and nine on multiple choice questions designed to measure various levels of abstraction. They concluded that third grade children favored concrete responses while sixth grade and ninth grade children favored functional and abstract responses. Asch and Nerlove (1967) found that acquisition of multiple meanings of words (e.g., run) occurs in a stepwise process which progresses from acquisition of concrete meanings as separate entities to more abstract meanings, and finally to the understanding that one label represents each of the meanings. Ervin-Tripp (1967) has emphasized in her extensive research of child language that conceptual maturation moves from concrete referents to hierarchies of superordinates which may have rather vague features (e.g., mammal, vertebrate) and nonvisible referents (e.g. politics, energy).

Clark's semantic feature hypothesis (1971) suggests, on the other hand, that superordinate lexical features are learned previous to, rather than following, more specific features. For example, in learning the words *before* and *after*, children may first associate both words with the concept of time, and use the words synonymously. Later, after differentiating between sequence and simultaneity, they understand that the words are opposites. Clark and Clark (1977) suggest that a possible explanation for the seeming discrepancy between learning orders (i.e., subordinate-to-superordinate versus superordinate-to-subordinate) may lie in the nature of the items being acquired. Superordinate first learning may apply predominantly to relational terms (e.g., before-after), while subordinate first learning occurs with lexical items on a concrete/abstract continuum (e.g., dog-mammal).

The influence of affect on word learning has been noted by Haggard (1980) in her study of conditions that precipitate word learning. She identified four specific developmental conditions in which elementary children learned new words independently: 1) because the word had an appealing sound or was perceived to be "adult," 2) the word occurred in an incident involving strong emotion, 3) the word had immediate usefulness, and 4) the word was common in peer group usage. Beyond the elementary years, the hierarchy is reversed, with peer group usage the most frequent condition. Haggard also found that rehearsal of the new word in a safe environment, such as among family and friends, influenced the acquisition of new words once meaning was determined.

Oral language acquisition extends from preschool through the elementary school grades. Phonological and morphological development are well established upon school entrance. Syntactical control increases through the elementary years, with greater sentence subordination and complexity occurring in the higher grades. Lexical growth appears to follow a concrete to abstract continuum, with the exception of relative terms, and to be influenced by social conditions and affect.

Written Language Acquisition

Preliterate writing. Recent interest in children's early writing has led to revised views of preschool children's language competence (Clay, 1983), and their concepts about written language (Harste, Burke and Woodward, 1982). The work of Clay (1975, 1983), Ferreiro (1978a, 1978b), and Dyson (1982) indicates that, beginning with pictorial representation, children attempt to connect speech with written language and understand the relationship of graphic symbols to sounds. Whether they use standard symbols or not, preliterate youngsters produce contextually appropriate writing, such as vertically aligned grocery lists and paragraphed letters to a grandparent (Harste, Burke, and Woodward, 1981). In their study of preschool children's written production, Harste, Burke, and Woodward (1982) conclude that 1) written language, like oral language, is learned naturally; 2) children in literate societies are involved at an early age in understanding and controlling print; and 3) children's perceptions of print are organized, systematic, and identifiable.

Closely related to investigations into children's early writing has been the study of children's invented spellings. Read (1971, 1975) and C. Chomsky (1971, 1979) found that invented spellings are systematic, rule governed, and consistent. Read's extensive work on the|origin|of invented spellings indicates that many such rules grow directly from children's attempts to map speech to print. In addition, developmental stages of spelling growth have been identified in which children move through prephonemic, early phonemic, letter name, and transitional stages to standard spelling (Beers and Henderson, 1977; Henderson and Beers, 1980; Gentry, 1978; Temple, Nathan, and Burris, 1981).

Stages of writing development. Various studies have examined the development of children's writing during elementary school years (Loban, 1963, 1976; Hunt, 1970; O'Donnell, Griffin and Norris, 1967). Generally, the complexity of children's written production increases steadily throughout elementary school, with early writing bearing close resemblance to spoken language. As with oral language development, progression appears to move from multiple conjoined sentences to embedded. A detailed study by Harrell (1957) compared selected language variables in the speech and writing of children aged nine, eleven, thirteen, and fifteen using a short movie as the speech and writing stimulus. The investigator found that the length of the compositions and clauses used in oral and written expression increased with age, with a large percentage of subordinate clauses being used by the older children in both written and spoken composition. The children were found to use a larger percentage of subordinate clauses in writing than in speaking. A larger percentage of adverbial clauses, except those of time and cause, were used in the children's speech. The developmental increase of each language variable in relation to age was found to be greater for written compositions than for oral.

Also of interest in the O'Donnell, Griffin, and Norris (1967) research was the finding of distinct variation in the syntax of speech and writing in grades three, five, and seven. At third grade, oral expression was deemed superior to written expression in sentence complexity, while at grades five and seven the reverse was true. These findings are similar to those of the previously mentioned Harrell study and suggest that by the intermediate grades children have some production control over stylistic variations which require more complex constructions in written expression.

By examining research which contrasts the language development of children possessing hearing deficiency with that of normal children, the relationship between oral language experiences and written language production is brought into sharper focus. Heider and Heider (1940) secured written compositions, based on a motion picture, from a large number of deaf and hearing children ranging in age from 11 to 17 years and 8 to 14 years, respectively. Although the deaf children were three years older, their compositions were found to resemble the less mature hearing children. The deaf children were found to use fewer numbers of words and clauses than the hearing children, while the hearing children used more compound and complex sentences with a larger number of words in coordinate and subordinate clauses, thus indicating a more advanced development in language production.

The written language of normal and hearing impaired children has been examined in Templin's research (1950). Children with hearing deficiencies were found to use more words in their explanations of natural phenomena than did hearing children of the same age, grade, and intelligence. This finding was interpreted to reflect less adequate control over vocabulary, and perhaps syntax, rather than representing a more complex type of expression. The hearing impaired children apparently needed more words to express a concept due to inability to express their ideas through elaborated sentences and more abstract vocabulary.

Both the Heider and Heider and the Templin studies point to a significant relationship between oral and written language development. The opportunity for oral language experience through hearing would appear to exert direct influence on performance in written language.

Danielewicz's extensive review (1984) suggests that children progress through stages of writing development in which they 1) *unify* spoken and written language, making few distinctions between the two; 2) *distinguish* between spoken and written language by reducing coordinating conjunctions; 3) *strip* features of spoken language from written production; and 4) *add* features typically associated with written language.

Written language development extends from preliterate writing through formal written production. While the stages of development are not sharply defined, a clear progression is noted in differentiation among spoken and written language, spelling, and syntactic complexity.

Factors Influencing Oral and Written Language Development

Various background variables have been credited with enhancement of language performance. John and Goldstein's verbal mediation research (1964) reveals that children's verbal interaction with mature speakers is of importance in making provision for testing tentative notions about word meanings.

Such opportunity would appear to produce greater verbal control and enable children to rely on words as mediators facilitating thought. Vygotsky (1962) has suggested that the availability of adults for dialogue with children is of great import to language acquisition. This consideration also receives support from Davis' early research (1937), which revealed that in families of only children language facility was found to develop more rapidly than in families of children with siblings; and children with siblings were found to develop language facility faster than twins.

Cazden's work (1965) with two and three year old children indicated that the use of full grammatical sentences in response to children's verbal expression and the expansion of their telegraphic speech to full adult grammatical sentences resulted in an increased level of performance on several measures of grammatical development when contrasted with a control group. The "richness of verbal stimulation" appeared to be important in extending grammatical control.

The effect of factors in the home environment on language achievement is evidenced in Milner's investigation (1963). Following the selection of high and low achievers in first grade reading, an indepth interview was carried out exploring the children's use of language in the home. Milner found that the high achieving children had an enriched verbal environment with more books available and were read to more often by highly esteemed adults than were the low achieving children. The high scoring children also engaged in conversation with their parents more often than the low scoring children. Milner noted further that in many of the homes of low scoring children a positive family atmosphere was not evident nor did the children have an adult interaction relationship established. There appeared to be little opportunity for these children to interact verbally with adults possessing adequate speech patterns and who were of high personal value to the children.

Recent studies have examined the relationship of various home and community factors on oral and written language development. These findings suggest that children from homes in which "children are to be seen and not heard" are not verbally assertive with adults (Ward, 1971), resulting in limited child-initiated verbal interaction. Children from middle class homes, however, are assertive and even "forward" with adults, and use language for clarification and extension of experience (Brown and Bellugi, 1964; Brown, 1973). In addition, middle class parents frequently imitate children's speech and provide expanded models of language during telegraphic sentence stages (Brown and Bellugi, 1964). Speidel (1982) notes that in middle class homes questioning routines are used to give information and teach concepts, e.g, "See the cow? What is the cow doing?"

whereas in low income Hawaiian-Creole homes, questions are used to notify children of a mistake or an error. As a consequence, Hawaiian-Creole children have difficulty participating in direct question episodes in the school environment. Tough (1977), in a longitudinal study of advantaged and disadvantaged children, found that advantaged children used language more frequently to project into the future, imagine, examine alternative explanations, and report on past and present experiences than did their counterparts.

It appears that children from language enriched homes have greater opportunity for success in literacy acquisition when the home language and literacy attitudes are similar to those of the school. Labov (1968) notes that children from black ghetto homes are highly verbal, but that rules of address, politeness, and adult-child verbal interaction are quite different from those of the school (1970). Gallimore, Boggs, and Jordan (1974) found that Hawaiian-Creole children were "manifestly competent" in home and community, where information giving and concept development are transmitted during group conversation or verbal play, but not at school where information sharing rules are distinctly different.

An important aspect of language learning is the acquisition of a wide range of language behaviors which allow children to function easily in home, community, and school settings. This range has been described by various researchers. Bernstein (1961, 1964) categorizes language into "restricted" and "elaborated" codes. Restricted code assumes shared knowledge, is often telegraphic, and uses limited subordination. Elaborated code is decontextualized, richer in explanation, and more syntactically complex. Halliday (1975) describes seven models, or functions, of language: instrumental, regulatory, interactional, personal, imaginative, heuristic, and informative. Further, Halliday posits that acquisition of the complete range is necessary for full communication.

Flexibility of language functioning develops as children acquire different language "registers" which include what is appropriate to talk about, when, with whom, how, and with what speech patterns (Smith 1981). Within the school setting, at least three types of functions, or registers, appear to be necessary. These are described with their oral and written forms in Figure 1.

Language Function	Oral Form	Written Form
Informal Personal Exchange	Greetings	Personal notes to friends
	Communications of feelings	Unedited written experiences
	Control of others' behavior	Memos and directions
Formal Informational Exchange	Classroom discussion	Edited experience stories
	Classroom lectures	Edited academic reports
	Public speeches	School textbooks
Literary Exchange	Drama and theater	Poetry, narrative, drama

Figure 1.   Classroom language functions.

Once a variety of registers is acquired, register switching allows adjustment to situational needs. Of particular importance to this discussion is acquisition of registers unique to school, language instruction (DeStefano, 1978), and the language of written text (Olson, 1977). The work cited suggests that children from language enriched backgrounds achieve control over a wider range of language registers than do children from less enriched backgrounds.

The Relationship of Oral and Written Language Acquisition to Reading

Reading-Decoding. Menyuk (1984) concludes that an interaction between language development and reading occurs once formal reading instruction begins. New categories of language are acquired and this knowledge is then applied in new domains. With regard to the phonological and morphological knowledge children bring to formal instruction, DeStefano (1978) cautions that it is important to determine whether children are operating from the adult rule system or their own, and to distinguish between their ability to perceive the rule system and apply it. These same cautions would appear to be equally useful for spelling and written production.

Linguists such as Venezky (1967), Wardhaugh (1968), and Reed (1966) have strongly recommended that it is necessary to consider letter patterns beyond the simple sound-letter correspondence level if a more consistent relationship between oral and written language forms is to be realized. This recommendation is based on the linguistic unit known as the morphophoneme, the intermediate (between phoneme and morpheme) sound-spelling unit. The importance of this unit is obvious at once in the examination of the words supreme and supremity; obscene, obscenity. In both cases we observe a consistent shift in the sound value /iy/ to /i/ in adding the suffix *ity*. The same principle is present in the letter pattern using the final *e* marker, e.g., sit /i/, site /ay/.

Consideration also needs to be given to the possible value of utilizing phonological or sound segmentation rather than morphological or word-affix segmentation in teaching decoding skills. An experiment by Rodgers (1967) asked children to repeat words containing two syllables, e.g., toas-ter, and the same words divided between the two morphemes, e.g., toast-er. He found that the children were more successful in redividing words along syllabic or phonological breaks than along the morphological breaks, thus supporting phonological segmentation.

The work by Gibson and her colleagues (1962) has indicated that children develop higher-order generalizations in the early stages of reading and that these generalizations follow English spelling patterns. The children in the experiment appeared to perceive regularities in sound and spelling patterns and transfer these to decoding unfamiliar trigrams even though taught by what the researchers refer to as the "whole word" approach. The described research thus suggests the possible value and need to consider decoding units which extend beyond sound-letter correspondences and account for more regularity and larger perceptual units in the English spelling system.

Study of nonstandard dialects provides evidence that such dialects are highly regular language systems (Lobov, 1968; Ruddell, 1974). This regular nature is evident in the l-lessness common to the nonstandard black dialect and results in consistent production of homonyms so that *toll* becomes *toe*, and *fault* becomes *fought*. The simplification of consonant clusters in final positions such as /st/ —> /s/ and the loss of /t/ and /d/ results in homonyms so that *past* becomes *pass*, *meant* becomes *men*, and *hold* becomes *hole*. Bilingual Hispanic children may have difficulty with vowel contrasts which distinguish the words b*i*t /i/ and b*e*at /iy/, b*e*t /e/ and b*ai*t /ey/; and initial consonant contrasts such as *s*ue /š/ and *z*oo /z/. Navajo children have difficulty with initial consonant distinctions in words like *v*ote /v/ and *b*oat /b/; and *ch*ip /č/ and *g*yp /ǰ/.

These variations in the phonological system may result in meaning confusion between dialect and standard English speakers in situations where sentence context is not sufficient to clarify the intended meaning. If we are to understand the relationship between the phonological system and the graphological system, it becomes clear that dialectal variation must be accounted for. Otherwise, the reading program makes false assumptions about the language performance of the nonstandard speaker and the teacher may attempt to develop inappropriate sound-letter correspondences.

The language differences of the nonstandard speaker also result in significant grammatical variations. The previously discussed l-lessness, for example, may affect future forms where *you'll* becomes *you*, *he'll* becomes *he*, and *they'll* becomes *they*. Thus, when reading the sentence, "He will go." as "He go.", children are consistently translating the sentence in their dialect. An example used by Shuy (1969) is the written sentence "John asked if Mary wore a coat." which is frequently read by the black child as, "John asked did Mary wear a coat." In this instance the substitution of *did* for *if* and *wear* for *wore* does not represent an error in reading in terms of the child's dialect. If, however, the child read "John asked Mary if did she wear a coat." or "John asked Mary if she wear a coat.", the alterations do vary from the consistent dialect form and would represent a reading difficulty. Consistent performance may thus be interpreted to indicate a high degree of language competence.

Of additional importance is the translation of oral language forms to written language equivalent required of children during initial reading instruction. For example, *hafta*, *gonna*, *hadda*, *oughta*, *hasta*, and *wanna* are quite appropriate in informal conversational settings, but in written language are realized as *have to*, *going to*, *had to*, *ought to*, *has to*, and *want to* (Lindsay, 1969). The contractions *I'll*, *she'll*, *he'll*, and *they'll* are commonly used in oral language situations; however, the written equivalents *I will*, *she will*, *he will*, and *they will* appear in many children's textbooks from the child's earliest encounter with printed matter.

Reading-comprehension. From the early study of mistakes in paragraph reading of sixth grade children, Thorndike (1917) noted that understanding a paragraph is dependent upon the reader's selection of the right elements and synthesizing them in the right relations. Children's ability to comprehend material whether written or spoken would seem to be a function of their ability to see the relationships between key elements in the sentence. Thus, relating various subordinating elements to the central idea of the sentence is of basic importance for comprehending the discourse.

Using a "disarranged phrase test," Gibbons (1941) studied the relationship between third grade children's ability to understand the structure of sentences and their reading achievement. She found a high correlation (.89) between the ability to see relationships between parts of a sentence and the ability to understand the sentence when intelligence was partialled out. A significant correlation (.72) was also found between the ability to see relationships between parts of sentences and total reading achievement.

The importance of familiarity with syntactic patterning to reading achievement is evident in MacKinnon's research (1959). In a detailed study of beginning readers, he observed that children attempted to substitute syntactic patterns which they had previously read and were familiar with in place of unfamiliar patterns in their attempt to read unfamiliar materials. Ruddell's study of fourth grade readers (1965) examined the effect on reading comprehension of written patterns of language structure which occur with high and low frequency in children's oral language. By controlling the vocabulary difficulty, sentence length, and subject matter content in a series of reading passages, the relationship between reading comprehension and pattern complexity was examined. Reading comprehension scores on passages written with high frequency patterns of language structure were found to be significantly superior to comprehension scores on passages written with low frequency patterns of language structure.

Children's understanding of sentence structure would be expected to enhance their ability to narrow alternate word meanings and thus contribute to comprehension. For example, the word *that* not only cues a noun which follows but may also clarify or emphasize the semantic nature of the noun, e.g., "*That* yellow canary ate the cat." versus "*Some* yellow canary ate the cat." Miller (1962) and Miller, et al. (1951) have demonstrated that words in context following a similar grammatical pattern are perceived more accurately than in isolation. Additional support for the importance of context in narrowing semantic possibilities is found in the research of Goodman (1965). He has shown that although children may be unable to read words in isolation, they deal successfully with the same words in a running context. These findings support the importance of contextual association which provides sufficient delimiting information to enable the child to determine the semantic role of a word and, further, to recognize and comprehend it in a sentence.

A longitudinal study by Ruddell (1966, 1968) has demonstrated that the sentence and paragraph meaning comprehension of first and second grade children can be significantly enhanced by emphasizing the meaning relationships between key structural elements within and between sentences. Additionally, Baele

(1968) found that by the end of third grade the children who had participated in the treatment stressing the relationship between key structure elements were expressing themselves in written form with longer communication units and with greater clausal depth, thus indicating control over more complex constructions and subordination in the written language performance.

Schema theorists suggest that comprehension occurs as the reader uses prior knowledge, represented as schemata, to make predictions, form hypotheses, and understand new information (Adams and Collins, 1979; Rumelhart and Ortony, 1977; Anderson, 1977; Rumelhart, 1984). The relationship between oral and written language development and comprehension is evident in the previously cited work by Tough (1977) in which children from language-rich home backgrounds regularly engaged in reporting on past and present experiences, examining alternatives, and projecting into the future. Kress (1955) found that achieving readers were superior to nonachievers in their versatility and flexibility, their ability to draw inferences from relevant clues, and their ability to shift set when new standards were introduced. There is considerable research to support the relationship between language comprehension and individuals' ability to change, modify, and reorganize previously formed concepts (Singer, 1966).

Kress further reported that achieving readers demonstrated more initiative in exhausting solutions and were found to persist in problem solving under changing conditions in contrast to the nonachieving readers. Durkin's extensive work (1961, 1966a) with preschool children suggests that early readers are individuals who are serious and persistent, are curious in nature, and possess the ability to concentrate. The research of Piekarz (1956) identified high level readers as individuals who provide significantly more responses in interpreting a reading passage, a trait indicating greater involvement and participation. High level readers were also found to be more objective and impersonal in synthesizing the information sought.

Knowledge of text structure and expectations for bookreading are additional important schemata for comprehension. Various researchers (Durkin, 1966b; Clay, 1979; Butler and Clay, 1979) have suggested that children who have been read to prior to school entry are more likely to succeed in learning to read and write. These children approach print with high meaning expectations and possess knowledge of and familiarity with story structure and the language of text. Heath (1982) found that children from communities with different attitudes toward written language transferred commmunity and home literary patterns to learning behaviors at school. Maintown children received early initiation to books, written and oral narrative, bookreading behaviors, and questioning routines. Roadville children were expected to accept the power of print through association with alphabet letters and workbook like activities. Trackton children lived in a highly oral community where storytelling and verbal attention getting skills were prized, and few children's books and bookreading activities were found in the home. Heath concluded that Maintown children entered school not only familiar with bookreading routines, but with comprehension strategies as well.

A common relationship between language and reading skill acquisition is found in the children's search for generalizations stemming from hypothesis formation and testing. Children appear to progress from sound-letter correspondence to higher order perceptual units which follow regular English spelling generalizations. Reading instruction must also account for consistent phonological and syntactical variations used by nonstandard speakers if decoding and meaning problems are to be avoided.

Knowledge of and familiarity with the form and function of text appear to be potential factors in the development of reading comprehension. Familiarity with lexical, syntactical, and structural elements of text increases children's ability to perceive accurate relations within text and formulate hypotheses upon which predictions about new information may be made. Further, in providing experiences with print and establishing the value of literacy, the home environment exerts strong influence in literacy acquisition.

Summary and Recommendations

In conclusion, upon entry to formal education, children display language performance which reflects a high degree of competence. Five significant factors appear to characterize initial language acquisition and subsequent development of language and reading skill. First, children are active theory builders and hypothesis testers; as such, their current rule system may or may not match the rule systems used by adults at home and school. Second, the driving force behind language performance and reading growth is children's need to obtain meaning — to make sense of the world. Third, language performance is directly related to language environment, including the available language models and opportunities for language interaction. Fourth, oral and written language acquisition are parallel and interactive in development. And fifth, oral and written language development are directly related to and interactive with reading acquisition and development.

This research review provides strong support for the interactive nature of oral and written language and the reading process. Additional research examining the nature of this interaction is of critical importance in formulating a theory of reading with strong explanatory power. Toward this end, the following areas of investigation are suggestive of needed direction for inquiry:

1. Research examining the relationship between children's preliterate experiences with text and reading acquisition.
2. Research examining the relationships among children's perception of reading instruction, text, and reading acquisition.
3. Longitudinal study of the process through which children develop lexical control during the elementary school years.
4. Longitudinal study of the relationship between lexical control and reading comprehension.

5. Qualitative research examining the relationship between children's meta-linguistic awareness of oral and written language functions and reading acquisition.
6. Ethnographic research studying the relationship between the literacy support systems in home and community environment and reading and writing acquisition.

REFERENCES

Adams, M.J., and A. Collins. "A Schema-Theoretic View of Reading." In R.O. Freedle (Ed.), *New Directions in Discourse Processing*. Norwood, NJ: Ablex, 1979.

Anderson, R.C. "The Notion of Schemata and the Educational Enterprise." In R.C. Anderson, R.J. Spiro, and W. Montague (Eds.), *Schooling and the Acquisition of Knowledge*. Hillsdale, NJ: Erlbaum, 1977, 415-431.

Anderson, R.C., and P. Freebody. "Vocabulary Knowledge." In J.T. Guthrie (Ed.), *Comprehension and Teaching: Research Reviews*. Newark, DE: International Reading Association, 1981.

Anisfeld, M.A., and G.R. Tucker. "English Pluralization Rules of Six Year Old Children," *Child Development*, 39 (1967), 1201-1217.

Asch, S.E., and H. Nerlove. "The Development of Double Function Terms in Children: An Exploratory Investigation." In J.P. DeCecco (Ed.), *The Psychology of Language, Thought, and Instruction*. New York: Holt, Rinehart and Winston, 1967, 283-291.

Athey, I. "Syntax, Semantics, and Reading." In J.T. Guthrie (Ed.), *Cognition, Curriculum, and Comprehension*. Newark, DE: International Reading Association, 1977, 71-98.

Baele, E.R. "The Effect of Primary Reading Programs Emphasizing Language Structure as Related to Meaning upon Children's Written Language Achievement at the Third Grade Level," unpublished doctoral dissertation, University of California at Berkeley, 1968.

Beers, J., and E.H. Henderson, "A Study of Developing Orthographic Concepts among First Graders," *Research in the Teaching of English, 11*, 1977, 133-148.

Berko, J. "The Child's Learning of English Morphology," *Word*, 1958, 140-177.

Bernstein, B. "Elaborated and Restricted Codes: Their Social Origins and Some Consequences," *American Anthropologist*, 66 (1954), 55-69.

Bernstein, B. "Social Structure, Language, and Learning," *Educational Research*, 3 (1961), 163-176.

Brown, R., and U. Bellugi. "Three Processes in the Child's Acquisition of Syntax." In E.H. Lenneberg (Ed.), *New Directions in the Study of Language*, Cambridge, MA: MIT Press, 1964, 131-162.

Brown, R., and C. Fraser. "The Acquisition of Syntax." In U. Bellugi and R.W. Brown (Eds.), *The Acquisition of Language*, Monographs for the Society for Research in Child Development, 29 (1964), 43-79.

Brown, R. *A First Language: The Early Stages*. Cambridge, MA: Harvard University Press, 1973.

Butler, D., and M.M. Clay. *Reading Begins at Home*. Exeter, NH: Heinemann Educational Books, 1979.

Cazden, C.B. "Environmental Assistance to the Child's Acquisition of Grammar," unpublished doctoral dissertation, Harvard University, 1965.

Cazden, C.B. "The Acquisition of Noun and Verb Inflections," *Child Development*, 39 (1968), 433-448.

Chomsky, C.S. *The Acquisition of Syntax in Children from 5 to 10*. Cambridge, MA: MIT Press, 1969.

Chomsky, C.S. "Write First, Read Later," *Childhood Education*, 47 (1971), 269-299.

Chomsky, C.S. "Invented Spelling in the Open Classroom," *Word*, 27 (1975), 499-518.

Chomsky, C.S. "Approaching Reading through Invented Spelling." In L.B. Resnick and P.A. Weaver (Eds.), *Theory and Practice of Early Reading*. Hillsdale, NJ: Erlbaum, 1979, 43-65.

Clark, E.V. "On the Acquisition of the Meaning of *Before* and *After*, *Journal of Verbal Learning and Verbal Behavior*, 10 (1971), 256-275.

Clark, H.H., and E.V. Clark. *Psychology and Language*. New York: Harcourt Brace Jovanovich, 1977.

Clay, M.M. "Reading Errors and Self-Correction Behaviour," *British Journal of Education,* 30 (1969), 47-56.

Clay, M.M. *What Did I Write?* Auckland, New Zealand: Heinemann Educational Books, 1975.

Clay, M.M. *Reading: The Patterning of Complex Behavior,* second edition. Auckland, New Zealand: Heinemann Education Books, 1979.

Clay, M.M. "Early Writing and Reading: Reciprocal Gains." In M. Clark and T. Glynn (Eds.) *Reading and Writing for the Child with Difficulties.* Occasional publication No. 8, *Educational Review,* University of Birmingham, 1980.

Clay, M.M. "Getting a Theory of Writing." In B.M. Kroll and G. Wells (Eds.) *Explorations in a Development of Writing.* New York: John Wiley and Sons, 1983.

Danielewicz, J.M. "Developmental Differences between Children's Spoken and Written Language," unpublished paper, University of California at Berkeley, 1984.

Davis, E.A. *The Development of Linguistic Skill in Twins, Singletons with Siblings, and Only Children from Ages Five to Ten Years.* Minneapolis: University of Minnesota Press, 1937.

DeStefano, J.S. *Language, the Learner and the School.* New York: John Wiley and Sons, 1978.

De Villiers, J.G., and P.A. De Villiers. "A Cross-Sectional Study of the Development of Grammatical Morphemes in Child Speech," *Journal of Psycholinguistic Research,* 2 (1973), 267-278.

Durkin, D. "Children who Learn to Read Before Grade One," *Reading Teacher,* 13 (1961), 163-166.

Durkin, D. "The Achievement of Preschool Readers: Two Longitudinal Studies," *Reading Research Quarterly,* 1 (1966a), 5-36.

Durkin, D. *Children Who Read Early.* New York: Teachers College Press, 1966b.

Dyson, A.H. (1982) "Reading, Writing, and Language: Young Children Solving the Written Language Puzzle," *Language Arts,* 59 (1982), 829-839.

Ervin, S.M., and W.R. Miller "Language Development." In H. Stevenson (Ed.), *Child Psychology,* the 62nd Yearbook of the National Society for the Study of Education. Chicago: University of Chicago Press, 1963, 108-143.

Ervin-Tripp, S.M. "Language Development," *Review of Child Development Research.* New York: Russell Sage Foundation, 1967, 55-105.

Feifel, H., and I.B. Lorge. "Qualitative Differences in the Vocabulary Responses of Children," *Journal of Educational Psychology,* 43 (1962), 170-174.

Ferreiro, E. *The Relationship between Oral and Written Language: The Children's Viewpoints.* New York: Ford Foundation, 1978a.

Ferreiro, E. "What is Written in a Written Sentence: A Developmental Answer," *Journal of Education,* 160 (1978b), 25-39.

Fraser, C., U. Bellugi, and R. Brown. "Control of Grammar in Imitation, Comprehension and Production," *Journal of Verbal Learning and Verbal Behavior,* 2 (1963), 121-135.

Gallimore, R., J.W. Boggs and C. Jordan. *Culture, Behavior and Education: A Study of Hawaiian-Americans.* Beverly Hills: Sage Publications, 1974.

Gentry, J.R. "Early Spelling Strategies," *Elementary School Journal,* 79 (1978) 88-92.

Gibbons, H.D. "Reading and Sentence Elements," *Elementary English Review,* 18 (1941), 42-46.

Gibson, E.J., et al. "The Role of Grapheme-Phoneme Correspondences in the Perception of Words," *American Journal of Psychology,* 75 (1962), 554-570.

Gibson, E.J. and H. Levin. *The Psychology of Reading.* Cambridge, MA: MIT Press, 1975.

Goodman, K.S. "A Linguistic Study of Cues and Miscues in Reading," *Elementary English,* 42 (1965), 639-643.

Haggard, M.R. "Vocabulary Acquisition During Elementary and Postelementary Years: A Preliminary Report," *Reading Horizons,* 21 (1980), 61-69.

Halliday, M.A.K. *Learning How to Mean.* London: Edward Arnold, Ltd., 1975.

Harrell, L.E., Jr. "An Inter-Comparison of the Quality and Rate of the Development of the Oral and Written Language in Children, *"Monographs of the Society for Research in Child Development,* 22 (1957).

Harste, J.C., C.L. Burke, and V.A. Woodword. *Children, Their Language and Their World: Initial Encounters with Print.* NIE Final Report (NIE-G-79-0132), 1981.

Harste, J.C., C.L. Burke, and V.A. Woodward. "Children's Language and World: Initial Encounters with Print." In J. Langer and M.T. Smith-Burke (Eds.), *Reader Meets Author/ Bridging the Gap.* Newark, DE: International Reading Association, 1982, 105-131.

Heath, S.F. "What No Bedtime Story Means: Narrative Skills at Home and School," *Language and Society,* 2 (1982), 49-76.

Heider, F.K., and G.M. Heider. "A Comparison of Sentence Structure of Deaf and Hearing Children," *Psychological Monographs,* 52 (1940), 42-103.

Henderson, E.H., and J.W. Beers (Eds.), *Developmental and Cognitive Aspects of Learning to Spell.* Newark, DE: International Reading Association, 1980.

Holdaway, D. *The Foundtions of Literacy.* Auckland, New Zealand: Heinemann Educational Books, 1979.

Hunt, K.W. "Syntactic Maturity in School Children and Adults," *Monographs of the Society for Research in Child Development,* 35 (1970).

John, V.P. and L.S. Goldstein. "The Social Context of Language Acquisition," *Merrill-Palmer Quarterly of Behavior and Development,* 10 (1964), 265-274.

Kress, R.A. "An Investigation of the Relationship between Concept Formation and Achievement in Reading," unpublished doctoral dissertation, Temple University, 1955.

Labov, W. *A Study of Nonstandard English.* Urbana, IL: National Council of Teachers of English, 1968.

Labov, W. "The Logic of Nonstandard English," in F. Williams (Ed.), *Language and Poverty: Perspective on a Theme.* Chicago: Markham, 1970, 153-189.

Lenneberg, E. "Speech As a Motor Skill with Special Reference to Nonaphasic Disorder," *Monographs of the Society for Research in Child Development,* 29 (1964), 115-127.

Lenneberg, E. *Biological Foundations of Language.* New York: John Wiley and Son, 1967.

Lindsey, M.R. "A Descriptive Exploration of the Growth and Development of Spontaneous Oral Vocabulary of Elementary School Children," unpublished doctoral dissertation, University of California, 1969.

Loban, W.D. *The Language of Elementary School Children.* Champaign, IL: National Council of Teachers of English, 1963.

Loban, W.D. *Language Development: Kindergarten through Grade Twelve,* Urbana, IL: National Council of Teachers of English, 1976.

MacKinnon, A.R. (1959). *How Do Children Learn to Read?* Vancouver: Clopp Clark, 1959.

McCarthy, D.A. "Language Development in Children." In L. Carmichael (Ed.), *Manual of Child Psychology.* New York: Wiley, 1954, 492-630.

Menyuk, P. "Syntactic Structures in the Language of Children," *Child Development,* 34 (1963), 407-422.

Menyuk, P. "Children's Learning and Production of Grammatical and Nongrammatical Phonological Sequences," *Child Development,* 39 (1968), 849-859.

Menyuk, P. *The Acquisition and Development of Language.* Englewood Cliffs, NJ: Prentice-Hall, 1971.

Menyuk, P. "Language Development and Reading," In J. Flood (Ed.), *Understanding Reading Comprehension.* Newark, DE: International Reading Association, 1984, 101-121.

Messer, S. "Implicit Phonology in Children," *Journal of Verbal Learning and Verbal Behavior,* 6 (1967), 609-613.

Miller, G.A. "Some Psychological Studies of Grammar," *American Psychologist,* 17 (1962), 748-762.

Miller, G.A., G.A. Heise, and W. Lichten. "The Intelligibility of Speech As a Function of the Context of the Test Material," *Journal of Experimental Psychology,* 41 (1951), 329-335.

Milner, E. "A Study of the Relationship between Reading Readiness in Grade One School Children and Patterns of Parent-Child Interaction," *The 62nd Yearbook of the National Society for Study of Education.* Chicago: University of Chicago Press, 1963, 108-143.

Morehead, D.M. "Processing of Phonological Sequences by Young Children and Adults," *Child Development,* 42 (1971), 279-289.

Newfield, M.U., and B.B. Schlanger. "The Acquisition of English Morphology by Normal and Educable Mentally Retarded Children," *Journal of Speech and Hearing Research,* 11 (1968), 693-706.

O'Donnell, R.C., W.J. Griffin, and R.C. Norris. *Syntax of Kindergarten and Elementary School Children: A Transformational Analysis.* Champaign, IL: National Council of Teachers of English, 1967.

Olson, D.R. "From Utterance to Text: The Bias of Language in Speech and Writing," *Harvard Educational Review,* 47 (1977), 257-281.

Piaget, J. "The Genetic Approach to the Psychology of Thought." In J.P. DeCecco (Ed.), *The Psychology of Language, Thought and Instruction.* New York: Holt, Rinehart and Winston, 1967.

Piekarz, J.A. "Getting Meaning from Reading," *Elementary School Journal,* 56 (1956), 303-309.

Read, C. "Preschool Children's Knowledge of English Phonology," *Harvard Educational Review,* 41 (1971), 1-34.

Read, C. *Children's Categorization of Speech Sounds in English,* Research Report #17. Urbana, IL: National Council of Teachers of English, 1975.

Reed, D.W. "A Theory of Language, Speech and Writing." In Leonard Courtney (Ed.), *Linguistics and Reading.* Highlights of the 1965 Preconvention Institutes. Newark, DE: International Reading Association, 1966, 4-25.

Rodgers, T.S. "Linguistic Considerations in the Design of the Stanford Computer Based Curriculum in Initial Reading," Institute for Mathematical Studies in the Social Sciences, Technical Report No. 111, USOE Grant OE5-10-050, 1967.

Ruddell, R.B. "Effect of the Similarity of Oral and Written Patterns of Language Structure on Reading Comprehension," *Elementary English,* 42 (1965), 403-410.

Ruddell, R.B. "Reading Instruction in First Grade with Varying Emphasis on the Regularity of Grapheme-Phoneme Correspondences and the Relation of Language Structure to Meaning," *Reading Teacher,* 19 (1966), 653-660.

Ruddell, R.B. *Second and Third Year of a Longitudinal Study of Four Programs of Reading Instruction with Varying Emphasis on the Regularity of Grapheme-Phoneme Correspondences and the Relation of Language Structure to Meaning,* 1968. U.S. Department of Health, Education and Welfare, Office of Education Cooperative Research Projects Nos. 3099 and 78085.

Ruddell, R.B. and B.W. Graves. "Socioethnic Status and the Language Achievement of First Grade Children," *Elementary English,* 1967, 730-739.

Ruddell, R.B. *Reading-Language Instruction: Innovative Practices.* Englewood Cliffs, NJ: Prentice-Hall, 1974.

Rumelhart, D.E. "Understanding Understanding." In J. Flood (Ed.), *Understanding Reading Comprehension.* Newark, DE: International Reading Association, 1984, 1-20.

Rumelhart, D.E., and A. Ortony. "The Representation of Knowledge in Memory." In R.C. Anderson, R.J. Spiro, and W. Montague (Eds.), *Schooling and the Acquisition of Knowledge.* Hillsdale, NJ: Erlbaum, 1977, 99-136.

Russell, D.H., and I.Q. Saadeh, "Qualitative Levels in Children's Vocabularies," *Journal of Educational Psychology,* 43 (1962), 170-174.

Shuy, R.W. "Some Language and Cultural Differences in a Theory of Reading." In K. Goodman and J. Fleming (Eds.), *Psycholinguistics and the Teaching of Reading.* Newark, DE: International Reading Association, 1969, 34-47.

Sinclair-de Zwart, H. "Developmental Psycholinguistics." In D. Elkind and J.H. Flavell (Eds.), *Studies in Cognitive Development.* New York: Oxford University Press, 1969.

Singer, H. "Conceptualization in Learning to Read: New Frontiers in College-Adult Reading." In G.B. Schick and M.M. May (Eds.), *The 15th Yearbook of the National Reading Conference.* Milwaukee, Wisconsin: 1966, 116-132.

Slobin, D.I. "Cognitive Prerequisites for the Acquisition of Grammar." In C.A. Ferguson and D.I. Slobin (Eds.), *Studies of Child Language Development.* New York: Holt, Rinehart and Winston, 1973, 175-208.

Smith, F. "Demonstrations, Engagement and Sensitivity: A Revised Approach to Language Learning," *Language Arts,* 1981, 103-112.

Smith, M.K. "Measurement of the Size of General English Vocabulary through the Elementary Grades and High School," *Genetic Psychology Monographs,* 24 (1941), 311-345.

Smith, M.E. "An Investigation of the Development of the Sentence and the Extent of Vocabulary in Young Children," *Studies in Child Welfare,* 5. Iowa City, IA: State University of Iowa, 1926, 28-71.

Speidel, G.E. "Responding to Language Differences," *Oral Language in a Successful Reading Program for Hawaiian Children,* Technical Report No. 105 of the Kamehameha Early Education Program, 1982.

Strickland, R.G. *The Language of Elementary School Children: Its Relationship to the Language of Reading Textbooks and the Quality of Reading of Selected Children,* Bulletin 38 of the School of Education. Bloomington, IN: Indiana University, 1962.

Temple, C., R. Nathan, and N. Burris. *The Beginnings of Writing.* Boston: Allyn and Bacon, 1981.

Templin, M.C. *The Development of Reasoning in Children with Normal and Defective Hearing.* Minneapolis: University of Minnesota Press, 1950.

Templin, M.C. (1957) *Certain Language Skills in Children,* University of Minnesota Institute of Child Welfare Monographs. Minneapolis: University of Minnesota Press, 1957.

Thorndike, E. "Reading as Reasoning: A Study of Mistakes in Paragraph Reading," *Journal of Educational Psychology,* 8 (1971), 323-332.

Tough, J. *The Development of Meaning.* New York: John Wiley and Sons, 1977.

Venezky, R.L. "English Orthography: Its Graphical Structure and Its Relation to Sound," *Reading Research Quarterly,* 2 (1967), 75-106.

Vygotsky, L.S. *Thought and Language.* Cambridge and New York: MIT Press, 1962.

Ward, M.C. *Them Children, A Study in Language Learning.* Holt, Rinehart and Winston, 1971.

Wardhaugh, R. "Linguistics-Reading Dialogue," *Reading Teacher,* 21 (1968), 432-441.

Whorf, B.L. "Linguistics As an Exact Science." In J.B. Carroll (Ed.) *Language, Thought, and Reality.* Cambridge, MA: The MIT Press, 1956, 220-232.

Coming to Understand Things We Could Not Previously Understand[1]

JOHN D. BRANSFORD
KATHLEEN E. NITSCH
Vanderbilt University

The purpose of this chapter is to discuss aspects of the comprehension problem that seem relevant to educational and clinical issues. The most pertinent problem seems to be how people come to understand things they could not previously understand or how they come to understand things in new ways. We therefore focus on how one moves beyond a particular state of knowing and understanding (the growth problem) and how particular changes permit subsequent understanding (the transfer problem). In short, we ask how people learn to know and comprehend better.

Questions about learning to comprehend seem directly relevant to educational and clinical settings. For example, effective clinicians and educators use a variety of (intuitively based) techniques for promoting growth and transfer. They may ask questions, provide examples, relate new inputs to already familiar domains by way of analogy, and encourage particular types of drill and practice. As psychologists begin to clarify how people come to understand things in new ways and to clarify what the nature of the changes are that permit such transfer, we should become better able to evaluate techniques for intervention. Furthermore, we might begin to improve upon techniques currently in use.

Exploring the Development of Expertise

The basic problem under consideration can be viewed as an attempt to understand better the processes involved in the development of expertise in particular domains of knowing (see Bransford, Nitsch, and Franks, forthcoming, for further discussion). Some simple examples can be used to clarify the types of problems to which this chapter is addressed. The first example involves the domain of reading comprehension. Marks, Doctorow, and Wittrock (1974) varied the relative familiarity of 20 percent of the words in a story in order to create two

Reprinted from J.F. Kavanaugh and W. Strange (Eds.), *Speech and Language in the Laboratory, School, and Clinic.* Copyright 1978 by MIT Press. Used by permission of the authors and the MIT Press.

versions that could be read by elementary school children. Story comprehension and retention were nearly doubled when the selected words in the story were changed from less familiar terms (such as lad) to more familiar terms (such as boy). This experiment provides a vivid illustration of the importance of mapping into the current state of a comprehender's knowledge in order to ensure adequate comprehension. From the present perspective, the important question involves the processes by which terms such as "lad" can become as meaningful. Through what procedures can students be helped to comprehend inputs in more accurate, efficient, and automatic ways?

Similar questions can be asked about other aspects of comprehension, for example, the ability of adult speakers of English to know that the sentence *John hit Mary* is more closely related to *Mary was hit by John* than is *Mary hit John.* Beilin and Spontak (1969) and Olson (1972) report that elementary school children have considerable difficulty making such intersentential judgments. However, they are quite good at selecting a picture that is an accurate description of each of the mentioned sentence types. What do they know that permits accurate sentence-picture but not sentence-sentence judgments and how do they develop the linguistic expertise characteristic of a normal adult?

The final example derives from an informal study we conducted. Freshmen in an introductory psychology seminar were provided with excerpts from a passage by Karl Buhler that discussed certain aspects of language comprehension (the passage was taken from Blumenthal, 1970, pp. 50-57). The students were asked to read and attempt to understand the passage so that they could answer essay questions to be provided later. Examination of these essays revealed that most of the students were able to understand what the passage said, but they were unable to do much with the information. For example, most were generally unable to generate novel examples relevant to Buhler's discussion or to state the relevance of Buhler's ideas for clarifying experiences in everyday life. What is involved in helping such students come to understand a domain in a manner that permits transfer, that permits a clarification of subsequent experiences they may have?

The preceding examples raise questions regarding the problem of coming to understand things one did not previously understand or of coming to understand things in new ways. Our purpose is to sketch an abstract framework that might be fruitful for conceptualizing such problems of growth and transfer. We shall argue that appeals to variables such as frequency of exposure and practice, especially when they refer to the formation of stronger and more durable "memory traces," seem less than adequate for characterizing processes leading to growth and transfer. Similarly, appeals to the induction of "rules" or "higher order units" also seem less than adequate because such accounts provide little discussion of the conditions necessary for their acquisition.

Our discussion of the growth problem will focus on learner-environment relationships that seem necessary in order to learn effectively from exposure and practice and on the "remodeling" of the system (Bransford, Nitsch, and Franks, forthcoming) necessary in order to "know about" information. The acquisition of higher order cognitive information that one knows will also be shown to affect what some consider to be lower order processes, for example, to affect the perception of speech in white noise.

The remainder of the chapter is organized as follows. First, the minimal unit for analyzing comprehension is considered and defined as a situation-input relationship rather than a mere input (a sentence); one wishes to understand his momentary situation, not simply the input. Second, situational prerequisites to understanding are discussed. What types of cognitive and perceptual support are necessary in order for someone to understand an input? The development of language comprehension is viewed as a process of moving away from the need for explicit-cognitive-perceptual support. The next section attempts to tie the above two points together. It focuses on the reciprocal influences of one's current knowledge on comprehension of subsequent inputs, as well as the effect of inputs on one's knowledge. Here an "abductive" (cf. Peirce, 1932) framework is proposed for conceptualizing the problems of helping someone come to understand things in new ways. The final section discusses implications of the proposed framework for programs of evaluation and intervention.

Discovery and the Minimal Unit for Analyzing Comprehension

This section begins by discussing experiences of insight and discovery as paradigmatic exemplars of the process of coming to know something in a new way. It is argued that insight is not a matter of comprehending new (for the organism) as opposed to old input information. Indeed, it is not the input information per se that is the primary target of one's comprehension activities; it is the relevant aspects of one's momentary cognitive-perceptual situation that one wishes to understand. The minimal unit of analysis is therefore defined as a situation plus input; never a mere input. The latter assumption has implications for clarifying the relationship between meaning and understanding. In addition, it leads to questions about what is being studied when the comprehension of individual sentences in the linguistic or experimental laboratory is investigated.

An Example of Discovery

Recently, one of the authors played a simple game of discovery with two elementary school students.[2] The game consisted of drawing a pattern (a schematic face) with a stick. The task was to discover the critical aspects of the "teacher's" movements and to copy them exactly. Following each unsuccessful attempt the children were told that their imperfect performances were wrong but no specific corrective feedback was provided. Through repeated juxtapositions of observations and attempts to mimic, the children gradually articulated all the necessary movements. The last and most difficult discovery was that the teacher was drawing with his left hand. (The children were right handed and naturally drew this way.)

During the game, the children were excited as they struggled to master the task. With each subsequent demonstration by the teacher, they expressed excitement that they had now discovered the "crucial" detail. They would jump up with a "Now I've got it," only to find that additional details still remained to be discovered. There was excitement when the game was finally mastered, but this excitement was short lived. It was no fun to continue correctly drawing the pattern over and over. The children might have done so if rewarded each time with some appropriate token, but the excitement of discovery still would have vanished as quickly. Indeed, once the children had mastered the game, they expressed a very simple but urgent request: "Change the rules so we can try again."

To understand the excitement of mastery, one must focus on the growth of understanding. The excitement is in the discovery of something new, not the mere repetition of something old. The discovery of something new can be breathtaking. Consider Helen Keller's discovery that entities have names, Archimedes' shout of "Eureka" when he noticed that his body displaced the water in his bath and that the same principle could be used to measure the mass of objects, the excitement generated in students by a fresh idea or perspective, the excitement of a child who grasps a new word or concept and tries it out in a number of instances, the excitement of a scientist who discovers something new. An analysis of such phenomena places constraints on what understanding entails.

The Relationship between Insight and Old Versus New Facts

How might one characterize comprehension that leads to discovery and insight? Does it simply involve understanding new (to the comprehender) rather than old facts? Archimedes shouted "Eureka" upon seeing water rise in the tub when he entered it. Note that people see essentially the same thing every day, yet seeing the water rise rarely fosters an insight. Similarly, imagine understanding a sentence like *A pliers can be used as a weight*. To most of us this information is also less than breathtaking. Yet imagine that someone attempting to solve Maier's (1930) two-string problem either generates or hears this information. This information will allow this person to restructure and clarify the perceived situation and an insight occurs.

A distinction between old and new facts does not illuminate the factors involved in insightful comprehension. Information may be old (and even quite familiar), yet it can lend clarification and insight to one's immediate situation. It is the situation one seeks to understand, not simply the input. For example, the reader undoubtedly knows the word *parachute*. It is old and its occurrence on the page probably suggests little more than the recognition of familiarity (or perhaps an image). But imagine a different situation: You have been trying to understand the utterance *The haystack was important because the cloth ripped* (Bransford and McCarrell, 1974). The clue *parachute* now permits a restructuring of the situation; an "aha" experience occurs. (Buhler, reprinted in Blumenthal, 1970). Similarly, the punch line of a joke can restructure one's knowledge and produce laughter, but it is not the punch line in isolation that is funny. The humor stems from the restructuring of the cognitive situation that had been specified by the telling of the first part of the joke.

Consider a more general illustration of the relationship between situations and old information. We have all undoubtedly experienced conversations where the nature of a problem under discussion was ill defined and fuzzy. A discussant may suggest something that clarifies the issue, yet the suggestion frequently consists of information that everyone already knows. A typical example for an academic discussion might be "Look, we seem to be assuming that correlation implies causation." In such instances it is not uncommon to think, "Of course, why didn't I think of that?"

How can one feel that a comment is clarifying and insightful when that comment consists of already known information like "correlation does not imply causation?" The preceding question appears paradoxical only when the more general problem of comprehension is tacitly equated with the special case of understanding and isolated input. For example, imagine that you are stranded in the desert and need water. You know some is near, but where? A few desert animals go by and you notice tracks of others; but you need water, not food. Besides you are too weak to catch them. You could know that desert animals need water, but the potential meaning of this fact for your present situation may never occur to you. If it does, it transforms your understanding of the present situation. Following the animal tracks is a better bet than blindly searching on your own.

To understand comprehension, we must focus on the relationship between an input and one's immediate cognitive-perceptual situation. It is the situation one seeks to understand. The minimal unit of analysis must therefore be a situation plus an input. Lashley (1951, p.112) emphasizes the importance of this type of analysis:

> My principal thesis today will be that the input is never into a quiescent or static system, but always into a system which is already actively excited and organized. In the intact organism, behavior is the result of interaction of this background of excitation with input from any designated stimulus. Only when we can state the general characteristics of this background of excitation, can we understand the effects of a given input.

Relationships between Understanding and Concepts of Meaning

Lashley's orientation has implications for characterizing the problem of meaning as well as for clarifying what is being studied when comprehension is investigated in the laboratory. Since comprehension is usually assumed to involve meaning, the two concepts appear intimately related. However, by focusing on the relationship between situations and inputs, some ambiguities in concepts of meaning are revealed.

Assume that you are in an experiment. Your task is to state whether or not you understand the inputs presented when the inputs include words like *gex*, *zebra*, and *bagpipe*. You will probably state that you understand the latter two words but not the first. Now assume a different situation. Your task is to understand the utterance *The notes were sour because the seam split* (Bransford and McCarrell, 1974). You will hear various cues and should mark whether you now understand. In this situation, neither *gex* nor *zebra* is likely to facilitate understanding. The cue *bagpipes*, however, will help. Of course, you will know the meaning of *zebra*, but your task is not to indicate whether you understand the input. Your task is to indicate whether the input helps you understand.

The latter task appears to be quite representative of everyday comprehension situations. For example, our previously mentioned discussant in a meeting may claim "We're assuming that correlation implies causation." The statement may be readily comprehended, but does it help you understand? What counts is whether the input helps you clarify the immediate problem. If it doesn't, you will say something like "I don't understand your point" or "I don't see what you mean."

What does the preceding discussion suggest about the relationship between meaning and understanding? It is easy to accept the assertion that comprehension involves "grasping meaning." However, there are important differences between knowing the meaning of a word or sentence and using information to understand a particular situation. Understanding involves grasping the significance of an input for the situation at hand (Bransford, McCarrell, and Nitsch, 1976; Nitsch, 1975). The problem of significance extends to nonverbal as well as verbal inputs (for further discussion see Bransford and McCarrell, 1974; Brewer, 1974; Franks, 1974), yet there clearly seems to be something called "linguistic meaning." Fillmore's (1971, p. 274) approach to linguistic meaning seems fruitful:

> The difficulties I have mentioned exist, it seems to me, because linguistic semanticists, like the philosophers and psychologists whose work they were echoing, have found it relevant to ask, not *What do I need to know in order to use this form appropriately and to understand other people when they use it?* but rather, *What is the meaning of this form?* And having asked that, linguists have sought to discover the external signs of meanings, the reflexes of meanings in the speech situation, and the inner structure of meanings. It is apparent that the wrong question has been asked.

This discussion focuses on the concept of significance or understood meaning rather than on linguistic meaning. This does not deny the crucial importance of linguistic meaning for understanding. It will be argued later that some level of understood meaning is a prerequisite for acquiring linguistic meaning in the first place.

Situation-Input Relationships in Experimental Research

The minimal unit of analysis has been defined as a situation plus input. All experimental research on comprehension occurs in some situation, yet this aspect is seldom analyzed. If understanding depends on situation-input relations, the nature of the experimental situation will have important effects on the results obtained in the experiment.

Consider a typical experiment where subjects hear individual sentences like *The boy hit the ball* or *John hit Mary.* It is extremely easy for adults to understand such sentences. It is tempting to assume that this type of task taps the simplest, most basic level of linguistic understanding. Note, however, that an experimenter does not simply walk into the room and begin uttering *The boy hit the ball.* If he or she did, the subjects would be extremely confused. The most important type of understanding that takes place in an experiment involves understanding the instructions so that one can define one's immediate situation. This affects how the experimental inputs are understood.

In most experiments the stimulus sentences are understood to have a very special significance; they are objects to be comprehended, rated, or remembered. They are viewed as examples of sentences that might be uttered by someone for some reason at some time and place. Treating a sentential input as an example of a potential utterance is very different from using an input to clarify a particular situation. For example, one can understand the isolated sentence *Desert animals need water.* This is quite different from understanding the potential meaning or significance of this fact for surviving in a desert. Note further that subjects frequently seek clarification after an experiment. Some ask all kinds of questions in an attempt to understand. These subjects are not trying to understand the sentences previously presented as stimuli; they are trying to understand the experiment. An experimenter's words of explanation will now be understood to the degree that they clarify the subject's previous experiences in the experiment.

There are important differences between comprehension in experimental situations and many everyday communications situations. The most striking contrast is between the experimental situation and the conditions under which language is originally acquired. One does not sit down with a two year old child and say "O.K. Billy, *The boy hit the ball, John hit Mary.*" A child would never acquire language in this manner. Children learn by understanding the significance of utterances relative to their cognitive-perceptual situation at the time (see MacNamara, 1972; Nelson, 1974; Bloom, 1978). Even older children have a strong tendency to understand information in terms of their immediate situation. For example, an adult will respond "true" to the proposition "Either it is raining outside or it is not." In contrast, children seek empirical support for the truth value of the statement: They will look to see whether it is actually raining or not (Osherson and Markman, 1975). Similarly, consider Scribner's (1975) studies comparing schooled and unschooled Kpelle villagers in their ability to understand classical syllogisms (see also Brown, forthcoming). Unschooled villagers refused to consider a problem such as "All Kpelle men are rice farmers. Mr. Smith (western name) is not a rice farmer. Is he a Kpelle man?" They had to know Mr. Smith in order for the task to make sense to them.

Schooled adults also normally attempt to understand the significance of inputs in terms of their immediate situation. They can treat inputs as examples of possible utterances and as objects of logical analysis, but it is easy to forget that this involves a special mode of understanding. For example, *Bill has a red car* is readily understood in an experimental context, but try walking into someone's office and simply uttering that statement. In such cases, people are extremely confused by the utterance. They know what was said but not what was meant (Bransford, McCarrell, and Nitsch, 1976).

What, then, is being studied in experiments that investigate the comprehension of individual, isolated sentences (or diagnose people on this basis)? Surely it is not the most basic and simplest level of language comprehension. Instead, the experimenters are relying on people's abilities to specify or invent particular situations in which an input could make sense. A number of studies suggest that sophisticated comprehenders do indeed spontaneously invent situations in which sentences might be meaningful (Bransford, Barclay, and Franks, 1972; Brewer, 1974; Johnson, Bransford, and Solomon, 1973; Schweller, Brewer, and Dahl, in press). Furthermore the ability to do so appears to be a prerequisite for effective comprehension (Bransford and Johnson, 1972, 1973; Bransford and McCarrell, 1984; Dooling and Lachman, 1971). The ability to specify or invent situations in which inputs can be meaningfully interpreted is clearly important. However, these studies do not necessarily specify how people got to the point where they are able to do this or how they understand given that they are immersed in a particular cognitive-perceptual situation. The effects of one's situation on comprehension of inputs is discussed in the next section.

The focus of this discussion has been on a general characterization of the problem of understanding. A basic question has been "What is it that one wants to understand?" Generally one seeks to understand one's experience or momentary cognitive-perceptual situation. It is the situation that is the primary focus of one's comprehension activities, not merely the input. Identical inputs (such as *A pliers can be used as a weight; We're assuming that correlation implies causation)* can therefore be insightful, mundane, or anomolous depending on one's situation. Already known information can be just as insightful as novel information. It is in coming to understand something in a new way that the inherent excitement of understanding occurs. Of course, the use of the term cognitive-perceptual situation presupposes considerable understanding on the part of the listener. Indeed, new understanding is built on previous understanding. It is those general processes that permit the growth of understanding that we eventually want to understand.

There are important differences between everyday comprehension situations and those that frequently occur in the experimental (and linguistic) laboratory. In the experimental situation, individual sentences are treated as objects of analysis, as examples of something that might be said. The ability to understand under such circumstances is clearly important, but it is surely not the most basic mode of understanding. This ability is the result of basic processes that we seek to understand. Children would never acquire language under experiment like conditions. Such situations rarely permit adults to understand something in a new way. It is therefore important to focus on situational prerequisites for understanding. What types of situational support are necessary for understanding certain types of syntactic structures, statements, or lexical items? Furthermore, what types of support must be provided in order to move one beyond one's particular level of knowing and understanding? Some of these questions are examined in the next section.

Before proceeding it may be helpful to clarify the differences between this and the following section. Here the question of how the comprehension of inputs can clarify and restructure one's understanding of one's immediate situation was emphasized. The next section will emphasize the opposite side of the coin: How one's immediate situation affects comprehension of a subsequent input. Following this, we will attempt to put the coin back together by emphasizing the reciprocal nature of the influence of input on situation and situation on input. That is, an input may both clarify one's situation yet be clarified by the situation.

Cognitive and Perceptual Support Necessary for Understanding

In this section the emphasis is on the situational support necessary to understand subsequent inputs rather than on the effects of the input toward clarifying one's situation. As will be argued in a later section, this division between situation and input influences is actually artificial, but it seems descriptively useful nonetheless. Some relations between situations and linguistic inputs for the adult comprehender are discussed first, followed by a consideration of some of the additional situational support often necessary for younger children to comprehend effectively. In general, early comprehension skills seem to be context specific or situation specific. That is, young comprehenders seem to require considerable situational support in order to understand utterances. More sophisticated comprehenders appear better able to supply such information on their own.

Syntactic Difficulty As Situationally Defined

In the 1960s linguistic theories emphasized the primacy of the sentence (Chomsky, 1965, 1972). Linguistic theories of this decade dealt with intersentential relationships, but these were relationships of transformational relatedness for individual sentence types. For example, *John hit Mary* and *Mary was hit by John* were assumed to differ in terms of surface structure but to be similar in deep structure (Katz and Postal, 1964). In contrast, sentences like *John is eager to please* and *John is easy to please* were assumed to share a similarity in surface structure while their deep structural descriptions were markedly different (Chomsky, 1965). For example, one can say *It is easy to please John* but not *It is eager to please John*.

Chomsky's theories clearly revolutionized thinking about the nature of both language and understanding (see Dixon and Horton, 1968). Yet in subsequent years many linguists' analyses of deep structure led them to make it "deeper and deeper" (McCawley, 1974; Ross, 1974). For example, on the basis of linguistic analysis, Ross (1970) argued that the deep structural representation of declarative sentences contain the information "I say to you that...." Such analyses begin to converge on what has been termed here the situation underlying linguistic communication (for example, that it always presupposes a speaker or a writer). There are, of course, numerous additional situational aspects as well. For example, the notions of sentence relatedness considered in Chomsky's theories are different from the intuitive coherence or relatedness of sentences in a normal flow of conversation ("I bought a new bike. The tires are bright red."). Interest in the constraints differentiating coherent and noncoherent flows of conversation is reflected in current attempts to construct text grammars rather than sentence grammars (Frederiksen, 1972, 1975; Kintsch, 1974; Schank, 1972; van Dijk, 1973; see Lakoff, 1971 on constraints on conjoining sentences). Text grammars reflect a concern with the relationship of a sentence to the more global macrostructure of a text.

Like the linguistic theory from which it took its impetus early psycholinguistic research focused on the individual sentence. For example, active sentences were found to be easier to comprehend and remember than passives, affirmatives easier than negatives (Gough, 1965, 1966). Psychological complexity was almost universally assumed to have a direct correspondence to the derivational complexity of the sentences (as computed according to then-current versions of linguistic theory). However, subsequent investigators questioned the validity of such indices of psychological complexity (see Fodor, Bever, and Garrett, 1974 for an overview). In addition, more attention was focused on the function of certain types of grammatical constructions. The same grammatical structure may be more or less appropriate depending on the context or situation in which it appears.

A number of studies explored contextual or situational constraints on ease of comprehension. For example, Wason (1961) investigated contexts of plausible denial. Slobin (1966) and Olson and Filby (1972) investigated situations that were conducive of the processing of passive sentences, and Huttenlocher, Eisenberg and Strauss (1968) showed that the same sentence may differ in ease of comprehension depending on the contextual situations to which it refers. Clark and Haviland (forthcoming; see also Clark, 1973) recently discussed a number of these results in terms of a "given-new contract." Following Halliday's (1967) linguistic analysis, they assume that sentences contain both given and new (for the comprehender) information. Thus, a sentence like *It was John who saw Mary* presupposes that *someone saw Mary* is already known as given and that *it was John* is new. If the sentence that precedes *It was John who saw Mary* in a conversation happens to be *Someone saw Mary,* the second sentence in the conversation seems appropriate and is readily comprehended (assuming that the prosodic stress was on John). The given information in this sentence is congruent with the information that the listener in fact already knew. In contrast, assume that a comprehender has just heard the utterance *John saw someone.* Under these conditions the sentence *It was John who saw Mary* seems inappropriate and is less quickly comprehended. A more acceptable and more easily understood sentence would be *It was Mary who was seen by John.* In this latter sentence, *John saw someone* is given and *Mary* is new.

The basic point of these studies is that syntactic structure has semantic implications and that syntactic appropriateness is determined relative to the situation in which a sentence is uttered. Even the appropriateness of using "the" versus "a" and the ease of comprehending the resulting utterances depends on the preexisting communicative situation (Chafe, 1972; Clark, 1973; Osgood, 1971). As Glucksberg and Danks (1975) argue, the results of most studies of comprehension difficulty that involve sentence-sentence and picture-sentence verifications indicate differential difficulties in decision times rather than differential difficulty in processing certain types of linguistic constructions. Furthermore, decision difficulty varies as a function of the situation in which an input occurs (Olson and Filby, 1972).

Assumptions about "inherent" syntactic difficulty have also been questioned from a somewhat different perspective. Some investigators have argued for the communicative efficiency of moderately complex, embedded sentences as compared to sets of grammatically simple sentences (Bransford and Franks, 1973; Pearson, 1969). Such communicative efficiency is obscured if one simply compares comprehension and memory for simple as opposed to more complex sentences. However, assume that one establishes a goal of communicating a particular constellation of semantic information, that is, the goal is to get someone to understand that there is a tall boy who hit a red ball. It seems obvious that use of a set of syntactically simple sentences is not necessarily the most efficient form for communicating such information. Compare, for example, *The tall boy hit the red ball* with *The boy was tall, The boy hit the ball, The ball was red.* Pearson (1969) reports data on children's comprehension indicating greater efficiency of certain types of embedded sentences relative to sets of grammatically simpler forms.

Further Investigations of Situational Support

Most of the previously mentioned research took place in an experimental context. Studying the case of comprehending a sentence in the context of a previous input is one step toward more natural communication conditions, but the subjects may still regard inputs as examples of sentences that might be uttered by someone at some time for some purpose. In settings other than the experimental laboratory, knowledge of who is speaking, when they are speaking, and why they are speaking is frequently necessary in order to understand adequately. This knowledge forms part of one's situation that may affect how the inputs are understood.

Brewer and Harris (1974) present data illustrating that sentences heard under conditions approximating those of ordinary conversation are understood differently from the same sentences heard in an experimental context. They approximated conversational situations by having the person uttering the sentence actually present and by having him converse as if he were presenting his own views at that particular time and place. In the experimental condition, subjects simply listened to sentences as in a normal experiment (where they are understood as possible sentences that someone might say). Free recall was used as an index of what was understood. Subjects in the experimental condition made many errors during recall. For example, the sentence *Marijuana grows wild in this county* was frequently recalled as *Marijuana grows wild in* the *or* that *county*. Such results are not surprising given that the sentences were viewed simply as examples of potential utterances. Without a well-specified temporal-spatial framework, words like *this* (and even *county*) may be understood at a linguistic level, but this does not ensure that the significance of these inputs for a particular domain is understood (Bransford, McCarrell, and Nitsch, 1976; Nitsch, 1975). In the conversational condition, subjects did have a well-defined temporal-spatial framework and their recall results differed radically. For example, subjects rarely misrecalled *that* or *the* for *this*.

The importance of situational support for understanding can also be illustrated with verb tenses. Consider a newspaper headline like *War Breaks Out in Europe*. The headline is in a quasi-present tense, but the significance of this information depends on the cognitive-temporal framework from which it is viewed. If one realizes one is reading an old newspaper, the significance of this headline is historical. If it is today's paper, the significance of the present tense is very different indeed.

Many experimentally presented sentences fail to suggest a well-defined cognitive-temporal framework. Therefore whether a subject mentioned in a sentence already has, is, or will be doing something has very little meaning; and all kinds of tense confusions occur in recall (see Clark and Stafford, 1969). If cues are added to make the tenses more meaningful, recall errors diminish greatly. For example, Harris and Brewer (1973) compared subjects' recall of sentences like

The astronauts will see a UFO with recall sentences like *Tomorrow, the astronauts will see a UFO*. In the first condition results were similar to those of Clark and Stafford (1969). In the latter situation tense shifting during recall was markedly reduced. Of course, in a normal conversation tense is usually meaningful even without using words like *yesterday* and *tomorrow.* If used in normal conversation, these words have a more well defined significance as well.

Development and Comprehension Skills

The preceding examples illustrate how one's situation can affect linguistic comprehension. Identical syntactic structures may be easy or difficult to understand depending on the situation, and linguistic elements may vary in understood meaning as a function of the situation in which they occur. (See also Anderson and Ortony, 1975; Barclay et al., 1974 on the flexibility of understood meanings.) Of course, no one doubts the fundamental influence of context on comprehension. However, it is still easy to believe that comprehension of context-free words and sentences is a prerequisite for any deeper level of understanding. From this perspective one must first comprehend the individual word or sentence and then elaborate it as a function of context. There are strong reasons for questioning this assumption, particularly as it applies to the development of linguistic expertise.

Consider the fact that adult speaker-listeners can recognize deep structural equivalences among different surface structures (for example that *John hit Mary* is similar to *Mary was hit by John).* Is this ability purely a function of linguistic knowledge or is it somehow more cognitively based? Experiments by Olson (1972, 1974), mentioned previously, are very important in this context. Olson (1972) presented young school children with sentences like *John hit Mary* and asked them to verify whether these were like other statements (for example *Mary hit John* and *Mary was hit by John).* Children's performance in this task was very poor. They were much better at deciding whether a picture was congruent with a sentence they had heard. In subsequent studies Olson (1974) explored the conditions under which children of the same age could make accurate sentence-sentence verifications. When he systematically increased the richness of the children's situation or knowledge context, performance consistently improved. Performance was lowest when arbitrary names (John and Mary, for example) were used; it was improved by simply including known characters, even though the events remained arbitrary. The addition of a story context in which both characters and their relations were nonarbitrary further facilitated the children's performances. In short, the nature of the cognitive situation in which the sentences were embedded affected the children's ability to deal with so-called syntactic (active-passive) relationships among the sentences. These results support the notion that as one moves to younger subjects language comprehension becomes even more situation bound.

Predictably, the most extreme dependence on the situation occurs during the early stages of language acquisition. As MacNamara (1972, p. 1) suggests, "The infant uses meaning as a clue to language, rather than language as a clue to meaning" (see also De Villiers and De Villiers, 1974; Dore et al., 1976; Nelson, 1974; Wells, 1974). In general, the infant must have some clue to the intended significance of a speaker's utterance in order to determine what the words mean (or even that they are used to mean; note, for example, Keller, 1903). This dependence on nonlinguistic situational support exists at many levels of language acquisition. For example, Bloom (1974) notes that her daughter first recognized the word "birds" in the context of a mobile above her dressing table and the word "music" in the context of the record player in her room. Bloom states, "She did not recognize the words 'birds' and 'music' in any situations other than her mobile and her record player for many months" (p. 289).

Reich (1976) discusses a related situation. He played a game called "Where?" with his eight-month-old child, Adam. He would say "Where is mommy?" and Adam would crawl to his mother, "Where's the bed?" and Adam would crawl to the bed. Reich's discussion focused on Adam's understanding of "shoes." When asked, "Where's the shoes?", Adam would crawl to his mother's closet and play with the shoes that were lined up on the rack (the game was played in the bedroom). When Adam was placed by the open door of his father's closet and asked, "Where's the shoes?", he would not play with those shoes but instead would proceed to his mother's closet and play with hers. Indeed, when a pair of his mother's shoes was placed near him in the middle of the bedroom and he was asked, "Where's the shoes?", Adam would still go to the shoes in his mother's closet. Adam's understanding of shoes involved a whole action sequence that was strongly linked with his mother's closet. Only gradually did Adam begin to understand that shoes could include those in daddy's closet, those in the middle of the floor, and those that someone was wearing at the time.

Situation-specific linguistic abilities can be illustrated in the domain of speech production as well as comprehension. For example, Bloom, Hood, and Lightbown (1974; cited in Bloom, 1974) played a "Simple Simon" game of imitation with Peter (age thirty-two months, two weeks) in which they presented sentences such as the following: *This is broken, I'm trying to get this cow in here, I'm gonna get the cow to drink milk, you make him stand up over there.* Peter's imitations were (respectively) as follows: *What's broken, Cow in here, Get the cow to drink milk, Stand up there.* As Bloom (1974) notes, such imitation data suggest that Peter had not yet developed certain levels of linguistic competence (he apparently lacked a consistent use of the copula *is* and lacked causal connnectives like *trying, gonna,* and *make*). However, each of the sentences that the experimenter had presented for imitation were examples of utterances that Peter himself had spontaneously produced at a previous time. For example, Peter had said "I'm gonna get the cow to drink milk" while returning to a toy cow with some toy barrels fetched from a sack. Similarly, Peter said, "You make him stand up over there" while trying to get the experimenter to spread an animal's legs so that it could stand in a spot Peter had cleared. These data provide a striking illustration of the importance of external and internalized situational knowledge on linguistic performance (see Slobin and Welsh, 1973). Labov (1970) has supplied similar illustrations of the critical importance of situational considerations in his criticism of research purporting to show a linguistic deficit in the language abilities of many black Americans (see also Cole and Bruner, 1971).

In general, initial comprehension abilities seem closely tied to particular situational settings and domains of knowledge. Chapman (this volume) provides an excellent discussion of situation-dependent comprehension. It seems doubtful that the ability to understand adequately sentences out of context is a prerequisite to deeper levels of understanding. Instead, the ability to understand isolated sentences seems to result from processes underlying the development of linguistic expertise. Factors influencing one's abilities to comprehend without the need for explicit situational support will be discussed in the next section.

To summarize, initial abilities to understand through the medium of language appear to be situationally dependent. The ability to understand isolated word and sentences seems to develop from more primary, conceptually dependent ways of knowing (see Bever, 1970; Bloom, 1974; Chapman, 1974; MacNamara, 1972; Nelson, 1974; Sinclair-deZwart, 1969 for further discussion). Comprehension is therefore not a unitary phenomenon. For example, children may be able to understand and communicate in some circumstances (in situations with rich social-perceptual support) yet have great difficulty in others. Assessments of comprehension difficulties may actually reveal problems of understanding and communicating in certain types of situations rather than reveal intrinsic linguistic deficits (Bloom, 1974; Labov, 1970).

The studies cited in this section suggest that externally and internally defined situations can affect comprehension of inputs. They can affect one's ability to recognize a word (Bloom, 1974), produce utterances (Bloom, Hood, and Lightbown, 1974), judge intersentential relationships (Olson, 1974), or affect the speed with which one can comprehend (Clark, 1973). This section therefore focused on situational prerequisites to comprehension, while the previous section focused on the influence of inputs on one's comprehension of the immediate situation. One's momentary situation can both clarify and be clarified by inputs. The next section sketches a framework for growth that integrates these two influences. Through this assimilative-accommodatory process (in Piagetian terms) one can move to a point where one can understand things in new ways.

Toward a Framework for Conceptualizing Growth

The framework sketched in this section for schematizing the growth problem, the problem of how one comes to understand things that one did not previously understand or how one comes to understand things in new ways, focuses on the reciprocal influences of situation on input and input on situation. Emphasis is placed on those situation-input relations that take one beyond one's current state of knowing and allow better comprehension of subsequent events. Our views of the types of changes or growth that permit such transfer will be contrasted with views assuming that learning simply involves amassing a storehouse of more and more knowledge or facts (see also Bransford, Nitsch, and Franks, forthcoming).

Schematizing the Growth Problem

It seems intuitively reasonable to assume that one needs appropriate knowledge in order to understand inputs. For example, Einstein's knowledge of relativistic physics permitted him to understand events in ways different from someone who lacks that knowledge. Someone else who acquires this knowledge should also be able to understand. It is tempting to conceptualize growth as the accumulation of more and more knowledge, but there are problems with such descriptions. When it is said that someone has come to understand something because he or she was given the knowledge to understand it, it is presupposed that the person can and does understand the new knowledge that was given. Entailed in this presupposition is the problem that needs to be explained. Similarly, the statement that some knowledge is easier to acquire than other knowledge because the former is more meaningful also presupposes that which needs explanation. As Jenkins (1974) warned, meaningfulness is not a property of stimuli. How might the growth process be conceptualized in order to make these issues clearer?

In a previous section it was argued that the minimal unit for analyzing comprehension must involve the relationship between one's current cognitive-perceptual situation (or perspective) and subsequent inputs. The proposed growth schema is organized around an analysis of situation-input relations in order to emphasize that one not only learns from experience, one also learns to experience. One's momentary situation or perspective affects how inputs are experienced, which determines what is learned from the experience. The reciprocal influences of situation on input (assimilation) and input on situation (accommodation) are assumed to lead to a remodeling or redefinition of one's current perspective so that subsequent inputs can now be understood (and learned from) in new ways. This schematization is therefore neither solely empiricistic nor rationalistic. It is neither solely deductive nor inductive, but perhaps more equivalent to Peirce's (1932) notion of abduction. The schema highlights the relatively gradual "bootstrapping" nature of the growth process and focuses attention on the situational support necessary to learn effectively from exposure and practice. It also directs attention to questions about the nature of the changes in the system that permit transfer to occur.

Exemplification As an Illustration of Abduction

The abduction schema is best illustrated by considering one of the most intuitively powerful means for helping someone come to understand something, the use of examples.[3] Listeners frequently know what speakers said yet need one or more examples in order to grasp adequately the intended message. Research by Pollchik (1975) documents the powerful effects that examples can have for helping people come to understand textual material in a manner that permits transfer, that permits them to understand subsequent statements and examples in new ways.

As an illustration of the process of exemplification, assume that one wished to use examples to communicate the concept of abduction (sketched above) to college sophomores. Initially, they hear the description of the concept stating that the minimal unit of analysis is a situation-input relation, that situations clarify inputs and inputs further clarify situations, and that this approach to learning is an abductive characterization of the growth process. Given this information, they might understand what was said. However, if someone simply stopped with this description, the students would be likely to ask, "So what?" They would need to know something more in order to understand what the concept could mean. Similarly, the students could memorize the description and hence be able to talk and think about it at some level. However, what significance would this knowledge have? How could it become something they use to think "in terms of" (Bransford, Nitsch, and Franks, forthcoming) or "know with" rather than something they merely "know about"?

A basic process involved in communicating the abduction concept (or any new concept) is essentially to point to certain phenomena and say, "There, that's an example of what I mean. There's another, and another." This process of pointing to phenomena looks like nothing more than simple ostensive definition. It is easy to interpret the resulting learning processes as one of forming associations between a concept label (such as abduction) and various referents. However, assumptions about the formation and storage of word-referent associations are insufficient for understanding the growth processes by which information can become useful for clarifying subsequent events.

Consider what is involved in utilizing exemplification to help communicate the abduction concept. The descriptive information about the concept is assumed to become part of an individual's situation or perspective. This initial information affects how the individual understands the inputs or examples that are pointed to, while the examples in turn further clarify the concept. It is through the reciprocal influences of concept on examples and examples on concept (or situation on input and input on situation) that one gradually becomes able to use the concept (in this case abduction) and hence understand subsequent inputs in new ways.

The effects of initial knowledge of a concept on examples is analogous to the effects of labels on droodles. Assume that one tells a comprehender to notice the umbrella in the drawing presented in Figure 1. A listener is likely to say, "I don't see what you mean." However, if the drawing is presented as an example of a bear climbing up the opposite side of a tree, one perceives the drawing differently—a restructuring occurs.

The abduction schema can be viewed as a potential alternative to other basic paradigms for conceptualizing acquisition, for example, paired-associate learning or the establishment of word-referent associations. From the present perspective, assumptions that people learn the meaning of a word like "dog" (or a word like "abduction") by associating the label with concrete referents ignore two important points. First, learners' momentary perspective affects how they understand the referents (or examples) and hence what they learn from them. Second, what is learned is not simply a list of examples that are attached to a concept label. One also learns what the examples are examples of. Thus, knowledge of the concept becomes refined (made more precise and more useful) in the process of comprehending the examples.

Consider the first point. Imagine that a speaker says, "Notice the sepia," while pointing to a complex painting (Hester, 1977). A listener who does not know that sepia refers to a color (and more specifically, to a brownish color), will have difficulty understanding the significance of the pointing act and hence fail to see what the speaker intends. As Wittgenstein (1953) argued, even ostensive definition (saying "This is red" while pointing to something colored red) presupposes that one has some knowledge of what the ostensibly defined thing is supposed to be an example of (in this case, color). Knowledge of the category color affects one's understanding of the object of the pointing gesture, which in turn clarifies one's understanding of the color red.

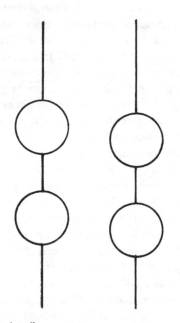

Figure 1. An example of a droodle.

This emphasis on the perspective from which one views examples becomes especially important when attempting to understand initial language acquisition. One must focus on those nonlinguistic actions and events that children understand in their social-perceptual environment in order to clarify the perspective from which they grasp the significance of linguistic utterances. For example, Hoffman (1968; cited in MacNamara, 1972) discusses some of the errors that frequently occur during the language acquisition period. A seventeen month old child used the word *hot* as the name for *stove*. Perhaps as the child was about to touch the stove an adult had said "hot." To this child, the significance of the utterance could easily have been understood as the name for *stove*. Of course if the adult had instead said "no, no, hot" and displayed considerable affect, the child might well have understood that the significance of the word *hot* was not as a name for an object. Social-perceptual information (from the external environment) is an integral part of a child's momentary perspective. This in turn affects the child's understanding of linguistic utterances (Bates, 1976; Bloom, this volume; Chapman, this volume; Nelson, 1974, forthcoming).

The abduction schema stresses that one's momentary situation or perspective not only affects comprehension of subsequent inputs (examples), but that the inputs further clarify one's perspective. It is through this reciprocal, assimilative accommodatory process (cf. Piaget's notion of equilibration) that one becomes able to use a concept and hence better understand subsequent events. This latter assumption reflects the second previously noted contrast between abduction and association paradigms, that one learns more than a mere list of examples attached to a concept label. As Bransford and Franks (1976) note, it is easy to assume that examples are beneficial simply because they are usually concrete and hence more easily learned and remembered. However, such explanations of the process of exemplification focus only on the acquisition and storage of facts or inputs. The abduction schema stresses that what is learned is not simply a list of facts or examples but rather a concept that transcends any enumeration of its exemplars (see Cassirer, 1923). Through practice at thinking in terms of or knowing with a concept, one gradually develops usable knowledge in the form of an abstract framework or perspective or guide articulation of subsequent events. It is this acquired framework or perspective that indicates such things as what counts as distinctive features and what aspects of events are momentarily important or nonimportant (see Bransford and Franks, 1976 for further discussion). In short, by coming to know with this abstract framework, one is able to understand subsequent events in new and more adequate ways.

An Experimental Investigation of Exemplification

Mary Lessick Hannigan (1976) recently completed a dissertation that explores some problems involved in becoming able to use a concept or schema. Her studies can be viewed as an analog of the previous discussion concerning the use of examples to help students understand the abduction concept. There it was suggested that initial knowledge of the concept affects understanding of the examples, which in turn further clarifies the concept. Furthermore, the resulting changes were assumed to affect transfer, and transfer was assumed to involve something more than storage of the list of examples that was heard. Hannigan's measures of learning and transfer also explore the degree to which certain experiences can result in more direct apprehension of subsequent inputs. Her primary dependent measure was the ability to detect sentences embedded in white noise.

Group one in Hannigan's study (the no-framework group) heard a list of seventy sentences and were asked to rate them on ease of comprehension. Examples of her acquisition sentences are as follows: The man set up housekeeping in the airplane, The man threw the curtain over the metal bar. The man propped the door against the rock wall. The man thrashed the leaves with his cane. The man put the chair at the base of the tree. The man piled the bricks under the tree. The man opened his briefcase. The man turned the bell upside down. The man made a sack out of the sheet. All of these sentences are understandable in isolation. Indeed, Hannigan's subjects rated them as very easy to comprehend.

The subjects in group two (the framework group) heard the identical set of seventy acquisition sentences. However, they were asked to understand each sentence as a description of survival on a deserted island and also as an illustration of one of seven particular aspects (subcategories) of survival (such as making shelter). The subjects were instructed to imagine that anything mentioned in a sentence was actually on the island, so ratings of comprehensibility should simply indicate their ability to see how a certain activity could be related to a particular subtopic. The examples and particular subtopics are as follows: *Making a shelter*. The man set up housekeeping in the airplane. The man threw the curtain over the metal bar. The man propped the door against the rock wall. *Reaching for food on a branch above your head*. The man thrashed the leaves with his cane. The man put the chair at the base of the tree. The man piled the bricks under the tree. *A container for carrying food*. The man opened his briefcase. The man turned the bell upside down. The man made a sack out of the sheet.

Understanding the preceding sentences from the perspective of survival clearly influences one's comprehension of them. This illustrates the effects of situations on the comprehension of subsequent inputs, yet inputs further clarify initial perspectives as well. In order to investigate the degree to which examples can further clarify initial concepts or schemas, Hannigan included a third group in her study, the framework-after group. These subjects heard all seventy sentences without any topic or subtopics (their task was equivalent to the no-framework subjects). They were told about the survival topic and subtopics immediately after sentence acquisition (prior to testing). If comprehending the examples provided further clarification for the initial concept, the framework-after procedure should not provide sufficient opportunity for subjects to move beyond their normative knowledge of survival (and its seven subcategories). These subjects should therefore perform less adequately than the framework group.

Following acquisition, Hannigan compared the performance of subjects in the no-framework, framework, and framework-after conditions. As a test, she took advantage of the finding that meaningful sentences are better identified under conditions of white noise than are less meaningful sentences (Miller, Heise, and Lichten, 1951). She reasoned that subjects in the framework group should now be able to understand novel but appropriate sentences that deal with aspects of survival (for example, *The man got up on the box*). If these sentences were, in fact, more meaningful for the framework group, they should be better detected in white noise.

During the test all subjects heard the same sentences embedded in white noise. Their performance was compared to a baseline group that received no initial experimental inputs prior to the detection test. Test sentences included olds (those heard by all groups except baseline), novel appropriates (appropriate in that they could be seen as related to the previous survival theme), and novel inappropriates (inappropriate in that they could not readily be seen as related to the survival theme). For example, *The man put the eraser under the table* was a novel inappropriate. The subjects' task was to listen to each sentence embedded in white noise and attempt to repeat it aloud as best they could.

For old sentences, accuracy of repetition in the no-framework, framework, and framework-after groups was superior to the baseline group. In addition, the framework group was better on olds than were the other two groups. All three groups were equivalent to the baseline subjects on the novel inappropriate sentences. However, the most important data involved performance on the novel appropriate test sentences. On these, the no-framework and framework-after groups were no better than the baseline group. In contrast, the framework group performed much more accurately at repeating the novel appropriate sentences. The subjects in this group were slightly less accurate on these than on olds. Nevertheless, the framework group was as accurate on novel appropriates as the no-framework group was on olds.

Subsequent experiments revealed that subjects in the no-framework and framework-after groups exhibited excellent recognition memory for the old sentences (tested without white noise). They had not simply failed to learn the inputs. However, the mere accumulation of inputs does not necessarily allow one a degree of clarity sufficient to understand something in a new way at a later point in time.

Hannigan also explored the degree to which the framework group's ability to transfer to novel appropriate sentences in white noise depended on making contact with related stored acquisition sentences. For example, the subjects may have originally heard *The man propped the door against the wall* as an example of *Making shelter* during acquisition. The novel appropriate sentence *The man leaned the car hood against the tree* is more similar to this acquisition sentence than any other. Other *Making shelter* acquisition sentences involved different types of relations (throwing a curtain over a metal box, setting up housekeeping in an airplane) that were in turn similar to other novel appropriates.

Hannigan reasoned that if transfer to a novel appropriate depended on making contact with a similar acquisition sentence, there should be strong dependencies between subjects' abilities to detect a particular acquisition sentence (an old) and its novel appropriate counterpart. Her analyses revealed no such dependencies, suggesting that memory mediation was not the basis for transfer. This is not particularly surprising since one must interpret the novel appropriate sentences in a specific manner in order to perceive adequately their similarity to the acquisition sentences. The no-framework group subjects showed no transfer yet received identical acquisition sentence-novel appropriate counterparts. The ability to comprehend novel appropriate sentences in a particular manner is presumably what was learned by the framework subjects. This apparently provided the basis for transfer, not contact with stored acquisition sentences.

Contextual Constraints on Knowing

Hannigan's experimental paradigm raises interesting possibilities for investigating further the processes involved in acquiring knowledge in a form useful for clarifying subsequent experiences. Her framework group illustrates processes of exemplification, but the general principles of abduction apply to other communicative techniques as well. Consider the use of metaphor and analogy. Here a speaker utilizes already known information about some domain X in order to clarify some subsequent domain Y. Learners' understanding of the Y domain is thus influenced by their momentary perspective (which includes X). At the same time, information about Y may further clarify and articulate previous information about X (Hesse, 1966; Verbrugge, 1977).

Similar analyses can be made of well-structured discourse and text. The understood significance of any sentence is influenced by the text or discourse structure in which it is embedded, yet each sentence may further clarify this overall structure. The basic purpose of effective communicative techniques is to marshal a listeners' momentary assets so that these can be used to understand subsequent inputs, which can in turn clarify and restructure their initial knowledge. Hannigan's results suggest that such clarifications are not simply a function of having stored particular propositions in memory. Her framework subjects appeared to acquire a more abstract framework or perspective that guided their comprehension of subsequent inputs. Similar analyses of what is learned may be necessary in order to characterize how people can learn from discourse and texts in a manner that permits them to transfer to subsequent events.

Hannigan's experiments also provide a reference point for identifying additional factors that must be considered in order to understand better the growth of comprehension abilities. At least two additional factors appear relevant to this discussion. The first involves a fine grained analysis of the process by which people develop usable knowledge of a concept. The second involves the contextual constraints under which particular acts of knowing can occur.

Hypotheses regarding the first factor have been discussed elsewhere (Bransford and Franks, 1976; Bransford, Nitsch, and Franks, forthcoming). During early stages of acquisition, knowledge of a concept seems to be closely tied to the original situation in which it was exemplified. For example, Bransford and Franks (1976) discuss students' early knowledge of a concept like operant shaping. They note that an instructor's initial requests for a definition frequently elicited statements like the following: "It's like when you want a rat to press a bar and you give him food for first orienting to the bar, then gradually approaching it...." The ability to apprehend the meaning of the concept seemed to depend on mediating steps involving retrieval of context-specific conditions under which the concept was originally learned (Bransford and Franks, 1976; Bransford, Nitsch, and Franks, forthcoming).

The question of the contextual constraints under which concepts can be used is closely related to the preceding discussion. This question involves contextual constraints on the range of possible conditions under which one can spontaneously carry out certain acts of knowing. For example, Hannigan's framework and framework-after subjects were explicitly informed that many of their test sentences would be related to the concept of survival on a deserted island. It is interesting to consider the limited extent to which their laboratory-gained knowledge might spontaneously affect their comprehension of subsequent, real-world experiences. Pushing this question even further, could certain contextual conditions be necessary in order even to recognize the meaning of a previously learned concept?

The following example suggests that the identification of a concept can be context dependent. One of the authors supplied members of an introductory freshman seminar with a list of concepts that had been discussed during the semester. An example was *ablation*. No one in the class knew its meaning until the instructor said, "Of course you do, think of when we discussed ways to study how various parts of the brain affect behavior." Given this contextual support, over half the class "lit up" and said "oh yea" (or some reasonable paraphrase). They could then discuss the concept. This observation seems analogous to studies of early language acquisition discussed above where the ability to perform certain acts of comprehension (recognition or production) seems context dependent. Additional observations suggest that many concepts employed by adults may be context or domain specific as well. For example, concepts or principles used to describe wartime activities may become ambiguous or anomalous when applied to everyday activities (*We had to destroy the city in order to save it*), and psychological concepts that seem perfectly clear in the context of laboratory experiments may become ambiguous when applied to everyday life. On the positive side, one may import a concept used in one domain (such as physics) to another domain (such as psychology) and thereby clarify a number of inadequately understood phenomena. The processes by which people expand (*decontextualize*) their comprehension abilities seems to be an extremely important area to understand.

Why should people contextualize their knowledge in the first place? We suggest two possible reasons. The first is that people must learn information in some context and may have difficulty resisting contextual influence (see Tulving and Thomson 1973 on *encoding specificity*). This seems especially true for younger children. The second reason stems from some informal pilot studies on vocabulary acquisition. If one must learn a number of new concepts, interference among them is minimized when the concepts are dissimilar. Presenting each concept in a distinct domain of application seems to facilitate the acquisition process. However, the ability to generate a definition or example of a newly acquired concept does not necessarily indicate the degree to which one can sufficiently use it in order to clarify a new domain or situation. For example, our informal data indicates that if people acquire the meaning of "lem" (a berb) in the context of antique dealers, they have great difficulty in initially using it to understand sentences about cowboys or sailors, despite the fact that the basic concept is readily applicable.

Further study of the processes by which people expand or decontextualize their ability to know with concepts and principles might have important educational implications. Note, for example, that traditional flash card drills may not be the most beneficial method for promoting the growth of flexibly usable knowledge. Our pilot studies indicate that subjects can become quite adept at recognizing new words (for instance *lem*) and at stating their definitions and providing examples. However, each act of recognition can involve the recreation of a particular domain of application (such as the subject always thinking of the verb *lem* in terms of antique dealers). This appears to inhibit the ability to apply the concept to some new domain (such as sailors). Such limits on flexibility become important when one considers skilled acts of comprehension, for example, reading. Skilled readers do not simply recognize words; instead they understand the significance of inputs for clarifying the topic of concern. Readers must also be able to read about numerous topics and so need a flexible ability to use the words they know.

Although further research is clearly needed, it is possible that traditional flash card techniques might be more useful if inputs were presented in some meaningful context and students were asked to judge whether the inputs were appropriate in that context (for example, Could these items be used on a picnic?). Such a procedure could make one's apprehension of inputs an activity that is related to the purpose of an overall theme or topic, as in reading and comprehending. By varying the contextual settings in the exercise, students might be helped to develop a flexible ability to use what they know.

Knowing What to Do in Order to Understand

Previous discussion focused on abduction as an abstract characterization of the processes by which one can come to understand things differently (and more adequately). However, questions about those processes that may provide the major contributions to the development and maintenance of expertise have not been discussed. These questions involve the problem of learning how to structure situations actively in order to bring oneself to a point where adequate understanding is possible. For example, the development of comprehension skills seems to be more closely related to the ability to ask relevant questions (of oneself and others) than to the ability to state factual content. What are the prerequisites for actively doing something (for example, asking questions) in order to understand better?

One prerequisite would seem to be realizing that a particular domain is indeed comprehensible. In his book *How Children Fail,* Holt (1964) argues that many children do not even realize that certain domains (such as mathematics) could be comprehensible. Such children exhibit different patterns of problem-solving activities from those who have some grasp of the notion that these domains should make sense (see also Bransford, Nitsch, and Franks, forthcoming, for discussion).

A second prerequisite appears to be the possession of criteria for evaluating the adequacy of one's present understanding. For the case of linguistic comprehension, such criteria must involve much more than the ability to distinguish between acceptable and anomalous statements. One can understand a statement at some level yet inadequately grasp a speaker or writer's intended meaning. Theoretically there is a need to differentiate the problem of the correctness or veridicality of comprehension from the problem of the feeling of understanding. Comprehenders who feel they understand will not perform any additional activities that might be necessary in order to grasp the point that the speaker actually intends.

Consider the following passage generated by Bransford, Johnson, and Mc-Carrell (cf. Bransford and McCarrell, 1974, p. 214):

> The man was worried. His car came to a halt and he was all alone. It was extremely dark and cold. The man took off his overcoat, rolled down the window, and got out of the car as quickly as possible. Then he used all his strength to move as fast as he could. He was relieved when he finally saw the lights of the city, even though they were far away.

College subjects heard this passage and were asked if they felt they adequately understood it. All said "Yes." However, their confident feelings of understanding could be easily dispelled. When the subjects were asked questions such as "Why did the man take off his overcoat?" and "Why did he roll down the window?" they suddenly realized they did not adequately understand the passage. For example, some subjects noted that taking off the coat seemed strange since the passage stated that the weather was cold. Given the above mentioned questions, some subjects (but a very few in this study) suddenly realized that the man's car must have fallen into the water. This reinterpretation of the story permitted the coat and window questions to be easily answered. Without these questions, however, all subjects seemed content with their initial feelings that they had indeed understood.

The criteria utilized in assessing feelings of understanding seem flexible.

They vary as a function of the cognitive-perceptual situation in which inputs occur as well as with the nature of the input itself. For example, subjects in Hannigan's no-framework group rated the acquisition sentences as more comprehensible than did subjects in the framework group, despite the fact that subjects in the latter group were far superior in the transfer test. We have conducted a study indicating that college subjects in an experimental context rate the sentence *Bill has a red car* as very easy to understand. Are particular criteria for understanding employed when one is in an experimental task?

Contrast the comprehension of sentences in an experimental context with one in which the situation is a social context. As mentioned above, Bransford, McCarrell, and Nitsch (1976) carried out such experiments. One involved the sentence *Bill has a red car*. In the experiment, a colleague (hereafter C) was sitting in his office. A friend (hereafter E) walked in and uttered *Bill has a red car*. C's reactions were interesting:

> He looked very surprised, paused for about three seconds, and finally exclaimed "What the hell are you talking about?" After a hasty debriefing session C laughed and told the E what had gone on in his head. First, C thought that E was talking about a person named Bill that C knew. Then C realized that E could not in all probability know that person; and besides, Bill would never buy a red car. Then C thought that E may have mixed up the name and really meant to say J (a mutual friend of C and E). The C knew that J had ordered a new car, but he was surprised that it was red and that it had arrived so soon. The C also entertained a few additional hypotheses — all within about three seconds of time. After that he gave up, thereupon uttering "What the hell are you talking about?" (p. 340).[4]

It is instructive to consider the differences in comprehending *Bill has a red car* in the experimental as opposed to the social situation. In the first instance the subjects comprehended; in the second the subject did not. Do we simply classify the second instance as an error or failure and the first as a success? Is it better to understand than to fail to understand?

Note the subject's activities in the social situation. He had some well-specified criteria about what he needed to know in order to feel that he understood the speaker. For example he was not willing to accept that Bill was someone unknown to him; he wanted to know which particular Bill. He even realized the possibility that the speaker had not said what he meant. In short, the colleague tacitly entertained questions of clarification like "Wait a minute, I don't understand who Bill is. Did you mean to say another name rather than Bill?" In contrast, subjects in the experimental situation seemed perfectly comfortable with their shallow understanding of the *Bill* sentence. The information they received was sufficient given their cognitive-perceptual situation at the time.

It seems clear that the sophistication of one's comprehension activities does not necessarily correlate with success versus failure to understand at any particular moment. There is a need to explore what sophisticated comprehenders do in order to generate interesting questions regarding particular (and perhaps previously accepted) domains of knowledge. It is possible that such styles of knowing might then be facilitated by effective teaching.

We have taken some very modest and simple steps in this direction. We asked how college freshmen might be helped to learn from and evaluate written material. Blumenthal's (1970) translation of Buhler's theory of comprehension was selected as the textual material. We asked whether certain personal experiences might provide a framework for understanding the significance of Buhler's theory as well as evaluating its adequacy. Our assumption was that more accomplished comprehenders might spontaneously relate what they read to other domains of knowledge (such as personal experiences) and hence understand more adequately. Before presenting Buhler's text, the students were provided with one of two different experiences. They were then instructed to attempt to understand the Buhler text in relation to their particular experience and the differences in what they learned were assessed.

Prior to reading the text, all students heard a potentially incomprehensible passage (Bransford and Johnson's, 1971; 1973, *washing clothes* passage) and were asked to recall it. However, students in group one heard the passage with the topic and hence did not realize it might be incomprehensible. Students in group two heard the passage first without the topic and then a second time with it. They therefore experienced a failure of comprehension followed by the ability to comprehend. Students from group one were told to notice the paraphrasing that occurred in their recall. Those in group two were told to notice the feeling of not understanding followed by the ability to understand.

All students were told to attempt to relate what they would read from the Buhler passage to their prior experiences with the *washing clothes* passage. Buhler's discussion dealt with paraphrase (consonant with group one experiences) but mainly with prerequisites to comprehension (consonant with group two experiences). Hence the passage was superficially applicable to both sets of experiences, but more directly relevant to group two. Students read the passage at their own rate (overall reading times did not differ) and were then given essay questions related to what they had read.

Blind scoring of the essays revealed that students in group two were superior to group one. Group two students were better able to generate novel examples and to relate the passage to their general life experienes. Furthermore, these students spontaneously generated more questions about the degree to which Buhler's theory explained other phenomena of comprehension. The act of understanding the text in terms of real life experiences had a positive impact on their ability to go beyond the text. One of the essay questions asked subjects to state their feelings about the experiment plus passage experience. The following is a spontaneous comment from one of the group two students:

> The idea of the shared field (a concept from the Buhler passage) especially struck me after the description (the washing clothes passage) we listened to earlier. The paragraph (the washing clothes passage) did not make sense to me but once I was

given a context—sharing the same field as the person that wrote the description—it made sense. This idea of a shared field or experience seems so obvious, but was one I had never really thought about.

I also knew what was meant by the separation of word perception and sentence comprehension because the same thing happened to me while listening to the clothes-washing passage. I understood every word yet was confused.

Also going through that experience helped me to understand the article. It was a very abstract article and if I hadn't had a concrete example to identify with, most of it would have been meaningless to me. As it was, when something was described that happened to me, the whole thing had more meaning.

The above mentioned investigation suggests that one aspect of skilled comprehension involves acts of relating inputs to other domains and experiences. Effective comprehenders may do this spontaneously. Questions about ways to help people learn what to do in order to further their understanding seem important to pursue.

In this section, an abduction framework for conceptualizing problems of growth and transfer was proposed. It was argued that one not only learns from experience, one learns *to* experience. One's momentary situation or perspective affects the ways in which one experiences subsequent inputs, which in turn further clarify one's perspective. Through this reciprocal, assimilative-accommodatory process, one's perspective may be redefined or remodeled, thereby allowing one to understand subsequent inputs in new ways.

Acts of exemplification were analyzed in terms of the abduction framework. An example is both clarified by one's perspective and further clarifies that perspective. Similar analyses can be made for the communicative efficiency of analogies, well-structured discourse, and well-written texts. The abduction schema was contrasted with other traditional paradigms for conceptualizing acquisition, for example, paired-associate learning and the acquisition of word-referent associations. The latter seem inadequate for conceptualizing preconditions for meaningful acquisition (see MacNamara, 1972) as well as for characterizing what is learned (one does not simply learn a list of concept-example associations). Hannigan's (1976) studies were cited as experimental investigations of the processes by which subjects can come to understand things differently. Her analyses suggested that transfer (for the framework group) was not mediated by contact with stored examples that the subjects had previously learned.

Two additional problems involved in the growth of understanding were considered. The first involved contextual constraints on people's abilities to perform certain acts of knowing. Contrary to many models (Collins and Loftus, 1975; Smith, Shoben, and Rips, 1974), knowledge may not exist in one unified (and completely interrelated) semantic or conceptual memory. Both children and adults sometimes appear to need explicit contextual or situational support in order to utilize effectively aspects of their knowing abilities. The processes by which people expand (decontextualize) their abilities to use certain types of information was cited as an important problem to pursue.

The second problem considered involved the processes by which comprehenders learn to structure situations actively in order to facilitate their own understanding. It was suggested that the development of comprehension skills
seems more related to the ability to ask appropriate questions than the ability to
state factual content. The criteria utilized to modulate feelings of understanding
seem to be flexible and depend on one's current perspective or situation. Research is needed in order to assess what accomplished comprehenders do in order to understand inputs effectively. Appropriate educational techniques ·that
facilitate acquisition of such activities might then be devised.

Toward a Framework for Understanding Assessment and Intervention

We have discussed problems of comprehension from a global perspective.
The guiding question has been how one can come to understand things that one
could not previously understand or how one can come to understand things in
new ways. It has been emphasized that the minimal unit of analysis must always
be in terms of the relationship between one's cognitive-perceptual situation and
inputs. One implication of this orientation is that meaning is not something possessed by stimuli or input or something stored solely within the organism. Meaning resides in organism-environment relations. From this perspective, growth
does not result from the mere accumulation of inputs and their meanings. To help
persons change or grow, one must focus on those relationships between their
current cognitive perceptual situation and inputs that permit them to acquire information in a form useful for understanding subsequent inputs in new ways.

In the introduction to this chapter it was noted that effective teachers use a
variety of intuitively based techniques for helping students come to understand
things. Theoretical psychology should ideally provide a framework that helps
clarify those intuitions about effective and ineffective modes of facilitation and
intervention. Some reasons why theoretical psychology (at least the adult, cognitive literature) fails to provide a coherent framework suitable for this purpose has
been discussed elsewhere (Bransford, Nitsch, and Franks, forthcoming). In general, the failure revolves around the lack of explicit concern with problems of
growth. This chapter represents an attempt to focus more directly on growth
problems. In this section some potential implications for the school and clinic are
presented. Like the discussion of comprehension, these implications will be at a
macrolevel.

An Example of Intervention

Anita Willis, an undergraduate student at Vanderbilt, recently completed a
project aimed at teaching new vocabulary items to a boy diagnosed as developmentally delayed. Although we were not involved in the project, we were struck
with Willis's observations and tentative conclusions. She warns that her study
was informal and that she lacks hard data to back up her observations, but her

experiences provide valuable hints about what someone might look for in order to understand intervention processes in more detail.

Willis worked with a male who was three years, nine months of age and had been diagnosed as developmentally delayed. At the beginning of the intervention project the boy's behavior was very erratic. He engaged in considerable self-stimulation behavior and exhibited an extremely short attention span, although this varied depending on the task and mood. The boy was easily excited and often difficult to calm down. He did have some receptive vocabulary; Willis's goal was to help him learn some new words.

Willis utilized the training technology generally referred to as behavior modification. She was aware that, as powerful a technique as this is, its success depends on the sophistication of its user. She therefore began by observing the thirteen children in her toddler group and noted their reactions in and out of behavioral modification sessions. She felt that the children did not really understand what their teachers wanted them to learn. For example, she noted that the children frequently performed an activity inappropriately yet clapped their hands mimicking the social praise they had received in training sessions. Furthermore she observed that children frequently performed a task correctly yet remained uncertain (as evidenced by a blank face or a questioning look) until the teacher clapped or in some way praised the child. At this point the child would realize that he or she had responded correctly and his or her facial expression would change. How might one bring children to a point where they have their own criteria for knowing whether their actions are appropriate? How might one make events more meaningful for children?

Willis decided to teach the child to understand words like *comb*, *brush*, and *mirror*. One might do this by placing objects on a table and teaching the child to respond correctly to requests like "Hand me the comb," but Willis did not proceed in this way. Instead she fashioned a minienvironment consisting of a small room equipped with such items as a comb and brush and a mirror on the wall in which the boy could see himself. She wanted to help the boy come to understand this environment and to teach him more about language in this context.

Willis noted that in the beginning of the sessions the boy exhibited extremely erratic behavior and was very inattentive. The objects seemed to have no meaning to him and he kept them in his mouth more often than not. However with each session the boy became more attentive. He kept the objects out of his mouth more and more and was observant when Willis used the comb and brush. Soon he was combing Willis's hair as well as his own. She notes that he became increasingly conscious of his image in the mirror and watched himself using the comb and brush. Throughout these sessions Willis would say things that were meaningful in the context of the child's actions (such as "You're using the comb very well") and would reinforce the child when he could respond to requests (such as "Where's the brush?"). All this training was done in an environment that was becoming increasingly meaningful to the child.

In the final session Willis tested the child's ability to understand the words and requests she had taught him. For example, she made requests like "Please hand me the brush." The child carried out the correct actions without hesitation. Willis was more impressed by the look on the child's face when he performed the actions than the mere correctness of these actions. These facial expressions demonstrated to Willis that the boy knew he was performing correctly. He still enjoyed and responded to the social praise from Willis, but the look of understanding occurred before Willis provided social praise.

Intervention and Simple Tasks

At a global level, Willis's procedure can be viewed as an attempt to simulate some of those conditions under which language acquisition occurs naturally. She first helped the child come to understand a particular nonlinguistic situation. Given this cognitive-perceptual situation, the significance of linguistic utterances could be better understood and could further clarify the boy's situation as well (including the nature of his relationship with Willis). Note, however, that she created an extremely simple environment for the child. The child was able to come to understand this environment and his place in it, but it may have been very difficult for him to come to understand an environment that was more complex. The notion of beginning with a simplified situation and building on it seems intuitively obvious, and it follows from the present emphasis on situation-input relations. However, this usage of simplicity differs in important ways from many other uses of the term.

McCarrell and Brooks (1975) provide an insightful analysis of prevalent theoretical conceptions of simple versus complex processes. They note that many theories view development as hierarchical in nature. Development is characterized as progressing from simple to more complex ways of processing information, and the simpler processes are assumed to be prerequisites for the more complex. The important point is that these simpler processes are viewed as involving something like copying. For example, McCarrell and Brooks cite Gagne (1970), who identifies the representational copying of stimulus-response connections as a prerequisite for higher learning; Berlyne (1965), who claims that basic associations provide the building blocks for subsequent thought and actions; and Jensen (1970; 1972), who distinguishes between level one and level two abilities. Level one abilities are assumed to involve only minimal processing of data and establish simple and direct stimulus-response correspondences. Level two abilities involve more sophisticated elaborations of inputs.

McCarrell and Brooks's analysis highlights some basic assumptions underlying many theories of development. From their perspective as well as our present orientation, such assumptions are highly questionable. The argument is not against intuitive assumptions about building blocks or prerequisites for further understanding. Instead, the argument is against equating these building blocks with basic processes of copying or forming simple stimulus-response connections. It is not at all clear that these are the basic processes that are prerequisites to higher order understanding and thought.

Note, for example, that Willis's project involved an attempt to eliminate the painstaking procedure of acquiring meaningless associations. She did not experimentally contrast the effectiveness of her procedure with other possible approaches, but there is sufficient literature to suggest that meaningful entities are learned much more readily. For example, Johnson et al. (1974) show that repetitions produce greater recall increments over trials if one is exposed to meaningful as opposed to less meaningful materials. Similarly, recent research in animal learning (see Garcia and Koelling, 1966; Seligman and Hager, 1972) suggests that the speed of learning can vary tremendously depending on the degree to which stimulus response pairings are ecologically significant or meaningful to the organism. This ecological significance is frequently due to the genetic preattunement of the organism (which forms part of its situation), yet it can depend on previous experiences as well (Birch, 1945). Finally, the data from Bloom, Hood, and Lightbown (1974) showed that their subject, Peter, was quite poor at simply copying or repeating a set of target sentences, even though these sentences were ones that he had spontaneously produced at a previous time. He had produced these in a meaningful context, but in the copying task this contextual information was not supplied.

One can understand why notions like nonelaborative copying might be mistakenly viewed as a prerequisite for higher order thinking and understanding. For example, if unsophisticated college sophomores are presented with a statement like *The Tao that can be spoken is not the great Tao,* the best they might be expected to be able to do is repeat the sentence or perhaps paraphrase it at a linguistic level. In contrast, a more sophisticated student of Eastern philosophy could elaborate on the statement and better explain what it means. It therefore looks as if copying occurs before more elaborative and meaningful understanding. However, this latter analysis ignores the fact that understanding also affects copying and memorizing. For example, considerable development must take place in order to know how to memorize explicitly (Brown, 1975; Flavell and Wellman, forthcoming), and it is easier to remember things that one understands. The fact that there are prerequisites for effective copying suggests that copying per se cannot be the most basic process upon which everything else is dependent.

From this perspective, one's ability to deal with information depends on the relationship between the inputs and one's momentary cognitive-perceptual situation. If one's situation includes knowledge of Eastern philosophy, one will be able to expand on a statement about the Tao. Yet even the less sophisticated student's ability to copy these sentences presupposes knowledge of language as well as an understanding of the nature of memory tasks. Surely one would not want to claim that the student who could only repeat the sentence had some deficiency in more elaborative thought processes. What one can do depends on the relationship between an input and one's current cognitive-perceptual situation.

Problems in Assessing "Where People Are"

In the context of the above mentioned college students, it seems absurd to talk about cognitive deficits. No one would consider using such data as evidence that one student could think better than the other. However, assumptions about cognitive deficits are frequently made in situations that seem directly analogous to the *Tao* example noted above.

Assume that one is attempting to assess children's abilities to think (solve problems) at various age levels. Younger children will usually perform more poorly than older children. It is therefore easy to believe that they must develop more complex thought processes before they can perform adequately in these tasks. Similarly, it is easy to assume that children who perform below their normal age group are deficient in certain cognitive skills (see Cole and Bruner, 1971) for a criticism of similar assumptions affecting cross-cultural research). According to the present orientation, such conclusions require serious reconsideration. Are current inabilities to perform a result of inherent deficits in thought processes or of differences in the relationships between inputs and a person's current cognitive-perceptual situation? Until the latter can be carefully analyzed, we have no idea of what deficit means.

Research by Odom and his colleagues (Odom and Mumbauer, 1971; Odom, Astor, and Cunningham, 1975) is very important in this context. In essence, their position is that one must carefully analyze a child's current situation in order to understand what he or she can do. Their method is to determine those aspects of the environment that are perceptually salient to individual children. Salience does not refer simply to what children can discriminate perceptually; it refers to those dimensions of stimulation that an individual child automatically notices and to which he or she attends. By first independently assessing saliency preferences for each child, Odom and his colleagues have been able to measure children's abilities to perform tasks (for example, a Piagetian matrix problem) that contain critical information that is either congruent or incongruent with children's saliency preferences. Their data strongly suggest that children as young as four years can perform in highly effective and sophisticated manners when task solutions require attention to dimensions that are highly salient for the individual child.

It is intriguing to compare Odom's results with the conclusion reached by de Groot (1966) in his studies comparing expert or master chess players with lesser skilled players. Why were experts so much better than lesser experts at determining the best move? His original hypothesis was they "thought more elaborately or deeply," but he found no evidence to support this conclusion. Instead he concluded that experts actually perceived the total chess board in a much more adequate manner. Their superiority in problem solving was due to the fact that they began at a much "higher place."

We know that increasing experience and knowledge in a specific field (chess, for instance) has the effect that things (properties, etc.) which, at earlier stages, had to be abstracted, or even inferred are apt to be immediately perceived at later stages. To a rather large extent, *abstraction is replaced by perception*, but we do not know much about how this works, nor where the borderline lies....As an effect of this replacement, a so called "given" problem situation is not really given since *it is seen differently* by an expert than it is perceived by an unexperienced person, but we do not know much about these differences (deGroot, 1966, pp. 33-34).

The preceding discussion in conjunction with arguments by Cole and Bruner (1971) as well as Labov (1970) suggests the need for serious clarification and reconsideration of deficit hypotheses and the normatively based tests by which people's abilities are assessed. Of course, people *do* differ in their current abilities to perform particular acts of knowing in certain situations and in their current abilities to learn from certain types of instruction. However, it is not clear that this is due to some inherent deficit in their ability to think and learn. The boy Willis worked with was unable to learn language as effectively as normal children. But this does not mean that he could not learn under appropriate conditions. By beginning where he was, he could be helped to come to understand a simplified environment and further understanding could be built on that understanding. If Willis had not begun where the boy was, he might easily have remained helplessly lost.

Many have observed that experienced teachers become intuitively sensitive to assessing where students are and teach on this basis. For example, questions asked by students can reveal what they must be assuming in order to ask these questions at all. Frequently, however, education and intervention take the form of boring, meaningless drill that fails to take the student beyond his current state of knowing. An additional problem is that students may become lost because instructional materials do not allow children to use what they already know in order to understand effectively. Imagine, for example, a paragraph describing various activities of six people. If adults hear such a passage, they find it almost impossible to keep who did what straight. However, when time is taken to learn about the people and their names first, the story is readily understood. One's current knowledge must provide a basis for learning something new. Bloom (1978) presents data indicating that children's language acquisition proceeds in such a manner. She notes that new linguistic constructions appear to be learned and applied initially in the context of linguistic and conceptual knowledge that is already well known to the child. Rather than employ intervention strategies based on normative tests and procedures, it might be more fruitful to identify those domains in which an individual performs adequately and work from there.

Summary and Conclusions

The major purpose of this chapter has been to sketch a general framework for conceptualizing problems of understanding. Since one's understanding of events changes, it seemed important to consider the problem from a perspective that is sensitive to this dynamic aspect (the problem of growth). Therefore our guiding question has been "How can we come to understand things that we did not previously understand?" or "How can we come to understand things in new ways?" The reasons for choosing to discuss understanding at this macrolevel are congruent with the types of arguments expressed in this paper. A global framework seems necessary in order to understand the meaning or significance of particular events (more specifically, the significance of various experimental results). One's framework frequently remains tacit. By attempting to make frameworks explicit, one can hope to evaluate more effectively the assumptions they entail. (See the physicist Bohm, 1969 on the assumptive nature of knowing and understanding.)

The basic theme has been that understanding is a function of the reciprocal relationships between inputs and one's current cognitive-perceptual situation. The minimal unit of analysis must therefore be a situation plus an input, never the mere input. At many levels the importance of situation-input relations is obvious: What we say to young children and what we deem appropriate to teach at various age levels reflect our appreciation of the importance of these relations. As long as these assumptions remain tacit however it is easy to ignore many factors that may be crucial to understanding understanding. For example, it easy to overlook the importance of the instructions in a sentence comprehension experiment. These instructions help define the subjects' situation so that sentences can be understood as examples of utterances that might be stated by someone, at some time, for some purpose. If one overlooks the specialized nature of the process involved in understanding sentences in this manner, it would then be easy to assume that such activities constitute the simplest and most basic form of comprehension. Higher order comprehension would then follow from this basic mode of understanding via processes of deductive inference. Someone incapable of higher order comprehension might therefore be assumed to have cognitive deficits of some kind.

Assumptions about the basic level of comprehension involved in understanding an isolated sentence like *The boy hit the ball* ignore the influence of situations on inputs. For example, a young child requires explicit social-perceptual situational support in order to understand linguistic utterances. The college freshmen presented with the term *ablation* needed certain support (such as the teacher's statement "Recall when we were discussing ways to study brain functions....") in order to identify its meaning. Available situational support is necessary to realize that one needs to know something further in order to understand a speaker adequately (as in the *Bill has a red car* example). Similarly, Hannigan's subjects needed situational support (such as the survival framework) in order to understand better the significance of sentences. Situational support is also necessary in order to realize that the sentence *I had a book stolen* (cf. Chomsky 1965) is syntactically ambiguous in many ways.

As one becomes acquainted with various domains, one's need for explicit situational support decreases. For example, adults can understand numerous sentences in relative isolation. Aspects of their linguistic knowledge have become decontextualized. Similarly, the above mentioned college freshmen may eventually grasp the meaning of *ablation* without the need for such explicit situational support. Essentially, more sophisticated comprehenders (experts in a particular field) are able to supply this support on their own. The processes by which one develops expertise were discussed in terms of the concept of abduction. Acts of exemplification were analyzed in terms of this abductive schema. Hannigan's (1976) studies were used to illustrate factors involved in acquiring knowledge in a form useful for clarifying subsequent events.

One's current situation or perspective is a function of relatively invariant, partially decontextualized information plus momentary, context-specific assumptions and expectations. Many theories attempt to characterize the relatively stable or normative aspects of one's knowledge that affect how one understands. For example, theories of semantic or lexical memory attempt to describe the relatively stable structure of lexical knowledge. Such theories are characterizations of the results of previous processes of growth and decontexturalization. For example, Bolinger (1965, p. 567) refers to lexical memory as a "frozen pantomime" whose entries are "nosegays of faded metaphors." Indeed aspects of the growth process seem analogous to progressions from "live" to "dead" metaphor. One may first need to view explicitly domain Y from the perspective of an already known X. Gradually, the need to recall X in order to use concept Y may be eliminated. The live metaphor through which one initially understood a situation gradually becomes dead (Hanson, 1970; Hesse, 1966; Verbrugge, 1977).

Normative theories of knowledge (such as semantic memory theories) are extremely important. They provide reference points for what knowledgeable people know. For example, normative theories of lexical memory can be used to assess what "normal" children know at various age levels (Anglin, 1970, 1976). They can identify basic concepts and suggest reasons for their basic nature (Rosch et al., 1976). They can suggest shifts in modes of organization, for example from functional or paradigmatic modes of organization in young children to syntagmatic modes of organization (Nelson, forthcoming). In short, normative theories can provide information that places important constraints on theories of growth and development. The most salient example of the importance of such constraints is illustrated by Chomsky's theories (1972) of an "ideal, adult speaker-hearer." Based on Chomsky's analysis of language, large classes of potential theories were seen as inadequate because they could not possibly account for the types of information available to adult speaker-hearers (see Dixon and Horton, 1968; Fodor, Bever, and Garrett, 1974).

The value of normative theories is enhanced by considering what they do not tell us as well as what they do tell us. For example, they do not necessarily tell us how people arrived at a particular level of knowing or how they can move beyond that level (Bransford, Nitsch, and Franks, forthcoming). Indeed, linguists have frequently been plagued by disagreements about basic data. These data involve speaker-hearer's intuitions about such things as grammaticality, acceptability, and intersentential relations. Yet intuitions about these questions frequently differ. If experienced linguists move to a point where they become more sensitive to linguistic subtleties than normal speaker-hearers, it seems reasonable to assume that their judgments about intuitive acceptability may differ as well.

Probably the most difficult problem in learning from normative theories involves understanding their relationships to the actual form of people's knowing and understanding abilities. It is easy to slip into the mode of assuming that a lexical structure or set of grammatical rules is actually embodied in a person's head. One is then tempted to ask how someone can contact a particular structure or move through it (see Bransford and Franks, 1976; Bransford et al., 1977, for further discussion). Normative theories are invaluable for representing information. However, representations are used by comprehenders to understand something. A representation of what someone knows is not necessarily equivalent to the form of that person's knowledge, which is assumed to be stored somewhere. Yet it is frequently assumed that representations are "in the head" and that the ability to know the meaning of something involves contacting some stored "meaning representation."

There are a number of reasons for questioning the assumption that the assessment of meaning involves contact with some stored meaning representation. The most basic reason is that one can come to understand things in new ways. How could one understand something new if meaning simply involved contact with old, stored representations? Assumptions about novel concatenations of old meaning elements are not sufficient because the elements themselves change in meaning. Indeed, how could children ever acquire linguistic meanings if meaning involved making contact with representations of meanings that were stored?

It has been suggested here that meaning resides neither in the input nor in the organism. Instead, meaning resides in the situation-input (organism-environment) relation. Both the environment and one's knowledge can be said to provide support for meaning or set the stage for meaning (Bransford and Franks, 1976), but meaning does not necessarily result from contacting a meaning representation stored in the head (see also Gibson, 1977; Mace, 1977; Shaw and McIntyre, 1974; Shaw and Pittenger, 1977, on Gibson's concept of affordances and its congruence with the position adopted here).

Problems in assuming that meaning involves contact with a stored trace can be clarified by noting that the meaning of an input can affect the speed with which it can be recognized. This frequently seems paradoxical because meaning somehow seems to affect recognition, yet one must recognize an input in order to find its meaning (see Turvey, 1974). However, it is only paradoxical if one assumes that comprehending the meaning of something involves finding a stored meaning trace. An input has meaning only by virtue of its relationship to the organism's current situation. A normatively meaningful input is therefore one that maps into the organism's current cognitive-perceptual situation. The latter exists prior to the input and will affect its recognition, just as a relatively decontextualized knowing system allows an adult to recognize an isolated sentence like *The boy hit the ball.* However, if a person's knowledge is not in a relatively decontextualized state, the input will not be normatively meaningful (the *ablation* example). One will therefore need additional contextual support in order to recognize the input readily.

The most important aspect of viewing meaning as residing the organism-environment relationship is the effect it has on thinking about growth processes. As perspectives change, understood meanings change. However, if meaning is a function of situation-input relations, effective change will take place only by beginning with a person's momentary situation and working from there.

REFERENCES

Anderson, R.C., and Ortony, A. 1975. On putting apples into bottles – a problem of polysemy. *Cognitive Psychology, 7,* 167-180.

Anglin, J.M. 1970. *The growth of word meaning.* Cambridge, Mass: MIT Press.

Anglin, J.M. 1976. Word, object, and conceptual development. New York: Norton.

Barclay, J.R., Bransford, J.D., Franks, J.J., McCarrell, N.S., and Nitsch, K. 1974. Comprehension and semantic flexibility. *Journal of Verbal Learning and Verbal Behavior, 13,* 471-481.

Bates, E. 1976. *Language and context: The acquisition of pragmatics.* New York: Academic Press.

Beilin, H., and Spontak, G. 1969. Active-passive transformations and operational reversibility. Paper presented at the biennial meeting of the Society for Research in Child Development, Santa Monica, Ca., March.

Berlyne, D.E. 1965. *Structure and direction in thinking.* New York: John Wiley and Sons.

Bever, T.G. 1970. The influence of speech performance on linguistic structures. In G.B. Flores d'Arcais and W.J.M. Levelt (Eds.), *Advances in psycholinguistics.* Amsterdam: North-Holland Publishing, 4-30.

Birch, H.G. 1945. The relation of previous experience to insightful problem solving. *Journal of Comparative Psychology, 38,* 367-383.

Bloom, L. 1974. Talking, understanding, and thinking. In R.L. Schiefelbusch and L.L. Lloyd (Eds), *Language perspectives: Acquisition, retardation, and intervention.* Baltimore, Md.: University Park Press, 285-311.

Bloom, L. 1978. The integration of form, content, and use in language development. In J. Kavanagh and W. Strange (Eds.), *Speech and language in the laboratory, school, and clinic.* Cambridge, Mass.: MIT Press.

Bloom, L., Hood, L., and Lightbown, P. Imitation in language development: If, when, and why. *Cognitive Psychology,* 6, 380-420.

Blumenthal, A.L. 1970. *Language and psychology.* New York: John Wiley and Sons.

Bohm, D. 1969. Further remarks on order. In C.H. Waddington (Ed.), *Towards a theoretical biology,* Vol. 2. Chicago: Adline, 41-60.

Bolinger, D. 1965. The atomization of meaning. *Language, 41,* 553-573.

Bransford, J.D., and Franks, J.J. 1973. The abstraction of linguistic ideas: A review. *Cognition: International Journal of Cognitive Psychology, 1,* 211-249.

Bransford, J.D., and Franks, J.J. 1976. Toward a framework for understanding learning. In G. Bower (Ed.), *The psychology of learning and motivation,* Vol. 10. New York: Academic Press, 93-127.

Bransford, J.D., and Johnson, M.K. 1972. Contextual prerequisites for understanding: Some investigations of comprehension and recall. *Journal of Verbal Learning and Verbal Behavior, 11,* 717-726.

Bransford, J.D., and Johnson, M.K. 1973. Considerations of some problems of comprehension. In W. Chase (Ed.), *Visual information processings.* New York: Academic Press, 383-438.

Bransford, J.D., and McCarrell, N.S. 1974. A sketch of a cognitive approach to comprehension. In W. Weimer and D. Palermo (Eds.), *Cognition and the symbolic processes.* Hillsdale, N.J.: Lawrence Erlbaum Associates, 189-229.

Bransford, J.D., Barclay, J.R., and Franks, J.J. 1972. Sentence memory: A constructive versus interpretive approach. *Cognitive Psychology, 3,* 193-209.

Bransford, J.D., McCarrell, N.S., and Nitsch, K.E. 1976. Contexte, compréhension et flexibilité sémantique: quelques implications théoriques et méthodologiques. In S. Ehrlich and E. Tulving (Eds.), *La mémoire sémantique*. Paris: Bulletin de Psychologie, 335-345.

Bransford, J.D. Nitsch, K.E., and Franks, J.J. Forthcoming. Schooling and the facilitation of knowing. In R.C. Anderson, R.J. Spiro, and W.E. Montague (Eds.), *Schooling and the acquisition of knowledge*. Hillsdale, N.J.: Lawrence Erlbaum Associates.

Bransford, J.D., McCarrell, N.S., Franks, J.J., and Nitsch, K.E. 1977. Toward unexplaining memory. In R.E. Shaw and J.D. Bransford (Eds.). *Perceiving, acting and knowing: Toward an ecological psychology*. Hillsdale, N.J.: Lawrence Erlbaum Associates, 431-466.

Brewer, W.F. 1974. The problem of meaning and the interrelations of the higher mental processes. In W. Weimer and D. Palermo (Eds.), *Cognition and the symbolic processes*. Hillsdale, N.J.: Lawrence Erlbaum Associates, 263-298.

Brewer, W.F., and Harris, R.J. 1974. Memory for deictic elements in sentences. *Journal of Verbal Learning and Verbal Behavior, 13*, 321-327.

Broudy, H. Types of knowledge and purposes of education. In R.C. Anderson, R.J. Spiro, and W.E. Montague (Eds.), *Schooling and the acquisition of knowledge*. Hillsdale, N.J.: Lawrence Erlbaum Associates, 1977.

Brown, A.L. 1975. The development of memory: Knowing, knowing about knowing, and knowing how to know. In H.W. Reese (Ed.), *Advances in child development and behavior,* Vol. 10. New York: Academic Press, 103-152.

Brown, A.L. Forthcoming. Development, schooling and the acquisition of knowledge about knowledge. In R.C. Anderson, R.J. Spiro, and W.E. Montague (Eds.), *Schooling and the acquisition of knowledge*. Hillsdale, N.J.: Lawrence Erlbaum Associates.

Cassirer, E. 1923. *Substance and function*. Chicago, Ill.: Open Court Publishing.

Chafe, W.L. 1972. Discourse structure and human knowledge. In J.B. Carroll and R.O. Freedle (Eds.), *Language comprehension and the acquisition of knowledge*. Washington, D.C.: Winston, 41-70.

Chapman, R.S. 1974. "Developmental relationship between receptive and expective language." In R.L. Schiefelbusch and L.L. Lloyd (Eds.), *Language perspectives: Acquisition, retardation, and intervention*. Baltimore, Md.: University Park Press, 335-344.

Chapman, R.S. This volume. Comprehension strategies in children.

Chomsky, N. 1965. *Aspects of a theory of syntax*. Cambridge, Mass.: MIT Press.

Chomsky, N. 1972. *Language and mind*. New York: Harcourt Brace Jovanovich.

Clark, H.H. 1973. Comprehension and the given-new contract. Paper presented at the conference on the role of grammar in interdisciplinary linguistic research, University of Bielefeld, Bielefeld, Germany,

Clark, H.H., and Haviland, S.E. Comprehension and the given-new contract. In R. Freedle (Ed.), *Discourse production and comprehension*. Hillsdale, N.J.: Lawrence Erlbaum Associates.

Clark, H.H., and Stafford, R.A. 1969. Memory for semantic features in the verb. *Journal of Experimental Psychology, 80*, 326-334.

Cole, M., and Bruner, J.S. 1971. Cultural differences and inferences about psychological processes. *American Psychologist, 26*, 867-876.

Collins, A.M., and Loftus, E.F. 1975. A spreading activation theory of semantic processing. *Psychological Review, 82*, 407-428.

de Groot, A.B. 1966. Perception and memory versus thought. In B. Kleimutz (Ed.), *Problem solving: Research, method, and theory.* New York: John Wiley and Sons, 19-50.

De Villiers, J.G., and De Villiers, P.A. 1974. Competence and performance in child language: Are children really competent to judge? *Journal of Child Language, 1*, 11-22.

Dixon, T.R., and Horton, D.L. (Eds.). 1968. *Verbal behavior and general behavior theory.* Englewood Cliffs, N.J.: Prentice-Hall.

Dooling, D.J., and Lachman, R. 1971. Effects of comprehension on retention of prose. *Journal of Experimental Psychology, 88*, 216-222.

Dore, J., Franklin, M.B., Miller, R.T., and Ramer, A.L.H. 1976. Transitional phenomena in early language acquisition. *Journal of Child Language, 3*, 13-28.

Fillmore, C.J. 1971. Verbs of judging: An exercise in semantic description. In C.J. Fillmore and D.T. Langendoen (Eds.), *Studies in linguistic semantics*. New York: Holt, Rinehart and Winston, 273-290.

Flavell, J.H., and Wellman, H.M. Forthcoming. Metamemory. In R.V. Kail, Jr., and J.W. Hagen (Eds.), *Perspectives on the development of memory and cognition.* Hillsdale, N.J.: Lawrence Erlbaum Associates.

Fodor, J.A., Bever, T.G., and Garrett, M.F. 1974. *The psychology of language: An introduction to psycholinguistics and generative grammar.* New York: McGraw-Hill.

Franks, J.J. 1974. Toward understanding understanding. In W. Weimer and D. Palermo (Eds.), *Cognition and the symbolic processes.* Hillsdale, N.J.: Lawrence Erlbaum Associates, 231-261.

Frederiksen, C.H. 1972. Effects of task-induced cognitive operations on comprehension and memory processes. In J.B. Carroll and R.O. Freedle (Eds.), *Language comprehension and the acquisition of knowledge.* Washington, D.C.: V.H. Winston, 211-245.

Frederiksen, C.H. 1975. Acquisition of semantic information from discourse: Effects of repeated exposures. *Journal of Verbal Learning and Verbal Behavior, 14,* 158-169.

Gagne, R.M. 1970. *The conditions of learning* (Rev. ed.) New York: Holt, Rinehart and Winston.

Garcia, J., and Koelling, R.A. 1966. Relation of cue to consequence in avoidance learning. *Psychonomic Science, 4,* 123-124.

Gibson J.J. Forthcoming. The theory of affordances. In R.E. Shaw and J.D. Bransford (Eds.), *Perceiving, acting and knowing: Toward an ecological psychology.* Hillsdale, N.J.: Lawrence Erlbaum Associates, 67-82.

Glucksberg, S., and Danks, J.J. 1975. *Experimental psycholinguistics: An introduction.* Hillsdale, N.J.: Lawrence Erlbaum Associates.

Gough, P.B. 1965. Grammatical transformations and speed of understanding. *Journal of Verbal Learning and Verbal Behavior, 4,* 107-111.

Gough, P.B. 1966. The verification of sentences: The effects of delay of evidence and sentence length. *Journal of Verbal Learning and Verbal Behavior, 5,* 492-496.

Halliday, M.A.K. 1967. Notes on transitivity and theme in English: II. *Journal of Linguistics, 3,* 199-244.

Hannigan, M.L. 1976. The effects of frameworks on sentence perception and memory. Unpublished Ph.D. dissertation, Vanderbilt University, Nashville, Tenn.

Hanson, N.R. 1970. A picture theory of theory meaning. In R.G. Colodny (Ed.), *The nature and function of scientific theories.* Pittsburgh, Pa.: University of Pittsburgh Press, 233-274.

Harris, R.J., and Brewer, W.F. 1973. Deixis in memory for verb tense. *Journal of Verbal Learning and Verbal Behavior, 12,* 590-597.

Hesse, M.B. 1966. *Models and analogies in science.* South Bend, Ind.: University of Notre Dame Press.

Hester, M. 1977. Visual attention and sensibility. In R.E. Shaw and J.D. Bransford (Eds.), *Perceiving, acting and knowing: Toward an ecological psychology.* Hillsdale, N.J.: Lawrence Erlbaum Associates, 135-169.

Hoffman, M. 1968. Child language. Unpublished Master's thesis, McGill University, Department of Psychology, Montreal, Canada.

Holt, J. 1964. *How children fail.* New York: Dell Publishing Co.

Huttenlocher, J., Eisenberg, K., and Strauss, S. 1968. Comprehension: Relation between perceived actor and logical subject. *Journal of Verbal Learning and Verbal Behavior, 7,* 527-530.

Jenkins, J.J. 1974. Can we have a theory of meaningful memory? In R.L. Solso (Ed.), *Theories of cognitive psychology: The Loyola Symposium.* N.J.: Lawrence Erlbaum Associates, 1-20.

Jensen, A.R. 1970. A theory of primary and secondary familiar mental retardation. In N.R. Ellis (Ed.), *International review of research in mental retardation,* Vol. 4. New York: Academic Press, 51-66.

Jensen, A.R. 1972. *Genetics and education.* New York: Harper and Row.

Johnson, M.K., Bransford, J.D. and Solomon, S. 1973. Memory for tacit implications of sentences. *Journal of Experimental Psychology, 98,* 203-205.

Johnson, M.K. Doll, T.J., Bransford, J.D., and Lapinski, R.H. 1974. Context effects in sentence memory. *Journal of Experimental Psychology, 98,* 358-360.

Katz, J.J., and Postal, P.M. 1964. *An integrated theory of linguistic descriptions.* Cambridge, Mass.: MIT Press.

Keller, H. 1903. *The story of my life.* New York: Doubleday, Page.

Kintsch, W. 1974. *The representation of meaning in memory.* Hillsdale, N.J.: Lawrence Erlbaum Associates.

Labov, W. 1970. The logical nonstandard English. In F. Williams (Ed.), *Language and poverty.* Chicago: Markham Press, 153-189.

Lakoff, R. 1971. If's, and's, and but's about conjunction. In C.J. Fillmore and D.T. Langendoen (Eds.), *Studies in linguistic semantics*. New York: Holt, Rinehart and Winston, 63-72.

Lashley, K.S. 1951. The problem of serial order in behavior. In L.A. Jeffress (Ed.), *Cerebral mechanisms in behavior*. New York: John Wiley and Sons, 112-136.

Mace, W.M. 1977. James Gibson's strategy for perceiving: Ask not what's inside your head, but what your head's inside of. In R.E. Shaw and J.D. Bransford (Eds.), *Perceiving, acting, and knowing: Toward an ecological psychology.* Hillsdale, N.J.: Lawrence Erlbaum Associates, 43-65.

MacNamara, J. 1972. Cognitive basis of language learning in infants. *Psychological Review, 79*, 1-13.

Maier, N.R.F. 1930. Reasoning in humans. I. On direction. *Journal of Comparative Psychology, 10*, 115-143.

Marks, C.B., Doctorow, M.J., and Wittrock, M.C. 1974. Word frequency and reading comprehension. *Journal of Educational Research, 67*, 259-262.

McCarrell, N.S., and Brooks, P.H. 1975. Mental retardation: Comprehension gone awry. Research colloquium sponsored by the John F. Kennedy Center for Research on Education and Human Development, Nashville, Tenn., September.

McCawley, J.D. 1974. On what is deep about deep structures. In W. Weimer and D. Palermo (Eds.), *Cognition and the symbolic processes*. Hillsdale, N.J.: Lawrence Erlbaum Associates, 125-128.

Miller, G.A., Heise, G.A., and Lichten W. 1951. The intelligibility of speech as a function of the context of the text materials. *Journal of Experimental Psychology, 41*, 329-335.

Nelson, K. 1974. Concept, word, and sentence. Interrelations in acquisition and development. *Psychological Review, 81*, 267-285.

Nelson, K. Forthcoming. Cognitive development and the acquisition of concepts. In R.C. Anderson, R.J. Spiro, and W.E. Montague (Eds.), *Schooling and the acquisition of knowledge*. Hillsdale, N.J.: Lawrence Erlbaum Associates.

Nitsch, K.E. 1975. Toward a conceptualization of the problem of meaning. Major area paper, Vanderbilt University, Nashville, Tenn.

Odom, R.D., and Mumbauer, C.C. 1971. Dimensional salience and identification of the relevant dimension in problem solving. *Developmental Psychology, 4*, 135-140.

Odom, R.D., Astor, E.C., and Cunningham, J.G. 1975. Effects of perceptual salience on the matrix task performance of four- and six-year-old children. *Child Development, 46*, 758-762.

Olson, D.R. 1972. Language use for communicating, instructing and thinking. In J.B. Carroll and R.O. Freedle (Eds.), *Language comprehension and the acquisition of knowledge*. Washington, D.C.: V.H. Winston, 139-168.

Olson, D.R. 1974. Towards a theory of instructional means. Invited address presented to the American Educational Research Association, Chicago, April.

Olson, D.R., and Filby, N. 1972. On the comprehension of active and passive sentences. *Cognitive Psychology, 3*, 361-381.

Osgood, C.E. 1971. Where do sentences come from? In D.D. Steinberg and L.A. Jakobovitz (Eds.), *Semantics: An interdisciplinary reader in philosophy, linguistics, and psychology.* London: Cambridge University Press, 497-529.

Osherson, D.N., and Markman, E. 1975. Language and the ability to evaluate contradictions and tautologies. *Cognition, 3*, 213-226.

Pearson, P.D. 1969. The effects of grammatical complexity on children's comprehension, recall, and conception of semantic relations. Unpublished Ph.D. thesis, University of Minnesota, Minneapolis.

Peirce, C.S. 1932. In C. Hartshorne and P. Weiss (Eds.), *Collected papers of C.S. Peirce*, Vol II. *Elements of Logic*. Cambridge, Mass.: Harvard University Press.

Pollchik, A. 1975. The use of embedded questions in the facilitation of productive learning. Unpublished doctoral dissertation, Vanderbilt University, Nashville, Tenn.

Reich. P.A. 1976. The early acquisition of word meaning. *Journal of Child Language, 3*, 117-123.

Rosch, E., Mervis, C.B., Gray, W., Johnson, D., and Boyer-Braem, P. 1976. Basic objects in natural categories. *Cognitive Psychology, 8*, 382-439.

Ross, J.R. 1970. On declarative sentences. In R.A. Jacobs and P.S. Rosenbaum (Eds.), *Readings in English transformational grammar*. Waltham, Mass.: Ginn, 222-272.

Ross, J.R. 1974. Three batons for cognitive psychology. In W. Weimer and D. Palermo (Eds.), *Cognition and the symbolic processes*. Hillsdale, N.J.: Lawrence Erlbaum Associates, 63-124.

Schank, R.C. 1972. Conceptual dependency: A theory of natural language understanding. *Cognitive Psychology, 3,* 552-631.

Schweller, K.G., Brewer, W.F., and Dahl, D.A. In press. Memory for illocutionary forces and perlocutionary effects of utterances. *Journal of Verbal Learning and Verbal Behavior.*

Scribner, S. 1975. Recall of classical syllogisms: A cross-cultural investigation of error on logical problems. In R. Falmange (Ed.), *Reasoning: Representation and process in children and adults,* Hillsdale, N.J.: Lawrence Erlbaum Associates, 153-174.

Seligman, M.E.P., and Hager, J.L. (Eds.). 1972. *Biological boundaries of learning.* New York: Appleton-Century-Crofts.

Shaw, R.E., and McIntyre, M. 1974. Algoristic foundations to cognitive psychology. In W. Weimer and D. Palermo (Eds.). *Cognition and the symbolic processes.* Hillsdale, N.J.: Lawrence Erlbaum Associates, 305-362.

Shaw, R.E., and Pittenger, J. 1977. Perceiving the face of change in changing faces: Implications for a theory of object perception. In R.E. Shaw and J.D. Bransford (Eds.), *Perceiving, acting, and knowing: Toward an ecological psychology.* Hillsdale, N.J.: Lawrence Erlbaum Associates, 103-132.

Sinclair-de Zwart, H. 1969. Developmental psycholinguistics. In D. Elkind and J.H. Flavell (Eds.), *Studies in cognitive development: Essays in honor of Jean Piaget.* New York: Oxford University Press, 315-336.

Slobin. D.I. 1966. Grammatical transformations and sentence comprehension in childhood and adulthood. *Journal of Verbal Learning and Verbal Behavior, 5,* 219-227.

Slobin, D.I., and Welsch, C.A. 1973. Elicited imitation as a research tool in developmental psycholinguistics. In C.A. Ferguson and D.I. Slobin (Eds.), *Readings in child language acquisition.* New York: Holt, Rinehart and Winston, 485-497.

Smith, E.E., Shoben, E.J., and Rips, L.J. 1974. Structure and process in semantic memory: A feature model for semantic decisions. *Psychological Review, 81,* 214-241.

Tulving, E., and Thomson, D.M. 1973. Encoding specificity and retrieval processes in episodic memory. *Psychological Review, 80,* 352-372.

Turvey, M.T. 1974. Constructive theory, perceptual systems, and tacit knowledge. In W. Weimer and D. Palermo (Eds.), *Cognition and the symbolic processes.* Hillsdale, N.J.: Lawrence Erlbaum Associates, 165-180.

van Dijk, T.A. 1973. Models for text grammars. *Linguistics, 105,* 35-68.

Verbrugge, R.R. Resemblances in language and perception. In R.E. Shaw and J.D. Bransford (Eds.), *Perceiving, acting, and knowing: Toward an ecological psychology.* Hillsdale, N.J.: Lawrence Erlbaum Associates, 365-389.

Wason, P.C. 1961. The contexts of plausible denial. *Journal of Verbal Learning and Verbal Behavior, 4,* 7-11.

Wells, G. 1974. Learning to code experience through language. *Journal of Child Language, 1,* 243-269.

Wittgenstein, L. 1953. *Philosophical investigations.* Oxford: B. Blackwell.

NOTES

[1] Also, see discussion of this paper by Robin S. Chapman, "Comprehension Strategies in Children," in the same volume. The discussion instantiates the theory that input requires situational cues for comprehension to be successful.

[2] We thank Todd and Tommy Boehm for sharing their enthusiasm with us in this game.

[3] Exemplification is not to be equated with abduction because the latter concept has a broader range of application. One can make an abductive analysis of other communicative techniques in addition to those that explicitly utilize examples. One can analyze the nature of analogy, well-structured discourse that is relevant to a particular audience, or well-written texts. Nevertheless, most of this discussion will center around exemplification. This discussion will set the stage for clarifying the relation between abductions and analogies or texts.

[4] The page number cited for this quotation refers to the published version of this manuscript in French translation. Copies of the article are available in English from the authors.

The Effect of Oral and Written Patterns of Language Structure on Reading Comprehension

ROBERT B. RUDDELL
University of California at Berkeley

Research concerned with readability control has focused to a large degree on one or more of the following elements: Some simple or complex measure of vocabulary, sentence length, number of prepositional phrases, number of pronouns, number of affixes, and number of syllables per hundred words (2). The multiple-correlation coefficients derived by correlation of specific elements with independent comprehension measures have produced coefficients ranging from .51 (5) to .72 (7). It is evident from these findings that the specific factors considered account for only 26 to 51 percent of the variance in the conprehension scores. A large proportion of the variance is thus unaccounted for by the factors considered.

The suggested importance of patterns of language structure as a variable of comprehension in written material is noted in the professional writing and research in the language arts during recent years. Dale and Chall (4), Flesch (6), Lorge (8), Robinson (9), and Steinberg and Jenkins (10) have emphasized the need for consideration of the organization of language structure in the development and control of readability of written materials. Strickland's recent report on the language of elementary school children recommended that the effect on reading ease of structural similarity in written language patterns and children's oral language patterns should be given consideration in readability research (11).

Hypotheses

The purpose of this study was to investigate the effect of the similarity of oral and written patterns of language structure on reading comprehension of fourth grade children.

Two research hypotheses were proposed for this investigation:

1. The degree of comprehension with which written passages are read is a function of the similarity of the written patterns of language structure to oral patterns of language structure used by children.

Reprinted from *The Reading Teacher*, 18 (January 1965), 270-275.

2. The comprehension scores on reading passages that utilize high frequency patterns of oral language structure will be significantly greater than the comprehension scores on reading passages that utilize low frequency patterns of oral language structure.

Six exploratory questions were designed to investigate the effect of subject background variables on the comprehension scores on the written material.

The occupational status of the father and the educational background of the parents were two of these variables. The other background variables were the intelligence, the mental age, the chronological age, and the sex of the subjects.

Methodology

Six reading passages were written for the study by utilizing patterns of language structure in the same proportional frequency in which they occurred in the oral language of fourth grade children. Three of the reading passages encompassed patterns of oral language structure representing the range of high frequency patterns (e.g., "A spaceman/could fix/the small hole."). The remaining three reading passages used patterns of oral language structure representing the range of low frequency patterns (e.g., "The leader/gave/the men/short breaks/ because they needed rest."). The similarity of the oral patterns of language structure used in the reading passages was determined by the similarity index. This index was derived by assigning the empirically determined frequency values of the oral patterns of language structure of fourth grade children to identical written patterns of language structure in a reading passage and totaling the assigned frequency values. The frequency values were based on data collected in a study by Strickland (*11*).

The reading passages were equated in difficulty by controlling the variables of vocabulary difficulty and sentence length using the Dale-Chall readability formula (*3*). Specific subject-matter content was controlled in the passages by limiting the story content to specific topics in the subject matter area of science. Cloze comprehension tests were constructed for each of the reading passages. They were made by deleting the fifth word from the beginning of each of the reading passages, and every fifth running word thereafter throughout each of the 254-word reading passages.

Children from the fourth grade elementary school population in the Bloomington Metropolitan School District, Bloomington, Indiana, were selected to constitute the population sample. The schools involved were chosen because they were the identical schools from which the original fourth grade oral language recordings were obtained for analysis in the study by Strickland (*11*).

The cloze comprehension tests were administered to a randomly selected sample by the investigator. Of the 140 pupils selected, 131 were present for the testing sessions. Pertinent data on the occupational and educational status of the subjects' parents were collected on a special information card with the help of the classroom teachers. Data on the intelligence, mental ages, and chronological ages of the children were obtained from the Otis Quick Scoring Mental Ability Test, New Edition, Beta, Form Em, which had been administered two weeks before the administration of the cloze comprehension tests. Scores on the paragraph meaning section of the Stanford Achievement Test, Intermediate I, were also made available to the investigator. This test had been administered the week preceding the administration of the cloze comprehension tests.

Reliability coefficients for the cloze comprehension tests were calculated by using the split-half reliability coefficient method and were corrected by the Spearman-Brown formula. These coefficients ranged from .85 to .90 on individual tests and from .95 to .96 on pooled tests which utilized high frequency patterns of oral language structure and low frequency patterns of oral language structure.

A form of construct validity was used in validating the cloze comprehension tests as measures of reading comprehension. This validity was determined by correlating the cloze comprehension scores with the scores from the paragraph meaning section of the Standard Achievement Test, Intermediate I. Validity coefficients were found to range from .61 to .72 with individual tests and from .71 to .77 on the pooled tests utilizing high frequency patterns of oral language structure and low frequency patterns of oral language structure. These correlations compare favorably with the correlational findings of Bormuth (1) and Taylor (12), in which individual cloze and multiple-choice comprehension tests scores on the same material were correlated. In regard to the construct validity, it was determined that the obtained coefficients were relatively high, in that the two sets of comprehensive scores were derived from different content and subject-matter areas.

It was concluded that the cloze comprehension tests were sufficiently reliable and valid to provide tests for the research hypotheses and the investigation of the exploratory questions of the study.

The data related to the two research hypotheses were analyzed by using a one-way analysis of variance with a repeated measurement design. The statistic Epsilon was used in estimating the strength of relationships in terms of correlation coefficients. The data related to the six exploratory questions were treated by using a two-way analysis of variance with a repeated measurement design.

Results

The comprehension scores on reading passages differing in similarity index values were significantly different beyond the .01 level, thus substantiating the first hypothesis. The findings are noted in Table 1.

Table 1

ANALYSIS OF VARIANCE OF CLOZE COMPREHENSION SCORES FOR PASSAGE
VARYING IN SIMILARITY INDEX VALUES

Sources of Variation	Degrees of Freedom	Sum of Squares	Mean Square	F Ratio
Between subjects	130	29,205.11	224.66	
Within subjects	655	9,763.17	14.91	
Reading passages	5	3,048.03	609.61	59.01*
Residual	650	6,715.14	10.33	
Total	684	38,968.28		

* Significant at the .01 level.

Estimates of the strength of relationship as calculated by Epsilon between the similarity factor and scores on reading comprehension resulted in a significant correlation coefficient of .55.

The data related to the second research hypothesis indicated that comprehension scores on the written material designed with high frequency patterns of oral language structure and comprehension scores on written material designed with low frequency patterns of oral language structure were significantly different beyond the .01 level. See Table 2.

Table 2

ANALYSIS OF VARIANCE OF CLOZE COMPREHENSION SCORES FOR PASSAGE
CONTAINING HIGH FREQUENCY AND LOW FREQUENCY PATTERNS OF
LANGUAGE STRUCTURE

Sources of Variation	Degrees of Freedom	Sum of Squares	Mean Square	F Ratio
Between subjects	130	87,615.34	673.96	
Within subjects	131	9,340.50	71.34	
Passage frequency (High and Low)	1	4,345.37	4,345.37	113.10*
Residual	130	4,995.13	38.42	
Total	261	96,955.84		

* Significant at the .01 level.

Estimates of the strength of relationship between the high and low frequency patterns of language structure and scores on reading comprehension resulted in a significant correlation coefficient of .68.

The exploratory questions indicated that significant differences existed at the .01 level between comprehension scores when considered in relation to the following background variables of the subjects: the occupational status of the father; the educational background of the parents; and the intelligence, the mental age and the chronological age of the subjects. No significant difference was found in comprehension scores in relation to the sex variable; however, an interaction significant at the .05 level was found. This interaction would seem to suggest that boys have disproportionally greater difficulty than girls in comprehending material written with low frequency patterns of oral language structure.

Conclusions

The following conclusions would seem to be warranted.

1. Reading comprehension is a function of the similarity of patterns of language structure in the reading material to oral patterns of language structure used by children.

2. Reading comprehension scores on materials that utilize high frequency patterns of oral language structure are significantly greater than reading comprehension scores on materials that utilize low frequency patterns of oral language structure.

As to the exploratory questions, it was concluded that the occupational status of the father, the educational background of the parents and the intelligence, mental age, and chronological age of the subjects are significantly related to reading comprehension on reading materials that utilize high and low frequency patterns of oral language structure. Sex differences are not significantly related to reading comprehension, though there is some suggestion that boys have disproportionally greater difficulty than girls in comprehending reading material written with low frequency patterns of oral language structure.

Recommendations

The following research studies are suggested in furthering a deeper understanding of the relationship of oral and written patterns of language structure in reading comprehension.

1. The development of a more extensive series of reading passages that utilize the patterns of oral language structure used in this study and other patterns of oral language structure occurring with different emission frequencies to verify the findings of this study.

2. An investigation of the effect of similarity of oral and written patterns of language structure on reading comprehension at other grade levels.

3. A more extensive study of the effect of low frequency patterns of oral language structure on reading comprehension of boys as compared to that of girls in verifying the interaction finding of this study.

4. A qualitative study of oral patterns of language structure used in this study in terms of the deviation of each pattern from the structure of the basic kernel sentence. The relationship of the degree of deviation of syntactic patterns from the basic sentence kernel to reading comprehension could then be investigated.

5. A study of the effect of special oral and written training on a selected number of high and low frequency patterns of language structure on reading comprehension over materials that utilize identical patterns of language structure.

6. A comparative longitudinal study of children's reading success using materials with controlled patterns of language structure which have been found to be used in their oral language as contrasted with children's reading success using materials that provide for little control of the patterns of language structure.

REFERENCES

1. Bormuth, John R. "Cloze Tests as Measures of Readability and Comprehension Ability." Unpublished doctoral dissertation, School of Education, Indiana University, 1962.
2. Chall, Jeanne S. *Readability: An Appraisal of Research Application.* Bureau of Educational Research Monograph No. 34. Columbus: Ohio State University, 1958.
3. Dale, Edgar, and Chall, Jeanne S. "A Formula for Predicting Readability," *Educational Research Bulletin*, 27 (January 1948), 11-20, 28.
4. Dale, Edgar, and Chall, Jeanne S. "The Concept of Readability," Elementary English, 26 (January 1949), 19-26.
5. Dale, Edgar, and Tyler, Ralph W. "A Study of the Factors Influencing the Difficulty of Reading Materials for Adults of Limited Reading Ability," *Library Quarterly*, 4 (July 1934), 384-412.
6. Flesch, Rudolf. "A New Readability Yardstick," *Journal of Applied Psychology*, 32 (June 1948), 221-233.
7. Flesch, Rudolf. "Measuring the Level of Abstraction," *Journal of Applied Psychology*, 34 (December 1950), 384-390.
8. Lorge, Irving. "Readability Formulae – An Evaluation," *Elementary English*, 26 (February 1949), 86-95.
9. Robinson, Francis F. "The Effect of Language Style on Reading Performance," *Journal of Educational Psychology*, 38 (March 1947), 149-156.
10. Steinberg, Erwin R., and Jenkins, William A. "Needed Research in the Teaching of the Elementary School Language Arts," *Elementary English*, 34 (December 1962), 790-793.
11. Strickland, Ruth G. *The Language of Elementary School Children: Its Relationship to the Language of Reading Textbooks and the Quality of Reading of Selected Children.* Bulletin of the School of Education, Vol. 38, No. 4. Bloomington: Indiana University, July 1962.
12. Taylor, Wilson L. "Cloze Readability Scores as Indices of Individual Differences in Comprehension and Aptitude," *Journal of Applied Psychology*, 41 (February 1957), 19-26.

A Linguistic Study of Cues and Miscues in Reading

KENNETH S. GOODMAN
University of Arizona

This is a report of the conclusions to date of a descriptive study of the oral reading of first, second, and third grade children. It is a study in applied linguistics since linguistic knowledge and insights into language and language learning were used.

Assumptions

In this study, reading has been defined as the active reconstruction of a message from written language. Reading must involve some level of comprehension. Nothing short of this comprehension is reading. I have assumed that all reading behavior is caused. It is cued or miscued during the child's interaction with written language. Research on reading must begin at this point of interaction. Reading is a psycholinguistic process. Linguistic science has identified the cue systems within language. The child learning to read his native language has already internalized these cue systems to the point where he is responding to them without being consciously aware of the process. To understand how children learn to read, we must learn how the individual experiences and abilities of children affect their ability to use language cues. We must also become aware of the differences and similarities between understanding oral language which uses sounds as symbol-units and written language which depends on graphic symbols.

Cue Systems in Reading

Here is a partial list of the systems operating to cue and miscue the reader as he interacts with written material. Within words there are:

Letter-sound relationships

Shape (or word configuration)

Known "little words" in bigger words

Reprinted from *Elementary English*, 42 (1965). 639-643. Copyright 1965 by the National Council of Teachers of English. Reprinted by permission of the publisher.

Whole known words

Recurrent spelling patterns

In the flow of language there are:

Patterns of words (or function order)

Inflection and inflectional agreement (examples: The boy runs. The boys run.)

Function words such as noun markers (the, a, that, one)

Intonation (which is poorly represented in writing by punctuation)

The referential meaning of prior and subsequent language elements and whole utterances

Cues external to language and the reader include:

Pictures

Prompting by teacher or peers

Concrete objects

Skill charts

Cues within the reader include:

His language facility with the dialect of his subculture

His idiolect (his own personal version of the language)

His experiential background (the reader responds to cues in terms of his own real or vicarious experiences)

His conceptual background and ability (a reader can't read what he can't understand).

Those reading attack skills and learning strategies he has acquired or been taught.

Procedures

The subjects of this study were 100 children in grades 1, 2, and 3 who attend the same school in an industrial suburb of Detroit. Every second child on an alphabetic list of all children in these grades was included. There were an equal number of boys and girls from each room.

For reading materials, a sequence of stories was selected from a reading series not used in the school. With the publisher's permission the stories were dittoed on work sheets. A word list from each story was also duplicated.

An assistant called each subject individually out of the classroom. The subject was given a word list for a story at about his grade level. If the child missed many words, he was given a list for an earlier story. If he missed few or none he was given a more advanced story. Each child eventually had a word list of comparable difficulty. The number of words which each child missed on the lists, then, was a controlled variable.

Next the child was asked to read orally from the book the story on which his word list was based. The assistant noted all the child's oral reading behavior on the work sheets as the child read. The assistant refrained from any behavior which might cue the reader. Finally, each subject was to close his book and retell the story as best he could. He was not given advance notice that he would be asked to do this. The reading and retelling of the story was taped. Comparison between the structure of the language in the book and in the retold stories is underway utilizing the system of the Loban and Strickland studies.[1] It is not complete and will not be reported here.

Words in Lists and in Stories

One concern of the research was the relative ability of children to recognize words in the lists and read the words in the stories. The expectation was that children would read many words in stories which they could not recognize in lists. I reasoned that, in lists, children had only cues within printed words while in stories they had the additional cues in the flow of language. I was not disappointed.

Table I
Average Words Missed in List and in Story

	List	Also Missed in Story		
	Average	Average	Percent	Ratio
Grade 1	9.5	3.4	38%	2.8:1
Grade 2	20.1	5.1	25%	3.9:1
Grade 3	18.8	3.4	18%	5.5:1

Table II
Ability to Read Words in Context Which Were Missed on List

	Less Than 1/2	More Than 1/2	More Than 2/3	More Than 3/4	More Than 4/5	N
Grade 1	11%	89%*	69%	49%	26%	35
Grade 2	3%	97%	81%	66%	50%	32
Grade 3	6%	94%	91%	76%	67%	33

* Cumulative percents of subjects

As is shown in Table I, the children in this study were able to read many words in context which they couldn't read from lists. Average first graders could read almost two out of three words in the story which they missed on the list. The average second grader missed only one-fourth of the words in the story which he failed to recognize on the list. Third graders were able to get, in the stories, all but 18 percent of the words which they did not know in the list.

As Table II shows, except for a small group of first graders and a very few second and third graders, all the children in this study could read correctly in the story at least half of the words that they could not recognize on the lists. Sixty-nine percent of first grade children could "get" two-thirds or more of their list errors right in reading the story. Sixty-six percent of the second graders could read three-fourths or more of their errors in the story. The comparable group of third graders could get better than four out of five. The children in successive grades in this study were increasingly efficient in using cue systems outside of words.

Table III
Total Errors and Substitution Errors on Lists

| | List Errors | Included Substitutions | | |
	Average	Average	Percent	Ratio
Grade 1	9.5	4.9	52%	1.9:1
Grade 2	20.1	11.5	57%	1.7:1
Grade 3	18.1	14.3	79%	1.3:1

At the same time, as Table III shows, children in successive grades were making greater attempts to use word attack skills, here defined as responses to *cue systems within words*. About half of the listed errors of first graders were omissions. The children did not attempt to figure the words out by using any available cues. Second grade children showed an increased tendency to try to "get" the word. This is shown by the somewhat higher percent of substitutions among the list errors of second grade children. Third graders showed a pronounced increase in the percent of substitutions among their list errors. Children in successive grades used word attack skills with increased frequency though not necessarily with increased efficiency.

Table IV
One-Time Substitutions for Known Words in Stories

	Average Substitutions	Average Lines Read	Substitutions Per Line Read
Grade 1	3.7	50.2	.074
Grade 2	14.9	126.2	.118
Grade 3	16.9	118.7	.142

There was no instance of a child getting a word right on the list but missing it consistently in the story. But often children made an incorrect substitution in the reading of the story in individual occurrences of known words. As Table IV indicates, second and third graders made more than twice as many one-time substitutions per line read as first graders. Third graders made more substitutions per line than second graders. Three possible causes of these one-time substitutions may be (1) overuse of cues within words to the exclusion of other cues, (2) miscuing by book language which differs from the language as the child knows it, and (3) ineffective use of language cues.

Regressions in Reading

This study also was concerned with regressions in reading, that is repeating one or more words. No statistics are needed to support one observation: virtually every regression which the children in this study made was for the purpose of correcting previous reading.

When a child missed a word on a list, unless he corrected it immediately he seldom ever went back. In reading the story, however, children frequently repeated words or groups of words, almost always to make a correction. Regressions themselves, then, were not errors but attempts (usually but not always successful) to correct prior errors.

Table V
Regressions in Reading

	First Grade		Second Grade		Third Grade	
	Per Child	Per Line Read	Per Child	Per Line Read	Per Child	Per Line Read
Word Only						
To correct word	2.40	.048	10.11	.090	10.30	.087
To correct intonation on word	.09	.002	.49	.004	1.42	.012
Total	2.49	.050	10.60	.094	11.72	.099
*Phrase**						
To correct word by repeating phrase	1.54	.031	5.77	.052	7.54	.061
To rephrase	.29	.006	1.97	.018	1.03	.009
To change intonation	.52	.011	2.83	.026	2.76	.023
Total	2.35	.048	10.57	.096	11.33	.093

* For these purposes a phrase is considered *any* two or more consecutive words.

If regressions are divided into two groups, word regressions—those which involve one word immediately repeated—and phrase regressions—those which include repeating two or more words—the two types each represent almost exactly half the regressions at each of the grade levels. (See Table V)

Regressions seem to function in children's reading about like this: If the child makes an error in reading which he realizes is inconsistent with prior cues, he reevaluates the cues and corrects his error before continuing. Otherwise, he reads on encountering more cues which are inconsistent with his errors. Eventually he becomes aware that the cues cannot be reconciled and retraces his footsteps to find the source of the inconsistency. Thus, regressions in reading are due to redundant cues in language. They are self-corrections which play a vital role in children's learning to read. In two cases errors go uncorrected: (1) if the error makes no difference to the meaning of the passage, and (2) if the reader is relying so heavily on analytical techniques using only cues within words that he has lost the meaning altogether.

A Preliminary Linguistic Taxonomy

In a third phase of the study I categorized all errors of the subjects according to linguistic terminology. This analysis produced the *Preliminary Linguistic Taxonomy of Cues and Miscues in Reading.* The Taxonomy will be published in a separate article.

It should be noted that the 100 subjects of this study, though all attend the same school and have learned to read with a fairly consistent methodology, exhibited virtually every kind of reading difficulty and deviation which I could predict linguistically.

Implications of This Study

There are several implications to be drawn from the description of the oral reading of these children. Some practices in the teaching of reading are made suspect.

1. Introducing new words out of context before new stories are introduced to children does not appear to be necessary or desirable.

2. Prompting children or correcting them when they read orally also appears to be unnecessary and undesirable in view of the self-correction which language cues in children.

3. Our fixation on eye fixations and our mania for devices which eliminate regressions in reading seem to be due to a lamentable failure to recognize what was obvious in this study: that regressions are the means by which the child corrects himself and learns.

4. Shotgun teaching of so-called phonic skills to whole classes or groups at the same time seems highly questionable in view of the extreme diversity of the difficulties children displayed in this study. No single difficulty seemed general enough to warrant this approach. In fact, it is most likely that at least as many children are suffering from difficulties caused by overusing particular learning strategies in reading as are suffering from a lack of such strategies.

5. The children in this study found it harder to recognize simple words than to read them in stories. Eventually I believe we must abandon our concentration on words in teaching reading and develop a theory of reading and a methodology which puts the focus where it belongs: on language.

NOTE
[1] Walter Loban, *The Language of Elementary School Children.* Champaign; National Council of Teachers of English, 1963 and Ruth Strickland, *The Language of Elementary School Children,* Bulletin of the School of Education, Indiana University, 38, July 1962.

Toward an Interactive Reading Instructional Model: Explanation of Activation of Linguistic Awareness and Metalinguistic Ability in Learning to Read

HALLIE KAY YOPP
HARRY SINGER
University of California at Riverside

Learning to read requires the activation of multiple systems in the learner (Singer, 1984a). Among them are linguistic awareness and metalinguistic ability (Mattingly, 1977). Linguistic awareness is not well defined, but among its manifestations is ability to perceive and segment words, syllables, and phonemes from the speech stream (Liberman et al., 1977).

Metalinguistic ability consists of knowledge about one's own language and ability to direct, regulate, monitor, and evaluate. As children develop their metalinguistic and linguistic awareness abilities, they are increasingly able to judge, analyze, and eventually remedy faulty sentences (Gleitman, 1977).

Although metalinguistic and linguistic awareness abilities increase with age, a current controversy in readiness for learning to read is whether development of these linguistic systems is a prerequisite for success in learning to read (Singer, 1981, 1984a). Some evidence has been adduced for this relationship. Phoneme segmentation ability, one index of linguistic awareness, predicts later reading achievement. Ability to segment by phonemes in kindergarten has been correlated with reading performance in second grade (Shankweiler and Liberman, 1976), while a test of phoneme segmentation in kindergarten substantially contributed to the multiple regression equation predicting success in first grade reading (Calfee, 1977). Error patterns of beginning and disabled readers also have been cited as evidence for a causal link between phoneme segmentation ability and learning to read (Liberman and others, 1977). Indeed, Liberman et al. hypothesize that the inability to segment the language is a major source of reading difficulty. Although the data regarding the relationship between phoneme segmentation ability and reading achievement are predominantly correlational (Ehri, 1979; Singer, 1981; Yaden, 1984), Yopp (1984) has offered empirical support for a causal relationship. Her findings reveal that children with the strongest phoneme segmentation ability learned to perform sounding and blending tasks quite

135

successfully while children with only chance level phoneme segmentation ability were virtually unable to sound and blend novel words following instruction.

If linguistic awareness is necessary for reading acquisition, then we have to determine why there is variation as to when children can successfully begin to learn to read. Some research indicates that children can make progress in learning to read at ages earlier than five or six while other investigators report that children younger than six have difficulty in learning to read. Singer's (1984b) analysis of such studies does show considerable variation in age and prerequisites for success in beginning reading; he attributes the variation to differences in the demands of the reading task, the level of learning required (Gagne, 1965), and the criterion for successful achievement. Those who have taught preschoolers (Moore, 1961; Davidson, 1931) may have been successful because their instruction placed hardly any metalinguistic and linguistic awareness demands upon their students, while those investigators who suggest that students require a higher mental age than age six (Morphett and Washburne, 1931) or greater linguistic sophistication (Perfetti and Beck, 1983; Gough, Juel, and Roper-Schneider, 1983) used instructional procedures that placed greater demands upon the students' resources. The students did not have to activate and rely upon their own linguistic systems; they only had to have the capacity to learn associations to letters or words, a form of learning this is relatively low in the hierarchy of the conditions of learning (Gagne, 1965). In contrast, rule-governed learning, which is higher in the learning hierarchy, and is necessary for "real reading" (Perfetti and Beck, 1983) or for "ciphering" (Gough et al., 1983), places greater demands upon students' cognitive and linguistic resources; in this condition of learning students had to generalize their learning beyond what was directly taught. That is, the learners had to decipher novel words to be successful in learning to read. Their reading was not restricted to directly taught associations. This contrast in learning conditions explains why Yopp (1984) found that phoneme segmentation ability was necessary for success in sounding and blending tasks, but was not as critical for sight word tasks.

Also, as Holmes (1962) pointed out, younger students in the studies were taught in individual or small group situations. The low teacher-student ratios allowed the instructors to employ a less demanding mode of learning in which the instructors activated their own metalinguistic and linguistic awareness abilities. That is, the instructors segmented or synthesized the words and the instructors provided the sounds for the letters or words. The students only had to hookup or connect the stimuli with the appropriate response (Samuels, 1971). In short, this use of learning may be necessary for forming sound patterns in readers' lexicons and establishing pathways between the visual stimuli and the corresponding sounds stored in the readers' lexicons. Thus, the learning situations at the younger ages did not require students to activate metalinguistic or linguistic awareness systems to succeed in the learning task. Students only had to mobilize their capacity for associative learning.

In contrast, the older students, taught in groups, had to activate their meta-linguistic and linguistic awareness systems to succeed in their more demanding rule-based learning, a mode of learning that also places a greater premium upon the higher level cognitive abilities of synthesis and analysis.

We can summarize by stating that students may not have to activate their linguistic systems or higher level cognitive abilities in learning to read, if instructional conditions do not require their use. In other words, whether a particular system within the reader is or is not mobilized does not depend only upon interaction between reader's resources and the characteristics of the text, as depicted in the Interactive Model of Reading (Rumelhart, 1976; Adams and Collins, 1979) shown in Figure 1.

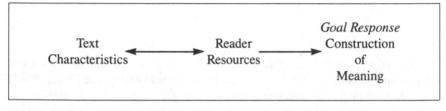

Figure 1. Interactive model of reading.

When the interaction occurs in an instructional setting, it also depends upon the instructor who exerts control over the stimulus task and the kind of response required by the reader or learner. In short, in the classroom situation where reading acquisition is occurring, a more adequate model would include not only the interaction between the demands of the stimulus-task and the resources of the reader or learner, but also between both of them and the resources of the instructor. Thus, we have included the teacher as a necessary component in our Interactive Reading Instructional Model (Singer, 1984b).

The Interactive Reading Instructional Model

The model, depicted in Figure 2, indicates that the demands of the stimulus-task and reader resources interact to attain a goal response that provides for feedback or knowledge of results, but each of the components and the interaction itself are under the influence of the instructor. Inclusion of the instructor explains why reading can be taught successfully at premetalinguistic and prelinguistic awareness age levels: when students are younger and fewer, their teachers tend to assume more of the metalinguistic and linguistic awareness demands and utilize lower level learning conditions. Conversely, as class size, age, and resources of readers or learners increase, their instructors tend to shift more of the linguistic and cognitive demands upon the student. In response to these demands, the student must activate the necessary resources, if they are available; or develop them, if they are not yet available but can be developed under appropriate instructional conditions.

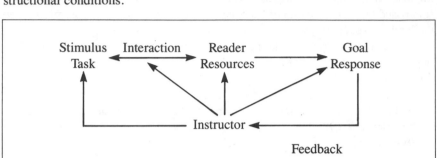

Figure 2. Interactive reading instructional model.

Therefore, whether metalinguistic and linguistic awareness abilities are a cause, concomitant, or consequence of learning to read (Yopp and Singer, 1984) is not dependent on only the stimulus demands (e.g., whole words, blending of letters) nor on only reader resources, but also on their interaction with the resources of the instructor. Thus, the instructor can exert control over the success or failure of beginning readers who vary in age and developmental attainments.

Experimental Evidence for the Model

The purpose of this study was to test a hypothesis drawn from the Interactive Reading Instructional Model. The model emphasizes the role played by the teacher in the acquisition of reading. If the teacher is, indeed, a significant component in the reader-task interaction, then we should find that children are more successful at certain tasks when the teacher provides assistance for their metalinguistic ability and linguistic awareness. We predict that even children lacking "prerequisite" abilities for a certain task will be successful if the metalinguistic and linguistic awareness demands of the task are placed more on the teacher and less on the students. Based upon this model, the importance of phoneme segmentation ability in reading acquisition should vary depending upon whom the burden of metalinguistic and linguistic awareness demands in the sounding and blending process is placed. That is, a child lacking phoneme segmentation ability can be successful in such an instructional approach if the metalinguistic and linguistic awareness demands of the task are placed on the teacher, rather than the student. Therefore, we hypothesize that children of varying levels of segmentation ability will perform significantly better on sounding and blending tasks when they are given some metalinguistic and linguistic awareness assistance than when they are not given assistance.

Subjects

Thirty-five kindergarten children from an Orange County, California, public school participated in this study. The children represented a range of ethnic and socioeconomic groups.

Procedure

Forty children were originally screened according to three tasks. First, it was necessary that all children know the sound-symbol correspondences in isolation. We tested for this knowledge by using flash cards of the alphabet letters and asking the children individually to identify the sounds of each of the letters. Second, the children had to be unable to perform the task they were to be taught during the experimental phase of this study, that is, they had to be unable to "sound and blend" novel words. Thirty-five of the forty children met these criteria and qualified for further participation in this study. All of these children then took part in the next few stages of this experiment.

Phoneme Segmentation Task

The phoneme counting task developed by Liberman et al. (1974) was used to assess each child's ability to segment by phonemes. Under gamelike conditions, each child was asked to tap the number of sounds he heard in a one, two, or three sound utterance. After a series of training trials, subjects were given 42 test items. A subject's score was the total number of items for which a correct number of taps were given. All students were tested individually. This task took approximately 10 minutes per child.

Results of the segmentation task revealed that students' segmentation ability varied widely (from 4-39 correct out of 42 items). Performance on this task allowed us to classify students according to the following segmentation ability levels: chance level (0-19 correct, that is, within one standard deviation of possible correct by chance), emerging segmentation ability (20-30 items correct, that is, from above one standard deviation of possible correct by chance up to the third standard deviation, approximately 75 percent of the items correct) and strong segmentation ability (31-42 items correct, that is, beyond the third standard deviation, approximately 75 percent or more of the items correct).

Phonics Instruction and Test

In small group conditions (approximately 7 per group), all children received instruction on sounding and blending of three-letter, cvc words. Children were told that the reason their teachers had taught them sound-symbol correspondences was so that anytime they came to a word they did not know, they could figure it out. They could use a process called "sounding and blending." The following words were used for purposes of demonstration: lip, fit, pig, dad, hill, rat. Each of these words was analyzed into its component sounds and then blended together. The experimenter demonstrated the process and then asked students en mass to try it on new, similar words. This task is similar to Gough, Juel, and Roper-Schneider's (1983) second stage of word recognition: ability to generalize to novel words. Children were told that they would be called individually to see how well they could figure out some new words. Instruction lasted for approximately 15-20 minutes, and was followed by an unrelated intervening task (music period), which in turn was followed by individual testing. During testing the children were presented with new words on flash cards and asked to read (figure out) the words.

Two types of testing occurred. First, each child was presented with the new words (hip, pill, big, fat, bag, ham) and asked to read (figure out) the words without any assistance by the teacher. Credit was given for the word if the child could correctly and independently identify it. If the children responded correctly to the first word, the next word was given. If the children could respond correctly on their own, we could say they were using their own resources to figure out the new word. If the children responded incorrectly or with "I don't know" then they were given assistance by the experimenter. During this second type of testing (that is, testing with assistance), the experimenters were using their resources to guide the children. The experimenters made comments such as "What sound does the first letter make? How about the second? Can you put these sounds together?" In other words, without giving the answer, experimenters reminded the students of the linguistic and cognitive strategies they could use in figuring out the word.

Results

Reading Tasks

Table 1 shows the group means for each of the six cells. These results are graphically depicted in Figure 3. A two way ANOVA for repeated measures was performed on the data in the two sounding and blending conditions across the three phoneme segmentation ability levels. A main effect for phoneme segmentation ability ($F = 29.5$, $p < .0001$) was found. Children strong in phoneme segmentation ability were the most successful at the sounding and blending reading tasks, followed by children with emerging phoneme segmentation ability. Children with only chance level phoneme segmentation ability were the least successful at the tasks. Each of these groups differed significantly according to Scheffe's test of pairwise comparisons.

A main effect was also found for reading task ($F = 42.22$, $p < .0001$). Children of all phoneme segmentation ability levels were able to sound and blend significantly more words when they were given metalinguistic and linguistic assistance than when they were asked to perform the task with no assistance.

Table 1
Mean Level of Reading Achievement for Students of Three Levels of Phoneme
Segmentation Ability Receiving No or Some Metalinguistic Assistance

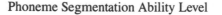

Sounding and Blending Task

Phoneme Segmentation Ability Level	No Assistance		With Assistance		t
	Mean	S.D.	Mean	S.D.	
Chance	.27	.47	1.36	1.5	2.63*
Emerging	1.36	1.15	3.29	1.59	5.01**
Strong	3.60	1.17	4.80	.63	4.81**

* p < .025
** p < .001

Phoneme Segmentation Ability Level

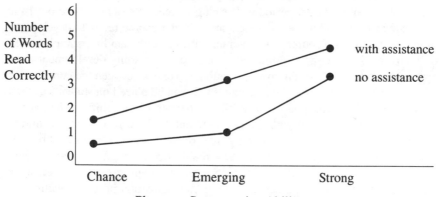

Phoneme Segmentation Ability

Figure 3.   Number of words read aloud under three levels of phoneme segmentation ability and two conditions of teacher assistance.

Discussion

Two important findings come from this study. First, we see that children with the strongest phoneme segmentation ability learned to perform sounding and blending tasks most successfully. Children with only chance level phoneme segmentation ability were virtually unsuccessful at sounding and blending novel words following instruction. These data support the notion of a causal link between linguistic awareness and success in reading.

The second, more pertinent finding is that beginning readers can perform significantly better when they are given metalinguistic and linguistic awareness assistance in the reading task. This finding is a consequence of the activation and use of the teacher's resources in the interaction between reader resources and stimulus demands in reading acquisition. As depicted in the Interactive Reading

Instructional Model, the teacher can exert control over the success or failure of beginning readers by varying the demands of the stimulus task, the resources that must be activated by the reader, and the level of learning and criterion required for successful progress in learning to read.

This model not only explains the experimental evidence of this study, but also the results of previous studies in which age and age-related prerequisites for success in learning to read varied from age three (Moore, 1961), four (Davidson, 1931), six years and six months (Morphett and Washburne, 1931), and later than six years (Liberman et al., 1977; Perfetti and Beck, 1982; Gough et al., 1983). The evidence indicates that an adaptation of Bruner's (1960) dictum can be valid for reading readiness instruction: we can successfully teach a child at any age the initial steps of reading acquisition provided our instructional conditions and demands upon the learner do not exceed the learner's level of cognitive and linguistic development.

Although the teacher can and tends to assume the linguistic and cognitive requirements in the initial period of learning to read, a teacher phase-out from this responsibility and phase-in of students as they become ready to develop and mobilize their own resources and interact with more demanding stimulus-tasks on their own is necessary in order to pace students' reading development at an appropriate rate. In short, an inverse relationship exists between the contribution of the teachers' resources and the demands that can be placed on students as their resources develop. The role of the teacher is to control this shift. If the pace of the shift is commensurate with the development of these resources and toward higher levels of learning as required by "real reading" in the sense stated by Perfetti and Beck (1982, p. 2) or the generalizeable word recognition stage formulated by Gough et al. (1983), then students are likely to progress with a feeling of cumulative success toward independence in the acquisition phase of reading development.

REFERENCES

Adams, M.J., and A. Collins. "A Schema-Theoretic View of Reading." In R. Freedle (Ed.), *New Directions in Discourse Processing*. Norwood, NJ: Ablex, 1979.
Bruner, J. *The Process of Education*. Cambridge, MA: Harvard University Press, 1960.
Calfee, R.C. "Assessment of Independent Reading Skills." In A.S. Reber and D. Scarborough (Eds.), *Towards A Theory of Reading*. New York: Halsted Press, 1977.
Davidson, H.P. "An Experimental Study of Bright, Average, and Dull Children at the Four-Year Mental Level," *Genetic Psychology Monographs*, 9 (1931), 119-287.
Ehri, L. "Linguistic Insight: Threshold of Reading Acquisition." In T.G. Waller and G.E. MacKinnon (Eds.), *Reading Research: Advances in Theory and Practice*. New York: Academic Press, 1979.
Gagne, R.M. *Conditions of Learning*, second edition. New York: Holt, Rinehart, and Winston, 1965.
Gleitman, L. Discourse at the University of Victoria Conference on Linguistic Awareness, Victoria, B.C., Canada, June 1977.
Gough, P., C. Juel, and D. Roper-Schneider. "A Two Stage Conception of Initial Reading Acquisition." In J Niles and L.A. Harris (Eds.), *Searches for Meaning in Reading Language Processing and Instruction*. Rochester, NY: National Reading Conference, 1983.

Holmes, J.A. "When Should and Could Johnny Learn to Read?" In J.A. Figurel (Ed.), *Challenge and Experiment in Reading*. Newark, DE: International Reading Association, 1962.

Liberman, I., D. Shankweiler, F. Fischer, and B. Carter. "Explicit Syllable and Phoneme Segmentation in the Young Child," *Journal of Experimental Child Psychology*, 18 (1974), 201-212.

Liberman, I., D. Shankweiler, A. Liberman, C. Fowler, and F. Fischer. "Phonetic Segmentation and Recoding in the Beginning Reader." In A. Reber and D.L. Scarborough (Eds.), *Toward a Psychology of Reading*. Hillsdale, NJ: Erlbaum, 1977.

Mattingly, I.G. "Reading, the Linguistic Process, and Linguistic Awareness." In J.F. Kavanagh and I.G. Mattingly (Eds.), *Language by Ear and by Eye: The Relationships between Speech and Reading*. Cambridge, MA: MIT Press, 1972.

Moore, O.K. "'Tis Time He Should Begin to Read," *Carnegie Corporation of New York Quarterly*, 9 (1961), 1-3.

Morphett, M., and C. Washburne. "When Should Children Begin to Read?" *Elementary School Journal*, 31 (1931), 496-503.

Perfetti, C.A., and I. Beck. "Learning to Read Depends on Phonetic Knowledge and Vice Versa," paper presented at the National Reading Conference's Annual Meeting, Clearwater, Florida, 1982.

Rumelhart, D.E. "Toward an Interactive Model of Reading." In S. Dornic (Ed.), *Attention and Performance*, VI. Hillsdale, NJ: Erlbaum, 1976.

Samuels, S.J. "Success and Failure in Learning to Read: A Critique of the Research." In F.B. David (Ed.), *The Literature of Research in Reading with Emphasis on Models*. Final Report: Targeted Research and Development Program in Reading, U.S. Office of Education, New Brunswick, NJ: Rutgers University, 1971.

Shankweiler, D., and I. Liberman. "Misreading: A Search for Causes." In J.F. Kavanagh and I.G. Mattingly (Eds.), *Language by Ear and by Eye: The Relationships between Speech and Reading*. Cambridge, MA: MIT Press, 1972.

Singer, H. Review of *Reading Research: Advance in Theory and Practice*. Volume I by T. Gary Waller and G.E. MacKinnon. New York: Academic Press, 1979. *The Reading Teacher*, 35 (1981), 114-119.

Singer, H. "Learning to Read and Skilled Reading: Multiple Systems Interacting within and between the Reader and the Text." In John Downing and R. Valtin (Eds.), *Language Awareness and Learning to Read*. New York: Springer-Verlag, 1984a.

Singer, H. "Toward an Interactive Reading Instructional Model: The Role of the Instructor in Determining Task Difficulty and Reader Resources Required for Success in Beginning Reading Instruction." In J. Niles (Ed.), *Issues in Literacy: A Research Perspective*. Thirty-Fourth Yearbook of the National Reading Conference. Rochester, NY: National Reading Conference, 1985.

Yaden, D.B., Jr. "Reading Research in Metalinguistic Awareness: Findings, Problems, and Classroom Application." *Visable Language*, 18 (1984), 5-47.

Yopp, H., and H. Singer. "Are Metacognitive and Metalinguistic Abilities Necessary for Beginning Reading Instruction?" In J. Niles and L.A. Harris (Eds.), *Thirty-Third Yearbook of the National Reading Conference*. Rochester, NY: National Reading Conference, St. Petersburg, Florida, 1984.

Yopp, H. "Phoneme Segmentation Ability: A Prerequisite for Phonics and Sight Word Achievement in Beginning Reading." In J. Niles (Ed.), *Issues in Literacy: A Research Perspective*. Thirty-Fourth Yearbook of the National Reading Conference. Rochester, NY: National Reading Conference, 1985.

Visual Perception

Trends in Perceptual Development:
Implications for the Reading Process[1]

ELEANOR J. GIBSON
Cornell University

Just about 13 years ago I was spending a year at the Institute for Advanced
Study in Princeton, New Jersey, working with great determination, but
not as great confidence, on a book on perceptual learning and development. I had planned this book, struggled with problems of theory construction and pursued relevant research (not only my own but other
people's) ever since my arrival at Cornell in 1949. I had thought of it much
earlier when I was a graduate student. Still, it wasn't going as smoothly as I
had hoped. One day two of my Cornell colleagues telephoned and said
they wanted to come to Princeton and talk about a new joint research
proposal to study basic psychological processes involved in reading. I said
no, this was the year of the book. But they came anyhow and argued that
perceptual development was undoubtedly a major factor in the acquisition of reading skill and that reading was an appropriate as well as a useful
area in which to apply the theory I had been developing.

A few weeks of thought convinced me that they were right, and I
began planning experiments that were under way less than a year later.
For the most part the book lay fallow as far as writing went until 1964,
when I started it all over again at the Center for Advanced Study in the
Behavioral Sciences. This time I knew where I was going and it pretty
much wrote itself. Since 1960 I have had twin projects that seem to
dovetail very neatly—seeking to understand the principles of perceptual
learning and development and trying to apply them to the reading
process.

The purpose of this paper is to explain how the theory and the
experiments are related. Since I cannot describe the theory in detail in a
brief paper, I have decided to try to show how the experiments are related
to the three trends in perceptual development that I discussed in the last

Reprinted from Anne D. Pick (Ed.), *Minnesota Symposia on Child Psychology, 8,* 1974, 24-54.
Copyright 1974 by the University of Minnesota, University of Minnesota Press, Minneapolis. Reprinted with permission.

chapter of my book. They were generated by a long foregrounding in theoretical concepts and factual descriptions of the development of perception of objects, the spatial layout, events, pictures, and symbols, and so these trends serve as a summary that I find exceedingly useful. The three trends were identified as: 1) increasing specificity of correspondence between information in stimulation and the differentiation of perception; 2) increasing optimization of attention; 3) increasing economy in the perceptual process of information pickup.

Other trends in cognitive development, in a wider sense, could be pointed out, and they might be equally or nearly as relevant for understanding the process of learning to read. One that seems to me especially important is the increasing ability to be *aware* of one's own cognitive processes, from the segmentation of the phonetic stream all the way up to the understanding of strategies of learning and problem solving. There seems to be a kind of consciousness-raising that goes along with many aspects of cognitive development, and it turns out, I think, to be associated with attaining mature reading skills. But I shall confine myself to the three trends I mentioned and to some of the research associated with them.

Increasing Specificity

Perceptual learning, as I see it, is characterized by an increased specificity of correspondence between stimulation and the precision of the responding organism's discrimination. My husband and I argued many years ago that the essence of perceptual learning was differentiation rather than enrichment and this kind of learning was not adding something like a response or an image to sensations but rather was a change in *what* was responded *to* uniquely and specifically (Gibson & Gibson, 1955). Early experiments with Dr. Anne Pick and Dr. Harry Osser (Gibson, Gibson, Pick, & Osser, 1962) pursued this trend and demonstrated the progress of the discrimination of letter-like forms and the way in which confusions decreased and unique identifications increased with age. In later research (Gibson, Osser, Schiff, & Smith, 1963; Gibson, Schapiro, & Yonas, 1968) I sought to specify the distinctive features that are used in letter discrimination and to compare them for several age groups. All of this work was at the perceptual level, and I would of course acknowledge that reading, although based on perception, is a very complex cognitive process.

For this reason I have been speculating further, perhaps overboldly, about the role of differentiation in reading. I am inclined to think that the problem of perceptual differentiation is accompanied by the growth of meaning, first at a perceptual level and later at a more abstract semantic level. The process of differentiating things and events in the world requires the abstraction of contrastive distinctive features and invariants. Objects, events, and their functional relations in the world are differentiated so that perceptions of them come to correspond with information in stimulation at a pretty early age. But the symbolic notations for these objects, events, and relations (*words* both spoken and written) come into more specific correspondence with their referents only later and more gradually. I propose the hypothesis that the meanings of words, like the meanings of things and events, are gradually differentiated and *converge,* eventually, with the meanings of things (and pictures of things, which are also differentiated very early [Hochberg & Brooks, 1962; Ryle, 1966]).

The meaning itself, I think, is *abstract*—neither imagistic nor linguistic. Semantic meaning may in its origins be an abstraction from the distinctive features (themselves abstracted) that permit perceptual differentiation (cf. Clark, 1973). Lexical features of words must in some sense correspond with distinctive features of things and of the events in which they are constituents, but the lexical features presumably are arrived at later. I believe that only much later are they *accessed* as immediately as are distinctive features of perceived objects, especially when the word is written. These arguments are consistent with and may help to explain the observation that immediacy of access to meaning from written verbal input is a characteristic of developmental progress in reading.

An experiment was designed on the basis of the argument just presented (Gibson, Barron, & Garber, 1972). The method was to compare over a wide range of ages the judgments of sameness or difference of a pair of pictures, a pair of words, and a pair consisting of a word and a picture. We predicted that the reaction time of the younger subjects especially would be faster when the items they were judging were presented in the same mode than when the modes were mixed (picture with word). We further predicted a developmental decline in the difference between single mode and mixed mode latencies, with the mixed mode latency converging toward the single mode conditions. The reasoning was that if matching can only be done on the basis of meaning and if the meanings of the word and the thing gradually come to have the same abstract representation with the same access time, then the difference between single mode and dual mode comparisons should progressively decline with age.

Since we wished our subjects to make a comparison on the level of meaning rather than on physical match, sets of words were prepared in two kinds of type (upper and lower case), a condition that has been found to discourage the processing of only graphic features (Posner & Mitchell, 1967), although processing could still stop at a naming stage. Two versions of each picture were also prepared representing similar, but not physically identical, objects—for instance two fish pictured from different angles or differing in a few noncritical details. Simple outline drawings of 12 objects (fish, bird, dog, cup, sock, boat, frog, lamb, cat, key, iron, plane), each in two versions, were prepared on slides, and the names of the objects were set in two kinds of type. The slides were combined appropriately in three conditions: PP, in which pairs of pictures of the same object or two different objects were to be compared; WW, in which pairs of words, either the same word or two different words, were to be compared; and WP, in which a picture and a word indicating the same object or two different ones were to be compared.

The experiment thus had three display conditions, with types of display presented in random order. Half of the displays required a same judgment and half required a different judgment. Each S saw all three types of display, prepared on slides and projected simultaneously with position (right or left) counterbalanced. Subjects were drawn from the second, fourth, and sixth grades and from a college group of summer school students.

Median latencies for each display condition and for each type of response (same or different) were computed for each subject. Means of these medians for the different age groups are presented in Table 1. An analysis of variance showed that the main effects of age and display conditions were significant, but there was not a significant difference overall between same and different responses. It should be noted, however, that *same* responses are shorter in seven out of eight cases for the *unimodal* displays. This trend is in accord with the typical finding in many previous experiments (cf. for example, Gibson, Schapiro, & Yonas, 1968).

The interaction between grade and display, the result of particular interest to us, was significant (p<.025). There was a relative decline with age in the difference between the dual mode (WP) condition and the other two. A difference score was calculated by the formula WP - $\frac{WW + PP}{2}$ and is plotted for the three age groups in Figure 1. The rationale of this formula was that bimodal comparison would take longer than unimodal in either mode but that as meaning of a word and its pictured counterpart converged toward the same abstract semantic features the difference would decrease. From the second to the sixth grade the predicted downward trend is evident in the responses of different. The trend is absent, however, for the responses of same.

A second interaction, a triple interaction of grade, display, and type of response (same or different), was also significant (p<.001). An interpretation of this interaction was suggested in a comparison of some first-order effects at different grade levels. For the second-grade subjects the PP condition had a shorter latency than the WW condition. Fourth and sixth graders did not differ in latency for the PP and WW conditions; but the adults had a longer latency on the PP comparison than on the WW

MINNESOTA SYMPOSIA ON CHILD PSYCHOLOGY

Table 1

MEAN LATENCIES FOR EACH GRADE AS A FUNCTION OF DISPLAY CONDITION AND
TYPE OF RESPONSE (IN MSCE)

Grade	Picture-Picture Display		Word-Word Display		Word-Picture Display	
	Same	Different	Same	Different	Same	Different
Two	1,957	1,987	2,044	2,133	2,141	2,281
Four	1,364	1,343	1,318	1,330	1,479	1,418
Six	1,114	1,194	1,132	1,162	1,224	1,221
College	821	856	783	842	939	893

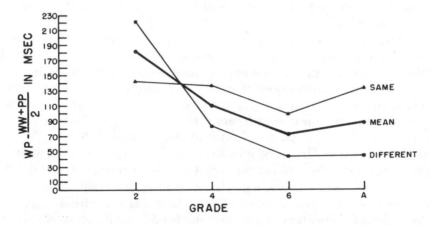

Figure 1.   Difference in latency between the WP condition and the mean of the PP and WW
conditions across grades.

comparison. When same responses and different responses were compared for the WP condition, an age difference again appeared. The
responses of same were shorter for second graders but the responses of
different were shorter for college students. (The apparent difference for
fourth graders was not significant.) There appears to be a radical difference in the processing of WP displays by second graders, and by adults.

What can we say about these differences that might throw light on the
development of processing the meaning of written words? The speculation is as follows. Perhaps for the second grader the WW condition elicits
the naming of words. When the second grader is faced with a WP display,
he looks at the picture first, since pictures are salient and highly meaningful for him but written words are less so. He names the picture to himself

in order to compare the name with the word. If the word coincides with the name, his reading will be facilitated and thus the same judgments will be faster (as they were, by 140 msec.).[2] But for adults words have become highly salient; they arouse a meaning before the word is spoken. The abstract meaning of the word can be compared directly with the abstract meaning of the picture. If they are different, no further processing is necessary. The picture need not be named because the meaning was accessed before the name (Moore, 1919).

What sort of process might the hypothesized comparison entail for the adult? The meaning of a word, I assume, is a set of abstract lexical features, such as animate, nonhuman, house pet, furry, etc., derived from earlier comparisons of real things. These features for the word could be compared with semantic features for the picture. In the WP condition of the present experiment, this comparison might take place serially. Template or "wholistic" processing seems implausible, if not impossible, with two modes of presentation. Thus a mismatch would be identified earlier than a match, and the judgments of different would be faster than the judgments of same. The other features need not be checked out, nor need the *name* of the picture even be processed for a judgment of different. Why should same judgments, on the other hand, be faster in the unimodal comparisons? We can only speculate that unimodal same comparisons can be made on a more wholistic or superficial basis, especially when the set of items has become known, because some physical features, like the tails of the fish or the similarity of two letters (e.g., C and c, S and S) might suffice for the making of a match.

This view of the picture-word comparison of the adult predicts that a different pair would require a greater amount of time for a decision, the more features the members of the pair share (e.g., deciding that *cat* and *dog* are different should take longer than *cat* and *iron*). Insofar as our data afford a comparison, the results are in accord with the prediction, but the data are too few to provide a convincing test. Dr. R. W. Barron is at present replicating the experiment with a proper test of the hypothesis. We should not expect to find this result for children at the second-grade level, for we suspect that they would do an entirely different kind of processing (naming the picture and comparing it with the word) before they have attained a well-developed set of abstract lexical features that is easily accessed by the printed word.

Some of the assumptions we are making are shared by other psychologists. That meaning is abstract, neither imagistic nor linguistic, has been defended not only by the Wurzburg school (cf. Moore, 1919) but more recently as well. Chase and Clark (1972) say for instance: "Our results suggest that the comprehension of both pictures and sentences must ultimately be represented in the same mental symbolic system. We do not mean by this that the ultimate representation of pictures and sentences is identical to linguistic descriptions of deep structure, but rather that there is a deep or conceptual structure that is common to both sentences and pictures. . . . Our conception is that meaning is to be found in a modality-free symbolic memory, but can be converted into modality-specific images when this is wanted" [p. 225].

The assumption that denotative meaning can be analyzed as a set of lexical features or abstract "semantic markers" was proposed by Katz and Fodor (1963). The notion of abstract semantic features is thus not new, nor is the notion that there is a correspondence between distinctive features of objects and the set of semantic features that comprise lexical meanings. That idea was suggested by Rubenstein (1971) as follows: "If they are the same, we would have a single set of features which would serve as locators for lexical entries both when the input is conceptual as well as when it is perceptual. To play both these roles these features would have to be abstract, that is, not lexical entries themselves . . ." [p. 50]. A similar view has been proposed by Clark (1973), who was particularly interested in the development in children of the semantic features of words.

Now we have come full circle to the hypothesis with which I started: that meanings of words converge developmentally toward a more specific correspondence with the meanings of things and events. I conceive of the meanings of both as sets of abstract features, but they are abstracted for objects early in life, while the development of abstract meanings for words progresses later as language and then reading skills are acquired. The immature reader does not access the abstract meanings directly from the word as he reads it. He probably decodes it to a phonetic representation and matches words (the name of this object and the word he has decoded), in contrast to the adult who has become capable of matching word and picture meanings directly via comparison of amodal, abstract features that have progressed to a high degree of correspondence. These ideas as presently formulated are doubtless more provocative than convincing, but I think the time has come to grope with the problem of how the printed word elicits meaning.

Optimization of Attention

One of the most striking aspects of perceptual development is the improvement of strategies for extracting the relevant and wanted information. Selection of critical features improves progressively, as does the apparent ability to ignore noisy, irrelevant information. The descriptive applicability of this trend to the acquisition of reading skill is so obvious that I hardly need argue it. But I would like to be more explicit. To do so it is necessary to talk a little first about what's in a word—what kinds of information it provides. That a written word has *graphic* information is an essential characteristic of a writing system. A written word has potential *acoustic* information too. We can read it aloud or *sotto voce* to ourselves or we can imagine how it sounds. It can carry *syntactic* and *morphological* information: it is a part of speech like a noun or a verb and it may be inflected to indicate that it is a modifier or a particular tense or plural rather than singular. Most important, a word carries *semantic* information. Our interest in communication is to get across our meaning to someone else or to discover the meaning of what the other one is saying or writing.

Optimization of attention in reading is uniquely characterized, I think, by the reader's ability to extract that aspect of the information that is most useful to him and to ignore or give secondary priority to the rest. I do not think the other information is often completely ignored; an example in point would be Rothkopf's (1971) finding that subjects who were instructed to read to learn facts from a text and who knew they were to be tested on their reading, retained some information about where a reference to a given fact had appeared in the text. Nevertheless, an optimal reading strategy usually assigns some priorities to certain aspects of the information which results in selective reading.[3]

The aspect of the information that should be selectively attended to depends on the reader's task—the purpose he has assigned himself or the instructions given him by his teacher or perhaps his boss. He may want to get the closing prices at the end of the day for 10 Wall Street stocks, which will result in a scan-and-pause strategy; he may be reading to learn his lines for a play, which will result in alternation of reading and rehearsal, with rather strong attention to phonetic aspects of the material so that he can try out intonations.

One can think of reading tasks which give priority to every one of the aspects of written text that I have mentioned. I have done experiments on only a few of them, but one task I have investigated in detail with the help of my colleagues and students is the task of scanning down a list to find a target such as a letter or a word. The experiments considered as a whole illustrate quite well the highly selective attention of the scanner to one kind of information so as to optimize the efficiency of the scan.

The first of these experiments was carried out in collaboration with Dr. A. Yonas (Gibson & Yonas, 1966a). We used a scan-and-search task modeled on that of Neisser (1963), with a few alterations to make it more feasible for children. Second-grade children and college students scanned down a list for a single letter target randomly inserted in different list positions to cover all positions equally over a series of trials. Although the children had much slower scan rates than the college students, the children did scan quite systematically, as is shown by the correlation between list position and time for scan. The correlation increases for college students, however, so attention in the scanning does become more systematic with age. Scanning rate, as well, becomes enormously faster with development.

There is strong evidence that in this task the subjects attend with high priority to graphic information. Gibson and Yonas (1966a) compared the effect of high and low graphic similarity of context letters to a target letter. Embedding a target letter in a context of letters containing many of the same distinctive features slows the scanning rate greatly, compared to the rate for finding the same letter embedded in a set with different features. This effect holds for both seven-year-old children and adults, but the interference in one experiment was relatively greater for the children, suggesting that adults may have developed greater efficiency in attending to minimal, optimal distinctive features in this task. Given an opportunity for practice, subjects learn to scan for a single very economical graphic feature as Yonas (1969) and Schapiro (1970) showed in appropriate transfer experiments.

Gibson and Yonas (1966b) also investigated the effect of extra-modal auditory interference on the scanning task. While scanning the list visually, the subject heard over earphones a voice pronouncing letters with names similar in sound to the target letter. Somewhat to our surprise there was no effect at all on the scanning rate of adults or even of seven-year-old children. Acoustic features of letters, or the sound of their names at least, appeared to be virtually ignored in this task. Obviously pronouncing all the letters subvocally while scanning for the target would slow the scanning rate, so this attentive strategy is highly economical. Kaplan, Yonas, and Shurcliff (1966) provided confirmation for this conclusion in a different experiment in which they compared the effect of high and low acoustic similarity of context letter names to the name of the target letter. The target was embedded in a context of letters that rhymed with it (e.g., B, V, D, T) or in a context of nonrhyming letters. Unlike graphic similarity of context, there was no effect on rate of scan of rhyming similarity. Acoustic similarity can, however, produce confusion and interference in another task, notably short-term memory, in which the subject attends particularly to the acoustic information, presumably as an aid to rehearsal.

The lack of interference from competing auditory stimulation in the second-grade children might seem to argue against developing optimization of attentional strategies. But in another thesis experiment, performed by Shepela (1971), improvement of attentional strategies with bimodal input was found when somewhat younger age groups were compared. She performed a detection experiment, a developmental study of "bimodal vigilance," with kindergarten and second-grade children. They detected a given target presented at intervals within a rapid succession of other items under both unimodal and bimodal conditions. The unimodal condition consisted of either a succession of pictures accompanied by the instruction to press a key whenever a picture of a bird appeared or a succession of spoken words presented over earphones with the instruction to press the key whenever the word "bird" was heard. The bimodal condition combined the two types of presentation but target occurrence for the two modes was not redundant. For the kindergarten children, target detection was significantly impaired under the bimodal condition, but for the second-grade children there was no impairment at all compared to unimodal presentation at the same rates. These children were able to attend successfully to both modes of input when the task required it.

It is interesting to ask whether semantic information is picked up in a scanning task. That it *can* be is suggested by findings from experiments in which the subject is required to search for a target *word* which is embedded in a list of other words. Neisser and Beller (1965) asked Ss to search for a word naming a member of a category, such as an animal (e.g., cat, dog, tiger). They were not given a specific target and the target item shifted from trial to trial. The scanning rate was fast, even though the S presumably had to examine each word individually for meaning. The rate, about 300 words per minute, is almost identical to the speed of scan found in a comparable experiment by Gibson, Tenney, and Zaslow (1971) and compares very favorably with the rate of scanning for a single letter. The rate of scan for a single letter tends, in fact, to be considerably slower, depending of course on the type of context, whether the target is repeated or changed, and on practice. Does this comparison imply that in scanning meaning is picked up faster than graphic information? Probably not. A word can be picked up as a whole, but random strings of letters must be scanned letter by letter. In a thesis by Clare (1969) it was shown that pronounceability (orthographic acceptability) of a target item significantly facilitated the search for the item as compared to a random string of letters; so the strategy of searching for a "whole" item, a string of letters that can be picked up as a unit, appears to be the important factor. The fact that context words were poorly remembered perhaps bears this out, but context letters in letter search are poorly remembered too. Unfortunately we have no data at present on children's rate of scan for words as compared with letters, so we do not know how early this attentive strategy develops.

Gibson, Tenney, and Zaslow (1971) investigated the effect on search rate of common categorical meaning in context items (e.g., all items are names of fruit) as opposed to a different category of meaning for target items (e.g., all targets are names of animals). The question was whether semantic structure would facilitate the rate of search for a target word.

The target word was embedded in a set of categorically related words. In a preliminary experiment, the S was presented with the specific target word before each scan began, but this procedure resulted in S's resorting to graphic information (scanning for the first two letters of the target, for instance), which was (or was considered to be by the Ss) more economical than processing meaning. The procedure was changed to Neisser and Beller's, and the subject was instructed to look for a target belonging to a category, either a name of an aminal or a part of the body. (Only one category was used for a subject.) We hoped that this procedure would force S to process for meaning and would allow the categorical structure of the context, when present, to influence the search rate. It did not, however. Categorical structure among context words afforded no faster rate of scan than did randomly selected words carefully matched for word length, initial letters, word frequency, and so on. We were forced to conclude that meaning plays a minor role in a scanning task. "Wholeness" of the items results in fewer units for S to process, but apparently the presence of meaning is not the source of facilitation.

Other tasks, in contrast to search and scanning, are characterized by high utility for meaning, especially categorical meaning. A well-known example of such a task is relatively long-term, as opposed to short-term, memory. Findings from numerous experiments attest to the utility of a common category or categories in a list of words to be remembered. Subjects remember more and tend to cluster by category. In a number of experiments the development with age of attention to common categories and the utilization of them for improved recall has been investigated. Children are not as adept at using categories for this purpose as are adults, but findings about age and categorizing vary with a number of parameters in the experiments.

I would like to summarize one study concerning the development of the use of categories, a very recent Ph.D. thesis by Tenney (1973). Tenney's problem, specifically, was to study the development of strategies of cognitive organization. She wanted to relate the development of the awareness of categories to the spontaneous adaptive use of them. She employed a task designed for this purpose, asking her subjects to tell her words that would be easy to remember along with one (a "key word") that she would give them. She told them that she would write down the words and that she would ask them to remember the words later. Therefore the child could choose what material he would recall, even making use of idiosyncratic strategies if he appreciated the importance of organizational principles and could select and attend to them.

There were three experimental conditions but the subjects took part in only one. One was the *category* condition in which subjects were given a key word such as "blue" by the E and were told to give three words belonging to the same category, which was defined for them. There were 12 categories (such as colors, days of the week, names), all of which had previously been shown to be known by young children. The second condition was the self-directed condition in which the Ss freely generated lists specifically for the purpose of easy recall, again having been given the same 12 key words by E but without any suggestion of a category or strategy. In the third condition, the *incidental* condition, the Ss were never informed of the purpose of the task; instead they generated the lists by free-associating to the 12 key words. The subjects were drawn from kindergarten and from the third and sixth grades. They participated in two sessions scheduled a week apart. During the first session they generated their lists of words (36 words in all for each S, including the key words). In the second session they were tested for recall. The S was read a list of 12 words drawn from the lists he had generated before being asked to recall this selected list. Half of the Ss were asked to recall a clusterable list and the other half a nonclusterable list.

Tenney's experiment was so rich in results that I can only present the gist of them. When the *self-directed* condition was compared with the *incidental* condition, there was a significant age interaction. The older children used deliberate strategies for selecting words for recall, but the younger children settled for the first three words that occurred to them. Sound relationships were very apparent in the lists they generated in both conditions. The use of sound relationships declined significantly with age. The older children made greater use of categories than did the younger children no matter what the condition, although there was category structure in the younger children's lists in the *category* condition.

As for recall, the effect of age on clustering was especially interesting in light of its interaction with condition. There was no significant difference with age in clustering in the category condition. The kindergarten children were helped by the instruction to categorize and were able to make use of it. Nor was there a significant difference among children of different ages in the incidental condition. Clustering by incidental free associations was insignificant at all ages. But in the *self-directed* condition, organization by structural principle—some kind of spontaneous categorizing—increased steadily with age. The kindergarteners showed no more clustering in this condition than in the *incidental* condition, but the older children clustered well above chance. The sixth graders clustered significantly more in this condition than when they were instructed to categorize. There was a strong developmental trend from ease of organization by category structure in response to E's suggestion to ease of organization by a self-directed structure. This seems to me to be a prime example of optimization of attentional strategies with increasing age. The younger children had little insight into how things could be remembered easily, although they could use categorical structure when it was presented to them. But the older subjects deliberately selected words according to a plan of their own, in this case one based on meaningful categorical relationships.

Tenney's results not only illustrate the optimization of attentional strategies with development, they also illustrate the third developmental trend, the trend in perceptual development that I called the increasing economy of information pickup. In the present case, the wording might be broadened to read the increasing economy of cognitive processing. The experiments to be discussed in the following section range, again, from what would ordinarily be termed perceptual tasks to cognitive tasks of presumably greater complexity such as problem solving.

Increasing Economy of Information Pickup and Cognitive Processing

There are two important and contrasting ways of increasing the economy of extracting information. The way that has the greatest utility depends on the task. One is the detection and use of the *smallest possible distinctive feature* that will permit a decision. This strategy is particularly efficient in a scanning task or in a task requiring perceptual categorizing of the Sternberg type. For instance, if there is a positive and a negative set to be distinguished in a reaction time experiment, an S will learn with practice to make his decision on the basis of the *minimal* feature difference that separates the two sets into unique categories. This type of learning has been documented in Ph.D. theses by Yonas (1969) and by Barron (1971). Evidence that the tendency to find the minimal most economical feature for perceptual categorizing increases with development is nonexistent, so far as I know. One reason for this lack may be that the tendency to make decisions on the basis of minimal useful information is present as early as we can make reliable observations of the behavior. Yonas (1969) observed children as well as adults in his experiment and found an enormous quantitative difference in reaction time for categorizing letters but found no interaction between age and the reduction of time with a minimal feature distinction. When the condition permitted greater economy of processing, the children exhibited the trend. One is tempted to conclude that cognitive processing tends toward the "least cost" at any age. What develops, I think, is S's ability to select minimal distinctive features that are of increasing validity and subtlety; but the research remains to be done.

The second way of increasing economy is the use of superordinate structure and rule systems to create increasingly larger units. The detection of higher-order structure in the stimulus array is the essence of efficient cognitive processing, and a skilled reader makes use of the rule systems available in written language at many levels—the orthographic level, the syntactic and morphological levels, and the semantic level. Redundancy and constraints within words and between words provide the rules for unit formation, and a reader learns to process textual information in the *largest possible units that are appropriate for his task.* I am not the first to say this, although I believe I have worked longer than most trying to document the trend and find out how it works. Huey remarked on it in 1908 as follows: "We are brought back to the conclusion of Goldscheider and Müller that we read by phrases, words, or letters as may serve our purpose best. But we see, too, that the reader's acquirement of ease and power in reading comes through increasing ability to read in larger units" [p. 116].

Huey might have mentioned Cattell as well. Although Cattell did not note that the reader chooses the unit that serves his purpose best, he showed (Cattell, 1885) that it takes longer to read a letter than to read a word and that a word is recognized in at least as short an exposure interval as is a letter. Since then it has been demonstrated that a letter embedded in a word can be identified at shorter exposure durations than a letter exposed alone (Baron & Thurston, 1973; Reicher, 1969; Wheeler, 1970). Words can be recognized at a distance in type too small to permit the recognition of an individual letter (Erdmann & Dodge, 1898). And detection of a word target in a search-and-scanning task is faster than detection of a letter target (Gibson, Tenney, & Zaslow, 1971; Neisser & Beller, 1965).

It is the principle of extracting and processing higher-order structure that is particularly applicable to the reading process. I would like to show how work of mine and my students relates to this principle and how we have tried to locate the relevant structural variables. What are the structural principles for unit formation? Cattell thought that the "word-superiority effect," as it is often referred to, was the result of the word's familiarity and meaning. But there are other possibilities that, as it turns out, deserve even more serious consideration. There are rules or predictable relations within words and there are relations, syntactical rules, and meaningful relations between words in phrases, sentences and passages of discourse. It is these relations with which I am concerned in this section.

Use of Orthographic Regularities within the Word

English has conditional rule systems for spelling that are morphophonemic in nature. Syllables may be morphemic units, but whether a syllable is a morpheme or not, it is a unit with some describable rules. It must have a vocalic center, which may or may not be preceded or followed by a consonant or a consonant cluster. The consonants, and especially the consonant clusters, are often constrained as to whether they can appear in initial or final position. English, compared to many other languages, makes wide use of consonant clusters, and these are nearly always constrained. According to Fries (1963) of the more than 150 consonant clusters in frequent use in English, all but three are constrained to initial or final position. Consider such examples as *script, strict, cling, twelfth.* Other vowels can be inserted in the center of the monosyllable and it retains legal English orthography as long as a vowel is present. But in no case can the final and initial consonant cluster be exchanged without violating English spelling patterns. This feature of English spelling provides enormous redundancy of a useful nature in the sense that there is more than one source of information (beyond the single letter) for what the word can be.

There is also redundancy of a different kind in sets of English spelling patterns that are easily classified and contrasted, thus yielding useful rule-like systems. Fries (1963) has categorized these and the following are examples:

bat → bate	bit → bite	cot → cote
cat → cate	fit → fite	dot → dote
fat → fate	kit → kite	got → gote
mat → mate	mit → mite	mot → mote

There are many such repetitive patterns in English and they provide for easy generalization in reading new English words, once the youthful reader has learned the principle. According to Garner (1962), there is more redundancy within words than between them, so it is not a waste of time to study the development of pickup of higher-order structure at the word level, even though we ordinarily read in larger units like phrases and clauses. I will describe research from our laboratory on intraword redundancy which is grouped by four experimental paradigms that supplement one another.

Tachistoscopic word recognition. The first of these experiments was performed by Gibson, Pick, Osser, and Hammond in 1962. Nonwords, termed pseudowords, were generated using constrained initial and terminal consonant clusters with a vowel between to provide two contrasting lists called (at that time) pronounceable and unpronounceable, respectively. The pronounceable items were monosyllabic (e.g., SLAND) and orthographically legal but they did not have referential meaning. The unpronounceable items were constructed by exchanging the initial and final consonant clusters (e.g., NDASL). The items, 25 of each, were presented to Ss tachistoscopically in a mixed order. Numerous replications of the experiment in which parameters such as exposure time, repetition, type of judgment (e.g., identification, recognition in a multiple choice set), and method of scoring were varied have yielded the same result as did the original experiment. The legal pseudowords are perceived better than the illegal ones.

The original experiment was performed on adults. We followed it up with an experiment on children who had just finished first or third grade (Gibson, Osser, & Pick, 1963). Sets of three-letter words and nonsense syllables were constructed to yield a real word in the first grader's reading vocabulary, a legal nonword made by permuting the letters of the word, and an illegal nonword (e.g., *ran, nar, rna*). The words and legal nonwords were all of the CVC pattern. Twenty four- and five-letter nonwords, ten of them legal ones and ten their illegal counterparts, were added. The items were presented tachistoscopically in a randomized sequence and the children spelled out what they saw (an undesirable way of getting the response, since it could encourage letter-by-letter looking, but seemingly unavoidable). For the three-letter items, words were read best overall, legal pseudowords next best, and illegal pseudowords least well. The two types of longer pseudowords were not differentiated from each other by first graders. All of them, whether legal or illegal, were read poorly. But the third graders read the legal combinations of longer pseudowords better than illegal ones. Accuracy did not approach that of adult Ss, but the difference between the two types was discriminated by some of the third graders.

We began by calling the legal pseudowords "pronounceable," implying thereby that ease of pronunciation had something to do with their superiority. Later when we recast our thinking in terms of an orthographic rule system, with all of its potential constraints and regularities, the pronounceability of the items became a less appealing choice and it certainly was not the only possible facilitator. An experiment was therefore run comparing deaf and hearing Ss of college age (Gibson, Shurcliff, & Yonas, 1970). The subjects were given instructions in sign language and wrote down what they saw. A new comparison group of hearing Ss of similar age was run. The deaf Ss, chosen for maximal and congenital or extremely early hearing loss, perceived fewer words correctly overall than did the hearing Ss, but the difference between the two sets of words was just as significant and just as striking for the deaf as for the hearing, suggesting that orthographic rules, rather than ease of pronouncing, accounted for the difference.

Each deaf S wrote a paragraph about how he had learned to read. We gained little from the factual content of these paragraphs, but the almost total absence of spelling errors was notable, although there were frequent grammatical and morphological errors. Evidently generalized spelling patterns and rules can be learned without the benefit of hearing accompanying sound mappings.

In an attempt to compare the roles of meaning and of pronounceability (as we were still calling it) on recognition and on recall, Gibson, Bishop, Schiff, and Smith (1964) prepared sets of nonword trigrams that varied in both meaningfulness and pronounceability. There were three types: one had referential meaning and formed a set of well-known initials (e.g., IBM); the second was a reordering of the initials in a CVC pronounceable arrangement (e.g., BIM); and the third was a reordering of the initials in a non-CVC unpronounceable arrangement (e.g., MBI). Recognition thresholds for the three types of items were obtained by increasing the brightness contrast of an item until it was read correctly. The lowest threshold was obtained for the pronounceable items. The difference was highly significant compared to both of the other types. The meaningful items did have an advantage, however, over the unpronounceable meaningless items; therefore meaningfulness of an item was apparently effective, even though its utility for this method of reading was not as great as was the unit structure of the spelling pattern. When the same items were tested for recall, the utility of the two features (meaningfulness and structure) was reversed; meaningfulness was more effective for enhancing recall.

Morphological features of a word such as classes of morpheme provide another system that might assist in forming structural units. I thought at first, naively it now seems, that adding a well-known inflectional ending to a base word would create a subordinate unit and thus make it easier to read and afford a longer letter span than a noninflected word of equal total length. Gibson and Guinet (1971) investigated the effect of adding a verb inflection (present tense *s*, past tense *ed*, or progressive *ing*) to monosyllabic base words of three kinds—real verbs such as *rain*, legal permutations such as *nair*, and illegal ones such as *nrai*. The bases varied in length from three to six letters. The words were presented tachistoscopically to third- and fifth-grade children and to adults. The extension of word length by inflection did not increase the length of the word that could be read (e.g., when an inflected word like *trying* was compared with a noninflected word like *listen*, the inflected word had no advantage). The results for nonwords indicated that an inflected ending, per se, was perceived as an intact unit when compared with a segment of the word of equivalent length without morphological significance. Older children noticed and commented on inflections more often than did younger children.

A base morpheme would seem to have priority for the reader; but an inflection also has integrity. These two features of a word, we concluded, provide different kinds of information, and the information is probably extracted independently. That the meaning of the base morpheme is processed separately from that of the tense marker was suggested by the tendency for *S*s to confuse inflected endings and sometimes to substitute one for another. With a fast exposure the *S* in such a case perceived the base morpheme and noted that it was inflected but did not have time to process the inflection accurately. Thus there may be two kinds of meaning within the word, each with its own rules.

Scanning experiments. Scanning experiments—searching for a word or letter target—have provided a small amount of evidence for the use of intraword structural constraints. As we remarked earlier, word-search is faster than letter-search and a pronounceable legal nonword is a better target than an illegal one (Clare, 1969). Gibson, Tenney, Barron, and Zaslow (1972) sought to determine whether or not context letter strings that were well structured orthographically would permit a faster search rate than poorly structured strings of context letters. The *S*s scanned for a single-letter target embedded in lists with or without good orthographic structure in the context items (e.g., *sland* versus *ndasl; clept* versus *ptecl*). The identical target letter was assigned to all lists. Subjects were fifth-grade children and adults. In neither age group did orthographically well-structured context facilitate the discovery of the target letter. Apparently any advantage of a structured background that could be processed in units larger than a letter was cancelled by the necessity of further processing for a specific target letter. The pickup of orthographic structure was apparently not the most economical strategy in this high-speed scanning task and was not used; the *S*s settled for graphic features.

If built-in structure were made economical for a search task, it should, according to our view, be used. Zaslow (1972), in a senior honors thesis, designed a search task in which a structural feature of orthography had potential utility. She selected consonant clusters constrained as to position within the word (e.g., *CL* would be a possible initial cluster only, whereas *PT* would be a possible final cluster only) and assigned such clusters (half initial and half final) as targets for search, using a different target for each list. In one condition the target was in its legal constrained position in a pronounceable five-letter string (e.g., *CLEPT*); the target assigned might be either CL or PT. The 29 context items were also five-letter pronounceable strings, all different but formed in the same way (e.g., *GLINK, FRAND*, etc.). In the other condition unpronounceable target and context items were constructed by reversing the consonant clusters (e.g., *PTECL*) and the same targets were assigned. Thus in one condition a given target item was located in a legal position in a string embedded in similarly formed strings. In the other condition the identical target was located in the reverse, illegal position in a string embedded in similar orthographically illegal strings. The subjects were unaware of the method of list construction.

The Ss (college students) located the targets faster when they were in their properly constrained positions. They thus generalized this knowledge of consonant constraint to advantage, even though the letter strings were not words. The experiment bears out the previous findings that good orthographic structure is a critical factor in the word-superiority effect, and it also confirms the notion that consonant constraint is an important feature of orthographic structure.

Judging word-likeness. Word recognition under enforced, very brief exposure is not a usual condition of reading, so it is interesting to ask whether other types of judgment will reveal the generalizability of the word-superiority effect. A method employed by several of my students has proved successful in extending some of the conclusions stated above. The S is presented with a pair of nonwords, one orthographically regular and one not, and asked to judge "which is more like a real word." Rosinski and Wheeler (1972) presented pairs of nonwords taken from the lists of Gibson et al. (1962, 1963) to children from the first, third, and fifth grade. The words varied in length from three to six letters. The first graders performed at chance level, but the third and fifth graders ranged from 69 to 80 percent correct in their choices. Word length in this experiment did not have a significant effect. Nine of the 16 first graders were located the following year and retested. They still did not discriminate between the word types.

Golinkoff (1972) repeated this experiment with several changes. The pairs of nonwords used by Rosinski and Wheeler had not been matched in the sense of being counterparts of one another; for instance a pair might be CLATS versus SPIGR. We thought that contrasting arrangements of the same letters would provide better control and would also be more likely to elicit a discrimination. Pairs of nonsense words ranged from three to six letters each in length. The poorly structured item in the four- to six-letter pairs had a consonant cluster illegally placed in either initial or final position (e.g., TARB - RBAT; GRET - TEGR). There were three conditions of the experiment, two of them adding redundant auditory information to the visually presented items. In one of them, the S heard the word pronounced over a tape recorder as he looked at the printed item. In the other he was asked to read the words aloud as he looked at them. All the Ss were drawn from second grade, toward the end of the school year. The children, over all conditions, discriminated the two types of nonword better than chance (74 percent correct), but neither of the auditory conditions differed from the nonauditory condition. Redundant sound did not facilitate judgment, either because the children pronounced the word subvocally when they were told only to look at it or because judgment of orthographic legality is based on purely visual information. Word length, as in the Rosinski and Wheeler experiment, made no difference, but there was some tendency to make more accurate judgments when the misplaced cluster appeared at the beginning of the word rather than at the end.

Golinkoff (1973) repeated her experiment, with modifications, with *S*s from first and second grade (late in the school year). There were three conditions of word presentation: visual, auditory, and redundant visual and auditory. The results revealed an interaction of age with condition. First-grade children performed only slightly better than chance with visual or auditory presentation alone, but they performed significantly better (72 percent correct) when the presentation was bimodal. But the second graders were significantly better with visual presentation alone (82.5 percent correct, as compared to 65 percent for auditory presentation and 70 percent for bimodal presentation). Thus combining auditory and visual presentation appeared to help in the beginning stages of learning to read, but toward the end of second grade, visual information for word-likeness had become of predominant importance. Golinkoff correlated performance on the word-likeness test with reading scores on the Metropolitan Achievement Test (given at the end of the year) and found a significant relationship (r = .50). We infer that ability to generalize knowledge of English orthography does reflect reading ability measured in other ways.

Learning experiments. Taken together, the preceding experiments suggest that normally children are learning and generalizing at least some aspects of the orthographic rule system in the second grade. How are they doing it? The research strategy by which I attempted to answer this question was a combination of training with a series of small problems requiring abstraction of a common spelling pattern and a learning set procedure. A typical problem consisted of eight words or word-like letter strings, each printed on a card, which the child was to sort into two piles. Half of the words had two letters in common in a given position; the other four contained the two letters but they were never arranged in the same way. When the common pattern was present, the other letters always differed. A typical sorting problem might be:

mean	name
beat	belt
leap	laep
read	road

The words were presented in random order and *E* corrected sorting errors, but the child made the abstraction for himself as in a concept learning experiment. He was not required to proceed for more than a specified number of trials (four trials in the first experiment) if he did not succeed in sorting correctly, but he was given a new problem. One problem followed another, six a day over five days of training in the first experiment (Gibson, Farber, & Shepela, 1968). The first children tested were in kindergarten and the experiment was not only grueling both for experimenters and for children, but it was a monumental failure. Only one child developed a learning set, showing gradually increasing success over problems. The next year we tried a slightly modified procedure with first-grade children with only a little more success. The patterns that stood out maddeningly to the experimenter seemed to have no salience at all for the children.

An answer frequently suggested by kindly critics was "why don't you just tell them?" So we did. Lowenstein (1969) ran a sorting experiment with the same problems over three days with children nearing the completion of first grade. There were three groups of children, and each group was given different instructions. The control group was run like the earlier experiments; the only instructions given were to "sort the mail, and put all yours here." A card for each pile was laid out for him and the procedure went on as before. The full-information group was told by the experimenter, "You will always know your mail because it will have these two letters in it, in this place." The common feature (constrained letter pair) was pointed out for each problem for the first two days. The third group was told, "You will know your mail because it will have the same two letters in the same place," but they were never shown the letter pair. The full-information group performed significantly better than the other two groups for the first two days, nearly everyone doing perfect sorts on the second day. On the third day, no further instructions were given. The group given the partial hint continued to improve, greatly exceeding the control group. But the full-information group deteriorated to the level of the control group. They had learned nothing from "being told." Apparently, S had to search actively and think for himself in order to learn something generalizable. Other psychologists, including Vygotsky and Piaget have emphasized that concepts are not "the sum of certain associative bonds formed by memory" and that they cannot be taught by drilling. To quote Vygotsky: "Practical experience also shows that direct teaching of concepts is impossible and fruitless. A teacher who tries to do this usually accomplishes nothing but empty verbalism, a parrotlike repetition of words by the child, simulating a knowledge of the corresponding concepts but actually covering up a vacuum" (Vygotsky, 1962, p. 83).

It occurred to me at this point that the sorting task might not make clear enough the economy of using a common feature or "collative principle." I decided to try another learning task, a simple one in which the economy of using a common feature is very obvious. We (Gibson, Poag, & Rader, 1972) set up a two-stage verbal discrimination task, comparing discrimination learning and generalization when there was or was *not* a common feature useful for learning the task in stage 1. All *S*s were to learn which of two buttons to press for each of four words when the words were presented one at a time. They were given feedback on each trial. They were run to a criterion of 10 perfect trials or stopped after 60 trials. One group of *S*s was presented with two rhyming pairs of words (king and ring; yarn and barn). The members of a rhyming pair were assigned the same button by *E*, so *S* had only two associations to learn if he noticed and used the rhyme or common spelling pattern. The other group of *S*s had four words that had no obvious common feature (nose, king, bell, yarn), and therefore they had to learn four associations.

Stage 2 was identical for the two groups. Four new words were presented, consisting of two rhyming pairs (boat and coat; cake and rake). It was predicted that an *S* who had the opportunity to use rhyme in stage 1 would learn to do so and would generalize the principle to stage 2, starting a criterion run of 10 perfect trials on trial 5. The other group, by comparison would be handicapped. The *S*s were second- and fifth-grade children.

Condition	Grade 1		Grade 5	
	Stage 1	Stage 2	Stage 1	Stage 2
GrE (common feature)	20.0%	26.6%	53.0%	60.0%
GrC (no common feature)	0.0	13.0	6.6	53.0

The results are summarized in the accompanying tabulation. When a common feature was present, grade five *S*s performed significantly better in both stages than did grade two *S*s; but they did not perform better when there was no common feature (G_rC, stage 1). There was development with age of an ability to perceive and to use the economical principle, but there was no improvement in associative learning as such. What was the effect of training within the experiment? Did anyone *learn* to use the common feature in the course of stage 1 and then generalize the principle to stage 2? The answer is no. There was no significant change from stage 1 to stage 2 for either of the age groups having a common feature in stage 1; nor did those groups excel significantly compared to the other groups in stage 2. Put another way, the *S* either applied the rule at once in the training stage or he never did. In terms of development, the ability to do this increases; but apparently it does not increase by virtue of the kind of training given in this experiment. Massed practice with differential reinforcement, even in this simple task, did not help to disclose a principle.

It seems to me now that abstraction of spelling patterns with consequent transfer is the result of much exposure to them and takes place slowly over time. I think that this process is mainly one of perceptual abstraction which occurs with as little awareness on the learner's part as is the case with learning grammar and with as little dependence on external reinforcement. The S s in the word-likeness experiments were seldom able to justify their choices in any intelligible way, even when the majority were correct. The successful S s in the discrimination learning experiment, especially the fifth graders, did frequently remark on the common features of the word pairs. The question is, did the learning experiments just described test the same ability as did the tachistoscopic and word-likeness experiments? The S s in the verbal discrimination learning task could have been given a follow-up test in which they would have been asked to judge word-likeness; the results of the two methods could then have been correlated. Unfortunately when the idea occurred to me, it was too late to retrieve the S s.

I now see this work as needing to proceed in two directions: one, to continue to attempt to enhance experiences of observing spelling patterns, since I still think there must be ways of helping the abstraction to "roll out" of its diverse contexts; and two, to pin down more carefully the patterns and the rules that are actually effective in creating the "word-superiority" effect and its generalization in adult readers. Without the latter knowledge we cannot know exactly which features of orthographic structure we should attempt to enhance. It is also possible that there is some optimal developmental progression in internalizing the rule system that could be exploited in presenting reading matter so as to reveal higher-order structure.

Use of Interword Redundancy in a Verbal Task

Most of my students' and my own experiments on the economical use of structure in reading have been aimed at structure within the word, but I am keenly aware that a skilled reader makes use of syntactic and semantic relations between words. So does an unskilled reader; but I am not sure when he begins to use these relations to extract information, rather than merely to guess at what may follow. Must he perhaps learn to deal with words themselves as units first? It is possible, of course, that learning to use all types of structure goes on at the same time in reading. Adults and children by third grade or so appear to make use of phrase structure and other grammatical relations as tested by the eye-voice span (Levin & Kaplan, 1970). These S s were reading aloud, of course, and were producing all the words in a sequence; the interpretation of the results is not entirely clear, beyond the fact that the S s have a knowledge of grammar. I sought for a novel verbal task, therefore, that would reveal the extent to which children who presumably know something about word structure would be able to draw on interword relations to increase their economy of verbal problem solving. The task I chose was anagram solution, since a good deal is known about how adults solve anagrams.

If there is syntactic or semantic order in the array of information in an anagram task, will it be used economically by children in the third and fourth grade when they should be freed from letter-by-letter reading? Gibson, Tenney, and Sharabany (1971) performed experiments with children at this age level, investigating the effect of syntactic and semantic structure on anagram solution. In the first experiment the effect of syntactic structure and sentence meaning on the solution of a set of five anagrams was investigated. The anagrams, when solved, yielded a sentence such as "Sally helps Mom clean house." There were three groups of Ss. The anagrams were presented to one group (SS, for sentence structure) one at a time in proper sentence order. There were six sets of this type, each set was arranged on a board so that one followed another. The letters, taken from a magnetized Scrabble set, could be moved around by the S during solution. One anagram was uncovered at a time and was left uncovered during solution. If an anagram had not been solved at the end of 90 seconds, the E arranged it in word order and S went on to the next anagram. The question was whether S would discover the sentence structure during the first few sets and look for structure in the remaining sets, thus facilitating solution.

A second group (NS, no structure) was given the same anagrams to solve, but they were not presented in sentence order. A third group (SS-NS) was presented with the first four sets in sentence order, but the last two sets were in scrambled order. If the sentence had been discovered during the first four sets, S might have been expected to continue to search for sentence structure that was no longer present. This group was given help in finding the sentence structure by being asked to read in order the words they had already solved before they uncovered each new anagram on a given board.

The mean summed times for solution of the first four sets varied for the three groups, being shortest for group SS-NS, next shortest for group SS, and longest for group NS. Only the difference between group SS-NS and the other two groups was significant, however. We were obliged to conclude that for these children the sentence structure was not detected and was not used without the hint given by reading the preceding words aloud. There was no interference for group SS-NS when compared to group NS on the last two scrambled sets, which were identical with those presented to group NS. However, 15 of the 16 Ss in group SS-NS took longer on board five than they had on board four, whereas the majority of the NS group improved their time, a difference which confirms the evidence that group SS-NS had previously been using the structure to facilitate solution. The fact that members of group SS almost uniformly failed to notice that the words made a sentence may be owing to the nature of the anagram task or to their immaturity. In a pilot experiment with adults in which more complex sentences were used, solution was facilitated when the anagrams were in sentence order. However, further confirmation of this result is needed.

In a second experiment the effect of semantic structure, specifically category membership, on anagram solution was investigated. That the solution of anagram problems by adults is facilitated by categorical relations has long been known (Rees & Israel, 1935). Since S must identify a solution as being a meaningful word, it stands to reason that knowing that the word will be an animal or a kind of fruit, etc., will assist solution. Six categories which were known to be familiar to third- and fourth-grade children were used. There were five anagrams for each category, and again five anagrams were presented on a board. There were two groups; in one the anagrams belonging to the same category were presented together on a board (group CS, category structure), whereas in the other the categories were scrambled so that none of the boards contained words of all one category (group NS, no structure).

Group CS had shorter mean times for all six boards, as Figure 2 shows. The curves suggest an increasing effect of category with practice, but the interaction was not significant; the facilitation was present and significant for group CS on the first board. The advantage appeared by the third anagram on a board and increased thereafter (a significant condition by trial interaction). Eleven of the 30 Ss in the CS group commented spontaneously on the presence of the category.

The results make it plain that the semantic relationship of belonging to a common category can be used by fourth graders for economical solution of a novel verbal problem. But to speculate a bit, we have some reason to think that the children's solution strategies may have differed from the adults' strategies. I would like to indulge in this speculation because it brings me back to meaning and how it is processed—the problem with which I began.

Several strategies for solving anagrams are possible, the simplest being a purely trial-and-error approach of moving the letters about and waiting for a word to pop out by trying to pronounce an arrangement to see if it sounds like a word. The children on the whole appeared to be doing this (admittedly we lack hard evidence, as yet). When an acceptable pronunciation turned up that was not a word (e.g., KLIM when the word was MILK), they were likely to be stuck. How then did presence of a category help them? Safren (1962) suggested that when a set of anagrams is related by meaning, "associative strength activates existing response sets" to facilitate solution. It seemed that something like this did happen with the children; if a child perceived a relation between the first two anagrams, he went through a category list, trying the words in turn on the anagram to see if they would fit, as the following typical comments illustrate: "I'm trying to think of another silverware, but I can't." "It must be another color. I'm trying them." This method of solution, even if not cognitively very sophisticated, did often give results and the strategy would be reinforced.

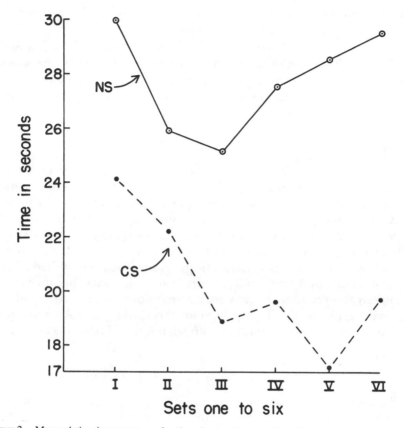

Figure 2. Mean solution time per set as a function of order of presentation of the set.

Adults observed in our laboratory gave comments suggesting quite a different strategy. They deliberately put consonant clusters or consonants at possible places and vowels or vowel clusters in the center to achieve orthographic acceptability, and then they checked for semantic acceptability. Knowledge of a category would facilitate recognition of a word, since much of the processing of lexical features would be eliminated and there would also be no need of going through a whole category list. Word meaning for an adult, as I suggested earlier, may usefully be thought of as the pattern of abstract conceptual features that uniquely characterizes a word.

Whether meaning is more concrete for a child, I do not know; but I infer from the first experiment described in this paper that access to abstract meaning upon reading a word is not so direct for a child as it is for a mature reader, and that the child sounds the word, as he appeared to do with the anagrams, before getting to meaning.

In any case, the children did use category knowledge in a way that facilitated anagram solution. I believe we can conclude that a person will use the most economical cognitive strategy that is possible for his developmental level and that there is progress in developing more sophisticated and higher-order strategies.

Conclusion

This rather lengthy summary of a good deal of the research (my own and a number of my students') of the last ten years or so has forced me to take stock of my successes and my failures and to own up to a fair number of failures and gaps in the evidence. But it leaves me convinced that opportunistic research on unrelated problems is never as rewarding to either the researcher or to the consumer as is research set in a theoretical framework that provides a systematic program. I might have had a better program, but I find that I still see increasing specificity, optimization of attention, and economy of processing the information in stimulation as giving a useful direction to developmental research on problems of reading skill, namely, in determining both what it is and how it is attained.

REFERENCES

Baron, J., & Thurston, I. An analysis of the word-superiority effect. *Cognitive Psychology,* 1973, 4, 207-228.

Barron, R. W. Transfer of information processing strategies in a choice reaction time task. (Doctoral dissertation, Ohio State University.) Ann Arbor, Mich.: University Microfilms, 1971.

Cattell, J. M. Uber die Zeit der Erkennung und Bennenung von Schriftzeichen, Bildern und Farben. *Philosophische Studien,* 1885, 2, 635-650.

Chase, W. G., & Clark, H. H. Mental operations in the comparison of sentences and pictures. In L. W. Gregg (Ed.), *Cognition in learning and memory.* New York: Wiley, 1972. Pp. 205-232.

Clare, D. A. A study of principles of integration in the perception of written verbal items. Unpublished doctoral dissertation, Cornell University, 1969.

Clark, E. V. What's in a word? On the child's acquisition of semantics in his first language. In T. Moore (Ed.), *Cognitive development.* New York: Academic Press, 1973.

Erdmann, B., & Dodge, R. *Psychologische Untersuchungen über das Lesen, auf Experimenteller Grundlage.* Halle: M. Niemeyer, 1898.

Fries, C. C. *Linguistics and reading.* New York: Holt, 1963.

Garner, W. R. *Uncertainty and structure as psychological concepts.* New York: Wiley, 1962.

Gibson, E. J., Barron, R. W., & Garber, E. E. The developmental convergence of meaning for words and pictures. In appendix to final report, *The relationship between perceptual development and the acquisition of reading skill.* Project No. 90046, Grant No. OEG-2-9-420446-1071(010), Cornell University and United States Office of Education, 1972.

Gibson, E. J., Bishop, C. H., Schiff, W., & Smith, J. Comparison of meaningfulness and pronunciability as grouping principles in the perception and retention of verbal material. *Journal of Experimental Psychology,* 1964, 67, 173-182.

Gibson, E. J., Farber, J., & Shepela, S. Test of a learning set procedure for the abstraction of spelling patterns. In *The analysis of reading skill: A program of basic and applied research.* Final report, Project No. 5-1213, Contract No. OE 6-10-156, 1968.

Gibson, E. J., Gibson, J. J., Pick, A. D., & Osser, H. A developmental study of the discrimination of letter-like forms. *Journal of Comparative and Physiological Psychology,* 1962, 55, 897-906.

Gibson, E. J., & Guinet, L. Perception of inflections in brief visual presentations of words. *Journal of Verbal Learning and Verbal Behavior,* 1971, 10, 182-189.

Gibson, E. J., Osser, H., & Pick, A. D. A study in the development of grapheme-phoneme correspondences. *Journal of Verbal Learning and Verbal Behavior,* 1963, 2, 142-146.

Gibson, E. J., Osser, H., Schiff, W., & Smith, J. An analysis of critical features of letters, tested by a confusion matrix. In Final report on *A basic research program on reading.* Cooperative Research Project No. 639, Cornell University and United States Office of Education, 1963.

Gibson, E. J., Pick, A. D., Osser, H., & Hammond, M. The role of grapheme-phoneme correspondence in the perception of words. *American Journal of Psychology,* 1962, 75, 554-570.

Gibson, E. J., Poag, K., & Rader, N. The effect of redundant rhyme and spelling patterns on a verbal discrimination task. In appendix to final report on *The relationship between perceptual development and the acquisition of reading skill.* Project No. 90046, Grant No. OEG-2-9-420446-1071(010), Cornell University and United States Office of Education, 1972.

Gibson, E. J., Schapiro, F., & Yonas, A. Confusion matrices for graphic patterns obtained with a latency measure. In *The analysis of reading skill: A program of basic and applied research.* Final report, Project No. 5-1213, Cornell University and United States Office of Education, 1968. Pp. 76-96.

Gibson, E. J., Shurcliff, A., & Yonas, A. Utilization of spelling patterns by deaf and hearing subjects. In H. Levin & J. P. Williams (Eds.), *Basic studies on reading.* New York: Basic Books, 1970.

Gibson, E. J., Tenney, Y. H., Barron, R. W., & Zaslow, M. The effect of orthographic structure on letter search. *Perception and Psychophysics,* 1972, 11, 183-186.

Gibson, E. J., Tenny, Y. H., & Sharabany, R. Is discovery of structure reinforcing? The role of semantic and syntactic structure in anagram solution. In final report, *The relationship between perceptual development and the acquisition of reading skill.* Project No. 90046, Grant No. OEG-2-9-420446-1071(010), Cornell University and United States Office of Education, 1971. Pp. 48-64.

Gibson, E. J., Tenny, Y. H., & Zaslow, M. Is discovery of structure reinforcing? The effect of categorizable context on scanning for verbal targets. In final report, *The relationship between perceptual development and the acquisition of reading skill.* Project No. 90046, Grant No. OEG-2-9-420446-1071(010), Cornell University and the United States Office of Education, 1971.

Gibson, E. J., & Yonas, A. A developmental study of visual search behavior. *Perception and Psychophysics,* 1966, 1, 169-171. (a)

Gibson, E. J., & Yonas, A. A developmental study of the effects of visual and auditory interference on a visual scanning task. *Psychonomic Science,* 1966, 5, 163-164. (b)

Gibson, J. J., & Gibson, E. J. Perceptual learning: Differentiation or enrichment? *Psychological Review,* 1955, 62, 32-41.

Golinkoff, R. M. Children's use of redundant auditory information in the discrimination of nonsense words. Unpublished paper, Cornell University, December, 1972.

Golinkoff, R. M. Children's discrimination of English spelling patterns with redundant auditory information. Paper presented at the American Educational Research Association, 1974.

Hochberg, J. E., & Brooks, V. Pictorial recognition as an unlearned ability: A study of one child's performance. *American Journal of Psychology,* 1962, 75, 624-628.

Huey, E. B. *The psychology and pedagogy of reading.* New York: Macmillan, 1908. Republished by M.I.T. Press, 1968.

Kaplan, G., Yonas, A., & Shurcliff, A. Visual and acoustic confusability in a visual search task. *Perception and Psychophysics,* 1966, 1, 172-174.

Katz, J. J., & Fodor, J. A. The structure of a semantic theory. *Language,* 1963, 39, 170-210.

Levin, H., & Kaplan, E. L. Grammatical structure and reading. In H. Levin & J. P. Williams (Eds.), *Basic studies on reading.* New York: Basic Books, 1970. Pp. 119-133.

Lowenstein, A. A. Effects of instructions on the abstraction of spelling patterns. Unpublished master's thesis, Cornell University, 1969.

Luria, A. R. Speech development and the formation of mental processes. In M. Cole & I. Maltzman (Eds.), *A handbook of contemporary Soviet psychology.* New York: Basic Books, 1969. Pp. 121-162.

Moore, T. V. Image and meaning in memory and perception. *Psychological Monographs,* 1919, 27 (Whole No. 119).

Neisser, U. Decision time without reaction time: Experiments in visual scanning. *American Journal of Psychology,* 1963, 76, 376-385.

Neisser, U., & Beller, H. K. Searching through word lists. *British Journal of Psychology,* 1965, 56, 349-358.

Posner, M. I., & Mitchell, R. F. Chronometric analysis of classification. *Psychological Review,* 1967, 74, 392-409.

Rees, H. J., & Israel, H. E. An investigation of the establishment and operation of mental sets. In J. J. Gibson (Ed.), *Studies in psychology from Smith College. Psychological Monographs,* 1935, 46 (Whole No. 6). Pp. 1-26.

Reicher, G. M. Perceptual recognition as a function of meaningfulness of stimulus material. *Journal of Experimental Psychology,* 1969, 81, 275-280.

Rosinski, R. R., & Wheeler, K. E. Children's use of orthographic structure in word discrimination. *Psychonomic Science,* 1972, 26, 97-98.

Rothkopf, E. Z. Incidental memory for location of information in text. *Journal of Verbal Learning and Verbal Behavior,* 1971, 10, 608-613.

Rubenstein, H. *An overview of psycholinguistics.* Grant Report, Lehigh University, Bethlehem, Pa., 1971. To be published in *Current Trends in Linguistics,* Vol. 12. The Hague: Mouton.

Ryle, A. L. A study of the interpretation of pictorial styles by young children. Unpublished doctoral dissertation, Harvard School of Education, 1966.

Safren, M. A. Associations, sets, and the solution of word problems. *Journal of Experimental Psychology,* 1962, 64, 40-45.

Schapiro, F. Information extraction and filtering during perceptual learning in visual search. Unpublished doctoral dissertation, Cornell University, 1970.

Shepela, S. T. A developmental study of bimodal vigilance. Unpublished doctoral dissertation, Cornell University, 1971.

Tenney, Y. H. The child's conception of organization and recall: The development of cognitive strategies. Unpublished doctoral dissertation, Cornell University, 1973.

Vygotsky, L. S. *Thought and language.* Cambridge and New York: M.I.T. Press and Wiley, 1962. Edited and translated by Eugenia Hanfmann and Gertrude Vakar.

Wheeler, D. D. Processes in word recognition. *Cognitive Psychology,* 1970, 1, 59-85.

Yonas, A. The acquisition of information-processing strategies in a time-dependent task. Unpublished doctoral dissertation, Cornell University, 1969.

Zaslow, M. The effect of orthographic structure on letter search: A reexamination. Senior Honors Thesis, Cornell University, 1972.

NOTES

[1] The writer wishes to acknowledge support from the National Institute of Mental Health and from the United States Office of Education during the period of work covered in this paper. Acknowledge-

ment and deepest appreciation are due to the many (onetime) students who contributed so heavily to the research described. Some of the research was done in collaboration with the author but much of it was done independently as theses and research reports.

[2] A recent experiment by Garber (personal communication) confirms the fact that reading a word at this age is facilitated if it is preceded by a picture identifiable by the same word.

[3] Compare this idea with a statement by Luria: "The characteristic feature of the adult's verbal meanings is that *the word preserves in itself all systems of connections inherent in it,* beginning with the very elementary and visual and ending with the very complex and abstract. Depending on the task, any of the systems of connections can become dominant. Without this ability, flexible thinking is impossible" (Luria, 1969, p. 137).

A Theory of Reading: From Eye Fixations to Comprehension[1]

MARCEL ADAM JUST
PATRICIA A. CARPENTER
Carnegie-Mellon University

Although readers go through many of the same processes as listeners, there is one striking difference between reading and listening comprehension—a reader can control the rate of input. Unlike a listener, a reader can skip over portions of the text, reread sections, or pause on a particular word. A reader can take in information at a pace that matches the internal comprehension processes. By examining where a reader pauses, it is possible to learn about the comprehension processes themselves. Using this approach, a process model of reading comprehension is developed that accounts for the gaze durations of college students reading scientific passages.

The following display presents an excerpt from the data to illustrate some characteristics of eye fixations that motivate the model. This display presents a protocol of a college student reading the first two sentences of a passage about the properties of flywheels. The reader averages about 200 words per minute on the scientific texts. In this study, the reader was told to read a paragraph with understanding and then recall its content. Consecutive fixations on the same word have been aggregated into units called *gazes*. The gazes within each sentence have been sequentially numbered above the fixated word with the gaze durations (in msec) indicated below the sequence number.

One important aspect of the protocol is that almost every content word is fixated at least once. There is a common misconception that readers do not fixate every word, but only some small proportion of the text, perhaps one out or every two or three words. However, the data to be presented in this article (and most of our other data collected in reading experiments) show that during ordinary reading, almost all content words are fixated. This applies not only to scientific text but also to narratives written for adult learners. The current data are not novel in this regard. The eye fixation studies from the first part of the century point to the same conclusion (Buswell, 1937, chap. 4; Dearborn, 1906, chap. 4; Judd and

Reprinted from *Psychological Review*, 87 (1980), 329-354. Copyright 1980 by the American Psychological Corporation. Reprinted by permission of the publisher and the authors.

Eye fixations of a college student reading a scientific passage. Gazes within each sentence are sequentially numbered above the fixated words with the durations (in msec) indicated below the sequence number.

1	2	3	4	5	6	7	8	9	1	2
1566	267	400	83	267	617	767	450	450	400	616
Flywheels	are	one	of the	oldest	mechanical	devices	known	to	man.	Every internal-

3	5	4	6	7	8	9	10	11	12	13
517	684	250	317	617	1116	367	467	483	450	383
combustion	engine	contains	a	small	flywheel	that	converts	the	jerky	motion	of	the	pistons	into	the

14	15	16	17	18	19	20	21
284	383	317	283	533	50	366	566
smooth	flow	of	energy	that	powers	the	drive	shaft.

Buswell, 1922, chap. 2). When readers are given a text that is appropriate for
their age level, they average 1.2 words per fixation. The words that are not always fixated tend to be short function words, such as *the*, *of*, and *a*. The number
of words per fixation is even lower if the text is especially difficult or if the reader
is poorly educated. Of course, this is not the case when adults are given simple
texts, such as children's stories; under such circumstances, these same studies
show an increase to an average of two words per fixation. Similarly, readers skip
more words if they are speed reading or skimming (Taylor, 1962). These old
results and the current results are consistent with the report of McConkie and
Rayner (1975; Rayner, 1978) that readers generally cannot determine the meaning of a word that is in peripheral vision. These results have important implications for the present model; since most words of a text are fixated, we can try to
account for the total duration of comprehension in terms of the gaze duration on
each word.

The protocol also shows that the gaze duration varies considerably from
word to word. There is a misconception that individual fixations are all about 250
msec in duration. But this is not true; there is a large variation in the duration of
individual fixations as well as the total gaze duration on individual words. As the
preceding display shows, some gaze durations are very long, such as the gaze on
the word *Flywheels*. The model proposes that gaze durations reflect the time to
execute comprehension processes. In this case the longer fixations are attributed
to longer processing caused by the word's infrequency and its thematic importance. Also, the fixations at the end of each sentence tend to be long. For example, this reader had gaze durations of 450 and 566 msec on each of the last words
of the first two sentences. The sentence-terminal pauses will be shown to reflect
an integrative process that is evoked at the ends of sentences.

The link between eye fixations data and the theory rests on two assumptions.
The first, called the immediacy assumption, is that a reader tries to interpret each
content word of a text as it is encountered, even at the expense of making guesses
that sometimes turn out to be wrong. Interpretation refers to processing at several
levels such as encoding the word, choosing one meaning of it, assigning it to its
referent, and determining its status in the sentence and in the discourse. The

immediacy assumption posits that the interpretations at all levels of processing are not deferred; they occur as soon as possible, a qualification that will be clarified later.

The second assumption, the eye-mind assumption, is that the eye remains fixated on a word as long as the word is being processed. So the time it takes to process a newly fixated word is directly indicated by the gaze duration. Of course, comprehending that word often involves the use of information from preceding parts of the text, without any backward fixations. So the concepts corresponding to two different words may be compared to each other, for example, whereas only the more recently encountered word is fixated. The eye-mind assumption can be contrasted with an alternative view that data acquired from several successive eye fixations are internally buffered before being semantically processed (Bouma and deVoogd, 1974). This alternative view was proposed to explain a reading task in which the phrases of a text were successively presented in the same location. However, the situation was unusual in two ways. First, there were no eye movements involved, so the normal reading processes may not have been used. Second, and more telling, readers could not perform a simple comprehension test after seeing the text this way. By contrast, several studies of more natural situations support the eye-mind assumption that readers pause on words that require more processing (Just and Carpenter, 1978; Carpenter and Daneman, Note 1). The eye-mind assumption posits that there is no appreciable lag between what is being fixated and what is being processed. This assumption has also been explored in spatial problem-solving tasks and has been supported in that domain as well as in reading (Just and Carpenter, 1976). The immediacy and eye-mind assumptions are used to interpret gaze duration data in the development of the reading model.

The article has four major sections. The first briefly describes a theoretical framework for the processes and structures in reading. The second section describes the reading task and eye fixation results accounted for by the model. The third section presents the model itself, with subsections describing each component process of the model. The fourth section discusses some implications of the theory for language comprehension and relates this theory of reading to other approaches.

Theoretical Framework

Reading can be construed as the coordinated execution of a number of processing stages such as word encoding, lexical access, assigning semantic roles, and relating the information in a given sentence to previous sentences and previous knowledge. Some of the major stages of the proposed model are depicted schematically in Figure 1. The diagram depicts both processes and structures. The stages of reading in the left-hand column are shown in their usual sequence of execution. The long term memory on the right-hand side is the storehouse of

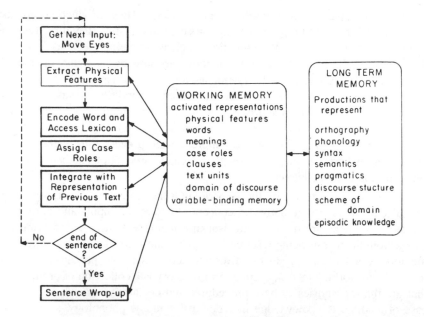

Figure 1.   A schematic diagram of the major processes and structures in reading comprehension. (Solid lines denote data flow paths, and dashed lines indicate canonical flow of control.)

knowledge, including the procedural knowledge used in executing the stages on the left. The working memory in the the middle mediates the long term memory and the comprehension processes. Although it is easy to informally agree on the general involvement of these processes in reading, it is more difficult to specify the characteristics of the processes, their interrelations, and their effects on reading performance.

The nature of comprehension processes depends on a larger issue, namely the architecture of the processing system in which they are embedded. Although the human architecture is very far from being known, production systems have been suggested as a possible framework because they have several properties that might plausibly be shared by the human system. Detailed discussions of production systems as models of the human architecture are presented elsewhere (Anderson, 1976; Newell, 1973, 1980). The following three major properties are of particular relevance here.

1. Structural and procedural knowledge is stored in the form of condition-action rules, such that a given stimulus condition produces a given action. The productions "fire" one after the other (serially), and it is this serial processing that consumes time in comprehension and other forms of thought. In addition to the serial productions, there are also fast, automatic productions that produce spreading activation among associated concepts (Anderson, 1976; Collins and Loftus, 1975). These automatic productions operate in parallel to the serial pro-

ductions and in parallel to each other (Newell, 1980). These productions are fast and automatic because they operate only on constants; that is, they directly associate an action with a particular condition (such as activating the concept *dog* on detecting *cat*). By contrast, serial productions are slow because they operate on variables as well as constants; they associate an action with a class of conditions. A serial production can fire only after the particular condition instance is bound to the variable specified in the production. It may be the binding of variables that consumes time and capacity (Newell, 1980).This architectural feature of two kinds of productions permits serial comprehension processes to operate in the foreground, whereas in the background, automatic productions activate relevant semantic and episodic knowledge.

2. Productions operate on the symbols in a limited capacity working memory. The symbols are the activated concepts that are the inputs and outputs of productions. Items are inserted into working memory as a result of being encoded from the text or being inserted by a production. Retrieval from long term memory occurs when a production fires and activates a concept, causing it to be inserted into working memory. Long term memory is a collection of productions that are the repositories of both procedural and declarative knowledge. In the case of reading, this knowledge includes orthography, phonology, syntax, and semantics of the language, as well as schemas for particular topics and discourse types (Schank and Abelson, 1977). A new knowledge structure is acquired in long term memory if a new production is created to encode that structure (Newell, 1980). This occurs if the structure participates in a large number of processing episodes.

One important property of working memory is that its capacity is limited, so that information is sometimes lost. One way in which capacity can be exceeded (causing forgetting) is that the level of activation of an item may decay to some subthreshold level through disuse over time (Collins and Loftus, 1975; Hitch, 1978; Reitman, 1974). A second forgetting mechanism allows for processes and structures to displace each other, within some limits (Case, 1978). Heavy processing requirements in a given task may decrease the amount of information that can be maintained, perhaps by generating too many competing structures or by actively inhibiting the maintenance of preceding information. There is recent evidence to suggest that working memory capacity (as opposed to passive memory span) is strongly correlated with individual differences in reading comprehension performance, presumably because readers with greater capacity can integrate more elements of the text at a given time (Daneman and Carpenter, in press).

3. Production systems have a mechanism for adaptive sequencing of processes. The items in working memory at a given time enable a given production to fire and insert new items, which in turn enable another production, and so on. In this way, the intermediate results of the comprehension process that are placed in working memory can influence or sequence subsequent processing. There is no need for a superordinate controlling program to sequence the mental actions.

The self-sequencing nature of productions is compatible with the model depicted in Figure 1. The composition of each stage is simply a collection of productions that share a common higher level goal. The productions within a stage have similar enabling conditions and produce actions that serve as conditions for other productions in the same stage. The productions within a stage need not be bound to each other in any other way. Thus the ordering of stages with a production system is accomplished not by direct control transfer mechanisms but an indirect self-sequencing accomplished by one production helping to create the conditions that enable the "next" production to fire.

This architecture permits stages to be executed not only in canonical orders but also in noncanonical orders. There are occasions when some stages of reading seem to be partially or entirely skipped; some stages seem to be executed out of sequence, and some "later" stages sometimes seem to be able to influence "earlier" stages (Levy, in press). Stages can be executed earlier than normal if their enabling conditions exist earlier than normal. For example, if a context strongly primes a case role, then the case assignment could precede the lexical access of a word. Having read *John pounded the nail with a* _____ , a reader can assign the last word to the instrumental case on the basis of cues provided by the words *pound* and *nail*, before encoding *hammer*. This organization can permit "context effects" in comprehension, where a strong preceding context shortens reading time on a given word or clause. This might occur if a processing stage that is normally intermediate between two others is partially or entirely eliminated. It could be eliminated if the preceding stage plus the context provided sufficient enabling conditions for the later stage. Analogously, a misleading context could lengthen comprehension time by providing elements that enable conflicting processes.

The production system organization can also explain how "later" stages can influence "earlier" stages, so that higher level schemas can affect word encoding, for example. If the productions of the normally later stage are enabled earlier than usual, then their outputs can serve as inputs to the normally earlier stage. The ordering of stages does not have to be entirely reversed to obtain this top-down influence. It may be sufficient for just a portion of the productions of the "later" stage to fire in order to influence the "earlier" stage.

In this view of processing stages, several stages can be executed cotemporaneously in the sense that firings of productions of two or more stages may be interleaved. Consequently, data and control can be transferred back and forth among different stages, somewhat similarly to computer programs organized into coroutines. Coroutines are two or more subprograms that have equal status (i.e., there is no master-slave relationship). When one coroutine obtains control, it executes until it detects a condition indicating it should relinquish control, and then another coroutine executes, and so on. One interesting difference between coroutines and the production system model is that coroutines generally transfer data between each other only along specified paths, used especially for this purpose. By contrast, productions "transfer" data by placing it in the working memory, so that all processes have access to it. In this sense, the working memory serves as a message center, and communication among stages is by means of the items in working memory. This is distinct from one stage feeding its output directly to another stage.

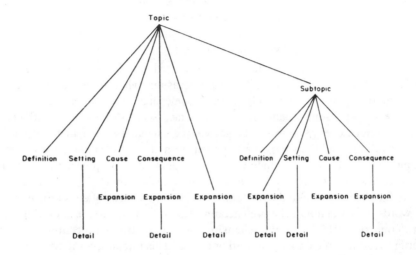

Figure 2.   A schematic diagram of the major textgrammatical categories of information in the scientific paragraphs.

Research

Texts

This section describes the texts that were used in the reading research because their properties, both local and global, have a large influence on the processing. The global organization of a narrative text has been shown to influence how a reader recalls the text (Kintsch and van Dijk, 1978; Mandler and Johnson, 1977; Meyer, 1975; Rumelhart, 1977b; Thorndyke, 1977). The experiment reported next shows that the organization has at least part of its effect when the text is being read. Scientific texts were selected from *Newsweek* and *Time* because their content and style are typical of what students read to learn about technical topics. The passages discussed a variety of topics that were generally unfamiliar to the readers in the study. When readers were asked to rate their familiarity with the topic of each passage on a 5-point scale, the modal rating was at the "entirely unfamiliar" end of the scale. There were 15 passages, averaging 132 words each. Although the texts are moderately well written, they are on the borderline between "fairly difficult" and "difficult" on Flesch's (1951) readability scale, with

17 words per sentence and 1.6 syllables per word. The following is an example of one of the passages:

> Flywheels are one of the oldest mechanical devices known to man. Every internal-combustion engine contains a small flywheel that converts the jerky motion of the pistons into the smooth flow of energy that powers the drive shaft. The greater the mass of flywheel and the faster it spins, the more energy can be stored in it. But its maximum spinning speed is limited by the strength of the material it is made from. If it spins too fast for its mass, any flywheel will fly apart. One type of flywheel consists of round sandwiches of fiberglass and rubber providing the maximum possible storage of energy when the wheel is confined in a small space as in an automobile. Another type, the "superflywheel," consists of a series of rimless spokes. This flywheel stores the maximum energy when space is unlimited.

The content of the passages was analyzed by segmenting the text into idea units and categorizing these units by means of a simple text grammar. First, all of the 15 passages were segmented into text units called *sectors*, producing 274 sectors. The average sector length was seven words. Each sector was judged to be a single meaningful piece of information, whether it consisted of a word, phrase, clause, or sentence. The general criteria for segmentation into sectors were similar to those used by Meyer and McConkie (1973), who related such text units to recall performance.

A simplified grammar was developed to categorize the sectors of the texts. The grammar (shown schematically in Figure 2) classifies the text units into a structure that is quasihierarchical. This abbreviated grammar captures most of the regularities in our short passages (see Vesonder, 1979, for a more complete grammar for longer scientific passages). The initial sentences generally introduced a topic—a scientific development or event. The beginnings of the passage sometimes gave details of the time, place, and people involved with the discovery. Familiar concepts were simply names, whereas unusual concepts were accompanied by an explicit definition. The main topic itself was developed through specific examples or through subtopics that were then expanded with further descriptions, explanations, and concrete examples. Consequences, usually toward the end of the passage, stated the importance of the event for other applications. Table 1 shows how each text unit or sector in the "Flywheel" passage was classified according to these categories. Each of the 274 sectors was asssigned to one of the five levels of the grammar by one of the authors. The levels of the grammar were further confirmed by a pretest involving 16 subjects who rated the importance of each sector in its passage on a 7 point scale. The mean importance ratings differed reliably among the five levels $F (4, 270) = 40.04$, $p < .01$. Specifically, the means decreased monotonically through the five postulated levels. Hence, the grammar potentially has some psychological reality, and its relevance to reading will be demonstrated with the eye fixation data. The next section presents the data collection and analysis procedures, followed by the model and results.

Table 1
A Classification of the "Flywheel" Passage Into Text-Grammatical Categories

Category	Sector
Topic	Flywheels are one of the oldest mechanical devices
Topic	known to man
Expansion	Every internal-combustion engine contains a small flywheel
Expansion	that converts the jerky motion of the pistons into the smooth flow of energy
Expansion	that powers the drive shaft
Cause	The greater the mass of a flywheel and the faster its spins,
Consequences	the more energy can be stored in it.
Subtopic	But its maximum spinning speed is limited by the strength of the material
Suptopic	it is made from.
Expansion	If it spins too fast for its mass,
Expansion	any flywheel will fly apart.
Definition	One type of flywheel consists of round sandwiches of fiberglas and rubber
Expansion	providing the maximum possible storage of energy
Expansion	when the wheel is confined in a small space
Detail	as in an automobile.
Definition	Another type, the "superflywheel," consists of a series of rimless spokes.
Expansion	This flywheel stores the maximum energy
Detail	when space is unlimited.

Methods and Data Analysis

The readers were 14 undergraduates who read 2 practice texts followed by the 15 scientific texts in random order. Although the readers were asked to recall each passage immediately after reading it, they also were told to read naturally without memorizing. They were also asked not to reread the passage or parts of it. The texts were presented on a television monitor using uppercase and lowercase letters and a conventional paragraph layout. To initiate the reading of a passage, the reader had to look at a fixation point (located where the first word of the paragraph would later appear) and press a "ready" button. If the reader's point of regard (as measured by the eye tracker) was within $1°$ of the fixation point, then exactly 500 msec later the passage appeared in its entirety on the screen. The passage appeared instantaneously (i.e., within one video frame) and remained there until the reader signaled that he had finished reading by pushing a response button.

The reader's pupil and corneal reflections were monitored relatively unobtrusively by a television camera that was 75 cm away. The monitoring system, manufactured by Applied Science Laboratories, computed the reader's point of regard (as opposed to eye or head position) every 16.7 msec. The accuracy of the tracker was verified before and after each passage was read by having the reader look at a fixation point and determining whether the obtained point of regard was within $1°$ of that point. This procedure indicated that accuracy was maintained during the reading of 195 of the 210 experimental passages in the entire experiment; the data from the 15 inaccurate trials were discarded.

Data reduction procedures converted the 60 observations per sec into fixations and then into gazes on each word. While the data were being acquired, a new "fixation" was scored as having occurred if the point of regard changed by more than $1°$ (the size of a three-letter syllable). The durations of blinks that were preceded and followed by fixations on the same location were attributed to the reading time on that location. Another program aggregated consecutive fixations on the same word into gazes and computed the duration of gaze on each of the 1,936 words in the 15 passages. Fixations on interword spaces were attributed to the word on the right because the perceptual span is centered to the right of the point of regard, at least for readers of left-to-right languages (McConkie and Rayner, 1976; Schiepers, 1980). The durations of saccades, blinks that occurred between words, regressions, and rereading were not included in the data analysis. Because of the instructions not to reread, these categories account for relatively little of the total reading time, approximately 12 percent in all. The mean duration of gaze on each word was computed by averaging over readers; these 1,936 mean gaze durations constitute the main dependent measure of interest.

The model presents a number of factors that influence various reading processes; some factors have their effect on individual words and some on larger units, such as clauses. The data were fit to the model with a multiple linear regression in which the independent variables were the factors postulated to affect reading time and the dependent variable was the mean gaze duration on each word. Since the model also applies at the level of clauses and phrases, a second regression analysis was done at the phrase/clause level. The independent variables for the latter analysis were the factors postulated to affect reading time at the clause level, and the independent variable was the mean gaze duration on each of the 274 sectors described previously.

The psychological interpretation of the independent variables in the two regression analyses will be described in detail in the sections that follow. The equation for the analysis of the gaze duration on individual words was

$$GW_i = \sum a_m X_{im} + \epsilon_i,$$

where GW_i is the gaze duration on a word i, a_m is the regression weight in msec for independent variable X_m, X_{im} are the independent variables that code the following seven properties of word i:

(a) length, (b) the logarithm of its normative frequency, (c) whether the word occurs at the beginning of a line of text, (d) whether it is a novel word to the reader, (e) its case grammatical role (one of 11 possibilities), (f) whether it is the last word in a sentence, (g) whether it is the last word in a paragraph.

The equation for the analysis of the gaze duration on individual sectors was

$$GS_j = b_0 + \sum b_n Z_{jn} + \epsilon_j$$

where GS, is the gaze duration on sector j, and b_n is the regression weight in msec for independent variable Z_n. The Z_{jn} are the independent variables that code the following eight properties of sector j:

(a) its text grammatical level, multiplied by the number of content words; (b) length; (c) the sum of the logarithm of the frequencies of its component words; (d) the number of line-initial words it contains; (e) the number of novel words it contains; (f) the sum of the case role regression weights of its component words; (g) whether it is the last sector in a sentence; (h) whether it is the last sector in a paragraph.

Results

The mean gaze duration on each word (239 msec) indicated reading rates that are typical for texts of this difficulty. If the 239 msec per word is incremented by 12 percent to allow for saccades, blinks, and occasional rereading, the reading rate is 225 words per min. The standard deviation of the 239-msec gaze mean was 168 msec, indicating considerable variability in gaze duration from word to word. The results of the regression analyses are shown in Table 2. The table is divided into three sections, corresponding to the three major processing stages postulated by the model, encoding and lexical access, case role assignment, and interclause integration. The regression weights shown in Table 2 for the word-by-word analysis (above the double line) are derived from a regression equation involving 17 independent variables (11 of which are the case role indicator variables). The standard error of estimate of this model was 88 msec, and the R^2 value was .72. The results of the interclause integration stage make use of both the word-by-word analysis and the sector-by-sector analysis. (The latter analysis will be explained in more detail in the section on interclause integration.) Since the gaze durations on successive words and phrases are time-series data, it is interesting to note that there was no reliable positive serial correlation among the residuals in the word-by-word regression or the sector-by-sector regression.

The Reading Model

The next five subsections describe the major stages shown in Figure 1: Get next input, encoding and lexical access, case role assignment, interclause integration, and sentence wrap-up. Each subsection describes the processes in that stage together with the factors that affect the duration of those processes, and hence the gaze durations.

Get Next Input

This is the first stage of a cycle that finds information, encodes it, and processes it. When the perceptual and semantic stages have done all of the requisite processing on a particular word, the eye is directed to land in a new place where it continues to rest until the requisite processing is done, and so forth. The specification of what constitutes "all of the requisite processing" is contained in a list of conditions that must be satisfied before the reader terminates the gaze on the current word and fixates the next one. These conditions include a specification of the goals of normal reading. For instance, one condition may be that a meaning of the word be accessed and another condition may be that a case role be assigned. These conditions can also reflect more specific reading goals. A reader who is trying to memorize a text may have as a condition that the word or phrase be transferred to long term memory. By setting the conditions appropriately, the reader can adjust his processes to the situation at hand. When the goal conditions for processing a word are satisfied, the resulting action is get next input.

The command to get next input usually results in a saccade to the next part of the text, one or two words forward. The process that selects the placement of the next forward fixation does not have to be very complex or intelligent. The choice of where to place the next forward fixation appears to depend primarily on the length of the next word or two to the right of the current fixation (McConkie and Rayner, 1975). The length information, which is encoded parafoveally, is then used to program a rightward saccade. However, if only the right margin is visible in the parafovea, then the eye is directed to the first word of the next line, producing a return sweep. In this case the information in peripheral vision is not adequate for accurate targeting. The return sweep is typically too short; the eye often lands on the second word of the new line for a brief amount of time (50 or 75 msec) and then makes a corrective saccade leftward to the first word of the line (Bayle, 1942). On occasion, a comprehension stage may require a review of previously read text to reencode it or process it to deeper levels. In those cases, the get next input stage results in a regressive saccade to the relevant portion of the text.

Table 2
Application of the Regression Model to the Gaze Duration on Each Word (Above Double Line) and to Each Sector (Below Double Line)

Processing stage	Factor	Regression weight (msec)
Encoding and lexical access	no. of syllables	52**
	log frequency	53**
	beginning of line	30**
	novel word	802**
Case role assignment	agent (86)	51**
	instrument (110)	53**
	direct or indirect object (174)	25*
	adverb/manner (35)	29
	place or time (64)	23
	possessive (genitive) (39)	16
	verb (368)	33**
	state/adjective (451)	44**
	rhetorical word (15)	70**
	determiner (243)	26**
	connective (351)	9
Interclause integration	last word in sentence	71**
	last word in paragraph	157**
	Integration time per content word from regression analysis of data aggregated into sectors	
	topic (22)	72**
	definition/cause/consequence (23)	94**
	subtopic (48)	78**
	expansion (68)	73**
	detail (113)	60**

Note. Frequency of occurrence of case roles is in parentheses.
* $t = p < .0.05$; ** $t = p < .01$.

The duration of the get next input stage is short, consisting of the time for a neural signal to be transmitted to the eye muscles. In monkeys, this takes about 30 msec (Robinson, 1972). This duration must not be confused with the typical 150 to 200 msec latency of a saccade to a visual stimulus that has spatial or temporal uncertainty (Westheimer, 1954). These latencies include stimulus detection, interpretation, and selection of the next fixation target. In normal reading, there is very little uncertainty about direction of the next saccade (it is almost always rightward for forward fixations, except for the return sweeps), nor is there much uncertainty about distance. On the average, the saccade distance may be simply the mean center-to-center distance between words, a distance that does not vary much, relative to the physically possible variation in eye movements. Thus it is reasonable to suppose that the preprograming time is very short here, consisting usually of a "go" signal and the time it takes that signal to be translated into a motor movement, about 30 msec (Robinson, 1972). The actual movements, the saccades, constitute about 5-10 percent of the total reading time. Recent analyses suggest that the saccade itself may destroy the visual persistence of the information from the preceding fixation so that it does not mask the input from the new fixation (Breitmeyer, 1980). Consequently, it is reasonable to assume that stimulus encoding can commence soon after the eye arrives at a new location.

Word Encoding and Lexical Access

The reading process involves encoding a word into an internal semantic format. It is assumed that prior to this encoding, the transduction from the printed word to the visual features has already taken place, and that the features have been deposited into the working memory. Perceptual encoding productions use the visual features as conditions; their action is to activate the representation of the word. Once the representation of the word has been sufficiently activated, its corresponding concept is accessed and inserted into working memory. The concept serves as a pointer to a more complete representation of the meaning, which consists of a small semantic network realized as a set of productions. The major nodes of the network are the possible meanings of the word, the semantic and syntactic properties of the meanings, and information about the contexts in which they usually occur (see Rieger, 1979, for a related proposal). The word meanings are represented as abstract predicates, defined by their relations to other predicates.

The productions that encode a word generally trigger on orthographically based subword units such as syllables (Mewhort and Beal, 1977; Spoehr and Smith, 1973; Taft, 1979). However, there are times when alternative codes, including orthographic, phonological, and whole-word codes, are used (Baron, 1977; Kleiman, 1975; LaBerge and Samuels, 1974). Since the syllablelike encoding is believed to be the dominant mode, the data were analyzed in terms of the number of syllables in each word. Encoding time increased by 52 msec for each syllable, as shown in Table 2.

The mechanism underlying lexical access is the activation of a word's meaning representation by various sources. There are three ways that a concept's level of activation can be temporarily increased above its base level. One activation mechanism is perceptual encoding; the encoded representation of a word can activate its meaning. A second source is the parallel productions that produce spreading activation through the semantic and episodic knowledge base of the reader. The third source is activation by the serial productions that do the major computations in all of the stages of processing. When a concept has been activated above some threshold by one or more of these sources, a pointer to its meaning is inserted into working memory. The activation level gradually decays to a subthreshold level unless some process reactivates it. If the word soon reoccurs in the text while the concept is still activated, lexical access will be facilitated because the activation level will still be close to threshold. When the activation level does decrease, it decreases to an asymptote slightly higher than the old base level. In this way, the system can learn from both local and long term word repetitions. Frequently used words will have a high base level of activation, and consequently will require relatively less additional activation to retrieve them. Thus, frequent words should take less time to access than infrequent words (Morton, 1969). Similarly, the various possible interpretations of each word will have different base activation levels, such that the more common interpretations have higher base activation levels. For example, although the word *does* has at least two very different meanings, the "third-person-singular verb" interpretation would have a higher base activation because it is more common than the "female deer" interpretation (Carpenter and Daneman, Note 1). The more common interpretation would then be accessed faster, since less additional activation would be required to bring the activation level to threshold. This model of lexical access can account for word frequency effects, priming effects, and repetition effects in reading.

The gaze duration showed both frequency and repetition effects. Frequency was analyzed by relating gaze duration to the logarithm of the normative frequency of each word, based on the Kučera and Francis (1967) norms. It was expected that gaze duration would decrease with the logarithm of the word's frequency; that is, small differences among infrequent words would be as important as much larger differences among frequent words (Mitchell and Green, 1978). For algebraic convenience, the normative frequencies were increased by one (to eliminate the problem of taking the logarithm of zero), and the logarithm was computed and then subtracted from 4.85, the logarithm of the frequency of the most frequent English word. The analysis indicated a clear relation between this measure of frequency and gaze duration. As shown in Table 2, gaze duration increased by 53 msec for each log unit decrease in word frequency. A moderately frequent word like *water* (with a frequency of 442) was accessed 140 msec faster than a word that did not appear in the norms.

At one extreme of the frequency dimension are words that a reader has never encountered before. In scientific passages, the novel words tend to be technical terms. To read these words, a reader cannot depend on contacting some prior perceptual and semantic representation; neither exists. The reader must construct some perceptual representation (perhaps phonological as well as orthographic), associate this with the semantic and syntactic properties of the concept that can be inferred from the passage, and then possibly construct a lexical entry. These processes seem to take a great deal more time than ordinary encoding and access processes. Two judges identified seven words in the texts (that had zero frequency) as probably entirely novel to the readers. Novelty was coded as an indicator variable, and it was found that these words took an additional 802 msec on average to process, as shown in Table 2. However, there was considerable variability among the words; their gaze durations ranged from 913 msec (for *staphyllococci*) to 2,431 msec (for *thermoluminescence*).

Once a word has been encoded and accessed, it should be easier to access it when it occurs again. Other research has suggested that frequency and repetition have their primary effect on lexical access rather than encoding (Dixon and Rothkopf, 1979; Glanzer and Ehrenreich, 1979; Scarborough, Cortese, and Scarborough, 1977), although the possibility of some small effects on the encoding process does exist. According to the model, repetition effects should occur in reading because the first time a word meaning is accessed, it should temporarily achieve a higher activation level similar to the level of a more frequent word. This mechanism particularly predicts repetition effects for infrequent words, whose activation levels are low to start with, but not for the highly frequent words that occur in natural text. Generally, repetition effects are larger for low-frequency words (Scarborough et al., 1977). "Low frequency" in the Scarborough study was defined as less than 28 occurrences per million, the boundary of 28 emerging from a median split of the frequencies of their stimuli. So the analysis of repetition effects was limited to words with frequencies of 25 occurrences per million or less. There were 346 such instances in the text; 251 were initial occurrences and 95 were repetitions. The repetitions were words with the same morphological stem, disregarding affixes. An analysis of covariance on this subset of the data examined the effects of repetitions covarying out the number of syllables. The adjusted mean gaze durations were 49 msec longer on the initial appearance of these words than on the subsequent appearances, $t(343) = 2.21$, $p < .03$. Most of this effect (43 msec) was obtained on the second appearance of a word. These results indicate that once an infrequent word appears in a text, processing time on that word is decreased on subsequent appearances.

Lexical access is complicated by the fact that some words have more than one meaning, so the appropriate interpretation must be selected, or at least guessed at. When a polysemous word is accessed, the word representation that is retrieved is a pointer to a semantic network that includes the multiple representations. The interpretation that is selected is the one with the highest activation level, and several factors can affect the activation. First, some interpretations start off with a higher activation level; for instance, the "third-person-singular" interpretation of *does* has a higher base activation level than the "deer" interpretation. Second, the automatic productions that produce spreading activation can contribute selectively to the activation level of one particular interpretation. The spreading activation can emanate from the preceding semantic and syntactic context, from the reader's knowledge of the domain, and from knowledge of the discourse style. Third, the output of other stages operating on the same word may activate a particular interpretation. For example, although *hammer* can be interpreted as a noun or a verb, a sentence context that suggests an instrument to the case role assignment stage (e.g., *John hit the nail with a* _____) may help activate the noun interpretation. Fourth, when a word with many highly related meanings occurs in an impoverished context, there may be no single interpretation with higher activation than the others, and the superordinate concept may be the selected interpretation of the word. This probably occurs for words that have many closely related interpretations, such as *get* and *take*.

The selection of only one interpretation of each word, posited by the immediacy assumption, provides a measure of cognitive economy. Selecting just one interpretation allows the activation of the unselected interpretations to decay, preventing them from activating their associates. Thus, the contextual effects would remain focused in the appropriate semantic domain. This permits a limited-capacity working memory to cope with the information flow in a spreading activation environment that may activate many interpretations and associations for any lexical item. This method of processing also avoids the combinatorial explosion that results from entertaining more than one interpretation for several successive words.

This aspect of the model is consistent with some recent results on lexical access that indicate that although multiple meanings of a word are initially activated, only one meaning remains activated after a few hundred milliseconds. In one experiment, the subjects simultaneously listened to a sentence and pronounced a visually presented word. When an ambiguous word (*rose*) was presented auditorily in a syntactic context (e.g., *They all rose*), the speed of pronouncing a simultaneous visual probe related to either meaning (stood or flower) was faster than in a control condition (Tanenhaus, Leiman, and Seidenberg, 1979). In another experiment, the subjects listened to a sentence and performed a lexical decision task on visually presented stimuli. When an ambiguous word (*bug*) was presented in a semantic context (*John saw several spiders, roaches, and bugs*), the speed of a simultaneous lexical decision related to either meaning (insect or spy) was faster than a control (Swinney, 1979). In both studies, the facilitation of the inappropriate meaning was obtained only within a few hundred milliseconds of the occurrence of the ambiguous word. If the probe was delayed longer, the inappropriate interpretation was no faster than the control. These results suggest that both meanings are available when an ambiguous word is being accessed, but the inappropriate meaning is lost from working memory after a short time.

As the interpretation of the text is constructed, a corresponding representation of the extensive meaning—the things being talked about—is also being built. If the referents of the words in a passage cannot be determined, the text will be more difficult to understand. One example of this problem is highlighted in a passage from Bransford and Johnson (1973) concerning a procedure that involved arranging "things into groups. Of course, one may be sufficient depending on how much there is. . ." (p. 400). Subjects who were not given the title *washing clothes* thought the story was incomprehensible. The referential representation helps the reader disambiguate referents, infer relations, and integrate the text.

The immediacy assumption posits that an attempt to relate each content word to its referent occurs as soon as possible. Sometimes this can be done when the word is first fixated, but sometimes more information is required. For example, although the semantic interpretation of a relative adjective like *large* can be computed immediately, the extensive meaning depends on the word it modifies (e.g., *large insect* vs. *large building*). The referent of the entire noun phrase can be computed only after both words are processed. The immediacy assumption does not state that the relating is done immediately on each content word, but rather that it occurs as soon as possible. This is an important distinction that will be made again in the discussion on integrative processes.

Assigning Case Roles

Comprehension involves determining the relations among words, the relations among clauses, and the relations among whole units of text. This section describes the first of these processes, that of determining the relations among the words in a clause (or in Schank's, 1972, terms, determining the dependencies among the concepts). These relations can be categorized into semantic cases, such as agent, recipient, location, time, manner, instrument, action, or state (Chafe, 1979; Fillmore, 1968). The case role assignment process usually takes as input a representation of the fixated word, including information about its possible case roles and syntactic properties. For example, hammers tend to be instruments rather than locations or recipients, and information about a word's usual case role can be an important contributor to the assignment process. But this normative information generally is not sufficient to assign its case role in a particular clause. Consequently, the assignment process relies on heuristics that use the word meaning together with information about the prior semantic and syntactic context, as well as language-based inferences. The output of the process is a representation of the word's semantic role with respect to the other constituents in its clause.

Just as certain meanings suggest particular case roles, so, too, can the context prime a particular case role. Consider the sentence *John was interrogated by the* _____ . The semantic and syntactic cues suggest that the missing word will be an agent, such as *detective*. The strength of the context becomes evident if the primed case does not occur, for example, *Johns was interrogated by the window*. The prior semantic context can precede the affected case assignment by more than a few words. In the sentences *The lawyer wanted to know where in the room John had been interrogated* and *Mary told him that John was interrogated by the window*, the thematic focus of the first sentence on a location alters the interpretation of *by* and facilitates a locative case role assignment for *window*.

The specific heuristics that are used in case role assignment have received some attention (see Clark and Clark, 1977, for some examples). Many proposals contain the suggestion that readers use the verb as a pivotal source of information to establish the necessary and possible case roles and then fit the noun phrases into those slots (Schank, 1972). But the immediacy assumption posits that the case role assignment for an item preceding the verb is not postponed in anticipation of the verb. Similar to the lexical access stage, the case assignment stage makes a best guess about a word's case when the word is fixated, rather than making the decision contingent on subsequent words. So, the model would not accord any special status to verbs. Another suggested heuristic (that children appear to use) is to assign a sequence consisting of animate noun-verb-noun to the case roles of agent-action-object (Bever, 1970). Like all heuristics, this one sometimes fails, so young children sometimes misinterpret passive sentences (Fraser, Bellugi, and Brown, 1963). This heuristic may be employed by adults, but in a modified version that conforms to the immediacy assumption. Rather than waiting for the three major constituents before assigning case roles, the reader should assign an animate noun to the agent role as soon as it is encountered, in the absence of contrary prior context.

The immediate assignment of a case role implies that readers will sometimes make errors and have to revise previous decisions. For example, an adult who assigns the role of agent to an animate noun and then encounters a passive verb will have to revise the agent assignment. (Presumably, young children do not make this revision.) The immediacy of the case assignment process is evident in the reading of sentences, such as *Mary loves Jonathan*. . . . The immediacy assumption suggests that a reader would assign to *Jonathan* the role of recipient; this would in turn result in an incorrect assignment if the sentence continued *Mary loves Jonathan apples*.

Because case roles are assigned within clauses, the assignment process must include a segmentation procedure to determine clause boundaries within sentences. Sentences can sometimes be segmented into clauses on the basis of explicit markers, such as a subordinating conjunction (e.g., *because*, *when*). More often, the reader cannot tell with certainty where one clause ends and another starts until beyond the clause boundary (or potential boundary). A general strategy for dealing with such cases has been suggested, namely to assign a word to the clause being processed, if possible (Frazier and Fodor, 1978). For example, the word *soil* in the sentence *When farmers are plowing the soil . . .* can continue the initial clause (*When farmers are plowing the soil, it is most fertile*) or start a new one (*When farmers are plowing the soil is most fertile*). The suggested strategy is to continue the initial clause until contrary information is encountered. Interestingly, the strategy discussed by Frazier and Fodor (1978) presupposes the immediacy assumption; the segmentation decision arises because case roles are assigned as soon as the words are encountered.

There is no direct mapping between particular case roles and the duration of the assignment process. For example, there is no a priori reason to expect that assignment of instruments takes more or less time than locations. The time for a particular assignment might depend more on the context and properties of the word than on the particular case role being assigned. Detailed specification of the process is not within the scope of this article; it probably requires a large-scale simulation model to examine the complex interactions of different levels of processing. Nevertheless, we examined whether all things being equal, different case role assignments tend to take different amounts of time.

The analysis included the usual case roles just noted (Fillmore, 1968), as well as other categories such as determiners and adjectives that are not cases but still play a part in the parsing and assignment process. Each word was classified into 1 of 11 categories; verb, agent, instrument, indirect or direct object, location or time, adverb, adjective or state, connective (preposition or conjunction), possessive, determiner, and rhetorical word (such as *well*). Some cases were pooled (such as location and time) because they were relatively infrequent in the text and because they have some conceptual similarity. The case roles were coded as indicator variables and were all entered into the regression with the intercept forced to zero.

The results of the case role assignment analysis, shown in Table 2, indicate that there are some variations among the cases. As expected, verbs did not take particularly long (33 msec), and in fact, although the time was significantly different from 0, it was not greater than the agent or instrument cases (51 msec and 53 msec respectively). Four cases had parameters that were not significantly different from 0, connectives (9 msec), adverb/manner (29 msec), place or time (23 msec), and possessive (16 msec). These parameters could reflect some properties of particular word classes, in addition to parsing and case role assignment processes. For example, if a connective (e.g., *and* or *but*) simply takes less time to access than other words, the advantage should appear in this parameter. However, the parameters are not due solely to length or frequency, since these variables make a separate contribution to the regression equation. Although this analysis does not examine any of the contextual effects thought to be of some importance in the case assignment process, it does indicate roughly the relative amount of time spent assigning various categories of words to their case roles in a clause. Later theories will have to account for the precise pattern of case assignment durations in terms of specific operations that use prior context and word meanings to assign the various cases.

Interclause Integration

Clauses and sentences must be related to each other by the reader to capture the coherence in the text. As each new clause or sentence is encountered, it must be integrated with the previous information acquired from the text or with the knowledge retrieved from the reader's long term memory. Integrating the new sentence with the old information consists of representing the relations between the new and the old structures.

Several search strategies may be used to locate old information that is related to the new information. One strategy is to check if the new information is related to the other information that is already in working memory either because it has been repeatedly referred to or because it is recent (Carpenter and Just, 1977a; Kintsch and van Dijk, 1978). Using this strategy implies that adjacency between clauses and sentences will cause a search for a possible relation. For instance, the adjacent sentences *Mary hurt herself* and *John laughed* seem related (John must be a cad) even though there is no explicit mention of the relation. This strategy also entails trying to relate new information to a topic that is active in working memory. This is a good strategy, since information in a passage should be related to the topic.

A second strategy is to search for specific connections based on cues in the new sentence itself. Sentences often contain old information as well as new. Sometimes the old information is explicitly marked (as in cleft constructions and relative clauses), but often it is simply some argument repeated from the prior text. The reader can use this old information to search his or her long term text representation and referential representation for potential points of attachment between the new information and the old (Haviland and Clark, 1974). This second strategy may take more time than the first. In fact, it takes longer to read a sentence that refers to information introduced several sentences earlier than one that refers to recently introduced information (Carpenter and Just, 1977a).

There are two main points at which integration can occur. First, as each ensuing word of the text is encountered, there is an attempt to relate it to previous information (Just and Carpenter, 1978). Second, a running representation of the clause is maintained, with an updating as each word of the clause is read. This running clause representation consists of the configuration of clause elements arranged according to their case relations. This second type of integration involves an attempt to relate the running clause representation to previous information at each update. Integration occurs whenever a linking relation can be computed. Consider the sentence *Although he spoke softly, yesterday's speaker could hear the little boy's question*. The point of this example is not so much that the initial integration of *he* and *speaker* is incorrect, but that the integration is attempted at the earliest opportunity. This model implies that integration time may be distributed over fixations on different parts of a clause. Moreover, the duration of the process may depend on the number of concepts in the clause; as these increase, the number of potential points of contact between the new clause and previous information will increase. There is also evidence for integration triggered by the end of the sentence; this process is discussed next in more detail.

Integration results in the creation of a new structure. The symbol representing that structure is a pointer to the integrated concepts, and this superordinate symbol is then available for further processing. In this way, integration can chunk the incoming text and allow a limited working memory to deal with large segments of prose. The macrorules proposed by Kintsch and van Dijk (1978) can be construed as productions that integrate.

Integration can also lead to forgetting in working memory. As each new chunk is formed, there is a possibility that it will displace some previous information from working memory. Particularly vulnerable are items that are only marginally activated, usually because they were processed much earlier and have not recently participated in a production. For instance, the representation of a clause will decay if it was processed early in a text and was not related to subsequent information. This mechanism can also clear working memory of "lower level" representations that are no longer necessary. For example, the verbatim representation of a previously read sentence may be displaced by the processes that integrated the sentence with other information (Jarvella, 1971). By contrast, the semantic elements that participate in an integration production obtain an increased activation level. This increases the probability that they will become a permanent part of long term memory.

The main types of interclause relations in the scientific passages correspond to the text-grammatical categories described previously, such as definitions, causes, consequences, examples, and so forth. Text roles that are usually more important to the text and to the reader's goals, such as topics or definitions, are integrated differently than less important units, such as details. The more central units will initiate more retrievals of relevant previous knowledge of the domain (schematic knowledge) and retrievals of information acquired from the text but no longer resident in the working memory. In addition, more relations will be computed between the semantically central propositions and previous information because centrality inherently entails relations with many other units. By contrast, details are often less important to the reader's goals and to the text. Moreover, when a detail is to be integrated, the process is simpler because details are often concrete instantiations of an immediately preceding statement (at least in these scientific texts), so they can be quickly appended to information still present in the working memory. Thus, higher level units will take more time to integrate because their integration is usually essential to the reader's goals, and because integration of higher units involves more relations to be computed and more retrievals to be made.

The nature of the link relating two structures may be explicitly denoted either in the text (with connectives like *because*, *therefore*, and *for instance*) or it may have to be inferred on the basis of schematic knowledge of the domain. For example, the causal relation between the sentences *Cynthia fell off the rocking horse* and *She cried bitter tears* is inferred from the reader's knowledge about the temporal and causal relation between falling and hurting oneself (Charniak, Note 2).

The model predicts that the gaze duration on a sector depends on its text-grammatical role and on the number of concepts it contains. Because integration can occur at many points in a sector, the gaze duration associated with integration cannot be localized to a particular word. Thus, to do the clause level of analysis, the gaze durations on the individual words of a sector were cumulated, producing a total of 275 sector gaze durations as the dependent variable. The independent variables were the aggregates of the word-level variables, except for case roles. The independent variable that coded the case-role effect for a sector was the sum of the case-coefficients (obtained from the word-by-word regression analysis) for each of the words in the sector. A new independent variable coded the text-grammatical role of a sector and its number of content words; it was the interaction of the indicator variables that represented the five text-grammatical levels and the number of content words in the sector, with content words defined as in Hockett (1958).

The results indicate that the integration time for a given sector depends on its text-grammatical role. The portion of Table 2 below the double line shows the integration time per content word for each type of sector. Generally, more important or central sectors take longer to integrate. The model describes this effect in terms of the integrative processes initiated by the semantics of the different types of information and their relevance to the reader's goals. An analysis of covariance examined the effect of text roles covarying out the number of syllables. The adjusted mean gaze durations differed reliably, $F (4, 268) = 8.82, p < .01$; paired comparisons indicated that details took significantly less time than all other roles, and expansions took significantly less time than topics and definitions/causes/consequences (all $ps < .01$). These results quantitatively and qualitatively replicate those reported previously for a slightly different paradigm (Carpenter and Just, in press). The previously obtained coefficients for the five text-grammatical categories were 65, 106, 81, 76, and 47 msec per content word, respectively, corresponding to the newly obtained 72, 94, 78, 73, and 60. The model accounts very well for the sector level data. The R^2 value was .94, and the standard error of estimate was 234. The mean gaze duration on a sector was 1,690 msec, with a standard deviation of 902 msec, and the mean sector length was 4.9 words.[2]

One cost of immediate interpretation, case role assignment, and integration is that some decisions will prove to be incorrect. There must be mechanisms to detect and recover from such errors. The detection of a misinterpretation often occurs when new information to be integrated is inconsistent with previous information. Thus, misinterpretation detection may be construed as inconsistency detection. For example, the sentence *There were tears in her brown dress* causes errors initially because the most frequent interpretation of *tears* is not the appropriate one here, and the initial interpretation is incompatible with *dress*. The eye fixations of subject reading such garden path sentences clearly indicate that readers do detect inconsistencies, typically at the point at which the inconsistency is first evident (Carpenter and Daneman, Note 1). At that point, they use a number of error-recovery heuristics that enable them to reinterpret the text. They do not start reinterpreting the sentence from its beginning. The heuristics point them to the locus of the probable error. Readers start the backtracking with the word that first reveals the inconsistency, in this case, *dress*. If that word cannot be reinterpreted, they make regressions to the site of other words that were initially difficult to interpret, such as ambiguous words on which a best guess about word meaning had to be made. The ability to return directly to the locus of the misinterpretation and to recover from an error makes the immediacy strategy feasible.

Sentence Wrap-Up

A special computational episode occurs when a reader reaches the end of a sentence. This episode, called sentence wrap-up, is not a stage of processing defined by its function, but rather by virtue of being executed when the reader reaches the end of a sentence. The processes that occur during sentence wrap-up involve a search for referents that have not been assigned, the construction of interclause relations (with the aid of inferences, if necessary), and an attempt to handle any inconsistencies that could not be resolved within the sentence.

The ends of sentences have two important properties that make them especially good places for integration. First, within-sentence ambiguities are usually clarified by the end of the sentence. For example, if a sentence introduces a new object or person whose identity cannot be inferred from the preceding context, some cue to their identity is generally given by the end of the sentence. For that reason, if readers cannot immediately determine the referent of a particular word, then they can expect to be told the referent or given enough information to infer it by the end of the sentence. Indeed, readers do use the ends of sentences to process inconsistencies that they cannot resolve within the sentence (Carpenter and Daneman, Note 1). The second property is that the end of a sentence unambiguously signals the end of one thought and the beginning of a new one. It can be contrasted with weaker cues that signal within-sentence clause boundaries such as commas, relative pronouns, and conjunctions that can signal other things besides the end of a clause. Since ends of sentences are unambiguous, they have the same role across sentences, and they may be processed more uniformily than the cues to within-sentence clause boundaries.

There is ample empirical support for the integrative processing at the ends of sentences. Previous eye fixation studies show that when a lexically based inference must be made to relate a new sentence to some previous portion of the text, there is a strong tendency to pause at the lexical item in question and at the end of sentence that contains it (Just and Carpenter, 1978). Readers were given paragraphs containing pairs of related sentences; the first noun in the second sentence was the agent or instrument of the verb in the first sentence:

(1a) *It was dark and stormy the night the millionaire was murdered.*
(1b) *The killer left no clues for the police to trace.*

In another condition, the integrating inference was less direct:

(2a) *It was dark and stormy the night the millionaire died.*
(2b) *The killer left no clues for the police to trace.*

It took about 500 msec longer to process Sentence 2b than 1b, presumably due to the more difficult inference linking *killer* to *die*. There were two main places in which the readers paused for those 500 msec, indicating the points at which the inference was being computed. One point was on the word *killer*, and the other was on the end of the sentence containing *killer*. Another eye fixation study showed that integration linking a pronoun to its antecedent can occur either when the pronoun is first encountered or at the end of the sentence containing the pronoun (Carpenter and Just, 1977b).

Reading-time studies also have shown that there is extra processing at the end of a sentence. When subjects self-pace the word-by-word or phrase-by-phrase presentation of a text, they tend to pause longer at the word or phrase that terminates a sentence (Aaronson and Scarborough, 1976; Mitchell and Green, 1978). The pause has been attributed to contextual integration processes, similar to the proposed interclause integration process here. Yet another source of evidence for sentence wrap-up processes is that verbatim memory for recently comprehended text declines after a sentence boundary (Jarvella, 1971; Perfetti and Lesgold, 1977). The model attributes the decline to the interference between sentence wrap-up processes and the maintenance of verbatim information in working memory. Finally, another reason to expect sentence wrap-up processes is that we have observed pauses at sentence terminations in an eye fixation study similar to the one reported here (Carpenter and Just, in press). However, the current study provides stronger evidence because the text was presented all at once.

The results indicate that readers did pause longer on the last word in a sentence. As Table 2 shows, the duration of the sentence wrap-up period is 71 msec.

It is possible that wrap-up episodes could occur at the ends of text units smaller or larger than a sentence. For example, the data of Aaronson and Scarborough (1976) suggest that there are sometimes wrap-up processes at the ends of clauses. It is also possible that wrap-up could occur under some circumstances at the ends of paragraphs. The decision of when and if to do a wrap-up may be controlled by the desired depth of processing. For example, skimming may require wrap-up only at paragraph terminations, whereas understanding a legal contract may require wrap-up at clause boundaries. In fact, the clause-boundary effects obtained by Aaronson and Scarborough are sensitive to the subjects' reading goals. The current analysis indicated that the final word in the paragraph might also be a wrap-up point; it received an additional 157 msec of fixation. However, since readers also pressed a button to indicate that they had finished reading the passage, this parameter might be influenced by their motor response.

Finally, the model included one other factor that involves a physical property of reading, namely the return sweep of the eyes from the right-hand side of one line of text to the left-hand side of the next line. Return sweeps are often inaccurate, landing to the right of the first word in a line. The inaccuracy is often corrected by a leftward saccade to the first word. As a result of this error and recovery, the first word on a line eventually receives an increased gaze duration, relative to a line-medial word. Almost all readers we have studied display the undershoot, but there are considerable individual differences in whether they compensate for it by making an extra leftward fixation to the first word. In fact, some researchers have associated these corrective leftward movements with poor readers (Bayle, 1942). To test for increased gaze durations on line-initial words, an indicator variable coded whether a word was the first one on a line. As Table 2 shows, these words received an additional 30 msec of fixation.

Fit of the Model

To see how well the model accounts for the data, one can informally compare how closely the estimated gaze durations match the observed gaze durations. The display that follows shows the estimated (in italics) and observed (in msec) gaze durations for two sentences from the "Flywheel" passage. The estimated durations can be computed by an appropriate combination of the weights give in Table 2. These estimates take into account the processes of encoding, lexical access, case-role assignment, sentence wrap-up, and the beginning of the line effect; they do not include integration time for text roles, since there is no way to distribute this time on a word-by-word basis. In spite of this, the match is satisfactory, and as mentioned earlier, the standard error of estimate was 88 msec overall.

Observed mean gaze durations (msec) on each word of a text sample and estimates (italicized, from the word-by-word regression analysis.

169	215	165	295	290	73	196	504	29	482	0	328	431	51
165	*236*	*75*	*409*	*304*	*75*	*249*	*438*	*75*	*413*	*80*	*338*	*349*	*78*
. . . One	type	of	flywheel	consists	of	round	sandwiches	of	fiberglas	and	rubber	providing	the

369	326	308	22	272	253	128	199	69	336	32	41	267	197	70	164	195
354	*318*	*297*	*75*	*378*	*138*	*77*	*239*	*128*	*326*	*87*	*102*	*206*	*209*	*112*	*87*	*127*
maximum	possible	storage	of	energy	when	the	wheel	is	confined	in	a	small	space	as	in	an

340	323	182	72	626	276	46	21	346	60	467	519
465	*334*	*236*	*77*	*513*	*304*	*75*	*102*	*289*	*75*	*361*	*319*
automobile.	Another	type,	the	"superflywheel,"	consists	of	a	series	of	rimless	spokes . . .

Table 3 presents an analogous comparison from the sector-by-sector analysis; this includes integration time. Again, the estimates from the model match the observed data quite well. The standard error of estimate was 234 msec overall.

Another way to evaluate the goodness of fit is to compare the regression results to those of another model that lacks most of the theoretically interesting independent variables and contains only the variable that codes the number of syllables. For the word-by-word analysis, this rudimentary model produces an R^2 of .46, compared to .72 for the complete model. For the sector-by-sector analysis, the rudimentary model accounts for a large portion of the variance between the gaze durations on sectors ($R^2 = .87$). This is not surprising, since there is considerable variation in their lengths. The complete sector-by-sector model accounts for 94 percent of the variance, or 54 percent of the variance unaccounted for by the reduced model.

Table 3

Observed and Estimated Gaze Durations (msec) on Each Sector of the "Flywheel" Passage, According to the Sector-By-Sector Regression Analysis of the Group Data

Sector	Observed	Estimated
Flywheels are one of the oldest mechanical devices	1,921	1,999
known to man.	478	680
Every internal-combustion engine contains a small flywheel	2,316	2,398
that converts the jerky motion of the pistons into the smooth flow of	2,477	2,807
energy that powers the drive shaft.	1,056	1,264
The greater the mass of a flywheel and the faster it spins,	2,143	2,304
the more energy can be stored in it.	1,270	1,536
But its maximum spinning speed is limited by the strength of the material	2,440	2,553
it is made from.	615	780
If it spins too fast for its mass,	1,414	1,502
any flywheel will fly apart.	1,200	1,304
One type of flywheel consists of round sandwiches of fiberglass and rubber	2,746	3,064
providing the maximum possible storage of energy	1,799	1,870
when the wheel is confined in a small space	1,522	1,448
as in an automobile.	769	718
Another type, the "superflywheel," consists of a series of rimless spokes.	2,938	2,830
This flywheel stores the maximum energy	1,416	1,596
when space is unlimited.	1,289	1,252

The regression equations were also fit to the gaze durations of each of the 14 readers individually. The subjects varied in their reading skill, with self-reported Scholastic Aptitude Test scores ranging from 410 to 660, which were correlated with their reading speeds in the experiment, ranging from 186 words per min. to 377 words per min. $r(12) = .54, p < .05$. The mean R^2 of the 14 readers was .36 on the word-by-word analysis and .75 on the sector-by-sector analysis. This indicates substantial noise in each reader's word-by-word data. Some of the regression weights of the readers indicated considerable individual differences with respect to certain processes. For example, 4 of the 14 readers spent no extra time on the last word of a sentence. Another parameter of great variability among readers was the extra time spent on novel words, which ranged from 94 msec to 1,490 msec.

Although the sector-by-sector regression analysis uses an independent varia-ble (the sum of the case role coefficients) that is estimated from the same data, this procedure does not do violence to the results. To estimate the effect of this procedure, the 14 subjects were divided randomly into two subgroups, and the case-role coefficients were obtained for each subgroup in a word-by-word analy-sis. Then these coefficients were aggregated and used as independent variables in a sector-by-sector analysis, such that one subgroup's coefficients were used in the analysis of the other subgroup's sector gaze durations. The results indicated no difference of any importance between the two subanalyses, and generally confirmed that using the case role coefficients from the word analysis in the sec-tor analysis was an acceptable procedure.

Some of the variables that were reliable in the word-by-word analysis were not reliable in the sector analysis. For example, sectors that included a line-initial word did not have reliably longer durations, and sectors that included the end of a sentence took 57 msec longer, but the reliability of the effect was marginal ($p < .08$). The sum of the logarithms of the frequencies of the words in a sector did not reliably affect gaze duration on the sector. These differences between the two levels of analysis indicate that some effects that are word specific are not reliable or large enough to be detected when the data are aggregated over groups of words. Nevertheless, some of these effects can be detected at the sector level if the appropriate analysis is done. For example, the reason that the frequency ef-fect was not reliable is that the aggregation of the logarithms smooths over the differences between infrequent words and frequent words. A regression analysis of the sector data shows a reliable word frequency effect if the independent vari-able encodes the number of infrequent words (arbitrarily defined as less than 25 in Kučera and Francis, 1967) occurring for the first time. This latter analysis indicates 82 msec extra spent for each infrequent word, and has an R^2 of .94. (Carpenter and Just, in press, reported a 51 msec effect for this variable.)

Recall Performance

The recall of a given part of a text should depend in part on what happens to the information as it is read. A clause that is thoroughly integrated with the rep-resentation of the text should tend to be stored in long term memory, and there-fore should be recalled better. There are two factors that determine how well a clause will be integrated. First, those sectors on which more integration time has been spent, like topics and definitions, should be recalled better. As predicted the integration parameter for a text role (i.e., the five weights at the bottom of Table 2) reliably affected the probability that a sector would be recalled, $t (271) = 2.01, p < .05$. A second factor affecting integration is the number of times an argument of a clause is referred to in the text; each repetition involving that argu-ment may initiate another integration episode that increases its chances of being recalled (Kintsch and van Dijk, 1978). A rough index of this kind of repetition was obtained by counting the number of times the arguments of each sector were repeated in subsequent sectors. The frequency of reference to the arguments did increase the probability of recalling a sector, $t(271) = 5.90, p < .01$.

The recall measure just reported was the proportion of the 14 subjects that recalled each of the 274 sectors. Two independent judges assigned 100 percent, 50 percent, or 0 percent credit for the recall of each sector, depending on whether it had been fully, partially, or not at all correctly recalled. Synonyms and paraphrases were given full credit if they were close to the gist of the sector. If only a part of a sector was recalled, then partial credit was given. The two judges were in full agreement about 80 percent of the time and in partial agreement (i.e., within 50 percent) on 94 percent of the judgments; disagreements were resolved by a third judge.

Text units that were higher in the text grammar were generally recalled better, $F(4, 269) = 5.67, p < .01$. There was a monotonic increase in the probability of recall as a function of a sector's level in the text grammar. Recall probabilities were lowest for details (.31), then increased for expansions (.34), subtopics (.39), definitions/causes/consequences (.41), and topics (.53). This replicates previous text-role effects observed with other types of texts (Meyer, 1975; Thorndyke, 1977). The model partially explains this result in terms of the processes that occur during comprehension. In addition, retrieval processes may play a role in this effect. For example, there may be many retrieval paths from less important concepts that lead to topics, but not vice versa. Also, a complete model of recall will have to consider how the recall of particular facts is affected by the reader's previous knowledge. Although the passages were generally unfamiliar, particular facts surely differed in their familiarity, and this could have a powerful effect on recall (Spilich, Vesonder, Chiesi, and Voss, 1979). Finally, there could be response output effects in recall. In summary, the results show that a model of the comprehension processes can be used to partially account for recall performance. To totally explain recall will require a precise account of the role of prior long term knowledge and the role of retrieval and reconstruction processes in recall.

Discussion

This section discusses three aspects of the theory: first, the implications of the immediacy assumption for language processing in general; second, how variation in reading modes can be handled by the theory; and third, the relation of the current theory to other theories of reading.

The Immediacy Assumption

The model's ability to account for fixation durations in terms of the processes that operate on words provides some validation for the immediacy and eye-mind assumptions. Readers interpret a word while they are fixating it, and they continue to fixate it until they have processed it as far as they can. As mentioned before, this kind of processing eliminates the difficulties caused by the potential ambiguity in language. It avoids the memory load and computational explosion that would result if a reader kept track of several possible meanings, case roles, and referents for each word and computed the final interpretation at the end of a clause or a sentence. This architectural feature also allows a limited-capacity processor to operate on a large semantic network without being bombarded by irrelevant associations. After a single interpretation has been selected, the activation of the unselected meanings can be dampened to their base levels so that they will not activate their semantic associates any further. This minimizes the chances that the reader will be conceptually driven in many directions at the same time.

The cost of this kind of processing is fairly low because the early decisions usually are correct. This is accomplished by taking a large amount of information into account in reaching a decision. The processes have specific heuristics to combine semantic, syntactic, and discourse information. Equally important, the processes operate on a data base that is strongly biased in favor of the common uses of words and phrases, but one that also reflects the effects of local context. The cost is also low because the reader can recover from errors. It would be devastating if there were no way to modify an incorrect interpretation at some later point. However, there are error-recovery heuristics that seem fairly efficient, although the precise mechanisms are only now being explored (Carpenter and Daneman, Note 1).

The fact that a reader's heuristics for interpreting the text are good explains why the garden path phenomenon is not the predominant experience in comprehension; it only happens occasionally. Perhaps the most common, everyday garden path experiences occur when reading newspaper headlines; for example, *Carter Views Discussed* and *Judge Admits Two Reporters*. The incorrect initial interpretations occur because headlines are stripped of the syntactic and contextual cues that guide the processing of normal text. Similarly, many jokes and puns explicitly rely on the contrast between two interpretations of an ambiguous word or phrase (Shultz and Horibe, 1974). Even garden path sentences sometimes seem funny. The humor in all of these cases resides in the incongruity between the initial interpretation and the ultimate one. Garden path sentences are also infrequent because writers usually try to avoid ambiguities that might encourage or allow incorrect interpretations. These kinds of sentences are useful tools for studying comprehension because they indicate where the usual comprehension strategies fail. But the fact that they are not frequent indicates that a reader's heuristics usually are sufficient.

Variation in Reading

There is no single mode of reading. Reading varies as a function of who is reading, what they are reading, and why they are reading it. The proposed model for the reading of scientific texts in this task is only one point in a multidimensional space of reading models. However, such variation can be accommodated within the framework presented in this article.

The reader's goals are perhaps the most important determinant of the reading process. A reader who skims a passage for the main point reads differently than someone who is trying to memorize a passage, or another person who is reading for entertainment. Goals can be represented in several aspects of the theory, but the main way is to require that each goal is satisfied or at least attempted before proceeding on to the next word, clause, or sentence. These goals correspond to the major products of each stage of comprehension and to the specific demands of a particular task. For example, an obvious goal associated with lexical access might be that one interpretation is selected. An added goal associated with the task of memorizing a passage may require rehearsing phrases or constructing explicit mnemonics before going on to the next phrase or sentence. But goals can be deleted as well as added. A speed reader may well eliminate goals for syntactic coherence, because the strategy of skipping over many words will destroy the syntax. Variations in goals can be detected with the current theory and analytic techniques. For example, it is possible to determine how much time is spent integrating different kinds of text roles in different tasks. When readers anticipate a recognition comprehension test, rather than recall, they spend less time integrating details (Carpenter and Just, in press).

Reading also depends on the text, the topic, and the reader's familiarity with both. A well-written paragraph on a familiar topic will be easier to process at all stages of comprehension. The lexical items will be easier to encode, the concepts will be more easily accessed, the case and text roles will be easier to infer, and the interrelations will be easier to represent. All of these dimensions of variation can be accommodated, measured, and evaluated within the theoretical framework. Moreover, any adequate theory must be sufficiently flexible to encompass such variation.

Even reading of the same text under the same circumstances will vary from person to person. There are several plausible sources of individual differences in the theory. One interesting source is the operational capacity of the working memory. Readers with a large working memory should be able to retain more of the text in the memory while processing new text, so their integration of the information may be more thorough. A promising first exploration of this hypothesis has found a very strong correlation between working memory capacity and various aspects of reading comprehension tests (Daneman and Carpenter, in press). By contrast, traditional measures of passive short term memory capacity do not have a strong correlation with reading comprehension. Operational capacity may depend on the automaticity of basic reading processes such as encoding and lexical access. Poor readers may devote more time and attention to these processes (Hunt, Lunneborg, and Lewis, 1975; Perfetti and Lesgold, 1977) and consequently have less capacity for maintaining previous information and integrating the new information (Case, 1978).

Theories of Reading

Previous theories of reading have varied in their choice of dependent measures, the levels of information represented in the theory, and the implementation of top-down effects. It is useful to consider how the current theory compares to these alternative proposals along these three dimensions.

One important feature of the current theory is its attempt to account for reading time on individual words, clauses, and sentences. This approach can be distinguished from research that is more centrally concerned with recall, question answering, and summarizing (e.g., Rumelhart, 1977b). The dependent measure is not an incidental aspect of a theory; it has important implications for which issues the theory addresses. The present focus on processing time has resulted in a theory that accounts for the moment-by-moment, real-time characteristics of reading. By contrast, the theory pays less attention to retrieval and reconstruction, two later occurring processes that are important to an account of summarization.

Another feature of the theory is the attempt to account for performance at several levels of processing. Previous theories have tended to neglect certain stages. For example, the reading models of LaBerge and Samuels (1974) and Gough (1972) focus on the word-encoding processes, whereas the model of Kintsch and van Dijk (1978) focuses on integration. This is not to say that these models do not acknowledge other aspects of processing, but simply that they describe detailed mechanisms for one aspect of reading and no comparable mechanisms for other stages. The current theory has attempted to span the stages of reading by describing mechanisms for the word-encoding and lexical-access stages, as well as the parsing and text integration stages. Moreover, it has attempted to describe some formal similarities by placing them all within the architecture of a production system.

A final but important distinction among reading theories is the manner in which they accommodate top-down and bottom-up factors in reading (see Rumelhart, 1977a). Some reading theories, particularly those addressed to word encoding, omit mechanisms to account for top-down or contextual effects (e.g., Gough, 1972). At the other extreme, there have been some theories that appear to place a major burden of comprehension on contextual effects. Some of these are recent schema-based theories of language comprehension (Schank and Abelson, 1977). Others are the older top-down models, developed out of analysis by synthesis theory; these models suggested that readers form explicit predictions about the next word and fixate it merely to confirm the hypothesis (Goodman and Niles, 1970). The current model falls somewhere between the extremes. It allows for contextual influences and for the interaction among comprehension processes. Knowledge about a topic, syntactic constraints, and semantic associates can all play a role in activating and selecting the appropriate concepts. However, the printed words themselves are usually the best information source that the reader has, and they can seldom be entirely replaced by guesses from the preceding context. Thus the top-down processes can influence the bottom-up ones, but their role is to participate in selecting interpretations rather than to dominate the bottom-up processes. Finally, the production system architecture permits a degree of coordination among different processes, so that any stage can be influenced by any cotemporaneously or previously executed stage.

Future Directions

The current theory suggests two major avenues of reading research. One direction is to construct computer simulations that are driven by reading performance data. The postulated human heuristics can be implemented in a computer program to examine the resulting complex interactions among knowledge sources. Reading-time data may be sufficiently constraining to select among various alternative heuristics. We are currently implementing aspects of the model presented here as a production system in collaboration with a colleague, Robert Thibadeau, to develop greater specification and more stringent tests of the model.

Although the production system framework is not essential for the interpretation of the empirical results in the present study, it has other benefits. First, it provides an architecture that can accommodate the flexibility and interaction that has been observed among the processes in reading and still express typical or canonical processing. Even though this theoretical framework is minimally specified, it seems sensible to start at this point and allow successive generations of data to constrain it, as Newell (1980) suggests. Finally, when expressed as a computer simulation, the model retains correspondence to postulated human processes and structures. Collections of serial productions may correspond to heuristic processes employed in comprehension. The firing of parallel productions can be identified with spreading activation in long term memory. The production system's working memory can be identified with the reader's working memory. Thus, the production system can be viewed as a useful theoretical vehicle, or excess baggage, depending on one's intended destination.

The second avenue includes further empirical research on the real time characteristics of reading. Eye movement and reading-time methodologies can reveal reading characteristics with other types of texts, tasks, and readers. The useful property of these methodologies is that they can measure reading time on successive units of text. One method is to present the successive words of a sentence one at a time, allowing the reader to control the interword interval (Aaronson and Scarborough, 1976). This procedure is only one end of a continuum defined by what units are presented. Rather than single words, they could be phrases, clauses, sentences, or entire passages (Carpenter and Just, 1977a; Mitchell and Green, 1978; Kieras, Note 3). In this way, it will be possible to gain more information about human performance characteristics and then use these data to develop a more complete theory of reading.

REFERENCE NOTES

1. Carpenter, P.A., and Daneman, M. *Lexical access and error recovery in reading: A model based on eye fixations*. Unpublished manuscript, Carnegie-Mellon University, 1980.
2. Charniak, E. *Toward a model of children's story comprehension* (Tech. Rep. 266). Cambridge, Mass.: MIT Artificial Intelligence Laboratory, 1972.
3. Kieras, D.E. *Modelling reading times in different reading tasks with a simulation model of comprehension* (Tech. Rep. 2). Tucson: University of Arizona, 1979.

REFERENCES

Aaronson, D., and Scarborough, H.S. Performance theories for sentence coding: Some quantitative evidence. *Journal of Experimental Psychology: Human Perception and Performance*, 1976, *2*, 56-70.

Anderson, J.R. *Language, memory, and thought*. Hillsdale, N.J.: Erlbaum, 1976.

Baron, J. Mechanisms for pronouncing printed words: Use and acquisition. In D. LaBerge and S.J. Samuels (Eds.), *Basic processes in reading: Perception and comprehension*. Hillsdale, N.J.: Erlbaum, 1977.

Bayle, E. The nature and causes of regressive movements in reading. *Journal of Experimental Education*, 1942, *11*, 16-36.

Bever, T.G. The cognitive basis for linguistic structures. In J.R. Hayes (Ed.), *Cognition and the development of language*. New York: Wiley, 1970.

Bouma, H., and deVoogd, A.H. On the control of eye saccades in reading. *Vision Research*, 1974, *14*, 273-284.

Bransford, J.D., and Johnson, M.K. Considerations of some problems of comprehension. In W.G. Chase (Ed.), *Visual information processing*. New York: Academic Press, 1973.

Breitmeyer, B.G. Unmasking visual masking: A look at the "why" behind the veil of "how." *Psychological Review*, 1980, *87*, 52-69.

Buswell, G.T. How adults read. *Supplementary educational monographs (45)*. Chicago: University of Chicago Press, 1937.

Carpenter, P.A., and Just, M.A. Integrative processes in comprehension. In D. LaBerge and S.J. Samuels (Eds.), *Basic processes in reading: Perception and comprehension*. Hillsdale, N.J.: Erlbaum, 1977. (a)

Carpenter, P.A., and Just, M.A. Reading comprehension as eyes see it. In M.A. Just and P.A. Carpenter (Eds.), *Cognitive processes in comprehension*. Hillsdale, N.J.: Erlbaum, 1977. (b)

Carpenter, P.A., and Just, M.A. Cognitive processes in reading: Models based on readers' eye fixations. In A.M. Lesgold and C.A. Perfetti (Eds.), *Interactive processes in reading*. Hillsdale, N.J.: Erlbaum, in press.

Case, R. Intellectual development from birth to adulthood: A neo-Piagetian interpretation. In R. Siegler (Ed.), *Children's thinking: What develops?* Hillsdale, N.J.: Erlbaum, 1978.

Chafe, W.L. *Meaning and the structure of language*. Chicago: University of Chicago Press, 1970.

Clark, H.H., and Clark, E.V. *Psychology and language*. New York: Harcourt Brace Jovanovich, 1977.

Collins, A.M., and Loftus, E.F. A spreading activation theory of semantic processing. *Psychological Review*, 1975, *82*, 407-428.

Daneman, M., and Carpenter, P.A. Individual differences in working memory and reading. *Journal of Verbal Learning and Verbal Behavior*, in press.

Dearborn, W. *The psychology of reading* (Columbia University contributions to philosophy and psychology). New York: Science Press, 1906.

Dixon, P., and Rothkopf, E.Z. Word repetition, lexical access, and the process of searching words and sentences. *Journal of Verbal Learning and Verbal Behavior*, 1979, *18*, 629-644.

Fillmore, C.J. The case for case. In E. Bach and R.T. Harms (Eds.), *Universals in linguistic theory*. New York: Holt, Rinehart and Winston, 1968.

Flesch, R.F. *How to test readability*. New York: Harper, 1951.

Fraser, C., Bellugi, U., and Brown, R. Control of grammar in imitation, comprehension, and production. *Journal of Verbal Learning and Verbal Behavior*, 1963, *2*, 121-135.

Frazier, L., and Fodor, J. The sausage machine: A new two-stage parsing model. *Cognition*, 1978, *6*, 291-325.

Glanzer, M., and Ehrenreich, S.L. Structure and search for the internal lexicon. *Journal of Verbal Learning and Verbal Behavior*, 1979, *18*, 381-398.

Goodman, K.S., and Niles, O.S. *Reading process and program*. Urbana, Ill.: National Council of Teachers of English, 1970.

Gough, P.B. One second of reading. In J.F. Kavanagh and I.G. Mattingly (Eds.), *Language by eye and by ear*. Cambridge, Mass.: MIT Press, 1972.

Haviland, S.E., and Clark, H.H. What's new? Acquiring new information as a process in comprehension. *Journal of Verbal Learning and Verbal Behavior*, 1974, *13*, 512-521.

Hitch, G.J. The role of short-term working memory in mental arithmetic. *Cognitive Psychology*, 1978, *10*, 302-323.

Hockett, C.F. *A course in modern linguistics*. New York: Macmillan, 1958.

Hunt, E., Lunneborg, C., and Lewis, J. What does it mean to be high verbal? *Cognitive Psychology*, 1975, *2*, 194-227.

Jarvella, R.K. Syntactic processing of connected speech. *Journal of Verbal Learning and Verbal Behavior*, 1971, *10*, 409-416.

Judd, C.H., and Buswell, G.T. Silent reading: A study of the various types. *Supplementary Educational Monographs (23)*. Chicago: University of Chicago Press, 1922.

Just, M.A., and Carpenter, P.A. Eye fixations and cognitive processes. *Cognitive Psychology*, 1976, *8*, 441-480.

Just, M.A., and Carpenter, P.A. Inference processes during reading: Reflections from eye fixations. In J.W. Senders, D.F. Fisher, and R.A. Monty (Eds.), *Eye movements and the higher psychological functions*. Hillsdale, N.J.: Erlbaum, 1978.

Kintsch, W., and van Dijk, T.A. Toward a model of text comprehension and production. *Psychological Review*, 1978, *85*, 363-394.

Kleiman, G.M. Speech recoding in reading. *Journal of Verbal Learning and Verbal Behavior*, 1975, *14*, 323-339.

Kučera, H., and Francis, W.N. *Computational analysis of present-day American English*. Providence, R.I.: Brown University Press, 1967.

LaBerge, D., and Samuels, S.J. Toward a theory of automatic information processing in reading. *Cognitive Psychology*, 1974, *6*, 293-323.

Levy, B.A. Interactive processes during reading. In A.M. Lesgold and C.A. Perfetti (Eds.), *Interactive processes in reading*. Hillsdale, N.J.: Erlbaum, in press.

Mandler, J.M., and Johnson, N.S. Remembrance of things parsed: Story structure and recall. *Cognitive Psychology*, 1977, *9*, 111-151.

McConkie, G.W., and Rayner, K. The span of the effective stimulus during a fixation in reading. *Perception and Psychophysics*, 1975, *17*, 578-586.

McConkie, G.W., and Rayner, K. Asymmetry of the perceptual span in reading. *Bulletin of the Psychonomic Society*, 1976, *8*, 365-368.

Mewhort, D., and Beal, A.L. Mechanisms of word identification. *Journal of Experimental Psychology: Human Perception and Performance*, 1977, *3*, 629-640.

Meyer, B. *The organization of prose and its effect on recall*. Amsterdam: North-Holland, 1975.

Meyer, B., and McConkie, G.W. What is recalled after hearing a passage? *Journal of Educational Psychology*, 1973, *65*, 109-117.

Mitchell, D.C., and Green, D.W. The effects of context on immediate processing in reading. *Quarterly Journal of Experimental Psychology*, 1978, *30*, 609-636.

Morton, J. Interaction of information in word recognition. *Psychological Review*, 1969, *76*, 165-178.

Newell, A. Production systems: Models of control structures. In W.G. Chase (Ed.), *Visual information processing*. New York: Academic Press, 1973.

Newell, A. Harpy, Production systems and human cognition. In R. Cole (Ed.), *Perception and production of fluent speech*. Hillsdale, N.J.: Erlbaum, 1980.

Perfetti, C.A., and Lesgold, A.M. Discourse comprehension and sources of individual differences. In M.A. Just and P.A. Carpenter (Eds.), *Cognitive processes in comprehension*. Hillsdale, N.J.: Erlbaum, 1977.

Rayner, K. Eye movements in reading and information processing. *Psychological Bulletin*, 1978, *85*, 618-660.

Reitman, J.S. Without surreptitious rehearsal, information in short-term memory decays. *Journal of Verbal Learning and Verbal Behavior*, 1974, *13*, 365-377.

Rieger, C.J. Five aspects of a full-scale story comprehension model. In N.V. Findler (Ed.), *Associative networks*. New York: Academic Press, 1979.

Robinson, D.A. Eye movements evoked by collicular stimulation in the alert monkey. *Vision Research*, 1972, *12*, 1795-1808.

Rumelhart, D.E. Toward an interactive model of reading. In S. Dornic (Ed.), *Attention and performance VI*. Hillsdale, N.J.: Erlbaum, 1977. (a)

Rumelhart, D.E. Understanding and summarizing brief stories. In D. LaBerge and S.J. Samuels (Eds.), *Basic processes in reading: Perception and comprehension*. Hillsdale, N.J.: Erlbaum, 1977. (b)

Scarborough, D.L., Cortese, C., and Scarborough, H.S. Frequency and repetition effects in lexical memory. *Journal of Experimental Psychology: Human Perception and Performance*, 1977, *3*, 1-17.

Schank, R.C. Conceptual dependency: A theory of natural language understanding. *Cognitive Psychology*, 1972, *3*, 552-631.

Schank, R.C., and Abelson, R.P. *Scripts, plans, goals and understanding: An inquiry into human knowledge structures*. Hillsdale, N.J.: Erlbaum, 1977.

Schiepers, C. Response latency and accuracy in visual word recognition. *Perception and Psychophsics*, 1980, *27*, 71-81.

Shultz, T., and Horibe, F. Development of the appreciation of verbal jokes. *Developmental Psychology*, 1974, *10*, 13-20.

Spilich, G.J., Vesonder, G.T., Chiesi, H.L., and Voss, J.F. Text processing of domain-related information for individuals with high and low domain knowledge. *Journal of Verbal Learning and Verbal Behavior*, 1979, *18*, 275-290.

Spoehr, K.T., and Smith, E. The role of syllables in perceptual processing. *Cognitive Psychology*, 1973, *5*, 71-89.

Swinney, D.A. Lexical access during sentence comprehension: (Re)consideration of context effects. *Journal of Verbal Learning and Verbal Behavior*, 1979, *18*, 645-659.

Taft, M. Recognition of affixed words and the word frequency effect. *Memory and Cognition*, 1979, *7*, 263-272.

Tanenhaus, M.K., Leiman, J.M., and Seidenberg, M.S. Evidence for multiple stages in the processing of ambiguous words in syntactic contexts. *Journal of Verbal Learning and Verbal Behavior*, 1979, *18*, 427-440.

Taylor, S.E. An evaluation of forty-one trainees who had recently completed the "reading dynamics" program. *Eleventh yearbook of the National Reading Conference*, 1962, 41-55.

Thorndyke, P.W. Cognitive structures in comprehension and memory of narrative discourse. *Cognitive Psychology*, 1977, *9*, 77-110.

Vesonder, G.T. *The role of knowledge in the processing of experimental reports*. Unpublished doctoral dissertation, University of Pittsburgh, 1979.

Westheimer, G.H. Eye movement responses to a horizontally moving visual stimulus. *Archives of Ophthalmology*, 1954, *52*, 932-943.

NOTES

[1] Since this article was selected for reprinting in this volume, a chapter with more detailed theory and analysis of data has been published. See P.A. Carpenter and M.A. Just, "What Your Eyes Do While Your Mind is Reading." In K. Rayner (Ed.), *Eye Movements in Reading: Perceptual and Language Processes*. New York: Academic Press, 1983.

[2] It might be argued that the variables coding the text-grammatical roles ought to be independent of the number of content words. One might argue that a definition, for example, takes a fixed amount of time to integrate, regardless of the number of content words it contains. Although the model predicts a length-sensitive duration, the analysis can also be done with five simple indicator variables to encode the five levels of the grammar. This analysis produced a fit that was almost as good ($R^2 = .93$). The weights (assuming a zero intercept) were 250, 341, 257, 214, and 118 msec for the five categories, from topics to details. Although this alternative is not ruled out by the data, we will continue to retain the view that integration time depends on the number of content words involved.

[3] The research was supported in part by Grant G-79-0119 from the National Institute of Education and Grant MH-29617 from the National Institute of Mental Health.

The First Two Rs

The way different languages reduce speech to script affects how visual information is processed in the brain

Ovid J. L. Tzeng
University of California at Riverside

William S.-Y. Wang
University of California at Berkeley

School days, school days, dear old golden rule days;
Readin' and 'ritin' and 'rithmetic,
Taught to the tune of a hickory stick.

The last line of this children's song calls to mind the old fashioned classroom with its stern discipline, which has by now all but vanished from the American scene. It also highlights an interesting fact — that reading and writing are skills that do not come naturally, the way speech does. Typically, by the time he has reached school age, a child has effortlessly soaked up from his environment all the basic structures of the language spoken around him, whether it be English, Chinese, or Telugu. Learning the written language, however, is frequently quite an arduous process. Millions of people in the world are illiterate for lack of adequate educational opportunity. A significant number of American children have problems with reading and writing, even with the help of the best facilities. This contrast between the two forms of language — speech versus script — is all the more striking given that written language is invariably based on spoken language.

In evolutionary terms, speech emerged considerably earlier than writing, when our ancestors roamed the grasslands for food and searched out caves for shelter many hundred thousand years ago. Agriculture began to replace hunting as the dominant human life-style some twelve thousand years ago. The earliest precursors of writing appeared shortly after this transition, even though these did not develop into full-fledged writing systems until several thousand years later (Wang 1982).

Reprinted by permission, *American Scientist*, "The First Two R's," by Ovid J.L. Tzeng and William S.-Y. Wang, 71: 238-43 (1983).

Early forerunners of writing include clay tokens, varying in size and shape as well as in marks and perforations, that were used for simple record-keeping. Such tokens found at sites along the Iran-Iraq border date back ten millennia or so; Schmandt-Besserat (1978) proposed that they gave rise to Sumerian ideographs. Incisions found on Neolithic pottery made some seven thousand years ago at Banpo, China, are believed to be the direct precursors of the Chinese script (Ho 1976). The pottery and the tokens apparently were produced in response to the needs of agricultural life.

Whereas the sounds of speech fade rapidly in time and are limited in space, a written message endures and can be carried from place to place. The invention of writing, which occurred independently in distant parts of the world at many times, even occasionally in the modern era, must rank among mankind's highest intellectual achievements. Without writing, human culture as we know it today is inconceivable.

All the major systems of writing are based on spoken language, though in ways that differ importantly from each other. To see these differences more clearly, we need to explain what is meant by the following terms that are used to describe units in all spoken languages: feature, segment, syllable, morpheme, and word (Wang 1971). A writing system, or a script, may be categorized according to how these five types of units are represented in its symbols. Actually, most writing systems are really composite in that they typically use two or more different types of these units (Wang 1981).

Features are elementary components of individual spoken sounds, but are not full segments of speech themselves. Some familiar phonetic features correspond to diacritic symbols in script, such as the cedilla in French, which changes the letter c from a k sound to an s sound (as in *ça*), or the tilde in Spanish, which changes a dental n sound into a palatal n sound (as in se*ñ*or).

The familiar type of alphabetic scripts that prevail in the West today are based roughly on the segment. That is, a letter in the script corresponds to a consonant or vowel segment in the spoken language. The shape of the letters may vary, of course, as they do between the Cyrillic and Latin alphabets. The correspondence between the letter and the segment is seldom perfect: in English, the single letter x may represent the two segments ks, and the two letters th, actually represent only one segment. Nonetheless, the ideal match is one letter for one segment. Another aspect typical of such scripts is that words, rather than morphemes or syllables, are separated by spaces.

In speech, the segments combine to form syllables. A syllable is a natural unit of pronunciation, typically containing a vowel and its surrounding consonants. Writing systems in which the symbols correspond to syllables are called syllabaries. In the Japanese *kana* syllabary, for instance, the symbol カ represents the syllable *ka*. There are two styles of writing *kana*: the printed style is called *katakana,* and the more cursive style *hiragana*.

An interesting script that makes composite use of features, segments, and syllables is *hangul,* devised in Korea in the middle of the fifteenth century during

Figure 1. The Korean *hangul* writing system, invented in the middle of the fifteenth century during the reign of King Sejong, makes more systematic use of the phonetic features of the spoken language than any other orthography. The plaque shown here, from the base of King Sejong's statue in Seoul, contains 17 symbols in the top row that represent consonant sounds, and 11 symbols in the bottom row that represent vowel sounds. (Photo courtesy of Namgui Chang.)

the reign of King Sejong (Fig. 1). While the letters correspond principally to speech segments, their design is organized to reflect their phonetic features. Furthermore, the letters are arranged in square frames, each frame corresponding to a syllable. In contrast to English, where the words are separated by spaces, in *hangul* it is thus the syllables that are written apart. In a sense, *hangul* is simultaneously an alphabet and a syllabary. It is an ingenious invention and deserves much further study from a psycholinguistic point of view.

Morphemes are the basic units of meaning that combine to make up words. For instance, *boy, boyish,* and *boyishness* contain one, two and three morphemes, respectively, even though each is a single word. Roughly speaking, words are minimal combinations of morphemes that occur as independent utterances; thus, *boy* is a word, but *ish* is not. The Chinese script is the only major writing system now in use in which a significant number of the symbols, called logographs, preserve a direct relation to the morphemes themselves rather than only to the pronunciation of these morphemes (Wang 1973). These logographs have spread beyond the boundaries of China. They are used extensively in Japan, in conjunction with *kana,* and in Korea, together with *hangul.* For several centuries, they were the primary script in Vietnam as well.

A few Chinese logographs are derived from stylized pictures, such as a simple drawing of a mountain or of a bird. After many centuries of simplification and standardization of the script, however, the likeness is often no longer obvious. Some other logographs are made up of pieces from which the meaning can be inferred. The symbol for *good*, for instance, is a combination of those for *woman* and *child;* the logograph for *inch* is the same as that for *hand* with a dot added below that shows the location of the pulse on the wrist—the inference here is that the distance between the two is an inch. However, over 80 percent of the logographs in the Chinese script are formed on a different principle. These logographs have two parts, one referring to the meaning, the other referring to the pronunciation. As an example, the left half of the logograph for *ocean* means *water* while the right half indicates that it is pronounced like the logograph *yang*. Thus, these logographs have a composite function—they may be best characterized as morpho-syllabic.

The Process of Reading

One of the major activities in learning to read is exploring the correspondence between the written script and the spoken language (Tzeng and Singer, 1981). Since this correspondence in an alphabetic writing system differs from that in a logographic system, the processing strategies developed by skilled readers in order to meet the cognitive requirements of the two types of systems also differ. These strategies are so entrenched in the reading system that after many years of constant practice their activation becomes all but automatic.

For example, a reader of English cannot keep from applying a system of abstract rules to tackle the correspondence between written letters and spoken segments, whereas a reader of Chinese automatically scans the configuration of the logographs. Thus, the diversity of writing systems provides excellent opportunities for investigators of human cognition to examine how children of different linguistic backgrounds develop different processing strategies to meet the various demands imposed by different writing systems. Once we understand the flexibility and limits of the adjustments involved, we will be in a better position to theorize about basic reading processes and to design remedial programs to help reading-disabled children.

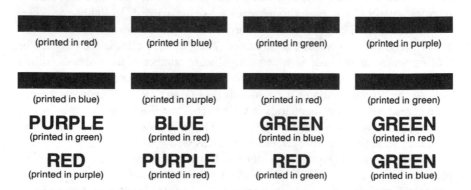

Figure 2.* Can words interfere with naming objects? You can test this by naming the colors of the blocks in the top two rows as quickly as possible, and then naming the colors of the English words in the next two rows—without reading the words themselves—as quickly as possible. The greater difficulty in performing the second half of this procedure, which is called the Stroop interference task, is an index of how directly the written words are coupled to their meanings.

* The Figure 2 which was included in the original article in *American Scientist* was in color, thus allowing for a demonstration of the Stroop interference task. The colors which were used for the blocks and words in the original article are indicated by the color words (shown beneath the blocks and words) in parentheses in the Figure 2 which is included with this chapter.

It has been known for quite some time that a fluent reader cannot avoid activating the semantic code of a printed word once he sees the word (Stroop 1935). This phenomenon can be demonstrated very easily with an experimental procedure called the Stroop interference task, in which color names are written in an ink of a different color, as shown in Figure 2. Subjects are asked to name the colors of the ink; as a control, they are also asked to name the colors of a series of different color patches on which no words appear. The results are usually clearcut. It takes much longer to name a series of colors with the distracting words than it does to name a series of unmarked color patches. This is a valid effect that has been found in every language examined (Biederman and Tsao 1979).

An interesting question arises at this point: Does the magnitude of interference—i.e., the time taken to name the color with the distracting word minus the time needed to name the color of the unmarked patch—differ across the various scripts? The answer is a decisive yes. Logographic scripts produce greater interference than either syllabaries or alphabets.

The Stroop task can be extended to pairs of languages. For a long time, researchers have realized that the interference is reduced for a bilingual reader if the words in color and the responses from among which the reader is asked to choose are printed in different languages known to the subject (Preston and Lambert 1969). We replicated this finding in our laboratories for several pairs of languages (Fang et al. 1981). Our results further show that there is a systematic relation between the amount of interference and the degree of similarity between the two scripts used. This relation can be seen in the data summarized in Table 1.

Table 1
Mean Reduction of Stroop Interference with Two Languages

Languages Used	Reduction (msec/item)
Chinese-English	213
Kanji-English	121
Hungarian-English	112
Hiragana-English	108
Spanish-English	68
German-English	36
French-English	33

Source: Fang et al. 1981

The ordering of the last three items in the table is particularly revealing. Why should switching between Spanish and English reduce the interference more than switching between French and English? It is certainly not immediately obvious that Spanish and English are orthographically more dissimilar than French and English. However, if we examine the spellings of color terms in these languages, as shown in Table 2, then the difference between the Spanish and English words is easily seen to be greater.

Table 2
Similarities in Names of Colors Used in Bilingual Experiments

Language		Names of colors used		
English	red	blue	green	brown
German	rot	blau	grün	braun
French	rouge	bleu	vert	brun
Spanish	rojo	azul	verde	cafe
Hungarian	piros	kék	zöld	barna
Chinese	紅	藍	綠	福

The systematic variation observed in the degree of interference across these several different scripts suggests that the linguistic code used in reading cannot be simply semantic. Rather, the findings indicate that the reader processes semantic, phonological, and orthographic information as an integrated whole.

Can the above results be an artifact of naming the colors aloud? To eliminate this possibility, we conducted another type of experiment that was in essence a variant of the Stroop task, but that required no oral response. We projected a pair of numbers, such as 6 and 9, onto a screen and asked subjects to choose the larger number by pressing a key. The two numbers were written either at the same size, or with the greater number smaller than the lesser number. That is, the 6 appeared larger on the screen than did the 9, as shown in Figure 3. A Stroop-like interference can be demonstrated here, in that it takes longer to make a correct choice when the greater number is smaller (Besner and Coltheart 1979). What would happen if we wrote out the words instead of using Arabic numerals? Oddly enough, the interference disappeared when we used English words. However, when a parallel experiment was done with Chinese logographs instead of alphabetic letters, the interference was again observed.

Figure 3. When a lesser number is written in a larger size than a greater number, the incongruence between the number and its size causes a subject to take longer to decide which number is greater. However, the amount of the effect, or interference, varies according to how the numbers are written. Using Arabic numerals and Chinese logographs causes more interference than using English or Spanish words.

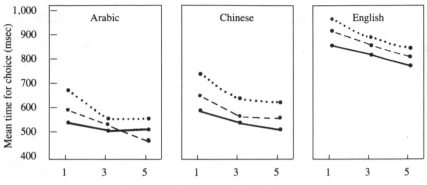

Figure 4. Native speakers of Chinese who learned English later in life were subject to interference when they had to choose the greater of two numbers presented in English words, as well as when Arabic numerals or Chinese logographs were used. In other words, the difference in the time they took to choose the greater number when it was smaller than the lesser number (*dotted line*) and the time they needed when the numbers were the same size (*dashed line*) or the lesser number was smaller (*solid line*) was significant in all three situations.

We carried the experiment a step further, presenting a group of Chinese native speakers who had learned English as young adults with all three types of stimuli: Arabic numerals, English words, and Chinese logographs. As before, we observed the interference with both Arabic and Chinese stimuli. Unexpectedly, however, these readers also showed an interference with the English words (Figure 4).

How do we account for this last finding? Could it simply be due to the fact that these subjects learned English later in life? Or is it because they were transferring the processing strategy for logographs to alphabetic spelling? To choose between these two hypotheses, we next worked with a group of native Spanish speakers who also learned English as young adults. They were asked to perform the same task with Arabic numerals, English words, and Spanish words (Figure 5).

The results are unequivocal: significant interference occurred only with the Arabic numerals, not with Spanish or English words. Therefore the interference observed with English words for the Chinese-English bilingual readers was not due to their later learning of that language, since we did not observe a similar effect with the Spanish-English readers. The remaining hypothesis, then, is that the Chinese-English subjects had transferred their reading habits from logographs to English words.

The evidence we have reviewed so far, from both the color and number Stroop experiments, supports the contention that the relation between script and speech underlying all types of writing systems plays an important role in reading behavior. A reader of a particular script must assimilate the orthographic charac-

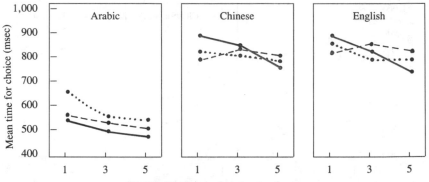

Figure 5. Native speakers of Spanish who learned English as young adults reacted similarly when they had to choose the greater of two numbers written in English and in Spanish, and demonstrated interference only when the numbers were in Arabic numerals. The interference found with the Chinese readers in Figure 4 is therefore not a result of having learned a language later in life, but rather of applying methods used to process logographs to processing alphabetic scripts. As in Figure 4, a dashed line indicates that the two numbers were the same size, a solid line that the greater number was bigger, and a dotted line that the greater number was smaller.

teristics of that system. That is to say, if the configuration of a logograph is important in deciphering it, then the reader has to pay special attention to the position of every element it contains. As a consequence, we should expect the processing of logographs to involve more visual memory than the processing of alphabetic script.

Differing Patterns of Memory

With this hypothesis in mind, we set out to compare the memory performance of native English speakers and native Chinese speakers. We presented a series of nine items to subjects either auditorily with a tape recorder or visually by means of a slide projector. In the visual presentations, the items were in either English words or Chinese logographs. The subjects were asked to recall the nine items according to their positions in the series, and the probability of recall was plotted according to the item's position. The resulting data can be seen in Figure 6.

Previous findings from other laboratories indicate that it is usually easier to remember items at the end of a list if they are presented auditorily than if they are given visually (Crowder 1976). The data from both groups of readers in this study show that this effect occurs with the last two items. The interesting difference between the two groups is that the Chinese readers recalled the other items in the series consistently better when these were presented visually rather than auditorily, whereas no such difference was found for the English readers. Visual presentation was superior for Chinese readers regardless of whether they were

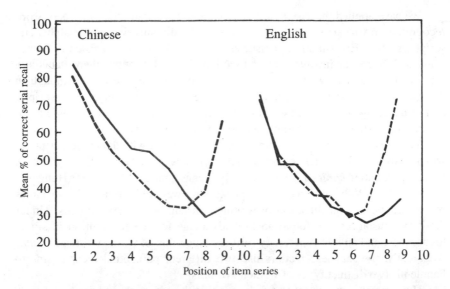

Figure 6. Readers of Chinese and English are alike in recalling the last items in a series better if the items are presented auditorially (*dotted line*), rather than visually (*solid line*). However, earlier items are recalled better in Chinese when they are presented visually, whereas in English there is no difference between auditory and visual presentation. This finding highlights the influence of the script on memory processes.

asked to recall the items orally or in writing. This finding suggests that processing logographs involves more visual memory than does processing alphabetic scripts, thus confirming the hypothesis raised earlier. In fact, it further suggests that the influence of the sensory characteristics of the visual information may not be restricted to the very early stages of processing, and that reading different kinds of script uses different mechanisms of memory that are specific to the individual script.

This greater involvement of visual memory in processing logographs can also be demonstrated with a different type of test. In recent years, experimental psychologists have been using a special apparatus called the tachistoscope (or T-scope) to investigate the specialization of functions and capabilities of each of the two cerebral hemispheres (Hardyck et al. 1977) Basically, a T-scope is a device that enables the experimenters to present visual images for very brief periods of time. When a subject focuses on a point in the center of a lighted square within the T-scope, each half of the visual field is projected to the opposite hemisphere of the brain. Thus, stimuli presented to the right visual field (RVF) are first processed in the left hemisphere, and stimuli to the left visual field (LVF) in the right hemisphere. By correlating the levels of performance on different tasks to the locations of the stimulus, most investigators agree that the left hemisphere is better able to analyze sequences, whereas the right hemisphere is better at matching visual patterns (Patterson and Bradshaw 1975).

We have applied the visual half-field technique to study the process of word recognition in various scripts. The results are hardly surprising. For alphabetic scripts, such as English and Spanish, an RVF superiority is consistently found, suggesting a greater involvement of functions in the left hemisphere. This RVF superiority obtains as well for scripts like Arabic and Hebrew, even though in these cases the letters run right to left across the page. In contrast to these scripts, an LVF advantage is observed when we present Chinese readers with single logographs, suggesting that their right hemisphere is more active.

The most striking results come from experiments with Japanese script, in which a word can be written either with the symbols of the *kana* syllabary or with logographs, called *kanji* (this term literally means Chinese characters; Hung and Tzeng, 1981). With native Japanese speakers we were able to hold the variables of subject, word, and direction of writing constant across experiments. Under these circumstances, we found an LVF advantage for the recognition of single logographs, and an RVF superiority for the recognition of words written in *kana*. Apparently, the Japanese readers use two different perceptual mechanisms to handle the two distinct types of written symbols.

However, it is important to emphasize that these data should not be taken to suggest that Chinese and Japanese readers store thousands of logographs in their right hemispheres and let their left hemispheres handle the spoken language. Rather, what has been demonstrated in all these experiments is that visual processing is more critical in the task of recognizing logographs, and that the involvement of the right hemisphere is therefore greater.

It is also worth noting that recognizing a single logograph is only a step toward comprehending a written sentence. Chinese and Japanese readers have to put several logographs together to form a "linguistic" word—e.g., the three characters 圖 書 館 which literally mean picture book hall, make up the word *library*. Thus the recovery of meaning from a word involves much more than just simple recognition of individual logographs. This stage of processing requires a greater involvement of the left hemisphere, and one would expect an RVF superiority in the *T*-scope experiment for such tasks. The reversal from an LVF superiority to an RVF superiority in reading combinations of logographs was exactly what we found in another series of studies (Tzeng et al., 1979).

This suggests that in reading different scripts, the initial perceptual pathways may be different, but later processing may converge on similar linguistic techniques. It is of great theoretical importance to ask at what stage the convergence occurs and what is the nature of the resulting linguistic code.

Findings made in our laboratories (Hung and Tzeng, 1981) and in others (Seidenberg and Tanenhaus, 1979) indicate that the answer is clear-cut. As soon as our eyes focus on a written symbol, the visual information, combined with the contextual information, is automatically transformed into an abstract "word" code that carries phonological, orthographic, and semantic information. There is no dispute among psychologists concerning the availability of orthographic and semantic data. However, there is a controversy over whether the phonological data are absorbed during or after reading, and whether they are necessary at all (Banks et al., 1981).

We prefer to think that recoding the visually presented script into a phonological format is an automatic and inevitable process (Tzeng et al., 1977). Recent experiments on word recognition have yielded much evidence to support this view. Polich and his colleagues (in press) have shown that a phonological anomaly interferes with word recognition at a very early stage of processing. This is true for the recognition of Chinese words, although not for single characters. It is also true for the recognition of Hebrew words, from which vowels are usually deleted. And readers of Serbo-Croatian script, in which words can be written in either Roman or Cyrillic letters, automatically recode the words into two different phonological formats (for instance, "POTOP" means inundation in Roman and rotor in Cyrillic letters), even when they are reading only one alphabet (Lukatela and Turvey, 1980).

These results tell us that in every type of writing system, a reader always has access to the phonological information. It is not true that reading Chinese logographs does not require such information. A native speaker of Mandarin Chinese has difficulty reading a Cantonese newspaper, which uses the same logographs but with different pronunciations. It may be more difficult for a Chinese or Japanese child to learn to convert script to sound automatically, owing to the fact that information about pronunciation is not always specified in the logographs. That is why reciting aloud plays so important a role in the early acquisition of reading skills in both China and Japan.

So far we have been concerned with fluent readers of various writing systems. It has been suggested that different neurolinguistic pathways are used to transform different scripts into a common linguistic code. Can this suggestion be corroborated by neurophysiological data? Happily, the answer is a positive one. In general, lesions in the temporal cortex are associated with greater impairment of reading and/or writing of scripts that are based on phonemes, whereas lesions in the posterior, occipito-parietal areas are associated with greater impairment in logographics scripts (Hung and Tzeng, 1981).

The most striking data come from the examination of Japanese aphasic patients with respect to their ability to use *kanji* and *kana* scripts. Sasanuma (1974) in Tokyo has reported that the ability of such patients to use these two types of script can be selectively impaired. Typically, the processing of *kana* is adversely affected in the context of Broca's aphasia, a disorder that disrupts speech; however, a decrease in the ability to process *kanji* is characteristic of Gogi aphasia, a disorder that makes it difficult to decipher the meaning of words. Thus the pathological data seem to be consistent with those from normal readers, an unusal feat in our search for the biological basis of cognition.

The interactions between the processing demands imposed by various scripts and the patterns of the visual-field effect in T-scope experiments show, on the one hand, the flexibility of our information-processing system to adapt to various orthographic principles. On the other hand, and of equal importance, they reveal the cooperative and integrative nature of our neurolinguistic activities in reading.

In recent years the discovery of hemispheric specialization has led many students of the brain to characterize the two hemispheres in such ways as "dominant versus nondominant," "Western versus Eastern," and "active versus passive," as if the hemispheres were two separate brains with two separate minds. Such a characterization of the brain's function is certainly misleading. There is no doubt that hemispheric specializations are important properties of the brain. However, it is the collaboration and balance of the various neural components working together as an integrated whole that is the most important hallmark of human cognition.

The diversity of scripts and the associated information-processing strategies reveal the intricate interaction between symbol and thought that touches the very core of the nature of cognition. Inevitably, we are led to wonder to what extent the ensuing differences in cognitive styles are ultimately responsible for more global differences among cultures. It seems that, here again, we are at once the creator and the product of our media.

REFERENCES

Banks, W.P., E. Oka, and S. Shugarman. 1981. Recoding of printed words to internal speech: Does recoding come before lexical access? In *The Perception of Print: Reading Research in Experimental Psychology,* ed. O.J.L. Tzeng, and H. Singer. Hillsdale, NJ: Erlbaum.

Besner, D., and M. Coltheart. 1979. Ideographic and alphabet processing in skilled reading of English. *Neuropsychologia,* 17: 467-72.

Biederman, I., and Y.C. Tsao. 1979. On processing Chinese ideographs and English words: Some implications from Stroop test results. *Cog. Psychol.,* 11:125-32.

Crowder, R.G. 1976. *The Principles of Learning and Memory.* Hillsdale, NJ: Erlbaum.

Fang, S.P., O.J.L. Tzeng, and L. Alva. 1981. Intralanguage vs. interlanguage Stroop effects in two types of writing systems. *Memory and Cognition,* 6:609-17.

Hardyck, C., O.J.L. Tzeng, and W.S.-Y. Wang. 1977. Cerebral lateralization effects in visual half-field experiments. *Nature,* 269:705-07.

Ho, P.T. 1976. *The Cradle of the East.* Chicago: University of Chicago Press.

Hung, D.L., and O.J.L. Tzeng. 1981. Orthographic variation and visual information processing. *Psycholog. Bull.,* 90:377-414.

Lukatela, G., and M.T. Turvey. 1980. Some experiments on Roman and Cyrillic alphabets. In *Orthography, Reading and Dyslexia,* ed. J.F. Kavanagh and R.L. Venezky. University Park Press.

Patterson, K., and J. Bradshaw. 1975. Differential hemisphere mediation of nonverbal visual stimuli. *J. Exp. Psycho.: Human Perception and Performance,* 1:246-52.

Polich, J.M., G. McCarthy, W.S.-Y. Wang, and E. Donchin. In press. When words collide: Orthographic and phonological interference during word processing. *Biol. Psychol.*

Preston, M.S., and W.E. Lambert. 1969. Interlingual interference in a bilingual version of the Stroop color-word test. *J. Verbal Learning and Verbal Beh.,* 8:295-301.

Sasanuma, S. 1974. Impairment of written language in Japanese aphasics. *J. Chinese Linguistics,* 2:141-57.

Schmandt-Besserat, D. 1978. The earliest precursor of writing. *Sci. Am.,* 238:50-59.

Seidenberg, M., and M.K. Tanenhaus. 1979. Orthographic effects on rhyme monitoring. *J. Exp. Psychol.: Human Learning and Memory,* 5:546-54.

Stroop, J.R. 1935. Studies of interference in serial verbal reaction. *J. Exp. Psychol.,* 18:643-62.

Tzeng, O.J.L., D.L. Hung, B. Cotton, and W.S-Y. Wang. 1979. Visual lateralization effect in reading Chinese. *Nature,* 282:499-501.

Tzeng, O.J.L., D.L. Hung, and W.S.-Y. Wang. 1977. Speech recoding in reading Chinese characters. *J. Exp. Psychol: Human Learning and Memory,* 3:621-30.

Tzeng, O.J.L., and H. Singer, eds. 1981. *The Perception of Print: Reading Research in Experimental Psychology.* Hillsdale, NJ: Erlbaum.

Wang, W.S.-Y. 1971. The basis of speech. In *The Learning of Language,* ed. C.E. Reed. East Norwalk, CT: Appleton-Century-Crofts.

Wang, W.S.-Y. 1973. The Chinese language. *Sci. Am.*, 228:50-60.

Wang, W.S.-Y. 1981. Language structure and optimal orthography. In *The Perception of Print: Reading Research in Experimental Psychology,* ed. O.J.L. Tzeng and H. Singer. Hillsdale, NJ: Erlbaum.

Wang, W.S.-Y., ed. 1982. *Human Communication: Language and Its Psychobiological Bases.* New York: W.H. Freeman.

Word Recognition

Learning to Read

ELEANOR J. GIBSON
Cornell University

Educators and the public have exhibited a keen interest in the teaching of reading ever since free public education became a fact (*1*). Either because of or despite their interest, this most important subject has been remarkably susceptible to the influence of fads and fashions and curiously unaffected by disciplined experimental and theoretical psychology. The psychologists have traditionally pursued the study of verbal learning by means of experiments with nonsense syllables and the like—that is, materials carefully divested of useful information. And the educators, who found little in this work that seemed relevant to the classroom, have stayed with the classroom; when they performed experiments, the method was apt to be a gross comparison of classes privileged and unprivileged with respect to the latest fad. The result has been two cultures: the pure scientists in the laboratory, and the practical teachers ignorant of the progress that has been made in the theory of human learning and in methods of studying it.

That this split was unfortunate is clear enough. True, most children do learn to read. But some learn to read badly, so that school systems must provide remedial clinics; and a small proportion (but still a large number of future citizens) remain functional illiterates. The fashions which have led to classroom experiments, such as the "whole word" method, emphasis on context and pictures for "meaning," the "flash" method, "speed reading," revised alphabets, the "return" to "phonics," and so on, have done little to change the situation.

Yet a systematic approach to the understanding of reading skill is possible. The psychologist has only to treat reading as a learning problem, to apply ingenuity in theory construction and experimental design to this fundamental activity on which the rest of man's education depends. A beginning has recently been made in this direction, and it can be expected that a number of theoretical and experimental studies of reading will be forthcoming (*2*).

Reprinted from *Science*, 148 (1965) 1066-1072 with the permission of the author and the American Association for the Advancement of Science.

Analysis of the Reading Process

A prerequisite to good research on reading is a psychological analysis of the reading process. What is it that a skilled reader has learned? Knowing this (or having a pretty good idea of it), one may consider how the skill is learned, and next how it could best be taught. Hypotheses designed to answer all three of these questions can then be tested by experiment.

There are several ways of characterizing the behavior we call reading. It is receiving communication; it is making discriminative responses to graphic symbols; it is decoding graphic symbols to speech; and it is getting meaning from the printed page. A child in the early stages of acquiring reading skill may not be doing all these things, however. Some aspects of reading must be mastered before others and have an essential function in a sequence of development of the final skill. The average child, when he begins learning to read, has already mastered to a marvelous extent the art of communication. He can speak and understand his own language in a fairly complex way, employing units of language organized in a hierarchy and with a grammatical structure. Since a writing system must correspond to the spoken one, and since speech is prior to writing, the frame work and unit structure of speech will determine more or less the structure of the writing system, though the rules of correspondence vary for different languages and writing systems. Some alphabetic writing systems have nearly perfect single-letter-to-sound correspondences, but some, like English, have far more complex correspondence between spelling patterns and speech patterns. Whatever the nature of the correspondences, it is vital to a proper analysis of the reading task that they be understood. And it is vital to remember, as well, that the first stage in the child's mastery of reading is learning to communicate by means of spoken language.

Once a child begins his progression from spoken language to written language, there are, I think, three phases of learning to be considered. They present three different kinds of learning tasks, and they are roughly sequential, though there must be considerable overlapping. These three phases are: learning to differentiate graphic symbols; learning to decode letters to sounds ("map" the letters into sounds); and using progressively high-order units of structure. I shall consider these three stages in order and in some detail and describe experiments exploring each stage.

Differentiation of Written Symbols

Making any discriminative response to printed characters is considered by some a kind of reading. A very young child, or even a monkey, can be taught to point to a patch of yellow color, rather than a patch of blue, when the printed characters YELLOW are presented. Various people, in recent popular publications, have seriously suggested teaching infants to respond discriminatively in this way to letter patterns, implying that this is teaching them to "read." Such responses are not reading, however; reading entails decoding to speech. Letters are, essentially, an instruction to produce a given speech sound.

Nevertheless, differentiation of written characters from one another is a logically preliminary stage to decoding them to speech. The learning problem is one of discriminating and recognizing a set of line figures, all very similar in a number of ways (for example, all are tracings on paper) and each differing from all the others in one or more features (as straight versus curved). The differentiating features must remain invariant under certain transformations (size, brightness, and perspective transformations and less easily described ones produced by different type faces and handwriting). They must therefore be relational, so that these transformations will not destroy them.

It might be questioned whether learning is necessary for these figures to be discriminated from one another. This question has been investigated by Gibson, Gibson, Pick, and Osser (3). In order to trace the development of letter differentiation as it is related to those features of letters which are critical for the task, we designed specified transformations for each of a group of standard, artificial letter-like forms comparable to printed Roman capitals. Variants were constructed from each standard figure to yield the following 12 transformations for each one: three degrees of transformation from line to curve; five transformations of rotation or reversal; two perspective transformations; and two topological transformations (see Fig. 1 for examples). All of these except the perspective transformations we considered critical for discriminating letters. For example, contrast V and U; C and U; O and C.

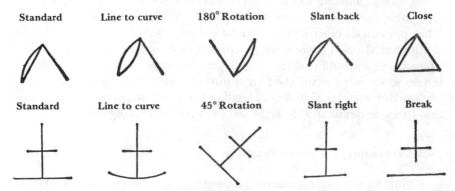

Figure 1.   Examples of letter-like figures illustrating different types of transformation.

The discrimination task required the subject to match a standard figure against all of its transformations and some copies of it and to select only identical copies. An error score (the number of times an item that was not an identical copy was selected) was obtained for each child, and the errors were classified according to the type of transformation. The subjects were children aged 4 through 8 years. As would be expected, the visual discrimination of these letter-like forms improved from age 4 to age 8, but the slopes of the error curves were different, depending on the transformation to be discriminated (Fig. 2). In other words, some transformations are harder to discriminate than others, and improvement occurs at different rates for different transformations. Even the youngest subjects made relatively few errors involving changes of break or close, and among the 8-year-olds these errors dropped to zero. Errors for perspective transformations were very numerous among 4-year-olds and still numerous among 8-year-olds. Errors for rotations and reversals started high but dropped to nearly zero by 8 years. Errors for changes from line to curve were relatively numerous (depending on the number of changes) among the youngest children and showed a rapid drop among the older—almost to zero for the 8-year-olds.

The experiment was replicated with the same transformations of real letters on the 5-year-old group. The correlation between confusions of the same transformations for real letters and for the letter-like forms was very high ($r = +.87$), so the effect of a given transformation has generality (is not specific to a given form).

What happens, in the years from 4 to 8, to produce or hamper improvement in discrimination? Our results suggest that the children have learned the features or dimensions of difference which are critical for differentiating letters. Some differences are critical, such as break versus close, line versus curve, and rotations and reversals; but some, such as the perspective transformations, are not, and must in fact be tolerated. The child of 4 does not start "cold" upon this task, because some of his previous experience with distinctive features of objects and pictures will transfer to letter differentiation. But the set of letters has a unique feature pattern for each of its members, so learning of the distinctive features goes on during the period we investigated.

Table 1

Number of Errors Made in Transfer Stage By Groups with Three Types of Training

Group	Type of training		Errors
	Standards	Transformations	
E1	Same	Different	69
E2	Different	Same	39
C	Different	Different	101

If this interpretation is correct, it would be useful to know just what the distinctive features of letters are. What dimensions of difference must a child learn to detect in order to perceive each letter as unique? Gibson, Osser, Schiff, and Smith (4) investigated this question. Our method was to draw up a chart of the features of a given set of letters (5), test to see which of these letters were most frequently confused by prereading children, and compare the errors in the resulting "confusion matrix" with those predicted by the feature chart.

A set of distinctive features for letters must be relational in the sense that each feature presents a contrast which is invariant under certain transformations, and it must yield a unique pattern for each letter. The set must also be reasonably economical. Two feature lists which satisfy these requirements for a specified type face were tried out against the results of

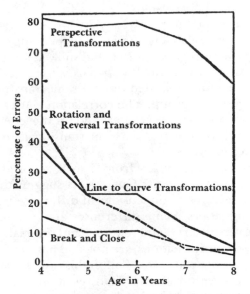

Figure 2.   Error curves showing rate of improvements in discriminating four types of transformation.

a confusion matrix obtained with the same type (simplified Roman capitals available on a sign-typewriter).

Each of the features in the list in Fig. 3 is or is not a characteristic of each of the 26 letters. Regarding each letter one asks, for example, "Is there a curved segment?" and gets a yes or no answer. A filled-in feature chart gives a unique pattern for each letter. However, the number of potential features for letter-shapes is very large, and would vary from one alphabet and type font to another. Whether or not we have the right set can be tested with a confusion matrix. Children should confuse with greatest frequency the letters having the smallest number of feature differences, if the features have been chosen correctly.

We obtained our confusion matrix from 4-year-old children, who made matching judgments of letters, programed so that every letter had an equal opportunity to be mistaken for any other, without bias from order effects. The "percent feature difference" for any two letters was determined by dividing the total number of features possessed by either letter, but not both, by the total number possessed by both, whether shared or not. Correlations were then calculated between percent feature difference and number of confusions, one for each letter. The feature list of Fig. 3 yielded 12 out of 26 positive significant correlations. Prediction from this feature list is fairly good, in view of the fact that features were

Features	A	B	C	E	K	L	N	U	X	Z
Straight segment										
Horizontal	+			+	+					+
Vertical		+		+	+	+	+			
Oblique /	+			+					+	+
Oblique \	+			+			+	+		+
Curve										
Closed		+								
Open vertically								+		
Open horizontally			+							
Intersection	+	+		+	+			+		
Redundancy										
Cyclic change		+		+						
Symmetry	+	+	+	+	+			+	+	
Discontinuity										
Vertical	+				+				+	
Horizontal				+		+	+			+

Figure 3. Example of a "feature chart." Whether the features chosen are actually effective for discriminating letters must be determined by experiment.

not weighted. A multidimensional analysis of the matrix corroborated the choice of the curve-straight and obliqueness variables, suggesting that these features may have priority in the discrimination process and perhaps developmentally. Refinement of the feature list will take these facts into account, and other methods of validation will be tried.

Detecting Distinctive Features

If we are correct in thinking that the child comes to discriminate graphemes by detecting their distinctive features, what is the learning process like? That it is perceptual learning and need not be verbalized is probable (though teachers do often call attention to contrasts between letter shapes). An experiment by Anne D. Pick (6) was designed to compare two hypotheses about how this type of discrimination develops. One might be called a "schema" or "prototype" hypothesis, and is based on the supposition that the child builds up a kind of model or memory image of each letter by repeated experience of visual presentations of the letter; perceptual theories which propose that discrimination occurs by matching sensory experience to a previously stored concept or categorical model are of this kind. In the other hypothesis it is assumed that the child learns by discovering how the forms differ, and then easily transfers this knowledge to new letter-like figures.

Pick employed a transfer design in which subjects were presented in step 1 with initially confusable stimuli (letter-like forms) and trained to discriminate between them. For step 2 (the transfer stage) the subjects were divided into three groups. One experimental group was given sets of stimuli to discriminate which varied in new dimensions from the *same standards* discriminated in stage 1. A second experimental group was given sets of stimuli which deviated from *new standards*, but in the same dimensions of difference discriminated in stage 1. A control group was given both new standards and new dimensions of difference to discriminate in stage 2. Better performance by the first experimental group would suggest that discrimination learning proceeded by construction of a model or memory image of the standards against which the variants could be matched. Conversely, better performance by the second experimental group would suggest that dimensions of difference had been detected.

The subjects were kindergarten children. The stimuli were letter-like forms of the type described earlier. There were six standard forms and six transformations of each of them. The transformations consisted of two changes of line to curve, a right-left reversal, a 45-degree rotation, a perspective transformation, and a size transformation. Table 1 gives the errors of discrimination for all three groups in stage 2. Both experimental groups performed significantly better than the control group, but the group that had familiar transformations of new standards performed significantly better than the group given new transformations of old standards.

We infer from these results that, while children probably do learn prototypes of letter shapes, the prototypes themselves are not the original basis for differentiation. The most relevant kind of training for discrimination is practice which provides experience with the characteristic differences that distinguish the set of items. Features which are actually distinctive for letters could be emphasized by presenting letters in contrast pairs.

Decoding Letters to Sounds

When the graphemes are reasonably discriminable from one another, the decoding process becomes possible. This process, common sense and many psychologists would tell us, is simply a matter of associating a graphic stimulus with the appropriate spoken response—that is to say, it is the traditional stimulus-response paradigm, a kind of paired-associate learning.

Obvious as this description seems, problems arise when one takes a closer look. Here are just a few. The graphic code is related to the speech code by rules of correspondence. If these rules are known, decoding of new items is predictable. Do we want to build up, one by one, automatically cued responses, or do we want to teach with transfer in mind? If we want to teach for transfer, how do we do it? Should the child be aware that this is a code game with rules? Or will induction of the rules be automatic? What units of both codes should we start with? Should we start with single letters, in the hope that knowledge of single-letter-to-sound relationships will yield the most transfer? Or should we start with whole words, in the hope that component relationships will be induced?

Carol Bishop (7) investigated the question of the significance of knowledge of component letter-sound relationships in reading new words. In her experiment, the child's process of learning to read was simulated by teaching adult subjects to read some Arabic words. The purpose was to determine the transfer value of training with individual letters as opposed to whole words, and to investigate the role of component letter-sound associations in transfer to learning new words.

A three-stage transfer design was employed. The letters were 12 Arabic characters, each with a one-to-one letter-sound correspondence. There were eight consonants and four vowels, which were combined to form two sets of eight Arabic words. The 12 letters appeared at least once in both sets of words. A native speaker of the language recorded on tape the 12 letter-sounds and the two sets of words. The graphic form of each letter or word was printed on a card.

The subjects were divided into three groups—the letter training group (L), the whole-word training group (W), and a control group (C). Stage 1 of the experiment was identical for all groups. The subjects learned to pronounce the set of words (transfer set) which would appear in stage 3 by listening to the recording and repeating the words. Stage 2 varied. Group L listened to and repeated the 12 letter-sounds and then learned to associate the individual graphic shapes with their correct sounds. Group W followed the same procedure, except that eight words were given them to learn, rather than letters. Learning time was equal for the two groups. Group C spent the same time-interval on an unrelated task. Stage 3 was the same for the three groups. All subjects learned to read the set of words they had heard in stage 1, responding to the presentation of a word on a card by pronouncing it. This was the transfer stage on which the three groups were compared.

At the close of stage 3, all subjects were tested on their ability to give the correct letter-sound following the presentation of each printed letter. They were asked afterward to explain how they tried to learn the transfer words.

Figure 4 shows that learning took place in fewest trials for the letter group and next fewest for the word group. That is, letter training had more transfer value than word training, but word training did produce some transfer. The subjects of group L also knew, on the average, a greater number of component letter-sound correspondences, but some subjects in group W had learned all 12. Most of the subjects in group L reported that they had tried to learn by using knowledge of component correspondences. But so did 12 of the 20 subjects in group W, and the scores of these 12 subjects on the transfer task were similar to those of the letter-trained group. The subjects who had learned by whole words and had not used individual correspondences performed no better on the task than the control subjects.

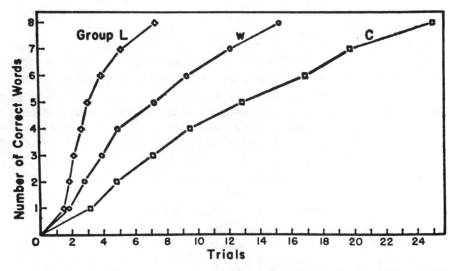

Figure 4.   Learning curves on transfer task for group trained originally with whole words (W), group trained with single letters (L), and control group (C).

It is possible, then, to learn to read words without learning the component letter-sound correspondences. But transfer to new words depends on use of them, whatever the method of original training. Word training was as good as letter training if the subject had analyzed for himself the component relationships.

Learning Variable and Constant Component Correspondences

In Bishop's experiment, the component letter-sound relationships were regular and consistent. It has often been pointed out, especially by advocates of spelling reform and revised alphabets (8), that in English this is not the case. Bloomfield (9) suggested that the beginning reader should, therefore, be presented with material carefully programed for teaching those orthographic-phonic regularities which exist in English, and should be introduced later and only gradually to the complexities of English spelling and to the fact that single-letter-to-sound relationships are often variable. But actually, there has been no hard evidence to suggest that transfer, later, to reading spelling-patterns with more variable component correspondence will be facilitated by beginning with only constant ones. Athough variable ones may be harder to learn in the beginning, the original difficulty may be compensated for by facilitating later learning.

A series of experiments directed by Harry Levin (10) dealt with the effect of learning variable as opposed to constant letter-sound relationships, on transfer to learning new letter-sound relationships. In one experiment, the learning material was short lists of paired-associates, with a word written in artificial characters as stimulus and a triphoneme familiar English word as response. Subjects (third-grade children) in one group were given a list which contained constant graph-to-sound relationships (one-to-one component correspondence) followed by a list in which this correspondence was variable with respect to the medial vowel sound. Another group started with a similarly constructed variable list and followed it with a second one. The group that learned lists with a variable component in both stages was superior to the other group in the second stage. The results suggest that initiating the task with a variable list created an expectation or learning set for variability of correspondence which was transferred to the second list and facilitated learning it.

In a second experiment, the constant or variable graph-sound relation occurred on the first letter. Again, the group with original variable training performed better on the second, variable list. In a third experiment adult native speakers of English and Spanish were compared. The artificial graphs were paired with nonsense words. Again there was more transfer from a variable first list to a variable second list than from a constant to a variable one. Variable lists were more difficult, on the whole, for the Spanish speakers, perhaps because their native language contains highly regular letter-sound relationships.

A "set for diversity" may, therefore, facilitate transfer to learning of new letter-sound correspondences which contain variable relationships. But many questions about how the code is learned remain to be solved, because the true units of the graphic code are not necessarily single letters. While single-letter-sound relations in English are indeed variable, at other levels of structure regularity may be discovered.

Lower- and Higher-Order Units

For many years, linguists have been concerned with the question of units in language. That language has a hierarchical structure, with units of different kinds and levels, is generally accepted, though the definition of the units is not easily reached. One criterion of a unit is recodability—consistent mapping or translation to another code. If such a criterion be granted, graphic units must parallel linguistic units. The units of the writing system should be defined, in other words, by mapping rules which link them to the speech code, at all levels of structure.

What then are the true graphic units? What levels of units are there? Exactly how are they mapped to linguistic units? In what "chunks" are they perceived? We must first try to answer these questions by a logical analysis of properties of the writing and speech systems and the correspondences between them. Then we can look at the behavior of skilled readers and see how units are processed during reading. If the logical analysis of the correspondence rules is correct, we should be able to predict what kinds of units are actually processed and to check our predictions experimentally.

Common sense suggests that the unit for reading is the single grapheme, and that the reader proceeds sequentially from left to right, letter by letter, across the page. But we can assert at once and unequivocally that this picture is false. For the English language, the single graphemes map consistently into speech only as morphemes—that is, the names of the letters of the alphabet. It is possible, of course, to name letters sequentially across a line of print ("spell out" a word), but that is not the goal of a skilled reader, nor is it what he does. Dodge (11) showed, nearly 60 years ago, that perception occurs in reading only during fixations, and not at all during the saccadic jumps from one fixation to the next. With a fast tachistoscopic exposure, a skilled reader can perceive four unconnected letters, a very long word, and four or more words if they form a sentence (12). Even first graders can read three-letter words exposed for only 40 milliseconds, too short a time for sequential eye movements to occur.

Broadbent (13) has pointed out that speech, although it consists of a temporal sequence of stimuli, is responded to at the end of a sequence.

That is, it is normal for a whole sequence to be delivered before a response is made. For instance, the sentence "Would you give me your _____?" might end with any of a large number of words, such as "name" or "wallet" or "wife." The response depends on the total message. The fact that the component stimuli for speech and reading are spread over time does not mean that the phonemes or letters or words are processed one at a time, with each stimulus decoded to a separate response. The fact that O is pronounced differently in BOAT and BOMB is not a hideous peculiarity of English which must consequently be reformed. The O is read only in context and is never responded to in isolation. It is part of a sequence which contains constraints of two kinds, one morphological and the other the spelling patterns which are characteristic of English.

If any doubt remains as to the unlikelihood of sequential processing letter by letter, there is recent evidence of Newman (14) and of Kolers (15) on sequential exposure of letters. When letters forming a familiar word are exposed sequentially in the same place, it is almost impossible to read the word. With an exposure of 100 milliseconds per letter, words of six letters are read with only 20 percent probability of accuracy; and with an exposure of 375 milliseconds per letter, the probability is still well under 100 percent. But that is more than 2 seconds to perceive a short, well-known word! We can conclude that, however graphemes are processed perceptually in reading, it is not a letter-by-letter sequence of acts.

If the single grapheme does not map consistently to a phoneme, and furthermore, if perception normally takes in bigger "chunks" of graphic stimuli in a single fixation, what are the smallest graphic units consistently coded into phonemic patterns? Must they be whole words? Are there different levels of units? Are they achieved at different stages of development?

Spelling Patterns

It is my belief that the smallest component units in written English are spelling patterns (16). By a spelling pattern, I mean a cluster of graphemes in a given environment which has an invariant pronunciation according to the rules of English. These rules are the regularities which appear when, for instance, any vowel or consonant or cluster is shown to correspond with a given pronunciation in an initial, medial, or final position in the spelling of a word. This kind of regularity is not merely "frequency" (bigram frequency, trigram frequency, and so on), for it implies that frequency counts are relevant for establishing rules only if the right units and the right relationships are counted. The relevant graphic unit is a functional unit of one or more letters, in a given position within the word, which is in correspondence with a specified pronunciation (17).

If potential regularities exist within words—the spelling patterns that occur in regular correspondence with speech patterns—one may hypothesize that these correspondences have been assimilated by the skilled reader of English (whether or not he can verbalize the rules) and have the effect of organizing units for perception. It follows that strings of letters which are generated by the rules will be perceived more easily than ones which are not, even when they are unfamiliar words or not words at all.

Several experiments testing this prediction were performed by Gibson, Pick, Osser, and Hammond (*18*). The basic design was to compare the perceptibility (with a very short tachistoscopic exposure) of two sets of letter-strings, all nonsense or pseudo words, which differed in their spelling-to-sound correlation. One list, called the "pronounceable" list, contained words with a high spelling-to-sound correlation. Each of them had an initial consonant-spelling with a single, regular pronunciation; a final consonant-spelling having a single regular pronunciation; and a vowel-spelling, placed between them, having a single regular pronunciation when it follows and is followed by the given initial and final consonant spellings, respectively—for example, GL/UR/CK. The words in the second list, called the "unpronounceable" list, had a low spelling-to-sound correlation. They were constructed from the words in the first list by reversing the initial and final consonant spellings. The medial vowel spelling was not changed. For example, GLURCK became CKURGL. There were 25 such pseudo words in each list, varying in length from four to eight letters. The pronunciability of the resulting lists was validated in two ways, first by ratings, and second by obtaining the number of variations when the pseudo words were actually pronounced.

The words were projected on a screen in random order, in five successive presentations with an exposure time beginning at 50 milliseconds and progressing up to 250 milliseconds. The subjects (college students) were instructed to write each word as it was projected. The mean percentage of pronounceable words correctly perceived was consistently and significantly greater at all exposure times.

The experiment was later repeated with the same material but a different judgment. After the pseudo word was exposed, it was followed by a multiple-choice list of four items, one of the correct one and the other three the most common errors produced in the previous experiment. The subject chose the word he thought he had seen from the choice list and recorded a number (its order in the list). Again the mean of pronounceable pseudo words correctly perceived significantly exceeded that of their unpronounceable counterparts. We conclude from these experiments that skilled readers more easily perceive as a unit pseudo words which follow the rules of English spelling-to-sound correspondence; that spelling patterns which have invariant relations to sound patterns function as a unit, thus facilitating the decoding process.

In another experiment, Gibson, Osser, and Pick (*19*) studied the development of perception of grapheme-phoneme correspondences. We wanted to know how early, in learning to read, children begin to respond to spelling-patterns as units. The experiment was designed to compare children at the end of the first grade and at the end of the third grade in ability to recognize familiar three-letter words, pronounceable trigrams, and unpronounceable trigrams. The three-letter words were taken from the first-grade reading list; each word chosen could be rearranged into a meaningless but pronounceable trigram and a meaningless and unpronounceable one (for example, RAN, NAR, RNA). Some longer pseudo words (four and five letters) taken from the previous experiments were included as well. The words and pseudo words were exposed tachistoscopically to individual children, who were required to spell them orally. The first-graders read (spelled out) most accurately the familiar three-letter words, but read the pronounceable trigrams significantly better than the unpronounceable ones. The longer pseudo words were seldom read accurately and were not differentiated by pronunciability. The third-grade girls read all three-letter combinations with high and about equal accuracy, but differentiated the longer pseudo words; that is, the pronounceable four- and five-letter pseudo words were more often perceived correctly than their unpronounceable counterparts.

These results suggest that a child in the first stages of reading skill typically reads in short units, but has already generalized certain regularities of spelling-to-sound correspondence, so that three-letter pseudo words which fit the rules are more easily read as units. As skill develops, span increases, and a similar difference can be observed for longer items. The longer items involve more complex conditional rules and longer clusters, so that the generalizations must increase in complexity. The fact that a child can begin very early to perceive regularities of correspondence between the printed and spoken patterns, and transfer them to the reading of unfamiliar items as units, suggests that the opportunities for discovering the correspondences between patterns might well be enhanced in programing reading materials.

I have referred several times to *levels* of units. The last experiment showed that the size and complexity of the spelling patterns which can be perceived as units increase with development of reading skill. The other levels of structure, both syntactic and semantic, contain units as large as and larger than the word, and that perception of skilled readers will be found, in suitable experiments, to be a function of these factors is almost axiomatic. As yet we have little direct evidence better than Cattell's original discovery (*12*) that when words are structured into a sentence, more letters can be accurately perceived "at a glance." Developmental studies of perceptual "chunking" in relation to structural complexity may be very instructive.

Where does meaning come in? Within the immediate span of visual perception, meaning is less effective in structuring written material than good spelling-to-sound corrrespondence, as Gibson, Bishop, Schiff, and Smith (20) have shown. Real words which are both meaningful and, as strings of letters, structured in accordance with English spelling patterns are more easily perceived than nonword pronounceable strings of letters; but the latter are more easily perceived than meaningful but unpronounceable letter-strings (for example, BIM is perceived accurately, with tachistoscopic exposure, faster than IBM). The role of meaning in the visual perception of words probably increases as longer strings of words (more than one) are dealt with. A sentence has two kinds of constraint, semantic and syntactic, which make it intelligible (easily heard) and memorable (21). It is important that the child develop reading habits which utilize all the types of constraint present in the stimulus, since they constitute structure and are, therefore, unit-formers. The skills which the child should acquire in reading are habits of utilizing the constraints in letter strings (the spelling and morphemic patterns) and in word strings (the syntactic and semantic patterns). We could go on to consider still superordinate ones, perhaps, but the problem of the unit, of levels of units, and mapping rules from writing to speech has just begun to be explored with experimental techniques. Further research on the definition and processing of units should lead to new insights about the nature of reading skill and its attainment.

Summary

Reading begins with the child's acquisition of spoken language. Later he learns to differentiate the graphic symbols from one another and to decode these to familiar speech sounds. As he learns to decode, he must progressively utilize the structural constraints which are built into it in order to attain the skilled performance which is characterized by processing of higher-order units—the spelling and morphological patterns of the language.

Because of my firm conviction that good pedagogy is based on a deep understanding of the discipline to be taught and the nature of the learning process involved, I have tried to show that the psychology of reading can benefit from a program of theoretical analysis and experiment. An analysis of the reading task—discriminatory and decoding aspects as well as the semantic and syntactical aspects—tells us *what* must be learned. An analysis of the learning process tells us *how*. The consideration of formal instruction comes only after these steps, and its precepts should follow from them.

REFERENCES

1. See C. C. Fries, *Linguistics and Reading* (Holt, Rinehart, and Winston, New York, 1963), for an excellent chapter on past practice and theory in the teaching of reading.

2. In 1959, Cornell University was awarded a grant for a Basic Research Project on Reading by the Cooperative Research Program of the Office of Education, U.S. Department of Health, Education, and Welfare. Most of the work reported in this article was supported by this grant. The Office of Education has recently organized "Project Literacy," which will promote research on reading in a number of laboratories, as well as encourage mutual understanding between experimentalists and teachers of reading.

3. E. J. Gibson, J. J. Gibson, A. D. Pick, H. Osser, *J. Comp. Physiol. Psychol.* **55**, 897 (1962).

4. E. J. Gibson, H. Osser, W. Schiff, J. Smith, in *A Basic Research Program on Reading*, Final Report on Cooperative Research Project No. 639 to the Office of Education, Department of Health, Education, and Welfare.

5. The method was greatly influenced by the analysis of distinctive features of phonemes by R. Jacobson and M. Halle, presented in *Fundamentals of Language* (Mouton, The Hague, 1956). A table of 12 features, each in binary opposition, yields a unique pattern for all phonemes, so that any one is distinguishable from any other by its pattern of attributes. A pair of phonemes may differ by any number of features, the minimal distinction being one feature opposition. The features must be invariant under certain transformations and essentially relational, so as to remain distinctive over a wide range of speakers, intonations, and so on.

6. A. D. Pick, *J. Exp. Psychol.*, in press.

7. C. H. Bishop, *J. Verbal Learning Verbal Behav.* **3**, 215 (1964).

8. Current advocates of a revised alphabet who emphasize the low letter-sound correspondence in English are Sir James Pitman and John A. Downing. Pitman's revised alphabet, called the Initial Teaching Alphabet, consists of 43 characters, some traditional and some new. It is designed for instruction of the beginning reader, who later transfers to traditional English spelling. See I. J. Pitman, *J. Roy. Soc. Arts* **109**, 149 (1961); J. A. Downing, *Brit. J. Educ. Psychol.* **32**, 166 (1962); _____, "Experiments with Pitman's initial teaching alphabet in British schools," paper presented at the Eighth Annual Conference of International Reading Association, Miami, Fla., May 1963.

9. L. Bloomfield, *Elem. Engl. Rev.* **19**, 125, 183 (1942).

10. See research reports of H. Levin and J. Watson, and H. Levin, E. Baum, and S. Bostwick, in *A Basic Research Program on Reading* (see *4*).

11. R. Dodge, *Psychol. Bull.* **2**, 193 (1905).

12. J. McK. Cattell, *Phil. Studies* **2**, 635 (1885).

13. D. E. Broadbent, *Perception and Communication* (Pergamon, New York, 1958).

14. E. Newman, *Am. J. Psychol.*, in press.

15. P. A. Kolers and M. T. Katzman, paper presented before the Psychonomic Society, Aug. 1963, Bryn Mawr, Pa.

16. Spelling patterns in English have been discussed by C. C. Fries in *Linguistics and Reading* (Holt, Rinehart, and Winston, New York, 1963), p. 169 ff. C. F. Hockett, in *A Basic Research Program on Reading* (see *4*), has made an analysis of English graphic monosyllables which presents regularities of spelling patterns in relation to pronunciation. This study was continued by R. Venezky (thesis, Cornell Univ., 1962), who wrote a computer program for obtaining the regularities of English spelling-to-sound correspondence. The data obtained by means of the computer permit one to look up any vowel or consonant cluster of up to five letters and find its pronunciation in initial, medial, and final positions in a word. Letter environments as well have now been included in the analysis. See also R. H. Weir, *Formulation of Grapheme-Phoneme Correspondence Rules to Aid in the Teaching of Reading*, Report on Cooperative Research Project No. 5-039 to the Office of Education, Department of Health, Education and Welfare.

17. For example, the cluster GH may lawfully be pronounced as an F at the end of a word, but never at the beginning. The vowel cluster EIGH, pronounced /A/ (/ej/), may occur in initial, medial, and final positions, and does so with nearly equal distribution. These cases account for all but two occurrences of the cluster in English orthography. A good example of regularity influenced by environment is [c] in a medial position before I plus a vowel. It is always pronounced /S/ (*social, ancient, judicious*).

18. E. J. Gibson, A. D. Pick, H. Osser, M. Hammond, *Am. J. Psychol.* **75,** 554 (1962).

19. E. J. Gibson, H. Osser, A. D. Pick, *J. Verbal Learning Verbal Behav.* **2,** 142 (1963).

20. E. J. Gibson, C. H. Bishop, W. Schiff, J. Smith, *J. Exp. Psychol.,* **67,** 173 (1964).

21. G. A. Miller and S. Isard, *J. Verbal Learning Verbal Behav.* **2,** 217 (1963); also L. E. Marks and G. A. Miller, *ibid.* **3,** 1 (1964).

Conceptualization in Learning to Read

HARRY SINGER
University of California at Riverside

Children have learned to read by means of a wide variety of methods and materials. During the history of American reading instruction (Smith, 71), the unit of initial instructional emphasis has varied by increasing in a surprisingly systematic way from the letter (alphabet method) to word parts (phonic method) to the whole word (word method) and finally to the sentence and paragraph (language arts method).[1] But, there is still only a paucity of knowledge about how children actually do learn to read (Mac-Kinnon, 52).

However, it is known that regardless of any of the strategies that have been employed for teaching reading, the average pupil in progressing through the grades does cumulatively learn to recognize words that have not been specifically taught. That is, the pupil develops general word recognition ability, the ability to transform printed stimuli into mental processes so that meaning can be associated with these stimuli. For example, even though the basal reader method emphasizes the development of a sight word vocabulary, pupils recognize at successively higher grade levels an increasingly greater percentage of words than those to which they have been systematically exposed (Gates, 23). Apparently, experience in supplemental reading and the developmental word recognition lessons of the basal reader have been successful in teaching pupils more than just the correspondence among the seen, heard, and spoken words when they are learning to read orally by means of the controlled basal reader vocabulary. In fact, scrutiny of the lesson plans in the teacher's manual which accompanies the basal reader reveals that pupils are explicitly taught to abstract and generalize recurring word parts, such as initial consonants, blends, phonograms, syllables, and affixes. Consequently, either by instructional design or by utilizing their own learning "strategies" (Bruner et al., 8), pupils could thus acquire a mediational response system for selecting, perceiving, and processing printed verbal

Reprinted from George B. Schick and Merrill M. May (Eds.), *New Frontiers in College-Adult Reading*, Fifteenth Yearbook of the National Reading Conference, 1966, 116-132. Reprinted with permission.

stimuli. The symbolic responses or concepts in this mediational response system can then be mobilized in varying combinations for recognizing many more printed words than those employed in the original formation of the mediational response system. Since the pupil would not need to develop a separate mediational response for each printed word that he can recognize, the possibility of "cognitive strain" would be reduced (Bruner, et al., 8). Of course, if the formation of a conceptualized mediational response system is not attained, then the pupil's rate of learning to recognize words would be relatively slow because he would be limited to recognition of just those words for which he had developed specific responses.

Whether reading is taught through a basal reader method or through some other method, a complex conceptual system and mental organization would have to be postulated to explain how individuals do learn to read. Because there are many factors which enter into the development of general reading ability (Holmes, 30, 32, 35; Holmes and Singer, 36, 37, 38; Singer, 66), each method of teaching reading can be relatively successful because it stresses one or another of the many variables that are related to attainment of speed and power of reading (Holmes, 32). However, all the necessary elements for reading are present in the materials employed by each method so that pupils in learning to read through any of these methods could have used their capabilities for selecting their own unit of perception, their own conceptualized mediational response systems, and developed their own mental organization for attaining speed and power of reading (Holmes and Singer, 36; Singer, 63, 66). Probably the acquisition of such response systems could be facilitated by an instructional strategy which capitalizes upon the cognitive capabilities of the learner (Singer, 67).

Some Related Research

Although many factors have to be postulated in order to account adequately for the attainment of reading behavior, the formation and use of concepts are, in fact, related to a significant portion of the variance in each subsystem of reading (Singer, 63, 64). From the many studies on conceptualization and the relationship between conceptualization and reading ability, which have been reviewed elsewhere (Singer, 63), only one investigation that is quite germane to a theoretical formulation of the role of conceptualization in learning to read will be reviewed again in this paper. Also, two more recent reports on the relationship between conceptual ability and reading achievement will be summarized.

Capacity for conceptualization was specifically related to reading achievement by Kress (43). After matching 25 pairs of children who were between the ages of 8 and 11, above average in intelligence and comparable on all subscales except the Similarities subscale of the Wechsler-Bellevue Intelligence Test, but who were significantly different on a word recognition test and the Stanford Achievement Test (Paragraph Meaning), Kress administered to each subject a battery of clinical tests of concept formation, which included the Goldstein-Scheerer, the Hanfmann-Kasanin, and the Wisconsin Card Sorting Tests. Responses to the WISC Similarities test were scored for concrete, functional, and abstract levels. Kress summarized the results of these concept formation tasks by stating that in contrast to the "achieving readers," the "non-readers" tend to lack a) versatility and flexibility, b) originality in establishing suitable hypotheses for testing, c) initiative for exhausting all solutions, d) persistence in problem solving under changing conditions, e) ability to draw inferences from relevant clues, f) ability to shift set when new standards are introduced, g) ability to analyze the factors present, h) adequate labels for common concepts, and i) adequate concepts for dealing with language. On the other hand, the non-readers tend to exhibit a) a tendency to cling to previous acceptable solutions, b) an abnormal need for success and avoidance of failure, c) a dependence on the physical characteristics of the objects, and d) a tendency to be more concrete and less abstract in conceptual functioning.

Jan-Tausch (41) also concluded that "retarded readers are retarded because of limitations to concrete thinking," but he conceded that other causes of reading retardation, such as poor vision, hearing, ego development, and instruction could be inferred from his data.

Recently, Robinson (60) hypothesized that rigidity in perception and conceptualization might be an important factor in reading retardation. She suggested that while most individuals are flexible in perceptual and conceptual modes, some pupils might rely mainly upon a single perceptual and conceptual style which, if non-modifiable, would require adaptation of instructional methods in order for these pupils to be successful in learning to read.

The evidence clearly indicates that there is a relation between conceptualization and learning to read, which is usually not a function of the method of teaching reading. Therefore, any theory which purports to explain how individuals learn to read would need to state explicitly the way in which the formation and use of concepts might enter into the development and dynamics of general reading ability. The following is an attempt at such a theoretical formulation. Also, an attempt will be made to integrate this theoretical formulation with the substrata-factor theory of reading.

Conceptual Ability in the Substrata-Factor Theory of Reading

In the process of learning to read, an individual develops and utilizes his ability to select and organize symbolic stimuli into perceptual units. Through conceptualization, the process of discriminating, abstracting, generalizing and organizing common elements (Hull, 39), relationships (Smoke, 72), or crucial aspects of a complex figure (Osgood, 56), an individual reduces a variety of stimuli into fewer categories, which simplify and facilitate his learning task by easing the "cognitive strain" (Bruner et al., 8). Gradually he thereby builds up a conceptual-readiness (Leeper, 48; Russell, 61; Vinacke, 75) to respond to stimuli with a symbolic mode of reaction (Heidbreder, 29) or mediated response (Osgood, 56; Morris, 53). The concept that is formed could vary in span (Zaslow, 78), consistency (Reed, 58), or level of generality (Hanfmann and Kasanin, 26; Goldstein et al., 25; Reichard, et al., 59; Zaslow, 78). These categories are internally linked together into a hierarchical system (Long and Welch, 49, 50) which enables an individual to organize broader units of response on a higher-order conceptual level and through such a superordination process to synthesize disparate elements (Bruner and Oliver, 10). An individual can then utilize this hierarchical system to select and respond to a perceptual unit. Through this circularity of perceptual processes and conceptualization, reinforced by successful practice, a coherent and flexible system develops, in which all the parts—when the individual attains maturity—psychosynchromesh as the individual compounds and recompounds them into working systems. These working systems are momentary organizations to meet the demands of the task-stimuli of the reading material and the reader's purpose (Holmes, 31). Thus, an individual acquires the ability to transform printed symbols into a complex of mental processes, known as his *word-recognition-substrata,* to which meaning can be associated.

If an individual lacks the capacity to conceptualize because of brain damage (Goldstein, et al., 25; Nielsen, 55; Werner and Garrison, 76), personality disorganization (Cameron, 12), or if his level of conceptual capability is inadequate at the time of instruction (Barnard, 3; Kress, 43; Piaget, 57; and Zaslow, 78), then the stimuli of the printed page during the process of learning to read may not be merged into concepts but remain a "succession of object like beads on a string" (Russell and Groff, 62). Furthermore, if a teacher believes that early reading experiences consist of acquiring "mechanics" of reading, then the teacher may aim to develop this ability by calling upon memorization, rather than higher thought processes (Gans, 19), but if a teacher does stress conceptualization by grouping stimuli into common elements, pupils will tend to attain greater transfer (Gates, 20); or, despite the organization of instruction, pupils who have the capability may still achieve the necessary generalizations (Carroll, 13, 14).

Concomitantly with the development of a word-recognition-substrata, an individual learns to associate meanings, the residuals of his experiences with the referents of the symbolic stimuli, to the transformation of the printed symbols. These associations are fused or arranged into thought sequences and integrated into a broader working system of symbolic reasoning. If a communications network is developmentally established and integrated, then there can be cumulative transfer of meaning from the kinesthetic to the auditory and the visual modalities (Holmes, 33). Consequently, a conceptual system could be formed by selecting and interrelating meanings across these modalities. Then, this conceptual system could be mobilized for responding to stimulus input through the kinesthetic, auditory, or visual modalities (Singer, 63; Singer and Balow, 70).[2]

Defined from the above theoretical analysis, reading is a processing skill that consists of a) transformation of printed stimuli into a word-recognition-substrata, b) association of meaning to the transformed stimuli, c) synchromeshing of a) and b) into a harmonious working system. This working system is a momentary organization of substrata processes that is controlled by the demands of the task-stimuli, the individual's level of maturity in reading, his purposes, his values (Holmes, 34; Athey, 2), and his biological support system (Davis, 15). Thus, through a succession of working systems, the individual is able to attain speed, comprehension, and power in reading. Interference, faulty functioning, or failure in any of the above subsystems, a), b), or c), serves to reduce achievement in speed and/or power of reading.

The remainder of this paper will be divided into three sections to explain in greater detail how conceptualization may operate in the interrelated subsystems of 1) word recognition, 2) word meaning, and 3) reasoning-in-context. In each of these broadly defined subsystems of general reading ability, flexibility in conceptualization will also be explicated.

Word Recognition

In the early stages of learning, the individual is confronted with a wealth of unfamiliar details which require fine discriminations for consequent perceptual accuracy and conceptual adequacy. Errors in responses to words at this primary level of development can often be attributed to perceptual immaturity, inadequate functioning of perceptual processes, incompletely developed word recognition concepts, or some combination of these factors. For example, a child may not be able to discriminate the fine differences between *e* and *o*, especially when these letters occur in the middle of a word and have to be discriminated from the other letters, as well as from each other, as in the words *net* and *not*. Or he may not have a correct kinesthetic or orientational concept of the so-called reversal letters of *b, d, p, q, u,* and *n.* Further errors may result from inadequate auditory discrimination of vowels, as in *pan* and *pin,* in which the slight change in pitch may not reach the level of awareness for some children.

The kinds of errors and their frequencies might not only arise from determinants within the individual, but also from interaction between these determinants and the method of instruction (Bond, 5; Fendrick, 18). If an individual with a sensory deficiency is exposed to a method of instruction which requires proficiency in that same sensory mode but is not able to compensate through a self-acquired method nor has had instruction adapted to his major mode of learning, he is likely to accumulate a disability in reading, in addition to a *negative* learning set in this area.

In diagnosing word recognition errors, care must be taken not to confuse various levels within a particular mode. For example, an individual may have good auditory acuity, that is, a peripheral auditory system in good functioning order, but his auditory conceptual system may not be operating adequately or at a sufficiently mature level to enable an individual to learn to respond well through that mode. In other words, an individual may have satisfactory acuity, but lack of ability to organize the auditory stimuli, as Kyme (44) has demonstrated. Although Kyme's study was in the area of musicality or aesthetic judgment, there is some evidence that there may be analogous levels of functioning for language in the auditory modality (Singer, 63). The discrepancy between peripheral and central functioning or integration in the auditory mode may also be true in the kinesthetic and visual modes.

Characteristics of Task-Stimuli and Modes of Conceptualization

Because of the nature of printed stimuli of language and his capabilities, the individual can learn to conceptualize such verbal stimuli through emphasis upon different modes, such as auditory, visual, kinesthetic, or a combination. That is, some aspects of printed language can be sounded out and auditorily grouped, such as *see, tea,* tidy; other parts of words may have identical letter configurations, such as *light, sight, right,* and can be organized into visual concepts; and all printed stimuli have characteristic lines or curves which the eye can follow and integrate into a general response because of kinesthetic features (Hebb, 28), such as the up-and-down-and-across characteristics in *tree, ate,* boat.[3]

However, any one word does not necessarily fit into a particular conceptual category, nor do two individuals necessarily develop the same conceptual responses or organization of responses. When a word does fall into multi-categories, an individual may form and draw upon several concepts and coordinate them into a working system to solve the word recognition task. For example, the word "right" may have an auditory unit or phonogram, "ri;" a visiogram, "gh" (silent); and a phonogram, "t," for one person, but another individual may have developed a larger gestalt, "r" and "ight." Still another person may perceive this word by its entire configuration and respond to it by means of a "whole word" process. Whatever concepts are formed, an individual will have to organize them into a working system to meet the demands of the task-stimuli.

Flexibility in word recognition. Conceptualizations in different modes enable a reader to recognize words in a variety of ways. Multimodal conceptualization of responses to words is necessary since words and parts of words do not fit into any one mode. Thus, if an individual starts to sound out a word, he may find that he has to stop at *a particular* boundary-point within the word because the next part could not be integrated as an auditory component; then, if he has the necessary visual or kinesthetic concept, he can utilize it. Finally he has to blend or synthesize all his responses together to form the whole word. In some instances a reader may fill in a missing word by calling upon his word sense. The conditions necessary for flexibility are a) a variety of processes that can be organized into a working system appropriate to the task-stimuli, b) a mental process which enables an individual to sense the necessity for shifting from one process to another, or to resolve discrepancies that may arise from a narrow response unit by calling upon a broader conceptual response, c) a fairly evenly developed cross-section of abilities, and d) a growing feeling of confidence in and mastery over the processes involved in learning to read.

Obviously, if an individual has only one approach, he can not shift to another. If he encounters a barrier to his one technique, he must stop because he has no other approach to circumvent the barrier or to make it permeable. For example, an individual may have a phonetic approach which works very well with c-a-t and such words, if properly applied, but which will not function with r-i-g-h-t. Or an individual may be able to sound out "ri," but reaches a barrier for "gh" if he systematically tries to sound out each letter. However, he may be able to circumvent this barrier if he knows "ight" as a phonovisiogram or he may be able to break the barrier if he knows the visiogram "gh" (silent) and passes on to the last letter of the word.

Even if an individual does have a broad word-recognition-substrata of phonics, syllabification, affixes, blending, and rhyming processes, he must also have some mechanism which institutes a reorganization of his word-recognition-substrata. If he does not reorganize, then he might persistently bump against the barrier. Sometimes in oral reading a child may be observed as he reaches such a barrier; instead of shifting to another approach, he backs up to the beginning of the sentence, as though he were going to get a running start of context clues to overcome the barrier by sheer ideational force.

The mechanism or process which institutes the switching or reorganization process might be termed "flexibility-in-manipulating-verbal-symbols." A necessary component of this process is the ability to generalize or conceptualize within limits appropriate to the task-stimuli of each mode. At the extremes of this conceptual span are the overgeneralizer and the undergeneralizer (Zaslow, 78).

The overgeneralizer, the person whose generalization within a particular mode is very broad, will tend to be frustrated in certain situations. For example, he may recognize correctly meat and seal, but not bread, if his generalization includes *all* vowel combinations of "ea," instead of only those which do not follow "r." Bright children may be in this classification early in learning (Carroll, 13, 14).

The undergeneralizer, the person whose concept in a particular mode is narrow, will tend to have difficulty in recognizing words, even though they are in his hearing or meaning vocabulary, which he might have recognized if his concept were broader. For example, the undergeneralizer might recognize seat, but not be able to recognize beat, even though he is able to substitute consonants, that is, he may not have developed a category for "*eat*." He might consequently think that the word recognition processes for each word are unique. This approach is probably characteristic of certain brain-damaged individuals who lack capacity for conceptualization.

The flexible generalizer, the person whose concept is inclusive but within appropriate boundaries, will tend to apply his concept when appropriate but shift to another readily when the first does not apply. For example, he may have acquired the concept that when two vowels are together, as in boat, the first vowel says its name and the second is silent, but he knows there are exceptions, such as "pneumatic" or "oil."

Differences in mode of conceptualization. Differences exist not only *between* individuals in each mode, but also within the *same* individual. Kling (42), for example, computed a correlation for college students of .03 between auditory and visual discriminations for nonverbal stimuli.

Comparison of individuals on any one aspect of word recognition results in a distribution whose shape reflects the general level of maturity for that process. At the fourth grade, for instance, knowledge of letter sounds is negatively skewed (Gates, 22) because this ability has already reached maturity in most of the subjects. But syllabification, a process still being developed at the fourth grade, yields a normal curve of distribution.

Measurements made repeatedly on the same individual in all three modes would probably reveal intraindividual differences in learning mode; over a period of time, these measurements would theoretically reveal a gradient-shift from kinesthetic-to-auditory-to-visual dominance in mode of learning ability (Holmes, 31). However, individuals, in general, do not necessarily need to develop to perfection in any one word recognition process. Instead, by means of a combination of fairly well developed skills in the various processes or modes, they can achieve sufficient accuracy in word recognition so that they are not handicapped at all *in transforming any word into mental processes for the purpose of arousing and associating meaning.* [4]

Emotional and personality factors. The degree of stress which an individual feels he is under while reading will tend to influence the breadth of his "cognitive map" (Tolman, 73). For example, in reading orally he might feel unduly self-conscious and consequently be very sensitive to his errors. These feelings, in turn, could feed back into and constrict his mental processes. This constriction would then operate against fluency in reorganization or selection of alternate routes required by the characteristics of the task-stimuli. But, under less emotion-provoking conditions, such as in silent reading, when he found himself blocked in one approach, he is more likely, if he has the necessary abilities, to fluently reorganize his word-recognition-substrata and mobilize a working system that is more appropriate for solving the particular word recognition task. Of course, a basic assumption for this flexibility is that the individual had been taught or had learned multiple routes to the goal of success in word recognition.

However, sometimes experiences in emotion-provoking situations may perseverate or be aroused in silent reading situations. For example, a child might have learned from a perfectionist, a teacher or parent or both, and as a consequence might feel that he is unable to read whenever he could not transform all the stimuli into corresponding oral responses that perfectly match the characteristics of the stimuli. Then, in reading silently, even at the 95 percent level of word recognition accuracy or at a level at which he could accurately attain ideas from the material, he would still not read with a feeling of enjoyment or satisfaction, for he would tend to recall the voice-of-conscience whenever he stumbled or slurred over a word.

At the other extreme, a permissive or laissez-faire atmosphere, could also result in inaccurate responses to printed words. In this environment an individual might not acquire the necessary motivation to make fine discriminations between and within words. Furthermore, the individual in this learning atmosphere might not receive sufficient correction for his errors. Because of this lack of motivation and feedback, the individual might be hindered from developing a learning set (Harlow, 27) for improving his word recognition abilities.

Fixation in development of word recognition. If an individual's ability in one area is disproportionately better developed than his abilities in other word recognition processes, he is likely to use his most developed ability, whether or not it is appropriate to the task-stimuli; that is, he might leap-before-looking, so to speak. Consequently, such an individual would continually experience frustration, until his other word recognition abilities had developed to the point where they could be mobilized into a working system for attaining word recognition.

However, some individuals might become fixated at a particular level of development in word recognition. For example, such an individual might use a combination of context, whole word recognition, or spelling, if the first two did not work. Because this combination could work for many words, he might not feel the necessity for expanding his repertoire of word recognition abilities.

Although a "gradient-shift" (Holmes, 31) might be a general characteristic of development towards maturity in which an individual reorganizes his word recognition processes and shifts from an inefficient to a more efficient and effective method of processing stimuli (Gates, 21; Singer, 66), a fixated individual would not fit into this developmental process. The manifestation would show up mostly in speed of reading. However, there could also be an interference in comprehension or in continuity of thought because an excessive concentration of energy had been utilized in overcoming word-barriers and because a maximum span of attention had been surpassed.

Summary on word recognition. Normal development of a word recognition subsystem is dependent upon adequately functioning kinesthetic, auditory, and visual perception and conceptual processes, plus an integrated and flexibly operating intercommunications network among these processes (Holmes, 33; Singer, 63). Facilitation of this development results not only from conceptualization of responses to printed stimuli, but also from considerable practice and experience in a moderately motivating and emotionally satisfying atmosphere for learning to read. Under these organismic and environmental conditions, an individual could form highly organized and flexible word-recognition-substrata which function so harmoniously and rapidly that the processes mobilized for this subsystem not only psychosynchromesh but also require a minimum of mental energy. Therefore, a maximum of mental energy could be devoted to the reasoning-in-context aspects of reading.

However, when a strange or unfamiliar word does appear, an individual has to mark time in his mental processing of the content and switch most of his mental energy to the operation of his word-recognition-substrata. This reduces his speed of reading and may interfere in his comprehension to the extent that he will have to re-read (Bayle, 4). When he has built a bridge over this gap in the continuity of his word-recognition-processing, the reader can then switch most of his mental energy back to his reasoning-in-context substrata or processes that are mobilized for attaining the central thought, integrating dispersed ideas, inferring from explicit or implicit premises in a passage, and such processes that go beyond word recognition and association of meaning to the recognized words.

Word Meaning

If an individual can recognize words, but not have any meaning to associate with these words, the result is known as "word calling." That is, an individual could learn to recognize a word as a whole word, or grasp the word from context, or utilize some combination of word-recognition-processes to transform it, but be unable to associate meaning to it, not because of some lack of association process (Holmes, 33) but because he simply has not had experience, direct or vicarious with the referent or referents of the word. Consequently, meanings for words should be developed concomitantly or even ahead of their appearance in reading material so that the word-recognition-substrata and the meaning-substrata can be integrated. However, in general, at about age 11, development of word recognition surpasses the development of meaning (Gates *et al.*, 24).

Some linguistic elements, such as affixes and roots, have generalized meaning, which can be utilized not only for unlocking the meaning of a word by analyzing it into its constituent elements and then synthesizing these elements (Hunt, 40) but also can be integrated into the word-recognition-substrata. Consequently these linguistic elements have a dual function.

In the early stages of learning to read, pictures may also enter into the two subsystems of word recognition and word meaning. They may serve as clues for word recognition and enable an individual to recall and associate a word with its object-referent. But, the picture is only a cue to some intermediate verbal transformation. That is, the individual must learn to make a verbal response to the picture and this verbal response then mobilizes the necessary word recognition or word meaning reaction.

Prior to the sixth grade, auditory cues for responses to pictures, as measured by a "reading capacity" test (Durrell and Sullivan, 17; Alden, 1), lead the individual to mobilize a quantitatively if not qualitatively different mental organization from that which is mobilized for response to a visual verbal type of reading test, such as the Gates Reading Survey (Singer, 63, 69). After the fifth grade, the two subsystems of listening comprehension and reading achievement, as assessed by the above types of tests, tend to merge. A possible hypothesis for this merger consists of two components: normally during the early stages of learning to read, the individual a) gradually develops his word-recognition-substrata and b) slowly acquires a greater degree of intercortical facilitation and communication between his auditory and visual modalities. When the developmental gradients of these two processes merge at the sixth grade level, the individual can not only transform printed stimuli into ideas at any level, concrete, functional, or verbal-conceptual, in accordance with the context and his level of intelligence, but he can also receive increased stimulation

from his auditory modality. Therefore, he can better associate his listening vocabulary with his word recognition processes and his reading vocabulary.

Reasoning-in-Context

As an individual develops word-recognition-substrata to overcome
the barrier presented by words in the form of printed symbols, he becomes increasingly able to use reading as a means of acquiring facts,
forming concepts, and relating them as generalizations (Brownell and
Hendrickson, 7). That is, he uses his reasoning-in-context substrata, an
organized working system of mental abilities and processes, to learn from
the printed page.

In a modern instructional program, word-recognition-substrata,
word-meaning-substrata, and reasoning-in-context substrata are developed simultaneously. But, as a result of mental capability, training, and
practice, the time and mental energy required for word-recognition-
substrata in the process of reading gradually decrease while the time and
energy employed for word-meaning-substrata and reasoning-in-context
substrata gradually increase. This development eventually reaches a point
where the mature and competent reader is relatively unconscious of the
organization and dynamics of his word-recognition-substrata as he reads.
He is almost unaware of the processes because his word recognition
subsystems are effectively mobilized, efficiently synchromeshed, and,
when necessary, flexibly and readily reorganized in response to the
stimuli of the printed page and his motivation in reading. Consequently
he can then focus his mental energy upon comprehending the ideas
conveyed by the words. Thus, he can read rapidly and fluently, unhin-
dered by barriers to word recognition, and only limited by his word-
meaning-substrata and his ability to reason-in-context.

Conceptual ability enters not only into the formation of word-
recognition-substrata but also operates in word-meaning-substrata and in
reasoning-in-context-substrata. For, as he reads, an individual can inductively form concepts (Werner and Kaplan, 77), hierarchically integrate previously formed concepts (Long and Welch, 49), deductively
"verify and strengthen the structure of a concept" (Russell, 61:162),
reorganize a concept (Brownell, 6) or create concepts (Leeper, 48). An
individual can thus use reading as one means of developing his concepts
from "simple to complex, concrete to abstract, undifferentiated to differentiated, discrete to organized, and from ego-centric to more social"
(Russell, 61:249).

Speed and/or power of reading require not only fluency in word
recognition but also flexibility in conceptual organization (Murphy, 54), in

addition to other types of flexibility (Laycock, 45, 46, 47). That is, to comprehend some passages an individual not only has to conceptualize, but he also has to change, modify or reorganize a previously formed concept. For example, a young child could have learned through his experience that home is a place where parental conflict exists. When he reads a story about parental relationships, he might find that the ideas in this story do not coincide with his concept of home. If he persists with this experientially-determined generalization, he might not "get it," re-read the passage to clarify the meaning (Bayle, 4), or even continue to read with the conflict unresolved. Consequently, lack of conceptual flexibility could adversely affect his speed and/or power of reading. For either reading component, the effect may be exhibited more at the judgmental or evaluative than at the factual level (McKillop, 51).

Another element of flexibility is the ability to shift from one concept to another in the process of reading. That is, a competent reader selects the relevant words and organizes them into concepts; he also uses previously formed concepts in responding to the material. The flexible reader modifies his conceptual span and appropriately shifts from one idea to another. If he has an overly broad span, he will probably attempt to include too much of the material into his concept and encounter confusion; if he has a narrow span, he will tend to exclude material and perhaps not arrive at a concept but only a sequence of events. In either extreme, the reader will not form the intended idea. In general, the ability to form an optimum span and adequate conceptual level is a function of mental age and normal developmental processes (Zaslow, 78).

Thus, in learning to read, an individual with the necessary capacities can develop a conceptualized mediational response system. Then, in accordance with his purposes and the demands of the task-stimuli, he can mobilize this system together with other subsystems into a mental organization for attaining speed and power of reading. Although each individual forms a working system that is composed of his unique strengths and weaknesses, he must mobilize at least minimum amounts of certain common subsystems, if he is to read at all (Holmes and Singer, 36, 38). Consequently, each individual's working system varies around a basic, developmental working system that is the common route to maturity in speed and power of reading (Buswell, 11; Holmes, 30; Singer, 63, 66; Holmes and Singer, 36, 38).

Summary and Implications

A theoretical formulation of the role of conceptualization in the acquisition of reading behavior was presented and an attempt was made to integrate this theoretical formulation with the substrata-factor theory of reading.

Theory is designed not only for explanation, but also for prediction (Singer, 68). Already plans have been made to test at the kindergarten level the predictive validity of an instructional strategy based upon the above theoretical formulation (Singer and Balow, 70). Eventually, a longitudinal investigation should be undertaken to test the developmental implications of this theory of conceptualization in learning to read. In the meantime, the theory can be used as a cognitive guide for teaching reading (Singer, 64, 65, 66, 67).

REFERENCES

1. Alden, Clara L., Helen B. Sullivan, and D. D. Durrell, "The Frequency of Special Reading Disabilities," *Education*, 62:32-39, September, 1941.
2. Athey, Irene, *Reading Personality Patterns at the Junior High School.* Unpublished doctoral dissertation, University of California, Berkeley, 1965.
3. Barnard, Maryline, *Reading Disability and Levels of Perceptual Efficiency: An Experimental Study.* Unpublished doctoral dissertation, University of Southern California, 1958.
4. Bayle, Evalyn L., "Nature and Causes of Regressive Eye Movements in Reading," *Journal of Educational Psychology*, 11:16-35, September, 1942.
5. Bond, Guy L., *The Auditory and Speech Characteristics of Poor Readers,* Teachers College Contributions to Education, No. 657, 1935.
6. Brownell, W. A., "Learning as Reorganization: An Experimental Study in Third Grade Arithmetic," *Duke University Research Studies in Education*, No. 3, 1939.
7. Brownell, W. A., and G. Hendrickson, "How Children Learn Information, Concepts, and Generalizations," *Yearbook of the National Society for the Study of Education*, 49: Part 1, 1950.
8. Bruner, J., *A Study of Thinking*, New York: Wiley, 1956.
9. Bruner, J., "The Course of Cognitive Growth," *American Psychologist*, 19:1-15, January, 1964.
10. Bruner, J. and Oliver, Rose., "Development of Equivalence Transformations in Children," *Monographs of the Society for Research in Child Development*, 28:125-143, 1963.
11. Buswell, Guy T., *Fundamental Reading Habits: A Study of Their Development*, Supplemental Educational Monographs, No. 21, 1922.
12. Cameron, N., "Reasoning, Regression, and Communication in Schizophrenics," *Psychological Monographs*, 50: No. 1, 1938.
13. Carroll, Herbert A., "Generalization of Bright and Dull Children: A Comparative Study with Special Reference to Spelling," *Journal of Educational Psychology*, 21:489-499, October, 1930.
14. Carroll, Herbert A., *Generalization of Bright and Dull Children*, New York: Teachers College Contributions to Education, Columbia University, Bureau of Publications, No. 439, 1930.
15. Davis, Frank R., "The Substrata-Factor Theory of Reading: Human Physiology as a Factor in Reading." In J. A. Figurel (Editor), *Proceedings of the Ninth Annual Conference of the International Reading Association*, 1964, 292-296.
16. Durrell, D. D., "The First Grade Cooperative Studies: History." In J. A. Figurel, *Reading and Inquiry. Proceedings of the Tenth Annual Convention of the International Reading Association*, Newark, Delaware, 1965.
17. Durrell, D. D., and Helen B. Sullivan, *Manual for Durrell-Sullivan Reading Capacity Test*, New York: World Book, 1937.
18. Fendrick, P., *Visual Characteristics of Poor Readers.* Teachers College Contributions to Education, No. 656, 1935.

19. Gans, Roma, *A Study of Critical Reading Comprehension in the Intermediate Grades*, Teachers College Contributions to Education, No. 811, 1940.

20. Gates, Arthur I., *Generalization and Transfer in Spelling*. New York: Teachers College, Columbia University, Bureau of Publications, 1935.

21. Gates, Arthur I., *The Improvement of Reading*, New York: MacMillan, 1947.

22. Gates, Arthur I., *The Manual of Directions for Gates Reading Diagnostic Test*. New York: Teachers College, Columbia University, Bureau of Publications, 1953.

23. Gates, Arthur I., "The Word Recognition Ability and the Reading Vocabulary of Second and Third Grade Children," *Reading Teacher*, 15:443-448, May, 1962.

24. Gates, Arthur I., G. L. Bond, and D. H. Russell, "Relative Meaning and Pronunciation Difficulties of the Thorndike 20,000 Words," *Journal of Educational Research*, 32:161-167, November, 1938.

25. Goldstein, K., and M. Scheerer, "Abstract and Concrete Behavior: An Experimental Study with Special Tests," *Psychological Monographs*, 53: No. 2, 1941.

26. Hanfmann, Eugenia, and J. A. Kasanin, "Conceptual Thinking in Schizophrenics," *Nervous Mental Disorders Monographs*, No. 67, 1942.

27. Harlow, Harry, "The Formation of Learning Sets," *Psychological Review*, 56:51-65, 1949.

28. Hebb, D. O., *Organization of Behavior*, New York: John Wiley, 1949.

29. Heidbreder, Edna, "Toward a Dynamic Psychology of Cognition," *Psychological Review*, 52:1-22, January, 1945.

30. Holmes, Jack A., *Factors Underlying Major Reading Disabilities at the College Level*, Unpublished doctoral dissertation, University of California, Berkeley, 1948.

31. Holmes, Jack A., *The Substrata-Factor Theory of Reading*, Berkeley, California Book, 1953. (Out of Print)

32. Holmes, Jack A., "Factors Underlying Major Reading Disabilities at the College Level," *Genetic Psychology Monographs*, 49:3-95, February, 1954.

33. Holmes, Jack A., "The Brain and the Reading Process." In Claremont College, *Reading is Creative Living, Twenty-Second Yearbook of the Claremont Reading Conference*. Claremont, California: Curriculum Laboratory, 1957, 49-67.

34. Holmes, Jack A., "Personality and Spelling Ability," *University of California Publications in Education*, 12:213-292, 1959.

35. Holmes, Jack A., "The Substrata-Factory Theory of Reading: Some Experimental Evidence." New Frontiers in Reading, *Proceedings of the Fifth Annual Conference of the International Reading Association*. New York: Scholastic Magazines, 1960, 115-121.

36. Holmes, Jack A., and Harry Singer, *The Substrata-Factor Theory: The Substrata Factor Differences Underlying Reading Ability in Known Groups*. Final report covering contracts 538 and 538A, Office of Education, U.S. Department of Health, Education, and Welfare, 1961.

37. Holmes, Jack A., and Harry Singer, "Theoretical Models and Trends Toward More Basic Research in Reading," *Review of Educational Research*, 34:127-155, April, 1964.

38. Holmes, Jack A. and Singer, Harry, *Speed and Power of Reading in High School*. U.S. Department of Health, Education, and Welfare: Office of Education. A publication of the Bureau of Educational Research and Development. Superintendent of Documents, Catalog No. FS 5.230:30016. U.S. Government Printing Office, Washington, D.C. 20402, 1966.

39. Hull, Clark L., "Quantitative Aspects of the Evolution of Concepts," *Psychological Monographs*, No. 123, 1920.

40. Hunt, Jacob T., "The Relation Among Vocabulary, Structural Analysis, and Reading," *Journal of Educational Psychology*, 44:193-202, April, 1953.

41. Jan-Tausch, James, "Concrete Thinking as a Factor in Reading Comprehension." In J. A. Figurel (Editor), *Challenge and Experiment in Education*, Proceedings of the Seventh Annual Conference of the International Reading Association, 1962, 161-164.

42. Kling, Martin, *Auditory and Visual Discriminations*, Unpublished Master's thesis, University of California, Berkeley, 1956.

43. Kress, R. A., *An Investigation of the Relationship Between Concept Formation and Achievement in Reading*, Unpublished doctoral dissertation, Temple University, 1955. *Dissertation Abstracts*, 16:573-574, 1956.

44. Kyme, George H., *The Value of Aesthetic Judgments in the Assessment of Musical Capacity*, Unpublished doctoral dissertation, University of California, Berkeley, 1954.

45. Laycock, Frank, *An Experimental Study of Flexibility in Reading Rate Among Candidates for College Matriculation*. Unpublished doctoral dissertation, University of California, Berkeley, 1947.

46. Laycock, Frank, "Flexibility in Reading Rate and Einstellung," *Perceptual and Motor Skills*, 8:123-129, June, 1958.

47. Laycock, Frank, "The Flexibility Hypothesis in Reading and the Work of Piaget." In J. A. Figurel (Ed.), *Challenge and Experiment in Education*, Proceedings of the Seventh Annual Conference of the International Reading Association, New York: Scholastic Magazines, 1962, 241-243.

48. Leeper, R. W., "Cognitive Processes," In S. S. Stevens (Ed.), *Handbook of Experimental Psychology*. New York: Wiley, 1958, 730-757.

49. Long, L., and L. Welch, "The Higher Structural Phases of Concept Formation in Children," *Journal of Psychology*, 9:59-95, January, 1940.

50. Long, L., and L. Welch, "Influences of Levels of Abstractness on Reasoning Ability," *Journal of Psychology*, 13:41-59, January, 1942.

51. McKillop, Anne S., *The Relationship Between the Reader's Attitude and Certain Types of Reading Responses*. New York: Teachers College, Columbia University, Bureau of Publications, 1952.

52. MacKinnon, Archie R., *How Do Children Learn to Read?* Toronto: Copp, Clark, and Company, 1959.

53. Morris, C. W., *Signs, Language and Behavior*, New York: Prentice-Hall, 1946.

54. Murphy, P. G., "The Role of the Concept in Reading Ability," *Psychological Monographs*, 44:21-73, 1933, No. 3.

55. Nielsen, J. M., *A Textbook of Clinical Neurology*, New York: Paul B. Hoeber, 1951.

56. Osgood, Charles, *Method and Theory in Experimental Psychology*, New York: Oxford University, 1956.

57. Piaget, J., "Principal Factors Determining Intellectual Evolution from Childhood to Adult Life." In *Factors Determining Human Behavior, Harvard Tercentenary Conference of Arts and Sciences*, Cambridge: Harvard University, 1937, 32-48.

58. Reed, H. B., "Factors Influencing the Learning and Retention of Concepts—I. The Influence of Set." *Journal of Experimental Psychology*, 36-71-87, 1946.

59. Reichard, Suzanne, M. Schneider and D. Rapaport, "The Development of Concept Formation in Children," *American Journal of Orthopsychiatry*, 14:156-162, January, 1944.

60. Robinson, Helen M., "Perceptual and Conceptual Style Related to Reading," In J. A. Figurel (Ed.), *Improvement of Reading Through Classroom Instruction*, Proceedings of the Ninth Annual Conference of the International Reading Association, 1964, 26-28.

61. Russell, David H., *Children's Thinking*, New York: Ginn, 1956.

62. Russell, David H., and Patrick J. Groff, "Personal Factors Influencing Perception in Reading," *Education*, 75:600-603, May, 1955.

63. Singer, Harry, *Conceptual Ability in the Substrata-Factor Theory of Reading*, Unpublished doctoral dissertation, University of California, 1960.

64. Singer, Harry, "Substrata-Factor Theory of Reading: Theoretical Design for Teaching Reading," In J. A. Figurel (Ed.), *Challenge and Experiment in Reading*, Proceedings of the Seventh Annual Conference of the International Reading Association, New York: Scholastic Magazines, 1962, 226-232.

65. Singer, Harry, "Substrata-Factor Evaluation of a Precocious Reader," *Reading Teacher,* 18:288-296, January, 1965.

66. Singer, Harry, *Substrata-Factor Reorganization Accompanying Development in Speed and Power of Reading.* Final report on Project No. 2011, U.S. Office of Education, 1965.

67. Singer, Harry, "A Theory of Human Learning for Teaching Reading: A Discussion of Professor Arthur Staats's 'Integrated Functional Learning Theory for Reading,' " in Albert J. Kingston (Ed.), *Use of Theoretical Models in Research,* Newark, Delaware: International Reading Association, 1966.

68. Singer, Harry, "Symposium on the Substrata-Factor Theory of Reading: Research and Evaluation of Critiques," In J. A. Figurel (Ed.), *Reading and Inquiry,* Tenth Annual Convention of the International Reading Association, Newark, Delaware: International Reading Association, 1965.

69. Singer, Harry, "Validity of the Durrell-Sullivan Reading Capacity Test," *Educational and Psychological Measurement,* 125:479-491, Summer, 1965.

70. Singer, Harry, and Irving H. Balow, *Evaluation of a Horizontal vs. Vertical Reading Readiness Program,* Research Proposal for Extramural Funds, University of California, Riverside, 1965. (Multilith)

71. Smith, Nila B., *American Reading Instruction,* Newark, Delaware: International Reading Association, 1965.

72. Smoke, Kenneth, "An Objective Study of Concept Formation," *Psychological Monographs,* 42, No. 4 (Whole No. 191), 1932.

73. Tolman, Edward, "Cognitive Maps in Rats and Men," *Psychological Review,* 55:189-208, 1948.

74. Triggs, Frances O., "The Development of Measured Word Recognition Skills, Grade Four Through the College Freshman Year," *Educational and Psychological Measurement,* 12:345, 349, Autumn, 1952.

75. Vinacke, W. E., "The Investigation of Concept Formation," *Psychological Bulletin,* 48:1-31, 1951.

76. Werner, H., and Doris Garrison, "Perceptual Behavior of Brain-Injured and Mentally Defective Children: An Experimental Study by Means of the Rohrschach Technique," *Genetic Psychology Monographs,* 31:51-110, 1945, No. 2.

77. Werner, H., and Edith Kaplan, "The Acquisition of Word Meaning: A Developmental Study," *Monographs of the Society for Research in Child Development,* 15, No. 1 (Whole No. 51), 1950.

78. Zaslow, Robert W., *A Study of Concept Formation in Brain Damaged Adults, Mental Defectives and Normals of Different Age Levels,* Unpublished doctoral dissertation, University of California, Berkeley, 1957.

NOTES

[1] Such a wide range of approaches to teaching reading in the first grade now exists that 27 somewhat different studies at this grade level were supported by the U.S. Office of Education at a total cost of approximately $600,000 (Durrell, 16).

[2] Bruner's (9) identification of enactive, iconic, and symbolic modes of representation is similar to the above formulation of kinesthetic, auditory, and conceptual modalities.

[3] An appropriate name for kinesthetically formed images of printed stimuli, the writer suggests, is "kinesthetograms."

[4] This hypothesis may explain Triggs's (74) otherwise puzzling results. Triggs reported that mean scores from a cross-sectional investigation on syllabication and rhyming, subtests of the Diagnostic Reading Test, rose steadily through the twelfth grade. Performance on these variables dropped slightly from grade 12 to college, however, while comprehension still continued to improve.

Word Recognition

S. JAY SAMUELS
University of Minnesota

For the past century, psychologists have exhibited consistent curiosity about the word recognition processes. During this period, there have been heated controversies among researchers concerning answers to a number of important questions about word recognition. For example, some of these sharp differences of opinion have centered on questions such as: What is the size of the visual span? Does a good reader take in more letters in a single fixation than a poor reader? What is the visual unit used in word recognition? Does phonological recoding take place in word recognition? When reading scripts in different languages such as English in contrast to Chinese, are different neural pathways in the brain used? Do different scripts impose different cognitive demands on memory systems? These are just a few of the questions for which one can find a variety of answers, and these questions will be addressed in this article.

If psychology is a science in which there is reliability of measurement, one wonders why researchers have provided us with such conflicting answers to our questions. How can the information derived from careful experimentation lead to such divergent views? In the first part of this article on word recognition, I will attempt to explain the underlying reasons which led to these sharp differences about word recognition. Next, I will propose an alternative approach to the study of word recognition which has the potential for resolving some of the conflicts. Third, I will address a number of major questions about the nature of word recognition. Finally, there will be a brief presentation of findings about word recognition with scripts which are not based on the alphabetic principle, such as those used by the Chinese. For those who wish additional information on word recognition, I recommend two outstanding reviews on this topic: the first is Gough's (1984) and the second is Henderson's (1982).

Why We Have Controversies Regarding the Word Recognition Process

To understand why we have divergent views on important questions about the word recognition process, we have to go back to 1879, a date which many consider to be the birth of modern academic psychology. It was in this year that Wundt established the first psychological laboratory in Leipzig, Germany. According to Wundt, the proper goal of psychology was to gain an understanding of how the human mind worked. The method he advocated for this task was introspection. Unfortunately, despite the brilliant and innovative research of this early period of psychological research, psychology faced several important problems, not the least of which was the low esteem with which it was held by the majority of the academic community.

Consequently, one of the major objectives of the early psychologists was to improve the status of their discipline. The 1913 and 1925 publications of J.B. Watson, the father of behaviorism, were designed to elevate psychology to the realm of a respected science. Watson's publications had a tremendous impact on psychology and contributed in large measure to our current theoretical conflicts. According to Watson, in order to elevate the status of psychology, psychologists had to imitate the goals and methods of the highly respected "hard" sciences, and in order to do this, psychologists had to depart from the teachings of Wundt. Three goals were outlined by Watson. First, psychology had to abandon the introspective methods advocated by Wundt because introspective methods were unreliable. Second, psychologists were to focus on stimuli and responses which were external to the human mind, because these could be measured with accuracy and consistency. Third, and most important to our understanding of why there are such differences of opinion on issues such as the word recognition processes, psychologists were advised to search for universal laws of behavior which could generalize across species and contexts, just as those in the hard sciences were searching for the general laws of the universe.

In quest of the Holy Grail of universal laws, psychologists investigated reinforcement, punishment, and extinction using species as diverse as pigeons, rats, and humans and devices as different as Skinner boxes, mazes, and memory drums, rewarding with food and conditioned reinforcers, all in the belief that general principles and laws could be found that would hold true across species, tasks, and contexts. Unfortunately, although this quest for universal laws in psychology seems destined for the cemetery of unfulfilled dreams, its ghost lives on to haunt us to this day. By the early 1960s, reports were entering the psychological literature indicating limitations to universal psychological principles. Breland and Breland (1961) described how the application of operant conditioning principles failed to break a raccoon of its habit of washing its face prior to eating because its genetic programing was more powerful than the operant training technology. Other researchers reported that behaviors that can be reinforced are those which occur naturally with that species, while other behaviors that are not natural seem to be suppressed by reinforcement.

Discoveries that certain behaviors could not be trained in particular species led Johnston (1981) to write: "...the general process view of learning, which guided research into learning for the first half of this century, has come under attack from several quarters in recent years. One form of criticism has come from the proponents of the so-called biological boundaries approach to learning. These theorists have presented a variety of data showing that supposedly general laws of learning may in fact be limited in their applicability to different species and learning tasks, and they argue that the limitations are drawn by the nature of each species' adaptation to the particular requirements of its natural environment" (p. 125).

A somewhat different criticism of the attempt to hammer out a psychology of universal principles on the anvil of experimental science comes from those who note that many of the conflicts in psychology and education result from failure to pay attention to the interactive nature of the variables which are found in all experiments. In every experiment there are four variables which interact and influence each other. These variables are the materials used in the study, the experimental task which the subject must perform, an individual difference variable representing the skill level which the subject brings to the task, and context. If any one of the variables is changed, there is a high probability that the outcome of the study will be altered.

To illustrate how experimental outcomes are altered by changing one of the four interacting variables, we can examine some examples drawn from what we know about word recognition (Samuels and Kamil, 1984). Imagine how the size of the visual unit used in recognizing words might change depending on the task. Let us assume that the reader is skilled and the text contains common words. When the task is proofreading for spelling errors, the unit of word recognition is probably the letter, whereas when reading for meaning the unit is probably the word. The skill of the reader appears to influence the size of the unit used in word recognition in that as reader skill increases there is a commensurate increase, up to some limit, in the size of the visual recognition unit. Not only is word recognition influenced by reader skill and the task being performed, but as every teacher and user of readability formulas knows, the reading process is influenced by the difficulty of the materials. When low frequency uncommon words are used, comprehension is not as good as when high frequency common words are used. Finally, context also exerts an effect on word recognition. For example, words may be presented in isolation or in context, as in "blood" vs. "red blood"; "sky" vs. "blue sky"; or "pepper" vs. "salt and pepper." Context seems to facilitate both accuracy and speed of word recognition. Thus, with these examples we have seen how each of the four variables—individual differences in reader skill, the task one is asked to perform, the materials, and context—can exert an effect on word recognition.

From this brief discussion of how alterations in the major interactive factors in an experiment can influence experimental outcomes, it becomes clear why we have conflicts on many psychological issues, including the word recognition process. As long as psychologists try to discover universal laws which can generalize across species, tasks, materials, and contexts, we will continue to have these problems. We cannot gather data on word recognition from college students and assume that our generalizations will be valid for children. Nor can we limit ourselves to one text, task, or context and hope to draw conclusions which will have broad generality.

If we wish to make continued progress in our field, we will have to abandon our attempt to find simple, universal laws which can generalize across a variety of populations, conditions, and tasks. Instead, we will have to specify the conditions under which particular processes occur. Our experiments will have to examine the developmental trends which occur in reading, and we will have to systematically investigate how the reading process is altered when we vary materials, tasks, and contexts. Only by engaging in these painstaking investigations will we be able to resolve some of the conflicts which we now face, and only then will we have a better understanding of the reading process.

Factors Which Influence Word Recognition

The perceptual span. The number of letters or words that can be taken in in a single fixation has obvious implications for any account of how words are recognized. Researchers such as Gibson and Levin (1975), Haber (1978), and Patberg and Yonas (1978) have suggested that the size of the perceptual span increases along with reading ability, and that the difference between skilled and less skilled readers may be understood in terms of the size of the perceptual span. However, other researchers such as McConkie and Rayner (1976) and Underwood and Zola (1984) contest these conclusions.

A number of different methods have been used to study the extent of the perceptual span. One of the simplest methods has been to divide the number of words read by the number of eye fixations. When this method is used, researchers have found that with increasing skill across grades one through twelve, there is an increase in the size of the span, with beginning readers averaging .5 words a fixation and adult readers about 1.5 words (Harris, 1941; Spragins, Lefton, and Fisher, 1976; Taylor, Frackenpohl, and Pettee, 1960). The shortcoming with this method is that an assumption is made that with each fixation there is no overlap of print; when, in fact, there may be considerable overlap. If the assumption is false, then conclusions drawn from the use of this method may be incorrect.

Another method used to study perceptual span uses a tachistoscope, a device which can expose printed matter for a predetermined time period. The brief exposure of the material, usually about 250 milliseconds, which is an approximation of the duration of an eye fixation when reading, is used to simulate a reading fixation. With this method, Marcel (1974) found that good readers reported more information than did poor readers. However, the limitation encountered with tachistoscopic presentation is that following the exposure, the amount of visual information on the retina of the eye fades extremely rapidly. By the time the experimental subject cognitively processes the information and reports what was seen, much of the information has been lost (Sperling, 1960).

Eye-voice span (EVS) also has been used to measure perceptual span. This technique involves having the subject read aloud and estimating how far behind where the eyes are looking the voice is trailing. One method involves removing the light from the page when the subject says a particular word during the oral reading and measuring how many more words can be read. Another method uses an eye tracker and simultaneously records where the eye is looking and what is being read. The EVS technique was reported as early as 1897 by Quantz, who found that the span varied from individual to individual, with better readers having a larger EVS. With the EVS technique, Morton (1970) found that good readers have a larger EVS than poor readers, and Levin and Kaplan (1970) have stated that good readers see more in a fixation. With nongrammatical strings of words the EVS across all ages is 2.19 words and for grammatical strings it is 3.91 words. With grammatical strings, the EVS for second graders is 3.19 words and for adults it is 5.02 words (Gibson and Levin, 1975, p. 363). Since the time duration between the blacking out of a page and the time the oral reading stops is of the order of 640-700 milliseconds, and the usual fixation when reading is about 250 milliseconds, a not unreasonable assumption is that the voice may be trailing by two eye fixations. Once again, a limitation of this method is that successive eye fixations may have considerable overlap, and the eye may be no more than one eye fixation ahead of the voice.

A fourth method used to measure perceptual span has the subject focus on a point while words are presented at brief durations to the left and right of the point. Although McKeever and Huling (1970) reported no difference in the size of the field with good and poor readers, a later study by Bouma and Legein (1977) found that the visual field is smaller for poor readers than for good readers. When English words are shown, more reading material is seen in the right visual field than in the left. For a time, the explanation offered for this asymmetry was that the structure of the brain favored printed material to the right side of the point of focus. But when Miskin and Forgays (1952) presented English words (written from left-to-right) and Yiddish words (written from right-to-left) to either side of a fixation point, they found that with Yiddish words more was seen to the left of fixation and with English more was seen to the right of fixation. Obviously, the visual asymmetries were not the result of how our brains are constructed but the result of an internal scanning mechanism that is under reader control. For English, the mechanism goes from left to right and for Hebrew, from right to left.

Another strategy which has been used to study perceptual span alters the text in some way, such as omitting the spaces between words by filling the spaces with a character. A number of studies have supported the hypothesis that better readers are using information from a larger span than poor readers (Fisher, Lefton, and Moss, 1978; Spragins, Lefton, and Fisher, 1976; Patberg and Yonas, 1978).

The most sophisticated technique for studying the perceptual span uses a computer controlled visual display which can alter the text at any distance to the right and left of fixation while the subject is reading. By noting at what distance from the point of focus changes in the regular text produces disruption in reading, the researchers are able to infer the size and symmetry of the span. Using college students, Underwood and McConkie (1984) found that text alterations more than four letter spaces to the left of fixation or eight or more spaces to the right had no effect on reading. This finding, that the recognition span is asymmetric, supports the earlier report of McConkie and Rayner (1976), and indicates that the perceptual span of college students who were reading newspaper articles is about twelve letter spaces. Underwood and Zola (1984) had fifth graders who were reading at grade 5.5 or higher or 4.5 or below read texts at a readability level of grade three. Contrary to what others have reported, Underwood and Zola found no difference in the size of the span between good and poor readers, the size being about two letter spaces to the left of fixation and up to six or seven spaces to the right, a span which is somewhat smaller than that found for college students.

That the perceptual span is about nine letter spaces and that there does not seem to be a difference in the size of the span between good and poor readers may appear to contradict findings in the next section on the visual unit used in word recognition. To understand this discrepancy, I should point out that there is a difference between the amount of visual information from the page that the eye takes in and the amount that the brain can process for meaning. Anderson and Dearborn (1952, p. 135) wrote: "Other studies have established the fact that good readers have a wider span than poor readers, but only if meaningful materials are used. These studies have not demonstrated that good and poor readers differ appreciably in the size of their span for nonsense material. Such results indicate that the real problem is not that poor readers suffer a narrow span per se, but they do not get the same meaning from material as good readers." Thus, the difference between good and poor readers may not be in the size of the perceptual span but in the amount of meaning that can be obtained in a fixation, a distinction which may be useful for understanding why there are differences between the size of the perceptual span and the visual unit of word recognition.

Visual unit of word recognition. The size of the visual unit used in word recognition is a topic over which there has been considerable difference of opinion for about a century. In 1885 Cattell designed an ingenious device known as a tachistoscope which exposed printed matter for a brief period of time. Using highly skilled readers, he had them read words or letters which were exposed for only 10 milliseconds. At that exposure duration, he found they could recognize only three to four unconnected letters, or two unconnected words, or four contextually connected common words. He concluded that words are read as wholes, not letter by letter. His conclusion was of great interest to educators in the United States who during this pre-1900 period were engaged in a pedagogical battle over the spelling method of reading instruction versus the look-and-say method. Educators who favored the look-and-say method used Cattell's finding to support their whole word method, completely ignoring the fact that findings drawn from highly skilled readers might be completely inappropriate for beginning readers.

Even during the infancy of academic psychology, researchers disagreed about the unit of word recognition. Erdmann and Dodge (1898) concluded that the unit was the whole word, because in their experimental work they found that when a word is degraded, whole words can be recognized whereas the component letters can not. Zeitler (1900), on the other hand, came down on the side of letter processing, and thought that the belief that one was reading an entire word was an illusion resulting from long practice and familiarity with reading. With the characteristic insight which has made Huey's (1908, p. 81) book on the *Psychology and Pedagogy of Reading* a classic text read to this day, he commented "...the more unfamiliar a sequence of letters may be, the more the perception of it proceeds by letters. With increase of familiarity, fewer and fewer clues suffice to touch off the recognition of the word or phrase, the tendency being toward reading in word wholes. So reading is now by letters, now by groups of letters or by syllables, now by word wholes, all in the same sentence sometimes, or even in the same word, as the reader may most quickly attain his purpose."

The controversy continues to this day. One of the more influential studies in support of holistic processing was done by Reicher (1969). In his study which used skilled readers, a tachistoscope flashed a common four-letter word such as CART and the word was followed immediately by a masking stimulus. It is assumed that the masking stimulus will halt any further processing of the previously presented word. Following the mask, two test letters such as "T" and "P" were shown and the subject's task was to decide which of the two letters had appeared in the word. What was especially clever about this study was that either of the test letters made a meaningful word as in "CART" or "CARP". The control condition was to present letter "T" by itself, followed by the mask, and then the two test letters appeared "T" and "P." Thus, the comparison was one of finding out if letter perception was better when the letter was in the word or when it was in isolation. Surprisingly, letter perception was superior in a word than in isolation. Other studies have substantially supported the word superiority effect (Wheeler, 1970; Thompson and Massaro, 1973).

Additional studies on the word superiority effect produced new and important information which helps us to understand Reicher's finding. Johnston and McClelland (1973) and Juola, Leavitt, and Choe (1974) found that the word superiority effect disappeared when no mask was used. Furthermore, the mask had greater interference effects on the single letter than on the whole word (Bjork and Estes, 1973; Massaro and Klitzke, 1979). Thus, the word superiority effect can be considered an artifact produced by the mask. Once again, we see that variation in one of the four variables which influence an experiment can have serious effects on the experimental outcome.

Gough, whom many consider to be the leading advocate of the component-letter process view of reading, states in his excellent review of word recognition, "But, it is surely significant, if not ironic, that the best accounts currently available of the word superiority effect, an effect thought to show that word recognition could not be mediated by letter recognition, assume that it is....Thus, the current state of our understanding of word recognition accuracy is that word recognition is mediated by letter recognition." Several of Gough's studies support his conclusion. In one study, skilled readers were presented words one at a time which varied in length. The reader's task was to say the word as soon as it was recognized and speed of recognition was measured. Stewart, James, and Gough (1969) found that the amount of time between the presentation of the word and the beginning of its pronunciation increased steadily along with word length in letters, from 615 milliseconds for three-letter words to 693 milliseconds for ten-letter words, suggesting that each increase of a letter added an additional 10-20 milliseconds to the word recognition processing time.

In another study by Gough and Stewart (1970), readers were given a string of letters and their task was to decide if the letter-string comprised a word. Again, one of the variables which was manipulated was word length and reaction time was measured. They found that four-letter strings were recognized as words about 35 milliseconds faster than six-letter words, a finding which was consistent that each additional letter adds an additional 10-20 milliseconds of processing time. Assume that the average word is seven letters long. With read-out at the rate of 10-20 milliseconds a letter, and with the duration of a fixation lasting for about 250 milliseconds, Gough estimates that reading speed should be about 300 words a minute.

Gough (1972) offers a succinct description of stages in word recognition. Following a fixation, the visual information from the page forms an image — or icon — on the retina of the eye. This information is read out of the icon as letters at the rate of about 10-20 milliseconds a letter. Any grouping of the letters into digraphs, syllables, or spelling patterns would occur at a later stage of processing. Thus, this process begins with the formation of an icon. Next, there is a stage when the letters are read out, and a stage when the letters are organized and grouped into patterns and then processed for meaning. Gough's description of stages in word recognition resembles Gilbert's (1959), who stated that the fixation pause served three functions. First, information is transmitted more efficiently when the eye is at rest than when it is in motion. Second, if two visual inputs come too close together in time, the second input can mask and erase the first input. Third, processing the input for meaning takes time, and part of the fixation pause is devoted to comprehension.

Still other methods have been used to understand what the visual unit is in word recognition. At the University of Minnesota we have been studying the unit of word recognition using a method which is conceptually similar to that used by Cattell and Gough. The reasoning behind this method is that if words are read letter by letter, then long words should take more time to recognize than short words, but if words are read as holistic units, then the amount of time it takes to recognize a word should be independent of its length. In our studies, we present words which vary in length from three to six letters, and the subject's task is to indicate with a button press if the word is an animal word. These words are common words which are carefully selected so that each word-length category is controlled for word frequency. Our first study presented words in isolation to college students and we measured accuracy and response latency on the button press. With this task, the subjects must identify the word, process its meaning, and make a decision as to whether it falls into the designated "animal" category. We found no difference in response latency for three to six letter words for the words which were presented in regular print, implying that the words were processed as holistic units. However, when the words were shown in mirror-image, we found an increase in response latency along with increase in word length, indicating that the mirror image words were being processed by their component letters (Terry, Samuels, and LaBerge, 1976). This study indicated that skilled readers had two ways to process the words, as holistic units when the words were familiar and through their component letters when the script was unfamiliar.

A second study examined developmental trends in the size of the visual unit used in word recognition. In this study, exactly the same task was given only now the subjects were in grades two, four, six, and college and all the words were in regular print. We found component letter processing in grade two, a transition between component and holistic processing for grade four, and holistic processing in grade six and college (Samuels, LaBerge, and Bremer, 1978). Thus, with increase in skill, the size of the visual unit of recognition increased. By grade six, holistic processing was occurring and the only difference between the sixth graders and the college students was that the more skilled college students were faster at recognizing the words.

Whereas the two studies just described presented words in isolation, a third study examined the effect of context or no context (Example: LOUD SOUND vs. xxxx SOUND), grade level (grades two and four), and reader skill (poor vs. good readers) on the unit of word recognition (Patberg, Dewitz, and Samuels, 1981). Rather than use a button push, this study used voice onset to measure word recognition latency. We found that good and poor second grade readers used component letter processing in the context and no context condition. Good fourth grade readers used holistic processing in all conditions. The most interesting results came from the poor fourth grade readers who, like the fourth graders in the Samuels, LaBerge, and Bremer (1978) study, seemed to be in a transition between component and holistic processing. The poor fourth grade readers did component letter processing in the no context condition, whereas in the context condition they switched to holistic processing. To summarize these studies on the unit of word recognition, they indicate that beginning readers are limited to the use of component letter processing while the skilled reader has the option to use either holistic or component letter processing.

In the studies which present words in isolation, it is obvious that for the beginning reader the most significant recognition cues are the component letters in the word. However, it is not so clear what the cues are for the skilled reader who does holistic processing. While the data indicates that the word is processed holistically, one might speculate about what cues are embedded within the word which might lead to its recognition. Several likely candidates come to mind. Embedded in the word are letter, configuration, and length cues; recent research by Haber, Haber, and Furlin (1983) indicate that adults use all of these cues. However, a study by Feitelson and Razel (1984) found that configuration cues were of little use to beginning readers. In all probability, when skilled readers encounter common words which have been learned to automaticity, there is simultaneous rather than sequential processing of the embedded information, which would account for the finding of holistic processing.

Of course, one can wonder why it is that when skilled readers are presented words in isolation and the words vary in length some of the studies reported letter-by-letter and others reported holistic processing. Subtle differences in the task requirements between the experiments may hold the answer to this question. In Gough's procedure a spoken response was required whereas in some of the experiments done at Minnesota a button push on a semantic categorization task was required. Second, in a semantic categorization task (Example: Are these animal words?), the words presented come from a very restricted range of the total body of English words, and the subject in the experiment is primed, as it were, to anticipate words from a particular semantic category. In Gough's procedure, which only requires a spoken response, the words presented come from an enormously larger population of words and so, no priming occurs. Again, we note how variations in any of the interactive factors in an experiment may influence its outcomes.

Context effects on word recognition. While on the surface there seems to be agreement over context effects on word recognition, just a bit of digging reveals some rather sharp differences of opinion about its importance. To reveal the nature of these differences, I will examine beginning and skilled stages of reading.

Goodman's study (1965) of word recognition for words in isolation and in context must be classified as one of the most influential studies ever published on beginning reading. In this study students in grades one, two, and three were first asked to read a list of words in which each word was in isolation. Then the students were asked to read the same words when they were part of a story. Word recognition errors were recorded for words in isolation and in context. Goodman's tables show that many words missed in isolation were read correctly in context and the facilitating effect of context increased along with grade level. In this study, however, there is an important procedural flaw. In every case, the student first read words in isolation and then read the same words in context. Is it not possible that the first reading in isolation provided the necessary practice for the words in context and that the improvement in the context condition is partly the result of the previous practice? A subsequent study by Negin (1977) tested this possibility. He found that first reading a list of words did produce a practice effect. Without the practice effect, context provided some help but not as much as Goodman reported.

Biemiller's (1970) study indicates that context plays a role in early reading. Based on his observations of reading errors of first grade children, he proposed three stages in reading development. First, there was a context dependent stage where word substitution errors fit the context of the sentence but not the orthographic-phonological form of the target. Second, there was a nonresponse stage, and finally, a stage where substitution errors are context driven and have some relationship to the printed word (the printed word is "lamp" and the student says "light").

Weber (1970), who also worked with first graders, found that when errors were made, if the error did not upset the meaning of the sentence, it was usually ignored, but when errors created an ungrammatical sentence, about 60 percent of them were self-corrected. What differentiated good and poor readers was that when an ungrammatical sentence was created, good readers corrected the error about twice as often as did the poor readers.

In a study of the effect of context on word recognition, Samuels, Begy, and Chen (1975) had college students and fourth graders recognize tachistoscopically flashed words which were in isolation or in context. As in the Weber (1970) study, Samuels found if an error was made, the skilled college reader was more aware of it than was the less skilled fourth grader. This study also examined the word recognition abilities of good and poor fourth grade readers. Given context and a word fragment from the target word (Example: high chxxx, black shxxx, bright lxxxt), the good readers were better able to generate the target word. However, it should be pointed out that this process of generating a target word was a very slow process. In beginning reading, where many of the words in a text are likely to be new to the student, the ability to use multiple sources of information such as context, letter information, and configuration cues may provide valuable help in word recognition. Another finding of interest in this study was that context does not always have a facilitating effect because it can miscue a word recognition response. If the student anticipated "cold snow" and instead the text was "cold sky," the subject often gave the anticipated response without even realizing that an error had been made. On the other hand, if the anticipated context and the text matched, speed of word recognition was significantly faster.

Similar findings on facilitation and inhibition were found in a recent study in which second and sixth graders named words preceded by either congruous, neutral, or incongruous contexts, that were either one or three sentences long. West, Stanovich, Feeman, and Cunningham (1983) found that naming time for a target word was facilitated or inhibited, depending on the type of preceding context. Naming time was not influenced by the length of the prior context, suggesting that contextual effects are intrasentence. The fact that context effects were larger for second than for sixth graders has important implications for the understanding of the role of context, as we shall see shortly.

Investigations which have studied the effect of context have generally found a facilitating effect on accuracy and speed with unskilled readers, providing there is a match between one's anticipation and the text and the student is able to use multiple sources of information such as letters, configuration, and length cues. One may wonder what the effect of context is with skilled readers who have developed automatic high-speed word recognition skills. In general, results with skilled readers are similar to those found with children (Tulving and Gold, 1963; Meyer, Schvaneveldt, and Ruddy, 1975), that is, depending on the congruence between an anticipation and the text, context may either facilitate or impair recognition accuracy and speed.

While laboratory studies with skilled readers indicate that context can have a facilitating effect on word recognition, it would be incorrect to think that in real reading, as done outside the experimental situation, similar facilitation would also occur. In studies where both the context and target are tachistoscopically presented and the subject must say the target word, the context may remain on the screen for a considerable period allowing the time necessary to generate a prediction of what may follow, and following the flash of the target word, there is time again to make a decision. In real reading, the skilled reader does not ordinarily attempt to predict the next word from context nor does one stop to think if the anticipated word actually matches the word in the text. It is only when there is a comprehension breakdown that we regress to attempt to locate the source of the problem.

Another method used to study contextual effects on word recognition utilizes what is called a lexical decision task. With this method a printed stimulus is shown (Example: NURSE) and a button is pushed to indicate if it is a word. Accuracy and response latency are recorded. The target word, NURSE, may be preceded by context (Example: DOCTOR-NURSE) or it may be presented in isolation. Use of this method has demonstrated that context may facilitate or retard recognition, depending on the match between one's expectation and the target word (Meyer et al., 1975). One should be cautious about generalizing findings from lexical decision tasks to a real reading situation, however, because the semantic priming which takes place in this task would not ordinarily occur in a real reading situation. As Gough (1984, p. 245) points out, every investigation of context effects has used noun targets which appear at the end of a string of words, a situation which is not representative of the real world of real texts. In addition, a study by Gough (1983) on the predictability of content words in real text found that one could predict with accuracy only about 10 percent of the time.

Despite the weaknesses of the experiments, we have learned a substantial amount about the role of context on word recognition. The usefulness of context increases when there is difficulty recognizing the target word either because the student is a poor reader or the target word is degraded in some way. On the other hand, if the reader is skilled and the target word is easily discriminated, there is no need to depend on context. Thus, there seems to be a trade off between the reliance on context and reliance on information from the target word itself. In recognition of this interaction between information from context and information from the target word, Stanovich (1980) has proposed an interactive-compensatory model of word recognition which states that the reader will utilize contextual information in order to compensate for difficulties in word recognition. This explains why context has a greater role to play in the lower grades where the students are not highly skilled in word recognition. The skilled reader faced with the task of recognizing familiar words has little need to rely on context partly because predictions are unreliable and the time it takes to generate a prediction is usually greater than the time necessary to recognize the target word.

Au and Singer (1985) had good and poor readers identify target words in predictable context, incongruous context, and in isolation. When the target words were equally familiar for both good and poor readers there were no differences in the processes they used to identify them. Adams and Huggins (1985) reached a similar conclusion.

Phonological recoding in word recognition. While I sit at my desk and look across the campus I can see students, buildings, and trees. My recognition of these objects seems to be direct, with no need to recode to inner speech. On the other hand, as I read difficult technical material or even, at times, my morning newspaper, I get the impression that I am subvocalizing. Whether phonological recoding is a necessary component of the word recognition process is an issue which has received considerable attention.

Although subvocalization and phonological recoding are conceptually similar they are not identical. Subvocalization refers to inner speech while reading which may range from whispering to silent inner speech which can be recorded only with electromyographic (EMG) instrumentation placed directly on the vocal cords. Phonological recoding, on the other hand, refers to a theory of how meaning is accessed from print (Rubenstein, Lewis, and Rubenstein, 1971). According to this theory, the journey from print to meaning is a two step process. Step one consists of recoding the sequence of letters in a word to their abstract representations as phonemes. Step two consists of searching one's mental dictionary for a match between the phonological recoding and the dictionary entry. When the two are matched, the word is recognized. Thus, the difference between the two terms is that one refers to a physical act which is directly measurable while the other refers to abstract hypothetical constructs.

Research on inner speech has a long history. As far back as 1908 Huey stated that although subvocalization was a component of the reading process, it should not be considered an essential element because people could read with understanding while engaging in behaviors which were thought to inhibit inner speech, such as whistling. However, it is possible to whistle and subvocalize while reading, so this procedure does not provide an appropriate test. More recently, both Edfeldt (1960) and McGuigan (1970), who used the EMG technique, found that subvocalization occurred regularly with reading and it increased along with the text difficulty.

In the belief that subvocalization reduces reading speed, there have been attempts to suppress it by providing uncomfortable auditory feedback to a reader; the more subvocalizing there is, the more painful the feedback (McGuigan, 1970). Studies showed that the subvocalization could be suppressed but the effect was temporary. As soon as the feedback was omitted or the difficulty of the material was increased, the students reverted back to inner speech while reading. With easy passages, suppressing the subvocalization did not seem to interfere with comprehension, but with difficult material, comprehension suffered when inner speech was suppressed.

There have been several studies which throw some light on the phonological recoding hypothesis. One method employs what on the surface appears to be a purely visual search task. A page of text is given and the subject is asked to cross out every letter "e" on the page. Corcoran (1967) found that silent letter "e" as in "the" or "skate" was missed nearly four times as often as a pronounced "e" as in "seat." In a subsequent study, the letter "e" was deleted from text and the subject was asked to insert them where they were missing. Again, Corcoran (1967) found that significantly more silent "e"s were missed than pronounced "e"s. It seems that in a purely visual task, subjects were recoding, and it was easier to detect the "e" when it was pronounced.

Another method has utilized homophones. These are real words which are spelled differently but sound alike, as in *blue/blew* or *steak/stake* or we may have a sentence such as "The bouy and the none sore a pear of bear feat in there rheum." A pseudohomophone is a nonword (Example: *sprane* or *nife*) which when pronounced, sounds like an English word. The rationale for using homophones to test the phonological recoding hypothesis is that if the two-stage phonological recoding hypothesis is correct, it should make no difference how a word is spelled because once the printed letter string is phonologically recoded to an English word and the word is in the mental lexicon, then we should be able to understand the sentence or word. The test of the phonological recoding hypothesis requires that we present pseudohomophones and see if they are accepted as real words.

In a lexical decision task, it should be harder to reject letter strings like *sprane* and *nife* as nonwords (because when recoded they sound like real words) than letter strings such as *sprede* or *nade* (because when they are recoded they do not sound like real words). In a lexical decision task using pseudohomophones like *sprane* and controls like *sprede*, Rubenstein et al. (1971) found support for the phonological recoding hypothesis because it took longer to reject the pseudohomophones than the controls. While this study provides some support for the recoding hypothesis, it does not tell the whole story because in the sentence about "The bouy and the none..." even though the sentence is pronounced normally, the spelling seems to interfere with comprehension. If access to the lexical code is mediated only through the phonological code, why does the unusual spelling impair comprehension? Is it possible that in word recognition we have a "two to go" situation where both the visual and phonological codes must be appropriate for the intended meaning? Leaving conjecture aside, the studies reviewed in this section strongly suggest that subvocalization and phonological recoding occur in normal reading. The questions of whether there can be direct access to meaning through the visual code without phonological mediation is still unanswered, and if it does occur, under what conditions? At one time it was thought that nonalphabetic Oriental written languages such as Chinese might provide a suitable model for direct access to meaning, but as we shall see, even these scripts require phonological recoding.

Word Recognition in Nonalphabetic Languages

Unfortunately, we become so immersed in our environments that we tend to forget that large segments of the world read using scripts which are very different from our own. Our models of word recognition are based almost exclusively on alphabetic languages, and in order to understand word recognition processes, we must examine how it occurs in nonalphabetic scripts such as the Chinese and Japanese use.

As creators of our symbol systems we also become the product of these systems. The variability found between scripts used to communicate thoughts may reflect more than mere culture. The scripts may reflect extraordinary important differences in cognitive styles, brain functioning, and ease of symbolic manipulation. Depending on which symbol system we use, our thinking may be blocked because the symbols used to represent concepts may be clumsy and require a great deal of our mental resources in order to hold them in memory and perform operations on them. For example, both the Roman number IX and the Arabic number 9 express the same concept, yet the Arabic symbols have proven to be more useful for mathematical thinking. Just as numerical symbol systems have proven to be more or less useful, the scripts used in reading can be evaluated across a variety of dimensions. Are there scripts which promote ease of initial learning? Are there scripts which are associated with reduced incidence of reading failure? Are there scripts which once mastered, facilitate comprehension? Are there scripts which are easier to learn to write? Are there scripts which lend themselves well to typing and commercial printing? And finally, are there scripts which can be understood across a variety of quite distinct dialects?

Just as there are different kinds of maps which represent political boundaries or surface features of the land, writing systems also can be differentiated by the manner in which the printed symbols represent or map on to the spoken language. Writing systems such as English are based on the alphabetic principle and individual letters or letter clusters represent surface features of the language such as individual speech sounds. These individual sounds, by themselves, carry no meaning. With the Chinese writing system, each symbol maps not onto a tiny speech segment but directly onto a concept or idea.

There are certain advantages as well as disadvantages associated with a script based on the alphabetic principle. In English, the student needs only to learn the letter-to-sound combinations for the twenty-six letters of the alphabet along with their digraphs (sch as in sch ool or gh as in rou gh) and the student can begin to sound out words. Learning to write letters of the alphabet is a relatively simple task, especially when beginning writing uses manuscript rather than the cursive form. Since only twenty-six letters are required, you can produce a typewriter keyboard which is of manageable size. An important disadvantage, however, to the use of alphabetic scripts is that since the letters map onto sounds used in a particular language, the written code can be understood only by people who speak the same language.

The Chinese have an ancient writing system. Incisions found on pottery, bones, and shells dug up in Bampo, a seven thousand year old neolithic village in Xian Province, have been identified as the direct precursor of modern Chinese script (Ho, 1976). As seen in Figure 1, going from left to right, one can trace the evolution of Chinese writing. At first the symbols reflected meaning as directly as possible by having the symbols look like the concept. There are some obvious disadvantages to this symbol system. Not everyone is a good artist, and abstract concepts are difficult to express. It is also obvious that the modern script is more abstract than the ancient script. Each abstract logograph or symbol maps directly onto meaning. For example, a symbol which looks like a tree (Y) has that concept. Two tree-like symbols side by side (YY) represent a wood, while three tree-like symbols (YYY) represent a forest. In addition to logographs, the Chinese also use pinyin to represent their spoken language. Pinyin, based on the alphabetic principle, uses English letters to represent the speech sounds used in Chinese words. Although several years ago the Chinese considered using pinyin to teach beginning reading, at the present time it is not in widespread use.

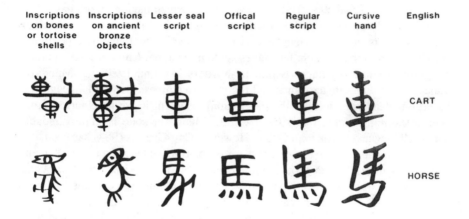

Inscriptions on bones or tortoise shells	Inscriptions on ancient bronze objects	Lesser seal script	Offical script	Regular script	Cursive hand	English
						CART
						HORSE

Figure 1. Shows evolution of Chinese script.

Ideograph /Phonetic/

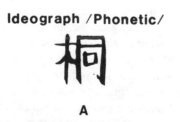

A

/Tong/

B

Figure 2A. The character shows both parts of a Chinese word. The part on the left of the character indicates its meaning, while the part to the right indicates its pronunciation.

Figure 2B. This element indicates only the pronunciation of the character.

There are some formidable problems connected with the use of a logographic symbol system. First, the Chinese dictionary has about 47,000 logographs; 3,000 of them are in common use. These 3,000 characters constitute the basic vocabulary necessary for being literate. To the beginning reader, the ability to visually discriminate and memorize this basic vocabulary presents a tremendous visual discrimination and memory task. Second, writing Chinese is also complicated. There are not many words which contain fewer than five strokes. Most contain eleven to twelve strokes, and the most complicated contain as many as thirty strokes. Developing a compact typewriter which can be used with some measure of speed has also been a problem. Since each Chinese word is represented by a separate symbol, and there are several thousand in common use, the keyboard of a Chinese typewriter is inconveniently large and typing speed is slow, at least by Western standards.

There is one area, however, where the Chinese logograph appears to have an advantage over alphabetic scripts. The advantage which the logograph has is that because the Chinese symbols represent concepts and ideas rather than the surface sound structure of any one language or dialect, the logograph should be understandable across the different languages spoken in China. China has seven mutually unintelligible languages within its borders. Around 1920, the Mandarin dialect became the lingua franca and the modern Chinese written language was based on Mandarin. Because the pictographic element in Chinese script represents meaning directly, this single written Mandarin code is understandable across all languages spoken in China. However, Chu-Chang (1984) has been able to demonstrate that to the extent that there is congruence between the written and spoken language, there is good comprehension, but if there is a mismatch, comprehension is impaired. Chu-Chang's experiments led her to conclude that even in a logographic writing system, there is speech recoding and that the logographic script is not as easily understood across different languages as had been thought previously.

There is evidence that there is speech recoding with logographic scripts. Approximately 80-90 percent of Chinese symbols are pictophonetic, consisting of a pictographic element to the left of the symbol which maps to meaning and a phonetic element to the right which represents an approximate pronunciation. Look at Figure 2 for example. The pictorial symbol on the left of Figure 2A means that it is a kind of tree, while the phonetic element to the right of 2A means that the word should be pronounced "tong," as in the symbol shown in Figure 2B. Tzeng and Wang (1983) have stated that in every writing system a reader always has access to the phonological information. A native speaker of Mandarin Chinese has difficulty reading a Cantonese newspaper, which uses the same logographs, but with different pronunciations. They claim that it may be more difficult for a Chinese or Japanese child to learn to convert script to sound automatically, owing to the fact that information about sound is not precisely given. The desire to develop automatic access to the pronunciation of the words is the reason for the emphasis on oral reading in Oriental schools. While it seems phonological recoding occurs with all codes, there is evidence that more takes place with alphabetic than with logographic codes (Treiman, Baron, and Luk, 1981).

It seems logical that learning to read with a logographic code as opposed to an alphabetic code would impose different demands on the human information processing system. Learning to read in Chinese should impose a heavier demand on visual discrimination and memory than learning an alphabetic code. In order to test these assumptions, native Chinese readers were compared with native English readers on the ability to recall the position of nine items in a series. Tzeng and Wang (1983) found that the Chinese were superior with the visually presented than with the auditorily presented list, while no such preference was found with the English speaker, thus supporting the hypothesis that learning to read with different scripts requires different strategies for recall of visual and auditory information.

The final issue in this section on reading in nonalphabetic languages pertains to how reading a logographic in contrast with an alphabetic script utilizes different parts of the brain. In order to study how different parts of the brain might be used to read with different kinds of scripts, Hung and Tzeng (1981) had Japanese words flashed either to the right or left of a fixation point. In terms of how words are processed by the hemispheres of the brain depending on whether they are to the right or left of a fixation point, words presented to the right of fixation are first processed in the brain's left hemisphere and words presented to the left of fixation are first processed in the brain's right hemisphere. Japanese writing uses two different writing systems. It uses logographs which represent meaning and a syllabary which is based on the alphabetic principle. When native Japanese speakers had the two types of words flashed to the left or right visual field, Hung and Tzeng found word recognition was better for logographs in the left visual field and for the syllabary in the right visual field. Thus, there is a right hemisphere advantage for the speech based syllabaries, indicating that different types of writing systems are favoring either left or right brain hemispheres. Somewhat similar findings come from the study of Japanese patients who have had brain injuries resulting in aphasia. Sasanuma (1974) found that patients with an injury to Broca's speech area of the brain lost the ability to read the alphabetic based syllabary but they could still read the logographs, whereas patients who had an injury to the back of the brain lost the ability to process the logographs but they could still read the syllabary. Clinical and experimental evidence reported by Hung and Tzeng as well as that provided by Sasanuma leads one to conclude that depending on the writing system one uses, different parts of the brain are called into use. Even this brief review of some of the factors which influence word recognition reveals that while we have learned a considerable amount about this process, there is much that we have yet to learn.

REFERENCES

Adams, M.J., and Huggins, A.W.F. The growth of children's sight vocabulary: A quick test with educational and theoretical implications. *Reading Research Quarterly*, 3 (1985), 262-281.
Anderson, I.H., and Dearborn, W.F. *The Psychology of Teaching Reading.* New York: Ronald Press, 1952, 135.
Au, R., and Singer, H. Developmental interactive word recognition hypotheses: Word recognition accuracy for third graders under variations in word familiarity and contextual conditions.

Paper submitted for publication, 1985.

Biemiller, A. The development of the use of graphic and contextual information as children learn to read. *Reading Research Quarterly,* 6 (1970), 75-96.

Bjork, E.L., and Estes, W.K. Letter identification in relation to linguistic context and masking conditions. *Memory and Cognition,* 1 (1973), 217-223.

Bouma, H., and Legein, C.P. Foveal and parafoveal recognition of letters and words by dyslexics and by average readers. *Neuropsychologia,* 15 (1977), 69-80.

Breland, K., and Breland, M. The misbehavior of organisms. *American Psychologist,* 16 (1961), 681-684.

Chu-Chang, M. Speech recoding revisited: Evidence from learning to read Chinese logographs, unpublished manuscript, Washington, D.C., 1984.

Corcoran, D.W.J. An acoustic factor in proofreading. *Nature,* 214 (1967), 851-852.

Edfeldt, A.W. *Silent Speech and Silent Reading.* Chicago: Chicago University Press, 1960.

Erdmann, B., and Dodge, R. Psychologische Untersuchungen über das Lesen, auf Experimenteller Grundlage. Halle, 1898.

Feitelson, Dina, and Razel, Micha. Word superiority and word shape effects in beginning readers. *International Journal of Behavioral Development,* 7 (1984), 359-370.

Fisher, D.F., Lefton, L.A., and Moss, J.H. Reading geometrically transformed text: A developmental approach. *Bulletin of the Psychonomic Society,* 11 (1978), 157-160.

Gibson, E.J., and Levin, H. *The Psychology of Reading.* Cambridge, MA: MIT Press, 1975.

Gilbert, L.C. Speed of processing visual stimuli and its relation to reading. *Journal of Educational Psychology,* 55 (1959), 8-14.

Goodman, K.S. A linguistic study of cues and miscues in reading. *Elementary English,* 42 (1965), 631-643.

Gough, Philip B. One second of reading. In J.F. Kavanagh and I.G. Mattingly (Eds.), *Language by Ear and by Eye.* Cambridge: MIT Press, 1972.

Gough, Philip B. Context, form, and interaction. In K. Rayner (Ed.), *Eye Movements in Reading: Perceptual and Language Processes.* New York: Academic Press, 1983.

Gough, Philip B. Word Recognition. In P. David Pearson (Ed.), *Handbook of Reading Research.* New York: Longman, 1984.

Gough, P.B., and Stewart, W.C. Word vs. nonword discrimination latency. Paper presented at Midwestern Psychological Association, 1970.

Haber, L.R., Haber, R.N., and Furlin, K.R. Word length and word shape as sources of information in reading. *Reading Research Quarterly,* 1983, 165-189.

Haber, R.N. Visual perception. *Annual Review of Psychology,* 29 (1978), 31-59.

Harris, T.L. A laboratory study of the relation of selected factors to the span of recognition in silent reading, doctoral dissertation, University of Chicago. Chicago: University of Chicago Press, 1941.

Henderson, Leslie. *Orthography and Word Recognition.* New York: Academic Press, 1982, 397.

Ho, P.T. *The Cradle of the East.* Chicago: University of Chicago Press, 1976.

Huey, Edmund B. *The Psychology and Pedagogy of Reading.* New York: Macmillan, 1908.

Hung, D.L., and Tzeng, O.J.L. Orthographic variations and visual information processing. *Psychological Bulletin,* 1981.

Johnston, J.C., and McClelland, J.L. Visual factors in word perception. *Perception and Psychophysics,* 14 (1973), 365-370.

Johnston, T.D. Contrasting approaches to a theory of learning. *Behavioral and Brain Sciences,* 4 (1981), 125-173.

Juola, J.F., Leavitt, D.D., and Choe, C.S. Letter identification in word, nonword, and single letter displays. *Bulletin of the Psychonomic Society,* 4 (1974), 278-280.

Levin, H., and Kaplan, E.L. Grammatical structure and reading. In H. Levin and J.P. Williams (Eds.), *Basic Studies on Reading.* New York: Basic Books, 1970.

Marcel, T. The effective visual field and the use of context in fast and slow readers of two ages. *British Journal of Psychology,* 65 (1974), 479-492.

Massaro, D.W., and Klitzke, D. The role of lateral masking and orthographic structure in letter and word recognition. *Acta Psychologica,* 43 (1979), 413-426.

McConkie, G.W., and Rayner, K. Asymmetry of the perceptual span in reading. *Bulletin of the Psychonomic Society,* 8 (1976).

McGuigan, F.J. Covert oral behavior during the silent performance of language tasks. *Psychological Bulletin,* 74 (1970), 309-326.

McKeever, W.F., and Huling, M.D. Lateral dominance in tachistoscopic word recognitions of children at two levels of ability. *Quarterly Journal of Experimental Psychology,* 22 (1970), 600-604.

Meyer, D.E., Schvaneveldt, R.W., and Ruddy, M.G. Loci of contextual effects on word recognition. In P.M.A. Rabbitt and S. Dornic (Eds.), *Attention and Performance.* New York: Academic Press, 1975.

Miskin, M., and Forgays, D.G. Word recognition as a function of retinal locus. *Journal of Experimental Psychology,* 43 (1952), 43-48.

Morton, J. The effects of context upon speed of reading, eye movements, and eye voice span. *Quarterly Journal of Experimental Psychology,* 16 (1964), 340-354.

Negin, Gary. The effects of reading ability and material difficulty on student's abilities to recognize words in isolation and in context, doctoral dissertation, 1977, University of Minnesota.

Patberg, J., Dewitz, P., and Samuels, S.J. The effect of context on the perceptual unit used in word recognition. *Journal of Experimental Psychology,* 13 (1981), 33-48.

Patberg, J.P., and Yonas, A. The effects of the reader's skill and the difficulty of the text on the perceptual span in reading. *Journal of Experimental Psychology: Human Perception and Performance,* 4 (1978), 545-552.

Reicher, G.M. Perceptual recognition as a function of the meaningfulness of stimulus material. *Journal of Experimental Psychology,* 81 (1969), 275-280.

Rubenstein, H., Lewis, S.S., and Rubenstein, M.A. Evidence for phonemic recoding in visual word recognition. *Journal of Verbal Learning and Verbal Behavior,* 10 (1971), 645-657.

Samuels, S.J., Begy, G., and Chen, C.C. Comparison of word recognition speed and strategies of less skilled and more highly skilled readers. *Reading Research Quarterly,* 1975, 72-86.

Samuels, S.J., and Kamil, M. Models of the reading process. *Handbook of Reading Research,* 1984, 185-221.

Samuels, S.J., LaBerge, D., and Bremer, C.D. Units of word recognition: Evidence for developmental changes. *Journal of Verbal Learning and Verbal Behavior,* 17 (1978), 715-720.

Sasanuma, S. Impairment of written language in Japanese aphasics: Kana versus kanji processing. *Journal of Chinese Linguistics,* 2 (1974), 141-157.

Sperling, G. The information available in brief visual presentation. *Psychological Monographs,* 43 (1960), 93-120.

Spragins, A.B., Lefton, L.A., and Fisher, D.F. Eye movements while reading and searching spatially transformed text: A developmental examination. *Memory and Cognition,* 4 (1976), 36-42.

Stewart, M.L., James, C.T., and Gough, P.B. Word recognition latency as a function of word length. Paper presented at Midwestern Psychological Association, 1969.

Taylor, S.E., Frackenpohl, H., and Pettee, J.L. EDL Research and Information Bulletin No. 3. Huntington, NY: Educational Developmental Laboratories, 1960.

Terry, P., Samuels, S.J., and LaBerge, D. The effects of letter degradation and letter spacing on word recognition. *Journal of Verbal Learning and Verbal Behavior,* 15 (1976), 577-585.

Thompson, M.C., and Massaro, D.W. The role of visual information and redundancy in reading. *Journal of Experimental Psychology,* 98 (1973), 49-54.

Treiman, R.A., Baron, J., and Luk, K. Speech reading in silent reading: A comparison of Chinese and English. *Journal of Chinese Linguistics,* 9 (1981), 116-125.

Tulving, E., and Gold, C. Stimulus information and contextual information as determinants of tachistoscopic recognition of words. *Journal of Experimental Psychology,* 66 (1963), 319-327.

Tzeng, Ovid J.L., and Wang, William S-Y, The first two Rs. *American Scientist,* 71 (1983), 238-243.

Underwood, N.R., and McConkie, G.W. Perceptual span for letter distinctions during reading. Unpublished manuscript, University of Illinois at Urbana-Champaign, 1984.

Underwood, N.R., and Zola, D. The span of letter recognition of good and poor readers. Unpublished manuscript, University of Illinois, 1984.

Weber, R.M. A linguistic analysis of first grade reading errors. *Reading Research Quarterly,* 5 (1970), 427-451.

West, R.F., Stanovich, K.E., Feeman, D.J., and Cunningham, A.E. The effect of sentence context on word recognition in second and sixth grade children. *Reading Research Quarterly,* 1983, 6-15.

Wheeler, D.D. Processes in word recognition. *Cognitive Psychology,* 1 (1970), 59-85.

Zeitler, Julius. Tachistoskopische versuche über das lesen. *Wundt's Philosoph. Studien,* Bd. 16, H. 3, 380-463.

An Interactive Activation Model of Context Effects in Letter Perception: Part 1. An Account of Basic Findings

JAMES L. MCCLELLAND
DAVID E. RUMELHART
University of California at San Diego

As we perceive, we are continually extracting sensory information to guide our attempts to determine what is before us. In addition, we bring to perception a wealth of knowledge about the objects we might see or hear and the larger units in which these objects co-occur. As one of us has argued for the case of reading (Rumelhart, 1977), our knowledge of the objects we might be perceiving works together with the sensory information in the perceptual process. Exactly how does the knowledge that we have interact with the input? And how does this interaction facilitate perception?

In this two-part article we have attempted to take a few steps toward answering these questions. We consider one specific example of the interaction of knowledge and perception—the perception of letters in words and other contexts. In Part 1 we examine the main findings in the literature on perception of letters in context and develop a model called the interactive activation model to account for these effects. In Part 2 (Rumelhart and McClelland, 1982) we extend the model in several ways. We present a set of studies introducing a new technique for studying the perception of letters in context, independently varying the duration and timing of the context and target letters. We show how the model fares in accounting for the results of these experiments and discuss how the model may be extended to account for a variety of phenomena. We also present an experiment that tests—and supports—a counterintuitive prediction of the model. Finally, we consider how the mechanisms developed in the course of exploring our model of word perception might be extended to perception of other sorts of stimuli.[1]

Basic Findings on the Role of Context in Perception of Letters

The notion that knowledge and familiarity play a role in perception has often been supported by experiments on the perception of letters in words (Bruner,

Reprinted from *Psychological Review*, 88 (1981), 375-407. Copyright 1981 by the American Psychological Association. Reprinted by permission of the publisher and the authors.

1957; Neisser, 1967). It has been known for nearly 100 years that it is possible to identify letters in words more accurately than letters in random letter sequences under tachistoscopic presentation conditions (Cattell, 1886; see Huey, 1908, and Neisser, 1967, for reviews). However, until recently such effects were obtained using whole reports of all of the letters presented. These reports are subject to guessing biases, so that it was possible to imagine that familiarity did not determine how much was seen but only how much could be inferred from a fragmentary percept. In addition, for longer stimuli, full reports are subject to forgetting. We may see more letters than we can actually report in the case of nonwords, but when the letters form a word, we may be able to retain as a single unit the item whose spelling may simply be read out from long term memory. Thus, despite strong arguments to the contrary by proponents of the view that familiar context really does influence perception, it has been possible until recently to imagine that the context in which a letter was presented influences only the accuracy of postperceptual processes and not the process of perception itself.

The perceptual advantage of letters in words. The seminal experiment of Reicher (1969) suggests that context does actually influence perceptual processing. Reicher presented target letters in words, unpronounceable nonwords, and alone, following the presentation of the target display with a presentation of a patterned mask. The subject was then tested on a single letter in the display, using a forced choice between two alternative letters. Both alternatives fit the context to form an item of the type presented, so that, for example in the case of a word presentation, the alternative would also form a word in the context.

Forced-choice performance was more accurate for letters in words than for letters in nonwords or even for single letters. Since both alternatives made a word with the context, it is not possible to argue that the effect is due to postperceptual guessing based on equivalent information extracted about the target letter in the different conditions. It appears that subjects actually come away with more information relevant to a choice between the alternatives when the target letter is a part of a word. And, since one of the control conditions was a single letter, it is not reasonable to argue that the effect is due to forgetting letters that have been perceived. It is hard to see how a single letter, once perceived, could be subject to a greater forgetting than a letter in a word.

Reicher's (1969) finding seems to suggest that perception of a letter can be facilitated by presenting it in the context of a word. It appears, then, that our knowledge about words can influence the process of perception. Our model presents a way of bringing such knowledge to bear. The basic idea is that the presentation of a string of letters begins the process of activating detectors for letters that are consistent with the visual input. As these activations grow stronger, they begin to activate detectors for words that are consistent with the letters, if there are any. The active word detectors then produce feedback, which reinforces the activations of the detectors for the letters in the word. Letters in words are more perceptible, because they receive more activation than representations of either single letters or letters in an unrelated context.

Reicher's basic finding has been investigated and extended in a large number of studies, and there now appears to be a set of important related findings that must also be explained.

Irrelevance of word shape. The effect seems to be independent of the familiarity of the word as a visual configuration. The word advantage over nonwords is obtained for words in lowercase type, words in uppercase type, or words in a mixture of uppercase and lowercase (Adams, 1979; McClelland, 1976).

Role of patterned masking. The word advantage over single letters and nonwords appears to depend upon the visual masking conditions used (Johnston and McClelland, 1973; Massaro and Klitzke, 1979; see also Juola, Leavitt, and Choe, 1974; Taylor and Chabot, 1978). The word advantage is quite large when the target appears in a distinct, high-contrast display followed by a patterned mask of similar characteristics. However, the word advantage over single letters is actually reversed, and the word advantage over nonwords becomes quite small when the target is indistinct, low in contrast, and/or followed by a blank, nonpatterned field.

Extension to pronounceable pseudowords. The word advantage also applies to pronounceable nonwords, such as REET or MAVE. A large number of studies (e.g., Aderman and Smith, 1971; Baron and Thurston, 1973; Spoehr and Smith, 1975) have shown that letters in pronounceable nonwords (also called pseudowords) have a large advantage over letters in unpronounceable nonwords (also called unrelated letter strings), and three studies (Carr, Davidson, and Hawkins, 1978; Massaro and Klitzke, 1979; McClelland and Johnston, 1977) have obtained an advantage for letters in pseudowords over single letters.

Absence of effects of contextual constraint under patterned-mask conditions. One important finding, which rules out several of the models that have been proposed previously, is the finding that letters in highly constraining word contexts have little or no advantage over letters in weakly constraining word contexts under the distinct-target/patterned-mask conditions that produce a large word advantage (Johnston, 1978; see also Estes, 1975). For example, if the set of possible stimuli contains only words, the context _HIP constrains the first letter to be either an s, a c, or a w; whereas the context _INK is compatible with 12 to 14 letters (the exact number depends on what counts as a word). We might expect that the former, more strongly constraining context would produce superior detection of a target letter. But in a very carefully controlled and executed study, Johnston (1978) found no such effect. Although constraints do influence performance under other conditions (e.g., Broadbent and Gregory, 1968), they do not appear to make a difference under the distinct-target/patterned-mask conditions of the Johnston study.

To be successful, any model of word perception must provide an account not only for Reicher's (1969) basic effect but for these related findings as well. Our model accounts for all of these effects. We begin by presenting the model in abstract form. We then focus on the specific version of the model implemented in our simulation program and consider some of the details. Subsequently, we turn to detailed considerations of the findings we have discussed in this section.

The Interactive Activation Model

We approach the phenomena of word perception with a number of basic assumptions that we want to incorporate into the model. First, we assume that perceptual processing takes place within a system in which there are several levels of processing, each concerned with forming a representation of the input at a different level of abstraction. For visual word perception, we assume that there is a visual feature level, a letter level, and a word level, as well as higher levels of processing that provide "top-down" input to the word level.

Second, we assume that visual perception involves parallel processing. There are two different senses in which we view perception as parallel. We assume that visual perception is spatially parallel. That is, we assume that information covering a region in space at least large enough to contain a four-letter word is processed simultaneously. In addition, we assume that visual processing occurs at several levels at the same time. Thus, our model of word perception is spatially parallel (i.e., capable of processing several letters of a word at one time) and involves processes that operate simultaneously at several different levels. Thus, for example, processing at the letter level presumably occurs simultaneously with processing at the word level and with processing at the feature level.

Third, we assume that perception is fundamentally an *interactive* process. That is, we assume that "top-down" or "conceptually driven" processing works simultaneously and in conjunction with "bottom-up" or "data driven" processing to provide a sort of multiplicity of constraints that jointly determine what we perceive. Thus, for example, we assume that knowledge about the words of the language interacts with the incoming featural information in codetermining the nature and time course of the perception of the letters in the word.

Finally, we wish to implement these assumptions by using a relatively simple method of interaction between sources of knowledge whose only "currency" is simple excitatory and inhibitory activations of a neural type.

Figure 1 shows the general conception of the model. Perceptual processing is assumed to occur in a set of interacting levels, each communicating with several others. Communication proceeds through a spreading activation mechanism in which activation at one level spreads to neighboring levels. The communication can consist of both excitatory and inhibitory messages. Excitatory messages increase the activation level of their recipients. Inhibitory messages decrease the activation level of their recipients. The arrows in the diagram represent excitatory connections, and the circular ends of the connections represent inhibitory connections. The intralevel inhibitory loop represents a kind of lateral inhibition in which incompatible units at the same level compete. For example, since a string of four letters can be interpreted as at most one four-letter word, the vari-

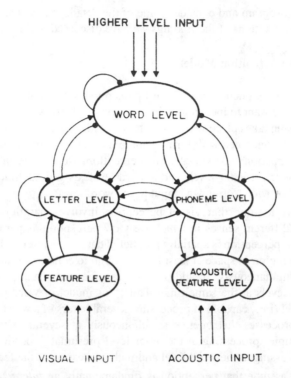

Figure 1. A sketch of some of the processing levels involved in visual and auditory word perception,
        with interconnections.

ous possible words mutually inhibit one another and in that way compete as possible interpretations of the string.

It is clear that many levels are important in reading and perception in general, and the interactions among these levels are important for many phenomena.
However, a theoretical analysis of all of these interactions introduces an order of
complexity that obscures comprehension. For this reason, we have restricted the
present analysis to an examination of the interaction between a single pair of
levels, the word and letter levels. We have found that we can account for the
phenomena reviewed above by considering only the interactions between letter
level and word level elements. Therefore, for the present we have elaborated the
model only on these two levels, as illustrated in Figure 2. We have delayed consideration of the effects of higher level processes and phonological processes,
and we have ignored the reciprocity of activation that may occur between word
and letter levels and any other levels of the system. We consider aspects of the
fuller model including these influences in Part 2 (Rumelhart and McClelland,
1982).

Specific Assumptions

Representation assumptions. For every relevant unit in the system we assume there is an entity called a *node*. We assume that there is a node for each word we know, and that there is a node for each letter in each letter position within a four-letter string.

The nodes are organized into levels. There are *word level* nodes and *letter level* nodes. Each node has connections to a number of other nodes. The nodes to which a node connects are called its *neighbors*. Each connection is two-way. There are two kinds of connections: *excitatory* and *inhibitory*. If two nodes suggest each other's existence (in the way that the node for the word *the* suggests the node for an initial *t* and vice versa), then the connections are excitatory. If two nodes are inconsistent with one another (in the way that the node for the word *the* and the node for the word *boy* are inconsistent), then the relationship is inhibitory. Note that we identify nodes according to the units they detect, printing them in italics; stimuli presented to the system are in uppercase letters.

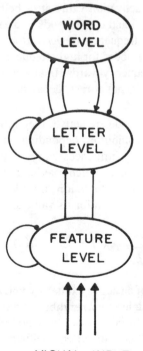

Figure 2. The simplified processing system.

Connections may occur within levels or between adjacent levels. There are no connections between nonadjacent levels. Connections within the word level are mutually inhibitory, since only one word can occur at any one place at any one time. Connections between the word level and letter level may be either inhibitory or excitatory (depending on whether the letter is a part of the word in the appropriate letter position). We call the set of nodes with excitatory connections to a given node its *excitatory neighbors* and the set of nodes with inhibitory connections to a given node its *inhibitory neighbors*.

A subset of the neighbors of the letter t is illustrated in Figure 3. Again, excitatory connections are represented by the arrows ending with points, and inhibitory connections are represented by the arrows ending with dots. We emphasize that this is a small subset of the neighborhood of the initial t. The picture of the whole neighborhood, including all the connections among neighbors and their connections to their neighbors, is much too complicated to present in a two-dimensional figure.

Activation assumptions. There is associated with each node a momentary activation value. This value is a real number, and for node i we will represent it by $a_i(t)$. Any node with a positive activation value is said to be *active*. In the absence of inputs from its neighbors, all nodes are assumed to decay back to an inactive state, that is, to an activation value at or below zero. This resting level may differ from node to node and corresponds to a kind of a prior bias (Broadbent, 1967) determined by frequency of activation of the node over the long term. Thus, for example, the nodes for high-frequency words have resting levels higher than those for low-frequency words. In any case, the resting level for node i is represented by r_i. For units not at rest, decay back to the resting level occurs at some rate θ_i.

When the neighbors of a node are active, they influence the activation of the node by either excitation or inhibition, depending on their relation to the node. These excitatory and inhibitory influences combine by a simple weighted average to yield a net input to the unit, which may be either excitatory (greater than zero) or inhibitory. In mathematical notation, if we let $n_i(t)$ represent the net input to the unit, we can write the equation for its value as

$$n_i(t) = \sum_j \alpha_{ij} e_j(t) - \sum_k \gamma_{ik} i_k(t), \quad (1)$$

where $e_j(t)$ is the activation of an active excitatory neighbor of the node, each $i_k(t)$ is the activation of an active inhibitory neighbor of the node, and α_{ij} and γ_{ik} are associated weight constants. Inactive nodes have no influence on their neighbors. Only nodes in an active state have any effects, either excitatory or inhibitory.

The net input to a node drives the activation of the node up or down, depending on whether it is positive or negative. The degree of the effect of the input on the node is modulated by the node's current activity level to keep the input to the node from driving it beyond some maximum and minimum values (Grossberg, 1978). When the net input is excitatory, $n_i(t) > 0$, the effect on the node, $\epsilon_i(t)$, is given by

$$\epsilon_i(t) = n_i(t)(M - a_i(t)), \qquad (2)$$

where M is the maximum activation level of the unit. The modulation has the desired effect, because as the activation of the unit approaches the maximum, the effect of the input is reduced to zero. M can be thought of as a basic scale factor of the model, and we have set its value to 1.0.

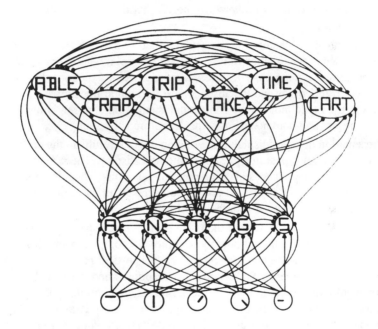

Figure 3. A few of the neighbors of the node, for the letter T in the first position in a word, and their interconnections.

In the case where the input is inhibitory, $n_{i(t)} < 0$, the effect of the input on the node is given by

$$\epsilon_i(t) = n_i(t)(a_i(t) - m), \qquad (3)$$

where m is the minimum activation of the unit.

The new value of the activation of a node at time $t + \triangle t$ is equal to the value at time t, minus the decay, plus the influence of its neighbors at time t:

$$a_i(t + \Delta t)$$
$$= a_i(t) - \Theta_i(a_i(t) - r_i) + \epsilon_i(t). \quad (4)$$

Input assumptions. Upon presentation of a stimulus, a set of featural inputs is made available to the system. Each feature in the display will be detected with some probability p. For simplicity it is assumed that feature detection occurs, if it is to occur at all, immediately after onset of the stimulus. The probability that any given feature will be detected is assumed to vary with the visual quality of the display. Features that are detected begin sending activation to all letter nodes that contain that feature. All letter level nodes that do not contain the extracted feature are inhibited.

It is assumed that features are binary and that we can extract either the presence or absence of a particular feature. So, for example, when viewing the letter *R* we can extract, among other features, the presence of a diagonal line segment in the lower right corner and the absence of a horizontal line across the bottom. In this way the model honors the conceptual distinction between knowing that a feature is absent and not knowing whether a feature is present.

Presentation of a new display following an old one results in the probabilistic extraction of the set of features present in the new display. These features, when extracted, replace the old ones in corresponding positions. Thus, the presentation of an *E* following the *R* described above would result in the replacement of the two features described above with their opposites.

On making responses. One of the more problematic aspects of a model such as this one is a specification of how these relatively complex patterns of activity might be related to the content of percepts and the sorts of response probabilities we observe in experiments. We assume that responses and perhaps the contents of perceptual experience depend on the temporal integration of the pattern of activation over all of the nodes. The integration process is assumed to occur slowly enough that brief activations may come and go without necessarily becoming accessible for purposes of responding or entering perceptual experience. However, as the activation lasts longer and longer, the probability that it will be reportable increases. Specifically, we think of the integration process as taking a running average of the activation of the node over previous time:

$$\bar{a}_i(t) = \int_{-\infty}^{t} a_i(x)e^{-(t-x)r}dx. \quad (5)$$

In this equation, the variable x represents preceding time, varying between $-\infty$ and time t. The exponential portion of the expression weights the contribution of the activation of the node in previous time intervals. Essentially, its effect is to reduce the contribution of prior activations as they recede further back in time.

The parameter r represents the relative weighting given to old and new information and determines how quickly the output values change in response to changes in the activations of the underlying nodes. The larger the value of r, the more quickly the output values change. *Response strength,* in the sense of Luce's choice model (Luce, 1959), is an exponential function of the running average activation:

$$s_i(t) = e^{\mu \bar{a}_i(t)}. \qquad (6)$$

The parameter μ determines how rapidly response strength grows with increases in activation. Following Luce's formulation, we assume that the probability of making a response based on node i is given by

$$p(R_i, t) = \frac{s_i(t)}{\sum_{j \in L} s_j(t)}, \qquad (7)$$

where L represents the set of nodes competing at the same level with node i.

Most of the experiments we will be considering test subjects' performance on one of the letters in a word or other type of display. In accounting for these results, we have adopted the assumption that responding is always based on the output of the letter level, rather than the output of the word level or some combination of the two. The forced choice is assumed to be based only on this letter-level information. The subject compares the letter selected for the appropriate position against the forced-choice alternatives. If the letter selected is one of the alternatives, then that alternative is chosen in the forced choice. If it is not one of the alternatives, then the model assumes that one of the alternatives would simply be chosen at random.

One somewhat problematical issue involves deciding when to read out the results of processing and select response letters for each letter position. When a target display is simply turned on and left on until the subject responds, and when there is no pressure to respond quickly, we assume that the subject simply waits until the output strengths have reached their asymptotic values. However, when a target display is presented briefly followed by a patterned mask, the activations produced by the target are transient, as we shall see. Under these conditions, we assume that the subject learns through experience in the practice phase of the experiment to read out the results of processing at a time that allows the subject to optimize performance. For simplicity, we have assumed that readout occurs in parallel for all four letter positions.

The Operation of the Model

Now, consider what happens when an input reaches the system. Assume that at time t_0 all prior inputs have had an opportunity to decay, so that the entire system is in its quiescent state, and each node is at its resting level. The presentation of a stimulus initiates a process in which certain features are extracted and excitatory and inhibitory pressures begin to act upon the letter-level nodes. The activation levels of certain letter nodes are pushed above their resting levels. Others receive predominantly inhibitory inputs and are pushed below their resting levels. These letter nodes, in turn, begin to send activation to those word-level nodes they are consistent with and inhibit those word nodes they are not consistent with. In addition, within a given letter position channel, the various letter nodes attempt to suppress each other, with the strongest ones getting the upper hand. As word-level nodes become active, they in turn compete with one another and send feedback down to the letter-level nodes. If the input features were close to those for one particular set of letters and those letters were consistent with those forming a particular word, the positive feedback in the system will work to rapidly converge on the appropriate set of letters and the appropriate word. If not, they will compete with each other, and perhaps no single set of letters or single word will get enough activation to dominate the others. In this case the various active units might strangle each other through mutual inhibition.

At any point during processing, the results of perceptual processing may be read out from the pattern of activations at the letter level into a buffer, where they may be kept through rehearsal or used as the basis for overt reports. The accuracy of this process depends on a running average of the activations of the correct node and of other competing nodes.

Simulations

Although the model is in essence quite simple, the interactions among the various nodes can become complex, so that the model is not susceptible to a simple intuitive or even mathematical analysis. Instead, we have relied on computer simulations to study the behavior of the model and to see if it is consistent with the empirical data. A description of the actual computer program is given in the Appendix.

For purposes of these simulations, we have made a number of simplifying assumptions. These additional assumptions fall into three classes: (a) discrete rather than continuous time, (b) simplified feature analysis of the input font, and (c) a limited lexicon.

The simulation operates in discrete time slices, or ticks, updating the activations of all of the nodes in the system once each cycle on the basis of the values on the previous cycle. Obviously, this is simply a matter of computational convenience and not a fundamental assumption. We have endeavored to keep the time slices "thin" enough so that the model's behavior is continuous for all intents and purposes.

Any simulation of the model involves making explicit assumptions about the appropriate featural analysis of the input font. We have, for simplicity, chosen the font and featural analysis employed by Rumelhart (1970) and by Rumelhart and Siple (1974), illustrated in Figure 4. Although the experiments we have simulated employed different type fonts, we assume that the basic results do not depend on the particular font used. The simplicity of the present analysis recommends it for the simulations, though it obviously skirts several fundamental issues about the lower levels of processing.

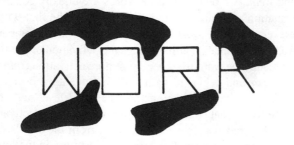

Figure 4. The features used to construct the letters in the font assumed by the simulation program, and the letters themselves. (From "Process of Recognizing Tachistoscopically Presented Words" by David E. Rumelhart and Patricia Siple, *Psychological Review*, 1974, *81*, 99-118. Copyright 1974 by the American Psychological Association. Reprinted by permission.)

Finally, our simulations have been restricted to four-letter words. We have equipped our program with knowledge of 1,179 four-letter words occurring at least two times per million in the Kučera and Francis (1967) word count. Plurals, inflected forms, first names, proper names, acronyms, abbreviations, and occasional unfamiliar entries arising from apparent sampling flukes have been excluded.

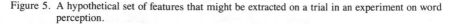

Figure 5. A hypothetical set of features that might be extracted on a trial in an experiment on word perception.

This sample appears to be sufficient to reflect the essential characteristics of the language and to show how the statistical properties of the language can affect the process of perceiving letters in words.

An Example

Let us now consider a sample run of our simulation model. The parameter values employed in the example are those used to simulate all the experiments discussed in the remainder of Part 1. These values are described in detail in the following section. For the purposes of this example, imagine that the word WORK has been presented to the subject and that the subject has extracted those features shown in Figure 5. In the first three letter positions, the features of the letters W, O, and R have been completely extracted. In the final position a set of features consistent with the letters K and R have been extracted, with the features that would disambiguate the letter unavailable. We wish now to chart the activity of the system resulting from this presentation. Figure 6 shows the time course of the activations for selected nodes at the word and letter levels, respectively.

At the word level, we have charted the activity levels of the nodes for the words *work*, *word*, *wear*, and *weak*. Note first that *work* is the only word in the lexicon consistent with all the presented information. As a result, its activation level is the highest and reaches a value of .8 through the first 40 time cycles. The word *word* is consistent with the bulk of the information presented and therefore first rises and later is pushed back down below its resting level, as a result of competition with *work*. The words *wear* and *weak* are consistent with the only letter active in the first letter position, and one of the two active in the fourth letter position. They are also inconsistent with the letters active in Positions 2 and 3. Thus, the activation they receive from the letter level is quite weak, and they are easily driven down well below zero, as a result of competition from the other word units. The activations of these units do not drop quite as low, of course, as the activation level of words such as *gill*, which contain nothing in common with the presented information. Although not shown in Figure 6, these words attain near-minimum levels of about -.20 and stay there as the stimulus stays on. Returning to *wear* and *weak,* we note that these words are equally consistent with the presented information and thus drop together for about the first 9 time units. At this point, however, the word *work* has clearly taken the upper hand at the word level, and produces feedback that reinforces the activation of the final *k* and not the final *r*. As a result, the word *weak* receives more activation from the letter level than the word *wear* and begins to gain a slight advantage over *wear*. The strengthened *k* continues to feed activation into the word level and strengthen consistent words. The words that contain an R continue to receive activation from the *r* node also, but they receive stronger inhibition from the words consistent with a K and are therefore ultimately weakened, as illustrated in the lower panel of Figure 6.

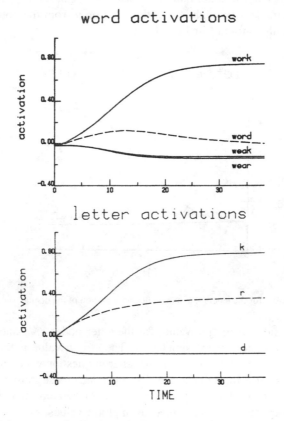

Figure 6. The time course of activations of selected nodes at the word and letter levels after extraction of the features shown in Figure 5.

The strong feature-letter inhibition ensures that when a feature inconsistent with a particular letter is detected, that letter will receive relatively strong net bottom-up inhibition. Thus in our example, the information extracted clearly disconfirms the possibility that the letter D has been presented in the fourth position, and thus the activation level of the *d* node decreases quickly to near its minimum value. However, the bottom-up information from the feature level supports either a K or an R in the fourth position. Thus, the activation of each of these nodes rises slowly. These activations, along with those for W, O, and R, push the activation of *work* above zero, and it begins to feed back; by about Time Cycle 4, it is beginning to push the *k* above the *r* (because WORR is not a word). Note that this separation occurs just before the words *weak* and *wear* separate. It is the strengthening of *k* due to feedback from *work* that causes them to separate.

Ultimately, the *r* reaches a level well below that of *k* where it remains, and the *k* pushes toward a .8 activation level. As discussed below, the word-to-letter inhibition and the letter-to-letter inhibition have both been set to 0. Thus, k and r both co-exist at moderately high levels, the r fed only from the bottom up, and the k fed from both bottom up and top down.

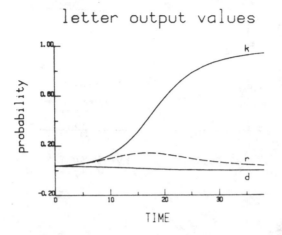

Figure 7. Output values for the letters r, k, and d after presentation of the display shown in Figure 5.

Finally, consider the output values for the letter nodes r, k, and d. Figure 7 shows the output values for the simulation. The output value is the probability that if a response was selected at time t, the letter in question would be selected as the output or response from the system. As intended, these output values grow somewhat more slowly than the values of the letter activations themselves but eventually, as they reach and hold their asymptotic values, come to reflect the activations of the letter nodes. Since in the absence of masking subjects can afford to wait to read out a response until the output values have had a chance to stabilize, they would be highly likely to choose the letter κ as the response.

Although this example is not very general in that we assumed that only partial information was available in the input for the fourth letter position, whereas full information was available at the other letter positions, it does illustrate many of the important characteristics of the model. It shows how ambiguous sensory information can be disambiguated by top-down processes. Here we have a very simple mechanism capable of applying knowledge of words in the perception of their component letters.

Parameter Selection

Once the basic simulation model was constructed, we began a lengthy process of attempting to simulate the results of several representative experiments in the literature. Only two parameters of the model were allowed to vary from experiment to experiment: (a) the probability of feature extraction and (b) the timing of the presentation of the masking stimulus if one was used.

The probability of feature extraction is assumed to depend on the visual characteristics of the display. In most of the experiments we will consider, a bright, high-contrast target was used. Such a target would produce perfect performance if not followed by a patterned mask. In these cases probability of feature extraction was fixed at 1.0 and the timing of the target offset and coincident mask onset typically was adjusted to achieve 75% correct performance over the different experimental conditions of interest. In simulating the results of these experiments, we likewise varied the timing of the target offset/mask onset to achieve the right average correct performance from the model.

In some experiments no patterned mask was used and performance was kept below perfect levels by using a dim or otherwise degraded target display. In these cases the probability of feature extraction was set to a value less than 1.0, which produces about the right overall performance level.

The process of exploring the behavior of the model amounted to an extended search for a set of values for all the other parameters that would permit the model to simulate, as closely as possible, the results of all of the experiments to be discussed later in Part 1, as well as those to be considered in Part 2 (Rumelhart and McClelland, 1982). To constrain the search, we adopted various restrictive simplifications. First, we assumed that all nodes have the same maximum activation value. In fact, the maximum was set to 1.0, and served to scale all activations within the model. The minimum activation value for all nodes was set at -.20, a value that permits rapid reactivation of strongly inhibited nodes. The decay rate of all nodes was set to the value of .07. This parameter effectively serves as a scale factor that determines how quickly things are allowed to change in a single time slice. The .07 value was picked after some exploration, since it seemed to permit us to run our simulations with the minimum number of time slices per trial, at the same time as it minimized a kind of reverberatory oscillation that sets in when things are allowed to change too much on any given time cycle. We also assigned the resting value of zero to all of the letter nodes. The resting value of nodes at the word level was set to a value between -.05 and 0, depending on word   frequency.

We have assumed that the weight parameters, α_{ij} and γ_{ij} depend only on the processing levels of nodes i and j and on no other characteristics of their identity. This means, among other things, that the excitatory connections between all letter nodes and all of the relevant word nodes are equally strong, independent of the identity of the words. Thus, for example, the degree to which the node for an initial t excites the node for the word *tock* is exactly the same as the degree to which it excites the node for the word *this*, in spite of a substantial difference in frequency of usage. To further simplify matters, the word-to-letter inhibition was also set to zero. This means that feedback from the word level can strengthen activations at the letter level but cannot weaken them.

The output from the detector network has essentially two parameters. The value .05 was used for the parameter r, which determines how quickly the output values change in response to changes in the activations of the underlying nodes.

This value is small enough that the output values change relatively slowly, so that transient activations can come and go without much effect on the output. The value 10 was given to the parameter μ in Equation 6 above. The parameter is essentially a scale factor relating activations in the model to response strengths in the Luce formulation.

The values of the remaining parameters were fixed at the values given in Table 1. It is worth noting the differences between the feature-letter influences and the letter-word influences. The feature-letter inhibition is 30 times as strong as the feature-letter excitation. This means that all of the features detected must be compatible with a particular letter before that letter will receive net excitation (since there are only 14 possible features, there can only be a maximum of 13 excitatory inputs whenever there is a single inhibitory input). The main reason for choosing this value was to permit the presentation of a mask to clear the previous pattern of activation. On the other hand, the letter-word inhibition is actually somewhat less than the letter-word excitation. When only one letter is active in each letter position, this means that the letter level will produce net excitation of all words that share two or more letters with the target word. Because of these multiple activations, strong word-word inhibition is necessary to "sharpen" the response of the word level, as we will see. In contrast, no such inhibition is necessary at the letter level. For these reasons, the letter-letter inhibition has been set to 0, whereas the word-word inhibition has been set to .21.

Table 1

PARAMETER VALUES USED IN THE SIMULATIONS

Parameter	Value
Feature-letter excitation	.005
Feature-letter inhibition	.15
Letter-word excitation	.07
Letter-word inhibition	.04
Word-word inhibition	.21
Letter-letter inhibition	.00
Word-letter excitation	.30

Comments on Related Formulations

Before turning to the application of the model to the experimental literature, some comments on the relationship of this model to other models extant in the literature are in order. We have tried to be synthetic. We have taken ideas from our own previous work and from the work of others in the literature. In what follows, we attempt to identify the sources of most of the assumptions of the model and to show in what ways our model differs from the models we have drawn on.

First of all, we have adopted the approach of formulating the model in terms similar to the way in which such a process might actually be carried out in a neural or neural-like system. We do not mean to imply that the nodes in our system are necessarily related to the behavior of individual neurons. We will, however, argue that we have kept the kinds of processing involved well within the bounds of capability for simple neural circuits. The approach of modeling information processing in a neural-like system has recently been advocated by Szentagothai and Arbib (1975) and is represented in many of the articles presented in the volume by Hinton and Anderson (1981) as well as many of the specific models mentioned below.

One case in point is the work of Levin (1976). He proposed a parallel computational system capable of interactive processing that employs only excitation and inhibition as its currency. Although our model could not be implemented exactly in the format of their system (called Proteus), it is clearly in the spirit of their model and could readily be implemented within a variant of the Proteus system.

In a recent article McClelland (1979) has proposed a cascade model of perceptual processing in which activations on each level of the system drive those at the next higher level. This model has the properties that partial outputs are continuously available for processing and that every level of the system processes the input simultaneously. The present model certainly adopts these assumptions. It also generalizes them, permitting information to flow in both directions simultaneously.

Hinton (Note 1) has developed a *relaxation* model for visual perception in which multiple constraints interact by means of incrementing and decrementing real numbered strengths associated with various interpretations of a portion of the visual scene in an attempt to attain a maximally consistent interpretation of the scene. Our model can be considered a relaxation system in which activation levels are manipulated to get an optimal interpretation of an input word.

Anderson and his colleagues (Anderson, 1977; Anderson, Silverstein, Ritz, and Jones, 1977) and Kohonen and his colleagues (Kohonen, 1977) have developed a pattern recognition system which they call an *associative memory* system. Their system shares a number of commonalities with ours. One feature the models share is the scheme of adding and subtracting weighted excitation values to generate output patterns that represent cleaned-up versions of the input patterns. In particular, our α_{ij} and γ_{ij} correspond to the matrix elements of the associative memory models. Our model differs in that it has multiple levels and employs a nonlinear cumulation function similar to one suggested by Grossberg (1978), as mentioned above.

Our model also draws on earlier work in the area of word perception. There is, of course, a strong similarity between this model and the logogen model of Morton (1969). What we have implemented might be called a hierarchical, nonlinear, logogen model with feedback between levels and inhibitory interactions among logogens at the same level. We have also added dynamic assumptions that are lacking from the logogen model.

The notion that word perception takes place in a hierarchical information processing system has, of course, been advocated by several researchers interested in word perception (Adams, 1979; Estes, 1975; Johnston and McClelland, 1980; LaBerge and Samuels, 1974; McClelland, 1976). Our model differs from those proposed in many of these papers in that processing at different levels is explicitly assumed to take place in parallel. Many of the models are not terribly explicit on this topic, although the notion that partial information could be passed along from one level to the next so that processing could go on at the higher level while it was continuing at the lower level had been suggested by McClelland (1976). Our model also differs from all of these others, except that of Adams (1979), in assuming that there is feedback from the word level to the letter level. The general formulation suggested by Adams (1979) is quite similar to our own, although she postulates a different sort of mechanism for handling pseudowords (excitatory connections among letter nodes) and does not present a detailed account.

Our mechanism for accounting for the perceptual facilitation of pseudowords involves, as we will see below, the integration of feedback from partial activation of a number of different words. The idea that pseudoword perception could be accounted for in this way was inspired by Glushko (1979), who suggested that partial activation and synthesis of word pronunciations could account for the process of constructing a pronunciation for a novel pseudoword.

The feature-extraction assumptions and the bottom-up portion of the word recognition model are nearly the same as those employed by Rumelhart (1970, Note 2) and Rumelhart and Siple (1974). The interactive feedback portion of the model is clearly one of the class of models discussed by Rumelhart (1977) and could be considered a simplified control structure for expressing the model proposed in that paper.

Application of the Simulation Model to Several Basic Findings

We are finally ready to see how well our model fares in accounting for the findings of several representative experiments in the literature. In discussing each account, we will try to explain not only how well the simulation works but why it behaves as it does. As we proceed through the discussion, we will have occasion to describe several interesting synergistic properties of the model that we did not anticipate but discovered as we explored the behavior of the system. As mentioned previously, the actual parameters used in both the examples that we will discuss and in the simulation results we will report are those summarized in Table 1. We will consider the robustness of the model, and the effects of changes in these parameters, in the discussion section at the end of Part 1.

The Word Advantage and the Effects of Visual Conditions

As we noted previously, word perception has been studied under a variety of different visual conditions, and it is apparent that different conditions produce different results. The advantage of words over nonwords appears to be greatest under conditions in which a bright, high-contrast target is followed by a patterned mask with similar characteristics. The word advantage appears to be considerably less when the target presentation is dimmer or otherwise degraded and is followed by a blank white field.

Typical data demonstrating these points (from Johnston and McClelland, 1973) are presented in Table 2. Forced-choice performance on letters in words is compared to performance on letters embedded in a row of number signs (e.g, READ vs. #E##). The number signs serve as a control for lateral facilitation or inhibition. This factor appears to be important under dim-target/blank-mask conditions.

Table 2

EFFECT OF DISPLAY CONDITIONS ON PROPORTION OF CORRECT FORCED CHOICES IN WORD AND LETTER PERCEPTION (FROM JOHNSTON & MCCLELLAND, 1973)

	Display type	
Visual condition	Word	Letter with number signs
Bright target/patterned mask	.80	.65
Dim target/blank mask	.78	.73

Target durations were adjusted separately for each condition, so that it is only the pattern of differences within display conditions that is meaningful. The data show that a 15 percent word advantage was obtained in the bright-target/patterned-mask condition and only a 5 percent word advantage in the dim-target/blank-mask condition. Massaro and Klitzke (1979) obtained about the same size effects. Various aspects of these results have also been corroborated in two other studies (Juola et al., 1974; Taylor and Chabot, 1978).

To understand the difference between these two conditions it is important to note that in order to get about 75 percent correct performance in the no-mask condition, the stimulus must be highly degraded. Since there is no patterned mask, the iconic trace presumably persists considerably beyond the offset of the target. It is our assumption that the effect of the blank mask is simply to reduce the contrast of the icon by summating with it. Thus, the limit on performance is not so much the amount of time available in which to process the information as it is the quality of the information made available to the system. In contrast, when a patterned mask is employed, the mask produces spurious inputs, which

can interfere with the processing of the target. Thus, in the bright-target/pat-
terned-mask conditions, the primary limitation on performance is the amount of
time that the information is available to the system in relatively legible form
rather than the quality of the information presented. This distinction between the
way in which blank masks and patterned masks interfere with performance has
previously been made by a number of investigators, including Rumelhart (1970)
and Turvey (1973). We now consider each of these sorts of conditions in turn.

Word perception under patterned-mask conditions. When a high-quality display is followed by a patterned mask, we assume that the bottleneck in performance does not come in the extraction of feature information from the target
display. Thus, in our simulation of these conditions, we assume that all of the
features presented can be extracted on every trial. The limitation on performance
comes from the fact that the activations produced by the target are subject to
disruption and replacement by the mask before they can be translated into a permanent form suitable for overt report. This general idea was suggested by Johnston and McClelland (1973) and considered by a number of other investigators,
including Carr et al. (1978), Massaro and Klitzke (1979), and others. On the
basis of this idea, a number of possible reasons for the advantage for letters in
words have been suggested. One is that letters in words are for some reason
translated more quickly into a nonmaskable form (Johnston and McClelland,
1973; Massaro and Klitzke, 1979). Another is that words activate representations
removed from the direct effects of visual patterned masking (Carr et al., 1978;
Johnston and McClelland, 1973, 1980; McClelland, 1976). In the interactive
activation model, the reason letters in words fare better than letters in nonwords
is that they benefit from feedback that can drive them to higher activation levels.
As a result, the probability that the activated letter representation will be correctly encoded is increased.

To understand in detail how this account works, consider the following example. Figure 8 shows the operation of our model for the letter E both in an
unrelated (#) context and in the context of the word READ for a visual display of
moderately high quality. We assume that display conditions are sufficient for
complete feature extraction, so that only the letters actually contained in the target receive net excitatory input on the basis of feature information. After some
number of cycles have gone by, the mask is presented with the same parameters
as the target. The mask simply replaces the target display at the feature level,
resulting in a completely new input to the letter level. This input, because it contains features incompatible with the letter shown in all four positions, immediately begins to drive down the activations at the letter level.

After only a few more cycles, these activations drop below resting level in
both cases. Note that the correct letter was activated briefly, and no competing
letter was activated. However, because of the sluggishness of the output process,
these activations do not necessarily result in a high probability of correct report.
As shown in the top half of Figure 8, the probability of correct report reaches a
maximum after 16 cycles at a performance level far below the ceiling.

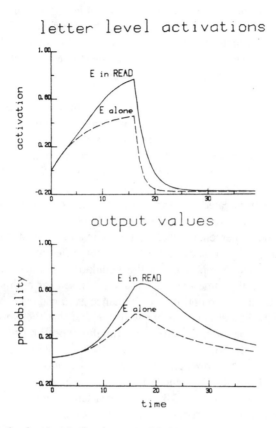

Figure 8. Activation functions (top) and output values (bottom) for the letter *E*, in unrelated context and in the context of the word *READ*.

When the letter is part of the word (in this case, READ), the activation of the letters results in rapid activation of one or more words. These words, in turn, feed back to the letter level. This results in a higher net activation level for the letter embedded in the word.

Our simulation of the word advantage under patterned-mask conditions used the stimulus list that was used for simulating the blank-mask results. Since the internal workings of the model are completely deterministic as long as probability of feature extraction is 1.0, it was only necessary to run each item through the model once to obtain the expected probability that the critical letter would be encoded correctly for each item under each variation of parameters tried.

As described previously, we have assumed that readout of the results of processing occurs in parallel for all four letter positions and that the subject learns through practice to choose a time to read out in order to optimize performance. We have assumed that readout time may be set at a different point in different conditions, as long as they are blocked so that the subject knows in advance what type of material will be presented on each trial in the experiment. Thus, in simulating the Johnston and McClelland (1973) results, we allowed for different readout times for letters in words and letters in unrelated contexts, with the different times selected on the basis of practice to optimize performance on each type of material.

A final feature of the simulation is the duration of the target display. This was varied to produce an average performance on both letters embedded in number signs and letters in words that was as close as possible to the average performance on these two conditions in the 1973 experiment of Johnston and McClelland. The value used for the run reported below was 15 cycles. As in the Johnston and McClelland study, the mask followed the target immediately.

The simulation replicated the experimental data shown in Table 2 quite closely. Accuracy on the forced choice was 81 percent correct for the letters embedded in words and 66 percent correct for letters in an unrelated (#) context.

It turns out that it is not necessary to allow for different readout times for different material types. A repetition of the simulation produced a 15 percent word advantage when the same readout time was chosen for both single letters and letters in words, based on optimal performance averaged over the two material types. Thus, the model is consistent with the fact that the word advantage does not depend on separating the different stimulus types into separate blocks (Massaro and Klitzke, 1979).

Perception of letters in words under conditions of degraded input. In conditions of degraded (but not abbreviated) input, the role of the word level is to selectively reinforce possible letters that are consistent with the visual information extracted and that are also consistent with the words in the subject's vocabulary. Recall that the task requires the subject to choose between two letters, both of which (on word trials) make a word with the rest of the context. There are two distinct cases to consider. Either the featural information extracted from the to-be-probed letter is sufficient to distinguish between the alternatives, or it is not. Whenever the featural information is consistent with both of the forced-choice alternatives, any feedback will selectively enhance both alternatives and will not permit the subject to distinguish between them. When the information extracted is inconsistent with one of the alternatives, the model produces a word advantage. The reason is that we assume forced-choice responses are based not on the feature information itself but on the subject's best guess about what letter was actually shown. Feedback from the word level increases the probability of correct choice in those cases where the subject extracts information that is inconsistent with the incorrect alternative but consistent with the correct alternative and a number of others. Thus, feedback would have the effect of helping the subject select the actual letter shown from several possibilities consistent with the set of extracted features. Consider again, for example, the case of the presentation of WORD discussed above. In this case, the subject extracted incomplete information about the final letter consistent with both R and K. Assume that the forced choice the subject was to face on this trial was between a D and a K. The account supposes that the subject encodes a single letter for each letter position before facing the forced choice. Thus, if the features of the final letter had been extracted in the absence of any context, the subject would encode R or K equally often, since both are equally compatible with the features extracted. This would leave the subject with the correct response some of the time. But if R were chosen instead, the subject would enter the forced choice between D and K without knowing the correct answer directly. When the whole word display is shown, the feedback generated by the processing of all of the letters greatly strengthens the K, increasing the probability that it will be chosen over the R and thus increasing the probability that the subject will proceed to the forced choice with the correct response in mind.

Our interpretation of the small word advantage in blank-mask conditions is a specific version of the early accounts of the word advantage offered by Wheeler (1970) and Thompson and Massaro (1973) before it was known that the effect depends on masking. Johnston (1978) has argued that this type of account does not apply under patterned mask conditions. We are suggesting that it does apply to the small word advantage obtained under blank-mask conditions like those of the Johnston and McClelland (1973) experiment. We will see below that the model offers a different account of performance under patterned-mask conditions.

We simulated our interpretation of the small word advantage obtained in blank-mask conditions in the following way. A set of 40 pairs of four-letter words that differed by a single letter was prepared. The differing letters occurred in each position equally often. From these words corresponding control pairs were generated in which the critical letters from the word pairs were presented in nonletter contexts (#s). Because they were presented in nonletter contexts, we assumed that these letters did not engage the word processing system at all.

Each member of each pair of items was presented to the model four times, yielding a total of 320 stimulus presentations of word stimuli and 320 presentations of single letters. On each presentation, the simulation sampled a random subset of the possible features to be detected by the system. The probability of detection of each feature was set at .45. As noted previously, these values are in a ratio of 1 to 30, so that if any one of the 14 features extracted is inconsistent with a particular letter, that letter receives net inhibition from the features and is rapidly driven into an inactive state.

For simplicity, the features were treated as a constant input, which remained on while letter and word activations (if any) were allowed to take place. At the end of 50 processing cycles, which is virtually asymptotic, output was sampled. Sampling results in the selection of one letter to fill each position; the selected letter is assumed to be all the subject takes away from the target display. As described previously, the forced choice is assumed to be based only on this letter identity information. The subject compares the letter selected for the appropriate position against the forced-choice alternatives. If the letter selected is one of the alternatives, then that alternative is selected. If it is not one of the alternatives, then one of the two alternatives is simply picked at random.

The simulation produced a 10 percent advantage for letters in words over letters embedded in number signs. Probability-correct forced choice for letters embedded in words was 78 percent correct, whereas for letters in number signs, performance was 68 percent correct.

The simulated results for the no mask condition clearly show a smaller word advantage than for the patterned mask case. However, the model produces a larger word advantage, which is observed in the experiment (Table 2). As Johnston (1978) has pointed out, there are a number of reasons why an account such as the one we have offered would overestimate the size of the word advantage. First, subjects may occasionally be able to retain an impression of the actual visual information they have been able to extract. On such occasions, feedback from the word level will be of no further benefit. Second, even if subjects only retain a letter identity code, they may tend to choose the forced-choice alternative that is most similar to the letter encoded—instead of simply guessing—when the letter encoded is not one of the two choices. This would tend to result in a greater probability of correct choices and less of a chance for feedback to increase accuracy of performance. It is hard to know exactly how much these factors should be expected to reduce the size of the word advantage under these conditions, but they would certainly bring it more closely in line with the results.

Perception of Letters in Regular Nonwords

One of the most important findings in the literature on word perception is that an item need not be a word in order to produce facilitation with respect to unrelated letter or single letter stimuli. The advantage for pseudowords over unrelated letters has been obtained in a very large number of studies (Aderman and Smith, 1971; Baron and Thurston, 1973; Carr et al., 1978; McClelland, 1976; Spoehr and Smith, 1975). The pseudoword advantage over single letters has been obtained in three studies (Carr et al., 1978; Massaro and Klitzke, 1979; McClelland and Johnston, 1977).

Our model produces the facilitation for pseudowords by allowing them to activate nodes for words that share more than one letter in common with the display. When they occur, these activations produce feedback which strengthens the letters that gave rise to them just as in the case of words. These activations occur in the model if the strength of letter-to-word inhibition is reasonably small compared to the strength of letter-to-word excitation.

To see how this takes place in detail, consider a brief presentation of the pseudoword MAVE followed by a patterned mask. (The pseudoword is one used by Glushko, 1979, in developing the idea that partial activations of words are combined to derive pronunciations of pseudowords.) As illustrated in Figure 9, presentation of MAVE results in the initial activation of 16 different words. Most of these words, like *have* and *gave*, share three letters with MAVE. By and large,

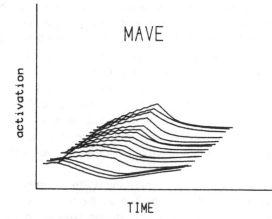

Figure 9. Activation at the word level upon presentation of the nonword *MAVE*.

these words steadily gain in strength while the target is on and produce feedback to the letter level, sustaining the letters that supported them.

Some of the words are weakly activated for a brief period of time before they fall back below zero. These typically are words like *more* and *many*, which share only two letters with the target but are very high in frequency, so they need little excitation before they exceed threshold. But soon after they exceed threshold, the total activation at the word level becomes strong enough to overcome the weak excitatory input, causing them to drop down just after they begin to rise. Less frequent words sharing two letters with the word displayed have a worse fate still. Since they start out initially at a lower value, they generally fail to receive enough excitation to reach threshold. Thus, when there are several words that have three letters in common with the target, words that share only two letters with the target tend to exert little or no influence. In general then, with pronounceable pseudoword stimuli, the amount of feedback—and hence the amount of facilitation—depends primarily on the activation of nodes for words that share three letters with a displayed pseudoword. It is the nodes for these words that primarily interact with the activations generated by the presentation of the actual target display. In what follows we will call the words that have three letters in common with the target letter string the neighbors of that string.

The amount of feedback a particular letter in a nonword receives depends, in the model, on two primary factors and two secondary factors. The two primary factors are the number of words in the neighborhood that contain the target letter and the number of words that do not. In the case of the M in MAVE, for example, there are seven words in the neighborhood of MAVE that begin with M, so the *m* node gets excitatory feedback from all of these. These words are called the "friends" of the *m* node in this case. Because of competition at the word level, the amount of activation that these words receive depends on the total number of words that have three letters in common with the target. Those that share three letters with the target but are inconsistent with the *m* node (e.g., *have*) produce inhibition that tends to limit the activation of the friends of the *m* node, and can thus be considered its "enemies." These words also produce feedback that tends to activate letters that were not actually presented. For example, activation from *have* produces excitatory input to the *h* node, thereby producing some competition with the *m* node. These activations, however, are usually not terribly strong. No one word gets very active, and so letters not in the actual display tend to get fairly weak excitatory feedback. This weak excitation is usually insufficient to overcome the bottom-up inhibition acting on nonpresented letters. Thus, in most cases, the harm done by top-down activation of letters that were not shown is minimal.

A part of the effect we have been describing is illustrated in Figure 10. Here, we compare the activations of the nodes for the letters in MAVE. Without feedback, the four curves would be identical to the one single letter curve included for comparison. So although there is facilitation for all four letters, there are definitely differences in the amount, depending on the number of friends and enemies of each letter. Note that within a given pseudoword, the total number of friends and enemies (i.e., the total number of words with three letters in common) is the same for all the letters.

letter level

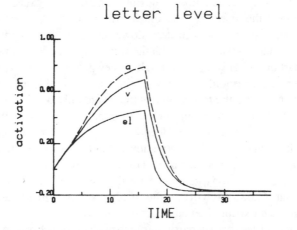

Figure 10. Activation functions for the letters *a* and *v* on presentation of *MAVE*. (Activation function for *e* is indistinguishable from function for *a*, and that for *m* is similar to that for *v*. The activation function for a single letter (sl), or a letter in an unrelated context is included for comparison.)

There are two other factors that affect the extent to which a particular word will become active at the word level when a particular pseudoword is shown. Although the effects of these factors are only weakly reflected in the activations at the letter level, they are nevertheless interesting to note, since they indicate some synergistic effects that emerge from the interplay of simple excitatory and inhibitory influences in the neighborhood. These are the *rich-get-richer effect* and the *gang effect*. The rich-get-richer effect is illustrated in Figure 11, which compares the activation curves for the nodes for *have, gave,* and *save* under presentation of MAVE. The words differ in frequency, which gives the words slight differences in baseline activation. What is interesting is that the difference gets magnified; so that at the point of peak activation, there is a much larger difference. The reason for the amplification can be seen by considering a system containing only two nodes, *a* and *b*, starting at different initial positive activation levels, *a* and *b* at time *t*. Let us suppose that *a* is stronger than *b* at *t*. Then at *t*+1, *a* will exert more of an inhibitory influence on *b*, since inhibition of a given node is determined by the sum of the activations of all nodes other than itself. This advantage for the initially more active nodes is compounded further in the case of the effect of word frequency by the fact that more frequent words creep above threshold first, thereby exerting an inhibitory effect on the lower frequency words when the latter are still too weak to fight back at all.

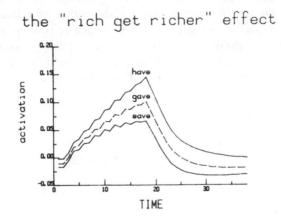

Figure 11. The rich-get-richer effect. (Activation functions for the nodes for *have, gave,* and *save* under presentation of *MAVE.*)

Even more interesting is the gang effect, which depends on the coordinated action of a related set of word nodes. This effect is depicted in Figure 12. Here, the activation curves for the *move, male,* and *save* nodes are compared. In the language, *move* and *make* are of approximately equal frequency, so their activations start out at about the same level. But they soon pull apart. Similarly, *save* starts out below *move* but soon reaches a higher activation. The reason for these effects is that *male* and *save* are both members of gangs with several members, whereas *move* is not. Consider first the difference between *male* and *move*. The reason for the difference is that there are several words that share the same three letters with MAVE as *male* does. In the list of words used in our simulations, there are six. These words all work together to reinforce the *m*, and *a*, and the *e* nodes, thereby producing much stronger reinforcement for themselves. Thus, these words make up a gang called the *ma_e* gang. In this example, there is also a *_ave* gang consisting of 6 other words, of which *save* is one. All of these work together to reinforce the *a*, *v*, and *e*. Thus, the *a* and *e* are reinforced by two gangs, whereas the letters *v* and *m* are reinforced by only one each. Now consider the word *move*. This word is a loner; there are no other words in its gang, the *m_ve* gang. Although two of the letters in *move* receive support from one gang each, and one receives support from both other gangs, the letters of *move* are less strongly enhanced by feedback than the letters of the members of the other two gangs. Since continued activation of one word in the face of the competition generated by all of the other partially activated words depends on the activations of the component letter nodes, the words in the other two gangs eventually gain the upper hand and drive *move* back below the activation threshold.

As our study of the MAVE example illustrates, the pattern of activation produced by a particular pseudoword is complex and idiosyncratic. In addition to the basic friends and enemies effects, there are also the rich-get-richer and the gang effects. These effects are primarily reflected in the pattern of activation at the word level, but they also exert subtle influences on the activations at the letter level. In general though, the main result is that when the letter-to-word inhibition is low, all four letters in the pseudoword receive some feedback reinforcement. The result, of course, is greater accuracy of reporting letters in pseudowords compared to single letters.

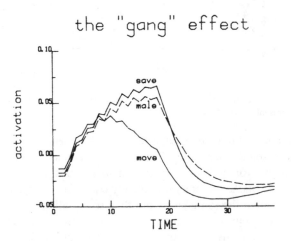

Figure 12. The gang effect. (Activation functions for *move, male,* and *save* under presentation of *MAVE*).

Table 3

ACTUAL AND SIMULATED RESULTS OF THE MCCLELLAND & JOHNSTON (1977) EX-
PERIMENTS (PROPORTION OF CORRECT FORCED CHOICE)

Result class	Target type		
	Word	Pseudoword	Single letter
Actual data			
High BF	.81	.79	.67
Low BF	.78	.77	.64
Average	.80	.78	.66
Simulation			
High BF	.81	.79	.67
Low BF	.79	.77	.67
Average	.80	.78	.67

Note. BF = bigram frequency.

Comparison of performance on words and pseudowords. Let us now consider the fact that the word advantage over pseudowords is generally rather small
in experiments where the subject knows that the stimuli include pseudowords.
Some fairly representative results, from the study of McClelland and Johnston
(1977), are illustrated in Table 3. The visual conditions of the study were the
same as those used in the patterned-mask condition in Johnston and McClelland
(1973). Trials were blocked, so subjects could adopt the optimum strategy for
each type of material. The slight word-pseudoword difference, though representative, is not actually statistically reliable in this study.

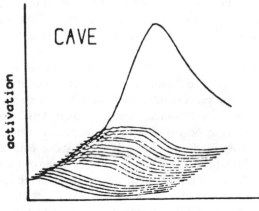

Figure 13. Activity at the word level upon presentation of *CAVE*, with weak letter-to-word inhibition.

a in different contexts

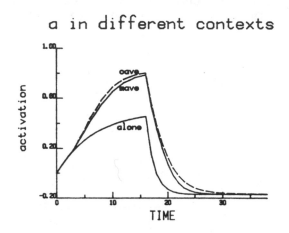

Figure 14. Activation functions for the letter *a*, under presentation of *CAVE* and *MAVE* and alone.

Words differ from pseudowords in that a word strongly activates one node at the word level, whereas a pseudoword does not. While we would tend to think of this as increasing the amount of feedback for words as opposed to pseudowords, there is the word-level inhibition that must be taken into account. This inhibition tends to equalize the total amount of activation at the word level between words and pseudowords. With words, the word shown tends to dominate the pattern of activity, thereby keeping all the words that have three letters in common with it from achieving the activation level they would reach in the absence of a node activated by all four letters. This situation is illustrated for the word CAVE in Figure 13. The result is that the sum of the activations of all the active units at the word level is not much different between the two cases. Thus, CAVE produces only slightly more facilitation for its constituent letters than MAVE, as illustrated in Figure 14.

In addition to the leveling effect of competition at the word level, it turned out that in our model, one of the common design features of studies comparing performance on words and pseudowords would operate to keep performance relatively good on pseudowords. In general, the stimulus materials used in most of these studies are designed by beginning with a list of pairs of words that differ by one letter (e.g., PEEL-PEEP). From each pair of words, a pair of nonwords is generated, differing from the original word pair by just one of the context letters and thereby keeping the actual target letters—and as much of the context as possible—the same between word and pseudoword items (e.g., TEEL-TEEP). A previously unnoticed side effect of this matching procedure is that it ensures that the critical letter in each pseudoword has at least one friend, namely the word from the matching pair that differs from it by one context letter. In fact, most of the critical letters in the pseudowords used by McClelland and Johnston (1977) tended to have relatively few enemies, compared to the number of friends. In general, a particular letter should be expected to have three times as many friends as enemies. In the McClelland and Johnston stimuli, the great majority of the stimuli had much larger differentials. Indeed, more than half of the critical letters had no enemies at all.

The puzzling absence of cluster frequency effects. In the account we have just described, facilitation of performance on letters in pseudowords was explained by the fact that pseudowords tend to activate a large number of words, and these words tend to work together to reinforce the activations of letters. This account might seem to suggest that pseudowords that have common letter clusters, and therefore have several letters in common with many words, would tend to produce the greatest facilitation. However, this factor has been manipulated in a number of studies, and little has been found in the way of an effect. The McClelland and Johnston (1977) study is one case in point. As Table 3 illustrates, there is only a slight tendency for superior performance on high cluster frequency words. This slight tendency is also observed in single letter control stimuli, suggesting that the difference may be due to differences in perceptibility of the target letters in the different positions, rather than cluster frequency per se. In any case, the effect is very small. Other studies have likewise failed to find any effect of cluster frequency (Spoehr and Smith, 1975; Manelis, 1974). The lack of an effect is most striking in the McClelland and Johnston study, since the high and low cluster frequency items differed widely in cluster frequency as measured in a number of ways.

In our model, the lack of a cluster frequency effect is due to the effect of mutual inhibition at the word level. As we have seen, this mutual inhibition tends to keep the total activity at the word level roughly constant over a variety of different input patterns, thereby greatly reducing the advantage for high cluster frequency items. Items containing infrequent clusters tend to activate few words, but there is less competition at the word level, so that the words that do become active reach higher activation levels.

The situation is illustrated for the nonwords TEEL and HOET in Figure 15. Although TEEL activates many more words, the total activation is not much different in the two cases.

The total activation is not, of course, the whole story. The ratio of friends to enemies is also important. And it turns out that this ratio is working against the high cluster items more than the low cluster items. In McClelland and Johnston's stimuli, only one of the low cluster frequency nonword pairs had critical letters with any enemies at all! For 23 out of 24 pairs, there was at least one friend (by virtue of the method of stimulus construction) and no enemies. In contrast, for the high cluster frequency pairs, there was a wide range, with some items having several more enemies than friends.

To simulate the McClelland and Johnston (1977) results, we had to select a subset of their stimuli, since some of the words they used were not in our word list. The stimuli had been constructed in sets containing a word pair, a pseudo-

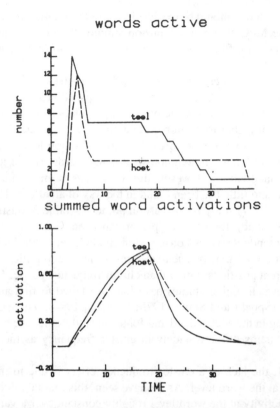

Figure 15. The number of words activated (top) and the total activation at the word level (bottom) upon presentation of the nonwords *TEEL* and *HOET*.

word pair, and a single letter pair that differed by the same letters in the same position (e.g., PEEL-PEEP TEEL-TEEP; __L __P). We simply selected all those sets in which both words in the pair appeared in our list. This resulted in a sample of 10 high cluster frequency sets and 10 low cluster frequency sets. The single letter stimuli derived from the high and low cluster frequency pairs were also run through the simulation. Both members of each pair were tested.

Since the stimuli were presented in the actual experiment blocked by material type, we separately selected an optimal time for readout for words, pseudowords, and single letters. Readout time was the same for high and low cluster frequency items of the same type, since these were presented in a mixed list in the actual experiment. As in the simulation of the Johnston and McClelland (1973) results, the display was presented for a duration of 15 cycles.

The simulation results, shown in Table 3, reveal the same general pattern as the actual data. The magnitude of the pseudoword advantage over single letters is just slightly smaller than the word advantage, and the effect of cluster frequency is very slight.

We have yet to consider how the model deals with unrelated letter strings. This depends a little on the exact characteristics of the strings. First let us consider truly randomly generated consonant strings. Such items typically produce some activation at the word level in our model, since they tend to share two letters with several words (one letter out of four is insufficient to activate a word, since three inhibitory inputs outweigh one excitatory input). These strings rarely have three letters in common with any one word. Thus, they only tend to activate a few words very weakly, and because of the weakness of the bottom-up excitation, competition among partially activated words keeps any one word from getting very active. So, little benefit results. When we ran our simulation on randomly generated consonant strings, there was only a 1 percent advantage over single letters.

Some items which have been used as unpronounceable nonwords or unrelated letter strings do produce a weak facilitation. We ran the nonwords used by McClelland and Johnston (1977) in their Experiment 2. These items contain a large number of vowels in positions that vowels typically occupy in words, and they therefore activate more words than, for example, random strings of consonants. The simulation was run under the same conditions as the one reported above for McClelland and Johnston's Experiment 1. The simulation produced a slight advantage for letters in these nonwords, compared to single letters, as did the experiment. In both the simulation and the actual experiment, forced-choice performance was 4 percent more accurate for letters in these unrelated letter strings than in single letter stimuli.

On the basis of this characteristic of our model, the results of one experiment on the importance of vowels in reading may be reinterpreted. Spoehr and Smith (1975) found that subjects were more accurate when reporting letters in unpronounceable nonwords that contained vowels than in those composed of all consonants. They interpreted the results as supporting the view that subjects parse letter strings into "vocalic center groups." However, an alternative possible account is that the strings containing vowels had more letters in common with actual words than the all consonant strings.

In summary, the model provides a good account of the perceptual advantage for letters in pronounceable nonwords, and for the lack of such an advantage in unrelated letter strings. In addition, it accounts for the small difference between performance on words and pseudowords and for the absence of any really noticeable cluster frequency effect in the McClelland and Johnston (1977) experiment.

The Role of Lexical Constraints

The Johnston (1978) experiment. Several models that have been proposed to account for the word advantage rely on the idea that the context letters in a word facilitate performance by constraining the set of possible letters that might have been presented in the critical letter position. According to models of this class, contexts that strongly constrain what the target letter should be result in greater accuracy of perception than more weakly constraining contexts. For example, the context __HIP should facilitate the perception of an initial s more than the context __INK. The reason is that __HIP is more strongly constraining, since only three letters (s, c, and w) fit in the context to make a word, compared to __INK, where nine letters (D, F, K, L, M, P, R, S, and W) fit in the context to make a word. In a test of such models, Johnston (1978) compared accuracy of perception of letters occurring in high- and low-constraint contexts. The same target letters were tested in the same positions in both cases. For example, the letters s and w were tested in the high-constraint __HIP context and the low-constraint __INK context. Using bright-target/patterned-mask conditions, Johnston found no difference in accuracy of perception between letters in the high- and low-constraint contexts. The results of this experiment are shown in Table 4. Johnston measured letter perception in two ways. He not only asked the subjects to decide which of two letters had been presented (the forced-choice measure), but he also asked subjects to report the whole word and recorded how often they got the critical letter correct. No significant difference was observed in either case. In the forced choice there was a slight difference favoring low-constraint items, but in the free report there was no difference at all.

Table 4

ACTUAL AND SIMULATED RESULTS (PROBABILITY CORRECT) FROM JOHNSTON
(1978) EXPERIMENTS

	Constraint	
Result class	High	Low
Actual data		
Forced choice	.77	.79
Free report	.54	.54
Simulation		
Forced choice	.77	.76
Free report	.56	.54

Although our model does use contextual constraints (as they are embodied in specific lexical items), it turns out that it does not predict that highly constraining contexts will facilitate perception of letters much more than weakly constraining contexts under bright-target/patterned-mask conditions. Under such conditions, the role of the word level is not to help the subject select among alternatives left open by an incomplete feature analysis process, as most constraint-based models have assumed, but rather to help strengthen the activation of the nodes for the letters presented. Contextual constraints, at least as manipulated by Johnston, do not have much effect on the magnitude of this strengthening effect.

In detail, what happens in the model when a word is shown is that the presentation results in weak activation of the words that share three letters with the target. Some of these words are friends of the critical letter in that they contain the actual critical letter shown, as well as two of the letters from the context (e.g., *shop* is a friend of the initial s in SHIP). Some of the words, however, are enemies of the critical letter in that they contain the three context letters of the word but a different letter in the critical letter position (e.g., *chip* and *whip* are enemies of the s in SHIP). From our point of view, Johnston's (1978) constraint manipulation is essentially a manipulation of the number of enemies the critical letter has in the given context. Johnston's high- and low-constraint stimuli have equal numbers of friends, on the average, but (by design) the high-constraint items have fewer enemies, as shown in Table 5.

Table 5

FRIENDS AND ENEMIES OF THE CRITICAL LETTERS IN THE STIMULI USED BY JOHNSTON (1978)

Critical letter position	High constraint			Low constraint		
	Friends	Enemies	Ratio	Friends	Enemies	Ratio
1	3.33	2.22	.60	3.61	6.44	.36
2	9.17	1.00	.90	6.63	2.88	.70
3	6.30	1.70	.79	7.75	4.30	.64
4	4.96	1.67	.75	6.67	3.50	.66
Average	5.93	1.65		6.17	4.27	

In the simulation, the friends and enemies of the target word receive some activation. The greater number of enemies in the low-constraint condition is responsible for the small effect of constraint that the model produces. What happens is that the enemies of the critical letter tend to keep nodes for the presented word and for the friends of the critical letter from being quite as strongly activated as they would otherwise be. The effect is quite small for two reasons. First, the node for the word presented receives four excitatory inputs from the letter level, and all other words can only receive at most three excitatory inputs and at least one inhibitory input. As we saw in the case of the word CAVE, the node for the correct word dominates the activations at the word level and is predominantly responsible for any feedback to the letter level. Second, while the high-constraint items have fewer enemies, by more than a two-to-one margin, both high- and low-constraint items have, on the average, more friends than enemies. The friends of the target letter work with the actual word shown to keep the activations of the enemies in check, thereby reducing the extent of their inhibitory effect still further. The ratio of the number of friends over the total number of neighbors is not very different in the two conditions, except in the first serial position.

This discussion may give the impression that contextual constraint is not an important variable in our model. In fact, it is quite powerful. But its effects are obscured in the Johnston (1978) experiment because of the strong dominance of the target word when all the features are extracted and the fact that we are concerned with the likelihood of perceiving a particular letter rather than performance in identifying correctly what whole word was shown. We will now consider an experiment in which contextual constraints played a strong role, because the characteristics just mentioned were absent.

The Broadbent and Gregory (1968) experiment. Up to now we have found no evidence that either bigram frequency or lexical constraints have any effect on performance. However, in experiments using the traditional whole report method, these variables have been shown to have substantial effects. Various studies have shown that recognition thresholds are lower, or recognition accuracy at threshold higher, when relatively unusual words were used (Bouwhuis, 1979; Havens and Foote, 1963; Newbigging, 1961). Such items tend to be low in bigram frequency and at the same time high in lexical constraint.

In one experiment, Broadbent and Gregory (1968) investigated the role of bigram frequency at two different levels of word frequency and found an interesting interaction. We now consider how our model can account for their results. To begin, it is important to note that the visual conditions of their experiment were quite different from those of McClelland and Johnston (1977), in which the data and our model failed to show a bigram frequency effect, and of Johnston (1978), in which the data and the model showed little or no constraint effect. The conditions were like the dim-target/blank-mask conditions discussed above, in that the target was shown briefly against an illuminated background, without being followed by any kind of mask. The dependent measure was the probability of correctly reporting the whole word. The results are indicated in Table 6. A slight advantage for high bigram frequency items over low bigram frequency was obtained for frequent words, although it was not consistent over different subsets of items tested. The main finding was that words of low bigram frequency had an advantage among infrequent words. For these stimuli, higher bigram frequency actually resulted in a lower percent correct.

Table 6
ACTUAL AND SIMULATED RESULTS OF THE BROADBENT AND GREGORY (1968) EXPERIMENT (PROPORTION OF CORRECT WHOLE REPORT)

	Word frequency	
Result class	High	Low
Actual data		
High BF	.64	.43
Low BF	.64	.58
Simulation		
High BF	.41	.21
Low BF	.39	.37

Note. BF = bigram frequency

Unfortunately, Broadbent and Gregory used five-letter words, so we were unable to run a simulation on their actual stimuli. However, we were able to select a subset of the stimuli used in the McClelland and Johnston (1977) experiment that fit the requirements of the Broadbent and Gregory design. We therefore presented these stimuli to our model, under the presentation parameters used in simulating the blank-mask condition of the Johnston and McClelland (1973) experiment above. The only difference was that the output was taken, not from the letter level, as in all of our other simulations, but directly from the word level. The results of the simulation, shown in Table 6, replicate the obtained pattern very nicely. The simulation produced a large advantage for the low bigram items, among the infrequent words, and produced a slight advantage for high bigram items among the frequent words.

In our model, low-frequency words of high bigram frequency are most poorly recognized, because these are the words that have the largest number of neighbors. Under conditions of incomplete feature extraction, which we expect to prevail under these visual conditions, the more neighbors a word has the more likely it is to be confused with some other word. This becomes particularly important for lower frequency words. As we have seen, if both a low-frequency word and a high-frequency word are equally compatible with the detected portion of the input, the higher frequency word will tend to dominate. When incomplete feature information is extracted, the relative activation of the target and the neighbors is much lower than when all the features have been seen. Indeed, some neighbors may turn out to be just as compatible with the features extracted as the target itself. Under these circumstances, the word of the highest frequency will tend to gain the upper hand. The probability of correctly reporting a low-frequency word will therefore be much more strongly influenced by the presence of a high-frequency neighbor compatible with the input than the other way around.

But why does the model actually produce a slight reversal with high-frequency words? Even here, it would seem that the presence of numerous neighbors would tend to hurt instead of facilitate performance. However, we have forgotten the fact that the activation of neighbors can be beneficial as well as harmful. The active neighbors produce feedback that strengthens most or all of the letters, and these in turn increase the activation of the node for the word shown. As it happens, there turns out to be a delicate balance for high-frequency words between the negative and positive effects of neighbors, which only slightly favors the words with more neighbors. Indeed, the effect only holds for some of these items. We have not yet had the opportunity to explore all the factors that determine whether the effect of neighbors in individual cases will on balance be positive or negative.

Different effects in different experiments. This discussion of the Broadbent and Gregory (1968) experiment indicates once again that our model is something of a chameleon. The model produces no effect of constraint or bigram frequency under the visual conditions and testing procedures used in the Johnston (1978) and McClelland and Johnston (1977) experiments but does produce such effects under the conditions of the Broadbent and Gregory (1968) experiment. This flexibility of the model, of course, is fully required by the data. While there are other models of word perception that can account for one or the other type of result, to our knowledge the model presented here is the only scheme that has been worked out to account for both.

Discussion

The interactive activation model does a good job of accounting for the results in the literature on the perception of letters in words and nonwords. The model provides a unified explanation of the results of a variety of experiments and provides a framework in which the effects of manipulations of the visual display characteristics used may be analyzed. In addition, as we shall see in Part 2 (Rumelhart and McClelland, in press), the model readily accounts for a variety of additional phenomena. Moreover, as we shall also show, it can be extended beyond its current domain of applicability with substantial success. In Part 2 we will report a number of experiments demonstrating what we call "context enhancement effects" and show how the model can explain the major findings in the experiments.

One issue that deserves some consideration is the robustness of the model. To what extent do the simulations depend upon particular parameter values? What are the effects of changes of the parameter values? These are extremely complex questions, and we do not have complete answers. However, we have made some observations. First, the basic Reicher (1969) effect can be obtained under a very wide range of different parameters, though of course its exact size will depend on the ensemble of parameter values. However, one thing that seems to be important is the overpowering effect of one incompatible feature in suppressing activations at the letter level. Without this strong bottom-up inhibition, the mask would not effectively drive out the activations previously established by the stimulus. Second, performance on pronounceable nonwords depends on the relative strength of letter-word excitation compared to inhibition and on the strength of the competition among word units. Parameter values can be found which produce no advantage for any multiletter strings except words, whereas other values can be found that produce large advantages for words, pseudowords, and even many nonword strings. The effects (or rather the lack of effects) of letter-cluster frequency and constraints likewise depend on these parameters.

It thus appears that relatively strong feature-letter inhibition is necessary, but at the same time, relatively weak letter-word inhibition is necessary. This discrepancy is a bit puzzling, since we would have thought that the same general principles of operation would have applied to both the letter and the word levels. A possible way to resolve the discrepancy might be to introduce a more sophisticated account of the way masking works. It is quite possible that new inputs act as position-specific "clear signals," disrupting activations created by previous patterns in corresponding locations. Some possible physiological mechanisms that would produce such effects at lower processing levels have been described by Weisstein, Ozog, and Szoc (1975) and by Breitmeyer and Ganz (1976), among others. If we used such a mechanism to account for the basic effect of masking, it might well be possible to lower the feature-letter inhibition considerably. Lowering feature-letter inhibition would then necessitate strong letter-letter inhibition, so that letters that exactly match the input would be able to dominate those with only partial matches. With these changes the letter and word levels would indeed operate by the same principles.

Perhaps it is a bit premature to discuss such issues as robustness, since there are a number of problems that we have not yet resolved. First, we have ignored the fact that there is a high degree of positional uncertainty in reports of letters — particularly letters in unrelated strings, but occasionally also in reports of letters in words and pseudowords (Estes, 1975; McClelland,1976; McClelland and Johnston, 1977). Another thing that we have not considered very fully is the serial position curve. In general, it appears that performance is more accurate on the end letters in multiletter strings, particularly the first letter. In Part 2 we consider ways of extending the model to account for both of these aspects of perceptual performance.

Third, there are some effects of set on word perception that we have not considered. Johnston and McClelland (1974) found that perception of letters in words was actually hurt if subjects focused their attention on a single letter position in the word (see also Holender, 1979,and Johnston, 1974). In addition, Aderman and Smith (1971) found that the advantage for pseudowords over unrelated letters only occurs if the subject expects that pseudowords will be shown; and more recently, Carr et al. (1978) have replicated this finding, while at the same time showing that it is apparently not necessary to be prepared for presentations of actual words. Part 2 considers how our model is compatible with this effect also. We will also consider how our model might be extended to account for some recent findings demonstrating effects of letter and word masking on perception of letters in words and other contexts.

In all but one of the experiments we have simulated, the primary (if not the only) data for the experiments were obtained from forced choices between pairs of letters, or strings differing by a single letter. In these cases, it seemed to us most natural to rely on the output of the letter level as the basis for responding. However, it may well be that subjects often base their responses on the output of the word level. Indeed, we have assumed that they do in experiments like the Broadbent and Gregory (1968) study, in which subjects were told to report what word they thought they had seen. This may also have happened in the McClelland and Johnston (1977) and Johnston (1978) studies, in which subjects were instructed to report all four letters before the forced choice on some trials. Indeed, both studies found that the probability of reporting all four letters correctly for letters in words was greater than we would expect given independent processing of each letter position. It seems natural to account for these completely correct reports by assuming that they often occurred on occasions where the subject encoded the item as a word. Even in experiments where only a forced choice is obtained, on many occasions subjects may still come away with a word, rather than a sequence of letters.

In the early phases of the development of our model, we explicitly included the possibility of output from the word level as well as the letter level. We assumed that the subject would either encode a word, with some probability dependent on the activations at the word level or, failing that, would encode some letter for each letter position dependent on the activations at the letter level. However, we found that simply relying on the letter level permitted us to account equally well for the results. In essence, the reason is that the word-level information is incorporated into the activations at the letter level because of the feedback, so that the word level is largely redundant. In addition, of course, readout from the letter level is necessary to the model's account of performance with nonwords. Since it is adequate to account for all of the forced-choice data, and since it is difficult to know exactly how much of the details of free-report data should be attributed to perceptual processes and how much to such things as possible biases in the readout processes and so forth, we have stuck for the present with readout from the letter level.

Another decision that we adopted in order to keep the model within bounds was to exclude the possibility of processing interactions between the visual and phonological systems. However, in the model as sketched at the outset (Figure 1), activations at the letter level interacted with a phonological level as well as the word level. Perhaps the most interesting feature of our model is its ability to account for performance on letters in pronounceable nonwords without assuming any such interactions. We will also see in Part 2 (Rumelhart and McClelland, 1982) that certain carefully selected unpronounceable consonant strings produce quite large contextual facilitation effects, compared to other sequences of consonants, which supports our basic position that pronounceability per se is not an important feature of the perceptual facilitation effects we have accounted for.

Another simplification we have adopted in Part 1 has been to consider only cases in which individual letters or strings of letters were presented in the absence of a linguistic context. In Part 2 we will consider the effects of introducing contextual inputs to the word level, and we will explore how the model might work in processing spoken words in context as well.

NOTES

[1]Hinton, G.E. Relaxation and its role in vision. Unpublished doctoral dissertation, University of Edinburgh, Scotland, 1977.

[2]Rumelhart, D.E. A multicomponent theory of confusion among briefly exposed alphabetic characters Tech. Rep. 22. San Diego: University of California, Center for Human Information Processing, 1971.

REFERENCES

Adams, M.J. Models of word recognition. *Cognitive Psychology*, 1979, 11, 133-176.

Aderman, D., and Smith, E.E. Expectancy as a determinant of functional units in perceptual recognition. *Cognitive Psychology,* 1971, 2, 117-129.

Anderson, J.A. Neural models with cognitive implications. In D. LaBerge and S.J. Samuels (Eds.), *Basic Processes in reading: Perception and comprehension.* Hillsdale, NJ: Erlbaum, 1977.

Anderson, J.A., Silverstein, J.W., Ritz, S.A. and Jones, R.S. Distinctive features, categorical perception, and probability learning: Some applications of a neural model. *Psychological Review,* 1977, 84, 413-451.

Baron, J., and Thurston, I. An analysis of the word superiority effect. *Cognitive Psychology,* 1973, 4, 207-228.

Bouwhuis, D.G. *Visual recognition of words.* Eindhoven, The Netherlands: Greve Offset B.V., 1979.

Breitmeyer, B.G., and Ganz, L. Implications of sustained and transient channels for theories of visual pattern masking, saccadic suppression, and information processing. *Psychological Review,* 1976, 83, 1-36.

Broadbent, D.E. Word-frequency effect and response bias. *Psychological Review,* 1967, 74, 1-15.

Broadbent, D.E., and Gregory, M. Visual perception of words differing in letter digram frequency. *Journal of Verbal Learning and Verbal Behavior,* 1968, 7, 569-571.

Bruner, J.S. On perceptual readiness. *Psychological Review,* 1957, 64, 123-152.

Carr, T.H., Davidson, B.J., and Hawkins, H.L. Perceptual flexibility in word recognition: Strategies affect orthographic computation but not lexical access. *Journal of Experimental Psychology: Human Perception and Performance,* 1978, 4, 674-690.

Cattell, J.M. The time taken up by cerebral operations. *Mind,* 1886, 11, 220-242.

Estes, W.K. The locus of inferential and perceptual processes in letter identification. *Journal of Experimental Psychology: General,* 1975, 1, 122-145.

Glushko, R.J. The organization and activation of orthographic knowledge in reading words aloud. *Journal of Experimental Psychology: Human Perception and Performance,* 1979, 5, 674-691.

Grossberg, S. A theory of visual coding, memory, and development. In E.L.J. Leeuwenberg and H.F.J.M. Buffart (Eds.), *Formal theories of visual perception.* New York: Wiley, 1978.

Havens, L.L., and Foote, W.E. The effect of competition on visual duration threshold and its independence of stimulus frequency. *Journal of Experimental Psychology,* 1963, 65, 5-11.

Hinton, G.E., and Anderson, J.A. (Eds.). *Parallel models of associative memory.* Hillsdale, NJ: Erlbaum, 1981.

Holender, D. Identification of letters in words and of single letters with pre- and postknowledge versus postknowledge of the alternatives, *Perception and Psychophysics,*1979, 25, 213-318.

Huey, E.B. *The psychology and pedagogy of reading.* New York: Macmillan, 1908.

Johnston, J.C. A test of the sophisticated guessing theory of word perception. *Cognitive Psychology,* 10, 1978, 123-154.

Johnston, J.C. The role of contextual constraint in the perception of letters in words. Unpublished doctoral dissertation, University of Pennsylvania, 1974.

Johnston, J.C., and McClelland, J.L. Visual factors in word perception. *Perception and Psychophysics,* 1973, 14, 365-370.

Johnston, J.C., and McClelland, J.L. Perception of letters in words: Seek not and ye shall find. *Science,* 1974, 184, 1192-1194.

Johnston, J.C., and McClelland, J.L. Experimental tests of a hierarchical model of word identification. *Journal of Verbal Learning and Verbal Behavior,* 1980, 19, 503-524.

Juola, J.F., Leavitt, D.D., and Choe, C.S. Letter identification in word, nonword, and single letter displays. *Bulletin of the Psychonomic Society,* 1974, 4, 278-280.

Kohonen, T. *Associative memory: A system-theoretic approach.* West Berlin: Springer-Verlag, 1977.

Kucera, H., and Francis, W. *Computational analysis of present-day American English.* Providence, RI: Brown University Press, 1967.

LaBerge, D., and Samuels, S. Toward a theory of automatic information processing in reading. *Cognitive Psychology,* 1974, 6, 293-323.

Levin, J.A. *Proteus: An activation framework for cognitive process models (ISI/WP-2).* Marina del Rey, CA: Information Sciences Institute, 1976.

Luce, R.D. *Individual choice behavior.* New York: Wiley, 1959.

Manelis, L. The effect of meaningfulness in tachistoscopic word perception. *Perception and Psychophysics,* 1974, 16, 182-192.

Massaro, D.W., and Klitzke, D. The role of lateral masking and orthographic structure in letter and word recognition. *Acta Psychologica,* 1979, 43, 413-426.

McClelland, J.L. Preliminary letter identification in the perception of words and nonwords. *Journal of Experimental Psychology: Human Perception and Performance,* 1976, 1, 80-91.

McClelland, J.L. On the time relations of mental processes: An examination of systems of processes in cascade. *Psychological Review,* 1979, 86, 287-330.

McClelland, J.L., and Johnston, J.C. The role of familiar units in perception of words and non-words. *Perception and Psychophysics,* 1977, 22, 249-261.

Morton, J. Interaction of information in word recognition. *Psychological Review,* 1969, 76, 165-178.

Neisser, U. *Cognitive psychology.* New York: Appleton-Century-Crofts, 1967.

Newbigging, P.L. The perceptual reintegration of frequent and infrequent words. *Canadian Journal of Psychology,* 1961, 15, 123-132.

Reicher, G.M. Perceptual recognition as a function of meaningfulness of stimulus material. *Journal of Experimental Psychology,* 1969, 81, 274-280.

Rumelhart, D.E. A multicomponent theory of the perception of briefly exposed visual displays. *Journal of Mathematical Psychology,* 1970, 7, 191-218.

Rumelhart, D.E. Toward an interactive model of reading. In S. Dornic (Ed.), *Attention and perform-ance IV.* Hillsdale, NJ: Erlbaum, 1977.

Rumelhart, D.E., and McClelland, J.L. An interactive activation model of context effects in letter perception: Part 2. The contextual enhancement effect and some tests and extensions of the model. *Psychological Review,* 1982, 89, 60-94.

Rumelhart, D.E., and Siple, P. The process of recognizing tachistoscopically presented words. *Psychological Review,* 1974, 81, 99-118.

Spoehr, K., and Smith, E. The role of orthographic and phonotactic rules in perceiving letter pat-terns. *Journal of Experimental Psychology: Human Perception and Performance,* 1975, 1, 21-34.

Szentagothai, J., and Arbib, M.A. *Conceptual models of neural organization.* Cambridge, MA: MIT Press, 1975.

Taylor, G.A., and Chabot, R.J. Differential backward masking of words and letters by masks of varying orthographic structure. *Memory and Cognition,* 1978, 6, 629-635.

Thompson, M.C., and Massaro, D.W. Visual information and redundancy in reading. *Journal of Experimental Psychology,* 1973, 98, 49-54.

Turvey, M. On peripheral and central processes in vision: Inferences from an information-processing analysis of masking with patterned stimuli. *Psychological Review,* 1973, 80, 1-52.

Weisstein, N., Ozog, G., and Sdzoc, R. A comparison and elaboration of two models of metacon-trast. *Psychological Review,* 1975, 82, 325-343.

Wheeler, D. Processes in word recognition. *Cognitive Psychology,* 1970, 1, 59-85.

Appendix

Computer Simulation of the Model

The computer program for simulating the interactive activation model was written in the c programing language to run on a Digital PDP 11/45 computer under the UNIX (Trade Mark of Bell Laboratories) operating system. There is now a second version, also in c, which runs under UNIX on a VAX 11/780. When no other jobs are running on the VAX, a simulation of a single experimental trial takes approximately 15-30 sec.

Data Structures

The simulation relies on several arrays for each of the processing levels in the model. The input is held in an array that contains slots for each of the line segments in the Rumelhart-Siple font in each position. Segments can be present or absent, or their status can be indeterminate (as when the input is made deliberately incomplete). There is another array that holds the information the model has detected about the display. Each element of this array represents a detector for the presence or absence of a feature. When the corresponding feature is detected, the detector's value is set to 1 (remember that both absence and presence must be detected).

At the letter level, one array (the activation array) stores the current activation of each node. A second array (the excitatory buffer) is used to sum all of the excitatory influences reaching each node on a given tick of the clock, and a third array (the inhibitory buffer) is used to sum all of the inhibitory influences reaching each node. In addition there is an output array, containing the current output strength of each letter level node. At the word level, there is an activation array for the current activation of each node, as well as an excitatory buffer and an inhibitory buffer.

Knowledge of Letters and Words

The links among the nodes in the model are stored in a set of tables. There is a table in the program that lists which features are present in each letter and which are absent. Another table contains the spellings of each of the 1,179 words known to the program.

Input

Simulated visual input is entered from a computer terminal or from a text file. Several successive displays within a single "trial" may be specified. Each display is characterized by an onset time (tick number from the start of the trial) and some array of visual information. Each lowercase letter stands for the array

319

of features making up the corresponding letter. Other characters stand for particular mask characters, blanks, and so forth. As examples, "_" stands for a blank,
and "0" stands for the $\boxtimes$ mask character. Thus the specification:

$$
\begin{array}{ll}
0 & \text{mav-} \\
12 & \text{mave} \\
24 & \text{0000}
\end{array}
$$

instructs the program to present the visual array consisting of the letters M, A,
and V in the first, second, and third letter positions, respectively, at Cycle 0; to
present the letter E in the fourth position at Cycle 12; and to present an $\boxtimes$ mask
at Cycle 24. It is also possible to specify any arbitrary feature array to occur in
any letter position.

Processing Occurring During Each Cycle

During each cycle, the values of all of the nodes are updated. The activations
of letter and word nodes, which were determined on Cycle t - 1, are used to
determine the activations of these nodes on Cycle t. Activations of feature nodes
are updated first, so that they begin to influence letter nodes right away.

The first thing the program does on each cycle is update the input array to
reflect any new changes in the display. On cycles when a new display is presented, detectors for features in letter positions in which there has been a change
in the input are subject to resetting. A random number generator is used to determine whether each new feature is detected or not. When the new value of a particular feature (present or absent) is detected, the old value is erased. Probability
of detection can be set to any probability (in many cases it is simply set to 1.0, so
that all of the features are detected).

For each letter in each position, the program then checks the current activation value (i.e., the value computed on the previous cycle) in the activation array.
If the node is active (i.e., if its activation is above threshold), its excitatory and
inhibitory effects on each node at the word level are computed. To determine
whether the letter in question excites or inhibits a particular word node, the program simply examines the spelling of each word to see if the letter is in the word
in the appropriate position. If so, excitation is added to the word's excitatory
buffer. If not, inhibition is added to the word's inhibitory buffer. The magnitudes
of these effects are the product of the driving letter's activation and the appropriate rate parameters. Word-to-letter influences are computed in a similar fashion.

The next step is the computation of the word-word inhibition and the determination of the new word activation values. First, the activations of all the active
word nodes are summed. The inhibitory buffer of each word node is incremented
by an amount proportional to the summed activation of all other word nodes
(i.e., by the product of the total word level activation minus its own activation, if
it is active, times the word-word inhibition rate parameter). This completes the

influences acting on the word nodes. The value in the inhibitory buffer is subtracted from the value in the excitatory buffer. The result is then subjected to floor and ceiling effects, as described in the article, to determine the net effect of the excitatory and inhibitory input. This net effect is then added to the current activation of the node, and the decay of the current value is subtracted to give a new current value, which is stored in the activation array. Finally, the excitatory and inhibitory buffers are cleared for new input on the next cycle.

Next is the computation of the feature-to-letter influences. For each feature in each letter position, if that feature has been detected, the program checks each letter to see if it contains the feature. If it does, the excitatory buffer for that letter in that position is incremented. If not, the corresponding inhibitory buffer is incremented. After this, the letter-letter inhibition is added into the inhibitory buffers following a similar procedure as was used in computing the word-word inhibitory effects. (Actually, this step is skipped in the reported simulations, since the value of letter-letter inhibition has been set to zero.)

Next is the computation of the new activation values at the letter level. These are computed in just the same way as the new activation values at the word level. Finally, the effect of the current activation is added into the letter's output strength, and the excitatory and inhibitory buffers are cleared for the next cycle.

The order of some of the preceding steps is arbitrary. What is important is that at the end of each cycle, the activations of all the word nodes have been updated to reflect letter activations of the previous cycle and vice versa. The fact that newly detected input influences the letter detectors immediately is not meaningful, since waiting until the next cycle would just add a fixed delay to all of the activations in the system.

Output

To simulate forced-choice performance, the program must be told when to read out the results of processing at the letter level, what position is being tested, and what the two alternatives are. In fact the user actually gives the program the full target display and the full alternative display (e.g., LEAD-LOAD), and the program compares them to figure out the critical letter position and the two choice alternatives. Various options are available for monitoring readout performance of the simulation. First, it is possible to have the program print out what the result of readout would be at each time cycle. Second, the user may specify a particular cycle for readout. Third, the user may tell the program to figure out the optimal time for readout and to print both the time and the resulting percent correct performance. This option is used in preliminary runs to determine what readout time to use in the final simulation runs for each experiment.

On each cycle for which output is requested, the program computes the probability that the correct alternative is read out and the probability that the incorrect alternative is read out, based on their response strengths as described in the text. Probability-correct forced choice is then simply the probability that the correct alternative was read out, plus .5 times the probability that neither the correct nor the incorrect alternative was read out.

Observation and Manipulation

It is possible to examine the activation of any node at the end of each cycle. A few useful summaries are also available, such as the number of active word nodes and the sum of their activations, the number of active letter nodes in each position, and so on. It is also possible to alter any of the parameters of the model between cycles or to change a parameter and then start again at Time 0 in order to compare the response of the model under different parameter values.

Running a Simulation

When simulating an experiment with a number of different trials (i.e., a number of different stimulus items in each experimental condition), the information the computer needs about the input and the forced-choice alternatives can be specified in a file, with one line containing all of the necessary information for each trial of the simulation. Typically a few test runs are carried out to choose an optimal exposure duration and readout time. Then the simulation is run with a single specified readout time for each display condition (when different display types are mixed within the same block of trials in the experiment being simulated, a single readout time is used for all display conditions). Note that when the probability of feature detection is set to 1.0, the model is completely deterministic. That is, it computes readout and forced-choice probabilities on the basis of response strengths. These are determined completely by the knowledge stored in the system (e.g., what the system knows about the appearance of the letters and the spellings of the words), by the set of features extracted, and by the values of the various parameters.

NOTE

[1] Preparation of this article was supported by National Science Foundation Grants BNS-76-14830 and BNS-79-24062 to J. L. McClelland and Grant BNS-76-15024 to D. E. Rumelhart, and by the Office of Naval Research under contract N00014-79-C-0323. We would like to thank Don Norman, James Johnston, and members of the LNR research group for helpful discussions of much of the material covered in this article.

Comprehension

Comprehension of Text Structures

P. David Pearson
University of Illinois

Kaybeth Camperell
University of Wisconsin

In this paper, we will review theoretical and empirical developments in the comprehension of text structure over the past twenty years. Following that review, we will offer some suggestions about what this area of scholarship has to say about educational practice. The suggestions will be of two types: a) tentative suggestions about educational practices that educational publishers and/or teachers ought to consider in preparing texts for students and lesson plans to help them cope with variations in text structure, and b) suggestions to educational researchers concerning classroom research which seem reasonable in the light of basic research about text structure influences.

What Would It Mean to Find that Text Structure Influences Comprehension?

Perhaps a good starting point for a review concerned with the influence of text structure on prose comprehension is to ask of what consequence any conceivable findings might be. For example, suppose our review were to demonstrate that 90 percent of the variation in students' comprehension of prose materials was due to the influence of variation in text structure. Suppose we could demonstrate that by holding content (the ideas, concepts, and relations among concepts) of a passage constant and altering the surface structure in which the ideas are communicated we could move a student from 25 percent comprehension of the passage to 75 percent comprehension. What would we recommend? Clearly, we would immediately inform the publishing industry that we had made a breakthrough in communication technology and write manuals on how to communicate ideas effectively in prose.

Suppose, alternatively that we found that variation in text structure had virtually no effect on comprehension. Suppose we found, in the hypothetical experi-

Reprinted from *Comprehension and Teaching: Research Reviews*, John T. Guthrie (Ed.). Newark, Delaware: International Reading Association, 1981.

ment above, that such alterations yielded a modest 5 percent instead of a 50 percent gain in comprehension of passages. We would probably drop our heads a little and recommend that our colleagues look elsewhere for any answers to the question of how to improve our communication efficiency—look at the nature of the concepts themselves and relations among them, perhaps.

Suppose that we found that variations in text structure made a big difference for young students but that the differences between various levels of complexity decreased as a function of age. We would likely advise our publisher to avoid certain grammatical structures or text organization patterns until some optimal age level at which, presumably, students have gathered enough linguistic experience to handle their complexity.

Suppose that we found, along with this hypothetical developmental effect, that we could overcome the deleterious effect of certain text structures on younger students by offering them direct instruction in dealing with those structures. We would advise teachers that if they are going to present young students with text embodying those structures, they will have to teach students how to handle them.

Findings like the hypothetical cases described above, while not quite so dramatic as our make-believe examples, have emerged from time to time over the past twenty or thirty years, sometimes but not always accompanied by recommendations like those we have suggested. That text structure influences comprehension, therefore, is not really at issue; what is at issue is the precise way in which the influence is exerted, why the influence exists, and what the influences have to say about practical matters of teaching and writing instructional materials.

What Counts as Text Structure

Before we can review the literature on the influence of text structure, we need to define what we mean by variations in text structure. We will approach our definition through examples. Consider examples (1-4) below.

1. The lad rode the steed to victory.
2. The steed was ridden to victory by the lad.
3. The young man rode the horse to a first place finish.
4. The horse was ridden to a first place finish by the young man.

Each of the four sentences exhibits a different surface form for the same underlying idea, yet there are only two different grammatical structures represented, the active and the passive. Hence the difference between (1) and (2) or between (3) and (4) can be regarded as a variation in text structure. However the differences between (1) and (3) or (2) and (4) are better characterized as lexical, or possibly semantic, variations. In the language of transformational generative grammar, we would say that (1) and (2) have the identical deep structure (underlying meaning), as do (3) and (4).[1] By intuition we would probably agree that there is only a slight difference in the two deep structures attributable to connotative differences in the meanings of lad-young man, victory-first place finish, and steed-horse. But the basic point is that we will regard alterations in the grammatical structure of sentences, which do not alter any semantic meanings or relations, as examples of text structure manipulations.

Now consider examples (5-8).

5. Henry lost the quarterback job because his arm gave out.

6. Because his arm gave out, Henry lost the quarterback job.

7. Henry lost the quarterback job. His arm gave out.

8. Henry's arm gave out. He lost the quarterback job.

The difference between (5) and (6) is like the difference between (1) and (2) above—simple grammatical transformation, in this case preposing a subordinate clause. The difference between (5) and (7) is not as simple. It is debatable whether or not the causal relation between the two clauses is preserved in (7), unless we resort to the Gricean principle of cooperation between author and reader (Grice, 1975) which posits that no author would arrange the two sentences in (7) adjacent to one another unless he was inviting the reader to infer that the one explained the other. Notice that the invitation to make the causal inference is even stronger in (8), presumably because of the covariation between causal and sequential ordering. Whether variations like those between (5) and (7) qualify as grammatical variation is not clear. But to us they definitely qualify as variation in some aspect of text structure. In certain systems of text analysis they would be regarded as alterations in the rhetorical structure (e.g., Meyer, 1975), cohesion structure (Halliday and Hasan, 1976), or logical structure (e.g., Frederiksen, 1975) of the discourse. Such variations are abundant in naturally occurring discourse, as exemplified in (9-11).

9a. If you want to be a Badger, then come along with me.

9b. Do you want to be a Badger? Come along with me.

10a. After Matthew ate lasagne, he bought a new TV.

10b. Matthew ate lasagne. (Then) he bought a new TV.

11a. Although Susan ran as fast as she could, she lost the race.

11b. Susan ran as fast as she could. But she lost the race.

11c. Susan ran as fast as she could. Alas! She lost the race.

Moving from smaller to larger units of discourse, other kinds of structural variation enter the picture. For example, the structural difference between (12) and (13) has been characterized as a staging variation (Grimes, 1975).

12. Robins build nests in trees. Pheasants build nests in bushes. Eagles build nests in rocks. Birds build nests in a variety of places.

13. Birds build nests in a variety of places. Robins build nests in trees. Pheasants build nests in bushes. Eagles build nests in rocks.

In this case, the meaning of the two texts is similar if not identical; however the position of the rule and its examples is reversed. Notice that this type of variation is a paragraph analogue of positional transformations (active/passive or preposing clauses) at the sentence level.

Thus far we have considered variations in text structure that have only minor influence on the semantic meaning of a text. Furthermore, the structural variations considered occur between or among rather small units of discourse — sentence components or sentences. Such analyses can be regarded as examinations of the microstructure of text.

Other, and particularly more recent, conceptualizations of text structure have ignored the perspective of examining structural variations that preserve meaning in favor of a perspective that examines the hierarchical aspects of text structure. Such schemes usually begin with a parsing of an entire text using either a case grammar (e.g., Meyer, 1975) or a propositional (e.g., Frederiksen, 1975; Kintsch, 1974) scheme to identify relations within and between sentences. Then the entire text is analyzed into a hierarchical structure. Ideas (usually in the form of propositions — basically a clause with an active or stative verb) are scaled according to their structural importance within the hierarchy. For expository texts, importance translates roughly into how "main" or superordinate the idea is. For narrative texts, importance means centrality to the story. Thus, characters, goals and settings are high in the hierarchy while particular episodes or motivations may be fairly low.

Implicit if not explicit in such analyses are two expectations: first, that height in the hierarchy will somehow predict and/or explain the comprehensibility of memorability of particular text segments, and second that surface structures that violate canonical structure will decimate comprehension and recall. Such schemes can be regarded as examinations of the macrostructure of text.

With these two aspects of text structure — microstructure and macrostructure — we have defined the scope of our investigation. Our next step is to examine the empirical studies that have been conducted to evaluate the importance of text structure in comprehension.

Microstructure 1: The Primacy of the Sentence

To psychologists academically reared in the verbal learning tradition of the forties and fifties, the revolution incited by Noam Chomsky's penetrating review of behavioral views of language processing (1959) and his alternative views proposed in *Syntactic structures* (1957) and *Aspects of the theory of syntax* (1965), must have seemed a bold departure from the conventional wisdom. The very notion that one could study units of discourse as large and complex as a sentence was revolutionary to researchers more comfortable with lists of nonsense trigrams or quingrams or associations among single words.

Nonetheless, Chomsky's views widened research possibilities for students of verbal behavior. Beginning with the work of Miller and his associates (e.g.,

Miller, 1962; Miller and Isard, 1963) several researchers in the mid-sixties conducted studies of sentence comprehension. The most common finding among such studies (e.g., Gough, 1965; Slobin, 1966) was that the transformational distance between the underlying meaning of a sentence (its deep structure) and its phonetic realization in speech or graphic realization in writing (its surface structure) was an accurate predictor of the speed or difficulty subjects experience in processing the sentence. In other words, performance could be predicted by variation in the grammar itself. Hence kernel sentences (simple active declaratives) were understood more rapidly than passives, interrogatives, or negatives, which presumably required more cognitive energy to process because more transformations had to be traversed in traveling from surface to deep structure. Findings such as these led to a derivational theory of complexity, i.e., that the derivation of a sentence's surface structure from its underlying deep structure predicted its processing difficulty.

Such studies were appealing to reading educators concerned specifically with reading comprehension. First, they provided needed methodological tools. Finally, there was a way of operationalizing sentence complexity. The notion of a transformation provided a countable index of complexity. In fact, Fagan (1971) and Pearson (1974-1975) used a derivational theory of complexity to generate and scale materials used to assess children's comprehension of sentence structure.[2]

Second, these studies corroborated what was known from (or at least implied by) the thirty year old history of readability research: that long complex sentences were associated with passages that rated high in readability and low in comprehensibility.

Unfortunately, the derivational theory of complexity lived only a short life. It was attacked on two different fronts, both as a linguistic theory and as a psychological theory.

The work of Fillmore (1968) on case grammar and generative semanticist framework of linguists like Lakoff (1971) called into question the transformationalists' preoccupation with syntactic relations at the expense of semantic relations.

In psychology, studies such as those conducted by Bransford and Franks (1971) and Sachs (1967) offered data contradictory to the derivational theory of complexity. Implicit in the theory is an assumption that comprehension occurs by analyzing a sentence into its basic constituents (that is how you get from surface to deep structure). Bransford and Franks' evidence suggested that comprehension was better characterized by synthesizing constituents into some semantically integrated chunk. Sachs' data indicated that memory for any aspects of sentence structure faded quite rapidly, while memory for the semantic "gist" of a sentence was remarkably stable. Working with children, Pearson (1974-1975) obtained results corroborating the work of Bransford and Franks and Sachs.

In some ways, however, the issue was soon to become a moot point because somewhere in the early seventies researchers turned their attention away from the sentence as a unit of linguistic analysis in favor of stories, passages, and expositions—with a concomitant emphasis on macrostructure rather than microstructure. Later we will examine that line of research; first, however, we must add two pieces to the microstructure puzzle.

Microstructure 2: Linguistic Connectives

The small but interesting body of research dealing with linguistic connectives speaks incidentally to issues of structural variation. This stems from the fact that when a connective is used in a sentence, it often has the effect of increasing the grammatical complexity of the sentence; connectives are involved in the formation of compound sentences and subordinate clauses such as those beginning with *because, although, before,* etc. In a sense, an examination of linguistic connectives is a sensible bridge from the studies looking at the sentence as a unit of analysis to those (in a later section) which emphasize the larger organizational patterns of text. Linguistic connectives usually establish or cue logical relations among propositions or sentences.

Walmsley (1977) defines linguistic connectives as follows:

> A linguistic connective (or logical or language connective—the terms appear to be used according to the orientation of a writer's discipline) may be defined as a "co-ordinating, qualifying or adverbial conjunction used to link a simple proposition with another idea (either a proposition or a concept) to form a complex proposition." Alternatively, it may be defined as a syntactic structure signalling underlying logico-semantic relations (see Olds, 1968). Connectives may link propositions within or between sentences; they may comprise a single word (e.g., *and*), or a phrase (e.g., *in addition to*). (p. 319)

Some researchers have examined the developmental changes that occur across ages in children's understanding of connectives and the relations between the propositions they link (e.g., Beilin et al., 1975; Neimark, 1970; Neimark and Slotnick, 1970; Paris, 1973). Not surprisingly, children's understanding improves with age; however, the research in this tradition, because of the nature of the task and isolated (not contextually embedded) stimuli, offers little advice concerning their role in reading larger units of discourse.

Robertson (1968) conducted one of the few educationally oriented studies. Her examination of basal readers used in the intermediate grades revealed that about one in three sentences in her sample employed some sort of connective. Student comprehension of connectives increased from grade four through grade six and was related to listening and reading ability.

Katz and Brent (1968) found that both first and sixth grade children preferred descriptions of causal relations that were made explicit by the use of a connective. This is consistent with the findings of Pearson (1974-1975) who reported that fourth grade students, given a choice as to the surface form in which a causal relation could be stated, preferred to have the relation stated in a grammatically complex subordinated form which included specific cues (*because, so*) denoting causal relationships. Pearson speculated that connectives and complexity (they go together) provided "...a more *unified* conception of the causal relation" (Pearson, p. 174) and that it is the function of connectives to make the causal relationship more explicit. These speculations were strengthened by the findings of a follow-up study in which students were asked to read individual sentences in which a causal relationship was either made explicit by inclusion of a causal connective or left implicit by omitting the connective. Results showed that in almost two-thirds of the cases in which subjects were asked to read sentences containing an unmarked (i.e., implicit) causal relationship, a connective *was included in recall*, thus unifying the relationship and making it explicit. Furthermore, if a sentence was not recalled in a cued, unified form, there was a 50 percent chance that it would not be recalled at all. These findings suggest that connectives have a strong effect on the salience of causal relationships expressed in sentences and may serve to facilitate the integration of ideas in memory.

Finally, Marshall and Glock (1978-1979) found that explicitly stated logical (i.e., causal and relational) structures facilitated the recall of propositional content or discourse for "not-so-fluent" (community college) readers. Recall for "truly-fluent" (college) readers for the same passages was more complete than for community college students and was not affected by the presence or absence of explicitly stated relationships. Structure of recall for good readers reflected a greater degree of differentiation among elements of the underlying structure of the text than did the recall of poorer readers who focused primarily on content. Marshall suggests that these differences are due to the fact that good readers have more well established schemata that can be used to interpret and store the meaning of discourse whereas poorer readers have less complete structure and, therefore, must depend to a greater extent on information explicitly encoded in the surface structure of text.

Microstructure 3: Sentence-Combining

Perhaps the most obvious attempt to determine the influence of direct instruction in the microstructure of text on comprehension has been in the tradition of sentence-combining instruction. Beginning with the observation that attempts to teach formal grammar have little positive effect on students' writing ability (Braddock, Lloyd-Jones, and Schoer, 1963; Mellon, 1969), researchers originally looked to sentence-combining as a way of influencing syntactic maturity in writing (Combs, 1975; Mellon, 1969; O'Hare, 1973). More recently, however, researchers have attempted to determine the effects of sentence-combining training on reading comprehension (Combs, 1975; Fisher, 1973; Hughes, 1975; Hunt and O'Donnell, 1970; Straw, 1979).

Basically, sentence-combining activities require students to integrate into a single sentence information expressed in two or more sentences as in (14) and (15).

14. The boy hit the ball. The boy was tall. The ball was small. He hit it through a window.

15. The tall boy hit the small ball through a window.

The rationale for believing that such instruction could alter writers' syntactic maturity seems obvious; the reason for suspecting a concomitant influence on reading comprehension stems from a view of the language arts that what influences growth in one language capacity will influence growth in another.

While positive effects have been reported on some limited measures of reading comprehension (Combs, 1975; Fisher, 1973; Hughes, 1975), only a study by Straw (1979) has looked at the effects of sentence-combining as they transfer to listening, reading, and writing. Straw found that a sentence-combining training condition affected growth in all three language capacities. However, growth in reading comprehension was limited to an investigator constructed cloze test; it did not affect growth on a standardized test. Interestingly, a complementary sentence-reduction task affected growth in reading comprehension (to a lesser degree than did sentence-combining) but not growth on the writing and listening measures. For purposes of our review, Straw's effects are noteworthy even though the treatment effects do not transfer to a standardized test. There is no good reason to believe that a typical standardized test will be sensitive to such instructional treatments. His results do suggest that attention to microstructure, specifically allowing students to actively manipulate it, pays at least short range dividends in comprehension growth.

These results seem compatible with those in the review of linguistic connectives. Note that linguistic connectives often serve the function of combining ideas that could be expressed in separate sentences. Ironically, then, these two areas of research suggest, in contrast to the earlier work in transformational grammar, that attention to cohesion rather than atomization of sentence elements pays greater dividends.

Macrostructure 1: Narratives

The main purpose of this section is to review research evaluating the influence of the overall structure of narratives on students' comprehension and recall of information presented in texts. Several writers (e.g., Mandler and Johnson, 1977; Rumelhart, 1975; Stein and Glenn, 1977; Thorndyke, 1977) have developed formalisms for analyzing the relations among propositions in stories. Propositions can be related in two ways: by their relative position within the hierarchy of a story and by their rhetorical function.

Like phrase structure grammars applied to sentences (e.g., Chomsky, 1957, 1965), in which rewrite rules dictated a sentence's decomposition (e.g., Sentence = > Noun Phrase + Verb Phrase, Noun Phrase = > Determiner + Noun + [Sentence], Verb Phrase = > Verb + [Sentence]), so story schemata or story grammars specify a set of rewrite rules for decomposing the relations among propositions in a story. Thus a story can be rewritten as STORY = > SETTING + THEME + PLOT + RESOLUTION; setting can be rewritten as SETTING = > CHARACTERS + LOCATION + TIME, etc. When all the rewrite rules have been applied to a story, what results is an inverted tree diagram for a story, which looks quite similar to a phrase structure parsing of a sentence, except that the basic units are sentences or propositions rather than words.

In essence, this tree structure creates a hierarchy. What appear at the top of the hierarchy are the setting of the story (including characters, location, etc.), the basic theme, a few of the key episodes in the plot, and a resolution of the problem that motivated the characters to whatever actions they undertook to begin with. At lower levels in the hierarchy will be subplots. For example, suppose a character needed to get a car to drive to a beach so that he could dig clams for an important dinner. The activities in the story that were associated with getting the car would appear lower in the hierarchy because they were instrumental in *allowing* a higher level event (getting to the beach) to occur. Further suppose that in order to rent a car, the character had to phone several friends to borrow money. Those events would appear at an even lower level. Such hierarchical relations exist among propositions throughout the story; often the implied link between a higher and an immediately lower level event is causation or enablement (a very weak sister to causation – A allowed or enabled B to occur but did not really compel B to occur).

In addition, some grammars have established intracategory connectors to allow for explicit logical connection between events or states at the same level in the hierarchy. Stein and Glenn (1977), for example, include AND, THEN, and CAUSE links. Hence rhetorical or logical connection between events and states is carried in two ways: vertically by implied hierarchical relations and horizontally by explicit links in the grammar.

Story grammarians have postulated two possible consequences of story grammars. Assuming that students internalize, through constant exposure to stories of various degrees of well-formedness, something like a schema for stories, then comprehension and recall of stories ought to be influenced by two kinds of variation. First, information in higher level nodes ought to be recalled more frequently than that in lower level nodes because of greater centrality to the basic actions and motivations of the characters. Second, violations in the well-formedness of stories (e.g., the degree to which the order of key events is reversed or scrambled, placing motivations out of synchronization with actions, placing setting information at the end of a story, etc.) ought to decrease comprehension and recall.

The first of these predictions has been emphasized by Rumelhart (1975, 1977). He has established a set of story summarization rules to predict the probability that a proposition will be recalled; basically a proposition is predicted to be recalled if a proposition lower in the hierarchy was recalled. He found that the conditional probability that a proposition would be recalled given that it was predicted to be recalled was .95. Rumelhart also interprets the data from the work of Thorndyke (1977) and Meyer (1975) as supporting his hierarchical hypothesis.

Other researchers (e.g., Mandler and Johnson, 1977; Stein and Nezworski, 1978; Thorndyke, 1977) have emphasized the effects in violation of canonical story structure. Thorndyke (1977) found that story recall was debilitated increasingly by a) moving the theme or goal to the end of the story, b) removing the theme altogether, and c) more or less randomly permuting the sentences in the story. Kintsch, Mandel, and Kozminsky (1977) asked college students to read well- and ill-formed (scrambled paragraphs) stories in time-limited or unlimited conditions. Then the students wrote summaries of the 1400 word stories. In the unlimited reading time condition, there was a 23 percent increase in reading time due to scrambling but no differences in writing time, length, or quality of story summaries. However in the limited time condition, better summaries were written for well-formed stories. Kintsch et al. felt that subjects in the unlimited time condition imposed a story structure on the scrambled text at the point of comprehension rather than simply at the point of summarization; hence the difference in reading but not summarizing time. Without time to restructure the ill-formed story, comprehension suffered, resulting in inferior summaries. Stein and Nezworski (1978) found results similar to those of Thorndyke (1977). Well-formed stories elicited better story recall than stories containing slightly disordered, randomly ordered, or unrelated statements. Furthermore, unrelated statements elicited the greatest number of inferences into recall, reflecting subjects' attempts to make sense out of an incoherent text, a finding reminiscent of Bartlett's (1932) early results on cross-cultural intrusions into story recall.

The developmental (cross-age) data collected by Stein and Glenn (1977) and Mandler and Johnson (1977) also support the notion of story schemata. As children grow older they tend to recall increasingly more of the lower level information in the story. Young children tend to recall only a few of the higher level propositions such as a character, an initiating event, and an outcome.

While story schemata have been criticized for their emphasis on prediction rather than explanation and the fact that they predict too many behaviors (Thorndyke and Yekovich, in press), their basic validity as formalizations of what people learn when they learn about how writers put stories together seems to us to be well-founded.

Instructional Research on Story Schemata

We were able to locate only three studies dealing even tangentially with issues of direct instruction about how stories are structured. Bower (1976) had subjects read a biography about a fictitious poet. Then half the subjects read two biographies with similar macrostructures while half read two unrelated texts. When they were asked to recall the original biography, experimental subjects (the three biographies) recalled more of the macrostructure (which was similar in all three) but interconfused details of the second and third with the first. The similarity of the three passages created macrostructure facilitation and detail interference. Thorndyke (1977) found that subjects who read a second story with the same structure as, but different characters from, the first story recalled more second story information than those whose second stories had the same characters as, but a different structure from, the first.

Neither of these studies can be considered instructional in anything but an incidental sense. However, a study by Gordon (1980) speaks directly to story structure instruction. Over a period of eight weeks she trained fifth grade students to apply a simplified story schema to basal reader stories that they read as a part of their normal reading instruction. On a transfer story, these students recalled significantly more, particularly of certain categories of high-level information, than a placebo or an untreated control group. She interpreted the findings as supporting the notion that direct instruction in story schemata provides students with a transferable framework for storing and retrieving textually presented information.

Macrostructure 2: Exposition

Research and theory about the macrostructure of expository text is not quite so abundant as that for narrative. Attempts have been made by Kintsch (1974), Frederiksen (1975), and Meyer (1975) to develop general schemes for representing relations among units of text. Kintsch and Frederiksen give more emphasis to a scheme that could serve as either a model of text structure or the structure of knowledge in memory; Meyer's system is, admittedly, more concerned with representing text per se. Because of space limitations and because it places greater emphasis on text macrostructure, we have chosen to concentrate on Meyer's system, recognizing full well that we can justify our decision only by asserting that we intend our review to represent an example from a class of text structure schemes.

Adhering closely to the theory of Grimes (1975) for connected discourse and to Fillmore's (1968) case grammar, Meyer has developed a text structure system that emphasizes relations among propositions in a text. She has lexical propositions that show the case relations between words within simple sentences and clauses. And she has rhetorical propositions which establish the relations between and among sentences, paragraphs, and longer units of text. Rhetorical predicates are labels used to specify the relationships within these propositions. Rhetorical predicates order the ideas in a text into hierarchical relationships, and they allow Meyer to develop a richer, higher-level organization than either Kintsch or Frederiksen.

Meyer's parsing of a passage looks much like an outline of the passage, except that all the ideas from the passage are included. Top-level discourse structures in the outline are simply the relations that occur in the top third of the diagram. Height in the system is indicated by "leftness" of a proposition in the content outline.

A basic thesis of Meyer's is that height in the hierarchy predicts how well propositions will be comprehended and recalled. She designed an experiment in which a target paragraph was embedded high within the hierarchy of passage 1 but low in passage 2. The serial position of the paragraph was identical across passages. While she found no overall recall differences between the two passages, the target paragraph was recalled better when it was staged higher in the hierarchy. These immediate recall differences increased with a week's delay. Similar differences were noted in the cued recall of the target passage after a week's interval.

Meyer (1977a, 1977b) extended her research to determine whether or not sixth grade students were sensitive to these hierarchical differences in content structure. Meyer predicted that students classified as low in ability would recall more information from low levels of the content structure than from high levels in the content structure.

Immediately after listening to a short article about parakeets, students answered fifteen main idea and fifteen detail questions about the article. The main idea questions were derived from idea units high in the structure of the passage, and the detail questions were derived from idea units low in the structure of the passage. Results indicated that all of the students, regardless of ability level, answered more main idea questions than detail questions. Brighter students remembered significantly more information from both levels of the structure than other students, but even low-ability students answered more main idea questions correctly than detail questions. Meyer concluded that children, like adults, remember more information from high levels of the content structure of a text and that a content structure representation can be useful in generating different types of comprehension questions for prose materials. Meyer cautions, however, that the results of this study might not generalize to low-ability students with reading or learning disabilities under reading versus listening conditions.

In order to explore the effects of different types of top-level discourse structures on recall, Meyer and Freedle (1979) had graduate students read articles with identical middle- and low-level structures and content. The passages differed in the way similar introductory information was organized in the top-level of their content structure diagrams. The four types of structures (rhetorical predicates she calls them) compared in the study were: adversative (contrastive pattern), covariance (cause-effect pattern), response (problem-solution pattern), and attributive (list-like pattern). The investigators predicted that information in passages organized with adversative, covariance, and response structures would be remembered better than information from the passage organized with an attributive structure.

Subjects participating in the study were graduate students working on advanced degrees in education. They were divided into four groups, and each group listened to a passage organized by one of the four rhetorical predicates. An immediate free-recall test, a delayed free-recall text, and a delayed short-answer test were administered to all subjects. The short-answer test consisted of questions which tapped memory for information that was identical in each of the four passage conditions. Recall protocols were scored for the number of idea units recalled and for the type of rhetorical structure subjects used to organize their recall protocols. The short-answer test was simply scored for the number of correct answers.

Subjects who listened to passages organized with adversative (contrastive) and covariance (cause-effect) structures remembered significantly more information than subjects who listened to passages organized with attribution (list-like) and response (problem-solution) structures. Moreover, subjects who listened to the adversative passage answered significantly more of the short-answer questions correctly than subjects who listened to the other passages. Subjects who listened to passages with adversative and covariance structures also used these types of relationships to organize their recall   protocols.

From these findings, Meyer and Freedle concluded that differences in the type of structure used to organize textual information significantly affected the amount of information graduate students learned and remembered. Adversative and covariance organizations enhanced recall over attribution and response organizations.

Using a schema theory orientation, Meyer and Freedle had predicted that adversative, covariance, and response structures would provide better organization for learning than an attributive, list-like structure. Each of the four types of structure is used in expository texts to let readers know information will be presented about a topic; but adversative, covariance, and response structures ostensibly provide readers with additional schemata to help them understand and remember the information. For example, an adversative structure indicates that the information will be about opposing views; covariance structures indicate that the information will be about causal relations; and response structures indicate that the information will be about problems and solutions. Attributive structures are more loosely organized, however, and do not provide additional information.

The prediction that adversative and covariance structures would facilitate recall was supported. The prediction about the response structure, however, was not confirmed. Meyer and Freedle explain this unexpected finding in terms of social-psychological facts and notions of perspective. The subjects participating in the study were school teachers who may have been offended by the solution in the response passage as it involved firing coaches. Thus, the teachers seemed to reject the schema provided by the author, read the text from their own perspective or personal viewpoint, and thereby processed the text differently than was expected.

The most important finding in this study was that certain types of top-level discourse structures did facilitate recall more than others. Meyer and Freedle interpret the results of this study as showing that the most efficient strategy students can adopt in typical school-learning or lab-learning situations is to identify and use the author's organizational framework to guide and structure their attempts to understand and remember information from textual materials. Students who are familiar with the way texts are typically organized can use that knowledge to comprehend and remember by relating the organizational structure, or schema, of the text to their prior knowledge (stored schemata) about how texts are organized and what to expect from texts organized in certain ways.

Meyer, Brandt, and Bluth (1978) investigated the effects of identifying and using the organizational structure of texts on recall. They predicted that readers who adopted the strategy of identifying the author's organizational structure (the author's schema) would be able to recall more information than students who did not adopt this strategy. Ninth grade students classified as good, average, poor, and "difference" (high vocabulary but low comprehension scores) readers participated in the study. They read and recalled two different expository passages. One passage was organized with a response predicate and the other with an adversative predicate. Thus, the passages differed in their top-level rhetorical structures and, also, in whether or not signaling devices were present in the texts.

Signaling devices, as defined by Meyer (1975), are ways in which authors emphasize aspects of the semantic content or structure of a text. The title of the passage and words such as "in contrast to" were types of signaling used in the adversative passage. An explicit statement of the problem and solution relations as well as signaling words such as "first," "second," etc. were the types of signaling included in the response passage. Meyer et al. predicted that signaling devices would benefit poor and "difference" readers in processing the texts as it was assumed that these readers did not normally use the organizational structure of texts to understand and remember information.

Immediate and delayed free-recall tests were scored for the number of idea units recalled and the degree of similarity between the organization of the recall protocols and that of the original passages. Results indicated that good readers organized their protocols with the same structure as that used in the passages they read and that they recalled significantly more information than students who did not adopt this strategy. This result was obtained with good readers even when signaling devices were not present in the texts they read. The strategy of using the author's "schema" to organize recalled information was a better predictor of recall than either standardized comprehension or vocabulary test scores; multiple regression analyses indicated that use of this strategy accounted for 44 percent of the variance in recall on the immediate-recall test and 68 percent of the variance in recall on the delayed test.

Signaling appeared to facilitate recall of low and average comprehenders on the immediate test but not on the delayed-recall test. On the immediate test, the students classified as poor, average, and "difference" readers who read the response passage with signaling organized their recall protocols with the same pattern of relationships as those in the original passage; they also recalled significantly more information than similarly classified students who read the without-signaling version of the passage. However, signaling had no effect on the recall of students who read the without-signaling and adversative versions of the passage.

In a subsequent study, Bartlett (1978) taught a group of ninth grade students to identify various types of top-level structures common to expository texts and to use the structures to organize their recall protocols. The students were taught how to identify and to use covariance, adversative, attribution, and response structures during a week-long training period. Apparently, students trained to use the strategy of identifying an author's top-level structure were able to recognize these structures in texts significantly better than students who did not receive training. Thus, some evidence exists to suggest that students can be taught to identify top-level discourse structures and that such training improves comprehension.

Implications for Reading Practice

It is always somewhat dangerous to leap too boldly across the gap from research, especially basic research, to educational practice. A more cautious approach is to suggest that research findings from laboratory or other basic research settings should be regarded as grist for applied research studies which should be carried out in real school environments before we make any conclusive recommendations for changes in materials or teaching strategies (e.g., Bronfenbrenner, 1976). Nonetheless, we see several areas in which the leap seems so reasonable and inviting that we make it, caution notwithstanding.

Recommendations to People Who Prepare Reading Materials

1. The research on children's comprehension of story structure suggests to us that from the outset of grade one, children ought to be reading stories that are highly predictable in terms of their conformity to canonical story schemata. We recognize that the need to control vocabulary in the earliest of stories makes it difficult for writers to create well-formed stories. Yet we are convinced that it is these young children who need the predictability the most. Consider the case of a first grade student who is trying to make sense out of the unfamiliar orthography of English writing. The child is already confronted with one source of potential confusion (figuring out what sounds the letters make); to embed that task in a context that can be another source of confusion (stories that violate story schemata) seems to compound the problem.

2. The research on the influence of connectives, structures of cohesion, and sentence-combining activities suggests that complexity may sometimes add to rather than always detract from the likelihood that comprehension will occur.

Cohesive forms of statements appear to make explicit what is otherwise left to children's inferential powers. Textbook writers need to be aware of this fact. Above all they should not be led to the false conclusion that writing becomes more readable when complex sentences are chopped in half (even though such a practice will reduce a passage's readability scores).

Recommendations to Educators (and Writers of Instructional Practice Materials)

3. The salutary on sentence-combining training has been replicated several times. It seems reasonable to recommend that students be given an opportunity to learn an important fact about the English language: that there is always more than one way to express a given idea. Awareness of this fact also apparently leads to growth in syntactic maturity and listening, particularly if the focus is on creating cohesive statements.

4. If teachers want students to "get the author's message," they are well advised to model for students how to figure out what the author's general framework or structure is and then allow students to practice discovering it on their own. They should be cautioned, however, that not all reading has as its purpose "getting the author's message"; sometimes students need to read to update their own knowledge, in which case they are probably better off working within their own schemata rather than an author's schema (Spiro, 1977).

We close this section with a disclaimer: These are not the only suggestions which could be derived from the research base on comprehension of text structure, only those that seemed most reasonable to use. Also, these may not be the most important implications to be derived for practice from research; it may be that the research based on the structure of knowledge in memory or the interaction between text structure and knowledge structure or the process of learning to monitor one's own comprehension may prove more fruitful for instruction. They simply do not fall under the scope of this review.

Implications for Instructional Research in Reading

1. We need to know more about the point in time when children are able to handle certain complex kinds of syntactic structures. There was a time in the late sixties when the conventional wisdom concerning syntactic development seemed to suggest that, by the age of six, children had mastered nearly all the syntactic structures they would use as adults. Then the work of C. Chomsky (1969), Bormuth, Manning, Carr, and Pearson (1971), Olds (1968), and others pointed out that even by age ten children still had trouble within many structures. Somehow the rush toward semantic and macrostructural concerns in the mid-seventies buried what was an incomplete and fruitful line of research. We still need to finish the job.

2. After the issue of development comes instructions: Are those structures which cause difficulty even for the ten-year-old amenable to direct instruction and systematic practice?

3. The work of Meyer and her associates suggests that good readers are better at following an author's rhetorical plan of organization than are poor readers. The next step is to demonstrate that poor readers who received direct instruction in deciphering an author's organizational plan improve in their ability to produce greater veridical comprehension and recall of text.

4. In this regard, we need to know more about the relative efficiency of different rhetorical plans of organization (e.g., adversative, covariance, attributional, etc.) in communicating content in various disciplines (science versus history versus geography). It may be that certain plans are uniquely suited to certain types of content.

5. The work of Gordon (1980) should be extended to younger age levels to see if the salutory effects of story schema training will assist even younger students. In this regard, we should mention the exciting but emerging work of a group of researchers in Boston (Rubin, 1980) who are using a story schema framework to help young children get off to a faster start in writing as well as reading stories.

6. Finally let us offer one general suggestion for instructional research derived from constructs emanating from basic research. When we look at research on teaching and learning variables, we have been awestruck by the persistence and ubiquity of two terms: engaged time on task and direct instruction (e.g., Becker, 1977; Berliner, 1975; Rosenshine, 1976). We finally seem to be getting the message that kids learn what they are taught and get to practice. Thus far, the research seems to have shown these effects in more mundane aspects of reading such as word identification. But there is no reason to believe that they wouldn't aid comprehension as well, even though we have evidence that few teachers teach comprehension (Durkin, 1978-1979). In fact, the work of Straw (1978) and Gordon (1980) reported earlier, as well as a recent study by Hansen (1979) seem to provide direct evidence that students learn new strategies for comprehending text when they are taught and practiced systematically. The point is simple: when we identify a variable, including a text structure variable, that looks like it might make a difference in comprehension, we ought to adopt a frontal assault strategy when considering its instructional power — teach about it systematically and make certain students have a chance to practice it. The time for a renaissance of the methodological study is now — now that we have better ideas of what to look at.

A final caution: we don't expect that the products of this new methodological research will be altogether new and surprising. In fact, we expect that many will elicit reactions of "reinventing the wheel," or "that's just common sense." Such reactions will please us. Common sense is all too common and all too sensible to be overturned by a single line of research. But the real value in the new research will be the contextual and theoretical base from which it emanates. Hence we will be in a better position to answer the question, "Why did it work?"

REFERENCES

Bartlett, B.J. *Top-level structure as an organizational strategy for recall of classroom text*. Unpublished doctoral dissertation, Arizona State University, 1978.

Bartlett, F.C. *Remembering: A study in experimental and social psychology*. Cambridge, England: Cambridge University Press, 1932.

Becker, W.C. Teaching reading and language to the disadvantaged—what we have learned from field research. *Harvard Educational Review*, 1977, *47*, 518-543.

Beilin, H., et al. *Studies in the cognitive basis of language development*. New York: Academic Press, 1975.

Berliner, D.C. *Impediments to the study of teacher effectiveness* (Tech. Rep. No. 75-11-3). San Francisco, Calif.: Far West Laboratory for Educational Research and Development, November 1975.

Bormuth, J.R. Readability: A new approach. *Reading Research Quarterly*, 1966, *1*, 79-132.

Bormuth, J.R., Manning, J.C., Carr, W., and Pearson, P.D. Children's comprehension of between- and within-sentence syntactic structures. *Journal of Educational Psychology*, 1971, *61*, 349-357.

Bower, G.H. Experiments on story understanding and recall. *Quarterly Journal of Experimental Psychology*, 1976, *28*, 511-534.

Braddock, R., Lloyd-Jones, R., and Schoer, L. *Research in written composition*. Urbana, Ill.: National Council of Teachers of English, 1963.

Bransford, J.D., and Franks, J.J. The abstraction of linguistic ideas. *Cognitive Psychology*, 1971, *2*, 331-350.

Bronfenbrenner, U. The experimental ecology of education. *Educational Researcher*, 1976, *5*, 5-15.

Chomsky, C. *The acquisition of syntax in children from 5 to 10*. Cambridge, Mass.: MIT Press, 1969.

Chomsky, N. *Syntactic structures*. The Hague: Mouton, 1957.

Chomsky, N. A review of *Verbal Behavior* by B.F. Skinner. *Language*, 1959, *35*, 26-58.

Chomsky, N. *Aspects of the theory of syntax*. Cambridge, Mass.: MIT Press, 1965.

Clark, H.H., and Clark, E. *Psychology and Language*. New York: Harcourt Brace Jovanovich, 1977.

Combs, W.E. *Some further effects and implications of sentence-combining exercises for the secondary language arts curriculum*. Unpublished doctoral dissertation, University of Minnesota, 1975.

Durkin, D. What classroom observations reveal about reading comprehension instruction. *Reading Research Quarterly*, 1978-1979, *14*, 481-533.

Fagan, W.T. Transformations and comprehension. *The Reading Teacher*, 1971, *25*, 169-172.

Fillmore, C.J. The case for case. In E. Bach and R. Harms (Eds.), *Universals in linguistic theory*. New York: Holt, Rinehart and Winston, 1968.

Fisher, K.D. *An investigation to determine if selected exercises in sentence-combining can improve reading and writing*. Unpublished doctoral dissertation, Indiana University, 1973.

Fodor, J.A., and Garrett, M.F. Some syntactic determinants of sentential complexity, *Perception and Psychophysics*, 1967, *2*, 289-296.

Frederiksen, C.H. Representing logical and semantic structure of knowledge acquired from discourse. *Cognitive Psychology*, 1975, *7*, 371-458.

Gordon, C.J. *The effects of instruction in metacomprehension and inferencing on children's comprehension abilities*. Unpublished doctoral dissertation, University of Minnesota, 1980.

Gough, P.B. Grammatical transformations and speed of understanding. *Journal of Verbal Learning and Verbal Behavior*, 1965, *4*, 107-111.

Grice, H.P. Logic and conversation. In P. Cole and J.L. Morgan (Eds.), *Syntax and semantics, 3, Speech acts*. New York: Seminar Press, 1975, 41-58.

Grimes, J.E. *The thread of discourse*. The Hague: Mouton, 1975.

Halliday, M.A.K., and Hasan, R. *Cohesion in English*. London, England: Longman, 1976.

Hansen, J.A. *The effects of two intervention techniques on the inferential ability of second grade readers*. Unpublished doctoral dissertation, University of Minnesota, 1979.

Hughes, T.O. *Sentence-combining: A means of increasing reading comprehension*. Kalamazoo: Western Michigan University, Department of English, 1975.

Hunt, K.W., and O'Donnell, R. *An elementary school curriculum to develop better writing skills*. U.S. Office of Education Grant No. 4-9-08-903-0042-010. Tallahassee: Florida State University, 1970.

Katz, E., and Brent, S. Understanding connections. *Journal of Verbal Learning and Verbal Behavior*, 1968, *7*, 501-509.

Kintsch, W. *The representation of meaning in memory*. Hillsdale, N.J.: Erlbaum, 1974.

Kintsch, W., Mandell, T.S., and Kozminsky, E. Summarizing scrambled stories. *Memory and Cognition*, 1977, *5*, 547-552.

Lakoff, R. Ifs, and's, and but's about conjunction. In C.J. Fillmore and D.T. Langendoen (Eds.), *Studies in linguistic semantics*. New York: Holt, Rinehart and Winston, 1971.

Mandler, J.M., and Johnson, N.S. Remembrance of things parsed. Story structure and recall. *Cognitive Psychology*, 1977, *9*, 111-151.

Marshall, N. *Comprehension of connected discourse: A study into the relationships between the structure of text and information recalled*. Unpublished paper, Arizona State University, 1976.

Marshall, N., and Glock, M. Comprehension of connected discourse: A study into the relationships between the structure of text and information recalled. *Reading Research Quarterly*, 1978-1979, *16*, 10-56.

Mellon, J. *Transformational sentence combining: A method for enhancing the development of syntactic fluence in English composition* (NCTE Research Rep. No. 10). Urbana, Ill.: National Council of Teachers of English, 1969.

Meyer, B.J.F. *The organization of prose and its effects on memory*. Amsterdam: North-Holland Publishing, 1975.

Meyer, B.J.F. The structure of prose: Effects on learning and memory and implications for educational practice. In R.C. Anderson, R. Spiro, and W.E. Montague (Eds.), *Schooling and the acquisition of knowledge*. Hillsdale, N.J.: Erlbaum, 1977. (a)

Meyer, B.J.F. What is remembered from prose: A function of passage structure. In R.O. Freedle (Ed.), *Discourse production and comprehension* (Vol. 1). Norwood, N.J.: Ablex, 1977. (b)

Meyer, B.J.F. *Structure of prose: Implications for teachers of reading* (Research Report No. 3). Tempe: Arizona State University, Prose Learning Series, Spring 1979.

Meyer, B.J.F., and Freedle, R. *The effects of different discourse types on recall*. Princeton, N.J.: Eduational Testing Service, 1979.

Meyer, B.J.F., Brandt, D.M., and Bluth, G.J. *Use of author's schema: Key to ninth graders' comprehension*. Paper presented at the meeting of the American Educational Research Association, Toronto, March 1978.

Miller, G.A. Some psychological studies of grammar. *American Psychologist*, 1962, *17*, 748-762.

Miller, G.A., and Isard, S. Some perceptual consequences of linguistic rules. *Journal of Verbal Learning and Verbal Behavior*, 1963, *2*, 217-228.

Neimark, E.D. Development of comprehension of logical connectives: Understanding of "or." *Psychonomic Science*, 1970, *21*(4), 217-219.

Neimark, E.D., and Slotnick, N.S. Development of the understanding of logical connectives. *Journal of Educational Psychology*, 1970, *61*(6), 451-460.

O'Hare, F. *Sentence-combining: Improving student writing without formal grammar instruction* (NCTE Research Rep. No. 15). Urbana, Ill.: National Council of Teachers of English, 1973.

Olds, H.F. *An experimental study of syntactical factors influencing children's comprehension of certain complex relationships* (Rep. No. 4). Cambridge, Mass.: Harvard University, Center for Research and Development on Educational Differences, 1968.

Paris, S.G. Semantic and constructive aspects of sentence memory in children. *Developmental Psychology*, 1973, *9*(1), 109-113.

Pearson, P.D. The effects of grammatical complexity on children's comprehension, recall, and conception of certain semantic relations. *Reading Research Quarterly,* 1974-1975, *10*, 155-192.

Reder, L.M. *Comprehension and retention of prose: A literature review* (Tech. Rep. No. 108). Urbana: University of Illinois, Center for the Study of Reading, 1978.

Robertson, J. Pupil understanding of connectives in reading. *Reading Research Quarterly*, 1968, *3*, 387-417.

Rosenshine, B. Classroom instruction. In N.L. Gage (Ed.), *The psychology of teaching methods* (7th NSSE Yearbook). Chicago: University of Chicago Press, 1976.

Rubin, A. *Making stories, making sense* (Reading Ed. Rep. No. 00). Urbana: University of Illinois, Center for the Study of Reading, 1980.

Rumelhart, D.E. Notes on a schema for stories. In D.G. Bobrow and A.M. Collins (Eds.), *Representation and understanding: Studies in cognitive science*. New York: Academic Press, 1975.

Rumelhart, D.E. Understanding and summarizing brief stories. In D. LaBerge and S.J. Samuels (Eds.), *Basic processes in reading: Perception and comprehension*. Hillsdale, N.J.: Erlbaum, 1977.

Sachs, J.S. Recognition memory for syntactic and semantic aspects of connected discourse. *Perception and Psychophysics*, 1967, 2, 437-442.

Slobin, D.I. Grammatical transformations and sentence comprehension in childhood and adulthood. *Journal of Verbal Learning and Verbal Behavior*, 1966, *5*, 219-227.

Spiro, R. Remembering information from text: The "state of schema" approach. In R.C. Anderson, R. Spiro, and W. Montague (Eds.), *Schooling and the acquisition of knowledge*. Hillsdale, N.J.: Erlbaum, 1977.

Stein, N.L., and Glenn, C.G. *A developmental study of children's construction of stories*. Paper presented at the SRCD meetings, New Orleans, March 17-20, 1977.

Stein, N.L., and Nezworski, T. *The effects of organization and instructional set on story memory* (Tech. Rep. No. 129). Urbana: University of Illinois, Center for the Study of Reading, 1978.

Straw, S.B. *An investigation of the effects of sentence-combining and sentence-reduction instruction on measures of syntactic fluency, reading comprehension, and listening comprehension of fourth-grade students*. Unpublished doctoral dissertation, University of Minnesota, 1978.

Straw, S.B. Measuring the effect of sentence-combining instruction on reading comprehension. In D. Daiker, A. Kerek, and M. Morenberg (Eds.), *Sentence combining and the teaching of English*. Akron, Ohio: L. and S. Books, 1979.

Thorndyke, P.W. Cognitive structures in comprehension and memory of narrative discourse. *Cognitive Psychology*, 1977, *9*, 77-110.

Thorndyke, P., and Yekovich, F. A critique of schemata as a theory of human story memory. *Poetics,* in press.

Walmsley, S. Children's understanding of linguistic connectives: A review of selected literature and implication for reading research. In P.D. Pearson (Ed.), *Reading: Theory, research, and practice*. 26th Yearbook of the National Reading Conference. Clemson, S.C.: National Reading Conference, 1977.

NOTES

[1]Many theorists would arge that the underlying meaning of the active/passive pairs is not identical. Clark and Clark (1977) using a topic-comment formulation would argue that the focus differs from active to passive: In 1), what is emphasized is some new information about the lad, i.e., that he rode the steed to victory, whereas in 2) the emphasis centers on new information about the horse, i.e., that it was ridden to victory by the lad. We concur. If we adopt a strict equivalence-in-meaning criterion, then the concept of paraphrase (multiple surface structure representations for a single deep structure) cannot exist. Nonetheless, we would probably find that 95 percent of the population would agree that the same basic notions are being communicated in active/passive pairs.

[2]An almost incidental but nonetheless important methodological tool was the question transformation. Bormuth (1966, 1969, 1971), Pearson (1974-1975), and Bormuth, Manning, Carr, and Pearson (1971) and many researchers since then have used the question transformation as an objective device for generating literal comprehension question probes from text.

Vocabulary Knowledge

RICHARD C. ANDERSON
PETER FREEBODY
University of Illinois at Urbana-Champaign

Our aim in this paper is to summarize what is known about the role of vocabulary knowledge in reading comprehension. Though word identification skills are important in reading, this paper is concerned exclusively with *knowledge of word meanings*. An assessment of the number of meanings a reader knows enables a remarkably accurate prediction of this individual's ability to comprehend discourse. Why this is true is poorly understood. Determining why is important because what should be done to build vocabulary knowledge depends on why it relates so strongly to reading. The deeper reasons why word knowledge correlates with comprehension cannot be determined satisfactorily without improved methods of estimating the size of people's vocabularies. Improved assessment methods hinge, in turn, on thoughtful answers to such questions as what is a word, what does it mean to know the meaning of a word, and what is the most efficient way of estimating vocabulary size from an individual's performance on a sample of words.

Vocabulary Knowledge and Linguistic Ability

Measures of vocabulary knowledge are potent predictors of a variety of indices of linguistic ability. The strong relationship between vocabulary and general intelligence is one of the most robust findings in the history of intelligence testing. Terman (1918), for instance, reported a correlation of .91 between mental age (as assessed by the Stanford Revision of the Binet-Simon Scale) and the vocabulary subscale. On this basis he suggested that the vocabulary measure alone constitutes a good estimate of performance on the entire scale and thus could be used as a short measure. Since then, this suggestion has been tested with various age groups. Table 1 summarizes representative evidence. In these studies, correlations between vocabulary subtest scores and total test scores on a number of different IQ and achievement tests have ranged from .71 to .98.

Reprinted from *Comprehension and Teaching: Research Reviews*, John T. Guthrie (Ed.). Newark, Delaware: International Reading Association, 1981.

Table 1

CORRELATIONS OF VARIOUS VOCABULARY TESTS WITH TESTS OF GENERAL
INTELLIGENCE

Vocabulary Measure	Intelligence Measure	Subjects	N	r	Source
Terman, 1916	Binet (1916)	School children	631	.91	Terman (1918)
Terman, 1916	Binet (1916)	School children	269	.87	Mahan & Witmer (1936)
Terman, 1937	Binet (1916)	School children	65	.92	Spache (1943)
Terman, 1937	Binet (1916)	School children	1161	.98	Elwood (1939)
Terman, 1937	Binet (1916)	School children	753	.86	White (1942)
Terman, 1937	Binet (1916)	Standardization sample, ages 8-18	710	.71 to .86	McNemar (1942)
Wechsler	Wechsler	Adult males	1000	.82	Lewinski (1948)
Wechsler	WISC	Standardization sample, ages 7.5, 10.5, 13.5	600	.71 .87 .78	Wechsler (1949)
Raven	Binet	School children	150	.93	Raven (1948)
Dupuy	Various tests	School children	2397	.76	Dupuy (1974)
Stanford Achievement Tests (1973) (vocabulary with total achievement test scores)	Standardization samples Grade 2 3 4 5 6 8		275,000 over grades and geog. locale	.82 .79 .80 .80 .83 .89	Stanford Achievement Tests (1973)

Note. Adapted from Miner (1957).

An equally consistent finding has been that word knowledge is strongly related to reading comprehension. Davis (1944a, 1968) factor analyzed nine comprehension tests and found a main factor for word knowledge on which a vocabulary test loaded about .8. Thurstone (1946) reanalyzed Davis' original data and found three major factors: vocabulary knowledge, ability to draw inferences from a paragraph, and ability to grasp the main idea of a paragraph. In the years that followed, several factor analytic studies identified a "reading comprehension" factor (Botzum, 1951; Clark, 1972; Fruchter, 1948; Wrigley, Saunders and Newhaus, 1958). The range of factor loadings for vocabulary tests in these studies was .41 to .93.

This strong relationship has been found to hold across a wide range of language groups. Thorndike (1973) collected data from over 100,000 students from 15 countries, across three age groups; he found median correlations between vocabulary knowledge and reading comprehension, corrected for test reliability, of

Table 2

CORRELATIONS OF WORD KNOWLEDGE WITH READING COMPREHENSION IN
FIFTEEN COUNTRIES

Country	Age Group		
	10 yrs.	14 yrs.	17 yrs.
Belgium (Fl)	.537	.591	.500
Belgium (Fr)	.588	.619	.481
Chile	.543	.508	.577
England	.735	.698	.497
Finland	.617	.654	.395
Hungary	.594	.533	.389
India	.569	.387	.320
Iran	.498	.427	.294
Israel	.651	.674	– –
Italy	.580	.587	.446
Netherlands	.620	.624	.310
New Zealand	– –	.685	.536
Scotland	.716	.719	.579
Sweden	.559	.598	.584
United States	.735	.693	.679

Note. From Thorndike (1973).

.71 (10 year olds), .75 (14 year olds), and .66 (17-18 year olds). Thorndike concluded that the results indicate "how completely reading performance is determined by word knowledge at different levels and in different countries" (p.62). The uncorrected correlations are reproduced in Table 2.

Analyses of readability (cf. Bormuth, 1966) also demonstrate the preeminent role of word knowledge. In a study of the factors that make prose difficult to read, Coleman (1971) examined morphological, syntactic, and semantic properties of words and sentences. While he found sentence complexity to be a fairly important variable, he was able to conclude that "any measure of word complexity (number of letters, morphemes, or syllables; frequency of usage) will account for about 80 percent of the predicted variance" (p. 184). Klare (1974-1975), in a review of readability, also concluded that a two-variable formula is sufficient for most practical purposes: one variable related to word difficulty and the other to syntactic or sentence difficulty. He went on to conclude that the word variable is consistently more highly predictive of difficulty than is the sentence variable. As would be expected, some index of vocabulary difficulty has typically been given the heaviest weight in readability formulas.

Why Is Vocabulary Knowledge a Major Factor in Linguistic Ability?

There are three more or less distinct views of why vocabulary knowledge is such an extraordinary correlate of linguistic ability. We will call the first the *instrumentalist* position: individuals who score high on a vocabulary test are likely to know more of the words in most texts they encounter than low scoring individuals. The heart of the instrumentalist hypothesis is that knowing the words enables text comprehension. In other words, this hypothesis claims that vocabulary knowledge is directly and importantly in the causal chain resulting in text comprehension. Unlike the two positions described below, the instrumentalist hypothesis has nothing to say about where vocabulary knowledge comes from but only that, once possessed, it helps the reader understand text.

According to the second position, vocabulary tests measure verbal *aptitude*. A person who scores high on such a test has a quick mind. With the same amount of exposure to the culture, this individual has learned more word meanings. He or she also comprehends discourse more readily than the person who scores low on a vocabulary test. The essential claim of the aptitude hypothesis is that persons with large vocabularies are better at discourse comprehension because they possess superior mental agility. A large vocabulary is not conceived to be involved in a direct way in better text understanding in this model. Rather vocabulary test performance is merely another reflection of verbal ability and it is verbal ability that mainly determines whether text will be understood.

The third position is the *knowledge* hypothesis. Peformance on vocabulary tests is seen as a reflection of the extent of exposure to the culture. The person who scores high has deeper and broader knowledge of the culture. The essential idea is that it is this knowledge that is crucial for text understanding. Rather than being directly important, possessing a certain word meaning is only a sign that the individual may possess the knowledge needed to understand a text. For instance, the child who knows the word *mast* is likely to have knowledge about sailing. This knowledge enables that child to understand a text that contains sentences which do not even involve the word *mast*, such as, "We jibed suddenly and the boom snapped across the cockpit."

Of course, *jibe, boom,* and *cockpit* are specialized words, too. It might be wondered whether the instrumental hypothesis and the knowledge hypothesis are really different. Strong versions of the two positions are distinguishable, at least. The instrumental position, as we choose to characterize it, stresses individual word meanings. The knowledge view emphasizes conceptual frameworks or "schemata"; individual word meanings are merely the exposed tip of the conceptual iceberg.

Which of these three positions is most tenable? The main point to be made is that there are neither the theoretical tools nor the data to justify a conclusion at the present time. A second important point is that it would be naive, indeed, to assume that one of the positions will turn out to be entirely right and the other two entirely wrong.

The most fully developed position is that vocabulary knowledge reflects verbal aptitude. As the studies reviewed earlier indicate, vocabulary tests intercorrelate highly with a variety of other kinds of tests reflecting "intelligence." On its face, this fact is hard to understand solely in terms of the instrumentalist or knowledge positions. Probably by metaphorical extension of notions of physical agility, it is customary to speak of people of high intelligence as having "quick" minds. Recently Earl Hunt and his associates have been trying to prove that this is more than a metaphor (cf. Hunt, 1978). They theorized that people of high verbal ability are literally faster than other people at elemental verbal coding and recoding operations. One task used to assess speed of mental operations developed by Posner (cf. Posner and Mitchell, 1967) involves the subjects' deciding whether pairs of upper or lowercase letters match. In one condition, subjects had to judge if two letters have the same name (e.g., aA), and in the other condition, the decision is whether the letters are physically identical (e.g., AA). The subjects' responses are timed. It is argued that a time measure derived from this task is a pure index of the speed of some elemental verbal operations, since the subject needs to "look up" in memory the names of the two letters and compare them. Hunt and his collaborators have found that this measure correlates about .30 with standardized tests of verbal ability. This is a relationship that could not have been predicted and is not readily explained by the other hypotheses being entertained.

Nevertheless, the case is far from conclusive. The general ability tests used in Hunt's studies probably placed subjects under at least some implicit time pressure. This could have given fast workers an advantage. If so, the studies may have revealed that fast people are fast rather than that fast people are smart. Consistent with this interpretation are the results of a factor analysis of representative paper and pencil ability measures and laboratory reaction time tasks completed by Hunt, Lunneborg, and Lewis (1975). The measures of speed of really elemental processes, such as letter matching time, loaded on a factor that appears to represent clerical speed and accuracy instead of on the factor representing general intelligence. A study of Kirby and Das (1977) also indicated that processing speed is a separable factor in tests of verbal and spatial abilities. This conclusion seems to be a sound one since Thorndike (1973) found, in his study of reading comprehension in 15 countries, only modest correlations between performance on reading speed and comprehension tests. The median corrected correlations were .42 for 10 year olds and .47 for 14 year olds.

With respect to the instrumentalist position, as the evidence reviewed earlier indicates, word difficulty is highly predictive of readability. Does this fact clinch the argument in favor of the instrumental hypothesis? No, since it is possible that variation among texts in vocabulary difficulty is merely symptomatic of deeper differences in knowledge prerequisites. To prove that knowing the meaning of individual words has an important instrumental role in understanding text would require more than correlational evidence. It would need to be shown a) that the substitution of easier or more difficult words in a text makes that text easier or more difficult to comprehend, and b) that people are helped to comprehend a text if they learn the meanings of the unfamiliar words it contains. A cursory look at the literature bearing on these points suggests that the assumptions of the instrumentalist position are unquestioned tenets rather than hypotheses in need of verification.

There is some research in which texts have been altered so as to vary word familiarity (see Chall, 1958, for a review of the early studies). In a recent set of experiments, Wittrock, Marks, and Doctorow (1975; see also Marks, Doctorow, and Wittrock, 1974) replaced 15 percent of the words in several passages with either high-frequency or low-frequency synonyms.

There is some confusion in the Wittrock et al. paper over the word frequency manipulations. While this detracts from the findings, the conclusions may hold for "easy" and "hard" words. Sixth graders of every level of reading skill evidenced better comprehension of texts containing easy words than texts containing hard words, whether they were reading or listening. Furthermore, children who began with an easy text later showed improved comprehension of the hard version of the same text. Performance on a vocabulary test suggested that children who had first received the easy version of a passage were able to learn some of the low-frequency words in the hard version.

Other recent evidence is less favorable to the instrumentalist position. Tuinman and Brady (1974) were unable to increase fourth, fifth, and sixth grade students' comprehension of texts that contained a substantial proportion of difficult words by direct instruction on those words, even though such instruction significantly increased the students' performance on the vocabulary items themselves. These authors concluded that the instrumental hypothesis seems to be ruled out. Jenkins, Pany, and Schreck (1978; see also Pany and Jenkins, 1977) were also unable to establish that vocabulary instruction improves reading comprehension. Several different methods for teaching word meanings were explored. All were at least somewhat better than no instruction. The method which proved most effective with both average and learning disabled children involved intensive drill and practice on the words in isolation. However, even when children had definitely learned the meanings of twelve difficult words, they did no better than uninstructed children who definitely did not know these words on a cloze test or in retelling a brief story containing the twelve difficult words. We do not know how to reconcile the conflicting results bearing on the instrumental hypothesis other than to conclude, as reviewers of educational research must so often conclude, that more research is needed.

Turning to the third position, there is now a truly substantial case that background knowledge is crucial for reading comprehension (cf. Anderson, 1978). However, there is thin evidence to support the view that vocabulary scores primarily reflect such background knowledge. We shall cite just one study which suggests that the idea is plausible. Steffensen, Joag-Dev, and Anderson (1979) asked natives of the U.S. and of India to read passages describing an American and an Indian wedding. The results showed that the native passages were read more rapidly and recalled in greater detail. There were more culturally appropriate elaborations of the native passages and more culturally inappropriate distortions of the foreign ones. The vocabulary of the two passages was closely controlled. For instance, there were only two words in the Indian passage, *sari* and *dhoti*, referring to articles of women's and men's clothing, respectively, that would have been unfamiliar to any of the American subjects. These two words did not figure in any important way in the passage, so failure to know them could have had no more than a negligible effect. Still, a two item vocabulary test, examining knowledge of *sari* and *dhoti*, would have been an excellent predictor of performance on the Indian passage. All Indian subjects would have known both words. Some Americans would have known *sari* but very few would have known *dhoti*. It is apparent that the test would have neatly divided subjects in terms of the extent of their knowledge of Indian culture, which was obviously the underlying reason for the large observed differences between Indians and Americans in comprehension, learning, and memory.

Instructional Implications of Different Hypotheses about Vocabulary Knowledge

It is important to know which of the three hypotheses about vocabulary knowledge is most nearly correct because the views have radically different implications for the reading curriculum. At one extreme, some who endorse the verbal aptitude hypothesis are fatalistic about whether any environmental factor can have a major influence on children's reading. They tend to recommend family planning instead of curriculum innovation as the final solution to the reading problem. Of course the verbal aptitude position does not require the belief that heredity is predominant. Alternatively, there are those who maintain that verbal ability grows in proportion to the volume of experience with language. The greater the opportunities to use language the faster and more efficient become the elemental processing operations. In turn, speed and efficiency permit greater benefit from each successive language encounter. More detailed accounts of this sort of position can be found in the well-known paper by LaBerge and Samuels (1974) and a recent paper by Perfetti and Lesgold (1979).

The latter formulation of the verbal aptitude hypothesis leads to the recommendation that educators should try to maximize the amount of reading children do. However, this is not very newsworthy. It is a practice that would be endorsed no matter what the theoretical persuasion. The distinctive emphasis in the verbal aptitude position is on speed and efficiency of processing. This emphasis gives rise to the recommendation that beginning readers and poor readers receive extensive drill and practice on "fundamentals" of reading. According to Perfetti and Lesgold (1979), the drill activities should include even more practice than typically provided in word vocalization, more practice in speeded word recognition, and more practice in immediate memory for the literal content of text. It should be noted that these suggestions are offered in the spirit of a hypothesis. Perfetti and Lesgold acknowledge that, so far at least, attempts to facilitate text comprehension by providing speeded word drills have not proved very successful (see especially Fleisher and Jenkins, 1977).

While, like everyone else, the advocate of the instrumental hypothesis favors lots of reading and varied language experience, the distinctive feature of this view is that it invites direct vocabulary building exercises. Becker (1977) has argued strongly for the instrumentalist position. He maintained that once decoding skills have been mastered, the chief remaining factor in determining whether a child will be a successful reader is vocabulary knowledge. He claimed that schools have never had reading programs that systematically build vocabulary. Children from middle class backgrounds pick up word meanings anyway. But the same is less true, Becker argues, of children coming from lower class homes, which often fail to provide support for the continuous vocabulary and concept growth important to school work. Consistent with this assumption is some recent work by Hall and Tirre (1979), who found that lower class parents, particularly lower class black parents, use substantially fewer of the words found in standardized intelligence tests when speaking with their children than do middle class parents.

Becker proposed a reading curriculum in which every child would learn about 7,000 basic words from direct instruction. The figure 7,000 comes from one estimate of the number of basic words known by the average high school senior (Dupuy, 1974). Becker acknowledged that there are families of words with related meanings, thereby permitting the child some generalization beyond the words that are specifically taught. By and large, though, he believed that learning one vocabulary item gives little advantage in learning the next one. For instance, he illustrated morphological instruction on the following set of unrelated words: *help, support, insist, toil, resist, recognize, assist.* Even his so-called "concept side" of the instruction entailed a component analysis of isolated words. So if this assumption is correct, direct teaching of a vocabulary of even 7,000 basic words would be an enormous task. Becker estimated that about 25 basic words would have to be taught per week from the third through the twelfth grade (p. 539).

The distinctive curriculum implication of the knowledge hypothesis is that generally new vocabulary ought to be learned in the context of acquiring new knowledge (cf. Goodman, 1976, p. 487). Every serious student of reading recognizes that the significant aspect of vocabulary development is in the learning of concepts not just words. The additional point that the knowledge position brings to the fore is that concepts come in clusters that are systematically interrelated. Returning to an earlier example, the concept of *mast* cannot be acquired independent of concepts such as *boat* and *sail.* Thus, it would seem to be sensible for people to learn the jargon in the context of learning about sailing and the anatomy of sailboats. According to the knowledge hypothesis, if a child were really naive, trying to teach a single sailing concept and word in isolation from the set of related concepts and words would be inefficient in the best case and completely fruitless in the worst case.

A thought experiment suggests the more general point about the role of knowledge in vocabulary learning. Suppose you wished to teach some French vocabulary to, let us say, two groups of English speaking Canadian children, evenly matched on aptitude and achievement. One group is from a downtown urban area, the other is from a small fishing village. The body of words you wish to teach is concerned with fishing (*trawlers, rods, nets, casting, bait, currents*). Would you expect one group to learn the words more quickly and easily than the other? Why? We do not know of research that has dealt systematically with these questions. One somewhat relevant study was carried out by Allen and Garton (1968). They found that physics students were much better than art students in recognizing physics words. They concluded that, for art students, physics words are semantically indistinct and thus have to be recognized on a more piecemeal basis. Familiarity with an area of knowledge increased the familiarity of the physics words.

Knowledge can be sliced in various ways. Thus far in this section, we have considered sets of words related because they are used in talking about the same topic. Words also may be conceptualized in terms of families related to one another because they convey related sets of distinctions. Consider an example involving verbs of visual perception.[1] The basic verb is *see*. If you notice that *look* involves a deliberate act of seeing, it can be appreciated that *glimpse* refers to a short act of seeing whereas *glance* refers to a short act of looking. *Stare*, on the other hand, refers to a prolonged act of looking. The variations in sense among these verbs can be understood in terms of just two semantic features, intention and duration. Further distinctions would be required to encompass other verbs of visual perception such as *notice* and *examine*.

We would consider that a lesson that helped children sharpen and extend the distinctions involved in visual perception words to be consistent with the spirit of the knowledge position. What the knowledge position would not countenance is a separate vocabulary lesson that included *glance, mast,* and a miscellany of other words. Herein lies a difference from the instrumentalist position, which does not seem to us to preclude exercises involving lists of unrelated words.

Johnson and Pearson's (1978) book, *Teaching Reading Vocabulary*, appears to represent predominantly the knowledge position, though it is an eclectic treatment that also reflects influences from the other two views. Johnson and Pearson advocated teaching a basic sight vocabulary using "intensive direct instruction in the early grades and with older children who do not read well!" (p. 28). They also endorsed both direct and indirect means for teaching phonics, promoting morphological analysis, causing vocabulary knowledge to expand, and teaching the use of the dictionary and thesaurus. Johnson and Pearson devoted a chapter to the use of contextual clues to figure out the meanings of unfamiliar and ambiguous words. Otherwise most of the exercises and games suggested throughout the book involve sets of words outside the context of stories or textbook chapters. However, the words usually involved sets of interrelated distinctions, such as were illustrated above with verbs of visual perception. Almost every activity was designed to expand children's sensitivity to these distinctions. There is an apparent discrepancy between the goals of the activities, which are concerned with conceptual distinctions and relations, and the format of the activities, which is based largely on isolated words. If the knowledge perspective were strictly adhered to, vocabulary instruction would not be thought of as a separate subject in school.

For the sake of clarity of exposition, we have presented the aptitude, instrumental, and knowledge positions in uncomplicated and somewhat overdrawn form. We must emphasize again that no serious scholar in reading or related fields rigidly adheres to any one of these positions. In particular Hunt, who has been identified with the aptitude hypothesis, has explicitly and emphatically stated that vocabulary size also is a reflection of an individual's accumulated knowledge of the world. Becker, whom we labeled an instrumentalist, heartily endorses some of the implications of both the aptitude and the knowledge views. Reading has been a fractious field. If a policy were followed of avoiding controversy where none genuinely exists, the quality of intellectual exchange and the sociopolitical climate might improve to the point where someone within the next decade could write a book entitled "Learning to Read: The Great Consensus."

What Does It Mean to Know the Meaning of a Word?

It is not clear that, if Ludwig Wittgenstein and Bertrand Russell were left alone in a room for three hours, they could decide that they really knew the meaning of *dog*. As Labov (1973, p. 341) said, "Words have often been called slippery customers, and many scholars have been distressed by their tendency to shift their meanings and slide out from under any simple definition."

An ordinary adult engaging in an ordinary conversation will be absolutely sure he knows the meanings of almost all of the words he hears. Notice that the restriction to ordinary use is an important aspect of this confidence. Consider the term *gold*, for example. The person who is sure he knows the meaning of this word in an ordinary use will quickly retreat when in the company of jewelers, mining engineers, geological survey assayists, or metallurgists.

What does a person know when he knows the meaning of a word in its ordinary, everyday, garden-variety sense? This issue is addressed in what we will refer to as the Standard Theory of semantics, according to which the meaning of a word can be analyzed into features (also called components, attributes, or properties), each of which represents one of the distinctions conveyed by the word. Necessary or essential features are usually distinguished from features that are merely characteristic. For instance, having a back could be said to be a necessary feature of *chair* since an object that is otherwise a chair except for the lack of a back is really a stool instead of a chair. On the other hand, the ability to fly is only a characteristic feature of *bird* since some birds (penguins) don't fly at all and others (chickens) do so very poorly.

To define a term, in the strong sense, is to list the features necessary to capture the essence of the thing (or event or quality) designated by the word. Saying this another way, a proper definition indicates the attributes a thing must have in order to be designated by a word; if any of these necessary properties were missing that word would not apply. Before we choose this as our criterion in the testing of children's word knowledge, however, we might wish to examine how well it applies to adults' normal use and understanding of words.

How able are people to define the words they are sure they know? "Not very" is the answer if one insists upon the strong sense of define. Consider *gold* again. Upon being asked to define *gold*, the ordinary citizen might say that gold 1) is precious, b) is a metal, and c) has a particular yellowish (i.e., golden) hue. The problem is that none of these is a necessary feature. Not all gold is a golden color. If, say, the Chinese were to discover a mountain of gold, the substance would no longer be precious. Not even the attribute of being a metal can be considered to be an eternal, immutable property of gold for, unlikely though it is, there might be a scientific breakthrough in which it was discovered that gold is not a metal.

A unicorn is a beast with such and such defining characteristics. Of course there are no beasts with these properties; which is to say that unicorns do not exist. By the same logic, if being precious and being a metal are defining features of gold, it follows that if the Chinese were to discover a mountain of the substance or scientists were to determine that the substance is not a metal, one would be forced to conclude that gold did not exist. As Putnam (1975) has noted, this is a very odd conclusion, because there would still be this "stuff" lying around that people used to call gold. We have a right to be suspicious of a semantic theory that backs us into such a peculiar corner.

Another example will illuminate the point even more starkly. When it comes to fine points of meaning, ordinary folks turn to experts as the final arbiters—to jewelers and metallurgists for the exact meaning of *gold*, to the Supreme Court for the proper interpretation of words in the Constitution, and so on. For the sake of the argument, it may be supposed that the American Psychiatric Association is the final arbiter of the meaning of *homosexual*. For years, this august group defined homosexuality as a disease of sexual orientation. Recently, however, the association declared that homosexuality is not a disease. Anita Bryant may not have agreed with that conclusion, but at least she understood it. If the characterization of homosexuality as a disease had been taken seriously as a defining feature, upon reconsidering its position, the American Psychiatric Association would have had to assert, "There is no such thing as homosexuality." That conclusion would simply have left Ms. Bryant puzzled.

There are other serious problems with Standard Theory. Notably, the members of a class called by the same name frequently do not all share a single set of common properties. Wittgenstein (1953; see also Rosch, 1973; Rosch and

Mervis, 1975) argued that things designated by the same word generally are related by "family resemblance." He intended an analogy to a human family whose members look and act alike. Mother and one son may have a prominent nose. Father and daughter may have the same hair color. And so on. But there may be no single respect in which they are all alike, no single feature which they all share. Wittgenstein claimed family resemblance was the most accurate characterization of the relationships among the various uses of most common words. To illustrate his point, he analyzed uses of the term *game*, noting the similarities and differences between team games, board games, and children's games. Others have shown the fuzziness and context sensitivity of the meanings of terms such as *cup* (Labov, 1973); *eat* (Anderson and Ortony, 1975); *red* (Halff, Ortony, and Anderson, 1976); and *held* (Anderson, Pichert, Goetz, Schallert, Stevens, and Trollip, 1976).

A great deal more could be said about semantic theory. (For authoritative, current treatments, see Clark and Clark, 1977, especially chapters 11-14; Fillmore, 1975; and Miller and Johnson-Laird, 1976.) The main point of this brief excursion into the meaning of meaning is to caution against holding up a standard of word comprehension for children that adults could not meet.

Depth of Word Knowledge

It is useful to distinguish between two aspects of an individual's vocabulary knowledge. The first may be called "breadth" of knowledge, by which we mean the number of words for which the person knows at least some of the significant aspects of meaning. Later sections of this paper will be concerned mainly with breadth of knowledge.

Treated in this section is a second dimension of vocabulary knowledge, namely the quality of "depth" of understanding. We shall assume that, for most purposes, a person has a sufficiently deep understanding of a word if it conveys to him or her all of the distinctions that would be understood by an ordinary adult under normal circumstances.

Eve Clark (1973) has marshalled an array of evidence which shows that the meaning a young child has for a word is likely to be more global, less differentiated than that of an older person. With increasing age, the child makes more and more of the adult distinctions. In other words, when first acquired, the concept a child has for a word need not include all of the features of the adult concept. Eventually, in the normal course of affairs, the missing features will be learned.

While there are some differences in theoretical interpretation and some findings appear to hinge on procedural details (Brewer and Stone, 1975; Glucksberg, Hay, and Danks, 1976; Nelson, 1977; Richards, 1976), most of the research done to date supports the conclusion that there is progressive differentiation of word meanings with increasing age and experience.

Just one illustration will be provided of the kind of evidence that points to this conclusion. Gentner (1975) completed a theoretical analysis of verbs of possession which indicated that *buy, sell,* and *spend* entail a more complex set of distinctions than *give* and *take*. Notice that giving involves the transfer of something from one person to another. Selling likewise involves the transfer of something from one person to another, but it involves an additional transaction as well, the transfer of money from the buyer to the seller. The complementary relationship holds between buying and taking.

Gentner expected children to acquire the full, adult meanings of these verbs in order of complexity. Children ranging from four to eight years of age were asked to make dolls act out transactions from directions involving each verb. For example, the children were requested to "make Ernie sell Bert a (toy) car." The four-year-olds performed flawlessly with directions containing *give* and *take*, but never correctly executed instructions that involved *spend, buy,* or *sell*. The eight-year-olds exhibited nearly perfect understanding of every direction except the ones containing *sell*. Overall, the results were exactly as expected: the adult meanings of verbs of possession are acquired in order of complexity.

Gentner's analysis (1975, p. 242) of the children's errors suggests that the younger ones treated the complex verbs as though they were simpler forms. She explained, "...the commonest incorrect response was some form of one-way transfer...the young child acting out *buy* and *sell* completely disregards the money transfer that should be part of their meanings, yet performs the object transfer in the correct direction. He reacts to *buy* as if it were *take*. He treats *sell* as if it were *give*." When asked to "make Bert spend some money," even the youngest child correctly handles the money transfer but neglects to have Bert get anything for the money he "spends." The child treats *spend money* as though it meant give money away.

Through some quirk of the sociology of science, the indepth study of word knowledge has been the special province of psycholinguists studying language development in young children. There is a substantial body of literature on selected vocabulary of children from about two through eight years of age. The literature involving older children and adults is meager.

In our judgment, vocabulary knowledge continues to deepen throughout lifetimes; that is, as they grow older, most people continue to learn nuances and subtle distinction conveyed by words that in some sense they have known since childhood. There is no hard data to support this conjecture. However, an illustration will show that many adults still have something to learn about even fairly common words. It is easy to find educated adults who confuse *infer* and *imply*. A person will say something along the lines, "I intended, by stating these arguments, to infer that...." Of course, this individual should have said *imply*. Speakers imply. Listeners infer. The complication, which no doubt makes the distinction difficult, is that speakers may report inferences they have made as well as get implications across to listeners.

Breadth of Word Knowledge

It is disturbing to examine available estimates of the average vocabulary size of various age groups. Table 3 summarizes studies that have been carried out to estimate total basic or "root" word knowledge. It can be seen that the estimates vary wildly.

It is not obvious how to evaluate the different sampling methods and response criteria that have been employed in research attempting to estimate vocabulary size. Recently, for instance, the distinguished psycholinguist, George Miller (1978), stated:

> Although the rapid rate of syntactic acquisition has inspired much respectful discussion in recent years, the rate of lexical growth is no less impressive. The best figures available indicate that children of average intelligence learn new words at a rate of more than 20 per day. It seems necessary to assume therefore, that at any particular time they have hundreds of words roughly categorized as to semantic or topical relevance but not yet worked out as to precise meaning or use. (p. 1003)

Miller did not specify whether he was referring to "basic" words. If he was, then he is positing a mean annual word acquisition rate of over seven thousand words, or about fifty thousand over the elementary and middle school years. This seems unlikely even in the light of the highest estimates summarized in Table 3. Miller may have been including compounds and derivatives. However, to our knowledge, no systematic examination of children's ability to understand these forms has been completed. Miller's statement highlights two points. First, in its original context, the statement is a crucial step in an argument about lexical development. Accurate estimates of the growth of word knowledge are an important element in discussions of lexical and conceptual development and the relationship between them. Second, how do we assess what are the "best figures available"?

In 1940, Seashore and Eckerson remarked that, even though the field of vocabulary testing is a "fairly old one" (p. 35), substantial problems of measurement remained. By now, in the time span of educational research, we might want to call the field "ancient," and virtually all of those original problems persist.

There are important practical reasons for attempting to make accurate assessments of total word knowledge. Language and reading programs aim to increase students' vocabularies. The number of words presented to students varies, in part, according to what is regarded as the most authoritative thinking and research on vocabulary size and growth (Clifford, 1978). More reliable estimates would indicate the appropriateness of the assumptions of a program, and perhaps highlight periods of growth to be capitalized upon. More generally, reliable estimates would indicate whether direct language instruction can plausibly account for a substantial proportion of the child's language growth, or whether word knowledge is acquired for the most part independently of formal instruction. To

Table 3

SOME PREVIOUS ESTIMATES OF TOTAL VOCABULARY SIZE AT SELECTED GRADES

Grade	Source	Estimate
1st	M.E. Smith (1926)	2,562
	Dolch (1936)	2,703
	Ames (1964)	12,400
	M.K. Smith (1941)	17,000
	Shibles (1959)	26,000
3rd	Dupuy (1974)	2,000
	Holley (1919)	3.144
	Terman (1916)	3,600
	Brandenburg (1918)	5,429
	Kirkpatrick (1907)	6,620
	Cuff (1930)	7,425
	M.K. Smith (1941)	25,000
7th	Dupuy (1974)	4,760
	Terman (1916)	7,200
	Holley (1919)	8,478
	Kirkpatrick (1907)	10,666
	Brandenburg (1918)	11,445
	Cuff (1930)	14,910
	Bonser, et al. (1915)	26,520
	M.K. Smith (1941)	51,000
College sophomore	Seashore (1933)	15,000
	Kirkpatrick (1907)	19,000
	Seashore & Eckerson (1940)	60,000
	Gerlach (1917)	85,300
	Gillette (1927)	127,800
	Hartman (1946)	200,000

Note. Adapted from Seashore and Eckerson (1940) and Bayer (1976).

refer again to a concrete proposal, Becker's (1977) idea that underachieving children should be taught via direct instruction the vocabulary most high school seniors possess would be difficult, but perhaps feasible, if the children had to learn 25 new words a week. It would be out of the question if they had to learn 25 words each school day.

Next we will present some of the central issues in broad gauged measurement of word knowledge. The discussion of these issues will reveal many of the reasons why estimates of vocabulary size have fluctuated so widely. Two general questions need to be considered. First, how is a sample of words to be selected? Second, what kind of response from a subject will be regarded as evidence that a word is in the individual's vocabulary?

Selecting a Sample of Words

In determining what is to count as a word, the researcher needs to decide whether it is of interest to discern the subject's ability to use derivatives and compounds (plurals, participles, tense markers, comparatives, etc.). Some authors, notably Seashore (1933), have preferred to calculate separate estimates for "special" terms and derivatives. Others, for example Dupuy (1974), have attempted to concentrate solely on "basic" words. Dupuy, the author of one of the most recent and thorough studies of word knowledge, sampled randomly from *Webster's Third New International Dictionary* (1961) and then applied three criteria to each word selected. The word had to be a main entry; a single word form (i.e., not a derivative or compound); and could not be technical, slang, foreign, or archaic.

The systematic nature of this sampling creates its own equally systematic biases. Some children may have acquired the generative rule for, say, negation by prefix (for example, *unable* or *dishonest*) and others may not have (Silvestri and Silvestri, 1977). Do we wish to exclude this element of vocabulary knowledge from the measure? Adults acquire a number of special or technical terms in their areas of expertise or interest, so exclusion of technical terms denies many subjects the opportunity of indicating their knowledge of a large number of words.

What counts as a word will depend upon the researcher's principal purposes. However, affixes and derivatives are important elements of word knowledge, and several questions related to their role are of considerable interest. In what way does knowledge of basic or root word forms relate to knowledge of the compound forms? Are entries organized conceptually in the personal dictionary such that the probability of knowing a compound word is the same as that of knowing all its family members, basic form included? Or is the chance of knowing a compound some combination of the frequencies of the particular compounding elements? Much is to be gained from research into these issues.

Whatever criteria are applied, there can be no doubt that there are many thousands of words in English. Dupuy (1974) estimated that there are about a quarter of a million main entries in *Webster's Dictionary* (1961). Of these, he calculated that about 12,300 are basic words.

A source and method of selecting from that source is required which will lead to the most accurate estimates of total word knowledge. The most obvious way to start is to sample randomly from an unabridged dictionary. Dupuy (1974), for instance, selected one word from every page of the dictionary (the third word from the top of alternating columns), and then applied the three criteria mentioned earlier for selecting the basic words out of this group. This procedure produced a final sample of 123 basic words.

Once a random sample of words has been selected, a test is constructed to assess how many of the words a person knows. Then, in principle, estimating the person's vocabulary size is straightforward. For instance, Dupuy's Basic Word Vocabulary Test contains 1 percent of the 12,300 basic words he calculated are in *Webster's*. Therefore, the absolute size of the basic word vocabulary can be approximated by multiplying the score on this test by 100. A person whose score is 60, after correction for guessing, would be judged to have a basic vocabulary of 6,000 words.

One disadvantage of this method is self-evident. Estimated vocabulary size depends heavily on the size of the dictionary. With respect to Dupuy, while he sampled initially from a large unabridged dictionary, a word had to appear as a major entry in each of three other small dictionaries in order to be counted as a basic word. A total of 979 words, 41 percent of the sample, were discarded on the basis of this rule. The result was a very conservative estimate of the number of basic words in American English and is one reason Dupuy's estimates of basic vocabulary size are so much smaller than those of other investigators. Of course, many of these words were very rare, but others such as *cloudlet, escaping, breezes, invited, starling,* and *unilateral* would be familiar to most people.

Already discussed is the issue of what to do with derivative and compound forms. A liberal policy will lead to large estimates of vocabulary size. A conservative policy will produce smaller ones. Dupuy was conservative. He eliminated 7.7 percent of the words in his sample on the grounds that they were compounds of derivatives, including a great many familiar ones, such as *grandchild, package,* and *toothache*.

There are other, more subtle considerations in selecting a random sample of words from a dictionary. Some procedures for sampling from an unabridged dictionary can introduce systematic error since all entries do not occupy the same amount of space on a page. This disproportion typically favors the words in more common use since these are the most elaborated, particularly in an unabridged dictionary where very many derivatives may be listed (Williams, 1932; Lorge and Chall, 1963). Consequently, while the words may seem to have been randomly selected, the frequency distribution of the sample may be substantially different from that of the population. This may partly account for the very large estimates of Seashore and Eckerson (1940) and Smith (1941).

A further problem is that projecting a vocabulary size from performance on a random sampling of words is inefficient. If the subject provides the meaning of *bibulous*, then using up test time by asking for the meaning of *bicycle* is wasteful. When estimating subjects' total vocabulary size is the researcher's major aim, then efficiency of items covered per unit of examinee time is an important consideration.

One obvious response to these problems is to select the sample from a frequency distribution of words. Terman and Merrill (1937) arranged their sample of words in order of "difficulty." When the subject failed at six consecutive words, the vocabulary test was stopped. Dupuy (1974) recommended a similar procedure. Time can be saved by such a procedure, but vocabulary size is likely to be underestimated. Furthermore, heavy stress is placed on the assumption that the frequency distribution of the sample mimics that of the population. If this assumption fails, then multiplication of the subject's score by the appropriate constant will produce a poor estimate of total words known.

The characteristics of the two major current word frequency compilations available (Carroll, Davies, and Richman, 1971; Kucera and Francis, 1967) suggest a potential problem with frequency sampling. These analyses indicate that the distribution of words is highly unbalanced, a conclusion reached over 25 years ago by Horn (1954), who calculated that about 2,000 types will account for about 95 percent of "running words in adult writing"; 3,000 for 96.9 percent; 4,000 for 97.8 percent; and 10,000 for 99.4 percent. At the low frequency end of the scale, there is a tail that approaches infinity. Even in a huge corpus, a vast number of words appear only once, twice, or not at all. Of the 86,741 word types listed by Carroll, Davies, and Richman from a corpus of over 5 million tokens, 35, 079, or 40.44 percent, appeared once. Kucera and Francis found 44.72 percent of the words appeared once in a sample of over one million tokens. So, if the test is short, the subjects run the risk of not being able to show that they know several medium frequency words, since there will be such a large proportion of rare words in the sample. A resolution of this issue is important, since a frequency-based sampling technique seems the most accessible method for overcoming the problems of simple random sampling.

Frequency is a parameter which probably is very strongly related to probability that a word will be known. There is evidence supporting this hypothesis from a number of areas: multiple choice performance on standardized tests (Kibby, 1977), recall of word meanings following presentation of pictures (Carrol and White, 1973; Duncan, 1977), and word recognition times following tachistoscopic presentation (Cohen, 1976; Rubenstein, Garfield, and Millikan, 1970). The only discrepant finding has been that of Davis (1944b) who found only a slight relationship between word difficulty and frequency. He explained this result in terms of the role of compound words: While the root of the word may be very common and well-known, a certain affix-root compound may be very infrequent but almost equally well-known if the affix is familiar. A more analytic approach to the relationship of this index of frequency of usage to probability of knowledge would entail the use of "family" frequency, that is, the frequency of the root word and all its compounds and derivatives. We might expect that the relationship of this index of frequency of usage to probability of knowledge would be more orderly.

Indeed, we are willing to go further and speculate that the relationship between family frequency and probability of knowing a word resembles the curve presented in Figure 1. In terms of breadth of knowledge, we would expect a ceiling at the upper end of the frequency scale: most people know all of the very common words. Other aspects of the curve would differentiate individuals: The point at which the curve dropped from the plateau level, and the slope of the function probably are the two parameters that would capture the important individual differences. Even for children, we might best think of the curve leveling out as the words become very infrequent, since it is likely that, from their hobbies, interests, or the occupation of their parents, most children would know some very rare words. Nevertheless, we have drawn the lower portion of the curve as a broken line since we are less sure about the relationship in this area.

In summary, a good test of word knowledge would present the subject with a large number of words, sampled liberally from the whole range of word frequency. Techniques should be developed which allow accurate estimation of the relationship of a given subject's probability of knowing a word and the frequency of the word's morphological family.

Criteria for Determining that a Word Is in a Person's Vocabulary

Four sorts of test formats have been employed in attempts to assess breadth of vocabulary knowledge: a) multiple choice; b) constructed answer in which the subject attempts to give a definition, a synonym, an illustration, or use the word in a sentence or phrase; c) yes/no judgments, in which the subject checks the words in a list that he or she knows; and d) matching where the subject pairs off words with their synonyms. Sims (1929) compared these four types using data obtained from students in fifth through the eighth grades. The correlation matrix Sims reported is reproduced in Table 4. Sims concluded that, although the checking method was as reliable as the others, it did not seem to offer acceptable construct validity. Only seventy words were used, however, and Sims failed to

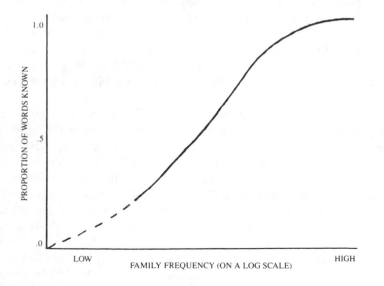

Figure 1. Possible relationship between likelihood word meanings are known and frequency of usage.

counterbalance for order or delay between tests. While there may be some questions about the trustworthiness of Sims' results, there is intuitive sense in the
notion that the constructed answers, multiple choice, and matching tasks have
more in common with one another than they have with a checking task that is not
corrected for guessing.

Table 4

CORRELATIONS BETWEEN FOUR TYPES OF VOCABULARY TESTS

	1	2	3	4
1. Checking (yes/no)	.92*			
2. Multiple choice	.54	.84*		
3. Matching	.64	.85	.93*	
4. Constructed answer	.56	.74	.82	.92*

Note. From Sims (1929).
* Split-half reliability coefficients.

The question that needs examination is which of these methods will be of
most theoretical and practical value as a measure of vocabulary. Three of these
types will be discussed in the light of several issues. Since the points raised about
the multiple choice format apply even more cogently to matching, the latter will
not be dealt with separately.

Multiple choice methods. People often possess partial knowledge of words.
In these instances the items' distractors become crucial. An individual may select
the correct synonym for *platitude* from the choices: a) duck-billed mammal, b)
praise, c) commonplace remark, d) flatness. He may make the correct selection
because he has heard the word used in reference to an utterance and with a negative connotation. This information, however, may not enable him to select correctly from a) commonplace remark, b) nonsense, c) irrelevant question, d)
insult. The set of choices constrains the individual's response to different degrees, and different policies for generating distractors will, of course, lead to
differences in performance.

Lepley (1955, 1965), for example, constructed two forms of a synonym test,
one employing distractors from the same semantic category as the target, and
another which used distractors from semantically diverse categories. Lepley
(1965) found equal split-half reliability (.93 and 94) but only a .66 correlation
between performance on the two scales, and significantly superior performance
on the version requiring only gross discriminations. The correlation is surprisingly low given the common format and the fact that the superficial demand characteristics were the same. Lepley's results illustrate the influence of the distractor
set.

The multiple choice format is currently the most widely used in standardized
vocabulary testing (e.g., California Achievement Tests, 1977; Metropolitan
Achievement Tests, 1970; Stanford Achievement Tests, 1973). The principal
complaint raised here so far is that the distractors cannot avoid constraining the

subject's response. If the purpose of the test is to provide data on relative performance only, not on absolute level of performance, then the distractors can be, and usually are, chosen to maximize the discriminating power of the item. If one is interested in vocabulary size, then this policy will not do.

Many vocabulary tests (e.g., Stanford, 1973) use sentence completion in a multiple choice format. Many of the problems already mentioned apply even when the test simulates a real encounter with the target word. In addition, the question of the effects of various amounts of contextual support on estimated vocabulary size, with groups of words that vary in frequency of usage, has not been studied. There is research that suggests that individuals vary not only in the size of their reading vocabularies but also in their ability to use context to deduce the meanings of unknown and partly known words (Mason, Knisely, and Kendall, 1978; Pearson and Studt, 1975).

A tricky problem with the multiple choice format is that young children may not consider all the distractors (Asher, 1978; Brown, 1975; Vurpillot, 1968). They will often choose the first or second alternative if it makes reasonable enough sense. The test-taking strategies of older children on multiple choice tests are not yet well characterized, but there quite probably are strategic components of good performance which serve to increase spuriously the relationship between a multiple choice vocabulary test and other achievement or intelligence tests in the same format. An insidious possibility is that some of the apparent growth in vocabulary knowledge over the elementary school years is really attributable to the acquisition of more sophisticated test-taking skills.

In conclusion, the multiple choice format is the most popular one. It makes relatively efficient use of examinee time and must be reasonably valid, otherwise the strong relationships between performance on such tests and other measures of linguistic competence, summarized at the beginning of this paper, would not have been obtained. The chief complication with the multiple choice format, when one wants absolute measures of vocabulary knowledge, is how to choose distractors. A further problem is that multiple choice tests may make demands on strategic knowledge in which young and poor readers are deficient.

Constructed answer measures. To overcome the problem of selecting distractors, several researchers, notably Seashore (1933), Smith (1941), Terman and Merrill (1937), have used a constructed answer format in which the subject reads or hears the target word and then writes or tells a definition of it, uses it in a sentence, gives a synonym for it, or in some other way provides an indication of its sense and reference. Subjects can be encouraged to do any one of these things just so long as the experimenter is convinced the word is "known." This format is capable of dealing with a variety of levels of knowing a word and avoids the issue of distractors. There are, however, two substantial problems with constructed answer measures: The problem of scoring the answers and the problem of response bias.

In the written format, in particular, a constructed answer measure is confounded by factors such as spelling ability, sentence construction ability, and even the ability to write legibly, all of which may discourage a subject from elaborating on a word used or understood in conversation. A slightly more subtle problem, and one that is more difficult to control, resides in the fact that, if a liberal criterion is used and the subject is allowed a range of possible responses to a target word, then a particular strategy for responding may be adopted. The problem is that some words would be more easily explicated in a particular form. The word *noun* may be more easily explained through illustration than by definition, for instance. The research of Anglin (1970) and Wolman and Baker (1965) indicates that, up to the age of about 10-12 years, children tend to provide concrete definitions-by-illustration rather than by an inclusive term or synonym. It is entirely possible that, depending on scoring criteria, the preference at a different age for certain explanatory strategies could produce spurious estimates of the rate of vocabulary growth.

A really vexing problem is how liberally to score answers. How does one score synonyms in relation to apt illustrations or perfect usage in a sentence? In many instances, partial knowledge is displayed. In one of our own recent testing sessions, it became clear that many fifth grade students had partial knowledge of the word *forbid*. Several students knew that it had something to do with not being permitted to do something but did not have as part of their knowledge the fact that *forbid* is used in imperative speech acts. We soon realized that, in this case, we needed to ask for its use in a sentence. We have found other more subtle and difficult cases of partial knowledge. For the word *propelled*, there was no problem in the students' recognition of the word because of their knowledge of propeller. When probed about the function of a *propeller*, many came close to generating the notion of propulsion on the theory that it would be strange to have a big round blade going around on the front of a plane unless it served some fairly fundamental purpose—and what planes do is move.

Some words have no near-synonyms. There are other instances when the only synonym is a less frequent word than the target. In such cases, the subject is being asked to produce a rare word in order to show that a common word is known.

There are some almost irresistible tendencies displayed by an examiner when administering a test with a constructed answer format. After a few children have been tested, the examiner develops a sense of which words are easy and which are difficult. It requires conscious effort to avoid expecting more explanation of the difficult words and less for the easy words. If every subject has known *chair* and the current subject pats the seat of his stool as a response, then the tendency is to award full marks. If he pats the wall for *edifice*, however, he might not score so well. Similarly there is an urge to expect more elaborated responses from older subjects. The preschooler who tells you that an *automobile* "goes brrrrrmmm" will strike you more favorably than the college sophomore who gives you the same answer. In addition, the experimenter will witness explanations of words which entail subtle nonverbal as well as verbal cues. Young children typi-

cally employ hand movements, facial expressions, and gestures in their communications especially when dealing with words that are a little difficult for them.

The horns of the dilemma are these. Stringent, operational, adult-like standards for evaluating whether a response indicates a word is known will confound
what is supposed to be a measure of breadth of vocabulary knowledge with expository ability. Looser, more flexible standards will confound the measure with
the subjective judgment of the examiners which may change from word to word,
subject to subject, and occasion to occasion.

So the liabilities of the constructed answer method are both logistical and
substantial. It is inefficient per unit of testing and scoring time, and it seems to
rely on often subtle intuitions on the part of the examiner, especially when the
subject displays partial knowledge of an item.

Yes/no format. The final format to be considered is that of "checking," which
we prefer to term a yes/no method. In this format the subject simply indicates
whether the meaning of a word is known. Two of the major difficulties that have
arisen consistently in the discussion of the other two major formats are the problem of response bias, and the need to present the subject with a large number of
words chosen from a wide frequency range. The checking format can satisfy the
second criterion admirably but problems of validity arise. Sims (1929) concluded:

> The writer is inclined to believe that a good guess as to whether or not a child knows
> the meaning of a word is almost as satisfactory a method of determining vocabulary
> as checking tests. The relative simplicity of such a measure, the case of preparation
> and administration should not blind one to its invalidity. (p. 96)

Chall and Dale (1950) reported that the average tendency to overestimate word
knowledge in the yes/no format over and above the definition format amounted to
about 11 percent, and was more pronounced for rare words.

It ought to be no real surprise that a yes/no test uncorrected for decisions in
the face of partial knowledge would give inflated estimates of vocabulary size and
would correlate poorly with other measures. Consider the yes/no task from the
point of view of the test taker. Some individuals may deny that they know the
word *gold* because they do not know its atomic weight, while others will agree
they know it because they have a feeling that it can be used to refer to a color.

The problem of correcting yes/no test scores for guessing is not insuperable.
Stating the issue more precisely, guessing is only part of the problem. The real
issue, as the *gold* example illustrates, is one of eliminating variation in the degree
of confidence different individuals must have before they are willing to say, "Yes,
I know that word."

Signal detection theory (Swets, 1964) affords a conceptual and computational framework that may allow estimation of amount of word knowledge independent of judgmental standards. This theory was originally developed for use in
psychophysical experimentation. In this setting, typically the subject is informed

that he will hear a short burst of background noise and that there may be a tone sounded as well. The subject's task is to report whether a tone (the signal) was present. Research has established that it is possible to get a very accurate estimate of a person's capacity to detect the signal by correcting for whatever tendency he or she has to report "hearing" the signal when it is not actually there. Pastore and Schreirer (1974) have summarized research showing that this paradigm can be applied to the analysis of a broad range of perceptual and cognitive tasks. With respect to vocabulary assessment, the work of Zimmerman, Broder, Shaughnessy, and Underwood (1977) has suggested that, by using close-to-English nonsense letter strings as the "noise only" stimuli, signal detection methods might be applied to word knowledge.

We are currently analyzing data collected from elementary and high school subjects on large numbers of words. The students responded yes or no to a mixture of many English words and almost as many nonsense words. Later they completed standardized multiple choice questions on the real word. Our preliminary analyses have indicated that yes/no scores adjusted according to signal detection theory, and other corrections for guessing and risk-taking, correlate highly with multiple choice performance. We later interviewed the subjects individually about a subset of the words. The data suggest that a value derived from the yes/no task gives a better estimate of true word knowledge than performance on the standardized multiple choice test.

The fact that words have multiple meanings poses a problem for the yes/no task, since presumably a person will check "yes" if he or she knows *any* meaning of a word. This is not a small problem. According to Lovell (1941), 43 percent of the words used by Seashore and Eckerson (1940) had multiple meanings. Recently, Balch (cited in Johnson and Pearson, 1978, p. 17) has reported that from 23 percent to 42 percent of the words in six widely used basic vocabulary lists have multiple meanings. In other recent research, Mason, Knisely, and Kendall (1978) have shown that children are much less likely to know the secondary than the primary meaning of words used in their secondary sense in a popular basal series. It is apparent that the yes/no format is not suitable for distinguishing which of the meanings of a word are known. When that is the goal, some other method of assessment is required.

In summary, the great attraction of the yes/no format is that it permits the presentation of a very large number of words in a given interval of examinee time. Compared to the multiple choice format, it reduces somewhat the burden of preparing distractors and, compared to constructed answer formats, it sidesteps vagaries of scoring. The notable problem with the yes/no task is that scores of individuals will be influenced markedly by differences in tendency to take risks in the face of uncertainty. If this problem can be solved, the yes/no task might be very useful for assessment of breadth of word knowledge.

Conclusion

While current research demonstrates the importance of such factors as a reader's perspective on a text (Pichert and Anderson, 1977) and text structure (Mandler and Johnson, 1977; Meyer, 1975), it is also clear that word knowledge is a requisite for reading comprehension: people who do not know the meanings of very many words are most probably poor readers. There are serious gaps in our understanding of why this is true and of how word knowledge grows throughout the life span. Filling those gaps promises to be both an intellectual and a practical challenge of considerable importance. We judge that a critical first step is the development of improved methods of assessing breadth of vocabulary knowledge. It is only after some refinement has been achieved at this level that models of lexical development and instructional programs can be based on realistic expectations about the acquisition of word meanings.

We conclude our review of vocabulary knowledge and vocabulary size with the realization that, since the turn of the century, a tremendous amount of energy has been put into answering the question, "How many words does an individual know?" We have come to wonder if this question is properly framed. The nature of language may make it unanswerable and thus, for scientific purposes, irrelevant. Empirical methods may be able to generate useful indices such as that discussed earlier—the relationship of the individual's knowledge of words to word frequency. However, to produce a single value from performance on a sample to represent total vocabulary size may be an exercise that relies too heavily on the assumptions of a static population of isolated words and on an overly restrictive view of how we generate and use words in context.

REFERENCES

Allen, L.R., and Garton, R.F. The influence of word knowledge on the word frequency effect in recognition memory. *Psychonomic Science*, 1968, *10*, 401-402.

Ames, W.S. The understanding vocabulary of first grade pupils. *Elementary English*, 1964, *41*, 64-68.

Anderson, R.C. Schema-directed processes in language comprehension. In A.M. Lesgold, J.S. Pellegrino, S.D. Fokkema, and R. Glaser (Eds.), *Cognitive psychology and instruction*. New York: Plenum, 1978.

Anderson, R.C., and Ortony, A. On putting apples into bottles: A problem of polysemy. *Cognitive Psychology*, 1975, *7*, 167-180.

Anderson, R.C., Pichert, J.W., Goetz, E.T., Schallert, D.L., Stevens, K.W., and Trollip, S.R. Instantiation of general terms. *Journal of Verbal Learning and Verbal Behavior*, 1976, *15*, 667-679.

Anglin, J.M. *The growth of word meaning*. Cambridge, Mass.: MIT Press, 1970.

Asher, S.R. *Referential communication* (Tech. Rep. No. 90). Urbana: University of Illinois, Center for the Study of Reading, June 1978.

Bayer, M.L. *Primary grade understanding vocabulary as measured by an orally administered Basic Word Vocabulary Test*. Unpublished master's thesis, Rutgers University, 1976. (ED 131 417)

Becker, W.C. Teaching reading and language to the disadvantaged—what we have learned from field research. *Harvard Educational Review*, 1977, *47*, 518-543.

Bonser, F.G., Burch, L.H., and Turner, M.R. Vocabulary tests as measures of school efficiency. *School and Society*, 1915, *2*, 714-718.

Bormuth, J.R. Readability: A new approach. *Reading Research Quarterly*, 1966, *1*, 79-132.

Botzum, W.A. A factorial study of reasoning and closure factors. *Psychometrika*, 1951, *16*, 361-386.

Brandenburg, G.C. Psychological aspects of language. *Journal of Educational Psychology*, 1918, *9*, 313-332.

Brewer, W.F., and Stone, B.J. Acquisition of spatial antonym pairs. *Journal of Experimental Child Psychology*, 1975, *19*, 199-307.

Brown, A.L. Recognition, reconstruction and recall of narrative sequences by preoperational children. *Child Development*, 1975, *46*, 156-166.

California Achievement Tests. Monterey, Calif.: CTB/McGraw-Hill, 1977.

Carroll, J., and White, M. Age-of-acquisition nouns for 200 picturable nouns. *Journal of Verbal Learning and Verbal Behavior*, 1973, *12*, 563-576.

Carroll, J.B., Davies, P., and Richman, B. *Word frequency book*. Boston: Houghton Mifflin, 1971.

Chall, J.S. *Readability: An appraisal of research and application*. Columbus: Ohio State Press, 1958.

Chall, J.S., and Dale, E. Familiarity of selected health terms. *Educational Research Bulletin*, 1950, *39*, 197-206.

Clark, E.V. What's in a word? On the child's acquisition of semantics in his first language. In T.E. Moore (Ed.), *Cognitive development and the acquisition of language*. New York: Academic Press, 1973.

Clark, H.H., and Clark, E.V. *Psychology and language*. New York: Harcourt Brace Jovanovich, 1977.

Clark, N.L. *Hierarchical structure of comprehension skills* (2 vols.). Hawthorn, Vict., Austral.: ACER, 1972.

Clifford, G.J. Words for school: The applications in education of the vocabulary researches of E.L. Thorndike. In P. Suppes (Ed.), *Impact of research on education: Some case studies*. Washington, D.C.: National Academy of Education, 1978.

Cohen, J. Tachistoscopic word recognition as a function of word abstractness/concreteness, word frequency, and IQ. *Perceptual and Motor Skills*, 1976, *42*, 471-476.

Coleman, E.B. Developing a technology of written instruction: Some determiners of the complexity of prose. In E.Z. Rothkopf and P.E. Johnson (Eds.), *Verbal learning research and the technology of written instruction*. New York: Columbia University, Teachers College Press, 1971.

Cuff, N.B. Vocabulary tests. *Journal of Educational Psychology*, 1930, *21*, 212-220.

Davis, F.B. Fundamental factors of comprehension in reading. *Psychometrika*, 1944, *9*, 185-197(a).

Davis, F.B. The interpretation of frequency ratings obtained from *The Teacher's Wordbook*. *Journal of Educational Psychology*, 1944, *35*, 169-174(b).

Davis, F.B. Research in comprehension in reading. *Reading Research Quarterly*, 1968, *3*, 499-545.

Dolch, E. How much word knowledge do children bring to grade 1? *Elementary English Review*, 1936, *13*, 177-183.

Duncan, C.P. Effects of frequency on retrieval from a semantic category, *Bulletin Psychonomic Society*, 1977, *10*, 57-59.

Dupuy, H.P. *The rationale, development and standardization of a basic word vocabulary test*. Washington, D.C.: U.S. Government Printing Office, 1974. (DHEW Publication No. HRA 74-1334)

Elmwood, M.I. A preliminary note on the vocabulary test in the revised Stanford-Binet Scale. *Journal of Educational Psychology*, 1939, *30*, 632-634.

Fillmore, C.J. The future of semantics. In R. Austerlitz (Ed.), *The scope of American linguistics*. Amherst, Mass.: Ridder Press, 1975.

Fleisher, L.S., and Jenkins, J.R. *Effects of contextualized and decontextualized practice conditions on word recognition* (Tech. Rep. No. 54). Urbana: University of Illinois, Center for the Study of Reading, July 1977.

Fruchter, B. The nature of verbal fluency. *Educational and Psychological Measurement*, 1948, *8*, 33-47.

Gentner, D. Evidence for the psychological reality of semantic components: The verbs of possession. In D.A. Norman, D.E. Rumelhart, and the LNR research group (Eds.), *Explorations in cognition*. San Francisco: Freeman, 1975.

Gerlach, F.M. *Vocabulary studies—false definition test*. Colorado: College Studies in Education and Psychology, No. 1, 1917.

Gillette, J.M. Extent of personal vocabularies and cultural control. *Science Monthly*, 1927, *29*, 451-467.

Glucksburg, S., Hay, A., and Danks, J.H. Words in utterance contexts: Young children do not confuse the meaning of *same* and *different*. *Child Development*, 1976, *47*, 737-741.

Goodman, K.S. Behind the eye: What happens in reading. In H. Singer and R.B. Ruddell (Eds.), *Theoretical models and processes of reading*, second edition. Newark, Del.: International Reading Association, 1976.

Halff, H.M., Ortony, A., and Anderson, R.C. A context-sensitive representation of word meanings. *Memory and Cognition*, 1976, *4* (4), 378-383.

Hall, W.S., and Tirre, W.C. *The communicative environment of young children: Social class, ethnic and situational differences* (Tech. Rep. No. 125). Urbana: University of Illinois, Center for the Study of Reading, May 1979.

Hartman, G.W. Further evidence on the unexpected large size of recognition vocabularies among college students. *Journal of Educational Psychology*, 1946, *37*, 436-439.

Holley, C.E. *Holley sentence vocabulary scale - grades 3-12*. Bloomington, Ill.: Public School Publication Co., 1919.

Horn, E. *Teaching spelling*. Washington, D.C.: AERA, National Education Association, 1954.

Hunt, E. Mechanics of verbal ability. *Psychological Review*, 1978, *85*, 109-130.

Hunt, E., Lunneborg, C., and Lewis, J. What does it mean to be high verbal? *Cognitive Psychology*, 1975, *7*, 194-227.

Jenkins, J.R., Pany, D., and Schreck, J. *Vocabulary and reading comprehension: Instructional effects* (Tech. Rep. No. 100). Urbana: University of Illinois, Center for the Study of Reading, August 1978.

Johnson, D.D., and Pearson, P.D. *Teaching reading vocabulary*. New York: Holt, Rinehart and Winston, 1978.

Kibby, M.W. A note on the relationship of word difficulty and word frequency. *Psychological Reports*, 1977, *41*, 12-14.

Kirby, J.R., and Das, J.P. Reading achievement, IQ, and simultaneous-successive processing. *Journal of Educational Psychology*, 1977, *69*, 564-570.

Kirkpatrick, E.A. Vocabulary test. *Popular Science Monthly*, 1907, *70*, 157-164.

Klare, G.R. Assessing readability. *Reading Research Quarterly*, 1974-1975, *10*, 62-102.

Kucera, H., and Francis, W.N. *Computational analysis of present-day American English*. Providence, R.I.: Brown University Press, 1967.

LaBerge, D., and Samuels, S.J. Toward a theory of automatic information processing in reading. *Cognitive Psychology*, 1974, *6*, 293-323.

Labov, W. The boundaries of words and their meanings. In C.J. Bailey and R. Shuy (Eds.), *New ways of analyzing variation in English*. Washington, D.C.: Georgetown University Press, 1973.

Lepley, W.M. Rationale, construction and preliminary try-out of the synonym vocabulary test. *Journal of Psychology*, 1955, *39*, 215-225.

Lepley, W.M. The synonym vocabulary test: Form III. *Journal of Psychology*, 1965, *59*, 109-112.

Lewinski, R.J. Vocabulary and mental measurement: A quantitative investigation and review of research. *Journal of Genetic Psychology*, 1948, *72*, 247-281.

Lorge, I., and Chall, J. Estimating the size of vocabularies of children and adults: An analysis of methodological issues. *Journal of Experimental Education*, 1963, *32*, 147-157.

Lovell, G.D. Interrelations of vocabulary skills: Commonest versus multiple meanings. *Journal of Educational Psychology*, 1941, *21*, 67-72.

Mahan, H.C., and Witmer, L. A note on the Stanford-Binet vocabulary test. *Journal of Applied Psychology*, 1936, *20*, 258-263.

Mandler, J.M., and Johnson, N.S. Remembrance of things parsed: Story structure and recall. *Cognitive Psychology*, 1977, *9*, 11-151.

Marks, C.B., Doctorow, M.J., and Wittrock, N.C. Word frequency and reading comprehension. *Journal of Educational Research*, 1974, *67*, 159-262.

Mason, J.M., Knisely, E., and Kendall, J. *Effects of polysemous words on sentence comprehension* (Tech Rep. No. 85). Urbana: University of Illinois, Center for the Study of Reading, May 1978.

McNemar, Q. *The revision of the Stanford-Binet Scale*. Boston: Houghton-Mifflin, 1942.

Metropolitan Achievement Tests. New York: Harcourt Brace Jovanovich, 1970.

Meyer, B.J.F. *The organization of prose and its effects on memory.* Amsterdam: North Holland, 1975.

Miller, G.A. The acquisition of word meaning. *Child Development,* 1978, *49,* 999-1004.

Miller, G.A., and Johnson-Laird, P.M. *Language and perception.* Cambridge, Mass.: Belknap Press, 1976.

Miner, J.B. *Intelligence in the U.S.* New York: Springer, 1957.

Nelson, K. Cognitive development and the acquisition of concepts. In R.C. Anderson, R.J. Spiro, and W.E. Montague (Eds.), *Schooling and the acquisition of knowledge.* Hillsdale, N.J.: Erlbaum, 1977.

Pany, D., and Jenkins, J.R. *Learning word meanings: A comparison of instructional procedures and effects on measures of reading comprehension with learning disabled students* (Tech. Rep. No. 25). Urbana: University of Illinois, Center for the Study of Reading, March 1977.

Pastore, R.E., and Schreirer, C.J. Signal detection theory: Considerations for general application. *Psychological Bulletin,* 1974, *81,* 945-958.

Pearson, P.D., and Studt, A. Effects of word frequency and contextual richness on children's word identification abilities. *Journal of Educational Psychology,* 1975, *67,* 89-95.

Perfetti, C.A., and Lesgold, A.M. Coding and comprehension in skilled reading and implications for reading instruction. In L.B. Resnick and P.A. Weaver (Eds.), *Theory and practice of early reading* (Vol. 1). Hillsdale, N.J.: Erlbaum, 1979.

Pichert, J.W., and Anderson, R.C. Taking different perspectives on a story. *Journal of Educational Psychology,* 1977, *69,* 309-315.

Posner, M.I., and Mitchell, R. Chronometric analysis of classification. *Psychology Review,* 1967, *74,* 392-409.

Putnam, H. The meaning of 'meaning.' In H. Putnam (Ed.), *Mind, language and reality.* New York: Cambridge University Press, 1975.

Raven, J.C. The comparative assessment of intellectual ability. *British Journal of Psychology,* 1948, *39,* 12-19.

Richards, M.R. *Come* and *go* reconsidered: Children's use of deictic verbs in contrived situations. *Journal of Verbal Learning and Verbal Behavior,* 1976, *15,* 655-665.

Rosch, E. On the internal structure of perceptual and semantic categories. In T.E. Moore (Ed.), *Cognitive development and the acquisition of languages.* New York: Academic Press, 1973.

Rosch, E., and Mervis, C.B. Family resemblances: Studies in the internal structure of categories. *Cognitive Psychology,* 1975, *1,* 573-605.

Rubenstein, H., Garfield, L., and Millikan, J. Homographic entries in the internal lexicon. *Journal of Verbal Learning and Verbal Behavior,* 1970, *9,* 487-494.

Seashore, R.H. Measurement and analysis of extent of vocabulary. *Psychological Bulletin,* 1933, *30,* 709-710.

Seashore, R.H., and Eckerson, L.D. The measurement of individual differences in general English vocabularies. *Journal of Educational Psychology,* 1940, *31,* 14-38.

Shibles, B.H. How many words does a first grade child know? *Elementary English,* 1959, *31,* 42-47.

Silvestri, S., and Silvestri, R. Developmental analysis of the acquisition of compound words. *Language, speech and hearing services in the school,* 1977, *8,* 217-221.

Sims, V.M. The reliability and validity of four types of vocabulary test. *Journal of Educational Research,* 1929, *20,* 91-96.

Smith, M.E. An investigation of the development of the sentence and the extent of vocabulary in young children. *University of Iowa Studies in Child Welfare,* 1926, *3,* 92.

Smith, M.K. Measurement of the size of general English vocabulary through the elementary grades and high school. *General Psychological Monographs,* 1941, *24,* 311-345.

Spache, G. The vocabulary tests of the revised Stanford-Binet as independent measures of intelligence. *Journal of Educational Research,* 1943, *36,* 512-516.

Stanford Achievement Tests. New York: Harcourt Brace Jovanovich, 1973.

Steffensen, M.S., Joag-Dev, C., and Anderson, R.C. A cross-cultural perspective on reading comprehension. *Reading Research Quarterly,* 1979, *15* (1), 10-29.

Swets, J.A. (Ed.). *Signal detection and recognition by human observers.* New York: Wiley, 1964.

Terman, L.M. *The measurement of intelligence.* Boston: Houghton-Mifflin, 1916.

Terman, L.M. Vocabulary test as a measure of intelligence. *Journal of Educational Psychology,* 1918, *9,* 452-466.

Terman, L.M., and Merrill, M.A. *Measuring intelligence.* Boston: Houghton-Mifflin, 1937.

Thorndike, R.L. *Reading comprehension education in fifteen countries*. New York: Wiley, 1973.

Thurstone, L.L. A note on a reanalysis of Davis' reading tests. *Psychometrika*, 1946, *11*, 185-188.

Tuinman, J.J., and Brady, M.E. How does vocabulary account for variance on reading comprehension tests? A preliminary instructional analysis. In P. Nacke (Ed.), *23rd NRC Yearbook*. Clemson, S.C.: National Reading Conference, 1974.

Vurpillot, E. Judging visual similarity: The development of scanning strategies and their relation to differentiation. *Journal of Experimental Child Psychology*, 1968, *6*, 632-650.

Wechsler, D. *Manual, Wechsler intelligence scale for children*. New York: Psychological Corporation, 1949.

White, M.L. Mental age norms for vocabulary scores on the 1937 Stanford-Binet. *Psychological Records*, 1942, *5*, 159-169.

Williams, H.M. Some problems of sampling in vocabulary tests. *Journal of Experimental Education*, 1932, *1*, 131-133.

Wittgenstein, L. *Philosophical investigations*. New York: Macmillan, 1953.

Wittrock, N.C., Marks, C., and Doctorow, M. Reading as a generative process. *Journal of Educational Psychology*, 1975, *67*, 484-489.

Wolman, R.N., and Baker, E.N. A developmental study of word definitions. *Journal of General Psychology*, 1965, *107*, 159-166.

Wrigley, C., Saunders, D.R., and Newhaus, J.O. Application of the quatrimax method of rotation to Thurstone's P.M.A. study. *Psychometrika*, 1958, *23*, 115-170.

Zimmerman, J., Broder, P.K., Shaughnessy, J.J., and Underwood, B.J. A recognition test of vocabulary using Signal-Detection Measures, and some correlates of word and nonword recognition. *Intelligence*, 1977, *1*, 5-31.

NOTE

[1] We are indebted to Charles Fillmore for this example.

Role of the Reader's Schema in Comprehension, Learning, and Memory

RICHARD C. ANDERSON
University of Illinois

The past several years have witnessed the articulation of a largely new theory of reading, a theory already accepted by the majority of scholars in the field. According to the theory, a reader's *schema*, or organized knowledge of the world, provides much of the basis for comprehending, learning, and remembering the ideas in stories and texts. In this paper I will attempt to explain schema theory, give illustrations of the supporting evidence, and suggest applications to classroom teaching and the design of instructional materials.

A Schema-Theoretic Interpretation of Comprehension

In schema-theoretic terms, a reader comprehends a message when he is able to bring to mind a schema that gives a good account of the objects and events described in the message. Ordinarily, comprehension proceeds so smoothly that we are unaware of the process of "cutting and fitting" a schema in order to achieve a satisfactory account of a message. It is instructive, therefore, to try to understand material that gives us pause, so that we can reflect upon our own minds at work. Consider the following sentence, drawn from the work of Bransford and McCarrell (1974):

The notes were sour because the seam split.

Notice that all of the words are familiar and that the syntax is straightforward, yet the sentence does not "make sense" to most people. Now notice what happens when the additional clue, "bagpipe," is provided. At this point the sentence does make sense because one is able to interpret all the words in the sentence in terms of certain specific objects and events and their interrelations.

Let us examine another sentence:

The big number 37 smashed the ball over the fence.

This sentence is easy to interpret. *Big Number 37* is a baseball player. The sense of *smash the ball* is to propel it rapidly by hitting it strongly with a bat. The fence is at the boundary of a playing field. The ball was hit hard enough that it flew over the fence.

Suppose a person with absolutely no knowledge of baseball read the Big Number 37 sentence. Such a person could not easily construct an interpretation of the sentence, but with enough mental effort might be able to conceive of large numerals, perhaps made of metal, attached to the front of an apartment building. Further, the person might imagine that the numerals come loose and fall, striking a ball resting on top of, or lodged above, a fence, causing the ball to break. Most people regard this as an improbable interpretation, certainly one that never would have occurred to them, but they readily acknowledge that it is a "good" interpretation. What makes it good? The answer is that the interpretation is complete and consistent. It is complete in the sense that every element in the sentence is interpreted; there are no loose ends left unexplained. The interpretation is consistent in that no part of it does serious violence to knowledge about the physical and social world.

Both interpretations of the Big Number 37 sentence assume a real world. Criteria of consistency are relaxed in fictional worlds in which animals talk or men wearing capes leap tall buildings in a single bound. But there are conventions about what is possible in fictional worlds as well. The knowledgeable reader will be annoyed if these conventions are violated. The less knowledgeable reader simply will be confused.

It should not be imagined that there is some simple, literal level of comprehension of stories and texts that does not require coming up with a schema. This important point is illustrated in a classic study by Bransford and Johnson (1972) in which subjects read paragraphs, such as the following, written so that most people are unable to construct a schema that will account for the material:

> If the balloons popped the sound wouldn't be able to carry since everything would be too far away from the correct floor. A closed window would also prevent the sound from carrying, since most buildings tend to be well insulated. Since the whole operation depends upon a steady flow of electricity, a break in the middle of the wire would also cause problems. Of course, the fellow could shout, but the human voice is not loud enough to carry that far. An additional problem is that a string could break on the instrument. Then there could be no accompaniment to the message. It is clear that the best situation would involve less distance. Then there would be fewer potential problems. With face to face contact, the least number of things could go wrong (p. 719).

Subjects rated this passage as very difficult to understand, and they were unable to remember much of it. In contrast, subjects shown the drawing on the left side of Figure 1, found the passage more comprehensible and were able to remember a great deal of it. Another group saw the drawing on the right in Figure 1. This group remembered no more than the group that did not receive a drawing. The experiment demonstrates that what is critical for comprehension is a schema ac-

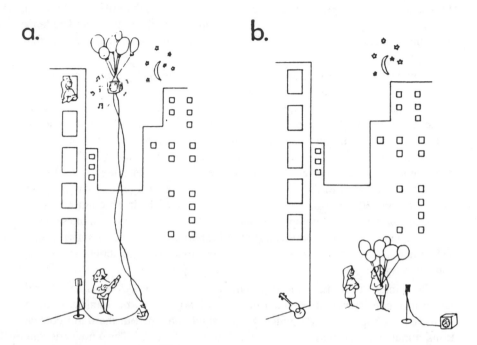

Figure 1. Illustrations from Bransford and Johnson (1972). Version "a" represents the appropriate context and version "b" represents the inappropriate context. See text for accompanying passage.

counting for the *relationships* among elements; it is not enough for the elements to be concrete and imageable.

Trick passages, such as the foregoing one about the communication problems of a modern day Romeo, are useful for illustrating what happens when a reader is completely unable to discover a schema that will fit a passage and, therefore, finds the passage entirely incomprehensible. More typical is the situation in which a reader knows something about a topic, but falls far short of being an expert. Chiesi, Spilich, and Voss (1979) asked people high and low in knowledge of baseball to read and recall a report of a half-inning from a fictitious baseball game. Knowledge of baseball had both qualitative and quantitative effects on performance. High-knowledge subjects were more likely to recall and embellish upon aspects of strategic significance to the game. Low-knowledge subjects, in contrast, were more likely to include information incidental to the play of the game.

Schema theory highlights the fact that often more than one interpretation of a text is possible. The schema that will be brought to bear on a text depends upon the reader's age, sex, race, religion, nationality, occupation—in short, it depends upon the reader's culture. This point was illustrated in an experiment completed by Anderson, Reynolds, Schallert, and Goetz (1977), who asked people to read the following passage:

> Tony slowly got up from the mat, planning his escape. He hesitated a moment and thought. Things were not going well. What bothered him most was being held, especially since the charge against him had been weak. He considered his present situation. The lock that held him was strong but he thought he could break it. He knew, however, that his timing would have to be perfect. Tony was aware that it was because of his early roughness that he had been penalized so severely—much too severely from his point of view. The situation was becoming frustrating; the pressure had been grinding on him for too long. He was being ridden unmercifully. Tony was getting angry now. He felt he was ready to make his move. He knew that his success or failure would depend on what he did in the next few seconds.

Most people think the foregoing passage is about a convict planning his escape from prison. A special group of people, however, see the passage an entirely different way; these are men who have been involved in the sport of wrestling. They think the passage is about a wrestler caught in the hold of an opponent. Notice how the interpretation of *lock* varies according to perspective. In the one case, it is a piece of hardware that holds a cell door shut; in the other it may be a sweaty arm around a neck. Males enrolled in a weight lifting class and females enrolled in a music education class read the foregoing passage and another passage which most people interpret as about several people playing cards, but which can be interpreted as about a rehearsal session of a woodwind ensemble. The results were as expected. Scores on a multiple choice test designed to reveal interpretations of the passages showed striking relationships to the subjects' background. Physical education students usually gave a wrestling interpretation to the prison/wrestling passage and a card playing interpretation to the card/music passage, whereas the reverse was true of the music education students. Similarly, when subjects were asked to recall the passages, theme-revealing distortions appeared, even though the instructions emphasized reproducing the exact words of the original text. For example, a physical education student stated, "Rocky was penalized early in the match for roughness or a dangerous hold," while a music education student wrote, "he was angry that he had been caught and arrested."

The thesis of this section is that comprehension is a matter of activating or constructing a schema that provides a coherent explanation of objects and events mentioned in a discourse. In sharp contrast is the conventional view that comprehension consists of aggregating the meanings of words to form the meanings of clauses, aggregating the meanings of clauses to form the meanings of sentences, aggregating the meanings of sentences to form the meanings of paragraphs, and so on. The illustrations in this section were intended to demonstrate the insufficiency of this conventional view. The meanings of the words cannot be "added up" to give the meaning of the whole. The click of comprehension occurs only when the reader evolves a schema that explains the whole message.

Schema-Based Processes in Learning and Remembering

According to schema theory, reading involves more or less simultaneous analysis at many different levels. The levels include graphophonemic, morphemic, semantic, syntactic, pragmatic, and interpretive. Reading is conceived to be an interactive process. This means that analysis does not proceed in a strict order from the visual information in letters to the overall interpretation of a text. Instead, as a person reads, an interpretation of what a segment of a text might mean is theorized to depend both on analysis of the print and on hypotheses in the person's mind. Processes that flow from the print are called "bottom-up" or "data driven" whereas processes that flow in the other direction are called "top-down" or "hypothesis driven," following Bobrow and Norman (1975). In the passage about Tony, who is either a wrestler or a prisoner, processing the word *lock* has the potential to activate either a piece-of-hardware meaning or a wrestling-hold meaning. The hypothesis the reader has already formulated about the text will tip the scales in the direction of one of the two meanings, usually without the reader's being aware that an alternative meaning is possible. Psychologists are at work developing detailed models of the mechanisms by which information from different levels of analysis is combined during reading (see Just and Carpenter, 1980; Rumelhart and McClelland, 1980).

The reader's schema affects both learning and remembering of the information and ideas in a text. Six functions of schemata that have been proposed (Anderson, 1978; Anderson and Pichert, 1978) are briefly explained.

A schema provides ideational scaffolding for assimilating text information. The idea is that a schema provides a niche, or slot, for certain text information. For instance, there is a slot for the main entree in a dining-at-a-fine-restaurant schema and a slot for the murder weapon in a who-done-it schema. Information that fits slots in the reader's schema is readily learned, perhaps with little mental effort.

A schema facilitates selective allocation of attention. A schema provides part of the basis for determining the important aspects of a text. It is hypothesized that skilled readers use importance as one basis for allocating cognitive resources — that is, for deciding where to pay close attention.

A schema enables inferential elaboration. No text is completely explicit. A reader's schema provides the basis for making inferences that go beyond the information literally stated in a text.

A schema allows orderly searches of memory. A schema can provide the reader with a guide to the types of information that need to be recalled. For instance, a person attempting to recall the food served at a fine meal can review the categories of food typically included in a fine meal: What was the appetizer? What was the soup? Was there a salad? And so on. In other words, by tracing through the schema used to structure the text, the reader is helped to gain access to the particular information learned when the text was read.

A schema facilitates editing and summarizing. Since a schema contains within itself criteria of importance, it enables the reader to produce summaries that include significant propositions and omit trivial ones.

A schema permits inferential reconstruction. When there are gaps in memory, a rememberer's schema, along with the specific text information that can be recalled, helps generate hypotheses about the missing information. For example, suppose a person cannot recall what beverage was served with a fine meal. If he can recall that the entree was fish, he will be able to infer that the beverage may have been white wine.

The foregoing are tentative hypotheses about the functions of a schema in text processing, conceived to provide the broadest possible interpretation of available data. Several of the hypotheses can be regarded as rivals—for instance, the ideational scaffolding hypothesis and the selective attention hypothesis—and it may be that not all of them will turn out to be viable. Researchers are now actively at work developing precise models of schema-based processes and subjecting these models to experimental test.

Evidence for Schema Theory

There is now a really good case that schemata incorporating knowledge of the world play an important role in language comprehension. We are beginning to see research on differentiated functions. In a few years it should be possible to speak in more detail about the specific processing mechanisms in which schemata are involved.

Many of the claims of schema theory are nicely illustrated in a cross-cultural experiment, completed by Steffensen, Joag-Dev, and Anderson (1979), in which Indians (natives of India) and Americans read letters about an Indian and an American wedding. Of course, every adult member of a society has a well-developed marriage schema. There are substantial differences between Indian and American cultures in the nature of marriages. As a consequence, large differences in comprehension, learning, and memory for the letters were expected.

Table 1 summarizes analyses of the recall of the letters by Indian and American subjects. The first row in the table indicates the amount of time subjects spent reading the letters. As can be seen, subjects spent less time reading what for them was the native passage. This was as expected since a familiar schema should speed up and expedite a reader's processing.

The second row in Table 1 presents the number of idea units recalled. The gist measure includes not only propositions recalled verbatim but also acceptable paraphrases. The finding was precisely as expected. Americans recalled more of the American text, whereas Indians recalled more of the Indian passage. Within current formulations of schema theory, there are a couple of reasons for predicting that people would learn and remember more of a text about a marriage in their own culture: A culturally appropriate schema may provide the ideational scaffolding that makes it easy to learn information that fits into that schema, or, it may be that the information, once learned, is more accessible because the schema is a structure that makes it easy to search memory.

Table 1

MEAN PERFORMANCE ON VARIOUS MEASURES
(FROM STEFFENSEN, JOAG-DEV, AND ANDERSON, 1979)

| Measure | Nationality | | | |
| | Americans | | Indians | |
	American Passage	Indian Passage	American Passage	Indian Passage
Time (seconds)	168	213	304	276
Gist Recall	52.4	37.9	27.3	37.6
Elaborations	5.7	.1	.2	5.4
Distortions	.1	7.6	5.5	.3
Other Overt Errors	7.5	5.2	8.0	5.9
Omissions	76.2	76.6	95.5	83.3

The row labeled *Elaborations* in Table 1 contains the frequency of culturally appropriate extensions of the text. The row labeled *Distortions* contains the frequency of culturally inappropriate modifications of the text. Ever since Bartlett's day, elaborations and distortions have provided the intuitively most compelling evidence for the role of schemata. Many fascinating instances appeared in the protocols collected in the present study. A section of the American passage upon which interesting cultural differences surfaced read as follows:

> Did you know that Pam was going to wear her grandmother's wedding dress? That gave her something that was old, and borrowed, too. It was made of lace over satin, with very large puff sleeves and looked absolutely charming on her.

One Indian had this to say about the American bride's dress: "She was looking all right except the dress was too old and out of fashion." Wearing an heirloom wedding dress is a completely acceptable aspect of the pageantry of the American marriage ceremony. This Indian appears to have completely missed this and, has inferred that the dress was out of fashion, on the basis that Indians attach importance to displays of social status, manifested in such details as wearing an up-to-date, fashionable sari.

The gifts described in the Indian passage that were given to the groom's family by the bride's, the dowry, and the reference to the concern of the bride's family that a scooter might be requested were a source of confusion for our American subjects. First of all, the "agreement about the gifts to be given to the in-laws" was changed to "the exchange of gifts," a wording which suggests that gifts are flowing in two directions, not one. Another subject identified the gifts given to the in-laws as favors, which are often given in American weddings to the attendants by the bride and groom.

In another facet of the study, different groups of Indians and Americans read the letters and rated the significance of each of the propositions. It was expected that Americans would regard as important propositions conveying information about ritual and ceremony whereas Indians would see as important propositions dealing with financial and social status. Table 2 contains examples of text units that received contrasting ratings of importance from Indians and Americans. Schema theory predicts that text units that are important in the light of the schema are more likely to be learned and, once learned, are more likely to be remembered. This prediction was confirmed. Subjects did recall more text information rated as important by their cultural cohorts, whether recalling what for them was the native or the foreign text.

Table 2
EXAMPLES OF IDEA UNITS OF CONTRASTING IMPORTANCE TO AMERICANS AND INDIANS

American Passage		Indian Passage	
Idea Units More Important to Americans	Idea Units More Important to Indians	Idea Units More Important to Americans	Idea Units More Important to Indians
Then on Friday night *they had the rehearsal* at the church *and the rehearsal dinner,* which lasted until almost midnight. *All the attendants wore dresses that were specially designed to go with Pam's.* Her mother wore yellow, which looks great on her with her bleached hair, *and George's mother wore pale green.*	*She'll be lucky if she can even get her daughter married, the way things are going.* Her mother wore yellow, which looks great on her *with her bleached hair,* and George's mother wore pale green. Have you seen the diamond she has? *It must have cost George a fortune because it's almost two carats.*	Prema's husband had to wear a dhoti *for that ceremony and for the wedding the next day.* *There were only the usual essential rituals:* the curtain removal, the parents giving the daughter away, walking seven steps together, etc., *and plenty of smoke from the sacred fire.* There must have been about five hundred people *at the wedding feast. Since only fifty people could be seated at one time, it went on for a long time.*	*Prema's in-laws seem to be nice enough people.* They did not create any problem in the wedding, *even though Prema's husband is their only son.* *Since they did not ask for any dowry,* Prema's parents were a little worried about their asking for a scooter before the wedding, *but they didn't ask for one.* *Prema's parents were very sad when she left.*

Note. Important idea units are in italics.

Of course, it is one thing to show, as Steffensen, Joag-dev, and Anderson did, that readers from distinctly different national cultures give different interpretations to culturally sensitive materials, and quite another to find the same phenomenon among readers from different but overlapping subcultures within the same country. A critical issue is whether cultural variation within the United States could be a factor in differential reading comprehension. Minority children could have a handicap if stories, texts, and test items presuppose a cultural perspective that the children do not share. An initial exploration of this issue has been completed by Reynolds, Taylor, Steffensen, Shirey, and Anderson (1981), who wrote a passage around an episode involving "sounding." Sounding is an activity predominantly found in the black community in which the participants try to outdo each other in an exchange of insults (Labov, 1972). In two group studies, and one in which subjects were individually interviewed, black teenagers tended to see the episode as involving friendly give-and-take, whereas white teenagers interpreted it as an ugly confrontation, sometimes one involving physical violence. For example, when attempting to recall the incident, a black male wrote, "Then everybody tried to get on the person side that joke were the best." A white male wrote, "Soon there was a riot. All the kids were fighting." This research established that when written material has an identifiable cultural loading there is a pronounced effect on comprehension. It remains to be seen how much school reading material is culturally loaded.

In the foregoing research, schemata were manipulated by selecting subjects with different backgrounds. Another approach for getting people to bring different schemata to bear is by selecting different passages. Anderson, Spiro, and Anderson (1978) wrote two closely comparable passages, one about dining at a fancy restaurant, the other about a trip to a supermarket. The same eighteen items of food and beverage were mentioned in the two texts, in the same order, and attributed to the same characters. The first hypothesis was that subjects who received the restaurant passage would learn and recall more food and beverage information than subjects who received the supermarket passage. The reasoning was that a dining-at-a-fine-restaurant schema has a more constrained structure than a trip-to-a-supermarket schema. That is to say, fewer food and beverage items will fit the former schema; one could choose soda pop and hot dogs at a supermarket, but these items would not be ordered at a fine restaurant. Moreover there are more cross-connections among items in a restaurant schema. For example, a steak will be accompanied by a baked potato, or maybe french fries. In two experiments, subjects who read the restaurant text recalled more food and beverage items than subjects who read the supermarket text.

The second prediction was that students who read the restaurant text would more often attribute the food and drink items to the correct characters. In a supermarket it does not matter, for instance, who throws the brussel sprouts into the shopping cart, but in a restaurant it does matter who orders which item. This prediction was confirmed in two experiments.

A third prediction was that order of recall of foods and beverages would correspond more closely to order of mention in the text for subjects who read the restaurant story. There is not, or need not be, a prescribed sequence for selecting items in a grocery store, but there is a characteristic order in which items are served in a restaurant. This hypothesis was supported in one experiment and the trend of the data favored it in a second.

Another technique for manipulating readers' schemata is by assigning them different perspectives. Pichert and Anderson (1977) asked people to pretend that they were either burglars or home buyers before reading a story about what two boys did at one of the boys' homes while they were skipping school. The finding was that people learned more of the information to their assigned perspective. For instance, burglars were more likely to learn that three 10-speed bikes were parked in the garage, whereas home buyers were more likely to learn that the house had a leaky roof. Anderson and Pichert (1978; see also Anderson, Pichert, and Shirey, 1979) went on to show that the reader's perspective has independent effects on learning and recall. Subjects who switch perspectives and then recall the story for a second time recall additional, previously unrecalled, information important to their new perspective but unimportant to their original perspective. For example, a person who begins as a home buyer may fail to remember that the story says the side door is kept unlocked, but may later remember this information when told to assume the role of a burglar. Subjects report that previously unrecalled information significant in the light of the new perspective "pops" into their heads.

Recent unpublished research in my laboratory, completed in collaboration with Ralph Reynolds and Paul Wilson, suggests selective allocation of attention to text elements that are important in the light of the reader's schema. We have employed two measures of attention. The first is the amount of time a subject spends reading schema-relevant sentences. The second is time to respond to a probe presented during schema-relevant sentences. The probe is a tone sounded through earphones; the subject responds by pushing a button as fast as possible. The logic of the probe task is that if the mind is occupied with reading, there will be a slight delay in responding to the probe. Our results indicate that people assigned a burglar perspective, for instance, have slightly longer reading times and slightly longer probe times when reading burglar-relevant sentences. Comparable results have been obtained by other investigators (Cirilo and Foss, 1980; Haberlandt, Berian, and Sandson, 1980; Just and Carpenter, 1980).

Implications of Schema Theory for Design of Materials and Classroom Instruction

First, I urge publishers to include teaching suggestions in manuals designed to help children activate relevant knowledge before reading. Children do not spontaneously integrate what they are reading with what they already know (cf. Paris and Lindauer, 1976). This means that special attention should be paid to preparation for reading. Questions should be asked that remind children of relevant experiences of their own and orient them toward the problems faced by story characters.

Second, the teachers' manuals accompanying basal programs and content area texts ought to include suggestions for building prerequisite knowledge when it cannot be safely presupposed. According to schema theory, this practice should promote comprehension. There is direct evidence to support knowledge-building activities. Hayes and Tierney (1980) asked American high school students to read and recall newspaper reports of cricket matches. Performance improved sharply when the students received instruction on the nature of the game of cricket before reading the newspaper reports.

Third, I call for publishers to feature lesson activities that will lead children to meaningfully integrate what they already know with what is presented on the printed page. From the perspective of schema theory, prediction techniques such as the Directed Reading-Thinking Activity (Stauffer, 1969) can be recommended. The DRTA would appear to cause readers to search their store of knowledge and integrate what they already know with what is stated. It must be acknowledged, however, that the empirical evidence for the efficacy of the DRTA is flimsy at present (Tierney and Cunningham, in press). Recently, Anderson, Mason, and Shirey (in preparation) have illustrated that under optimum conditions strong benefits can be obtained using a prediction technique. A heterogeneous sample of third graders read sentences such as, "The stupid child ran into the street after the ball." Children in the prediction group read each sentence aloud and then indicated what might happen next. In the case of the sentence above, a frequent prediction was that the child might get hit by a car. A second group read the sentences aloud with an emphasis on accurate decoding. A third and a fourth group listened to the sentences and read them silently. The finding was that the prediction group recalled 72 percent of the sentences, whereas the average for the other three groups was 43 percent.

Fourth, I urge publishers to employ devices that will highlight the structure of text material. Schema theory inclines one to endorse the practice of providing advance organizers or structured overviews, along the lines proposed by Ausubel (1968) and Herber (1978). Ausubel, who can be regarded as one of the pioneer schema theorists, has stated that "the principal function of the organizer is to bridge the gap between what the learner already knows and what he needs to know before he can successfully learn the task at hand" (1968, p. 148). There have been dozens of empirical studies of advance organizers over the past 20 years. Thorough reviews of this bulky literature by Mayer (1979) and Luiten, Ames, and Ackerson (1980) point to the conclusion that organizers generally have a facilitative effect. Nevertheless, from within current formulations of schema theory, there is room for reservations about advance organizers. Notably, Ausubel's insistence (cf. 1968, pp. 148, 333) that organizers must be stated at a high level of generality, abstractness, and inclusivenss is puzzling. The problem is that general, abstract language often is difficult to understand. Children, in particular, are more easily reminded of what they know when concrete language is used. As Ausubel himself has acknowledged (e.g., 1968, p. 149), "To be useful . . . organizers themselves must obviously be learnable and must be stated in familiar terms."

A final implication of schema theory is that minority children may sometimes be counted as failing to comprehend school reading material because their schemata do not match those of the majority culture. Basal reading programs, content area texts, and standardized tests lean heavily on the conventional assumption that meaning is inherent in the words and structure of a text. When prior knowledge is required, it is assumed to be knowledge common to children from every subculture. When new ideas are introduced, these are assumed to be equally accessible to every child. Considering the strong effects that culture has on reading comprehension, the question that naturally arises is whether children from different subcultures can so confidently be assumed to bring a common schema to written material. To be sure, subcultures within this country do overlap. But is it safe simply to *assume* that when reading the same story, children from every subculture will have the same experience with the setting, ascribe the same goals and motives to characters, imagine the same sequence of actions, predict the same emotional reactions, or expect the same outcomes? This is a question that the research community and the school publishing industry ought to address with renewed vigor.

REFERENCES

Anderson, R.C. Schema-directed processes in language comprehension. In A. Lesgold, J. Pellegrino, S. Forkkema, and R. Glaser (Eds.), *Cognitive psychology and instruction*. New York: Plenum, 1978.

Anderson, R.C., Mason, J., and Shirey, L.L. The reading group: An experimental investigation of a labyrinth. *Reading Research Quarterly*, 1984, *20*, 6-38.

Anderson, R.C., and Pichert, J.W. Recall of previously unrecallable information following a shift in perspective. *Journal of Verbal Learning and Verbal Behavior*, 1978, *17*, 1-12.

Anderson, R.C., Pichert, J.W., and Shirey, L.L. *Effects of the reader's schema at different points in time*. Technical Report No. 119. Urbana: University of Illinois, Center for the Study of Reading, April 1979. (ED 169 523)

Anderson, R.C., Reynolds, R.E., Schallert, D.L., and Goetz, E.T. Frameworks for comprehending discourse. *American Educational Research Journal*, 1977, *14*, 367-382.

Anderson, R.C., Spiro, R.J., and Anderson, M.C. Schemata as scaffolding for the representation of information in connected discourse. *American Educational Research Journal*, 1978, *15*, 433-440.

Ausubel, D.P. *Educational psychology: A cognitive view*. New York: Holt, Rinehart and Winston, 1968.

Bobrow, D.G., and Norman, D.A. Some principles of memory schemata. In D.G. Bobrow and A.M. Collins (Eds.), *Representation and understanding: Studies in cognitive science*. New York: Academic Press, 1975.

Bransford, J.C., and Johnson, M.K. Contextual prerequisites for understanding: Some investigations of comprehension and recall. *Journal of Verbal Learning and Verbal Behavior*, 1972, *11*, 717-726.

Bransford, J.D., and McCarrell, N.S. A sketch of a cognitive approach to comprehension. In W.B. Weimer and D.S. Palermo (Eds.), *Cognition and the symbolic processes*. Hillsdale, NJ: Erlbaum, 1974.

Chiesi, H.L., Spilich, G.J., and Voss, J.F. Acquisition of domain-related information in relation to high- and low-domain knowledge. *Journal of Verbal Learning and Verbal Behavior*, 1979, *18*, 257-274.

Cirilo, R.K., and Foss, D.J. Text structure and reading time for sentences. *Journal of Verbal Learning and Verbal Behavior*, 1980, *19*, 96-109.

Haberlandt, K., Berian, C., and Sandson, J. The episode schema in story processing. *Journal of Verbal Learning and Verbal Behavior*, 1980, *19*, 635-650.

Hayes, D.A., and Tierney, R.J. *Increasing background knowledge through analogy: Its effects upon comprehension and learning.* Technical Report No. 186. Urbana: University of Illinois, Center for the Study of Reading, October 1980. (ED 195 953)

Herber, H.L. *Teaching reading in content areas* (2nd ed.). Englewood Cliffs, NJ: Prentice-Hall, 1978.

Just, M.A., and Carpenter, P.A. A theory of reading: From eye fixations to comprehension. *Psychological Review*, 1980, *87*, 329-354.

Labov, W. *Language in the inner city: Studies in the black English vernacular.* Washington, DC: Center for Applied Linguistics, 1972.

Luiten, J., Ames, W., and Ackerson, G. A meta-analysis of the effects of advance organizers on learning and retention. *American Educational Research Journal*, 1980, *17*, 211-218.

Mayer, R.E. Can advance organizers influence meaningful learning? *Review of Educational Research*, 1979, *49*, 371-383.

Paris, S.G., and Lindauer, B.K. The role of inference in children's comprehension and memory. *Cognitive Psychology*, 1976, *8*, 217-227.

Pichert, J.A., and Anderson, R.C. Taking different perspectives on a story. *Journal of Educational Psychology*, 1977, *69*, 309-315.

Reynolds, R.E., Taylor, M.A., Steffenson, M.A., Shirey, L.L., and Anderson, R.C. *Cultural schemata and reading comprehension.* Technical Report No. 201. Urbana: University of Illinois, Center for the Study of Reading, April 1981.

Rumelhart, D.E., and McCelland, J.L. *An interactive activation model of the effect of context in perception* (Part 2). CHIP Technical Report. La Jolla: University of California, Center for Human Information Processing, 1980.

Stauffer, R.G. *Teaching reading as a thinking process.* New York: Harper and Row, 1969.

Steffensen, M.S., Joag-Dev, C., and Anderson, R.C. A cross-cultural perspective on reading comprehension. *Reading Research Quarterly*, 1979, *15*, 10-29.

Tierney, R.J., and Cunningham, J.W. Research on teaching reading comprehension. In P.D. Pearson (Ed.), *Handbook of reading research.* New York: Longman, 1984.

Schema Activation and Schema Acquisition: Comments on Richard C. Anderson's Remarks

JOHN D. BRANSFORD
Vanderbilt University

Professor Anderson has done an excellent job of presenting the essentials of schema theory and of highlighting a number of its implications. My comments on his paper are divided into two points. First, I want to reemphasize some of Anderson's major arguments and elaborate on several of their implications. I shall then discuss some potential shortcomings of many versions of schema theory and suggest some modifications that seem relevant to the issue of understanding how people learn from texts.

Several of Anderson's points about schema theory can be reviewed by considering the processes involved in understanding, and later remembering, a simple statement such as the following: "Jane decided not to wear her matching silver necklace, earrings, and belt because she was going to the airport." In order to comprehend this statement, one must go beyond the information that was given, and postulate a reason for the connection between airports and Jane's style of dress. People who are familiar with airports—who have a well-developed "airport schema"—might assume that Jane decided not to wear her silver jewelry because of the metal detectors in airports. In Anderson's terminology, their schemata provide a basis for interpreting and elaborating on the information they heard.

Anderson also argued that schemata affect processes at the time of output as well as at input. For example, adults who attempt to recall the original "airport" statement three days later may rely on their knowledge of airports for a selective search of memory and then state that "Jane decided not to wear some metal jewelry because it could cause unnecessary delays at the airport." Note that this type of response reveals the comprehender's assumptions about important elements. It is the fact that the jewelry was metal that was most important and not, for example, that it was expensive or pretty. Anderson also emphasized this function of schemata: They provide a basis for determining the important elements in a message or text.

Reprinted from *Learning to Read in American Schools: Basal Reader and Context Texts*. Edited by R.C. Anderson, J. Osborn, and R.J. Tierney. Copyright 1984 by Lawrence Erlbaum Associates. Reprinted by permission.

Overall, Anderson discussed six functions of schemata. They provide a basis for (a) assimilating text information, (b) making inferential elaborations that fill in the gaps in messages, (c) allocating attention to important text elements, (d) searching memory in an orderly fashion, (e) formulating a summary of information, and (f) making inferences that can enable one to reconstruct an original message despite having forgotten some of the details. It may be possible to add to Professor Anderson's list of "schema functions," but the six functions he cited are sufficient to illustrate why the knowledge possessed by the learner has pervasive effects on performance. I might add that Anderson was not simply arguing that the activation of appropriate knowledge is a useful thing to do; he was asserting that it is a fundamental aspect of the act of comprehending and remembering. One clear implication of this position is that some children may appear to have poor comprehension and memory skills *not* because they have some inherent comprehension or memory "deficits," but because they lack, or fail to activate, the background knowledge that was presupposed by a message or a text.

It is instructive to note that there are many levels at which a child may lack the background knowledge necessary to understand a text. At one extreme, the child may have no information about a concept; he or she may know nothing about airports, for example. At another level, a child may know something about a concept (for example, airports) yet still fail to understand many statements that involve this concept. As an illustration, consider once again the simple statement about Jane's trip to the airport and her decision about her silver jewelry. A child may know that airports are "places where planes take off and land" yet have no knowledge that airports contain metal detectors. The child therefore knows something about airports, but his or her "airport schema" is still less articulated than that of most adults. The child's knowledge may be sufficient for understanding some types of statements about airports (e.g., John went to the airport because his aunt was coming to visit) yet insufficient for others (e.g., the earlier statement about Jane). The question of what it means for children to be "familiar" with the words used in a story is therefore more complicated than might be apparent at first glance.

Imagine another child who knows that airports are places where planes land and take off, and also knows that airports are often crowded and may be havens for thieves. This child may form the following interpretation of the statement about Jane and the airport: "Jane did not wear her expensive jewelry because she was afraid that someone might take it." This interpretation is quite different from one that focuses on the fact that airports have metal detectors. According to the "crowded airport" interpretation, the important elements are that the jewelry is valuable, visible, and easily accessible, rather than the fact that the jewelry is metal and hence may trigger a security alarm. Relatively subtle differences in people's schemata (in this case their "airport schemata") can therefore have important effects on the interpretations they make.

Consider some of the problems that can arise when two people form different interpretations of the same message. For example, imagine that a teacher forms a "metal detector" interpretation of the statement about Jane and that a child forms a "thief" interpretation. In a one-to-one conversation, these two individuals might well discover their differences in interpretation and agree that both are reasonable. However, extended one-to-one conversations are often impossible in an educational setting. Teachers are frequently forced to use assessment questions in order to evaluate students' comprehension. These questions may be supplied either by the author of a text or by the teacher. In either case, the phrasing of the question may reflect the question asker's initial interpretations of a message. For example, a question such as "Why didn't Jane wear something metal?" may stem from a "metal detector" interpretation, whereas the question "Why didn't Jane wear her expensive jewelry?" tends to reflect a "thief" interpretation. My colleagues and I have found that even relatively subtle mismatches between a learner's initial interpretations and a teacher's or a tester's way of phrasing questions can cause considerable decrements in memory performance (Barclay, Bransford, Franks, McCarrell, and Nitsch, 1974). If my phrasing of a question is not congruent with a child's initial interpretation of an event, I may erroneously conclude that the child did not learn.

Mismatches between the phrasing of questions and a child's initial interpretations affect not only teachers' assessments of children's learning abilities; I am convinced that they also affect children's assumptions about their own abilities. Several years ago, Marcia Johnson and I conducted a study with college students that is relevant to this point (Bransford and Johnson, 1973). We created a passage about a man walking through the woods; nearly all our students interpreted the story as describing a hunter. They did not realize that the passage could also be interpreted from the perspective of an escaping convict. As Anderson noted, the perspective one takes on a story affects one's interpretation of the significance of information. For example, the story included information about it being muddy, hence the man's boots sunk in deeply. He then came to a little stream and walked in it for awhile. From the perspective of a hunter, this information suggests that the boots may have become caked with mud and that the man tried to clean them by walking in the stream. From the perspective of an escaping convict, however, the same information suggests that the man was leaving footprints and must take precautions in order to avoid being tracked.

We asked one group of college students to read the story I have described but said nothing about the possibility of interpreting it as an escaping convict. They therefore assumed that it was about a hunter, and the story made sense from this point of view. After reading the story, we supplied students with questions and explained that these should help them retrieve the information they had studied. However, the questions were written from the perspective of the escaping convict interpretation. For example, one question was "What was the concern with the trail and what was done to eliminate it?" Not surprisingly, these questions did not help students remember relevant aspects of the story; instead they caused confusion. Many of the students thought about the questions for a considerable amount of time and eventually concluded that they had completely misinterpreted the story. Several apologized for having made such an error. In reality, however, they had not "misinterpreted" the story; their original interpretations had been perfectly reasonable. We eventually told the students this, of course, because it would have been unfair to let them think that they had been in error. The point I want to stress, however, is that these mismatches between initial interpretations and the phrasing of questions can occur inadvertently in almost any situation. Furthermore, learners who do not realize why their performance suffered may mistakenly attribute their difficulties to their own inabilities to learn.

The preceding examples illustrate only a few of many important implications of schema theory, but I now want to consider some possible shortcomings of many versions of this theory. I refer to these as *possible* shortcomings because I am uncertain whether they are shortcomings of the actual theory or shortcomings that stem from my personal interpretation of schema theory (i.e., my "schema theory schema" may be only partially developed). At any rate, I believe that there are some issues concerning schema theory that need to be explored, especially when one begins to ask how teachers and authors might use this theory to help them avoid some of the text-student mismatches and question-student mismatches that have been discussed.

One possible approach to the problem of mismatches is to analyze carefully the materials presented to children and then to simplify them so that mismatches are much less likely to occur. There are some obvious merits to this approach, but it involves some potential problems as well. These problems revolve around the issue of what it means to "simplify" texts.

Several years ago, I participated in a conference where the topic of simplifying texts arose during one of the discussion periods. One of the participants at the conference expressed some concerns about the reading materials that his children had received in the elementary grades (see Kavanagh and Strange, 1978, pp. 329-330). He felt that the content of the stories (e.g., about a milkman, mailman, etc.) was extremely dull. When he asked the teachers why the children received such uninteresting materials, he was told that the children were familiar with the "community helpers." The teachers had not read about schema theory, so they did not say, "These stories are written to be congruent with the children's preexisting schemata." Nevertheless, the teachers were emphasizing the importance of providing children with materials that were congruent with the knowledge they already possessed.

The conference participant went on to say that his children did not like to read stories about topics that were extremely familiar; they were much more interested in reading about novel situations. In addition, he asked how theories that emphasize the importance of assimilating information to preexisting knowledge can account for the fact that it is possible to understand stories about novel situations. I think that this is a crucial question to ask schema theorists. It is especially crucial for those schema theorists who argue that comprehension involves the activation of a preexisting schema that provides a coherent account of the givens in a message. Many schema theorists have very little to say about the processes by which novel events are comprehended and new schemata are acquired.

In his presentation, Professor Anderson mentioned two types of situations involving schemata. One involves the activation of preexisting schemata. The second, which he noted was more interesting, involves the construction of new schemata. Since a major goal of education is to help students develop new skills and knowledge — to help them become able to understand things that they could not understand previously — the issue of schema construction or schema acquisition is extremely important. Nevertheless, nearly all the experiments used to support schema theory involve situations where students are prompted to activate preexisting schemata. For example, students may be prompted to activate a "washing clothes" schema, "prisoner" schema, "fancy restaurant" schema, "homebuyer" schema, and so forth. We have seen that these schemata provide important support for both comprehension processes and memory processes. However, experiments involving these schemata "work" only because the students in the experiments have already acquired the necessary schemata. If a person knew nothing about washing clothes, for example, it would do no good to simply tell him or her that this is the topic of the washing clothes passage. Similarly, imagine that a child is told that "Jane did not wear her silver jewelry because she was going somewhere" and is then given the cue, "She is going to the airport." A child who knows only that airports are places where planes take off and land is still going to have difficulty understanding this statement. In situations such as this, we confront the problem of helping students develop new schemata or of helping them refine the structure of schemata that they have already acquired (e.g., Bransford and Nitsch, 1978; Bransford, Nitsch, and Franks, 1977; Brown, 1979).

Imagine that we want to help a child develop a more sophisticated "airport schema." We will assume that the child knows that airports are places where planes take off and land, yet is unaware that there are metal detectors in airports. A basic and time-honored procedure for helping the child acquire this new information is to tell him or her about it. One might therefore supply information such as "There are metal detectors in airports" either prior to the child's reading a text or in the text itself.

There are many reasons why a statement such as "There are metal detectors in airports" may not be helpful to a child. An obvious reason is that a child may not be familiar with the concept of metal detectors. However, assume that our child is familiar with this general concept. He or she may still not benefit from the statement that "There are metal detectors in airports." The child needs to understand what the detectors are for and who uses them. Without this information, the child may assume that there are stores in airports that sell things, and hence conclude that most airports have "metal detector" stores. This is not the interpretation we want the child to make.

It seems clear that effective teachers or writers would do much more than simply state "There are metal detectors in airports." They would elaborate by helping the child realize that pilots guide planes to particular locations, that someone could try to force a pilot to fly to a different location, that this act may involve a gun or knife, that these objects can be detected by metal detectors, that the detectors at the airport are designed to keep people from taking knives and guns aboard the plane, and so forth. The amount of explanation needed will depend on the preexisting knowledge base of the learner. (E.g., a relatively knowledgeable child may need only be told that "There are metal detectors in airports in order to discourage hijacking.") The point I want to emphasize is that the goal of this instruction is to help the child develop a more sophisticated schema rather than simply to activate a schema that already exists. The teacher or author is attempting to help the child activate various preexisting "pockets" of knowledge that previously had been unrelated, and to help the child reassemble these "pockets" of knowledge into an integrated schema. This schema should then provide support for comprehending and remembering subsequent events. For example, the child's interpretation of "the metal-detector repairman received a phone call and rushed to the airport" may now be more likely to involve the assumption that he was rushing to repair a machine rather than rushing to catch a plane or to meet someone arriving by plane.

At a general level, an emphasis on the importance of helping students activate sources of preexisting knowledge that can be reassembled into new schemata is consistent with Ausubel's (1963, 1968) theory of meaningful learning. For example, he advocates the use of "advanced organizers" in order to prepare students for texts. I think it's fair to say, however, that many aspects of this theory need greater articulation; in particular, the guidelines for writing advanced organizers are relatively vague. One of the difficulties of constructing these guidelines is that advanced organizers must differ depending on whether one is dealing with a problem of schema activation or schema construction. An advanced organizer that is relatively general can be effective if learners have already acquired the schemata necessary for understanding a text; these general statements can prime concepts that learners might fail to activate spontaneously. When one is dealing with problems of schema construction or acquisition, however, advanced organizers composed of general statements will not suffice.

Earlier, I emphasized some of the specific elaborations or explanations that may be required to help a child incorporate information about metal detectors into his or her airport schema. It seems valuable to explore this issue further by examining the processes involved in acquiring knowledge about a more complex domain. Imagine, therefore, that someone is familiar with the general terms "vein" and "artery," yet wants to learn more about them. (This is analogous to knowing something about airports, yet needing additional information.) Assume that the person reads a passage which states that arteries are thick, are elastic, and carry blood that is rich in oxygen from the heart; veins are thinner, are less elastic, and carry blood rich in carbon dioxide back to the heart. To the biological novice, even this relatively simple set of facts can seem arbitrary and confusing. Was it veins or arteries that are thin? Was the thin one or the thick one elastic? Which one carries carbon dioxide from the heart (or was it to the heart)?

Even the biological novice who is familiar with the terms "veins" and "arteries" may have difficulty learning the information in this passage. The problem the learner faces is that the facts and relationships appear arbitrary. It is possible to create an analogous situation by using concepts that are familiar to everyone. For example, imagine reading 10 statements such as those listed below and then answering questions about them from memory:

> The tall man bought the crackers.
> The bald man read the newspaper.
> The funny man liked the ring.
> The hungry man purchased the tie.
> The short man used the broom.
> The strong man skimmed the book.

College students do quite poorly when they are presented with these statements and are then asked memory questions such as "Which man bought the crackers?" (Stein and Bransford, 1979; Stein, Morris, and Bransford, 1978). The students rate each sentence as comprehensible, yet have difficulty remembering because the relationship between each type of man and the actions performed seem arbitrary. The biological novice is in a similar position because he or she sees no particular reason why an artery should be elastic or nonelastic, thick or thin. Note that to a child, a statement such as "Airports have metal detectors" can also seem arbitrary. The child may therefore have difficulty retaining the new information about airports; hence it will be available for future use. This problem of retention becomes even more acute if we make the reasonable assumption that children are introduced to a number of new ideas during the course of a day. For example, they may receive new information about airports, fancy restaurants, dinosaurs, countries, and so forth. If these new facts seem arbitrary, it can be difficult to remember which things go with what.

In order to make the facts less arbitrary, we need to give a learner information that can clarify their significance or relevance (see Bransford, Stein, Shelton, and Owings, 1980). For example, what's the significance of the elasticity of arteries? How does this property relate to the functions that arteries perform? Note that our imaginary passage states that arteries carry blood from the heart—blood that is pumped in spurts. This provides one clue about the significance of elasticity—arteries may need to expand and contract to accommodate the pumping of blood. It can also be important to understand why veins do *not* need to be elastic. Since veins carry blood back to the heart, they may have less of a need to accommodate the large changes in pressure resulting from the heart pumping blood in spurts.

The process of clarifying the significance of facts about veins and arteries can be carried further. Since arteries carry blood *from* the heart, there is a problem of directionality. Why doesn't the blood flow back into the heart? This will not be perceived as a problem if one assumes that arterial blood always flows downhill, but let's assume that our passage mentions that there are arteries in the neck and shoulder regions. Arterial blood must therefore flow uphill as well. This information might provide an additional clue about the significance of elasticity. If arteries expand from a spurt of blood and then contract, this might help the blood move in a particular direction. Arteries might therefore perform a function similar to one-way valves.

My colleagues and I have argued that there are at least two important consequences of activities that enable a learner to understand the significance or relevance of new factual content (e.g., Bransford, Stein, Shelton, and Owings, 1980). First, people who understand the significance of facts develop knowledge structures that enable them to deal with novel situations. As an illustration, imagine that a biological novice reads a passage about veins and arteries and is then given the task of designing an artificial artery. Would it have to be elastic? A person who has merely memorized the fact that "arteries are elastic" would have little basis for answering the question. In contrast, the person who understands the significance or relevance of elasticity is in a much better position to approach the problem. For example, this person might realize the possibility of using a relatively nonelastic material that is sufficient to withstand the pressure requirements of spurting blood, plus realize the possibility of equipping the artificial artery with one-way valves that direct the flow of blood. This individual may not be able to specify all the details for creating the artificial artery, of course, but he or she at least has some appreciation of various possibilities and has an idea of the types of additional information that need to be discovered or acquired.

Activities that enable people to understand the significance of new factual content also facilitate memory. Facts that initially had seemed arbitrary and confusing become meaningful; the information is therefore much easier to retain. As an illustration, consider once again the earlier statements about the different types of men. I noted that college students have a difficult time remembering which man did what because the relationship between the type of man and the actions performed seem arbitrary. These same statements become easy to remember if students are supplied with information, or are helped to generate information, that renders these relationships less arbitrary (Stein and Bransford, 1979). For example:

> The tall man purchased the crackers that had been lying on the top shelf.
> The bald man read the newspaper in order to look for a hat sale.
> The funny man liked the ring that squirted water.
> The hungry man purchased the tie so that he could get into the fancy restaurant.
> The short man used the broom to operate the light switch.
> The strong man skimmed the book about weightlifting.

Elaborations such as these help people understand the significance or relevance of linking a particular type of man to a particular activity. They are therefore able to answer memory questions such as "Which man purchased the tie?", "Which man used the broom?" etc. In a similar manner, people who understand the significance of various properties of veins and arteries (e.g., the significance of the elasticity of arteries) are able to remember which properties go with what, and the child who understands the significance of having metal detectors in airports is better able to remember this fact.

It is important to note, however, that there are constraints on the type of additional information, or elaboration, that will enable students to understand the significance or relevance of new facts. As an example, consider the following list:

> The tall man purchased the crackers from the clerk in the store.
> The bald man read the newspaper while eating breakfast.
> The funny man liked the ring that he received as a present.
> The hungry man purchased the tie that was on sale.
> The short man used the broom to sweep the porch.
> The strong man skimmed the book before going to sleep.

These statements include elaborations that make sense semantically, but the elaborations do not help one understand why a particular type of man performed a particular activity. College students who receive a list of 10 sentences such as those above do *worse* than students who received the first list (the list *without* any additional elaboration; Stein and Bransford, 1979). My colleagues and I refer to elaborations such as those just noted as *imprecise* elaborations. In contrast, *precise* elaborations (such as those provided earlier) clarify the significance or relevance of facts (Stein and Bransford, 1979; Stein, Morris, and Bransford, 1978). Imprecise elaborations can make sense semantically; that is, they need not be nonsense. Nevertheless, they can actually produce poorer memory than a set of arbitrary statements that receive no elaborations at all. Note that there are many potential elaborations of facts about veins and arteries, airports, etc., that would also be imprecise. For example, a statement such as "Arteries are elastic so that they can stretch" does not help one understand why they need to be elastic, and a statement such as "There are metal detectors in airports that are used to check passengers" does not help one understand what is being checked nor why.

An emphasis on the degree of precision necessary to help people understand the significance of facts is important for analyzing the issue of what it means to "simplify" texts. A text can be composed of relatively simple words and simple syntax yet still seem quite arbitrary. My colleagues and I asked metropolitan Nashville teachers to provide us with samples of some of the passages their elementary school students are asked to read, and found a large number that seem arbitrary. For example, one passage discussed the topic of "American Indian Houses." It consisted of statements such as "The Indians of the Northwest Coast lived in slant-roofed houses made of cedar plank....Some California Indian tribes lived in simple, earth-covered or brush shelters....The Plains Indians lived mainly in tepees," etc. The story provided no information about why certain Indians chose certain houses. For example, it said nothing about the relationship between the type of house and the climate of the geographical area, nor about the ease of finding raw materials to build houses depending on the geographical area. Furthermore, the story said nothing about how the style of house was related to the lifestyle of the Indians (e.g., tepees are relatively portable). If students either did not know, or failed to activate this extra information, the passage was essentially a list of seemingly arbitrary facts.

Other passages we examined discussed topics such as tools, animals, machines, and so forth. In each case, the passages contained a number of facts, yet frequently failed to provide the information necessary to understand the significance of the facts. For example, a passage describing two types of boomerangs — a returning versus a nonreturning boomerang — provided information about each boomerang's shape, weight, length, function, and so forth. However, it failed to systematically help the reader understand how the structure of each boomerang was related to its function (e.g., how the shape affected whether it returned to the thrower or not, how the weight was a factor in determining whether a boomerang could be used to hunt small versus large game, and so forth). The passages about animals also failed to help students focus on relationships between structure and function. For example, camels have a number of properties that help them adapt to certain aspects of desert life, including desert sandstorms. Facts such as "camels can close their nose passages" and "camels have thick hair around their ear openings" become more significant when one understands how they reduce problems caused by blowing sand. Students who are unable to make these connections on their own experience difficulty because the facts seem arbitrary. They also fail to develop a level of understanding that can provide support for learning subsequent materials. For example, a student who realizes how various properties of camels protect them during sandstorms is in a better position to understand a subsequent story about desert travelers who wear scarves over their faces even though it is hot.

It is important to note that passages such as the ones I have described do not necessarily seem arbitrary to someone who has already developed expertise in these areas. The expert not only already knows the facts but also understands their significance or relevance. Even new facts (e.g., camels can close their nose passages) can seem meaningful to the person whose preexisting schemata provide a basis for understanding their significance (e.g., a person may already know that camels are adapted to survive in desert sandstorms). Adults who construct or evaluate passages for children are usually in a "schema activation" mode, but children who read these passages are usually confronted with the problem of constructing new schemata or of developing more detailed schemata. This is as it should be; the goal of the educator is to help children develop new skills and knowledge. However, we need to recognize that schema activation and schema construction represent two different problems. Our attempts to simplify texts can be self-defeating if we inadvertently omit the kinds of precise elaborations necessary for understanding the significance of the information. Indeed, we may sometimes need to introduce children to relatively sophisticated concepts that can provide a basis for more precise understanding. For example, the general concept of adaptation (of structure-function relationships) provides a powerful schema that supports the comprehension of new facts in a number of domains (e.g., structure-function relationships are important for understanding biological systems such as veins and arteries, tools such as different types of boomerangs, animals and environments such as camels and their desert habitats, and so forth). The careful introduction of core concepts such as this one may facilitate learning to a considerable degree.

Summary and Conclusions

I began by reemphasizing Professor Anderson's arguments about schema theory because they are extremely important. For example, Dr. Anderson's discussion of the six functions of schemata provided a powerful argument for the pervasive effects of students' preexisting knowledge. I elaborated on two implications of his argument. One implication was that students may have developed partial schemata that are sufficient for understanding some types of statements but not for understanding others. We therefore need a more precise analysis of what it means for students to be "familiar" with the words in a text. The second implication was that preexisting schemata affect the interpretation of teachers and authors as well as the interpretation of students, and that a person's interpretation can affect the way that he or she phrases test questions. If there is a mismatch between the phrasing of a question and a student's interpretation of a passage, decrements in performance can occur.

Most of my comments were directed at differences between schema activation and schema construction. Professor Anderson noted that these represented two different (although related) problems. Most of the experiments he discussed dealt with schema activation because this represents the current state of the experimental literature. I emphasized schema construction because a major task for the educator is to help children develop new knowledge and skills.

The concept of precision provided the framework for my discussion of schema construction. To the novice, new facts can seem arbitrary unless they are precisely elaborated in a way that clarifies their significance or relevance. New facts that are not elaborated, or that are imprecisely elaborated, are difficult to remember and hence are not available for future use. In contrast, precisely elaborated facts can be integrated into new schemata that can provide support for the comprehension of subsequent texts. I also noted that texts can be composed of simple words and syntax, yet can still seem arbitrary to the novice; the notion of what it means to "simplify" texts, therefore, warrants careful consideration. Indeed, we may need to introduce children to relatively sophisticated "core concepts" that can provide a basis for understanding the significance of a wide variety of new facts.

The final point I want to emphasize involves an issue which I have not mentioned but which I feel is extremely important. I have noted that texts which are not precisely elaborated can seem arbitrary to the novice, but I don't believe that children's materials should always be elaborated explicitly. The reason is that children must learn to identify situations where they need more information in order to understand precisely, and they must learn to supply their own elaborations. More generally, I believe that they must learn about themselves as learners. This includes an understanding of how different texts and text structures influence their abilities to comprehend new information and to remember it at later points in time.

My colleagues and I have been working with fifth graders who are proficient at decoding but who differ in their abilities to learn from texts. In contrast to the successful learners in our samples, our less successful learners have very little insight into the factors that make things easy or difficult to comprehend and remember, and they rarely attempt to use information that is potentially available to understand the significance or relevance of new facts. Their ability to learn is therefore impaired. We have created sets of materials that enable these students to experience the effects of their own learning activities and that enable them to learn to modify their activities. We find that these exercises can improve their performance considerably. In order to do this, however, we purposely create materials that are arbitrary, help the students evaluate these materials and experience their effects on memory, and then help them learn what to do to make the same materials significant or relevant. This seems necessary in order to help the students learn to learn on their own. The learning-to-learn issue is beyond the scope of Professor Anderson's paper and mine; Armbruster and Brown will discuss this issue later. I simply wanted to mention the issue at this point in order to emphasize that the procedures necessary to make texts easy to learn are not necessarily identical to those necessary to help children learn to learn on their own.

REFERENCES

Ausubel, D. *The psychology of meaningful verbal learning*. New York: Grune and Stratton, 1963.
Ausubel, D. *Educational psychology: A cognitive view*. New York: Holt, Rinehart, and Winston, 1968.
Barclay, J.R., Bransford, J.D., Franks, J.J., McCarrell, N.S., and Nitsch, K. Comprehension and semantic flexibility. *Journal of Verbal Learning and Verbal Behavior*, 1974, *13*, 471-481.
Bransford, J.D., and Johnson, M.K. Considerations of some problems of comprehension. In W. Chase (Ed.), *Visual information processing*. New York: Academic Press, 1973.
Bransford, J.D., and Nitsch, K.E. Coming to understand things we could not previously understand. In J.F. Kavanagh and W. Strange (Eds.), *Speech and language in the laboratory, school, and clinic*. Cambridge, MA: MIT Press, 1978.
Bransford, J.D., Nitsch, K.E., and Franks, J.J. Schooling and the facilitation of knowing. In R.C. Anderson, R.J. Spiro, and W.E. Montague (Eds.), *Schooling and the acquisition of knowledge*. Hillsdale, NJ: Erlbaum, 1977.
Bransford, J.D., Stein, B.S., Shelton, T.S., and Owings, R.A. Cognition and adaptation: The importance of learning to learn. In J. Harvey (Ed.), *Cognition, social behavior and the environment*. Hillsdale, NJ: Erlbaum, 1980.

Brown, A.L. Theories of memory and the problems of development: Activity, growth, and knowledge. In L.S. Cermak and F.I.M. Craik (Eds.), *Levels of processing and human memory*. Hillsdale, NJ: Erlbaum, 1979.

Kavanagh, J.F., and Strange, W. (Eds.). *Speech and language in the laboratory, school and clinic*. Cambridge, MA: MIT Press, 1978.

Stein, B.S., and Bransford, J.D. Constraints on effective elaboration: Effects of precision and subject generation. *Journal of Verbal Learning and Verbal Behavior*, 1979, *18*, 769-777.

Stein, B.S., Morris, C.D., and Bransford, J.D. Constraints on effective elaboration. *Journal of Verbal Learning and Verbal Behavior*, 1978, *17*, 707-714.

Story Comprehension and Fables

JOHN T. GUTHRIE
University of Maryland

In any reading program excepting the most bizarre, children read stories. Exactly what do teachers expect children to understand and remember from stories they read or stories teachers read to them? How much should children comprehend and remember, and what kind of growth in story comprehension should teachers expect?

Gordon Bower, of Stanford University, has proposed a set of simple rules that illuminate the structure of many stories and the processes of human understanding. Bower's report comes from his Presidential address to the Experimental Division of the American Psychological Association in September 1976. A picture of the structure is presented here.

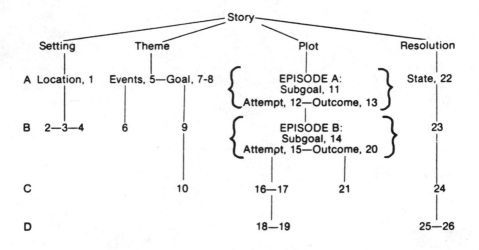

Adapted from *The Reading Teacher*, 30 (1977) and 31 (1978).

Story Structures

The first rule simply defines a story as consisting of a setting, theme, plot, and a resolution, which usually occur in that sequence. The second rule is that the setting consists of characters and usually the location and time of a story. The third rule is that the theme of a story consists of the main goal of the main character. The goal may be to rescue the beautiful damsel from the dreadful dragon. The plot of a story consists of a series of episodes designed to help the main character reach his goal. Each episode consists of a subgoal, an attempt to reach the goal, and a resolution of the attempt. For instance, our hero wants to get a horse to ride to the dragon's cave. His attempt may consist of asking the king for a horse, and the resolution occurs when the king grants him one. After several episodes, an outcome occurs which matches the goal of the main character, ushering in a final resolution. These rules apply to many stories, folktales, and dramas, and give us a common framework for understanding them.

Story Understanding

What can be done with the grammar for stories that Bower has proposed? We can make predictions about how people understand stories. Bower predicted and found that sentences located high in the hierarchy of the story structure are remembered much better than sentences low in the hierarchy. In this schematic, propositions in Level A were ten times more likely to be recalled than propositions in Level D. What people remember about stories is powerfully determined by the structural importance of the information to the story as a whole. Since people rely so heavily upon these structures to remember stories, Bower predicted that stories without a theme and a structure will be judged as incoherent and difficult to recall. Indeed, he found that none of the propositions in a paragraph of random sentences was remembered as well as the propositions that were lowest in the hierarchy and hardest to remember in a coherent story. Texts and tales that violate the rules of story grammar are perceived as incomprehensible and are harder to remember.

Bower's work on story comprehension has been done with adults. What about children? Jean Mandler and her associates at the University of California at San Diego have studied the development of story understanding. They found that first graders, fourth graders, and adults all remembered settings and resolutions quite well. The beginnings of stories and their final conclusions were extremely salient for children as young as six years. Children differed from adults by being less able to recall episodes within the plot. In particular, they had a harder time remembering attempts to reach the subgoal of an episode and the outcome of the attempts. Children are least able to comprehend reactions and causes, for example, the reactions of the main character to achieving or failing to achieve a goal or the cause of his actions. Since these features usually must be inferred by the reader, they entail more complex cognitive operations than remembering other aspects of stories.

This account of research on understanding stories has borrowed heavily from Bower and Mandler and has oversimplified their ideas; those researchers have borrowed from Rumelhart, who borrowed from Bartlett, who conducted his studies in 1932 in England. The significance of these studies is that they symbolized a radical, renewed commitment among many psychologists to investigate how people build mental models of their world.

Comprehension Instruction

The little research that has been done on understanding stories shows clearly that children expect a story to have a structure. They perceive the story in terms of its structure, and remember it accordingly. As children grow older and are exposed to more stories, their expectations become more differentiated and precise. At the very least, educators should help children fulfill their expectations about stories. We can do this by giving children stories that have sufficient structure for them to grasp. We should relieve children of the burden of coping with themelessness. We can help children achieve their expectations by questioning them appropriately. Questions drawn haphazardly from facts in the story are of course misleading to children. Asking children about the "main idea" is equally misleading. Research has shown that there is no such thing as one main idea in a story. There are multiple components to the story structure, and children perceive these components even in first grade. They know better than to expect one main idea. Comprehension of a story is not comprehension of haphazard facts or a main idea, but it is comprehension of the structure. That is to say, it is comprehension of the setting, theme, plot, and resolution; their components; and their interrelationships. Teachers can improve children's understanding of what they read by checking the questions in the materials they are currently using, eliminating any haphazard questions and using questions that will help reconstruct the story. Most important: Recognize the ability of even six year olds to search for and use abstract story structure as a basis for comprehension and memory.

Fables

This explanation of story structure and its implications for comprehension continues with the analysis of a fable.

Once upon a time there lived a psychologist, a man who understood all about fairy tales. He could tell a good fairy tale from a bad one and explain how children came to understand fairy tales. He took it upon himself to talk to teachers about fables. He dreamed with glee of the teachers' delight when they were told the secret of how children comprehend these stories. The psychologist started, "We will begin our lesson from a fable according to Aesop."

The Shepherd Boy and the Wolf

1 A shepherd boy went out to the hills every day with his father's sheep. *2* The pasture was a lonely spot beside a dark forest, and the hours passed slowly. *3* The boy often longed for some company to make the time pass faster. *4* He began to think it might even be fun if a wolf came to attack the sheep. *5* Then everyone would come rushing, and there would be some excitement for a change.

6 One day the boy decided to give the alarm just to see what would happen. *7* Hiding behind a tree, he shouted loudly, "Wolf! Wolf!"

8 The men in the village snatched up their clubs and guns and came running as fast they could. *9* But when they reached the pasture they saw no wolf. *10* The sheep were grazing peacefully, and the shepherd boy was laughing. *11* 'It was only a joke,' he explained. *12* "I wanted to see what would happen if I called for help."

13 Then one day a wolf really did creep into the pasture and fall upon the sheep. *14* The frightened boy ran down the hill, screaming, "Wolf! Wolf!" as loudly as he could.

15 But the men in the village thought it was just another silly trick. *16* They smiled at each other and shook their heads. *17* They were not going to be fooled again.

18 So the wolf enjoyed himself, feasting upon the poor sheep.

19 When he finally vanished into the dark forest, the boy gathered what was left of his flock and returned to the village. *20* He was sad and ashamed, but he had learned his lesson.

One way of explaining this story is to divide it into several sections. One means for this is Perry Thorndyke's model consisting of the setting, theme, plot, and resolution of the story. These elements are placed in the diagram which follows. Each number in the diagram represents a sentence from the fable. The most important sentences appear at Level A and less important at Level B, with the least important at Level C.

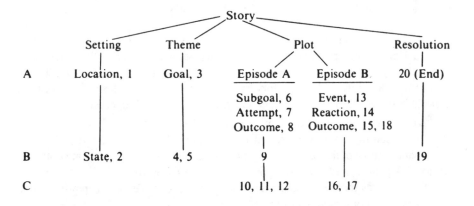

A summary of the fable can be constructed by combining the most important sentences, those at the A Level. With some editing, we arrive at:

A lonely shepherd boy longed for some company. He called "Wolf!" just to see what would happen, and the villagers came running. When a wolf appeared and fell upon the sheep, the villagers did not respond to his calls. He returned home sad and ashamed.

If a child were given this fable and wrote this summary of it, we might say he comprehended and remembered it. This we may call the semantic level of representation of the fable. All of the major portions of the story seem to be present and accounted for.

Examined more closely, the semantic representation is inadequate. The resolution in the diagram we have been using is, "He was sad and ashamed, but he had learned his lesson" (20). It is clearly the ending to the story in some sense. But it is not a resolution to the goal of the story. The goal is communicated from the sentence that says, "The boy often longed for some company to make the time pass faster." It is Sentence 3 and listed under the theme of the story. Being sad and ashamed does not satisfy the boy's longing for company. At least as we have diagramed it, this semantic representation does not quite grasp the story. Also, on the basis of raw intuition, we suspect that this summary is not what the story is really about. The thrust of the story is in some other direction.

From a feeling of incompleteness, we are impelled to a symbolic reconstruction of the fable. We must invent a new way for telling what the story means. We bring to the story a wealth of ideas and beliefs. Among them is the presumption that honesty is rewarded, and deception is punished. On the basis of this belief, the story can be reconstructed in symbolic form as illustrated.

Symbolic Reconstruction	Sentences from Story
Honesty is rewarded. Deception is punished.	
Honesty is violated.	A boy deceives the villagers.
reaction to the violation	The villagers ignore him.
consequence of the reaction	Boy doesn't get help when needed.
Rule of honesty is restored.	The boy suffers.

It can be noticed in the symbolic form of the story that the resolution occurs only in terms of the original presumption. Only because we generally believe that deception should be punished does the boy's suffering bring a resolution. There is nothing inherently within the story that can justify the boy's loss of sheep. Our general belief about honesty is needed to finally piece it all together.

Allow me to illustrate how a nine year old boy remembered this story. The story was read to him in May. About five months later, he was asked, "Can you tell what the story of the boy and the wolf was about?" He replied, "You shouldn't try to trick people, and if you do, you might get into big trouble." To see how this child's recall was more than semantic, note how the sections of his answer match the symbolic reconstruction of the fable.

"You shouldn't try to trick people,	Deception is punished.
and if you do,	Honsty was violated.
you might get into big trouble.	Honesty was restored.

For this boy, the presumption that deception is generally punished was remembered as an aspect of the story. Because it is necessary to the symbolic reconstruction, it was remembered as part of the story. It was never presented directly along with the story except in the mind of the child. The child's memory was not a replica of the story — it was a reconstruction that was consistent with his prior beliefs and his sense of logic.

After the psychologist had finished his explanation, one teacher made a response. "I certainly understand how we relate our background values to fables. But don't people often have strong feelings about characters in stories? When I read this fable to my class of second graders, they all felt very sorry for the boy. I did, too, since he was so lonely and didn't get any help from the villagers. Can you explain why we sometimes feel so strongly about people in fables?"

The psychologist looked blankly at the teacher, disappointed that his explanation had not been more exhilarating. He returned to his studies disconsolate.

A Schema-Theoretic View of Reading

MARILYN JAGER ADAMS
University of Illinois at Urbana-Champaign

ALLAN COLLINS
Bolt, Beranek and Newman

At one level, reading can be described as the process of translating graphemic strings into spoken words. However, what we really mean by reading is not the ability to decode words but the ability to extract the meaning, both explicit and implicit, from the written text. It depends on the intricate coordination of our visual, linguistic, and conceptual information-processing systems. If we are to understand reading, we must find a way to break it down into a set of more tractable subskills and to identify their interrelations.

The standard approach is to begin with the ultimate goal of the reader and then to determine its prerequisite. At the highest level, the reader has successfully read a passage if he understands it both as it was intended by the author and in terms of its impact on himself. This presumes that the reader has extracted the information provided by the text, which in turn, depends upon his having comprehended the individual sentences, which depends upon his having correctly processed the clauses and phrases of those sentences, which depends upon his having recognized the component words of those units, which depends upon his having recognized their component letters.

When reading is analyzed in this way, the component levels of processing appear to be organized hierarchically. The attainment of any given level presumes the execution of all subordinate or less complex levels; moreover, the converse is not strictly true. Whereas the reading of a written passage depends on the reading of its sentences, words, and letters, the dependency is, in some sense, unidirectional. An individual letter may be perfectly legible whether or not it is embedded in a word, a sentence, or a passage. Similarly, we are fully capable of reading individual words and sentences in the absence of a larger context. This asymmetry has been exploited by traditional analyses of reading. For teachers, it provides a rational structure for instructional programs: start at the bottom, with

Marilyn Jager Adams and Allan Collins. "A Schema-Theoretic View of Reading." In R.O. Freedle (Ed.), *New Directions in Discourse Processing*, Vol. 2. Norwood, NJ: Ablex, 1979. Used by permission.

single letter recognition, and successively work up through the higher level skills. For researchers, it provides a means of empirically isolating the processes involved at any given level in the structure: the effects of higher order processes on the level in question are supposed to be null, and the effects of lower processes can be empirically identified and subtracted out.

The problem with this approach is that when we are reading a meaningful passage, we are not reading its component letters, words, and sentences in the same way as when they are presented in isolation. Rather, processing at each level is influenced by higher, as well as lower order information. Thus, individual letters become more perceptible when they are embedded in words (Reicher, 1969, Wheeler, 1970). Individual words are recognized more easily when they are embedded in meaningful sentences (Tulving and Gold, 1963, Schuberth & Eimas, 1977). Unfamiliar words may be processed more easily if they are embedded in a familiar story (Wittrock, Marks, and Doctorow, 1975). Sentences that more coherently integrate the underlying semantic relations may be assimilated more easily than those that do not, irrespective of their syntactic complexity (Pearson, 1974; Haviland and Clark, 1974).

These sorts of interactions tremendously ease the task of the skilled reader. Because of them, he is not obliged to grind through every graphemic detail of the written representation. Instead he may opt to process lower order information only as is necessary for checking his higher order hypotheses about the content of the passage. By contrast, these sorts of interactions greatly complicate the task of analyzing the reading process. They challenge the wisdom of bottom-up instructional strategies, and they all but nullify the generality of empirical findings based on "isolated" processes. Moreover, they leave us without a good working model of the reading process.

Recently, however, through the combined efforts of cognitive psychologists, linguists, and specialists in artificial intelligence, a new set of formalisms for analyzing language comprehension has begun to emerge. These theories are, at core, related to the old notion of a schema (Bartlett, 1932; Kant, 1781; Woodworth, 1938). In the current literature, they are variously referred to as frames (e.g., Charniak, 1975; Minsky, 1975) and scripts (e.g., Schank and Abelson, 1975; Lehnert, 1977), as well as schemata (e.g. Becker, 1973; Bobrow and Norman, 1975; Rumelhart and Ortony, 1976). We would argue that schema theory for the first time provides a structure powerful enough to support the interactions among different levels of processing in reading.

In the remainder of this chapter, we will first provide a general description of schema-theoretic models and the way they work, and then examine some extensions of the models to the study of reading. A disclaimer is in order at this point. Many schema-theoretic models have been, are being, and will be developed, and there are some fundamental differences among them. In view of this, we have not tried to provide a faithful description of any one model. Instead we gloss over controversies and differences between models in the hope of providing a coherent tutorial glimpse of the overall effort.

Schema Theory and Language Comprehension

A fundamental assumption of schema-theoretic approaches to language comprehension is that spoken or written text does not in itself carry meaning. Rather, a text only provides directions for the listener or reader as to how he should retrieve or construct the intended meaning from his own, previously acquired knowledge. The words of a text evoke in the reader associated concepts, their past interrelationships, and their potential interrelationships. The organization of the text helps him to select among these conceptual complexes. The goal of schema theory is to specify the interface between the reader and the text—to specify how the reader's knowledge interacts and shapes the information on the page and to specify how that knowledge must be organized to support the interaction.

Structural Organization of Schema-Theoretic Models

A schema is a description of a particular class of concepts and is composed of a hierarchy of schemata embedded within schemata. The representation at the top of the hierarchy is sufficiently general to capture the essential aspects of all members of the class. For example, if the conceptual class represented by a schema were "going to a restaurant" (Schank and Abelson, 1975), its top level representation would include such information as that a restaurant is a commercial establishment where people pay money to have someone else prepare their food and clean up after them. At the level beneath this global characterization, are more specific schemata (e.g., going to a diner, going to a fast hamburger operation, and going to a swanky restaurant). In general, as one moves down the hierarchy, the number of embedded schemata multiplies while the scope of each narrows, until, at the bottom most level, the schemata apply to unique perceptual events. Each schema at each level in the hierarchy consists of descriptions of the important components of its meaning and their interrelationships, where these descriptions are themselves schemata defined at the appropriate level of specifity. The power of this structure derives from the fact that the top level representation of any schema simultaneously provides an abstraction of and a conceptual frame for all of the particular events that fall within its domain.

Because the top level description of a schema must pertain to every member of its class, many of its components may be but vaguely specified. For example, in the restaurant schema very few properties of *the place to be served* could be extended to all possible members of the class, be they any variety of booths, tables or counters; accordingly, very few properties could be explicitly attached to their superordinate descriptions. On the other hand, the most general schema for the place to be served in a restaurant effectively contains all of the service arrangements one has experienced, or equivalently, the collective features of those service arrangements weighted in terms of their likelihood in different contexts. Thus, while no specific value is anticipated, a stereotype is defined; in the absence of further information, the concept is still meaningful.

Because the schema specifies the interrelationships between its underlying components, once any element is specified, it can be understood in the proper context. For example, if a counter is mentioned within the restaurant schema, it can immediately be understood as a place at which food can be served and not as an abacus or a parrying boxer's blow. Moreover, the introduction of a counter might be sufficient to eliminate swanky restaurants from consideration, thereby indirectly narrowing the probable range for other, as yet unspecified, components of the restaurant schema.

Any important element or schema within a schema may be thought of as a *slot* (Minsky, 1975) that can accept any of the range of values that are compatible with its associated schemata. The comprehension of a specific situation or story involves the process of instantiation whereby elements in the situation are bound to appropriate slots in the relevant schema. This process not only serves the purpose of filling out the details of the schema, but also of temporarily connecting it to characteristics of the bound schemata. Thus, if there is a nervous old man in the story who takes the order in the restaurant, he will be bound to the waiter role. If subsequently the waiter knocks over a glass of water, this fact will be related back to the nervous quality of the old man currently assigned to the waiter role. Often, a text will not explicitly provide the element to be bound to a particular slot even though it is an integral component of some relevant schema. In these cases, the reader may assign *default* values. The default assignment will be determined by the values associated with its slot. The precision of the default description will depend on the specificity of those values. If one knew that the restaurant in the story was swanky, the default assignment might be that the customer sat at the table; if one also knew it was an authentic Japanese restaurant, the default assignment might be that the customer sat on cushions rather than a chair; if the story were about a particular, familiar Japanese restaurant, the default assignment might be very elaborate.

The Processing of Information

Within schema theory, the process of interpretation is guided by the principle that all data must be accounted for (Bobrow and Norman, 1975). Every input event must be mapped against some schema, and all aspects of that schema must be compatible with the input information. This requirement results in two basic modes of information processing. The first mode, *bottom-up processing,* is evoked by the incoming data. The features of the data enter the system through the best fitting, bottom-level schemata. As these schemata converge into higher level schemata, they too are activated. In this way, the information is propagated upwards through the hierarchy, through increasingly comprehensive levels of interpretation. The other mode, *top-down processing,* works in the opposite direction. Top-down processing occurs as the system searches for information to fit into partially satisfied, higher order schemata.

An important aspect of a schema-theoretic account of reading comprehension, is that top-down and bottom-up processing should be occurring at all levels of analysis simultaneously (Rumelhart, 1976). The data that are needed to instantiate or fill out the schemata become available through bottom-up processing; top-down processing facilitates their assimilation if they anticipated or are consistent with the reader's conceptual set. Bottom-up processing insures that the reader will be sensitive to information that is novel or that does not fit his ongoing hypotheses about the content of the text; top-down processes help him to resolve ambiguities or to select between alternative possible interpretations of the incoming data. Through the interactions between top-down and bottom-up processing, the flow of information through the system is considerably constrained. Even so, these processes are not, in themselves, enough to ensure apt comprehension.

The notion that the human mind is guided by a central, limited capacity processor is by now taken for granted within many psychological theories of information-processing. The general acceptance of this notion among psychologists has been principally due to empirical demands. Recently, however, Bobrow and Norman (1975) have argued that some such construct must be incorporated into any schema-theoretic type of system, be it person or machine, if its responses to its environment are to be rational and coherent.

Bobrow and Norman's argument is based on three observations. First, in order for a system that is so diffuse and receptive to maintain coherence, it must be imbued with purpose. In their words (p. 146), "Without purpose, the system will fail to pursue a line of inquiry in any directed fashion." Moreover, too many purposes can be the same as none. Their second observation is related: individual purposes are by definition, single-minded. In order to select among different, and possibly conflicting purposes, the system must have some more global self-awareness or, in Bobrow and Norman's words, "a central motivational process." Third, some mechanism which has access to all memory schemata must guide the interpretive process. This is necessary in order to decide when a schema has been adequately filled out for the current purpose, to evaluate the goodness of fit of the data to the schemata, and to detect and appropriately connect metaphorical or analogical references. These observations led Bobrow and Norman to conclude that the schemata must culminate in some central, omniscient processor—a grand self schema, if you will. The primary responsibility of this processor is to adaptively allocate the limited resources for active processing among the various activities of the system.

Taking this notion back to the schema-theoretic model, we see that there are two basic ways in which the processing capabilities of the system may be limited (Norman and Bobrow, 1975). First, there may be some difficulty in mapping input data to the memory structure with the result that their normally automatic, bottom-up propagation through the system is obstructed; in this case, the system is *data-limited*. Second, the various, simultaneous demands for active control may exceed the system's capacity to cope; in this case, the system is *resource-limited* and the execution of some of the ongoing activities will be compromised. Both kinds of limitations are relevant to the reading process.

Norman and Bobrow (1975) have distinguished two types of data-limits on processing. The definitive characteristic of each is that no amount of effort on the interpreter's part will eliminate the problem. The first, *signal data-limits,* occurs when the quality of the input confuses the mapping process as, for example, when one is listening for faint a signal in a noisy environment. Examples of signal data-limits in the reading dominion range from the deciphering of poor handwriting to the comprehension of a wholly incoherent passage. For the second kind of data-limits, *memory data-limits,* the quality of the input may be impeccable, but the mapping processing is obstructed for lack of appropriate memory structures. Both of us would, for example, suffer from memory data limit in trying to understand Japanese speech; since we know no Japanese, we could not, with any amount of effort, succeed. With respect to reading, problems related to memory data-limits are pervasive. For the beginning reader, they may occur at the level of single letter recognition. For more experienced readers, they may persist at the levels of word recognition, syntactic analysis, and, of course, in any dimension of semantic interpretation.

As an example of resource-limited processing, Bobrow and Norman describe the familiar situation in which one is simultaneously driving a car and carrying on a conversation. Both activities can be managed as long as they are proceeding as expected. If one, however, absorbs inordinate attention, it does so at the expense of the other. Surprising news may result in bad driving; a busy intersection may provoke a pause in the driver's speech or distract him from listening. The analogy exists in the reading situation — we can tolerate more or less distraction while reading, depending on the difficulty of our material or our reasons for reading it.

But, with respect to reading, the more critical problems related to resource-limited processing arise when activities subserving the same end compete for attention. If their respective demands cannot be met, the comprehension process breaks down. A good reader may encounter this problem when, for example, he is trying to read a legal document or a scientific paper that is outside of his area of expertise; he may devote a lot of energy toward understanding the words and sentences, only to find that he has not understood the meaning of the paragraph. For young readers, this kind of problem may be especially frequent since many of the subskills and concepts presumed by a text may not yet be well learned or integrated.

Schema Theory and Reading Comprehension

A crucial idea for a schema-theoretic account of reading comprehension is that it involves the coordinated activity of schemata at all levels of analyses. As schemata at the lower levels (e.g., visual features) are activated they are bound to thus evoke schemata at the next, higher level (e.g., letters); as these schemata are activated they, in turn, trigger their own superordinate schemata (e.g., words). In this way, through bottom-up processing, the input data are automatically propagated up the hierarchy toward more meaningful or comprehensive levels of representation. At the same time, schemata at higher levels are competing to fill their slots with elements from the levels beneath through top-down processing. Again, the theory is that, for the skilled reader, both top-down and bottom-up processing are occurring simultaneously and at all levels of analysis as he proceeds through the text (Rumelhart, 1976).

A necessary assumption here is that schemata exist at all levels of abstraction (Abelson, 1975; Rumelhart and Ortony, 1976). At the letter level, the schematic descriptions may be relatively concrete and specific. For example, the schema for an uppercase K might consist of three subschemata: (1) a vertical line on the left; (2) an oblique line extending upwards from near the center of the vertical line to a point to the right of and perpendicular to the top of the vertical line; and (3) a second oblique line extending downwards from somewhere along the bottom half of the first oblique line to a point directly beneath the top end of the first oblique line and perpendicular to the bottom of the vertical line.

At the other extreme, schematic descriptions may be very abstract and general. As an example, consider Rumelhart and Ortony's (1976) tentative version of the problem solving schema. In it there are three variables: a Person P, an Event E, and a Goal G. The schema has a two step structure:

1. E causes P to want G;
2. P tries to get G until P gets G or until P gives up.

Each of the elements like cause, want, and try in this schema are themselves schemata, just as the letters in the schemata for words are themselves schemata. Rumelhart and Ortony's version of the *try* schema has two variables which are bound in the problem solving schema: a Person P, a Goal G. The proposed steps are:

1. P decides on an action A which could lead to G;
2. While any precondition A for A is not satisfied, P tries to get A;
3. P does A.

The problem solving and trying schemata reflect what Newell and Simon (1963), have called means-ends analysis. In means-ends analysis, whenever a goal cannot be obtained directly, an appropriate subgoal is set up. This subgoal may itself be recursively dissolved into sub-subgoals, until a stepwise means has been found to attain the original goal. We would argue, as have Newell and Simon (1963), that just such problem solving pervades many human motivations and actions. It follows that a full understanding of many stories by and about people, depends on being able to interpret their events in terms of something like the problem solving and trying schemata that Rumelhart and Ortony (1976) have outlined.

The power of a schema-theoretic account of reading derives from the assumption that lower level schemata are elements or subschemata within high level schemata. It is, above all, this aspect of the theory that allows perceptual elements to coalesce into meaning, that allows such abstract, higher order schemata, as the problem solving schema, to be appropriately and usefully accessed. Moreover, it is this aspect of the theory which provides a structure for conceptualizing the interrelationships between levels of processing.

In order to give a more detailed description of what is theoretically happening as one reads, it is easiest to consider different levels of processing as if those levels were separable (which they are not). In the next four sections of this chapter, we will deal successively with letter and word processing, syntactic processing, semantic processing, and processing at the interpretive level. In each case, the basic argument in favor of a schema-theoretic explanation of these processes is that they cannot be explained in terms of bottom-up processing and that the top-down influences seem to be too automatic and too well structured to be attributable to simple guessing.

We will describe these processes in terms of how a skilled reader might arrive at an understanding of the following fable:

Stone Soup

A poor man came to a large house during a storm to beg for food. He was sent away with angry words, but he went back and asked, "May I at least dry my clothes by the fire, because I am wet from the rain?" The maid thought this would not cost anything, so she let him come in.

Inside he told the cook that if she would give him a pan, and let him fill it with water, he would make some stone soup. This was a new dish to the cook, so she agreed to let him make it. The man then got a stone from the road and put it in the pan. The cook gave him some salt, peas, mint, and all the scraps of meat that she could spare to throw in. Thus the poor man made a delicious stone soup and the cook said, "Well done! You have made a wonderful soup out of practically nothing."

Aesop

Knowledge and Processing at the Letter and Word Levels

The first step toward understanding the Stone Soup story is that of recognizing the words. The processes involved in recognizing written words have been a topic of prolonged debate among educators and psychologists. On one side, there are those who argue that word recognition must be mediated by more elementary activities, like letter identification; on the other, there are those who argue that words are recognized wholistically.

The first position has many practical arguments in its favor. First, for example, the pattern analyzing mechanisms that must be posited would be far less cumbersome if the system worked on single letters or even their elementary features, than if it worked on whole word patterns. The importance of this argument is stressed when one considers the innumerable variety of type styles and scripts that are legible. Second, there must be some connection in the system between written and spoken language, and our alphabetic cipher provides a natural candidate for such a link. In addition, it provides a means by which unfamiliar written words that are familiar in their spoken expression, can be "decoded." However, the potential advantages of an alphabetic language are denied if letters are not functional stimuli in reading. Third, thorough instruction in letter-to-sound correspondences has been shown to be an important component of early reading curricula (Barr, 1974; Chall, 1967); by implication these correspondences, or some aspect of the analysis they involve, must be useful to the reading process.

In support of the other contention—that people recognize words wholistically—is the fact that people act like that's what they do. Certainly skilled readers are rarely aware of reading in a letter-by-letter fashion. Moreover, experimental studies have shown that whole words can be perceived at least as quickly and accurately as single letters (Cattell, 1886; Reicher, 1969; Wheeler, 1970).

The most reasonable solution to the dilemma is that the processing recognizing written words involved analyses at both the letter and the word level, and that these analyses occur simultaneously and interact with each other. Recently, Adams (1975) ran a series of experiments comparing the visual processing of words, pseudowords, and orthographically irregular nonwords, which yielded direct support for this explanation. She then proposed a model which is very much in the spirit of schema theory.

The basic assumption underlying Adams' model is that any set of internal units or schemata that are repeatedly activated at the same time, become associated such that the activation of one of them facilitates the activation of the others. The essential idea of the model is that the extraction of visual information proceeds in the same way for words, pseudowords, and orthographically irregular strings, and that their differential perceptibility is due to interactions between the schemata against which the visual information is mapped. These interactions are illustrated in Figures 1 and 2.

The circles in Figure 1 represent letter recognition schemata, the arrows represent associations between them. The circles correspond to schemata receiving activation from both an external stimulus and other activated schemata while the broken circles correspond to those receiving activation from other schemata only. The degree of interfacilitation should be determined by both the strength of the external input and the strength of the association where the latter is presumably a function of the letters' history of co-occurrence. The strengths of these

STIMULUS

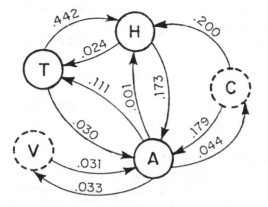

(a) THAT

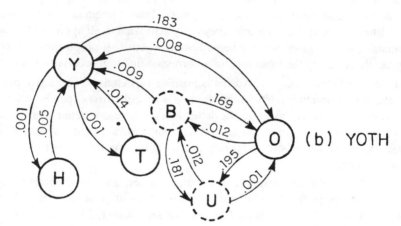

(b) YOTH

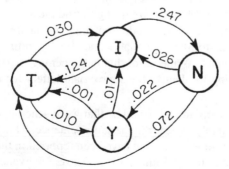

(c) IYTN

Figure 1. Associated letter network (from Adams, 1975).

interletter associations can therefore be estimated from transition probabilities, as has been done in this Figure.

This structure would predict a considerable perceptual advantage of words and pseudowords over orthographically irregular nonwords, especially given that the extraction of visual information proceeds in parallel. That is, interfacilitation between the component letters of words and pseudowords would be mutual and coincident with external input. With reference to the example in Figure 1A, the *T,* the *H,* and the *A* would all be simultaneously receiving external activation from the stimulus and internal activation from each other. By contrast, the activation of the component letters of nonword strings, as in Figure 1C, would depend almost entirely on external input; since the transition probabilities between the adjacent letters of irregular nonwords are quite small, their mutual facilitation must also be minimal.

In order to explain the perceptual advantage of real words over pseudowords a second, lexical level of analysis must be included in the model. The level is diagrammed in Figure 2. The connections between the lexical schemata and the letter schemata represent the associations between them. The weighting of these associations are supposed to depend on lognormal word frequency. As the individual letter schemata receive input, they relay activation to all appropriate word schemata, and as a given word schema becomes active, it proportionately and reciprocally facilitates the letter schemata corresponding to its component letters.

In terms of schema theory, Adams is positing two kinds of interactive processes that go on simultaneously in recognizing words: the first depends on interconnections between schemata at the letter level, where one letter triggers an expectation for another letter; the second depends on the structure within schemata at the word level, where competing words are looking for letters to fill their respective slots.

What happens concurrently at the feature, letter, and word levels as the reader scans through the Stone Soup story is something like this. The eye collects information about different visual features that are present. These are features that are automatically bound to slots that they fit in the letter schemata. Meanwhile, partially instantiated letter schemata are trying to find the appropriate visual features to fill their remaining slots. In addition, they are facilitating other letter schemata that correspond to likely neighbors and, finally, fitting themselves to slots in the word schemata. While all of this is happening, partially activated word schemata are trying to identify the appropriate letters for their own unfilled slots.

A natural extension of Adams' model would be that word schemata facilitate other word schemata that are likely to occur in the same sentence. This extension could explain the semantic priming effects that have been reported in the psychological literature (e.g., Schuberth and Eimas, 1977; Meyer, Schvaneveldt and Ruddy, 1975; Tulving and Gold, 1965). But when a person is reading connected discourse, syntactic and higher order semantic knowledge must also be influencing the identification of words. As described below, words themselves are subschemata within these higher levels schemata.

STIMULUS

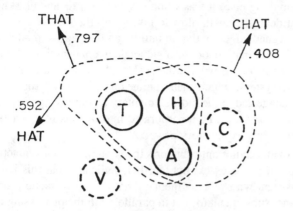

THAT
.797

CHAT
.408

.592

HAT

(a) THAT

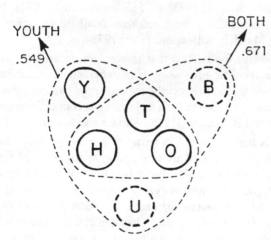

YOUTH
.549

BOTH
.671

(b) YOTH

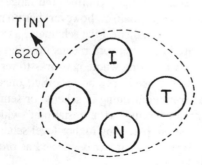

TINY
.620

(c) IYTN

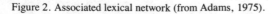

Figure 2. Associated lexical network (from Adams, 1975).

Knowledge and Processing at the Syntactic Level

Perhaps more than anything else, it was Chomsky's (1959) review of Skinner's verbal learning, that dealt the death blow to bottom-up theories of syntactic processing. Chomsky argued cogently that in building a descriptive model of linguistic behavior, the "...elimination of the independent contribution of the speaker and learner...can be achieved only at the cost of eliminating all significance from the descriptive system, which then operates at a level so gross and crude that no answers are suggested to the most elementary questions" (p. 30). In other words, top-down processes must be incorporated into models of syntactic processing if they are to have any explanatory power.

Recent experimental evidence not only supports the contention that syntactic analysis is guided by top-down processes, but, further, indicates that this happens in a way that is consistent with schema theory. That is, the syntactic processing of a phrase occurs not subsequent to, but in parallel with the processing of its lexical elements (Marslen-Wilson, 1973; 1975; Wannemacher, 1974). Moreover, the syntactic hypotheses interact with and thus facilitate the lower level processes (Marcel, 1974; Marslen-Wilson and Tyler, 1975).

One of the most powerful formalisms that researchers in artificial intelligence have developed for syntactic processing is the augmented transition network (ATN) grammar (Woods, 1970). Recently, experimental evidence has been accumulating that ATN theory provides at least a plausible account of human syntactic processing (Stevens and Rumelhart, 1975; Wanner and Maratsos, 1975).

The ATN formalism is best explained in terms of a small network that can parse a subset of English. There exists an ATN grammar for most of English (Woods, Kaplan, and Nash-Webber, 1972), but it is complicated to understand. Figure 3 shows a sample network for analyzing English sentences (s) from Woods (1970), and associated networks for analyzing noun phrases (NP) and prepositional phrases (PP). The arcs (or pointers) in the ATN formalism act like slots in the schema formalism. Thus, going out from the s state in Figure 3, any auxiliary will satisfy the lower arc. "Auxiliary" defines the range of values that can satisfy that arc (or slot). The ATN formalism, however, has no notion equivalent to default values in the schema formalism. Like schemata, ATN networks are embedded: going along an NP arc in any network means jumping to the NP network to analyze a noun phrase. By allowing whole networks to replace arcs, the network for analyzing noun phrases need only be specified once. This is the same kind of power that comes from embedding in schema or semantic network theory: one can have a schema for "trying" or a "restaurant" which can be referred to in a wide variety of different places by higher level schema, so it need only be specified once. ATN networks can in fact be viewed as procedural schemata for representing syntactic knowledge.

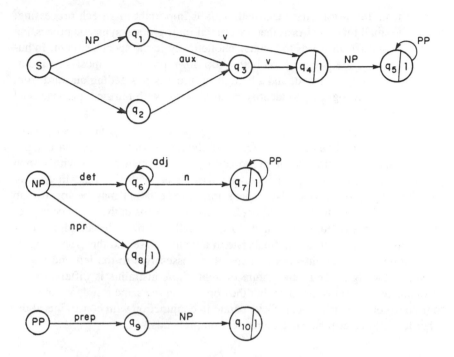

Figure 3. A sample transition network. S is the start state. g_4, g_5, g_6, g_7, g_8, and g_{10} are the final states (from Woods, 1970).

Woods (1970) describes how the ATN network in Figure 3 analyzes sentences as follows:

> To recognize the sentence "Did the red barn collapse?" the network is started in state S. The first transition is the aux transition to state q2 permitted by the auxiliary "did." From state q2 we see that we can get to state q3 if the next "thing" in the input string is an NP. To ascertain if this is the case, we call the state NP. From state NP we can follow the arc labeled det to state q6 because of the determiner "the." From here, the adjective "red" causes a loop which turns to state q6, and the subsequent noun "barn" causes a transition to state q7. Since state q7 is a final state, it is possible to "pop up" from the NP computation and continue the computation of the top level s beginning in state q3 which is at the end of the NP arc. From q3 the verb "collapse" permits a transition to the state q4, and since this state is final and "collapse" is the last word in the string, the string is accepted as a sentence [pp. 591-592].

Most ATN parsers that have been developed to date have been top-down processors: the parser starts out looking for a sentence in the s network, and the parser will fail if the input is not a well formed string according to the grammar. But there is nothing about the ATN formalism that is inherently top-down. In fact, Woods (1976) has recently developed an ATN parser that proceeds in bottom-up fashion from the words first identified. This is important in speech processing, where the small function words that are crucial for top-down syntactic processing are the most difficult words to identify phonetically in the speech stream. In human comprehension, we envision both a top-down process, as most ATN grammars are currently designed, and a bottom-up process proceeding outward from the first words recognized to identify noun phrases, verb phrases, prepositional phrases, etc.

At the syntactic level then, the reader's processing of the Stone Soup fable must be something like the following. From the top down the reader starts looking for a sentence. There is a high probability that a sentence starts with a noun phrase (i.e., arcs must have frequencies associated with them as in Adams' model in Figure 1), and so the reader's initial expectation may be for a noun phrase, which "A poor man" satisfies. But different words in the sentence trigger expectations in a bottom-up fashion: "a" is usually followed by an adjective or noun; "man" is likely to be the final state in a noun phrase and therefore triggers expectations for determiners, adjectives, and possessives to the left and a verb phrase to the right. Thus, the nature of syntactic constraints is different from word and letter level constraints, but they operate in the same top-down and bottom-up patterns. Furthermore, they operate in conjunction with constraints at the other levels to determine what the reader comprehends.

Knowledge and Processing at the Semantic Level

In reading the Stone Soup fable the skilled reader fills in many details that are not in the text. For example, 1) that the man came to the house because he was hungry and the maid sent him away, because she didn't want to give away her master's food; 2) that the poor man asked to dry himself by the fire because he thought the maid might let him in and he wanted to get into the house so he could get some food; 3) that the maid let him in because she felt sorry for him and did not realize his request was a ploy to get food; 4) that the man suggested making stone soup because he thought the cook might be fooled into thinking that a stone could be used to make soup and, if so, she would throw in scraps of food as she normally does in making soup; 5) that the cook agreed because she thought the man knew about a novel dish, and she did not realize he had invented the dish as a ploy to get food; 6) that the cook did not realize that the man had contributed nothing to the soup; and 7) that the reason the soup tasted good was because of the ingredients the cook added. None of these motivations and causal connections are in the passage itself.

There is a large amount of the reader's world knowledge that must be invoked in order to construct such an interpretation for the Stone Soup fable. Table 1 shows what some of that information might look like in schema-theoretic terms.

Table 1

SOME WORLD KNOWLEDGE SCHEMATA NEEDED FOR STONE SOUP FABLE

A maid

1. A woman servant P1 who cleans and takes care of residence I for master and/or mistress P2.
2. The goal of P1 is to please P2.
3. P2 pays P1 with money and/or by providing room and board.

How to please a master

1. A person P1 can please a master P2 by working hard, by being nice to P2, and by protecting P2's property.

How to obtain goods

1. If a person P1 has money M, P1 can buy goods G from a store I or person P2 possessing G.
2. If a person P1 has no money M, P1 can borrow M or P1 can steal goods G from a store I or person P2 possessing G, or beg for G from P2, or con P2 into giving G.

How to con somebody

1. If a person P1 has a goal G1, and
2. If another person P2 has a means M and a goal G2 to prevent P1 from obtaining G1, and
3. If P1 performs an action A which P2 thinks is directed toward a different goal G3 and which leads P1 to obtain G1 without P2 giving up either M or G2,
4. Then P1 cons P2 by doing A.

How to make soup X

1. A person P1 puts potable liquid in a pan.
2. P1 adds a large quantity of food X or a base for meat stock X like soup bones or scraps.
3. P1 adds spices and other bits of food F that are available.
4. P1 cooks over low heat for a long time.

The process of comprehending the passage at the semantic level must be something like the following. The fact that the man is poor triggers the notion that he does not have much money or wealth. The large house he comes to, therefore, must not be his own house. Begging is one means of obtaining food (see *how to obtain goods* in Table 1), and the fact that the man does not have money satisfies the precondition for begging. Because the reader tries to interpret actions in terms of the problem solving and trying schemata, he will bind the poor man to the person P in both schemata, and the begging of food to the action A in the trying schema that could lead to some goal G. Because no goal and no initiating event are specified in the story, the reader makes the default assumptions that the man is hungry (event E) and his goal G is to eat. It is the need to satisfy these slots in the problem solving schema that forces these assumptions. Obviously they could be wrong; the man might be seeking food for his dog or casing the house to rob it, but the default values are assumed unless and until the reader is forced to revise them.

When the poor man is sent away with angry words, the reader similarly makes a default assumption that a resident of the house sent the poor man away, not because the poor man offended the resident but in order to preserve property (i.e. food). When the poor man comes back for permission to dry his clothes, this doesn't fit the earlier goal of wanting to eat, so the reader assumes that the poor man's goal has changed to getting dry from the storm mentioned in the first sentence. The reference to the maid in the last sentence of the first paragraph binds her to the resident that sent the poor man away originally. To fill the slots in the problem solving schema, the reader assumes that the maid's goal in letting the beggar come in is to make him happy, out of general kindness to the poor. This is reconciled with her earlier refusal of food, because the action taken in this case does not violate the means by which she can please her master (see Table 1).

Inside, the man apparently adopts another new goal of teaching the cook how to make stone soup. The reader has no schema for making stone soup; it is news to the reader as well as the cook. But the reader, in order to understand the story, must have a schema like that in Table 1 as to how to make soup in general. One of the conditions for making soup is violated, namely that the basic ingredients be edible or meat bones or scraps. This triggers the reader to look for another goal for the poor man's actions. The fact that the cook put a lot of scraps into the soup means that she has supplied the base for the soup. This suggests that the man's original goal of getting food might be his goal in making stone soup. There is nothing in the story that says he eats the soup, but the cook says the soup tastes good, which implies that it has been made. The default value when people perform some task together is that both share the fruits of the labor, so that the reader should assume the poor man gets to eat the soup. Therefore, the reader can make sense of this episode in terms of the man's reaching his original goal of obtaining food.

Furthermore, if the reader is clever, he will see he can reduce the number of independent goals for the poor man to one, if the man's request to dry himself by the fire is interpreted as a subgoal to getting into the house, and getting into the house, in turn, a subgoal to getting food. This interpretation works because an alternative to begging for goods is conning someone for goods (see Table 1). The way the con operates here is that the man has the goal to get food, which the maid wants to prevent. By asking to dry himself by the fire the man takes an action which leads to getting food, but which the maid thought was directed to getting dry. Thus, she misinterpreted his action and was conned.

A still more difficult inference is to see that the man conned the cook as well as the maid. To make this inference the reader must infer that the cook also would have refused the man food. In the case of the maid, this is revealed by her actions. In the case of the cook, it must be inferred from the fact that she too would want to please her master by preserving his property. Furthermore, the reader must infer both that the cook believed that the man's goal was to make soup from a stone, and that his real goal was to get her to give him some food. We saw how the reader could realize that the man's goal was to obtain food. The clue that the cook did not understand the man's goal is only indirect; she marvels at his having made a wonderful soup out of practically nothing, which implies she does not see that it was she who contributed all of the substantial ingredients to the soup and that he and his stone added nothing. Therefore, she too was conned by the poor man.

Thus, the skilled reader can make sense of the actions and motivations in such a story through a variety of inferences and default assumptions. This involves the use of a wide variety of world knowledge from the schema for problem solving, to the schema for maids, to the schema for how to con somebody. Different readers may misunderstand the story in many different ways depending on which of these assumptions or inferences they fail to make or which they make incorrectly.

Knowledge and Processing at the Interpretive Level

An understanding of the interrelationships between the character and events in a story typically requires a host of complex inferences. But the goal of the skilled reader goes beyond that of following the story: in addition, he seeks to interpret or impose a structure on the passage as a whole. Processing at this level requires even more abstract knowledge and more complex inferences, since it depends less on the actual content of the text than it does on the goals of the reader and his perception of the author's intentions.

If the reader knows about fables, the Stone Soup story will be much easier for him to interpret. This is because fables are constructed according to a regular formula. A fable is a short story. Its characters, which are often animals, are stereotypes (e.g., maids are subservient, rabbits are frivolous, foxes are self-serving and cunning). Fables are generally based on the theme that life requires that we be flexible: the individual who is too nearsighted is liable to suffer the consequences—his goals will be thwarted or he will be outsmarted; the individual who is adaptive and resourceful will be successful even in the face of adversity. Any particular fable is intended to convey a more specific lesson or moral within this theme. The moral is often summarized by the last line of the fable. All of this knowledge would presumably be organized in a general fable schema.

For purposes of interpreting the Stone Soup story, the reader's first task is that of recognizing that it is a fable. If this information is not explicitly given, it may be signalled in bottom-up fashion from the structure of the story or from the fact that it was authored by Aesop. Once the fable schema has been suggested, top-down processes will be initiated in the effort to satisfy its slots. Most importantly, the fable schema must (1) find either a flexible successful character or a rigid, foiled character; and (2) interpret the events leading to this character's success or failure in terms of some general lesson of conduct. If the moral were summarized in the last line, as is often the case with fables, the reader would be half way there: he would need only to relate that synopsis back to the events in the story—the relevant characters would be brought out in the process. The moral is not summarized in the last line of the Stone Soup story, but the fable schema demands that there be one. The reader's task is therefore to use the event structure of the story to discover what the moral could be.

If the reader has made the inferences described in the previous section, then he should have constructed an event structure for the Stone Soup fable something like the following:

1. The goal of the poor man is to get some food.
2. The goal of the maid and the cook is to protect their master's goods.
3. The man's initial attempt to reach his goal is denied by the maid.
4. He devises a clever subterfuge to get part way to that goal.
5. He devises an even cleverer subterfuge to get the rest of the way to that goal.
6. The cook and the maid are conned into giving the man some food and, thus, betraying their master against their wills.

In this fable, Aesop seems to have filled two morals with one stone. While the poor man satisfies the flexible-and-successful description, the maid and the cook satisfy the rigid-and-foiled description. Moreover, both the success of the poor man and the plight of the servants can be translated into general lessons of conduct. The generality of these lessons is evidenced by the fact that they can be captured by other maxims: for the man, "Where there's a will, there's a way"; for the servants, "Beware of Greeks bearing gifts." If the reader has recognized these lessons, he has understood the story in the fullest sense.

Since schemata at the interpretive level are not compelled by the text, one can enjoy and feel like one understands a story perfectly well without them. One might be fully satisfied with the Stone Soup story without drawing out its lessons. Or one might be entertained by the story of *Candy* without interpreting it as a spoof on *Candide*. But interpretive schemata add a level of understanding that may be enlightening and often critical. We would argue that skilled readers have a variety of specialized schemata, like the fable schema, at the interpretive level that enable them to read such things as algebra problems, mysteries, political essays, allegories, recipes, contracts, and game instructions to their most useful ends.

Conclusion

The analysis of the Stone Soup fable at these four different levels illustrates how reading comprehension depends as much on the reader's previously acquired knowledge as on the information provided by the text. Moreover, comprehension depends on the reader's ability to appropriately interrelate his knowledge and the textual information both within and between levels of analysis. The power of schema-theoretic models of reading lies in their capacity to support these interactions through a single, stratified knowledge structure and a few basic processing mechanisms.

Top-down and bottom-up processing are fundamental mechanisms which apply at all levels of analysis. Bottom-up processing occurs when schemata that have been identified suggest other candidate schemata at the same level or the next level up. Examples of bottom-up processes at the four levels of analysis are:

a) Letters that have been identified suggest neighboring letters and candidate words.
b) A determiner such as "a" suggests that a noun or adjective will follow and that a noun phrase has been started.
c) Reference to "begging for food" suggests the schemata for "obtaining goods" and "trying."
d) The man's persistent, devious, and sucessful measure to get food suggest a candidate moral such as "Where there's a will, there's a way."

Top-down processing occurs when schemata that have been suggested try to find schemata from the same level or the next level down to fill out their descriptions. Examples of top-down processes at the four levels of analysis are:

a) A candidate word such as MAN looks for M, A, and N to fill its three slots.
b) A noun phrase looks for particular parts of speech, such as a determiner or a proper noun, to fill its initial slot.
c) The problem solving schema looks for a goal, such as eating, to account for the man begging for food.
d) The fable schema looks for a moral as the point of the story.

As top-down and bottom-up processes operate simultaneously at all different levels of analysis, they work to pull the various fragments of knowledge and information into a coherent whole.

Finally, neither the basic knowledge structure nor the processing mechanisms that have been described are supposed to be unique to a particular story or even to the reading process in general. Rather, within schema theory, the same knowledge structures and processes are supposed to underlie all cognitive processes. Clearly, people must have knowledge about maids, stories, problem-solving, and grammar like that described here. Such knowledge has many uses in addition to that of understanding text. Schema theory provides a way of integrating our understanding of text with our understanding of the world in general.

REFERENCES

Abelson, R.P. Concepts for representing mundane reality in plans. In D.G. Bobrow and A. Collins (Eds.), *Representation and understanding: Studies in cognitive science.* New York: Academic Press, 1975.
Adams, M.J. Perceptual components of the word apprehension effect. Unpublished doctoral dissertation, Brown University, 1975.
Barr, R. The effect of instruction on pupil reading strategies. *Reading Research Quarterly,* 1975, *10,* 555-582.
Bartlett, F.C. *Remembering.* Cambridge: University Press, 1932.
Becker, J.D. A model for the encoding of experiential information. In R. Schank and K. Colby (Eds.), *Computer models of thought and language.* San Francisco: W.H. Freeman and Company, 1973.

Bobrow, D.G., and Norman, D.A. Some principles of memory schemata. In D.G. Bobrow and A.M. Collins (Eds.), *Representation and understanding: Studies in cognitive science.* New York: Academic Press, 1975.

Cattell, J. McK. The time taken up by cerebral operations. *Mind, 1886, 11,* 220-242.

Chall, J. *Learning to read: The great debate.* New York: McGraw Hill, 1967.

Charniak, E. Organization and inference in a frame-like system of common knowledge. In proceedings of theoretical issues in natural language processing: An interdisciplinary workshop. Cambridge, MA: Bolt, Beranek and Newman, 1975.

Charniak, E. A partial taxonomy of knowledge about actions. *Proc. Fourth International Joint Conference on Artificial Intelligence.* Tbilisi, Georgia: USSR, 1975, 91-98.

Chomsky, N.A. A review of B.F. Skinner's *Verbal behavior. Language,* 35 (1959), 26-58.

Haviland, S.E., and Clark, H.H. What's new? Acquiring new information as a process in comprehension. *Journal of Verbal Learning and Verbal Behavior, 1974, 13,* 512-521.

Kant, E. *Critique of pure reason* (1st ed. 1781, with 2nd ed. 1787, translated by Kemp Smith). London: Macmillan and Company 1963.

Lehnert, W. Human and computational question answering. *Cognitive Science, 1977, 1,* 47-73.

Marcel, T. The effective visual field and the use of context in fast and slow readers of two ages. *British Journal of Psychology,*1974, *65,* 479-492.

Marslen-Wilson, W. Linguistic structure and speech shadowing at very short latencies. *Nature,* 1973, *244,* 522-523.

Marslen-Wilson, W. Sentence perception as an interactive parallel process. *Science,* 1975, *189,* 226-227.

Marslen-Wilson, W., and Tyler, L.K. Processing structure of sentence perception. *Nature,* 1975, *257,* 784-786.

Meyer, D.E., Schvaneveldt, R.W., and Ruddy, M.G. Functions of graphemic and phonemic codes in visual word recognition. *Memory and Cognition,* 1974, *2,* 309-321.

Minsky, M. A framework for representing knowledge. In P.H. Winston (Ed.), *The psychology of computer vision.* New York: McGraw-Hill, 1975.

Newell, A., and Simon, H.A. GPS, a program that simulates human thought. In E.A. Feigenbaum and J. Feldman (Eds.), *Computers and thought.* New York, McGraw-Hill, 1963.

Norman, D.A., and Bobrow, D.G. On data-limited and resource-limited processes. *Cognitive Psychology,* 1975, *7,* 44-64.

Pearson, P.D. The effects of grammatical complexity on children's comprehension, recall, and conception of certain semantic relations. *Reading Research Quarterly,* 1974-75, *10,* 155-192.

Reicher, G.M. Perceptual recognition as a function of meaningfulness of stimulus material. *Journal of Experimental Psychology,* 1969, *81,* 275-280.

Rumelhart, D.E. Toward an interactive model of reading. In S. Dornic (Ed.), *Attention and performance VI.* London: Academic Press, in press.

Rumelhart, D.E., and Ortony, A. Representation of knowledge. In R.C. Anderson, R.J. Spiro, and W.E. Montague (Eds.), *School and the acquisition of knowledge.* Hillsdale, NJ: Lawrence Erlbaum, 1977, in press.

Schank, R. and Abelson R. *Knowledge structures.* Hillsdale, NJ: Erlbaum, in press.

Schuberth, R.E., and Eimas, P.D. Effects of context on the classification of words and nonwords. *Journal of Experimental Psychology: Human perception and performance, 1977, 3,* 27-36.

Stevens, A.L., and Rumelhart, D.E. Errors in reading: Analysis using an augmented transition network model of grammar. In D.A. Norman and D.E. Rumelhart (Eds.), *Explorations in cognition.* San Francisco: W.H. Freeman, 1975.

Tulving, E., and Gold, C. Stimulus information and contextual information as determinants of tachistoscopic recognition of words. *Journal of Experimental Psychology, 1963, 66,* 319-327.

Wannemacher, J.T. Processing strategies in picture-sentence verification tasks. *Memory and Cognition, 1974, 2,* 554-560.

Wanner, E., and Maratsos, M. An augmented transition network model of relative clause comprehension. Unpublished, Harvard University 1975.

Wheeler, D.D. Processes in word recognition. *Cognitive Psychology,* 1970, *1,* 59-85.

Wittrock, M.C., Marks, C., and Doctorow, M. Reading as a generative process. *Journal of Educational Psychology,* 1975, *67,* 484-89.

Woods, W.A. Speech understanding systems. *Vol. IV Syntax and semantics,* Report No. 3438. Cambridge, MA: Bolt, Beranek, and Newman, 1976.

Woods, W.A. Transition network grammars for natural language analysis, *Communications of the ACM,* 1970, *13,* 591-606.

Woods, W.A., Kaplan, R.M., and Nash-Webber, B. The lunar sciences natural language information system: Final Report, BBN Report No. 2378. Cambridge, MA: Bolt, Beranek, and Newman, 1972.

Woodworth, R.S. *Experimental psychology.* New York: Henry Holt and Company, 1938

Spontaneous Instantiation of General Terms

MARIAM JEAN DREHER
University of Maryland at College Park

Current explanations of comprehension maintain that individuals understand encountered information by locating knowledge structures, or schemata, in their memory systems that will account for that information (e.g., Adams and Collins, 1979; Rumelhart, 1980). But selecting appropriate schemata is not enough. "Comprehension of a message entails filling the slots in the relevant schemata with particular cases in such a way as to jointly satisfy the constraints of the message and the schemata" (Anderson et al., 1976). The filling of the slots in schemata with particular cases is called instantiation, and this process is considered critical to the active construction that occurs during comprehension. Anderson (1977), for example, argues that "centrally involved in comprehending text...is the development of instantiated representations consistent with the message. All of the ingredients needed for concretization are not in the message itself. Therefore, more of the picture has to be drawn...by the reader; the detail has to be generated based on what is stored in memory" (p. 424).

This paper focuses on the one aspect of the instantiation process, the instantiation of general terms. Research on the instantiation of general terms has centered on an instantiation hypothesis formulated by Anderson et al. (1976). According to this hypothesis, when individuals encounter a general noun in context, they use the context and their prior knowledge to generate a particular instance of that noun. They then use that instantiation to represent the meaning of the general term in memory. For example, readers may generate *pig* for the general term *animal* in the sentence, *The animal rolled in the mud*.

To support their views on instantiation, Anderson et al. demonstrated that a cue representing the expected instantiation of a general noun in a sentence was a more effective recall cue than the general noun itself. For example, *actress* was more effective than *woman* for eliciting recall of *The woman was outstanding in the theater*, even though *woman* had actually occurred in the sentence and *actress* had not. To counter the explanation that the results were due to preexisting associations, control sentences were included such as *The woman worked near the theater*. For these control sentences, cues such as actress were less effective than the actually occurring nouns such as *woman*, because the context of the control sentences did not guide subjects to instantiate actress. Thus, Anderson et al. concluded that the evidence supported the instantiation hypothesis.

Other studies have also supported instantiation either by directly testing the

426

instantiation of general terms or by testing similar issues of context-sensitive representations of meanings (Anderson and McGaw, 1973; Anderson and Ortony, 1975; Barclay et al. 1974; Dreher and Singer, 1981; Garnham, 1979; Halff, Ortony, and Anderson, 1976). But all of these studies were conducted with college students. Dreher (1981) sought to determine whether the instantiation hypothesis would generalize to children. The available evidence on children indicated that first and fourth graders could instantiate when they were guided to do so (Anderson, et al. 1978). But there was no evidence on whether children, like college students, could instantiate *spontaneously*, or whether they stored an instantiation in memory as part of their representation of general terms in context.

To determine whether children instantiate spontaneously, Dreher conducted a study with intermediate grade children which employed an extension of the paradigm used with college students by Anderson et al. (1976). If the children instantiated spontaneously as did the college students in the Anderson et al. experiment, then their performance on target sentences such as *The fish attacked the swimmer* should have been better with particular cues (e.g., *shark*) than with general cues (e.g., *fish*). Instead, there was not a statistically significant difference in the effectiveness of particular and general cues for target sentences. Moreover, performance was best when particular cues such as *shark* were given for sentences that actually contained the particular term (e.g., *The shark attacked the swimmer*). This result suggested that the children could store and use a provided instantiation in sentences they read but that they did not spontaneously instantiate general terms.

However, it was possible to conceptually integrate Dreher's results with children and those of Anderson et al. (1976) with college students. In Dreher's study the instantiation hypothesis was not supported since the superiority of particular cues over general cues was not statistically significant for target sentences. Moreover, the opposing view—that abstract core meanings are encoded—was not supported either, since that position would have required general cues to be more effective than particular cues for target sentences. As a result, the hypothesis was formulated that intermediate grade children are at a point on a developmental trajectory between no spontaneous instantiation and the spontaneous instantiation found at the college level. This developmental trajectory hypothesis gains some support from the fact that the children were able to use an instantiation when it was provided and that they can instantiate when required to do so.

In order to determine whether the developmental trajectory hypothesis was valid, further research was necessary. The purpose of the current study was to test the validity of the developmental trajectory hypothesis by examining three conditions that might affect instantiation in children. First, if children are on a developmental trajectory toward instantiation, some intermediate-grade children could be expected to be further along the trajectory than others. Good readers, for example, might be more likely to instantiate spontaneously than poor readers. This result might be expected because instantiation is considered to play an important role in comprehension. For example, Anderson et al. explain that "people instantiate in order to give utterances a coherent interpretation" (1976, p. 675). If this explanation is correct, then good readers—being more successful comprehenders than poor readers—may engage in spontaneous instantiation while poor readers do not. When good and poor readers are not separated it may appear that no instantiation takes place and that, as Dreher (1981) suggested, the children may have been storing a word based representation of the sentences in memory (see Hayes-Roth and Thorndyke, 1979). Such a result would be in line with Wilson and Hammill's finding (1982) that ninth grade poor readers, contrasted with good readers, drew fewer inferences and were more likely to produce verbatim responses to a text.

Second, perhaps the failure to instantiate could be attributed to a memory burden. Therefore, the current study investigated whether children would be more likely to instantiate when asked to learn shorter rather than longer sentence lists.

Third, the type of directions given to children at the beginning of the task might influence their performance. Since there is an instructional emphasis in elementary school on literal recall of math and spelling facts, stories, and factual material, there was a possibility that children might not infer meaning unless instructed to do so. Consequently, directions which are designed to bias children toward meaningful processing might be more effective at eliciting instantiation than directions which simply ask children to read and learn sentences. Although it appeared likely that children would perform in the same way under both sets of directions, the hypothesis nevertheless required an empirical test.

Experiment 1: Method

Subjects. The subjects were 46 fifth graders and 47 sixth graders from a public school in a moderate to low income suburban area in southern California. Subjects' total reading scores from the *Comprehensive Test of the Basic Skills* from the preceding spring were used to select good and poor readers from the school's total population of fifth and sixth graders. Students who scored in the range represented by their grade placement at the time of testing (i.e., 4.0 to 4.9 and 5.0 to 5.9 respectively) were not included. The mean grade equivalent score was 7.3 for sixth grade good readers and 6.3 for the fifth grade good readers. The mean grade equivalent score was 3.8 for sixth grade poor readers and 3.5 for fifth grade poor readers. The subjects' teachers confirmed their classification as good or poor readers. A total of 24 good readers and 23 poor readers in sixth grade participated. At fifth grade, good and poor readers each numbered 23.

Materials. The materials consisted of twelve sets of three related sentences. Each sentence set contained target, control, and exemplar sentences. First, target sentences, such as *The fish attacked the swimmer*, were designed to lead students to one particular exemplar (e.g., *shark*). The target sentences had previously been shown to elicit the intended exemplar when intermediate grade students were required to instantiate (Dreher, 1981). Thus, the information necessary to instantiate the sentences was within the knowledge base of the subjects. Second, control sentences, such as *The fish stayed away from the swimmer* were not designed to lead to any particular exemplar. Control sentences were also tested in the previous work (Dreher, 1981). Third, exemplar sentences, such as *The shark attacked the swimmer*, were identical to the target sentences except that the subject nouns had been replaced by their expected instantiation. Each member of a sentence set was randomly assigned to one of three lists, with the constraint that each list contain equal numbers of each of the three types of sentences. Each list had two random orders.

Two types of cues were used for each sentence: 1) particular cues, such as *shark*, which represented the expected instantiation in the target sentences and 2) general cues, such as *fish*, which were the same as the subject nouns in the target and control sentences.

Because they had to be tailored to children, the materials used in the study are not identical to those used with college students in the Anderson et al. (1976) work. However, previous research has demonstrated that the materials used here are functionally equivalent for college students to those used by Anderson et al. (Dreher and Singer, 1981). Thus, developmental comparisons can be made.

Design and Procedure. Approximately equal numbers of fifth and sixth grade good and poor readers were randomly assigned to one of four groups. Each group participated separately in an empty classroom.

The procedure was essentially the same for all groups. Each child was randomly assigned to one of the three sentence lists which were presented in booklets with one sentence per page. The children studied each page for 12 seconds. A tape recorded tone signaled them to turn the page. After studying the sentences, they completed a five minute math computation task which lessened the likelihood that performance on the ensuing task would be based on recall from short term memory. Finally, the students completed a cued recall task at their own speed. For each sentence, they received both a particular and a general cue. The cues were presented in a booklet with one cue on each page. The children were to write the sentence which each cue solicited. So that they would not occur together, the two cues for each sentence were randomly assigned to different blocks with the constraint that each block of cues contained equal numbers of particular and general cues. The cues in each block occurred in two different random orders. The block order was counterbalanced.

Although all groups learned three types of sentences and received two types of recall cues, one difference was the type of direction each group received before the task. Groups 1 and 2 were told that we wanted to find out how people read and remember sentences, and that they were to read and remember as many sentences as they could. Groups 3 and 4 received exactly the same directions except that their directions contained an explicit instruction to concentrate on getting the meaning of a sentence rather than its exact words.

A second difference among the groups pertained to the length of the list of sentences. For each direction type, there were two task lengths. Groups 1 and 3

learned all the sentences, engaged in the interpolated task, and responded to a
cued recall. Groups 2 and 4 learned *half* the sentences, engaged in the interpolated task, and responded to a cued recall of the sentences learned; then after a
short break, they repeated the sequence with the other half of the sentences (split-
task condition). All students had the same total number of sentences to learn and
recall.

In the split-task, students were assigned to one of the lists of sentences. However, each of the lists had been randomly divided into two shorter lists with the
constraint that each shorter list contained equal numbers of the three kinds of
sentences. The two halves of each sentence list were presented in one order for
half the students in the split-task and in the reverse order for the remaining students. Each list half was accompanied by its own interpolated math task and its
own cued recall booklet.

The students' responses were scored according to the presence or absence of
the last word of the appropriate sentence as Anderson et al. (1976) had done with
their college subjects' responses. However, the children had been asked to write
the entire sentence because previous work (Dreher, 1981) indicated that some
children become confused when asked to respond only with the last words of a
sentence. These scoring procedures were shown to produce equivalent results in
previous work (Dreher and Singer, 1981). Verbatim responses as well as responses that preserved the meaning of the last word of a sentence were accepted.
Two judges scored the responses. Few disagreements were found and these were
resolved in conference.

Results and Discussion

A repeated measures analysis of variance was conducted to determine
whether cue type and sentence type interacted in accordance with the predictions
of the instantiation hypothesis and whether direction type, list length, and reading ability would affect the pattern of the cue x sentence interaction. A preliminary analysis had shown that the order in which the two halves of the split-task
condition were presented did not affect performance.

The cue type x sentence type interaction was statistically significant [F
$(2,154) = 62.67$, p. $< .001$]. No other factors or sets of factors were involved in
a statistically significant higher order interaction with the cue x sentence interaction.[1]

Thus, the three variables—direction type, list length, and reading level, examined in the current study—did not affect the pattern of the cue type x sentence
type interaction. But what is the pattern of the interaction and does it support the
instantiation hypothesis? The interaction can be examined in Table 1 which contains the mean proportion of last words recalled. In order to support the instantiation hypothesis the results should show that "particular terms are better cues than
general terms for target sentences but are worse cues for control sentences" (An-

derson et al., 1976, p. 669). Tukey HSD post hoc comparisons indicated support for the first portion of the criterion; particular cues were better than general cues for target sentences (p < .05). However, post hoc comparisons did not support the second part of the criterion; the difference between particular and general cues was not statistically significant for control sentences (p > .05).

Table 1

MEAN PROPORTION OF LAST WORDS RECALLED

| | Type of Sentence | | |
Type of Cue	Exemplar (The shark attacked the swimmer)	Target (The fish attacked the swimmer)	Control (The fish stayed away from the swimmer)
Particular (Shark)	.58	.41	.25
General (Fish)	.20	.30	.29

A comparison of these findings to the previous study (Dreher, 1981) reveals that the results of the post hoc tests are different, but that the *pattern* of the results is the same in both studies. Moreover, that pattern corresponds to the criterion for demonstrating spontaneous instantiation. Replication of a pattern of results is strong evidence for the reliability of an effect. Therefore, the results of Experiment 1 and the previous study, considered together, strongly suggest spontaneous instantiation.

However, to increase confidence in the evidence for spontaneous instantiation, another study was conducted to determine whether the pattern of the results would replicate a third time.

Experiment 2: Method

Subjects. The subjects were 60 fifth graders from the same school as in Experiment 1. None of the subjects had participated in Experiment 1. They were divided into good and poor readers by ordering their total reading scores on the Comprehensive Test of the Basic Skills from high to low and dividing the group in half. The 30 good readers had a mean reading score of 5.6 when tested the preceding spring. The 30 poor readers had a mean reading score of 3.5.

Materials. The materials consisted of target, control, and exemplar sentences, and particular and general cues as described in Experiment 1.

Design and Procedure. Because neither list length nor type of directions affected the results in Experiment 1, subjects in both conditions received the regular list length and the directions to concentrate on meaning as in Group 3. Subjects participated in groups of approximately 15. Otherwise, the design and procedure correspond to the basic paradigm described in Experiment 1.

Results and Discussion

A repeated measures analysis of variance indicated that the cue type and sentence type interaction was statistically significant [F(2,106)=32.49, p < .001] and that reading level did not enter into a higher order interaction with the cue x sentence interaction.[2] Thus, the cue x sentence interaction is the same regardless of reading level.

The pattern of the cue x sentence interaction, shown in Table 2, is exactly the same as in Experiment 1. And as in Experiment 1, Tukey HSD post hoc comparisons indicated that for both exemplar and target sentences, the difference between particular and general cues was statistically significant (p < .05); the difference in the effectiveness of the two types of cues on control sentences was not statistically significant (p > .05).

Table 2

MEAN PROPORTION OF LAST WORDS RECALLED (EXPERIMENT 2)

Type of Cue	Type of Sentence		
	Exemplar	Target	Control
Particular	.47	.29	.14
General	.08	.17	.17

These results replicate those of Experiment 1. Moreover, Experiments 1 and 2 share the identical pattern of results with the Dreher (1981) study. Thus, a consistent pattern has been obtained across three studies. This consistency is strong evidence for the reliability of the findings.

Summary and Conclusion

Although instantiation is held to be integral to the comprehension process (Anderson, 1977; Anderson et al., 1976), the evidence on instantiation in children has been limited to demonstrating that they can instantiate when guided to do so (Anderson et al., 1978; Dreher, 1981). Evidence of *spontaneous* instantiation has been obtained using college students (Anderson et al., 1976; Dreher and Singer, 1981), but no previous evidence has been available to show that children engage in spontaneous instantiation. Since effects demonstrated on college subjects cannot be automatically assumed to occur in children, the research reported here has dealt with children's ability to engage in spontaneous instantiation.

Using fifth and sixth grade children, Experiments 1 and 2 and the Dreher (1981) study all produced the same pattern of results. Moreover, the pattern has also been replicated in work with third graders (Dreher, 1983). Thus, this series of studies demonstrates a replicable pattern of results which is consistent with the hypothesis that spontaneous instantiation occurs in children. Accordingly, evidence now exists that both college students and children engage in spontaneous instantiation. However, there remain questions about how, when (Gumenik, 1977; Sanford, Garrod, and Bell, 1978), and under what conditions (Dreher, 1985; Whitney and Kellas, 1984) instantiation occurs.

REFERENCES

Adams, M.J., and Collins, A. A schema-theoretic view of reading. In R.O. Freedle (Ed.), *New Directions in Discourse Processing*, Vol. 1. Norwood, NJ: Ablex, 1979.

Anderson, R.C., and McGaw, B. On the representation of the meanings of general terms. *Journal of Experimental Psychology*, 101 (1973), 301-306.

Anderson, R.C., and Ortony, A. On putting apples into bottles: A problem of polysemy. *Cognitive Psychology*, 7 (1975), 167-180.

Anderson, R.C., Pichert, J.W., Goetz, E.T., Schallert, D.L., Stevens, K.V., and Trollip, S.R. Instantiation of general terms. *Journal of Verbal Learning and Verbal Behavior*, 15 (1976), 667-679.

Anderson, R.C., Stevens, K.C., Shifrin, Z., and Osborn, J.H. Instantiation of general terms. *Journal of Reading Behavior*, 10 (1978), 149-157.

Barclay, J.R., Bransford, J.D., Franks, J.J., McCarrell, N.S., and Nitsch, K. Comprehension and semantic flexibility. *Journal of Verbal Learning and Verbal Behavior*, 13 (1974) 471-481.

Clark, H.H. The language-as-fixed-effect fallacy: A critique of language statistics in psychological research. *Journal of Verbal Learning and Verbal Behavior*, 12 (1973), 335-359.

Dreher, M.J. The generalizability of the instantiation hypothesis to children. *Reading Research Quarterly*, 17 (1981), 28-42.

Dreher, M.J. Determining the onset of spontaneous instantiation in children. In J.A. Niles and L.A. Harris (Eds.), *Searches for Meaning in Reading/Language Processing and Instruction*, Thirty-Second Yearbook of the National Reading Conference, 1983.

Dreher, M.J., and Singer, H. The validity of the instantiation hypothesis. *Journal of Reading Behavior*, 13 (1981), 223-236.

Dreher, M.J. Cognitive processes underlying instantiation. Paper presented at the International Reading Association Convention, New Orleans, 1985.

Garnham, A. Instantiation of verbs. *Quarterly Journal of Experimental Psychology*, 31 (1979), 207-214.

Gumenik, W.E. The advantage of specific terms over general terms as cues for sentence recall: Instantiation or retrieval? *Memory and Cognition,* 7 (1977), 240-244.

Halff, H.M., Ortony, A., and Anderson, R.C. A context-sensitive representation of word meanings. *Memory and Cognition*, 4 (1976), 378-383.

Hayes-Roth, B., and Thorndyke, P.W. Integration of knowledge from text. *Journal of Verbal Learning and Verbal Behavior*, 18 (1979), 91-108.

Rumelhart, D.E. Schemata: The building blocks of cognition. In R.J. Spiro, B.C. Bruce, and W.F. Brewer (Eds.), *Theoretical Issues in Reading Comprehension*. Hillsdale, NJ: Erlbaum, 1980.

Sanford, A.J., Garrod, S., and Bell, E. Aspects of memory dynamics in text comprehension. In M.M. Gruneberg, P.E. Morris, and R.N. Sykes (Eds.), *Practical Aspects of Memory.* London: Academic Press, 1978.

Whitney, P., and Kellas, G. Processing category terms in context: Instantiation and the structure of semantic categories. *Journal of Experimental Psychology: Learning, Memory, and Cognition*, 10 (1984), 95-103.

Wilson, C.R., and Hammill, C. Inferencing and comprehension in ninth graders reading geography textbooks. *Journal of Reading*, 25 (1982), 424-428.

NOTES

This research was supported by a grant from the General Research Board of the University of Maryland. The computer time for this project was supported by the Computer Science Center of the University of Maryland.

[1]Because controversy exists over the appropriate analysis of data from experiments using language materials (Clark, 1973), a quasi-F analysis was also conducted. As in the regular F test, this analysis indicated that the cue type and sentence type interaction was statistically significant [min F' $(2,13)$ = 21.88, p < .001] and that the cue x sentence interaction was not affected by reading level, list length, or direction type.

[2]A quasi-F analysis also indicated a statistically significant cue type x sentence type interaction [min F' $(2,17)$ = 12.64, p < .001] and no effect of reading level on the cue x sentence interaction.

Scripts in Memory for Text

GORDON H. BOWER
Stanford University

JOHN B. BLACK
University of Illinois at Chicago Circle

TERRENCE J. TURNER
Department of Education, Queensland, Australia

We are interested in how people understand and remember narratives since this seems a promising way to investigate cognitive processes. A persistent problem for theories of narrative comprehension is to specify how people use their knowledge to expand upon what they are reading or hearing. Texts are usually elliptical and abbreviated, suggesting far more than they say explicitly. A conversational postulate to "avoid prolixity and boring redundancy" may force such brevity. To understand a text fully, then, a model of comprehension must have methods for expanding upon an abbreviated text. Further, the model needs an organized knowledge store surrounding the topic of the text, which serves as a base for the elaborations.

Schank and Abelson (1977) proposed their "script theory" as a partial solution to the elaboration problem. They propose that part of our knowledge is organized around hundreds of stereotypic situations with routine activities. Examples are riding a bus, visiting a dentist, placing an operator-assisted telephone call, asking for directions, and so on. Through direct or vicarious experiences, each person acquires hundreds of such cultural stereotypes along with his idiosyncratic variations. Schank and Abelson use the term "script" to refer to the memory structure a person has encoding his general knowledge of a certain situation-action routine. The script theory is a specific elaboration of the frame theory of Minsky (1975).

The parts of a script are illustrated by the restaurant script in Table 1. As with other scripts, the restaurant script has standard roles to be played, standard props or objects, ordinary conditions for entering upon the activity, a standard sequence of scenes or actions wherein one action enables the next, and some

Reprinted from *Cognitive Psychology*, 1979, *11*, 177-220. Used with permission of Academic Press and the authors.

normal results from performing the activity successfully. The information surrounding any one of these roles, props, or actions is assumed to be stored at varying levels of abstraction. For example, the Server Role in the restaurant must be a human, can be a male or female, and is usually dressed "appropriately" (e.g., is not wearing a suit of armor), and so on. The Server Role may be thought of as a list of alternative feature packages, with some features obligatory (e.g., must be alive), some optional (e.g., male or female), and some with weakly bound ranges (e.g., age and style of dress).

A person's scripts are supposedly used in several ways. First, they aid planning and execution of conventional activities. The entering conditions and normal outcomes of scripts are examined during planning: the planner selects from memory a script whose normal result matches the current goal (e.g., satisfy hunger), then tries to bring about the entering conditions so she can perform the script. Second, scripts enable understanding when the person observes or reads about someone performing another instance of a conventional activity. We shall focus on this second use of scripts.

Whenever a text mentions a script header (e.g., "The Restaurant") or a few lines that match parts of the memory script, the reader can "instantiate" the general script by filling in its variables (or "slots") according to the details mentioned. To illustrate, consider this vignette:

> John went to a restaurant.
> He ordered a lasagna.
> Later, he paid and left.

Table 1

THEORETICAL RESTAURANT SCRIPT (ADAPTED FROM SCHANK & ABELSON, 1977)

Name: *Restaurant*

Props:	Tables	*Roles:*	Customer
	Menu		Waiter
	Food		Cook
	Bill		Cashier
	Money		Owner
	Tip		

Entry Conditions:	Customer hungry	*Results:*	Customer has less money
	Customer has money		Owner has more money
			Customer is not hungry

Scene 1: *Entering*
Customer enters restaurant
Customer looks for table
Customer decides where to sit
Customer goes to table
Customer sits down

Scene 2: Ordering
             Customer picks up menu
             Customer looks at menu
             Customer decides on food
             Customer signals waitress
             Waitress comes to table
             Customer orders food
             Waitress goes to cook
             Waitress gives food order to cook
             Cook prepares food

Scene 3: Eating
             Cook gives food to waitress
             Waitress brings food to customer
             Customer eats food

Scene 4: Exiting
             Waitress writes bill
             Waitress goes over to customer
             Waitress gives bill to customer
             Customer gives tip to waitress
             Customer goes to cashier
             Customer gives money to cashier
             Customer leaves restaurant

The first line activates the restaurant script. John instantiates the role of the customer and lasagna is the food ordered. Because the brief text calls for the full script, the reader can elaborate many objects and connections that are implied but not stated. The availability of these connections is suggested by the reader's ability to answer such questions as: Did John eat? What did he eat? Did he talk to a waiter or waitress? Did he receive a bill? What for? Such elaborated connections are frequently useful in understanding later parts of the story. For example, if later in the story John is found to have tomato stains on his shirt or professes not to be hungry, readers can guess how this came about from the restaurant scene.

Our experiments investigate some psychological implications of Schank and Abelson's script theory. Experiments 1 and 2 examine the organization of people's knowledge about stereotyped activities. What actions, roles, and props do people mention and how do they group or cluster these into subscenes? Experiments 3 and 4 ask whether, in remembering a text mentioning a subset of script actions, people tend to remember numerous unmentioned parts of the underlying script. Experiment 5 examines whether in recalling a text people will tend to recall the script actions in their stereotypic order even though the actions are mentioned in another order in the text. Experiment 6 asks whether the reading of earlier actions in a script speeds up the reading and comprehension of later actions in that script. Finally, Experiment 7 examines memory for occasional events, inserted into script-based stories, which interfered with or deviated from the smooth running of the script.

Experiment 1: Script Generation

In this experiment, we collected "free association norms" for common scripts. If subjects did not agree about the essentials of a script, we would doubt the "cultural uniformity" assumption of script theory. However, it is not a foregone conclusion that everyone would describe a continuous action stereotype in the same way, using terms at the same level of specificity. There may not be a culturally uniform level of "basic action" description for scripts, as Rosch, Mervis, Gray, Johnson, and Boyer-Braem (1976) had found for basic object categories. Groups of undergraduates were asked to write scripts about common activities. The exact instructions to them turned out to be critical. If subjects were told to "write a completely common, boring story about a lecture or doctor visit" (which is one description of a script given by Schank and Abelson, 1977), their replies were quite variable. Our subjects in fact tended to write interesting stories about boring lectures or to describe frustrations caused by boring delays in waiting to see a doctor. Therefore, we revised the instructions to emphasize the subject's task of listing the central actions in a cultural stereotype.

Method

Materials. Each student generated events or actions for one situation. The five situations were attending a lecture, visiting a doctor, shopping at a grocery store, eating at a fancy restaurant, and getting up in the morning and getting off to school. Each subject received a blank sheet with appropriate instructions at the top. For example, the instructions for eliciting the lecture script were as follows:

> Write a list of actions describing what people generally do when they go to a lecture in a course. We are interested in the common actions of a routine lecture stereotype. Start the list with arriving at the lecture and end it with leaving after the lecture. Include about 20 actions or events and put them in the order in which they would occur.

Subjects. The subjects were Stanford undergraduates fulfilling a course requirement for their Introductory Psychology class. We handed out different scripts to differing numbers of subjects during one mass testing session with a group of 161 students. The numbers of subjects filling out and turning in the various scripts were as follows: grocery 37, getting up 35, restaurant 33, lecture 32, and doctor 24. The data were edited and tabulated according to frequency of citation of specific events, and their associated roles and props. Paraphrases and synonyms were lumped together.

Results

The issue is whether people agree in the actions they mention. The maximum diversity would be if all subjects generating a particular script mentioned once 20 or so completely unique events. But what is surprising is how much agreement there is in the "basic action" language that people use to describe the activities. This uniformity is reflected in how few of the events were mentioned by only one person. For example, in the restaurant script, of 730 actions mentioned in total (types times tokens), only four were completely unique (given by a single person). Similarly, the ratio of unique mentions to total events was 4/704 for Lecture, 26/814 for Grocery, 26/770 for Getting up, and 36/528 for Doctor (which had the fewest subjects and least chances for overlap). So there is at least someone who agrees with nearly every action that any subject writes for a script.

Furthermore, there is high reliability in the frequency with which particular actions of a script are mentioned. We divided each group in half and correlated the frequencies of mentioning specific actions by the two halves. The Pearson correlations were Restaurant .88, Lecture .81, Grocery .85, Getting up .87, and Doctor .80. Thus, the frequency norms are reliable, at least with a homogeneous group like Stanford undergraduates.

Each subject mentioned a sample of very common actions along with some less common ones, presumably reflecting his experiences and speaking style. Across subjects, there was a continuous gradation in frequency of mention of particular events. We may arbitrarily designate the group's stereotype or script to be those events mentioned by more than some criterion percentage of subjects. Examining the distributions of how many actions were mentioned by varying numbers of respondents, the distributions had similar shapes with a distinct gap near 25% agreement. So we selected 25% mention as a lenient criterion for inclusion of an action in Table 2. Table 2 reports for the five situations each action mentioned by at least one-fourth the respondents. The actions are listed in the serial order in which they are usually mentioned. Two other criteria were selected at natural breaks in the percent-agreement distribution for each situation. The items in italics were more popular, falling above a criterion of 40%-50% mention; actions in capitals were the most popular, having been mentioned by 55%-75% of subjects (varying with scripts).

The 22 to 25 entries for the different scripts appear to capture common experiences in our culture. The actions mentioned the standard characters in the script, the usual "props" and locations for the actions. The fewer actions at the more stringent criteria also seem to be the more central or important ones of the script, with the actions in all capitals being the most important. In recent pilot work, Masling, Barsalou, and Bower collected "importance ratings" for events within scripts. The most frequently mentioned events of Table 2 were also rated as centrally important to the script. Such a high frequency-high importance event seems to correspond to what Schank and Abelson (1977, p. 45) call a "main conceptualization," an event which is essential within its scene in that subordinate actions within that scene depend upon it, often enabling or resulting from it. These main conceptualizations are likely to appear in a summary or synopsis of a script-based text. Furthermore, mention of one of these central events should act as a powerful probe to call up the script from the reader's memory.

Table 2

EMPIRICAL SCRIPT NORMS AT THREE AGREEMENT LEVELS

GOING TO A RESTAURANT	ATTENDING A LECTURE	GETTING UP	GROCERY SHOPPING	VISITING A DOCTOR
Open door	ENTER ROOM	*Wake up*	ENTER STORE	*Enter office*
Enter	*Look for friends*	Turn off alarm	GET CART	CHECK IN WITH RECEPTIONIST
Give reservation name	FIND SEAT	Lie in bed	Take out list	SIT DOWN
Wait to be seated	SIT DOWN	Stretch	Look at list	Wait
Go to table	Settle belongings	GET UP	Go to first aisle	Look at other people
BE SEATED	TAKE OUT NOTEBOOK	Make bed	*Go up and down aisles*	READ MAGAZINE
Order drinks	*Look at other students*	*Go to bathroom*	PICK OUT ITEMS	*Name called*
Put napkins on lap	*Talk*	Use toilet	Compare prices	Follow nurse
LOOK AT MENU	Look at professor	*Take shower*	Put items in cart	*Enter exam room*
Discuss menu	LISTEN TO PROFESSOR	*Wash face*	Get meat	Undress
ORDER MEAL	TAKE NOTES	Shave	Look for items forgotten	*Sit on table*
Talk	CHECK TIME	DRESS	Talk to other shoppers	Talk to nurse
Drink water	Ask questions	Go to kitchen	Go to checkout counters	NURSE TESTS
Eat salad or soup	Change position in seat	Fix breakfast	*Find fastest line*	Wait
Meal arrives	Daydream	EAT BREAKFAST	WAIT IN LINE	Doctor enters
EAT FOOD	Look at other students	BRUSH TEETH	*Put food on belt*	Doctor greets
Finish meal	Take more notes	Read paper	Read magazines	Talk to doctor about problem
Order dessert	*Close notebook*	*Comb hair*	WATCH CASHIER RING UP	Doctor asks questions
Eat dessert	*Gather belongings*	*Get books*	PAY CASHIER	DOCTOR EXAMINES
Ask for bill	Stand up	Look in mirror	*Watch bag boy*	Get dressed
Bill arrives	Talk	Get coat	Cart bags out	Get medicine
PAY BILL	LEAVE	LEAVE HOUSE	Load bags into car	Make another appointment
Leave tip			LEAVE STORE	LEAVE OFFICE
Get coats				
LEAVE				

Items in all capital letters were mentioned by the most subjects, items in italics by fewer subjects, and items in small case letters by the fewest subjects.

Discussion

The script norms in Table 2 are the main outcome of this study. There was considerable agreement in the way subjects described events. For example, people wrote "He ate his soup" rather than "He picked up his soup spoon, dipped it into the cup of soup, lifted it out, blew on it to cool it, raised it to his lips, put the spoon in his mouth...." Presumably people use action-summary terms or basic-level action terms (see Rosch et al., 1976) to describe a continuum of events because they share a conversational postulate which says one ought to speak or write so as to be informative but not overly redundant (Grice, 1975). Because people know how to eat soup, it is ordinarily unnecessary and ill-mannered for a speaker to describe the steps in such detail. Perhaps it is these habits of speaking that lead our subjects into event descriptions at roughly the same basic level. Of course, a script itself is a familiar routine whose recital would normally be redundantly boring and gauche. But the experimental setting and our instructions for the generation task conveyed our interest in the subject's telling us all these normally boring details within a script.

We conceive of a standard activity like eating in a restaurant or visiting a dentist as a fuzzy concept for which there are many characteristic features but few, if any, defining features (see Smith, Rips, and Shoben, 1974; Rosch and Mervis, 1975; Zadah, 1965). Different instances of an activity seem to bear a "family resemblance" to one another, but they may possess no common features. For example, although eating would seem to be a general event of the restaurant script, one can be "in the restaurant script" without eating just as one can eat in many contexts besides the restaurant script (e.g., tasters, food judges). Events or actions are more or less diagnostic of a given activity or script. A diagnostic event or feature is statistically valid in the sense that its presence or absence correlates highly across situations with the presence or absence of the scriptal activity. A given script-instance should be judged as prototypical of the activity to the extent it combines highly valid features. As Rosch and Mervis have shown, the most prototypical exemplar is judged to resemble on average more other instances of the category and to bear less resemblance to instances of alternate categories. These properties of fuzzy concepts seem particularly appropriate to the notion of scripts.

The scripts of Table 2 should be useful for further experimental investigations. We have used them in investigations of memory for scripts and of comprehension of script-based texts. The scripts can be used like high-frequency association norms, much like the Battig and Montague (1969) category norms have been used in studies of word perception, priming, semantic judgments, and memory. As one example, an experiment in progress is checking to see whether a given action can be classified more rapidly as "fitting" a given script header if it is a high associate of the script. Further, one could check whether high-frequency action associates of a script are better recalled but more poorly recognized than low-frequency actions of the script. High-frequency actions, if not mentioned in a text, may later attract many false-positive recognitions because they were implicitly aroused during reading the text.

Experiment 2: Constituent Structure of Scripts

The events within a lengthy ordered script appear to be segmented naturally into several major chunks or constituents. The script is not an undifferentiated, linear chain, but rather seems organized into major scenes, with those composed of subsequences of actions. Thus, eating in a restaurant may have as major scenes entering, ordering, eating, paying, and leaving. But ordering requires being seated, getting and reading a menu, having a waitress come to take your order, and so on. To check our intuitions, we asked subjects if they thought there was a "natural segmentation" of the lower-level action sequences in a script. If they segmented the actions into chunks, we were then interested in whether they agreed on the location of the chunk boundaries.

Method

Ten texts were written by converting all of the actions in 10 underlying scripts into actual story statements. The texts ranged in length from 148 to 254 words. The scripts used were going to a restaurant, getting up in the morning, attending a lecture, going to a birthday party, going swimming, grocery shopping, making coffee, visiting a doctor, attending a movie, and playing football.

Thirty Stanford undergraduates were given a booklet containing the 10 stories, each on a different page. They were told that some people felt that each story had several natural parts; they were to read the stories, decide whether a story had some parts and, if so, identify these parts by placing a slash line in the texts marking the end of each part. They were given no hint as to how many slashes (chunk boundaries) to place in each text, if any.

Results

The main issue is whether people agree in their chunking judgments. That is, are there locations in the stories where most people put slashes to indicate a part boundary, and other locations where very few people put slashes? We first divided the story into script action statements, since subjects only placed slashes at such clause boundaries. We tabulated the frequency of slashes (chunk boundaries) at each site. Table 3 displays these slash frequencies in brackets after each clause for two of the ten texts.

To measure the agreement of the location of slashes, we divided the group in half and correlated their slash frequencies at the clause boundaries for the several story locations. The Pearson correlations for the different scripts were as follows: getting up .98, coffee .94, lecture .99, doctor .99, birthday .96, swimming .95, movie .98, football .98, shopping .96, and restaurant .98. Next, we per-

Table 3
THE CHUNK JUDGMENTS OF EXPERIMENT 2

The Doctor

Diane was feeling very bad today, [0] so she decided to go see the family doctor. [7] Therefore she had her husband take her to the doctor's office. [17]/ When she arrived at the doctor's office [1] she went into the waiting room. [1] Once inside she walked over and checked in with the receptionist [0] and then sat down to wait her turn. [4] As she waited she read some old medical magazines that were on the table [0] and looked at the colorful medical posters that adorned the wall [17]./ Finally the nurse came in and called her name, [0] so she went into the examination room with the nurse. [7] The nurse closed the door and asked her to take off her clothes. [0] The nurse then weighed her and took her blood pressure. [0] When these preliminaries were completed the nurse left [7] and a short while later the doctor came in. [5] The doctor was very nice to her, so she calmed down a little bit. [15] / As the doctor started to make various examinations of her [3] she wondered what he was doing [0] and what he was finding. [5] Finally he looked directly at her and told her that she had the flu and could expect to be laid up in bed for a few days. [0] Then he wrote a prescription for some pills [0] and left [22]./ She got dressed [0] and made another appointment with the receptionist [0] on her way out of the doctor's office.

The Restaurant

David noticed that his stomach was emitting hunger pains, [1] so he decided to go out to a restaurant to eat. [6] Therefore he drove to the local French restaurant. [19] / He arrived at the restaurant a little before the dinner rush hour, [1] so as he entered the restaurant [0] he noticed that there were plenty of empty tables. [0] He decided to sit at a window table, [5] so he went over [0] and sat down. [20] / A waitress came up [0] and gave him a menu. [1] He carefully perused the menu [0] and decided what he wanted. [4] The waitress came back [0] and he gave her his order. [13] / After a short wait [0] during which he nibbled on bread and butter [1], his dinner arrived. [13] / He proceeded to eat the dinner with gusto. [2] The food here was really excellent [0] and not too expensive either. [16] / Finally he finished [0] and asked the waitress for the check. [9] He left the waitress a tip on the table [0] and went over to the cashier. [2] He paid the cashier [1] and went home quite satisfied.

The numbers in brackets indicate the number of subjects (out of 30) who marked those actions as boundaries between parts of the story. Slashes mark the major constituent boundary locations (i.e., those marked by 10 or more people).

formed chi-square tests to determine whether the distributions of slashes differed from a uniform distribution. The chi-squares for all scripts were significant, with all p's $<$ .001.

We considered how to describe the group's agreement on number and location of chunk boundaries. We examined the number and location of story constituents selected by varying numbers of people. All 10 of the scripts yielded a roughly bimodal distribution: there were a few sites between action clauses where most of the subjects placed slashes (e.g., 18 to 20 subjects); then there were many locations where few subjects placed slashes (e.g., 3, 4, 5, and 6 subjects); finally, there were very few sites selected by a moderate number of subjects (e.g., 10 to 12). In 9 of the 10 scripts, the one-third percentage (10 subjects) fell in a natural gap in the slash distribution, so we selected one-third as the cutoff point. By this criterion the 10 scripts each have three to five constituent boundaries. Slashes locate these major constituent boundaries in the texts of Table 3.

One guide to determining the constituents of a sentence is that "a constituent is a group of words that can be replaced by a single word without change in function and without doing violence to the rest of the sentence" (Clark and Clark, 1977, p. 48). We find that we can substitute summary-actions for our empirically derived constituents in scripts. For example, in the Doctor story given in Table 3, we can replace the first constituent by "Diane went to the doctor's office," the second by "She waited," the third by "She went through the preliminaries," the fourth by "The doctor examined her," and the fifth by "She left the doctor's office." Note that if we try to move any boundary to encompass adjacent text actions, the one-action summaries no longer fit. The other script boundaries show similar properties, so our empirically derived script boundaries fit the summary criterion of a constituent.

Discussion

Clearly, our subjects agreed with our intuitions that a continuous script activity can be segmented into chunks or scenes. And they agreed with one another where the scene boundaries were located in the event sequence. Thus, the script is not a linear chain of actions at one level but rather a hierarchically organized "tree" of events with several levels of subordinate actions. That activities are decomposable into a hierarchy of subactions is a recurrent theme in cognitive psychology (e.g., see Bower, 1975; Goodman, 1970; Miller, Galanter, and Pribram, 1960; Pew, 1974).

Actions may be identified with their intended goals or subgoals. From this perspective, the activity hierarchy is really a goal tree, wherein a top goal is decomposed into a series of subgoals. Thus, the top goal of eating in a restaurant script can be decomposed into the subgoals of getting inside a restaurant, sitting down and ordering, eating the food received, paying the bill, and leaving. In turn, the subgoal of ordering the food can be decomposed into events of getting a menu, reading it, getting the waiter to your table and telling him what food you want. The relevance of such goal hierarchies is that they are frequently useful for answering questions about specific actions or events (see e.g., Schank and Yale A.I. Project, Note 4; Winston, 1977, p. 301 ff.). The following strategies often work:

> Why questions (e.g., why did you speak to the waiter?) often can be answered by moving one level up from the queried action in the hierarchy and stating that goal (e.g., "Because I was ordering"). Repeated Why's may force the respondent to the top of the tree, where sits the script-entry reason (i.e., I ate to reduce hunger; and I did that to stay alive).

> How questions can often be answered by moving one level down in the hierarchy from the queried action, and listing its subordinate actions. Thus, "How did you order?" can be answered by "I translated the French menu,

called over the waiter, and pointed to what I wanted." If the queried action has no subordinates in the tree, an acceptable answer is "I just did it" (as in answer to "How did you swallow your food?").

When questions (e.g., when did you read the menu?) can be answered by referring either to the goal-activity one level up and using *while* ("While I was ordering"); or by referring to preceding and succeeding actions at the same level. Thus, we can reply, "I read the menu just *after* the waiter left it on my table, and *before* I gave him my order."

Besides helping answer questions, the action hierarchy can be used by the person generating summaries of script-based texts. Any sequence of subordinate actions within a given chunk can be summarized by the superordinate action (Rumelhart, 1977; Schank and Yale A.I. Project, Note 4). Thus, "John read the menu, decided on his selection, and told the waiter what he wanted to eat" can be summarized as "John ordered."

Given this information about chunk structures in scripts, several psychological experiments would seem called for. Our own efforts along this line have been limited to date. One pilot study is that mentioned earlier by Masling, Barsalou, and Bower which had subjects rating the importance of various scenes to the goal of the script. The most important scenes within a text should be those most likely to survive in memory over a retention interval. Another pilot study of ours investigated the number of false alarms that occurred in recognition memory for unstated actions within a chunk for which either one or two other actions of that chunk were stated in a text the subject read. Contrary to expectation, the number of false alarms was lower to an unstated action when two actions within that chunk were also stated than when only one of those actions was stated. Other studies using the chunk-boundary norms could examine all-or-none recall of chunks, probe latency for recall of the "next successor" by a within-chunk vs. a prior-chunk action (see Ammon, 1968), and the process of purging or clearing out of short-term memory as a sequence of script-action sentences passes over a chunk boundary (see Jarvella, 1970, 1971). Clearly more research on the topic is needed.

Experiment 3: Script Recall

Next we investigate recall of texts composed of selected lines from an underlying script.[1] The question was whether in recalling such a text subjects will use the underlying script to fill in gaps of intervening actions not explicitly mentioned in the text. We might expect some such intrusions in recall since they correspond to the familiar phenomenon of changing the wording of a story when we retell it "in our own words."

The script idea gives us a way to think about paraphrases of a story. If a sequence of actions calls up an underlying script from memory which is then filled out according to the particulars of the text, then the "same story" can sometimes be retold by mentioning a different selection of its actions. If a b c d e f g represent the underlying script events and Text 1 comprises sentences instantiating a c e g, then Text 2 comprised of congruent instantiations of b d f could be judged to be an acceptable paraphrase of Text 1, despite having no events in common. Such a possibility is a consequence of conceiving of script instances as only bearing a family resemblance to one another. Similarity of two texts will probably be a systematic function of the amount and importance of their overlapping as opposed to their distinguishing features. It is an empirical matter to explore in detail which parts of a script-based text can be replaced or altered without changing the intuition that the second text is a paraphrase of (or closely similar to) the first. The importance of similar paraphrases for studies of memory is that we can expect the person's memory to be confused between two paraphrases of the same script, sometimes substituting or intruding in recall actions that were implied but not stated in the text.

We may expect subjects to remember for some minutes the events explicitly stated in the text. But as their "surface memory" of the text fades, they should intrude more assertions into recall which represent implications and which in theory were used to fill in the gaps between the script actions read originally. A model for this might suppose that after reading the person has both a veridical memory for the actually read statements (in "episodic memory") and an activated and completely filled out underlying script. In immediate recall, the person merely reproduces his veridical memory. But this memory fades over time and he relies then upon the fully completed script, which leads to unstated script actions being intruded into recall.

We were also interested in a second phenomenon which, if found, may prove harder to explain. We wondered whether we could increase the subject's belief that an unstated action had occurred in a script-based text by having him read *related* script stories in which the analogous or parallel actions were explicitly mentioned. The kind of parallel stories used are illustrated in Table 4, one for John visiting a doctor, the other for Bill visiting a dentist. These are different instances of an abstract script for visiting a health professional.

The actions enclosed by parentheses in Table 4 were not included in the texts read by the subjects, but are part of the Health Professional script. Notice that some of the actions left out in the Doctor text have their parallel actions explicitly stated in the Dentist text, and vice versa. For example, the Dentist text mentions nothing about Bill checking in with a receptionist, whereas the Doctor text mentions that John checked in with the Doctor's receptionist. We predicted that in a memory test people would tend to recall gap-filling events left out of a script story, and they would tend to do this more if they also read other instantiations of this script which did mention the analogous actions. The experiment below tests this specific prediction, that recall intrusions of gap-fillers will increase if other instances of the same script are also read.

Table 4
SAMPLE TEXTS USED FOR EXPERIMENTS 3 AND 4

The Doctor	*The Dentist*
Entry: John was feeling bad today.	Entry: Bill had a toothache.
1. John decided to go see the doctor.	1. (Bill decided to go see the dentist.)
2. (John arrived at the doctor's office.)	2. Bill arrived at the dentist's office.
3. (John entered the doctor's office.)	3. (Bill entered the dentist's office.)
4. John checked in with the doctor's receptionist.	4. (Bill checked in with the dentist's receptionist.)
• • •	• • •
7. John looked at some medical magazines.	7. (Bill read some dental magazines.)
• • •	• • •
12. (The nurse checked John's blood pressure and weight.)	12. The dental hygienist x-rayed Bill's teeth.
• • •	• • •

Sentences in parentheses were presented only during the recognition test in Experiment 4.

Method

Materials. There were nine basic scripts each with about 20 actions (and thus similar to the 25% cutoff level in Experiment 1). Each script was chosen to have at least three distinctive versions (e.g., the Health Professional script had the Doctor, Dentist, and Chiropractor versions). Hence the materials were a total of 27 specific script versions, so it was impractical to collect and analyze script norms to serve as a basis for all these materials (one would need around 30 subjects per action list for 27 action lists). Therefore these scripts were created by one of the experimenters (JB) and a colleague. We individually composed a list of common actions for each generic script, then compared our versions and reached a compromise prototype. Three stories were then written based on each script; each story was about eight lines long and represented a different instance of the script. Hence, the story pool contained nine clusters of three stories per cluster: attending a symphony, play, or movie; visiting a doctor, dentist, or chiropractor; playing a game of football, baseball, or golf; going swimming, skin diving, or surfing; getting ready in the morning to go to school, church, or work; attending a class lecture, sermon, or speech; shopping for bread, a coat, or a toaster; going to a birthday party, New Year's Eve party, or Halloween party; and making coffee, tea, or hot chocolate. Each subject read one story each for three of the nine scripts, two stories each for another three scripts (i.e., six stories), and three stories each for the other three scripts (i.e., nine stories). Hence, each subject read a total of 18 stories, presented in random order. Which story fell into which category was balanced across subjects. Each story was also given a title (e.g., The Doctor, Football, etc.).

To clarify complex relations among instantiations, the three texts for Visiting a Health Professional are given here.

The Doctor
John was feeling bad today so he decided to go see the family doctor. He checked in with the doctor's receptionist, and then looked through several medical magazines that were on the table by his chair. Finally the nurse came and asked him to take off his clothes. The doctor was very nice to him. He eventually prescribed some pills for John. Then John left the doctor's office and headed home.

The Dentist
Bill had a bad toothache. It seemed like forever before he finally arrived at the dentist's office. Bill looked around at the various dental posters on the wall. Finally the dental hygienist checked and x-rayed his teeth. He wondered what the dentist was doing. The dentist said that Bill had a lot of cavities. As soon as he'd made another appointment, he left the dentist's office.

The Chiropractor
Harry woke up with a bad pain in his back again. He decided to go see a chiropractor that very day. He had to wait a long time. Finally the chiropractic assistant finished and left him, and the chiropractor himself came in. The chiropractor carefully examined Harry by feeling all the bones in his back. Eventually Harry left the chiropractor's office.

Note, the stories are about seven or eight lines long, and they share only the common entering and leaving conditions. The middle six or so actions of each story were selected without replacement from the 20 actions comprising the master Health-Professional script. A third of the subjects would read all three of these texts scattered through the study phase; a third read a randomly selected two of them; and a third read a randomly selected one of them. The same routine was followed with each of the nine master scripts.

Procedure. The subjects were run in groups of two to eight. As a warmup, subjects first read for 10 min a coherent narrative that was completely unrelated to the material of this experiment. They were then given reading instructions, given their story booklet for the present experiment, and had 10 min to read and study it. This study time was sufficient for all subjects to read through their 18 stories. After reading, the subjects performed an intervening task for 20 min. This task involved their recalling in writing the narrative that they had read at the beginning of the session. After that they were instructed regarding recall of the 18 scripts of this experiment. The script titles were read as cues, and subjects wrote their recall of each corresponding text on a new sheet of paper. They were given 1 min to recall each of the eight-line stories. They were asked to be accurate and to reproduce each text verbatim insofar as possible, but they were to recall the gist of an event if they could not remember it verbatim.

Subjects. The subjects were 18 students at California State University at Sacramento who participated to fulfill a service requirement for their Introductory Psychology course.

Results

The recalls were scored for the presence or absence of the underlying script actions. We had no trouble deciding to which script action a given sentence in recall referred. We classified the actions in each person's recall into stated script actions, unstated script actions, and other actions that did not fit these two categories. The numbers of recalled actions filling into these three categories are displayed in Table 5. The rows of the table correspond to the conditions of one, two, or three story instances of a script.

Table 5
AVERAGE NUMBERS OF ACTIONS RECALLED PER SCRIPT VERSION IN EXPERIMENT 3

		Number of stated script actions	Number of unstated script actions	Other actions	Total actions recalled	Percent of total that are unstated script actions
Number of	1	3.03	0.80	0.39	4.22	19
script	2	2.27	1.26	0.35	3.88	31
versions	3	2.56	1.16	0.36	4.08	28

Before listing statistical tests, let us recognize the current controversy over whether investigators using language materials should use fixed or mixed effect analysis of variance (ANOVA) models to test hypotheses (Clark, 1973; Clark, Cohen, Smith, and Keppel, 1976; Wike and Church, 1976). In our case, the question is whether to treat the scripts as a random sample of all scripts and thus as a random effect in the ANOVA model, or to limit the conclusions to these 18 scripts and thus treat them as a fixed effect in the ANOVA model. We report statistical tests for both models. Happily, only rarely in this paper does the test influence the pattern of significances, and we will note whenever it does.

A first feature of the data in Table 5 is that stated script actions are recalled more than unstated script actions, which in turn are more frequent than other actions. These pairwise comparisons are statistically significant at .01 for the three- and two-instance rows, and at .05 for the one-instance row. Stated actions exceed unstated ones significantly, considering the differing materials exemplifying a condition as either a fixed or random effect (using an F test for a fixed effect ANOVA model or a quasi-F, F', test for a random effect ANOVA model). So, while we may conclude that unstated script actions appear in recall in appreciable amounts, subjects nonetheless display considerable "surface memory," at least at a 20 min retention interval, since they are producing two to three times more stated than unstated actions. The data in Table 5 are raw frequencies. To convert them to percentage of script actions given, one must divide the left hand entries by the number of stated actions (8) and the middle entries by the number of unstated actions (arbitrarily 12 here, though indeterminate in reality). Thus, the proportionate reproduction of stated versus unstated actions is even more pronounced than the raw frequency results.

Next consider the influence of having read two or three script instances upon intrusion of unstated script actions (the "gap fillers" in Table 4). Since recall levels varied somewhat across conditions, we expressed the intrusions of unstated script actions as a percentage of the total recall, and entered this in the last column of Table 5. Clearly, the percentage of unstated script intrusions increase when other story instances of the same script are present. Comparing the percentages of gap-fillers to all actions recalled, scripts with two story versions have many more than do scripts with one story version $[F(1, 18) = 10.68, p < .01]$; similarly, three story versions lead to more gap-fillers than does one story version. However, three and two do not differ in intrusion rate.

So, we may conclude that having another version of the same script mention an action increases the probability that the unmentioned analogous action is intruded in recalling a related story. We reserve theoretical discussion of this priming effect until after the results of Experiment 4 are presented. Unfortunately, the priming effect does not increase steadily as the number of script versions is increased. We have no explanation for this leveling off.

Considering recalls of the stories having one, two, and three instances of the underlying script, it is clear that they do not differ in the number of "other actions" recalled nor in the total recall. However, the conditions differ in recall of stated actions with the one-instance stories being higher. This effect is significant considering materials as a fixed effect $[F(2, 30) = 4.42, p < .05]$, but not when materials are considered as a random effect $(p > .05)$.

If reliable, the lower recall of stated actions with multi-instance texts suggests several interpretations. First, because multi-instance texts create more intrusions, there are more opportunities for "output interference," whereby output of an intrusion causes forgetting of a not-yet-recalled stated action (see Roediger, 1974). Second, if people normally avoid reporting redundantly close (and therefore uninformative) actions from a script, then the increased intrusions of implied actions in the multi-instance conditions would cause increased editing out and nonrecall of nearby stated actions.

Finally, examination of the "other actions" category in recall reveals that 40% of them are superordinate actions or terms summarizing lower-level script actions. For example, if the text said, "She took out the coffee pot, filled it with water, put it on the stove,..." a summarizing "other" statement would be, "She heated some water." Such summarizing statements are expected, considering the underlying script as a hierarchical tree with the summarizing terms referring to nodes at the higher levels of the tree.

An unexpected result is that the proportion of superordinate actions among the "other actions recalled" category is over twice as great (62.5%) for the recall of the one-instance stories as for the averaged recall of the two- and three-instance stories (28.3%). This effect is statistically reliable [$F(1, 5) = 19, p <$ .01]. However, we have no explanation for this curiosity.

Experiment 4: Script Recognition

The recalls in Experiment 3 showed the effect of interest, namely, a fairly high intrusion rate of unstated actions from the underlying script. Moreover, this intrusion rate when recalling a story could be raised by presenting the counterpart actions in a parallel story that is a different version of the same underlying script. Our next experiment aimed to demonstrate these effects more clearly using recognition memory. In the recognition test, the subjects saw a test sentence from the underlying script and assessed how well it matched anything within the specific subset of sentences stored in memory from when they had read the text. To the extent that studying a sentence describing an action activates associated actions in the underlying script, those associated actions will later appear to have been read. This prediction arises because, during testing, the person allegedly only knows the level of activation in memory corresponding to the test proposition, but is confused about the source of this activation, whether it is due to an explicit or implicit presentation. This failure to discriminate the source of activation is one supposed cause of false-positive recognition judgments.

Method

Materials. The learning materials were the same titled script stories used in Experiment 3. The presentation of the stories and the counterbalancing of materials across experimental conditions were the same as before.

Procedure. Subjects first read two unrelated, 600-word stories for 5 min. These stories were unrelated in content to the scripts of this experiment. Subjects then read the 18 script stories of this experiment, each with a title. They had 5 min to read these stories. They then spent 30 min writing recalls of the first two stories. Finally they were given the recognition test over the 18 script stories. The recognition test contained 16 test statements for each of the nine generic scripts (or 9 X 16 = 144 in total). These were blocked by story title. For each generic script the recognition test contained eight stated script actions, four unstated script actions, and four other actions that were false though not implausible. Typical false items mispaired actors and actions, or locations and actions, from the stories studied. When two or three story versions of the same generic script were used, the 16 recognition items were chosen evenly from the two or three stories. The subjects rated each test statement on a 7-point scale, with 1 denoting "Very sure I did not read this sentence," and 7, "Very sure I did read it."

Subjects. The subjects were 45 Stanford University students who were ful-filling an Introductory Psychology course requirement. They were tested in groups of two to eight.

Results

The primary results are the average recognition ratings for the various item types. These are shown in Table 6 for stories in the one, two, and three script version conditions. A high number indicates that the subjects believed the state-ment had been in the texts read a half hour earlier.

In general, ratings are highest for stated actions, intermediate for unstated script fillers, and lowest for novel false statements. These pair-wise comparisons are statistically significant at .01 within each row of Table 6; they are significant considering learning materials as either a fixed or random effect.

Table 6
AVERAGE RECOGNITION RATINGS PER TEST ITEM IN EXPERIMENT 4[a]

		Stated script actions (S)	Unstated script actions (U)	Other actions (O)	Ratio (R)
Number of	1	5.46	3.91	1.71	54.6
script versions	2	5.40	4.62	1.76	66.3
	3	5.59	4.81	1.86	68.6

[a] 7 means "Sure Old" and 1 means "Sure New."

Comparing conditions with varying numbers of instances, recognition rat-ings for stated items are equivalent. So the recognition accuracy measure does not uphold the small difference between one versus two or three versions found earlier with the recall measure. There is a slight difference in ratings of False items which is significant treating learning materials as a fixed effect [F (2, 84) = 5.33, $p < .01$] but not as a random effect [F' (2, 28) = 1.29, $p > .10$].

The most salient difference between the different instance conditions occurs with unstated script fillers. As predicted, false-positive recognition ratings for an unstated script filler increase as more instances are put into memory. The differ-ences in ratings on unstated script fillers for one, two, or three instances are highly significant; fixed effect ANOVA yields [F (2, 84) = 31.3, $p < .001$]; random-effect ANOVA yields [F' (2, 17) = 5.35, $p < .05$]. Individual compari-sons show that conditions one and two differ, and one and three differ by both F and F' tests. However, although two and three differ at the .05 level by a fixed-effect F test, they are not significant by a random-effect F'.

The ratio score in the last column of Table 6 scales ratings of script fillers relative to the hit rate on Stated actions and the false-positive rate on Falses. The ratio score is 100 (U-F)/(S-F), where S, U, and F stand for Stated trues, Unstated script fillers, and False items, respectively. The ratio scores differ reliably, mainly because the one-instance ratio is below the other two. The two- and three-instance conditions do not differ reliably in this ratio measure.

After the data were collected, we noticed that our test items for unstated script actions for two or three script instances were actually of three types. The types are illustrated by the example fillers in Table 4. One type of action confusion is shown in Lines 1, 2, 4, and 7 of Table 4; it involves mixing up, say, John's arriving in the Doctor's office with Bill's arriving at the Dentist's office. False alarms to such gap fillers would reveal the person mixing up actions, objects, and actors in a simple manner. Line 3 of Table 4 illustrates the second type of action confusion. These items are script actions that were not stated in any of the story versions read. The third type of action confusion is shown in Line 12 of Table 4; here the similarity of the sentences in the two stories stems from their exemplifying the same role or function in the abstract script. For example, the abstract health-professional script has an action in which an assistant performs some preliminary procedures on the patient. An instantiation of this role for the Doctor script is, "The nurse checked John's blood pressure and weight"; for the Dentist story an instantiation is, "The dental hygienist checked and x-rayed Bill's teeth." Clearly, taking John's temperature has little direct similarity to x-raying Bill's teeth. Rather, they are similar by virtue of the roles they play in the abstract script.

We wondered whether the effect of number of instances in increasing false alarming to gap fillers held true for all three types of recognition items. There were many more items of the first type than of the second and third; furthermore, the counterbalancing of story versions into the one-, two-, and three-instance conditions caused a marked loss of observations on any specific abstract inference. Putting aside these problems, however, we computed the average recognition ratings for the second and third types of unstated script actions mentioned above, for the one-instance condition versus the combined two- and three-instance conditions. For the direct inferences not stated in any text (second type above), the ratings for one versus two and three instances were 3.49 and 4.75, respectively (one versus two [$F(1, 28) = 28.06, p < .01$]; one versus three [$F(1, 28) = 18.15, p < .01$]; two versus three is not significant). For the abstract inferences (third type), the ratings for one versus two and three instances were 2.73 and 4.73, respectively (one versus two [$F(1, 28) = 7.84, p < .01$]; one versus three [$F(1, 28) = 12.11, p < .01$]; two versus three is not significant). There is a clear effect of other text instances on these two classes of confusion errors. The effect is as large as that obtained for simple actor-action mix-ups which comprise the majority of cases in the composite averages in Table 6. The fact that the third type of inference yields an equal-sized effect is remarkable since the basis for the similarity of two action-statements in this case is not their meaning per se, but rather the abstract role they fulfill in the two scripts. In closing, we would repeat that the comparison of the effect of number of instances for the three inference types is not balanced across materials, and we would be more confident if we had designed our experiment for this comparison. However, the current results suggest optimism that a properly balanced experiment would replicate the effects found here.

Discussion

Two major results of Experiments 3 and 4 require explanation. The first is that subjects intrude in recall and falsely recognize actions that are in the underlying scripts but were not stated in the texts. The second result is that these intrusions and false alarms increase if the subjects read more than one text that instances the same script. We will now contrast two models of memory for script-based texts and note whether they can account for these results. The models describe the way a script-based text interacts with a generic script in memory to create an episodic memory trace of the text. We will first discuss the representation of generic scripts and of episodic instances of them.

Figure 1 schematizes the knowledge structure for the "Visit Health Professional" script. At the top level, the script has a Name (or Header), a list of Roles, Props, Entry Conditions, and Actions. The Roles would be Patient, Receptionist, Professional Person, and Professional's Assistant. The Props would be an Office, Waiting Room, Magazines, Examination Room, etc. The Entry Conditions would be state descriptions such as "Patient feels bad." The Actions would be verb-based conceptualizations like "Patient arrives at office," "Patient checks in with receptionist," etc., or some representation even more abstract than these conceptualizations, such as the primitive actions suggested by Schank and Abelson (1977). The entries for the Roles, Props, Entry Conditions, and Actions in Figure 1 are enclosed in angle brackets to indicate that they are lists of constraints on whatever fills the role rather than actual instantiations of the variables.

As a person reads a script-based text that fits this Health Professional script, we assume that she sets up a new episodic memory structure to encode that particular story. We will contrast two different models of what the episodic memory contains, the Full Copy and the Partial Copy models. To illustrate the contrast, suppose the person reads a script-based text that begins as follows:

> John was feeling ill. He arrived at Doctor Smith's office. As he waited, he read a *Family Health* magazine. Then he went into an examination room where a nurse checked his blood pressure and weight....

In the Full Copy model, the reading of this text allegedly causes the person to set up an episodic memory structure which is a fully instantiated version of the complete script up to and including the point of the last script statement in the text. Thus, from the sample text, the script-applying mechanism knows how several "variables" of the abstract script in Figure 1 are to be "bound" or specified. Thus, the Patient (R1) is set equal to John; the Health Professional (R4) is set equal to "Doctor Smith"; and the Assistant (R3) is set equal to "Nurse." The Receptionist (R2) is not specified but will be filled with the prototypical value (e.g., a young

```
        Generic Visit Health Professional Script in the Knowledge Store

        Name = Visit Health Professional

                 ⎧ R1 = < Health Professional >
                 ⎪ R2 = < Receptionist >
        Roles =  ⎨ R3 = < Health Professional's Assistant >
                 ⎪ R4 = < Health Professional >
                 ⎩

                 ⎧ P1 = < Office >
                 ⎪ P2 = < Waiting Room >
        Props =  ⎨ P3 = < Chair >
                 ⎪ P4 = < Magazines >
                 ⎩
                          ⋮

                 ⎧ C1 = < Patient feel bad >
        Entry =  ⎨ C2 = < Patient have Money >
                 ⎩

                 ⎧ A1 = < Patient decide to go see Health Professional >
                 ⎪ A2 = < Patient arrive at office >
        Actions = ⎨ A3 = < Patient check in with Receptionist >
                 ⎪          ⋮
                 ⎪ A23 = < Patient leave office >
                 ⎩
```

Figure 1. Generic visit health professional script in the knowledge store.

woman in a white uniform). The actions of the script are then filled in as fully as possible according to these bound variables or according to their prototypical values. If a script action is explicitly mentioned in the text, then that action instantiates an action variable. If the action is not mentioned, then an appropriate default value or prototypical action congruent with explicit bindings is entered. This process is shown in part by Figure 2 where we have noted the text sentences plus a few surrounding script actions. (This figure omits the role and prop variables for simplicity.) To the right of each statement is a tag or marker, which is **(two asterisks) if that script line was in the text and which is * (one asterisk) if it was not in the text but was derived by filling in the corresponding generic action with the prototype congruent with the bound role and prop variables of this particular text. The asterisk count is the sole discriminative trace regarding which script lines were stated in the text versus which lines were derived.

A nice feature of the Full Copy model is that it can readily answer questions about script-based inferences from the stated text. If we suppose that the occurrence markers fade with time, then the person will eventually be unable to discriminate whether a script-based statement was or was not stated in the text. This explains the false-positive recognition results that we found.

```
Name = Visit Doctor

Prototype = Visit Health Professional

Entry =    C1 = John feeling bad                              **
           C2 = John has money                                *

           A1 =  John decided to visit Dr. Smith             *
           A2 =  John arrived at Dr. Smith's office          **
           A3 = John checked in with Receptionist
             .              .
             .              .
             .              .
           A7 =  John read "Family Health"                   **
Actions    A8 =  John went to Dr.'s exam room                *
             .              .
             .              .
             .              .
           A12 =  Nurse checked blook pressure and
                     weight of John                          **
           A13 =  Dr. Smith came into exam room              *
                     with John
             .              .
             .              .
             .              .
```

Figure 2. Full copy model episodic memory.

What about the influence on the "John at Doctor" memory of other texts such as "Bill visiting the Dentist"? According to the Full Copy theory, the "Bill visiting Dentist" text would cause another instantiation of the Health Professional script to be fully copied into episodic memory, comparable to the episodic structure in Figure 2. The new structure would have different variable bindings (e.g., "R4 = Dentist" rather than "Doctor Smith"). Unfortunately, within the Full Copy model, we have found no natural or parsimonious mechanism for creating confusions between memories of two script instances: they exist in distinct episodic compartments and do not interact. Consequently, the Full Copy model has no way to explain our second result, that other text instances of a script increase memory confusions about a given text.

A more adequate model is the Partial Copy model schematized in Figure 3. In this case, the reading of a script-based text sets up an episodic memory that leaves traces at two locations. First, the specific propositions of the texts are recorded into episodic memory structures, shown as boxes to the right in Figure 3. The unstated script actions are not instantiated at this time. Second, the abstract action corresponding to a text statement is marked in the knowledge store (to the left in Figure 3) as having been accessed and used during understanding of a text. This activation is indicated in Figure 3 by two asterisks attached to the memory node representing the abstract action. On the other hand, unstated actions of the script will be weakly activated (one asterisk) because they are part of the overall Health Professional script which has been aroused and is activating all its subordinate actions. This "top-down" activation from the script name (or header) to its subordinate actions corresponds to unconscious expectations regarding what conceptualizations the language understander is likely to encounter as the script-based text is read. In any event, stated actions are distinguished in memory from unstated script actions because (1) a copy of the stated action is in the episodic trace, and (2) the level of activation is higher on the abstract action node corresponding to a stated action.

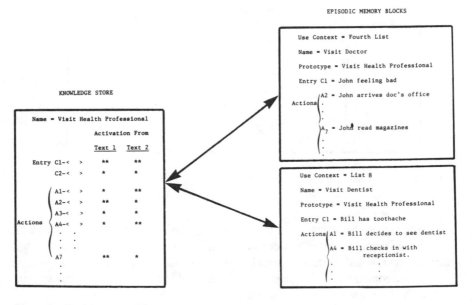

Figure 3.   Partial copy model.

In such a theory, the person would be able to answer questions about the plausible truth of unstated but implied events by deriving the answer at the time of the question using the generic script and instantiating it according to the variable bindings in the episodic memory for the text. Such derived answers would take longer than directly stored answers, a result found by Reder (Note 1) and Kintsch (1974), among others. However, this difference in reaction time could be predicted by the Full Copy model if actions filled in by implication are at a weaker strength than stated actions. Therefore, the major distinguishing feature of the two models is that the Full Copy model has no simple way to account for some interfering "cross-talk" between different instantiations of the same abstract script.

In the Partial Copy model, forgetting occurs in two ways. First, the propositions represented in the episodic trace are simply "erased" or "fade away," the loss of any one propositional trace occurring in an all-or-none manner with a fixed small probability in each unit of time. This process leads to exponential decay (or spottiness) over time of the propositional traces in the text's memory block. Second, and independently of loss of the episodic propositions, the activation on the superordinate action node in the abstract script also decays over time. The effect of the first decay process is that over time the subject will forget exactly what was stated in the script-based text, though he may be able to derive approximately what was stated from the difference in activation levels on the script-action nodes. The effect of both decay processes is to cause the person eventually to forget everything about the text he read.

In the Partial Copy theory, recognition memory is a three-stage process which is diagrammed in Figure 4. First, the memory scanner searches the appropriate episodic memory block (one of the episodic boxes in Figure 3), where it checks the test sentence for a match to the memories of the stated propositions remaining in this episodic memory block (which may be spotty from decay). If a match occurs here, then a fast, confident recognition judgment ("Yes, Old") ensues.[2] If no match occurs here, the scanner then goes up to the superordinate script-action corresponding to the test statement. If no superordinate script action corresponds to the probe, then the decision maker issues a confident "Did not read before" judgment. If a superordinate match does occur, then the scanner checks the level of activation on this node (the total number of asterisks on that line in Figure 3). If the activation here is high, that means that an instantiation of this abstract expression recently occurred in some context. Therefore, it is plausible that the text probe in fact corresponds to an action stated earlier but now forgotten. On these grounds, the decision process is likely to "accept" or "recognize" the test statement. On the other hand, if the activation on the superordinate node is low, then the test sentence should be rejected, judged to have been "not stated" in the text. The judgments given by the third stage are less confident than the judgments from the first two stages. This decision model resembles that of Atkinson and Juola (1973) except ours has more stages and its episodic and semantic memories are assumed to be searched in different orders. Hopefully, there will be simplifying special cases of this complex decision model.

Let us now examine how this Partial Copy model deals with our results on memory for several instantiations of the same abstract script. Figure 3 shows an episodic memory block for the "Bill visiting Dentist" text, as well as the block for the "John visiting Doctor" text. The stated propositions of two texts are recorded separately with the Prototype variable referring each instance back to the general script in the knowledge store. Note, however, each action in the Dentist text causes activation (asterisks) to accumulate at the superordinate script level in Figure 3. We suppose this activation on an action node summates regardless of its source. This accumulation of activation occurs not only for abstract actions stated in the second instance text but also, by spreading activation, for actions not

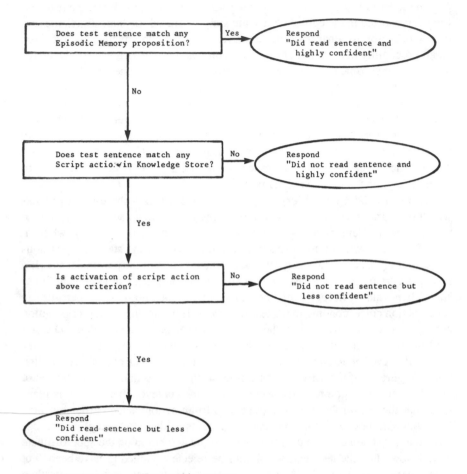

Figure 4. Partial copy model's recognition process.

stated in either instance of the text. (These correspond to the several types of script inferences distinguished in the Results section.) It is this accumulated activation on the superordinate action node which, according to this theory, causes the increase in false-positive responses to unstated actions as the number of related texts increases. An unstated test sentence will fail to match in the topical episodic store, will then be referred to the corresponding superordinate action, and the activation on that node is likely to be above the "acceptance" criterion if one of the other texts had recently instantiated this action. At this point, the decision maker knows only the level, not the source, of activation on the generic action node, so false-positive recognitions may occur. These later-stage responses would be expected to come out more slowly and with less confidence than early-stage responses. This model predicts our result that unstated inferences receive lower recognition ratings than do tests on stated propositions.

The Partial Copy model seems to provide a reasonable account of the salient features of our results. It also makes further predictions about verification latencies that seem consistent with existing data. We will, therefore, tentatively maintain the Partial Copy model. It is regrettably complex. But the data to be accounted for seem to warrant some complexities.

Experiment 5: Script Action Reordering

Some scripts have strongly ordered actions, whereas others have none. The scripts used in the previous experiments (the Restaurant, the Doctor, etc.) are temporally ordered and most actions either cause or set up the preconditions for ("enable") the next action to occur.

The memory script that represents ordered actions must record this order in some manner. If this structure is used to record any text mentioning these actions anew, the process would be biased towards storing this listing in the canonical order of the script. But suppose the person must remember an arbitrarily reordered version of the Restaurant or Doctor scripts. That should prove difficult because the canonical order in memory should serve as a source of negative transfer and proactive interference against learning and recall of the reordered version. Further, the interference during recall should be in a specific direction. In trying to remember, the person should rearrange the misordered actions of the arbitrary text so that they are reproduced closer to their canonical order in the underlying script.

This ordering prediction for scripts is a special case of the general idea that stock narrative schemata have ordered constituents. Thus, the general story schema may have an ordering like Setting, Initiating Event, Establishing Goal, Plan, Attempts, Consequence, and Resolution. Experiments have suggested that after reading misordered stories, readers are likely to remember them in their natural schematic order (see Kintsch, Mandel, and Kazminsky, 1977; Mandler, 1978; Stein and Glenn, 1978).

For comparison to learning of shuffled ordered scripts, we had subjects also learning arbitrary orders for what are naturally unordered scripts. An "unordered script" is a known set of actions or events for which there is no canonical order (in a particular subculture) – or if there is, the subject does not know it. For example, for most of us, the order of events passing in review in a Veteran's Day parade is haphazard; all such parades have bands, children on bikes, dogs, policemen on horses, ladies auxiliary marchers, and so on, but to our knowledge there is no conventional order. The same is true for the scheduling of circus performers in the main ring at a circus. Since these events have no canonical order, the learning of any arbitrary order for them should be equally difficult, and there is no predictable direction for the misordering errors. Therefore, comparing memory for an arbitrary sequence of an unordered script versus an ordered script, the best recall for order (or serial position) should be for actions from ordered scripts whose position in the arbitrary sequence correspond to their position in the canonical script. Intermediate serial-position recall should occur for any actions from unordered scripts. Least accurate serial-position recall should occur for actions from ordered scripts whose position in the arbitrary sequence differs from their position in the canonical script.

A first experimental attempt to create this effect produced negative results. We scrambled all 12 actions in ordered scripts, had subjects study them, and then reconstruct their serial order from memory. Their reconstructions were almost random, with none of the predicted drift toward the canonical order. The subjects told us what was wrong with this procedure, namely, they remembered that the script actions were "all mixed up" in the to-be-learned orders, so if they forgot the presented random order, they still tried to reconstruct an order which preserved the "all mixed up" property.

We avoided this task strategy in the experiment reported by presenting the scripts predominantly in their canonical order but with a few events rather far out of order. The hope was that if subjects forgot the order, they could still use the fact that the listed actions were predominantly in their canonical order to guide their reconstruction. This reconstructive guide would help rather than hinder the directional errors of interest.

Method

Subjects. The subjects were 12 Stanford undergraduates participating to fulfill a service requirement for their Introductory Psychology class. They were tested in groups of 4, 3, 3, 1, and 1, sitting around a large table. The experiment took about 45 min.

Materials. We composed five ordered scripts and five unordered scripts, each 12 sentences long. The ordered scripts were Birthday Party, Shopping for a Coat, Playing Football, Going to a Movie, and Attending a Lecture. The unordered scripts were Cleaning House, Shopping at the Supermarket, Veteran's Day Parade, Main Ring at the Circus, and Mechanic's Check-Up on Car. The Cleaning House and Birthday Party scripts were used alternately as primacy and recency buffers in the memory task, and data from them were discarded by plan. Each ordered script was paired with an unordered mate and the two scripts were yoked together in the sense of appearing close together in all input schedules. Also, an out-of-order action in the ordered script was compared in reconstruction to its yoked action presented in the same position in the unordered script.

The subjects read the 12 ordered actions in each of the 10 lists, then later tried to reconstruct all their orders. Setting aside the two lists assigned as primacy and recency buffers, the input position of the eight middle lists was counterbalanced over subjects by using four different input sequences. Thus, any given list (e.g., circus) appeared in Positions 2 or 3, 4 or 5, 6 or 7, and 8 or 9 for three subjects at each position.

The position of the 12 actions within the ordered scripts was assigned by the following procedure. From the canonical order four actions were selected at random for each script to be interchanged in their positions (the other eight remained fixed in their normal positions). A Latin Square was used to produce four orders of these selected four actions: one was the normal order and the other three became unique misorderings. Each of the three misordered versions was used with four different subjects. The summed number of steps required to move all of the four interchanged actions within a story back to their canonical positions averaged 13.5. The to-be-learned order of the unordered scripts was determined by random numbers; only one order was learned by all subjects.

The 12 action statements were typed on 12 3 X 5 inch cards and a title card was placed at the front of the deck. The experimenter arranged the cards in each deck in the order to be learned by the subject using that deck.

Procedure. Subjects were seated and instructed that they were to study 10 ordered lists of 12 actions per list, each typed on a deck of cards with a title at the front. They were told to remember the specific order in which the cards were arranged, so that they would be able to reconstruct that order exactly when they were given the scrambled deck of cards during later testing.

Ten decks of cards were then placed before each subject in the sequence he was to study them. They were in four colors to help him keep his place as he moved from one deck to another. The subject looked at the title card at the front of a given deck for 5 sec, then turned over the cards within that deck, one at a time, studying each statement for 5 sec paced by the experimenter tapping on the table using a stopwatch. Memory for the order of the statements was emphasized.

After all 10 lists had been studied, the experimenter thoroughly shuffled each deck of 12 action statements while instructing the subject on the serial reconstruction task. The subject was to take the shuffled cards of a deck, lay the 13 cards (12 plus a title) on the table before her, rearrange the cards into the serial order she believed she had studied (guessing when necessary), and finally record on a protocol sheet her reconstructed order using random numbers on the back of the cards for identifying them. The 10 lists were reconstructed in the same sequence as they had been studied. Testing took about 30 min.

In the statistical analysis, subjects and the four scripts within each condition served as random effects, whereas the type of script (ordered or unordered) and the sequence of presentation were fixed effects. We scored each sentence on the basis of its absolute position in the reconstructed order, comparing this to its position in the studied list and, if possible, to its canonical position in the underlying script.

Results

Comparing the probabilities that items are remembered in the same absolute position as their presentation, the predicted pattern emerges. Within ordered scripts, actions presented in their canonical location were remembered 50% at exactly that location, actions presented away from their canonical location were remembered only 18% at the presented location. For comparison, actions of the unordered (control) scripts were remembered 30% of the time at their presented position. For statistical analysis, the unordered script actions were divided into one set of four yoked to the four misordered actions in the ordered scripts and the remaining set of eight. We tested the interaction of ordered versus unordered scripts with correctly located versus mislocated actions. As the percentages above indicate, this interaction was highly significant [$F(1, 7) = 19.3, p < .005$]. That is, in ordered scripts, misordered actions were recalled less accurately than their yoked actions (in unordered scripts), but ordered actions were recalled more accurately than their yoked actions.

Next, we examined whether misordered actions of ordered scripts drifted back towards their canonical position during reconstruction. Each reconstructed item was given a score indicating the number of steps (serial positions) it had moved from its presented position in the direction toward its canonical location. (Movements in the opposite direction received negative signs.) The summed displacements of the four misordered items towards their canonical positions averaged 6.44 steps (out of 13.5 possible), whereas the comparable sum for the unordered control items was 0.92 steps. These differ reliably [$F'(1, 5) = 8.74, p < .05$]. Thus, the misordered items move about 48% of the distance towards their normal location in the underlying script.

We may conclude that the canonical order of a memory script helps people learn the order of any new textual instantiation which preserves the canonical order but hinders them if the new instantiation has misorderings. The script order in memory acts as a source of proactive interference or as a source for guessing when the presented order has been forgotten.

Texts that relate events out of their natural order, as we have done here, are not uncommon in literature. A storyteller is not constrained to preserve natural order in his narrative rendering. Some styles of storytelling, such as sports reporting (football, baseball), even have a standard misordering; one first tells the final score of the game, then recounts the significant events (e.g., big plays, penalties) in order of their importance, then perhaps recites the temporal succession of scoring plays. Thus, in telling some stories, we sometimes describe events in a manner other than reciting their temporal order, much as was done in the present study.

Experiment 6: Script Expectations and Comprehension Time

We have assumed that when an abstract script is aroused, it activates the memory nodes representing the script actions. Each such memory node is similar to a logogen (see Morton, 1969) which accepts and accumulates activation ("evidence") from prior context and from present sensory input. Activation of the overall script brings the activation level of script actions close to the firing threshold. Hence, relatively little sensory evidence directed to an action node is required in order for it to be perceived. Also, expected stimulus patterns should be identified rapidly because their logogens have been brought near firing threshold by the context alone.

The script-to-subactions activation just mentioned is a mechanism for creating generalized expectations; that is, the person expects other script actions to occur. A more refined proposal hypothesizes more specific activation local to an action node that has just been instantiated (i.e., read in the text). Specifically, this hypothesizes that the local activation caused by reading a given script action spreads to neighboring script actions in a forward direction, causing them in particular to be expected. We will call this the Local Spread hypothesis.

One method for testing this hypothesis compares the time a person takes to comprehend a sentence that is expected to one that is not. The method relies on the assumption that a sentence is perceived and understood more readily if it is expected (e.g., Haviland and Clark, 1974). The Local Spread hypothesis implies that a script line in a text should be read and comprehended more quickly if it is preceded in the text by a statement referring to an action that just precedes it in the underlying script. The text statement just preceding the target statement will be called the "priming statement" or "prime" for the target. The Local Spread hypothesis predicts that target comprehension time should be shorter the closer in the underlying script is the preceding action given as a prime and the greater the number of preceding primes.

This hypothesis and derivation was first thought of by Abelson and Reder, and they performed experiments (unpublished; Note 1) to investigate it. One experiment was inconclusive and the other gave mainly negative evidence against the Local Spread hypothesis.

We were unaware of these experiments when we planned and conducted the experiment below, looking for a distance effect. Our procedure differed from that of Abelson and Reder, and was somewhat more successful in getting the subject "farther into the scripts" before the target probe occurred.

Method

Materials. The script versions used were 18 from Experiments 3 and 4, which were three instances of six different abstract scripts, each text being eight statements long. Within each text the fourth and the seventh statements served as critical test sites. These were edited to be 12 words long. The construction of the texts and the test sites relative to the underlying script are illustrated in Figure 5. Every three subjects were tested with a different selection of statements (version) from each script, comprising the columns of Figure 5. The plus marks in the columns indicate the statements presented, always in the first-to-last script order. The symbols A_1 through A_{12} represent events of a hypothetical underlying script. The selected test sites in this instance are the sixth and eleventh elements of the underlying scripts. For different text versions the critical test sites are immediately preceded by a statement which, in the alleged underlying script, was either one, two, or three steps back ("distance"). Within a list, the priming distance at the second test site was different than that at the first site. Across the 18 lists for a given subject, the first and second sites were preceded six times each by priming sentences one, two, or three steps back. The last test site was never the last line of the text or the script.

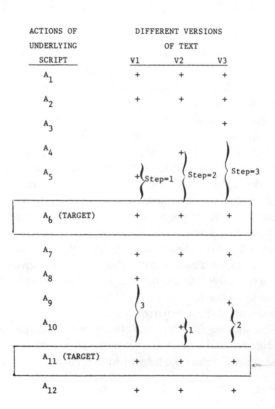

Figure 5. Schema for materials used in experiment 5.

After composing these texts we used the chunk (scene) norms of Experiment 2, to score whether the priming and target actions were within the same chunk, or were one or two chunks apart. The average chunk distances for Steps 1, 2, and 3 were 0.50, 0.50, and 1.08, respectively. Thus, chunk distance increases monotonically along with number of actions between prime and target statements.

Procedure. The texts were presented one line at a time on a 9.5 X 7 inch cathode ray tube (Hazeltine Model 1) connected to a Nova 820 laboratory computer. The subject pressed a button as soon as she read and understood each sentence. The button press removed the sentence and 1 sec later the next sentence was displayed. Comprehension time was defined as the time from the display of a sentence to the button press removing it. Subjects were unaware that their reading time per sentence was being recorded. To provide a reason for reading the sentences, subjects were told we were interested in how people make up titles to characterize stories. Our subjects thus made up an interesting title for each text as it was read. They wrote down their title when a message signaled the end of the text. This procedure enforced a delay of 15 to 30 sec between scripts. After writing their title, to start the next text, subjects pressed the button which displayed a warning asterisk and 1 sec later the first sentence appeared. Subjects read the texts combined with the step sizes of the primes in one of 18 different orders over the experiment, with three subjects per order.

Subjects. The subjects were 54 Stanford University undergraduates, half fulfilling an Introductory Psychology requirement and half recruited for pay. They were run in groups of one to three at separate computer terminals. Each subject sat at a table with her CRT screen about 18 inches away.

Results

The primary result is that a Step 1 prime produced faster comprehension of the target sentence than did Step 2 and Step 3 primes. The reaction times in msec are 2600 for Step 1, 2730 for Step 2, and 2681 for Step 3. The difference in the means is statistically significant [F (2, 106) = 3.43, $p <$ .05]. (Materials were nested within subjects by design so that F is the correct test here even with materials as a random effect.) There is a significant difference between Step 1 and Step 2 [F (1, 53) = 5.93, $p <$ .05]; but not between Step 3 and the other two. Inspection shows the distance effect to be small and nonmonotonic. We will return to discussing this later.

The other significant effect in the experiment is that comprehension time is slower for the later (seventh line) location (2818 msec) than for the early (fourth line) location (2424). This is highly significant [F (2, 53) = 51.39, $p <$ .001]; however, the location effect does not interact with the priming distance effect reported above. Although the target sentences in these two locations had been equated for number of words, we noted that they unfortunately differed in the number of syllables per sentence. In fact, when the reading time per syllable is calculated, the location effect reverses, with the first location having a comprehension time of 170 msec per syllable and the second location 152 msec per syllable [F (1, 53) = 16.71, $p <$ .001]. If syllables rather than words are the proper units for reading, this faster comprehension of the second location provides some support for the accumulation of activation across script lines.

The results show facilitation of reading at only the immediately adjacent action, without a graded effect of distance in the underlying script. While there is doubtless general activation of the whole script as individual events are read, the extra "local spread" of activation from the just-read action appears extremely local. The absence of a graded effect cannot be explained by appeal to a "chunk-distance" measure since that increases monotonically with our measure of number of intervening actions.

Discussion

Our failure to find a graded distance effect can be interpreted in several ways. One view suggests that the failure can be laid to uncontrolled variations in literary style or conversational fittingness of the texts with increasing prime-to-target distances. Some gaps are simply too large to bridge meaningfully; others convey the wrong impression of what is going on; others sound stilted or silly. Although we tried to avoid such stylistic blemishes in our materials, we cannot guarantee that style effects were inconsequential relative to the distance effects of interest.

An alternative interpretation is that there is no graded distance effect. After hearing an action, the reader expects its immediate successor more than others, but his within-script expectations are not further differentiated than that. Apparently, the latest version of the SAM program for applying scripts to texts (see Cullingford, Note 2; Schank and Yale A.I. Project, Note 4) has a predictive mechanism that operates in just this way.

A third view of the results is to suppose that a script is such a complex web of interconnected parts that the representation of temporal distance between actions bears little relationship to the node distance between them in the network. For example, scripts often have some causal or contingent connections which bridge large temporal gaps between early events and much later events. Thus, the size of a tip the customer leaves depends upon the quality of service he received much earlier in the restaurant script; what specifically the dentist does to you depends on your specific reason for visiting him. Further, two temporally distant actions may be close in node distance because they involve the same props and actors, whereas temporally close events may be farther apart in node space in that they refer to different roles, props, and within-script locations. Taking this view of scripts, then, it is misguided to expect local spread of activation to be indexed simply by temporal distance between two events.

Experiment 7: Remembering Deviations from Scripts

Although we are investigating script-based texts, we should remember that a script does not make an interesting story; in fact, it is miserably dull, containing all the predictable details of an activity. Script recital violates a conversational postulate that enjoins speakers and writers to be informative and not overly redundant. People read such boring texts only to assuage some psychology experimenter.

While actions within a script may be referred to in real stories, they serve only as a background or context within which something more interesting happens in the foreground. Thus, we may recite a restaurant script to note that while waiting for our food, a man at the next table had an epileptic seizure; or we note that when the soup arrived it had a fly in it, etc. Let us call these "interruptions" in the predictable flow of the normal script. The next experiment asks how well people remember such interruptions in comparison to the script actions.

Schank and Abelson (1977) noted several types of script interruptions called *obstacles*, *errors*, and *distractions*. In obstacles, some enabling condition for an imminent action is missing (e.g., You can't read the French menu), so some corrective action is taken (e.g., ask the waiter to translate for you). In errors, a script action leads to an unexpected or inappropriate outcome. For example, you order a hamburger, but the waitress brings a hot dog. The standard corrective action is to repeat the action: order the hamburger again. Distractions are unexpected events or states which set up new goals for the actor, taking him temporarily or permanently outside the script. For example, the waiter may spill soup on the customer, initiating a visit to the restroom for cleaning up.

Our intuition is that such interruptions will be remembered better than the routine script actions because they will appear subjectively more important and so will occasion more attention or deeper processing. The interruption is an unpredicted event, and so a script-based "von Restorf" effect (i.e., better memory for the surprising event) could be predicted. Further, from the viewpoint of the reader, the interruption seems to be the only "point" of the story.

Besides interruptions, other extraneous statements can occur in script-based texts. These include irrelevant statements about attributes of the props or characters of the script, or the thoughts and feelings of the character which have no essential place in the causal flow of events. An irrelevancy would seem to be something that can occur in parallel with essential actions without impeding the flow of events. Thus, while looking at the menu, the central character may notice the print type, or notice the waitress' red hair, etc. Since such irrelevancies neither aid nor block the goal-directed actions of a script, we would normally expect them to be remembered very poorly. Now, there surely are some irrelevancies that refer to events or properties which, if they were experienced, would have a vivid impact, and would be well remembered (e.g., "The waitress was stark naked"). The experiment below sidesteps this issue by having the irrelevancies as well as the script interruptions be relatively pallid and routine.

To summarize, then, we predict that interruptions will be remembered better than script actions and that irrelevancies will be remembered less than either.

Method

Materials. Six script-based stories were written about making coffee, attending a lecture, getting up in the morning, attending a movie, visiting a doctor, and dining at a restaurant. The texts were 22 to 26 sentences long. Setting aside the first few and last few sentences, the remainder of each text was divided into three groups of five to seven actions (avoiding divisions within a chunk). In each group we inserted one irrelevant remark and one interruption. Across the three groups within a text, there were one obstacle, one error, and one distraction. Across scripts, the six possible orders of the three interruption-types occurred once each. Thus, each text contained one each of an obstacle, error, and distraction, three irrelevancies; and about 20 relevant script sections. Each story was titled, and all six were stapled into a booklet.

Procedure. The subjects read the booklet of six stories for 5 min total, with only general comprehension instructions. They engaged in an intervening task for about 10 min as part of another study that involved rating the comprehensibility of unrelated sentences. After the rating task, subjects were asked to recall the stories in writing as close to verbatim as possible. They were cued with each story title and given as much time as needed (maximum of 5 min per story).

Subjects. The subjects were 24 Stanford undergraduates either fulfilling an Introductory Psychology requirement or receiving payment. They were run in groups of two to eight.

Results

The recall protocols were scored for presence of each text proposition (basically, clauses). The average percentages recalled were: interruptions 53%, script actions 38%, and irrelevancies 32%. The interruptions are recalled reliably more than are the script actions, with fixed effect $[F(1, 21) = 55.26]$ and mixed effect $[F'(1, 12) = 21.30$, both p's $< .001]$. The script actions are recalled somewhat better than the irrelevancies [with fixed $F(1, 21) = 6.36, p < .05$ but mixed F' $(1, 8) = 1.64, p > .10]$. The results are as predicted; interruptions were remembered best as though they were the point of the story, and irrelevancies were remembered poorest.

Calculating the percentages recalled of the three types of interruptions, obstacles were highest (60%), then the distractions (56%), with the errors recalled least (42%). Obstacles and distractions do not differ reliably but both are significantly higher than recall of the errors when materials are considered as a fixed effect $[F(1, 21)$ for obstacles is $15.11, p < .001$, and for distractions is $5.86, p < .05]$. However, the differences are not significant when different scripts are considered as a random effect [obstacles $F'(1, 10) = 4.83, p > .05$; and distractions $F'(1, 13) = 2.69, p > .10]$. Consequently, we are uncertain whether the recall profile of types of interruptions will generalize across variations in learning materials. Although the interruptions as a whole are recalled better than the script actions as noted above, the recall of the errors does not differ reliably from the recall of the script actions $[F(1, 21) = 1.56, p > .10]$.

Discussion

Recall of interruption types was ordered in the way we expected, with obstacles and distractions being remembered better than errors. In our texts, the errors were "minor": simply incorrect outcomes of events. Obstacles, on the other hand, involved real blocks to the progress of the script; the obstacle stopped the flow of events and had to be dealt with. Distractions were interesting incidents that suspended the script's goal, and temporarily replaced it with a more pressing goal for the character.

We can speculate about how such interruptions would be recorded in the episodic memory trace of the script-based text. The main trace would be the appropriate "Partial Copy" of the underlying script (see Figure 3) with the variables bound as specified by the text. An error is an outcome with an unexpected value inserted into a standard slot in the script. It is as though a prediction of an outcome (a "slot filler") has to be replaced by a different object or value. An obstacle, and the corrective actions it causes, would also be recorded in the episodic script memory, at the script location where it occurred to frustrate a subgoal. A distraction, on the other hand, could be recorded on a separate "goal chart" (see Schank and Abelson, 1977, Chapter 5), with its actions and outcome together with a pointer to the location in the episodic script where the distraction occurred. The timing of most distractions is not linked causally to any specific point in the script (e.g., the person at the next table could have a seizure at any time). Therefore, we might expect subjects to remember the location of distractions within a script-based text more poorly than they would the location of obstacles or errors. A pilot experiment found no tendency for memory to err by mislocating distractions nearer to (rather than farther from) a scene boundary.

General Discussion

We may view our results from two perspectives. The first considers them as empirical investigations of a previously unexplored domain of semantic knowledge; the second assesses their articulation with the general script theory of Schank and Abelson (1977).

From the empirical perspective, we have explored the properties of scripts considered as concepts about routine activities. Just as concepts like *birds* or *weapons* have culturally agreed upon attributes and instances, so do activities like *eating in a restaurant* or *visiting a doctor*. These activities have conventional roles, props, event sequences, standard entering conditions, and standard outcomes. Not only did our subjects largely agree on what these are but also on how to segment the event sequences into constituent scenes or chunks. We found that in remembering script-based texts, subjects confused what was said with what the script strongly implied. Further, subjects preferred to learn event sequences that preserved the scriptal order. In remembering a script-based text, subjects were best at recalling brief obstacles or distractions which blocked or temporarily suspended pursuit of the script goal, whereas properties or events irrelevant to that goal were least recalled. Such results serve as an opening into empirical explorations of the organization and use of script knowledge in text understanding and recall.

From the theoretical perspective, our results are generally consistent with current script theory (see Cullingford, Note 2; Schank and Abelson, 1977).

Some results are not specifically addressed by script theory (e.g., how different instantiations of a script interfere with one another in memory, or how people remember texts with out-of-order actions). Further, our results do not address many problems of language processing which script theory was proposed to solve. The theoretical writings and computer simulation programs (see Cullingford, Note 2) mainly concern the way scripts act as a predictive context for processing single sentences, for tying together sequences of sentences, and for answering questions about a text (see Lehnert, 1977). For example, for understanding single sentences, an active script will suggest the relevant meanings of ambiguous words, will help establish referents of terms, will merge referents, will fill in unspecified roles, and will predict likely conceptualizations to follow. The psychological counterparts of such processes probably occur in real-time as sentences are comprehended, and variations in factors affecting them (e.g., the ease of establishing referents) could affect comprehension time. However, except for Experiment 6 which examined within-script gradients of expectancy, we have not investigated how scripts influence comprehension in real-time.

Our results also do not address the extensive theorizing concerning goals and plans that underlays the script concept (see Meehan, Note 3; Schank and Abelson, 1977). Goal issues arise quickly in answering *why* questions about human actors (e.g., "Why did he leave the restaurant before he'd eaten?"). It is not obvious how the methods of experimental psychology can provide much relevant information on such issues beyond that provided by intuition and common sense. In any event, we have not tried to do so here. Because we have not examined issues of real-time comprehension or of goal-based question answering, our results make contact with only a small part of script theory.

Unresolved Issues About Scripts

Although our results have advanced the case for scripts and we find many attractive features of script theory, we would be remiss not to balance the picture by pointing out a few of the unresolved issues or critical questions about script theory. These represent conceptual puzzles that are on the research agenda.

A first question requiring some answer concerns how to elicit script knowledge. In Experiment 1, we instructed people in detail how to tell us about the major events of a routine activity and we obtained reasonable results; but the results surely will vary with the way instructions are phrased. Rather than recall, our subjects could have been asked to identify or recognize script-relevant actions from a large pool presented to them. There is little guarantee that all methods will yield the same conclusions. A problem is that recall or report methods can give only script knowledge that is accessible to conscious introspection. But just as a fish fails to report that he is surrounded by water, so do people surely have much tacit, nonintrospectible knowledge about stereotyped procedures and activities that they do not or cannot report (see Goffman, 1959, for details of unconscious social conventions). For example, traditional Japanese rarely think to mention that one takes off his shoes before entering a Japanese restaurant, though that feature immediately strikes a Westerner as unusual. Similarly, our Restaurant script does not mention when it is proper to sit at a table with a stranger, or how close the waiter stands while taking your order. In reciting a script, people assume and do not report tacit conventions regarding physical layouts and interpersonal commerce, even though such conventions are clearly exhibited when they enact the script.

This latter split between enacting versus verbalizing a script raises the more general question of how we are to decide whether someone is behaving according to a script and, if so, which script it is. Clearly, someone can go through the motions of a script enactment without having the knowledge that customarily underlays its performance. Thus, an uneducated person will appear to follow eating protocol at a formal state dinner by imitating those around him, or by following instructions from his dining companion. He is using immediately available cues or rules rather than memories of prior performance or prior rules as his guide. But the cues that control behavior are rarely conspicuous, so we will frequently err in inferring whether someone is following a memory script. Furthermore, we are prone to similar errors in deciding which of several scripts someone is following. Errors are introduced by the loose relation between intentions and actions. The source of errors can be illustrated by considering cases of deceit, con games, bluffs, and sham put-ons. In competitive situations, which many stories describe, a character may present an appearance or "front" of following one script (designed to mislead his adversary), whereas he is actually following another plan which will give him an advantage. Thus, in football, the quarterback fakes a line plunge before passing, hoping that the defenders will react to the apparent intention and leave themselves open for the pass. Such common examples show the difficulty of identifying which script someone is following from their surface behavior.

A second question about scripts concerns the level of detail that is recorded with each script, and how much of this is called forth when the script is instantiated. For example, in the Restaurant script, what kind of general and specific information is stored about the Service Person? Some features are mandatory (must be a living person), some are optional (male or female), some have a range of permissible values with a prototypical value (e.g., with 25-45 years), and others have a range without a clear prototype (e.g., hair color). Is all this information stored with the script and brought forth when it is instantiated? Possibly not. Rather, the script may only refer to an empty waiter or waitress role, which then points to a mental "dictionary" or lexicon which holds context-free information about these concepts and their prototypes. In instantiating the script, the features of the prototype will be "loosely bound" in the sense that the text can readily replace a guessed value.

A problem with separating the script from the lexicon is that we often want the two sources to interact and exchange expectations. For example, if at lunch we discover our Server is a (nude) topless waitress, we want inferences from that to propagate back to selection of a specific track (type) for the Restaurant script, namely, that we are in a Go-Go bar. Similarly, a fast-food restaurant and a haute cuisine French restaurant have different Server prototypes. It would seem, therefore, that each track of a script must have an associated file of prototypical values.

Schank and Abelson (1977) introduce the idea of a *track* to refer to a distinct subclass of script situations. For example, for the eating script, one has a track for eating various types of meals and snacks at McDonalds, at school, at a coffeehouse, a picnic, a hiking camp, a church benefit, an Algerian casbah, on a train or airplane, and so on, to the limits of his experience. Mention of each situation evokes memories which specify contextually appropriate prototypes for various roles, props, and events. But, one may ask, if episodic memories about track experiences provide this information, of what value is the general Restaurant script? Presumably, the general script identifies the cluster of common or frequent features of the tracks it subsumes (e.g., there is an exchange of money for prepared food). By virtue of these clusters, to say that one ate in a restaurant is to set up many common expectations in the listener.

A third problem for script or frame theories is to account for how special or novel contexts propagate throughout the script to modify the appropriate details. For example, if we watch theater actors in a play pretend to eat in a restaurant, or if a child enacts with dolls what goes on in a restaurant, how does the context of that pretend world get passed along to modify this instantiation of the real-world script? We do not expect the pretend food to be hot, or the money to be real, or there to be a real kitchen off stage, etc. The issue is to account theoretically for the way a context like "theater world" or "toy world" selectively cancels certain aspects of the script but not others. The issue is similar to how we know what properties to ascribe to a fake duck or a dollhouse.

A fourth problem for script theory (or any schema theory) is to decide at what level of abstraction the memory script is to be used and modified. For example, suppose you read a text about visiting a specific cardiologist. How are we to understand and record that text in memory? Is that an instance of the script called "visiting a cardiologist," or a doctor, or any health professional, or any professional, or any person, or the script called "going to Place X and talking to Person Y"? The concepts are all connected in a hierarchy, and properties true of an activity described at one level are also true of subordinate scripts in the subset tree. But when a text calls up a script from the reader's memory to begin instantiating its slots, at what level is that script?

A defensible answer is that successive clues from the text are sorted through a discrimination net to retrieve the most detailed script available in memory to encode the current text or situation. A problem with such a system is that according to schema theory, the understander must commit himself to some initial schema in order to understand sentences; yet the most diagnostic information may not appear in the text until later. That is, one can be misled down "garden path" stories. When gross errors of predictions are encountered, the system must be able to discard the currently active schema, substitute another, and then try to retrieve earlier inputs and reinterpret them in terms of the newly suggested schema. Thus, what started out as an "eat-in restaurant" script may turn into an "attend political fund-raiser banquet" or a "deliver food to restaurant" script. Any strongly predictive ("top-down") understander system, such as script theory, must have ways to modify a current script, to reject and replace it when it becomes inappropriate.

An alternative view of the comprehension process is that the reader progressively builds up a model or image of the situation the text is about; he conjectures an initial ill-defined model from the initial sentences, then uses successive lines of the text either to fill in the empty slots of that model or to revise it dynamically (e.g., see Feldman, 1975; Collins, Brown, and Larkin, 1978). In such a dynamic process, the important connections would not be specifiable in advance; the appropriate model for a text would be arrived at by successive revisions, by refinements according to constraints of the text, by applying problem-solving methods rather than by selecting a preformed template from a storeroom of static scripts. This dynamic modeling approach would claim that each situation is somewhat unique, with novel combinations of features and happenings, and that it is unlikely that a limited file of scripts would "cover" or subsume many particular instances. The script-file could appear to cover many instances only by ignoring their special or deviant features, or by endlessly amending or specializing the general script to describe the unique cases (see the "weird list" of Schank and Abelson, 1977, p. 166). Perhaps it would have been more efficient to combine information from several different scripts to describe the cases directly. But then, why bother to have static scripts to do this rather than just a network of concepts?

A fifth problem for script theory is to specify an induction algorithm by which new scripts can be learned from experience. If new situations can only be understood as instances of preformed scripts (perhaps with some deviations), how then can any new script be learned? The theory now seems to encompass *specialization* as a way to learn, as when we learn the McDonald's track as a special case of the general restaurant script. In turn, the restaurant script could be learned as a special instrument to enable the basic action of eating. Similarly, attending concerts, lectures, museums, and movies would be specialized instruments to the basic action of attending to (perceiving) something (see the semantically primitive acts enumerated by Schank, 1975, p. 40ff). This view suggests that many scripts will be clustered around the primitive action they enable. Thus, the restaurant, bar, and kitchen scripts cluster around ingestion; the bus, train, airplane, and bicycle scripts cluster around physically moving oneself, and so on. The elaboration of a given primitive action (say, eating) would seem to develop by specialization and by noting recurrent patterns of features (see, e.g., the concept learner of Hunt, Marin, and Stone, 1966). The result would be a tree or discrimination net in memory, with branches encoding different locations and styles of eating (the "tracks" of Schank and Abelson, 1977). The details of growing such a net have not been worked out.

Related to the issues of abstraction and learning, a sixth issue for script or frame theory is deciding where a new fact is to be stored and which scripts are to have access to it (see Anderson, 1976, p. 446). Suppose while at a lecture, I learn that the use of saccharin sweeteners can be harmful to my health, I gain nothing by simply recording that fact in my "Lecture" script. I must record it in such a manner to make it accessible to my "Bar" script to avoid drinking Thin-tonic, to my "Coffeehouse" script to avoid putting it in my coffee, to my "Birthday Party" script to avoid giving dietetic candies as presents to my friends, and so on. We would like the fact to be available diffusely across all relevant contexts, but that would seem difficult to achieve if it is buried in one particular script. Conceptual networks provide this sort of diffuse broadcasting of a new fact across multiple contexts. Perhaps script theory can gain some of this generality by altering facts in the lexicon (e.g., about drinks or foods that involve saccharin), so that all scripts using tokens of that lexical entry would be modified if that value is retrieved when the script is next executed. But it is not obvious how to do this in an efficient way.

A final problem for script and frame theories is that they currently have a clear way to deal with simultaneous execution of several scripts which have strong interactions. SAM and other script implementations (Cullingford, Note 2) seem to deal with one script and motive at a time, whereas people frequently act from multiple motives and within multiple constraints. To illustrate, suppose two businessmen who are chess enthusiasts are riding together on a train to a business convention. While eating in the dining car, they play a game of chess and also negotiate a business contract with one another. These men are engaging in at least five scripts more or less at the same time (or in rapid alternation): going to a convention, riding a train, eating dinner, playing chess, and negotiating a business contract. The activities have various embedding relations to one another; the train ride is the first part of the attending convention script, the dinner script is embedded within the train script, and the chess and negotiations proceed in parallel and embedded within the dinner script.

A language understander must be able to refer an incoming sentence to the appropriate script, and this could be done reasonably well by keeping a queue of foregrounded (active) scripts to which each input would be compared for a relevant match. It would not be difficult in current script programs to interrupt a script, save your location there, go do an embedded script for awhile, save your location there, return to the desired location in the first script and proceed from there for awhile, then return to the second script, and so on. What is harder to model are interactions between the goals and resource allocations among several simultaneous scripts. Thus, the outcome of the business negotiations can influence who pays the bill for dinner, or the seller may make low-quality moves to lose in chess in hopes of influencing the business deal, or at the most delicate decision-point in the business negotiations the buyer reveals a brilliant chess move to divert the seller's attention from the negotiations. These are cases in which a script action is performed for other than its usual reasons; they satisfy motives other than the standard ones, and along with bluffs and deceptions they comprise some of the role-taking complexities of real human commerce.

In closing this discussion, let us repeat that we consider scripts as a powerful and potentially valuable theoretical approach. The unresolved issues and theoretical puzzles raised here are not unique to script theory, but to any well-specified schema theory. We raise these issues to suggest the direction of future research.

REFERENCES

Ammon, P.R. The perception of grammatical relations in sentences. *Journal of Verbal Learning and Verbal Behavior*, 1968, *7*, 869-875.

Anderson, J.R. *Language, memory, and thought*. Hillsdale, NJ: Erlbaum, 1976.

Anderson, R.C. The notion of schemata and the educational enterprise: General discussion of the conference. In R.C. Anderson, R.T. Spiro, and W.E. Montague (Eds.), *Schooling and the acquisition of knowledge*. Hillsdale, NJ: Erlbaum, 1977.

Atkinson, R.C., and Juola, J.R. Factors influencing speed and accuracy in word recognition. In S. Kornblum (Ed.), *Attention and performance, IV*. New York: Academic Press, 1973.

Battig, W.R., and Montague, W.E. Category norms for verbal items in 56 categories: A replication and extension of the Connecticut norms. *Journal of Experimental Psychology*, 1969, *80*, Part 2, 1-46.

Bower, G.H. Cognitive psychology: An introduction. In W.K. Estes (Ed.), *Handbook of learning and cognitive processes*, Vol. 1. Hillsdale, NJ: Erlbaum, 1975.

Clark, H.H. The language-as-fixed-effect fallacy: A critique of language statistics in psychological research. *Journal of Verbal Learning and Verbal Behavior*, 1973, *12*, 335-339.

Clark, H.H., and Clark, E.V. *Psychology and language*. New York: Harcourt Brace Jovanovich, 1977.

Clark, H.H., Cohen, J., Smith, J.E.K., and Keppel, G. Discussion of Wike and Church's comments. *Journal of Verbal Learning and Verbal Behavior*, 1976, *15*, 257-266.

Collins, A., Brown, J.S., and Larkin, K.M. Inference in text understanding. In R.J. Spiro, B.C. Bruce, and W.F. Brewer (Eds.), *Theoretical issues in reading comprehension*. Hillsdale, NJ: Erlbaum, 1978.

Feldman, J. Bad-mouthing frames. In R. Schank and B.L. Nash-Webber (Eds.), *Theoretical issues in natural language processing*. Conference Proceedings. Cambridge, MA: MIT Press, 1975.

Goffman, E. *The presentation of self in everyday life*. Garden City, NY: Doubleday, 1959.

Goodman, A.I. *A theory of human action*. Englewood Cliffs, NJ: Prentice-Hall, 1970.

Grice, H.P. Logic and conversation. In P. Cole and J.L. Morgan (Eds.), *Syntax and semantics (Vol. 3): Speech acts*. New York: Seminar Press, 1975.

Haviland, S.E., and Clark, H.H. What's new? Acquiring new information as a process in comprehension. *Journal of Verbal Learning and Verbal Behavior*, 1974, *13*, 512-521.

Hunt, E.B., Marin, J., and Stone, P. *Experiments in induction*. New York: Academic Press, 1966.

Jarvella, R.J. Effects of syntax on running memory span for connected discourse. *Psychonomic Science*, 1970, *19*, 235-236.

Jarvella, R.J. Syntactic processing of connected speech. *Journal of Verbal Learning and Verbal Behavior*, 1971, *10*, 409-416.

Kintsch, W. *The representation of meaning in memory*. Hillsdale, NJ: Erlbaum, 1974.

Kintsch, W., Mandel, T.S., and Kazminsky, E. Summarizing scrambled stories. *Memory and Cognition*, 1977, *5*, 547-552.

Lehnert, W. Human and computational question answering. *Cognitive Science*, 1977, *1*, 47-73.

Mandler, J.M. A code in the node. *Discourse Processes*, 1978, *1*, 14-35.

Miller, G.A., Galanter, E., and Pribram, K.H. *Plans and the structure of behavior.* New York: Holt, Rinehart, and Winston, 1960.

Minsky, M. A framework for representing knowledge. In P.H. Winston (Ed.), *The psychology of computer vision.* New York: McGraw-Hill, 1975.

Morton, J. The interaction of information in word recognition. *Psychological Review,* 1969, *76,* 165-178.

Pew, R.W. Human perceptual-motor performance. In B.H. Kantowitz (Ed.), *Human information processing: Tutorials in performance and cognition.* Hillsdale, NJ: Erlbaum, 1974.

Roediger, H.L. III. Inhibiting effects of recall. *Memory and Cognition,* 1974, *2,* 261-269.

Rosch, E.R., Mervis, C.B., Gray, W.D., Johnson, D.M., and Boyer-Braem, P. Basic objects in natural categories. *Cognitive Psychology,* 1976, *8,* 382-439.

Rosch, E.R., Mervis, C.B., Gray, W.D., Johnson, D.M., and Boyer-Graem, P. Basic objects in natural categories. *Cognitive Psychology,* 1976, *8,* 382-439.

Rumelhart, D.E. Notes on a schema for stories. In D.G. Bobrow and A. Collins (Eds.), *Representation and understanding: Studies in cognitive science.* New York: Academic Press, 1975.

Rumelhart, D.E. Understanding and summarizing brief stories. In D. LaBerge and S.J. Samuels (Eds.), *Basic processes in reading: Perception and comprehension.* Hillsdale, NJ: Erlbaum, 1977.

Schank, R.C. *Conceptual information processing.* Amsterdam: North-Holland, 1975.

Schank, R.C., and Abelson, R.P. *Scripts, plans, goals, and understanding.* Hillsdale, NJ: Erlbaum, 1977.

Smith, E.E., Rips, L.J., and Shoben, E.J. Semantic memory and psychological semantics. In G.H. Bower (Ed.), *The psychology of learning and motivation,* Vol. 8. New York: Academic Press, 1974.

Stein, N.L., and Glenn, C.G. An analysis of story comprehension in elementary school children. In R. Freedle (Ed.), *Multidisciplinary perspectives in discourse comprehension.* Hillsdale, NJ: Erlbaum, 1978.

Wike, E.L., and Church, J.D. Comments on Clark's "The language-as-fixed-effect fallacy." *Journal of Verbal Learning and Verbal Behavior,* 1976, *15,* 241-255.

Winston, P.H. *Artificial intelligence.* Reading, MA: Addison-Wesley, 1977.

Zadah, L. Fuzzy sets. *Information and Control,* 1965, *8,* 338-353.

REFERENCE NOTES

1. Personal communications from Lynne Reder, March 1977; and Bob Abelson, January 1978.
2. Cullingford, R.E. *Script application: Computer understanding of newspaper stories.* Research Rep. No. 116, Department of Computer Science, Yale University, 1978.
3. Meehan, J. *The metanovel: Writing stories by computer.* Unpublished doctoral dissertation, Yale University, 1976.
4. Schank, R.C., and Yale A.I. Project. *SAM—A story understander.* Research Rep. No. 43, Department of Computer Science, Yale University, 1975.

NOTES

[1] Note our terminology. A *script* refers to a generic memory structure in a person's head (e.g., visiting a Health Professional). A script-based *text* or *story* is a list of sentences, read by the subject, most of which denote actions of an underlying script. A given script may be instanced by different texts (e.g., Diane visiting her doctor or dentist). An *instantiated* script is an episodic memory structure set up in the reader's head to encode and remember a particular script-based text; it is the "memory trace" of reading the story of Diane visiting her doctor.

[2] A possible earlier stage not elaborated in Figure 4 would have the text probe first analyzed for its theme or script; and if the script of the probe is not among the active script headers, then the probe might be rejected outright. The logical complications with such a process are several: first, not all probes will activate a determinate script, so a branching decision tree must be articulated farther; second, distinctive distractions (e.g., witnessing a murder while eating) may be highly memorable parts of a text yet not be related at all to any active script from the experimental texts. Since we have no data to inform the complications created by such a "script-checking" stage, we have not inserted it in the decision process of Figure 3.

Problem-Solving Schema with Question Generation for Comprehension of Complex Short Stories

HARRY SINGER
DAN DONLAN
University of California at Riverside

Comprehension consists of an interaction between the resources of the reader and the characteristics of the text (Adams and Collins, 1977; Rumelhart, 1977). This interaction shifts along a continuum from reader-based to text-based processing (Tierney and LaZansky, 1980; Tierney and Spiro, 1979), partly because of prior knowledge and partly because preexisting knowledge structures assimilate information contained in the text (Anderson, Spiro, and Montague, 1977; Ausubel, 1960). When the text is unfamiliar, processing becomes more text-based, which is less efficient (Taylor, 1979), partly because the reader has to create knowledge structures for assimilating information, which readers can do through the use of analogies embedded in text (Hayes, 1979) or metaphors (Ortony, 1981), inferences and summarization rules (Van Dijk and Kintsch, 1977), concept formation processes (Taba, 1965), and other metacognitive processes (Brown, 1981; Brown, Campione, and Day, 1980).

The purpose of this investigation was to determine whether readers, through direct instruction in how to pose questions about a story, could also acquire ability to use their knowledge about stories to focus on specific information in a particular story that would represent an *instance* of a generic variable slot (that is, recurring story elements like goal, problem, plan, etc.) In other words, if we taught students about these recurring story elements and showed them examples of story-specific questions that would elicit such elements, could they learn to develop and use such questions on their own? Furthermore, we wanted to know whether such instruction in a problem-solving schema with schema-general questions and practice in generating schema-specific questions for complex short stories would improve readers' comprehension as assessed by a test on story content. For example, a reader may have a problem-solving schema which consists of the knowledge that a story involves a *character* selecting a *plan* for achieving a *goal* and encountering and attempting an obstacle to reaching the *goal* (Adams and Collins, 1977). But the reader may not be applying this knowledge to the story, but simply perceiving and storing the words. In short, this reader is en-

Reprinted from *Reading Research Quarterly*, 17 (1982), 166-186.

gaged in an extreme form of text-based processing. We wanted to determine whether teaching this reader to state problem-solving schema in the form of general questions and story-specific questions would enable the reader to apply this knowledge of problem-solving to the story's content (Donlan and Singer, 1979). Specifically, would the general question of *What action does the main character initiate?* lead readers to think of the concept of action, and then would a story-specific question enable readers to select information from the story that would be an *instance* which would satisfy the general question? They would then be using general and story-specific questions for selecting and subsuming story content within their knowledge structures (in this example, within the concept of action). If the readers had learned to use questions to select or infer information from story content and remember the information with their knowledge of story structures, then we could infer that the instruction had helped the readers develop reading skills nearer the reader-based end of the interaction continuum.

Previous instruction to improve comprehension has used teacher-posed questions embedded in text (Frase, 1970; Rothkopf, Note 1), instruction to readers to generate questions (Frase and Schwartz, 1975; Helfeldt and Lalik, 1976; Manzo, 1970), direct instruction in knowledge-structures, such as story grammar (Dreher and Singer, 1980), or self-directed study in asking questions about main ideas and new instances of ideas or concepts (Andre and Anderson, 1978-1979). No previous research has taught students *both* knowledge structures for assimilating content and generation of content-specific questions for interacting with text. Readers have to have both the knowledge structures and a process for instantiating them if they are to use a reader-based process for interacting with text. Although readers can use several metacognitive processes for interacting with text (Brown, Campione, and Day, 1980), the self-questioning strategy was selected for this study because of previous research which has shown that the questioning process is an effective way of interacting with and learning from text (Anderson and Biddle, 1975), particularly if there is coherence among the questions posed, the structure and content of the text, and the goal or assessment of learning (Rothkopf, Note 1).

However, the goal of instruction is to have readers acquire not only knowledge but also a process for learning how to learn (Buswell, 1956): in this case how to learn from text by formulating and reading to answer self-posed questions (Singer, 1978, 1979). Although readers can learn to pose their own questions by imitating teacher-posed questions (Rosenthal, Zimmerman, and Durning, 1970), they can also do so via a more direct instructional strategy in which they actually generate their own questions (Frase and Schwartz, 1975: Helfeldt and Lalik, 1976; Manzo, 1970).

Generation of appropriate questions for selecting from the text and storing relevant and knowledge-enhancing information depends upon preexisting knowledge structures (Miyake and Norman, 1979). In short, a reader has to know enough to ask an appropriate question. Then the question helps the reader to select text information needed to instantiate a slot in a knowledge structure or to provide information for expanding or creating a knowledge structure. In other words, questions may extend a knowledge structure or form a bridge from one knowledge structure to another. For example, a schema-general question for the variable slot of *plot* in a story schema is "What is the leading character trying to accomplish?" This question leads to the subordinate knowledge structure of *plan* and to story-specific questions that relate *plan* to actual events in a story. In the story "Just Lather, That's All," the question that takes the reader to the specific plan-event in the story is "Will the barber kill the officer with a razor?" Thus, the questions select appropriate information from the text for instantiating knowledge structures, which in turn organize the information and transfer it to long term memory.

Some evidence is available (Dreher and Singer, 1980: Mandler and Johnson, 1977) that story-schema instruction in and of itself is not enough. In addition, readers must be able to monitor their own use of schema information. Therefore, the hypothesis we shall test is that readers can improve in comprehension of narrative prose by using more adequate and more appropriate knowledge structures for short stories and by using a process for generating general and story-specific questions for interacting with text. To test this hypothesis, we adopted a problem-solving schema that was adequate for assimilating vignettes and simple fables (Adams and Collins, 1977; Rumelhart, 1977, Rumelhart and Ortony, 1977; Thorndyke, 1977), but was inadequate for comprehending complex short stories. We augmented this problem-solving schema with a set of schema-general questions that could be used for generating story-specific questions (Donlan and Singer, 1979). Then we taught these structures and processes to eleventh graders and tested their ability to use them to comprehend short stories typically read at the high school level. We then compared the comprehension of the experimental group with another group taught to comprehend short stories through a traditional method, as we explain in greater detail.

Traditional Instruction vs. Schema-Based Self-Questioning for Comprehending Short Stories

Traditional Instruction

The use of questions posed by the teacher before reading appears to be the most widely used strategy for teaching reading comprehension (Singer and Donlan, 1980). The questions frequently direct the reader to focus on the story's theme, structure, or author. For example, Ray Bradbury's (1969) short story "All Summer in a Day" deals with emotions of school children awaiting the sun's first appearance in seven years. (In the story, the sun appears for only one hour and then is not seen again for another seven years.) One of the students, Margot, locked in a closet as a cruel children's prank, misses the sun's appearance. A teacher, focusing on this story's theme, might prepose these questions:

1. How is Margot different from the other children?
2. How do the children react to Margot?
3. What does this story tell you about human nature?

Students then read the story to find answers to the teacher's questions about the theme. Another teacher, stressing the story's structure, might prepose these questions:

1. Why is so much of the story devoted to dialogue?
2. Does Margot play an active or passive part in the story's climax?
3. Do you agree or disagree that the story's ending is abrupt and unsatisfying?

Another teacher, emphasizing the author, might prepose these questions:

1. Is this story typical or atypical of Ray Bradbury's work?
2. Compare "All summer in a Day" with another Ray Bradbury story you have read recently.
3. Why does Bradbury use science fiction settings to tell us about human nature?

After students read "All summer in a Day" they engage in discussion, writing, or other creative activity that involves both direct and indirect use of answers to the preposed questions. If the activities after reading do not relate to the preposed questions, students will soon view them as a hollow ritual.

The problem with preposed questions, even if they are germane to the story, is that students read to satisfy the teacher's purposes, not their own. A useful alternative is to teach students *to read to find answers to their own questions*.

But students' preposed questions vary greatly (Donlan and Singer, 1979). Sometimes they are not relevant to the main points of a story but, instead, focus on a detail or minor issue. And students may change their perspective while reading because of some compelling interest aroused by the story. For example, in Joseph Petracca's "Four Eyes," a sixth grade boy is caught in a conflict between his teacher, who thinks he needs eye glasses, and his father, who is determined he won't get them. But in reading this story, the students focused their questions on the personality of the teacher. Consequently the class's performance on a quiz was quite low; this low score was understandable. When students generate and read to answer questions that are not congruent with the goals of instruction, we can expect their test comprehension scores to be lower. To coin a phrase, the test did not have "reader-processing validity."

What teachers and students need to attain a high level of comprehension is coherence among (a) the questions asked and answered during the story, (b) the content and structure of the story, and (c) the goals of instruction such as posttest comprehension questions about the story. Thus, a problem-solving schema with schema-general questions, a process of making these questions story-specific, and a content-valid test were the components for coherence in the instructional plan for this study.

Instruction in Generating Questions from Schema

Many short stories are constructed to fit a problem-solving type of schema. In these stories, a leading character wants to accomplish something, a goal. The character adopts a plan to reach the goal. On the way to the goal, the character meets the first obstacle, which the character overcomes, circumvents, is defeated by, or else the character is forced to adopt an alternative plan or redirect his or her effort to an alternate goal. Successive obstacles present the same problems. If all obstacles are overcome, the character reaches a goal. The outcome of a story eventually occurs when the character is defeated or is successful. The theme of the story is what the author tells us about life as depicted by the interaction of the character, the goals, and the outcome. Thus, a short story is characterized by a plan, a goal, action, obstacles, and outcomes that represent success or failure (Adams and Collins, 1977: Rumelhart and Ortony, 1977).

This problem-solving schema and its accompanying schema-general questions were taught to high school students. The students were also taught to use the schema-general questions to generate story-specific questions and had to answer their own questions. Students had no difficulty in using this strategy. For example, from the following schema-general questions, students generated the adjacent story-specific questions:

Schema-General Questions	*Story-Specific Questions*
1. Who is the leading character?	1. Is this story going to be more about the officer or the barber?*
2. What is the leading character trying to accomplish in the story?	2. Will the barber kill the officer with the razor?
3. What stands in the way of the leading character reaching the desired goal?	3. Will the officer be a willing victim?

* These questions pertain to "Just Lather, That's All" by Hernando Tellez. See Table 2 footnote for complete citation.

A more complete list of schema-general questions developed for the experiment (Donlan and Singer, 1979) is reproduced in Table 1.

The effect of the two types of instruction on comprehension was then evaluated in an ecologically valid experimental design.

Experimental Design

Subjects. A sample of students, drawn from each of three eleventh grade English classes which met during the same time period, was randomly assigned

Table 1

SCHEMA-GENERAL QUESTIONS

I. The leading character
   A. Who is the leading character?
   B. What action does the character initiate?
   C. What do you learn about this character from this action?
II. The goal
   A. What does this leading character appear to be striving for?
   B. What do you learn about the character from the nature of the goal?
   C. What course of action does the character take to reach the goal?
   D. What do you learn about the character from the course of action chosen?
III. The obstacles
   A. What is the *first* obstacle the character encounters?
      1. How does the character deal with this obstacle?
      2. Does the character alter the goal because of this obstacle? How?
      3. What do you learn about the character from the way the obstacle is dealt with?
   B. What is the final obstacle the character encounters?
      1. How does the character deal with this obstacle?
      2. Does the character alter the goal because of this obstacle? How?
      3. What do you learn about the character from the way the obstacle is dealt with?
IV. The outcome
   A. Does the character reach the original goal or the revised goal or no goal?
   B. If the character is successful, what helped most?
      1. Forces within character's control. Which ones?
      2. Forces outside character's control. Which ones?
   C. If the character is defeated, what hindered the person most?
      1. Forces within the person's control which weren't dealt with?
      2. Forces outside the person's control which weren't dealt with?
V. The theme
   This story basically shows a person's struggle with...
   A. Himself or herself.
   B. Nature.
   C. Other people.

to two instructional groups. Fifteen students were in each group. However, we eliminated from the data analysis any student who missed two or more consecutive days of instruction; the samples then shrank to 14 subjects in one group and 13 in the other.

Instruction. Both groups were taught by one of the experimenters, who has had 11 years' experience in high school teaching. Highly experienced in different methods of instruction and in teaching literature, he was able to maintain the integrity of the two instructional procedures.

Materials. Six short stories, listed in Table 2, constituted the teaching materials. The stories are often used in the literature curriculum at the high school level, but they had not been used in the courses taken by students in either group taught in this study, and students in both groups indicated they had not previously read the stories. The readability levels of the stories, as indicated by the Flesch formula are also shown in Table 2. The average readability level of the five stories used in the last five trials or sessions is grade equivalent 6.8.

Procedure

Both groups were pulled out of their regular English classes for three weeks to receive "special" instruction. The schema group met on Mondays and Wednesdays and the traditional group on Tuesdays and Thursdays. The format of the six lessons for both groups was identical. Each lesson focused on a short story. Both groups received background information and vocabulary explanation for each story immediately before they read each story. Each student received a copy of the story to follow while listening to a recording of the story; the use of the recordings controlled for variations in reading rate. At a given point in the story, the recording was interrupted. The teacher then asked schema-group students to list in writing three questions which they wanted to answer as the story progressed. The traditional group was asked story-specific questons, such as "What do you think will happen to X?" "What will X do now?" or "Why do you think that might happen?" The teacher did not pass judgment on students' spontaneous answers. Next, in both groups, the recording played to the end of the story without further interruption. At this point, the teacher asked the schema-group students to write any additional questions which had occurred to them during the story and the traditional group wrote 50 to 75 word essays in response to questions about the story. (For example, *Describe the air crash from the point of view of someone standing on the ground.*) Next, both groups answered identical 10-item multiple-choice quizzes. Each succeeding day all papers were returned with scores and comments and discussed. Students in both groups kept graphs of their achievement on the daily quizzes. Only the self-generated questions from the schema group were returned to the teacher and kept for further analysis. Quizzes were scheduled so that neither group received evaluated papers before the other group had the same lesson. The experimenters maintained folders containing all of the student work. As a result, students from the two groups could not share concrete information about the disparate treatment procedures.

The daily quiz. Each lesson day, students in the two groups took 10-item multiple-choice quizzes based on five basic characteristics of a short story: (1) the leading character; (2) the character's goal; (3) obstacles; (4) outcomes of the character's struggle to achieve goals; and (5) the theme, the underlying idea which caused the author to write the story. These quizzes required students to use their acquired metacognitive processes of generating story-specific questions to select the appropriate response from the multiple choice test, which we assumed would be congruent with information selected and stored in memory during the process of reading.

Table 2 shows the six stories that were taught and the number of quiz questions asked in each of the five categories. An item analysis of each day's quiz was presented in class when the quizzes were returned.

The schema treatment. Five story elements were introduced and discussed, one each day. With each element, students were shown content-general questions from which they could generate content-specific questions about the stories they

Table 2

THE SIX STORIES TAUGHT TO BOTH GROUPS, THE NUMBER OF QUESTIONS ASKED IN EACH CATEGORY AFTER EACH SESSION, AND MEANS AND STANDARD DEVIATIONS ON EACH QUIZ

Lesson	Story	Readability Level	Quiz Questions						Schema Question		Traditional Teacher-Preposed	
			Character	Goal	Obstacles	Outcome	Theme	Total	M	SD	M	SD
1	"The 50-Yard Dash" by William Saroyan[a]	9.2	1	1	4	2	2	10	4.1	1.29	4.2	1.40
2	"Just Lather, That's All" by Hernando Tellez[b]	6.5	2	1	3	3	1	10	5.8	1.70	5.8	1.10
3	"Shoe Shine" by Jerome Weidman[c]	7.9	3	2	2	2	1	10	5.8	1.06	5.0	1.90
4	"All Summer in a Day" by Ray Bradbury[c]	5.5	2	1	3	3	1	10	8.2	1.08	7.5	0.50
5	"The Long Night" by Lowell D. Blanten[c]	6.0	2	2	4	1	1	10	7.7	2.00	5.0	1.20
6	"Four Eyes" by Joseph Petracca[c]	8.2	1	2	3	3	1	10	5.1	1.38	4.6	.83
Total			11	9	19	14	7	60				

a William Saroyan, My Name Is Aram. New York: Harcourt Brace Jovanovich, 1940.
b In J. Cline, R. Hill, V. Tallman (Eds.), Voices in Literature, Language, and Composition, B. Lexington: Ginn, 1972.
c In J. Cline, K. Williams, and D. Donlan (Eds.), Voices in Literature, Language, and Composition, I. Boston: Ginn, 1969.

were reading. Table 3 shows the lesson in which each story element was introduced along with selected content-general questions. Each day, students submitted lists of content-specific questions. Each student question was coded by the experimenter by type: for example, C for a question concerning character, or G for a question dealing with goal. Occasionally a question fit into two categories. When that happened one-half of a question was assigned to each of the two relevant categories.

Table 3

LESSONS IN WHICH SPECIFIC STORY ELEMENTS WERE INTRODUCED, WITH
CONTENT-GENERAL QUESTIONS FOR EXPERIMENTAL GROUP

Lesson	Specific Story Elements	Examples of Content-General Question
1	General introduction	No specific question.
2	Character	Who is the leading character?
3	Goal	What is the leading character trying to accomplish?
4	Obstacles	What obstacles does the character encounter enroute to a goal?
5	Outcome	Does the character reach the goal?
6	Theme	Why did the author write the story? What does the author want to show us about life?

The traditional treatment. In place of active questioning, students in the traditional group wrote essays that used data from the stories. The essays were built on the responses students had made to teacher-posed questions when the recording had been interrupted in the middle of the text. Essays were evaluated, but not graded, and returned to the student. Sample papers were read aloud, just as sample questions were read aloud in the schema group.

Analysis of the data. The mean raw scores and standard deviations on the criterion-referenced posttests for the two groups appear in Table 2. There was no statistically significant difference between the groups on the first two trials or sessions. Each session, which lasted for one day, covered a different story. On Sessions 3, 4, 5, and 6, the schema group scored consistently higher than the traditional group. The last session reveals a convergence in the two curves.

As in paired-associate learning, we considered the first session to be an informing trial. We transformed the scores on each of the remaining sessions into T-scores with a common mean of 50 and a common standard deviation of 10 so that we could properly add an individual's scores across tests. We then summed the T-scores and averaged each student's total T-score for the number of sessions the student had participated. We did a *t*-test on the difference between the means of the two groups' averaged T-scores. The results for a pooled variance estimate with a two-tail probability was t (1, 25) = 3.08, $p <$ .05.We obtained similar results for a separate variance estimate. Thus, instruction over six short stories resulted in a significant difference between the two groups.

T-tests for the separate sessions also revealed a significant difference between the two groups occurred but only in Session 5: t (1, 23) = 2.63, $p <$ .05 for a two-tailed test pooled variance estimate. The results were also significant for a separate variance estimate. In Session 6, the difference between the two groups was in the expected direction, but the difference was not significant.

Analysis was also made of the self-generated questions. They were classified into questions on story elements for each story, as shown in Table 4.

Table 4

STORY ELEMENTS TAUGHT AND CONTENT-SPECIFIC QUESTIONS GENERATED BY EXPERIMENTAL GROUP FOR STORY ELEMENTS IN EACH LESSON

| Lesson | Story Element Taught | Number of Students | Self-generated content-specific questions | | | | | | |
			Character	Goal	Obstacle	Outcome	Theme	Other	Mean
1	General	14	NC	NC	NC	NC	NC	NC	NC[a]
2	Character	13	*17.5(32)*[b]	5(9)	20.5(37)	7(13)	0	5(9)	4.2
3	Goal	12	11.5(20)	*14.5(25)*	11(19)	10(17)	0	11(19)	4.8
4	Obstacle	12	10(20)	8(16)	*19(37)*	6(12)	0	8(16)	4.2
5	Outcome	15	13.5(21)	9(14)	11.5(18)	*21(33)*	0	9(14)	4.3
6	Theme	12	2.5 (5)	.5(1)	16(34)	3(6)	*1(2)*	24(51)	3.9
	Total		55(20)	37(13)	78(28)	47(17)	1(.003)	57(21)	4.3

[a] No check was made for self-generated questions on this lesson.
[b] The first number indicates how many questions were asked for this story element. The number in parentheses is percent of total number of questions asked for this story. The underline shows this story element was taught in this lesson.

Inspection of this table indicates the students tended to ask the most questions for the story element taught in the particular lesson. (See italicized data in Table 4.) For example, in Session 2 characterization was taught. Next, the recorded story was played and interrupted at a given point, about 150 words into the story, and students were asked to write three questions which they wanted the story to answer as it progressed. The 13 students who participated in this lesson responded by generating a total of 55 questions: 17.5 (or 32 percent) of them were questions about the characters specific to the story. In Session 3, students learned about the goal element and generated 14.5 questions or 25 percent of their questions on this story element. In Session 4, 19 of their questions (37 percent) were questions about obstacles. In Session 5, 21 questions (33 percent) were about outcomes. But in Session 6, students were taught the story element of theme; subsequently they asked only one question (2 percent) on the theme.

The greatest number of questions were asked about obstacles (28 percent) and the least about theme (.003 percent). The evidence is inconclusive as to why this difference occurs. It may be easier to ask about obstacles than themes. Students asked about obstacles with the highest frequency in Session 2 (20.5 questions, 37 percent), even before they had been taught about obstacles. However, it is possible that obstacle questions are more likely to occur to readers early in a short story. It is also possible that both explanations are correct. The resolution of this issue must await further research.

What is clear is that readers did generate questions related to instruction. This evidence means that instruction led students to use reader-based resources for processing the text. This shift occurred because the schema-general and story-specific questions enabled the reader to select specific events from the content of the story and assimilate them under specific knowledge structures instead of only identifying and storing words in memory as they occur in the story. Whether this shift is temporary or carries over from one text to another cannot be determined from the data since the number of questions asked for each story was limited and the interruption to obtain reader-generated questions always occurred at about the same point in the story. Whether content-specific schema questions were also occurring at other points in the story was not tested in this study.

Discussion of Results

Previous instruction in story grammar has not been successful, probably because students already knew and could apply story grammar to well-structured stories, such as simple fables (Dreher and Singer, 1980; Mandler and Johnson, 1977). But when students have to apply schemata to complex short stories, in which the fit between the schema-structures and the story is not readily apparent, then effective instruction for acquiring story-general questions and generating story-specific questions for instantiating schema slots must continue over more than one story, so that students can learn these complex metacognitive processes and have practice in applying them. The results of the data for this study support this procedure; if we had used only one, two, or even three stories (or sessions), the differences between the two treatments would not have become apparent. Indeed, to claim that learning of any complex strategy has occurred, it is necessary to continue the instructional treatment over multiple trials and keep the test-tasks constant (Singer, 1973, 1977, 1981). It is fortunate we heeded this prescription because a clear gap in the difference between the two treatment groups did not become apparent until the third session and then remained throughout the rest of the sessions.

However, in the last session the results for the two groups tended to converge. In reading and reacting to this story, the group focused on a point that was of minor import to the story but of compelling interest to the group. In fact, this point became the dominant issue in the students' discussion of the story. Apparently in processing this story, the experimental group had shifted its perspective away from the problem-solving schema and story-specific questions related to this schema. A change in perspective means the students had shifted to use of another high-level schema for processing and for assimilating information from the story (Anderson and Pichert, 1977; Pichert and Anderson, 1977). Hence, students formulating questions from the general schema reduced the amount of information they had assimilated under their problem-solving schema for this story and consequently they had less information stored for answering questions based on it. Nevertheless, the difference between the group formulating questions from schema and the group answering teacher-posed questions was in the expected direction and the results, averaged over Sessions 2 through 6, including the perspective change, represented a significant difference between the two groups' comprehension of the short stories.

In traditional literature instruction, where teachers ask preposed questions and students read to answer them, comprehension tends to narrow because students are likely to focus only on the passages related to the preposed questions (Frase, 1967). Consequently, they assimilate less information than those students who learn to generate questions throughout the entire story (Singer, 1979).

Another dimension entered into the comprehension results for both groups. The fluctuations in the comprehension results were identical for the two groups and the rank order of the comprehension scores had a perfectly inverse correlation with the rank order of the reading difficulty levels of the stories. This finding tends to validate both the readability formula and the criterion-referenced comprehension tests used in this study.

The most difficult story was the last one. "Four Eyes." Perhaps the increase in difficulty led to the shift in perspective. On this story, the experimental group was trying to generate story-specific questions on the theme. This task itself is difficult and, given a more difficult story, the combination may have led to a shift in perspective towards an aspect of the story more familiar to them. This kind of shift may be tantamount to what occurs in reconstructive recall of a story (Brown, Smiley, Day, Townsend, and Lawton, 1977). Nevertheless, fluctuations in comprehension notwithstanding, the average mean differences in comprehension between the two groups for the last five trials was statistically significant.

These significant differences between our groups cannot be ascribed to teaching toward the test. An essential component in any instructional paradigm is a content-valid test for assessing the effects of instruction (Rothkopf, Note 1; Singer, Note 2). We used content-valid tests for both of our groups, each of which had the same opportunity to acquire the content assessed on the posttest. Indeed, both groups showed no significant differences on the first two posttests. The effects of the experimental instruction had not cumulated enough to have made a difference on these trials. This evidence supports our claim that we did not teach for the test; had we done so, such instructional bias would have been evident on the first two tests. We attribute this difference between the two groups on the content-valid tests to the experimental group's acquisition of ability to generate schema-based general and story-specific questions for assimilating, storing, and recalling content-related information.

The addition of question-generation ability to the problem-solving schema served to relate the nodes in an hierarchical organization of schemata for comprehending complex stories. This addition may explain why we got favorable results in contrast with previous instruction in story grammar which only taught knowledge structures and teacher-directed categorization under these structures (Dreher and Singer, 1980). Evidently readers not only need to have schemata but also need to learn how to use and apply this knowledge spontaneously to particular complex stories. Apparently acquisition of schema-general and story specific questions augmented the students' ability to select information to instantiate slots in their knowledge structures and thus significantly enhanced their comprehension.

Limitations

This study has several limitations:

1. The criterion-referenced test for each story had only 10 items, which tended to restrict its reliability. When we summed test scores across the stories, we were, in effect, lengthening the comprehension test and thereby increasing the probability of having a more reliable test. Under this test condition, the cumulative differences between the two groups were statistically significant.

2. At first glance it may appear that we did not test for maintenance of learning or for transfer. We think that this perception is not entirely warranted. We taught self-generation of questions on only one aspect and a different aspect of the problem-solving schema each session, but we tested for comprehension of all aspects on each test. Also, because each story was different, we assumed we were testing for maintenance and cumulative transfer of learning at each test session. If we had had more reliable individual tests, then our expectations of cumulative transfer across stories might have reached the criterion of statistically significant differences between our two groups prior to the fifth story. As it is, the fact that we did get a statistically significant difference on the fifth story and over all the stories tends to support our assumption. However, it is true that we did not test for further maintenance of learning or have another transfer test after our last treatment session.

3. Our final treatment session was on generation of questions about the theme of the story. We now think that question generation on this knowledge structure cannot be taught in one session unless the theme is already familiar to the students. Furthermore, we think that our students were not familiar with the theme of the particular story we used for teaching generation of questions about theme, and that is one possible reason why our students may have shifted their perspective on the story. In retrospect, we should not have included theme in our

instruction because it is not a compelling aspect of story comprehension (Adams and Collins, 1977). It is more dependent on prior knowledge and reasoning resources than any other aspect of story structure. This aspect of story comprehension requires a separate study, for which we already have made plans.

4. We did not test for comprehension through free recall. Until we do so, we must limit the claim for our instructional effects to a recognition type of comprehension.

5. We also realize that the design of our study did not let us determine whether our statistically significant effects were due to the enhancement and use of schemata alone or enhancement and use of schemata plus generation of questions. If we assume on the basis of previous research (Dreher and Singer, 1980; Mandler and Johnson, 1977) that both of our groups had and were already able to use schema for stories, and that we did not enhance or increase our group's use of schema for stories, then our study is reduced to a test for the effect on comprehension of self-generated versus teacher-posed questions. Since instruction in self-generated questions in the current study may have enhanced and increased the use of problem-solving schema for stories in our question-generation group, we are careful to claim in this study that the combination of the problem-solving schema with self-question generation constituted the effective treatment. In our next study, we plan to use a more elaborate 2 x 3 design to try to tease out the effects of schema explanation (schema explanation versus no explanation) and type of question (self-generated versus teacher-posed versus no questions).

Summary and Conclusions

A problem-solving schema with schema-general questions was developed and taught to a group of high school students along with a strategy for student-generation of story-specific questions. The comparison group received instruction with teacher-preposed questions about the story's theme, structure, and author. Both groups received instruction and criterion-referenced tests over six complex short stories that were appropriate for a high school curriculum. Over a two-week period of instruction, the results on the criterion-referenced tests revealed that the average mean difference between the two groups over Trials 2 through 6 was statistically significant. This result indicates that high school students can learn to apply to complex short stories a problem-solving schema, combining schema-general questions to fit complex stories and a strategy of generating story-specific questions from the schema-general questions. The function of the story-specific questions was to select events from the story to instantiate the problem-solving schema. Also, this combination of schemata or knowledge structures and student generating of general and story-specific questions during the process of reading, which we call "active comprehension," helped students improve in comprehension of short stories, probably by shifting them toward more efficient reader-based processing of text—that is, toward use of questions to select, organize, and subsume story events under specific schema slots, instead of merely perceiving words and storing them sequentially into memory.

The prevailing view, based on application of story grammar to simple fables, is that students as early as the elementary school level are already sophisticated about story grammar and its application to narrative prose. But this view must be modified.

Story grammar and problem-solving schema subsume only the compelling meaning of a story (Adams and Collins, 1977); they do not include more reader-based purposes (Guthrie, 1979) and sources of knowledge, such as symbolic re-constructions, affective responses, and other reader-based elaborations to text-based material (Guthrie, 1978; Reder, 1980). The results of this study also indicate that students at the high school level can acquire more adequate schemata and appropriate metacognitive processes for comprehension of complex short stories as measured by a content-valid comprehension test. Under these instructionally coherent conditions, comprehension of complex short stories improved significantly.

REFERENCES

Adams, M.J., and Collins, A. A schema-theoretic view of reading. Cambridge, Mass.: Bolt, Beranek and Newman, 1977.

Anderson, R.C., and Biddle, W.B. On asking people questions about what they are reading. In G.H. Bower (Ed.), *The psychology of learning and motivation*, Vol. 9. New York: Academic Press, 1975.

Anderson, R.C., and Pichert, J.W. *Recall of previously unrecallable information following a shift of perspective*, Technical Report No. 41. Urbana, Ill.: Center for the Study of Reading, April 1977.

Anderson, R.C., Spiro, R.J., and Montague, W.E. (Eds.). *Schooling and the acquisition of knowledge*. Hillsdale, N.J.: Erlbaum, 1977.

Andre, M.E.D.A., and Anderson, T.H. The development and evaluation of a self-questioning study technique. *Reading Research Quarterly*, 1978-1979, *14*, 605-623.

Ausubel, D. The use of advance organizers in the learning and retention of meaningful verbal material. *Journal of Educational Psychology*, 1960, *51*, 267-272.

Bradbury, Ray. All summer in a day. In J. Cline, K. Williams, and D. Donlan (Eds), *Voices in literature, language, and composition*. Boston: Ginn, 1969.

Brown, A. Writing and reading and metacognition. In M. Kamil (Ed.), *The Thirtieth Yearbook of the National Reading Conference*. Washington, D.C.: National Reading Conference, 1981.

Brown, A., Campione, J.C., and Day, J.D. *Learning to learn: On training students to learn from texts*, Technical Report No. 189. Urbana, Ill.: Center for the Study of Reading, 1980.

Brown, A., and Day, J.D. *Strategies and knowledge for summarizing tests. The development and facilitation of expertise.* Urbana, Ill.: Center for the Study of Reading, 1980.

Brown, A.L., Smiley, S.S., Day, J.D., Townsend, A.R., and Lawton, S.C. Intrusion of a thematic idea in children's comprehension and retention of stories. *Child Development,* 1977, *48*, 1454-1466.

Buswell, Guy T. Educational theory and the psychology of learning. *Journal of Educational Psychology*, 1956, *47*, 175-184.

Donlan, D., and Singer, H. Active comprehension of short stories. In M.P. Douglass (Ed), *Forty-Third Yearbook of the Claremont Reading Conference*. Claremont, Calif.: Claremont Reading Conference, Claremont Graduate School, 1979.

Dreher, J., and Singer, H. Story grammar instruction unnecessary for intermediate grade students. *The Reading Teacher,* 1980, *34,* 261-268.

Frase, L.T. Learning from prose material: Length of passage, knowledge of results, and position of questions. *Journal of Educational Psychology,* 1967, *58,* 266-272.

Frase, L.T. Boundary conditions for mathemagenic behaviors. *Review of Educational Research,* 1970, *40,* 337-348.

Frase, L.T., and Schwartz, B.J. Effect of question production and answering on prose recall. *Journal of Educational Psychology,* 1975, *67,* 628-635.

Guthrie, J.T. Research views: Fables. *The Reading Teacher,* 1978, *31,* 110-112.

Guthrie, J.T. Purpose and text structure. *The Reading Teacher,* 1979, *32,* 624-626.

Hayes, D.A. *The effect of text-embedded analogy upon comprehension and learning.* Unpublished doctoral dissertation, University of Arizona, 1979.

Helfeldt, J.P., and Lalik, R. Reciprocal student-teacher questioning. *The Reading Teacher,* 1976, *30,* 283-287.

Mandler, J.M., and Johnson, N.S. Remembrance of things parsed: Story structure and recall. *Cognitive Psychology,* 1977, *9,* 111-151.

Manzo, A.V. Improving reading comprehension through reciprocal questioning. Doctoral dissertation, Syracuse University, 1970. *Dissertation Abstracts International,* 1970, *30,* 5344A (University Microfilms No. 70-10, 364).

Miyake, N., and Norman, D.A. To ask a question, one must know enough to know what is known. *Journal of Verbal Learning and Verbal Behavior,* 1979, *18,* 351-364.

Ortony, A., Metaphor. In R. Spiro, W. Bruce, and W. Brewer (Eds.), *Theoretical issues in reading comprehension.* Hillsdale, N.J.: Erlbaum, 1981.

Pichert, J.W., and Anderson, R.C. Taking different perspectives on a story. *Journal of Educational Psychology,* 1977, *69,* 309-315.

Reder, L.M. Comprehension and retention of prose. *Review of Educational Research,* 1980, *50,* 15-53.

Rosenthal, R.L., Zimmerman, B.J., and Durning, K. Observationally induced changes in children's interrogative classes. *Journal of Personality and Social Psychology,* 1970, *16,* 681-688.

Rumelhart, D. Understanding and summarizing brief stories. In D. LaBerge and S.J. Samuels (Eds.), *Basic processes in reading: Perception and comprehension.* Hillsdale, N.J.: Erlbaum, 1977.

Rumelhart, D., and Ortony, A. The representation of knowledge in memory. In R. Anderson, R. Spiro, and W. Montague (Eds.), *Schooling and the acquisition of knowledge.* Hillsdale, N.J: Erlbaum, 1977.

Singer, H. Measurement of early reading ability: Norm-referenced standardized tests for differential assessment of progress in learning how to read and in using reading for gaining information. In P. Nacke (Ed.), *Twenty-Third Yearbook of the National Reading Conference,* 1973. (Abstract)

Singer, H. IQ is and is not related to reading. In Eric *Document Resumes,* July 1974, ED 088 004. Also in S. Wanat (Ed.), *Issues in evaluating reading,* Arlington, Va.: Center for Applied Linguistics, 1977.

Singer, H. Active comprehension: From answering to asking questions. *The Reading Teacher,* 1978, *31,* 901-908. Revised version in C. McCullough (Ed.), *Inchworm, inchworm: Persistent questions in reading education.* Newark, Del.: International Reading Association. 1979.

Singer, H. Hypotheses on reading comprehension in search of classroom validation. In M. Kamil (Ed.), *Thirtieth Yearbook of the National Reading Conference.* Washington, D.C.: National Reading Conference, 1981.

Singer, H., and Donlan, D. *Reading and learning from text.* Hillsdale, N.J.: Erlbaum, 1985.

Taba, H. The teaching of thinking. *Elementary English,* 1965, *42,* 534-542.

Taylor, B.M. Good and poor readers' recall of familiar and unfamiliar text. *Journal of Reading Behavior,* 1979, *11,* 375-380.

Thorndyke, P. Cognitive structures in comprehension and memory of narrative discourse. *Cognitive Psychology,* 1977, *9,* 77-110.

Tierney, R.J., and La Zansky, J. The rights and responsibilities of readers and writers: A contractual agreement. *Language Arts,* 1980, *57,* 606-613.

Tierney, R.J., and Spiro, R.J. Some basic notions about reading comprehension: Implications for teachers. In J. Harste and R.F. Carey (Eds.), *New perspectives on comprehension* (Monograph No. 3 in Language and Reading Series). Bloomington: Indiana University, 1979.

van Dijk, T., and Kintsch, W. Cognitive psychology and discourse: Recalling and summarizing stories. In W.U. Dressler (Ed.), *Current trends in textlinguistics.* Berlin, New York: DeGruyter, 1977.

REFERENCE NOTES

1. Rothkopf. E.Z. Adjunct aids, and the control of mathemagenic activities during purposeful reading. In W. Otto and S. White (Eds.), *Reading Expository Material.* New York: Academic Press, 1982.

2. Singer, H. *Towards an instructional theory for learning from text.* A discussion of E.Z. Rothkopf's "Adjunct aids, and the control of mathemagenic activities during purposeful reading." In W. Otto and S. White (Eds.), *Reading Expository Material.* New York: Academic Press, 1982.

NOTE

We wish to express our appreciation to Mark Jensen for his assistance in analyzing the data for this project, and to the students, teachers, and principal at Norco Senior High School who participated in this project. We also wish to acknowledge the support of the Research Committee of the University of California at Riverside, on travel funds to report this study.

Good and Poor Readers' Recall of Familiar and Unfamiliar Text

BARBARA M. TAYLOR
University of Minnesota

Recently, reading has been described as a complex, interactive process which involves both knowledge-based and text-based analysis (Adams and Collins, 1979; Frederiksen, 1979; Rumelhart, 1977). While it would be possible for a person to focus primarily on textual information and not prior knowledge while reading, comprehension inevitably would suffer.

Research on adults' and children's recall of prose in which prior knowledge was manipulated supports the notion that use of schemata facilitates discourse comprehension. Bransford and Johnson (1972) asked subjects to read a fairly incomprehensible story. Subjects who received prior knowledge about the passage in the form of a clarifying picture were able to recall more of the passage than subjects who did not see the picture. In a similar study, Dooling and Lachman (1971) found that subjects who were presented with a meaningful title prior to reading a metaphorical passage were able to recall more about the passage than subjects who did not see the title prior to reading. For example, comprehension of a vague passage about three sturdy sisters was facilitated by the title "Christopher Columbus." Brown, Smiley, Day, Townsend, and Lawton (1977) found that children who received background information about an unfamiliar topic prior to listening to a passage on the topic could recall more of the passage after listening to it than children who did not receive the background information. According to an interactive model of reading, subjects in all three of these studies were using prior knowledge about the topic of a passage to facilitate comprehension.

Frederiksen (1979) has suggested that readers are likely to revert to primarily text-based processing strategies when they encounter difficulties with text. Frederiksen reasoned that poor readers, frequently struggling with the text as they read, may have learned to use primarily text-based processing strategies in reading. Consequently, their comprehension of written text may be poor because they fail to make adequate use of prior knowledge as they read. Anderson (1977)

Reprinted from *Journal of Reading Behavior*, 1979, *11*, 375-388. Used with permission of the National Reading Conference and Barbara Taylor.

has also suggested that good and poor readers may differ in their ability to use schemata in reading.

A number of studies suggest that poor readers tend to rely on text-based processing instead of knowledge-based processing when reading. Clay and Imlach (1971) found that poor second grade readers paused after every 1.3 words in oral reading whereas their good reading peers paused after every 7.4 words. It appears that the poor readers were engaged in word-by-word text-based processing. Cromer (1970) found that poor college readers, unlike good college readers, comprehended text as well when it was presented one word at a time as when it was presented in normal form. This finding also suggests that poor readers tend to read in a word-by-word manner which is basically text-based in nature.

While past research supports the notion that poor readers tend to rely on text-based processing when they encounter text which is difficult for them to read, this research has not adequately addressed the question of whether poor readers are able to use knowledge-based strategies adequately if they encounter text which is not so difficult. The purpose of the present study was to gain insight into the reading strategies used by poor readers. Specifically, poor readers' ability to use knowledge-based processing strategies was investigated by comparing good and poor readers' recall of familiar and unfamiliar text which was not considered to be difficult for any of the subjects to decode. A basic assumption of this study was that good readers effectively use prior knowledge when reading easy material on a familiar topic. However, good readers presumably would be forced to use inefficient text-based strategies more than usual when processing text on an unfamiliar topic for which they had little prior knowledge (Spiro, 1979). Given two passages very similar in structure and readability level, good readers would be expected to comprehend less and therefore recall less after reading unfamiliar than familiar material. On the other hand, if poor readers rely primarily on text-based processing regardless of the familiarity of the text, and consequently have poor comprehension of familiar or unfamiliar material, they should show less difference than good readers in their ability to recall unfamiliar versus familiar material. However, if poor readers depend on knowledge-based processing when reading material which is familiar and easy to decode, they should be as bothered as good readers in terms of recall ability by text written on an unfamiliar topic.

Method

Subjects

Subjects included 31 third grade children reading on a third-fourth grade level (good readers). 31 fifth grade children reading on a third-fourth grade level (poor readers), and 20 fifth grade children reading on a fifth-sixth grade level (good readers). The third grade readers were randomly selected from all third grade children in four schools in a rural area in Virginia who were reading on a 3.0-4.5 grade level as determined by the comprehension test of the *Gates-MacGinitie Reading Tests, Primary C*. The fifth grade subjects reading on a third-fourth grade level included all fifth grade children in the four schools who had received a raw score corresponding to a 3.0-4.5 grade level on the same text. The third grade subjects had a mean raw score of 28.2 (3.5 grade level) and the poor fifth grade readers had a mean raw score of 28.4 (3.5 grade level) on the reading achievement text. The fifth grade subjects reading on a fifth-sixth grade level were randomly selected from all fifth graders at one of the four schools who were identified by their teachers as reading on a fifth or sixth grade level.

Material

The two passages used in this study included a third grade passage on a familiar topic, bird nest building, and a third grade passage on an unfamiliar topic, bee dancing. The readability level of the passages was determined by Fry's Readability Graph (Fry, 1968). Field testing was done to verify that the passages were on topics which were familiar or unfamiliar to third and fifth grade children. Thirty third grade children and thirty fifth grade children, who were randomly selected from the same four schools as the subjects in the study, were asked five questions on each of the topics of the two passages. Both the third and fifth grade children answered more than four out of five questions on the average on bird nest building and less than one question out of five on the average on bee dancing. Therefore, it was concluded that bird nest building was familiar and bee dancing was unfamiliar to third and fourth grade children as assumed.

The two passages, written by the investigator, contained approximately 125 words each and were very similar to each other except for familiarity of subject matter. The passages followed a similar pattern of main ideas and details, contained the same number of sentences, and contained similar numbers of idea units, unfamiliar words, and different concepts or nouns. The passages were segmented into propositions through a discourse analysis procedure adapted from the work of Grimes (1975) and Meyer (1975). Every predicate or argument of a proposition was considered to be a separate idea unit. There were about 60 idea units in each passage. A second person, trained in the discourse analysis procedure, analyzed the passages and agreed with 90 percent of the idea units which the investigator had identified.

Procedure

Each subject was tested individually by the investigator. First, the subject silently read and orally retold a practice passage on underground animal homes. Then, the subject silently read and orally retold each text passage presented in random order. All recalls were free recalls. In other words, subjects were not probed with questions. All retellings were taped. The retellings were transcribed and scored for number of idea units recalled for each passage. Paraphrased statements as well as verbatim statements were scored as correctly recalled. A second person scored ten retellings, selected at random, to establish inter-rater reliability. The Pearson r for scores assigned to the retellings by the scorer and investigator was .98.

Results

The means and standard deviations for idea units recalled by the three groups on the two passages are presented in Table 1 and graphically displayed in Figure 1. Recall was analyzed in a 3 (group) x 2 (familiarity) analysis of variance with repeated measures on the last factor. Results indicated a significant effect of group, $F(2, 79) = 14.54, p < .001$; a significant effect of familiarity, $F(1, 79) = 53.49, p < .001$; and a significant group x familiarity interaction, $F(2, 79) = 6.39, p < .01$. Newman-Keuls tests showed that both the good and poor fifth grade readers recalled more than the third grade children on the familiar passage, but the good and poor fifth grade readers' mean scores were not found to differ significantly on this passage ($p > .05$). While the fifth grade good readers recalled more than the third grade good readers or fifth grade poor readers on the unfamiliar passage, the third graders' and fifth grade poor readers' mean scores did not differ significantly on this unfamiliar passage ($p > .05$). Newman-Keuls tests of differences in mean recall scores for the three groups on the familiar and unfamiliar passages showed that all three groups recalled more on the familiar passage than on the unfamiliar passage. Further analysis was made of the differences in subjects' recall between the familiar and unfamiliar passages to investigate the source of the significant group-familiarity interaction, and, in fact, yielded the same significant F-value, $F(2, 79) = 6.39, p < .01$. These tests showed that the fifth grade poor readers' mean difference score of 10.3 idea units was greater than the third and fifth grade good readers' mean difference scores of 4.0 and 3.8 idea units ($p < .05$), respectively, which did not differ significantly from each other ($p > .05$).

It is not surprising that all subjects recalled less after reading the passage on an unfamiliar topic than the passage on a familiar topic. This finding supports the theoretical notion that reading is a schema-based process and comprehension is impaired when the use of prior knowledge is restricted. Prior knowledge about the subject matter of a text aids in processing as well as remembering that text.

While it appears that all groups of subjects found the unfamiliar passage more difficult to read and recall than the familiar passage, the results of the data analysis suggest that poor readers, in particular, had difficulty with this unfamiliar passage. The poor readers' mean difference score, derived from the difference in the amount recalled on the familiar and unfamiliar passages, was greater than the mean difference scores for both the third and fifth grade good readers. This

Table 1

RETELLING SCORES AND STANDARD DEVIATIONS FOR THIRD GRADE GOOD
READERS, FIFTH GRADE POOR READERS, AND FIFTH GRADE GOOD READERS ON
THE TWO TEST PASSAGES

		Familiar Passage	Unfamiliar Passage
Third Grade	$\overline{X}$	14.00	10.03
Good Readers	SD	6.43	6.00
	N	31	31
Fifth Grade	$\overline{X}$	19.81	9.55
Poor Readers	SD	7.02	6.24
	N	31	31
Fifth Grade	$\overline{X}$	22.85	19.05
Good Readers	SD	8.67	8.46
	N	20	20

does not support the notion that poor readers are always engaged in primarily text-based processing as they read and have poor comprehension regardless of whether material is familiar or unfamiliar. Instead of being less impaired in comprehension and ability to recall by unfamiliar material, as a text-based model of unskilled reading would predict, the poor readers were more impaired in their ability to recall after reading than the good readers when given a passage to read for which they had little prior knowledge, or schema. This finding supports the notion that poor readers, like good readers, depend on schema-based strategies to read and recall text whenever possible, as when reading easy, familiar material. Additionally, this finding suggests that poor readers' comprehension and ability to recall particularly suffers when they are restricted in their use of prior knowledge, as when reading unfamiliar material, and they are forced to resort primarily to inefficient, text-based processing.

The findings of this study, based on good and poor readers' recall of one familiar and one unfamiliar passage, cannot be generalized to other passages. However, important instructional implications would stem from similar findings identified through further research which support the notion that poor readers can recall as much as good readers after processing relatively easy, familiar text. Such findings would suggest that poor readers should be able to do an adequate job of reading for meaning in the classroom if given easy material to read which is on a relatively familiar topic.

In conclusion, the results of this study support the theoretical notion that efficient reading is a schema-based process. Prior knowledge is used by readers whenever possible to process and recall text. Furthermore, this knowledge-based processing does not appear to be limited to good readers. Poor readers, as well as good readers, seem to engage in knowledge-based processing strategies when reading material which is not too difficult.

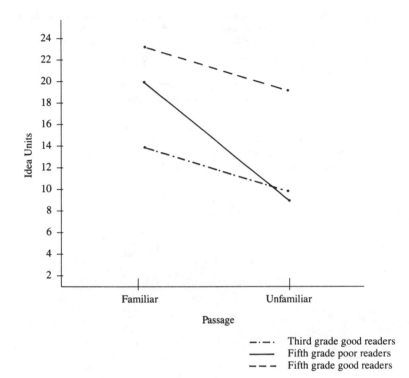

Figure 1. Mean number of idea units recalled by the third grade good readers, fifth grade poor readers, and fifth grade good readers on the two passages.

REFERENCES

Adams, M.J., and Collins, A.A. A schema-theoretic view of reading. In R. Freedle (Ed.), *New directions in discourse processing*. Norwood, N.J.: Ablex, 1979.

Anderson, R.C. *Schema-directed processes in language comprehension* (Technical Report No. 50). Urbana, Ill.: University of Illinois, Center for the Study of Reading, 1977.

Bransford, J.D., and Johnson, M.K. Contextual prerequisites for understanding: Some investigations of comprehension on recall. *Journal of Verbal Learning and Verbal Behavior*, 1972, *11*, 711-726.

Brown, A.L., Smiley, S.S., Day, J.D., Townsend, M.A., and Lawton, S.C. Intrusion of the thematic idea in children's comprehension and retention of stories. *Child Development*, 1977, *48*, 1454-1466.

Clay, M.M., and Imlach, R.H. Juncture, pitch, and stress as reading behavior variables. *Journal of Verbal Learning and Verbal Behavior*, 1971, *10*, 133-139.

Cromer, W. The difference model: A new explanation for some reading difficulties. *Journal of Educational Psychology*, 1970, *61*, 471-483.

Dooling, D.J., and Lachman, R. Effects of comprehension on retention of prose. *Journal of Experimental Psychology*, 1971, *88*, 216-222.

Frederiksen, C.H. Discourse comprehension and early reading. In L. Resnick and P. Weaver (Eds.), *Theory and practice of early reading*. Hillsdale, N.J.: Erlbaum, 1979.

Fry, E.B. A readability formula that saves time. *Journal of Reading*, 1968, *11*, 513-516.

Gates, A.I., and MacGinitie, W.H. *Gates-MacGinitie reading tests, primary c*. New York: Teachers College Press, 1965.

Grimes, J.E. *The thread of discourse*. The Hague, Netherlands: Mouton, 1975.

Meyer, B. *Organization of prose and its effects on recall*. Amsterdam: North Holland Publishing Company, 1975.

Rumelhart, D. Toward an interactive model of reading. In S. Dornic (Ed.), *Attention and performance*, VI. Hillsdale, N.J.: Erlbaum, 1977.

Spiro, R. *Etiology of reading comprehension styles*. Technical Report No. 124. Urbana, Ill.: University of Illinois, Center for the Study of Reading, 1979.

Metacognition

Metacognition: The Development of Selective Attention Strategies for Learning from Texts

ANN L. BROWN
University of Illinois

Introduction

In this paper, I will discuss some recent research from my laboratory concerned with strategies for studying. In so doing I will address various forms of behavior that could be called metacognitive (Baker and Brown, 1984a) but needn't be. My primary aim is to demonstrate the complex interaction of many forms of knowledge that take place when students are engaged in a variety of learning activities, including learning from reading.

Metacognition

First, however, what is metacognition and how does it relate to reading? In recent reviews of the literature, Linda Baker and I (Baker and Brown, 1984a, b) argued that it is necessary to distinguish between two types of metacognitive knowledge: 1) knowledge about cognition and 2) regulation of cognition. These two forms of metacognition are closely related. Attempts to separate them lead to oversimplification but such a separation does help us clarify the topic of discussion.

The first cluster is knowledge about cognition. Here the focus is on the knowledge readers have about their own cognitive resources and the compatibility between themselves as readers and the demands of a variety of reading situations. This form of self-knowledge is relatively stable, statable, fallible and late-developing. It is the form of knowledge that has traditionally been referred to as knowing that. It is *stable* because one would expect a reader who knows pertinent facts (such as that passages containing familiar words are easier to read than those containing unfamiliar words) to continue to "know" these facts when inter-

Reprinted from M.L. Kamil (Ed.), *Directions in Reading: Research and Instruction*. Washington, D.C.: The National Reading Conference, 1981, 21-43. Used with permission of the National Reading Conference and the author.

rogated appropriately. This form of knowledge is often *statable* in that the child can reflect on the cognitive processes involved in reading and discuss them with others. Of course, this form of knowledge is also *fallible* in that the child, or adult for that matter, can perfectly well "know" certain facts about reading that are not true!

The ability to reflect on one's own cognitive processes, to be aware of one's own activities while reading, writing, solving problems, etc. is a *late-developing* skill with important implications for the child's effectiveness as an active, planful learner. If children are aware of what is needed to perform effectively, then it is possible for them to take steps to meet the demands of a learning situation more adequately. If, however, children are not aware of their own limitations as learners or the complexity of the task at hand, then they can hardly be expected to take preventive actions in order to anticipate or recover from problems.

The second cluster of metacognitive activities, regulation of cognition, consists of processes that are relatively unstable, rarely statable, without considerable effort, and relatively age independent. It consists of the self-regulatory mechanisms used by an active learner during an ongoing attempt to solve problems. These indices of metacognition include *planning* one's next move, *checking* the outcome of any strategies one might use, *monitoring* the effectiveness of any attempted action, *testing*, *revising* and *evaluating* one's strategies for learning. These are not necessarily stable skills in the sense that although they are more often used by older children and adults, they are not always used by them, and quite young children may monitor their activities on a simple problem. Indeed, a case could be made that all learning involves monitoring to some degree. They are also not often statable, we know how to do a great many things that we cannot state explicitly; this is the form of knowledge often referred to as knowing how.

Expert readers monitor their comprehension and retention and evaluate their own progress in the light of the purposes for which they are reading. With repeated experience on these routine school activities, many of these cognitive monitoring processes become automatic. That is, although mature readers typically engage in comprehension monitoring, it is not often or even usually a conscious experience (Brown, 1980). When comprehension is proceeding smoothly, good readers proceed as if on automatic pilot, until a problem is detected. Some triggering event (Brown, 1980; Collins, Brown, Morgan, and Brewer, Note 1) alerts them to a comprehension failure. Then and only then does the understanding process slow down and become planful, demanding conscious effort. Study monitoring for the expert involves many automatic, overlearned components, although here the need for conscious forethought, planning, and checking is somewhat greater. Less successful students are much less aware of the need to be strategic, plan ahead, monitor and check their own understanding. They have not yet learned how to learn from texts (Baker and Brown, 1984a). Reading is not a primary or preferred mode of obtaining information and the task of studying is often interpreted to involve nothing more than passive, sometimes desperate, rereading. The self-regulatory activities that they can perfectly well apply to listening, for example, they are not yet able to apply to reading.

The importance of self-awareness and self-control while learning were recognized well before the current popularity of metacognitive theories; indeed, educational psychologists since the turn of the century (e.g., Dewey, 1910; Huey, 1968; Thorndike, 1917) were quite aware that reading involves the planning, checking, and evaluating activities now called metacognitive skills. For example, Dewey's system of inducing reflective thinking is essentially a call for metacognitive training. The aim was to induce active monitoring, critical evaluation and deliberate "seeking after meaning and relationships." Similarly, Thorndike claimed that reading was reasoning and involved a great many activities now called metacognitive.

> Understanding a paragraph is like solving a math problem. It consists of selecting the right elements of the situation and putting them together in the right relations, and also with the right amount of weight or influence or force for each. The mind is assailed as it were by every word in the paragraph. It must select, repress, soften, emphasize, correlate and organize, all under the influence of the right mental set or purpose or demand. (Thorndike, 1917, p. 329)

Although the term metacognitive may be new, the type of knowledge to which it refers has long been recognized.

Study Strategies and Selective Attention

Also not new is the main focus of the work I will concentrate on in this paper, study strategies. There is a long history of interest in the types of knowledge and strategies students bring to the task of learning from texts — notetaking, underlining, adjunct aids, question-asking, outlining, etc. (Anderson and Armbruster, 1980; Baker and Brown, 1984a). In the past, however, the work has been limited in several ways: first, the majority of prior work has concentrated almost exclusively on the study activity of adults, usually college students. Second, the majority of studies have been descriptive rather than explanatory or manipulative. And third, the most important limitation is that the majority of studies have shared a concentration on product rather than process. That is, the main metric has been some outcome measure such as the test scores of students who do or do not use a certain strategy. Little or no consideration is given to the activity of the studiers, i.e., what they are *actually doing* while studying. An example of this is the large number of experiments that have considered the product of the activity of notetakers, i.e., how well they do on tests, but have ignored the processes that the notetaker employs; even the notes themselves are not examined for evidence of the process that the taker of notes might be employing (Brown and Smiley, 1978).

Developmental psychologists have been concerned with the processes that learners employ when studying. However, their work also has its limitations; primarily the fact that the main concentration is on children learning strange kinds of material in even stranger settings. It is only recently that developmental psychologists have turned their attention to the school-like activity of studying texts (Brown and Smiley, 1978; Brown and Day, Note 2). One impetus for the work carried out in my laboratory has been an attempt to combine the interest in developmental processes of learning with the concentration of educational psychologists on learning in academic settings.

To be very brief, the major findings from the developmental literature that have influenced our work are: first, the notion of *Selective Attention*. As children mature they become adept at channeling their attention to the most informative aspect of information. They become able to ignore irrelevant or less informative aspects of material. This selective attention is influenced by three main factors: 1) *Strategies*, as children mature they show a marked tendency to introduce a variety of increasingly ingenious ploys to aid learning; 2) *Metacognition*, as previously discussed, as children mature they acquire more knowledge concerning methods and procedures for studying and the match between the task at hand and their available repertoire of strategies; and 3) *Content Knowledge*, obviously as children mature, they acquire more knowledge about the world around them. This increased content knowledge must influence how they selectively attend, and how they tailor their learning process.

Plan of the Chapter

The work from my laboratory has concentrated on examining the mutual compatibility and interdependence of these forms of knowledge and the effect they have on students' efficiency when learning from texts. In the remaining section of the paper I will give a brief description of four lines of work: 1) Selecting and studying the main idea by means of such strategies as note-taking and underlining; 2) filling in the details to support the main idea; 3) summary writing and 4) question asking. On the last two topics I will discuss initial attempts to train students to become more effective users of the necessary strategies.

Selecting and Studying the Main Ideas

The original work on text learning was conducted with Sandra Smiley. We began in 1972. At that time there was little existing developmental work on children's memory for stories, with the exception of the classic studies by Binet (Binet and Henri, 1894) and Piaget (1928). Influenced by Bartlett's work with adults, we chose folktales as our story material and for the first half of this paper I will discuss our work on children learning story materials. In the second half of the paper my concern will be children studying expository materials.

Students are commonly exhorted to concentrate on the main ideas when studying, but in order to be responsive to this suggestion, they must be aware of what the main points of a passage are. This is a gradually developing skill; and although children as young as six can often indicate the main character and sequence of events in a simple narrative, they often experience difficulty isolating central issues in more complex prose (Brown and Smiley, 1977; Smiley, Oakley, Worthen, Campione, and Brown, 1977). For example, we found that grade school children who were perfectly able to recall the main ideas of folk stories had much more difficulty rating sections of the stories in terms of their importance to the theme. We asked students, aged 8, 10, 12, and 18 years, to rate the idea units of complex folk stories in terms of their importance to the theme of a passage (Brown and Smiley, 1977). Only 18-year-olds could reliably distinguish the previously rated four levels of importance. Twelve-year-olds did not differentiate the two intermediate levels of importance, but they did assign their lowest scores to the least important and highest scores to the most important elements. Eight-year-olds made no reliable distinction between levels of importance in their ratings and even 10-year-old students could only distinguish the highest level of importance from all other levels. There was considerable agreement between independent groups of college students, and even 12-year-olds, concerning the importance of constituent idea units of a text passage; but 8- and 10-year-old subjects were unable to differentiate units in terms of their relative importance to the text. Thus, when the passage is relatively long (55 idea units) and complex (fifth grade reading level), even junior high school students experience some difficulty in identifying the important elements of text.

It is important to note, however, that recall of the passages at all ages was sensitive to the importance level of the units. After rating a story for the importance of its units, subjects were asked to read and recall another story. Although the older students remembered more than the younger children, the general pattern of results was consistent across the age range of 8 to 18 years, the least important units were recalled less frequently than all other units and the most important units were most often recalled. Even without prior awareness of the importance of constituent units, younger children still favor the important units in recall. Apparently we spontaneously abstract the main ideas of an oral or written communication even when no deliberate attempt to do so is instigated.

These initial findings have important implications for studying. In order to go beyond retention of just a few main points, i.e., to achieve a more complete "fleshed-out" memory of the text, one must engage in active strategies to ensure increased attention to important material that will not be retained automatically. This need for active intervention is particularly pressing if the contents of lengthy texts are to be retained over some period of time, a typical school learning situation. If young children have difficulty distinguishing what is important they will also have difficulty studying. Quite simply, one cannot selectively attend to importance in the absence of a fine sensitivity to what *is* important.

As children mature they become better able to identify what are the essential organizing features and crucial elements of texts. Thanks to this foreknowledge, they make better use of extended study time. For example, we found that when given an extra period of study (equal to three times their reading rate), children from seventh grade up improved their recall considerably for important events of text; recall of less important details did not improve. Children below seventh grade did not usually show such effective use of additional study time; their recall improved, if at all, evenly across all levels of importance. As a result, older students' recall protocols following study included all the essential elements and little trivia. Younger children's recall, though still favoring important elements, had many such elements missing (Brown and Smiley, 1978).

We believe that the older students benefit from increased study time as a direct result of their insights into their own cognitive processes while reading and their ability to predict ahead of time what are the important elements of the texts. Younger students, not so prescient, cannot be expected to distribute extra time intelligently; they do not concentrate on only the important elements of text, since they do not know in advance what they are.

To substantiate our belief that metacognitive control governs this developmental trend we observed the study actions of the students. In particular, we examined the physical records they provided—notes and underlining of texts. A certain proportion of children from fifth grade and up spontaneously underlined or took notes during study. At all ages, the physical records of spontaneous subjects favored the important elements; i.e., the notes or underlined sections concentrated on elements of the text previously rated as crucial to the theme (Brown and Smiley, 1978).

Students induced to adopt one of these strategies did not show a similar sensitivity to importance; they took notes or underlined more randomly. Although the efficiency of physical record keeping in induced subjects did improve with age, it never reached the standard set by spontaneous users of the strategy. Furthermore, the recall of spontaneous producers of the strategies was much superior. Even fifth graders who spontaneously underlined showed an adult-like pattern and used extra study to differentially improve their recall of important elements. This interesting difference between spontaneous and induced users of the note-taking or underlining strategy may explain the curious lack of effect so far found in adult studies concerned with these processes (Anderson, 1980). Previous studies have typically assigned students arbitrarily to treatment groups, thus, in effect, combining those who would or would not use the strategy on their own volition. This procedure tends to mask the efficiency of the strategy, an efficiency which is dependent on its subject-generated nature (Baker and Brown, 1984a; Brown and Smiley, 1978).

Filling in Details

Once they have ensured that the main ideas are well understood, efficient students will take steps to fill in the details. One method of achieving this is to test oneself to determine which details one has failed to recall and then to devote extra attention to the previously missed information. Even grade school children can initiate some efforts to test their current state of memory (Masur, McIntyre, and Flavell, 1973) and mildly retarded children can be taught to do so (Brown and Campione, 1977; Brown, Campione, and Barclay, 1979). But this can become a much more difficult task if the material is complex.

We examined the ability to concentrate on information one has previously failed to recall, in a laboratory task analogous to the process of studying (Brown, Smiley, and Lawton, 1977; Brown and Campione, 1979). Students from fifth through twelfth grade, together with college students, were asked to study prose passages until they could recall all the details in their own words. They were allowed repeated study trials. The passages were divided into constituent idea units rated in terms of their importance to the theme; there were four levels of rated importance. On each trial the students were allowed to select a subset of the idea units (printed on cards) to keep with them while they attempted recall. After recall and a rest period, the entire process was repeated.

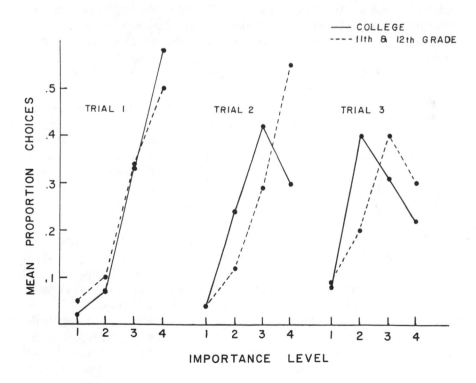

Figure 1. Retrieval cue selection over trials for the older students (from Brown & Campione, 1979).

Of interest are the idea units selected as retrieval aids to enhance recall. The data for college students and older high school students are shown in Figure 1. On the first trial the majority of students at all ages selected the most important units to help them recall. Children below high school age continued to do this, even though across trials they became perfectly able to recall the most important information without aid, but persistently failed to recall additional details. College students, however, modified their selection as a function of trials: on the first trial they selected predominantly important Level 4 units for retrieval aids. On the second trial they shifted to a preference for Level 3 units while on the third trial they preferred Level 2 units. On all three trials, Level 1 units were treated appropriately as trivia. As they learned more and more of the material, college students shifted their choice of retrieval cues to reflect their estimated state of knowledge.

Older high school students showed the same basic pattern as the college students, but they were one trial behind; they did not begin to shift to less important units until the third trial. This lag could be due to slower learning, i.e., both groups shifted when they reached the same criterion of learning but the younger students took an extra trial to reach that criterion. It could also be due to a slower selection of the effective study strategy of switching to less important units, i.e., both groups learned as much on each trial but it took high school students longer to realize they needed to shift cue selection. The latter appears to be the correct interpretation, for even when students were matched on the basis of degree of learning, the younger students still look longer to shift their choice of retrieval cues.

The ability to select suitable retrieval cues is a late-developing skill, because it requires a fine degree of sensitivity to the demands of studying. The successful user of the flexible retrieval plan illustrated in these studies must have (a) information concerning the current state of knowledge, i.e., what he knows of the text and what he does not yet know; (b) knowledge of the fine gradation of importance of various elements of texts, i.e., what is important to know and what can be disregarded; and (c) the strategic knowledge to select for retrieval cue information previously missed.

It is interesting to note that in some sense the very late development of this study skill is surprising. Students as young as third grade (Masur et al., 1973) and even fifth grade educably retarded students (Brown and Campione, 1977) can employ a primitive version of this strategy. Given a list of pictures to remember, they do select for extra study items they have failed to recall. But it is not until much later in their school careers that students can apply this strategy to the complex task of learning from texts. I believe that this is a ubiquitous problem for young studiers who must learn to apply strategies they can use perfectly well outside of reading tasks to the less familiar written medium. We are currently working on training students to use the appropriate selection strategy for filling in details by illustrating the activity on the simple list learning task and explicitly stating the obvious analogy to the text learning situation (Brown, Jones, and Mancuso, work in progress).

Summary Writing

Jeanne Day and I have been working on a series of studies concerning the development of the ability to write summaries of studies and expository materials (Brown, Campione, and Day, 1981; Brown and Day, Note 2; Day, 1980). As we have seen, adequate recall of anything more than simple short stories requires both effort and judgment. Recall, if it is to include more than a bare skeleton, demands strategies for concentrating on difficult and important elements (Brown and Campione, 1979); it requires judgment of what to include and what to omit. For these reasons, improved recall after studying complex texts is a relatively late developing skill (Brown and Smiley, 1978). Similarly, summarizing texts must also entail judgment and effort if more than the barest synopsis is required. Estimations of fine degrees of relative importance must be made and rules for condensation employed. Thus, we predicted that the ability to provide an adequate summary of a lengthy text would also be a late developing skill, a prediction well supported by the existing traditional educational literature (Germane, 1921a, 1921b; Stordahl and Christensen, 1956).

A problem with estimating children's ability to summarize is that it is essential that we are able to distinguish between the "automatic" by-product of comprehension, and the deliberate result of judgment and effort (Brown, 1975; Hasher and Zacks, 1979). If children as well as adults "automatically" extract the main gist when comprehending stories, there is a danger that we will obtain excellent summaries from children, not because they thought about their responses, but because they produced all the information they had available. It is necessary, therefore, to ensure that subjects can recall much of the information they are required to summarize. Two ways of accomplishing this are to use simple stories which are well-formed according to a story grammar view and that produce excellent recall (Johnson, 1978). But such well-formed stories are already excellent summaries, leaving little room for judgment and selection. The second alternative, the one we adopted, is to use more lengthy, complex stories and require that the students learn the texts to some criterion before preparing a summary. Under these circumstances, we can examine the development of children's judgments concerning what elements to omit or include but we would not have confounded memory and selection.

Six studies will be reported briefly. The first serves as a descriptive study of the development of the ability to summarize texts. Here we build upon our previous work on children's identification and use of important element of texts (Brown and Campione, 1979; Brown and Smiley, 1977, 1978; Brown, Smiley, and Lawton, 1977; Brown, Smiley, Day, Townsend, and Lawton, 1977). The second study is a more analytic examination of the condensation rules used by children and adults to achieve adequate synopses of texts. In the third study we examined experts' use of summarization rules using on-line "talk-aloud" protocols. Following our consideration of experts we turned our attention to novices; in the fourth study we examined the potential diagnostic power of our developmental norms by considering the performance of junior college students, a population known to experience problems in critical reading and effective studying. In the fifth and sixth experiments we attempted to train a variety of junior college students to improve their ability to summarize texts.

Summarizing the main idea. We asked students from fifth, seventh and eleventh grade, as well as college-age students, to learn a story so that they could remember all the information, even the details, in their own words. Only those students able to comply with this request (remember more than 80 percent of all four levels of importance in our stories) were allowed to continue in the study. After recalling the story, the students were then asked to write a summary in their own words. The number of words was not specified.

After they had finished the first summary (and a break), the children were told that the editor (person in charge of space) had cut their space because there was a very important story that must be covered. Their task now was to write the story again but in only forty words. To help them they were given large sheets of paper with forty spaces at the bottom where they were to write their summary. No explicit instructions concerning the use of the top half of the page (blank) were given. We thought that this might be a hint that the subjects should make a rough draft before attempting to fill in the spaces. In the final phase, the procedure was repeated except that the subject's space was cut back to twenty words.

A brief synopsis of the summarization performance of eleventh graders and college students is that they included in their summaries primarily level 3 and 4 (important) units. While some lower level units (1-2) were included in the free paraphrase, these dropped out as soon as space pressure was exerted. Even though the pattern of results was very similar for eleventh graders and college students, college students' greater efficiency was reflected in their ability to include more idea units in the same number of words.

The fifth grade pattern was somewhat different but intriguing in light of prior data from this age group. Remember that in our initial study (Brown and Smiley, 1977), fifth graders had been asked to rate the units of these stories for importance. The fifth graders' ratings differed from older children in that they were only able to distinguish level 4 units as more important to the theme than the remaining units. This difference in rating data has been found to influence the note-taking (Brown and Smiley, 1978), underlining (Brown and Smiley, 1978), and retrieval cue selection (Brown and Campione, 1979; Brown, Smiley, and Lawton, 1978) of fifth grade subjects. Whereas older subjects show a clear pattern of underlining, notetaking, and cue selection, reflecting all levels of importance of idea units, fifth graders only show a preference in their notes, underscored sections or selections for level 4 units over all the other units. This pattern of results has been taken as evidence of a close link between knowledge factors and performance. As the fifth graders only recognize level 4 units as more important, they concentrate only on these units when working on these texts. Older students distribute their attention as a function of the finer degrees of importance that they are able to recognize.

This same pattern was found here with the unconstrained summary. When left free to paraphrase in as many words as they wished, fifth graders included many more level 4 units in their summaries than any other level but showed no preference for level 3 over levels 1 or 2. However, as space pressure was exerted in the constrained summaries, the pattern changed in interesting ways. Constrained to forty words, the fifth graders dropped level 1 units; further limited to twenty words the fifth graders dropped level 2 units and thus ended up with a pattern indistinguishable from older subjects. This dropping of units as a function of their rated importance is the first evidence we have, in this extensive series of studies, that fifth graders are in any way sensitive to fine differences in importance between levels 1, 2 and 3 of these stories. When severely pressed for space even the younger children are sensitive to fine degrees of importance, a sensitivity that comparable age children do not show when studying the texts (Brown and Smiley, 1977, 1978) or rating them under a variety of conditions (Brown, Smiley, and Lawton, 1978; Brown and Campione, 1979). This is a nice illustration of the fact that estimating a child's knowledge or "awareness" is not a simple task; the degree to which a student will be judged "aware" depends on the indices used to measure that awareness (Baker and Brown, 1984a; Brown, 1978; Brown, 1980). Only when severely pressed for space do fifth graders indicate that the units of these texts differ in terms of their importance to the theme of the story.

In all phases of the initial summarization study we provided scratch paper and blank spaces for any attempts to rough draft the summaries before filling in the spaces. Students varied in the degree to which they spontaneously prepared rough drafts. A prototype rough draft would consist of a preliminary written version of the passage, often with the number of words indicated, then a rewrite, and sometimes more than one rewrite. The proposition of students attempting a rough draft increased with age (.13, .37, .46, and .63 respectively for grades five, seven, eleven and college students).

Another interesting index of planning was our informal observation that the younger children not only failed to make a rough draft but also appeared to run out of space, i.e., the children complained that they had no spaces left into which to fit the end of the story. To test this observation we divided the text into two halves so that the halves contained approximately the same number of idea units, distributed evenly over the levels of importance. We then calculated how many units of the first and second half of the story were included in the summaries of children who did and did not make rough drafts (referred to as the Plan and No Plan groups). There was a dramatic difference between planning and not planning subjects at the lower two ages. Those younger children who prepared a rough draft showed no effects of first half, second half in their summaries. Subjects not thinking ahead, however, favored the first half of the story. This confirms the anecdotal report that younger children ran out of space because they failed to leave room for the second half of the story. This was not true for older subjects or for younger subjects who made a rough draft. Younger children who failed to make a rough draft tended to run out of space before completing their summary. College students who do not produce a rough draft have sufficient control of their activity to enable them to produce an adequate representation of both halves of the story.

To summarize, by fifth grade, children are unable to attempt a summary of lengthy texts but clear developmental trends are found. College students and older high school students outperform younger children in their propensity to plan ahead, in their sensitivity to fine gradations of importance in the text, and in their ability to condense more idea units into the same number of words. As predicted, under circumstances when a summary (or a recall protocol) is not just a measure of automatic retention, the ability to recursively work on the information to render it as succinctly as possible requires judgment and effort, knowledge and strategies (Baker and Brown, 1984a, b; Brown and Smiley, 1978). As such, the ability to provide an adequate summary of a lengthy text is a late developing skill that continues to be refined throughout the school year (Brown and Day, Note 2).

Condensation rules for summary writing. At this point my colleagues and I became dissatisfied with our total reliance on the rated importance measure as an indication of efficiency. Although the rated importance metric was quite successful as a measure of where attention was being directed, it did not provide sensitive information concerning the sophisticated strategies students used to direct attention. For example, the younger students in the Brown and Smiley (1978) note-taking study produced a pattern of note-taking that differed qualitatively from the older students; their notes were closely related to the surface structure of the text, both in the order of occurrence of the idea units and in the near verbatim selection of words actually contained in the text. Older subjects not only showed a greater tendency to take notes and to take notes that were extremely sensitive to rated importance, they also demonstrated a greater ability to paraphrase and to rearrange order into topic clusters.

A very similar pattern emerged in our initial summarization study (Brown and Day, Note 2). Younger children tended to operate on material mainly by deleting or retaining surface elements of the texts. Older students relied on paraphrase and condensation rules to combine and rearrange idea units, to depart from the words actually present in the text. It was by such means that they were able to condense more idea units into fewer words. It is these strategies that the importance level rating procedure did not measure. And it is these activities that we wished to capture by a more sensitive metric.

After considering the qualitative differences between the younger and older students' summaries we identified a number of general rules that we believed to be the ones used by the more mature. To test this we asked expert summarizers (college rhetoric and journalism teachers) what rules they used to summarize. Although they were remarkably uninformative about the existence of set rules, a consideration of their "talk-aloud" protocols while actually summarizing confirmed that the rules we had identified were, indeed, the primary ones used by experts. In addition, contemporaneous with our work, Kintsch and van Dijk (1978) described a series of macrorules for comprehension of texts that had a great deal of similarity to our summarization rules. Thus, from both a practical and theoretical viewpoint, we had reason to believe in the psychological reality of our rule coding system.

Two of the six rules we identified involve the deletion of unnecessary material. One should obviously *delete* material that is *trivial*, and even grade school children are quite adept at this if the content of the material is familiar. One should also *delete* material that is important but is also *redundant*. Kintsch and van Dijk's system also includes these two deletion rules. Two of the rules of summarization involve the *substitution of a superordinate* term or event for a list of items or actions. For example, if a text contains a list such as: cats, dogs, goldfish, gerbils and parrots, one can substitute the term pets. Similarly, one can substitute a superordinate action for a list of subcomponents of that action, i.e., John went to London, for: John left the house, John went to the train station, John bought a ticket, etc., etc. These rules are roughly comparable to Kintsch and van Dijk's (1978) generalization rules. The two remaining rules have to do with providing a summary of the main constituent unit of text, the paragraph. The first rule is—*select a topic sentence*, if any, for this is the author's summary of the paragraph. We referred to this as the *selection rule*, but it is similar to Kintsch and van Dijk's integration rule. The final rule is—if there is no topic sentence, *invent* your own. These operations are roughly equivalent to Kintsch and van Dijk's (1978) construction rule. We would like to point out that although we identified these basic rules as specific strategies actually used by students when engaged in the formal task of summarizing, they are also rules used by the more mature students in the note-taking studies conducted earlier (Brown and Smiley, 1978). We agree with Kintsch and van Dijk that the *macrorules of deletion, superordination, selection* and *invention* are general rules underlying comprehension of texts.

These operations are used freely by experts when summarizing texts, but do less sophisticated readers realize that these basic rules can be applied? To map the developmental progression associated with the use of the basic rules we examined the ability of students from grades 5, 7 and 10 and various college students to use the rules while summarizing. We used specially constructed texts that enabled us to predict when each rule should be applied or at least would be applied by experts (college rhetoric teachers). Even the youngest children were able to use the two deletion rules with above 90 percent accuracy, showing that they understood the basic idea behind a summary—get rid of unnecessary material. On the more complex rules, however, developmental differences were apparent. Students became increasingly adept at using the topic sentence selection rules, with college students performing extremely well. However, the most difficult rule, invention, was rarely used by fifth graders, used on only a third of appropriate occasions by tenth graders and on only half of the occasions when it was appropriate, even by college students.

Although, within the Kintsch and van Dijk (1978) model, there is no reason to suspect that the five rules of summarization would be of different difficulty, our developmental pattern was quite clear. One explanation for the differential difficulty of the five rules is that they demand differing degrees of cognitive manipulation and they depart to a greater or lesser extent from the already existing strategy favored by the younger participants. We refer to this as the *copy-delete* strategy. Fifth graders tend to treat the task of summarizing as one of deciding if to include or delete elements that actually occur in the surface structure of the original text. This is the same general strategy employed by fifth and seventh grade note-takers (Baker and Smiley, 1978) and even second grade summarizers attempting to orally summarize simple stories (Johnson, 1978). The strategy is as follows: a) read text elements sequentially; b) decide for each element on inclusion or deletion; c) if inclusion is the verdict, copy it more or less verbatim from the text.

This simple strategy is used consistently in a variety of text processing tasks by 11-12 year old students and it works relatively well in that it gets the job done, it does result in a product that is recognizably a summary, an outline or a set of notes. It is because the simple copy-delete strategy is so generally applicable and meets with some success that it is difficult to get students to attempt more complex rules. Bereiter and Scardamalia (in press) have found that the simple "knowledge-telling" strategy in writing, preferred by 11-12 year olds, is also resistant to change, again because it is relatively successful and generally applicable.

Consider the five rules of deletion, superordination and topic sentence manipulation in terms of how far they depart from the copy-delete strategy. Obviously the easy deletion rules map straight onto the existing strategy. Copy-delete works quite well for superordination with the exception that the students must add a superordinate in place of a list. But in order to use the topic sentence rules appropriately the students must abandon either the sequential unit by unit approach (selection) or both the sequential approach and the copy-delete principle (invention). To use the selection rule the students must have some realization of the unique status of the topic sentence within paragraphs and write their summaries in support of topic sentences they have selected. This would demand disrupting the sequentiality rule and giving unique status to topic sentences, probably by selecting them first to form the scaffolding of the summary. This is the rule used by experts (Brown and Day, Note 2). The copy-delete rule still applies in that one can copy the selected topic sentence straight from the text.

The difficult invention rule is, I think, difficult because it departs most radically from the favored copy-delete ploy. Students must now add something of their own, a synopsis in their own words of the implicit meaning of the paragraph. The invention rule, therefore, requires that the students add information rather than just delete, select or manipulate sentences already provided for them. It is these processes that are the essence of good summarization, that are used with facility by experts and that are most difficult for novice learners.

Experts' summaries. Even college students did not apply the condensation rules perfectly, experiencing particular problems with the invention rule. We decided, therefore, to look at the performance of experts. Our experts were fourth year graduate students in English who had taught rhetoric classes. Their performance on the summary task is presented in Figure 2, together with the data from undergraduates at a four year college and junior college students.

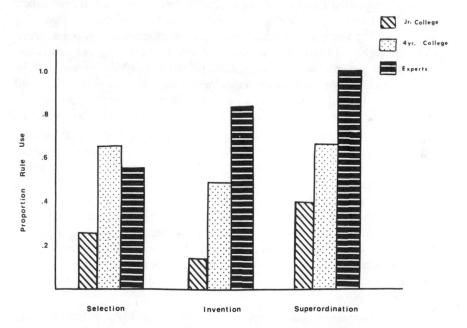

Figure 2. Use of the selection, invention and superordination rules by college students with varying degrees of expertise (from Brown & Day, Note 2).

The experts used the superordination rule perfectly compared to the 70% level set by college students. There were no differences between populations in the use of the selection rule. However, the experts used the difficult invention rule much more than did the college students (.84 vs. .49). Indeed, a case could be made that the experts performed perfectly because on the rare occasions that they did not receive a "correct score" for invention use, they had combined two paragraphs into one, thereby losing credit for one topic sentence use. (This tendency depressed their scores for the selection rule also.) Rarely did any of the other students combine paragraphs. Experts, however, favored the paragraph-combining strategy and attempted to use it whenever possible.

We also collected verbal protocols from the experts. In the open-ended interviews prior to actually summarizing, the experts showed a surprising lack of evidence that they knew any effective rules for summarization. Their description of what a good summary was, and what to tell students, was essentially similar to that contained in rhetoric textbooks (Bessey and Coffin, 1934). They stressed that a summary is a concise statement of the theme and that one should avoid unnecessary repetition, be concise, include only main ideas, etc., but there was no mention of a systematic set of rules for doing this.

During their attempt to summarize, however, the experts made frequent mention of the basic rules. Of the statements judged to be a reference to rule use, 58% were an explicit statement of one of the five rules. For example, one expert provided the following succinct statement of the superordination rule: "One thing I've done is drop the kinds of plants. Instead of writing daisies, poppies, marigolds, and lilies, all I've written is 'annual plants,' again leaving out details and talking about generalizations." And for the invention rule, she provided: "The paragraph is about the cycle of the annual plants that produce seeds, wait until rainfall, bloom, produce seeds again, etc. Although it doesn't say so, all you need is to state this cycle, then you can drop the rest" (Brown and Day, Note 2).

The experts were unable or unwilling to give a precise statement of the rules prior to attempting to summarize a text; they spoke in very general terms about finding "main ideas" and "being concise," etc. However, when actually faced with the task of summarizing a passage, they were much more explicit about the rules they were employing and the rules they stated were, for the most part, the basic rules of deletion, superordination and topic sentence manipulation. The only other dominant rule that was used by experts and repeatedly appeared in their protocols was the combining-paragraphs rule. Experts used the rule routinely, whereas less mature students rarely attempted to combine across paragraphs, seeming instead to be "captured" by the paragraph structure provided in the original passage.

Novices' summaries. Having examined experts' summarization performance, we turned our attention to novices. In order to examine the diagnostic value of our age norms, we repeated the summary study using junior college students, a population known for deficient skills of critical reading and studying, although a consideration of the traditional educational research literature would suggest that junior college students are not alone in their inability to adequately abbreviate text. Elementary school children (Germane, 1921a, 1921b), Air Force recruits (Stordahl and Christensen, 1956), and Harvard undergraduates (Perry, 1959) all demonstrate poor summarizing skills. In fact, summarizing is just one of several study techniques that these students fail to employ well (Anderson and Armbruster, 1980; Baker and Brown, 1984a). Educators complain that high school students (Beauchamp, 1923; Dynes, 1932; Germane, 1921b), recruits for the armed forces (Stordahl and Christensen, 1956; Weinstein, 1978), and even college undergraduates (McClusky and Dolch, 1924; Preston and Tufts, 1948) lack effective note-taking, outlining, and summarizing skills. An examination of the validity of these traditional claims, using our sensitive diagnosis of rule use, seemed timely. Our novices were junior college students enrolled in an English course that fulfilled the freshman rhetoric requirement at that college and at many 4-year universities. That is, students could receive credit for this course should they continue their education at a 4-year institution. The students were *not*, therefore, diagnosed as having any reading or writing problems on the basis of tests administered on entry to the college. In general, they were in a college preparation stream. English was their first language.

The novices performed extremely well on the deletion rules but departed significantly from the norms set by college students on the superordination, selection and invention rules (see Figure 2). In general, junior college students performed on a par with seventh graders in our developmental study. These data confirm the claims of educational psychologists that students from less academically privileged backgrounds perform poorly on a variety of text processing strategies, including summarization. Our data take us beyond this global claim by providing a more fine-grained analysis of where the students are experiencing particular problems. We see that the ability to delete trivial or redundant material is relatively intact, at least with the very simple expository materials used in these studies. The strategies needed for adequate manipulation of topic sentence rules are, however, much more problematic for these students. Junior college students, even those with no diagnosed reading or writing problems, perform on a level comparable to that of seventh graders from regular junior high schools (Brown and Day, Note 2). Given this depressing level of performance, it appears that there is ample room for improvement.

Training summarization skills. In her Ph.D. thesis, Jeanne Day undertook to train junior college students to use the condensation rules more appropriately. This was a complex study from which I will select only the highlights (for full details, see Day, 1980). There were two studies in the Day thesis; the first provided 3 days of training in small groups to junior college students of two levels of ability: *"Normal"* students with no reading or writing problems diagnosed and *Remedial Writer* students with diagnosed writing problems but no known reading problems. The second study provided intensive, one-on-one training to a more severely learning impaired group, *Remedial Readers*, who had both reading and writing problems.

Students were assigned to one of four instructional conditions that varied in how explicit the training was: 1) *Self-management:* the students were given general encouragement to write a good summary, to capture the main ideas, to dispense with trivia and all unnecessary words—but they were not told rules for achieving this end. This type of instruction is quite typical of the routine class-room practice for "teaching" summarization (Bessey and Coffin, 1934). 2) *Rules:* the students were given explicit instructions and modeling in the use of the rules. For example, they were given various colored pencils and shown how to delete redundant information in red, delete trivial information in blue, write in superor-dinates for any lists, underline topic sentences if provided and write in a topic sentence if needed. 3) *Rules Plus Self-Management:* the students in the third group were given both the general self-management instruction of Group I and the rules instruction of Group II, but they were left to integrate the two sets of information for themselves. 4) *Control Plus Monitoring:* the fourth and most explicit training condition involved training in the rules and additional explicit training in the monitoring of these rules—i.e., the students were shown how to check that they had a topic sentence for each paragraph (either underlined or written in), to check that all redundancies were deleted, all trivia erased, etc., and that any lists of items were replaced with superordinates; they were taught how to monitor that the rules had been used correctly and exhaustively.

The results of training were encouraging. The two deletion rules were easy to apply to these simple texts and, therefore, performance was nearly perfect before, during, and after training for both the Normal and Remedial Writers. Performance on the superordination rule was very good after only minimal in-struction and all students, regardless of ability, learned to use it well. Perform-ance on the selection rule was never as good as performance on the superordination rule. Nevertheless, after students were taught to select topic sen-tences, they continued to do so at a reasonable level of proficiency at least 2 weeks after training had ceased. Average writers were more adept at using the rule, but all students seemed to try. Finally, the invention rule was the most diffi-cult for all subjects. Training was helpful and did result in lasting improvement but it took the very explicit training (Rules Plus Monitoring) before the perform-ance of the remedial students reached that set by 4-year college students.

The Remedial Readers, students with the most serious problems, also showed improvement following training. They were readily prompted into using the deletion rules as effectively as average students do without training. The su-perordination rule was also learned easily and students maintained good use of the rule on the posttests. However, improvement in the use of the selection rule was slight and poor readers experienced major problems before, during, and af-ter training with the invention rule. Instruction in the hardest rules resulted in little improvement.

Apart from providing evidence that the basic skills of summarization can be taught, Day's study also demonstrated a form of aptitude by treatment interaction (Snow, 1980) in that the more experienced students tended to need less explicit instruction in order to improve their performance. For example, students diag-nosed as poor writers needed the very explicit training involving instruction in monitoring rule use before they reached a level of performance similar to that set by untrained 4-year college students. It was often the case that average and poor writers and poor readers did not differ on the pretests but, as can be seen in Figure 3, average writers benefited much more from training. Theoretically, we claim that the students of varying ability level had different "zones of proximal development" or "regions of sensitivity to instruction" (Brown, Campione, and Day, 1981; Brown and Ferrara, in press; Brown and French, 1979; Vygotsky, 1978). That is "readiness" to benefit from instruction differentiated the groups. Note that for these students, the starting level of competence was approximately equal; that is, initial performance level would not differentiate the groups. However, the zone of potential development, or how much can be achieved with aid, is higher for the average than for the remedial students.

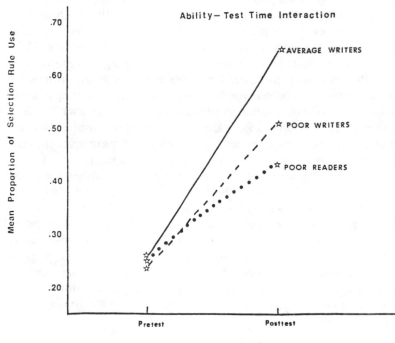

Figure 3. Junior college students' improvement in selecting topic sentences after training (from Day, 1980).

A second major finding in the Day study concerns the "explicitness" of instruction. The best performance was always obtained in the rules plus monitoring condition; the next best was the rules plus self-management group; the third best was the rules alone training; and insignificant gains were made by the self-management alone group. This ordering was found on training, on immediate and on delayed posttests. And it was obtained across rules. The consistency of this result is impressive.

In summary, training attempts were successful at improving the summarizing abilities of junior college students. The difficulty of the rules being taught and the ability level of the students interacted to determine how explicit training must be to effect improvement. In the absence of specific means to accomplish the goals, instruction of only very general self-management routines was not beneficial. Straightforward training in the specific strategies needed for problem solution led to better performance on the simpler rules. However, with the more difficult concepts, particularly with students with diagnosed reading and writing problems, explicit training in strategies for accomplishing the task coupled with routines to oversee and monitor their success, was clearly the best approach.

As a final note, we would like to reiterate that the rules of summarization that we have been studying are general comprehension strategies, not just a set of specific rules for summarizing per se (Kintsch and van Dijk, 1978). These rules are the essential operations that are basic to comprehension and it is variants of these rules that students need to make explicit as procedures for studying. Making the macrorules explicit, as we have done in our training procedures, is a generally useful study skill invaluable for improving one's ability to monitor one's own comprehension. For example, checking oneself while reading to see if one has pinpointed important material and discarded trivial information, to see if one can either identify an author's topic sentence or invent one if necessary, are all checks that comprehension is progressing smoothly. If, for example, one cannot produce an adequate synopsis of a paragraph (invention rule), this is a clear sign that comprehension is *not* proceeding smoothly and remedial action is called for (Baker and Brown, 1984a). Given the general applicability of the basic macrorules for a wide variety of study monitoring tasks and our initial success in training rudimentary use of the rules, we are optimistic that a general cognitive skill training program could be developed using the macrorules as cornerstones. Macrorules for comprehension (1) are important, (2) have a wide range of applicability, (3) are developmentally sensitive, (4) are educationally relevant, and (5) can be taught; all, we have argued, essential features of target skills for intensive cognitive skills training programs (Brown and Campione, 1981; Brown, Campione, and Day, 1981).

Self-Questioning Routines and Reciprocal Questioning

The final study I will report has just been completed and I will give only a brief synopsis of the results. The topic is a familiar one, self-questioning while reading.

One way to facilitate learning from text during reading is to engage in self-interrogation. Andre and Anderson (1978-1979) recently developed and tested a self-questioning study technique in which high school students were taught to locate sections of text containing important points and generate questions about them. They found that generating such questions facilitated learning better than simply reading and rereading text or making up questions without regard to important points. In addition, the training was more effective for students of lower ability, suggesting that the better students had developed effective self-questioning techniques of their own. Andre and Anderson suggest that self-questioning may be more effective than such passive strategies as rereading because it incorporates many metacognitive components. That is, it encourages the reader to (a) set purposes for study, (b) identify and underline important segments of the material, (c) generate questions which require comprehension of the text to be correctly answered, and (d) think of possible answers to the questions. The questioning strategy leads the student to an active monitoring of the learning activity and to the engagement of strategic action.

Student-generated questions are valuable not only as an aid to studying but also as an aid to comprehension itself. Singer's (1978) conception of "active comprehension" involves reacting to a text with questions and seeking answers with subsequent reading. He found that student-generated questions are more effective in promoting comprehension than teacher-generated questions even for children in elementary school. The ability to ask relevant questions of oneself during reading is, of course, crucial to comprehension monitoring and studying. Thus, training in effective question-asking may be an important first step in the development of monitoring skills. Collins, Brown, and Larkin (1980) suggest that many failures of comprehension are in fact due to a failure to ask the right questions; and a study by Nash and Torrance (1974) has shown that participation in a creative reading program designed to sensitize readers to gaps in their knowledge, such as inconsistencies and ambiguities, led to a significant improvement in the kinds of questions that first graders asked about their reading material.

A student in my laboratory, Annemarie Palincsar (Note 3), undertook to train four seventh grade minority children who were reported by their teachers to be adequate decoders (fifth-seventh grade) but poor comprehenders (second grade). The design of the study was influenced by the technology of applied behavior analysis. Palincsar had two interventions that she referred to as (1) corrective feedback and (2) strategy training. *Corrective feedback* consisted of asking children questions about a story they had read, and providing explicit information concerning the correct answer, the location of the answer in the text, and whether or not the material was implicitly (need to be inferred) or explicitly stated (Raphael, 1980). *Strategy training* (reciprocal questioning) was based on the *Re Quest* procedure developed by Manzo (1968). The student and the instructor take turns asking each other questions concerning the text. Palincsar concentrated on two of the types of comprehension fostering questions suggested by Collins and Smith (1981): hypothesis testing and prediction making. The instructor in this procedure both encourages the students to ask questions and, in turn, models the desired question type repeatedly.

Palincsar personally tested the children every day for approximately 40 days. During baseline (6-8 days), the students read grade-appropriate passages and then answered the comprehension questions on the text. Each day throughout the study, they continued to read a text privately and answer 10 questions; and it

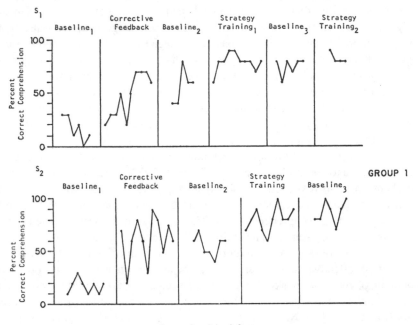

Figure 4. Improvement on comprehension measures during baseline and training sessions (from Palincsar, Note 3).

is the performance of two of the students on these texts that is shown in Figure 4. In the training session, however, performance on the privately read text was preceded by either the corrective feedback or the strategy training session.

During baseline, the students achieved a level of approximately 15% correct. Following baseline, the students in corrective feedback improved to a level of approximately 50% correct, although their performance was very variable. They maintained this level of performance in the second baseline (sessions with no training). When the strategy training (reciprocal questioning) was introduced, performance soared to an impressive 80%-90% correct level. Remember that these scores, shown in detail in Figure 4, were obtained on the privately read passages, i.e., different texts the students read after their interaction with the instructor. What was learned during the instructional sequence was used independently by the learners, both in the laboratory setting and in subsequent classroom behavior (Palincsar, Note 3). Modeling in how to ask appropriate questions greatly increased the students' independent comprehension scores, to the delight of their teachers.

We are greatly encouraged by the success of the reciprocal training procedure and are currently developing a version to use with younger, or less mature coders (Brown, Echols, and Palincsar, work in progress). We begin by introducing the question game as a "fun activity" outside the context of reading. The student and the tutor watch a video-film with predetermined interest to young children of the popular suspense-surprise mode (Lichtenstein and Brewer, 1980). The film is interrupted at preset (suspenseful) intervals and the students and the teacher take turns asking each other questions. The teacher models three types of questions (inferential reasoning, analogy seeking, and prediction and hypotheses generation). Students' questions are systematically evaluated to serve as an indication of their starting competence; changes over sessions indicate their susceptibility of the model's influence. If students persist in asking inappropriate questions (such as literal facts only), the tutor, on subsequent sessions, instigates explicit training by pointing out what kinds of questions she wants and how they help comprehension. Following training, trained students will be paired with naive peers and asked to play the reciprocal questioning game with them. Such a procedure should demonstrate what the trainee has learned.

After practice with the films, students are asked to use the technique during reading sessions (if and only if there was an adequate level of questioning during the film sessions). Student and tutor again question each other at predetermined points of the text. The performance of film-trained students will be compared to a matched group of students who did not receive this treatment.

Immediately following each interactive session, the students receive a comparable text and are asked to study it on their own — underlining and writing down questions for themselves if they so wish. Following private study, students are asked to answer comprehension questions on both the interacted on and private texts. These measures of retention and comprehension will reveal a great deal about the effects of training.

Again, following training on the reading task, we plan to have trained students play the reciprocal questioning game with untrained peers. We have prior success using this method as an index of what children have gained from training (Brown, 1980; Brown and Ferrara, in press). A nice illustration of how informative such a procedure can be was provided by Au (in preparation). She asked third-grade, native Hawaiian children to give a reading lesson to naive first graders, exactly as their teacher did. The children were recidivists from a program that placed heavy emphasis on comprehension training. Good readers asked their small tutees a variety of comprehension type questions ("Why do you think the mouse helped the lion?"). Intermediate readers asked far fewer questions, mainly of the literal or text-explicit kind ("What did the lion have in his foot?"). Poor readers rarely questioned their charges at all, concentrating on rereading, decoding, and pronunciation. Via such techniques, it is possible to evaluate the tutor's own understanding of the reading process.

Conclusion

This series of studies has been directed at uncovering the development of selective attention strategies for understanding and remembering prose. During the junior high and high school years, students develop and increasingly fine-tune a battery of serviceable skills for learning from texts. These include: under-lining (Brown and Smiley, 1978), taking notes on main ideas (Brown and Smiley, 1978), developing macrorules for comprehension, retention, and synopsis writ-ing (Brown and Day, Note 2; Day, 1980), outlining (Armbruster, 1979), self-questioning (Andre and Anderson, 1978; Palincsar, Note 3), concentrating on previously missed or difficult segments of text (Brown and Campione, 1977, 1979; Brown, Campione, and Barclay, 1979; Brown, Smiley, and Lawton, 1978), and the general propensity of treating studying as a purposive act of atten-tion-directing and self-questioning. All these skills tend to be relatively late in developing because they require a fine degree of sensitivity to the demands of learning from texts. Learners must develop rudimentary knowledge of 1) availa-ble strategies for directing attention; 2) their own characteristics as learners, in-cluding capacity limitations and background knowledge; 3) text characteristics, including important elements, structural features, etc.; and 4) the nature of the criterial task, or the test to which the learning must be put (Baker and Brown, 1984a, b; Brown, Bransford, and Ferrara, in press; Brown, Campione, and Day, 1981). The complex coordination of all these factors enables the student to plan, monitor, and evaluate his interaction with texts in an economical and efficient manner.

NOTE

The preparation of this manuscript and the research reported herein was supported by the following grants: HD 06864, HD 05951, and a Research Career Development Award HD 00111, from the Na-tional Institute of Child Health and Human Development, and under Contract No. HEW-NIE-C-400-76-0016. I would like to express my appreciation to the many students and colleagues who have collaborated in various stages of the research, notably Linda Baker, Craig Barclay, Joe Campione, Jeanne Day, Roberta Jones, Sallie Lawton, Annemarie Palincsar, and Sandra Smiley.

REFERENCES

Anderson, T.H. Study strategies and aids. In R.J. Spiro, B.C. Bruce, and W.F. Brewer (Eds.), *Theo-retical issues in reading comprehension*. Hillsdale, N.J.: Erlbaum, 1980.
Anderson, T.H., and Armbruster, B.B. Studying. In P.D. Pearson (Ed.), *Handbook of reading re-search*. New York: Longman, 1980.
Andre, M.E.D.A., and Anderson, T.H. The development and evaluation of a self-questioning study technique. *Reading Research Quarterly,* 1978-1979, *14,* 605-623.
Armbruster, B.B. *An investigation of the effectiveness of "mapping" text as a studying strategy for middle school students.* Unpublished doctoral dissertation, University of Illinois, 1979.
Baker, L., and Brown, A.L. Metacognitive skills of reading. In P.D. Pearson (Ed.), *Handbook of reading research*. New York: Longman, 1984a.
Baker, L., and Brown, A.L. Cognitive monitoring in reading and studying. In J. Flood (Ed.), *Under-standing reading comprehension*. Newark, Del.: International Reading Association, 1984b.
Beauchamp, W. A preliminary experimental study of the technique in the mastery of subject matter in elementary physical science. *Supplementary Educational Monographs*, *24*, University of Chicago, 1923.

Bereiter, C., and Scardamalia, M. From conversation to composition: The role of instructional-developmental process. In R. Glaser (Ed.), *Advances in instructional psychology* (Vol. 2). Hillsdale, N.J.: Erlbaum, in press.

Bessey, M.A., and Coffin, C.P. *Reading through precis*. New York: Appleton-Century, 1934.

Binet, A., and Henri, V. La mémoire des phrases (Mémoire des idées). *Année Psychologique*, 1894, *1*, 24-59.

Brown, A.L. The development of memory: Knowing, knowing about knowing, and knowing how to know. In H.W. Reese (Ed.), *Advances in child development and behavior* (Vol. 10). New York: Academic Press, 1975.

Brown, A.L. Knowing when, where, and how to remember: A problem of metacognition. In R. Glaser (Ed.), *Advances in instructional psychology*. Hillsdale, N.J.: Erlbaum, 1978.

Brown, A.L. Metacognitive development and reading. In R.J. Spiro, B.C. Bruce, and W.F. Brewer (Eds.), *Theoretical issues in reading comprehension*. Hillsdale, N.J.:Erlbaum, 1980.

Brown, A.L. Learning how to learn from reading. In J. Langer and T. Smith-Burke (Eds.), *Reader meets author/bridging the gap: A psycholinguistic and sociolinguistic perspective*. Newark, Del.: International Reading Association, 1982, 26-54.

Brown, A.L. Learning and development: The problems of compatibility, access and induction. *Human Development*, in press (b).

Brown, A.L., Bransford, J.D., and Ferrara, R.A. Learning, understanding and remembering. To appear in J.H. Flavell and E.M. Markman (Eds.), *Handbook of development psychology: Vol. 1, Cognition,* in preparation.

Brown, A.L., and Campione, J.C. Training strategic study time apportionment in educable retarded children. *Intelligence*, 1977, *1*, 94-107.

Brown, A.L., and Campione, J.C. The effects of knowledge and experience on the formation of retrieval plans for studying from texts. In M.M. Gruneberg, P.E. Morris, and R.N. Sykes (Eds.), *Practical aspects of memory*. London: Academic Press, 1979.

Brown, A.L., and Campione, J.C. Inducing flexible thinking: A problem of access. In M. Friedman, J.P. Das, and N. O'Connor (Eds.), *Intelligence and learning*. New York: Plenum Press, 1981.

Brown, A.L., Campione, J.C., and Barclay, C.R. Training self-checking routines for estimating test readiness: Generalization from list learning to prose recall. *Child Development*, 1979, *50*, 501-512.

Brown, A.L., Campione, J.C., and Day, J.D. Learning to learn: On training students to learn from texts. *Educational Researcher*, 1981, *10* (2), 14-21.

Brown, A.L., and Ferrara, R.A. Diagnosing zones of proximal development: An alternative to standardized testing? To appear in J.V. Wertsch (Ed.), *Culture, communication, and cognition: Vygotskian perspectives*. Boston: Cambridge University Press, in press.

Brown, A.L., and French, L.A. The zone of potential development: Implications for intelligence testing in the year 2000. *Intelligence*, 1979, *3*, 255-277.

Brown, A.L., and Smiley, S.S. Rating the importance of structural units of prose passages: A problem of metacognitive development. *Child Development*, 1977, *48*, 1-8.

Brown, A.L., and Smiley, S.S. The development of strategies for studying texts. *Child Development*, 1978, *49*, 1076-1088.

Brown, A.L., Smiley, S.S., Day, J.D., Townsend, M., and Lawton, S.C. Intrusion of a thematic idea in children's recall of prose. *Child Development*, 1977, *48*, 1454-1466.

Brown, A.L., Smiley, S.S., and Lawton, S.C. The effects of experience on the selection of suitable retrieval cues for studying texts. *Child Development*, 1978, *49*, 829-835.

Collins, A., Brown, J.S., and Larkin, K.M. Inference in text understanding. In R.J. Spiro, B.C. Bruce, and W.F. Brewer (Eds.), *Theoretical issues in reading comprehension*. Hillsdale, N.J.: Erlbaum, 1980.

Collins, A., and Smith, E.E. Teaching the process of reading comprehension. *Intelligence*, 1981.

Day, J.D. *Training summarization skills: A comparison of teaching methods*. Unpublished doctoral dissertation, University of Illinois, 1980.

Dewey, J. *How we think*. Boston: Heath, 1910 (2nd ed., Heath, 1933). In D.K. Dettermon and R.J. Sternberg (Eds.), *How and how much can intelligence be increased?* Norwood, N.J.: Ablex, in press.

Dynes, J.J. Comparison of two methods of studying history. *Journal of Experimental Education*, 1932, *1*, 42-45.

Germane, C.E. Outlining and summarizing compared with rereading as methods of studying. In G. Whipple (Ed.), *The Twentieth Yearbook of the National Society for the Study of Education*, Part II, 1921(a).

Germane, C.E. Value of the written paragraph summary. *Journal of Educational Research*, 1921(b), *3*, 116-123.

Hasher, L., and Zacks, R.T. Automatic and effortless processes in memory. *Journal of Experimental Psychology General*, 1979, *108*, 356-388

Huey, E.B. *The psychology and pedagogy of reading*. Cambridge, Mass.: MIT Press, 1968.

Johnson, N. *A structural analysis of the development of story recall and summarization*. Unpublished doctoral thesis, University of California, San Diego, 1978.

Kintsch, W., and van Dijk, T.A. Toward a model of text comprehension and production. *Psychological Review*, 1978, *85*, 363-394.

Lichtenstein, E.H., and Brewer, W.F. Memory for goal-directed events. *Cognitive Psychology*, 1980, *12*, 412-445.

Manzo, A.V. *Improving reading comprehension through reciprocal questioning*. Unpublished doctoral dissertation, Syracuse University, 1968.

Masur, E.F., McIntyre, C.W., and Flavell, J.H. Developmental changes in apportionment of study time among items in a multitrial free recall task. *Journal of Experimental Child Psychology*, 1973, *15*, 237-246.

McClusky, F.D., and Dolch, E.W. A study outline test. *School Review*, 1924, *34*, 757-772.

Nash, W.A., and Torrance, E.P. Creative reading and the questioning abilities of young children. *Journal of Creative Behavior*, 1974, *8*, 15-19.

Perry, W. Students' use and misuse of reading skills: A report to the faculty. *Harvard Educational Review*, 1959, *29*, 193-200.

Piaget, J. *Judgment and reasoning in the child*. New York: Harcourt, 1928.

Preston, R., and Tufts, E. The reading habits of superior college students. *Journal of Experimental Education*, 1948, *16*, 196-202.

Raphael, T.E. *The effects of metacognitive strategy awareness training on students' question answering behavior*. Unpublished doctoral thesis, University of Illinois, 1980.

Scardamalia, M., and Bereiter, C. *Fostering the development of self-regulation in children's knowledge processing*. Paper presented at NIE-LRDC Conference on Thinking and Learning Skills, Pittsburgh, October 1980.

Singer, H. Active comprehension: From answering to asking questions. *The Reading Teacher*, 1978, *31*, 901-908.

Smiley, S.S., Oakley, D.D., Worthen, D., Campione, J.C., and Brown, A.L. Recall of thematically relevant material by adolescent good and poor readers as a function of written versus oral presentation. *Journal of Educational Psychology*, 1977, *69*, 381-387.

Snow, R.E. Aptitude processes. In R.E. Snow, P.A. Federico, and W.E. Montague (Eds.), *Aptitude, learning, and instruction* (Vol. 1). Hillsdale, N.J.: Erlbaum, 1980.

Stordahl, K.E., and Christensen, C.M. The effect of study techniques on comprehension and retention. *Journal of Educational Research*, 1956, *49*, 561-570.

Thorndike, E.L. Reading as reasoning: A study of mistakes in paragraph reading. *Journal of Educational Psychology*, 1917, *8*, 323-332.

van Dijk, T.A., and Kintsch, W. Cognitive psychology and discourse: Recalling and summarizing stories. In W.U. Dressler (Ed.), *Trends in textlinguistics*. New York: de Gruyter, 1977.

Vygotsky, L.S. *Mind in society: The development of higher psychological processes*. (Eds.), M. Cole, V. John-Steiner, S. Scribner, and E. Souberman. Cambridge, Mass.: Harvard University Press, 1978.

Weinstein, C. Elaboration skills as a learning strategy. In H.F. O'Neil (Ed.), *Learning strategies*. New York: Academic Press, 1978.

REFERENCE NOTES

1. Collins, A., Brown, A.L., Morgan, J.L., and Brewer, W.F. *The analysis of reading tasks and texts*. Center for the Study of Reading Technical Report, University of Illinois, 1977.

2. Brown, A.L., and Day, J.D. *Strategies and knowledge for summarizing texts: The development of expertise*. Unpublished manuscript, University of Illinois, 1980.

3. Palincsar, A. *Corrective feedback and strategy training to improve the comprehension of poor readers*. Unpublished manuscript, University of Illinois, 1981.

Affect

Reading Research in the Affective Domain

IRENE ATHEY
Rutgers University

There is probably little disagreement today, even among the most fervent advocates of a cognitive-linguistic view of reading, that affective factors play a role both in reading achievement and reading behavior. Given this fact, it might be expected that theoretical models of the reading process would incorporate components that reflect motivational or attitudinal variables and would give them due emphasis in recognition of their presumed importance; and, indeed, some models have been constructed in such a way as to draw attention to the significance of affect in a comprehensive view of the reading process (Holmes, 1948, 1953; Ruddell, 1976; Singer, 1976).

Having said that, it must be acknowledged that, beyond appearing as a "box" in the figure depicting the model, affective factors receive little elaboration or explication. Holmes (1976), for example, who fully recognized the role of affective factors in reading, was unable to demonstrate their specific contribution to successful performance, and concluded that they must be shadowy variables lurking in the rather large proportion of variance not accounted for by cognitive and linguistic measures employed in his study. In view of the large number of measures Holmes included in his substrata analysis in an attempt to cover all possible sources of contribution to variance, it is remarkable that as much as 22 percent of the variance in comprehension (or "power of reading," as he called it) remained unexplained and had to be attributed "probably" to "sustained effort and desire to know," while 44 percent of the variance in speed of reading he thought was "probably" due to "motivational habit and desire for speed" (1976, p. 195). Similarly, in his analysis of power of reading in elementary school children, Singer (1965) found that cognitive-linguistic variables could account for 66 percent of the variance at Grade 3, 71 percent at grade 4, 69 percent at grade 5, and 73 percent at Grade 6, leaving approximately 30 percent of the variance in comprehension among elementary school subjects unexplained by such factors. Psychological profiles on the salient verbal and intellectual variables that emerged through the successive analyses also revealed that the most powerful readers at the third grade level were superior to the least powerful readers at the sixth grade level, and that the latter improved hardly at all between fifth and sixth grade. Singer attributes this fact to "inadequate learning and perhaps inappropriate instruction" (pp. 145-149). We would venture to suggest that learning may be inadequate for motivational reasons and instruction may be inappropriate because it fails to appeal to the values and interests of the learner.

Ruddell's systems-of-communication model reported in an earlier edition of this volume also includes "affective mobilizers" (a term used by Holmes to refer to constellations of beliefs, values, and attitudes that predispose an individual to persist in a field of endeavor). These affective mobilizers, like cognitive strategies, are part of a person's repertoire of capacities that may be drawn upon at any point during an ongoing activity. Operationalized as the objectives and goals of the individual, affective mobilizers include both lifetime goals and long term objectives as well as the immediate purposes at hand, since all are seen as influencing the person's store of concepts and in turn the semantic dimensions of language processing (Ruddell, 1976, p. 463). The content of these mobilizers and the timing and mode of their operation in the course of reading is still a matter of conjecture.

In an early study in this area, Athey and Holmes (1969) attempted to bring a modicum of precision to the question of the content of affective mobilizers. In this study, as in all his previous research, Holmes took the position that, while many variables (some of which may have no *obvious* bearing on reading) are involved, the importance of the part played by each varies from one individual to another, and even within the same individual from time to time, depending upon the immediate purpose in reading the material. This view makes sense if we consider the analogous situation whereby two individuals with identical IQ scores on the same test may achieve that score by means of very different profiles on the subsets measuring different abilities. While this fact may be of great interest and utility to the counseling psychologist or the caseworker, psychology as a scientific endeavor relies upon similarities among subjects that can form the basis for generalizations and ultimately scientific laws. If persons who can be grouped on the basis of one criterion, e.g. grade level or reading score, tend to exhibit similar affective mobilizers, then that fact in itself can be significant in furthering our understanding of the psychological processes underlying reading.

The criterion chosen for this study was the score on the Stanford Achievement Test, Paragraph Meaning (subtest). The choice of a measure of affective mobilizers, however, proved more difficult than the choice of a measure of reading competence. Historically, the dearth of suitable measures has been an impediment to reading research in the affective domain. Some reasons for this state of affairs have been postulated in an earlier document (Athey, 1965). Personality tests, for example, are usually constructed for diagnostic purposes rather than for tapping academic achievement. Since they are standardized on clinical samples, they are rarely applicable to normal school populations except for identifying children suspected of some form of pathology. Moreover, the fact that in all statistical analyses of reading affective factors tend to be overwhelmed by cognitive and linguistic factors suggests the need for more refined measures of affect than the gross personality and attitudinal measures currently available.

A major objective of the Athey and Holmes study was to construct new measures that could be shown to be related to academic achievement and were more refined in terms of including only that affective content proven to be relevant to reading.

To accomplish this task, groups of good and poor readers at the seventh, eighth, and ninth grade level were compared *item by item* on a large personality inventory specially designed for junior high school students to determine which items significantly differentiated between the groups. An interesting, and possibly unique, feature of this inventory was that, for every item, the respondent indicated not only his or her resemblance to the person portrayed in the item, but also whether he or she *wished* to resemble that person. Hence, in addition to tapping beliefs and attitudes about the self, school, etc., the items also elicited value statements pertaining to the ideal self, desirable characteristics of the school, etc.

Since affective items (and even tests) tend to be less stable than intellectual items, two cross-validations of the items at the ninth grade level were conducted. The items that survived this rigorous process were then submitted to a factor analysis in order to determine whether they tended to form clusters of values, beliefs, and attitudes (mobilizers).

Four clear factors emerged from this process. The first factor, which was labelled Social Independence, consisted of a constellation of items that seemed to reflect a degree of immaturity and a desire to remain somewhat dependent on family. For example, the poor readers expressed both a strong belief that they were not old enough to make their own decisions and an equally strong desire to remain in this condition. They thought of themselves as enjoying many friends and having fun, and wanted to be popular, agreeable, trusting, and sensitive to other people's feelings. In brief, this factor depicts the poor reader as sociable, unassertive, dependent, and oriented toward family and friends—and quite contented with this state of affairs.

The second factor was readily interpretable as reflecting the poor reader's low self-concept as a school achiever. Much as they would like to be leaders, the poor readers did not see themselves as exercising leadership; as being among the brightest, best-dressed, or most popular; as getting good marks; enjoying reading; or being liked by their teachers. In summary, Factor 2, Self-Concept, reflected a very negative view of self in relation to school in general and reading in particular.

Factor 3, which was basically a catalog of School Dislikes reiterated some of the same concerns. This seemed to be a bipolar factor representing different clusters of dislikes for good and poor readers. In general, the dislikes of poor readers tended to center around classmates, especially those who were snobbish, or started exclusive clubs. The poor reader also disliked having to recite in class and, more particularly, being laughed at while reciting. Good readers' dislikes, on the other hand, focused more on teachers—those who criticized their faults and errors, used sarcasm and ridicule, were not interested in their pupils, and sometimes punished their pupils for things they did not do. Good readers also objected to monotonous school work, and would welcome a chance to choose their own teachers. The orientation toward teachers as opposed to friends and classmates presents a rather striking difference between the attitudes and anxieties of good and poor readers.

The final factor, which was labelled Family Orientation and Anxieties, reiterated some of the same themes. Poor ninth grade readers claimed to spend much of their leisure time helping mother around the house, and wished their parents had more time to spend with them. They also averred that, if they were 16 years old, they would get a job and live at home. Good readers, by contrast, stated that they would prefer to continue their schooling. Additionally, good readers rejected the idea of imitating someone in a book or show, whereas poor readers tended to indulge in such fantasies much more readily.

The four factors had loadings of .137, .480, .072, and .445 respectively on the reading criterion and together accounted for about 13 percent of the variance. Since the correlations of the original inventory subtests with the reading criterion all hovered around zero, this figure represents a substantial improvement in predictive power, and demonstrates the superiority of using only items that are specifically geared to academic achievement. In this context, it should be noted that, although new subscales were constructed, they were created from old items. Presumably, new scales consisting of affective items that have been specially developed around some theory that seeks to explain the role of affective mobilizers in reading acquisition and functioning would have even greater explanatory potential. However, to the writer's knowledge, no investigator has sought to develop such scales, the probable reasons being that construct validity is hard to establish, and that most reading researchers are more interested in other aspects of reading.

If such a person were to appear, in what area of psychology, sociology, or other discipline should this researcher most profitably seek a theory or model? Mathewson (1976) believes that "by necessity, the attempt to construct a model dealing with affect in the reading process must be limited" (p. 655). He elects the field of experimental social psychology, and chooses as his central affective component from several possible candidates that of attitude, which has the advantage of having been rigorously defined and measured, but suffers from the lack of an active, energizing quality. Drawing upon the work of Berlyne (1950) and Harlow et al. (1950), Mathewson attempts to overcome this difficulty by adding the motivational components of curiosity and exploration, being careful to point out that there is no necessary, inherent relationship between attitudinal and motivational variables. For example, a student may have an unfavorable attitude toward a particular book's content or style, but may work hard to demonstrate the requisite knowledge of the book that will gain an A on the course. This example points up the necessity of subsuming temporary, or less important, objectives under long range goals. The student described is willing to suspend an unfavorable attitude toward the book, since experience with the book will be brief, whereas the grade will have more far-reaching effects on home relationships or career. On the other hand, it is easy to envisage a scenario where the book content is so repugnant or the writing style so opaque that the reader simply decides to devote no further effort to it. In the former case the motivation to do well in the course may be superseded by some higher value, e.g. the dislike of content that is perceived as racist. In the latter case, the effort required may be deemed too great relative to the perceived pay-off. Clearly, the balance among the attitudes and motives, as well as the peceptions on which they are based, may change over time, as when the student decides at mid-semester to settle for a *B* and to work harder on other courses. Of such conglomerations of values, attitudes, concepts, and perceptions are decisions made, and by such decisions is the course of our lives determined.

With the affective components of the model firmly in place, Mathewson proceeds to add, as "the locus of effect upon which attitude and motivation operate" (p. 659), comprehension and attention. He bases this inclusion on several studies (Bernstein, 1955; Groff, 1962; Shnayer, 1969) showing a positive, facilitating effect of attitude on comprehension, and the obvious prerequisite of attention before comprehension can occur. The resulting model, which he calls "The Acceptance Model," by presenting a systematic theoretical framework, is designed to "contribute to the understanding of how affective factors influence reading during the reading act…and to generate testable hypotheses concerning what will happen to comprehension when attitude and motivation are manipulated experimentally" (p. 663). Such a hypothesis might relate to the effects of attitude toward a particular form of reading material (e.g. content written in Black English dialect) upon comprehension, but it is clear that many others could be generated.

As noted previously, the affective domain is both large and relatively uncharted. Mathewson's choice, as he clearly recognized, focused on but one of the possible areas of inquiry, that of experimental social psychology, from which he selected certain variables, attitude toward reading and the higher-level motives of curiosity and exploration. While this choice represents a fruitful approach to the problem, immediately suggesting as it does a wealth of studies that might be conducted around these concepts, it does preclude other whole areas of theoretical inquiry that might also have much to offer. In the second edition of this volume, some of these theories were explored and will be touched on again in the present edition.

Self-Concept Theory

Why should a concept, which is clearly a construct belonging to the cognitive domain, be considered an affective variable? Osgood (1953) defines *concept* as "a common response (usually verbal) made to a class of phenomena the members of which display certain common characteristics" (p. 666). As a behaviorist, Osgood avoids mention of such nebulous entities as beliefs, attitudes, and feelings, though it is perfectly reasonable to assume that even concepts of concrete objects include such excess baggage, and it is very clear that feelings about certain abstract concepts such as the fatherland or justice may run so high that people are willing to die for them. The concept of the self is indeed such an amalgam of accurate and inaccurate perceptions, uninformed beliefs, deep-seated values, and a wide range of feelings—pride, confidence, smugness, abhorrence, anxiety—some of which are clearly articulated, but many of which may never have been verbalized and may even remain largely unconscious throughout the lifespan. The "class of phenomena" do indeed have a common characteristic; they all refer, or are believed to refer, to the self. But the "common response" is different in this case. Osgood was referring to the fact that many people who share similar backgrounds will have roughly the same concept of (i.e. respond in approximately the same way to) an object or its referent. But a person's self-concept is, by definition, unique to that individual, and is not shared by other people, and hence does not fit Osgood's definition of concept. It must also be assumed that the values, beliefs, and feelings associated with the self are more strongly held, and hence, probably more resistant to change than those associated with other concepts. In these two respects, then, the self-concept tends to differ from other concepts, and is thus considered an appropriate candidate for the affective sphere. (We will consider in due course the wisdom of this dichotomy, and whether it may have outlived its usefulness.)

The picture is further complicated by the fact that, as Super pointed out, the self-concept is not a single entity, but rather a system of concepts, pictures of the self assuming different roles in different types of situations. "Thus it should be noted that it is incorrect to write of the self-concept as though each person had just one; each person has a number of self-concepts, but one self-concept system at any point in time. This system may be well or poorly organized" (Super et al., 1963, p. 19).

The multiple nature of self-concepts was fully realized by William James, whose famous chapter on the self in *Principles of Psychology* (1890, Chapter X) set the stage for much contemporary theorizing. Recognition of this multiplicity is further reflected in some modern instruments such as the Tennessee Self-Concept Scale (Fitts, 1965), which include such subtests as Family Self, Social Self, Physical Self, Personal Self, Moral-Ethical Self, and so forth. It is incumbent on researchers who choose to work in this area to select measures that have at least this degree of refinement, and it is to be hoped that future tests will reflect an even greater degree of precision. In fact, the need to use specific, rather than global, measures applies not only to the entire affective domain, but is equally pertinent to reading (cf. Wigfield and Asher, 1984, p. 432).

Given the multiple nature of the self-concept, the question arises as to how the many self-concepts are organized to form the self-system. As Super noted, the constellation forming the self-concept system may be well or poorly organized, but what is meant by this is not entirely clear. One criterion of good organization might be the absence of contradictory self-concepts. The lack of such stability may result in the person successively assuming different, and sometimes, incompatible roles. Robert White's portrayal of Joseph Kidd in *Lives in Progress* (1966) provides a vivid example of instability of self-concept structure in a freshman college student. These, and possibly other salient criteria, are important indices that need to be included in our theorizing about the affective domain, especially when this theorizing is used to explain academic achievement.

Self-Consistency Theory

If we are to find a theory that speaks to the unit and stability of the self-concept system, the most likely place to find it is in an organismic theory such as Lewin's or Goldstein's (Hall and Lindzey, 1957, Chapters 6 and 8). A major disadvantage of organismic theories, however, is that, plausible as they may seem to the reader, it is usually very difficult to operationalize the key concepts in such a way as to provide an empirical test of the theory. In point of fact, the only theory that has given rise to a measure of self-organization is that enunciated by Prescott Lecky in his sole work, *Self-Consistency,* which appeared in 1950. Lecky viewed "all psychological phenomena as illustrations of the single principle of unity" (p. 152), namely, the need to maintain self-consistency among the perceptions, beliefs, and actions of the individual. Faced with conflicting data, the organism will 1) reject the conflicting information outright, 2) modify it to fit the prevailing belief structure, or 3) change the prevailing belief structure to accommodate the countervailing information. The factors that determine which of these outcomes will ensue are the strength of the prevailing belief structure, the extent to which the opposing information penetrates the core of cherished beliefs, and the degree to which the antithetical evidence is irresistible. If the belief structure is tightly knit and the threatening information impinges on the person's core value system, the most powerful and persuasive contradictory evidence may be rejected. On the other hand, fairly weak arguments may be readily assimilated if they threaten peripheral beliefs and values.

> Resistance is the opposite of assimilation and learning, and represents the refusal to reorganize the values, especially the ego values....To the educator, it appears as an obstacle to learning. But if we would really understand these resistances, we must see them not as neurotic or abnormal manifestations, but as wholly natural devices for avoiding reorganization (Lecky, 1950, p. 162).

Interestingly enough, the example Lecky chooses to illustrate the dynamics of his theory comes from the known preponderance of boys in elementary reading disability classes. Lecky's explanation of this phenomenon runs as follows:

> The boy from six to eight years old, just beginning to learn to read, is mainly concerned with maintaining the conception of himself as manly. He likes to play cowboy, G-man and Indian. He tries not to cry when he gets a bump. Yet this boy, when the reading lesson begins, must stand up before his companions and read that "the little red hen says 'Cluck! Cluck!'"—or something equally inconsistent with his standards of how he should behave. To be obliged to read such material aloud, espe-

cially in the presence of others, is not consistent with his view of masculine values. If a boy is trying to maintain a standard of manliness on the playground, he does not abandon that standard merely because he walks from the playground into the classroom. When books on railroads and airplanes are provided, they serve to support these values and are assimilated eagerly. The point is, of course, that the assumed defect in reading never was a defect, except from the standpoint of an unenlightened school system, but on the contrary was a manifestation of a wholesome, normal, and desirable resistance. (pp. 162-163)

Lecky would not maintain, of course, that this affront to masculinity is the sole, or even the major, cause of reading disability among boys but, given the complex causal patterns operating, it is plausible to conclude that reading material that is inconsistent with the perceived self is likely to be rejected, and that this rejection may well generalize to the whole of reading, especially when the child's experience with reading is, of necessity, limited. Asher and Markell's finding (1974) that boys performed as well as girls on high interest material provides some corroboration for Lecky's thesis, as does Daniel's anecdotal evidence that black children's reading performance improved as the result of an intensive program of high-interest reading. We have here a factor that can be readily modified, and publishers of elementary level reading materials would be well advised to consider the interests and self-concepts of their readers in addition to such indices as readability.

Any test of Lecky's theory will, of course, require the construction of a measure of its key concept of self-consistency. Lecky himself attempted to construct such a measure, the *Individuality Record,* which was designed to demonstrate the existence of a self-consistent attitudinal posture toward various aspects of the environment that would be especially evident within the limits of prescribed belief systems. After administering the inventory to 500 college freshmen, he concluded that:

> The scores indicate that confidence in social situations, cooperation, optimism, a friendly attitude toward other members of the family, companionship with the opposite sex, efficient work dispositions, freedom from nervous symptoms, and a feeling of physical well-being are closely interrelated and tend to increase or decrease together.... There is a coherence in the behavior of any single organism which argues against an explanation in terms of chance combinations of determiners and points to an organized dynamic system which tends toward self-determination. (p. 75)

If Lecky's hypothesis is correct with respect to young boys who are learning to read, then there should be some correlation between the severity of the reading problem and the degree and kind of "masculine" behavior exhibited (e.g. in play). If such a correlation were established, it would also be incumbent on the researcher to demonstrate that such behavior was less prevalent among boys who did not have a reading problem or to suggest reasons to account for the presence and absence of reading failure in the two groups of "masculine boys."

Lecky's theory should have wider implications than this, however. Reading may be conceived more broadly as an intellectual or academic activity, rather than as a "feminine" activity. Conceived this way, it may conflict equally with the value systems of some girls, as well as many boys. Research might be designed to show that a belief system which emphasized the inherent value and pleasure of reading would differentiate good and poor readers, regardless of intelligence or sex.

It should be noted in passing that, like most other personality inventories, Lecky's *Individuality Record* measures only aspects of the self-concept and coherence among those aspects, and does not address the question of values or desired (ideal) self-concept. Yet each self-concept in the self-concept system is tied to one of the values in the hierarchy that forms the individual's value system, and it is this fact that makes a particular self-concept more or less salient to the individual's beliefs and, hence, actions. As William James pointed out, the fact that a person has a poor self-concept in a particular area (e.g. golf) is unimportant if the person places little value on the activities and skills represented by that area. In the previously cited Athey and Holmes study, it was clear that the poor readers tended to place a high value on social relationships, and a relatively low value on excelling in schoolwork, whereas good readers were much more teacher- and work-oriented. McMichael (1980) suggests that children with poor academic skills tend to form social clusters that reinforce feelings of school alienation.

Hence, although values play a key role in Lecky's theory, it is not equally clear that his instrument measures values. However, a modified version of the *Individuality Record* could be devised to address these shortcomings. In fact, Lecky does not speak to the problem of how the "ideal" self, as opposed to the self-concept, is related to self-consistency, especially when a discrepancy exists between them. (Such a discrepancy is often viewed as a symptom of maladjustment among personality theorists.) Yet it would seem that data on the ideal self would provide important clues to the dynamics of the individual's belief system, whether an ideal self-discrepancy existed or not.

Such a discrepancy is but another example of the mechanisms whereby conflicting information is either assimilated or rejected. Reduction of the discrepancy is thus brought about by either modifying (probably lowering) the ideal to make it more attainable (i.e. the individual becomes more accepting of limitations) or the self-concept is raised so that it conforms more closely to the ideal (Fennimore, 1968). Such changes can give us much information about the individual's changing belief system over time. Where an ideal self-discrepancy persists, this may mean that the individual would like to emulate the ideal, other things being equal, but that other values have higher priority. The person would like to be cooperative, for example, but this desire conflicts with other values such as "getting ahead." In such cases, we have information about the position of a particular value in the total value system, e.g. whether it is central or peripheral to the system, how resistant it is likely to be to change, and so forth. These would be important considerations if, as seems probable, beliefs about the self and the ideal self were found to be related to reading.

It would be wrong to suggest that Lecky's ideas have languished over the years, though it may be true that they have not received the attention they deserve. There have been some attempts to test various hypotheses related to his theory. For example, working within Lecky's theoretical framework, Fillmer et al. (1971-1972) related the various subscales of the Tennessee Self-Concept Scale to reading scores on the Stanford Achievement Test and to measures of two- and three-dimensional perception. Significant relationships were found between reading and two of the self-concept measures, moral-ethical self and self-criticism. Several of the self-concept measures were highly related to visual perception. The authors suggest several reasons, all consonant with Lecky's theory, to account for these phenomena.

Another study that seems to have some bearing on the theory is that of Bakan (1971) who hypothesized that, when a student values academic achievement, that student's self-esteem is affected by the consistency with which he or she achieves. From a total of 639 junior high school students, she selected 112 with average GPAs and rank-ordered them in terms of the consistency of grades obtained over a four-year period. Both the achievement level and the self-concept of ability scores (Brookover scale) of the highly inconsistent group showed a greater decrement over time than the highly consistent group. This result is interesting because it suggests that all round average achievement has a greater positive effect on both self-concept and subsequent achievement than superior achievement in some areas compensated by inferior achievement in others. Apparently, junior high school students have not yet come to appreciate William James' aphorism that the sense of self-worth must reside in one or two chosen areas in which a person performs well. Weiner et al. (1971) also believe that children's reasoning about their achievements is tied to the consistency of their experiences with success and failure.

Khan (1969, 1970) and Khan and Roberts (1971), in a longitudinal study exploring affective correlates of academic achievement, found certain affective characteristics to have high factorial stability over time, and to predict achievement scores better than grades. The highest predictor for both sexes was a factor labelled *Achievement Anxiety* which appeared to reflect a low value for competition and striving for advancement.

Self-concepts form over time and are subject to a variety of influences. In conformance to the line of reasoning suggested earlier, it would seem that some self-concepts, e.g. those closer to the core value system, crystallize at a fairly early age and are impervious to change, probably because much of the content is unverbalized. It is well established, for example, that children have a fairly well-developed concept of sex role patterns of behavior and expectations even before the age of five. On the other hand, it seems likely that the concept of self as a student, or more specifically as a reader, would not begin to be formulated until somewhat later, and hence, would be more amenable to the influence of external factors. Some evidence for this conjecture may be found in a study by Eder (1983), in which first grade children's self-concepts were affected by temporary placement in a higher or lower group. Additionally, other studies (Bridgeman and Shipman, 1978; Eshel and Klein, 1981) have shown that although there are few differences between SES groups in young children, beyond school entrance the self-concept of ability of lower SES declines more sharply than among middle-class subjects. (For a review of school influences on reading see Wigfield and Asher, 1984.)

As Lecky pointed out, in addition to coherence among beliefs, self-consistency refers to the relative tenacity of values, beliefs, and attitudes. An important consideration, therefore, is the position of the individual's belief about his or her own academic ability in the hierarchy of beliefs and values, since the core beliefs would be most resistant to change. If this determination were to be made prior to a treatment program designed to change beliefs about reading, presumably those cases in which reading was a peripheral value would be most subject to change, but again, this hypothesis has not been tested.

Two conclusions seem to follow from the above discussion. First, research on the self-concept in relation to reading must be narrowly defined so as not to incorporate other, irrelevant aspects of the self. Second, examining the self-concept without simultaneously studying the values inherent in that self-concept is to ignore the more important aspect of the information. What persons aspire to be is probably as important a predictor of performance as what they believe themselves to be.

Competence Theory

In a classic paper entitled "Motivation reconsidered: The concept of competence" published in 1959, Robert White postulated a basic, lifelong drive in all animals, including man, for ordering and mastering the environment. This drive is so strong that, where order does not exist, the organism will tend to impose its own order on external phenomena (the parallel for internal phenomena would be self-consistency). Ordering the environment reduces the uncertainty about what may be expected to happen, gives the individual better powers of prediction and control, and hence reinforces feelings of security by reducing the anxiety associated with uncertainty. Mastering the environment satisfies a basic need to perceive oneself as having an influence on events that affect one, and thus, of being capable of reducing the uncertainty still further. Other writers (e.g. Erikson, 1950; Jahoda, 1958) have come to view this feeling of having the ability to control the environment (at least to some degree) as essential to, and a major index of, mental health.

The feeling of competence, according to White, is a source of satisfaction which is independent of extrinsic rewards, punishments, or social expectations. The need to organize and manipulate the environment is innate; but the ways in which it finds expression are determined by a person's experiences, especially experiences with significant others. The early years are especially critical in determining whether this drive will find expression through constructive channels or will be thwarted or repressed. Erikson (1950, 1959) has proposed a stage theory showing the basic requisites and interactions that produce a developing sense of mastery in relation to the environment. Since learning to read is an activity in which all "normal" members of our society are expected to participate, Erikson's theory is particularly appropriate for theory and research on the affective dimensions of reading, because it concentrates on the development and functioning of the normal or healthy personality, rather than upon behavioral aberrations.

Erikson conceives of the whole psychological span of human life as a series of eight periods or stages, the first four of which are pertinent to the present discussion. Each stage is characterized by its own peculiar developmental task, which is imposed partly by the individual's own maturation and partly by the expectations of the society in response to this maturation. The developmental task — or crisis, as Erikson calls it — has both a positive and a negative dimension, and the successful accomplishment of a particular stage depends upon achieving a workable balance between the two. For example, the first developmental task, which will lay the foundation for the emerging personality and is crucial to all subsequent tasks, is "the firm establishment of enduring patterns for the balance of basic trust over basic mistrust" (1959, p. 63). The healthy personality contains both elements (a person should know when to trust and when to mistrust the evidence of both perceptions and judgments), but trust predominates for the most part over mistrust. The outcome of each stage for a given individual depends upon the nature of experience during that stage. Thus, whether a child develops basic trust depends largely on the quality of the maternal relationship and upon the parents' conveying to the child "an almost somatic conviction that there is a meaning to what they are doing" (1950, p. 222). Children who fail to develop this "somatic conviction" may experience trouble later in detecting meaning in other patterns of experience such as the printed page. A drastic loss of mother love at the time when basic trust is being established may lead to acute infantile depression or to a mild depressive coloring of the personality for the whole remainder of life (Spitz, 1945).

The second psychosocial task, which occurs in the second or third year of life, is the establishment of autonomy over shame and doubt. The sense of autonomy is built on the child's newfound mastery over the physical environment through the use of movement and over the social environment through the use of language. However, these new abilities need room to grow and operate. Impatient or belittling adults can stunt the growth of autonomy and tip the balance in the direction of a lasting sense of shame or self-doubt. As in the case of basic trust, too much autonomy can be detrimental, since it will assuredly bring the individual into conflict with nature or society. Whatever the resolution of the crisis, this stage is critical to the formation of the child's self-concept.

At the age of four or five, the child must use this newly gained autonomy to initiate fresh activities and social interactions, and must be allowed to do so without constantly being made to feel guilty about actions performed in reality or in fantasy. For instance, children who spin "tall tales" are beginning to exercise an imagination that will stand them in good stead in later situations, (such as experiencing events vicariously through reading), and it is a profound disservice to nip this imagination in the bud under the mistaken impression that "truthfulness" is more important. Again, the way this crisis of initiative versus guilt is resolved will affect the child's later career as a "self-starter."

The fourth stage is probably the most interesting to teachers because it coincides with the elementary school period. This is the stage of "industry versus inferiority," in which the mastery of the skills deemed important by the society, and the establishment of a good relationship with those who teach those skills, are the central tasks and are crucial to the child's sense of identity. The enjoyment of work and a sense of pride in one's accomplishments and creations are the principal items of learning during this period. Perhaps even more salient to the present discussion is Erikson's diagnosis of what happens when the balance is tipped toward inferiority rather than industry. In such cases, the children become adolescents and adults who derive little satisfaction from sustained work, and are likely to drift from one job to another without ever developing a sustained career pattern. The vital importance of a steady diet of success in the early school years has been reiterated elsewhere (Resnick and Robinson, 1975; Wigfield and Asher, 1984).

Erikson elaborates on several other important features of the stages. First, it should be noted that no crisis is resolved once and for all, but is a continuing theme throughout life, that has more saliency at some periods than others. At any given age, the particular conflict designated by the theory is the dominant issue for that stage. Second, the stages occur in a fixed sequence, and the emergence of each new level of physical and social interaction is dependent on the degree to which the preceding stages have been successfully negotiated. This means that some children who have reached the age of school entrance or beyond may still be wrestling with residual conflicts from earlier stages and are thus ill-equipped to start establishing the work patterns typical of the "industry versus inferiority" period.

Erikson does not refer specifically to reading as one of the skills to be mastered, though it would seem to follow from his general description of this period, and few would deny that learning to read can assume crisis proportions in some children. The school's priorities today are such that learning to read could well be considered the *major* developmental task of the elementary years. As Margaret Mead (1958) pointed out, "At whatever point the society decides to stress a particular adjustment, it will be at this point that adjustment becomes acute to the individual" (p. 347). There can be no doubt that in the American culture, learning to read is a major adjustment, often quite discontinuous from previous experience, that the child must make to retain the respect and approval of parents, teachers, and friends. It is part of the process of "growing up," a *"sine qua non"* of maturity, and a product of socialization processes that is almost as important as learning to walk and talk.

If this interpretation of Erikson's theory is correct, it gives rise to a number of hypotheses with respect to the relationship of reading to certain aspects of psychosocial development. Specifically, the following hypotheses, if confirmed at the elementary school level, would support the validity of the interpretation:

1. Good readers may be expected to exhibit strong feelings of self-esteem, and a firm conviction of their own worth, while poor readers will display feelings of inferiority and inadequacy, especially in school and institutions requiring reading.
2. Good readers will obtain higher scores on measures of basic trust, autonomy, and initiative, or a composite of all three, than will poor readers.
3. Good readers will value and enjoy school work whereas poor readers will tend to value other activities in preference to school-related ones.
4. Good readers will identify (but not overidentify—see Erikson, 1959, pp. 87-88) with their teachers, while poor readers will reject teachers' identification models.
5. Good readers will be relatively free from anxiety and neurotic manifestations, while poor readers will have a higher anxiety level and will exhibit more symptoms of maladjustment, especially school maladjustment.

These are a few of the hypotheses that might be generated from Erikson's theory, and others may readily spring to mind. Research studies designed to test these hypotheses would call for the construction of valid measures of the psychological constructs Erikson posits as critical at each stage—basic trust, autonomy, etc.—since no suitable measures currently exist. Behavior rating scales might be the most appropriate method of measuring these particular constructs in young children.

Much of the research in this area tends to support this theorizing, even though the hypotheses were not cast in the Eriksonian framework, and hence the hypotheses were not stated in precisely these terms. For convenience, the studies have been summarized under rubrics that appear to fit the above constructs without distorting the researchers' original intentions: Autonomy, Environmental Mastery, Perception of Reality, Attitudes toward Learning, and Anxiety.

Autonomy

Autonomy may appear in the literature under a number of guises. The concept itself, as described by Erikson, would seem to include components of exploration, independence, self-confidence, constructive channeling of aggression, and pride in one's achievements. Improvement in one or more of these factors is frequently associated with enhanced school performance.

Shatter (1956) found that fourth grade boys who were retarded readers made significant gains in reading and in maturity, independence, and self-reliance as a result of a group therapy program. McGinnis (1965) found that parents of good readers manifested attitudes favoring growth of independence and exposed their children to democratic practices and to environmental activities calculated to encourage such growth. Winterbottom (1958) likewise found that mothers of 8- to 10-year old boys with high achievement motivation made more demands for independence. Conversely, Carrillo (1957) found poor readers to show lack of independence, avoidance of leadership opportunities, and a poor attitude to responsibility. On a nonverbal task requiring the subject to place self in relation to a triangle with points labelled *parents, teacher,* and *other children,* poor readers placed themselves within the triangle significantly more often than good readers (Henderson, Long, and Ziller, 1965).

Anderson (1972) hypothesized that Self-Directed Activity (SDA) as observed in 14 fourth grade "natural classroom environments" would lead to superior quality of response on the Directed-Reading-Thinking Activity devised by Stauffer. In addition to this finding, some interaction effects among sex, race, and teacher estimates of SDA were observed, suggesting that high SDA in girls is acceptable to the teacher, but in boys may be perceived as a threat to authority. The author concluded that approaches to reading which provide maximum opportunity for SDA are generally superior to those that do not.

Henderson and Long (1971) obtained scores on the Children's Self-Social Constructs Test and behavior ratings by teachers for 95 black children at school entrance. At the end of first grade significant differences were found on these measures among three groups differing in academic achievement: repeaters, promoted nonreaders, and readers. The readers displayed a pattern of mature, realistic independence. Berger (1978) has also remarked on the importance of promoting a positive identity and sense of independence among college students with reading problems. McClelland's theory (1961) emphasizes the need for experiences involving independent mastery as a prerequisite of achievement motivation.

Environmental Mastery

Blackham (1965) found ninth grade overachievers in reading to have a greater amount of intellectual energy at their disposal, to be more spontaneous and creative, and to be able to make finer intellectual discriminations. Tabarlet (1958) found fifth grade children two or more years retarded in reading to be inferior to normal readers in interpersonal skills, social participation, satisfactory work and recreation, and adequate outlook and goals. Carter (1964) reviewed the later careers of retarded readers of normal intelligence, and found that their vocational mobility and aspirations tended to remain horizontally oriented. Norman and Daley (1959) found clusters of items suggesting feelings of "environmental deprivation" and maltreatment to differentiate poor male readers in the sixth grade, while Spache concluded from two studies (1954, 1957) that the typical retarded reader in the primary grades had less insight into the human dynamics of a situation and manifested less solution-seeking behavior. Abrams (1964), likewise, concluded that nonreaders were more impulsive and less able to respond appropriately to environmental stimuli than good readers.

Perception of Reality

Environmental mastery would seem to be dependent to some extent to the degree to which the individual perceives the environment accurately and realistically. There is some suggestion in the literature that poor readers may be less aware of (Margulies, 1942) and more prone to entertain erroneous conceptions of their environment (Jackson, 1944) specifically of their teachers and peers (Holzinger, 1967). They have been found to be deficient in ego strength, defined as "the ability to gauge reality and synthesize behavior in appropriate goal-directed activity" (Barber, 1952). Ramsey (1962) and Lasswell (1967) have remarked that poor readers are less realistic in their estimates of themselves as readers, while Bouise (1955) and Van Zandt (1963) have demonstrated a similar lack of realism with respect to educational and vocational aspirations. In a series of carefully documented case studies, Shrodes (1949) has described changes in student self-awareness and growth of insight into the motivations governing behavior as results of a course in bibliotherapy.

Holzinger (1967) found that poor readers in the first grade scored significantly lower on peer and teacher perception, while those in the fourth grade, in addition to the above measures, were also significantly lower on self-perception. There is some suggestion that poor readers may be more interested in the world of fantasy than in the realities of the school situation. Gates (1936), for example, observed 26 cases of recessive behavior, including mind wandering and daydreaming, among 100 poor readers (recall the "book or show" item in the Athey and Holmes study).

Attitudes toward Learning

Since reading is the basis of most other school subjects, it seems logical to suppose that when the child finds reading a pleasurable experience, positive attitudes toward reading will rapidly become generalized to most other subjects. The expanding interest in other subjects should, in turn, lead to deeper love of reading as a primary source of information and enjoyment. The child's burgeoning curiosity may find many other avenues of expression besides reading, but in this society reading still remains one of the major vehicles for satisfying a desire for knowledge.

The available evidence tends to support the view that good readers are likely to be more intellectually oriented (Gates, 1936; Granzow, 1954; Witty, 1950), and to exhibit higher aspirations (Lasswell, 1967) and drive for achievement (Bauer, 1956), and to show more curiosity (Maw and Maw, 1962), and more positive attitudes toward school in general (Carter, 1964; Granzow, 1954) and reading in particular (Groff, 1962; Healy, 1965; Ketcham, 1966). Johnson (1959) found that by categorizing first grade children as "eager" or "reluctant" readers, he could predict reading success in the second grade, even though the two groups made comparable scores on initial reading readiness tests. Attitudinal factors have similar implications for remedial reading (Peter, 1963).

Biel (1945) and others have hypothesized that the known sex differences in the number of reading disability cases may be attributable in part to the difficulty boys experience in identifying with women teachers in the primary grades (cf. Lecky's self-consistency theory). Gowan (1955) and Fliegler (1957), after reviewing the literature on gifted underachievers, point out that the underachiever is usually characterized by an inability to identify with authority figures, or to create warm relationships with either teachers or peers. Dorney (1963) found that delinquent adolescent boys improved significantly in their attitude toward authority figures after a course of reading instruction.

As part of a longitudinal study of the relationship of preschool social-emotional functioning to later intellectual achievement, Kohn and Rosman (1972) examined two dimensions of their Social Competence Scale — Interest-Participation versus Apathy-Withdrawal and Cooperation-Compliance versus Anger-Defiance. An earlier study by Silverman (1968) confirmed the hypothesis that 103 nursery school children who scored high on Apathy-Withdrawal were having later learning difficulties as measured by a group achievement test administered in second grade. (The Anger-Defiance dimension was not predictive.) In the Kohn and Rosman study, nearly 300 children were followed for one year in day care centers and for two years in the first and second grades of New York City schools. The earlier finding was confirmed. By the end of second grade, girls (but not boys) high on Anger-Defiance were also exhibiting low achievement patterns. The importance of interest and participation in school-related activities demonstrated in this study is consonant with the earlier findings of Kagan and his colleagues (Kagan et al., 1958; Sontag et al., 1958).

Anxiety

The relationship between anxiety and performance appears to be U-shaped, either too little or too much anxiety serving as an impediment. The optimal level of anxiety probably varies with the individual and the type of task. Smith and Carrigan (1959) have suggested that anxiety is an important dimension in reading disability, its role being to excite some functions such as fluency, and to depress others such as word recognition and day-to-day memory. A number of investigators have found a significant negative relationship between reading comprehension and anxiety (Cowen et al., 1965; Frost, 1965; Neville, Pfost and Dobbs, 1967; Pacheco, 1964; Phelps, 1967) or neuroticism (Savage, 1966). Some authors have suggested that the influence of anxiety may lie in its interaction with other variables such as perceptual rigidity (Simula, 1964), introversion (Vehar, 1968), intelligence (Scarborough, Hindsman, and Hanna, 1961), socioeconomic status (Dukes, 1964), and disparity between reading and arithmetic performance (Lynn, 1957). Other writers have noted that the negative correlation between test anxiety and performance on achievement tests (especially reading) increases through the elementary school grades (Dusek, 1980; Hill, 1980).

Cotler (1969) evaluated the effects of positive and negative reinforcement and test anxiety on the reading performance of 189 boys in the fourth, fifth, and sixth grades. He concluded that "test anxiety or its equivalent can no longer be ignored as a relevant variable" in reading performance, whereas reinforcement (in this case money) was not a significant variable. In two further experiments, Cotler and Palmer (1970, 1971) found that anxiety and academic achievement were related in middle-class boys, but not girls or lower-class boys. Using the galvanic skin response (GSR) as an index of anxiety, Rugel (1971) found that the level of arousal in second and third graders increased as the reading task increased in difficulty from instructional to independent to frustration levels. At the college level, Maxwell (1971) has remarked on a syndrome among underachieving students whose most salient features are self-deprecation, lack of a clear system of goals and values, vulnerability to disparagement by others, immature relationships with parents, lack of insight into personal problems, and a pervasive anxiety or depression — in brief, all the dimensions hypothesized from Erikson's theory.

On the other hand, it should be noted that some researchers (e.g. Anderson, 1964; Shapiro, 1968) have failed to find any relationship between reading ability and anxiety, so the role of anxiety in reading success or failure remains in some doubt.

Social Learning Theory

Rotter's theory (1960) is based on his observations that certain accepted principles of reinforcement theory do not adequately reflect human behavior unless a concept of *expectancy* is added. Rewarding a behavior strengthens the behavior indirectly by strengthening the expectancy that the behavior will produce future rewards. In animals and very young children the expectation of reward is strongly linked to frequency of reward. In human beings, at least in those who have begun to form concepts and have some awareness of complex causes, many factors can influence the expectation of reward — past experience, current information, one's estimate of the probabilities of the situation, etc.

Rotter suggests that one of the most important factors contributing to this expectancy is the individual's belief in the extent to which he or she can affect the outcome. Clearly, this belief will vary from situation to situation, or so one might assume. But Rotter finds that some people have a general disposition to believe in their own efficacy to control events, while others seem to be (or to *think* they are) perpetually at the mercy of forces beyond their control. This "learned helplessness" (Dweck and Goetz, 1978) has been found to be characteristic of poor readers (Dweck and Repucci, 1973). As might be expected, anxiety is a frequent accompaniment to learned helplessness (Dweck, 1975).

Since Rotter first drew attention to the phenomenon, a body of literature on "locus of control" has accumulated. (For the interested reader, there are two reviews by Joe, 1971, and Throop and Macdonald, 1971.) Coleman et al. (1966) used a measure of internal-external control in their study on the *Equality of Educational Opportunity* and found that disadvantaged children students with high achievement scores were higher on the internal attitudes than the poor achievers. In general, "internals" seem to spend more time in academic activities and have higher educational aspirations than "externals" but the research has not been extended to the subject of reading. Entwisle (1971) has suggested that "control beliefs" may be especially important for reading, since middle-class parents teach their children from the beginning to expect order and meaning in their daily lives and to develop alternative strategies for dealing with problems that appear to violate this order, whereas poor children's early education may be deficient in these respects. The expectancy that reading will not only be a system with its own internal meaning and consistency, but also a tool to help solve other problems, must have important consequences for the excitement and desire to learn that children bring to reading. On the other hand, when reading is not seen as having these characteristics, it becomes "one more thing" imposed on unwilling victims by powerful authority figures.

Attitudes like these are probably first learned in the home. It would be unrealistic to expect that parents whose lives are wrapped in hopelessness will imbue their children with feelings of self-determination and conquest. If such attitudes are as important to reading as Entwisle and others suggest, it becomes a matter of urgency that the school develop strategies for changing the feelings of apathy and hopelessness that impede learning.

Several studies (e.g. Milner, 1963; Bee et al., 1969; Feshbach, 1975; Nottleman, 1978) have shown how the hidden curriculum of the middle-class home inculcates a general expectancy for success in solving problems and for achieving in school. Other studies have shown that internals spend more time in academic activities (Chance, 1965; Crandall, Katkovsky, and Crandall, 1965), consistently attain higher course grades and achievement scores (McGhee and Crandall, 1968), and have higher academic confidence and educational aspirations (Gurin et al., 1969; Lao, 1970).

The relationship of locus of control to reading remains relatively unexplored, though a few studies have begun to appear. Willey (1978) reported a significant relationship between reading and locus of control, while Cole and Garner (1984) found a combined locus of control and field independence measure to be a more precise predictor of self-concept than either measure alone, and to be highly related to reading in urban eighth grade students. These authors view locus of control as the primary influence and field independence a "mediating" influence.

Expectancy Theory

This theory differs from the previous one in that the expectancies here are those of other people *for* the individual, not the individual's expectations *about* other people. Rosenthal has taken the ancient adage that we all try to live up (or down) to other peoples' opinions of us, and has attempted to give it the status of a scientific principle that can be demonstrated with different actors in a variety of situations. The first such demonstration was recorded in *Pygmalion in the Classroom* (1968) in which children identified as "late bloomers" were later found to grow intellectually, the inference being that this growth was a direct result of their teachers' expectation that it would occur.[1] The phenomenon has been observed elsewhere (Brookover et al., 1967). Rubovitz and Maehr (1973) observed the behavior of student teachers who had been led to believe that certain students were "gifted" or "nongifted." They found that teacher behavior toward students did change as a function of expectations, but it was also affected by other variables such as the student's race (cf. Brophy and Good, 1974, Datta, Schaeffer, and Davis, 1968). The major difference was in the quality rather than the amount of attention given. A significant interaction was also found with teacher personality. The more dogmatic the teacher, the greater the tendency to react positively to "gifted" white students and negatively to "gifted" black students. It appears that teachers' expectations[2] do affect their behavior toward students, and hence, we may infer, students' perceptions of those expectations (this would provide the link with locus of control).

Palardy (1969) and Purkey (1970) discuss a number of research studies showing that students' self-perceptions are positively correlated with their perceptions of the teacher's feelings toward them. Moreover, the more positive the children's perceptions of their teacher's feelings, the better the academic achievement and the more desirable their classroom behavior tends to be. Mantaro (1971) found that the learner's perception of certain dimensions of the interpersonal relations between self and teacher (regard, empathy, and congruence) were positively related to both self-concept and reading performance.

Parents too have expectations that lead them to become more involved in their children's activities and to evaluate their performance more carefully (Katkovsky, Crandall, and Preston, 1964). While most parents hold high educational aspirations for their children (Brook, Whiteman, Peisach, and Deutsch, 1975), middle-class parents tend to make plans toward the achievement of those goals (Wolff, 1966), thus ensuring the important continuity between home and school.

Such studies are usually conceived within the framework of some other theory than expectancy theory. This fact underscores the relationships among the various theories and the interaction of the variables involved. Investigation may start from the vantage point of any one of these theories, but sooner or later the researcher must take cognizance of the effects of variables that play a key role in other theories. If this procedure leads to a study of the interaction of such variables, it must also lead to some integration of the theories, and hence to an increased understanding of the total dynamics of the behavior studies. To date, such integration has not occurred.

Cognitive Style Theory

The notion that people may differ in their style of conceptualization was introduced in a 1963 monograph by Kagan and his colleagues. The Conceptual Style Test (CST) was devised to separate those possessing the "analytic" attitude from those whose perceptual organization is of a more global nature. It requires the child to respond to a series of three-picture items by grouping the objects depicted in one of two possible ways.

The analytic-global distinction is further related to a number of personality dimensions, among which the reflectivity-impulsivity distinction seems particularly relevant to reading. Kagan suggests that the discrimination of stimuli called for in the reading task should favor analytic children over those who are "restless and impulsive, unable to accept the sedentary and reflective requirements of the reading situation." The suggestion appears warranted, in that those innercity children who most frequently manifest severe reading disabilities have been found to be hyperactive and impulsive. Subsequent research has attempted to verify this hypothesis and to assess the efficacy of programs designed to train children in the analytic attitude.

Reflective children do seem to adopt more efficient strategies, such as focusing on the stimulus attributes of a perceptual task, generating plausible hypotheses, and asking questions designed to elicit more relevant information, than do impulsive children (McKinney, 1973). Other writers agree that impulsive children "do not scan the field for distinctive features as systematically as do reflectives" (Ault, Crawford, and Jeffrey, 1972). Supporting evidence comes from Nuessle's finding (1972) of a relationship between developmental differences in focusing and developmental differences in reflectivity-impulsivity, and Kagan's study (1965) showing that reflective children learned letters and words more easily than impulsive children. Kagan further noted that children with reading disabilities were more likely to be impulsive than reflective (Kagan, 1966).

As might be expected, conceptual style has been found to correlate with response time. Kagan et al. (1964) have found stable individual differences in response time in about two-thirds of the samples tested, and there has been some speculation as to the reinforcement history of children manifesting these conceptual styles. Weiner and Adams (1974), for example, have suggested that reflective children are likely to have experienced failure, whereas frustration is the more probable antecedent of impulsive behavior. Accordingly, a number of programs have been devised to help children increase their response time and adopt a more reflective approach to cognitive tasks, with some measure of success (Briggs and Weinberg, 1973; Egeland, 1974; Kagan, Pearson, and Welch, 1966; Robertson and Keeley, 1974; Zelniker, Cochavi, and Yered, 1974).

As previously indicated, there has been some suggestion that conceptual style may be related to class or ethnic background. Wagner and Wilde (1973) found four intercorrelated dimensions of cognitive style to differentiate middle-class children from lower-class children. Ethnic background and sex, on the other hand, did not seem to be significant variables. Nor, does conceptual tempo appear to be related to intelligence (Messer, 1974), although this may not be true for specific populations.

Much research has been generated since the concept of cognitive style was first introduced into the literature, and new questions are constantly being posed about its relationship to other variables. To the extent that reading involves discrimination tasks and hypothesis-generating behavior, the research on cognitive style would seem to have direct implications for the reading field. There is a need to establish which components of reading are most susceptible to the influence of cognitive style, especially where styles may be modified by training. Bear in mind that the hypothesized relationships between reflectivity-impulsivity and accuracy of response did not hold for one third of the children studied who fell into the category of fast-accurate or slow-inaccurate. Not only should these children be studied further, but the advantage of being fast-accurate or even fast-inaccurate (as opposed to slow-accurate) in relation to different kinds of tasks warrants consideration. The student who is interested in this topic will find a sizable literature, but there are several reviews that may be consulted with advantage (Kagan and Kogan, 1970; Messer, 1974; Rosenfield, 1975). In brief, this appears to be one of the more fruitful areas for future research on reading and the affective domain.

Attribution Theory

Building on McClelland's (1961) achievement motivation theory, Weiner (1979) and his colleagues consider the major determinant of this motive to be individuals' reasoning about the causes of their successes and failures, since such reasoning is an expression of their values and affects their expectations (Covington and Omelich, 1979), which in turn influences the amount of effort they are willing to expend on a task. The affective concomitants of this reasoning vary as a function of the sources to which the achievement outcome is attributed (ability, external causes, chance). Although this theory emphasizes the role of cognition in achievement motivation, it is clear that affective constructs are also important predictors of achievement motivation.

Metacomprehension Theory

Comprehension is a process in which the perceiver brings a complex of knowledge, previous experience, values, and expectations to the task of translating the stimulus (clouds, voices, print) into a meaningful message (rain, argument, directions). Additionally, skilled "interpreters" (in this case, readers) monitor their performance at critical points throughout the process. This monitoring may be verbal or nonverbal. In fact, the primary criterion of whether a skill has become "automatic" (LaBerge and Samuels, 1976) may be the suppression of *verbal* monitoring. However, it is clear that, even when the task is proceeding smoothly, some form of monitoring is taking place since the reader is immediately alerted to a problem when the message begins to break down (e.g. the reader sees *con*tent for con*tent,* thereby interrupting the flow of meaning). At this point, verbal monitoring may be resumed, and the reader makes a strategic regression, perhaps to the beginning of the sentence.

Research on this subject (Brown, 1981, Flavell, 1981) suggests that the monitoring processes of good and poor readers are quite different. In the first place, poor readers are likely to have fewer skills that have reached the requisite level of automaticity, and fewer strategies for coping with problems that arise. Depending on the nature and severity of the disability, poor readers may exhibit little monitoring behavior or a greater degree of laborious, verbal monitoring. In the second place, it seems likely that the verbal monitoring of poor readers is also overloaded with affective responses that may or may not be relevant to the task, but in either case, serve as an impediment to the desired outcome.

Metacognitive monitoring, according to the above authors, includes the following activities: Assessment of task difficulty, an estimate of chances of success, identification of appropriate strategies, and continuous monitoring of progress. Athey (1982) has attempted to incorporate some of the previously mentioned affective variables (self-concept, anxiety) under the rubric of metacognitve monitoring, and to demonstrate how affective responses taking place during the course of these activities may facilitate or inhibit reading performance. For example, many of the responses generated while preparing for a test provide glimpses into the student's self-concept ("I never was good at history"), intellectual values ("I'd rather be playing baseball"), independence ("I don't believe the author has his facts straight"), anxiety ("If I don't do well on this exam, I'll fail the course"), and so forth. Clearly, all of these responses are "relevant" in a sense, but some are more helpful toward accomplishing what has to be done than others.

At this point, we will return briefly to Holmes' substrata-factor theory of reading. In addition to the psychological model described earlier, Holmes also speculated on the neurological counterparts of the substrata factors. In this context, Hebb's (1949) notion of brain-cell assemblies proved to be a useful way of thinking about how incoming information is processed and stored in the substrata factors. Affective responses such as those described above are generated at the time of input and become as integral to the assembly as cognitive, task-oriented responses.[3] With more experience, these subsystems of brain-cell assemblies become facilitated by firing in phase. In this way, diverse appropriate subsets of "information" learned under different circumstances at different times, and hence stored in different parts of the brain, may be brought simultaneously into awareness when triggered by appropriate stimuli. The cognitive and the affective become merely different aspects of the complex of knowledge and attitudes that comprise the substrata factor.

Conclusion

This chapter has presented a brief exposition of some of the theories that have given, or could give, rise to hypotheses related to achievement in general and/or reading in particular and of some of the research studies conducted within the framework of these theories. It does not claim to be exhaustive in either respect. On the one hand, probably any psychological theory could be used as a starting point for the derivation of testable hypotheses about some aspect of reading. On the other hand, the achievement-related research that could appropriately be included in any one of the sections is quite voluminous. The reader should, therefore, regard this chapter as a preliminary foray into some of the more promising lines of investigation from which to proceed in the quest for more fruitful theorizing and for new research directions.

REFERENCES

Abrams, J.C. A study of certain personality characteristics of nonreaders and achievers. Unpublished doctoral dissertation, Temple University, 1955.

Abrams, J.C. Further considerations on the ego functioning of the dyslexic child—a psychiatric viewpoint. In G.D. Spache (Ed.), *Reading Disability and Perception.* Proceedings of the 13th Annual Conference of the International Reading Association. Newark, DE: International Reading Association, 1969, 13(3), 16-21.

Akeret, R.U. Interrelationships among various dimensions of the self concept. In G. Lindzey and C.S. Hall (Eds.), *Theories of Personality: Primary Sources and Research.* New York: Wiley, 1965, 491-493.

Anderson, D.J. Manifest anxiety level and reading achievement: A study of the relationships between the manifest anxiety level and the reading achievement of fifth and sixth grade boys. Unpublished doctoral dissertation, New York University, 1964.

Anderson, W.W. Self-directed activity as a variable in reading instruction. *Reading World,* 1972, 12 (1), 3-14.

Asher, S.R., and Markell, R.A. Sex differences in comprehension of high and low interest material. *Journal of Educational Psychology,* 1974, 66, 680-687.

Athey, I.J. Reading-personality patterns at the junior high school level. Unpublished doctoral dissertation, University of California at Berkeley, 1965.

Athey, I.J., and Holmes, J.A. *Reading Success and Personality Characteristics in Junior High School Students.* Berkeley, CA: University of California Press, 1969.

Athey, I.J. Reading: The affective domain reconceptualized. In B.A. Hutson (Ed.), *Advances in Reading/Language Research* (Vol. 1). Greenwich, CT: JAI Press, 1982, 203-217.

Ault, R., Crawford, D., and Jeffrey, W.E. Visual scanning strategies of reflective, impulsive, fast-accurate, and slow-inaccurate children on the Matching Familiar Figures Test, *Child Development,* 1972, 43, 1412-1417.

Bakan, R. Academic performance and self concept as a function of achievement variability. *Journal of Educational Measurement,* 1971, 8(4), 317-319.

Barber, L.K. Immature ego development as a factor in retarded ability to read. Unpublished doctoral dissertation, University of Michigan, 1952.

Bauer, E.B. The interrelatedness of personality and achievement in reading. Unpublished doctoral dissertation, University of California at Berkeley, 1956.

Bee, H.L., Van Egeren, L., Streisguth, A.P., Nyman, B.A., and Leckie, M.S. Class difference in maternal teaching strategies and speech patterns. *Developmental Psychology,* 1969, 1, 726-734.

Bell, D.B., Lewis, F.D., and Anderson, R.F. Some personality and motivational factors in reading retardation. *Journal of Educational Research,* 1972, 65(5), 229-233.

Berger, A. Identity confusion and reading instruction. *Journal of the Reading Specialist,* 1968, 7(4), 170-174.

Berlyne, D.E. Novelty and curiosity as determinants of exploratory behavior. *British Journal of Psychology,* 1950, 41, 68-80.

Bernstein, M.R. Relationship between interest and reading comprehension. *Journal of Educational Research,* 1955, 49, 283-288.

Berretta, S. Self-concept development in the reading program. *Reading Teacher,* 1970, 24(3), 232-238.

Biel, J.E. Emotional factors in the treatment of reading difficulties. *Journal of Consulting Psychology,* 1945, 9, 125-131.

Blackham, G.J. A clinical study of the personality structures and adjustments of pupils underachieving and overachieving in reading. Unpublished doctoral dissertation, Cornell University, 1955.

Bodwin, R.F. The relationship between immature self concept and certain educational disabilities. Unpublished doctoral dissertation, Michigan State University, 1957.

Bouise, L.M. Emotional and personality problems of a group of retarded readers. *Elementary English,* 1955, 32, 544-584.

Bricklin, P.M. Self-related concepts and aspiration behavior of achieving readers and two types of nonachieving readers. Unpublished doctoral dissertation, Temple University, 1963.

Bridgeman, B., and Shipman, V.C. Preschool measures of self esteem and achievement motivation as predictors of third-grade achievement. *Journal of Educational Psychology,* 1978, 70, 17-28.

Briggs, C.H., and Weinberg, R. Effects of reinforcement in training children's conceptual tempos. *Journal of Educational Psychology,* 1973, 65, 383-394.

Brook, J.S., Whiteman, M., Peisach, E., and Deutsch, M. Aspiration levels of and for children: Age, sex, race, and socioeconomic correlates. *Journal of Genetic Psychology,* 1974, 124, 3-16.

Brookover, W.B., Erickson, E.L., and Joiner, L.M. *Self Concept of Ability and School Achievement: III. Relationship of Self Concept to Achievement in High School.* U.S. Office of Education, Cooperative Research Project. Final Report, Contract No. 1831, 1967.

Brophy, J., and Good, T.L. *Teacher-Student Relationships.* New York: Holt, 1974.

Brown, A.L. Metacognitive development and reading. In R.J. Spiro, B. Bruce, and W.F. Brewer (Eds.), *Theoretical Issues in Reading Comprehension.* Hillsdale, NJ: Erlbaum, 1981.

Carrillo, L.W. The relation of certain environmental and developmental factors to reading ability. Unpublished doctoral dissertation, Syracuse University, 1957.

Carter, P., Jr. A descriptive analysis of the adult adjustment of persons once identified as disabled readers. Unpublished doctoral dissertation, Indiana University, 1964.

Chance, J.E. Internal control of reinforcement and the school learning process. Paper read at the Annual Conference of the Society for Research in Child Development, Minneapolis, 1965.

Claiborn, W.L. Expectancy effects in the classroom: A failure to replicate. *Journal of Educational Psychology,* 1969, 60(5, Part 1), 377-383.

Cohn, M., and Cornelly, D. For better reading—a more positive self-image. *Elementary School Journal,* 1970, 70(4), 199-201.

Cole, E.G., and Garner, C.W. The relationship between locus of control field dependence and the academic self-concept and achievement of the disadvantaged. Unpublished paper, Rutgers University, 1984.

Coleman, J.S., Campbell, E.Q., Hobson, C.J., McPhartland, J., Mood, A.M., Wekinfield, F.D., and York, R.L. *Equality of Educational Opportunity.* Superintendent of Documents Catalog No. FS 5.238:38001. Washington, DC: U.S. Government Printing Office, 1966. (ED 012 275)

Cooper, H.M. Pygmalion grows up: A model for teacher expectation, communication, and performance. *Review of Educational Research,* 1979, 49, 389-410.

Cotler, S. The effects of positive and negative reinforcement on the reading performance of male elementary school children. *Genetic Psychology Monographs,* 1969, 80, 29-50.

Cotler, S., and Palmer, R.J. The relationships among sex, sociometric, self, and test anxiety factors and the academic achievement of elementary school children. *Psychology in the Schools,* 1970, 7(3), 211-216.

Cotler, S., and Palmer, R.J. Social reinforcement, individual difference factors, and the reading performance of elementary school children. *Journal of Personality and Social Psychology,* 1971, 18(1), 97-104.

Covington, M.V., and Omelich, C.L. It's best to be able and virtuous too: Student and teacher evaluative responses to successful effort. *Journal of Educational Psychology,* 1979, 71, 688-700.

Cowen, E.L., Zax, M., Klein, R., Izzo, L.D., and Trost, M.A. The relationship of anxiety in school children to school record, achievement, and behavioral measures. *Child Development,* 1965, 36, 685-695.

Crandall, V.C., Katkovsky, W., and Crandall, V.J. Children's belief in their control of reinforcement in intellectual-academic achievement situations. *Child Development,* 1965, 36, 91-109.

Cummings, R.N. A study of the relationship between self concepts and reading achievement at third grade level. Unpublished doctoral dissertation, University of Alabama, 1970.

Daniels, S. *How 2 Gerbils, 20 Goldfish, 200 Games, 2000 Books and I Taught Them How to Read.* Philadelphia: Westminister Press, 1971.

Datta, L., Schaeffer, E., and Davis, M. Sex and scholastic aptitude as variables in teachers' ratings of the adjustment and classroom behavior of Negro and other seventh-grade students. *Journal of Educational Psychology,* 1968, 59, 94-101.

Dennerll, D.E. Dimensions of self concept of later elementary children in relationship to reading performance, sex role, and socioeconomic status. Unpublished doctoral dissertation, University of Michigan, 1971.

Dorney, W.P. The effectiveness of reading instruction on the modification of certain attitudes toward authority figures of adolescent delinquent boys. Unpublished doctoral dissertation, New York University, 1963.

Dukes, B.M. Anxiety, self-concept, reading achievement, and creative thinking in four socioeconomic status levels. Unpublished doctoral dissertation, University of Alabama, 1964.

Dusek, J.B. The development of test anxiety in children. In I.G. Sarason (Ed.), *Test Anxiety: Theory, Research, and Applications.* Hillsdale, NJ: Erlbaum, 1980.

Dweck, C.S. The role of expectations and attributions in the alleviation of learned helplessness. *Journal of Personality and Social Psychology,* 1975, 11, 674-685.

Dweck, C.S., and Goetz, T.E. Attributions and learned helplessness. In J.H. Harvey, W.I. Ickes, and R.F. Kidd. (Eds.), *New Directions in Attribution Research* (Vol. 2). Hillsdale, NJ: Erlbaum, 1978.

Dweck, C.S., and Repucci, N.D. Learned helplessness and reinforcement responsibility in children. *Journal of Personality and Social Psychology,* 1973, 25, 109-116.

Eder, D. Ability grouping of students and academic self concepts: A case study. *Elementary School Journal,* 1983, 84, 149-161.

Egeland, B. Training impulsive children in the use of more efficient scanning techniques. *Child Development,* 1974, 45, 165-171.

Elashoff, J.D., and Snow, R.E. *A Case Study in Statistical Inference: Reconsideration of the Rosenthal-Jacobson Data on Teacher Expectancy.* Department of Health, Education, and Welfare, Report No. Tr-15, Bureau No. BR-5-0252, December 1970. (ED 046 892)

Entwisle, D.R. Implications of language socialization for reading models and for learning to read. *Reading Research Quarterly,* 1971 (Fall), 7(1), 111-167.

Erikson, E.H. *Childhood and Society.* New York: Norton, 1950.

Erikson, E.H. Identity and the life cycle. In G.S. Klein (Ed.), *Psychological Issues,* New York: Basic Books, 1959, 18-171.

Eshel, Y., and Klein, Z. Development of academic self concept of lower-class and middle-class primary school children. *Journal of Educational Psychology,* 1981, 73, 187-193.

Eysenck, H.J. A dynamic theory of anxiety and hysteria. *Journal of Mental Science,* 1955, 101, 28-51.

Eysenck, H.J. *Dynamics of Anxiety and Hysteria.* London: Routledge and Kegan Paul, 1957.

Fennimore, F. Reading and the self concept. *Journal of Reading,* 1968, 11(6), 447-451, 481.

Feshbach, N.D. Some interpersonal factors associated with successful and problem readers. Paper presented at the annual meeting of the Society for Research in Child Development, Denver, Colorado, 1975.

Fillmer, H.T., Busby, W.A., and Smittle, P. Visual perception and self concept: New directions in reading. *Journal of Reading Behavior,* 1971-1972, 4(3), 17-20.

Fitts, W.H. *Manual: Tennessee Self-Concept Scale.* Nashville, TN: Counselor Recordings and Tests, 1965.

Flavell, J.H. The nature and development of metacognition. Paper presented at Annual Conference of the American Educational Research Association, Los Angeles, 1981.

Fliegler, L.A. Understanding the underachieving gifted child. *Psychological Reports,* 1957, 3, 533-536.

Frerichs, A.H. Relationship of self-esteem of the disadvantaged to school success. *Journal of Negro Education,* 1971, 40(2), 117-120.

Frost, B.P. Intelligence, manifest anxiety, and scholastic achievement. *Alberta Journal of Educational Research,* 1965, 11, 167-175.

Gates, A.I. The role of personality maladjustment in reading disability. *Journal of Genetic Psychology,* 1941, 59, 77-83.

Gowan, J.C. The underachieving gifted child—a problem for everyone. *Exceptional Children,* 1955, 21, 247-249.

Granzow, K.R. A comparative study of underachievers, normal achievers, and overachievers in reading. Unpublished doctoral dissertation, Iowa State University, 1954.

Griffiths, A.N. Self concept in remedial work with dyslexic children. *Academic Therapy,* 1971, 6(2), 125-133.

Groff, P.J. Children's attitudes toward reading and their critical reading abilities in four content type materials. *Journal of Educational Research,* 1962, 55, 313-317.

Gurin, P., Gurin, G., Lao, R.C., and Beattie, M. Internal-external control in the motivational dynamics of Negro youth. *Journal of Social Issues,* 1969, 25, 29-53.

Hall, C.S., and Lindzey, G. *Theories of Personality.* New York: Wiley, 1957.

Hallock, G.A. Attitudinal factors affecting achievement in reading. Unpublished doctoral dissertation, Wayne State University, 1958.

Harlow, H.F., Harlow, M.K., and Meyer, D.R. Learning motivated by a manipulation drive. *Journal of Experimental Psychology,*1950, 40, 228-234.

Healy, A.K. Effects of changing children's attitudes toward reading. *Elementary English,* 1965, 42, 269-272.

Hebb, D.O. *The Organization of Behavior.* New York: Wiley, 1949.

Hedges, R.E. An investigation into the effects of self-directed photography experiences upon self concept and reading readiness achievement of kindergarten children. Unpublished doctoral dissertation, Syracuse University, 1971.

Henderson, E.H., and Long, B.H. Personal-social correlates of academic success among disadvantaged school beginners. *Journal of School Psychology,* 1971, 9(2), 101-113.

Henderson, E.H., Long, B.H., and Ziller, R.C. Self-social constructs of achieving and nonachieving readers. *Reading Teacher,* 1965, 19, 114-118.

Hill, K.T. Motivation, evaluation, and educational testing policy. In L.J. Fyans, Jr. (Ed.), *Achievement Motivation: Recent Trends in Theory and Research.* New York: Plenum, 1980.

Holmes, J.A. Factors underlying major reading disabilities at the college level. *Genetic Psychology Monographs,* 1954, 49, 3-95.

Holmes, J.A. The substrata-factor theory of reading: Some experimental evidence. In J.A. Figurel (Ed.), *New Frontiers in Reading.* Proceedings of the Fifth Annual Conference of the International Reading Association. New York: Scholastic Magazines, 1960, 115-121.

Holmes, J.A. Personality characteristics of the disabled reader. *Journal of Developmental Reading,* 1961, 4, 111-122.

Holmes, J.A. Basic assumptions underlying the substrata-factor theory. In H. Singer and R.B. Ruddell (Eds.), *Theoretical Models and Processes of Reading,* second edition. Newark, DE: International Reading Association, 1976, 597-618.

Holmes, J.A., and Singer, H. *Substrata-Factor Differences Underlying Reading Ability in Known Groups.* Report of a Cooperative Research Project to U.S. Office of Education, Contract Nos. 538, SAE-8176 and 538, SAE-8660, 1961.

Holzinger, M. Personality and behavioral characteristics of able and less able readers of elementary school age. Unpublished doctoral dissertation, University of Minnesota, 1967.

Jackson, J. A survey of psychological, social, and environmental differences between advanced and retarded readers. *Journal of Genetic Psychology,* 1944, 65, 113-131.

Jackson, R. Building reading skills and self concepts. *Reading Teacher,* 1972, 25(8), 755-758.

Jahoda, M. *Current Concepts of Positive Mental Health.* New York: Basic Books, 1958.

James, W. *Principles of Psychology* (Vol. 1). New York: Dover Publications, 1890.

Joe, V.C. Review of the internal-external control contract as a personality variable. *Psychological Reports,* 1971, 28, 619-640.

Johnson, D.E. Reading behavior, achievements, and attitudes of first grade boys. Unpublished doctoral dissertation, Stanford University, 1959.

Kagan, J. Reflection-impulsivity and reading ability. *Child Development,* 1965, 36, 609-628.
Kagan, J. Reflection-impulsivity: The generality and dynamics of conceptual tempo. *Journal of Abnormal Psychology,* 1966, 71, 17-24.
Kagan, J., and Kogan, N. Individual variation in cognitive processes. In P.H. Mussen (Ed.), *Carmichael's Manual of Child Psychology,* third edition, 1970, Vol. 1, 1273-1365.
Kagan, J., Moss, H.A., and Sigel, I.E. Psychological significance of styles of conceptualization. In J.C. Wright and J. Kagan (Eds.), *Basic Cognitive Processes in Children.* Monograph of the Society for Research in Child Development, 1963. Reprinted in *Cognitive Development in Children: Five Monographs of the Society for Research in Child Development,* 1970.
Kagan, J., Pearson, L., and Welch, L. Modifiability of an impulsive tempo. *Journal of Educational Psychology,* 1966, 57, 359-365.
Kagan, J., Rosman, B., Albert, J., and Phillips, W. Information-processing in the child: Significance of analytic and reflective attitudes. *Psychological Monographs,* 1964, 78, No. 1.
Kagan, J., Sontag, L.W., Baker, C.T., and Nelson, V.L. Personality and IQ change. *Journal of Abnormal and Social Psychology,* 1958, 56, 261-266.
Katkovsky, W.A., Crandall, V.C., and Preston, A. Parent attitudes toward their personal achievements and toward the achievement behavior of their children. *Journal of Genetic Psychology,* 1964, 104, 67-82.
Ketcham, C.A. Factors in the home background and reader self concept which relate to reading achievement. Unpublished doctoral dissertation, Lehigh University, 1966.
Khan, S.B. Affective correlates of academic achievement. *Journal of Educational Psychology,* 1969, 60(3), 216-221.
Khan, S.B. Affective correlates of academic achievement — a longitudinal study. *Measurement and Evaluation in Guidance,* 1970, 3(2), 76-80.
Khan, S.B., and Roberts, D.M. Factorial stability of academically relevant affective characteristics. *Measurement and Evaluation in Guidance,* 1971, 3(4), 209-212.
Kohn, M., and Rosman, B.L. Relationship of preschool social-emotional functioning to later intellectual achievement. *Developmental Psychology,* 1972, 6(3), 445-452.
Krim, L.F. Underachieving readers in an elementary school summer reading improvement program: A semantic-differential measure of their change in attitude toward school, self, and aspiration. Unpublished doctoral dissertation, University of Denver, 1968.
Lao, R.C. Internal-external control and competent and innovative behavior among Negro college students. *Journal of Personality and Social Psychology,* 1970, 14, 263-270.
Lasswell, A. Reading group placement: Its influence on enjoyment of reading and perception of self as a reader. Paper presented to the Annual Conference of the American Educational Research Association, New York, 1967.
Lecky, P. *Self-Consistency: A Theory of Personality.* New York: Island Press, 1951.
Lockhart, H.M. Personality and reading readiness. *Illinois School Research,* 1965, 2, 9-11.
Lumpkin, D.D. The relationship of self concept to achievement in reading. Unpublished doctoral dissertation, University of Southern California, 1959.
Lynn, R. Temperamental characteristics related to disparity of attainment in reading and arithmetic. *British Journal of Educational Psychology,* 1957, 27, 62-67.
Malmquist, E. Factors related to reading disabilities in the first grade of the elementary school. *Acta Universitatis Stockholmiensis,* Stockholm Studies in Educational Psychology, No. 2. Stockholm: Almquist and Wiksell, 1958.
Mantaro, C.A. An investigation of the relationship between interpersonal relationships perceived by a pupil to exist between himself and 1) his reading achievement, 2) his self concept. Unpublished doctoral dissertation, Syracuse University, 1971.
Margulies, H. Rorscharch responses of successful and unsuccessful students. *Archives of Psychology,* 1942, No. 271.
Mathewson, G.C. The function of attitude in the reading process. In R.B. Ruddell and H. Singer (Eds.), *Theoretical Models and Processes of Reading,* second edition. Newark, DE: International Reading Association, 1976, 655-676.
Maw, W.H., and Maw, E.W. Children's curiosity as an aspect of reading comprehension. *Reading Teacher,* 1962, 15, 236-240.
Maxwell, M. The role of attitudes and emotions in changing reading and study skills behavior of college students. *Journal of Reading,* 1971, 14(6), 359-364, 420-422.

McClelland, D.C. *The Achieving Society.* New York: Free Press, 1961.

McGhee, P.E., and Crandall, V.C. Beliefs in internal-external control of reinforcement and academic performance. *Child Development,* 1968, 39, 91-102.

McGinnis, D.J. A comparative study of the attitudes of parents of superior and inferior readers toward certain child-rearing practices. *National Reading Conference Yearbook,* 1965, 14, 99-105.

McKinney, J. Problem-solving strategies in impulsive and reflective second graders. *Developmental Psychology,* 1973, 8, 145.

McMichael, P. Reading difficulties, behavior, and social status. *Journal of Educational Psychology,* 72 (1980), 76-86.

Mead, M. Adolescence in primitive and modern society. In E.E. Maccoby, T.M. Newcomb, and E.D. Hartley (Eds.), *Readings in Social Psychology,* third edition. New York: Holt, 1958, 341-350.

Messer, S. Reflectivity-impulsivity: A review. Unpublished paper, 1974.

Miller, C.D. An exploratory investigation of self concepts of high achieving, average achieving, and low achieving groups of junior high pupils as perceived by the pupils and their teachers. Unpublished doctoral dissertation, University of Colorado, 1963.

Miller, W.H., and Windhauser, E. Reading disability: Tendency toward delinquency. *The Clearing House,* 1971, 46(3), 183-187.

Milner, E. A study of the relationship between reading readiness in grade one school children and patterns of parent-child interaction. *62nd Yearbook of the National Society of the Study of Education.* Chicago: University of Chicago Press, 1963, 108-143.

Neville, D., Pfost, P., and Dobbs, V. The relationship between test anxiety and silent reading gain. *American Educational Research Journal,* 1967, 4, 45-50.

Norman, R.D., and Daley, M.F. The comparative personality adjustments of superior and inferior readers. *Journal of Educational Psychology,* 1959, 50, 31-36.

Nottleman, E.D. Parent-child interaction and children's achievement-related behavior. Unpublished doctoral dissertation, University of Illinois, 1978.

Nuessle, W. Reflectivity as an influence on focusing behavior of children. *Journal of Experimental Child Psychology,* 1972, 14, 265-276.

Osgood, C.E. *Method and Theory in Experimental Psychology.* New York: Oxford, 1953.

Pacheco, A.D. Anxiety and reading achievement in sixth grade children. Unpublished doctoral dissertation, Colorado State University, 1964.

Palardy, J.M. For Johnny's reading sake. *Reading Teacher,* 1969, 22(8), 720-724.

Peter, Sister M. The role of intelligence, personality, and selected psychological factors in remedial reading progress. Unpublished doctoral dissertation, University of Rochester, 1963.

Phelps, R.E. The measurement of manifest anxiety in young children and its relationships to later reading achievement. Unpublished doctoral dissertation, University of Connecticut, 1967.

Pratz, O.R. A study of the affective correlates of academic achievement in school children of different countries. Unpublished doctoral dissertation, University of Texas at Austin, 1969.

Purkey, W.W. *Self Concept and School Achievement.* Englewood Cliffs, NJ: Prentice-Hall, 1970.

Ramsey, W. A study of salient characteristics of pupils of high and low reading ability. *Journal of Developmental Reading,* 1962, 5, 87-94.

Resnick, L.B., and Robinson, B.H. Motivational aspects of the literacy problem. In J.B. Carroll (Ed.), *Towards a Literate Society.* New York: McGraw-Hill, 1975.

Reynolds, S.C. The relationship between ability to read and the meaning and expression of emotion: A study of lower-class, institutionalized boys with antisocial behavior problems. Unpublished doctoral dissertation, Columbia University, 1970.

Robertson, D., and Keeley, S. Evaluation of a mediational training program for impulsive children by a multiple case study design. Paper presented at the American Psychological Association Conference. New Orleans, August 1974.

Rosenfield, S. Cognitive style and the reading process. Paper presented at the International Reading Association Conference, New York City, 1975.

Rosenthal, R., and Jacobson, L. *Pygmalion in the Classroom: Teacher Expectation and Pupils' Intellectual Development.* New York: Holt, Rinehart and Winston, 1968.

Rotter, J.G. Generalized expectancies for internal versus external control of reinforcement. *Psychological Monographs,* 1966, 80(1). (Whole No. 609)

Rubovits, P.C., and Maehr, M.L. Pygmalion black and white. *Journal of Personality and Social Psychology,* 1973, 25(2), 210-218.

Ruddell, R.B. Psycholinguistic implications for a systems of communication model. In H. Singer and R.B. Ruddell (Eds.), *Theoretical Models and Processes of Reading.* Newark, DE: International Reading Association, 1970, 239-258.

Ruddell, R.B. Language acquisition and the reading process. In H. Singer and R.B. Ruddell (Eds.), *Theoretical Models and Processes of Reading,* second edition. Newark, DE: International Reading Association, 1976.

Rugel, R.P. Arousal and levels of reading difficulty. *Reading Teacher,* 1971, 24(5), 458-460.

Savage, R.D. Personality factors and academic attainment in junior school children. *British Journal of Educational Psychology,* 1966, 36, 91-92.

Scarborough, O.R., Hindsman, E., and Hanna, G. Anxiety level and performance in school subjects. *Psychological Reports,* 1961, 9, 425-430.

Schoeller, A.W., and Pearson, D.A. Better reading through volunteer reading tutors. *Reading Teacher,* 1970, 23(7), 625-630, 636.

Schwyhart, F.K. Exploration of the self-concept of retarded readers in relation to reading achievement. Unpublished doctoral dissertation, University of Arizona, 1967.

Seay, L.C. A study to determine some relations between changes in reading skills and self-concepts accompanying a remedial program for boys with low reading ability and reasonably normal intelligence. Unpublished doctoral dissertation, Texas State College, 1960.

Sebeson, L. Self concept and reading disabilities, *Reading Teacher,* 1970, 23(5), 460-464.

Shapiro, M.A. Relationships among extraversion, neuroticism, academic reading achievement, and verbal learning. Unpublished doctoral dissertation, Rutgers University, 1968.

Shatter, F. An investigation of the effectiveness of a group therapy program, including the child and his mother, for the remediation of reading disability. Unpublished doctoral dissertation, New York University, 1956.

Shnayer, S.W. Relationships between reading interests and reading comprehension. In J.A. Figurel (Ed.), *Reading and Realism.* Newark, DE: International Reading Association, 1969.

Shrodes, C. Bibliotherapy: A theoretical and clinical experimental study. Unpublished doctoral dissertation, University of California at Berkeley, 1949.

Silverman, H. The prediction of learning difficulties and personality trends in preschool children. Unpublished doctoral dissertation, Columbia University, 1968.

Simula, V.L. An investigation of the effects of test anxiety and perceptual rigidity upon word recognition skill of second grade children. Unpublished doctoral dissertation, Indiana University, 1964.

Singer, H. *Substrata-Factor Reorganization Accompanying Development of General Reading Ability at the Elementary School Level.* U.S. Office of Education, Cooperative Research Project, Final Report, Contract No. 2011, 1965.

Smith, D.E.P., and Carrigan, P.M. *The Nature of Reading Disability.* New York: Harcourt Brace Jovanovich, 1959.

Smith, M.E. The effects of an experimental program to improve self concept, attitudes toward school, and achievement of Negro fourth, fifth, and sixth grade students. Unpublished doctoral dissertation, University of Michigan, 1970.

Smith, P.W. Self concept gain scores and reading efficiency terminal ratios as a function of specialized reading instruction or personal interaction. In J.A. Figurel (Ed.), *Reading and Realism.* Proceedings of the 13th Annual Convention of the International Reading Association. Newark, DE: International Reading Association, 1969, 13(1), 671-674.

Sontag, L.W., Baker, C.T., and Nelson, V.L. Mental growth and personality development: A longitudinal study. *Monographs for Research in Child Development,* 1958, 23(2).

Sopis, J.F. The relationship of self-image of a reader to reading achievement. Unpublished doctoral dissertation, New York University, 1965.

Spache, G.D. Personality characteristics of retarded readers as measured by the Picture-Frustration study, *Educational and Psychological Measurement,* 1957, 14, 186-192.

Spache, G.D. Personality patterns of retarded readers. *Journal of Educational Research,* 1957, 50, 461-469.

Stevens, D.O. Reading difficulty and classroom acceptance. *Reading Teacher,* 1971, 25(1), 52-55.

Super, D.O., Starishevsky, R., Matlin, N., and Jordaan, J.P. *Career Development: Self Concept Theory.* New York: College Entrance Examination Board, 1963.

Tabarlet, B.E. A study of mental health status of retarded readers. Unpublished doctoral dissertation, Louisiana State University, 1958.

Thorndike, R.L. Review of *Pygmalion in the Classroom. American Educational Research Journal,* 1968, 5, 708-711.

Throop, W.F., and Macdonald, A.P. Internal-external locus of control: A bibliography. *Psychological Reports,* 1971, 28, 175-190.

Toews, A. Emotions and reading difficulties. *School and Community,* 1972, 58(8), 35.

Toller, G.S. Certain aspects of the self-evaluations made by achieving and retarded readers of average and above average intelligence. Unpublished doctoral dissertation, Temple University, 1967.

VanZandt, W. A study of some home-family-community factors related to children's achievement in reading in an elementary school. Unpublished doctoral dissertation, Wayne State University, 1963.

Vehar, M.A. Extraversion, introversion, and reading ability. *Reading Teacher,* 1968, 21, 357-376.

Wagner, S., and Wilde, J.E. Learning styles: Can we grease the cogs in cognition? *Claremont Reading Conference,* 1973, 37, 135-142.

Wattenberg, W.W., and Clifford, C. Relation of self-concepts to beginning achievements in reading. *Child Development,* 1964, 35, 461-467.

Weiner, A.S., and Adams, W.V. The effect of failure and frustration on reflective and impulsive children. *Journal of Experimental Child Psychology,* 1974, 17, 353-359.

Weiner, B. A theory of motivation for some classroom experiences. *Journal of Educational Psychology,* 1979, 71, 3-25.

Weiner, B., Frieze, I., Kukla, A., Reed, A., Rest, S., and Rosenbaum, L.M. *Perceiving the Causes of Success and Failure.* Morristown, NJ: General Learning Corporation, 1971.

West, C.K., and Anderson, T.H. The question of preponderant causation in teacher expectation research. *Review of Educational Research,* 1976, 46, 613-630.

White, R.W. Motivation reconsidered; the concept of competence. *Psychological Review,* 1959, 66, 297-333.

Wigfield, A., and Asher, S.R. Social and motivational influences on reading. In P.D. Pearson, R. Barr, M.L. Kamil, and P. Mosenthal (Eds.), *Handbook of Reading Research.* New York: Longman, 1984, 423-452.

Wiggins, R.V. A comparison of children's interest in and attitude toward reading material written in standard and black English forms. Unpublished doctoral dissertation, Ohio State University, 1971.

Winterbottom, M.R. The relation of need for achievement to learning experiences in independence and mastery. In J.W. Atkinson (Ed.), *Motives in Fantasy, Action, and Society.* Princeton, NJ: Van Nostrand, 1958.

Witty, P.A. Reading success and emotional adjustment, *Elementary English Review,* 1950, 27, 296.

Wolff, R. The measurement of environment. In A. Anastasi (Ed.), *Testing Problems in Perspective.* Washington, DC: American Council on Education, 1966.

Zelniker, T., Cochavi, D., and Yered, J. The relationship between speed of performance and conceptual style: The effect of imposed modification of response latency. *Child Development,* 1974, 45(3), 779-784.

Zimmerman, L., and Allebrand, C.N. Personality characteristics and attitudes toward achievement of good and poor readers. *Journal of Educational Research,* 1965, 59, 28-30.

NOTES

[1] Students who plan to conduct research in this area should be aware of the methodological problems. See Claiborn (1969), Elashoff and Snow (1970), and Thorndike (1968) for critiques.

[2] For reviews of the literature on teacher expectations, see Cooper (1979) and West and Anderson (1976).

[3] If this hypothesis is correct, the affective concomitants of initial learning experiences become extremely important for later learning and performance.

Culture

Achieving School Failure: An Anthropological Approach to Illiteracy and Social Stratification

R.P. McDermott
Rockefeller University

Introduction

This chapter is divided into four sections. The first defines a problem and asks a question. The problem is that children from minority communities appear to regenerate their parents' pariah status by learning how to act in ways condemned by the larger host community. The question asks where this learning comes from and whether or not it represents a rational adaptation to socialization attempts by host schools.

The second section examines the production of pariah-host social organizations in terms of what both pariah and host members must know about the daily business of treating each other as pariahs and hosts. Early experiences in the politics of everyday life determine the categories children develop for use in deciding how to act in similar situations at future times. In other words, the politics of everyday life socialize the identities, statuses and abilities of children and, as such, are the source of the persistence of social organizations, including pariah groups, across generations.

The third section discusses an example. Specifically, the social organization of learning to read in a host teacher and pariah student classroom is examined in terms of the politics of everyday life. For black American children in white-administered schools, it is argued that competence in reading and competence in classroom politics are inversely proportional. Inability to read is positively condemned by the host population and assures oppression and the assignment of pariah status by the host community. Nevertheless, not learning to read is accompanied by all the social skills essential to a peer-defined political success within the classroom. In peer group terms, it represents more of an achievement than a disability.

Accordingly, the hypothesis examined is that a significant number of what are usually described as reading disabilities represent situationally induced inattention patterns which make sense in terms of the politics of the interethnic classroom. Pariah children learn not to read as one way of acquiring high status and strong identity in a host classroom.

The fourth section describes a starting point for culturally induced learning disabilities in terms of cultural or communicative code differences and conflicts. Specifically, it is hypothesized that minor differences in communicative codes can lead to disasters in everyday life. On the basis of communicative code conflicts, teachers classify their students into ability groups. Although in no way related in the first grade to potential reading or social leadership skills, the teacher's classificatory schema has great influence as a self-fulfilling prophecy. Many pariah children adapt to the senseless and degrading relational messages given them by unknowing teachers with different communicative codes by shutting down their attention skills in response to teacher tasks such as reading. Communicative code conflicts between black children and white teachers are discussed in detail, and the high rate of black school failure is tentatively explained.

The Ontogeny of Pariah Minorities

Most modern nations harbor one or more *pariah groups* "actively rejected by the host population because of behavior or characteristics positively condemned" by host group standards (Barth 1969:31). Host standards can be violated by an absurd collection of traits ranging from skin color and occupational specialties to culinary and sexual preferences. What is interesting is the persistence of both host group standards and pariah groups across generations. Even in the face of efforts by modern states to subdue the arbitrary and oppressive standards of host groups and to accommodate minority behavior patterns by programs of rationalization and equalization, pariah groups endure. For example, America has blacks, Native Americans, and Hispanic people; Japan has the Koreans (Mitchell 1967) and the racially indistinct Burakamin (DeVos and Wagatsuma 1966); Norway, the Lapps (Eidheim 1969); Northern Ireland, the Catholics; India, the outcasts; and Israel, the Oriental Jews. In all these groups, each generation of children will renew their parents' life styles, apparently oblivious to the condemnation and oppression that pariah status vis-à-vis the host group will bring down upon their heads.

How does this happen? How is pariah status acquired by each new generation? Despite years of special education, minority American children continue to speak low esteem dialects, fail in school, and attain occupational specialties which run afoul of public morality and legality.

Apparently, the acquisition of pariah behavior patterns is a very complex process rooted in everyday life and is not going to be altered by formal training in a classroom for a few hours a week. Indeed, most pariah behavior patterns need not be altered. Black language, for example, bears a pariah label, but it is a perfectly efficient mode of communication with special social functions within the black community (Labov 1969). To treat it as an inferior or deprived language is wrong. To meddle with its use by way of a language arts program in order to homogenize it with the host language is not only wrong, but also naive. It indicates that we understand very little about how people acquire models of and guides to behavior in their own society and how these models are used to generate social structures complete with stratification. This chapter will attempt a better understanding of the acquisition of social structure (Cicourel 1970a)—how children acquire what has to be known in order to act in a culturally or subculturally appropriate way in specific social situations (Frake 1962, 1973).

Two positions are usually taken on the acquisition of pariah social status. To the distant observer and the pariah group member, it seems an obvious case of host populations working to defeat the efforts of each and every pariah child to break the degradation that bonds him without reason from his first day out of the womb. The child is simply tagged as he enters the world in such a way that the tag is available for all to see. Negative differential behavior is then applied to all the tagged regardless of acquired skills. Racial markers can, of course, do this job most efficiently: witness black America. Similar systems have been attempted without racial markers. Tattooing is one possibility. The Japanese of the Tokugawa era attempted another by having all members of the pariah Burakumin wear leather squares on the outside of all their garments (Cornell 1970). The point is that pariah children are made visible to all, defined as deviant because of their visibility, and treated badly as a result.

There is a good reason for viewing the ascriptive system just described as too simple a representation of the acquisition of a particular status in a social structure. First, such clear-cut boundaries between host and pariah groups are seldom defined. Racial boundaries are not available in most societies in which there are pariah group problems. In fact, most observers must live in an area for a long time before they can start distinguishing between groups. The codes are subtle. Religion, language, dress and the minutiae of nonverbal communication very often function as markers for ascription. Even where biological boundaries can be drawn, as may be the case for outcastes in India, it takes either a native's eye or an anthropometrist's calipers to do the job (Beteille 1972). In such cases, identification involves much social work on the part of the interactants. The host population must be keyed to spotting certain cues, and the pariah population must in some way send off the cues which will allow them to be identified and abused.

A second problem with viewing status ascription as a simple tagging process is that in most contemporary societies such overt ascription is frowned upon by both legal constitutions and popular ideologies. Formal organizations which operate according to ascriptive criteria are officially prohibited. Japan and America stand out as two countries which have done a great deal to minimize overt ascription with universal schooling and uniform testing procedures for the placement of personnel in both the public and private sectors of their economies (Azumi 1969; Parsons 1959). Yet pariah boundaries remain firm, even within the school systems themselves (Shimahara 1971; Cicourel and Kitsuse 1963). Again it appears that something more than ascription is going on. How else could it be that, even after the demise of formal institutional powers to identify and operate against pariah people, pariah groups survive? The host population does not simply slot a child on the basis of its parentage and then keep a careful eye out for the child so that he never advances a slot. Rather, it seems as if the child must learn how to do it himself; he must learn a way of acting normally which the host population will be able to condemn according to the criteria the hosts have learned for evaluating, albeit arbitrarily, their own normal behavior. Pariah status appears almost as achieved as ascribed.

An alternative to the distant observer's view of the acquisition of pariah social status is the view of a host population native who usually sees in pariahs an obvious case of inferior persons begetting inferior persons. The argument is that pariah children acquire their low status because they are inferior. Unfortunately, each new pariah generation often reaffirms the soundness of the host's classificatory schema by apparently learning the codes of behavior essential to the schema's maintenance. Although there is no evidence that host classifications are accurate assessments of the natural order of people and their abilities, the host perception of pariah group behavior may not always be totally blinded by prejudice. Hosts may merely see what is there for them to see given the standards of evaluation that they use uniformly on all people regardless of race or ethnic identity. The question is, how is it that what is there for them to see is in fact there?

Consider an extreme example. The Burakumin minority in Japan has suffered a long history of political suppression due to its participation in condemned occupational specialties (Ninomiya 1933). Since the formal breakdown of the caste system during the Mejii Restoration a century ago, many Burakumin have attempted unsuccessfully to pass into the mainstream of Japanese life. At present, they are physically, linguistically, religiously, and, for the most part, occupationally indistinct from other

Japanese. They can be discovered only on the basis of either their present or past residence in known Burakumin ghettos. Accordingly, most Japanese teachers are unaware of a child's Burakumin status in the early grades (Shimahara 1971). Yet, by puberty, a Burakumin identity will be visible and of increasing importance, as there is an increasing differential in the performances of Burakumin as opposed to non-Burakumin pupils. They lag behind on I.Q. and achievement tests and daily attendance, and they are the first to engage in delinquent activities (DeVos and Wagatsuma 1966; Brameld 1968). How does host group prejudice work against an invisible group? Obviously, it does not. It may be that unconscious host group standards work against Burakumin children in some subtle ways, however, for the children are eventually made visible, sorted out and condemned. But this is not obvious to a liberal and enlightened Japanese teacher, who, through no apparent fault of his own, winds up doing exactly the same job that a prejudiced teacher might do: he winds up failing many more Burakumin than non-Burakumin. The host-group stand appears strong. The teacher has only reacted to what was available for him to see, namely, obviously inferior performances by many Burakumin children. Again, pariah status seems almost as achieved as ascribed.

This Burakumin example sheds great light on this ascription versus inherent acquisition issue. The Burakumin child experiences teachers as prejudiced beings who inflict failing biographies on Burakumin children. The children are perhaps correct given the subtleties of interclass or interethnic communication. They are incorrect in viewing their school records as products of a blind ascription, for their invisibility protects them from such a fate. Host teachers have equally confusing experiences with school failure. They are correct in not assuming complete blame for the high rate of Burakumin school failure. Nevertheless, they are incorrect in viewing school failure as the result of an inherent acquisition, the unfolding of an inferior genetic stock or, at best, the unfolding of an inferior socialization process that leaves the child deprived. First, the Burakumin do not represent a gene pool (Taira 1971). Second, the social disadvantage perspective is almost as simplistic as the ascription stand, for it has never been able to account for how children with failing school records do so well in complex settings outside of school. Learning to talk and learning to behave sensibly in everyday life are far more complex than the tasks learned in school, and most so-called disadvantaged children excel at both, at least to the extent that such children have been carefully studied. Disadvantage is indeed a too simple, and often biased, account of minority school failure. Burakumin children do not come to school disadvantaged; they leave school disadvantaged. The question is, without some ascriptive mechanism working against them, how does this school failure and consequent disadvantage come about? In other words, if neither ascription nor inherent acquisition can completely account for pariah school failure, then how can the acquisition of pariah status be conceived?

A third position is possible. From their respective vantage points, both the pariah and the host groups are correct. To the pariah group, host behavior is indeed oppressive. To the host group, pariah behavior is indeed inadequate. If we understand how the two groups find this out about each other, we will have located the central problem. What is it that pariah people do that has host people react in oppressive ways, even if they do not want to be oppressive? And what is it that host people do that has pariah people react in antithesis to host expectations, even as they struggle to behave adequately according to host standards? If such misunderstandings take place very often in the early grades, the results can be disastrous. Once a host teacher treats a child as inadequate, the child will find the teacher oppressive. Often, once a child finds a teacher oppressive, the child will start behaving inadequately. After such a point, relations between the child and the teacher regress—the objectionable behavior of each will feed back negatively into the objectionable behavior of the other.

It is in this context that a third position makes sense: a child must achieve his pariah status. It is neither ascribed to the child nor naturally acquired by him in the sense that puberty is acquired. First, some form of miscommunication between a child and his teacher must take place. If this is not repaired quickly, a mutually destructive or regressive one-to-one relationship (Scheflen 1960) will be established between the teacher and the child. When teacher-student communication is complicated by interethnic code differences, regressive relations occur with enough frequency to result in the children forming alternatives to the teacher's organization of the classroom. Within the confines of these new social organizations, the children work at becoming visible. As a result, they leave themselves open to even further condemnation. The teacher's role as the administrator in charge of failure becomes dominant. And the children's revolt grows. School work gets caught in this battle, and a high rate of school failure results. A great deal of social work must be performed by both teachers and students in order for so many failures to occur. Whether the records list all passing or all failing grades, student records represent achievements in the sense that many difficult battles in the politics of everyday life had to be fought in their making. Teachers do not simply ascribe minority children to failure. Nor do minority children simply drag failure along, either genetically or socially, from the previous generation. Rather, it must be worked out in every classroom, every day, by every teacher and every child in their own peculiar ways.

Viewing school failure as an achievement implies that school failure can be understood as a rational adaptation by children to human relations in host schools. The rest of this chapter will be aimed at showing just that.

The next section will consider, theoretically, how human relations are worked out face-to-face in the classroom. These relations have fantastic implications for the social organization of the classroom—who gets to interact with whom, when, and about what and who gets to learn from whom, when, and about what. In short, face-to-face relations help to organize status and abilities in the classroom. In the last two sections, the interference of interethnic human relations on learning to read is examined for black Americans.

The Social Organization of Status and the Politics of Everyday Life

It is considered a social fact (although actually it is either a native or a professional sociological model, but it is always treated as a fact) that there are different groups in the social organizations of modern states, and some of these are defined as pariah groups. It is this social fact that most social scientists want to explain. Beneath this fact, however, there are many other facts made of the little stuff of everyday life that helps produce larger social facts or patterns available for observation. A social organization is not a thing in itself as Durkheim would have us believe. Rather, it is an accomplishment, the product of great work in the everyday life of innumerable social actors. The term "social organization" is a shorthand term for the organization of social actions performed by social actors (Garfinkel 1956:181; cf. also, Miller, Galanter, and Pribram, 1960:98). The term social organization glosses all the hard work of social actors attempting to deal with each other. It hides all the achievements of everyday life. Social organizations are daily accomplishments, daily products of actors working out rational ways of dealing with each other.

If a social organization shows a division into pariah and host groups, then this is a division produced in everyday life; in their daily dealings, pariah and host people must classify each other into different groups and then treat each other in accordance with the dictates of their classification. Such a division cannot be taken by itself as a topic of our inquiry, for it is a mere gloss of the social acts that make it look like a fact. We must go deeper and ask how this fact is available for seeing and naming by either host or pariah members or the ethnographer. Let us examine, then, not that fact of such pariah-host relationships, the resource, but the fact of the fact, the topic; let us ask how it is that the persons involved in such relationships manage to organize and produce such relationships and to take them as the substance of everyday life (Beck 1972); let us "examine not the factual properties of status hierarchies, but the *fact* of the factual properties of status hierarchies" (Zimmerman and Pollner 1970:83). How is it then that host and pariah people, and the sociologists who study them, come to see their existence as related groups as facts?

The question we started with was how do the children of each generation acquire pariah status. This question has shifted somewhat in our
discussion, and we must now ask how children learn to uniformly produce
pariah-host statuses in their interactions with each other and their
teachers. The designated statuses are not simple, cut and dried slots into
which members of different groups are easily placed. *Statuses* do not
specify everything that occurs in an interaction; rather they are the labels
"used by the observer and actor as practical language games for simplifying the task of summarizing a visual field and complex stimuli that are
difficult to describe in some precise, detailed way" (Cicourel 1970b:21).
Status labels never reduce the complex stimulus fields so much that social
life becomes easy. There is always interaction work to be done; social life is
always in process.

One's place in a society is not easily acquired. Even if it is the lowest
place on the stratification ladder, it is not simply worn as a piece of
clothing. A selective way of seeing oneself in the position and of seeing
others in relation to oneself must be developed. As Becker has written, an
actor acquires a "symbolic mansion" established and maintained in interaction with other human beings; the symbols develop early in ontogeny
and prescribe for the actor what situations he should attend, "what he
should do in a particular social situation, and how he should feel about
himself as he does it" (Becker 1962:84). Statuses, therefore, must be
learned. Depending on how they are learned, a child develops specific
identities and abilities for use in specific situations. First they are learned
in the home in everyday interaction with family members. Many of these
first statuses, identities, and abilities undergo considerable alterations in
school on the basis of everyday interaction with class members and especially the teacher. School-specific social and intellectual skills must therefore be understood in terms of the politics of everyday life in the classroom. If the skills developed at home are relevant to what happens in the
classroom, or if new skills must be developed, they will be visible, and they
will make sense in terms of the politics of the classroom.

The *politics of everyday life* are built on messages of relationship passed
between two or more social actors. According to Bateson's classic distinction, communication involves not only the transfer of information, but
also the imposition of a relationship (Bateson 1972). A communicative act
not only has a content which it reports, it also has command aspects which
stipulate the relationship between the communicants. An army sergeant
sends out messages of relationship with his uniform and an annoyed wife
with her hands on her hips. These relational messages form the context
for the transfer of information by classifying its intent (Watzlawick,
Beaven, and Jackson 1967:54). Such a context is read by the interpreter of
a communicative act before the content of a message is attended. Thus,
with open arms one sets a context which can be interpreted as specifying a

love relationship, and everything said after that point will be measured for its value in this context; open arms with a gun in each hand asserts a different context and the information transferred, assuming one does not flee in fear of being shot, is understood differently. In both contexts the host may inform his guest that he has been anxiously awaiting his arrival, but the information transferred would be quite different depending upon the message of relationship sent off before any words were spoken.

Children are extremely well equipped by school age for entrance into the politics of everyday life. Messages of relationship are handled competently by neonates (Caudill and Weinstein 1969) and constitute the only form of communication allowed the child in its early years (Blurton-Jones 1972). Love, hate, support, antagonism, trust and deference are some of the relational messages transferred in daily life. Indeed, apparently few concerted practical activities are possible without the communication of such messages; even a slight eruption in their flow can cause a social breakdown (Garfinkel 1963). Children are especially expert in handling these messages as they have not yet developed competence in the verbal arts of saying what is not meant and interpreting what is not intended. Relational messages are more rooted in nonverbal channels which allow for more leakage and clues to deception than verbal channels (Ekman and Friesan 1969), and children decipher these without hindrance from message content.

At school age, the point at which children start acquiring their institutional biographies, relational messages continue in their dominance over information transfer. This is a decisive and delicate time in a child's life. School success, an essential ingredient in any child's avoidance of pariah status, is dependent upon high levels of information transfer. In these early stages of school, depending upon how the politics of everyday life are handled, the child defines his relations with his classmates and his teachers. These relations, remember, define the context of whatever information is to be transferred by a communicant. If the wrong messages of relationship are communicated, reading, writing, and arithmetic may take on very different meanings than they do for the child who is more successful in getting good feelings from the politics of the classroom. The wrong messages of relationship can result in learning disabilities. More will be said on this issue later. At present it is only essential to realize that children deal seriously in relationships, are profoundly affected by their abilities to do relational work, and acquire a social status and attendant skills on the basis of their successes and failures.

Let us try to describe the setting in which relational work is performed. Its general properties are really well known. Goffman (1963) has described the "primal sociological event" as one in which a person with an obvious stigma, no nose, for example, encounters a person without a stigma; in such a case, a tremendous amount of work must go into unspoken arrangements about how the two are to look at each other, at the nose, around the nose, or at the ground. Looking in this situation carries powerful relational messages. One has the power to induce confusion, embarrassment, anger, fright, trust, or love. The eyes will tell the stigmatized whether he has met a person with a similar stigma, with an acquaintance and understanding of the stigma, or with a fear or hate of the stigma. Goffman's point is that we all suffer from stigma of sorts. Every interaction is marked by some hiding and some probing. How much must be hidden, how much probing can go on, or indeed, whether hiding and probing are necessary at all, is dependent upon the messages of relationship exchanged. A policeman's uniform usually invokes hiding on ego's part and allows for probing on the policeman's part. Sexually suggestive clothing does the opposite. In the first case, ego shuts down, and in the second, an opening up is usually called forth. Situations in which these same cues invoke the opposite reactions can be imagined. The effort is to make as much sense as possible of the person's actions, to infer his intentions, and to then react sensibly given the intentions of both interactants (Schutz 1953).

The cues available in any situation are endless. People can send messages with their ecological setting, e.g., whether they are in a bar or a church (Barker 1968; J. McDermott 1969; Sommer 1969); with their posture (Scheflen 1964); with their spacing vis-à-vis their interpreter (Hall 1966); with their odor (Largey and Watson 1972); with their gaze (Kendon 1967); with their tone of voice (Crystal 1972; Laver 1968); with their sequencing of body and voice rhythms (Condon and Ogston 1966, 1971; Byers 1971; Kendon 1970, 1973); and so on. Everything available to the senses of the actors constitutes a possible contribution to the sense and rationality of an interaction.

More than the success of the interaction rides on how sensibly it can be made. Something important happens to the way in which the stigmatized person is going to interpret his next interaction; if one is treated to understanding and sympathy on one occasion, the next occasion will be attended and scanned for messages in a very different way than if the original interaction resulted in a fight. The selective perception skills that are carried from one situation to another of similar type, following Cicourel (1970b), are called status. In addition to his status, the stigmatized individual's feelings can undergo alteration. In talking about formative experiences during puberty, Erikson has noted that "it is of great relevance to the young individual's identity formation that he be responded to and be given function and status as a person whose gradual transformation makes sense to those who begin to make sense to him" (1968:156). Both status and identity are developed in daily interactions. A great deal is at stake in each and every one of them, for status and identity breakdowns are also developed in daily interactions.

An example of the social organization of status and identity in a classroom may be helpful here. Teachers often break their classes into ability groups in order to simplify their administration of the classroom. Not only the level of work engaged in, but also the people interacted with and the kind of feedback received from the teachers all depend upon the group to which the child is assigned. In this way, the teacher organizes the statuses and identities of the children in the class. What is most interesting is that the children seldom reject their assignment—even if they are assigned the lowest status in the classroom achievement hierarchy, they most often accept it as if it makes sense. If the child does not like his assignment, he may buckle down and work harder to catch the rest of the class. But revolt is seldom attempted. The reason is that the teacher generally assigns children to groups according to the same criteria that the children themselves use in their dealings with each other, and the same criteria that the children's parents and the rest of their community use in their dealings with the children. In short, the teacher handles the children in a way the children are used to being handled. Politically, the teacher, the children and the child's community are in harmony. Even if being placed in a low ability group is not good for the child's ego, the results of grouping, if it makes sense, will not be disastrous. The politics of everyday life in the classroom will be identical to the politics of everyday life outside the classroom, and the children's world will be in order.

The social organization of status and identity sometimes does not go so smoothly. Consider the case of an intense, bright child who arrives in school unable to keep up in reading because of some developmental lag specific to processing printed information. When this child is assigned to the lowest ability group, it makes no sense to him. He is treated as a gifted learner and a sociometric star outside the classroom; anything less than equivalent treatment in the classroom will be inadequate to the child's way of evaluating his place in the world. Of course, he revolts and "a negative motivational cycle" begins to take shape (Singer and Beardsley 1970). Later, the possibilities of a host group teacher successfully grouping minority children into the same ability groups that the minority community might inself perceive will be considered. From the high rate of revolt and "negative motivational cycles" in minority classrooms, the possibilities seem slim. The point here is that the politics of everyday life socially organize a classroom. Ability groupings help a teacher to isolate into accessible units children who are to receive fairly similar messages of relationship from the teacher. If the wrong children are assigned to the low ability groups, they will reject the messages of relationship forwarded from the teacher. They will demand a political reorganization of the classroom, one that is more commensurate with their statuses and identities outside the classroom. In the early weeks of a school year, the politics of the classroom feed the teacher's perception, and the classroom is organized accordingly. Then the children reorganize the class according to their own perceptions. If the teacher is insensitive to their demands, the remainder of the year can be occupied in small battles over each child's status and identity within the classroom. Whether or not anything is ever accomplished in the classroom depends upon how quickly these battles can be resolved. Thus, the development of abilities and disabilities also depends upon the politics of daily classroom life.

The specific division of abilities and disabilities among any pariah and host groups should be understood in terms of the politics of everyday life. It is in the very small political arenas constituted by dyads and only slightly larger groups that social organizations are produced. If we want to understand a large scale organizational division within a social organization, we must start asking how this division is produced. Pariah and host group members acquire different skills and produce the different behavior that makes for the organizational division between pariah and host groups. The division looks so real that we professional social scientists study it, and lay social scientists, or natives, perceive and use it as a model for their dealings with each other. In fact, the division is dependent for its existence on the daily differential use of abilities and disabilities by host and pariah group members. The employment of these abilities and disabilities depends upon man's delightful capacity to attend to, think about, and manipulate only certain selected aspects of his environment. Just what parts of an environment are attended and mastered depends upon the social meaning of the environment as recorded in the experiences of the developing child. For example, reading materials can or cannot be attended depending upon whether looking in a book is an acceptable activity in a particular social milieu and whether books contain information helpful to operating in a particular social environment. The social organization of reading materials will now be considered in more detail.

A Biobehavioral Ethnography of Reading Disabilities

Black children in America have a high rate of learning disabilities. Rates of functional black illiteracy are estimated around 50 percent (Thompson 1966) as compared to 10 percent for white Americans and only 1 percent for Japan (Makita 1968). The high rates of these disabilities do not point to a high rate of genetic inferiority, neurological damage, language deprivation, or any of the other intrapsychic causes suggested in social and behavioral science literature. Rather, the high rates of learning disorders point to learned patterns of selective inattention developed in the politics of everyday life in the classroom. Status and identity work is a dismal failure in early elementary school for many black children with white teachers and, as a result, they turn off, in the sense that they physiologically shut down. As a yoga or Zen master (Kasamatsu and Hirai 1966) may do for an entire environment, black children disattend reading materials and join their peers in the student subculture within the class. Reading disabilities and school failure result.

School failure is an important place to start an inquiry into the acquisition of pariah status, and social science literature on pariah group persistence across generations has often centered on school failure and its causes. Most of the work has centered on the children, independent of the schools they attend, as if there was something naturally wrong with their brains. To paraphrase crudely, the cause of pariah groups is that pariah children do not seem to think too well. This deprivation theme should be fairly offensive to social science; after all, has not a century of anthropology shown that to understand people is to discern difference and not deprivation? Yet the anthropological argument is difficult. Pariah children fail, and fail miserably. How can we claim that they are neither damaged nor deprived? One answer is that we have been measuring achievements with a biased set of standards. Achievements are realized only in particular situations. Rather than attempting to measure the development of absolute capacities that a child uses for all situations through time, perhaps we should center on the situations in which and for which particular skills are acquired. In other words, if we examine the classroom as a set of situations or an "occasion corpus" (Zimmerman and Pollner 1970), a child's failing performance on classroom tests might appear to be something of a situational achievement. Deprivation hypotheses are considerably weakened, if, instead of just looking at the skills stored in children's bodies, we look also at the social contexts in which the skills are turned into achievements.

Medicine, education, and psychology have all produced deprivation hypotheses for social scientists to adopt. Of late, pariah children have been described as genetically inferior (Jensen 1969). Another claim has it that an unspecified number suffer brain damage due to the poverty and ignorance that burdened their mothers in pregnancy and birth (Birch and Gussow 1970). Social science itself has had a hand in claiming that pariah children suffer perceptual handicaps (C. Deutsch 1968; Jensen 1966) and conceptual and linguistic handicaps (M. Deutsch 1963; Bernstein 1964; Entwisle 1971) due to low social class and its associated life-style. All these disciplines assume to discover facts out of context, raw facts about the world and the behavior of its inhabitants. Of course there are no such things. All behavior is context-bound. More important, all behavior is indexical or dependent upon our interpretation of the context in which the behavior is situated (Bar-Hillel 1954; Beck 1972; Cicourel, in press). Yet all assume that facts are available for all to see, and that these facts are invariable. In the case of learning disabilities, each discipline has assumed that whatever is located in the heads of the children studied is invariable. Whether a discipline uses a perceptual, cognitive, or language test, a projective technique or a sociometric status score, each has assumed that it describes the skills the individual has acquired for all occasions and tasks. That is, of course, incorrect. Each of these disciplines assumes too much.

My proposal is that each of these disciplines is describing the same social processes and merely indexing them differently. Scores on perceptual, intelligence, attitude, language competence, and even neurological tests are all remnants of the normal and practical work of persons in a particular situation. Ways of perceiving, thinking, feeling, talking, and the activities of the neural wetware processing our perceiving, thinking, feeling, and talking are all dependent upon the situations in which the person is placed. Testing offers a particular situation which may record little more than the way the subject defines the testing situation in response to the way in which the subject understands the tester's definition of the situation. In short, test scores always have discernible roots in the social world in which they take place (Cicourel, in press). We cannot expect tests to necessarily reveal very much about intrapsychic events and the capabilities of any subject. But tests can, if they are properly read, tell a great deal about interpsychic, social procedures in which a subject is engaged. For example, Cazden (1970) has described black children who do badly on language complexity tests in formal situations, and very well in informal situations; the opposite holds true for white children. What we can learn from such tests has nothing to do with a child's capacity to talk; but there is a great deal of information about social organization stored in this little test. Social organizations are made by people knowing approximately what to do in particular situations; a social organization is a cognitive phenomenon. When we look to tests for information about social organization, about the thinking underlying the social acts to be performed during the test, then they are very revealing.

Reading tests can significantly reveal the dynamics of social organization. Pariah children do very badly at them, almost certainly for social reasons. Reading is an act which apparently aligns the black child with the "wrong" forces in the social universe. In the classroom social organization produced by the politics of everyday life, reading takes its place as part of the teacher's "ecology of games" (Long 1958). To read is to accept these games and all the statuses and identities that accompany them. Not to read is to accept peer group games and their accompanying statuses and identities. In other words, given a particular social organization, reading failure is a social achievement. Conventional testing procedures could never reveal this trend. The battle grounds on which it is determined whether a child learns to read or not are drawn by the statuses and identities made available by the teacher and the peer group, in short, by social relations. If the teacher and the children can play the same games, then reading and all other school materials will be easily absorbed.

The success of educational settings directed by ethnic (Alitto 1969; Hostetler and Huntington 1971) and dialect (Fishman and Leuders-Salmon 1972) minorities for themselves illustrates this point nicely. If the children and the teacher generate their behavior from a shared set of interpretive procedures, efficient classroom learning can almost be assumed. This record contrasts, however, with educational settings designed and administered by outsiders to a community. Such settings often result in school failure. Centuries of failure in the white education of American Indians and blacks and Japanese failures in the education of Korean and Truk natives (Fisher 1961) illustrate this contrasting situation. If the classroom is divided into two separate worlds with teachers and students occupying different ecologies of games, school failure appears to be inevitable. The identities and statuses offered by a school system without roots in the community are apparently not worth seeking or are worth avoiding. For many children in such a situation, a social reorganization of the classroom becomes the main alternative to following the teacher's dictates.

An essential question at this point is how the politics of everyday life get inside a child's body and dictate what shall be perceived. This question can now easily be handled by recent advances in neuropsychology. Not all biology is reductionist, and there is good reason to attempt a view of social life by an examination of the biological foundations of behavior. Geertz alerted us to this possibility in his account of the dynamic, feedback relationship between biology and culture.

> As our central nervous system—and most particularly its crowning curse and glory, the neocortex—grew up in great part in interaction with culture, it is incapable of directing our behavior or organizing our experience without the guidance provided by systems of significant symbols . . . Such symbols are thus not mere expressions, instrumentalities, or correlates of our biological, psychological, and social existence; they are prerequisites of it. Without men, no culture, certainly; but equally, and more significantly, without culture, no men (1965:61).

Attention is the mechanism by which our bodies help us divide the world into significant and insignificant. As Wallace has suggested, man has created a rich and elaborate world for himself "by a process of selective attention to his total environment" (1965:277). Apparently, man suffers tremendous limitations in his ability to process all the information available to him at any one instant. Selection is a ubiquitous and unending process throughout our central nervous systems. Significance is stored not only in the social world, in the symbols out there, but in our equipment for decoding and interpreting the world. As Pribram has indicated, "societies are made up of persons whose brains shape the interactive matrix" (1969:37). What is organized in social organizations are individuals interpreting the world, human brains attending to some aspects of the social world and not to others.

A brief account of the psychophysiological concept of attention will hopefully suggest the importance of attention patterns for social scientists and detail for us how patterns of inattention can result in reading disabilities. The central nervous system has been increasingly conceived as a set of models depicting the world outside the body, in terms of which an organism attends, perceives, thinks, and acts (Sokolov 1969; Pribram 1971; MacKay 1972). Stimuli enter the body and if they are uninformative no attention will be paid to them. If the match is improper, the central nervous system will orient in search of new information which will either restore or redefine the model. In such a case, the organism is said to be "looking to see," and different parts of the brain will be activated in processing the new stimuli until harmony is again established (Pribram 1970). First a decision is made to look for a stimulus and only then is a second decision made as to whether or not the proper stimuli occur (Dewey 1896; N. Mackworth and Bagshaw 1970).

The human system is best discussed in terms of the feedback relations between pertinence, attention, and memory storage. Physiologists are not easily given to talking about pertinence centers in the brain, but they do talk about the efferent control of afferent stimuli on the basis of what central mechanisms deem to be the most pertinent information at any particular time. Central control of the models is called up from memory with plans. Furthermore, there is central control right down at the receptor sites as to what sort of information makes it to the brain for consideration and possible action (Pribram 1970, 1971; Rothblatt and Pribram 1972). The central nervous system is thus intimately involved in the organizational work that goes into the construction of significance in the world. The same symbols that are processed by our bodies are those processed in our social systems. Our bodies are the nodes in the communicative network that is society, and the work of these various nodes produces what has come to be seen as social organization. Statements of this proposition are unfortunately rare, but the trend is apparently changing (Bateson 1972; Beck 1971a,b). Nevertheless, we still have only a few anecdotes interrelating the organization of social events and the organization of neurological events. Pribram has given one delightful example:

> For many years there was an elevated railway line (the "el") on Third
> Avenue in New York that made a fearful racket: when it was torn down,
> people who had been living in apartments along the line awakened
> periodically out of a sound sleep to call the police about some strange
> occurrence they could not properly define. The calls were made at the
> times the trains had formerly rumbled past. The strange occurrences
> were, of course, the deafening silence that had replaced the expected
> noise (1971:50).

A model of the world for a particular time and place existed in the central
nervous systems of many people up and down the Third Avenue El.
When the environment did not supply the essential information, the
people began orienting and paying attention. In this case, our ecology
worked its way into our bodies and told us when to listen, namely at the
time when the El had previously roared by; our social system then worked
its way into our bodies and told us what to hear when we listened, perhaps
a thief or another strange occurrence requiring police assistance. Society
and ecology are merely two aspects of the environment with which we
communicate. They send us messages about the adequacy of the internalized models of the time and space criteria in terms of which we
perceive, think and act. We all live in a world of information which we
decode according to the dictates of context. Much of this context is
encoded in our memory and evidenced in our attention patterns.

There are many Third Avenue El trains in our lives. In every classroom in America, there is an organization of ecological and social happenings mediated by various neurologies with memory and attention biases
wired into the wetware. To study one is to study the other, to study the
brain is to study social organization, and vice versa. In this biobehavioral
inquiry into reading disabilities, however, both systems are obviously
involved. The epidemiological contours of reading disabilities run along
ethnic and cultural lines and suggest that they are indeed socially organized. Yet unlike most behavior that we see as socially organized,
reading skills or their diminution due to brain insult or socially induced
inattention, obviously, rather than implicitly, involve neurological organization. Indeed, the picture we are developing of reading as a "psycholinguistic guessing game" (Goodman 1970; Wanat 1971) fits exactly the
picture we have of the structure of the brain's activity in all behavior. In an
excellent paper, J. Mackworth has laid the two side by side: reading
involves

> a selective process that involves partial use of available language cues
> selected from the perceptual input on the basis of the reader's expecta-
> tion, an interaction between thoughts and language . . . ; the neuronal
> model anticipates the future probability and meaning of the next

stimulus. A neuronal mechanism checks the meaning and nature of an incoming stimulus against the predictions of the neural model. Thus construction of a neural model is an active process, involving a two-way exchange of messages from environment and brain (1972:704, 708).

Both the environment and the brain are socially constructed. When a child is unable to read, part of the environment is not being processed by the brain. Because the epidemiology of reading disabilities follows a social organization, it is possible to claim that the organization of the proper neurological models for reading also follows a social organization. A brief look at the social organization of classrooms for black children in America will indicate how their brains appear disabled for reading. *In the politics of everyday life, black children in America learn how not to read; they learn how not to attend to printed information and as a result show high rates of reading disabilities.* The implications of this high rate of illiteracy for the acquisition of pariah status is obvious.

Almost a half a century ago, attention was a major focus of classroom research. Primarily this old research attempted to document whether or not children were paying attention to their teachers by noting their gaze direction during lessons. This is not a very efficient method of studying attention, for receptor orientation gives little information about just what a child is attending to during a boring lecture. The literature is significant, however, in documenting contrasting receptor attention patterns between middle American host schools then and minority classrooms now. In their check of gaze direction, it was shown that more than 90 percent of the host children had their eyes fixed on their teachers or their work at any given time (Jackson 1968). This contrasts considerably with estimates obtained from the contemporary classrooms that share in the early century pedagogical style of the teacher directing all attention in the classroom. M. Deutsch (1963) has found that teachers in Harlem elementary schools spent more than half their day calling children to attention. Attention patterns indeed appear to define the "scene of the battle" in pariah group education (Roberts 1970). School does not seem to work for many teachers and pariah children, and formal roles and statuses are not identically defined by teachers and students. The call for attention appears far more often and seems to have far less effect than it did in the twenties when these earlier studies were carried out.

There is much social organization in these attention and inattention patterns. In primate studies, attention patterns have recently been used to delineate the social organization of dominance hierarchies (Chance 1967). The more one baboon visually attends to another baboon, the more responsible it is to the leader's every movement. Similarly, in the classroom where teachers and students produce leadership patterns for each other, attention is an issue. To attend to a teacher is to give the teacher a leadership role in the classroom: to attend to the peer group is to subvert the teacher's role. In the older studies, the primary fact is that all the children paid homage to the teacher's leadership role by attending, physically at least, to the teacher's activities. In schools populated by pariah children, this leadership role is much more subject to negotiation: some teachers can pull it off and some cannot; some children give their attention and others do not. It is in the context of this battle for attention that we must consider the nature of pariah reading disabilities. In many pariah classrooms, the politics of everyday life has been escalated into war games; there are teacher games and peer group games, and every student must make his choice. One takes sides by attending or not attending. Those who attend learn to read; those who do not attend do not learn how to read.

Attention patterns increasingly shift from teacher games to peer group games as a pariah child moves through elementary school. In addition to the often reported facts that pariah children learn less and misbehave more often as they get older, data on shifts in the perceptual, language structure and function, and attitude patterns of children in school are now available. The next few years promise to bring us far more information, not only on American blacks, the focus of all the work to be briefly discussed here, but on other pariah groups as well.

Perception

Much of the transmission of social know-how that occurs in the early years of school amounts to perceptual learning. Apparently different cultures learn how to perceive differently. This is especially the case for materials represented in two dimensions which apparently allow for more variability than the three-dimensional world of movement and action (Segall, Campbell, and Herskovits 1966; Forge 1970). Learning how to read involves a great deal of perceptual learning. Many children reverse their letters when first learning how to write, for there really is not much difference between p, d, g and b; o and e; u, n, m, v and w. Normals master these subtle differences, and disabled children continue to have difficulty distinguishing these forms after the first grade. Careful attention must be paid to differences in rotation, line-to-line curve, dimension and line-breaking transformations in order to make the proper distinctions between the letters which signal differences in word form and meaning. We develop these skills and store them deep in our nervous system. The more we read, the less work it takes to distinguish the different forms. The eye apparently learns just what to look for and orients only when a drastically misshapen form appears; the difficulties of proofreading illustrate just how well a good reader is programmed to read for meaning and to notice typographic irregularities only when they are given special attention.

Some black children do not permanently develop the essential skills for letter differentiation. In a test designed to analyze a child's competence at handling the perceptual transformations essential to letter discrimination, Gibson (1965) has shown that most children have trouble with rotation and line-to-curve transformations at age five. By age seven most children have mastered these transformations. This is the case for both black and white children. However, black children I tested at twelve years of age showed a mixed range in these skills; those who could read performed well, and those who could not read performed very poorly, scoring below younger black children on the same test. These children had apparently learned how not to see, or, more specifically, learned how not to look in order that they might not see. Reading apparently became a call for inattention, and they submerged the skills essential for a successful attending to reading materials.

Language Structure and Function

This shift in the perceptual properties of many black children is accompanied by subtle but highly significant changes in language structure and function. The brilliant work of Labov and his associates in Harlem has revealed that our language is indeed socially organized. The way in which our vocal chords allow for a passage of air to reverberate into the ears of other social actors depends greatly on just who the interactants are and how they are related. Depending upon who is doing the talking and who is doing the listening, not only will different points of information be passed, but the way of saying it may be remarkably different. Pariah children often learn to use one speech code or register for dealings with pariah people and another for host people; the differences in the code may be subtle lexemic markers as in Japan (Donoghue 1971), subtle phonemic shifts as between social classes and ethnic groups in New York City's Lower East Side (Labov 1964a), gross dialect shifts as between whites and blacks in America, or major language shifts as between French and English speakers in Canada or the Lapps and Norwegians in Norway (Eidheim 1969).

American blacks acquire a nonstandard or dialect English which is more often mutually intelligible with white English. When there is an intelligibility breakdown, the result can be disastrous. Gumperz gives the following example from a postbellum southern teacher's diary:

> I asked a group of boys one day the color of the sky. Nobody could tell me. Presently the father of one of them came by, and I told him of their ignorance, repeating my question with the same result as before. He grinned: "Tom, how sky stan'?" "Blue," promptly shouted Tom (1970:4).

This gross level of language interference was, of course, attributed by the teacher to the child's stupidity, and the teacher probably unconsciously related to the child the subordinate status that accompanies being "stupid" in a classroom.

For the most part, however, black and white verbal codes are mutually intelligible in content. Switching does not cause a problem at the structural level; rather the codes function to differentiate the games being played and the meaning attached to the behavior of various other actors in the game. Messages of relationship are differently stored in the codes. Indeed, using one and not the other is itself a powerful relational message. Switching codes causes a problem, then, for an actor's definition of situation. If an actor defines himself in terms of the ecology of games played by the peer group, then taking on the code which demands participation in the ecology of teacher and book games demands an existential leap and is neither easily nor healthily performed.

The differentiation of codes according to grammar alone deals only with what is systematically possible. Learning should not be blocked. Children merely learn new codes. The differentiation of codes on the basis of appropriateness is apparently a much more difficult chasm to bridge. When the social organization of communicative behavior is divided by two definitions of what is culturally appropriate, the one definition belonging to the teacher and the other to the pupils, communication across codes is much more limited than if codes are merely structurally at odds. It is not difficult to learn that "What color is the sky?" and "How sky stan'?" are equivalent, but, when your teacher deems you ignorant for using the one and your peer group shuns you for using the other, then the job of switching codes is difficult indeed.

The ecology of peer group games is well defined by the growth of a highly elaborate linguistic code restricted to peer group members. Labov has performed a masterful task in isolating these games in his delineation of the stages of acquisition of nonstandard English:

1. Up to age 5: basic grammatical rules and lexicon are taken from parents.
2. Age 5 to 12 the reading years: peer group vernacular is established.
3. Adolescence: "The social significance of the dialect characteristics of his friends become gradually apparent."
4. High school age: "The child begins to learn how to modify his speech in the direction of the prestige standard in formal situations or even to some extent in casual speech" (Labov 1964b:91).

The second and third stages are, of course, most important for a consideration of the implications of the school and the peer group registers for learning. The implications are not so obvious; what difference does it make if children use one register for interacting with teachers and reading materials and another for interacting with each other? The importance of these two registers lies in the fact that during the school years the two become mutually exclusive. As children participate more in their peer groups, the less importance is attached to school games. The more children participate in the ecology of games defined by their peers, the more deviant their linguistic registers; it is these linguistic features which help to mark off the peer group from the ecology of the schools.

Labov has documented these trends beautifully. Participation in peer groups, especially those with formal organizations such as street gangs, are accompanied by major phonological and grammatical shifts. One of the many charts presented in his Harlem study is reproduced here (Labov et al. 1968:182):

Percent of Standard Verb Agreement for Club Members, Lames and Whites

Present Tense Forms of Verb	Club Members	Lames	Whites
has (3rd sg.)	19	60	100
doesn't (3rd sg.)	03	36	32
were (2nd sg. + pl.)	14	83	100
does (3rd sg.)	00	13	100
says (3rd sg.)	04	00	100
(No. of subjects	31	10	8)

This illustrates the implications that peer group status has for the speech register employed by black adolescents. Lames do not participate in formally organized peer groups although they are in contact with the gangs and are part of the black speech community. In school, Lames are still open to interpreting favorably some cues from the teacher's ecology. The Inwood whites are of a low social class, but they do not show the extreme alienation patterns which characterize black children in school. Club members show the most extreme deviance from the standard English linguistic code, Inwood whites the least, and Lames fall in between. The same rank ordering can be made for the three groups' participation in school. This is not to say that linguistic difference causes alienation from school; rather it is a standard for nonacceptance of the ecology of games played in white schools. The rise in status of a black child in his peer group, the adoption of the peer group's linguistic register, and alienation from school all develop together.

In terms of this inquiry into reading disabilities, participation in peer group formal organizations and the employment of their linguistic registers are of great importance, for they correlate very well with reading scores. Labov and Robins (1969:57, 167) have shown perfectly the relation between the acquisition of reading skills and the participation in the peer group ecology of games. Not one out of 43 gang members was able to achieve a reading score on grade level and most are more than two years behind the national average. Participation in the peer group ecology of games appears indeed to be exclusive of a participation in the school ecology of games of which reading is a part. Printed materials appear to send few meaningful cues to those interested in improving their status among their peers.

Attitudes

Labov's findings are not limited to classrooms which harbor members of formally organized gangs in Harlem. In two classrooms in suburban New York City, the exact same trends were found. The children were not unaware of the trends, and their significance was readily apparent in the children's attitudes towards each other. This should not surprise us at all. In my high school, I remember that most of us could define others and make very accurate estimates of their grade point averages on the basis of clothes worn, speech patterns, and some postural cues. Our expertise was perhaps not as loaded as that of black children, for their expertise not only defines others but also determines who is to be popular or not. A series of sociometric tests administered in an all black, bottom track, sixth grade were consistent in placing nonreaders at the center of all peer group activities. Similar tests in an all black, nontracked, fifth grade also showed nonreaders at the center of most activities. Reading skills do not recommend an actor for leadership. Indeed, the acquisition of such skills can exclude an actor from the peer group ecology of games.

Ethnographic Summary

Many topics have been briefly touched in this short description of the black classroom, but its thrust can be summarized. Learning disabilities occur at very high rates in the American black population. The distribution of these disabilities overlaps with the distribution of social behavior that leads to the acquisition of nonmarketable and pariah biographies, behavior such as participation in street gangs and classroom subcultures specializing in disruption and failure. This nascent pariah population shows subtle shifts in its perceptual, linguistic, and attitude patterns. What the children are doing is learning to behave in new, culturally appropriate ways in educational settings, new ways which will determine their acquisition of pariah status vis-a-vis the host population. These new ways of behaving involve the development of new cues to be sent out in interaction with other humans, such as new phonemes and morphemes, and the development of new perceptual and evaluative skills, such as the abilities to hear new phonemes and perceive group leaders without confusion. What is being learned are new attention patterns, new ways of seeing, hearing, and construing the meaning of particular items of behavior shared with others in the subculture. When some items are attended, others are disattended, some of them actively so. Learning to behave in a culturally appropriate way in black classrooms in white school systems apparently involves learning to attend to cues produced in the peer group and learning to disattend teacher and school produced cues, such as shouts for attention or the introduction of tasks such as reading. These attention patterns are deeply programmed in the central nervous system. When the child attempts to attend to cues outside his learned competence, he fails. In this way, many black children fail in reading, and they appear neurologically impaired. Obviously, they are usually not impaired at all; they have merely learned to attend to different stimuli in a school situation. Ironically and tragically, for their successful and rational adaptation to the school situation, they are categorized as impaired and treated as inferiors. Thus they acquire pariah status.

Biculturation and the Acquisition of Pariah Status

Now that we have some notion of how a black classroom is organized in American schools and what black children must know in order to act in a subculturally appropriate way in the classroom, we must ask how this know-how is produced. Why is it that the social world of many black children is organized without a place for printed materials? Some observers might point to genes or to various kinds of deprivation leading to cognitive or motivational breakdowns. Others, especially radical educators (Holt 1969; Kohl 1967), black leaders, and P.T.A. groups, point to "underachieving schools" and the failure of teachers to do the job. Implicit in much of this rhetoric is the claim that racism is the primary factor in the failure of whites to educate black children; white teachers expect black children to fail and subtly induce their expectations into the children who indeed do fail.

These are the two alternatives offered by the literature: the children fail because there is something wrong with their heads; or the children fail because the schools are disasters and the teachers are racists. The first argument is far too simple. Gene pools (Montagu 1964) and cognitive and motivational systems are not easily located, and no one has shown why any of these systems fail in school and not in other settings in the social world. The second literature is a little more difficult to dismiss. Obviously, it is not only the schools that fail, for they serve different groups the same product with differential success. When racism is appended to the charge of school underachievement, the argument is intuitively more forceful. However, we have little idea just what racism means of late or, more importantly, how it works especially for the mostly well-meaning, hard-working, and ideologically nonracist teachers that staff our urban schools.

The proposal of this chapter is that reading disabilities are products of the way in which the people in the classroom use their categories for interaction to produce statuses and identities, or ways of attending stimuli, in the classroom setting. Although racist categories work their way into the production of the social organization of black-white relations, a teacher does not have to be a racist for the politics of everyday life to produce a classroom rigidly divided between teacher and peer group games. Any formal differences in the communicative styles of the teacher and the children can introduce havoc to their relations and the messages of relationship they consequently send to each other.

Consider the following important example. Two black Americans attending a Chicago college were introduced to each other. A film, shot at the rate of 24 frames per second, was made of their shaking hands. There was a definite rhythm to their handshake; for three frames their hands went up and for three frames down, and so on. Two Polish Americans at the same college produced a different but also fairly rhythmic interaction. One Pole and one black from each dyad produced a disastrous interaction (Leonard 1972): five up, one down, one up, two down, etc. There was no rhythm to their interaction. There they were, joined together at the hands, but with apparently little idea about what to do with each other. An analysis of the conversational false starts indicates that they also had little idea of what to say to each other. Rational and stigma-free interactions are difficult to make out of such material. Apparently, our communicative codes go into our bodies and establish rhythms and expectations about the rhythms of others. Interacting with a person with a slightly different code or rhythm can be a fatiguing and upsetting experience. On a one-to-one basis, these difficulties can be worked out or negotiated until the two interactants have managed consistent or rational ways of dealing with each other. In a classroom in which a teacher often stands one-to-thirty against a code of difference, negotiations are often not possible and at best limited (Byers, personal communications).

Communicative code differences in a classroom setting can have tremendous effects. A teacher out of phase with his students will undoubtedly fail in the politics of everyday life. Rational interaction with the group will hardly be possible. As a result, the teacher will fall back on his formal authority as a teacher, his so-called "role" to instruct the children in their classroom behavior. The children often reject this authority role and develop an idiosyncratic code. such as the nonstandard peer group code Labov has described. The children's actions make much sense. When rational interaction with a teacher is not possible, that is, when his position of authority makes no sense in terms of his relations with the children, they produce an alternative system and disown the teacher's authority. Reading skills get caught in this battle over which cues are to be attended—peer group cues or teacher cues.

This paper has suggested how a child learns to produce a pariah status in his work in everyday life. It has offered an example of this work in detailing how a large number of black children acquire statuses, identities, and behavioral patterns which produce a pariah biography. The statuses, identities, and behavioral patterns developed by black children in white school systems produce learning disabilities and enable the host population to exclude the black child from participation in the more lucrative institutions of American society. How are these statuses, identities and behavioral patterns produced? Three tasks remain if this question is to be answered.

Communicative Code Differences and the Inhibition of School Learning

First, examples of how minor differences in communicative codes can induce a selective inattention to school material must be given. One of the first reports of such interference was offered by Spindler (1959) in his work on the self-fulfilling prophecies of teachers unconsciously dominating classroom social organization. He showed how middle-class teachers attended to middle-class children and labeled them as the most talented and ambitious of the children in their classes. School success followed along identical lines, but more subtle evaluations of talent divided the populations along different lines. In this case, lower class children gave up trying and acquired failing "institutional biographies" (Goffman, 1963) because of an inability to give evidence of their intelligence in terms of the limited code that the teachers used to evaluate children.

A more specific example has been recently offered for a St. Louis elementary school with black teachers and black children. The effects of little things were in no way little in this school. Rist offers the following account of the classroom after it had been divided into three "ability groups," the fast, slow and nonlearners at Tables 1, 2, and 3, respectively:

> The organization of the kindergarten classroom according to the expectation of success or failure after the eighth day of school became the basis for the differential treatment of the children for the remainder of the

school year. From the day that the class was assigned permanent seats, the activities in the classroom were perceivably different from previously. The fundamental division of the class into those expected to learn and those expected not to permeated the teacher's orientation of the class (1970: 423).

Assignment to each of the tables was based on the teacher's subjective evaluations which, after dissection by Rist, were shown to be rooted in the teacher's evaluation of the children's physical appearance and interactional and verbal behavior. At Table 1 are centered children with newer and cleaner clothes and more of them on cold days, slightly lighter skin, and processed hair. Children with reciprocal traits were positioned at lower tables. Class leaders or direction givers also clustered at Table 1. The children at the low tables spoke less in class, in heavy dialect when they did, and almost never to the teacher. What is most unfortunate is that by the third grade the children at the lower tables were still at the lower tables. Once the child is tracked, it is almost impossible for him to break loose. The lower his table, the less he gets in instructional time. In addition, teacher expectations follow him from year to year. Apparently, the acquisition of a school biography is completed within the first week of school, and all on the basis of a teacher's ethnocentric evaluation of a child's mannerisms.

A similar analysis can probably be carried out for every year of schooling that a child undergoes. Each year, more are sorted out until the "select few" reach college. The word "select" should not be taken in its elitist sense. By the time they enter college, some people may be more select because their enculturation to school equips them to do college work. We should not make the mistake, however, of thinking that the select few were selected for any reason other than that they were most like their teachers. Given Labov's speech data, we can see that the children at Table 3 are not the interactional and verbal dullards that the teacher supposed them to be. By the sixth grade, assuming Labov's data are predictive, the children at Table 3 will talk the most and be the best dressers and the most popular individuals in every class. Their native equipment for leading and learning is in perfect shape, although by the sixth grade it is understandably directed away from school. Why these children are not selected in their early years by teachers has to do with how well prepared both they and their teachers are for working out the conflicting points in their communicative code. The children are often more adaptable than their teachers. They are able and willing to develop new codes; indeed, they do so every day in the playgrounds. However, if the new code is used to degrade the children, as is the case for the children in "lower" ability groups, they will take flight and cut themselves off from whatever rewards the new code has to offer them. If a modus vivendi is not reached in the early grades, the children at the lower tables will create their own subculture defined partly in opposition to the classroom culture attempted by the teacher.

Pariah children invariably share some minor traits which help them to identify each other and to distinguish themselves from the host population. A particular phoneme, lexeme, or body movement can do the job. Invariably, these traits are at most minuscule factors in cognitive development. Even a dialect barrier great enough to produce mutual unintelligibility is not enough to stop German children from speaking and reading High German (Fishman and Leuders-Salmon 1972). Dialect differences between black children and white school officials and books, often claimed as a source of reading failure (Baratz and Shuy 1969), apparently present little formal interference to the reading process (Melmud 1971). It depends on what is done with the differences. In host-pariah teacher-student relations, the differences are used to do a great deal, and are allowed to intervene in interactions to the extent that they cut off the possibility of sense being made between the pair. The child gets stuck in a low ability group for reasons he cannot understand and the teacher finds the child's behavior equally incomprehensible. In such a case the teacher grasps onto a formal definition of the teacher's role in order to make sense of the situation: the teacher develops status or interaction skills in accordance with the definition of the teacher as a person to be listened to and learned from under any circumstances. Faced with this senseless rigidity of the teacher's role, the child develops his status and identity in the alternative source offered by his peer group. Recall the disabled child assigned low status in the classroom despite a high degree of acceptance outside the classroom. The child shut down his learning skills and turned to abnormal behavior (Singer and Beardsley 1970). The same senseless assignment to ability groups is often made in the interethnic classroom. The host teacher has different standards of evaluation than the minority child. Accordingly, the wrong children are often assigned to the low ability groups. Their assignment does not make sense to them, and they understandably shut down their learning skills and revolt. The difference between what happens to the disabled child who perceives a senseless status assignment and a minority child in an identical situation is that the minority child is never alone. The teacher invariably makes mistakes on a number of the children, and the ensuing revolt can develop earlier and more powerfully when a large number of chilren is involved.

The children in an interethnic classroom have three choices. They can take school as a source of identity; thus, the children at Table 1. They can take the peer group as a source of identity and fight the system; thus, the children at Tables 2 and 3 transformed by late elementary school into the gangs Labov has described. The third and perhaps the worst choice is represented by the children at the lower tables who accept the teacher's definitions and passively fail through school into pariah status. They also fail in their identity work. For the children to dispute the messages of relationship offered by a teacher to the lower ability groups causes havoc in the classroom but solid ego development in the children's own community. For the children to passively accept subordinate status creates classroom calm, but a weak ego. Either way, learning is blocked; in the first case by active selective inattention and misbehavior, in the second case with motivational lag and selective inattention. Neither group learns to read.

Black-White Communicative Code Differences

A second task is to describe possible points of conflict in black and white communicative skills and the difficulties of biculturation or the acquisition of competence in both codes. Work on this topic is just beginning, but already there are indications that the use of time and space in black culture is distinct from the use of time and space in white culture. Regardless of what these codes are an adaptation to, the point is that blacks and whites slice up the world in slightly different ways. When the black child enters a host school, he is asked to alter his codes drastically for spacing his body vis-a-vis (Aiello and Jones 1971; Hall 1971; Scheflen 1971; Johnson 1971) and his timing in conversation (Lewis, 1970; Gumperz and Herasimchuk, 1972; Leonard, 1972). This is very important, for it is in terms of these time and space coordinates that people send each other messages of relationship. If these code differences are not worked out, the teacher and students will tie into or punctuate (Bateson 1972; Watzlawick et al. 1967) each other in all the wrong ways.

Punctuation breakdowns are the stuff of the self-fulfilling prophecies described above. The child moves or speaks in the wrong way at the wrong time according to the teacher's code, and he will be branded hyperactive, out of control, or stupid. The teacher will appear equally disoriented according to the child's code and may well be branded cold and unfair. Slight differences in time and space use do not have to result in such a disaster, but they often do.

In an exciting article, Byers and Byers (1972) have described how black-white code differences can lead to pupil-teacher breakdown. The teacher in question is considered unbiased and talented. Byers and Byers filmed her interaction with four four-year-old girls, two black and two white. In the sequence analyzed, she looks at the black and white children almost an identical number of times. However, the black children look at the teacher more than three times as often as the white children. One might postulate that the children are anxious about their performance, or perhaps they are hyperactive, etc. Byers and Byers have a much more interesting conclusion to offer, after they add the most important information that the white children established eye contact with the teacher almost twice as often as the black children who are straining three times as hard to catch the teacher's eyes. This is very crucial, for it is during eye contact that the teacher can send the children messages of reassurance and affection, messages such as, "I love you," "You are doing well," "How smart!", or at least, "You are making sense to me." Why do these black and white eyes punctuate each other in all the wrong ways?

Consider what social work is performed by a glance of the eyes. The eyes are engaged in gathering information about the content and report of any interaction that a body is engaged in. Constant surveillance makes people uncomfortable, perhaps because it is a statement of distrust, a sign of one's unwillingness to suspend belief that nothing threatening is about to occur. So the eyes are used in brief spurts only, in passing glances. What is more interesting is that these glances are very well timed to occur at moments of maximum information transfer. Eye glances are paced by conversational rhythms, intonation patterns, and body movements and are sequenced rather neatly to other rhythms between two people. The white girls in the interaction that Byers and Byers have described appear to know just when to look at the white teacher in order to gain access to her eyes and whatever relational messages she is to dispense. The black girls do not appear to have the same information. They appear to be working off a slightly different interaction rhythm. Of course, this is just as Leonard's (1972) analysis of the black-white handshake and Gumperz's and Herasimchuk's (1972) analysis of black-white intonation rhythms predicted. Interaction is indeed an action between people, and if not perfectly timed the interaction will fail. In the case of this teacher and these children, the white-white interaction is successful, and the white-black interaction fails. For all their interactional work, the two black girls receive little relational support, and it is not difficult to predict that they will someday direct their interactional work towards each other. In time, achievement will be located in the peer group, and not in the teacher.

More blatant examples of teacher-student battles over time and space use exist in every American classroom in which teachers generally monopolize 85 percent of class space and 100 percent of class time (Sommer 1969). From the first to the last grade, the teacher attempts to dictate when and where a child should speak or move. In ghetto schools, this often leads to constant and open warfare. Teachers spend an inordinate amount of a child's six years in elementary school fighting with the class about just who is going to say and do what at a particular moment; manuals guiding a new teacher in instructional methods in such a school detail at length exactly how a teacher must rigidly structure time and space (Trubowitz 1968; Board of Education 1966). The children fight this particular structure to the extent that it stifles them; if their function and status in the structure do not make sense to them, that is, if the politics of classroom life do not make sense, they reject the structure and all that comes with it, including literacy.

A large percentage of American blacks are especially adept at making the code shifts essential to smooth interactions with whites. This is no easy task, for enculturation into two cultures, or biculturation (Valentine 1971), can have its drawbacks for ego development. The bicultural child must acquire two sometimes mutually exclusive ways of knowing how to act appropriately, one way for when whites are present and another for when the interaction matrix is all black. Where code shifting is most difficult is apparently in the bureaucratic setting in which the white code, in addition to being the only acceptable medium of information exchange, is also the medium for the expression of host group power and host group access to the essential and even luxurious utilities of the ecosystem that is contemporary America. The police station, the welfare office, the job interview and the classroom are all situations which demand complete subservience to host group codes. In each of these situations, people are being processed rather than negotiated with in an attempt to establish rationality. The rationale is already set. The bureaucrat has it down and the pariah does not. The bureaucrat already has the role defined, and the pariah must fit in if he is to be processed successfully. Even when the bureaucrat attempts to negotiate a rational interaction—to approach his public as he would normal people in everyday life, he is unable to do so because of the sheer numbers of people that must be processed. The teacher, for example, must deal with 30 children at a time, and the give and take that characterizes everyday life become impossible. Consequently, the teacher's code becomes the classroom code, and children are evaluated in its terms.

In the classroom, the teacher has the power; the teacher has the tools to supply the institutional biography that the child needs to escape his pariah origins. Teachers are quick to point this out to children and daily tell them that there is no success without school. If the child attempts biculturation, he adapts to the teacher's code, accepts the teacher's messages of power and dominance, and works hard at school. Many black children do not go this route. They reject the teacher's code and transform their minor differences in time and space use into large differences defining the classroom as the scene of the battle between the races. Code differences do not have to develop in this fashion, but they most often do. It is a measure of the teacher's adaptability in the early grades. The more sensible student-teacher relations can be made in the early grades, the less difference code differences will make. If the teacher fights the children with his formal authority from the early grades on, the children will equate the teacher's code with senseless suppression; it will become a difference that makes a difference. The children will reject the new code and seek the more rewarding alternatives offered by the peer group.

Host group teachers do not produce code differences. Both the teacher and his students partake in long ethnic traditions in their first years of life, and they then bring these traditions to school. The question is, how are ethnic differences made to make a difference? In the earlier grades, teachers make the difference as they are apparently not as adaptable as their students. In later years, as peer group lines solidify and code differences become the focus of most classroom social and political work, the children enforce the distinction between the teacher's code and their own code. In making their code make a difference, they are learning how to produce pariah status vis-à-vis the host group; they are learning to appear like "one-of-those"; they are producing a pariah biography which will haunt them until the next generation again plays the politics of everyday life in the classroom.

Identity and Mobility

The third task cannot be properly dealt with until we have detailed accounts of the politics of everyday life for many pariah groups both here in America and in other cultures. The third task is to explain why blacks do not fare as well as other minorities in classroom politics. All ethnic groups, Jews, Japanese, or Italians, for instance, bring some differences to the classroom. Shouldn't they all lead to communicative breakdowns, degrading relational messages between students and teachers, and, finally, learning disabilities? Yes, and indeed they do. Some groups have worked out ingenious strategies for by-passing host group discriminatory powers. American Catholics, for example, appear to have always understood the complexities of moving through host schools. Accordingly, they have always maintained their own school systems which have functioned not only as socializing agents, but also as protection against the sorting efforts of host group members. Whether or not their diplomas were equivalent in quality to host diplomas, Irish, Italian, and other Catholic Americans have always equipped their children with the institutional biographies required for at least minimally upward mobility.

The strategies of each group for identity work in the face of unacceptable messages of relationship in the classroom are probably deeply rooted in its history. The reasons for its having to develop such strategies exist in the politics of the classroom. If group identity work is necessitated by a breakdown in teacher-student relations, strategies as to what will be attended to and what will be acted upon will be worked out among the students. Learning abilities and disabilities are developed in such a context. School learning is almost always set back; the question is whether the group opts for learning how not to learn, the case described in this paper, whether the group merely opts to learn only about its own materials, as is the case for Hasidic Jews and the Pennsylvania Dutch, or whether the group overcomes the degrading messages and does scholastically better than host children even according to host group standards. The last case is most intriguing because of the records achieved by American Jews and American Japanese. Both groups have soared over mobility barriers and appear to have well escaped pariah status because of their mastery of the American school system. Of course, both groups reached the American shores with tremendous entrepreneurial skills and established traditions of literacy. Nevertheless, the essential question remains unanswered; namely, what did the Jews and the Japanese know that other pariah groups did not know? Alternatively, it can be asked what the host group knew about Jews and Japanese that it apparently does not know about other minorities (Spindler, personal communication). The point is that ethnic identity work defines what is to be learned and how it is to be learned, what is to be read and the strategies used for the reading act. What is different about the ethnic identity work of one group rather than another? Such a question will keep the next generation of scholars busy. If we achieve an answer, we will know a great deal.

Summary

Pariah groups are continually regenerated by host and pariah children learning how to assign *meanings* to particular social acts and how to *act appropriately* on the basis of the meanings assigned. These meanings are programmed into the *central nervous system* as patterns of *selective attention* to the stimuli particular to some acts and not to others. Patterns of selective attention, glossed in everyday language as *abilities, statuses* and *identities,* shape a child's *institutional biography* and define whether the child, his abilities, statuses and identities, are to be assigned to a pariah or a host group in any situation.

The conclusion of this chapter is that the patterns of selective attention and inattention demonstrated by pariah children in school represent rational adaptations to the politics of everyday life in the classrooms. School failure and delinquency often represent highly motivated and intelligent attempts to develop the abilities, statuses, and identities that will best equip the child to maximize his utilities in the politics of everyday life. If the teacher is going to send degrading messages of relationship regardless of how the game is played, the child's best strategy is to stop playing the game.

The ability to read is taken up in some detail since it is one program which defines the boundary between pariah and host groups. Specifically, it is suggested that the politics of everyday life induce patterns of inattention for the reading task in particular groups. Host teachers and pariah children find each other occasionally unintelligible because of vocal and body language code differences and stereotypes. These differences are escalated into cues for intergroup conflict when degrading messages of relationship are appended by the teacher to the child's use of his own code for interpreting and generating behavior. The child is engaged in identity and status work and often rejects these messages as meaningless. The child then develops patterns of inattention to the teacher, the teacher's tasks such ae behaving "properly" and reading, and, eventually, most stimuli generated by the host group. The high rate of black American illiteracy and pariah group membership is explained in this way.

REFERENCES

Aiello, J., and S. Jones, 1971, "Field Study of the Proxemic Behavior of Young Children in Three Subcultural Groups," *Journal of Personality and Social Psychology* 19(7):351-356.

Allitto, S., 1969, "The Language Issue in Communist Chinese Education." In C. Hu, ed., *Aspects of Chinese Education*. New York: Teachers College Press.

Azumi, K., 1969, *Higher Education and Business Recruitment in Japan*. New York: Teachers College Press.

Baratz, J., and Shuy, R., eds., 1969, *Teaching Black Children To Read*. Washington, D.C. Center for Applied Linguistics.

Bar-Hillel, Y., 1954, "Indexical Expressions," *Mind* (n.s.) 63:359-379.

Barker, R., 1968, *Ecological Psychology*. Stanford, Calif.: Stanford University Press.

Barth, F., 1969, "Introduction." In F. Barth, ed., *Ethnic Groups and Boundaries*. Boston: Little, Brown and Company.

Bateson, G., 1972, *Steps to an Ecology of Mind*. New York: Ballantine Books.

Beck, H., 1971a, "The Rationality of Redundancy," *Comparative Political Studies* 3(4):469-478.

Beck, H., 1971b, "Minimal Requirements for a Biobehavioral Paradigm," *Behavioral Science* 16:442-456.

Beck, H., 1972, "Everyman Meets the Epistemologist." Paper presented at the 1972 Annual Meeting of the American Political Science Association.

Becker, E., 1962, *The Birth and Death of Meaning*. New York: The Free Press.

Bernstein, B., 1964, "Elaborated and Restricted Codes," *American Anthropologist* 66(6, part 2):55-69.

Beteille, A., 1972, "Race, Class and Ethnic Identity," *International Social Science Journal* 23(4):519-539.

Birch, H., and J. Gussow, 1970, *Disadvantaged Children: Health, Nutrition and School Failure*. New York: Harcourt Brace Jovanovich.

Blurton-Jones, N., 1972, "Nonverbal Communication in Children." In R. Hinde, ed., *Nonverbal Communication*. London: Cambridge University Press.

Board of Education, New York City, 1966, *Getting Started in the Elementary School*.

Brameld, T., 1968, *Japan: Culture, Education and Change in Two Communities*. New York: Holt, Rinehart and Winston, Inc.

Byers, P. 1971, "Sentics, Rhythms, and a New View of Man." Paper presented to the 138th Annual Meeting of the American Association for the Advancement of Science, Philadelphia, December 30, 1971.

Byers, P., and H. Byers, 1972, "Nonverbal Communication and the Education of Children." In C. Cazden, et al., eds., *Functions of Language in the Classroom*, New York: Teachers College Press.

Caudill, W., and H. Weinstein, 1969, "Maternal Care and Infant Behavior in Japan and America," *Psychiatry* 32:12-43.

Cazden, C., 1970, "The Situation: A Neglected Source of Social Class Differences in Language Use," *Journal of Social Issues* 26(2):35-60.

Chance, M., 1967, "Attention Structure as the Basis of Primate Rank Orders," *Man* (n.s.) 2(4):503-518.

Cicourel, A., 1970a, "The Acquisition of Social Structure." In J. Douglas, ed., *Understanding Everyday Life*. Chicago: Aldine.

Cicourel, A., 1970b, "Basic and Normative Rules in the Negotiation of Status and Role, *Recent Sociology* 2:4-45.

Cicourel, A., 1974, "Ethnomethodology." In T. Sebeok, ed., *Current Trends in Linguistics*, vol. 12. The Hague: Mouton.

Cicourel, A., and J. Kitsuse, 1963, *Educational Decision Makers*. New York: Bobbs-Merrill.

Condon, W., and W. Ogston, 1966, "Sound Film Analysis of Normal and Pathological Behavior Patterns," *Journal of Nervous and Mental Disease* 163(4):338-347.

Condon, W., 1971, "Speech and Body Motion Synchrony of the Speaker-Hearer." In D. Horton and J. Jenkins, eds., *The Perception of Language*. Chicago: Charles Merrill.

Cornell, J., 1970, " 'Caste' in Japanese Social Structure," *Monumenta Nipponica* 15(1-2):107-135.

Crystal, D., 1972, "Prosodic and Paralinguistic Correlates of Social Categories." In E. Ardener, ed., *Social Anthropology and Language*. London: Tavistock.

Deutsch, C., 1968, "Environment and Perception." In M. Deutsch, et al., eds., *Social Class, Race and Psychological Development*. New York: Holt, Rinehart and Winston, Inc.

Deutsch, M., 1963, "The Disadvantaged Child and the Learning Process." In A. Passow, ed., *Education in Depressed Areas*. New York: Teachers College Press.

DeVos, G., and H. Wagatsuma, eds., 1966, *Japan's Invisible Race*. Berkeley: University of California Press.

Dewey, J., 1896, "The Reflex Arc in Psychology," *Psychological Review* 3(4):357-370.

Donoghue, J., 1971, "An Eta Community in Japan: The Social Persistence of an Outcaste Group." In G. Yamamato and T. Ishida, eds., *Modern Japanese Society*. Berkeley: McCuthchan.

Eidheim, H., 1969, "When Ethnic Identity Is a Social Stigma." In F. Barth, ed., *Ethnic Groups and Boundaries*. Boston: Little, Brown and Company.

Ekman, P., and W. Friesen, 1969, "Nonverbal Leakage and Clues to Deception," *Psychiatry* 32(1):88-106.

Entwistle, D., 1971, "Implications of Language Socialization for Reading Models and for Learning to Read," *Reading Research Quarterly* 7(1):111-167.

Erikson, E., 1968, *Identity: Youth and Crisis*. New York: Norton.

Fisher, J., 1961, "The Japanese Schools for the Natives of Truk." In G. Spindler, ed., *Education and Culture*. 1963, New York: Holt, Rinehart and Winston, Inc.

Fishman, J., and E. Leuders-Salmon, 1972, "What Has Sociology To Say to the Teacher." In C. Cazden, et al., eds., *Functions of Speech in the Classroom*. New York: Teachers College Press.

Forge, A., 1970, "Learning to See in New Guinea." In P. Mayer, ed., *Socialization*. London: Tavistock.

Frake, C. O., 1962, "The Ethnographic Study of Cognitive Systems." In S. Tylor, ed., *Cognitive Anthropology*. New York: Holt, Rinehart and Winston, Inc., 1969.

Frake, C. O., 1975, "How to Enter a Yakan House." In M. Sanches and B. Blount, eds., *Sociocultural Dimensions of Language Use*. New York: Academic Press.

Garfinkel, H., 1956, "Some Sociological Concepts and Methods for Psychiatrists," *Psychiatric Research Reports* 6:181-196.

Garfinkel, H., 1963, "A Conception of, and Experiments with, 'Trust' as a Condition of Stable Concerted Actions." In O. Harvey, ed., *Motivation and Social Interaction*. New York: Roland Press.

Geertz, C., 1965. "The Impact of the Concept of Culture on the Concept of Man." In E. Hammel and W. Simmons, eds., *Man Makes Sense*. Boston: Little, Brown and Company.

Gibson, E., 1965, "Learning To Read," *Science* 148:1066-1072.

Goffman, E., 1963, *Stigma*. Englewood Cliffs, N.J.: Prentice-Hall, Inc.

Goodman, K., 1967, "Reading: A Psycholinguistic Guessing Game." In H. Singer and R. Ruddell, eds., *Theoretical Models and Processes of Reading*. Newark, N.J.: International Reading Association.

Gumperz, J., 1970, "Sociolinguistics and Communication in Small Groups," *Language-Behavior Research Laboratory Working Paper no. 38*. Berkeley, Calif.

Gumperz, J., and E. Herasimchuk, 1973, "The Conversational Analysis of Social Meaning." In R. Shuy, ed., *Sociolinguistics: Current Trends and Prospects*. Washington, D.C.: Georgetown University Press.

Hall, E., 1966, *The Hidden Dimension*. New York: Anchor Books.

Hall, E., 1971, "Environmental Communication." In H. Essor, ed., *Behavior and Environment*. New York: Plenum Press.

Holt, J., 1969, *The Underachieving School*. New York: Pitman.

Hostetler, J., and G. Huntington, 1971. *Children in Amish Society: Socialization and Community Education*. CSEC. New York: Holt, Rinehart and Winston, Inc.

Jackson, P., 1968, *Life in the Classroom*. New York: Holt, Rinehart and Winston, Inc.

Jensen, A., 1966, "Social Class and Perceptual Learning," *Mental Hygiene* 50:226-239.

Jensen, A., 1969, "How Much Can We Boost I.Q. and Scholastic Achievement?" *Harvard Educational Review* 39:1-123.

Johnson, K., 1971, "Black Kinesics," *Florida FL Reporter* 9(1,2):17-20, 57.

Kasamatsu, A., and T. Hirai, 1966, "An Electroencephalographic Study on the Zen Meditation," *Folia Psychiat, Neurolog, Japonica* 20:315-336.

Kendon, A., 1967, "Some Functions of Gaze-Direction in Social Interaction," *Acta Psychologica* 26:22-63.

Kendon, A., 1970, "Movement Coordination in Social Interaction," *Acta Psychologica* 32:100-125.

Kendon, A., 1973, "The Role of Visible Behavior in the Organization of Social Interaction." In M. von Cranach and I. Vine, eds., *Social Communication and Movement*. London: Academic Press.

Kohl, H., 1967, *36 Children*. New York: New American Library.

Labov, W., 1964a, "Phonological Correlates of Social Stratification," *American Anthropolgist* 66(4, part 2):164-176.

Labov, W., 1964b, "Stages in the Acquisition of Standard English." In R. Shuy, ed., *Social Dialects and Language Learning*. Champaign, Ill.: National Council of Teachers of English.

Labov, W., 1969, "The Logic of Nonstandard English," *Florida FL Reporter* 7(1):60-75, 169.

Labov, W., P. Cohen, C. Robins, and J. Lewis, 1968, *A Study of the Nonstandard English of Negro and Puerto Rican Speakers in New York City*, Cooperative Research Project No. 3288.

Labov, W., and C. Robins, 1969, "A Note on the Relation of Reading Failure to Peer-group Status in Urban Ghettos," *Florida FL Reporter* 7(1):54-57, 167.

Largey, G., and D. Watson, 1972, "The Sociology of Odors," *American Journal of Sociology* 77(6):1021-1034.

Laver, J., 1968, "Voice Quality and Indexical Information," *British Journal of Disorders of Communication* 3:43-54.

Leonard, C., 1972, "A Method of Film Analysis of Ethnic Communication Style." Paper presented to the American Ethnological Society Meetings, Montreal, April 6.

Lewis, L., 1970, "Culture and Social Interaction in the Classroom," Language-Behavior Research Laboratory Working Paper no. 38. Berkeley, Calif.

Long, N., 1958, "The Local Community as an Ecology of Games." In N. Polsby, et al., eds., *Politics of Social Life*, 1963. Boston: Houghton Mifflin Company.

MacKay, D., 1972, "Formal Analysis of Communicative Processes." In R. Hinde, ed., *Nonverbal Communication*. London: Cambridge University Press.

Mackworth, J., 1972, "Some Models of Reading Process: Learners and Skilled Readers," *Reading Research Quarterly* 7:701-733.

Mackworth, N., and M. Bagshaw., 1970, "Eye Catching in Adults, Children and Monkeys." *Perception and Its Disorders, ARNMD*, 48:201-203.

Makita, K., 1968, "The Rarity of Reading Disability in Japanese Children," *American Journal of Orthopsychiatry* 38:599-614.

McDermott, J., 1969, "Deprivation and Celebration: Suggestions for an Aesthetic Ecology." In J. Edie, ed., *New Essays in Phenomenology*. New York: Ballantine.

Melmud, R., 1971, "Black English Phonology: The Question of Reading Interference," Monographs of the Language-Behavior Research Laboratory. Berkeley: University of California.

Miller, G., E. Galanter, and K. Pribram, 1960, *Plans and the Structure of Behavior* New York: Holt, Rinehart and Winston, Inc.

Mitchell, R., 1967, *The Korean Minority in Japan.* Berkeley: University of California Press.

Montagu, A., ed., 1964, *The Concept of Race.* New York: Crowell-Collier and Macmillan.

Ninomiya, S., 1933, "An Inquiry Concerning the Origin, Development, and Present Situation of the *Eta* in Relation to the History of Social Classes in Japan," *Transactions of the Asiatic Society of Japna* (second series) 10:47-145.

Parsons, T., 1959, "The School Class as a Social System," *Harvard Educational Review* 29(4):69-90.

Pribram, K., 1969, "Neural Servosystem and the Structure of Personality," *Journal of Nervous and Mental Disease* 149(1):30-39.

Pribram, K., 1970, "Looking to See." *Perception and Disorders, ARNMD* 48:150-162.

Pribram, K., 1971, *Languages of the Brain.* Englewood Cliffs, N.J.: Prentice-Hall, Inc.

Rist, R., 1970, "Student Social Class and Teacher Expectations," *Harvard Educational Review* 40:411-451.

Roberts, J., 1970, *Scene of the Battle: Group Behavior in Urban Classrooms.* New York: Doubleday Company.

Rothblat, L., and K. Pribram, 1972, "Selective Attention: Input Filter or Response Selection," *Brain Research* 39:427-436.

Scheflen, A., 1960, "Regressive One-to-one Relationships," *Psychiatric Quarterly* 23:692-709.

Scheflen, A., 1964, "The Significance of Posture in Communication Systems," *Psychiatry* 27:316-331.

Scheflen, A., 1971, "Living Space in an Urban Ghetto," *Family Process* 10(4):429-450.

Schutz, A., 1953, "Common .Sense and Scientific Interpretation of Human Action." In M. Natanson, ed., *The Philosophy of the Social Sciences,* 1963. New York: Random House.

Segall, M., D. Campbell, and M. Herskovits, 1966, *The Influence of Culture on Visual Perception.* Indianapolis: Bobbs-Merrill.

Shimahara, N., 1971, *Burakumin: A Japanese Minority and Education.* The Hague: Martinus Nijhoff.

Singer, H., and B. Beardsley, 1970, "Motivating a Disabled Reader," Thirty-seventh yearbook of the Claremont College Reading Conference.

Sokolov, E., 1969, "Modeling Properties of the Nervous System." In M. Cole and I. Maltzman, eds., *Handbook of Contemporary Soviet Psychology.* New York: Basic Books.

Sommer, R., 1969, *Personal Space,* Englewood Cliffs, N.J.: Prentice-Hall, Inc.

Spindler, G., 1959, "The Transmission of American Culture." In G. Spindler, ed., *Education and Culture,* 1963. New York: Holt, Rinehart and Winston, Inc.

Taira, K., 1971, "Japan's Invisible Race Made Visible," *Economic Development and Cultural Change* 19(4):663-668.

Thompson, L., 1966, *Reading Disability.* Springfield, Ill.: Charles C. Thomas.

Trubowitz, S., 1968, *A Handbook for Teaching in the Ghetto School.* New York: Quadrangle.

Valentine, C., 1971, "Deficit, Difference and Bicultural Models of Afro-American Behavior," *Harvard Educational Review* 41(2):137-158.

Wallace, A., 1965, "Driving to Work." In M. Spiro, ed., *Context and Meaning in Cultural Anthropology.* New York: The Free Press.

Wanat, S., 1971, *Linguistic Structure and Visual Attention in Reading,* Research Reports. Newark, Delaware: International Reading Association.

Watzlawick, P., J. Beaven, and D. Jackson, 1967, *Pragmatics of Human Communication.* New York: Norton.

Zimmerman, D., and M. Pollner, 1970, The Everyday World as a Phenomenon. In J. Douglas, ed., *Understanding Everyday Life.* Chicago: Aldine.

Social Context of Learning to Read

COURTNEY B. CAZDEN
Harvard University

To adults, reading is a solitary activity, a kind of internal language process that contrasts with interpersonal talk. The contrast is not complete: We read song sheets aloud and together; we exchange notes during a lecture, thus using reading as well as writing for immediate interactional ends; and we listen alone to talk on the radio or TV, thus making a solitary activity of the comprehension of speech. But usually we talk with others and read alone.

Not so with children, especially children just learning to read in the primary grades. Learning to read, like mature reading later on, is certainly a cognitive process; but it is also a very social activity, deeply embedded in interactions with teacher and peers. Hopefully, as we understand those interactions more fully, we will be able to design more effective environments for helping children learn. This paper reviews research on children learning to read in classroom interactions in four parts: influences on time engaged in reading; differences in the focus of instruction; the complexities of reading group lessons; and peer interactions in the older grades.

Influences on Time Engaged in Reading

One obvious way in which classroom interactions affect learning is through their effect on how much time children actually spend engaged in reading tasks. Three descriptions by Piestrup (1973), McDermott (1978), and Au (in press, in preparation), are sociolinguistic and ethnographic analyses of audio or video-taped lessons. Two descriptions by Hess and Takanishi (1974) and Cazden (1973) are more traditional studies in which observers did on-the-spot coding.

Piestrup's research (1973) is on sources of interference between the language of black children and their teachers. In an analysis of 104 reading instruction episodes audiotaped in 14 first grade classrooms with predominantly black children, Piestrup identified two kinds of interference which she labelled structural and functional. Whether the mismatch is only a temporary misunderstanding or a

This is an expanded version of a paper by the same title which appears in L.B. Resnick and P.A. Weaver (Eds.), *Theory and Practice of Early Reading*. Reprinted by permission of Lawrence Erlbaum Associates, Inc.

more serious barrier depends on the teacher's understanding of the problem and her response to it. In the following episode about a workbook lesson, the teacher explicitly and effectively dealt with a structural (dialect) conflict:

T "...how would you harm the colt?"

C_1 Tear it.

T Huh?

C_1 Tear it.

T Th—th—Oh! Do you, do you know what a colt is, now?

C_1 Oh, kill it, kill it!

T No, what's a colt?

C_1 Somethin' you wear.

T There's an "l" in it. "Coat" is c-o-a-th—don't laugh, that's all right. "Colt" is very hard for city children, because they haven't been out on the farm, and they don't know about it. It's a baby, a baby colt.

C_3 A baby colt.

C_1 Oh yeah!

T Remember the story? An' it's a c-o-l-t. "Coat" is c-o-a-t, and there's no "l" in it, but listen to—Keisha—colt, colt, colt. Now do you know what a colt is?

C_4 Yeah, I know.

T What is it?

C_2 A baby horse.

T Yes, uh-huh, how could you harm a baby horse?

(Piestrup, 1973, pp. 3-5)

Interference is termed functional rather than structural when the mismatch comes from the functions language is used for rather than from structural features of the language itself. In the following excerpt from oral reading, the children shift away from discussion of remote content to verbal play; the teacher is ignored and fails to get their attention back to the reading task:

T "Off"

C_1 "Off to the—

T OK. It says "wood."

C_1 —wood.

T We would say woods—this book was written in England.

C_1 Now, I'm through. I ain't gonna read this page again.

T OK. Well, we're gonna turn the page and we're just gonna read the next page.

C_1 Uh uh! Darren 'sposed to be first.

T Well, I'm waiting for Darren to come back. Come on, Darren.

C_2 He just playin' aroun' _____
   (not clear).

C$_1$ He crack his knuckles, in the buckles.

C$_3$ Uh-uh.

T   OK, Zip and Wendy ran to the woods, and here's the —

C$_1$ I got a tow truck. My mama bought me one.

T   — father.

C$_1$ An' I got me a car to hook it on. It got a hook —

(Piestrup, 1973, pp. 6-7)

The two teachers out of the group of fourteen who were able to accommodate most effectively to both structural and functional sources of interference, termed "Black Artful" by Piestrup, had teaching episodes that were both lively and focused on reading, and their children had the highest reading scores at the end of first grade. Piestrup concludes that "the ways teachers communicate in the classroom are crucial to children's success in learning to read" (p. 170).

McDermott (1978) has done an intensive microanalysis, frame by frame, of videotapes of two 30-minute reading groups (top group and bottom group) in one first grade classroom. During those 30 minutes around the reading table, children in the top group spend three times as much time on task as children in the bottom group, and McDermott has tried to understand how this happens. First, the procedure for allocating turns to read is different in the two groups. In the top group, the number of pages in the story is allocated equally among the children, and each child reads his share in order around the table. In the bottom group, there's no fixed order and each turn is negotiated according to who requests a turn and who the teacher thinks can read the page in question. Interruptions are more frequent in the bottom group (40 vs. 2 for the top group) and more disruptive because continuation of reading is more dependent on the teacher for assigning the next turn. Some of these interruptions are even initiated by the teacher herself:

> On one occasion, for example, she organizes the children to call for a turn to read their new books, "Raise your hands if you can read page 4." The children straighten themselves up in their chairs, form neat lines along the sides of the reading table, and either raise their hands for a turn or at least look at their books or the teacher. As their hands reach their highest point, the teacher looks away from the reading group to the back of the room. She yells at one child in the top group, and then another child in the top group. The three children in the bottom group who raised their hands, lower them to the table. Another little boy who didn't have his hand raised thrusts his chair back away from the reading table and the teacher and balances it on its two back legs. The other two children in the group simply look down at their books. The teacher returns and says, "Nobody can read page 4? Why not?" Eventually the children recover, and someone gets a turn. But it all takes time.
> (McDermott, 1978)

How does this contrast come about? Possibly the teacher has been told somewhere that calling on children in a random order helps keep the attention of potentially more disorderly children. More importantly, McDermott (1978) suggests:

> What is driving this whole system? I don't think it is the negative expectations of the teacher. Rather, the children in the bottom group represent pedagogical and interactional problems for the teacher. Pedagogically, there is no doubt that it is easier for the teacher to practice reading with the children in the top group than to struggle with the process of teaching decoding to the children in the bottom group. And interactionally, there is the pressure of the competition between the groups and the scarred identities of the children in the bottom group. Even within the bottom group we hear claims of one child against another. ("Oh, you can't read." "Better than you.") Or we can point to a child in the bottom group who constantly calls for turns to read while, at the same time, appears to struggle to make sure that she does not get eye contact with the teacher.

> In response to all these problems, the teacher and the children in the bottom group make adaptations. In response to all these pressures they struggle to solve the pedagogical and interactional problems of coming to school not knowing how to read, of having a teacher who expects them to know how to read, of having a teacher who doesn't know how to overcome that they do not know how to read while she has twenty other children walking around the room, and of overcoming the pressure of having the other children taunt them for their performances. In response to all this, they make very specific adaptations. One adaptation is to make sure that no one child is isolated to read something too difficult. So the teacher uses the two different turn taking systems with the different groups, and this adaptation has the consequences already explicated.

McDermott (1978) concludes:

> Success in learning is best predicted by the time a child spends on a task; some may learn faster than others, but with time, almost any child can learn what has to be learned in school, if there are the proper organizational constraints for getting the child on task for the necessary amount of time. The question of why some children achieve more than others has been transformed into a question about the environments in terms of which some children get consistently organized to attend to school tasks in classrooms while others do not....

> Certain children, who, for whatever reasons come to school behind their peers in the development of classroom skills, constitute both pedagogical and interactional problems for most teachers. Most teachers say of them that they are harder to teach; part of that reaction is that they need more of the teacher's time if they are to catch up with their peers. In addition, they must learn under the pressure of knowing that they are behind, generally in a classroom which allocates status in part on the basis of the children's intellectual ranking in the classroom....

> Thus, the small differences between children in the early years of school expand quickly to the drastic forms of differential performance which become obvious in later years. At the root of these differences is not so much the extreme complexity of the school tasks, nor the differences in the learning potentials of the different children, but the differential environments we offer the children for getting organized and on task so that learning can take place.

I think we have to acknowledge that what McDermott has exposed would be found elsewhere if we dared to take as close a look.

Fortunately, we have reports of one success story too. The Kamehameha Early Education Program (KEEP) is in a privately supported school for ethnically Hawaiian children, whose reading achievement in regular classrooms traditionally has been very low. In 1976 a new reading program was introduced at KEEP, and reading scores of the first grade children increased from an average of the 19th percentile in the preceding three years to the 69th percentile (Jordan, Weisner, Tharp, and Au, 1978).

According to Au (in press), the new reading lessons have three component parts, which she labels ETR, for *E*xperience, *T*ext and *R*elationships: The teacher begins by evoking comments from the children about their *experiences* that relate to the story (which is usually from a basal reader); she then assigns a page or two of *text* to be read silently and questions the children about the text; finally, she draws out *relationships* between the text and their experiences.

So far, except for the careful attention to evoking the children's personal experiences to engage their attention and provide schemata for comprehension, this sequence does not sound different enough to account for such striking gains. Au believes that the success lies not only in the cultural congruence of the content but, as with Piestrup's Black Artful teachers, in the cultural congruence of the context as well. Briefly, the rapid interactions between teacher and children, and the cooperative interaction among the children who build on one another's responses, produce lesson talk with striking similarities to "talk-story," a form of collaborative narrative of personal experience that is a special speech event in Hawaiian culture. Au (in preparation) is now documenting in more detail, from an analysis of videotaped lessons, how this talk happens and how the teacher channels the talk-story-like ways of speaking toward academic ends. Quantitatively, the children are certainly more engaged in reading tasks in the new program; but qualitatively the focus of their attention has been changed as well.

Hess and Takanishi (1974) observed student "engagement" in eight 30-minute observations in 39 elementary school classrooms in low-income communities to find out what teachers did to "turn on" their students to academic work in mathematics and language arts. Overall, they found that student engagement was strongly and consistently related to teacher behavior, but not to classroom architecture, nor to student characteristics such as sex and ethnicity. Two demonstrations of intra-teacher consistency in their data are impressive. First, two teachers were observed during two consecutive years. Although they had completely different classes and reported that they felt large differences between the two years, the mean level of engagement in their classes remained almost identical. Second, during the second year of the study, an entire school being observed moved from a self-contained classroom building to one with open-space architecture. The overall level of engagement across these very different physical environments was identical (82 and 83 percent), and the rank order of teachers in terms of percent engagement in their classrooms was .85.

Contrary to expectations, Hess and Takanishi found that these levels of student engagement were not consistently related across teachers to "specific teacher strategies" such as the frequency of specific questions or of feedback; instead they were strongly related to more "global instructional strategies" such as instructional group size (more engagement in small groups), and direction of student attention (more engagement when directed toward the teacher than toward other students or materials alone). The authors conclude with a recommendation that teacher-training programs concentrate on skills in classroom social organization rather than on more specific teaching behaviors. This is an important caution for competency-based training as it is usually conducted.

An observational study, done at the request of Children's Television Workshop, also measured children's engagement—or attention as we called it (Cazden, 1973). We wanted to find out what environmental variables affected the viewing behavior of children watching *The Electric Company* in their elementary school classrooms. Viewing behavior was defined as both visual attention and verbalizations. We observed ten primary grade classrooms during the 30-minute show five or six times each. Two independent measures of attention were used: a scan of the entire class at 30-second intervals to count those visually oriented toward the TV screens, and continuous monitoring and recording of the visual attention of individual students on an event-recorder. Monitoring individual attention on the event-recorder was extremely reliable (.94 interobserver agreement), and group attention averages from the 30-second scans had high validity (average within classroom correlation of .94 between measures of group and individual attention). Coding verbalizations was more difficult (interobserver reliability attained only .84). The ten classrooms were selected to represent a range in classroom "structure," defined here as a continuum from classrooms where attention to the show was expected and enforced by the teacher ("high" structure) to classrooms where a range of competing activities was available ("low" structure). As expected, we found that classroom structure was positively related to both group attention (correlation .87) and individual attention (correlation .95). High structure affected all children, increasing their attentiveness and responsiveness to *The Electric Company,* so that poor readers in high structure classrooms had higher attention scores than better readers in low structure classrooms.

With the exception of one classroom, structure also correlated highly with average number of reading responses (correlation of .90 for nine classes, but only .38 for all ten). In the one exception, the most highly structured classroom was highest in amount of attention paid by the students but lowest in average number of reading responses. Since there was nothing in the level of reading ability in the classroom that would explain this anomaly, we think that some aspect of this teacher's classroom control (which we could not understand from our limited observations) discouraged overt reading responses.

Because *The Electric Company* is designed especially for children reading below grade level, we were also interested in the relationship between viewing behavior and reading level. Children's reading ability can be categorized according to their relative standing in their class (high, middle or low reading group) or ranked more absolutely according to standardized test scores. Average attention of children in the lowest quartile of achievement test scores was 79.1 percentile. While this was not as high as the 86.5 percentile and 90.2 percentile attention of the two middle quartiles (25-75 percentiles), it was higher than the 65.8 percentile attention of the best readers and was encouraging evidence that the show was reaching its intended audience. More interesting and surprising was a finding that, without exception, children of the same tested reading level showed less attention and more fluctuations in their attention (more distractions) when they are among the lowest readers in their classroom than when they are in relatively higher reading groups. The data are shown below for the six second grade classrooms for which fall standardized test scores were available.

ATTENTION AND FLUCTUATION OF CHILDREN IN HIGH AND LOW READING GROUPS

Class Standing	Comprehension Quartiles[a]			
	1-25	26-50	51-76	76-100
	Percent attention			
High	0. (0)	89.5(10)	90.9(9)	73.2(11)
Low	79.1(20)	79.0 (4)	87.3(2)	49.4 (5)
	Number of fluctuations			
High	0. (0)	51.2(10)	30.6(9)	44.4(11)
Low	50.6(20)	58.6 (4)	57.5(2)	64.6(5)

Note. The data are from Cazden, 1973.
[a] Numbers in parentheses indicate the number of children in each cell.

Because our sample was not designed for matching numbers of children in each of these cells, firm conclusions cannot be drawn. But in these admittedly limited data, lower relative standing in class (in terms of reading group assignments) adversely affects children's attention to televised reading material. Seen in this way, a variable such as reading level (usually considered a child variable in its absolute sense) becomes an environmental variable as well through the child's relative standing in the classroom group.

Differences in the Focus of Instruction

Time on task is a powerful variable, but it is not the only one. One more qualitative variable is where the attention of children and teacher is focused during reading instruction. We know that learning to read requires mastering a complex set of concepts and skills at many levels of a hierarchical system. Analytically, we can separate a series of nested units — from the meaningless sounds symbolized by letters, to larger and larger meaningful units of words, phrases, clauses, paragraphs and stories; and we can isolate the conventions of punctuation, capitalization and layout on a page that support the communication of meaning (remember that the division of print into lines is one visual feature that does not carry meaning except in poetry and that children must therefore learn to ignore). But such analytical separation says nothing about how children should be helped; it does not determine in what order their attention should be focused on different units in the hierarchy, nor how an eventual integration can best be achieved.

The simplest contrast in focus is between decoding skills and meaning. We know we cannot tell what actually happens from the manuals on a teacher's desk or the methods she professes to use. For example, in one of the first grade reading studies supported by the Office of Education Cooperative Research Project, Chall and Feldman (1966) went behind "method A vs. method B" comparisons to examine what teachers actually did to implement those methods. Observational studies of teachers showed no significant relationship between the ranking of the teacher's professed method emphasis (whether "sound-symbol" or "meaning") and the method emphasis observed in her classroom (p. 573).

If attention to phonic skills and to meaning is included in reading group lessons, then that combination can create problems of shifting focus and complex interactions that will be discussed further below. Here I want to report research that describes classrooms in which these foci are separated—by children, by type of instructional event, or by language.

Separation of Focus by Children

In the classroom studied by McDermott, the focus differed from one group in the classroom to another.

> [In the top group] occasionally, the children create problems by word calling instead of reading for meaning, and the teacher's main pedagogical task is to convince the children that there is living language complete with propositions with illocutionary force on the page. Thus, one child reads, "But Ricky said his mother..." in a dull monotone, and the teacher corrects her, "Let's read it this way, 'But Ricky, said his mother'."
>
> With the bottom group, the teacher has rather different problems. Accordingly, the teacher and the children constitute rather different environments for each other in the different groups. The children in the bottom group do not read as well as the children in the top group, and the teacher attends less to the language on the book's pages and more to the phonics skills needed to interpret any given word in the text. Thus, there are many more stopping places in the children's reading, and the story line which is to hold the lesson together is seldom alluded to and never developed. (McDermott, 1978)

This same contrast between focus on meaning for better readers and focus on phonic skills for poorer readers is found in two other studies by Gumperz

(1972) and Allington (1978). Gumperz reports observations in a first grade classroom in a racially integrated California district:

> We observed a reading session with a slow reading group of three children, and seven fast readers.... With the slow readers she [the teacher] concentrated on the alphabet, on the spelling of individual words.... She addressed the children in what white listeners would identify as pedagogical style. Her enunciation was deliberate and slow. Each word was clearly articulated with even stress and pitch.... Pronunciation errors were corrected whenever they occurred, even if the reading task had to be interrupted. The children seemed distracted and inattentive....
>
> With the advanced group on the other hand reading became much more of a group activity and the atmosphere was more relaxed. Words were treated in context, as a part of a story.... There was no correction of pronunciation, although some deviant forms were also heard. The children actually enjoyed competing with each other in reading and the teacher responded by dropping her pedagogical monotone in favor of more animated natural speech. (Gumperz, 1972)

Allington's study (1978) suggests that this contrasting focus is not just a chance characteristic of two classrooms that happened to be studied by McDermott and Gumperz. Allington audiotaped oral reading segments of reading lessons with the best and the poorest readers in 20 primary classrooms in three school districts. He analyzed how the teachers responded to children's oral reading errors and found dramatic differences between the two reading groups across the 20 classrooms, differences which fit exactly the pictures described more qualitatively by McDermott and Gumperz. First, there was a difference in the rate of teacher corrections of the errors (68 percent of poor readers' errors were corrected, but only 24 percent of good readers' errors). Second, there were differences in the timing of the correction: teachers were more likely to interrupt poor readers at the point of error (88 percent of poor readers' errors vs. only 70 percent of good readers' errors) rather than waiting for the next phrase or clause boundary. Finally, there were differences in the cues provided by the teachers to help the children read the right word: for the poor readers, the cues were more apt to be graphemic/phonemic (26 percent vs. only 17 percent of the cues for good readers), while the cues for good readers were more apt to be semantic/syntactic (31 percent vs. 14 percent for poor readers).

The critical question raised by these reports is whether such differentiated teacher behavior is helpful or not. Marie Clay speaks from New Zealand of the goals of education as helping children become "self-improving systems" (personal communication). In other words, the goal is not to create children who never make mistakes, but rather children who have the capacity to notice their own mistakes and have strategies for correcting them. She has found that children in the first grade who do the most self-correcting are the children who become the better readers in late grades (Clay, 1973). Does being interrupted make self-correcting more or less likely to develop? And if a cue from the teacher is needed, what kind of a cue should it be?

Allington's paper is titled, "Are good and poor readers taught differently? Is that why poor readers are poor readers?" The implication is clear that he believes it is possible (as do I) that these teacher behaviors to low group children may increase their problems in the long run. Prompt interruptions seem too much like a "law and order" approach to errors, as if the teacher is acting out of fear that the errors, like the children themselves, may get out of control. But just because it is the long run that counts, we need longitudinal studies that follow teacher behaviors and children's progress over time. (I am grateful to Rebecca Barr for this caution.) Only then can we separate constructive individualization from destructive bias.

Separation of Focus by Instructional Event

A very different kind of separation of foci of attention is by instructional events distributed throughout the school day. As part of a larger study of children's functional language competence in kindergarten and the primary grades conducted at the Center for Applied Linguistics, Griffin (1977) has described the set of events in which reading happens in one first grade classroom. These include: reading a recipe for hot cross buns that leads to a discussion of the meaning of "lukewarm" and experiments with feeling lukewarm milk later in the day; and story time when the teacher reads aloud, stopping frequently for talk about what is going to happen next. Griffin notices that comprehension skills of vocabulary and prediction were built in such nonreading group times of the day; whereas in the reading groups themselves, phonics was the overriding concern. This separation was so consistent that definite expectations about appropriate responses had been learned by the children. If the teacher shifted momentarily to a meaning cue during a reading group, the children were apt to respond with a phonic-based response anyway. For example:

> One child was reading, in a very halting style: "The pigeon flies far...." He paused. The teacher repeated the sentence in a more fluent style with correct intonation and then gave the child a prompt: "The pigeon flies far.... Think. Think what it would say! The pigeon flies far...." A second child chimes in saying, " 'A' says it name. *Away.*" (Griffin, 1977, p. 381)

In considering the merits of such a separation by instructional events, we must remember that it can only work in classrooms where there is a rich set of nonreading group events in which reading takes place. One tragic result of the pressures of the back-to-basic movements may be less time available for experiences like reading recipes and hearing stories in which vocabulary building and comprehension education can so meaningfully occur.

Separation of Focus by Language

In the most extreme case, a focus on meaning and a focus on phonics may be separated in a single classroom not only by reading events, but by languages as well. While this review does not attempt to cover research on learning to read in two languages, my own observations in a bilingual first grade classroom in Chicago are relevant here.[1]

In the fall, the teacher's reading instruction was in Spanish only, using a traditional syllabic approach (ma me mi mo mu). Around Christmas when she felt that the children's oral English had developed sufficiently, the teacher started a phonic-based reading program in English. As she described that attempt afterward, it just didn't work; the children resisted and she finally stopped. About that time, in a graduate class she was taking, she read Sylvia Ashton-Warner's *Teacher* and felt immediately that those ideas fit her philosophy and her children. The result was that by February, when I visited again, instruction in Spanish reading via syllables coexisted, for all children, with instruction in English reading via "key words." Moreover, the teacher was consistent in the cues she gave the children in the two contexts. In Spanish she focused their attention on the syllabic components on which they had had extensive practice:

Fe li pe to ma u na fo to.

In English, she helped with a meaning cue: when a child couldn't read *butter* on his key word card, she asked, "What do you put on your toast?"

At first thought, such separation may seem detrimental to learning. Intuitively, it seems harder for children to get decoding and meaning cues together in a single mental act if they are taught separately in different parts of the school day, or even in different languages. On the other hand, maybe a clear and consistent focus of attention is helpful, especially for beginning readers, as long as both are included somehow, for all the children.

The Complexities of Reading Group Lessons

Primary grade reading groups are complex interactional scenes—complex because of the triangular relationship between a reader, a text being read, and the participation of teacher and peers; because of the many levels of organization of the text that may move unpredictably in and out of the focus of the teacher's instruction; and because oral reading serves simultaneously as practice for the child and a context for evaluation by the teacher. Two research reports, by Dickinson, Kozak, Nelson, and Epstein (1977) and Heap (1978, 1979) say more about these complexities.

Dickinson et al. described differences in single vs. multiple foci, and attendant differences in time spent off-task, in a math lesson and a reading group lesson with first grade children in a single K-1 classroom. In the math lesson, the children were individually manipulating attribute blocks into intersecting sets. There was a repeated and, therefore, predictable sequence of teacher directives about placement of the blocks, questions to the children about what they had done, and finally a concluding statement about what they had found out. In successive sequences, the two parts of each directive (e.g., "Place the blue blocks in this circle" and " Place the yellow blocks in this circle") were spoken with decreasing intervening time, and successive questions to the children elicited progressively more information. In the reading group, in contrast, there was more variation and less predictability in both the focus of attention and the interactional structure. The teacher asked individual children to take turns reading aloud, but talk about the book title, table of contents, page numbers, and capital vs. lower case letters was interspersed in seemingly unpatterned ways.

There were so many other differences between the two groups that no firm conclusions can be drawn—differences in activity, group size, and whether the group included all children present or only a subset. While the reading group was smaller, it did not include all the children in the room at the time and so was more subject to interruptions and divided teacher attention. It would take more controlled research to determine how much the interactional simplification of the math group alone contributed to the greater on-task engagement.

The possible instructional value of such interactional simplification is not a new idea. Some of the success of Distar may be due to this feature. Such simplification has also been advocated in a discussion of the design of Sesame Street (Gibbon, Palmer, and Fowles, 1975). A familiar example of holding the instructional frame constant while varying the content is the Sesame Street categorization game, "One of these things is not like the other." Gibbon et al. explain the reason for this design:

> Varying the content while keeping the format constant promotes familiarity with format conventions that are potentially useful for instructional purposes. The format of any program segment functions as a kind of "frame" for the instructional content, a complex of auditory and visual conventions that the child can master through repeated exposure. For example, the viewer can learn to expect that a particular format will usually deal with a particular category of stimulus (letter, word number, concept) and with a particular intellectual activity (memorizing, sorting or classifying, guessing, combining). A particular sequence of events or types of events will reliably occur; a particular type of feedback to the viewer's implicit or explicit responses will be delivered. Moreover, a viewer's familiarity with a given format can help him determine at what point in the presentation the important information will come, how much of it there will be, perhaps even whether it is likely to be too easy, too difficult, or about right for him. Among the main instructional advantages afforded by these various forms of cueing is that they will entice the viewing child to attend to what is new in each succeeding application of the format, since it will "stand out" against the familiar background more than if the entire presentation were novel. As a result, learning and concept formation are enhanced. (Gibbon, Palmer, and Fowles, 1975, pp. 225-226)

Reading groups as traditionally enacted in primary school classrooms are inherently complex in content and interactional structure because learning to read requires so many different kinds of learnings. We need interactional analyses of alternative organizations of reading events in which these learnings are separated or combined.

Heap (1978, 1979) is studying the "social organization of reading activities" in 20 classrooms. He has finished only one year of a five-year project, and so only preliminary reports are available. In these reports, he has identified three "social organizational problems" in primary grade reading instruction; two will be familiar to teachers, and all three raise important questions about the relationship between social organization and individual cognition.

The two familiar problems are problems in evaluating a child's response. On the one hand, a child's correct answer in a reading group lesson may be an artifact of other resources that the group provides. As Heap describes a specific example, "As a task organized to make reading skills observable and evaluable, the reading lesson provided an unforeseen resource, reading aloud, for a participant to continue to participate in the task" (Heap, 1979, p. 4) by answering comprehension questions even though her book had been closed. On the other hand, a child's reading errors may be due to obstacles created by that same reading group organization—for example, anxiety about the social performance of reading aloud in front of peers.

The third organizational problem is more complex. Here is Heap's example, from the comprehension section of a second grade reading group lesson after the first part of "Rumpelstiltskin" had been read:

Teacher No. Who helped Mineen?
Child   Rumpelstiltskin.
Teacher Yeah the little man. We don't know his name is Rumpelstiltskin yet do we?
         The little man. Okay, what was the first thing the prince said—sorry, that
         the girl gave to Rumpelstiltskin, to the little man. We better call him the
         little man because we don't know really he's Rumpelstiltskin yet. (Heap,
         1978, p. 2).

The story was titled "Rumpelstiltskin"; the teacher had written that name on the board as a new vocabulary word at the beginning of the lesson; and she knew that several of the children had seen a movie version of the story the previous year. Yet she still corrected the child, and self-corrected herself, from saying "Rumpelstiltskin" to the vaguer "little man." As Heap says, it is only true that "we don't know his name is Rumpelstiltskin yet" in a very special sense: within the limits of and the terms of a convention, a game, that disengages reading and answering questions about that reading from everything else the child knows, from everything outside the boundary of the text itself.

These "organizational problems" that Heap has described are not unique to reading groups. Any exercise of any cognitive process—for us, as for children—takes place in some context: of particular task format, physical conditions, social organization, conventional rules, etc.; and characteristics of that context will contribute either supports or obstacles to the cognitive tasks performed within it. Cognition is always in some context; and it can't be taught or evaluated apart from some particular context either. (I am indebted to Michael Cole for many conversations on this point.) Because of the importance of reading groups as a context for both instruction and evaluation in the primary grades, we need to examine that context—and the "games" we play within it—with particular care. Yet because reading groups are so traditional and so familiar, that examination is especially hard for participants to do for themselves. To complete the circle back to the first study by Hess and Takanishi reported at the beginning of this review, classroom teaching must be considered as a complex orchestration of social life in which diverse individual cognitive processes can most effectively be developed, and we need to understand teaching from both the social and the cognitive points of view.

Peer Group Interaction in the Older Grades

This review has focused on learning to read in the primary grades—partly because of my own interests and experiences as a teacher (Cazden, 1976) and researcher with younger children, partly because most of the recent sociolinguistic and ethnographic research has focused on the primary grades as the place where children are first inducted into the school "culture" and where their academic "identities" are first formed. I assume that classroom interactions are not less important for reading instructions in the intermediate and secondary grades, but that the relevance takes different forms. One important form is the relationship between the instructional process and interactions among peers.

Consider the implications of just one study: Labov's research on the relationships among the incidence of nonstandard Black English (BE) dialect features, peer group membership, and reading failure (Labov and Robins, 1969; Labov, in press). Labov and his colleagues analyzed the incidence of BE features in the speech of black adolescents in fourth through tenth grade, identified the speakers as either central or peripheral members of peer group in the street culture by sociometric interviews and participant observation, and then correlated these data with performance on standardized reading tests.

One linguistic indicator of BE dialect is saying *have* for *has* in the third singular present. Labov (in press) reports the frequency of the standard form *has*, and then comments on the group differences:

> ...club members used only 19 percent of the *has* form; the lames [isolates from the street culture] used 60 percent; and white working-class adolescents 100 percent.... These [dialect] differences are slight: they are small differences in the probability of a rule being applied. They reflect patterns of communication and ideology, but in no way could they be conceived of as the causes of differences in reading achievement.

Differences in reading achievement existed. All 46 club members, core participants in the street culture, reached a virtual plateau in reading achievement at the fifth grade level, while the 32 lames continued to progress, one-third of them at or above grade level. According to Labov, the dialect differences are not in themselves the cause of these reading problems; they are rather the indicators of group membership and of a value system that accompanies such membership that is in conflict with the school.

Support for Labov's argument comes from the co-occurrence of events around the fifth grade watershed year. This is the time when peer group formation differentiates members and lames in life on the street outside of school, and also differentiates their reading achievement within. More generally, fifth grade is the point at which, across the country, poor children's reading scores decline relative to their richer peers':

> A new state report [by the state legislative analyst's office] says the achievement gap between richer and poorer children in the California schools appears to be widening...[this decline] seems to be part of a national trend, with the decline beginning around the fifth grade and increasing later. (*Palo Alto Times*, 11/3/78)

While these reading achievement data are usually interpreted in terms of the changing character of reading texts and tasks in the intermediate grades, it seems probable that, for some students, value conflicts accentuate the problem.

The connection between this research and the focus of this review comes in Labov's (in press) discussion of possible remedies.

> The techniques of learning and studying imposed by our schools are avowedly individualistic and competitive. Each student is expected to learn by himself, and as I noted at the outset, interaction in the classroom is fundamentally confined to dealing directly with the teacher....
>
> The skills that are highly developed in vernacular culture depend upon a different strategy. Sports, formal and informal, depend upon close cooperation of groups. The same holds for music....Individuals practice by themselves, but the major steps in learning are done in tempo with the group....
>
> If we continue to repress vernacular culture, and try to extract one or two individuals from their cultural context, we will continue the pattern of massive educational failure that we now observe in the schools. The other route is to understand the interests and concerns of the youth who come to school and use that understanding in a positive way. (Labov, in press)

This "positive way" will have to make possible less individualistic ways of learning to read, so that the power of group interactions can be used directly as contexts for learning. (See Steinberg and Cazden, in press, for one report of peer teaching in an intermediate grade.) Unfortunately, in discussions of teaching, the term "classroom interaction" has become limited to interactions in which the teacher is involved. We need to expand its meaning back to include all interactions in which learning takes place—not only with the teacher, but among students as well.

REFERENCES

Allington, E.L. *Are good and poor readers taught differently? Is that why poor readers are poor readers?* Paper presented at the annual meeting of the American Educational Research Association, Toronto, March 1978.

Au, K.H. Using the experience-text-relationship method with minority children. *The Reading Teacher*, 1979, *32*, 677-679.

Au, K.H. *A test of the social organizational hypothesis: Relationships between participation structures and learning to read.* Unpublished doctoral dissertation, University of Illinois, in preparation.

Cazden, C.B. *Watching children watch "The Electric Company": An observational study in ten classrooms.* Final report to Children's Television Workshop, August 1973.

Cazden, C.B. How knowledge about language helps the classroom teacher—or does it: A personal account. *The Urban Review,* 1976, *9,* 74-90.

Chall, J., and Feldman, S. *A study in depth of first grade reading: Analysis of the interactions of proposed methods, teacher implementation and child background.* Cooperative Research Project No. 2728, U.S. Office of Education, 1966.

Clay, M.M. *Reading: The patterning of complex behavior.* Auckland, N.Z.: Heinemann, 1973.

Dickinson, D., Kozak, N., Nelson, E., and Epstein, M. *Examination of differences in the dynamics of small and large group instruction.* Unpublished term paper, Harvard Graduate School of Education, 1977.

Gibbon, S.Y., Jr., Palmer, E.L., and Fowles, B.R. Sesame Street, The Electric Company and reading. In J.B. Carroll and J.S. Chall (Eds.), *Toward a literate society.* New York: McGraw-Hill, 1975.

Griffin, P. How and when does reading occur in the classroom? *Theory into Practice,* 1977, *16,* 376-383.

Gumperz, J.J. Verbal strategies in multilingual communication. In *Georgetown University Round Table on Languages and Linguistics 1970.* Washington, D.C.: Georgetown University Press, 1972.

Heap, J.L. *Rumpelstiltskin: The organization of preference in a reading lesson.* Paper presented at the annual meeting of the Canadian Sociology and Anthropology Association, London, Ont., June 1978.

Heap, J.L. *The social organization of reading evaluation: Reasons for eclecticism.* Toronto: Ontario Institute for Studies in Education, April 1979.

Hess, R.D., and Takanishi, R. *The relationship of teacher behavior and school characteristics to student engagement* (Tech. Rep. No. 42). Stanford, Calif.: Stanford Center for Research and Development in Teaching, 1974.

Jordan, C., Weisner, T., Tharp, R.G., and Au, K.H. *A multidisciplinary approach to research in education: The Kamehameha Early Education Program* (Tech. Rep. No. 81). Honolulu: The Kamehameha Schools, 1978.

Labov, W. Competing value systems in the inner-city schools. In P. Gilmore and A. Glatthorn (Eds), *Ethnography and education: Children in and out of school.* Philadelphia: University of Pennsylvania Press, in press.

Labov, W., and Robins, C. A note on the relation of reading failure to peer-group status in urban ghettos. *The Teachers College Record,* 1969, *70,* 395-405.

McDermott, R.P. Pirandello in the classroom: On the possibility of equal educational opportunity in American culture. In M.C.Reynolds (Ed.), *Futures of exceptional children: Emerging structures.* Reston, Va.: Council for Exceptional Children, 1978.

Piestrup, A.M. *Black dialect interference and accommodation of reading instruction in first grade* (Monographs of the Language Behavior Research Laboratory No. 4). Berkeley: University of California, 1973.

Steinberg, Z., and Cazden, C.B. Children as teachers—of peers and ourselves. *Theory into practice,* in press.

NOTE
[1] These observations are part of a research project on "The social and cultural organization of interaction in classrooms of bilingual children," supported by NIE grant 780099 to Frederick Erickson and Courtney B. Cazden.

Anglo and Chicano Comprehension of Ethnic Stories

NANCY ROGERS-ZEGARRA
Wake Forest University

HARRY SINGER
University of California at Riverside

Reading comprehension consists of an interaction between text-based and reader-based information (Adams and Collins, 1977; Rumelhart, 1977). An hypothesis drawn from this interaction view of reading comprehension is that when texts reflect only the Anglo experience, Chicanos are at a disadvantage and vice versa. The purpose of this investigation was to test this hypothesis by assessing the comprehension of the two groups when (a) the text passages are drawn from both Anglo and Chicano experiences and (b) both groups are equated for general reading ability. More specifically, the hypothesis was tested that when Chicano students are equal in general reading ability to their Anglo peers, they have an advantage when assessed on inferences based on scriptal knowledge of Mexican-American culture and are at least equal when assessed on inferences based on scriptal knowledge of American culture. The reason the hypothesis may be tenable is that Chicanos participate in their own culture, of course, more so than Anglos do. However, Anglos, especially those in southern California, do become somewhat knowledgeable about Chicano culture. Therefore, they have some knowledge-base to draw upon for interacting with ethnic literature reflecting the Mexican-American culture. Chicanos also tend to experience the major cultural events in American culture as much as Anglos do and consequently have a knowledge-base for interacting with texts that is likely to equal Anglos when reading stories based on significant events in the general American culture.

Previous comparisons of Anglo and Chicano students' reading abilities have been based upon standardized reading achievement tests. These tests attempt to minimize or eliminate assessment of text- and reader-based interactions. They especially try to avoid asking scriptal questions in testing comprehension; scriptal questions require the reader to draw upon background knowledge and use it in

Reprinted from M.L. Kamil (Ed.), *Directions in Reading: Research and Instruction*. Washington, D.C.: The National Reading Conference, 1981, 205-210. Used with permission of the National Reading Conference and the authors.

interaction with text-based information to arrive at correct answers (Pearson and Johnson, 1978). Indeed, some reader-based knowledge is necessary in reading printed materials of any kind because all the information necessary for comprehending a text passage is not contained within a text. Those readers who cannot mobilize the missing information from their knowledge repertoire are at a disadvantage (Marshall, 1976). This knowledge repertoire consists of three types of information: scripts, which are culturally determined sequences of events (Schank and Abelson, 1977); propositions, which are statements about the world (Kintsch, 1974; Winograd, 1972); and semantic maps, which consist of a concept with its properties, hyponyms, superordinates, and relationships with other concepts or semantic maps (Pearson and Johnson, 1978).

Because of the interaction between text-based and reader-based information, assessment of comprehension can vary on a continuum from text-based to reader-based interactions. Consequently, there can be a band of acceptable responses to comprehension of passages (Tierney and Spiro, 1979; Tierney and LaZansky, 1980). Although the interaction between text and prior knowledge is always present, requirements for use of prior knowledge may change according to (1) type of information being used, (2) purpose in reading, and (3) differences in individuals' processing levels (Spiro, 1979). What makes the interaction evident are responses to scriptal questions. Therefore, in this study the variations were type of questions (literal, implicit, and scriptal), type of information being read (Anglo and Chicano ethnic stories), and hence the degree to which prior knowledge must be drawn upon to interact with text-based information in answering the comprehension questions. Research related to these types of comparisons will be briefly reviewed.

Review of Related Literature

Bartlett (1932) found that readers in England comprehended an American Indian folktale, "The War of the Ghosts," by modifying their recall and interpretation of events in the story so that the events gradually became more consistent with the schemata (knowledge structures) already present in the reader's background knowledge.

When readers come from different cultural backgrounds, they may interpret the same story differently at the time of initial comprehension. Steffenson, Joagdev, and Andersen (1978) reported that East Indians and Americans interpreted an East Indian and an American wedding ceremony according to their own cultural backgrounds.

Even when readers come from the same cultural background, it is possible for them to interpret passages differently, depending on which high-level schemata are activated, as Pichert and Anderson (1977) and Anderson and Pichert (1978) demonstrated when they gave different perspectives to randomly selected college students, a "house buyer" perspective to one group and a "burglar" perspective to the other group.

Spontaneous selective storage of information from a text is likely to differ during learning sessions when individuals vary in their belief systems, as Levine and Murphy (1943) discovered. They had college students with pro- and anti-communistic social philosophies read the same passage dealing with the Soviet Union. The students read and reproduced the same passage twice over a time span varying from 15 minutes to 4 weeks. The rate of learning the anti-Soviet passage was greater for the anti-communistic students, but the decline in rate of retention for the different amounts of information each group had learned was about the same for both groups when tested weekly over a five-week period.

Since cultures are not homogeneous, even within a nation, groups of individuals can be identified whose perspectives on issues and events will vary considerably. Consequently, their scriptal or reader-based comprehension of the same passage will differ. One such contrast is urban versus rural children. Reynolds, Taylor, Steffenson, Shirey, and Anderson (1980) found that at the eighth grade level differences in comprehension of urban students, white and black, when compared with rural white students were related to variation in the students' background knowledge for a story. Goodman (1978) also concluded that variation in prior knowledge and experience accounted for differences in reading comprehension of groups of elementary school children who were non-native and dialectal speakers drawn from four different cultural backgrounds.

Cultural differences can occur not only for interpretation of stories, but also for particular words. These variations in interpretation can have dramatic effects in everyday life. For example, Chicanos interpreted medical benefits for the "family" as including not only the nuclear but also the extended family. Consequently, their extended family showed up for medical treatment, which led their employers to a hasty modification of the wording of the contract for medical benefits. Thus, some of the differences in reading comprehension between Chicanos and their Anglo peers, even for text-based literal and inferential comprehension, can be attributed to differences in cultural perspectives and background knowledge.

But none of the cross-cultural studies reviewed here equated the comparison groups on general reading ability. Moreover, none of the studies attempted to determine whether the two comparison groups were equal in text-based literal and inferential comprehension. These methodological limitations were rectified in the design of this study.

Experimental Design

Independent Measures

A total of 173 students, consisting of two ethnic groups, Anglos and Chicanos, drawn from grades 5 and 8 from four schools located in Riverside, California, participated in the study. Two grade levels were used because students' background knowledge of American and Mexican-American cultures should improve with age. Moreover, the older students, Anglo and Chicano, should have a greater degree of knowledge about *both* cultures.

At each grade level, each of the two ethnic groups was equated on standardized tests of reading achievement. Since the standardized reading tests emphasize text-based literal and implicit types of comprehension, the two groups should be equal when assessed on literal and implicit types of comprehension for ethnic stories. Each group was then further subdivided into two groups of readers: high (two years on the average above grade level) and low (two years on the average below grade level).

Since previous research has shown that students from higher socioeconomic backgrounds perform better on comprehension tests, the readers were also classified according to two socioeconomic levels on the occupational index, high (professionals) versus low (nonprofessionals).

Thus, the study employed a 2 x 2 x 2 x 2 experimental design. It consisted of two ethnic groups (Anglos versus Chicanos), two grade levels (5 and 8), two reading levels (high versus low), and two socioeconomic levels (high versus low).[1]

Dependent Measures

Thirty-six multiple-choice questions were constructed for three levels of comprehension, following Pearson and Johnson's criteria (1978). Answers to the literal questions are provided in the story. Answers to the implicit questions can be inferred from text-based information. However, the scriptal questions require the reader to use prior knowledge in interaction with text-based information in order to arrive at correct answers. Thus, there were three dependent measures, consisting of twelve comprehension questions for each type of comprehension. These questions were equally divided among the two types of ethnic stories.

Materials: Ethnic Stories

Twelve stories were written, six based on Mexican culture and six on Anglo culture. The Mexican culture stories concerned holidays and customs unique to Mexican-Americans in the Southwestern United States (eg., Las Posadas or El dia de los Muertos). The Anglo stories dealt mainly with holidays or customs unique to North American Anglo life (e.g., the Fourth of July celebration and April Fool's Day).

All of the stories were written at approximately an equal level of difficulty. The range of readability varied from the fourth grade to the seventh grade level of difficulty as assessed by the Fry readability formula. This range of variation is within the formula's standard error of measurement. The stories ranged in length from 250 to 1,000 words, but were balanced for length for both groups.

Four adult representatives, two Anglos and two Chicanos, rated the stories for ethnic content. Each pair of raters agreed that the stories consisted of content that was familiar.

Procedure. All the stories were read aloud to the students. Each student also had a copy of each story and therefore could follow along, reading silently. Thus, any word recognition difficulties were minimized, while comprehension was maximized (Goldstein, 1940).

Results

For *literal questions*, the analysis of variance was significant only for reading level ($F = 31.97$, df 1,157, $p < .001$). The better readers at both grade levels were superior at recalling or locating information directly stated in the text.

For *implicit questions*, significant differences were found for grade ($F = 25.07$, df 1,157, $p < .001$) and reading level ($F = 25.29$, df 1,157, $p < .001$). These results were also expected because older students are generally better in recalling information and at making inferences from text-based information.

For *scriptal questions*, the results were again significant for grade ($F = 19.16$, df 1,157, $p < .001$) and reading levels ($F = 12.73$, df 1,157, $p < .001$). The older and better readers were not only superior in drawing inferences, but also had greater background knowledge to draw upon for answering scriptal questions. However, a trend for ethnicity ($F = 2.70$, df 1,157, $p = .10$) and a trend toward interaction ($F = 3.72$, df 1,157, $p < .056$) for ethnicity and reader level occurred. The better readers among the Chicano students, regardless of grade level, had significantly higher scriptal comprehension for text involving content based on Chicano culture than did the Anglo high and low readers and the Chicano low readers. Chicano students also performed as well as Anglos on scriptal questions for Anglo literature. These results indicate that the Chicanos have bicultural knowledge to draw upon in reading either type of literature. This knowledge is superior to Anglos for answering scriptural questions on the Chicano literature and equal to Anglos for answering questions on the Anglo literature.

Socioeconomic level was not statistically significant in any of the analyses, probably because equating the groups on reading level and using professional level as a dividing point for high versus low socio-economic levels washed out differences attributable to socioeconomic levels.

Summary and Implications

The results of this study indicated that when Chicanos and Anglos from grades 5 and 8 are matched on general reading ability as assessed by standardized tests the older and better readers from both ethnic groups were significantly better than the younger readers on all types of comprehension. Within each grade level, the Chicanos were equal to the Anglos on text-based literal and implicit types of comprehension, but the Chicanos, and particularly the better readers among the Chicanos across grade levels, were superior to the Anglos on scriptal questions for Anglo-based stories.

This study indicates that in order to have a comprehensive assessment of reading ability, it is necessary to measure all three types of comprehension: literal, implicit, and scriptal. The study also demonstrates the importance of assessing students on different types of ethnic literature because when Chicanos are equated with Anglos on general reading ability, those students with a bicultural background tend to perform as well on text-based comprehension and can exhibit their advantage in text- and reader-based interactions over their Anglo peers for Chicano-based literature. At the same time, Anglos who have the opportunity to read multiethnic literature and participate in the non-Anglo culture also tend to expand their background knowledge and are better able to answer scriptal questions, as shown by the better performance of the older over the younger students for both types of literature. This expansion occurs in Southern California where events for both Anglo and Chicano cultures are celebrated in the schools and in the community. Thus, both groups benefit from development of bicultural schemata in many ways and particularly in comprehension of Anglo and Chicano ethnic stories.

REFERENCES

Adams, M.J., and Collins, A. *A schema-theoretic view of reading*. Technical Report No.32. Urbana, Illinois: Center for the Study of Reading, University of Illinois, 1977.

Anderson, R.C., and Pichert, J.W. Recall of previously unrecallable information following a shift in perspective. *Journal of Verbal Learning and Verbal Behavior*, 1978, 17, 1-12.

Bartlett, F.C. *Remembering*. Cambridge: University Press, 1932.

Goldstein, H. *Reading and listening comprehension at various controlled rates*. Teachers College Contributions to Education, No. 821. New York: Bureau of Publications, Columbia University, 1940.

Goodman, K.S. *Reading of American children whose language is a stable rural dialect of English or a language other than English*. Final Report. Washington, DC: National Institute of Education, U.S. Department of Health, Education and Welfare, 1978.

Joag-dev, C., and Steffensen, M.S. *Studies of the bicultural reader: Implications for teachers and librarians*. Reading Education Report No. 12. Urbana, Illinois: Center for the Study of Reading, University of Illinois, 1980.

Kintsch, W. *The representation of meaning in memory*. Hillsdale, New Jersey: Erlbaum-Wiley, 1974.

Levine, J.M., and Murphy, G. The learning and forgetting of controversial material. *Journal of Abnormal and Social Psychology*, 1943, 38, 507-517.

Marshall, N. *The structure of semantic memory for text*. Unpublished doctoral dissertation, Cornell University, 1976.

Pearson, P.D., and Johnson, D.D. *Teaching reading comprehension*. New York: Holt, Rinehart and Winston, 1978.

Pichert, J.W., and Anderson, R.C. Taking different perspectives on a story. *Journal of Educational Psychology*, 1977, 69, 309-315.

Reynolds, R., Taylor, M., Steffensen, M.S., Shirey, L., and Anderson, R.C. *A study of the effect of cultural knowledge on reading comprehension: A comparison of black and white.* Urbana, Illinois: Center for the Study of Reading, University of Illinois, 1980.

Rogers-Zegarra, N. *Anglo and Chicano literal, implicit and scriptal comprehension of ethnic stories.* Doctoral dissertation, University of California, 1981.

Rumelhart, D.E. Toward an interactive model of reading. In S. Dornic (Ed.), *Attention and performance VI.* Hillsdale, New Jersey: Erlbaum, 1977.

Schank, R.C., and R.P. Abelson. *Scripts, plans, goals, and understandings.* Hillsdale, New Jersey: Erlbaum, 1977.

Spiro, R. *Prior knowledge and story processing: Integration, Selection, and Variation.* Technical Report No. 138. Urbana, Illinois: Center for the Study of Reading, University of Illinois, 1979.

Steffensen, M.S., Joag-dev, C., and Anderson, R.C. *A cross-cultural perspective on reading comprehension.* Technical Report No. 97. Urbana, Illinois: Center for the Study of Reading, University of Illinois, 1978.

Tierney, R.J. and LaZansky, J. The rights and responsibilities of readers and writers: A contracted agreement. *Language Arts*, 1980, 57, 606-613.

Tierney, R.J., and Spiro, R.J. Some basic notions about reading comprehension: Implications for teachers. In J. Harste and R.F. Carey (Eds.), *New perspectives on comprehension.* Monograph No. 3 in Language and Arts Series. Bloomington, Indiana, 1979.

Winograd, T. Understanding natural language. *Cognitive Psychology,* 1972, 3 (whole issue).

NOTE

[1] The data used in this report are part of the information collected for a more detailed investigation (Rogers-Zegarra, 1981).

Section Three

MODELS OF READING

Introduction to Models of Reading

We have selected six types of models for this section: developmental, information processing, interactive, inferential, transactional-psycholinguistic, and affective. In this introduction, we shall explain definitions of *theories* and *models*, criteria for evaluating them, and ways to gain insight into their structures, dynamics, and utility. Throughout this introduction, we will draw examples from the theories and models to be presented in this section.

Definitions

Although the terms *theories* and *models* are used interchangeably, they are not identical. A theory is an explanation for a phenomenon, such as reading. A model is a way of depicting a theory's variables, mechanisms, constructs, and their interrelationships. A theory is dynamic, that is, it describes the way in which a model operates; for example, how an individual processes print or attains a product, such as comprehension. Although it is possible to design models with moving parts or create filmed versions of models in operation, models are usually depicted statically, a momentary view of a dynamic process. Consequently, it is necessary to understand how a model works.

Evaluation of Theories and Models

Theories and models should first be understood in relationship to their *purposes,* i.e., what they are trying to accomplish, and then judged on how adequately they have accomplished it. For example, substrata-factor theory's purpose is to explain how individuals attain speed and/or power of reading: they organize and reorganize hierarchically interrelated factors at several substrata levels according to their changing purposes and the demands of the reading task. This explanation is based on the assumption that the mind is capable of this type of organization and dynamic interaction.[1] The models for the theory attempt to account for individual differences in speed and/or power of reading and show how an average individual's substrata factors could be organized to attain it. The question then is whether the models serve the purposes of the theory and represent an organization of factors that account for individual differences in reading ability at particular grade levels.

Another example: Gough's information processing model attempts to explain the sequence of mechanisms and processes that information progresses through in a reader from first seeing the printed stimulus phrase, "one second of reading," to oral encoding or uttering the phrase aloud. Gough's purpose in constructing this model was to integrate evidence from a multitude of research studies on how information is processed and the mechanisms that have to be postulated to account for the processing. An assumption made in information processing research is that reaction time is an index to the location of a mechanism; a longer reaction time indicates that a mechanism occurs later in a sequence. This assumption underlies the construction of linear models. Although Gough's information processing model does not represent interactions among the mechanisms and processes, it does represent the research on the mechanisms involved in reading. It also highlights the mechanisms that still need to be discovered. Hence, his model has didactic and heuristic value.[2]

Explanation: Theories and models should be tested to determine whether they explain how an individual perceives a word, processes a sentence, and comprehends both narrative and expository prose. If they cannot explain the processing of one or more of these constituents of printed materials, then we would judge they were not an *adequate* or *comprehensive* theory or model of reading. For example, automaticity theory explains conditions under which attention can be allocated to comprehension, not how comprehension itself is attained.

Even if a theory or model only purports to apply to a part of written communication, we would expect to make *predictions* from it on how individuals respond to print. For example, Rumelhart's interactive model of reading would predict that recognition of words in context would activate perceptual, syntactic, and semantic processes simultaneously, while recognition of words in isolation would not activate semantic or syntactic processes, unless the reader provided his own contextual elaboration. In short, Rumelhart's interactive model assumes that all the processes can act on text simultaneously; they can also mutually and reciprocally interact with each other and with cues in the text.

We also expect theories and models to be *internally consistent,* that is, not self-contradictory. Ruddell and Speaker's knowledge utilization and control model involves interaction between the reader and the text. For example, their model explains that the text interacts with the reader's knowledge sources through his control mechanisms to arrive at a text representation or meaning for the text. If their model were to explain that text representation occurs in a linear sequence, it would be self-contradictory.

A theory should be *productive,* that is, it should generate hypotheses that will explain new phenomena. Van Dijk and Kintsch's theory and model for comprehending and recalling stories explain that readers use the macrostructures, the higher level knowledge structures of stories, such as *theme, complication,* and *resolution,* that inform the reader about the story or discourse as a whole, and omit the microstructures, the supporting propositions, in summarizing a story. If the macrostructure of a story is missing because it has been intentionally omitted from the text, as Bransford and Johnson did in their experimental work, then individuals will find it most difficult to even comprehend the story; and, of course, they could not summarize it without knowing or being able to construct its macrostructure.[3]

If hypotheses drawn from a theory have been confirmed or found to be tenable, the *weight of the evidence* provides support for and creates confidence in the theory. For example, Goodman has demonstrated that oral responses which depart from those expected from text data can be attributed to expectancies in the reader, either stimulated by previous information in the text or by the direction taken by the reader's thought processes; thus, he has adduced evidence that supports his view that these responses are not errors, but are *miscues* made by the reader in search of meaning. Mathewson's affective model is based on an experiment that indicates attitudes are related to reading comprehension. The point we want to emphasize is that we should ask whether a theory or model has evidence to support it.

Note that the type of evidence used to support a theory or construct a model varies considerably. Substrata-factor theory relies on statistical analysis of test variables; hence, its statistical models can also be called psychometric models.[4] Gough uses laboratory evidence, particularly reaction time data. Goodman analyzes miscues. Schema theorists manipulate narratives and obtain recall protocols from which they make inferences that confirm hypotheses drawn from their theories and models. In short, the evidence adduced for support tends to focus on different stimulus tasks, from letters to connected discourse, and different response outputs, from reaction times to printed words to delayed recall of narratives.[5]

Why do theorists utilize different methods for testing hypotheses about their theories or models? Because they are trying to explain different aspects of reading. Substrata-factor theorists ask this question: What factors account for individual differences in speed and power of reading? Information theorists want to know what sequence, processes, and mechanisms must be postulated to account for research data, particularly in word recognition, and whether attention is allocated to word recognition or comprehension processes. Interaction theorists want to know whether knowledge sources (semantics, syntax, lexical, and orthographic knowledge) operate in parallel and in compensatory ways.[6] Activation schema theorists want to know how the reader's schema (knowledge structures) and perspectives are activated and instantiated. Discourse processing theorists want to know how text data are organized and represented in memory, and how such sources of knowledge as sensory information, episodic memory, control processes, and long term memory affect the construction and retrieval of information.[7] Knowledge utilization and control theorists and affective theorists want to know the factors that determine what an individual will want to read and remember.

If hypotheses cannot be deduced from a theory or if there is no way of falsifying a theory's hypotheses, that is, empirically testing them and finding they may not be tenable, then the theory is not a *scientific theory*. This criterion also requires that theories be *communicable* and *objective*. That is, other researchers should be able to comprehend and test their hypotheses, not just the formulators of the theory.

Insight into Theories and Models

Theories and models can be systematically analyzed to find out what they are and how they work by applying a series of questions to them. As an example, we will apply these questions to LaBerge and Samuel's automaticity theory and model.

1. *What does the theory assume?* Automaticity theory assumes that attention is basic and necessary to information processing, it is finite, and it is susceptible to allocation by the reader. If attention is focused during reading entirely on word recognition processes, then the reader is not likely to comprehend the text. Conversely, if processes of word recognition are automatic or require minimal attention, then attention can be allocated maximally to comprehension processes.

2. *What is the model's structure or components?* The model consists of a sequence of three memory components: visual, primary, and semantic, plus an episodic memory (memory for events that have occurred, marked with time and place), and an attention allocation mechanism. The 1973 model was modified by adding feedback loops from semantic memory to visual and primary memory to account for the effect that context (semantics and syntax) have upon perception of printed words, e.g., *read* (present tense) and *read* (past tense) can only be properly pronounced when their syntactic properties are known. Words are also perceived more rapidly when the meaning of the word can be inferred from the context, e.g., *The car raced down the* __ __ __ __ .

3. *How does the model work?* The model explains attention allocation in the following way: If most attention is required for perception of print, a reader will not be able to attend to processes of comprehension, such as making inferences and interpretations; skilled readers can perceive print with minimal attention and hence can give maximal attention to comprehension processes.

4. *What is its utility?* The theory implies that if students are taught to perceive not only accurately, but beyond accuracy to automaticity, their comprehension is likely to improve.

5. *What are its limitations?* The theory and model emphasize word recognition; little explanation is provided on how comprehension is attained.

These questions should be applied to each theory and model. Then the theories and models should be compared for their similarities and differences to gain further understanding of them. One comparison can focus on the constructs, concepts, or terms used by two theories, such as substrata-factor and schema-interaction theories. For example, we can ask: Is a *substrata-factor* different from a *schema? Hierarchical structure* from *embedded schema? Mobilization* from *activation?* A *working system* from *activated schemata? Substrata factors mobilized in response to the reader's purposes and demands of the text* from *text and reader interactions? Mobilization of multiple and correlated factors* from *simultaneous and mutual interaction of processes?* Concepts from other pairs of theories can also be compared. Is *knowledge utilization* different from *activation of a schema to subsume information?* Or is a *transaction* different from *construction of meaning?*

Another comparison can examine the structures of models, their variables and their interrelationships. How do their structural differences affect their explanations of processing of printed stimuli? For example, compare interactive with linear models. The interactive models with their simultaneous processing of print at more than one level can better explain why an individual can achieve an interpretation of a sentence as soon as he gets to the end of it; linear processing models, such as Gough's, would require more processing time after the last printed stimulus has been taken into the reader's icon—at least one more second.

Comparisons can also be made on the dynamics or explanations of how models work:

1. Substrata-factor theory: Readers organize substrata factors (knowledge structures) into a working system for solving a problem in reading, such as recognizing a word, getting a word meaning, or reasoning in reading. Readers can reorganize their substrata-factors into other working systems at one level or another as their purposes or the demands of the task change. Thus, the working system is a momentary organization of knowledge structures in response to the changing purposes of the reader and the demands of the reading task.

2. Information processing models: Readers perceive and comprehend by processing information through a sequence of mechanisms and memory stores until the information is understood and stored in long term memory.

3. Schema-interaction theory: Readers activate schema at the orthographic, lexical, syntactic, and semantic levels for subsuming text data; these knowledge sources act simultaneously on text and in mutual interaction with each other. Comprehension occurs when slots in a schema or script are instantiated.[8]

4. Knowledge utilization and control theorists: The reader's affective system arouses attention to print and leads a reader to use his knowledge utilization and control mechanisms to effect an interaction between text input and knowledge sources that results in text representation, the meaning for a text.

5. Inferential model: Propositions in a text and, if necessary, inferred propositions to attain referential coherence are organized according to the reader's goal (in the form of a schema). The schema controls the macro-operators that transform the textbase into an hierarchical structure of macropropositions that represent the gist of the text and determine which micropropositions are relevant to the gist. This representation, stored in long term memory, is the reader's comprehension of the text.[9]

6. Affective model: The reader's attitudes, motives, affect, and physical feelings lead to a decision to read, which, in turn, influences the reader's primary and secondary reading processes resulting in the construction of meaning. The output of the primary and secondary processes may via a feedback route arouse curiosity for further reading. But, if a negative attitude toward the content has arisen, or if satiation has occurred, or if the reader's curiosity has been satisfied, the feedback will terminate reading.

A more personal way of evaluating theories or models is to ask whether they explain how you yourself read different types of material, at different levels of difficulty, and for different purposes.[10]

Summary

Evaluate a theory and its model(s) according to their purposes and their ability to satisfy these formal criteria: explanatory power, adequacy or comprehensiveness, predictiveness, internal consistency, objectivity and communicability, supporting evidence, utility, heuristic value, and susceptibility to self-correction. To understand a theory or model, determine its assumptions, structure, dynamics, utility, and limitations. Also compare the theories and models on their concepts, structures, explanations, and usefulness.

Test Questions

To test the explanatory power and comprehensiveness of theories and models, ask how they explain the following reading phenomena:

1. Acquisition of reading, including word identification, word meaning, and reasoning during the process of reading.

2. Processes of decoding (narrowly construed as *word recognition*, not as communication theory's broadly construed meaning of decoding as *comprehension*); recoding (only transforming information from the printed to the oral code without any attempt at constructing meaning); arriving at the meaning of a passage; organizing and storing information in memory; retrieving information from long term memory; encoding (transforming information into the reader's internal code) and mechanisms for oral output.

3. The mechanisms or processes involved in directing, monitoring, testing, and evaluating any aspect of reading, including word identification, word meaning, and comprehension, and making self-corrections.

4. How new knowledge is acquired or learned from text.

5. How affective, cognitive, and perceptual processes interact in response to the reader's changing purposes and demands of the text.

6. What readers do to attain comprehension. For example, compare the concepts of "extracting information from text" with "mobilizing a working system to solve a problem," or "constructing meaning for a text," or "instantiating slots in a schema or script."

7. What change(s) occurs in a model when a reader's purpose shifts from reading relatively easy material rapidly to reading difficult material slowly and more analytically. Or, from familiar to unfamiliar word meanings. Or, from words that are readily identifiable at sight to unfamiliar words that require other word identification processes. Or, from one type of content to another.

8. How skilled readers differ from beginning readers in processing text.

9. How you read and comprehend. Take these aspects of text: a word, sentence, or longer unit of discourse, such as a story; see if you can use the theories or models to explain how to process them.

10. Why individual students have difficulty in comprehending text. In other words, do the theories provide pedagogical insights? What implications for diagnosis and improvement of reading can be gleaned from the theories and models?

What guidance do they provide for instruction in word identification, word meaning, and comprehension?

We could not include all the theories, models, and research on reading in this text. The following are additional significant contributions which deserve careful examination.

RELATED REFERENCES

Richard C. Anderson, Jean Osborn, and Robert J. Tierney. *Learning to Read in American Schools: Basal Readers and Content Texts.* Hillsdale, NJ: Erlbaum, 1984.
Critical analysis of instructional texts, including basal readers, workbooks, and content area text books.
Fred Davis (Ed.). *Literature of Research in Reading with Emphasis on Models.* Targeted Research and Development Program in Reading. Report No. 2. U.S. Department of Health, Education, and Welfare. Washington, DC: Contract No. OEC-0-70-4790 (508), Project No. 0-9030, 1971.
The result of a year long review of the literature, this volume contains papers on language development, learning to read, and models related to the reading process.
Robert de Beaugrande. Design criteria for process models of comprehension. *Reading Research Quarterly*, 1981, 16, 261-315.
Establishes criteria for comparing models.
Lance M. Gentile, Michael L. Kamil, and Jay S. Blanchard (Eds.), *Reading Research Revisited.* Columbus, Ohio: Charles Merrill, 1983.
Critical review of classical theories and research.
Arthur C. Graesser. *Prose Comprehension Beyond the Word.* New York: Springer-Verlag, 1981.
Presents a schema-based framework for exploring comprehension and knowledge representation, with an emphasis on a schema pointer plus tag model of prose memory.
Leon Henderson. *Orthography and Word Recognition in Reading.* New York: Academic Press, 1982.
Description of writing systems and evaluation of English orthography, strategies for pronouncing printed words, and visual word recognition, including letter-mediated and holistic models of word recognition.
James Kavanagh and Ignatius Mattingly (Eds.). *Language by Ear and by Eye.* Cambridge, MA: MIT Press, 1973.
Chapters are on linguistic theory, writing systems, speech perception, auditory processing of speech, component processes in reading, and an information processing model (Philip Gough's model, reprinted in this section).
James F. Kavanagh and Richard L. Venezky. *Orthography, Reading, and Dyslexia.* Baltimore, MD: University Park Press, 1980.
Examines cross-national studies of orthography and reading, design and improvement of orthographies and literary program, orthographies in initial stages of the reading process, orthography in skilled reading, and dyslexia.
David E. Kieras and Marcel A. Just. *New Methods in Reading Comprehension Research.* Hillsdale, NJ: Erlbaum, 1984.
Methods for investigating comprehension, includes multiple regression, word-by-word reading, subject-paced reading tasks, rapid serial visual presentation, priming and on-line comprehension, eye-movements, thinking-out loud, naturalistic observation and interviews, and computer modeling.
David LaBerge and S. Jay Samuels (Eds.). *Basic Processes in Reading: Perception and Comprehension.* Hillsdale, NJ: Erlbaum, 1977.
Proceedings of a conference that included topics on perception and memory (W.K. Estes), neural models (J.A. Anderson), models of word identification (N.F. Johnson), information processing in vision (W. Schneider and R.M. Schiffrin), perception (E.J. Gibson), understanding and summarizing brief stories (D.E. Rumelhart), mechanisms for pronouncing words (J. Baron), integration processes in comprehension (P.A. Carpenter and M.A. Just), inferences in comprehension (H.H. Clark), and computer simulation of language acquisition systems (D.R. Anderson).

Harry Levin and Eleanor Gibson. *The Psychology of Reading.* Cambridge, MA: MIT Press, 1975.
Levin and Gibson review research and critically analyze several information processing models. They challenge the theoretical position that the fluent reader predicts and confirms prediction by sampling print; they ask such critical questions as, what specifically does the reader predict? How does the reader know what to sample and where to search for information to confirm or disconfirm predictions? Rejecting attempts to construct *the* model of *the* reading process, Levin and Gibson prefer to stress these principles of reading: reading involves selection of word features, active strategies, and economy in processing by reducing alternatives. The Levin-Gibson concept of "reduction of alternatives" raises these questions: What are the alternatives? How does the reader decide on what alternatives to act upon? What test is used by the reader to determine whether the alternative selected is appropriate?

Jean M. Mandler. *Stories, Scripts, and Scenes: Aspects of Schema Theory.* Hillsdale, NJ: Erlbaum, 1984.
Explains types of mental structures, story schemas and processing, and scripts and scenes.

Wayne Otto and Sandra White (Eds.). *Reading Expository Material.* New York: Academic Press, 1982.
Proceedings of a conference that focused on the reader, the text, interaction of the reader with the text, classroom implications, and the role of the teacher in developing comprehension of expository text.

P. David Pearson (Ed.). *Handbook of Reading Research.* New York: Longman, 1984.
Contains some 4,000 references on methodological issues, processes of reading, and instructional practices. One chapter is on models of the reading process.

Keith Rayner (Ed.). *Eye-Movements in Reading.* New York: Academic Press, 1983.
Book is divided into seven sections: 1) Eye movements and psychophysical processes (Chapters by Bruno G. Breitmeyer, Robert E. Morrison, Gary S. Wolverton and David Zola, and Paul A. Kolers); 2) eye movements and perceptual processes (George W. McConkie, Keith Rayner, J. Kevin O'Regan, and Arnold D. Well); 3) eye movements and context effects (Wayne L. Shebilske and Dennis Fisher, Albrecht W. Inhoff, Susan F. Ehrlich, Philip B. Gough); 4) eye movements and language processes (Lyn Frazier, Alan Kennedy, Kate Ehrlich, Charles Clifton, Jr.); 5) eye movements and language and language processes (Patricia A. Carpenter and Marcel Adam Just, Thomas W. Hogaboam, Rheingold Kliegl, and Richard K. Olson and Brian J. Davidson, Maria L. Slowiaczek); 6) eye movements in picture processing and visual search (Geoffrey R. Loftus, Calvin F. Nodine, Jonathan Vaughan, Mary C. Potter); and 7) eye movements and dyslexia (George T. Pavlidis, Richard K. Olson and Reinhold Kliegl and Brian J. Davidson, Ashby Jones and Lawrence Stark, Francis J. Pirozzolo, and Alexander Pollatsek).

S. Jay Samuels and Michael L. Kamil. Models of the reading process. In P.D. Pearson (Ed.), *Handbook of Research on Reading.* New York: Longman, 1984.
Summarizes and critically reviews models of reading.

Harry Singer. Theoretical models of reading: Implications for teaching and research. In H. Singer and R.B. Ruddell (Eds.), *Theoretical Models and Processes of Reading,* first edition. Newark, DE: International Reading Association, 1970.
Singer briefly reviews models organized under the categories of a) teaching, b) processing, and c) skills types of models. He finds that some models deal with only part of the reading process (perceptual, cognitive, neurological), while others are intended to be comprehensive. After discussing implications of models for research and teaching, he suggests variables, processes, and cultural contexts that need to be included in a comprehensive model of reading.

Rand J. Spiro, Bertram C. Bruce, and W.F. Brewer. *Theoretical Issues in Reading Comprehension.* Hillsdale, NJ: Erlbaum, 1980.
Theoretical issues in schema theory, text structures, language and knowledge of the world, inference, and comprehension strategies.

Keith E. Stanovich. Toward an interactive-compensatory model of individual differences in the development of reading fluency. *Reading Research Quarterly,* 1980, 16, 32-71.
Adduces evidence that top-down and bottom-up processing is not necessarily sequential. Any process or set of processes can compensate for deficiencies in any other process or processes.

Thomas G. Sticht, Lawrence J. Beck, Robert N. Hauke, Glenn M. Kleiman, and James H. James. *Auding and Reading: A Developmental Model.* Alexandria, VA: Human Resources Research Organization, 1974.

This model depicts four developmental stages in which cognitive developmental processes interact with environmental factors and an individual's basic adaptive processes to result in languaging, which includes oracy (auding and speaking) and literacy (reading and writing).

Ovid J.L. Tzeng and Harry Singer. *Perception of Print: Reading Research in Experimental Psychology.* Hillsdale, NJ: Erlbaum, 1981.

Contains models on word perception, plus two chapters on teaching word recognition and an eclectic model for reading instruction from preschool through high school.

Teun A. van Dijk and Walter Kintsch. *Strategies of Discourse Comprehension.* New York: Academic Press, 1983.

Van Dijk and Kintsch summarize their strategic, process oriented model in the following way: "The theory assumes that a verbal input is decoded into a list of atomic propositions [words] which are organized into larger units on the basis of some knowledge structure to form a coherent text base. From this text base a macrostructure is constructed which represents the most essential information in the text base. Not only the comprehender's knowledge, but also beliefs and goals play a crucial role in this process. In parallel with this hierarchical textbase a situation model is elaborated which integrates the comprehender's existing world knowledge with the information derived from the text that is being processed. Thus, the end product of comprehension is a multilevel processing record, which includes memory traces of the actual linguistic input, of the meaning of the text both at a local and global level, and of the effect the text had on the comprehender's world knowledge" (p. x).

NOTES

[1] See Jack A. Holmes. Basic assumptions underlying the substrata-factor theory. *Reading Research Quarterly,* 1965, 1, 5-27. After critical review of other statistical models and their neurological assumptions, Holmes explains a neurological model that is assumed by his own statistical model for reading.

[2] An updated but only summary version of this model can be found in Philip B. Gough and Michael J. Cosky, "One Second of Reading Again," in N.J. Castellan, D.B. Pison and G.R. Potts (Eds.), *Cognitive Theory,* Vol. 2. Hillsdale, N.J.: Erlbaum, 1977. In the review of research for the first model, Gough concluded that print is processed letter-by-letter. In this updated review, Gough and Cosky conclude, "...while there is evidence that is difficult to reconcile with the view that we read words by reading their letters, there is evidence that is hard to explain otherwise. In the end, we are caught in the middle" (p. 287). Also, see Gough's "One Second of Reading: Postscript," in this volume.

[3] See Richard Anderson's article on schema activation theory, this volume, for a summary and analysis of the Bransford and Johnson experiment. Also see Anderson's strong and weak forms of schema activation theory: "Some reflections on the acquisition of knowledge." *Educational Researcher,* 1984, 13 (9), 5-10.

[4] S. Jay Samuels and Michael L. Kamil in their chapter on "Models of Reading," in P.D. Pearson (Ed.), *Handbook of Reading Research,* listed in the references to this section, point out that the substrata factor model is a developmental *and* a psychometric model.

[5] See last article in this volume by Harry Singer on principles and pitfalls in conducting research on comprehension. Also see annotated reference to David Kieras and Marcel Just, this section, for methods of investigating comprehension.

[6] See Keith E. Stanovich. Toward an interactive-compensatory model of individual differences in the development of reading fluency. *Reading Research Quarterly,* 1980, 16, 32-71. Stanovich has postulated that knowledge sources do not act in a sequence from top-down (semantics to orthographic knowledge) or vice-versa, from bottom up. Instead any knowledge source can compensate for any other knowledge source, that is, semantic and syntactic knowledge sources (context) can facilitate or compensate for deficiencies in word identification, or word identification processes can compensate for lack of contextual facilitation or even for incongruous or misleading text.

[7] For an up-dated version of this model, see Teun A. van Dijk and Walter Kintsch. *Strategies of Discourse Comprehension.* New York: Academic Press, 1983. Van Dijk and Kintsch postulate that in parallel with the construction of an hierarchical textbase, the reader creates or updates a situational model, which consists of a combination of episodic and instantiated general information from semantic memory.

[8] See Marilyn J. Adams and Allan Collins's selection, "A schema-theoretic view of reading," this volume; their selection consists of an implicit model of text-data interacting with reader resources (letters, word parts, lexical, syntactic, semantic, and interpretive levels) under the influence of a limited capacity processor to result in construction of meaning.

[9] For information on analyzing texts into propositions, see Robert J. Tierney and James Mosenthal. Discourse comprehension and production: Analyzing text structure and cohesion. In J.A. Langer and M. Trika Smith-Burke (Eds.), *Reader Meets Author/Bridging the Gap*. Newark, DE: International Reading Association, 1982. Also, see J. Miller and W. Kintsch. Readability and recall of short passages: A theoretical analysis. *Journal of Experimental Psychology: Human Learning and Memory,* 1980, 6, 332-351.

[10] See Robert de Beaugrande's article, listed in references to this introduction to models, for a comprehensive set of criteria for evaluation and comparison of models.

Developmental Model

The Substrata-Factor Theory of Reading

HARRY SINGER
University of California at Riverside

Holmes (1953) pioneered a new era in research in reading with his formulation of a theory of reading. All the previous research in reading had been atheoretical. Neither Huey's (1908) book on *The Psychology and Pedagogy of Reading* nor Anderson and Dearborn's text (1952) on *The Psychology of Teaching Reading* had the term theory in the text or index (Holmes, 1953). The dominance of behaviorism with its rejection of mentalism and its emphasis on s-r psychology led educational psychologists and psychologists to avoid constructing theories about events that were not observable.

However, some precursors of the substrata-factor theory of reading can be found in the perceptual, linguistic, and cognitive studies done in the previous 75 years of research in reading. Moreover, some researchers and practitioners anticipated the formulation of the theory in their multicausality explanations of reading difficulty or success. We shall briefly review these precursors.

Precursors of the Substrata-Factor Theory of Reading

Perceptual Factors

The beginning of the scientific study of reading focused on perception. Javal (1879) began this line of inquiry by discovering that a reader's eye movements consisted of jerky forward movements, followed by relatively long pauses, and occasionally some backward movements. Later, using a camera to record corneal reflections of these movements, Buswell (1922; also in Anderson and Dearborn, 1952) plotted the average number of forward movements, pause durations, and backward movements for average groups of students in grades 2 to college that resulted from their reading of the same relatively easy material. He interpreted the curves as representing normal progress for the group as a whole, the most common route to the goal of maturity in reading around which individuals deviated. Buswell attributed the direction students travelled over the routes toward maturity in reading largely to methods of instruction because he found that the reading eye-movement behavior of first graders correlated with their methods of instruction. Thus, Buswell came close to formulating a theory of reading.

A shorter version of some of the ideas in this chapter appeared in "A Critique of Jack Holmes' Study: The Substrata Factor Theory of Reading and Its History and Conceptual Relationship to Interaction Theory," from *Reading Research Revisited,* edited by L. Gentile, M. Kamil, and J. Blanchard. Columbus, Ohio: Merrill, 1983. Used by permission.

Judd and Buswell (1922) came even closer to formulating an interactive theory of reading as a result of research on the effects that text variations and changes in readers' purposes have upon individuals' eye movement behavior in reading. They found that eye movement behavior in reading dynamically interacts with changes in the content and difficulty of the text, and with the reader's purposes in reading. Although both Judd and Buswell believed that all eye-movements during reading were symptomatic of central or cognitive processes, Buswell limited his definition of reading to perception of printed words; he attributed all else in reading to processes of thinking.

Linguistic Factors

Essentially in agreement with Buswell's definition of reading, Gates (1926, p. 438) obtained evidence that perception is not a unitary factor: he found that the average intercorrelation among perception of printed words, numbers, and geometric objects was only .35 for children in grades 1 to 6. Because of the specificity of perception, he concluded that "differences in reading ability may depend upon the specific skills pupils have of perceiving a certain kind of material, namely printed words...."

Gates (1921) was also the first to determine that speed and power of reading, although interrelated, nevertheless were separate components of general reading ability. This division can be related to the current automaticity theory of LaBerge and Samuels (1976; also in this volume). They separated skilled reading ability into two sets of processes: one set consists of spontaneous and unconscious operation of word identification processes, including perceptual, syntactic, and perhaps some meaning processes, such as instantiation or selection of contextually constrained meanings for more general terms (Anderson, Pichert, Goetz, Schallert, Stevens, and Trollip, 1976; Dreher, 1980, 1981a, 1981b; Dreher and Singer, 1981; see Dreher's article in this volume) and the other set encompasses more effort and more conscious operation of processes, such as reasoning during reading, or reflecting about information constructed from previous print or utilizing cognitive processes and knowledge structures in retrieving information stored in long term memory.

Mobilization of different sets of processes for different purposes in reading is part of the substrata-factor theory of reading. So is an hierarchical organization of abilities for attaining speed or power of reading. Gates (1947) approached this concept of hierarchical organization when he found that correlations between his tests and reading comprehension could be arrayed from a low of .10 for motor abilities to over .80 for phrase perception. In short, the correlations increased as his tests assessed functions that, according to substrata factor models, are structurally closer to speed or comprehension of reading.

Cognitive Factors

A shift in the definition of reading from an emphasis upon perception to cognition occurred when Thorndike (1917) defined reading as reasoning. Subse-

quently, numerous studies have shown that general intelligence, whether assessed as rate of learning (IQ) or ability to solve age-graded problems (mental
age), is highly related to reading achievement (Singer, 1960). However, when
reading ability is separated into its two overlapping developmental components,
reading acquisition or learning how to read and using reading to gain information
or learn from text, IQ has a decreasing relation to reading acquisition but an increasing relationship to ability to learn from text for a group of students as they
progress through school (Singer, 1973, 1977). In short, whether a predictor is
large or small depends not only on the functions it assesses, but also on the variability of the criterion it predicts. As the variability in a criterion decreases for a
group of students as they progress through school, as it does for reading acquisition, then correlations with its predictors will decrease; conversely, as variability
in a criterion increases, as it does for ability to learn from text or reading comprehension, then complex predictors, such as general intelligence, have an increasing correlation with it. However, neither IQ nor mental age alone account
for all individual differences in general reading ability.

Multicausality Views of Reading

Although Monroe pointed out that a multiplicity of factors are related to accuracy in oral reading and to comprehension in silent reading, she did not apply
higher order statistical analyses to her data, such as multiple correlation. However, she did use multiple regression type of thinking in her study on *Children
Who Cannot Read* when she concluded that "a reading defect may result in those
cases in which the number and strength of the impeding factors is greater than the
number and strength of the facilitating factors" (Monroe, 1932, p. 10).

Among the first to use factor analysis on a matrix of correlations resulting
from administration of a battery of tests of reading ability was Phelan (1940). She
discovered that three factors correlated with reading comprehension: rote memory for words, cognition, and perception for words.

Lazar (1942) did not conduct a research study, but used her insights as a
practitioner in the New York City Schools to point toward the conceptual and
research direction later taken by substrata factor theory when she wrote: "....the
origin of reading failure is to be sought in a constellation of causes...The factors
in a constellation differ in magnitude....The most constructive approach that can
be taken in the study of reading failure is to investigate these causes in their interdependence in order to find, if possible, which carry the most weight....No clear
and definite method exists for specifically isolating the most significant elements
from the combination of many."

A few years later, Holmes (1943) invented a statistical technique, substrata
analysis, to discover the constellation and magnitude of factors underlying general reading ability and formulated the substrata-factor theory of reading.

Overview of Research on the Substrata-Factor Theory

Research on the substrata-factor theory of reading began with Holmes's (1948) dissertation, "Factors Underlying Major Reading Disabilities at the College Level," published in *Genetic Psychology Monographs* (Holmes, 1954). Subsequently, he (1953) formulated the theory that explained the results of his doctoral research. Later, Holmes (1965) explicated the basic assumptions underlying his theory and formulated a neurological explanation for the organization and functioning of the mind.

Singer (1960) expanded the substrata-factor theory by incorporating into it the conceptual domain (Singer, 1966c, reprinted in this volume). He also constructed a battery of perceptual, linguistic, and conceptual tests that he used to confirm that the central hypothesis of the substrata-factor theory of reading could be generalized to the elementary school level. Later, Singer (1962) explained how substrata factor models could be used for teaching, diagnosis, and evaluation of reading ability. Next, Singer (1964, 1965) obtained evidence for the validity of the substrata-factor theory's developmental hypothesis.

Then Holmes and Singer (1961, 1966) tested a hypothesis derived from substrata-factor theory. The hypothesis stated that in attempting to solve a problem in reading, individuals will tend to maximize their strengths and minimize their weaknesses. Holmes and Singer did not confirm their hypothesis; they found that all individuals, regardless of their strengths or weaknesses, have to have and use at least minimal levels of word recognition abilities, if they are to read at all. A similar hypothesis was tested and a similar conclusion was reached by Anderson and Freebody (1983). In short, all individuals have to traverse some word recognition route before they can take alternative routes to achieve the same comprehension goal. These studies also confirm Gough's (1984, p. 225) premise: "Word recognition is the foundation of the reading process."

Athey and Holmes (1969, also reported by Athey in this volume) investigated personality factors and the affective domain in reading that Flavell (1981) would later label as "metacognitive experiences" (Athey, 1982). In the same year Kling (1969) showed that substrata-factor theory was compatible with general open-systems theory. Recently Katz (1980) and Katz and Singer (1983, 1984) tested a substrata-factor hypothesis at the first grade level.

Summary

Starting with the substrata-factor theory of reading in 1953, research in reading has become theory based. In testing the hypothesis derived from the substrata-factor theory of reading, statistical models of reading have been constructed at the elementary, secondary, and college levels. In 1965 a neurological theory was formulated and integrated with the substrata-factor theory of reading. The theory's developmental hypothesis has been found to be tenable as evidenced by statistical data and models constructed for grades 3 to 6 (Singer, 1964, 1965a, 1965c). The evidence represented by the statistically constructed models buttress the three integrated psychological, neurological, and developmental explanations of reading ability and reading development.

The substrata-factor theory of reading has had precursors in prior research studies and is a precursor itself for the schema-interactive theory that followed it (Singer, 1983; also see chapters by Adams and Collins and by Anderson in this volume). In the remainder of this chapter, I shall present the statistical models, the three theoretical formulations they represent, the specific hypotheses that have been tested, and conclude by pointing out applications of the theories and the models for teaching reading.

Statistical Model

Methodology

The best way to understand the substrata-factor statistical models is to know how they were constructed. Their construction followed the same progression of statistical procedures outlined by Peters and Van Voorhis (1940) in their text, *Statistical Procedures and Their Mathematical Bases*. These procedures are applicable to the construction of statistical models in any field of inquiry:

1. Use analysis of variance to determine which variables are significant.

2. Compute the relationships among the variables that are statistically significant.

3. Intercorrelate these variables and factor analyze the resulting correlation matrix. This step is consistent with science's criterion of parsimony.

4. Use the factors in a multiple regression equation to predict a criterion.

Selection of Variables

Holmes did the first step in the Peters and Van Voorhis progression by thoroughly reviewing the research literature to find which variables were significantly related to reading. Although he appreciated this research foundation, Holmes recognized the shortcomings of this prior research. He wrote: *"the justication for the present study rests on the problem of integrating the fragmentary bits of knowledge which have been screened from the foregoing review of the literature"* (Holmes, 1954, p. 17; italics in the original). Nevertheless, from the review, Holmes selected 37 independent variables, each of which had a significant zero-order correlation with the dependent variables of speed and/or power of reading. The independent variables fit into five categories: mental ability, linguistic ability (vocabulary, general information, spelling, phonetic association, word discrimination, affixes, word sense), small motor ability, oculomotor functional control (eye-movement behavior), and personality factors (assessed by the Bell Adjustment Inventory, Johnson Temperament Analysis, and California Test of Personality). Rate of reading was measured by the Van Wagenen Rate of Comprehension and Minnesota Speed of Reading Tests. Power of reading was determined by the total score on the Van Wagenen-Dvorak Diagnostic Examination of Silent Reading Abilities, which consists of the subtests of central thought, clearly stated details, interpretation, integration of dispersed ideas, and ability to draw inferences. This test qualifies as a power test because it does not curtail the time for reading relatively difficult passages and answering relatively difficult questions.

Holmes then went on to the second step of theory construction by administering the battery of tests to a sample of college students, whose resulting scores were intercorrelated to form a correlation matrix. He combined the third and fourth steps by using the Wherry-Doolittle Multiple Test Selection Technique. This technique selects the minimum number of variables that predict or account for the maximum variance in a criterion, such as speed or power of reading.

Multiple Correlation and Regression Analysis

The Wherry-Doolittle statistical procedure works in a stepwise fashion. First, one predictor is selected, usually the variable with the largest zero order correlation with the criterion. Then the covariance between this predictor and the criterion are taken out of the correlation matrix. Hence, the next largest predictor is independent of the first and accounts for some of the remaining variance in the criterion. This procedure is repeated for each predictor until no statistically significant prediction can be made. The procedure is analogous to an experimental selection of a large sample of students who differ on reading comprehension. Taking out the first predictor, such as vocabulary ability, is analogous to selecting out of the sample of students all those who are now alike with respect to vocabulary ability. However, they still differ in reading comprehension, but their variability in this component is now much less. Taking out the next predictor—say, mental age—is analogous to a further selection from the reduced sample to a new sample of all those who are alike in mental age. This second reduction leads to a group alike in both vocabulary and mental age. Since some difference in reading comprehension still remains among this group, you can take out another predictor, say, graphophonemic ability. The resulting group is an even more select sample of students who are alike in vocabulary, mental age, and graphophonemics. The process is repeated again for morphemics (ability to divide words into meaningful units and know their meaning). After this predictor has been taken out, some differences may still remain among the resulting sample. This difference may remain as unexplained variance, which means that no predictors can be found in the correlation matrix to explain it. This multiple selection procedure is depicted in Figure 1.

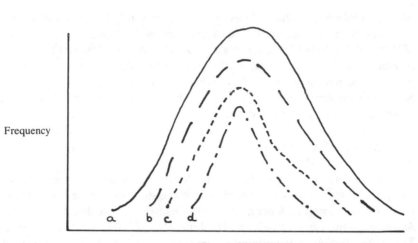

Figure 1. Frequency distribution showing that the range of variability decreases from curves a to d as successive predictors are statistically taken out of a matrix in a stepwise multiple correlation procedure or analogously as the selection criteria increase in choosing those who are alike on the criteria from a given distribution of individuals randomly selected from a population.

Multiple correlation usually stops at this first level. But at this junction, Holmes invented substrata analysis.

Substrata Analysis

In a simple yet brilliant contribution to statistical technique, Holmes extended the Wherry-Doolittle to a second level of analysis to determine which of the remaining variables in the matrix predicted each of the first-level predictors. He then went on to a third level of analysis. Holmes named this extension substrata analysis. It consists simply of a systematic succession of multiple correlations and regression equations in which the predictor variables at one level become subcriteria at the second level, and predictors for these subcriteria, in turn, become subcriteria for the next level. A schematic of substrata analysis through two levels is depicted in Figure 2.

This schematic indicates that P_1, P_2, and P_3 are first level predictors of criterion C_0, Speed of Reading. Then each of these predictors becomes criteria C_1, C_2, and C_3 for their predictors at the second level of analysis; P_{11}, P_{12}, and P_{13} for C_1; P_{21}, P_{22}, and P_{23} for C_2, and P_{31}, P_{32}, and P_{33} for C_3. Percent contribution to variance for each predictor is then computed by simple arithmetic from the regression equation for predicting a criterion or subcriterion. The percent variance of the predictors for each criterion, speed and power of reading, and for each subcriterion is the percent of a criterion or subcriterion's determined variance (R x 100) prorated among the predictors in its regression equation ($R = B_{01} r_{01} + B_{02}$

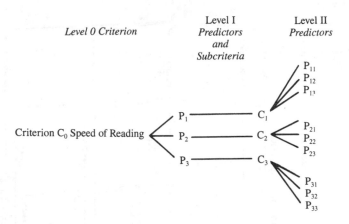

Figure 2. Schematic of substrata analysis through two levels.

$r_{02} + B_{03} r_{03} \ldots B_{on} r_{on}$). The substrata analysis stops when a point of diminishing returns has been reached, or when there is no rationale or no predictors left in the matrix for further analysis of a subcriterion (Singer, 1960; Holmes and Singer, 1966; Singer, 1969). Holmes (1948) then used substrata analysis to construct a statistical model at the college level.

College Level Model

The college level model is depicted in Figure 3. The structure of the model will be described according to the factors selected as predictors. Each of these factors consists of closely related sets of information. The model will be interpreted as a statistical analogue of the major structural hypothesis of the substrata factor theory of reading.

Structural description. The model is to be read in the following way: On the right hand side of the model, at the first substrata level, four factors predict power of reading: perception of verbal relations, intelligence, vocabulary in context, and fixations. These factors indicate that college students who are more powerful in reading are also better at relating ideas and solving abstract problems; can draw upon a better vocabulary repertoire; use context to select appropriate meanings for terms; and tend to process print in smaller units, perhaps more carefully and precisely, than college students who are less powerful in reading.

The next question is, what predicts vocabulary in context? The answer is shown at the second level in the model: general information, vocabulary in isolation, and prefixes predict vocabulary in context. In other words, for better performance in obtaining constrained word meanings, college readers can draw

FLOW SHEET FOR THE TASKS INVOLVED IN THE READING ACT
WITH BREAKDOWN FOR UNDERLYING FACTORS

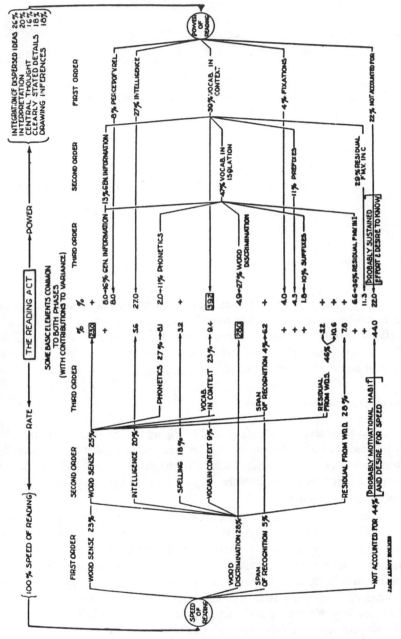

Figure 3. Substrata-factor model for the college level.

upon their better knowledge of the world, greater number of meanings for general terms, and better ability to analyze words into their constituents and know their meanings.

Then, what determines ability to perform better on vocabulary in isolation? The answer is shown at the third level in the model: general information (knowledge of the world), phonetics (ability to sound out printed words), word discrimination (ability to detect words quickly), and suffixes (ability to analyze and know the meanings of constituents of words) predict vocabulary in isolation.

The left hand side of the chart is read in the same way for the substrata analysis of speed of reading.

The variance not accounted for in first order prediction is at the bottom of the flow chart. Holmes thought that the remaining variance in power of reading might be "sustained effort and desire to know," and in speed of reading, "motivational habit and desire for speed." In other words, if a test for "sustained effort and desire to know" had been in the matrix of predictors, it might have accounted for the remaining variance in power of reading. That is, students who do well in power of reading are those who not only perform better on perception of verbal relations, intelligence, vocabulary in isolation, and in fixations, but also are willing to expend effort and really want to understand. In short, they are willing to stay with the reading task until they can comprehend it. (See Athey's chapter on Affect, this volume.)

The flow chart represents for an age group (such as college students) the factors that constitute the group's average working system around which individuals deviate. In other words, the flow chart depicts the factors or knowledge systems that, on the average, are likely to be organized to obtain power or speed of reading, or some underlying subcriterion.

A working system is a momentary organization of these factors or, stated in neurological terms, an intercerebral communication system that has been mobilized or activated by the interaction of the task and the reader's purpose to solve a problem in reading. The organization of the working system is determined by mobilizers, which arise from an individual's value system. Hence, an individual's values will determine the factors an individual will bring to bear upon a task. In short, how individuals will try to solve a problem and the effort they will expend is determined by their value system.

To summarize: The flow chart represents a cross-section of subabilities and processes that an average member of a particular group can mobilize into a working system for attaining speed and power of reading.

Hypothesis confirmed. The flow chart also confirms the major structural hypothesis of the theory: General reading ability of college students is a composite of speed and power of reading. Underlying each component is a multiplicity of related and measurable factors. Disabilities in reading should bear an inverse relationship to the quantitative levels of each such component and hence manifest detectable deficiencies in such underlying factors (Holmes, 1954).

Limitations in the Statistical Model

Although Wherry-Doolittle Multiple Test Selection results in statistically in-dependent predictors, their zero order correlations with the criterion are used in computing the predictive regression equation. In this equation, the predictors are no longer independent but are related because the zero order correlations are not only correlated with the criterion being predicted but also with one another. These correlations are implicit in the models. However, they are not a limitation; instead, they are consistent with the concept of 1) mutual and reciprocal facilita-tion and 2) simultaneous interaction among the predictors and between the pre-dictors and their criterion that occur in the dynamic process of reading.

Another limitation arises because both the statistical method and the norm-referenced tests apply to differences, not similarities, among students in a partic-ular grade level. For example, as students learn and become alike in finite or close-ended factors, such as symbol-sound correspondence, which almost all students can master (Bloom, 1971), given adequate instruction and time to learn (Carroll, 1963), the factor drops out as a predictor of reading achievement at the grade level at which most individuals have mastered it. However, the factor still can be mobilized in the process of reading, even though it does not appear in the statistically-constructed model at that grade level or at higher grade levels. Hence, to determine all the substrata factors that can be mobilized at a particular grade level, it is necessary to realize that substrata factors in the sequence of models in prior grades can also be activated. For example, we do not find that syntax is a first level predictor after grade one, nor graphophonemics after grade six. The syntactic ability of students tends to be asymptotic to maturity after age 6. That is, most students have acquired almost all their syntactic structures by that time. Tests of syntactic ability, such as those assessed in the Illinois Test of Psycholinguistic Abilities, will indicate little or no variability after grade one; hence syntax will not be a predictor in any statistically constructed models after grade one. However, it can still be mobilized in the process of reading. Likewise, letter-sound knowledge is a predictor in the lower grades, but at some point be-tween the first and the intermediate grades it drops out as a predictor because almost all students will have learned these relationships prior to the intermediate grade level. In contrast, semantics (vocabulary ability) is an open-ended factor; individual differences on this factor increase as students progress through the grades. Therefore, it remains as a first level predictor of reading achievement at each grade level. Another open-ended factor is reasoning-in-reading (mental age). Indeed, factor analytic studies show that reading comprehension loads to some degree on semantics and reasoning-in-reading at each grade level. By re-membering that a model at any grade level represents individual differences and subsumes the substrata-factor predictors in models for prior grades, this limita-tion of an individual difference model can be overcome.

Thus, the statistical model represents the structural hypothesis of the theory. The dynamics of the theory, or how the model works in the process of reading, constitutes the theory's psychological model.

Psychological Model

The substrata-factor theory states that in trying to attain speed or comprehension in reading, individuals mobilize their substrata-factors into a momentary working system to solve a problem. At one moment, the problem may be to identify a printed word, or select an appropriate meaning for a word, or make an inference or an interpretation for a passage. A different working system is mobilized for each of these problems. For example, if a reader cannot recognize a word as a whole word (sight word recognition), then readers must mobilize the underlying factors and processes for whole word recognition. Or if readers have to sound out a whole word, they have to mobilize the abilities and processes that underlie whole word sounds. This substrata factor organization can be seen on the statistical model. Look at the model for the fourth grade, Figure 4; on the right hand side of the chart, see Matching Sounds in Words. Underlying this factor are Spelling Recall and Blending Word Sounds. They are the substrata factors a reader can mobilize to sound out whole words. Spelling Recall consists of a complex of abilities and processes for identifying the parts of a printed word in a correct sequence. Blending Word Sounds involves synthesizing parts of a word into a whole word. Thus, readers can identify a whole word sound by mobilizing its underlying subabilities and processes.

As a reader's purposes, difficulty of the material, or type of content to be read change even within the same passage, the reader mobilizes, organizes, and reorganizes substrata factors into momentary working systems in response to each change. In short, a dynamic interaction occurs between the stimulus task and the organization of substrata factors within the individual. Or for the same task, the reader's purpose may change from reading material analytically to skimming it. As readers' purposes change, so do the substrata factors mobilized into their working systems change. In other words, the dynamic interaction results in moment-to-moment changes in the mobilization and organization of factors into working systems for responding to the changing demands of the task and/or the purposes of a reader. Thus, we can envision that as a reader's eyes jump across a line of print from one fixation to the next, at each fixation a reader is mobilizing different substrata factors into momentary working systems at one or more substrata levels to solve a task in reading. In Holmes's words (1953, Chapter 32, p. 1):

> The Substrata-Factor Theory of Reading is predicated on the fundamental hypothesis that the reading ability of an individual, in a particular field, is a dynamic and complex skill, compounding and recompounding for each new task an appropriate integration of a multiplicity of related and underlying factors. Upon this basic assumption the rationale of the generalized theory must stand or fall.

He added that:

> Different amounts of each factor...at different times, are momentarily unified or integrated into a working system of subabilities which are directed toward the solution of a problem. The problem organizes the abilities as the abilities determine what may be organized. That is, the particular kind of problem requires a certain organization of abilities, as the individual's possession of certain abilities limits what

he may organize...efficient reading...depends upon the synthesis of many subabilities. The synthesizing and integrating process is the crux of the reading process, i.e. the quick comprehension of the printed page. Whenever the smooth and rapid flow of thought-intake is interrupted in the reading process by incomprehension or confusion...then the reader must slow down and reread in his effort to resolve the problem by analysis...in power of reading the analytical process is more to the fore than is synthesis. Nevertheless, both speed and power of reading are dependent upon the integration of a set of subskills which cluster on at least three levels of complexity.

Implicit in the statistical and psychological models is a neurological model. This model explains the structure and functioning of the brain that enables an individual to mobilize the factors and processes into momentary working systems at various substrata levels to solve problems in reading and respond to changing tasks and purposes. Through these changing working systems an individual is able to attain speed and power of reading.

Neurological Model

Holmes (1965) introduced the neurological model and the basic assumptions underlying his theory of reading by first criticizing the neurological conceptualizations that are implicit in the factor analytic models of Spearman, Thurstone, and Thomson. He then explained his own neurological and statistical model. Later, Holmes (Holmes and Singer, 1966, pp. 178-179) succinctly stated two basic assumptions. His first assumption is that the "cognitive complex of the brain is thought of as constituting a cosmos of subability systems which become dynamically associated in a multitude of working systems in accordance with the requirements of the task and the purposes of the individual." The subsystems are composed of substrata factors. Each substrata factor consists of sets of information stored in cell assemblies (Hebb, 1949). This information has been acquired from instruction and learning in such broadly defined areas of reading as word recognition, word meaning, and reasoning-in-context (Singer, 1960) and from formal and informal instruction and experience in school and everyday living (Singer, 1981). As a result of maturation, instruction, and practice in reading, these cell assemblies are organized into substrata-factors, which can be mobilized to form neurological subsystems.

Holmes's second assumption, a statistical one, is that "a meaningful correlation in the present context merely reflects a mean mutual interaction of two sets of test scores which, in turn, represent the dynamic interplay of (a) two macrosystems, (b) a system within one of its subsystems...correlations simply reflect the interdependence of two cortical systems....The correlation...arises from the interaction of two organized bodies of information."

Thus, Holmes perceived the brain as consisting of microsystems of cell assemblies that may be conjoined or organized into hierarchically structured working systems, then reorganized into other working systems according to moment-to-moment changes in the tasks and purposes of the reader.

Next, Singer expanded the substrata-factor theory by formulating its developmental explanation. He then tested the generalizability of the main hypothesis of the substrata-factor theory of reading and subsequently the validity of the theory's developmental hypothesis. Thus, he constructed the theory's developmental model.

Developmental Model

The formation and development of substrata-factor systems can be explained in the following way. At maturity in reading, an individual's working system functions fluently and flexibly. But in the initial stages of learning to read, attempts by individuals to mobilize their developing subsystems into working systems for responding to the printed page are characterized by hesitancy, rigidity, and frequent lack of success because they do not yet have adequately developed subsystems nor the necessary mental structures and flexibility for changing appropriately from one working system to another (Laycock, 1962). Gradually, subsystems improve in variety, magnitude, and intercommunicability as a result of maturation, learning, and experience in mobilizing subsystems. Individuals thus develop the ability to shift from one mental organization to another, and can be more flexible in organizing and reorganizing subsystems. Consequently they can be more effective and efficient in the process of reading.

At first, however, the individual can only mobilize relatively simple working systems, consisting perhaps of only some associations to printed words or letters. If individuals continue to acquire, store, and utilize only simple associations, they will eventually reach a point of cognitive overload because of the complexity of printed English. Instead of a separate response for each nonidentical printed stimulus, an individual who has the capability and receives appropriate instruction can develop auditory, visual, and kinesthetic concepts that effectively reduce the complexity of printed English (Singer, 1966). By mentally grouping printed words according to some common characteristics, which then can be abstracted and generalized within limitations of printed English, individuals can conceptualize input stimuli and subsequently utilize their concepts for selective perception of and response to printed stimuli. For example, an auditory concept could be formed for the common element that is visually different in such words as *my*, *aisle*, *eye*, *tried* and *high;* a visual concept could be constructed for the common visual, but auditorily dissimilar element in such words as *cough* and *though*; and a kinesthetic concept could be abstracted from eye-movement response-sensations to the characteristic lines and curves for any letter, such as the up-and-down-and-across generalized characteristics of the letter *t* in *Tom*, *tree*, and a cursively written word *boat* (Hebb, 1949; Singer, 1960).

Because of their growing capabilities, individuals are increasingly able to conceptualize stimuli not only in their input, but also in their mediational processing systems. Therefore, as individuals progress through the grades, they become more capable of forming and mobilizing conceptual systems that are appropriate for responding to various stimulus categories and for integrating more widely dispersed ideas (Singer, 1960; Bruner and Olver, 1963). By integrating their experiences to printed words, individuals could thus develop conceptualized meaning-responses, even in the initial stage of reading. For example, an individual might have had a tangible experience with a toy boat in which he or she manipulated the boat and thus acquired kinesthetic, visual, and often gustatory images of the boat. Later, the individual might have heard someone refer to the object manipulated as a "boat." Still later he or she may have acquired further knowledge about boats. After learning to read, the individual may mobilize these images and information into an organized response to give meaning to the printed word. Of course, from the reading readiness stage on throughout the curriculum, reading instruction could be designed to facilitate the development of increasingly more abstract conceptualized responses to printed words (Singer and Balow, 1965).

Conceptualization or hierarchical organization can thus reduce "cognitive strain" (Bruner, Goodnow, and Austin, 1956) in an individual's perceptual, storage, retrieval, and response systems. If an individual also accumulates or fuses meaning while reading, he or she could utilize "word sense" (Holmes, 1948) or "sentence sense" (Lefevre, 1964) for judging whether his working system is adequate to the task or should be switched to a more appropriate organization for perceiving and reacting to printed words. Utilization of sentence sense may not only signalize the necessity of a shift from one mental organization to another, but may also act as an advance mobilizer for selecting responses to multiple meaning words. An advance mobilizer is particularly necessary for such word categories as homographs such as the noun /prod' uce/ and the verb /produce'/ and homophones such as /heir/ and /air/. If individuals cannot or do not utilize such conceptualization and meaning processes, then their rate of learning to read is likely to be slower and their working system for attaining speed and power of reading will tend to be more cumbersome and less effective and efficient.

With continued development, instruction, and practice in reading progressively more challenging material and concomitant increases in experience and mental maturation, individuals gradually form their substrata-factors into an hierarchical organization of word-recognition, word meaning, and reasoning-in-context subsystems (Singer, 1962). When the necessary subsystems have been developed and can be mobilized in proper order and magnitude, an individual attains working systems for speed and power of reading that function fluently and harmoniously. However, increased speed and power of reading are not only related to changes in magnitude and variety of available substrata-factors, but also to a more mature organization and a greater degree of integration among substrata-factors. Consequently, there is more interfacilitation among the substrata-factors that have been mobilized into a working system. Therefore, as individuals improve in reading ability, they are increasingly more able to mobilize rapidly and flexibly an hierarchical organization of subsystems in which a minimum of mental energy is devoted to their input systems and a maximum is expended upon their mediational and output systems.

As part of a developmental reorganization in their general working system that can be mobilized for attaining speed and power of reading, individuals, in general, go through a gradient-shift in modality dominance in which they rely more upon visual modes of perception, less upon auditory, and even less upon kinesthetic. At each stage, individuals utilize their growing capability to conceptualize within appropriate limits and gradually become versatile in shifting appropriately from one perceptual category and from one level of meaning to another. Moreover, as a result of practice and development of a wide repertoire of subskills and abilities, their word-recognition-substrata and word-meaning-substrata begin to psychosynchromesh, and individuals can then concentrate more of their mental energy upon their reasoning-in-context substrata. Gradually individuals not only improve in speed and power of reading, but also in the dominant process by which they attain these products of their general working system. At maturity, therefore, as a consequence of maturation, development, instruction, and practice, their working systems function smoothly with a dominance of visual over auditory processes for reasoning from printed symbols.

This developmental formulation of the theory provides insight that a model at any grade level is a cross-section of the multiplicity of factors and processes within the individual that are progressing along the routes to maturity in reading. Consequently, finding that the major structural hypothesis of the theory was also tenable at the fourth grade level, Singer (1960) constructed a model of the factors underlying power and speed of reading at the fourth grade level.

Fourth Grade Model

Structural description. The flow chart for the fourth grade model, shown in Figure 4, indicates the systems that underlie Power of Reading. In current terminology these systems, shown on the right hand side of the chart, are graphophonemics (matching word sounds); semantics (vocabulary); morphemics (suffixes); and reasoning ability, which includes conceptualization ability (mental age). For Speed of Reading, left side of chart, there are three systems: speed and span of perception (phrase perception discrimination), semantics (vocabulary), and reasoning (mental age). Each system is composed of a sequence of substrata factors. For example, underlying Phrase Perception Discrimination are three factors: Word Recognition in Context, Word Perception Discrimination, and a Residual of unexplained variance. In other words, if two individuals are alike in both Word Recognition in Context and Word Perception Discrimination, they might still differ somewhat in Phrase Perception Discrimination. If we could not determine what accounted for this difference from our battery of tests, we called the remaining difference the residual or unexplained variance. Underlying Word Perception Discrimination are also three factors: Spelling Recognition, Visual Verbal Abstraction, and a Residual.

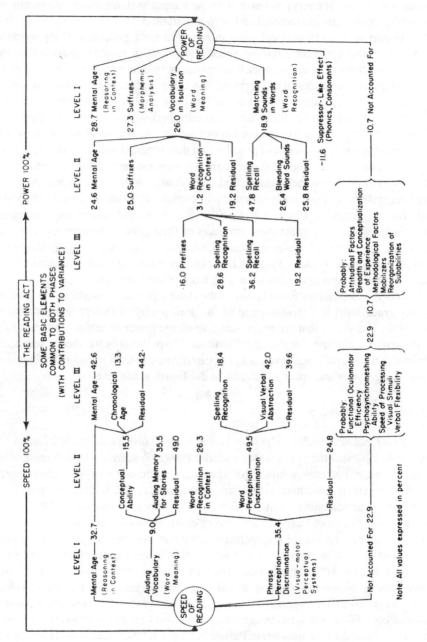

Figure 4.   Flow chart to show the results of the substrata analysis of speed and power of reading at the fourth grade level.

Progressing from the first to the third level requires mobilization and utilization of underlying factors and involves a cognitive process of analysis; proceeding from the third to the first level involves a process of synthesis. For example, Spelling Recognition and Visual Verbal Abstraction plus a Residual Factor become integrated or combine into a working system to solve a problem in Word Perception Discrimination. Likewise, Word Recognition in Context and Word Perception Discrimination plus a Residual Factor are organized into a working system for success in Phrase Perception Discrimination. At the highest level, Phrase Perception, Vocabulary, and Mental Age plus a Residual Factor work together to obtain Speed of Reading. Thus, the model indicates that a shift in the task from power to speed of reading, or from any criterion or subcriterion in the model, necessitates a change in the mental organization of the reader.

The degree of achievement attained in speed and power of reading is due to individual differences in the kinds and strengths of substrata-factors which individuals can mobilize into their working systems. However, there is more than one route to the goal of success in reading: two individuals may attain the same degree of achievement by means of qualitatively and/or quantitatively different organizations or working systems.

Conceptualization in the model. The substrata-factor theory was expanded to encompass conceptualization ability, the ability to form and use concepts. To test the hypothesis that conceptualization abilities are factors that underlie speed and power of reading, Singer (1960, 1966) constructed a series of tests to assess abstraction ability (auditory and visual verbal abstraction) and selected a test of mental age (Kuhlmann-Anderson Test of Intelligence) that emphasized conceptualization abilities and processes. Through these tests, Singer demonstrated among fourth graders that several factors underlie speed and power of reading, among them being 1) conceptualization (for example, self-generation of a concept such as *flower* from four exemplars—*rose, daisy, tulip,* and *pansy*—displayed in a list of ten otherwise unrelated items) and 2) perceptual abstraction and generalization ability (for example, auditory abstraction from words such as *ch*eese, mat*ch,* and *ri*ches, and visual abstraction from words such as *i*sle, s*i*t, and tr*i*o that have common elements).

Developmental Hypothesis

Singer (1965a) also tested a developmental hypothesis of the substrata-factor theory. This hypothesis states that as individuals learn to read, they develop substrata-factors that can be sequentially and hierarchically organized. To test this hypothesis, he administered a battery of tests to representative samples of some 250 students each in grades three, four, five, and six. Then he constructed statistical models for each grade. To show developmental changes from grades three to six, he used the first level predictors from each of these grades to construct developmental models for speed (Singer, 1965c) and power of reading (Singer, 1964). The model for power (1965c) of reading is shown in Figure 5; development of a particular subsystem is shown in Figure 6.

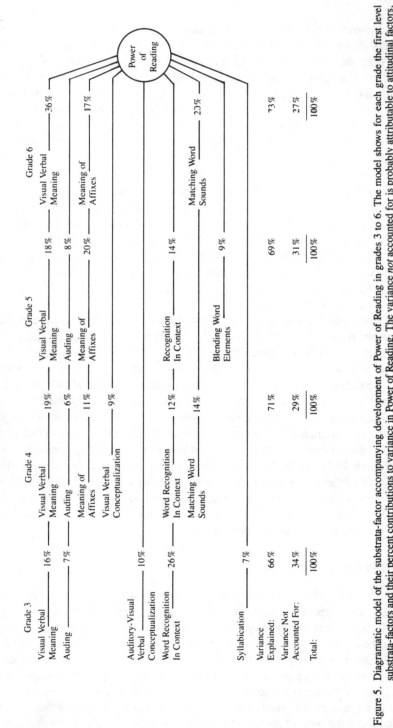

Figure 5. Diagramatic model of the substrata-factor accompanying development of Power of Reading in grades 3 to 6. The model shows for each grade the first level substrata-factors and their percent contributions to variance in Power of Reading. The variance *not* accounted for is probably attributable to attitudinal factors, verbal flexibility, and mobilizers (Singer, 1964).

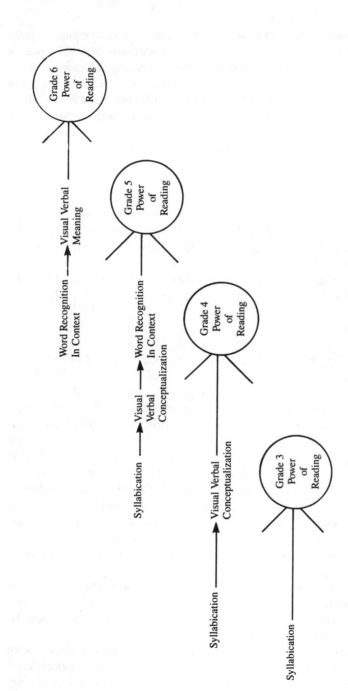
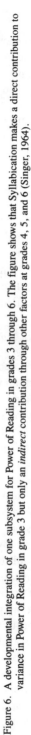

Figure 6. A developmental integration of one subsystem for Power of Reading in grades 3 through 6. The figure shows that Syllabication makes a direct contribution to variance in Power of Reading in grade 3 but only an *indirect* contribution through other factors at grades 4, 5, and 6 (Singer, 1964).

Singer interpreted these data as supporting the major developmental hypothesis: a sequential development of a hierarchical organization of factor does, in fact, accompany improvement in speed and power of reading. Moreover, a reorganization of substrata-factors tends to occur in which first level factors at lower grades become subsumed within substrata-factors at higher grade levels. However, some first level factors, such as Visual Verbal Meaning or Vocabulary for Speed and Power of Reading, and Speed of Word Perception for Speed of Reading are first level factors throughout the intermediate grades.

Hypothesis Testing

A requirement for a scientific theory is that hypotheses derived from it should be capable of being falsified. Two additional substrata-factor studies have been conducted that fit this requirement. The first study tested two hypotheses, a major and a minor, at the high school level, and only the major one was found to be tenable. The second study tested an hypothesis that was tenable at the first grade level. Each of these studies will be briefly reviewed.

High School Study

Holmes and Singer (1966) tested these theoretically derived hypotheses at the high school level:
1. Different known groups — boy versus girl, bright versus dull, fast versus slow, and powerful versus nonpowerful — will mobilize different substrata-factor hierarchies for the purpose of reading with speed and/or power. The result of the substrata analysis will be assumed to be the pattern of abilities underlying speed and/or power of reading in the "theoretically most representative individual of each such known groups." Differences in patterns between representative individuals will indicate "there is more than one way to solve an intellectual problem."
2. The minor hypothesis is that since students can bring to focus in the reading process only those skills and abilities in their particular repertoire, they must learn to read by learning to integrate that characteristic hierarchy or working system of substrata-factors which will maximize their strengths and minimize their weaknesses.

To test these hypotheses, 400 high school students took a battery of 56 variables, including mental, linguistic, visual perceptual, listening, and auditory-perceptual abilities. They were also assessed on academic attitudes, interests, emotional-social problems, and musicality.

The study reconfirmed the major structural hypothesis of the substrata-factor theory. The data also indicated that known groups may indeed mobilize different sets of subabilities to attain identical success in their speed and/or power of reading. Thus, there is more than one way to solve an intellectual problem or more than one route to success in reading achievement.

However, the minor hypothesis was not confirmed. Both the substrata analysis and the factor analysis data indicated the hypothesis had to be revised in the following way: To read "at all with speed and/or power of reading at the high school level, a student must be able to mobilize minimum amounts of certain basic audiovisual verbal processing abilities, particularly word recognition abilities, even though these may be among his weakest. However, as his proficiency increases, to surpass mounting competition, he must mobilize into his working system increasing amounts of his appropriate strengths, even though such assets may be only remotely associated with reading success for people in general, and even though these strengths may be relative weaknesses for his known group" (Holmes and Singer, 1966, pp. 158-159).

First Grade Study

The basic hypothesis tested in the First Grade Study (Bond and Dykstra, 1967) is that variation in methods of instruction would result in differences in reading achievement. Although methods that stressed phonics did make a difference in word recognition, the basic hypothesis was not tenable.

Katz and Singer (1976), drawing upon substrata-factor theory, reformulated the hypothesis: Differential emphases in methods of instruction result in differences in the development of subsystems for attaining reading comprehension. Since the first grade data were not adequate for testing this hypothesis, Katz (1980) did an experimental study to test the hypothesis. The study was conducted in two phases.

Instructional phase. Four teachers were employed by the experimenter to provide supplemental instruction to beginning readers (kindergarten and first grade students). These students within two schools had been randomly assigned to supplementary instruction in each of four subsystems: graphophonemics, morphophonemics, semantics, and syntax. After ten weeks of supplementary instruction, an analysis of variance design revealed significant systematic differences among the criterion-referenced tests given to all the groups. Each group was significantly superior to the others on the supplementary method it had been taught (Katz and Singer, 1981). Then the data for each group were analyzed further.

Statistical analysis phase. For each group a multiple regression equation was computed for determining its predictors of comprehension. The data, derived from criterion-referenced tests and the Metropolitan Reading Instructional Tests, revealed that each group's multiple-regression equation for predicting reading comprehension contained the same predictors, but each group's lowest predictor was in the very subsystem in which the group had received supplementary instruction. The lowest predictor achieved this status because the group was more *alike* on this predictor than the other predictors and was probably more likely to mobilize or activate it into a working system for identifying printed words.

The results of this study were interpreted as supporting the substrata-factor hypothesis: methods of instruction interact with students' capabilities to differentially develop subsystems underlying reading achievement. The subsystems of graphophonemics, syntax, and semantics developed at the first grade level are functionally related to differences in methods of instruction (Katz and Singer, 1984). This finding, in agreement with Buswell's early study (1922) and Barr's more recent investigation (1974-1975), has important implications for diagnosis and improvement of reading. It is implied that even during the first grade, students should be assessed to determine whether all the necessary subsystems for learning to read are being developed; if not, then a change in method may be the appropriate remedy. This remedy is consistent with Monroe's explanation (1932) that overemphasis on a particular method may be a cause of reading difficulty. This explanation may be the reason why Burt and Lewis (1946) found, in a large scale investigation of remedial reading in England, where groups of students were changed from one method to another that *a change in method per se* (italics, mine) was related to reading improvement. However, students' development in first grade should be assessed so that changes in instruction can be instituted before reading difficulties arise.

Katz (1980) also found, through principal components factor analysis, that at the end of first grade, the Metropolitan Reading Achievement Subtest, Comprehension, correlated only 0.27 with a word recognition factor, but 0.73 with a reasoning-in-reading factor heavily saturated with semantics and syntax. The low correlation between comprehension and word recognition perhaps occurred because all of the students in Katz's study had received considerable graphophonemics instruction in their regular classrooms and therefore were less variable in this factor than in the reading-in-reasoning factor.

Further research is necessary to fill in the gap in substrata models between grades one and three and to determine, through a longitudinal study, whether the methodologically induced differences in subsystems underlying achievement in the first grade lead toward convergence in the fourth grade. Singer (1970) predicted that variations in "stimulus models" for teaching reading might produce initial differences in the routes to reading comprehension, but that convergence is likely to occur in subsequent grades. Later, Guthrie (1973) inferred from his cross-sectional data that such convergence did occur. However, he did not perform a longitudinal study of groups that had started off with systematic instructional differences.

Thus, hypotheses can be derived from the substrata-factor theory and tested. The results have provided support for the theory. They also have implications for further research and for teaching reading.

Implications for Teaching Reading

Before stating some implications for teaching reading, I shall point out some qualifications to the implications in the form of disclaimers and restatement of some limitations.

Qualifications

1. The theory and the models were formulated to explain the structure and dynamics of reading. Hence, their primary contribution is to the psychology, not to the pedagogy of reading.

2. For a primary contribution to the pedagogy of reading, the theory and its models would have to be expanded to include the role of the instructor. Research would also have to be conducted to test the validity of hypotheses drawn from this expanded theory and its models. Some pedagogical models are already in the initial stages of development (Singer, 1984; Roehler and Duffy, 1984; also see chapter by Yopp and Singer, this volume).

3. Because the substrata-factor statistical models, constructed at various points in the developmental continuum indicate that the substrata-factors and their pattern of organization change with progress toward maturity in reading (Holmes, 1954; Singer, 1962, 1965c; Holmes and Singer, 1966), it is necessary to draw implications for teaching from a model constructed at or near the grade level for which instruction is being planned.

4. The models and their implications apply to the average reader for the grade level. Individuals within these grade levels vary interindividually and intraindividually in relation to the substrata-factors in a model. Consequently, a model may be useful for planning in general for a particular grade, but for determining whether instruction is needed for particular students, teachers will have to assess students separately on the specific factors. This provision is necessary even if two individuals have the same level of comprehension because they may still differ on their specific, underlying factors (Balow, 1962).

5. The section on "Limitations in the Statistical Model" pointed out the models and the factors within them represent differences, not similarities, among individuals. However, a model at any one grade level subsumes substrata-factors that precipitated in models at previous grade levels. Hence, factors in a model for a particular grade level and factors in models in all prior grade levels are available for mobilization into an average individual's working system to solve a problem in reading.

With these qualifications in mind, we will explain how the fourth grade model, shown in Figure 4, can be used as a theoretical design for teaching reading (Singer, 1962).

Theoretical Design for Teaching Reading

The model provides the teacher with a "cognitive map" of "what leads to what," to use Tolman's concepts (1948), in the general working system for attainment of speed and power of reading at the fourth grade level. The insight gained from this cognitive map enables the teacher to formulate objectives for this design.

Objectives

1. Instruction should at least encompass the instructionally modifiable elements represented in the model, such as vocabulary, morphemics (indicated by the Suffix factor), and graphophonemics (Matching Sounds in Words). Since intelligence is largely maturational, it would not be an instructional objective; indeed, its maturational basis is why it did not become a subcriterion to be predicted in the substrata analysis.

2. Instruction should provide for development of versatility in readers to organize and reorganize their working systems according to their changing purposes and demands of the task. The teacher can do so by varying purposes and demands, teaching students to develop and take different routes to the same goal, and instructing students to try these alternate ways of solving a problem in reading. For example, an unfamiliar word may constitute a barrier to a working system mobilized for whole word recognition. That is, the reader cannot recognize the word holistically. To eliminate this barrier to the goal of word recognition, a more analytical working system has to be mobilized. This switch may occur for a word like /right/ that the individual cannot recognize instantly. The individual then has to mobilize different factors and processes, such as symbol-sound correspondence for /ri/, knowledge that /gh/ is silent, and symbol-sound correspondences for /t/. Alternate routes to identifying the word *right* can also be taken such as, /r/ (symbol-sound correspondence) + /ight/ (phonogram). Thus, the teacher can help students develop flexibility in organization and reorganization of their working systems by instruction that results in a broad structure of subskills and processes; provides practice in switching from one working system to another, that is, taking different routes to the same goal; and creates an emotional atmosphere conducive to utilization of different routes to solving problems, or meeting the demands of the stimulus task, or satisfying the changing purposes of the reader enroute to the overall goal of attaining speed and power of reading.

3. Whenever possible, subskills for power and speed of reading should be developed in alternation. In agreement with the meaning of theory of learning, understanding or power of reading should be developed first, then efficiency or speed of response next. For example, after teaching a student to recognize a word accurately, perhaps by sounding out its parts and then blending them together, switch to visual recognition of that word in a visual word perception discrimination exercise.

Subgrouping. The model clearly indicates that a multitude of factors underlie speed and power of reading. Hence, subgrouping should be based not only on degree of achievement in the major criteria, speed and power of reading, but also on the level of performance in each of the subcriteria and their specific underlying elements. Some individuals, however, may deviate so markedly from the group that models at other grade levels would be more suitable for their instructional designs.

Development of word recognition ability. Although some beginning readers rely on memorization for word recognition, others apparently learn to utilize higher cognitive processes (Gough, Juel, and Roper-Schneider, 1983). To facilitate use of higher cognitive processes, materials could be organized for teaching pupils to conceptualize word recognition responses. For example, after teaching some sight words, the teacher could group these words according to a common auditory element, such as *c*at, *k*it, *c*ow or visual element, such as *it*, *hide*, and tax*i*, and instruct students to perceive, abstract, and generalize this common element. Words which do not contain this element could serve to limit the generalization and, perhaps, help the child develop necessary versatility in word attack. Thus, instead of learning a separate response for each stimulus word, students would gradually develop an adequate repertoire of mediated responses or generalizations to mobilize in varying combinations of working systems for recognizing any unknown word.

The fourth grade model indicates the factors and systems that underlie Phrase Perception Discrimination and Matching Sounds in Words. These systems can be built up; for example, instruction could be given in spelling processes and in blending symbol-sound correspondences. Then these processes could be integrated by providing students with practice in discriminating and giving whole word sounds to words that are visually dissimilar but auditorily similar such as w*oo*d and w*ou*ld. The model indicates a similar approach for speed of word recognition with an emphasis on development and integration of visual factors and processes.

Word meaning. Vocabulary is a first level predictor throughout the grades. Consequently, its development should have high priority in an instructional program. Responses to concrete, functional, and abstract levels of words need to be taught, and students should also develop range, depth, and breadth in their vocabularies (Russell, 1956) so that they can mobilize appropriate vocabulary meanings for instantiating general terms according to the contextual constraints of sentences (Anderson et al., 1976; Dreher, 1980; Dreher and Singer, 1981; also see Dreher's article in this volume).

But vocabulary is also an index of natural concepts, abstracted from experiences in and out of school, and organized into knowledge structures that can be mobilized and reorganized according to changing demands and purposes. For example, when reading the phrase "place setting," an individual can mobilize a situational concept of a combination of silverware and dinnerware, and when the phrase "sorting the silverware" occurs, the reader can mobilize another concept that involves separating the silverware according to types. Thus, vocabulary can be dynamically organized and reorganized.

Although concepts should be developed along various dimensions, such as span, clarity, richness, organization, and communicability (Russell, 1956), conceptual ability is dependent upon mental and chronological age, and upon organic and personality factors (Zaslow, 1957).

Diagnosis. The theory and the models depict how a substrata diagnosis can proceed in a systematic way. Start with a symptom at the first level, determine which system is not functioning as well as expected, then proceed through that system's substrata levels to determine where the specific difficulty may lie or to discover whether there are causal deficiencies or defects in the underlying factors. For example, a student may not be performing well in Power of Reading at the fourth grade level. The model at that grade level, Figure 4, indicates we should begin by assessing the student on the first level predictors for power of reading: Mental Age (ability to reason in reading), Suffixes (morphemics), Vocabulary in Isolation (semantic ability), and Matching Sounds in Words (graphophonemics). We should also make some estimate of the student's desire to know and understand. Suppose the student was performing as well as expected, except in vocabulary. We would then follow this system down to its predictors at the next level, say to Word Recognition in Context, and if this factor is below par, go on to the next lower level, to its underlying factors. Thus, within the limitations of the model, we would be determining where a difficulty lies in a particular system.

Evaluation. Evaluation is analogous to a complete medical checkup: A student takes the entire battery of tests that have been selected as indices to the substrata factors in the model. By comparing the student's performance with a psychograph, a profile of good and poor readers' performances on all the substrata factors at the grade level the student can read, we can note discrepancies from this norm group's psychograph and thus determine the student's relative strengths or weaknesses.

We followed this procedure by evaluating a five year old precocious reader named Marion (Singer, 1965). Figure 7 depicts Marion's performance in Power of Reading by a dashed line. The solid line on the left represents the performance of the nonpowerful readers (the average of the *lower* fourth of the class on Power of Reading at the fourth grade level) and the solid line on the right, the powerful readers (the average performance of the *upper* fourth of the class on Power of Reading). Although Marion is in kindergarten, her profile indicates her Power of Reading is better than the lower group's (a standard score of 43); so is her vocabulary ability and her abilities on matching and blending sounds. Her other abilities are closer to the line. We can infer from her pattern of abilities why she is able to read at the fourth grade level. She performs at the fourth grade level on all the predictors for Power of Reading; her greatest strength is in the graphophonemic system (matching sounds in words and blending sounds) and her relative weaknesses are in morphemic analysis (suffixes) and reasoning (mental age) *when compared with fourth graders.* Only by comparing her abilities with fourth graders, could we determine her relative strengths and weaknesses. If we had compared her with her own age group, kindergartners, Marion would have been at the highest level on all the tests and we would not have discerned the intraindividual differences in her substrata-factor pattern. (For a more detailed analysis of Marion's substrata-factor evaluation, see Singer, 1965b.)

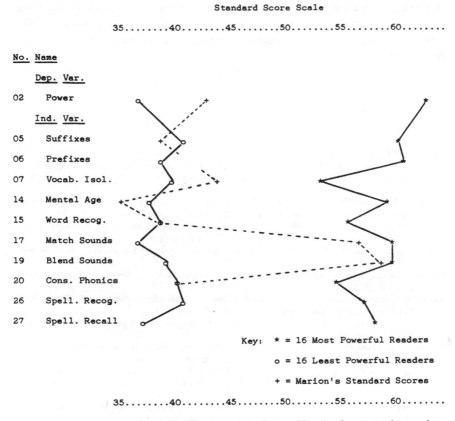

Figure 7. Psychograph of selected substrata elements for Power of Reading for a precocious reader.

Thus, teachers and reading clinicians can use the theory, models, and psychographs for explanation, for teaching plans, and for diagnosis and evaluation of an individual's attainment of speed and power of reading.

Summary and Conclusion

After some 75 years of atheoretical research in the field of reading, the substrata-factor theory of reading was formulated by Holmes (1953). The theory consists of integrated psychological, neurological, developmental, and statistical models (Downing, 1983). Hypotheses derived from the theory have been tested. Implications have been drawn for teaching and applications have been made to diagnosis and evaluation, from both the theory and its models.

Although other theories and models of reading have been formulated, substrata-factor theory is the only one that has statistically-constructed models to represent its major structural hypothesis and provide supporting data for its psychological, neurological, and developmental explanations of reading. Thus, the substrata-factor theory has had a productive and useful life and continues to be a powerful explanation of the structure, dynamics, and development of general reading ability.

REFERENCES

Anderson, I.H., and Dearborn, W.F. *The psychology of teaching reading.* New York: Ronald, 1952.
Anderson, R.C., Pichert, J.W., Goetz, E.T., Schallert, D.L., Stevens, K.V., and Trollip, S.R. Instantiation of general terms. *Journal of Verbal Learning and Verbal Behavior,* 1976, 15, 667-679.
Anderson, R.C., and Freebody, P. Effects of vocabulary difficulty, text cohesion, and schema availability on reading comprehension, *Reading Research Quarterly,* 1983, 13, 277-294.
Athey, I. Reading: The affective domain reconceptualized. In B.A. Hutson (Ed.), *Advances in reading/language research,* Vol. I. Greenwich, CT: JAI Press, 1982.
Balow, I.H. Does homogeneous grouping give homogeneous groups? *Elementary School Journal,* 1962, 63, 28-32.
Barr, R. The effect of instruction on pupil reading strategies. *Reading Research Quarterly,* 1974-1975, 10, 555-582.
Bloom, B.S. Mastery learning and its implications for curriculum development. In E. Eisner (Ed.), *Confronting curriculum reform.* Boston: Little, Brown, 1971.
Bond, G.L., and Dykstra, R. The cooperative research program in first grade reading instruction. *Reading Research Quarterly,* 1967, 2, 5-142.
Bruner, J., Goodnow, J., and Austin, G.A. *A study of thinking.* New York: Wiley, 1956.
Bruner, J., and Olver, R. Development of equivalence transformations in children. *Monographs of the Society for Research in Child Development,* 1963, 28, 125-143.
Burt, C., and Lewis, R.B. Teaching backward readers. *British Journal of Educational Psychology,* 1946, 16, 116-132.
Buswell, G.T. *Fundamental reading habits: A study of their development.* Supplementary educational monographs, No. 21. Chicago: University of Chicago Press, 1922.
Carroll, J.B. A model of school learning. *Teachers College Record,* 1963, 64, 723-733.
Davis, F. (Ed.). *Literature of research in reading with emphasis on models.* Targeted Research and Development Program in Reading, Report No. 2. Washington, DC: U.S. Department of Health, Education, and Welfare. New Brunswick, NJ: Rutgers University, 1971.
Downing, J. A commentary on Jack Holmes's substrata-factor theory of reading: Novelty, novelty, novelty. In L.M. Gentile, M.L. Kamil, and J.S. Blanchard, *Reading research revisited.* Columbus, OH: Merrill, 1983.
Dreher, M.J. The instantiation of general terms in children. Unpublished doctoral dissertation, University of California, 1980.
Dreher, M.J. The generalization of the instantiation hypothesis to children. *Reading Research Quarterly,* 1981, 17, 28-43.
Dreher, M.J. Schema theory: The validity of the instantiation hypothesis. *Journal of Reading Behavior,* 1981, 13, 223-236.
Flavell, J.H. Cognitive monitoring. In W.P. Dickson (Ed.), *Oral communication skills.* New York: Academic Press, 1981.
Gates, A.I. An experimental and statistical study of reading and reading tests. *Journal of Educational Psychology,* 1921, 12, 303-314.
Gates, A.I. A study of the role of visual perception, intelligence, and certain associative processes in reading and spelling. *Journal of Educational Psychology,* 1926, 17, 433-445.
Gates, A.I. *The improvement of reading.* New York: Macmillan, 1947.
Gough, P., Juel, C., and Roper-Schneider, D. A two stage conception of initial reading acquisition. In J. Niles and L.A. Harris (Eds.), *Searches for meaning in reading language processing and instruction.* Rochester, NY: National Reading Conference, 1983.

Guthrie, J. Models of reading and reading disability. *Journal of Educational Psychology,* 1973, 65, 9-18.

Hebb, D.O. *The organization of behavior.* New York: Wiley, 1949.

Holmes, J.A. *The substrata-factor theory of reading.* Berkeley, CA: California Book, 1953. (OP)

Holmes, J.A. Factors underlying major reading disabilities at the college level. Doctoral dissertation, University of California at Berkeley, 1948. *Genetic Psychology Monographs,* 1954, 49, 1-95.

Holmes, J.A. The substrata-factor theory of reading: Some experimental evidence. In J.A. Figurel (Ed.), *New frontiers in reading.* New York: Scholastic, 1960. (OP)

Holmes, J.A. Basic assumptions underlying the substrata-factor theory of reading. *Reading Research Quarterly,* 1965, 1, 5-28.

Holmes, J.A., and Athey, I. *Reading success and personality characteristics in junior high school students.* University of California Publications in Education, Vol. 18. Berkeley, CA: University of California Press, 1969.

Holmes, J.A., and Singer, H. *The substrata-factor theory: Substrata-factor differences underlying reading ability in known groups.* U.S. Office of Education, Final Report No. 538, SAE 8176, 1961.

Holmes, J.A., and Singer, H. Theoretical models and trends toward more basic research in reading. *Review of Educational Research,* 1964, 34, 127-155.

Holmes, J.A., and Singer, H. *Speed and power of reading in high school.* U.S. Department of Health, Education, and Welfare, Cooperative Research Monograph No. 14. Washington, DC: U.S. Government Printing Office, Catalog No. FS 5.230:30016, 1966.

Huey, E.B. *The psychology and pedagogy of reading.* New York: Macmillan, 1908.

Javal, E. Essai sur la physiologie de lecture. *Annales d' Oculistique,* 1879, 82, 242-253.

Judd, C.H., and Buswell, G.T. *Silent reading: A study of the various types.* Supplementary Educational Monographs, No. 23. Chicago: University of Chicago Press, 1922.

Katz, I.C. The effects of instructional methods on reading acquisition systems. Unpublished doctoral dissertation, University of California at Riverside, 1980.

Katz, I.C., and Singer, H. Effects of instructional methods on reading acquisition systems: A reanalysis of the first grade studies data. Paper presented at the International Reading Association's Convention, Anaheim, California, May 1976. In Educational Retrieval of Information Center, 1976.

Katz, I., and Singer, H. The substrata-factor theory of reading: Differential developmental of subsystems underlying reading comprehension in the first year. In J.A. Niles and L.A. Harris (Eds.), *New inquiry in reading research and instruction.* Thirty-First Yearbook of the National Reading Conference. Rochester, NY: National Reading Conference, 1982.

Katz, I., and Singer, H. The substrata-factor theory of reading: Subsystem patterns underlying achievement in beginning reading. In J.A. Niles (Ed.), *Thirty-Third Yearbook of the National Reading Conference.* Rochester, NY: National Reading Conference, 1984.

Kling, M. General open systems theory and the substrata-factor theory of reading. In A.J. Kingston (Ed.), *Use of theoretical models in research.* Newark, DE: International Reading Association, 1966. (OP)

Laycock, F. The flexibility hypothesis in reading and the work of Piaget. In J.A. Figurel (Ed.), *Challenge and experiment in reading.* New York: Scholastic, 1962.

Lazar, M. A diagnostic approach to the reading program, part 1. *Educational Research Bulletin,* No. 3. Bureau of Reference, Research and Statistics. New York: New York Board of Education, 1942.

Lefevre, C.A. *Linguistics and the teaching of reading.* New York: McGraw-Hill, 1964.

Monroe, M. *Children who cannot read.* Chicago: University of Chicago Press, 1932.

Peters, C.C., and Van Voorhis, W.R. *Statistical procedures and their mathematical bases.* New York: McGraw-Hill, 1940.

Phelan, Sister M.B. Visual perception in relation to variance in reading and spelling. *Educational Research Monograph,* 1940, 12, 1-48.

Roehler, L.R., and Duffy, G.G. Direct explanation of comprehension processes. In G.G. Duffy, L.R. Roehler, and J. Mason (Eds.), *Comprehension instruction: Perspectives and suggestions.* New York: Longman, 1984.

Rumelhart, D.E. *Toward an interactive model of reading.* Technical report No. 56. San Diego: Center for Human Information Processing, University of California, 1976.

Rumelhart, D.E. Schemata: The building blocks of cognition. In J.T. Guthrie (Ed.), *Comprehension and teaching.* Newark, DE: International Reading Association, 1981.

Russell, D.H. *Children's thinking.* New York: Ginn, 1956.

Singer, H. Conceptual ability in the substrata-factor theory of reading. Unpublished doctoral dissertation, University of California at Berkeley, 1960.

Singer, H. Substrata-factor theory of reading: Theoretical design for teaching reading. In J.A. Figurel (Ed.), *Challenge and experiment in reading.* New York: Scholastic, 1962.

Singer, H. Substrata-factor patterns accompanying development in power of reading, elementary through college levels. In E. Thurston and L. Hafner (Eds.), *The philosophical and sociological bases of education.* Fourteenth Yearbook of the National Reading Conference. Marquette, WI: National Reading Conference, 1964.

Singer, H. A developmental model for speed of reading in grades three through six. *Reading Research Quarterly,* 1965, 1, 29-49.

Singer, H. Substrata-factor evaluation of a precocious reader. *Reading Teacher,* 1965, 18, 288-296.

Singer, H. *Substrata-factor reorganization accompanying development in speed and power of reading at the elementary school level.* Cooperative Research Project No. 2011, U.S. Department of Health, Education and Welfare, Office of Education, 1965.

Singer, H. Conceptualization in learning to read. In G. Schick and M. May (Eds.), *New frontiers in college-adult reading.* Fifteenth Yearbook of the National Reading Conference. Marquette, WI: National Reading Conference, 1966.

Singer, H. Roundtable review: Reply to John Carroll's critique of the substrata-factor theory of reading. *Research in the Teaching of English,* 1969, 3, 87-102.

Singer, H. Stimulus models for teaching reading. In M. Clark and S. Maxwell (Eds.), *Reading: Influence on progress.* Proceedings of the Fifth Annual Study Congress of the United Kingdom Reading Association, 1970, 112-119.

Singer, H. Conceptualization in learning to read. In H. Singer and R.B. Ruddell (Eds.), *Theoretical models and processes of reading,* Second Edition. Newark, DE: International Reading Association, 1976.

Singer, H. *Preparing content reading specialists for the junior high school level: Strategies for meeting the wide range of individual differences in reading ability.* Final Report to the U.S. Office of Education, EPDA Project, 1973. (ED 088 003, CS000 924)

Singer, H. A century of landmarks in reading and learning from text at the high school level: Theories, research, and instructional strategies. *Journal of Reading,* 1983, 26 332-342.

Singer, H. Hypotheses on reading comprehension in search of classroom validation. In M. Kamil (Ed.), *Thirtieth Yearbook of the National Reading Conference.* Chicago: National Reading Conference, 1981.

Singer, H. A critique of Jack Holmes's study: The substrata-factor theory of reading and its history and conceptual relationship to interaction theory. In L.M. Gentile, M.L. Kamil, and J.S. Blanchard. *Reading research revisited.* Columbus, OH: Merrill, 1983.

Singer, H. An interactive reading instruction model. Paper presented at the Thirty-Third Annual Meeting of the National Reading Conference, St. Petersburg, Florida 1984.

Singer, H., and Donlan, D. *Reading and learning from text.* Hillsdale, NJ: Erlbaum, 1985.

Singer, H., and Ruddell, R.B. (Eds.).*Theoretical models and processes of reading,* First Edition, 1970; Second Edition, 1976. Newark, DE: International Reading Association, 1970, 1976.

Thorndike, E. Reading as reasoning: A study of mistakes in paragraph reading. *Journal of Educational Psychology,* 1917, 8, 323-332.

Tolman, E.C. Cognitive maps in rats and men. *Psychological Review,* 1948, 55, 189-208.

Wherry-Doolittle Technique. In H.E. Garrett, *Statistics in psychology and education.* New York: Longman Green, 1947.

Zaslow, R.W. Study of concept formation in brain damaged adults, mental defectives, and normals of different age levels. Unpublished doctoral dissertation, University of California at Berkeley, 1957.

Information Processing Model

One Second of Reading

PHILIP B. GOUGH
University of Texas

Suppose the eye of a moderately skilled adult reader (henceforth, the Reader) were to fall on this sentence, and that he were to read it aloud. One second after his initial fixation, only the first word will have been uttered.[1] But during that second, a number of events will have transpired in the mind of the Reader, each the evident result of processes of amazing complexity. If we knew the train of events, we would know what the processes must accomplish and thus something of their nature. If we knew this, we would know what the child must learn to become a Reader.

Accordingly, this paper is concerned with two topics. First, it tries to describe the sequence of events that transpire in one second of reading, in order to suggest the nature of the processes that link them. Second, it attempts to relate this description to some facts about the acquisition of reading. The description of the chain of events is intended to be exhaustive in the conviction that the complexity of the reading process cannot otherwise be fully appreciated. Thus it is detailed by choice, speculative by necessity, and almost certainly flawed. I hope these are virtues, for much of what is written about reading is either too vague to be tested or too banal to bother, and an analysis that can be attacked in detail can yield detailed knowledge. The consideration of research on reading in children, on the other hand, is anything but complete. Quite apart from the familiar methodological shortcomings which abound in this research, most of it is aimed at a level of description too gross to be of any use here. So rather than presenting an unavoidably dreary review of the literature, I have attempted to interpret the acquisition of reading in terms of the present model, and to fit selected experimental results into the resulting framework.

The Reading Process

Reading begins with an eye fixation. The Reader's eyes focus on a point slightly indented from the beginning of the line, and they remain in

Reprinted from J.F. Kavanagh and I.G. Mattingly (Eds.), *Language by Ear and by Eye.* Cambridge, MA: MIT Press, 1972, 331-358. With permission of the author and MIT Press.

that fixation for some 250 msec (Tinker 1958). Then they will sweep 1-4 degrees of visual angle (say 10-12 letter spaces) to the right, in a saccadic movement consuming 10-23 msec, and a new fixation will begin. Barring regressions, and ignoring return sweeps (which take 40-54 msec), this sequence will be repeated as long as reading continues [up to at least six hours according to Carmichael and Dearborn (1947)]. When the initial fixation is achieved, a visual pattern is reflected onto the retina. This sets in motion an intricate sequence of activity in the visual system, culminating in the formation of an icon.

Iconic Representation

The existence of the icon, a relatively direct representation of a visual stimulus that persists for a brief period after the stimulus vanishes, has been amply demonstrated (Sperling 1960, 1963). I take the icon to be a central event, presumably corresponding to neural activity in the striate cortex (cf. Haber & Standing 1969). I further assume that the icon is an "unidentified" or "precategorical" visual image, a set of bars, slits, edges, curves, angles, and breaks, perhaps corresponding to the output of simple cells like those identified by Hubel and Wiesel (1962).

Whatever the form of its contents, the iconic buffer has a substantial capacity. Sperling (1963) has shown that it can hold at least 17 of 18 letters presented in three rows of six. In the case of ordinary reading matter, it can be estimated that the useful content of the icon will include everything in an oval roughly two inches wide and an inch high, or about 20 letter-spaces of the line under fixation.[2]

The decay of the icon has been intensively studied (cf. Haber 1968, 1969). It is known to persist for several seconds if the stimulus is followed by darkness, but for less than half a second if in light (Sperling 1963). It can be erased or masked by a following patterned stimulus (Liss 1968; Spencer 1969).

The *formation* of the icon, on the other hand, has scarcely been studied at all. One reason is that it is excruciatingly difficult to investigate; the question of how long it takes to form an icon is no less than the question of how long it takes us to sense something. Simple threshold data are uninformative, for they only indicate how much (i.e., what duration of) visual energy is necessary to initiate the train of events which results in the icon. Masked threshold data tell no more, for they are naturally interpreted as indicating how long one icon exists before it is replaced by another. As far as I can see, the only relevant published data are to be found in studies of visually evoked potentials (e.g., Dustman and Beck 1965). If a flash of light is presented to the eye, it is reflected in detectable changes in electrical potential at the occipital cortex no less than 50 msec later;[3] Dustman and Beck (1965) have suggested that wave components with mean latencies of 57 and 75 msec are related to awareness of the light. Assuming that patterned visual information is processed no faster than a flash of light, we might infer (acknowledging the length of the leap) that the icon could not be formed in less than 50 msec, and that its full development may require closer to 100 msec.[4]

Given these assumptions, we are led to suppose that the Reader's initial fixation yields an icon containing materials corresponding to the first 15 to 20 letters and spaces of the sentence (e.g., "Suppose the eye of a"). This icon will become fully "legible" in something like 100 msec. It will last until it is replaced by the icon arising from the Reader's second fixation, some 250 msec later.

In the meantime, the lines, curves, and angles of the first icon will be recognized as familiar patterns. I assume they are identified as letters.

Letter Identification

Letter recognition is very rapid. There is striking evidence that even unrelated letters can be recovered from the icon at rates of 10-20 msec per letter.

One such datum was provided by Sperling (1963), who found that if a random matrix of letters was followed immediately by a patterned mask, the number of letters reported increased linearly with the duration of the matrix, one letter every 10 msec, up to a limit imposed by memory. Since premask stimulus duration is directly related to icon duration, this result presumably reflects the rate of readout of letters from the icon into a more durable register.

Given that simple recognition thresholds have been shown to be lower for words [and even pronounceable nonsense syllables (Gibson, Osser et al. 1963)] than for random strings like Sperling's, it would be interesting to see if their letters can be read out even more rapidly. To my knowledge, the relevant experiment has not yet been conducted.[5] But there are data that suggest a comparable rate of letter identification with meaningful materials.

First, Scharf, Zamansky et al. (1966) found the masked recognition threshold (using Sperling's own mask) for familiar five-letter words to be roughly 90 msec (under high luminance). This fact provides little comfort for any assumption that read-out of letters from the icon is more efficient for meaningful or pronounceable materials than for random strings of letters; Sperling's results show that under the same circumstances, four or five unrelated letters can easily be registered.

Second, Michael Stewart, Carlton James, and I (Stewart, James et al. 1969) found that visual recognition latency—the time between presentation of a word and the beginning of its pronunciation—increases steadily with word length in letters, from 615 msec for three-letter words to 693 msec for ten-letter words. The function is negatively accelerated; the increase in latency with length is greater with short words than long. But the data are compatible with the assumption that letters of words are read out of the icon at a rate of 10-20 msec per letter.

Third, W. C. Stewart and I (Gough and Stewart 1970) have measured how long it takes readers to decide that a given string of letters is a word or not. One of the variables we manipulated was word length. We found that four-letter words are acknowledged some 35 msec faster than six-letter words, again consistent with the assumption that each additional letter requires an additional 10-20 msec for readout from the icon.

These data, among others, suggest that letters are recovered from the icon *as* letters, that the evident effects of higher levels of organization (like spelling patterns, pronounceability, and meaningfulness) on word recognition and speed of reading should be assigned to higher, and later, levels of processing. It is worth noting that if this analysis is correct, then it can be, at best, a half-truth to say that we do not read letter by letter.

Suppose that letters are identified and read out of the icon at a rate of 10 to 20 msec per letter, starting the moment the icon is formed. Since the icon should endure for some 250 msec, between one and two dozen letters could be identified from it even if readout were strictly serial. With a conservative estimate of three fixations per second, and assuming the average word to contain seven letters, even the lower value of letter transfer (i.e., 12 per fixation) would yield a reading speed in excess of 300 words per minute.

I see no reason, then, to reject the assumption that we do read letter by letter.[6] In fact, the weight of the evidence persuades me that we do so serially, from left to right (cf. White 1969). Thus I will assume that the letters in the icon emerge serially, one every 10 or 20 msec into some form of character register.

How the letters get here and what form they take once they have arrived are intriguing questions. But more important is what is done with them. Clearly, letters are not the stuff of which sentences are made. They must be associated with meanings; they must be mapped onto entries in the mental lexicon. The specification of the mechanism by which this is accomplished is, as I see it, the fundamental problem of reading.

The Mapping Problem

There are two superficially appealing possibilities. First, one might assume that the lexicon is directly accessible from the character register, that the Reader goes "directly" from print to meaning. This possibility is appealing to some theorists (cf. Kolers 1970) at least in part because of the nonalphabetic (i.e., neither phonemic nor syllabic) character of many orthographies. Since readers of such orthographies have to learn thousands of arbitrary associations between printed and spoken words, they could as easily learn direct associations between the orthographic words and their meanings and circumvent the spoken word altogether. And if they can do it, so can we.

We can, indeed, but only at great (and quite unnecessary) expense. Every potential Reader has a lexicon that is accessible through phonological information; he can understand the spoken word. Presumably, then, each of his lexical entries contains a phonological representation, and he has a retrieval mechanism that can address the entry through that representation. If he learns to assign such a representation to the printed word, the mapping problem is solved, and he quickly becomes a Reader. If he does not, he must add an orthographic representation to each of the tens of thousands of lexical entries (to say nothing of constructing a completely new retrieval mechanism to make use of them). The Reader of a nonalphabetic orthography might do this, for his is Hobson's choice. But we have a significant alternative, for while the orthography of English is complex and its rules are numerous, no one has seriously proposed that the number of these rules approaches within a factor of 100 the size of our lexicons. If there is any principle of cognitive economy, it surely must demand that we do not acquire tens of thousands of supererogatory associations, and we must not go straight from print to meaning.

The second possibility is, in this respect, appropriate: it is that we go from print to meaning by way of speech. On this view, the Reader applies orthographic rules to the contents of the character register, converting them to speech, and then listens to himself. All the Reader must add to his cognitive equipment are the orthographic rules. Nothing needs to be added to the lexicon; no new retrieval system needs to be constructed.

The advantages of this hypothesis are obvious. It is a venerable one, and it has prompted any number of studies of subvocal activity during reading (Conrad 1972). But I find it untenable, for I do not believe that the device it proposes can work fast enough. Recall that M. Stewart, C. T. James, and I (1969) found that production latency for a three-letter word is in excess of 600 msec. A highly motivated and practiced subject can push this down to 500 msec. Subtracting the 32 msec our voice key consumes, the 10 msec or so it requires for a nervous impulse to travel from the midbrain to the larynx (Ohala 1970), and another 5 or 10 for it to get to the midbrain from the motor cortex, one is still left with well over 400 msec for an instruction to speak to be assembled. Even ignoring the additional time required for a circuit through some version (however abstract) of an auditory loop, a Reader would not understand a printed word for better than 400 msec after his eye fell on it.

Clearly, we do not know just how long it takes to understand a word. But what may be relevant evidence was obtained several years ago in a study by Rohrman and myself (Rohrman and Gough 1967). We asked subjects to decide if pairs of words were synonymous or not, and measured the latencies of their decisions. On some trials, we announced that a pair would be presented in two seconds by saying "set"; on others, the warning signal was one member of the pair to be judged. We found that giving the subject one member in advance reduced his decision latency by roughly 160 msec. If it is assumed that simultaneous presentation of the pair requires a serial search for the two meanings, and that giving one word in advance eliminates only the retrieval of its meaning from the total decision process, then this result indicates that the meaning of a printed word is located in something on the order of 160 msec. (This result is, in light of the present model, fascinating: if the icon of the word was formed in 100 msec, then it suggests that the meaning of a word is located as fast as its letters can be read out of the icon.) This interpretation is clearly open to question, but if the estimate is anywhere near the true value, then the Reader understands a word well before he can begin to utter it, and the speech-loop hypothesis cannot possibly hold.

In light of these considerations, I am led to a third hypothesis, one that claims the advantages of both (and the disadvantages of neither) at the small price of a charge of abstraction. Suppose it is assumed that the Reader maps characters, not onto speech, but rather onto a string of systematic phonemes, in the sense of Chomsky and Halle (1968). Systematic phonemes are abstract entities that are related to the sounds of the language—the phonetic segments—only by means of a complex system of phonological rules. Thus it is easy to imagine that formation of a string of systematic phonemes would necessarily take place at some temporal distance from (i.e., some time before) the posting of motor commands, and the prohibitive cost of passage through the speech loop would be eliminated. Moreover, since lexical entries must contain, in addition to their semantic and syntactic features, a lexical representation in systematic phonemes, it seems reasonable to assume that the speaker of a language employs, in the comprehension of speech, retrieval mechanisms that access the lexical entries through these lexical representations. If characters are converted into comparable representations, then available retrieval mechanisms could be engaged, and the search for meaning in reading would require no costly new apparatus.

Obviously, this hypothesis is highly speculative, and I can offer no experimental evidence in support of it.[7] But Halle (1969) and N. Chomsky (1970) argue persuasively for a similar view, and I know of nothing to preclude it. More important, it provides the basis for a coherent account of a central problem in the acquisition of reading, as I will attempt to show later.

Thus, I will assume that the contents of the character register are somehow transposed into abstract phonemic representations. If, as Chomsky and Halle argue, the orthography of English directly reflects this level of representation, little processing will be required; otherwise, more complex transformations [e.g., the grapheme-phoneme correspondence rules of Venezky (1970)] will yield a string of systematic phonemes that can be used to search the mental lexicon.

Lexical Search

Whether the preceding hypothesis is correct remains to be seen. But whether by this mechanism or by some other, lexical entries are ultimately reached; the Reader understands the words of the sentence. Too little is known about word comprehension to suggest how it is accomplished or even to constrain speculation in any serious way. So I will adopt what I take to be the simplest assumption: that the words of the sentence are understood serially, from left to right.

Apparent objections to this hypothesis lie in the prevalence of lexical ambiguity. First, if words are understood one at a time, then it seems likely that they will frequently be misunderstood, at least until context demands and receives assignment of a new reading. Second, it would seem that prior context would determine the course of lexical search, a procedure not incorporated in the present model.

The first is no real objection, for words often are misunderstood momentarily, and the presence of lexical ambiguity in a sentence demonstrably increases the difficulty of processing the sentence. For example, Foss (1970) has found that if subjects are asked to monitor a sentence for the presence of a given phoneme, their reaction time to the target is increased if it follows an ambiguous item. As to the second point, several experiments in our laboratories have failed to find evidence that the disruptive effect of ambiguity can be eliminated by prior context. Foss has found the same increase in phoneme monitor latency after an ambiguous word even when that word is preceded by a context that completely disambiguates it. In pilot studies, several of my students have found that it takes longer to decide if a pair of words are related when one is ambiguous than if it is not, even when the unambiguous word is presented first (e.g., *prison-cell* takes longer than *prison-jail*). Thus we have (as yet) found no evidence that disambiguation takes place until *after* lexical search.

Such evidence suggests that the abstract phonemic representation is assigned the first lexical entry that can be found. This is consistent with the results of Rubenstein, Garfield, and Millikan (1970) and Gough and Stewart (1970) which show that words are acknowledged to be words more rapidly if they are ambiguous than if they are not (with form and frequency equated). This result suggests that the various readings of a polysemous word are stored separately in the mental dictionary, rather than under a single heading (as they are in Webster's). Interestingly,

Rubenstein, Lewis, and Rubenstein (1971) have found that this result does not hold for systematically ambiguous items (i.e., items like *plow*, in which the ambiguity lies only in grammatical category); consistency demands the assumption that these constitute single entries with alternative syntactic features specified.

Thus, lexical search would appear to be a parallel process, with the race going to the swift. When the first entry is located, its contents are accepted as the reading of the word until it proves incompatible with subsequent data; in the case of a systematically ambiguous word, its grammatical category can remain unspecified until further information is provided. In either event, the contents of the lexical entry yielded by each successive word must be deposited somewhere to be organized into a sentence. Primary memory is a likely spot.

Primary Memory

A small-capacity buffer storage system where 4 to 5 verbal items are maintained for a matter of seconds is postulated in many current models of memory (cf. Norman 1970). An item entering this primary memory [PM] (Waugh and Norman 1965) is generally thought to be subject to any of four fates. If it is ignored, it will simply (and rapidly) decay; on the other hand, it can be renewed through rehearsal. When the PM is full, an item in residence must be displaced if a new item is to enter. Finally, it may be transferred or copied into a more permanent store, the secondary memory.

There is one impediment to the assumption that the PM is the temporary repository for the content of a lexical entry. It is widely assumed that the contents of the PM are primarily acoustic or articulatory or phonemic (e.g., Baddeley 1966; Conrad 1964), largely because it is readily shown that verbal items are easily confused on this basis in short-term memory. I find this argument shaky.

First, confusion based on supraphonological properties of items in short-term memory can be demonstrated quite easily. Cornbleth, Powitzky, and I have found that lists of six nouns are more easily remembered if all are singular or plural than if singulars and plurals are mixed in a list; a variety of controls show that the effect cannot be attributed to confusion at the phonological level. The same appears to be true of verbs and tense, *mutatis mutandis*. If confusion data suggest that phonological information is in the PM, then reasoning from appropriate data leads to the same conclusion regarding syntactic or semantic properties. Second, Craik (1968) has shown that the immediate memory span is virtually identical for words of one to four syllables. This clearly suggests that the capacity of the PM is not defined by acoustic, articulatory, or even phonemic parameters, for all of these surely must vary from one-syllable to four-syllable words.

These data, I think, justify the assumption that the contents of lexical entries, including phonological, syntactic, and semantic information, are deposited in the PM, presumably one entry to a cell. The PM thus would become the working memory for the mechanisms of sentence comprehension.

There are many observations consistent with the assumption that the PM and the comprehension device interact in some such fashion. Three might be noted. First, it is obvious that far more words may be retained in sentences than out of them; sentences are remembered better than lists. In the present model this would be explained by assuming that when words are processed into sentences, the resulting structure is allocated to a further storage system with a much greater capacity. I am inclined to identify it with the secondary memory of the memory theorists, and to propose that items pass into secondary memory only when they are related to one another, or integrated in some fashion akin to comprehension. But that is another matter. For the present purpose, it suffices to assume that when a sentence is understood, it is deposited in the Place Where Sentences Go When They Are Understood (PWSGWTAU).

Second, when the contents of the PM are integrated, the PM can be cleared and new items entered. Support for this notion comes from a series of recent experiments by John Mastenbrook and myself, in which we have found that if a subject is asked to recall a five-word sentence together with five unrelated words, his recall is significantly greater if the sentence is presented before the list than vice versa, independent of recall order. This is easily explained in the present model: if the list is registered first, PM is full when the sentence arrives, and it can be processed only at the cost of some items from the list, whereas if the sentence arrives first, it is quickly understood and the PM is cleared when the list arrives.

Third, the model predicts that any sentence whose initial words exceed the capacity of PM before they can be understood (i.e., before their grammatical relations can be discovered) will prove incomprehensible. This is just the case with sentences self-embedded to a degree of 2 or more.

The evidence, then, supports the assumption that the PM provides a buffer memory for the comprehension device. In my opinion, we have no good idea how that device works; the question is being studied and debated intensively (cf. Gough 1971). For the present purpose, it suffices to assume that some wondrous mechanism (which we might dub *Merlin*) operating on the information in the PM, tries to discover the deep structure of the fragment, the grammatical relations among its parts. If Merlin succeeds, a semantic interpretation of the fragment is achieved and placed in the ultimate register, the PWSGWTAU. If Merlin fails, we would assume that the fixation will be maintained to provide further processing time, or that a regressive eye movement would be called for. This is obviously consistent with the well-known facts about eye movements and difficulty of material (cf. Tinker 1958).

Assuming success, the obtained deep structure provides the basis for the formation of a superficial structure containing the formatives from PM; application of phonological rules to this structure will yield instructions for the pronunciation of the fragment, and the Reader will begin to speak.

At this moment, some 700 msec have passed since the Reader's eye fell on the sentence. By this time, he is probably into his third fixation, perhaps 30 spaces into the sentence. The material from the first fixation is in the ultimate register (the PWSGWTAU); that from the second fixation is crowding into the PM.

I have tried to summarize the history of the 700 msec in Table 1, where the contents of each of the proposed stages of processing are specified at 100-msec intervals. Obviously, most of the entries are little more than plausible guesses. But the table suggests just how much must have happened. Some 20 to 25 letters have been internalized as characters, and converted into abstract phonemes. Perhaps a half dozen lexical entries have been located, and their contents copied into PM. The grammatical relations between some portion of these have been discovered, and the construction of a deep structure has begun. The semantically interpreted items have been inserted into a surface phrase-marker, and that, in turn, has been translated into motor commands.

On the outside, the Reader has rotated his eyes a few millimeters and he has begun to move his mouth. But on the inside, there has been a rapid succession of intricate events. Clearly, this succession could only be the product of a complex information processing system. That which has been proposed herein is outlined in Figure 1. It contains components that are asked to perform amazing feats with amazing rapidity, and precisely in concert. It remains to be seen whether this model bears any resemblance to reality. But it does suggest the complexity of the system that must be assembled in the mind of the child who learns to read.

The Acquisition of Reading

The child comes to the task of learning to read with several of the necessary components, or at least with crude versions of them.

Obviously, he comes with a visual system, and it produces an icon. Whether or not the child's visual image is comparable to the adult's is a fascinating question; so far as I know, we know too little of the quantity

Table 1
Level of Representation as a Function of Time

Msec	Material under Fixation	Level of Processing: Lines, Curves, Angles	Level of Processing: Letters	Level of Processing: Systematic Phonemes
000	Suppose the eye	Suppose the eye		
100	" " "	"	s	
200	" " "	"	. . . pose th . . .	sŭb = p . . . .
300	ose the eye of a mod	"	. . . e the e . . .	. . . = pɔ̄z#ð . . . .
400	" " "	ose the eye of a mod	. . . e eye o . . .	. . . z#ð̃ɛ̆#i . . . .
500	of a moderately skil	"	. . . ye of a . . .	. . . i#t̆v#æ̃ . . . .
600	" " "	of a moderately skil	. . . e of a . . .	. . . v#æ̃#m . . . .
700	" " "	"	. . . oderate . . .	. . . #modɛ̆ . . . .
800	tely skilled adult r	"	. . . erately . . .	. . . ɛ̆ræ̃t# . . . .
900	" " "	tely skilled adult re	. . . led adu . . .	. . . #ly#s . . . .
1000	adult reader (hencef	"	. . . d adult . . .	. . . skɨld . . . .

Table 1 (continued)

Msec	Level of Processing: Lexical Entries	Level of Processing: Semantic Representation	Level of Processing: Phonetic Representation	Vocalization
000				
100				
200				
300	$\begin{bmatrix} +V_t \\ +\text{ment} \\ \cdot \\ \cdot \end{bmatrix}$			
400	$\begin{bmatrix} +\text{Art} \\ +\text{Def} \\ \cdot \\ \cdot \end{bmatrix} \begin{bmatrix} +V_t \\ +\text{ment} \\ \cdot \\ \cdot \end{bmatrix}$			
	$\begin{bmatrix} +N_c \\ +\text{Conc} \\ \cdot \\ \cdot \end{bmatrix} \begin{bmatrix} +\text{Art} \\ +\text{Def} \\ \cdot \\ \cdot \end{bmatrix} \begin{bmatrix} +V_t \\ +\text{ment} \\ \cdot \\ \cdot \end{bmatrix}$			
500		$\text{IMP}(_s \text{ you will suppose } [_s$		
600	$\begin{bmatrix} +\text{Prep} \\ +\text{Poss} \\ \cdot \\ \cdot \end{bmatrix} \begin{bmatrix} +N_c \\ +\text{Conc} \\ \cdot \\ \cdot \end{bmatrix} \begin{bmatrix} +\text{Art} \\ +\text{Def} \\ \cdot \\ \cdot \end{bmatrix}$	$\ldots \text{ suppose } [_s \text{ the eye } (_s$	səpʰowz	

Table 1 (continued)

Msec	Level of Processing: Lexical Entries	Level of Processing: Semantic Representation	Level of Processing: Phonetic Representation	Vocalization
700	$\begin{bmatrix} +\text{Art} \\ -\text{Def} \\ \cdot \end{bmatrix} \begin{bmatrix} +\text{Prep} \\ +\text{Poss} \\ \cdot \end{bmatrix}$	. . . the eye $(_s \text{ X } [_s$	ōwzðiyáy	"Su . . ."
800	$\begin{bmatrix} +\text{Adj} \\ +\text{Deg} \\ \cdot \end{bmatrix} \begin{bmatrix} +\text{Art} \\ -\text{Def} \\ \cdot \end{bmatrix} \begin{bmatrix} +\text{Prep} \\ +\text{Poss} \\ \cdot \end{bmatrix}$	. . . eye $(_s \text{X } [_s \,]$ has eye	zðiyáyəv	" . . . ppo . . ."
900	$\begin{bmatrix} +\text{Adv} \\ +\text{Deg} \\ \cdot \end{bmatrix} \begin{bmatrix} +\text{Art} \\ -\text{Def} \\ \cdot \end{bmatrix} \begin{bmatrix} +\text{Prep} \\ +\text{Poss} \\ \cdot \end{bmatrix}$	. . . X $[_s$ X be Y $(_Y$ mod$)$	ðiyáyəv	" . . . se . . ."
1000	$\begin{bmatrix} +\text{Adj} \\ +\text{Anim} \\ \cdot \end{bmatrix} \begin{bmatrix} +\text{Adv} \\ +\text{Deg} \\ \cdot \end{bmatrix} \begin{bmatrix} +\text{Art} \\ -\text{Def} \\ \cdot \end{bmatrix}$	. . . X be skilled $(_s$skil . . .	áyəvə	" . . . se . . ."

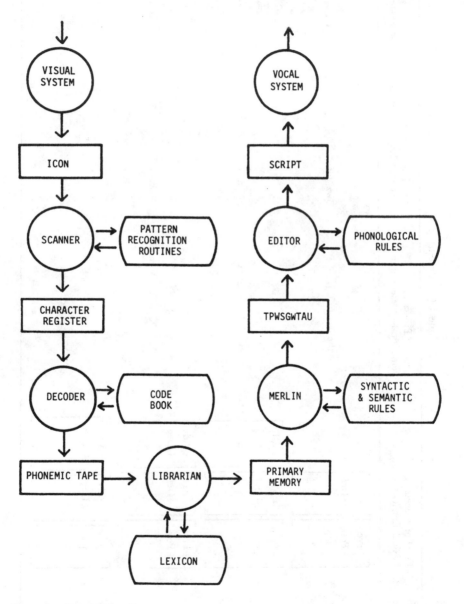

Figure 1.   A model of reading.

and quality of the child's icon to say. But there can be little doubt that he has one.

At the other extreme, the child clearly has the capacity to produce and understand sentences. He comes to school equipped with a lexicon, a comprehension device, and a phonological system; in terms of the present model, he incorporates a Librarian, a Merlin, and an Editor. None of these is as elaborate or extensive as they all will be when he reaches adulthood. His lexicon obviously contains fewer entries than it will, and there are indications that the entries it has are not as complete as they will be (cf. McNeill 1970, Chapter 8). His comprehension device (or at least the grammar it draws upon) is not that of an adult; there are a variety of syntactic structures which he does not yet reliably process (Berko 1958; Chomsky 1969). His phonological component, at least as it is engaged in speech production, is likely to show considerable deviation from the adult norm.

But at the same time, none of these shortcomings precludes the assembly of (at least) a primitive reading machine, for the child can readily make use of what he has. What is lacking is a character recognition device (the Scanner) and the device which will convert the characters it yields into systematic phonemic representations (the Decoder).

Character Recognition

There is no doubt that character recognition poses a problem for the child. We know pitifully little about form perception in children (cf. Reese and Lipsitt 1970, Chapter 11). But it seems clear that letters—"lank, stark, immovable, without form or comeliness, and as to signification, wholly void" (Mann 1841)—are not naturally identified. They can, of course, be discriminated (Caldwell and Hall 1969, 1970), but this is a far cry from the absolute identification demanded by the reading process. For example, while children will make relatively few mistakes in copying a pattern like a letter (Asso and Wyke 1971), indicating that they are quite capable of simultaneous discrimination, they find the same distinction inordinately difficult in a successive discrimination task (Rudel and Teuber 1963).

The difficulties posed for the child by letters that are mirror images of one another (e.g., "b-d, p-q") and, to a lesser extent, by those that are inversions (e.g., "b-p") have long been noted (cf. Monroe 1932). There have been a number of studies assessing methods of teaching children these distinctions (e.g., Hendrickson and Muehl 1962). And almost as often, this problem has been taken as a symptom of reading disability (cf. Orton 1937).

In one sense, it must be such a symptom. An inability to reliably identify "b" cannot fail to be a handicap in reading. But as E. Gibson has pointed out, the discrimination our orthography demands of the child runs directly counter to virtually all of his perceptual experience, in which objects differing only in orientation are equivalent. Moreover, Corballis and Beale (1971) have argued persuasively that such equivalence is deeply rooted in the bilateral symmetry of our anatomy. Thus these distinctions must pose a problem for every child, and there is every indication that this is the case.

Aside from orientation, the features that distinguish (or fail to distinguish) one letter from another in the child's icon are little understood. Gibson's studies of letter confusions in early readers and adults (Gibson, Schapiro et al. 1968) have suggested a set of features that may well be those used by the character recognition device. What remains to be disclosed, however, are the features by which the prereader will distinguish the same patterns. This knowledge would indicate which subcomponents of the character recognition device are available in the prereader, and which are not, and we might get some idea of what it takes to assemble the complete device.

It would be comforting to think that character recognition (or better, the lack of it) was the chief impediment to learning to read, for it can be taught (at least with patience). The unwary might be tempted to find support for this in the infamous fact that knowledge of the alphabet is the single best predictor of reading achievement (Bond and Dykstra 1967). But Samuels (1971) has reported the results of several studies that found no evidence that teaching the alphabet facilitates learning to read.

It remains to be seen, however, if the correlation is entirely spurious. Teaching of the alphabet, the ABC's, dates at least to the time of Socrates (Mathews 1966), and I find it difficult to believe that a tradition that appears to serve no other purpose would survive if it did not serve this one. Whether by means of alphabet books, blocks, or soup, character recognition must be mastered. It is obviously a necessary component of reading; equally obvious, it is not a sufficient one. Given character recognition, the fundamental problem arises, that which is commonly referred to as *decoding*.

Decoding

The Reader converts characters into systematic phonemes; the child must learn to do so. The Reader knows the rules that relate one set of abstract entities to another; the child does not. The Reader is a decoder; the child must become one. The decoding metaphor is familiar, and it would be difficult to argue that it is unappropriate. But if we take seriously the notion that characters are decoded to systematic phonemes, there is an interesting consequence. We can no longer think of the child as a clerk to whom we hand the code, for there is no direct way to display the rules constituting it. We cannot show him that this character goes with that systematic phoneme, for there is no way to isolate a systematic phoneme. We cannot tell him, "This goes with That," for we have no way of representing That.

In short, we cannot teach him the code. This is not to say that he cannot acquire it; every Reader before him has done so. But the child must master the code through a sort of cryptanalysis rather than through memorization. Viewed in this light, what is necessary for the child to learn to read is that he be provided with a set of pairs of messages known to be equivalent, one in ciphertext (writing) and one in plaintext (speech). They must be provided in sufficient quantity to enable him to arrive at a unique solution, and that is all.

A full solution of the code (i.e., one equivalent to that we ascribe to the Reader) can be achieved only if the child correctly identifies the alphabets of the plaintext and of the ciphertext. If we assume that the child has lexical representations in the form of systematic phonemes, the former should pose no special problem. (There is, however, some evidence to suggest that this may be a facile assumption (Savin 1972). It remains to be seen whether evidence of this sort is indicative of a different sort of phonological organization in the child, or the result of something much more superficial.)

If the child has mastered the character recognition problem as discussed above, then he has isolated the alphabet of the ciphertext, and his problem is reduced to a tractable one: that of searching for correspondences between the message pairs. But if, for some reason, he has not realized the unity of the letters, then he is faced with a cryptanalytic task of demonstrably greater difficulty, that of working out the cipher alphabet and the code simultaneously. In this connection, the Look-and-Say method obviously comes to mind. In light of the present analysis this method is not totally unreasonable. It provides the essential ingredients for the child's cryptanalysis (i.e., pairs of spoken and written messages). The trouble with it is that it does not appropriately define the problem for the child-cryptanalyst.

The Look-and-Say method confronts the child with a problem of paired-associate (PA) learning. We know that subjects confronted with the PA task will "solve" it as efficiently as they can; they will select some cue, some feature of each stimulus, and associate the defined response with that cue. That cue can be any feature or property of the stimulus item that distinguishes it from the others; in the case of visual material, it might be length, or area, or the presence of a curved line. I know of no reason to suppose that the child is different from the sophomore subject in this respect. Confronted with a word (the Look) to which he must associate a response (the Say), he should be likely to seize upon any feature of the word that differentiates it from the others he must master.

An egregious example of this can be found in a study reported by Coleman (1970) as part of his effort to collect a data base for a technology of reading. One of Coleman's concerns was to rank words that might be used in basic reading programs in order of the ease with which the child could learn to read them. So several hundred words were taught to different children by the look-say method, and the number of errors to criterion was taken as the basic datum. The words *kitten* and *no* were found to be the easiest of all. When it is noted that the words were presented in short lists, and that *kitten* is the only word as long as six letters, it is easy to see why these words were easy (and it is not that they are intrinsically so).

Given the manner in which lists are learned, it seems clear that the Look-and-Say method would not force the child to map characters onto phonemes until simpler strategies will no longer work, and that will not happen until the list reaches a substantial length. At this point, we would expect that some children will tackle the cryptanalysis and learn to read, but we should not be surprised to see others resign in frustration. And that, of course, is what is known to happen with the Look-and-Say method.

It is clearly preferable to confront the child with the mapping problem from the start, and to suggest to him that it is solvable. One way is through phonics. In this method (or better, class of methods), the child is explicitly directed to the ciphertext alphabet, and conceivably to the plaintext as well. The method requires that he pair letters (and clusters of letters) with spoken syllables; to the extent that he segments those syllables, such learning might provide material for the necessary cryptanalysis.

It is important to realize, though, that phonics does not teach the mapping required to become a Reader. What the Reader knows is the mapping between characters and systematic phonemes; what the child is taught in phonics is to name a letter (or letter pair) with a syllable that contains the appropriate systematic phoneme. When a child "sounds out" a new word, it is apparent to any auditor that the child is not converting letters into underlying phonemic representations. Rather he is searching for something that he can hear as a word.

In the present analysis, phonics is not a method of teaching the child grapheme-phoneme correspondence rules. The rules he learns are not the rules he must master, but rather heuristics for locating words through the auditory modality. The lexical representations of those words then provide data for the induction of the real character-phoneme rules. Skill in phonics gives the child a means of naming a word *in loco parentis;* it provides him with a valuable means of data collection.

The crucial variable in the cryptanalytic problem is the character of the data: the nature and number of message pairs. Other things equal, the shorter the messages, the fewer the potential solutions; so cryptanalysis is facilitated if the shortest possible messages are provided first. Virtually every method takes advantage of this fact by beginning reading instruction with short words. [It is interesting to note that Jacotot, one of the intellectual ancestors of Gestalt psychology, advocated beginning with a book and gradually working back to the letter, whatever that means (Mathews 1966).] Cryptanalysis is also facilitated if the messages are arranged such that covariation is apparent; if a change in a ciphertext is also accompanied by a change in the corresponding plaintext, the solution is obvious.

From this perspective, the various so-called Linguistic Methods [like those advocated by Bloomfield (1942) and Fries (1963)] appear to be optimal, for they offer the child a sequence of message pairs in which only one element is varied at a time. What is surprising, at least on first inspection, is that this method has not been shown to be superior. Indeed, there is no compelling evidence that any reasonable method of reading instruction yields results different from the others. This is encouraging, in one sense, for it means that children can manage to learn to read under any method, so long as they are provided the appropriate data, and the present hypothesis predicts just that. But it is also frustrating, for differential predictions are the stuff of which theories are made.

The trouble is, of course, that Methods are not methods. That is, a Method describes little more than an orientation on the part of a teacher, and perhaps the use of a particular basal reading series (Chall 1967). What are desperately needed are experimental studies of reading acquisition in detail, where we know what was presented to the child, when, in what manner, and how often.

There have been very few, and they are not very revealing. The first (that I know of) was conducted by Bishop (1964), using adult subjects. It was intended to compare the transfer effects of word and letter training. One group of subjects was taught to an eight-item paired-associate list, where each stimulus consisted of four Arabic characters (e.g., وں | ف) drawn from a set of twelve, and each response was a disyllabic Arabic word (e.g., /faru/). A second group was taught to name each of the twelve characters with its appropriate phoneme (i.e., they were given instruction in Arabic phonics). A third learned an irrelevant task. When all groups were then asked to learn a new eight-item PA list (in which the characters were recombined to form novel words), the phonics group learned it most rapidly. This is scarcely surprising (though it may have been when the study was conducted), for it seems clear that the whole-word group had little reason to detect correspondences, since other strategies requiring no intellectual effort would suffice perfectly well. (In fact, we might have expected to see negative transfer in this group, save for the fact that training and transfer stimuli had no initial characters in common.) What is more interesting is that the word group performed better than the control; some subjects evidently took on the cryptanalysis even though it was not necessary. But these subjects were college students, and it is not obvious that children would go to the same trouble.

A more promising study was conducted with kindergarteners by Jeffrey and Samuels (1967). They employed an artificial alphabet of six nonsense figures. Three (call them A, B, C), were identified with the consonants /m, s, b/, three (X, Y, Z) with the vowels /e, i, o/. One group of subjects, the Word Group, was taught a four-item PA list: AX-/mo/, BX-/so/, CY-/be/, CZ-/bi/. A Letter Group was taught four isolated correspondences: A-/m/, B-/s/, Y-/e/, and Z-/i/. A control group was taught an unrelated task.

Prior to training, all groups were familiarized with the alphabet, and given practice on "blending" the sounds to be used in the ultimate transfer list, AZ, BZ, BY, and AY. Then each group was given its training. On the transfer list, the phonics group performed significantly better than the others, which did not differ. In this study, the Letter Group was given what amounts to phonics instruction, and the Word Group might be thought of as representing a linguistic method. If this were so, the phonics instruction would seem to be the superior method of (at least) initial instruction. But there is a serious flaw in this analogy, for the Word Group was mistreated.

The Letter Group was exposed to just those four elements that would be involved in the transfer; the Word Group, on the other hand, confronted items composed of six. But more important, the organization of those elements fell short of that which could be expected to yield successful cryptanalysis.

The message pairs which the Word Group was allowed to use may be arranged in a matrix, arrayed by initial and final ciphertext element:

	X	Y	Z
A	/mo/	—	—
B	/so/	—	—
C	—	/be/	/bi/

This display makes clear the structure of the correspondence rules, and it is conceivable that they might be induced by someone who knew that CY can be decomposed to C and Y, and that /be/ consists of /b/ plus /e/. (In fact, the Word Group produced something like eight correct responses—of a possible 80—on the initial transfer trial, so more than one of the 20 must have induced something.) But there is nothing to demand it, for memorizing only four item-item correspondences will solve the problem. In fact, to achieve the solution of the code implicit in this matrix would require the identification of *six* rules. It is surely reasonable for the learner to prefer rote memory in this instance.

Such considerations lead to the hypothesis that the child would most readily learn the true system of correspondences when it provides the simplest solution to the cryptanalytic problem. For example, if, in a design like that of Jeffrey and Samuels, the child had been forced to learn not just four items, but all six lying outside a diagonal of this matrix, then the principled solution would be as simple as the associative one, and we would expect significantly greater transfer to novel items (i.e., the diagonal items).

This analysis suggests that the child's task bears a striking resemblance to those studied in adults under the rubric of miniature linguistic systems. Since the seminal experiments of Esper (1925, 1933), this literature has grown too large to review here (see Smith and Braine, 1972). But it provides abundant evidence for the principle proposed here: The greater the advantage afforded by induction of structure (over rote memory), the more frequent the induction. In the present case, we should expect to see that if Jeffrey and Samuels had not only more completely filled the matrix but enlarged it (in either dimension), the Word Method would have yielded dramatically better results (cf. Foss 1968; Palermo and Parrish 1971). And when one considers that the real task confronting the child involves a matrix in multiple dimensions, the consequences are even more apparent. There have been other studies of teaching methods (e.g., Hartley 1970)—in this experimental sense—but they add little to this picture.

How the child solves the decoding problem is a mystery, but many do. If one does, he should be able to understand and produce any word that conforms to the rules he has mastered. Yet it has long been observed that there are children who can read and pronounce words, children who can decode, but yet do not seem to *read* connected discourse. They "bark at print"; they are "word-callers" or "parrot-readers." Evidently, solving the decoding problem does not automatically make the child a Reader.

The Speed Problem

There is a natural interpretation of this problem within the present model. To understand a sentence, it does not suffice to obtain lexical entries, place them in the PM, and pronounce them. If the words of a sentence are to be integrated into a semantic reading, they must be deployed in the PM together.

To be sure, we adults can tolerate substantial delays between words without apparent disruption of comprehension; if the delays are brief enough, as in hesitation pauses, we may not even be aware of them. This is to be expected if the PM is indeed the repository for material waiting to be understood, for it will hold that material for a short while. But Martin (1968) has shown that pauses of as little as two seconds interfere with our ability to perceive sentences in noise, and we have found some evidence in pilot studies that repetition of words within sentences reduces our capacity to remember them.

It seems reasonable to suppose that the child's ability to comprehend sentences is affected in the same way. Furthermore, if—as some evidence suggests (Haith, Morrison, et al. 1970)—the child's PM is much smaller than our own, then pauses between words will prove even more disruptive for the child's comprehension. There is an obvious source of pauses in reading sentences: if words are identified slowly, then pauses are inevitable. There is abundant evidence that children do not identify words as rapidly as adults, and that the poor reader does not identify words as rapidly as the good one.

The hypothesis that temporal word spacing will significantly diminish sentence comprehension in the child would be easy to test. But I think that naturalistic observation of children reading aloud suggests that temporal spacing is a ubiquitous problem in early reading. If it takes too long to read a given word, the content of the immediately preceding words will have been lost from the PM, and comprehension will be prevented. If the word in question is read aloud, it will necessarily be read as a citation form, and the child's oral reading will sound like a list just because he is, in fact, reading a list.

To prevent this, the child who would understand must try to read rapidly, and if he cannot quickly identify a word, he must guess. The result will frequently be an oral reading error. These errors have been the subject of considerable study (Weber 1968), and seemingly contradictory conclusions have been drawn from them. On the one hand, it has been argued [e.g., by Goodman (1970) and elsewhere] that reading is normally a kind of guessing game, in which the reader uses the printed word for little more than hints as to whether he is thinking the right thoughts or not. In this view, oral reading errors are nothing but a manifestation of normal function, not a symptom of malfunction, and thus they should not be squelched. On the other hand, it has been argued (Biemiller, 1970), that at least in the early stages of reading, oral reading errors are an indication that the child is avoiding the decoding problem, and thus a sign that he is unable to identify what lies before him.

From the present point of view, Biemiller is closer to the truth. A guess may be a good thing, for it may preserve the integrity of sentence comprehension. But rather than being a sign of normal reading, it indicates that the child did not decode the word in question rapidly enough to read normally. The good reader need not guess; the bad should not.

In the model I have outlined, the Reader is not a guesser. From the outside, he appears to go from print to meaning as if by magic. But I have contended that this is an illusion, that he really plods through the sentence, letter by letter, word by word. He may not do so; but to show that he does not, his trick will have to be exposed.

REFERENCES

Asso, D., and M. Wyke, 1971. Discrimination of spatially confusable letters by young children. *J. Exp. Child Psych.* 11:11-20.

Baddeley, A. D., 1966. Short-term memory for word sequences as a function of acoustic, semantic, and formal similarity. *Quart. J. Exp. Psychol.* 18:362-365.

Berko, J., 1958. The child's learning of English morphology. *Word,* 14:150-177.

Biemiller, A., 1970. The development of the use of graphic and contextual information. *Reading Res. Quart.* 6:75-96.

Bishop, C. H., 1964. Transfer effects of word and letter training in reading. *J. Verbal Learning and Verbal Behavior* 3:215-221.

Bloomfield, L., 1942. Linguistics and reading. *Elementary English,* 18:125-130; 183-186.

Bond, G. L., and R. Dykstra, 1967. The cooperative research program in first-grade reading instruction. *Reading Res. Quart.* 2:4, 5-126.

Caldwell, E. D., and V. C. Hall, 1969. The influence of concept training on letter discrimination. *Child Development* 40:63-71.

Caldwell, E. D., and V. C. Hall, 1970. Concept learning in discrimination tasks. *Develop. Psych.* 2:41-48.

Carmichael, L., and W. F. Dearborn, 1947. *Reading and Visual Fatigue.* Boston: Houghton Mifflin.

Chall, J., 1967. *Learning To Read: The Great Debate.* New York: McGraw-Hill.

Chomsky, C., 1969. *The Acquisition of Syntax in Children from 5 to 10.* Cambridge, Mass.: M.I.T. Press.

Chomsky, N., 1970. Phonology and reading. In H. Levin and J. P. Williams (eds.), *Basic Studies on Reading.* New York: Basic Books, pp. 3-18.

Chomsky, N., and M. Halle, 1968. *The Sound pattern of English.* New York: Harper and Row.

Coleman, E. B., 1970. Collecting a data base for a reading technology. *J. Ed. Psych. Monographs* 61:4, Part 2, pp. 1-3.

Conrad, R., 1964. Acoustic confusions in immediate memory. *Brit. J. Psych.* 55:75-84.

Conrad, R., 1972. Speech and reading. In James F. Kavanagh and Ignatius Mattingly (Eds.), *Language by Ear and by Eye.* Cambridge: M.I.T. Press.

Corballis, M. C., and I. L. Beale, 1971. On telling left from right. *Sci. Amer.* 224:96-104.

Craik, F. I. M., 1968. Two components in free recall. *J. Verbal Learning and Verbal Behavior* 7:996-1004.

Dustman, R. E., and E. C. Beck, 1965. Phase of alpha brain waves, reaction time and visually evoked potentials. *Electroenceph. Clin. Neurophysiol.* 18:433-440.

Esper, E. A., 1925. A technique for the experimental investigation of associative interference in artificial linguistic material. *Language Monogr.,* vol. 1.

Esper, E. A., 1933. Studies in linguistic behavior organization: I. Characteristics of unstable verbal reactions. *J. Gen. Psych.* 8:346-379.

Feinberg, R., 1949. A study of some aspects of peripheral visual acuity. *Amer J. Optometry and Arch. of Amer. Acad. Optometry* 26:49-56, 105-119.

Foss, D. J., 1968. Learning and discovery in the acquisition of structured material. *J. Exp. Psych.* 77:341-344.

Foss, D. J., 1970. Some effects of ambiguity upon sentence comprehension. *J. Verbal Learning and Verbal Behavior* 9:699-706.

Fries, C. C., 1963. *Linguistics and Reading.* New York: Holt, Rinehart, and Winston.

Gibson, E. J., 1965. Learning to read. *Science,* 148:1066-1072.

Gibson, E. J., F. Schapiro, and A. Yonas, 1968. Confusion matrices for graphic patterns obtained with a latency measure. In *The Analysis of Reading Skill: A Program of Basic and Applied Research.* Final report, Project No. 5-1213, Cornell University and U.S.O.E., pp. 76-96.

Gibson, E. J., H. Osser, and A. Pick, 1963. A study in the development of grapheme-phoneme correspondences. *J. Verbal Learning and Verbal Behavior* 2:142-146.

Gilbert, L. C., 1959. Speed of processing visual stimuli and its relation to reading. *J. Ed. Psych.* 55:8-14.

Goodman, K. S., 1970. Reading: A psycholinguistic guessing game. In *Theoretical Models and Processes of Reading,* H. Singer and R. R. Ruddell (eds.), Newark, Del.: International Reading Association, pp. 259-272.

Gough, P. B., 1968. We don't read letter-by-letter? Paper presented at a Consortium on Psycholinguistics and Reading, Convention of the International Reading Association, Boston.

Gough, P. B., 1971. (Almost a decade of) experimental psycholinguistics. In *A Survey of Linguistic Science,* W. O. Dingwall (ed.), College Park: Linguistics Program, Univ. of Maryland.

Gough, P. B., and W. C. Stewart, 1970. Word vs. non-word discrimination latency. Paper presented at Midwestern Psychological Association.

Haber, R. N. (ed.), 1968. *Contemporary Theory and Research in Visual Perception.* New York: Holt, Rinehart and Winston.

Haber, R. N. (ed.), 1969. *Information-Processing Approaches to Visual Perception.* New York: Holt, Rinehart and Winston.

Haber, R. N., and L. B. Standing, 1969. Direct measures of short-term visual storage. *Quart. J. Exp. Psych.* 21:43-54.

Haith, M. M., F. J. Morrison, K. Sheingold, and P. Mindes, 1970. Short-term memory for visual information in children and adults. *J. Exp. Child Psych.* 9:454-469.

Halle, M., 1969. Some thought on spelling. In *Psycholinguistics and the Teaching of Reading.* K. S. Goodman and J. T. Fleming (eds.), Newark, Del.: International Reading Association.

Hartley, R. N., 1970. Effects of list types and cues on the learning of word lists. *Reading Res. Quart.* 6:97-121.

Hendrickson, L. N., and S. Muehl, 1962. The effect of attention and motor response pretraining on learning to discriminate b and d in kindergarten children. *J. Ed. Psych.* 53:236-241.

Hubel, D. H., and T. N. Wiesel, 1962. Receptive fields, binocular interaction and functional architecture in the cat's visual cortex. *J. Physiol.* 160:106-154.

Jeffrey, W. E., and S. J. Samuels, 1967. Effect of method of reading training on initial learning and transfer. *J. Verb. Learning and Verbal Behavior* 6:354-358.

Kolers, P. A., 1970. Three stages of reading. In *Basic Studies on Reading,* H. Levin and J. P. Williams (eds.), New York: Basic Books, pp. 90-118.

Liss, P., 1968. Does backward masking by visual noise stop stimulus processing? *Perception and Psychophysics* 4:328, 330.

McNeill, D., 1970. *The Acquisition of Language.* New York: Harper and Row.

Mann, 1841; cited by Mathews (1966), p. 77.

Martin, J. G., 1968. Temporal word spacing and the perception of ordinary, anomalous, and scrambled strings. *J. Verbal Learning and Verbal Behavior* 7:1954-157.

Mathews, M. M., 1966. *Teaching to Read: Historically Considered.* Chicago: University of Chicago Press.

Monroe, M., 1932. *Children Who Cannot Read.* Chicago: University of Chicago Press.

Norman, D. A. (ed.), 1970. *Models of Memory.* New York: Academic Press.

Ohala, J., 1970. Aspects of the control and production of speech. UCLA: Working Papers in Phonetics, vol. 15.

Orton, S. T., 1937. *Reading, Writing, and Speech Problems in Children.* New York: W. W. Norton.

Palermo, D. S., and M. Parrish, 1971. Rule acquisition as a function of number and frequency of exemplar presentation. *J. Verbal Learning and Verbal Behavior* 10:44-51.

Reese, H. W., and L. P. Lipsitt, 1970. *Experimental Child Psychology.* New York: Academic Press.

Rohrman, N. L., and P. B. Gough, 1967. Forewarning, meaning, and semantic decision latency. *Psychonomic Sci.* 9:217-218.

Rubenstein, H., L. Garfield, and J. A. Millikan, 1970. Homographic entries in the internal lexicon. *J. Verb. Learning and Verbal Behavior* 5:487-492.

Rubenstein, H., S. S. Lewis, and M. A. Rubenstein, 1971. Homographic entries in the internal lexicon: Effects of systematicity and relative frequency of meanings. *J. Verbal Learning and Verbal Behavior* 10:57-62.

Rudel, R. G., and H.-L. Teuber, 1963. Discrimination of direction of line in children. *J. Comp. Physiol. Psychol.* 56:892-898.

Samuels, S. J., 1971. Letter-name versus letter-sound knowledge in learning to read. *The Reading Teacher,* 24:604-608.

Savin, Harris B., 1972. What the child knows about speech when he starts to learn to read. In James F. Kavanagh and Ignatius Mattingly (Eds.), *Language by Ear and by Eye.* Cambridge: M.I.T. Press.

Scharf, B., H. S. Zamansky, and R. F. Brightbill, 1966. Word recognition with masking. *Perception and Psychophysics,* 1:110-112.

Smith, K. H., and M. D. S. Braine, 1972. Miniature languages and the problem of language acquisition. In *The Structure and Psychology of Language,* T. G. Bever and W. Weksel (eds.), New York: Holt, Rinehart and Winston.

Spencer, T. J., 1969. Some effects of different masking stimuli in iconic storage. *J. Exp. Psych.* 81:132-140.

Sperling, G., 1960. The information available in brief visual presentations. *Pschol. Monogr.,* 74: No. 11 (whole No. 498).

Sperling, G., 1963. A model for visual memory tasks. *Human Factors,* 5:19-31.

Stewart, M. L., C. T. James, and P. B. Gough, 1969. Word recognition latency as a function of word length. Paper presented at Midwestern Psychological Association.

Tinker, M. A., 1958. Recent studies of eye movements in reading. *Psych. Bull.* 55:215-231.

Venezky, R. L., 1970. *The Structure of English Orthography.* The Hague: Mouton.

Waugh, N. C., and D. A. Norman, 1965. Primary memory. *Psych. Rev.,* 72:89-104.

Weber, R., 1968. The study of oral reading errors: A survey of the literature. *Reading Res. Quart.* 4:96-119.

Wertheim, T., 1894. Ueber die indirekte Sehschärfe. *Z. Psychologie u. Physiologie der Sinnesorgane* 7:172-187.

White, M. J., 1969. Laterality differences in perception: A review. *Psych. Bull.* 72:387-405.

NOTES

[1] This estimate is based on my reading, as naturally as possible, 50 sentences drawn from the *Daily Texan* and presented tachistoscopically. The median interval between stimulus and response onset was just over 700 msec, and the average initial word required roughly 300 msec to produce.

[2] I am indebted to Kent Gummerman for this estimate. It is based on "a) acuity data for viewing in the horizontal meridian (Feinberg, 1949), b) Wertheim's (1894, p. 185) 'iso-acuity' ellipses that show

areas of equal acuity in all directions, and c) the conservative assumption that a letter can be resolved if the thickness of its component lines can be resolved by the eye" (Gummerman, personal communication).

3 There is an early component of the wave at approximately 43 msec, but Dustman and Beck feel that it is not correlated with stimulus awareness.

4 Presumably the latency of the icon will vary with the intensity of the stimulus (and perhaps with its complexity).

5 Gilbert (1959) came close when he presented linguistic segments (words and phrases) of various lengths for various durations, and examined the amount recovered as a function of length of material and exposure duration. But his materials were presented by film, so that control over stimulus quality and duration was crude, and he presents only a rough general description of his materials.

6 Elsewhere (Gough, 1968) I have tried to argue that the traditional arguments against this notion are without foundation.

7 Since this paper was delivered, Herbert Rubenstein has reported that subjects take longer to decide that a nonsense word which is homophonic with some English word is *not* a word than to make the same decision about nonsense items which are homophonic with any English lexical item. This result is, in my view, persuasive evidence for the hypothesis that the printed word is mapped onto a phonemic representation by the Reader.

One Second of Reading: Postscript

PHILIP B. GOUGH
University of Texas

This model is wrong. I take this to be a mark of virtue. It is easy to create a model which is "right"; all you need do is make one interactive or transactional enough such that everything in reading influences everything else. The result will be "right," because it will be impervious to disprove; it will yield no falsifiable predictions. But my view has always been that such models are not really right, they are simply empty, for a model which cannot be disproved is a model without content.

The purpose of a model is to summarize available knowledge and to lead to new knowledge by yielding novel predictions. It is by this standard that I find this model virtuous, for it embodied several claims which, though now demonstrably false or at least insufficient, have contributed to the growth of our knowledge of reading.

The claim that we read words letter-by-letter from left to right is one such claim: it is almost certainly wrong. But much, if not most, of what we know about word recognition has been learned in the effort to refute it. Alternative views (e.g., that the unit of word recognition is the visual feature, or the word itself) have not yielded testable predictions. So while I must now concede that my serial assumption was false, I remain committed to the view that the letter mediates word recognition.

The second claim for which this paper is notorious is that word recognition is mediated by phonological recoding. There is clearly a consensus that this, too, is inadequate (see, for example, McCusker, Hillinger, and Bias, 1981); it is widely agreed that skilled readers have direct or visual access to (at least) high frequency words. But we have learned much about word recognition in testing predictions derived from the phonological recoding hypothesis (see Gough, 1984). (In contrast, I argue that we have learned nothing from the direct access hypothesis: since it is nothing but the negation of the phonological recoding hypothesis, it yields no predictions of its own.) Moreover, while high frequency words account for a considerable fraction of words in print (word tokens), the vast majority of word types are infrequent. So I would still maintain that most words (i.e., types) are recognized through phonological recoding.

But perhaps the greatest virtue I would claim for the model is that it exemplifies the idea that the skilled reader reads what is on the printed page.

Reading may not be primarily visual; the average sharp-eyed Eskimo cannot read printed English. Psycholinguistic processes beyond word recognition abound in reading, and while my model paid lip service (see Merlin) to the problem of sentence comprehension, it clearly gave no heed to the very real and difficult problems of understanding text.

But neither is reading primarily psycholinguistic; the blind can read printed English no better than the Eskimo.

Most scholars resolve this tension by adopting an interactive view, that linguistic knowledge is skillfully combined with visual information to reconstruct the meaning intended by the author. But skilled readers, when seriously reading, not only succeed in extracting meaning from the printed page, they can (and I believe do) also succeed in accurately recognizing virtually every single word on that page (Alford, 1980; Stevens and Rumelhart, 1975). Moreover, eye-movement studies (e.g., Just and Carpenter, 1980) suggest that they do so by successively fixating all but the shortest of those words.

The hallmark of the skilled reader is the ability to recognize, accurately, easily, and swiftly, isolated words (and, even more so, pseudowords). We have argued elsewhere (Gough, 1981, 1983; Gough, Alford, and Holley-Wilcox, 1981) that this skill can only be attributed to the ability to decode, for while highly predictive context can and does facilitate word recognition, proving a strictly "bottom-up" model like mine wrong, most words are not predictable and so can only be read bottom-up. A successful model of reading must account for this ability. My model may have failed, but I still believe it pointed in the right direction.

REFERENCES

Alford, J.A., Jr. Lexical and contextual effects on reading time. Unpublished doctoral dissertation, University of Texas at Austin, 1980.

Gough, P.B. A comment on Kenneth Goodman. In M.L. Kamil (Ed.), *Directions in Reading: Research and Instruction*. Washington: National Reading Conference. 1981, 92-95.

Gough, P.B. Form, context, and interaction. In K. Rayner (Ed.), *Eye Movements in Reading*. New York: Academic Press, 203-211.

Gough, P.B. Word recognition. In P.D. Pearson (Ed.), *Handbook of Reading Research*. New York: Longman, 1984, 225-253.

Gough, P.B., Alford, J.A., Jr., and Holley-Wilcox, P. Words and contexts. In O.L. Tzeng and H. Singer (Eds.), *Perception of Print: Reading Research in Experimental Psychology*. Hillsdale, N.J.: Erlbaum, 1981, 85-102.

Just, M.A., and Carpenter, P.A. A theory of reading: From eye fixations to comprehension. *Psychological Review*, 87, 1980, 329-354.

McCusker, L.X., Hillinger, M.L., and Bias, R.G. Phonological recoding and reading. *Psychological Bulletin*, 89, 1981, 217-245.

Rayner, K. (Ed.) *Eye Movements in Reading*. New York: Academic Press, 1983.

Stevens, A.L., and Rumelhart, D.E. Errors in reading: Analysis using an augmented transition network model of grammar. In D.A. Norman and D.E. Rumelhart (Eds.), *Explorations in Cognition*. San Francisco: Freeman, 1975, 136-156.

Toward a Theory of Automatic
Information Processing in Reading

DAVID LABERGE
S. JAY SAMUELS
University of Minnesota

Among the many skills in the repertoire of the average adult, reading is probably one of the most complex. The journey taken by words from their written form on the page to the eventual activation of their meaning involves several stages of information processing. For the fluent reader, this processing takes a very short time, only a fraction of a second. The acquisition of the reading skill takes years, and there are many who do not succeed in becoming fluent readers, even though they may have quickly and easily mastered the skill of understanding speech.

During the execution of a complex skill, it is necessary to coordinate many component processes within a very short period of time. If each component process requires attention, performance of the complex skill will be impossible, because the capacity of attention will be exceeded. But if enough of the components and their coordinations can be processed automatically, then the load on attention will be within tolerable limits and the skill can be successfully performed. Therefore, one of the prime issues in the study of a complex skill such as reading is to determine how the processing of component subskills becomes automatic.

Our purpose in this paper is to present a model of the reading process which describes the main stages involved in transforming written patterns into meanings and relates the attention mechanism to processing at each of these stages. In addition, we will test the model against some experimental findings which indicate that the role of attention changes during advanced states of perceptual and associative learning.

This paper is divided into four sections in which we 1) briefly summarize the current views of the attention mechanism in information processing, 2) set forth a theory of automaticity in reading and evaluate it against some data, 3) discuss factors which may influence the develop-

Reprinted from *Cognitive Psychology*, 6, 1974, 293-323. With permission of the authors and Academic Press, Inc.

ment of automaticity, and 4) discuss some implications of the model for research in reading instruction.

Attention Mechanisms in Information Processing

In view of the fact that the present model places heavy emphasis on the role of attention in the component processes of reading, it may be well to review briefly the way the concept has been used by researchers in the recent past.

The properties of attention most frequently treated by investigators are selectivity and capacity limitation. Posner and Boies (1971) list alertness as a third component of attention, but this property has been investigated mostly in vigilance tasks and less often in the sorts of information processing tasks related closely to reading. The property of attention which has generated the most theoretical controversy is its limited capacity. When early dichotic listening experiments indicated that subjects select one ear at a time for processing messages, Broadbent (1958) proposed a theory which assumed that a filter is located close to the sensory surface. This filter allows messages from only one ear at a time to get through. However, later experiments indicated that well-learned significant signals such as one's own name (Moray, 1959) managed to get processed by the unattended ear. This led Treisman (1964) to modify the Broadbent theory and allow the filter to attenuate the signal instead of blocking it completely. In this way, significant, well-learned items could be processed by the unattended ear. Deutsch and Deutsch (1963), on the other hand, described a theory which rejected the placement of a selective filter prior to the analysis or decoding of stimuli and instead placed the selection mechanism at a point much later in the system, after the "importance" or "pertinence" (Norman, 1968) of the stimulus has been determined.

In the present model, it is assumed that all well-learned stimuli are processed upon presentation into an internal representation, or code, regardless of where attention is directed at the time. In this regard, the model is similar to the models of Deutsch and Deutsch and of Norman. However, the present theory proposes in addition that attention can selectively activate codes at any level of the system, not only at the deeper levels of meaning, but also at visual and auditory levels nearer the sensory surfaces. The number of existing codes of any kind that can be activated by attention at a given moment is sharply limited, probably to one. But the number of codes which can be simultaneously activated by outside stimuli independent of attention is assumed to be large, perhaps unlimited. In short, it is assumed that we can only attend to one thing at a time, but we may be able to process many things at a time so long as no more than one requires attention.

It is this capability of automatic processing which we consider critical for the successful operation of multicomponent, complex skills such as reading. As visual words are processed through many stages en route to meaningfulness, each stage is processed automatically. In addition, the transitions from stage to stage must be automatic as well. Sometimes a stage may begin processing before an earlier one finishes its processing. Examples of these interrelations between stages of processing are treated in the research of Sternberg (1969) and Clark and Chase (1972). In the skill of basketball, ball-handling by the experienced player is regarded as automatic. But ball-handling consists of subskills such as dribbling, passing, and catching, so each of these must be automatic and the transitions between them must be automatic as well. Therefore, when one describes a skill at the macrolevel as being automatic, it follows that the subskills at the microlevel and their interrelations must also be automatic.

Our criterion for deciding when a skill or subskill is automatic is that it can complete its processing while attention is directed elsewhere. It is especially important in such tests that one take careful account of all attention shifts. On many occasions, people appear to be giving attention to two or more things at the same time, when, in fact, they are shifting attention rapidly between the tasks. An example is the cocktail party phenomenon in which a person may appear to be following two conversations at the same time, but in reality he is alternating his attention.

The way we attempt to manage this problem in the laboratory is to test automaticity with procedures that control the momentary attention state of the subject (LaBerge, Van Gelder, & Yellott, 1970). Typically, we present a cue just prior to the stimulus the subject is to identify, and this induces a state of preparation for that particular stimulus. Most of the time he receives the expected stimulus, but occasionally he receives instead a test stimulus unrelated to the cue. The response to the unexpected test stimulus requires that the subject switch his attention as well as process the test stimulus. If the processing of the test stimulus requires attention, then the response latency will include both time for stimulus processing and time for attention switching. If, however, the stimulus processing does not require attention (i.e., it is automatic), then the response latency will not include stimulus processing time, assuming that the stimulus processing is completed by the time attention is switched.

Model of Automaticity in Reading

With these considerations of attention in mind, we turn to a description of a model of automatic processing in reading. This model is based on the assumption that the transformation of written stimuli into meanings involves a sequence of stages of information processing (Posner *et al.*, 1972). Although the overall model has many stages and alternative routes of information processing, we hope that the way it is put together will permit us to isolate small portions of the model at a time for experimental tests without doing violence to the model regarded as a whole. Our strategy here is to capture the basic principles of automaticity in perceptual and associative processing with simple examples drawn from initial processing stages of reading and then indicate how these examples generalize to more complex stages of reading.

We shall consider first the learning, or construction, of visual codes in reading, which includes the perception of letters, spelling patterns, words, and word groups. After presenting some relevant data, we will attempt to detail the rest of the model, showing how the visual stage fits into the larger picture. Then we will describe an experiment which attempts to demonstrate the acquisition of automaticity in the kind of associative learning utilized in the decoding and simple comprehension of words.

Model of Grapheme Learning

Now let us consider in some detail the learning of a perceptual code. It is assumed that incoming information from the page is first analyzed by detectors which are specialized in processing features such as lines, angles, intersections, curvature, openness, etc., as well as relational features such as left, right, up, down, etc. (Rumelhart, 1970). For present purposes, it is not necessary that we stipulate the exact mapping of these features onto properties of physical stimuli. In fact, to do so would emphasize a punctate view of the feature detectors, whereas we wish to provide for the possibility, following Gibson (1969), that relational aspects may be important in this kind of learning. However, it should be pointed out that it is sometimes difficult to define relational properties in a clear way.

In Figure 1 we present an abbreviated sketch of the role of visual perception in the reading model. In this schematic drawing, graphemic information enters from the left and is analyzed by feature detectors, which in turn feed into letter codes. These codes activate spelling-pattern codes, which then feed into word codes, and word codes may sometimes give rise to word-group codes. Some features activate spelling patterns and words directly (e.g., f_1 and f_2). These features detect characteristics such as word shape and spelling-pattern shape. This hierarchical coding scheme draws heavily on the notions of Gibson (1971), Bower (1972), Johnson (1972), and others, but particularly on the model described by Estes (1972).

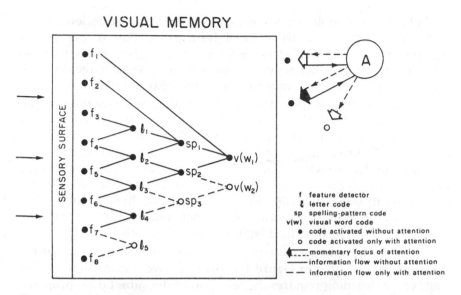

Figure 1.   Model of visual memory showing two states of perceptual coding of visual patterns. Arrows from the attention center (A) to solid-dot codes denote a two-way flow of excitation: attention can activate these codes and be activated (attracted) by them. Attention can activate open-dot codes but cannot be activated (attracted) by them.

The role of the attention center of Figure 1 is assumed to be critical early in the learning of a graphemic code, but expendable in later states of learning. Arrows from the attention center indicate a two-way flow of information between the center and each visual code in long-term memory. Every visual code in long-term memory is represented by the symbol O or ●. The open circle indicates codes that are activated only with the assistance of attention. The filled circles indicate codes which may be activated without attention. The lines leading from the visual codes to attention represent the flow of information that occurs when a code has been activated or "triggered" by stimuli. The lines leading from the attention center to visual codes represent the activation of these units by attention. When a stimulus occurs and activates a code, a signal is sent to the attention center, which can "attract" attention to that code unit in the form of additional activation. Only the well-learned, filled-circle codes can attract attention. If attention is directed elsewhere at the time a visual code is activated by external stimulation, attention will not shift its activation to that visual code, unless the stimulus is intense or unless the code automatically activates autonomic responses or other systems which mediate the "importance" (Deutsch & Deutsch, 1963) or "pertinence" (Norman, 1968) of that code to the attention center.

The many double arrows emanating from the attention center, therefore, indicate potential lines of information flow to every well-learned code in visual long-term memory. At any given moment, however, the attention center activates only one code. This characteristic of the model represents the limited-capacity property of attention.

As conceptualized here, attentional activation may have three different effects on information processing. First of all, it can assist in the construction of a new code by activating subordinate input codes. For example, in Figure 1, successive activation of features f_7 and f_8 is necessary to synthesize letter code l_5. Secondly, activation of a code prior to the presentaton of its corresponding stimulus is assumed to increase the rate of processing when that stimulus is presented (LaBerge *et al.*, 1970). Finally, activation of a code can arouse other codes to which it has been associated, as will be described later in connection with Figure 3.

Some of the most common patterns we learn to recognize are letters, which are represented in Figure 1 as l_1, l_2, etc. We assume that the first stage of this learning requires the selection of the subset of appropriate features from the larger set of features which are activated by incoming physical stimuli. For example, assume that a child is learning to discriminate the letters t and h. The length of the vertical line is not relevant to the discrimination of these two letters. Instead he must note the short horizontal cross of the t and the concave loop in the h. These are the distinctive features of these letters when considered against each other. In the model, we represent the selection of features of a given letter by the lines leading from particular features to a particular letter. In this example, the length of the vertical line is an irrelevant feature, but when these two letters are compared with other letters, for example the letter n, the length of the vertical line becomes a relevant feature. We assume that this kind of adjustment in feature selection continues as the rest of the alphabet is presented to the child. One feature that seems to be irrelevant for all letters is thickness of line. It would appear, then, that many features are selected for a given letter, and in many cases letters share features in common. Therefore, the relationship between the feature and letter code levels shown in Figure 1 is somewhat simplified for economy of illustration. Figure 1 shows only two lines leading from features into a given letter; typically a letter is coded from more than two feature detectors, and a given feature may feed into more than two letters.

As a first stage of perceptual learning, selection of relevant features is similar to the initial stages of concept learning tasks (e.g., Trabasso & Bower, 1968) in which the subject searches for the relevant dimension before he selects a response. The rate of learning to select the appropriate features of a pattern may be quite slow the first time a child is given letters to discriminate. However, after a child has experienced several discrimination tasks, he may develop strategies of visual search which permit him to move through this first stage of perceptual learning at an increasingly rapid rate.

In the second stage of perceptual learning, as conceived here, the subject must construct a letter code from the relevant features, a process which requires attention. By rapid scanning of the individual feature detectors, perhaps along with some application of Gestalt principles of organization (e.g., proximity and similarity), a higher-order unit is formed. If the pattern has too many features, organization into a unit code might not be manageable. This would mean that when the letter is itself organized into a superordinate code, it would consist of several components, instead of one unit. However, when the features do permit organization into a unitary code, this code is of a short-term nature at first and is quickly lost when the eye shifts to other patterns, or when attention activates another visual code. But every time the subject organizes the features into that particular letter code, some trace of this organization between features and letter code is laid down. The dashed lines in Figure 1 between features and a letter represent the early state of establishment of these traces, and the solid lines represent later states of trace consolidation.

In the early trials of learning we assume that attention activation must be added to external stimulation of feature detectors to produce organization of the letters into a unit. In the later trials, we assume that features can feed into letter codes without attentional activation, in other words, that the stimulus can be processed into a letter code automatically.

For example, contrast the perception of the familiar letter a with the unfamiliar Greek letter γ. Let us assume that the visual stimulus, a, first activates the feature detectors f_3 and f_4. These features automatically activate the letter code l_1, which corresponds to the letter a. When the Greek letter, γ, is presented, assume that features f_7 and f_8 are activated. However, these features do not excite the letter code l_5 by themselves. Nevertheless, when this unfamiliar letter is presented, the feature detectors f_7 and f_8 induce the attention center to switch attention activation to themselves, because they are already linked to the attention center (by learning or heredity). The resultant scanning or successive activation of these features by attention produces sufficient additional activation to organize and arouse the letter code l_5. Were the subject to activate and not organize the features, then the Greek letter would not be perceived as a unit but merely as a set of features, f_7 and f_8.

If the subject is induced to organize the separate features into a unit when it is presented to him, the lines linking features f_7 and f_8 will presumably become strengthened, until after many such experiences they eventually become as strong as those lines linking features f_3 and f_4 with letter code l_1, which represents a highly familiar pattern such as the letter *a.* When this is accomplished, the Greek letter, γ, can be perceived as a unit without requiring attention to the scanning of its component features.

When this unitization becomes automatic, there is nothing to prevent the subject from exercising the option of attending to the features of the Greek letter, much as he can choose to pay attention to the curved lines in the familiar letter *a* if he chooses. This optional attentional activation at either the feature level or the letter level is implied in the model by the placement of dots at both feature detectors and letter codes.

At this point it would appear appropriate to mention that there may exist another stage of learning located between feature selection and the unitizing stages of perceptual learning. Quite possibly the subject may learn to scan features more rapidly with practice, and eventually the scanning itself may become automatic. Experiments which measure the learning of patterns by shortened reaction time in matching tasks or by increased accuracy in tachistoscopic exposures would then be revealing the learning of a scanning path for features and not necessarily the gradual formation of a unit. One way to test for feature scanning as opposed to unit formation might be to estimate how much short-term memory capacity is taken up when a letter is presented. For example, to identify each letter by a series of feature tests may require about four or five binary decisions (Smith, 1971), implying that each letter is represented by as many components. Even if a subject stores only three or four letters visually in short-term memory, this means he would have to be storing 12-20 feature chunks, which seems unlikely given the limits set by Miller (1956) at seven plus or minus two.

One might be tempted to move the argument up one level in the visual hierarchy and maintain that letters are the visual units normally coded in reading. This would leave the formation of higher-order units to other systems such as the phonological system. This position is close to the one taken by Gough (1972), who makes a strong attempt to reconcile letter-by-letter visual scanning with the apparently high rates of word processing by fluent readers.

One could even move the argument up another level to consider spelling patterns as the typical units of visual perception in reading, a position preferred by Gibson (1971), although she maintains that these units must eventually be reorganized into still higher-order units.

The critical point being made here is that automaticity in processing graphemic material may not necessarily mean that unitizing has taken place. Scanning pathways may have been learned to the degree that they can be run off automatically and rapidly, whatever the size of the visual code unit involved. The present model as depicted in Figure 1 adapts itself to the view that a letter may be a cluster of discrete features which are scanned automatically. One simply equates the symbol l_1 with the term (f_3, f_4), to indicate that the code at the letter level is a cluster of feature units. The interpretation of automaticity is the same. For the dashed lines linking features with letters, the features cannot be adequately scanned without the services of attention; for the solid lines, the features are scanned automatically. For present purposes of exposition, however, we find it more convenient to refer to letters, spelling patterns, and words as unit codes, but we hope that the reader will keep in mind that there is an alternative view of what it is that is being automatized in perceptual learning of this kind.

Before extending the model to other stages of processing, such as sounding letters, spelling patterns, and words or comprehension of words, we will describe briefly an experiment which attempted to measure automaticity of perception and use it as an indicator of amount of perceptual learning of a graphemic pattern.

Indicators of automatic perceptual processing. One way to test recognition of a letter is to present two letters simultaneously and ask the subject to indicate if they match or not (Posner & Mitchell, 1967). In order to determine whether a person can automatically recognize a letter pattern, we must present a pair of patterns at a moment when he is not expecting them. The way this was done in a recent study (LaBerge, 1973b) was to induce the subject to expect a letter, e.g., the letter a, by presenting it first as a cue in a successive matching task. If the letter which followed the cue was also an a, he was to press a button, otherwise not. Occasionally, following the single letter cue a, the subject was given a pair of letters other than the letter expected, e.g., the stimulus (b b). If these letters matched, he was to press the button, otherwise not, regardless of what the cue was on that trial. In terms of Figure 1, the state of the subject at the moment he expects the letter a may be represented by the attention arrow activating l_1, which we shall assume corresponds to the letter code a. The perceptual analyzers are primed to process the stimulus a and when it occurs, the speed of recognition should be increased. However, when a pair of different letters, (b b), is presented, corresponding to l_4, for example, the attention arrow leading to l_4 now becomes activated and the arrow to l_1 deactivated. The time required for this change is often referred to as switching time and may be as large as 80 msec in some cases (LaBerge, 1973a). The important prediction by the model is that familiar letters corresponding to l_4 will have already processed features f_6 and f_7 into the letter code l_4 by the time attention is switched from l_1 to l_4, whereas unfamiliar letters such as l_5 will not have achieved this capability of processing features f_7 and f_8 into l_5 before attention is switched to l_5.

Therefore our indicator of automaticity in the perception of letter pattern is the extra time it takes to perceptually process a letter once attention has been shifted to that letter. If this time is negligible, then we conclude that the letter code is activated automatically from external stimulation of its features before attention was switched to it. If this time is substantial, then we conclude that attention was needed to synthesize the features into the letter code. Of course we do not have direct means of assessing the amount of attention time involved in perceptual coding. However, we do have good estimates of the total time it takes to code and match highly familiar letters in these tasks, which for adults we assume must be quite automatic by now. Using familiar letters as controls, we can measure the differences between match latencies for unfamiliar and familiar letters and use this as an estimate of the extra attention time required to process unfamiliar letters. Then, as further training is given, we may note the convergence of the latencies of the unfamiliar to the familiar letters and use this as an indicator of perceptual learning.

In the experiment by LaBerge (1973b), the unfamiliar letters were [↳ ↲↾↿] and the familiar letters used as controls were [b d p q]. Other groups of letter patterns, e.g., [a g n s], were used as cues to focus the subject's attention at the moment a pair of test letters was given according to the procedure just described. Referring to Figure 1, a letter from the familiar test group could be represented by a letter code such as l_4, and a letter from the unfamiliar test group by l_5. A letter from the group [a g n s] could be represented by l_1, which represents the momentary focus of attention. We expected that latencies of unfamiliar test letter matches would be longer than the familiar letter matches at first, but we expected that the amount of the difference would decrease with practice if perceptual learning were taking place.

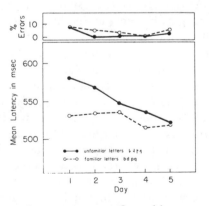

Figure 2.   Mean latency and percent errors of matching responses to unfamiliar and familiar letter patterns.

The results from the 16 college-age subjects are shown in Figure 2. The initial difference in latency between unfamiliar and familiar letters was 48 msec and the difference clearly decreased over the next four days. In terms of the model in Figure 1, we would say that the dashed lines between features f_7 and f_8 and l_5 were strengthened over days and approached the automatic level of learning of the lines connecting f_6 and f_7 with l_4.

The finding that unfamiliar letters improved with practice more than did familiar letters offers support for the hypothesis that something is being learned about the unfamiliar letters over the days of training. Evidence that subjects are learning automatic processing of the unfamiliar letters is supported by a special testing condition presented to another group of 16 subjects. In this condition, the familiar and unfamiliar patterns were presented both as cues and target stimuli so that we could assess the time taken to detect the letter when the subject expected that letter. In terms of the model in Figure 1, we assume for the unfamiliar letter that the attention arrow to l_5 is activated at the time the letter is presented. Similarly, when a familiar letter, l_4, is cued, the attention arrow is focused on l_4 in preparation for that letter to be presented.

A comparison of latencies of these successive matches showed that the time to make an unfamiliar match equals the time to make a familiar match. This means that under conditions when the subject is attending to these letters, differences between perceptual learning of letters are not revealed. Only under conditions when the subject is attending elsewhere at the moment when the test letter is presented do these differences emerge.

Taken together, the data from these two conditions strongly suggest that what is being learned over days is a perceptual process that operates without attention, namely an automatic perceptual process. Whether the process be a unitizing one or a quick scanning of features, or perhaps something else, is not decided by these data. The main conclusion is that what is being improved with practice is automaticity.

Apparently, acquiring automaticity is a slow process in contrast to the relatively quick rate of acquiring accuracy in paired associate learning (Estes, 1970). For a five-year old, one suspects that achievement of automatic recognition of the 26 letters of the alphabet may indeed be a slow learning process, assuming that the child is no better than the college adult at this task. It may be that the child can learn to distinguish letters with accuracy with relatively few exposures, but it is costing him a considerable amount of attention to do it. Apparently, considerably greater amounts of exposure to the graphemes are necessary before the child can carry out letter recognition automatically, a feat he must learn to do if he is to acquire new skills involving combinations of these letters.

For other studies which support the hypothesis that visual processing may occur without attention, the reader is referred to Eriksen and Spencer (1969), Posner and Boies (1971), Egeth, Jonides, and Wall (1972), and Shiffrin and Gardner (1972). An experiment by LaBerge,

Samuels, and Petersen (1973) treats perceptual learning of unfamiliar letter-like patterns which are more complex than the ones described here with similar results.

Theoretical Relationships between Visual and Phonological Systems

We turn now to a consideration of other processing systems which presumably operate on the inputs from visual codes. Of course the model we are describing step-by-step is not considered to be complete at this time. Rather we expect that it will have to be modified a good deal as the appropriate experimental tests are made. However, we hope that the present model will help clarify some of the locations of our ignorance and point the way to the kinds of experimental and theoretical operations most likely to remove that ignorance.

In Figure 3 we describe the structure of the phonological memory system and the more important lines of associative activation, both direct and indirect, leading from the visual codes. Evidence that recognition of visually presented words typically involves phonological recoding is given by Rubenstein et al. (1971) and Wicklund and Katz (1970). A model of the articulatory response system is also briefly sketched to represent direct links between phonological memory and the overt articulation of words. The structures in the visual memory system are abbreviated in Figure 3 for economy of exposition.

The phonological memory system is assumed to contain units closely related to acoustic and articulatory inputs. If we were to represent these systems separately, we would be strongly tempted to construct the acoustic system in a fashion similar to the visual system, with features, phonemes, syllables, and words structured in a hierarchy. The structure of the articulatory system is roughly suggested within the response system of Figure 3, in the form of a hierarchy of response output nodes arranged in a mirror image of the hierarchies for the sensory systems. For example, to respond with a word, one gives attention to $r(w_1)$ which then automatically feeds into the syllabic units $r(s_1)$ and $r(s_2)$, and perhaps from these into phonemes. For present purposes, we feel that we can trace the flow of information from the visual system to the phonological system without making specific assumptions about the precise relationships between the acoustic and articulatory systems. Following Gibson (1971), therefore, we lump these under the general heading of the phonological system.

The input to the phonological memory system is assumed to come from at least six sources: units in visual memory, response memory, semantic memory, and episodic memory, as well as from auditory stimulation and articulatory response feedback. Of course, additional activation

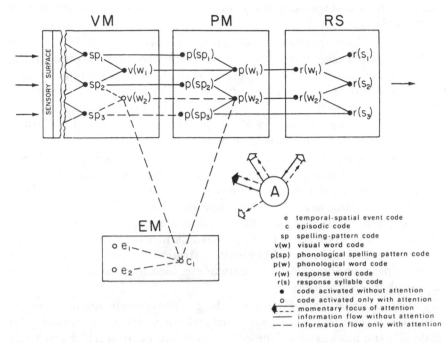

Figure 3. Representation of associative links between codes in visual memory (VM), phonological memory (PM), episodic memory (EM), and the response system (RS). Attention is momentarily focused on a code in visual memory.

can be provided from the attention center to any well-learned unit in phonological memory as is the case for units in visual memory. The sources of input of main interest here are the codes of the visual system. Associations between visual codes and their phonological counterparts are indicated by the lines drawn between the visual and phonological systems. Solid lines denote automatic associations; dashed lines denote associations that require additional activation by attention to generate an association. For example, a visually coded word $v(w_1)$, e.g., "basket," automatically activates its phonological associate, $p(w_1)$, e.g., /basket/, while another visual word code $v(w_2)$, e.g., "capstan," requires additional activation by attention before it can activate its phonological associate $p(w_2)$, e.g., /capstan/. Another way that the phonological code $p(w_1)$ can be activated by the visual system is by way of the component spelling patterns sp_1 ("bas") and sp_2 ("ket"), which may be associated with the phonological units $p(sp_1)$, (/bas/), and $p(sp_2)$, (/ket/). Once $p(sp_1)$ and $p(sp_2)$ are activated, they in turn activate and organize a blend into the phonological word unit, $p(w_1)$, (/basket/). This blend is accomplished by the two connecting lines presumably learned to automaticity by a great deal of practice in hearing and speaking these two syllabic components in the context of the word unit.

Thus we have specified two different locations in which the unitizing of a word might take place, one in the visual system and the other in the phonological system. For the experienced reader, the particular location used is optional. If he is reading easy material at a fast pace, he may select as visual units words or even word groups; if he is reading difficult material at a slow pace, he may select spelling patterns and unitize these into word units at the phonological level.

Exactly how these options are executed is a matter for speculation at present. Our best estimate of the role of the attention activator during fast reading is one in which no attention is given to the visual system, and the highest visual unit available is the one that automatically activates its corresponding phonological code. For slow reading, we suspect that the attention arrow is directed to the visual system where smaller units are given added activation, resulting in the activation of smaller phonological units. These phonological units then are blended automatically into larger phonological units.

The dashed lines in Figure 3 leading to the episodic memory system represent an indirect way that a visual code may activate a phonological code. This memory system, labeled "episodic" by Tulving (1972), is closely related to the temporal-contextual-information store of Shiffrin and Geisler (1973). It contains codes of temporal and physical events which can be organized with visual and phonological codes into a superordinate code, indicated here by c_1. These codes represent associations that are in the very earliest stages of learning. The dashed lines connected with the episodic code represent the fact that attention is required to activate the code. With further practice, direct lines may be formed between visual and phonological codes, for example the line joining $v(w_2)$ with $p(w_2)$. This link is represented by a dashed line to indicate that additional activation by attention still is necessary for the association to take place. The solid lines joining visual and phonological codes, of course, represent well-learned associations that occur without attentional activation. Of course, all three types of associations, episodic, nonautomatic direct, and automatic direct, are assumed to be at the accuracy level.

The initial association between a new visual pattern and its phonological response is considered to be a fast learning process (Estes, 1970). It may not occur on the first trial, but when it does occur, it appears to happen in an all-or-none manner. For this state of learning, progress is indicated customarily by percent correct or percent errors. When the subject has achieved a criterion of accurate performance, the visual code still requires attention whenever retrieval occurs through the episodic memory code or through a direct dashed-line connection, even if the perceptual coding of the visual stimulus itself is automatic. Further training beyond the accuracy criterion must be provided if the association is to occur without attention, represented by the solid lines. The letter-naming experiment soon to be described will serve as an illustrative example of the associative learning this model is intended to represent.

Theoretical Relationships between Visual, Phonological, and Semantic Systems

Once a visual word code makes contact with the phonological word code in reading, we assume that the meaning of the word can be elicited by means of a direct associative connection between the phonological unit, $p(w_1)$, and the semantic meaning unit, $m(w_1)$, as shown in Figure 4. Most of the connections between phonological word codes and semantic meaning codes have already been learned to automaticity through extensive experience with spoken communications. In fact, authors of children's books purposely select vocabularies in which words meet this condition. This takes the attention off the processing of meaning and frees it for decoding. However, for a child in the process of learning meanings of words, we assume that the linkage between a heard word and its meaning may be coded first in episodic memory. This is represented in Figure 4 by the organization of $p(w_3)$ and $m(w_3)$ and event e_1 and e_2 into the episodic code c_2. Additional exposures to a word along with activations of its meaning would begin to form a direct link between the phonological unit and its meaning, represented by the dashed line between $p(w_2)$ and $m(w_2)$. At these two states of learning, attention is needed to activate the association of a heard word into its meaning, but with enough practice, a word should elicit its meaning automatically, as illustrated by the solid line joining $p(w_1)$ with $m(w_1)$.

At this point we may mention that the association between the phonological form of a word and its meaning may go in the other direction, so that activation of a meaning unit could automatically excite a phonological unit. However, we are not prepared to specify in any detail how this is done. We simply wish to indicate that generating speech by activation of semantic structures also appears to be automatic, at least in the general sense in which we are using the term here.

We should note the possibility in the model that a visual word code may be associated directly with a semantic meaning code (Bower, 1970; Kolers, 1970). That is, a unit, $v(w_1)$, may activate its meaning, $m(w_1)$, without mediation through the phonological system. The fact that we can quickly recognize the difference in the meaning of such homonyms as "two" versus "too" seems to illustrate this assumption.

Indicators of automatic associative processing. The way we are currently measuring the role of attention in associative processing is similar in

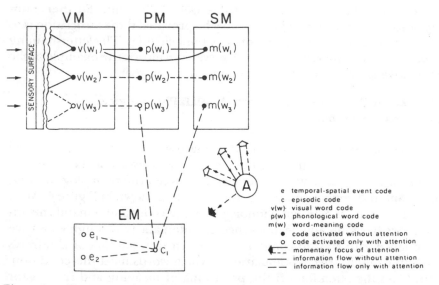

Figure 4.   Representation of three states of associative learning involving codes
in visual memory (VM), phonological memory (PM), semantic mem-
ory (SM), and episodic memory (EM). Attention is momentarily focused on a code in episodic memory.

principle to the method already described in this paper for testing automaticity of perceptual recognition. Here again, latency serves as the
critical indicator, since we are interested in learning trends after the
accuracy criterion has been met. The fact that response latency of a paired
associate decreases considerably after accuracy has been achieved has
been well-established by Millward (1964), Suppes *et al.* (1966), Judd and
Glaser (1969), and Hall (1972).

In a test of automatic associative processing used by LaBerge &
Samuels (1973), the subject is asked to name the letter he sees. In order to
strictly control the subject's attention at the moment the letter appears, we
give him another task to perform and then insert the letter at a moment
when he does not expect it. Eight subjects observed pairs of common
words presented successively and pressed a button when the second word
matched the first word. Conditions were arranged so that the first word of
each pair prepared the subject's attention for the following word. Occasionally, instead of presenting the same word for a match, we presented a
letter and asked the subject to name it aloud into a microphone which
activated a voice key. Since he expected to see a particular word at that
moment, we could test how much of the letter-naming process was carried
out before attention was shifted to the letter. Of course, this test of
automaticity required a control condition with letters whose names were
already at the automatic level of associative learning.

The two sets of letters were the same as the ones used in the perceptual learning study. The familiar set was [b d p q] and the unfamiliar set was [ʖ ɟ ʮ ꓩ]. The names for the familiar set were bee, dee, pea, and cue, and the names for the unfamiliar set were one, two, four, and five. The overall latency of naming a letter pattern presumably includes perceptual coding time, association time, and residual response time. However, we were interested in differences only in association time. After determining that the residual-response component was equal for the familiar and unfamiliar letters, we had only to equate the familiar and unfamiliar letters with respect to perceptual coding time. To do this we gave the subjects preliminary training on perceptual matching of the unfamiliar patterns until they were recognized as fast as familiar patterns. These matching tests were given under automatic test conditions already described. When the criterion had been met on matching tests, the subjects were given a card for about two minutes on which were drawn the new patterns along with their corresponding names. They then began a series of daily tests of naming these new letters along with tests in which familiar letters were named. After each day's test block, intensive training blocks were given in which a trial consisted of a small circle as a cue followed by one of the eight letters which the subject named. Figure 5 shows the results of this experiment over 20 days of testing and training.

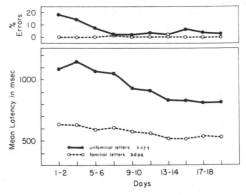

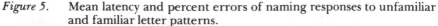

Figure 5.   Mean latency and percent errors of naming responses to unfamiliar and familiar letter patterns.

It is evident that the latency difference of a naming response to the new and old letters is quite large at first and converges over days of training. All eight subjects showed convergence. This convergence continues when accuracy appears to be stationary. Additional tests conducted under conditions in which the subject was attending to the naming operation prior to the stimulus onset showed no difference in latencies of familiar and unfamiliar letters. In view of these findings, we believe that

Figure 5 provides an indication of the gradual learning of automatic naming associations.

In Figure 6 is shown a model of three levels of associative learning for this experiment. Any one of the familiar letters may be designated as l_4 and its name by $n(l_4)$; any of the unfamiliar letters may be designated by l_6 and its name by $n(l_6)$. At first the subject may associate the unfamiliar letters with their names by some mnemonic strategy, rule, or image. This state of learning is represented by the lines which connect with the episodic code c_1. Later, as learning progresses, a direct link may be formed. This is indicated by the type of line joining l_5 with $n(l_5)$. Dashed lines, of course, indicate that attention must be focused on the letter to provide the additional activation needed to complete the association and excite the phonological name unit. The solid line joining the familiar letter l_4 with its name $n(l_4)$ represents an automatic association, which allows the stimulus activation of l_4 to then excite $n(l_4)$ while attention is directed elsewhere.

The results shown in Figure 5 are consistent with this model of automatic association. However, at the end of 20 days of practice, the

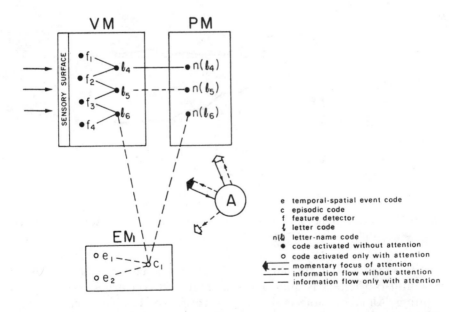

Figure 6.   Representation of three states of associative learning between codes in visual memory (VM), phonological memory (PM), and episodic memory (EM). Attention is momentarily focused on a code in visual memory.

college subjects did not name unfamiliar letters as fast as they named the familiar letters, a finding which leads us to conclude that the subjects were still using some degree of attention to make the association. Apparently, it would take a great many more days to bring letter naming of these rather simple letters to the level of automaticity already achieved by the familiar letters. We are tempted to generalize to classroom routines in elementary schools in which letter naming is directly taught and tested only up to the accuracy level. A child may be quite accurate in naming or sounding the letters of the alphabet, but we may not know how much attention it costs him to do it. This kind of information could be helpful in predicting how easily he can manage new learning skills which build on associations he has already learned.

We agree that higher-order reading skills are based more on sounding letters than naming them. Had we instructed the subjects to sound the letters instead of name them, we would regard the expected convergence of latency of the unfamiliar sounds to the latency of the familiar sounds as indicating the gradual development of automaticity in sounding letters. In this case, we would designate the sound of a visual letter code l_5 in Figure 6 as $p(l_5)$ instead of $n(l_5)$, etc. We assume that the three states of learning to associate a name with a letter would generalize to the case of learning to sound that letter and to sounding spelling patterns and words as well.

Turning to the association of word sounds with word meanings illustrated in Figure 4, it is possible to perform learning experiments using indicators of automaticity of associating meanings in much the same way as we did for associating names. The only major difference in procedure is that instead of asking the subjects to name a letter, we ask him to press a button if the word is a member of a particular category of meaning (Meyer, 1970).

General model of automaticity in reading. In Figure 7 all the memory systems relevant to this theory of reading are shown together. We may use this sketch to trace some of the many alternative routes that a visually presented word could take as it proceeds toward its goal of activating meaning codes. A given route is defined here not only in terms of the particular systemic code encountered along the way, but also in terms of whether or not attention adds its activation to any of these codes. A few of the possible optional processing routes may be described as follows:

Option 1: The graphemic stimulus is automatically coded into a visual word code $v(w_1)$, which automatically activates the meaning code $m(w_1)$. An example is "bear" or "bare" or any very common word which is not processed by Option 2.

Option 2: The graphemic stimulus is automatically coded into a visual word code $v(w_2)$, which automatically activates the phonological code

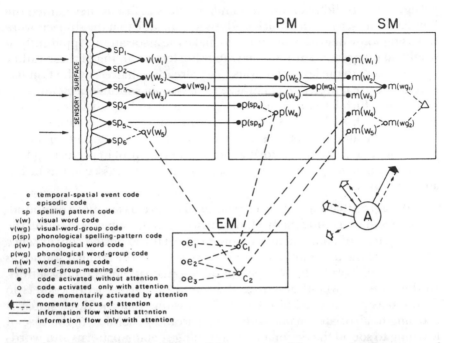

e	temporal-spatial event code
c	episodic code
sp	spelling pattern code
v(w)	visual word code
v(wg)	visual-word-group code
p(sp)	phonological spelling-pattern code
p(w)	phonological word code
p(wg)	phonological word-group code
m(w)	word-meaning code
m(wg)	word-group-meaning code
●	code activated without attention
○	code activated only with attention
△	code momentarily activated by attention
⬅---	momentary focus of attention
——	information flow without attention
– –	information flow only with attention

Figure 7.   Representation of some of the many possible ways a visually presented word may be processed into meaning. The four major stages of processing shown here are visual memory (VM), phonological memory (PM), episodic memory (EM), and semantic memory (SM). Attention is momentarily focused on comprehension in SM, involving organization of meaning codes of two word-groups.

$p(w_2)$. This code then automatically excites the meaning code $m(w_2)$. An example is any very common word which is not processed by Option 1.

Option 3: The graphemic stimulus is automatically coded into the visual word-group code $v(wg_1)$. This code automatically activates the phonological word-group code $p(wg_1)$, which in turn activates automatically the meaning code of the word group $m(wg_1)$. An example might be the words "beef stew" or "après ski."

Option 4: The graphemic stimulus is automatically coded into two spelling patterns sp_4 and sp_5. These units activate the phonological codes $p(sp_4)$ and $p(sp_5)$. These two codes are blended with attention into the phonological word code $p(w_4)$, which activates with attention the episodic code c_1. This code is then activated by attention to excite the meaning code $m(w_4)$. An example might be "skylab," for those who have had few experiences with the word.

Option 5: The graphemic stimulus is coded with attention into the visual word code $v(w_5)$. Attention activates this code to excite the episodic code c_2. When attention is shifted to c_2, it generates the meaning code $m(w_5)$. An example is the name of a character in a Russian novel which is too long to pronounce easily.

An act of comprehension is illustrated in Figure 7 by the focusing of attention on the organization of two word groups, one of which, $m(wg_1)$, has been automatically grouped, and the other, $m(wg_2)$, has required attention to be grouped. We assume that $m(w_2)$, $m(w_3)$, $m(w_4)$, and $m(w_5)$ can be organized to make sense to the subject only if he can manage to shift his attention activation quickly among these meaning codes to keep them simultaneously active. We are assuming that the process of organizing is promoted by fast scanning at the semantic level in much the same way that fast scanning of feature detectors promotes unitizing of features into new letter patterns at the usual level.

Options 1 and 2 illustrate what many consider the goal of fluent reading: the reader can maintain his attention continuously on the meaning units of semantic memory, while the decoding from visual to semantic systems proceeds automatically. The rest of the examples serve to emphasize that the reader often has the option of several different ways of processing a given word. When he encounters a word he does not understand, his attention may be shifted to the phonological level to read out the sound for attempts at retrieval from episodic memory. At other times he may shift his attention to the visual level and attempt to associate spelling patterns with phonological units, which are then blended into a word which makes contact with meaning. When the decoding and comprehension processes are automatic, reading appears to be "easy." When they require attention to complete their operations, reading seems to be "difficult."

One could say that every time a word code requires attention we are made aware of that aspect of the reading process. For example, when we encounter a word that does not make sense, we may speak it and thereby are momentarily aware of the sound of the words we are reading. Or if the word does not sound right to us, we may examine its spelling patterns, thereby becoming aware of its visual aspects. However, when reading is flowing at its best, for example in reading a mystery novel in which the vocabulary is very familiar, we can go along for many minutes imagining ourselves with the detective walking the streets of London, and apparently we have not given a bit of attention to any of the decoding processes that have been transforming marks on the page into the deeper systems of comprehension.

Development of Automaticity

Throughout this paper we have stressed the importance of automaticity in performance of fluent reading. Now we turn to a consideration of ways to train reading subskills to automatic levels. Unfortunately, very little systematic research has been directed specifically to this advanced stage of learning. Reviews of studies of automatic activity (Keele, 1968; Welford, 1968; Posner & Keele, 1969) deal mostly with automatic motor tasks and, to our knowledge, there are no studies which systematically compare training methods which facilitate the acquisition of automaticity of verbal skills. Therefore, our remarks here will be speculative, although we are currently putting forth efforts in the laboratory to shed light on this problem.

First of all, we would agree with most practitioners involved in skill learning that practice leads to automaticity. For example, recognizing letters of the alphabet apparently becomes automatic by successive exposures (see Figure 2). Sounding spelling patterns apparently becomes automatic by repetition of the visual and articulatory sequences. Even the meaning of a visual word would seem to achieve automatic retrieval through successive repetitions. Edmond Huey in 1908 emphasized the role of repetitions in the development of automaticity when he wrote, "To perceive an entirely new word or other combination of strokes requires considerable time, close attention and is likely to be imperfectly done, just as when we attempt some new combination of movements, some new trick in the gymnasium, or a new serve at tennis. In either case, repetition progressively frees the mind from attention to details, makes facile the total act, shortens the time, and reduces the extent to which consciousness must concern itself with the process" (Huey, 1908, p. 104).

In the case of perceptual learning, repetitions would seem to provide more than the consolidation of perceptions to the point where they can be run off quite quickly and automatically. Another thing that can happen during these repetitions is that the material can be reorganized into higher-order units even before the lower-order units have achieved a high level of automaticity. For example, when the child reads text in which the same vocabulary is used over and over again, the repetitions will certainly make more automatic the perceptions of each word unit, but if he stays at the word level he will not realize his potential reading speed. If, however, he begins to organize some of the words into short groups or phrases as he reads, then further repetitions can strengthen these units as well as word units. In this way he can break through the upper limit of word-by-word reading and apply the benefits of further repetitions to automatization of larger units. Apparently this sort of higher-order chunking progresses as the child gains more experience in reading. For example, Taylor et al. (1960) found that 1st grade children made as many as two fixations per word whereas 12th graders made one fixation for about every two words.

Reorganization into larger units requires attention, according to the model. We do not know specifically how to train a child to organize codes into higher units although some speed-reading methods make claims that sheer pressure for speed forces the person out of the word-by-word reading into larger units. Nevertheless, we feel reasonably sure that considerable application of attention is necessary if the reorganization into higher-order units is to take place. When a person does not pay attention to what he is practicing, he rules out opportunities for forming higher units because he simply processes through codes that are already laid down.

What may be critical in the determination of upper limits of word-group units is the number of word meanings that the subject can comprehend in one chunk in his semantic memory. Units at the semantic level may determine chunk size at the phonological level which, in turn, may influence how attention is distributed over visual codes. Stated more generally, this hypothesis says that the limiting size of the chunk at early levels is influenced by the existing chunk size at deeper levels. If this hypothesis holds up under experimental test, it would imply that the teaching of higher-order units for the reader should progress from deeper levels to sensory levels, rather than the reverse.

We have suggested that during the development of automaticity the person either may attempt to reorganize smaller units (e.g., words) into larger units (e.g., word phrases) or he may simply stay at the word unit level. It stands to reason that he has more confidence in his performance at the lower unit level where he has had the most practice. Whenever he attempts to reorganize word codes into larger units, he may temporarily slow down and perhaps make more errors. Therefore, to encourage chunking, we may have to relax the demand for accuracy. In general, teachers who stress accuracy too strongly may discourage children from developing sophisticated strategies of word recognition (Archwamety & Samuels, 1973). Thus, a child who has performed successfully at one level of processing may be reluctant to leave it and move to higher levels which could eventually improve reading speed.

In the case of association learning, automaticity presumably develops by the sheer temporal contiguity of the two codes. For example, sounding the word "dog" as it is visually presented with no attention to organization of the stimulus and the response may be sufficient for attainment of automaticity. Presumably, proficient readers continue to increase their speed on word-naming tests by sheer practice without special attention to organizing or reorganizing associations.

However, at the initial stages of association, well before automaticity begins to develop, organizational processes are probably involved during a repetition (Mandler, 1967; Tulving, 1962). While it is possible to form an initial associative link directly (rote learning), most likely the subject organizes the stimulus and response together with an event or with a rule and stores this code in episodic memory, as shown in Figure 3. Later, when the stimulus is presented, attention activates the stimulus code to excite the episodic code. This episodic code now "attracts" attention to activate it further and the code generates its subordinate codes, including the response code. This way of recalling a response requires attention activation and takes a relatively large amount of time. With further repetitions, the stimulus code should begin to short-circuit the episodic code and form a new direct link with the response code. At this point, the stimulus code may require some attention to activate the response code. However, the route through episodic memory remains as an option, and subjects probably use it as a check on the response obtained by the new direct route. With enough practice, of course, activation of the stimulus code excites the response code without attentional assistance.

We expect that the rate of growth of automaticity will depend upon a number of other factors. Two of these, namely distribution of learning and presentation of feedback, have been studied extensively in verbal learning and motor learning experiments. For both motor skill and verbal learning, it has generally been found that distributed practice is better than massed practice, although the optimal interval seems to be a matter of minutes, not days. Massed practice appears to be more favorable when one deals with meaningful material. If we can assume that organizational processing requires massed practice, then we would be inclined to predict that massed practice would be more beneficial for acquiring automatic perceptual processing where organization of codes into larger chunks seems critical. However, automatic associating of sounds or names with these perceptual chunks should involve little if any organization and therefore should profit more from distributed practice.

Since the important growth of automaticity takes place after the subject has achieved accuracy, overt feedback for correct and incorrect responses may be redundant because at this stage of learning the subject knows when he is correct or not (Adams & Bray, 1970). However, there is another type of feedback which may affect the rate of automaticity learning. While learning proceeds toward the automatic level, it might be appropriate to inform the subject of the time it took to execute his response. In fact, the research we have described on acquisition of automaticity routinely informs the subject of his response speed after each trial as well as at the end of a block of trials. Of course, latency feedback for a response to a particular stimulus will not be meaningful by itself, it must be related to some criterion baseline. For example, the time it takes to identify a new word should be compared to the time it takes to identify a word that is already at the automatic level. Thus, the critical metric is the difference between the two latencies. In practice, what we do is present a few old and well-learned patterns along with the new material we wish the subject to learn. At the end of a series of these trials, we show the subject the two latencies. Another way to present feedback is to give it after each response. When his response is faster than the mean on the previous block, he is given a light or sound to indicate a fast response. Aside from the incentive value of knowing how his response speed compares with a criterion, the feedback may influence the way he distributes attention before and immediately after stimulus presentation. This may in turn influence how he organizes the perceptual aspects of reading. As for the purely associative operations, we would suspect that latency feedback would be effective mainly in assuring that the subject continues to respond fast enough to maintain optimal temporal contiguity between stimulus and response codes.

Implications of the Model for Research in Reading Instruction

The model which has been presented here may have several helpful features for the researcher concerned with reading. It provides explanatory power by clarifying a number of phenomena which have puzzled educators for some time, and it suggests directions for pedagogical improvement.

One of the current questions in reading is whether it should be considered as a wholistic process or as a cluster of subskills. In support of the subskill view, Guthrie (1973) found that correlations among subskills were high for a group of good readers but low for poor readers, suggesting that they differ in the way they organize component skills. Jeffrey and Samuels (1966) found that children who were taught all of the subskills necessary for decoding words were able to do so without any guidance from a teacher, whereas children who were not taught a particular component were unable to decode.

From the point of view of a mature reader, however, the process appears to be a unitary one. In fact, it is customarily referred to by one label, namely "reading." When a teacher observes a bright child learning to read, he may see the child slowly attaining one skill. However, when the same teacher is confronted with a slow learner, he may observe the child slowly learning many skills. This comes about because the child often must be given extensive training on each of a variety of tasks, such as letter discrimination, letter-sound training, blending, etc. In this manner, a teacher becomes aware of the fact that letter recognition can be considered a skill itself, to be taught like we teach object-naming, for example, naming birds.

The fluent reader has presumably mastered each of the subskills at the automatic level. Even more important, he has made their integration automatic as well. What this implies is that he no longer clearly sees the dividing lines separating these skills under the demands of his day-to-day reading. In effect, this means that he is no longer aware of the component nature of the subskills as he was required to be when he was a beginning reader, learning skills one-by-one. Therefore, if you should ask a typically fluent reader how he perceives his reading process, he is likely to tell you that he views it as a wholistic one.

It seems from our consideration of this model that all readers must go through similar stages of learning to read but do so at different rates. The slower the rate of learning to read, the more the person becomes aware of these component stages. One of the hallmarks of the reader who learned the subskills rapidly is that he was least aware of them at the time, and therefore now has little memory of them as separable subskills. On the basis of this model, therefore, we view reading acquisition as a series of skills, regardless of how it appears to the fluent reader. Pedagogically, we favor the approach which singles out these skills for testing and training and then attempts to sequence them in appropriate ways.

In consideration of each stage, for example, learning to sound letter patterns, it would appear that there are two criteria of achievement: accuracy and automaticity. During the achievement of accuracy, we assume the student should have his attention focused on the task at hand to code the association between the visual letters and their sounds in episodic memory, or to establish direct associations (cf. Figure 6). Once he has learned letter-sound correspondences, he may or may not be ready to attack the next stage, namely to "blend" these sounds into syllables or words. To ascertain his readiness to move ahead, we must consider a further criterion, namely automaticity. If a good deal of attention is required for him to be accurate in sounding letter patterns, then "blending" will be more difficult to perform owing to the total number of things he must attend to and hold in short-term memory.

In practice, the letter-sound processing need not be fully automatic for him to make progress towards blending, since even the slowest learner has sufficient short-term memory capacity to store a few sounds while he works at blending them. Of course, the less time that his attention must be allocated to the letter-sound processing, the more time he can devote to the blending operation and the faster the progress in learning to blend. We could say that the child who either has a small short-term memory capacity or who has not yet developed the letter-sound skill to the automatic level has too many things to which he must switch his attention in order to carry out the operation of blending. This means that he will forget information crucial to the blending process, and therefore he is more likely to suffer unsuccessful experiences with this task. In short, accuracy is not a sufficient criterion for readiness to advance to skills which build on the subskills at hand. One should take into account the amount of attention required by these subskills as part of the readiness criterion.

Comprehension

We turn now to consider the way the model can be used to clarify some of the comprehension processes and to point to certain pedagogical consequences. In its present simple form, the model does not spell out higher-order linguistic operations such as parsing, predictive processing, and contextual effects on comprehension. If initial tests of the model are successful, it is hoped that it can be elaborated to represent more complex semantic operations such as these. For present purposes, we find it convenient to separate comprehension from word meaning. By word meaning we refer to the semantic referent of a spoken or written word, morpheme, or groups of words that denote a meaningful unit. By comprehension, on the other hand, we refer to the organization of these word meanings. To do this, the meaning units presumably are scanned one-by-one by attention and organized as a coherent whole. The momentary act of comprehension is represented in Figure 7 by the focus of attention on the coding of $m(wg_1)$ with $m(wg_2)$. If a subject maintains attention solely on single-meaning codes, this would constitute a rather low form of comprehension, much like viewing characters in a play one-by-one and ignoring their interactions. On the other hand, for high-level comprehension of passages, attention must be directed to organizing these meaning codes, and presumably this is where effort enters into reading just as it does in understanding difficult spoken sentences.

So long as word meanings are automatically processed, the focus of attention remains at the semantic level and does not need to be switched to the visual system for decoding, nor to the phonological level for retrieving the semantic meanings. On the other hand, attention could be focused on the decoding of visual words into their phonological form and spoken aloud without any attention to comprehension. In fact, this has been frequently observed with some beginning readers, and goes by the label of "word calling."

Another phenomenon which the model may clarify is reading for meaning, but without recall for what has just been read. The model indicates that meanings of familiar words and word groups may be activated automatically, leaving attention free to wander to other matters, perhaps to recent personal episodes. If the reader gives little attention to organizing meanings into new codes for storage, it is not surprising that he later finds he cannot recall what he has been reading.

The complexity of the comprehension operation appears to be as enormous as that of thinking in general. When a person is comprehending a sentence, he quite often adds his own associations to the particular organized pattern of meanings. In addition, the ways in which he might organize the meaning units from semantic memory may be influenced by strategies whose programs of operation are themselves stored in semantic memory. We assume that the act of adding material from one's own experiences to what one is reading is represented by switching to other codes in semantic and episodic memory. When this occurs, the item in semantic memory is used as a retrieval cue to access an association or strategy. The finished organizational product presumably is then stored in episodic or semantic memory. When this is successfully done, we say the person can remember what he has read.

REFERENCES

Adams, J. A., & Bray, N. W. A closed-loop theory of paired-associate verbal learning. *Psychological Review*, 1970, **77**, 385-405.

Archwamety, T., & Samuels, S. J. A mastery based experimental program for teaching mentally retarded children word recognition and reading comprehension skills through use of hypothesis/test procedures. Research Report #50, Research, Development and Demonstration Center in Education of Handicapped Children, Minneapolis, Minnesota, 1973.

Bower, G. H. A selective review of organizational factors in memory. In E. Tulving & W. Donaldson (Eds.), *Organization of memory*. London: Academic Press, 1972.

Bower, T. G. R. Reading by eye. In H. Levin & J. Williams (Eds.), *Basic studies in reading*. New York: Basic Books, 1970.

Broadbent, D. E. *Perception and communication*. London: Pergamon Press, 1958.

Clark, H. H., & Chase, W. G. On the process of comparing sentences against pictures. *Cognitive Psychology*, 1972, **3**, 472-517.

Deutsch, J. A., & Deutsch, D. Attention: Some theoretical considerations. *Psychological Review*, 1963, **70**, 80-90.

Egeth, H., Jonides, J., & Wall, S. Parallel processing of multielement displays. *Cognitive Psychology*, 1972, **3**, 674-698.

Eriksen, C. W., & Spencer, T. Rate of information processing in visual perception: Some results and methodological considerations. *Journal of Experimental Psychology Monographs*, 1969, **72** (2Pt.2), 1-16.

Estes, W. K. *Learning theory and mental development*. New York: Academic Press, 1970.

Estes, W. K. An associative basis for coding and organization in memory. In A. W. Melton & E. Martin (Eds.), *Coding processes in human memory*. New York: Wiley, 1972. Pp. 161-190.

Gibson, E. J. *Principles of perceptual learning and development*. New York: Appleton-Century-Crofts, 1969.

Gibson, E. J. Perceptual learning and the theory of word perception. *Cognitive Psychology*, 1971, **2**, 351-368.

Gough, P. B. One second of reading. In J. F. Kavanaugh and I. G. Mattingly (Eds.), *Language by ear and by eye*. Cambridge: M.I.T. Press, 1972.

Guthrie, J. T. Models of reading and reading disability. *The Journal of Educational Psychology*, 1973, **65**, No. 1, 9-18.

Hall, R. F., & Wenderoth, P. M. Effects of number of responses and recall strategies on parameter values of a paired-associate learning model. *Journal of Verbal Learning and Verbal Behavior*, 1972, **11**, 29-37.

Huey, E. B. *The psychology and pedagogy of reading*. New York: Macmillan, 1908.

Jeffrey, W. E., & Samuels, S. J. The effect of method of reading training on initial learning and transfer. *Journal of Verbal Learning and Verbal Behavior*, 1966, **57**, 159-163.

Johnson, N. F. Organizations and the concept of a memory code. In A. W. Melton & E. Martin (Eds.), *Coding processes in human memory*. New York: Wiley, 1972.

Judd, W. A., & Glaser, R. Response latency as a function of training method, information level, acquisition, and overlearning. *Journal of Educational Psychology Monograph*, 1969, **60,** No. 4, Part 2.

Keele, S. W. Movement control in skilled motor performance. *Psychological Bulletin*, 1968, **70,** 387-403.

Kolers, P. A. Three stages of reading. In H. Levin and J. Williams, (Eds.), *Basic studies in reading*. New York: Basic Books, 1970. Pp. 90-118.

LaBerge, D. Identification of the time to switch attention: A test of a serial and parallel model of attention. In S. Kornblum (Ed.), *Attention and performance* IV. New York: Academic Press, 1973a.

LaBerge, D. Attention and the measurement of perceptual learning. *Memory and Cognition*, 1973b, **1,** 268-276.

LaBerge, D., & Samuels, S. J. On the automaticity of naming artificial letters. Technical Report #7, Minnesota Reading Research Project, University of Minnesota, 1973.

LaBerge, D., Samuels, S. J., & Petersen, R. Perceptual learning of artificial letters. Technical Report #6, Minnesota Reading Research Project, University of Minnesota, 1973.

LaBerge, D., Van Gelder, P., & Yellott, J. I. A cueing technique in choice reaction time. *Perception and Psychophysics*, 1970, **7,** 57-62.

Mandler, G. Organization and memory. In K. W. Spence and J. T. Spence (Eds.), *The psychology of learning and motivation*. Vol. 1. New York: Academic Press, 1967.

Meyer, D. F. On the representation and retrieval of stored semantic information. *Cognitive Psychology*, 1970, **1,** 242-300.

Miller, G. A. The magical number seven plus or minus two: Some limits on our capacity for processing information. *Psychological Review*, 1956, **63,** 81-97.

Millward, R. Latency in a modified paired-associate learning experiment. *Journal of Verbal Learning and Verbal Behavior*, 1964, **3,** 309-316.

Moray, N. Attention in dichotic listening: Affective cues and the influence of instructions. *Quarterly Journal of Experimental Psychology*, 1959, **11,** 56-60.

Norman, D. A. Toward a theory of memory and attention. *Psychological Review*, 1968, **75,** 522-536.

Posner, M. I., & Boies, S. J. Components of Attention. *Psychological Review*, 1971, **78,** 5, 391-405.

Posner, M. I., Boies, S. J. Eichelman, W. H., & Taylor, R. L. Retention of visual and name codes of single letters. *Journal of Experimental Psychology Monograph*, 1969, **79,** No. 1, Part 2.

Posner, M. I., Lewis, J. L., & Conrad, C. Component processes in reading: A performance analysis. In J. F. Kavanaugh & I. G. Mattingly (Eds.), *Language by ear and by eye*. Cambridge: M.I.T. Press, 1972.

Posner, M. I., & Mitchell, R. A chronometric analysis of classification. *Psychological Review*, 1967, **74,** 392-409.

Posner, M. I., & Keele, S. W. Attention demands of movements. *Proceedings of the seventeenth congress of applied psychology*, Amsterdam: Zeitlinger, 1969.

Rubenstein, H., Lewis, S. S., & Rubenstein, M. A. Evidence for phonemic recoding in visual word recognition. *Journal of Verbal Learning and Verbal Behavior*, 1971, **10,** 645-647.

Rumelhart, D. E. A multicomponent theory of the perception of brie/fly exposed visual displays. *Journal of Mathematical Psychology*, 1970, **7,** 191-218.

Shiffrin, R. M., & Gardner, G. T. Visual processing capacity and attentional control. *Journal of Experimental Psychology*, 1972, **93,** 72-82.

Shiffrin, R. M., & Geisler, W. S. Visual recognition in a theory of information processing. In R. L. Solso (Ed.), *Contemporary issues in cognitive psychology:* The Loyola Symposium. New York: Wiley, 1973.

Smith, F. *Understanding reading*. New York: Holt, Reinhart & Winston, 1971.

Sternberg, S. The discovery of processing stages: Extensions of Donder's methods. In W. Koster (Ed.), *Attention and performance*, Vol. 2. Amsterdam: North Holland Publishing Co., 1969.

Suppes, P., Groen, G., & Schlag-Ray, M. A model for response latency in paired-associate learning. *Journal of Mathematical Psychology*, 1966, **3**, 99-128.

Taylor, S. E., Frackenpohl, H., & Pattee, J. L. Grade level norms for the components of the fundamental reading skill. Bulletin #3, New York: Huntington, Educational Development Laboratories, 1960.

Trabasso, T. R., & Bower, G. H. *Attention in learning: Theory and research*. New York: Wiley, 1968.

Treisman, A. Selective attention in man. *British Medical Bulletin*, 1964, **20**, 12-16.

Tulving, E. Subjective organization in free recall of "unrelated words." *Psychological Review*, 1962, **69**, 344-354.

Tulving, E. Episodic and semantic memory. In E. Tulving & W. Donaldson (Eds.), *Organization of memory*. New York: Academic Press, 1972.

Welford, A. I. *Fundamentals of skill*. London: Methuen, 1968.

Wicklund, D. A., & Katz, L. Short term retention and recognition of words by children aged seven and ten. Visual Information Processing, Progress Report No. 2, University of Connecticut, 1970.

NOTE

This research was supported by a grant (HD-06730-01) to the authors from the National Institute of Child Health and Human Development, and in part by the Center for Research in Human Learning through National Science Foundation Grant GB-17590.

Toward a Theory of Automatic
Information Processing in Reading: Updated*

S. JAY SAMUELS
University of Minnesota

In the social sciences, if models are to be useful they must meet three criteria. First, a good model is capable of summarizing and synthesizing large amounts of information collected in the past. Second, it is capable of helping one understand what is happening in the present. Third, it can help one formulate hypotheses and predictions about what will happen in the future. Thus, a good model has something useful to say about the past, the present, and the future.

Of the three characteristics of a good model, it is the ability to test predictions and hypotheses about the future that is most important to science, since it is through hypothesis testing that we are able to evaluate the degree of truthfulness of a model. Through observation and hypothesis testing, we discover which parts of a model hold up and can stand the tests of time and which parts need to be revised.

We shall see that, as new conceptualizations of the reading process were advanced and as empirical testing of the LaBerge and Samuels automaticity model was conducted, the model was revised. When the automaticity model was published in 1974, it appeared as a linear model. This meant that information flowed through the system in one direction only and that information processing taking place in the final stages had no opportunity to influence information processing taking place at the earlier stages. By 1977 I published an article in which the linear model was revised and feedback loops from semantic memory to earlier stages of processing were included (Samuels, 1977). The simple addition of feedback loops to the model meant that prior knowledge stored in semantic memory could interact with the earlier stages of processing. What was needed now was empirical tests of the original and revised models.

Shortly after the automaticity model was published, LaBerge and I began to test the visual memory component of the model. This component indicated that there were several different sized units used in word recognition. These visual units included component features of letters, letters, letter clusters, and whole

---

* The views expressed in this paper are those of S. Jay Samuels and may not correspond with those of David LaBerge with regard to the amount of influence on visual processing.

words. In our first study, in which we tested the size of the visual unit used in word recognition, we presented common words in isolation to college students (Terry, Samuels, and LaBerge, 1976). These words were presented either in regular or in mirror image print. When the mirror image words were presented, the college students had many of the same problems trying to decode them that a beginning reader has. When the adult was reduced to the level of a child in decoding, we found the letter was used as the visual unit, and every additional letter increased the time to read a word by about 20 milliseconds a letter. However, when the words were presented in regular print, they were recognized as holistic units. In this case, the unit of recognition was the entire word. These findings suggest that skilled college readers have several options available. When decoding is difficult they can use a letter-by-letter process but when decoding is easy they can use the entire word as the unit of word recognition.

In a subsequent study, we used students from grades two, four, six, and college (Samuels, LaBerge, and Bremer, 1978). These grade levels were chosen because they represent a range of reading skills from beginning to skilled. Again, the words were in isolation but they were all presented in regular print. Findings from this study supported what we had found in the previous study. The beginning readers in the second grade for whom decoding still presented somewhat of a problem were using the letter as the unit of word recognition, while the skilled sixth graders and college students were using the entire word. The only difference between the two levels was the college students were faster at word recognition. Developmentally, the fourth graders were between the second and sixth graders, using units larger than the letter but not quite the entire word.

I think the most interesting test of the revised model came when we tested good and poor readers in grades two and four on words presented in isolation and in context (Patberg, Dewitz, and Samuels, 1981). Context consisted of word pairs such as "green grass" and "blue sky" and words in isolation such as "grass" or "sky." We found that the less skilled second graders did letter-by-letter processing regardless of whether the word was in isolation or in context. The more highly skilled readers in second and fourth grades did holistic processing regardless of whether the word was in isolation or in context. The poor readers in the fourth grade, however, shifted strategies depending on whether the word was in isolation or in context. When the word was in isolation, they used letter-by-letter processing, but when the word was in context, they shifted to holistic processing. The significance of the finding of strategy shift indicates that prior knowledge of word associations which is stored in semantic memory at the last stage of the system may influence the size of the visual unit used to process words. This visual processing takes place in visual memory which is located at the beginning of the system. Thus, this study supports the addition of feedback loops from later stages to stages which occur earlier in the sequence.

This brief accounting of some of the empirical testing of the automaticity model illustrates two things. First, as new conceptualizations of reading as an interactive process occurred, such that different parts of the information processing system were in communication with each other, this was incorporated in the model. Second, the empirical tests supported our contention that different sized visual units are used in word recognition and identified when and how the different sized units were used. The experiments indicated that beginning readers were locked into letter-by-letter processing while skilled readers had the option to use either letter-by-letter or holistic processing, depending on the difficulty of decoding.

Will the revision of our model stand additional tests of time? The best we can expect is that replications will provide the same findings we found. But as different materials are used, as different experimental tasks are given, as different contexts are provided, and as students with different amounts of reading skill are used in the studies, it is probable that researchers will gain new insights into the reading process and new models will be devised.

REFERENCES

LaBerge, D., and Samuels, S.J. Toward a theory of automatic processing in reading. *Cognitive Psychology*, 6 (1974), 293-323.

Patberg, J., Dewitz, P., and Samuels, S.J. The effect of context on the size of the perceptual unit used in word recognition. *Journal of Reading Behavior*, 13 (1981), 33-48.

Samuels, S.J. Introduction to theoretical models of reading. In W. Otto, C. Peters, and N. Peters (Eds.), *Reading Problems: A Multidisciplinary Perspective*. Reading, Mass.: Addison Wesley, 1977.

Samuels, S.J., LaBerge, D., and Bremer, C. Units of word recognition: Evidence for developmental changes. *Journal of Verbal Learning and Verbal Behavior*, 17 (1978), 715-720.

Terry, P., Samuels, S.J., and LaBerge, D. The effect of letter degradation and letter spacing on word recognition. *Journal of Verbal Learning and Verbal Behavior*, 15 (1976), 577-585.

Interaction Model

Toward an Interactive Model of Reading

DAVID E. RUMELHART
University of California at San Diego

Introduction

Reading is the process of understanding written language. It begins with a flutter of patterns on the retina and ends (when successful) with a definite idea about the author's intended message. Thus, reading is at once a "perceptual" and a "cognitive" process. It is a process which bridges and blurs these two traditional distinctions. Moreover, a skilled reader must be able to make use of sensory, syntactic, semantic, and pragmatic information to accomplish his task. These various sources of information appear to interact in many complex ways during the process of reading. A theorist faced with the task of accounting for reading must devise a formalism rich enough to represent all of these different kinds of information and their interactions.

The study of reading was a central concern of early psychologists (see Huey, 1908). Now, after years of dormancy, reading has again become a central concern for many psychologists. It would seem that the advent of the information-processing approach to psychology has given both experimentalists and theorists paradigms within which to study the reading process. The formalisms of information processing, the flow charts, notions of information flow, etc., have served as useful vehicles for the development of first approximation models of the reading process. Unfortunately, the most familiar information-processing formalisms apply most naturally to models assuming a series of noninteracting stages of processing or (at best) a set of independent parallel processing units. There are many results in the reading literature that appear to call for highly interactive parallel processing units. It is my suspicion that the serial, noninteracting models have been developed not so much due to an abiding belief that interactions do not take place, but rather because the appropriate formalisms have not been available. It is the purpose of this chapter to adapt a formalism developed in the context of parallel computation to the specification of a model for reading and then show that such a model can account in a convenient way for those aspects of reading that appear puzzling in the context of more linear stage-oriented models. No

Research support was provided by grant NS 07454 from the National Institute of Health.

claim is made about the adequacy of the particular model developed. The primary claim is that this richer formalism will allow for the specification of more detailed models. These will be able to characterize aspects of the reading process which are difficult or impossible to characterize within the more familiar information-processing formulations.

I will first review two recent models of the reading process. Then, I will discuss some of the empirical evidence that is not conveniently accounted for by these models or their natural extensions. Finally, I will develop a reading model which makes use of a formalism allowing highly interactive parallel processing units, and then show that this model offers a reasonable account of the problematic results of Section III.

Current Models of Reading

Gough's Model

Gough (1972) has proposed a model of reading that is remarkable in the degree to which it attempts to give a complete information-processing account of the reading process. Gough attempts to pin down as completely as possible the events that occur during the first second of reading. A schematic diagram, representing the flow of information during the reading process is shown in Figure 1. According to Gough's model, graphemic information enters the visual system and is registered in an *icon* which holds it briefly while it is scanned and operated on by a *pattern recognition* device. This device identifies the letters of the input string. These letters are then read into a *character register* which holds them while a *decoder* (with the aid of a *code book*) converts the character strings into their underlying *phonemic* representation. The phonemic representation of the original character strings serves as input to a *librarian* which matches up these phonemic strings against the *lexicon* and feeds the resulting lexical entries into *primary memory* The four or five lexical items held in primary memory at any one time serve as input to a magical system (dubbed *Merlin*) which somehow applies its knowledge of the syntax and semantics to determine the deep structure (or perhaps the meaning?) of the input. This deep structure is then forwarded to its final memory register TPWSGWTAU (the place where sentences go when they are understood). When all inputs of the text have found their final resting place in TPWSGWTAU, the text has been read and the reading is complete.

I do not want to discuss the merits or demerits of Gough's particular model at this point. Instead, I point to the general form of the model. For Gough, reading consists of a sequentially ordered set of transformations. The input signal is first registered in the icon and then transformed from a character level representation to phonemic representation, lexical level representation and finally to deep structural representation. Thus, the input is sequentially transformed from low-level sensory information into ever higher-level encodings. Note, however, that the

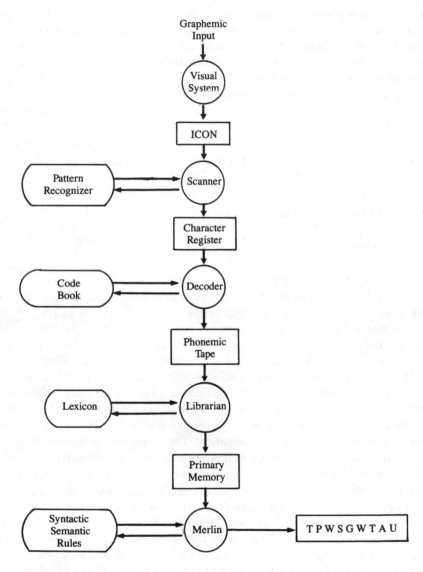

Figure 1. Gough's reading model. (After Gough, 1972.)

information flow is totally "bottom up." That is, the information is initiated with the sensory signal and no higher level of processing can affect any lower level. The reading process is strict letter-by-letter, word-by-word analysis of the input string. There is no provision for interaction within the system. The processing at any level can directly affect only the immediately higher level.

LaBerge-Samuels Model

In another paper, LaBerge and Samuels (1974) have developed an equally detailed (though somewhat more perceptually oriented) model of the reading process. Figure 2 gives a schematic representation of their model. The basic model consists of three memory systems holding three different representations of the input string. The Visual Memory System holds visually based representations of the features, letters, spelling groups, words, and word clusters. The Phonological Memory System holds phonological representations of spelling groups, words, and word groups. Finally, the Semantic Memory System holds the semantic representation of the words, word groups, and sentences that are read. The reading process begins with the registration of the visual signal on the sensory surface. The information is then analyzed by a set of specialized *feature detectors* which extract information about lines, angles, intersections, etc., from the physical stimulus. Most of these feature detectors, f_i, feed directly into letter codes, l_i. Thus, the activation of letter codes results naturally from the convergence of a set of feature detectors. These letter codes feed into spelling pattern codes, sp_i, which in turn feed into visual word codes, $v(w_i)$. Some features (e.g., f_2) map directly into spelling pattern codes and others (f_i) directly into visual word codes. Such features are sensitive to the overall configuration of the words and spelling patterns. There are a number of routes whereby words can be mapped into meanings.

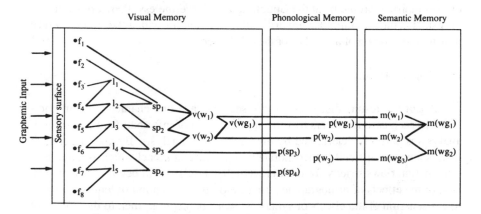

Figure 2. Reading in the LaBerge-Samuels model. (After LaBerge and Samuels, 1974.)

1. Visual word codes can feed directly into word meaning codes, $m(w_i)$. This route would be necessary for the discrimination of such homophonous word pairs as "pear" and "pair" or "chute" and "shoot."

2. The visual word codes can pass through a phonological word code, $p(w_i)$, and then into a word meaning code. This is perhaps the ordinary route of analysis within the LaBerge-Samuels model.

3. The model also allows for word groups, such as "time out," to be analyzed into visual word group codes, $v(wg_1)$ from these into phonetic word group
codes, $(p(wg_1)$ and finally into group meanings, $m(wg_1)$.

4. When a word has not been learned as a visual stimulus, information can
be translated directly from visual spelling patterns into phonological spelling patterns, $p(sp_1)$, from these into phonological word codes and finally into word
meaning codes. In addition, word meaning codes feed into word group meaning
codes.

Ultimately, when the entire set of inputs have been presented, a set of word
group meanings will emerge and the reader will be said to have understood the
input.[1]

Again, I do not want to discuss the particular merits or demerits of the La-
Berge-Samuels model. Rather, I again point out the general form of the model
and suggest that it takes that form, at least to some extent, because of the formalisms used to represent the ideas. The LaBerge-Samuels model, like the Gough
model, is a strictly bottom-up process.[2] Although there are alternative routes, the
basic sequence is from features to letters, to spelling patterns, to visual word
representations to phonological word representations to word meanings to word
group meanings. A series of stages, each corresponding to a level of analysis in
which no higher level can in any way modify or change the analysis at a lower
level. The LaBerge-Samuels model (unlike the Gough model) does allow certain
stages to be bypassed. This allows multiple paths of analysis and alleviates some
of the empirical problems of the Gough model. Nevertheless, there are a number
of results in the literature that are difficult to account for with either model. I turn
now to a discussion of a number of these problems.

Problematic Results

All of the results discussed in this section have one characteristic in common. In each case it appears that the apprehension of information at one level of
analysis is partially determined by higher levels of analysis. By and large, such
results are very difficult to incorporate in a processing model which assumes that
information flows strictly from lower to higher levels. I will begin with a discussion of the effects of orthographic structure on the perception of letters, proceed
to a discussion of the effects of syntax on word perception, then to the effects of
semantics on word and syntax perception and finally to the effects of general
pragmatic factors on the perception of meanings.[3]

The Perceptions of Letters Often Depend on the Surrounding Letters

The literature on reading abounds with evidence on this point. Perhaps the
most difficult of these results for a purely bottom-up model to account for are the
well-known context effects illustrated in Figure 3 (after Nash-Weber, 1975).

Here we see an ambiguous symbol. *W* , which is interpreted as a W in one context and interpreted as an E followed by a V in another context. It would appear that our interpretation of the sentence has determined our perception of the ambiguous symbol.

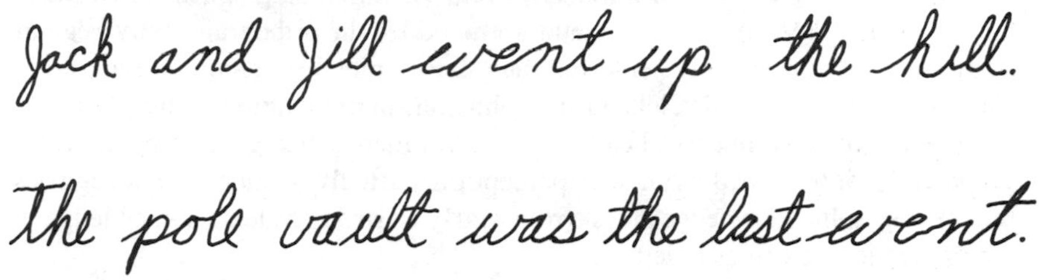

Figure 3. The dependence of letter perception of context. (After Nash-Weber, 1975.)

The problem with results such as these stems from the fact that we appear to have "word-level" or "phrase-level" perceptions determining our perceptions at the letter level, a higher-level perception affecting a lower-level one. These results can be accounted for by bottom-up models, but only at some cost. No final decision can be made at the letter level. Either a set of alternative possibilities must be passed on, or the direct feature information must be sent to the higher levels. In either of these cases the notion that letter perception precedes word perception becomes suspect. Word and letter perception occur simultaneously.

Perhaps the strongest objection to a demonstration like this one is that it is very unusual to find such ambiguous letters and that the norm involves characters which are perfectly discriminable. Although this may be true of printed text, it is not true of handwriting. Characters can often be interpreted only with reference to their context. Yet, I would not want to argue that the reading process is essentially different for handwritten than for printed material.

There are many other results which appear to call for this same conclusion. For example, more letters can be apprehended per unit time when a word is presented than when a string of unrelated letters is presented (Huey, 1908/1968). Letter strings formed either deleting a letter of a word or replacing one or two of the letters of the word is often clearly perceived as the original word (Pillsbury, 1897). Even when great care is taken to control for guessing, a letter is more accurately perceived when it is part of a word than when it is among a set of unrelated letters (Reicher, 1969). All of these results appear to argue strongly that letter perceptions are facilitated by being in words. Word-level perceptions affect letter-level perceptions. Here again, the only way that the types of models under consideration can account for these effects is to suppose that partial letter information is somehow preserved and the additional constraints of the word level are brought to bear on the partial letter information.

It is of some interest that these effects can be observed in letter strings which are not words, but which are similar to words in important ways. For example, the more the sequential transition probabilities among letters in a string approximate those of English, the more letters can be perceived per unit time (Miller, Bruner, and Postman, 1954). Similarly, even when guessing is controlled (as in the Reicher, 1969, experiment), letters embedded in orthographically regular strings are more accurately perceived than those embedded among orthographically irregular strings (McClelland and Johnston, in preparation). Thus, not only is a letter embedded in a word easier to see, but merely being a part of an orthographically well-formed string aids perception virtually as much. This suggests that orthographic knowledge plays a role nearly as strong as lexical knowledge in the perception of strings of letters.

Not only does orthographic structure have a positive effect on the perception of letters embedded in an orthographically regular string, but our apprehension of orthographically irregular strings is often distorted to allow us to perceive the string as being orthographically regular. This point is nicely illustrated in a recent experiment carried out in our laboratory by Albert Stevens. In this experiment subjects were presented with letter strings consisting of two consonants (i.e., an initial consonant cluster designated CC_i) followed by two vowels (a vowel cluster, designated VC) followed by two more consonants (a final consonant cluster CC_f). The initial consonant cluster was constructed from pairs of consonants that can occur at the beginning of English words in only one order (e.g., English words can begin with "pr," but not "rp"). Similarly the vowel clusters used occur as diphthongs in English in one order but not in the other (e.g., "ai" but not "ia"). The final consonant clusters were similarly chosen so that they occur at the end of English words in one order, but not the other (e.g., "ck" but not "kc"). Strings were then constructed in which each letter cluster was either in its legal or illegal order. Table 1 illustrates several examples of the various types of letter strings.

Subjects were given tachistoscopic presentations of the various letter strings and asked to name the letters they observed. Of particular interest are the times when they were presented illegal strings, but made them legal by transposing the letter pair in their reports. Figure 4 illustrates the comparison of interest. The figure compares the percentage of times an illegally ordered letter cluster is transposed into a legal cluster with the number of times a legal letter cluster is transposed into an illegal one. The results show that although initial consonant clusters are never transposed, illegal vowel clusters are transposed almost 25 percent of the time as compared to only about 3 percent transposition for the legal vowel clusters. Similarly final consonant clusters are transposed almost 14 percent of the time when they are illegal, but only about 3 percent of the time when they are legal. These results show clearly the effect that orthographic structure has on our perception of letter strings. The perception of a certain letter in a certain position depends on what we perceive in adjacent positions as well as on the sensory evidence we have available about that position in the string.

Table 1
EXAMPLES OF LEGAL AND ILLEGAL LETTER STRINGS

	CC_i			
	Legal VC		Illegal VC	
CC_f	Legal	Illegal	Legal	Illegal
legal	praick	priack	rpaick	rpiack
	stourt	stuort	tsourt	tsuort
illegal	praikc	priakc	rpaikc	rpiakc
	stoutr	stuotr	tsoutr	tsuotr

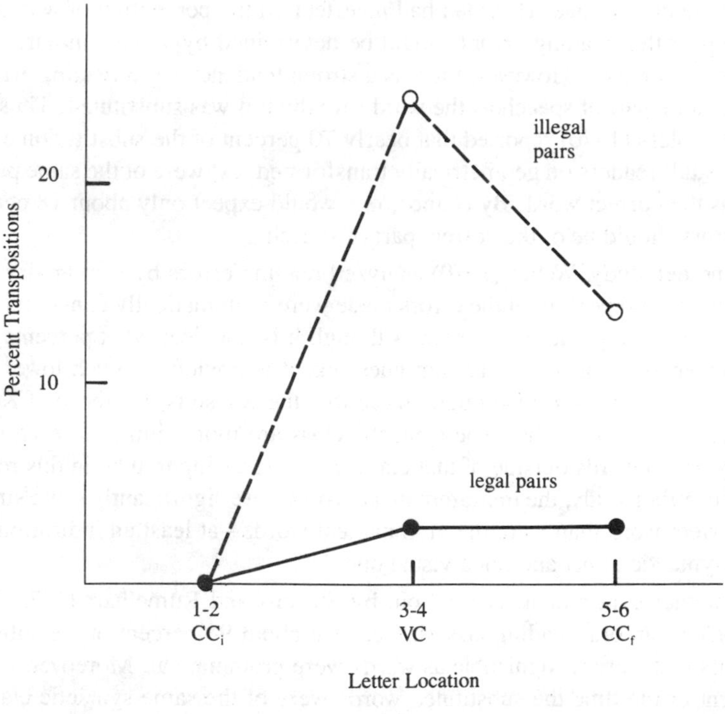

Figure 4. Transpositions as a function of letter location.

To summarize, then, it appears that no model which supposes that we first perceive the letters in a stimulus and then put them together into higher-order units can be correct. However, models like the Gough model and the LaBerge-Samuels model can survive such results if they assume that partial information is somehow forwarded to the higher levels of analysis and that the final decision as to which letters were present is delayed until this further processing has been accomplished.

Whereas it is not too difficult to see how, say, the LaBerge-Samuels model could account for the effects of orthographic structure on letter perception, it is somewhat more difficult to see how the effects of syntax and semantics can be mediated within such a model. I now turn to evidence for syntactic effects in reading.

Our Perception of Words Depends on the Syntactic
Environment in Which We Encounter the Words

Perhaps the best evidence for syntactic effects on the level of word perception comes from an analysis of oral reading errors. The most common error in oral reading is the substitution error—when an incorrect word is simply substituted for the correct one. If syntax had no effect on the perception of words, we would expect that reading errors should be determined by visual similarity and not by part of speech. However, there is a strong tendency for a reading error to be of the same part of speech as the word for which it was substituted. Thus, for example, Kolers (1970) reported that nearly 70 percent of the substitution errors made by adult readers on geometrically transformed text were of the same part of speech as the correct word. By chance, one would expect only about 18 percent of the errors should be of the correct part of speech.

In another study, Weber (1970) analyzed reading errors by first graders and found that over 90 percent of the errors made were grammatically consistent with the sentence to the point of the error. Although it is not clear what percentage to expect under assumptions of random guessing, it is obviously much lower than 90 percent in most texts. One might argue that these results and those of Kolers occur because words in the same syntactic class are more similar to each other than they are to words outside of that class. It is interesting to note in this regard that in the Weber study, the ungrammatical errors were significantly more similar to the correct word than were the grammatical words—at least an indication that this is a syntactic effect and not a visual one.

In another experiment, carried out by Stevens and Rumelhart (1975) with adult readers, an oral reading task showed that about 98 percent of the substitution errors that were recognizable as words were grammatical. Moreover, nearly 80 percent of the time the substituted words were of the same syntactic class as the class most frequently predicted at that part in a cloze experiment. Once again, it appears that we have a case of grammatical knowledge helping to determine the word read.

In addition, in an important experiment, Miller and Isard (1963) compared perceptibility of spoken words under conditions in which normal syntactic structure was violated with the case in which syntactic structure was intact. They found that many more words could be reported when the sentences were syntactically normal. Although I do not know of a similar study with written materials, it is doubtless that similar results would occur—another case of a higher level of processing determining the perceptibility of units at a lower level.

It is difficult to see exactly how the models under discussion would deal with results such as these. In the Gough model syntactic processing occurs only very late in the processing sequence — after information has entered short-term memory. It seems unlikely that he would want to assume that partial information is preserved that far in the process. It is not clear just where syntax should be put in the LaBerge-Samuels model. It is particularly difficult to represent productive syntactic rules of the sort linguists suggest in the LaBerge-Samuels formalism. As I will discuss subsequently, it would appear to be essential to be able to represent systems of rules to account for such results.

Our Perception of Words Depends on the Semantic Environment in Which We Encounter the Words

It is even more difficult to incorporate a mechanism for semantic effects on the word recognition process into a purely bottom-up model than it is to incorporate a mechanism for syntactic effects. There have recently been a number of studies which provide very nice demonstrations of semantic effects on word recognition.

In a series of experiments Meyer, Schvaneveldt, and Ruddy (Meyer and Schvaneveldt, 1971; Meyer, Schvaneveldt, and Ruddy, 1972; Meyer, Schvaneveldt, and Ruddy, 1974; Ruddy, Meyer, and Schvaneveldt, 1973; Schvaneveldt and Meyer, 1973) have reported convincing evidence of semantic effects on word recognition. The basic procedure in these experiments involved measuring reaction times to come to a lexical decision about a pair of words. The basic result is that the decision can be made much faster when the pair of words are semantically related (such as BREAD-BUTTER or DOCTOR-NURSE) than when they are unrelated (such as BREAD-DOCTOR and NURSE-BUTTER). The most plausible account of these results would seem to be that the process of perceiving the first word somehow allows us to process the second word more quickly just in case it is a semantically related word. Thus, we again have the processing at the semantic level modifying our processing at the word level.

In a series of experiments recently carried out in our laboratory Graboi (1974) demonstrated this same general effect using quite a different method. In one of his experiments Graboi employed a variation of Neisser's search procedure. First subjects were trained to search for occurrence of any one of five target words among a list of semantically unrelated nontargets. Half of the subjects searched for any one of the words labeled Experimental Target Set (see Table 2) scattered among lists constructed from the Unassociated Nontargets. The other half of the subjects searched for the words labeled Control Target Set against the same background. Notice that neither target set is semantically related to the nontarget background in which it is searched for. After 14 hours of training, the experimental group was searching their lists at a rate of 182.2 msec per word. The control group scanned at a rate of 180.0 msec per word. On the fifteenth hour of practice, the background lists were changed. Both groups now search for their targets against the Associated Nontarget background. Now the experimental group was searching for its targets against a background of nontargets, all semantically associated with the target set. The control group was also switched, but the Associated Nontargets were not semantically related to the control target set. After the change we find that the control group scans against the new background at about the same rate as they scanned the old one—179 msec per word scanned. The experimental group, however, scanning through words semantically related to the target set was slowed to a rate of 197.4 msec per word.

One might suppose that the subjects in the experimental group were just surprised to see related words in the background and a few long pauses accounted for the entire difference. However, on this account one would expect the difference soon to disappear. But this did not happen. Through five additional hours of searching (they searched through 2,000 words during one hour session) the difference between the control and experimental subjects remained at about 20 msec per word. It would thus appear that even when searching for particular words our expectations are based on meaning as well as visual form.

Using still another experimental procedure, Tulving and Gold (1963) and Tulving, Mandler, and Baumal (1964) both found that the prior presentation of a sentence context lowers the threshold at which a tachistoscopically presented word can be recognized.

Again we have a case of a higher level of processing (meaning) apparently effecting our ability to process at a lower level (the word level). Notice, moreover, that semantic relatedness can either make our processing more efficient (as with the Meyer et al., 1974 and Tulving and Gold, 1963 experiments) or it can interfere with our processing (as with the Graboi experiment, 1974). It is again difficult to see how a strictly bottom-up, stage-by-stage processing model can account for results such as these.

Our Perception of Syntax Depends on the Semantic Context in Which the String Appears

Although neither Gough nor LaBerge and Samuels have attempted to specify their models much beyond the level of words, a complete model of reading must, of course, account for the way semantics affects our apprehension of the syntax of a sentence we are reading. Experiments at this level are few and far between, but there are numerous examples which seem rather compelling on this general point.

Perhaps the most commonly observed effect of this sort involves the semantic disambiguation of syntactically ambiguous sentences. Consider the following sentences:
(1) a. They are eating apples.
     b. The children are eating apples.
     c. The juicy red ones are eating apples.

Table 2

ALTERNATIVE STIMULI IN THE TARGET AND NONTARGET SETS

	A. Associated Nontargets	
	WORM CHICK NESTS ROBIN CHIRP WINGS FLY	
Experimental	EAGLE PARROT SONG BLACK GRAY PURPLE	Control
target	BROWN GOLD BLUE RED YELLOW GREEN PAINT	target
set	SAVE SPEND COINS DIME BANK SILVER DOLLAR	set
	CASH PENNY PEARL BOOKS SCHOOL READ	
	CLASS WRITE TEACH EXAM NOTES GRADE	
	STUDY ORANGE NUTS GRAPE SWEET PLUM	
BIRD:	APPLE PEACH PEAR FRESH LEMON	:ROCK
COLOR:		:CHAIR
MONEY:	B. Unassociated Nontargets	:HOUSE
LEARN:	HUG PEN SLEEP NIGHT BRIDGE STAPLE LAMP	:SPORT
FRUIT:	RULER LEADER ROAR SUNNY PLACE CORNER	:CLOUD
	ALBUM ABOUT RATE WEEK POINT SWITCH	
	ANKLE TOWN DIAL SPOON TOWEL SHEET STOVE	
	CRUST BRUSH GLASS ROAD WHICH AFTER	
	PASS STORY SIGN CHURCH MURAL PHONE	
	BOOTH CARD STREET MOTOR RADIO KNOB	
	PLUG DRIVE LINE TASK PRINT SHIFT	

At the syntactic level all three sentences allow for at least two readings:

1. The reading in which the thing referred to by the first noun phrase is performing the act of eating some apples.

2. The reading in which the thing referred to by the first noun phrase is said to be a member of the class of "eating apples."

However, at a semantic level only the first one remains ambiguous—even it would be disambiguated if we had some notion as to the referent of *they*.

Schank (1973) has given a number of similar examples. Consider, for example:

(2) a. I saw the Grand Canyon flying to New York.

b. I saw the Grand Canyon *while I was* flying to New York.

c. I saw the Grand Canyon *which was* flying to New York.

Most readers immediately interpret Sentence (2a) as meaning the same as (2b) rather than Sentence (2c) simply on the grounds that it is semantically anomalous to imagine the Grand Canyon actually flying. On the other hand Sentence (3a) is ordinarily interpreted to mean the same as Sentence (3c) rather than Sentence (3b):

(3) a. I saw the cattle grazing in the field.

b. I saw the cattle *while I was* grazing in the field.

c. I saw the cattle *that were* grazing in the field.

In Examples (1), (2) and (3) semantics play the determining role as to which surface structure we apprehend. Thus, just as orthographic structure affects our ability to perceive letters and syntax and semantics affects our perception of words, so too does semantics affect our apprehension of syntax.

Our Interpretation of the Meaning of What We Read Depends on the General Context in Which We Encounter the Text

Just as the appropriate interpretation of our ambiguous symbol, $\mathcal{W}$, was determined by the sentence in which it was embedded, so too it often happens that the *meaning* of a word is dependent on the words surrounding it. Consider, for example, the following sentences:

(4) a. The statistician could be certain that the difference was significant *since all of the figures on the right hand side of the table were larger than any of those on the left.*

   b. The craftsman was certainly justified in charging more for the carvings on the right *since all of the figures on the right hand side of the table were larger than any of those on the left.*

Here our interpretation of the second clause is thus quite different depending on the nature of the first clause. In Sentence (4a) for example, the term *figure* is readily interpreted as being a number, the term *table* a place for writing numbers, and the relation *larger* can properly be interpreted to mean $>$. In Sentence (4b) on the other hand, the term *figure* presumably refers to a small statue, the term *table* refers to a physical object with a flat top used for setting things on, and the relation *larger* clearly means something like *of greater volume*. Here we have a case in which no determination about the meaning of these individual words can be made without consideration of the entire sentence. Thus, no decision can be made about the meaning of a word without consideration of the meaning of the entire sentence in which the word appears.

Not only is the interpretation of individual words dependent on the sentential context in which they are found, but the meaning of entire sentences is dependent on the general context in which they appear. The following example from Bransford and Johnson (1973) is a case in point:

(5)
Watching a Peace March from the 40th Floor

The view was breathtaking. From the window one could see the crowd below. Everything looked extremely small from such a distance, but the colorful costumes could still be seen. Everyone seemed to be moving in the same direction in an orderly fashion and there seemed to be little children as well as adults. The landing was gentle, and luckily the atmosphere was such that no special suits had to be worn. At first there was a great deal of activity. Later, when the speeches started, the crowd quieted down. The man with the television camera took many shots of the setting and the crowd. Everyone was very friendly and seemed glad when the music started. (p. 412)

In this passage, the sentence beginning *The landing was gentle...* appears to make no sense. No clear meaning can be assigned to it in this context. As such, when subjects were given the passage and later asked to recall it very few subjects remembered the anomalous sentence. On the other hand, when the passage was entitled *A Space Trip to an Inhibited Plant* the entire passage was given quite a different interpretation. In this case the anomalous sentence fits into the general interpretation of the paragraph very well. Subjects given the *Space Trip* title recalled the critical sentence three times as often as those given the *Peace March* title. Many other examples could be given. The dependence of meaning on context would appear to be the norm rather than the exception in reading.

To summarize, these results taken together appear to support the view that our apprehension of information at one level of analysis can often depend on our apprehension of information at a higher level. How can this be? Surely we cannot first perceive the meaning of what we read and only later discover what the sentences, words or letters were that mediated the meaning. To paraphrase a remark attributed to Gough (cited in Brewer, 1972): It is difficult to "see how the syntax [or semantics for that matter] can go out and mess around with the print" (p. 360). The problem I believe, arises from the linear stage formalism that has served so well. The answer, I suspect, comes by presuming that all these knowledge sources apply simultaneously and that our perceptions are the product of the simultaneous interactions among all of them.

An Interactive Model

Perhaps the most natural information-processing representation of the theoretical ideas suggested in the previous section is illustrated in Figure 5. The figure illustrates the assumption that graphemic information enters the system and is registered in a visual information store (VIS). A feature extraction device is then assumed to operate on this information extracting the critical features from the VIS. These features serve as the sensory input to a pattern synthesizer. In addition to this sensory information, the pattern synthesizer has available nonsensory information about the orthographic structure of the language (including information about the probability of various strings of characters), information about lexical items in the language, information about the syntactic possibilities (and probabilities), information about the semantics of the language and information about the current contextual situation (pragmatic information). The pattern synthesizer, then, uses all of this information to produce a "most probable interpretation" of the graphemic input. Thus, all of the various sources of knowledge, both sensory and nonsensory, come together at one place and the reading process is the product of the simultaneous joint application of all the knowledge sources.

Although the model previously outlined may, in fact, be an accurate representation of the reading process, it is of very little help as a model of reading. It is one thing to suggest that all of these different information sources interact (as many writers have), but quite another to specify a psychologically plausible hypothesis about how they interact. It is thus clear why serious theorists who have attempted to develop detailed models of the reading process (e.g., Gough, 1972; LaBerge and Samuels, 1974) have stayed away from a formulation of the sort illustrated in Figure 5. All that is interesting in the model takes place in the box labeled "Pattern Synthesizer." The flow chart does little more than list the relevant variables. We need a representation for the operation of the pattern synthesizer itself. To represent that, we must develop a means of representing the operation of a set of parallel interacting processes.

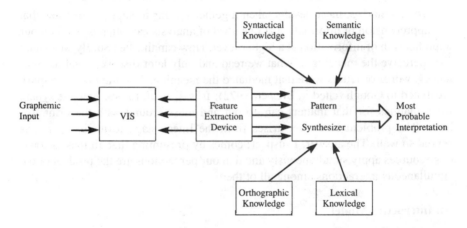

Figure 5. A stage representation of an interactive model of reading.

Flow charts are best suited to represent the simple serial flow of information. They are badly suited for the representation of a set of parallel highly interactive processes. However, with the advent of the parallel computer (at least as a conceptual device), computer scientists have begun to develop formalisms for the representation of parallel processes. It is interesting that the major problem in each case seems to have been the representation of the lines of communication among the otherwise independent processes.

Of the several different systems of communication that have been proposed, two were developed in the context of language processing by computer and seem to be most promising as a formalism for the development of a reading model. One of these was developed by Kaplan (1973) and is called the General Syntactic Processor (GSP). The second was developed by Reddy and his associates at Carnegie-Mellon University (see Lesser, Fennell, Erman, and Reddy, 1974) as an environment for a speech understanding program. This system is called HEAR-SAY II. These two systems have a good deal in common and solve the communication problem in much the same way—namely, both systems consist of sets of totally independent asynchronous processes which communicate by means of a global, highly structured data storage device. In Kaplan's system the communication center is called a *chart,* in the HEARSAY system it is called a *blackboard.* I use the more neutral term *message center* in my development below. This development is most closely related to the HEARSAY system and could well be considered as an application of the HEARSAY model to reading. However, I also draw on aspects of GSP and the model as I develop it has the Rumelhart and Siple (1974) model of word recognition as a special case.

Following HEARSAY, the model can be characterized as consisting of a set of independent *knowledge sources.* (These knowledge sources correspond to the sources of input to the pattern synthesizer in Figure 5.) Each knowledge source contains specialized knowledge about some aspect of the reading process. The message center keeps a running list of hypotheses about the nature of the input string. Each knowledge source constantly scans the message center for the appearance of hypotheses relevant to its own sphere of knowledge. Whenever such a hypothesis enters the message center the knowledge source in question evaluates the hypothesis in light of its own specialized knowledge. As a result of its analysis, the hypothesis may be confirmed, disconfirmed, and removed from the message center, or a new hypothesis can be added to the message center. This process continues until some decision can be reached. At that point the most probable hypothesis is determined to be the correct one. To facilitate the process, the message center is highly structured so that the knowledge sources know exactly where to find relevant hypotheses and so that dependencies among hypotheses are easily determined.

The Message Center

The message center can be represented as a three-dimensional space; one dimension representing the position along the line of text, one dimension representing the level of the hypothesis (word level, letter level, phrase level, etc.) and one dimension representing alternative hypotheses at the same level. Associated with each hypothesis is a running estimate of the probability that it is the correct hypothesis. Moreover, hypotheses at each level may have pointers to hypotheses at higher or lower levels on which they are dependent. Thus, for example, the hypothesis that the first word in a string is the word THE is supported by the hypothesis that the first letter of the string is "T" and supports the hypothesis that the string begins with a noun phrase.

Figure 6 illustrates a two-dimensional slice of the message center at some point during the reading of the phrase, THE CAR.

The figure illustrates hypotheses at five different levels (feature level, letter level, letter-cluster level, lexical level, and syntactic level). The diagram is only a two-dimensional slice inasmuch as no alternative hypotheses are illustrated. In practice, of course, many alternative hypotheses would be considered and evaluated in the course of reading this phrase. It should be pointed out that the tree-like structure should not be taken to mean that the tree was constructed either from a purely bottom-up process (starting with the features, then hypothesizing the let-

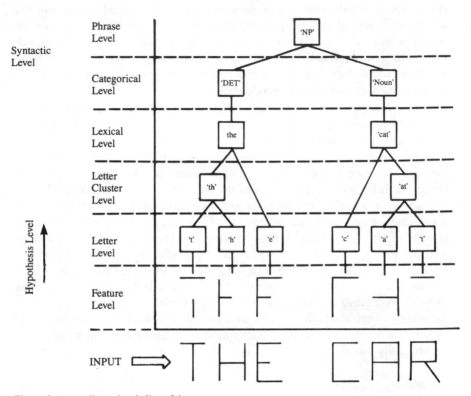

Figure 6. A two-dimensional slice of the message center.

ters, then the letter clusters, etc.), nor from a purely top-down analysis (starting with a view that we have a noun phrase and that noun phrases are made up of determiners followed by nouns, etc.). Rather, the hypotheses can be generated at any level. If it is likely that a line begins with a noun phrase, then we postulate a noun phrase and look for evidence. If we see features that suggest a "t" as the first letter we postulate a "t" in the first position and continue processing. If we later have to reject either or both of these hypotheses little is lost. The system makes the best guesses and checks out their implications. If these guesses are wrong it will take a bit longer, but the system will eventually find some hypotheses at some level that it can accept.

An example. To illustrate the operation of the system, consider the following experimental procedure. A subject is presented with a picture (e.g., Figure 7) and allowed to view it for a few seconds. Then he is given a tachistoscopic presentation of a noun phrase which he knows will refer to one of the objects in the picture. His job is to decide which object was referred to. This experimental procedure is designed to simulate the process of reading a phrase for meaning. (An experimental procedure of this sort is currently under development in our laboratory.) I will illustrate the current model by showing the changes we might expect in the message center as the phrase THE CAR is read after viewing Figure 7.

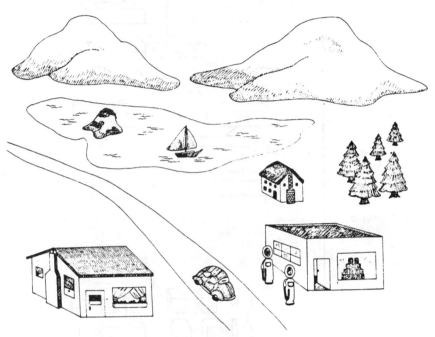

Figure 7. A scene. (Figure provided by Jean Mandler.)

Figure 8 shows the message center at an early point in the processing of this phrase. The subject knows from the instructions of the experiment that the phrase will refer to some object in the picture. Thus, the semantic-level "object" hypothesis can be entered and assigned a high likelihood value from the start. Moreover, through looking at the picture and perceiving certain aspects of it as salient, the subject will develop expectations as to the probable referent of the phrase. In this case, I have assumed that the subject set up special expectations for a phrase referring to *the lake* or to *the Volkswagen*.

Similarly, at the syntactic level, the subject can be quite certain that the input will form a noun phrase. Thus, the hypothesis "NP" is entered into the message center and assigned a high value. Noun phrases have a rather characteristic structure. About 25 percent of the time they begin with a determiner (DET). Thus, in the example, I have assumed that the hypothesis that the first word was a determiner was entered. Similarly, we can expect the second word of a noun phrase to be a noun about 20 percent of the time. Thus, I have entered the hypothesis that the second word is a noun. Now, in the case where the first word is a determiner, we could expect it to be the word "the" about 60 percent of the time and the word "a" about 20 percent. Thus, I have assumed that these two hypotheses have also been entered.

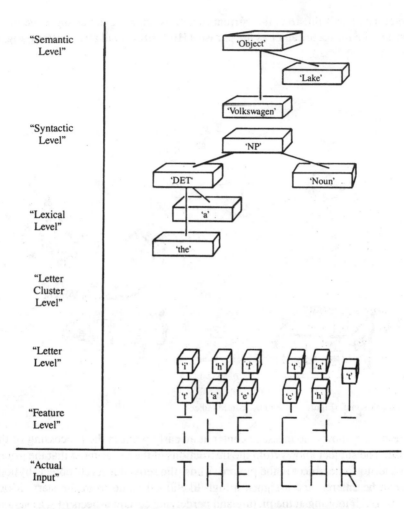

Figure 8. The message center shortly after processing has begun on THE CAR.

As all of these hypotheses are being entered in top-down fashion, hypotheses at the letter level are also being entered bottom-up on the basis of featural information. In the example, I have assumed that for each of the first five letter positions the two most promising letter possibilities were entered as hypotheses. For the sixth letter position, which contains very little featural information, I have assumed that only its most likely letter hypothesis has been entered.

Figure 9 illustrates the state of the message center at a later point in the processing. In the meantime, the lexical hypothesis "a" has led to a letter hypothesis which was then tested against the featural information and rejected. The hypothesization of an initial "t" has led to the hypothesization of an initial "th" at the letter cluster level—a hypothesis which is given added validity by the possible "h"

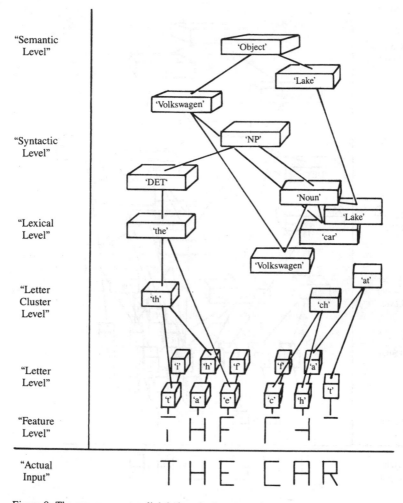

Figure 9. The message center slightly later in the processing sequence.

in the second position. The lexical-level hypothesis of the word "the" has also led to the hypothesization of the letter cluster "th" followed by the letter "e." The prior existence of these hypotheses generated from the bottom up has led to a mutual strengthening of all of the hypotheses in question and a resultant weakening of the alternative letter hypotheses at the first three letter positions.

While this processing was taking place, lexical hypotheses were generated from the semantic level as possible nouns. In this instance I have assumed that the semantic hypothesis "lake" has led to the lexical hypothesis that the word "lake" was in the string and that the semantic hypothesis "Volkswagen" has led to the lexical hypothesis "Volkswagen" and to the lexical hypothesis "car." Meanwhile, the letter hypotheses have led to alternative letter cluster hypotheses "ch" and "at."

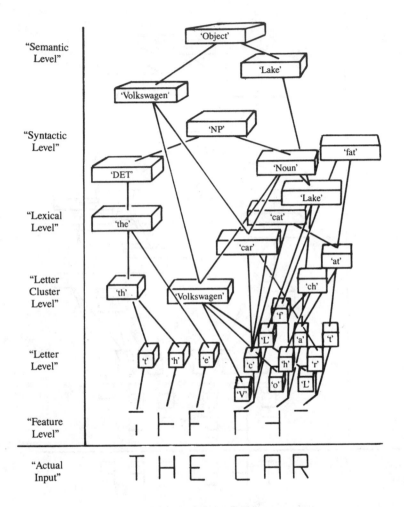

Figure 10. The message center well into the processing sequence.

Figure 10 illustrates the state of the message center at a still later point in the processing of the input. By this point the hypothesis that the first word is "the" has reached a sufficient value that further processing has ceased. No new hypotheses have been generated about the first word. On the other hand, lexical hypotheses on the second word have proliferated. The existence of the letter hypothesis "c" followed by the letter cluster hypothesis "at" has led to a hypothesization of the lexical item "cat" Similarly, the letter hypothesis "f" followed by "at" has led to hypothesizing the lexical item "fat." The lexical hypothesis "cat" is consistent with the "noun" hypothesis, thus strengthening the view that the second word is a noun. At the same time, the lexical hypotheses "lake," "Volkswa-

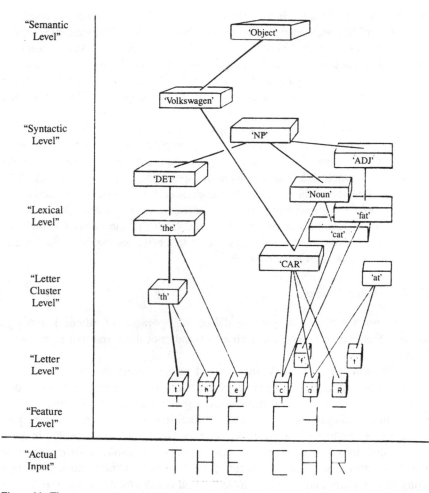

Figure 11. The message center near the end of processing. At this point the semantics of the input has been pretty well determined.

gen" and "car" have either strengthened existing letter hypotheses or have caused new ones to be generated. Notice, in particular, that the prior existence of the letter hypotheses "c" and "a" strengthened the semantically derived lexical hypothesis "car" which in turn strengthened the letter hypothesis "r"—even though the letter hypothesis "r" has not yet been evaluated in light of the featural information in the final position.

Finally, Figure 11 illustrates a state of processing after the letter hypotheses have been tested against the featural information. At this point, only three lexical hypotheses for the second word remain—"fat," "cat," and "car." The lexical hypothesis "fat" has led to the syntactic hypothesis that the second word is an adjective (ADJ) and the lexical hypothesis "cat" has led to the semantic level hypothesis that there should be a cat in the picture. Meanwhile, the semantic hypothesis "Volkswagen" has been strengthened by the findng that the final featural information is consistent with the hypothesis that the last letter is an "r." At this point the semantic hypothesis "Volkswagen" is probably high enough to lead to a response. If not, a test of the semantic hypothesis "cat" will lead to the rejection of that hypothesis and the consequent strengthening of the "Volkswagen" hypothesis and thus the lexical hypothesis "car" and the letter level hypotheses "c," "a" and "r."

It should be clear from this example how, in principle at least, one could build a model of reading that would actually employ constraints from all levels concurrently in the process of constructing an interpretation of an input string. Of course, this example is a long way from the specification of such a model. All I have illustrated here is the nature of the message center and how it is structured to facilitate communication among processes acting at various levels. Before a concrete model of reading can be specified, the nature of the various knowledge sources must be specified as well. I now turn to a brief discussion of the separation of the various knowledge sources.

The Knowledge Sources

I do not yet have a detailed model of the operation of all the knowledge sources. However, I do have ideas about a number of them and will now discuss them:

1. *Featural knowledge.* At this level, I am assuming that features are extracted according to the assumptions of the Rumelhart and Siple (1974) model. Moreover, I am assuming that these critical features are the basic level of processing. In a tachistoscopic experiment, all decisions must be made with respect to the set of features extracted during and shortly after the exposure. In free-reading situations the reader can go back and get more featural information if no hypothesis gets a sufficiently high rating or if some hypothesis does get a high rating at one point and is later rejected. Such occasions probably account for regressions in eye movements.

2. *Letter-level knowledge.* This knowledge source scans the feature inputs and whenever it finds a close match to a known letter, it posits a letter hypothesis. In addition, whenever a letter hypothesis appears from a higher level, this knowledge source evaluates that hypothesis against the feature information. In addition to information about letters in various fonts, the letter-level knowledge source presumably takes into account the probabilities of letters in the language. Thus, relatively more featural evidence would be necessary to postulate a "z" or "q" than an "e" or a "t."

3. *Letter-cluster knowledge.* This knowledge source scans the incoming letter-level hypotheses looking for letter sequences that are likely and form units in the language, or single letters which are frequently followed or preceded by another letter (e.g., as "q" is frequently followed by "u"). In either case a letter cluster is postulated. In the latter case a letter level hypothesis is also introduced.

(That is, if a "q" is found a "qu" is postulated at the letter-cluster level and a "u" is postulated at the letter level.) The value associated with any of these hypotheses depends on the values of the letter-level information on which it is based and on the frequency of such clusters in the language. In addition, the letter cluster knowledge source looks for the introduction of letter cluster hypotheses from the lexical level. Whenever it finds these it evaluates them by proposing the appropriate letter level hypotheses. For this knowledge source, as with all others, the most probable hypotheses that are unsupported from the following or that support no higher-level hypotheses are evaluated first.

4. *Lexical-level knowledge.* The lexical-level knowledge source operates in exactly the same way as the other knowledge sources. It scans the letter cluster and letter hypotheses for letter sequences which form lexical items, or which are close to lexical items. When it finds such information it posits the appropriate lexical-level hypotheses and any additional letter-cluster or letter-level hypotheses. When evaluating the goodness of any hypothesis it takes into account the goodness of the evidence on which it is based and the a priori frequency of that item in the language. In addition, whenever a lexical item is postulated from either the semantic or syntactic levels this knowledge source evaluates that hypothesis by postulating those letter-cluster and letter hypotheses that are not yet present. Those letter and letter-cluster hypotheses that are present are strengthened due to the convergence of lines of evidence. Other alternatives without such convergent information are relatively weakened.

5. *Syntactic knowledge.* Like all of the other knowledge sources this knowledge source is designed to operate in both a bottom-up and top-down mode. Thus, whenever a lexical hypothesis is suggested, one or more syntactic category hypotheses are entered into the message center. In general, not all syntactic category hypotheses consistent with the lexical form would be expected. Instead, those categories which are most probable, given that lexical item, would be entered first. Similarly, sequences of lexical category hypotheses would be scanned looking for phrase possibilities, etc. At the same time, the syntactic knowledge source would have the capacity to operate in a top-down fashion. Thus, for example, whenever a noun-phrase hypothesis was entered, the syntactic knowledge source would establish, say a determiner, syntactic-category hypothesis which in turn might initiate lexical-level hypotheses of determiner words like "a" and "the." Following Kaplan's (1973) GSP I assume that this top-down portion of the syntactic knowledge source would be well represented by an Augmented Transition Network (ATN) parser. (See Stevens and Rumelhart, 1975, for an application of an ATN to reading data.) Like all other levels, the syntactic hypotheses are given values dependent on the goodness of the evidence (or prior probabilities) of the hypotheses on which they are based. Moreover, a convergence of top-down and bottom-up hypotheses strengthens both.

6. *Semantic-level knowledge.* This is perhaps the most difficult level to characterize. Nevertheless, I assume that its operation is essentially the same as the others. Whenever strong lexical hypotheses occur, this knowledge source must

have the ability to look for semantic-level correlates to evaluate the plausibility of the hypothesis (at both the lexical and syntactic levels). Moreover, it must be able to develop hypotheses about the content of the input and generate lexical-level hypotheses as possible representations of this. The experimental procedure discussed in the previous section was designed as an attempt to reduce the complexity of the semantic component by supposing a relatively simple referential semantics.

Still, of course, after having outlined the functional characteristics of the various knowledge sources I am still far from the quantitative model I have in mind. However, it would appear that a HEARSAY type model such as this offers promise as a framework for the development of serious models of reading which nevertheless assumes a highly interactive parallel processing system.

A Mathematical Model of Hypothesis Evaluation

In this section I will specify in somewhat more detail the nature of the hypothesis evaluation process I envision. Figure 12 illustrates a simplified version of the message center from the primary example. This figure differs somewhat in format from the previous figures of this type in order to make clearer the sequential dependencies among hypotheses at the same level. Thus, the fact that an NP consists of a DET and NOUN and that the word "cat" consists of C + A + T is illustrated by the arrows connecting those constituents at the same level. Moreover, the dependency arrows have been drawn to only the left-hand member of such hypothesis sequences. In a sense, as we shall see below, the left-hand member is representing the entire sequence of hypotheses.

There are four different types of dependency relationships among hypotheses in this model. These types are illustrated in the figure. First, an hypothesis may have one or more *daughter* hypotheses. A daughter hypothesis is one at a lower level which is connected directly to a higher-level hypothesis. In the figure the hypothesis, "DET" has two daughter hypotheses: "the" and "a." The hypothesis "the" has a single daughter, "t." An hypothesis may have any number of daughters. Each daughter is an alternative way in which the higher hypothesis can be realized. Thus, "the" and "a" are alternative ways in which "DET" can be realized. For any hypothesis, h_i, I shall use the symbol D_i to designate its set of daughters.

The reciprocal relationship to daughter is *parent*. Any hypothesis may have one or more parent hypotheses. A parent hypothesis is one to which an hypothesis can lend direct support. Thus, in the figure "NOUN" is a parent of both "car" and "cat." Similarly, the letter hypothesis "c" has two different parents, "car" and "cat." Only hypotheses which are at the left most position of a sequence of hypotheses may have parents. Thus, the hypothesis "NOUN" has no parent. For each hypothesis, h_i, I shall designate the set of parents P_i.

In addition to parents and daughters, hypotheses may have *sisters*. Sisters are hypotheses in a sequence which either follow or precede a particular hypothesis at the same level. Sisters are not alternatives, but are consistent possibilities

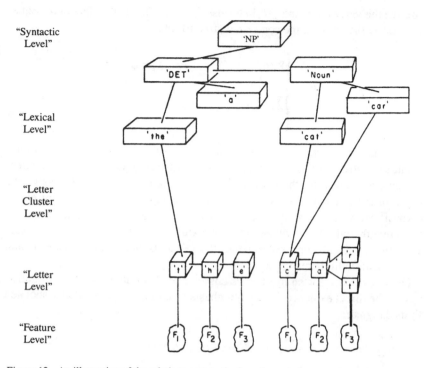

Figure 12. An illustration of the relations among the hypotheses in the message center.

of the same level. There are two sorts of sister hypotheses; *right sisters* and *left sisters*. Right sisters are hypotheses that follow a given hypothesis in a sequence of hypotheses. Thus, "NOUN" would be a right sister of "DET" and "r" and "t" are right sisters of the letter-level hypothesis "a." I designate the set of right sisters of h_i as R_i. Left sisters are those hypotheses which precede a given hypothesis in a string of hypotheses. Although it is possible for an hypothesis to have more than one left sister, no cases of this are illustrated in the figure. I designate the set of left sisters of hypothesis h_i as L_i.

We are now in a position to develop a measure for evaluating hypotheses. The measure that I will propose is essentially the Baysian probability that the hypothesis is true given the evidence at hand. The evidence favoring a particular hypothesis can be broken down into two parts: contextual evidence, dependent only on sister and parent hypotheses, and direct evidence dependent solely on the evidence derived from daughter hypotheses and ultimately featural evidence. Equation (1) illustrates the assumed multiplicative relationship between these two kinds of evidence:

$$s_i = \nu_i \cdot \beta_i.^4 \tag{1}$$

where s_i is the overall strength of the hypothesis h_i, ν_i is a measure of the direct evidence for h_i, and β_i is a measure of the contextual evidence for h_i. Now, we can define the values of v_i and β_i in terms of the parents, and sisters of h_i. Equation (2) gives the value of the contextual strength of h_i:

$$\beta_i = \begin{cases} \text{Pr}(h_i) & P_l = L_l = \phi \\ \sum_{s_k} \dfrac{\cdot \text{Pr}\,(h_i|h_k)}{v_i} \text{ otherwise,} \end{cases} \qquad (2)$$

where the sum is over all $h_k \in P_i$ or L_i. Thus, when h_i has no parents or left sisters, its contextual strength is given by its a priori probability. Otherwise, its contextual strength is given by the sum, over all of its left sisters and parents of the strength of the left sister or parent, h_k, times the conditional probability of the hypothesis given h_k. The sum is then divided by its own direct strength so that its direct strength will not contribute to its contextual strength (since as we shall see, its own direct strength contributes to the strength of its parents and left sisters and is represented multiplicatively in s_k).

Direct evidence for an hypothesis comes only from its daughters. Equation (3) gives the direct evidence for an hypothesis as a function of a value associated with its daughters:

$$v_i = \begin{cases} \sum C_{ik} \cdot \text{Pr}(h_k|h_i) & D_i \neq \phi \\ 1 & \text{otherwise} \end{cases} \qquad (3)$$

where the sum is over all $h_k \in D_i$ and where C_{ik} is the *cumulative evidence* for hypothesis h_i associated with the sequence of hypotheses whose left most member is the daughter h_k. Thus, in the diagram, the direct evidence for "car" is determined jointly by the direct evidence for "c," for "a" and for "r." The value of C_{ik} is given by the following equation:

$$C_{i,k} = \begin{cases} v_k & R_k = \phi \\ \sum_j v_k \cdot C_{i,j} \cdot \text{Pr}(h_j|h_i, h_k) & \text{otherwise} \end{cases} \qquad (4)$$

where the sum is over all $h_j \in R_k$. Thus, the cumulative evidence for hypothesis h_i associated with hypothesis h_k is determined by the product of the direct evidence for h_k and the cumulative evidence for its right sister. If its probable right sisters are very strong then the cumulative evidence is very strong and thus offers good support to its parent. Otherwise, it offers support against its parent.

Finally, we must give special attention to the first level hypotheses associated with featural level inputs. For any letter hypothesis h_i featural level inputs have cumulative values of C_{iF} given by:

$$C_{i,F} = [\text{Pr}(F)]^{-1} \qquad (5)$$

where F is the set of features observed in that location. This, in effect, is a normalizer designed to keep the strengths in the 0 to 1 range.

The equations (1)-(5) define a system of evaluation which makes near optimal use of the information available at any given point in time. Whenever a new hypothesis is postulated and a new connection is drawn, new values must be computed for the entire set of hypotheses. Resources can be allotted to the knowledge sources based upon their momentary evaluations. Effort can be focused on generating hypotheses from the top down whenever we have hypotheses with strong contextual strengths and few daughter hypotheses. Effort can be focused on the generation of hypotheses from the bottom up whenever there is strong direct evidence and few parents. Moreover, the strength values can be signals to stop processing and accept an hypothesis. When some criterion strength-value is obtained an hypothesis can be accepted and no further processing need be required. Then resources can be siphoned to other more critical areas.

Of course specifying equations such as these does not fully specify our model. We must specify all of the knowledge sources and how they postulate hypotheses. They do, I feel, illustrate the model under consideration can be quantified and can generate specific predictions—in spite of the enormous complexity of a highly interactive system.

REFERENCES

Bransford, J.D., and Johnson, M.K. Considerations of some problems of comprehension. In W.G. Chase (Ed.), *Visual information processing.* New York: Academic Press, 1973.

Brewer, W.F. Is reading a letter-by-letter process? In J.F. Kavanagh and I.G. Mattingly (Eds.), *Language by ear and by eye.* Cambridge, Mass.: MIT Press, 1972.

Gough, P.B. One second of reading. In J.F. Kavanagh and I.G. Mattingly (Eds), *Language by ear and by eye.* Cambridge, Mass.: MIT Press, 1972.

Graboi, D. Physical shape, practice and meaning in visual search. Unpublished doctoral dissertation, University of California, San Diego, 1974.

Huey, E.B. The psychology and pedagogy of reading. Cambridge, Mass.: MIT Press, 1968. (Originally published 1908.)

Kaplan, R.M. A general syntactic processor. In R. Rustin (Ed.), *Natural language processing.* New York: Algorithmics Press, 1973.

Kolers, P.A. Three stages in reading. In H. Levin and J.T. Williams (Eds.), *Basic studies in reading.* New York: Basic Books, 1970.

LaBerge, D., and Samuels, S.J. Toward a theory of automatic information processing in reading, *Cognitive Psychology,* 1974, 6, 293-323.

Lesser, V.R., Fennell, R.D., Erman, L.D. and Reddy, D.R. *Organization of the HEARSAY II speech understanding system.* (Working papers in Speech Recognition III.) Pittsburgh, Pa.: Carnegie-Mellon University, 1974, 11-21.

Luce, R.D. *Individual choice behavior.* New York: Wiley, 1959.

McClelland, J.L., and Johnston, J.C. The role of familiar units in perception of words and nonwords. *Perception and Psychophysics,* 1977, 22, 249-261.

Meyer, D.E., and Schvaneveldt, R.W. Facilitation in recognizing pairs of words: Evidence of a dependence between retrieval operations. *Journal of Experimental Psychology,* 1971, 90, 227-234.

Meyer, D.E., Schvaneveldt, R.W., and Ruddy, M.G. Activation of lexical memory. Paper presented at the meeting of the Psychonomic Society, St. Louis, November 1972.

Meyer, D.E., Schvaneveldt, R.W., and Ruddy, M.G. Functions of phonemic and graphemic codes in visual word recognition. *Memory and Cognition,* 1974, 2, 309-321.

Miller, G.A., Bruner, J.S., and Postman, L. Familiarity of letter sequences and tachistoscopic identification. *Journal of Genetic Psychology,* 1954, 50, 129-139.

Miller, G.A., and Isard, S. Some perceptual consequences of linguistic rules. *Journal of Verbal Learning and Verbal Behavior,* 1963, 2, 217-228.

Nash-Weber, B. The role of semantics in automatic speech understanding. In D.G. Bobrow and A. Collins (Eds.), *Representation and understanding.* New York: Academic Press, 1975.

Pillsbury, W.B. A study in apperception. *American Journal of Psychology,* 1897, 8, 315-393.

Reicher, G.M. Perceptual recognition as a function of meaningfulness of stimulus material. *Journal of Experimental Psychology,* 1969, 81, 274-280.

Ruddy, M.G., Meyer, D.E., and Schvaneveldt, R.W. Context effects on phonemic encoding in visual word recognition. Paper read at the meeting of the Midwestern Psychological Association, Chicago, May 1973.

Rumelhart, D.E., and Siple, P. Process of recognizing tachistoscopically presented words. *Psychological Review,* 1974, 81, 99-118.

Schank, R.C. Identification of conceptualizations underlying natural language. In R.C. Schank and K.M. Colby (Eds.), *Computer models of thought and language.* San Francisco: Freeman, 1973.

Schvaneveldt, R.W., and Meyer, D.E. Retrieval and comparison processes in semantic memory. In S. Kornblum (Ed.), *Attention and performance IV.* New York: Academic Press, 1973.

Stevens, A.L., and Rumelhart, D.E. Errors in reading: Analysis using an augmented network model of grammar. In D.A. Norman, D.E. Rumelhart, and the LNR Research Group, *Explorations in cognition.* San Francisco: Freeman, 1975.

Tulving, E., and Gold, C. Stimulus information and contextual information as determinants of tachistoscopic recognition of words. *Journal of Experimental Psychology,* 1963, 66, 319-327.

Tulving, E., Mandler, G., and Baumal, R. Interaction of two sources of information in tachistoscopic word recognition. *Canadian Journal of Psychology,* 1964, 18, 62-71.

Weber, R.M. First graders' use of grammatical context in reading. In H. Levin and J.T. Williams (Eds.), *Basic studies in reading.* New York: Basic Books, 1970.

NOTES

[1]LaBerge and Samuels were particularly interested in the role of attention and the notion of automaticity in reading. I have also omitted discussion of episodic memory since neither of these aspects of their model is relevant to my point here.

[2]Actually the aforementioned attention mechanism of the LaBerge-Samuels model offers *some* top-down capacity. However, within their model it is limited and serves to speed up certain weak bottom-up paths.

[3]I use the term *perception* rather freely here. In general, it is my opinion that the distinction between the perceptual and conceptual aspects of reading is not that useful. As I will suggest later, there appears to be a continuity between what has been called perception and what has been called comprehension. My use of the term perception in the present context is simply the use of the one term to cover the entire process.

[4]This is the same relationship between these two sorts of evidence assumed by Luce (1959) and which is incorporated into the Rumelhart and Siple (1974) model for word recognition.

The Interactive Reading Process: A Model

ROBERT B. RUDDELL
RICHARD B. SPEAKER, JR.
University of California at Berkeley

The reading process involves a complex set of interactions between a reader and a text to derive meaning. A model representing this process should serve several key functions. First, it should identify significant processing components critical to a theory of reading; second, it should specify predictable interactions between these components; and third, it should provide the basis for generating testable hypotheses for basic and applied research. The development of this paper has been guided by these functions in our effort to describe the psychological and linguistic processes involved in the reading act, to create a model or metaphor for this description, and to derive implications from the model for research and instruction.

Model Overview

Our model of the reading process incorporates four interactive components: 1) Reader Environment, 2) Knowledge Utilization and Control, 3) Declarative and Procedural Knowledge, and 4) Reader Product. These major components and their interactions will be described in the early part of our discussion and developed in depth in the remainder of the paper.

The *Reader Environment Component* of the model includes the immediate textual, conversational, and instructional features used by the reader in constructing meaning from text. The authors acknowledge that other environmental factors such as home influence (Ruddell and Haggard, this volume; Bloom and Green, 1984; Wigfield and Asher, 1984) are necessary to consider especially during reading acquisition, but due to limitations of space such factors are not the major focus of this model.

The *Knowledge Utilization and Control Component* influences the processing of text and the activation of information and procedures. The reader's Affective, Cognitive, and Metacognitive States—defined as the reader's goals and expectations, plan of action, and ability to monitor and evaluate, respectively—are included in this component of the model. In addition, Knowledge Utilization and Control includes the Text Representation. The Text Representation is the

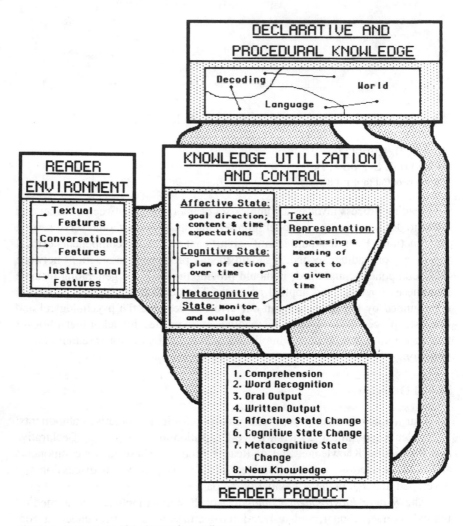

Figure 1. Components of the interactive reading process.

reader's interpretation of the text meaning and the record of the text processing to a given time. This record of the text processing episode is constructed during reading and is available for later retrieval.

The *Declarative and Procedural Knowledge Component* of the model includes the reader's store of schemata related to Decoding, Language, and World Knowledge and the procedures for using these knowledge forms (Anderson, 1980). Declarative knowledge includes the repertoire of information about decoding, language, and the world which is stored in memory. Procedural knowledge contains the strategies for processing text which must be appropriately activated for comprehension. This conception of Declarative and Procedural Knowledge follows that of Rumelhart (1981).

The *Reader Product Component* is the outcome of the interactions of Reader Environment, Knowledge Utilization and Control, and Declarative and Procedural Knowledge. Eight products are specified: Comprehension, Word Recognition, Oral Output, Written Output in the forms of Written Language and Representations, Affective State Change, Cognitive State Change, Metacognitive State Change, and New Knowledge. Products may occur simultaneously or be produced in sequence depending on the reader's goals and expectations, plan of action, and monitoring and evaluation. These major components of the model are depicted in Figure 1.

The components of the reading model function simultaneously during the reading process under the control of the Knowledge Utilization and Control Component. They interact in the construction of the Text Representation using information from the Reader Environment and Declarative and Procedural Knowledge to form Reader Product. There is no fixed sequence for the operation of the components; instead, they all are involved in the construction of the Text Representation and products from it over time. The operation of the components over time adds a crucial dimension to the model.

Three time perspectives are important in the reading process. First, since reading takes place during a time interval filled with complex processing, the study of this processing must account for the degree of completeness of the meaning representation formed by the reader at a given time and place in the text. During reading, the reader's Text Representation changes as a product is constructed. Information accretes as the reader activates previously learned information, evaluates ongoing comprehension and production, hypothesizes, forgets, reactivates and switches strategies. If the information is consistent with expectations only minor tuning of the reader's Text Representation is needed over time. However, if inconsistencies arise, a major restructuring of the meaning of the text must occur over time and the Text Representation may be altered radically.

The second time perspective is related to the degree of fit between the reader's time expectation and the actual reading time required to process a given text. A reader expects to spend a given amount of time to meet specific reading goals, such as learning the minutia of the information in the text, developing a general understanding, or gathering information for an assigned essay. Different goals affect the reader's persistence in reading the text and, in turn, the elaborateness of the resulting Text Representation. If the fit between the time expectation and real time is good, learning persistence and affect will remain high. Poor fit, however, will result in limited persistence, decreasing affect and little learning. In some cases where the fit is poor, the reader may change goals rather than spend the time needed to meet the original goal. Subsequent retrieval of the information will be directly related to the degree of learning persistence and the affect during the reading episode.

The third time perspective is quite different from the first two and affects the reading process over a period of years extending from the child's preschool years through adulthood. The reading process is conceptualized on a developmental learning continuum without precisely defined stages. During this time, the child's knowledge and linguistic abilities develop rapidly. Procedures for dealing with language become more efficient. Gradually, the ability to use chunks of visual language becomes automatic (LaBerge and Samuels, 1976). The learner accretes, tunes, and restructures declarative and procedural knowledge (Rumelhart and Norman, 1978) so that information can be more efficiently processed. The primary product of this process is comprehension of text, but other products develop as the learner progresses and acquires the procedural knowledge necessary to their construction.

The following discussion will review the literature on three model components: Reader Environment, Knowledge Utilization and Control, and Procedural and Declarative Knowledge. The fourth component, Reader Product, will be developed as the Interactive Model is presented in detail. The model will then be applied to text interpretation and followed by implications for research and instruction.

Literature Review

Reader Environment

Many features in the Reader Environment will influence reader performance and, in turn, Reader Product. These range from the impact of cultural background to turn-taking allocation procedures and the nature of the instruction (Ruddell, 1983). In our society, different social groups vary in the support systems provided for literacy development and place different priorities on the importance of literacy in the schools. Learning to read in a classroom embodies the culturally imposed pedagogic authority of the school as an institution (Bourdieu and Passeron, 1977).

The work of Erickson (1982), Coulthard and Sinclair (1974), and Au and Mason (1981) illustrates the impact of family, culture, and peer group on the learner. In particular, these researchers emphasize the possible mismatch between teacher and learner of different cultural backgrounds and the influence of this mismatch on expectations, communicative speech acts and nonverbal responses. This mismatch can lead to communication breaks which interfere with learning. The learner's cultural background affects expectations for literacy uses in the classroom and expectations for future use of literacy activities; because of this, the learner's use of the immediate environment may not focus on the importance of activities leading to literacy. As the child matures, the peer group becomes increasingly instrumental in determining the effectiveness of classroom interaction with the teacher.

While background shapes the responses of the learner and of the teacher, the school and instructional features are, for the most part, controlled by the institutionalized school system (Bourdieu and Passeron, 1977). School is the purveyor of a monoculture where specific language, e.g., standard English, specific behaviors, e.g. turn taking mechanisms such as floor holding by the teacher and question-answer routines, and specific socioeconomic values, e.g. middle class, coalesce to form a social system unlike any other social institution (Sacks, Schegloff, and Jefferson, 1974; McHoul, 1978; Mehan, 1980). Considering one of these factors, socioeconomic values, researchers have found that such values can prompt a teacher to stereotype children in ways detrimental to their achievement. Rist (1970) noted that arbitrary grouping based on social factors, such as appearance, hygiene and language, persisted from grade one into subsequent grades resulting in a "fulfillment of prophecy" effect and poor performance on literacy tests. Rosenthal and Jacobsen (1968) also reported on this phenomenon of inaccurate stereotyping from perceptions of ability.

For the purposes of this model, Reader Environment is delimited to the immediate learning environment of the reader. Three factors are considered most important in this environment. These are Textual Features, Conversational Features, and Instructional Features.

Textual Features. The Textual Features of the Reader Environment are defined as the linguistic structures of the text and its associated visible structures. Visible structures include the printed words, pictures, charts, graphs and such adjunct aids as headings, written questions at the beginning of sections, and concluding summaries. The text structure is viewed as hierarchical in nature whether based on Fillmore's (1968) case grammar (Meyer, 1975); Frederiksen, 1975) or on story grammars (Rumelhart, 1975; Mandler and Johnson, 1977; Stein and Glenn, 1978). It is important to note that such text structure analyses do not consider the relationship of other aspects of the text, such as pictures, to the overall structure.

Conversational Features. The Conversational Features of the Reader Environment are defined as the interaction patterns present in the Reader Environment which are involved in interpersonal communication (Sacks, Schegloff, and Jefferson, 1974; McHoul, 1978; Mehan, 1980). The features of these patterns include message form, message content, addressor, addressee, audience, outcomes, tone, manner (Hymes, 1974). These features are aspects of the conversational-interaction patterns which must be internalized by the learner if meaningful interaction is to occur. These Conversational Features are largely under the control of the teacher (Green and Harker, 1982).

Instructional Features. The Instructional Features are defined as those aspects of the Reader Environment related directly to the act of teaching. These include the plans, goals and objectives of the teacher, the structure of learning objectives and activities, and instructional implementation in the classroom. Advocates of mastery learning, for example, specify the importance of presenting a lesson, monitoring learner performance, giving feedback, and assessing learner ability (Bloom, 1982; Rosenshine, 1976; Levin and Long, 1981). While there is still considerable debate on the most effective methods of instruction (Chall, 1967, 1979; Mason, 1984; Barr, 1984; Johnson and Bauman, 1984; Rosenshine and Stevens, 1984), direct group instruction with academic emphasis and both guided and independent practice are considered to be important to the development of reading skill (Fisher, et al., 1978).

These three features of the Reader Environment, Textual Features, Conversational Features and Instructional Features, interact with the other components of the model through the Knowledge Utilization and Control Component.

Knowledge Utilization and Control

The skilled reader possesses a wide range of abilities and strategies which may be applied to the Textual, Conversational and Instructional Features of the Reader Environment. The reading process for the mature reader is flexible and not a unidirectional, verbal march through the language of the text. The permanent nature of the text provides the reader substantial flexibility in the construction of the Text Representation. The Conversational and Instructional Features are processed by the reader to assist in constructing meaning. The text processing may include regressions, pauses, switching strategies, goals and objectives, making decisions, inferences, evaluations, hypotheses, consulting the teacher or other texts, or abandoning the text as the reader desires.

The use of these processes requires some mechanism to direct them during reading. The capacity limits of the human memory system require that any theory of reading have some means to control the activation of information in memory. Only some portion of the reader's knowledge can remain active at a given time. Three internal states are proposed in this control: 1) Affective State, 2) Cognitive State, and 3) Metacognitive State. These internal control states interact and are responsible for the activation of information used in construction of the Text Representation. The following discussion provides research support for each of these states and defines the role of each in text processing.

Affective State. The reader's Affective State includes the reader's interests, attitudes, and values which determine goals and objectives for the reading of a passage. Mathewson's model (1976, this volume), designed to explain the influence of affect on reading, hypothesized that motivation and attitude influence attentional processes, comprehension and acceptance of the content of the text. Athey (1965) has demonstrated the importance of values in motivating the reading of junior high school students. Belloni and Jongsma (1978) found a significant interaction between seventh graders' interest and comprehension. They noted that the comprehension of low ability subjects reading high interest material was high even when the readability of the material surpassed the readers' frustrational level.

Despite these results, the effect of world knowledge cannot be easily separated from affective variables. A reader will usually know more about a topic of high interest. Osako and Anders (1983) pointed out that when attempts are made to separate knowledge from interest the variance explained by interest is small. Walberg and Tsai (1983) overcame this difficulty by providing a metastudy of attitude and reading achievement supplemented by a correlational study of 2,300 seventeen year olds sampled in the National Assessment of Educational Progress. Of the nine factors that Walberg and Tsai found significantly related to reading achievement, three were attitudinal. Good readers had good self-concepts as readers, enjoyed reading, and believed that there should be freedom to choose materials to read from such sources as the library. The researchers concluded that "achievement, attitude, and opportunities to read appear to naturally reinforce one another among students who do well on reading tests."

Several text variables may influence the Affective State. These include content, format, and form of the text (Mathewson, 1976). Readers will persevere and comprehend material that is considerably harder than material at their reading level if they have high interest in the content (Shnayer, 1969). The format of the book has been found to influence a reader's decision to persevere and to comprehend text. The reader's interest in the text may be modified by the presence or absence of pictures (Samuels, 1970; Samuels, Biesbrock, and Terry, 1974), print size and style (Mathewson, 1976), and even the nature of the book cover (Lowery and Grafft, 1968). The linguistic form of the text such as its dialect or syntax also appears to affect the reader's interest, acceptance, and comprehension of the text (Mathewson, 1974).

The Affective State serves to establish the reader's goal direction and expectations for content, processing time and product. Highly interesting text or text which has been judged as important to the reader's goal will receive maximum processing and persistence. With less interesting text or text judged to be of little importance, the reader will be less persistent, and limited processing will occur.

The reader's persistence will also be influenced by the fit between the reader's time expectations and the real or perceived processing time. The skilled reader will often be more effective in projecting the real time required to process a given text. For the less-skilled reader whose goals are limited to word recognition and oral reading (Canney and Winograd, 1979; Myers and Paris, 1978), the time spent with the text exceeds expectations, and the reader may become discouraged, shift goals and stop reading. With increasing difficulty, the desire to continue reading decreases and may result in low interest and a negative attitude toward the text. In this case, the reader's negative affect influences the acquisition of reading skill; little application and no practice of behaviors appropriate to proficient reading will occur. In severe cases, the learner's goal becomes the avoidance of texts whenever possible.

Cognitive State. The Cognitive State represents the reader's plan for the construction of the Text Representation and is influenced by goal direction and expectations. The plan incorporates the reader's schema for the reading process which activates the Procedural Knowledge that the reader uses during reading. The reader's plan limits the use of procedures to those which can be readily activated. Although the reader may have the Declarative Knowledge necessary to analyze a text structure, procedures for using this knowledge during reading may not exist. Thus, the reader's plan may not be sufficient to activate text-structure.

knowledge useful in understanding and storing the information from the text. For the beginning reader, the plan tends to focus on the decoding process (Canney and Winograd, 1979; Myers and Paris, 1978) and, as a result, the Text Representation will contain elaborate information about decoding. The product of this reader may be word recognition or oral reading with minimal concern for comprehension. Effective instruction, however, will encourage the reader to incorporate a "meaning plan" which will lead to a comprehension product. For the more skilled reader, the Text Representation elaborates meaning, and comprehension is the major product of reading.

The reader must develop a symbol processing system which will provide an efficient plan for the conceptualization of experience. Bruner, et al. (1956) have shown that cognitive strategy is of crucial importance to the conceptualization process. Basic to the reader's strategy is the development of procedures to chunk information. In decoding, the efficiency of the chunking processes determines the speed of decoding (LaBerge and Samuels, 1976; LaBerge, 1979; Gibson, 1971, 1974). If the reader's plan uses knowledge about text structures, the reader can store the information from the text in a Text Representation with a structure which closely parallels the text structure. This type of plan makes the Text Representation highly efficient for the retrieval of information at some later time. Kress (1955) concluded from a concept formation study of elementary school children that achieving readers were superior to nonachievers in versatility and flexibility, ability to draw inferences from relevant cues, and ability to shift set when new standards were introduced. Such flexibility indicates that individual differences in the reader's plans (Langer, 1978) develop early in the acquisition of knowledge. Singer (1966) concluded that an important dimension in comprehending language consists of changing, modifying and reorganizing a previously learned concept.

The cognitive strategies used by the reader will depend on the reader's goals which are part of the reader's Affective State; thus, the Cognitive State interacts with the Affective State as suggested by Matthewson (1976, this volume). Together these two states set the reader's expectations and process the incoming text by activating appropriate knowledge and procedures from the Declarative and Procedural Knowledge Component. If the reader is to be effective, the product of this processing must be evaluated against the reader's expectations. This requires metacognitive monitoring and evaluation.

Metacognitive State. The Metacognitive State consists of the self-monitoring and self-correcting strategies which the reader uses during the reading of a text. These strategies include critical and evaluative reading, hypothesis testing and self-questioning as the reader constantly evaluates the fit between meaning and the original goal. The effectiveness of the original plan in achieving this goal must also be evaluated by the Metacognitive State. Thus, the self-monitoring of the information in the Text Representation enables the reader to alter the processing plan to meet the original goal, to change goals or to terminate the reading process.

According to Brown (1982), the most efficient reader has an automatic comprehension monitoring system. Baker and Brown (1984) cite results indicating that younger or poorer readers are either unaware of the need to read for meaning or are unable to read for meaning due to the allotment of cognitive capacity to decoding. These readers do not take corrective action when they encounter problems in decoding or comprehension. Differences in the self-correction of oral reading miscues are also observed indicating that good readers are more able to self-monitor during reading (Goodman, 1970, 1973; Goodman and Goodman, 1977).

Younger and poorer readers appear unable to choose appropriate metacognitive decision making strategies in using text structure. Several studies have indicated that younger children are less aware of text features such as paragraph organization, expository text patterns and narrative substructures (Myers and Paris, 1978; Meyer, Brandt and Bluth, 1980; McGee, 1982; Goetz, Palmer and Haensley, 1983; Hiebert, Englert and Brennan, 1983). Olshavsky (1976-1977) and Goetz, et al. (1983) demonstrated that younger and poorer readers use the same strategies as the more skilled readers but use those strategies less frequently. Goetz, et al, also demonstrated that poorer readers are less able to identify sources of reading difficulty within a difficult text. This result was supported by McGee (1982) when less skilled readers were asked to retrieve information. She found that the match of text structure to the structure of recall protocols improved with age and skill. These results indicate that younger and poorer readers do possess at least some knowledge needed to make metacognitive decisions but they may not be able to use the knowledge when the processing demands of a text are high.

Recently, investigations have focused on the locus of metacognitive decisions. It has been hypothesized that readers make decisions about the importance of information in different segments of the text during reading. Eye movement studies have found that additional processing time is allocated at the end of the sentence (Carpenter and Just, 1981; Ehrlich and Rayner, 1983). Once the decision is made that a text segment is important, additional time appears to be allocated for processing that segment. Goetz, Schallert, Reynolds and Radin (1983) found evidence that readers spend more time on important sentences in a text as did Cirilo and Foss (1980).

Orienting tasks have been found to influence the allocation of processing time. Reynolds, Standiford, and Anderson (1979) found that college undergraduates spent additional time on information which was relevant to questions inserted in the text and performed better on those retrieval questions than a group without questions. Rothkopf and Billington (1979) reported a similar result for high school students who memorized a set of objectives before reading. Thus, some metacognitive decisions influence the time spent in processing selected segments of a text.

Metacognitive strategies monitor the product of reading and evaluate it against the goals and time expectations set in the Affective State. The beginning reader has difficulty monitoring and evaluating because of difficulty in making decisions about the relative importance of information. The skilled reader monitors the fit between goal and product and evaluates this fit continuously. Thus, for the effective reader, the Metacognitive State interacts with the Affective and Cognitive States to modify the choice of product, the reader's plans, and time expectations for constructing the product.

Text Representation. The reader's construction of the Text Representation requires the use of the Textual Features of Reader Environment and Declarative and Procedural Knowledge under control of the reader's affective goal, cognitive plan and metacognitive monitoring. The Text Representation is a model of the "text world" (De Beaugrande, 1981) which represents the reader's meaning structure for the text and the record of the text processing to a given time. Since the information in the Text Representation may exceed the reader's limited capacity, only some portion of the Text Representation will remain active during construction. During reading, however, the reader may reaccess information in the Text Representation necessary to build inferences from the text. The Text Representation is a theoretical construct which should not be construed as a literal storage buffer, but as a representation of the reader's interpretation of the text and its processing.

More information is contained in the Text Representation than is usually retrieved by the reader (Anderson and Pichert, 1978; Pichert and Anderson, 1977). The information from the text is elaborated by the processing the reader engages in during reading. This elaboration uses phonemic, structural, semantic and contextual information from the reader's Decoding, Language, and World Knowledge and information from the Textual, Conversational, and Instructional Features of the Reader Environment. In essence, the reader remembers not only the text interpretation, but also the processing leading to that interpretation (Craik and Tulving, 1975).

The structure of the Text Representation is based on the reader's ability to use text structure knowledge as well as the ability to elaborate. The development of these abilities is influenced by the reader's experiences with text and the expansion of Declarative and Procedural Knowledge. Low achieving learners are less likely than average or high achieving learners to elaborate information from text even when they possess the appropriate world knowledge (Stein, et al., 1982; Franks, et al., 1982). Low achievers apply text structure knowledge in fewer situations (McGee, 1982; Whaley, 1982; Hiebert, Englert and Brennan, 1983) and are less precise in their elaborations (Stein, et al., 1982). Training has been found to improve the abilities of the less successful learner to use both text structure and elaboration (Meyer, 1984; Franks, et al., 1982).

Declarative and Procedural Knowledge

Declarative and Procedural Knowledge so critical to the reading process contains three subcomponents: Decoding Knowledge, Language Knowledge, and World Knowledge. Declarative knowledge is the reader's collection of information facts, concepts and generalizations, the knowledge about decoding, language, and the world. Procedural knowledge is the reader's set of skills and strategies for performing activities in the environment. It is knowing how to do things (Anderson, 1980, p. 223). Both declarative and procedural knowledge are incorporated into the same memory structure or schema based on this schema-theoretic view of memory (Rumelhart and Ortony, 1977; Rumelhart, 1981; Adams and Collins, 1979).

Decoding Knowledge. Decoding Knowledge contains the reader's knowledge about the visual forms of language. The skills for the decoding of the visual information of a text and the strategies for chunking visual information constitute the essential procedural knowledge for decoding. Effective decoding requires the reader to possess schemata which integrate declarative and procedural knowledge about the decoding process. These schemata decode automatically when the words are familiar to the reader but can be activated deliberately when an unfamiliar word is encountered.

To account for the Decoding Knowledge in the processing of text, three areas must be considered. These are visual and phonological chunks, lexical access, and context effects. The concepts of chunking and automaticity (LaBerge and Samuels, 1976) are of great import to this discussion. A chunk is the unit of information being processed as a whole without analysis of its substructures (Gibson, 1965, 1971, 1974; Ruddell, 1974). Developing readers or readers who have encountered an unfamiliar word depend on chunks smaller than words and must devote attention to using the chunks to construct a recognizable word. The word recognition processes for a skilled reader are automatic as long as the words in the text are familiar. Automaticity in word recognition implies that attention can be devoted to processes other than recognition. Since the processing capacity of the reader is limited, automaticity of word recognition allows the reader to devote effort to the comprehension of the text's message or learning the new information presented.

Visual and phonological chunking is one of the central tasks of early reading and assists the child in discovering the nature of the correlation between printed units and their oral counterparts. Instructional approaches have placed varying degrees of emphasis on a variety of decoding units. These include careful control of "regularities" and "irregularities" in grapheme-phoneme correspondences, notably vowels; spelling sound units which are related to the morphophoneme; and a phonologically based unit known as the vocalic-center group which closely approximates the syllable and in certain instances the morpheme (Ruddell, 1976a). In essence, instructional approaches to reading focus the child's attention on different chunks of visual information ranging from single letters and letter clusters to whole words and words in context, the associating of these chunks with linguistic output and combining these chunks into meaningful messages.

   The development of reading skill must account for the acquisition of the visual aspects of the reading process. Jackson and McClelland (1981) posited an independent visual processing component separate from general language comprehension. They found that more skilled readers could access memory for visual symbols faster than less skilled readers on a variety of stimuli which included letter names, synonyms, homonyms, homophones, picture categories and letterlike stimuli which were given nonsense-syllable names. These researchers offer two alternate explanations for their findings which merit consideration: first, the rate difference could be inherent and it is possible that skilled readers were always faster at visual access; second, the rate difference may be due to practice differences in the skilled reader's experience with print. At least from an instructional view, the latter explanation is most tenable. Instruction may have little influence on any inherent rate differences but provides practice. Practice is crucial if the beginning reader is to automate skills needed for efficient reading.

   Ruddell (1976a) noted that the recommendation that initial words be introduced on the basis of grouped grapheme-phoneme consistencies had been proposed by Bloomfield (1933), Smith (1957), Soffietti (1955), Hall (1961), and Fries (1963). These researchers have expressed the opinion that the structures of the English orthographic system place a limitation on the acquisition of sound-symbol correspondences. Although the results have been inconsistent in investigations varying the degree of emphasis on sound-symbol correspondences and related generalizations, some early studies have revealed superior results for phonic emphasis at early grade levels, particularly in word recognition (Bear, 1958; Kelly, 1958; Sparks and Fay, 1957). The work of Hayes (1966), Ruddell (1968), Hahn (1966), Tanyzer and Alpert (1966), Mazurkiewicz (1966), and Downing (1965) have lent support to the value of greater consistency in the introduction of sound-letter correspondences. Additionally, the consistent replication of research findings discussed by Chall (1967, 1979) supports the logical expectation that an approach to decoding which helps the child grasp the nature of the English writing code would be of value.

   Samuels and Jeffery (1966; Jeffery and Samuels, 1967) emphasize the value of sound-letter correspondence chunks. In their research, pseudo letters were designed to represent English phonemes, and kindergarten subjects were taught to decode on either the basis of sound-letter correspondences or the basis of "whole words." Their findings indicated that subjects taught by the first method were more effective in transferring their skills to "new words" than those taught by the second method. In a replication study (1967), these researchers attributed some of their results to one aspect of their experimental treatment; subjects were taught to blend phonemes represented by pseudo letters. This finding is similar to that of Silberman (1964) whose subjects were unable to transfer correspondence information to new words unless they had received phonic-blend instruction. These findings may be interpreted to suggest that grapheme-phoneme and sound-blending instruction assist the chunking of graphophonic information into higher order chunks for more efficient use by a reader (Ruddell, 1976a).

More recent research indicates that skilled readers may automatically activate phonological information even when such information is redundant. While word sized chunks may be used in processing, smaller chunks may be activated during reading. Shimron and Navon (1982) demonstrated that recognition of isolated Hebrew words is facilitated in both children and adults when the optional vowel information is included in the orthography. Glushko (1981) reached essentially the same conclusion using regular words, exception words and pseudo words. However, Shimron and Navon (1982) pointed out that there are several possible explanations for this finding: first, redundancy may enhance processing by allowing various processors to work on the same information; second, the phonemic information may enhance the response-generation abilities of the system, lexical access, or both; finally, in the case of Hebrew, the visual nature of the graphophonic information may enhance visual access to the word's representation in memory.

If a decoding program is to account for the nature of the English writing system, it must consider spelling chunks or letter patterns which provide for prediction of sound correspondences on the morphographemic-morphophonemic level, a level beyond that of grapheme-phoneme correspondence. Venezky (1967), Wardhaugh (1968), and Reed (1966) have discussed this concern with reference to the morphophoneme. This chunk represents a level of structure between the phoneme and morpheme; for example, in considering the words "extreme" and "extremity," one might point to the second e grapheme and note that there is little regularity in its representation of the given sound. However, when one considers these two words on the morphophonemic level, a very regular pattern is immediately obvious which fits in a consistent pattern with such words as "obscene-obscenity" and "supreme-supremacy." Although some instructional materials for beginning reading have examples of the simplest of these alterations — such as that found in the final e marker (sit-site) — very little consideration has been given to detailed study and research in this area (Ruddell, 1976a).

Glushko (1981) has questioned the psychological reality of sound-spelling patterns in the decoding of words. He demonstrated, using latency data, that the use of a regular sound-spelling pattern can be explained by a more general activation system of lexical access. For example, he demonstrated that some regular words like "wave" have response latencies equal to irregular words like "have," so activation rather than the sound-spelling regularity provides an alternate explanation of the latency data. Glushko implied that an instructional program should not spend time on abstract rules for decoding as these rules do not appear to have a psychological reality. Instead, time should be spent with exemplars of the abstract rules so that the developing reader develops specific morphographic-morphophonemic knowledge.

Another decoding chunk is known as the vocalic-center group. Hansen and Rodgers (1968) posited that this chunk provides for high transfer value in the decoding process. This unit, defined as a vowel plus associated preceding and following consonants, is phonologically rather than semantically based; however, in most cases, it is isomorphic to the syllable. The rationale for considering such a unit is that chunks at this level are of greater significance than morphophological segmentation for the early reader (Ruddell, 1976a). The research of Gibson and her colleagues (Gibson, 1971, 1974; Gibson, Bishop, Schiff, and Smith, 1964; Gibson, Farber, and Shepela, 1967) has explored the psychological reality of this unit.

Gibson et al. (1964, 1967) demonstrated that children in the early stages of reading have developed higher-order generalizations which provide for decoding pseudo linguistic letter patterns following English spelling expectancies. Children appeared to perceive regularities in sound-letter correspondences and transfer these to unfamiliar trigrams even though taught by a "whole word" approach. This would indicate that the vocalic-center group might be preferable to graphemes and morphographemes in initial decoding instruction. The work of Gibson et al., has demonstrated that adults perceive pseudolinguistic trigrams more easily when they follow English spelling generalizations (e.g., BIF) than when they are less pronounceable (e.g., IBF) or more meaningful (e.g., FBI). Because the task of the reader is that of decoding written letter patterns and transferring them to some meaningful representation which may be phonologically based, pronounceable letter combinations would seem to be of significant value. On the other hand, meaningful trigrams, such as FBI, require the reader to work on three chunks rather than one. It was noted however, that the latter type of trigram was more likely to be recalled than a pronounceable unit which was attributed to prior existence of the trigram in memory. These researchers concluded that pronounceability was the better grouping principle for reading.

At this point the discussion has considered several decoding chunks and their psychological reality in developing decoding schemata. LaBerge and Samuels (1974; LaBerge, 1979) indicate that different chunk sizes may be used in skilled word recognition. For efficient reading, the size of chunk should be maximized and its recognition should be automatic. Thus, instruction should focus on a variety of chunks which can be used by the reader in word recognition.

Lexical access research is most often characterized by a debate over access to the reader's lexicon, particularly whether the access is by use of a phonological or verbal code, or whether the lexicon can be accessed via visual or nonphonological codes. A variety of models of lexical access have been proposed and supported. Katz and Feldman (1981) hypothesized two possible routes to the lexicon: first, graphemic information could be coded into verbal chunks which are then concatenated by the appropriate phonological and morphemic rules into word codes represented in the lexicon; second, graphemic information could be visually chunked using automated visual chunking rules and stored in a temporary visual buffer. From this buffer, the appropriate word code in the lexicon is accessed. While Katz and Feldman appear to be calling for a two process access procedure for the lexicon, they have proposed that the two representations of the access procedure are isomorphic, and therefore must be considered phonological.

Evidence for separate coding systems comes from the research of Baddeley (1979; Baddeley and Lewis, 1981; Salame and Baddeley, 1982) and Klapp, Marshburn and Lester (1983). Baddeley demonstrates two coding systems activated in short-term memory while Klapp et al. demonstrate that there must be more than two systems. These researchers make the point that several systems are available for the maintenance of information and its processing. For reading, this notion of multiple systems would imply that the reader can maintain and use several sources of information at one time.

Rumelhart and McClelland (1981) proposed that information is processed in parallel with each level of analysis inhibiting and enhancing other levels. A similar hypothesis for lexical access with facilitation by visual, phonological, syntactic and semantic information was proposed by Danks and Hill (1981). They suggested that many word codes are activated by any given input and the internal state of the system. But, despite many activations, word codes are rapidly eliminated until only one is left. This rapid elimination does not require complete visual information unless more than one lexical item remains activated at the end of the elimination phase of processing. If this is the case, additional, time-consuming processing must occur; this is likely to include the search for sufficient information to identify a single word code. Danks and Hill found that modifications of lexical, syntactic and semantic information caused disruptions of oral reading in children and adults which indicated that all levels of the information contributed to the processing.

In summary, several models of lexical access have been proposed. The rationale and research at this time favors multiple coding systems for lexical access. The answer to the debate on phonological versus visual coding seems most likely to be answered by a model of reading which admits both types of access to the lexicon.

Context effects which are not readily accounted for in models of lexical access (Jacoby, 1983a, b), have been shown to influence word recognition. If a word is in a meaningful context, its recognition is facilitated (Stanovich, 1980, 1981, 1982; Stanovich and West, 1983; West, Stanovich, Freeman, and Cunningham, 1983). West, Stanovich, Freeman, and Cunningham demonstrated that the context enhances the recognition of a word by two mechanisms. First, there is a rapid automatic spread of activation of knowledge related to the context which uses visual, lexical, syntactic and semantic information. This form of activation is not conscious and does not require processing capacity. Second, there is a slower process which involves conscious expectations and predictions and requires processing capacity. Highly efficient readers process text rapidly, and, therefore, must depend heavily on the automatic spread of activation (Stanovich and West, 1983). The younger, less efficient reader, however, processes text more slowly and may depend on both conscious prediction and spread of activation. The apparent conflicting finding that learners who show a facilitation for word recognition but poor comprehension when the context is favorable

(Stanovich, 1980) may be explained by the use of automatic spread of activation without the use of conscious expectations and predictions.

The second mechanism, conscious expectation and prediction, is more amenable to instruction than the spread of activation. The conscious use of context to provide information and meaning is a strategy that should aid learners in deriving meaning from text (Goodman, 1976). Carnine, Kameenui, and Coyle (1984) provided support for the notion that older students are more likely to use context clues than younger. In addition, Carnine, et al., conducted a training study which showed that fourth, fifth, and sixth grade students improved their ability to use context in test situations when they had received systematic practice in using context strategies.

In summary, the efficiency of the reader will be limited by the conscious processing of visual chunks in decoding the text. The knowledge for using visual information must be developed and automated if the beginning reader is to become efficient. Declarative and Procedural Knowledge contains a variety of visual chunks of information which can be consciously used by the skilled reader when dealing with an unfamiliar word. Lexical access takes place using both visual and verbal coding of information. Once word recognition becomes automatic, the reader can devote more attention to comprehension and produce a more meaningful Text Representation. It seems clear that word recognition is facilitated by meaningful context.

Language Knowledge. Language Knowledge includes lexical, syntactic, and text structure knowledge necessary to the understanding and production of language. The development of phonology and morphology is discussed in depth in other references (Ruddell and Haggard, this volume; Ruddell, 1974, 1976b; Slobin, 1979), and due to space limitations will not be considered here. The Language Knowledge schemata range from the identification and production of lexical and syntactic forms to the recognition and use of narrative and expository text structure. This knowledge enables the reader to represent selected aspects of World Knowledge, so lexical information is closely connected to world knowledge schemata.

Reading is a linguistic process and requires Language Knowledge if the reader is to form a representation of the text. This process makes use of the reader's syntactic, lexical and text structure knowledge. As Carroll (1976) has emphasized, the essential skill in reading is similar to the essential skill in comprehending spoken discourse – getting the meaning of the message. The reader's awareness of the meaning cues used by the writer will facilitate this process. This skill requires the active use of the reader's language systems; it also requires the reader to hold the linguistic information in the Text Representation long enough to analyze it (Jarvella, 1971).

The development of language is, thus, essential to reading acquisition. The child's environment is constantly a source of both oral and written linguistic information which must be used to expand and elaborate linguistic knowledge (Cazden, 1965, 1979). Developmental psycholinguists (Slobin, 1979; Ochs and

Schieffelin, 1982), have demonstrated the universality of language acquisition in a variety of social settings. Harste, Burke, and Woodward (1982) have shown that the reading awareness of children develops before formal schooling. They suggest that the separation of oral language development from written language development is an artificial one and that further investigation is needed into the parallel development of language concepts relating oral and written language. These researchers view literacy as part of the continuum of speech acts available to the functioning adult in a literate society.

Syntactic knowledge develops in advance of the child's reading skill. Scolon (1979) demonstrated a subtle form of syntax before two word utterances while Dore (1979) showed that preschool children have considerable command of illocutionary function and conversational procedure. He argued that a model of language development needs to consider conversational competence. Chomsky (1969, 1972) studied the relationship between children's comprehension of oral sentences and exposure to reading. She found that stages of language development were positively associated with several measures of early reading based on literary background inventory, interview scores, and levels of books named by parents. Loban (1966, 1967, 1976) reported that a child's language continues to develop throughout schooling while Ruddell (1965) demonstrated the effect of syntactically similar oral and written language patterns on comprehension. Taken together, these studies indicate that the development of syntactic knowledge is a process that starts very early and directly influences the comprehension of text. The knowledge of syntax allows the reader to organize information into larger chunks than single words. Thus, with increasing syntactic knowledge, the reader develops the ability to chunk words into larger meaningful segments.

Lexical knowledge—the knowledge of vocabulary and word meanings—is important to the reading process. Johnson, Toms-Bronowski, and Pittleman (1981) cited results supporting the importance of informational chunking in the development of lexical knowledge. They speculated that words are clustered in hierarchically structured categories which are interconnected with other related word concept structures.

Generally results of vocabulary training on reading comprehension have indicated that increasing vocabulary knowledge can improve comprehension (Mezynski, 1983). Haggard (1980) found, however, that situations other than reading were identified with vocabulary acquisition. She reported four categories of situations which precipitated vocabulary acquisition in children and adults in an introspective study which required adults to recall their acquisition of vocabulary as children and adults. Respondents remembered acquiring a word because the new word 1) sounded adult or interesting, 2) was used in a highly emotional situation, 3) was immediately useful, or 4) was used by peers. The first two reasons were given most often for acquisition during elementary school years while the last two were most frequently given as reasons for acquisition of words as a postelementary student. The most frequent strategy used in acquiring new words was discovering the new word's meaning. Some respondents also indicated they rehearsed the new word by using it in conversation with family or friends. Rarely was acquisition reported due to classroom instruction. No acquisition was reported from reading alone although some respondents noted that they encountered the newly acquired word frequently after acquisition.

Text structure knowledge is an important part of Language Knowledge. The developing reader gradually becomes familiar with the general forms of oral and written text and develops representations for them, in the form of text structure schemata. Using these schemata, the reader recognizes the probable structure of the text and forms expectations for the structure of the content. On the most global level, the reader decides whether the text is narrative or expository. The narrative subschemata can have slots which must be instantiated with characters, story setting, characters' problems and goals, episodes, attempts to resolve problems and resolutions. The expository subschemata have slots for different expository structures such as cause/effect patterns, descriptive/informational patterns, problem/solution patterns and comparison/contrast patterns. When a reader recognizes the structure of a text, the Text Representation may be structured based on that pattern, and knowledge about the pattern is used as a cue to access the most appropriate information.

Several models of text structure have been formulated which lead to hypotheses about the nature of text structure schemata. Some models apply only to narrative (Mandler and Johnson, 1977; Thorndyke, 1977; Stein and Glenn, 1977; Rumelhart, 1975, 1977) while others afford a wider range of applicability (Frederiksen, 1975; Meyer, 1975; Kintsch and van Dijk, 1978; Turner and Greene, 1977). Since most of these models posit a hierarchical text structure, one consistent finding for skilled readers is the importance of the levels effect (Miller and Kintsch, 1980; Thorndyke, 1977; Meyer, 1975; Britton et al., 1979, 1980; Mandler and Johnson, 1977). This effect demonstrates that text information high in the text hierarchy is more likely to be recalled than information low in the hierarchy. In the case of narrative structure, more important information such as setting, initiating events, and consequences is more likely to be recalled than less important information exemplified by internal responses of a character or reaction (Nezworski, Stein, and Trabasso, 1982).

Evidence for a developmental sequence of text structure schemata is mixed. In developing readers, the superiority of higher order over lower order information is not as marked as in skilled readers (McGee, 1982; Freebody and Anderson, 1983a,b). Although Baker and Stein (1981) reviewed several studies which indicate even young children recall the most important ideas best, they posited that this superiority does not differentiate text structures below the highest level in the hierarchy. McGee (1982) found results which provide some evidence for a developmental trend. Third grade good readers recalled a greater proportion of subordinate ideas than superordinate ideas; fifth grade poor readers recalled an equal proportion of each; and fifth-grade good readers recalled a greater proportion of superordinate than subordinate ideas. In her analysis of children's use of a story schema in recall, she found no evidence that third graders used any story structure, poor fifth grade readers used partial story structure, and good fifth-grade readers used the full structure for the relatively simple passages of the study. However it should be noted that McGee's research fails to disambiguate instructional emphasis from developmental trends.

Whaley's research (1982) shows a developmental trend in the application of story schema at grades three, six, and eleven. Nezworski, Stein, and Trabasso (1982) found that kindergarten and third grade children remembered information from the more important story categories. Further, the children shifted important information from a story category of low importance to a category of high importance. While some evidence is present to support a developmental sequence in using text structure, this area deserves careful attention and future research (Pearson and Camperell, 1981).

The recognition that text has a structure should be useful to both the developing and the skilled reader. It seems reasonable that part of the knowledge that separates the more skilled readers from the less skilled at any age has to do with their ability to recognize and use text structures. At the earliest levels, the development of a concept of story structure undergoes qualitative change from unorganized lists of information to sequences and primitive narratives to focused chains of events until full narrative forms emerge (Applebee, 1978). Later development is in the application of the knowledge of text structure in a variety of situations. Meyer, Brandt, and Bluth (1980) found that text structure was used in both immediate and delayed recall by good ninth grade readers but was used only in immediate recall by average ninth grade readers. On the other hand, poor readers use a list description strategy for recalling information from text when a more complex retrieval strategy would have been more effective in structuring the retelling.

A highly efficient retrieval strategy involves the use of a text structure to assist recall (Britton et al., 1979, 1980). This implies that the average and above readers studied by Meyer et al. (1980) had developed a schema for retrieving texts but that the superior readers could apply the structure in more situations. Poorer readers either lacked the text structure schema entirely or were unable to use it as a retrieval mechanism.

Evidence suggests that students can identify certain text structures and that text structure instruction enhances recall. Englert and Hiebert (1984) indicated that third and sixth grade subjects could identify passages based on a sequential or enumerational structure more readily than passages based on comparison-contrast or description. While high reading ability college students are better able to identify enumeration and comparison-contrast structures than low ability students, these two groups are approximately equivalent on sequence and description structures (Hiebert, et al., 1983). Meyer (1979, 1984) cited results that indicate learners can be taught to identify and use text structure. Barnett (1984) found that only minimal instruction in text structure before reading a well structured text was sufficient to improve recall of information. Furthermore, for text structure information to be useful, text structure knowledge must be developed before reading the text so that the reader can use the text structure to assist in the construction of the Text Representation (Barnett, 1984).

In summary, all aspects of language impinge upon the reading process. Language Knowledge enhances comprehension by allowing the reader to use syntactic, lexical, and text structure knowledge learned from oral language and text. Lexical knowledge can be acquired either through teacher directed instruction or through learner instigated inquiry. Oral language abilities of children and adults continue to grow as more sophisticated linguistic structures occur in the environment. As exposure to more complex oral and written language forms increases, the child becomes more likely to use them in oral and written language, comprehension, and production. The use of text structure knowledge becomes important to the storage and retrieval of information from a Text Representation. The efficient reader must use automatic decoding and language processes during reading as a base for reading but one major factor in reading must be added — the reader's World Knowledge.

World Knowledge. World Knowledge contains information about the reader's world experience ranging from facts and beliefs to actions and procedures for functioning in specific situations. It contains the store of semantic information and the strategies for using it which are essential to the reading process. World knowledge schemata are the devices for recognizing and structuring the conceptual information derived from the text.

The most vital task during reading is the reader's construction of a representation of the text's meaning. To construct a Text Representation, the reader must use information from World Knowledge. Schema theory has provided insight into the relationship between constructing a Text Representation and World Knowledge by explaining the organization of information in the reader's memory. A schema is a memory structure which represents a generic concept based on prototypes (Rumelhart, 1981; Rumelhart and Ortony, 1977). It can remain stable or can be changed by future learning. A schema is considered to have four properties: 1) procedural information which allows the activation of the schema and the instantiation of the schema with information from the text, 2) inheritance which allows properties from higher level schemata to be inherited by their embedded subschemata, 3) default values which allow inferences to be made when all information is not available from another source such as a text, and 4) an organizational structure which is basically hierarchical (Norman, 1979; Yekovich and Thorndyke, 1981). The research of Bower, Black, and Turner (1979) supported the notion that readers use prototypical scriptlike episodes to aid comprehension and retrieval of information.

Activation of appropriate World Knowledge from Declarative and Procedural Knowledge is necessary for the comprehension of text (Anderson, 1977). Early work by Bransford and Johnson (1972) indicated that comprehension of text does not occur unless a relevant schema can be activated. Anderson, et al. (1977) demonstrated that the activation of a specific schema from World Knowledge influences the interpretation of a text and the later retrieval of the Text Representation. They examined this effect by having readers of two very different backgrounds, physical education and music, read and recall passages which allowed different interpretations depending on the schema activated by the reader. Accurate predictions of the reader's interpretation were made depending on the reader's background of experience. The perspective taken by a reader during reading was found to influence information retrieved (Anderson and Pichert, 1978; Pichert and Anderson, 1977).

In instructional settings, both the teaching of World Knowledge and activation of appropriate world knowledge schemata should be major concerns. Reading comprehension can be improved if appropriate world knowledge is taught before reading a text (Stevens, 1982). Langer (1984) examined the effect of classroom activities for activating World Knowledge before reading on below average, average and above average sixth grade readers. She found that activation activities increased scores for average readers on textually implicit subordinate and textually explicit superordinate questions. Above average readers' performance was better on implicit questions under an activation condition than a motivation condition but the performance of these readers did not differ significantly from the nonintervention condition. The below average readers were not affected by any treatments. Since the passages were the same for all readers, it would appear that the below average readers needed additional instruction before reading. Langer concluded that activation of appropriate world knowledge schemata was important to comprehension but that teaching concepts needed by learners before reading may be necessary if they lack sufficient world knowledge.

In summary, the use of Declarative and Procedural Knowledge in the comprehension of a text is influenced not only by Decoding Knowledge which must become automatic, but also by Language and World Knowledge. The beginning reader may have difficulty applying Language and World Knowledge to a text because a substantial part of the processing capacity in the Text Representation has been devoted to Decoding Knowledge, and the Cognitive State may not incorporate the use of Language and World Knowledge into its plan. If meaning is to be derived, the reader must draw on Language Knowledge to identify lexical items and text structure knowledge to construct the Text Representation. The lexical items associated with the text must activate appropriate world knowledge to construct the Text Representation, while the schemata in the Text Representation activate additional lexical, syntactic, and text structure knowledge.

The reader's ability to integrate Decoding Knowledge, Language Knowledge and World Knowledge develops over time. In the mature reader, the three subcomponents of Declarative and Procedural Knowledge will function simultaneously under the direction of the internal control states. When the reader experiences difficulty in a text, the control states are modified through metacognitive evaluation; the resulting new goals and plans can activate strategies and information from Decoding, Language, and World Knowledge to deal with the difficulty. For example, if an early reader attempts to read the sentence "The *cat* plays with the yarn," some visual and auditory analysis must occur. The reader may use a linear plan to recognize the letters and to associate them with sounds which can be pronounced before each word is recognized. Lexical, syntactic, and narrative text structures—all aspects of Language Knowledge—provide sentence and story clues. If the appropriate Decoding and Language Knowledge are applied, the words are recognized and represented. The reader's World Knowledge about cats is activated and the reader may image a prototypical cat along with actions the cat will engage in. If these prototypical actions have lexical and narrative text representation in Language Knowledge, the early reader can describe the possible activities of a cat and predict what might be included in a text about a cat. On the other hand, the reader may interpret the sentence, using an illustration, as "The kitten played with the ball." In this case, the reader's miscues are the result of relying heavily on Language and World Knowledge, rather than Decoding Knowledge.

For the skilled reader, Decoding Knowledge is automatic, and the presentation of the same text accesses the Language and World Knowledge. The skilled reader's schema for "cat" contains the visual and auditory forms of the word, a script for the cat's actions, and the language necessary to represent these actions. When reading about a cat, this knowledge is incorporated in the reader's Text Representation. As the reader continues, the text information about cats becomes elaborated and a more complete structure for the text is constructed in the Text Representation.

The effective reader thus establishes a specific goal, formulates a plan, and evaluates progress toward this goal. Affective, cognitive, and metacognitive strategies are critical to both the control of the reading process and the use of Declarative and Procedural Knowledge. Both are involved in creating the Text Representation. The role of these components in forming Reader Product will be discussed under Product Construction and Evaluation, as the interactive model is developed.

The Interactive Reading Model

Model Interactions

The interactive model is organized around five interactions which link the components. These five interactions, as shown in Figure 2, are:
- Environment Interaction (A)
- Knowledge Interaction (B)
- Product Construction and Evaluation Interaction (C)
- Affective/Cognitive/Metacognitive Control Interaction (A/C/M Control Interaction) (D)
- New Knowledge Interaction (E)

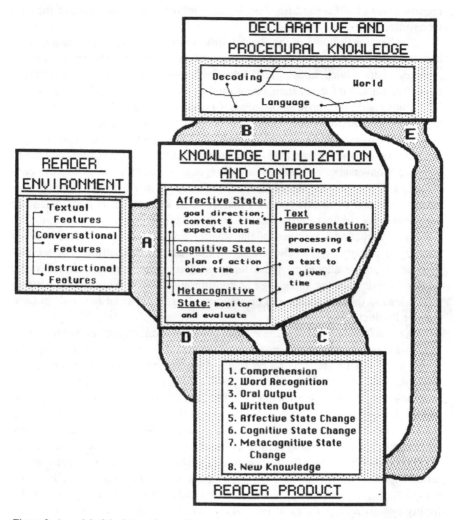

Figure 2. A model of the interactive reading process.

These interactions occur simultaneously during the reading process rather than in some fixed sequence. Each interaction, however, is controlled by the Knowledge Utilization and Control Component of the model.

Environment Interaction. The Environment Interaction (A in Figure 2) links the Reader Environment Component with Knowledge Utilization and Control Component. This interaction provides the basic input mechanism of the model. Any feature of the Reader Environment which is to be processed enters the Text Representation via the Environment Interaction. As the features of the environment are used, interpreted, elaborated, and stored in the Text Representation, the control system itself is modified due to the monitoring and evaluating of the Metacognitive State.

The Textual Features of the Reader Environment are the linguistic and visible structures of the text. The visible structures would include the printed words, pictures, chapter titles, headings, or subtitles for sections of the text, size of type, paper and ink colors, and arrangement on the page. If the reader has appropriate Declarative and Procedural Knowledge, these structures are used in the construction of the Text Representation and, in turn, products from the text.

The Conversational Features of the Reader Environment consist of any spoken discourse in the environment. When the discourse is about the text and the fit between Conversational Features and Language Knowledge is good, the construction of the Text Representation is facilitated. When the discourse is unrelated to the text or the fit between features and knowledge is poor, adequate construction of the Text Representation will be inhibited.

The Instructional Features of the Reader Environment are defined as any strategy or activity used by the teacher in the instructional setting. The reader's goal and plan are altered by these features. Under the teacher's direction, the reader must develop the knowledge of appropriate classroom interaction patterns which lead to the construction of appropriate Text Representations and, in turn, Reader Product.

In the Affective State, the reader sets goal direction, expectations for a product, and expectations for the time needed to create the product. These expectations are based on the text to be read, its situational context in the reader environment, and the declarative and procedural knowledge already activated and located in the Text Representation. The Affective State can be modified during the reading process based on the metacognitive evaluation of the fit between the goals and expectations of the Affective State and the product of the Text Representation. If the overriding feature of the environment is instructional, say the reading is assigned, the Affective State will be based on external rather than internal expectations. Completing the assignment within the allotted time becomes the goal. If the environment is not instructional, say the reader has selected a highly interesting text for pleasure reading, the Affective State will be based on internal expectations using knowledge from the Declarative and Procedural Knowledge Component. If the text offers features such as pictures which are highly appealing to the beginning reader, the reader is more likely to persist in reading than if the text lacks pictures. The Text Representation of the reader may incorporate images of the pictures which can be used by the reader at the time of retrieval. If the text includes complex tables and graphs, the sophisticated reader may search for specific information and persist only long enough to derive the information sought. While images of the tables and graphs may be incorporated into the Text Representation, they may not be used at time of retrieval; instead the reader may rely on the information derived from the tables and graphs which is verbally coded in the Text Representation.

In the Cognitive State, the reader sets a plan of action for reading the text under the influence of the current goals and expectations formulated in the Affective State. Cognitive strategies from Procedural Knowledge are activated so that the reader can follow the plan of action set by the Cognitive State. This plan influences the use of input from the environment and from knowledge sources. If the beginning reader fails to understand that reading is a meaning based process, the reader's goal will be limited to word recognition and will fail to incorporate Language and World Knowledge. The strategies used and recorded in the Text Representation will, then, be related to recognition rather than comprehension. Also, the Metacognitive State will be limited by the reader's goal and plan, and the evaluation of the Text Representation will be based solely on the formation of an internal representation used for decoding the print into words. For the more proficient reader or even a beginning reader with a meaning-oriented schema for reading, the Cognitive State will activate conceptually driven procedures for deriving meaning.

In the Metacognitive State, the reader formulates an internal state to monitor and evaluate the Text Representation based on the goals and expectations of the Affective State and the plan of the Cognitive State. Thus, the Metacognitive State is sensitive to the relationship between the Text Representation and the goals and plan set by the Affective and Cognitive States. The Metacognitive State is also influenced by changes in the environment. For example, new instructional directions by a teacher may force a change of the Affective and/or the Cognitive States. The reader must then alter the reading goal and plan. This, in turn, will require different metacognitive monitoring of the Text Representation and a reinterpretation of the text.

In the Text Representation, the reader constructs a representation of the text and records the processing that is used to form a representation of the text's meaning. The construction of the Text Representation depends heavily on the Knowledge Interaction.

*Knowledge Interaction.*The Knowledge Interaction (B in Figure 2) links the reader's Knowledge Utilization and Control Component to the reader's Declarative and Procedural Knowledge Component. The knowledge that must be used by the control system to construct a Text Representation resides in the Decoding, Language, and World Knowledge of the reader. For the effective reader, many of the procedures for analyzing the input from Reader Environment are automatic and leave a minimal record in the Text Representation. The mature reader's decoding, for example, is, for the most part, automatic unless the reader encounters an unusual and difficult word. Decoding the unfamiliar word leaves a record of its processing which is more elaborated in its visual and phonological structure than a word which is automatically decoded. For the beginning reader, the record of decoding can become so salient in the Text Representation that interference in retrieval of the text meaning results.

Decoding, Language, and World Knowledge schemata are considered to be highly interrelated. The efficient reader's World Knowledge about a topic such as amphibians contains images and language about amphibians and even visual representations of the words along with the procedures for activating that knowledge. With most texts, several types of information converge to activate the appropriate schema for a text. Thus, lexical access is provided by general schema activation procedures rather than a separate procedure. The lexicon is subsumed as a part of the schematic structure of knowledge rather than a separate component of the knowledge system.

During the construction of the Text Representation, two types of processing events must be distinguished. These two types will be designated as usual and unusual processing events. Usual processing events occur when the reader readily decodes and activates the appropriate schemata for the comprehension of a text. When the reader retrieves information from this Text Representation, the salient features of the schemata activated during the construction of the Text Representation will be recalled along with the significant elaborations the reader incorporated into the structure of the Text Representation. Thus, the information recalled from the text is predictable based on the schema activated. Each episode in narration should have some action or actor to be remembered while each new topic in exposition should have some salient relationship to previous topics. In essence, retrieval of information from the Text Representation is only a partial report of the information.

The fate of the unusual processing event is affected by the further processing received. An unusual processing event could include the processing of a new episode in the story structure, a new topic or subtopic in exposition, a new relationship between concepts in the text or information which is difficult to comprehend due to a lack of Language or World Knowledge. An unusual processing event will experience one of three possible fates depending on the goal, plan, and evaluation of the reader: 1) it can be dismissed as unimportant, 2) it can be put on hold waiting for additional input and processing, 3) it can be processed further without additional input. Each of these three options will influence the relationship between the unusual processing event and the structure of the whole Text Representation. In turn, the relationship of the event to the whole of the Text Representation will influence the retrieval of the information contained in the record of the unusual event. Each case will be discussed in some detail.

In the first case, the unusual event is dismissed as unimportant by the evaluation of the Metacognitive State of the reader. This evaluation is based on the Affective and Cognitive States and the schemata which have been activated and used in structuring the Text Representation. Events in this case receive no further processing and are not likely to be retrievable except when explicitly cued. It is extremely unlikely that this type of event will become salient in the Text Representation.

In the second case, the event is put on hold pending additional input from the text. The reader's Metacognitive State provides direction either to continue reading or to regress in the text. If the additional input is not useful in processing the event, it will suffer the same fate as the event that was dismissed in the first case with one qualification. The Text Representation contains a record that the event was held for some time. Thus, this event is slightly more elaborated and thus more likely to be retrieved. If additional processing occurs as the result of the additional input, the case two event can become easily retrievable if it is salient in the Text Representation.

In the third case, the unusual event becomes the source of additional processing that does not require additional input from the text. Here no schema becomes readily available to form an interpretation of the event and the reader's metacognitive decision requires that Declarative and Procedural Knowledge be searched for additional usable knowledge and procedures. The final interpretation may be far from the one intended by the author of the text, but the processing of the event is terminated. If the search for an applicable schema requires further processing, the event may be elaborated by a constellation of attempts to process it. If the problem is resolved by accessing and accepting a schema, the relation of that schema to the others contained in the Text Representation will determine the event's retrievability.

Transcripts of oral elaborations made during reading of narratives were collected by Speaker (1984) for the purpose of examining the retention of unusual processing events. Unusual processing events were classified into three categories: decoding, language and scriptual processing difficulties. Decoding difficulties were rare while language and scriptual difficulties were found to occur more frequently. As the model predicts, processing difficulties which were resolved by the reader tend to be recalled with high frequency, 92 percent of the time. On the other hand, processing difficulties which were not resolved by the reader were rarely recalled, only 8 percent of the time.

Product Construction and Evaluation Interaction. The Product Construction and Evaluation Interaction (C in Figure 2) links the reader's Knowledge Utilization and Control Component, which includes the Text Representation, with the Reader Product Component. Eight products of the reading episode are Comprehension, Word Recognition, Oral Output, Written Output in the form of Written Language and Representations, Affective State Change, Cognitive State Change, Metacognitive State Change, and New Knowledge. Again, the products formed during the reading act depend on the goal(s) set by the reader's Affective State which in turn may depend on environmental factors such as instruction from a teacher who assigned a text for a specific purpose. The plan for achieving the goal(s) must incorporate strategies for product construction. As previously discussed, these strategies are activated from the Declarative and Procedural Knowledge Component. Finally, the product is evaluated using the Metacognitive State. In all cases, the Text Representation is the immediate source of the information used in constructing the product.

Comprehension is the primary product of skilled reading, requiring the construction of meaning from text. This internal product is represented in the Text Representation and developed under the control of the internal states. For the beginning reader, the Text Representation may include little salient information related to meaning because much of the elaboration is based on Word Recognition Product rather than Comprehension. In skilled reading, most of the processing and elaboration pertains directly to the comprehension of the text, so comprehended information is most easily retrieved. In the instructional setting, comprehension is measured using other products such as Oral or Written Output.

It is important to note that capacity limitation is only one explanation of comprehension difficulty predicted by the model. Comprehension Product is formulated as an integral part of the Text Representation. However, only part of the Text Representation may remain active during construction of meaning. This follows, to some degree, the formulation of Kintsch and van Dijk (1978). In the case of the beginning reader, the most highly elaborated information in the Text Representation may be the processing related to decoding even though the reader has the capacity to elaborate meaning. Since this elaboration tends to make decoding information more salient than comprehension, it will tend to be difficult for the beginning reader to demonstrate comprehension. Consequently, early reading instruction must place an emphasis on elaborating the meaning of the text. For the skilled reader, the salience of decoding information disappears unless the vocabulary of the text is extremely difficult, so comprehension is easy to demonstrate.

Word Recognition is an internal product which is important for both the beginning and the skilled reader. For the novice reader, the Cognitive State plan focuses heavily on decoding processes in the construction of the Text Representation. For the skilled reader, word recognition of familiar words is automatic, and little elaborated word recognition information remains in the Text Representation. The most salient features of the Text Representation, thus, involve meaning.

Oral Output has two major forms, oral reading and spoken discourse about a text. Both require that the Text Representation be used as a source of information. Goals and expectations of the Affective State must account for word recognition, comprehension, and oral output while the plan for accomplishing goals must incorporate strategies to construct oral output. Finally, the product is evaluated by the Metacognitive State.

For oral reading, the Metacognitive State must monitor the relationship between the output from the Text Representation and the text. The Text Representation is accessed during the construction process and errors due to incomplete representation of the text may occur. Since the reader's goal is to read orally, the Text Representation may not elaborate meaning of the text to the degree that would occur if the reader had planned to answer questions about the text. Word recognition should be more highly elaborated in the constructive processes during oral reading than would be the case for other situations.

The beginning reader relies heavily on the decoding processes during oral reading. Visual chunks of text are used in processing while activated language and world knowledge operate conceptually to guide the interpretation and decoding process. Once the young reader has activated a world knowledge schema and its associated language schema, the reader becomes bound to that conceptual processing. The Metacognitive State cannot alter the established schema easily. The beginning reader has difficulty shifting from an activated interpretation of the text because the metacognitive knowledge and strategies for flexible self-monitoring have not been fully developed. Even so, the self-correction of mis-cues, observed with the early reader, is based on the reader's monitoring using the activated schemata in the Text Representation.

The skilled reader's Metacognitive State uses Declarative and Procedural Knowledge more effectively than is the case for the beginning reader. Monitor-ing can shift between internal and external sources of information so that cross checking between the text and the currently active portion of the Text Representa-tion can occur. Since the Metacognitive State is able to use several sources of data simultaneously, a shift of schema is more likely to occur when some interpreta-tion mismatch occurs.

Spoken discourse about a text provides access cues to some of the structure of the Text Representation. It is usually based on a more complete Text Representation than oral reading but may suffer from retrieval effects such as difficulty in retrieving any but the highest level of schema based information. However, as the discourse progresses, the Conversational Features of the teacher-student interaction in the Reader Environment may provide the individual with new cues which assist in re-trieving information from the Text Representation. The beginning reader when moni-toring conversation may not be able to effectively use and retain information long enough to have a turn in the discourse. Thus, the procedural knowledge embodying conversational competence and the memory capacity of the young reader will affect the production of spoken discourse about a text. The older, skilled reader uses the highly developed metacognitive flexibility and conversational competence to enhance oral discourse responses related to text.

Written Output consists of two forms, Written Language and Written Repre-sentations. Written Language is in the visible language medium and, therefore, requires goals, plans and monitoring which differ from spoken discourse. Lan-guage Knowledge for a written product is from the Declarative and Procedural Knowledge Component and must include written forms and conventions rather than oral. Although these conventions in some cases will parallel oral forms, they are not identical to them. Written Output is not restricted to narration and exposition; it also includes note-taking, outlining, and question-answering. Writ-ten Representations include maps, graphs, diagrams, and pictures which are used to represent a text. These representations help organize the Text Representation and aid in retrieval of information. Thus, the Written Output is interactive with the Text Representation.

The Text Representation is the immediate source of the information which is used for Written Output. The control states for the experienced reader-writer must activate appropriate schemata from Declarative and Procedural Knowledge for the formation of the Text Representation and, in turn, Written Language and Representations. Selected information from the Text Representation is reconstructed in written form to be read by another reader or for later use by the writer. For the beginning reader-writer, the goals and expectations, plan of action, monitoring and evaluation needed to form written products are relatively undeveloped. Reading for the purpose of constructing a written product has not been experienced with a frequency which provides for retrieval and use of information for written output.

Change of Control State consists of three change products. These are Affective State Change, Cognitive State Change, and Metacognitive State Change. A change in one state will require adjustment in each of the remaining states. For example, a reader may establish the goal of understanding and remembering information from a text for a difficult test. Assuming, however, the reader discovers the information in the text is extremely unfamiliar, indicating the absence of Language and World Knowledge schemata, the reader will be required to modify time expectations for creating a Text Representation which will incorporate adequate information for the test. As a result, the Affective State goal must be modified to allow additional time for processing of the information to be learned. The Cognitive State must, in turn, incorporate a plan for reading and studying the difficult text while the Metacognitive State must evaluate and monitor the processing of the text in light of the new goals, expectations and plans. Thus, the three control states can change rapidly, altering the original goal, plan and monitoring to accommodate new information from the Reader Environment, draw on different Declarative and Procedural Knowledge, and create a revised Text Representation, resulting in different product(s).

New Knowledge is a product based on the Text Representation which becomes part of the Declarative and Procedural Knowledge Component. For the beginning reader, the new knowledge will include Decoding, Language, and World Knowledge. For the skilled reader, new Decoding Knowledge will be rare while the acquisition of Language and World Knowledge will continue. For example, the New Knowledge for a parent based on reading a familiar story to a preschool child may include a new interpretation of the story or new emotional responses stemming from the parent-child interaction. By contrast, reading *War and Peace* in a modern literature course may result in New Knowledge about the characters, plot, setting, history of the period presented in the novel and individual emotional responses to the novel.

A/C/M Control Interaction. The A/C/M Control Interaction (D in Figure 2) links the Reader Product and Knowledge Utilization and Control. Through this interaction, the reader is constantly modifying the Affective, Cognitive, and Metacognitive control states based on Reader Product. This interaction, thus, influences the control processes and, in turn, the Text Representation and Reader Product(s).

New Knowledge Interaction. The final interaction, the New Knowledge Interaction (E in Figure 2) links Reader Product with the Declarative and Procedural Knowledge Component of the model. This interaction ensures that the new knowledge is integrated in the reader's memory and retained in Decoding, Language, and World Knowledge.

Application of the Model to Text

The application of the interactive model to text is illustrated below using a brief passage entitled "Magic Craft." The passage is followed by one interpretation of the constructive reading processes using the model components and their interactions. The reader is asked to read silently, to comprehend the passage, and to reflect on the processes used during the reading of this passage.

Magic Craft

Through the thick, smoked glass viewport, she surveyed the dark bars and grey walls. A layer of fuliginous residue covered the bottom, but she chose to do nothing about it.

A knob was turned, and some of the bars changed from black to radiating red. The space beyond the viewport became hotter and hotter. The residue began to smoke, adding an unpleasant smell to the closed space. She worried about this, but decided it was too late to do anything about it. An alarm rang but it quickly stopped. Just a nuisance, she thought.

The heat light flashed and went off. She pulled on thickly insulated gloves, opened the protective heat door, and moved some of the bars, carefully positioning them. Finally, the oven was hot, and she put the pans of bread in to bake.

The reader's understanding of the analysis for processing the passage will be facilitated by referring to the interactive reading model presented in Figure 2.

Text: *Magic Craft*.

1. Reader Environment
In the context of a paper about a reading model, the reader finds the title of a passage; the title consists of a noun phrase consisting of an adjective, *magic* and a noun, *craft* (Textual Features). There are no Conversational Features present unless some discussion occurred. The instructions included reading the passage silently to comprehend; there is a didactic intent by the authors of this chapter (Instructional Features).

2. Knowledge Utilization and Control
The goals are to recognize words, to form a comprehension product during silent reading, and to understand the relationship of the passage to the model; the reader suspects something will be unusual about the passage (Affective State). The plan is to read the passage from its title to its end and modify this plan as any difficulties are encountered; decoding is automatic; language knowledge about titles is activated (Cognitive State). Monitoring and evaluation strategies are activated by the plan (Metacognitive State).

The two words of the title are represented, and an interpretation may be formed (Text Representation). The ambiguity of the title is noticed; the evaluation may alter the goal and plan (Metacognitive State). The ambiguity fulfills the reader's expectation that the passage will present some difficulty and activates several hypotheses using Declarative Knowledge.

3. Declarative and Procedural Knowledge

The words of the title are automatically decoded (Decoding Knowledge). They fit appropriate categories for a title; both narrative and expository text structure schemata are activated (Language Knowledge). The meanings of *craft* activate several possible schemata which are included in the Text Representation; these include the Science Fiction Schema, the Magic Schema, and the Arts and Crafts Schema (World Knowledge).

4. Reader Product

The original products were to be Word Recognition (automatic), Comprehension, and New Knowledge related to the application of the model. The metacognitive evaluation produced change in the internal states. Predictions are formulated that can be evaluated against future input to the Text Representation (Comprehension).

Text: *Through the thick, smoked glass viewport, she surveyed the dark bars and grey walls. A layer of fuliginous residue covered the bottom, but she chose to do nothing about it.*

1. Reader Environment

The sentences form the Textual Features. There were no conversational Features. There is a didactic intent by the authors (Instructional Feature).

2. Knowledge Utilization and Control

The goal now includes differentiating among competing hypotheses for the interpretation of the title (Affective State). The plan adds precise reading to identify clues the authors may have hidden (Cognitive State). Monitoring and evaluation strategies continue operating (Metacognitive State). The first sentence is recognized and their syntactic relationships activated from Language Knowledge (Text Representation).

The word *she* is evaluated and precludes the likelihood of an expository passage. The goal and plan change to emphasize the narrative text structure schema as the organizational structure of the Text Representation (Metacognitive State). Since the narrative text structure requires the instantiation of a character and setting, the unnamed female character located in a roomlike location with a windowlike opening is interpreted as fulfilling these requirements (Text Representation). An ambiguity of the setting may be noticed; the character could be inside looking out or outside looking in (Metacognitive State).

The word *fuliginous* is not recognized automatically so Decoding Knowledge is deliberately used to syllabicate the word; the reader may pronounce the word orally (Text Representation). If lexical access cannot be achieved, new strategies for arriving at the meaning of the sentence and the word *fuliginous* are activated (Metacognitive State). The internal control states are changed to activate such strategies as using context, or using a dictionary to identify meaning, or the reader may put the unusual processing event on hold pending further input (Cognitive State).

3. Declarative and Procedural Knowledge

Decoding Knowledge for the first sentence is automatic as is lexical access; the second sentence requires deliberate use of decoding and lexical access procedures. The narrative text-structure schema is fully activated, and the expository text-structure schema loses its active state (Language Knowledge). The word *craft* from the title may still admit several interpretations. This will depend on whether a decision has been made on the setting and the reader's ability to keep the various schemata activated (World Knowledge).

4. Reader Product

The products are Word Recognition (automatic and deliberate), Comprehension, New Knowledge, and change in the internal control states. The reader may expect the story to misdirect the reader's interpretation (Comprehension, Metacognitive State Change).

Text: *A knob was turned, and some of the bars changed from black to radiating red. The space beyond the viewport became hotter and hotter. The residue began to smoke, adding an unpleasant smell to the closed room. She worried about this, but decided it was too late to do anything about it. A warning alarm sounded. Just a nuisance, she thought.*

1. Reader Environment

Again, the sentences form the Textual Features. There are no Conversational Features. The didactic intent of the authors remains (Instructional Feature).

2. Knowledge Utilization and Control

The goal is to differentiate among competing hypotheses for the interpretation during silent reading (Affective State). The plan is to read precisely to identify the misdirections hidden by the authors (Cognitive State). Monitoring and evaluation strategies continue (Metacognitive State). The sentences are automatically represented (Text Representation). Ambiguity is noted in the deletion of the agent in the first of these sentences generating changes in internal control states and hypotheses, or default values to fill the slot of agent (Metacognitive State, Text Representation). The residue is reevaluated as more important to the story, possibly causing a regression to reread the second sentence of the first paragraph (Metacognitive, Affective, and Cognitive States). The reader may elaborate events by adding emotions of the character; a sense of urgency may be attributed to her (Text Representation).

3. Declarative and Procedural Knowledge

Decoding Knowledge is automatic. The narrative text-structure schema assigns an event and its consequence with either the known character or an undetermined character as agent (Language Knowledge). The turning of the knob caused extreme heat as inferred from the color change of the bars. The Escape-Attempt Schema may be activated by the word *bars*, but this schema is probably canceled when some of the bars glow with heat and evidence that the character is looking into a space which is becoming hotter. The heat produces smoke and possibly fire. The alarm could be a smoke alarm, an escape alarm, or a kitchen timer if the Baking Schema has been activated (World Knowledge).

4. Reader Product

The products are Word Recognition (automatic), Comprehension, New Knowledge, and change of internal control states to deal with an uninstantiated agent and character motivations. The reader may still expect the story to misdirect the reader's interpretation (Comprehension, Metacognitive State Change).

Text: *The heat light flashed and went off. She put on thickly insulated gloves, opened the protective heat door, and moved some of the bars, carefully positioning them. Finally, the oven was hot, and she put the pans of bread in to bake.*

1. Reader Environment

The sentences, again, form the Textual Features. No Conversational Features were present. The didactic intent of the authors remains (Instructional Feature).

2. Knowledge Utilization and Control

The goal remains to differentiate among competing hypotheses for the interpretation during silent reading (Affective State). The reader's plan is to hold several hypotheses in the Text Representation until one is confirmed (Cognitive State). The reader is aware that the passage ends with this paragraph (Metacognitive State). The sentences are automatically represented (Text Representation). The reader decides that the passage is about the mysteries of baking bread in a not-so-clean oven (Text Representation). The reader may reread to confirm this evaluation (Metacognitive State).

3. Declarative and Procedural Knowledge

Decoding Knowledge is automatic. Lexical items are identified and confirmed in the narrative text structure schema (Language Knowledge). The Preheat the Oven Script of the Baking Schema is activated and confirmed (World Knowledge).

4. Reader Product

The products are Word Recognition (automatic), Comprehension, and New Knowledge. The word *craft* is interpreted to mean baking. The setting is a kitchen with electric oven. The reader reorganizes the Text Representation by quickly rereading the passage and notes that the model components interact, operating simultaneously to produce products (New Knowledge).

This application of the model illustrates the highly interactive nature of the four model components.

Implications for Research and Instruction

New research directions and recommendations for instructional practice may be derived from the interactive reading model. Researchers have just begun to investigate the interactions specified by the model.

To better understand the Environment Interaction (A), researchers must investigate the relationship between the textual, conversational, and instructional features of the environment, and knowledge use and control. Some of these features seem to be automatically incorporated into the reader's Text Representation, others do not. For example, mature readers appear to make more effective use of text structure than beginning readers; however, we have little understanding of the relationship between the text and instructional features and the development of text structure knowledge. How do features in the reader environment influence the reader's knowledge of text structure? How do features in the reader's environment facilitate or inhibit retrieval and processing of text structure?

Knowledge interaction (B) has been the source of considerable research in reading. Readers use declarative and procedural knowledge to represent and to understand text, using Affective, Cognitive, and Metacognitive Control States. How do these control states develop? And how do they interact with Declarative and Procedural Knowledge to promote or inhibit the construction of a Text Representation? In brief, how is memory used during reading? What knowledge is necessary for effective product construction? If knowledge of text structure is essential to the construction of the Text Representation, how should such knowledge be taught? And when should it be taught?

The Product Construction and Evaluation Interaction (C) has not been sufficiently addressed in reading research. Research is needed to improve our understanding of the processing relationship between Text Representation and Reader Product(s). Additional work should examine the similarities and differences in constructing products, such as oral and written output, under various instructional conditions.

Research into the A/C/M Control Interaction (D) has focused for the most part on the cognitive aspects of learning. Affective and Metacognitive States have only recently received research emphasis. The effect of changes in these control states on text processing should be examined during reading and from a developmental perspective. Researchers should not only assess reader's abilities using the more traditional, cognitively oriented performance products such as standardized tests, but also incorporate observations and introspective approaches to better understand affective and metacognitive changes. Research on the role of the Affective State in reading disability deserves special attention. Because established patterns of failure with text have produced negative affect toward reading, disabled readers' affect should show marked improvement with reading success.

The New Knowledge Interaction (E) has received emphasis in research. The reader is expected to apply decoding, language and world knowledge in comprehending text and to retain new declarative and procedural knowledge. Research is needed to better understand how the construction of different products influences the retention of information from text. Current memory research suggests that greater elaboration in the processing of text improves retention, but this effect needs to be examined in a variety of classroom settings with learners of differing abilities.

Future research must give careful attention to the relationship between the research paradigm used and the research question being investigated. The strict experimentalist paradigm, which has characterized much of past reading research, has often failed to adequately specify the Reader Environment, resulting in limited application of findings to classroom instruction. By contrast, the current vogue of more phenomenalistic research has often succeeded in capturing a particular learning environment and the interactions which occur there, but is limited in generalizability to other environments and learners. The selective use of both experimental and phenomenalistic methodologies is necessary if we are to effectively match research questions with methodologies and to generate research findings possessing greater ecological validity.

Implications for instruction, based on the model, fall into two interaction categories, those related to the Environment Interaction (A) and those related to Product Construction and Evaluation (C). The model also holds explanatory power leading to a better understanding of the effectiveness of instructional strategies already used by teachers. It may also be used as a framework for the evaluation of instructional activities viewed in relation to the whole reading process rather than as a list of isolated subskills.

The central focus of the model is on the Knowledge Utilization and Control Component. A major instructional goal should be to aid the reader in developing conscious control of the reading process. The structure of the Reader Environment is vital to this end. Instructional emphasis should be placed on careful selection of activities with attention to strategies leading to effective text processing. The learner must know what to expect and how to successfully apply Declarative and Procedural Knowledge in the construction of the Text Representation and in turn Reader Product. The teacher should use a wide variety of instructional activities which demonstrate strategies for efficient reading and assist the learner in incorporating these strategies into Declarative and Procedural Knowledge.

The learner should be actively involved in the processing of text if affect is to remain high. This involvement should include setting goals and expectations for content, time and product. Attention must be given to the development of cognitive strategies to assist in the elaboration of information and metacognitive strategies for evaluating the fit between goal and Text Representation or Reader Product. The learner must develop the awareness that Language and World Knowledge are necessary for the understanding of text and that peers, teacher and other texts can be used as information sources when difficulty is encountered. The boosting of affect, and the development of cognitive and metacognitive strategies are important instructional goals which foster a learner who pays greater attention, has greater perseverance and interacts with text, teacher and peers.

The teacher's awareness of the nature of different reader products and the understanding of the relationship between each product and the reader's goal, plan, monitoring and text processing should lead to the design of more effective instruction. For example, comprehension and written output differ in that comprehension is an essential part of the Text Representation while writing requires the information in the Text Representation to be integrated and restructured for self or another reader.

In closing, the interactive model of the reading process offers a metaphor for a complex mental process. The model is based on the interaction of four key components directed by the Knowledge Utilization and Control Component. Implicit is the assumption that the Text Representation is constructed over time and reflects the elaboration and structuring of information from a variety of sources including the text, internal control states, declarative and procedural knowledge and products. Implications derived from the model can serve to provide new direction for research and the development of instructional strategies.

REFERENCES

Adams, M., and Collins, A. A schema-theoretic view of reading. In R. Freedle (Ed.), *New directions in discourse processing*. Norwood, NJ: Ablex, 1979.
Anderson, J.R. *Cognitive psychology and its implications*. San Francisco: W.H. Freeman, 1980.

Anderson, R.C. The notion of schemata and the educational enterprise. In R.C. Anderson, R.J. Spiro, and W.E. Montague (Eds.), *Schooling and the acquisition of knowledge*. Hillsdale, NJ: Erlbaum, 1977.

Anderson, R.C., and Freebody, P. Vocabulary Knowledge. In J.T. Guthrie (Ed.), *Comprehension and teaching: Research reviews*. Newark, DE: International Reading Association, 1981.

Anderson, R.C., and Pichert, J.W. Recall of previously unrecallable information following a shift in perspective. *Journal of Verbal Learning and Verbal Behavior, 17* (1978),1-12.

Anderson, R.C., Reynolds, R.E., Schallert, D.L., and Goetz, E.T. Frameworks for comprehending discourse. *American Educational Research Journal, 14* (1977), 367-381.

Anderson, R.C., Spiro, R.J., and Anderson, M.C. Schemata as scaffolding for the representation of information in connected discourse. *American Educational Research Journal, 15* (1978), 433-440.

Applebee, A. *The child's concept of story: Ages two to seventeen*. Chicago: University of Chicago Press, 1978.

Athey, I.J. *Reading personality patterns at the junior high school level*. Unpublished doctoral dissertation, University of California at Berkeley, 1965.

Au, K., and Mason, J.M. Social organizational factors in learning to read. *Reading Research Quarterly, 17* (1981), 115-152.

Baddeley, A. Working memory and reading. In P.A. Kolers, M.E. Wrolstad, and H. Bouma (Eds.), *The processing of visual language*. New York: Plenum Press, 1979.

Baddeley, A., and Lewis, V. Inner active processes in reading: The inner voice, the inner ear, and the inner eye. In A.M. Lesgold and C.A. Perfetti (Eds.), *Interactive processes in reading*. Hillsdale, NJ: Erlbaum, 1981.

Baker, L., and Brown, A.L. Metacognitive skills and reading. In P.D. Pearson (Ed.), *Handbook of reading research*. New York: Longman, 1984.

Baker, L., and Stein, N. The development of prose comprehension skills. In C.M. Santa and B.L. Hayes (Eds.), *Children's prose comprehension*. Newark, DE: International Reading Association, 1981.

Barnett, J.E. Facilitating retention through instruction about text structure. *Journal of Reading Behavior, 16* (1984), 1-14.

Barr, R. Beginning reading instruction: From debate to reformation. In P.D. Pearson (Ed.), *Handbook of reading research*. New York: Longman, 1984.

Bear, D.E. Phonics in first grade: A comparison of two methods. *Elementary School Journal, 59* (1958), 394-402.

Belloni, L.F., and Jongsma, E.A. The effects of interest on reading comprehension of low achieving students. *Journal of Reading, 22* (1978), 106-109.

Bloom, B. *Human characteristics and school learning*. New York: McGraw-Hill, 1982.

Bloom, D., and Green, J. Directions in the social linguistic study of reading. In P.D. Pearson (Ed.), *Handbook of reading research*. New York: Longman, 1984.

Bloomfield, L. *Language*. New York: Holt, Rinehart and Winston, 1933.

Bourdieu, P., and Passeron, J. *Reproduction in education, society, and culture*. London: Sage, 1977.

Bower, G.H., Black, J.B., and Turner, T.J. Scripts in memory for text. *Cognitive Psychology, 11* (1979), 177-220.

Bransford, J.D., and Johnson, M.K. Contextual prerequisites for understanding: Some investigations of comprehension and recall. *Journal of Verbal Learning and Verbal Behavior, 11* (1972), 717-726.

Britton, B.K., Meyer, B.J.F., Hodge, M.H., and Glynn, S.M. Effects of the organization of text on memory: Tests of the retrieval and response criterion hypotheses. *Journal of Experimental Psychology: Human Learning and Memory, 6* (1980), 611-629.

Britton, B.K., Meyer, B.J.F., Simpson, R., Holdredge, T.S., and Curry, C. Effects of the organization of text on memory: Tests of two implications of a selective attention hypothesis. *Journal of Experimental Psychology: Human Learning and Memory, 5* (1979), 496-506.

Brown, A. Learning how to learn from reading. In J.A. Langer and M.T. Smith-Burke (Eds.), *Reader meets author/bridging the gap*. Newark, DE: International Reading Association, 1982.

Bruner, J., Goodnow, J., and Austin, G. *A study of thinking*. New York: Wiley Press, 1956.

Canney, G., and Winograd, P. *Schemata for reading and reading comprehension performance*. Champaign: University of Illinois, Center for the Study of Reading, Technical Report No. 120, 1979.

Carnine, D., Kameenui, E.J., and Coyle, G. Utilization of contextual information in determining the meaning of unfamiliar words. *Reading Research Quarterly, 19* (1984), 188-204.

Carpenter, P.A., and Just, M.A. Cognitive processes in reading: Models based on readers' eye fixations. In A.M. Lesgold and C.A. Perfetti (Eds.), *Interactive processes in reading*. Hillsdale, NJ: Erlbaum, 1981.

Carroll, J.B. The nature of the reading process. In H. Singer and R.B. Ruddell (Eds.), *Theoretical models and processes of reading,* second edition. Newark, DE. International Reading Association, 1976.

Cazden, C.B. *Environmental assistance to the child's acquisition of grammar*. Unpublished doctoral dissertation, Harvard University, 1965.

Cazden, C.B. Learning to read in classroom interaction. In C.B. Resnick and P.A. Weaver (Eds.), *Theory and practice of early reading*. Hillsdale, NJ: Erlbaum, 1979.

Chall, J.S. *Learning to read: The great debate*. New York: McGraw-Hill, 1967.

Chall, J.S. The great debate: Ten years later, with a modest proposal for reading stages. In L.B. Resnick and P.A. Weaver (Eds.), *Theory and practice of early reading, Volume 1*. Hillsdale, NJ: Erlbaum, 1979.

Chomsky, C. *The acquisition of syntax in children from 5 to 10*. Cambridge: MIT Press, 1969.

Chomsky, C. Stages in language development and reading exposure. *Harvard Educational Review, 42* (1972), 1-33.

Cirilo, R.K., and Foss, D.J. Text structure and reading time for sentences. *Journal of Reading Behavior, 19* (1980), 96-109.

Coulthard, R.M., and Sinclair, J.M. *Towards an analysis of English used by teachers and pupils*. London: Oxford University Press, 1975.

Craik, F.I.M., and Tulving, E. Depth of processing and the retention of words in episodic memory. *Journal of Experimental Psychology: General, 104,* (1975), 268-294.

Danks, J.H., and Hill, G.O. An interactive analysis of oral reading. In A.M. Lesgold and C.A. Perfetti (Eds.), *Interactive processes in reading*. Hillsdale, NJ: Erlbaum, 1981.

De Beaugrande, R. Design criteria for process models of reading. *Reading Research Quarterly, 16* (1981), 261-315.

Dore, J. Conversation and preschool language development, In P. Fletcher and M. Garman (Eds.), *Language acquisition*. Cambridge: Cambridge University Press, 1979.

Downing, J.A. The i.t.a. reading experiment. *Reading Teacher, 18* (1965), 105-110.

Ehrlich, K., and Rayner, K. Pronoun assignment and semantic integration during reading: Eye movements and immediacy of processing. *Journal of Verbal Learning and Verbal Behavior, 22* (1983), 75-87.

Englert, C.S., and Hiebert, E.H. Children's developing awareness of text structures in expository materials. *Journal of Educational Psychology, 76* (1984), 65-74.

Erickson, F. Talking down: Some cultural sources of miscommunication in interracial interviews. In A. Wolfgang (Ed.), *Research in nonverbal communication*. New York: Academic Press, 1982.

Fillmore, C.J. The case for case. In E. Bach and R.T. Harms (Eds.), *Universals in linguistic theory*. New York: Holt, Rinehart and Winston, 1968.

Fisher, C.W., Filby, N.N., Marliave, R., Cahen, L.S., Dishaw, M.M., Moore, J.E., and Berliner, D.C. *Teaching behaviors, academic learning time, and student achievement: Final report of phase III-B, Beginning Teacher Evaluation Study*. San Francisco: Far West Educational Laboratory for Educational Research and Development, 1978.

Franks, J.J., Vye, N.J., Auble, P.M., Mezynski, K.J., Perfetto, G.A., Bransford, J.D., Stein, B.S., and Littlefield, J. Learning from explicit versus implicit texts. *Journal of Experimental Psychology: General, 111* (1982), 414-422.

Frederiksen, C. Representing logical and semantic knowledge acquired from discourse. *Cognitive Psychology, 7* (1975), 371-458.

Frederiksen, J.R. Sources of process interactions in reading. In A.M. Lesgold and C.A. Perfetti (Eds.), *Interactive processes in reading*. Hillsdale, NJ: Erlbaum, 1981.

Freebody, P., and Anderson, R.C. Effects of vocabulary difficulty, text cohesion, and schema availability on reading comprehension, *Reading Research Quarterly, 18* (1983a), 277-294.

Freebody, P., and Anderson, R.C. Effects on text comprehension of differing proportions and locations of difficult vocabulary. *Journal of Reading Behavior, 15* (1983b), 19-40.

Fries, C.C. *Linguistics and reading*. New York: Holt, Rinehart and Winston, 1963.

Gibson, E.J. Learning to read. *Science, 148* (1965), 1066-1072.

Gibson, E.J., Perceptual learning and the theory of word perception. *Cognitive Psychology, 2* (1971), 351-368.

Gibson, E.J. Trends in perceptual development: Implications for the reading process. In A.D. Pick (Ed.), *Minnesota symposium on child psychology, 8* (1974), 24-54.

Gibson, E.J., Bishop, C., Schiff, W., and Smith, J. Comparison of meaningfulness and pronounceability as grouping principles in the perception and retention of verbal material. *Journal of Experimental Psychology, 67* (1964), 173-182.

Gibson, E.J., Farber, J., and Shepela, S. Test of a learning set procedure for the abstraction of spelling patterns. *Project Literacy Reports, 8* (1967), 21-30.

Glushko, R.J. Principles for pronouncing print. In A.M. Lesgold and C.A. Perfetti (Eds.), *Interactive processes in reading*. Hillsdale, NJ: Erlbaum, 1981.

Goetz, E.T., Palmer, D.J., and Haensly, P.A. Metacognitive awareness of text variables in good and poor readers. In J.A. Niles and L.A. Harris (Eds.), *Searches for meaning in reading, languages processing, and instruction*, 32nd yearbook of the National Reading Conference, 1983a, 129-134.

Goetz, E.T., Schallert, D.L., Reynolds, R.E., and Radin, D.I. Reading in perspective: What real cops and pretend burglars look for in a story. *Journal of Educational Psychology, 75* (1983b), 500-510.

Goodman, K.S. Miscues: Windows on the reading process. In K.S. Goodman (Ed.), *Miscue analysis: Applications to reading instruction*. Urbana, IL: National Council of Teachers of English, 1973.

Goodman, K.S. Behind the eye: What happens in reading. In H. Singer and R.B. Ruddell (Eds.), *Theoretical models and processes of reading*, second edition. Newark, DE: International Reading Association, 1976.

Goodman, K.S., and Goodman, Y.M. Learning about psycholinguistic processes by analyzing oral reading, *Harvard Educational Review, 47* (1977), 317-333.

Green, J.L., and Harker, J.O. Reading to children: A communicative process. In J.A. Langer and M.T. Smith-Burke (Eds.), *Reader meets author/bridging the gap*. Newark, DE: International Reading Association, 1982.

Haggard, M.R. Vocabulary acquisition during elementary and postelementary years: A preliminary report. *Reading Horizons, 21* (1980), 61-69.

Hahn, H.T. Three approaches to beginning reading instruction. *Reading Teacher, 19* (1966), 590-594.

Hall, R.A., Jr. *Sound and spelling in English*. New York: Chilton Books, 1961.

Hansen, D.N., and Rodgers, T.S. Exploration of psycholinguistic units in initial reading. In K. Goodman (Ed.), *The psycholinguistic nature of the reading process*. Detroit: Wayne State University Press, 1968.

Harste, J.C., Burke, C.L., and Woodward, V.A. Children's language and world: Initial encounters with print. In J.A. Langer and M.T. Smith-Burke (Eds.), *Reader meets author/bridging the gap*. Newark, DE: International Reading Association, 1982.

Hayes, R.B. i.t.a. and three other approaches to reading at first grade. *Reading Teacher, 19* (1966), 627-630.

Hiebert, E.H., Englert, C.S., and Brennan, S. Awareness of text structure on recognition and production of expository discourse. *Journal of Reading Behavior, 15* (1983), 63-79.

Hymes, D. *Foundations in sociolinguistics: An ethnographic approach*. Philadelphia: University of Pennsylvania Press, 1974.

Jackson, M.D., and McClelland, J.L. Exploring the nature of a basic visual-processing component of reading. In O.J.L. Tzeng and H. Singer (Eds.), *Perception of print: Reading research in experimental psychology*. Hillsdale, NJ: Erlbaum, 1981.

Jacoby, L.L. Perceptual enhancement: Persistent effects of past experience. *Journal of Experimental Psychology: Learning, Memory, and Cognition, 9* (1983a), 21-38.

Jacoby, L.L. Remembering the data: Analyzing interactive processing in reading. *Journal of Verbal Learning and Verbal Behavior, 22* (1983b), 485-508.

Jarvella, R.J. Syntactic processing of connected speech. *Journal of Verbal Learning and Verbal Behavior, 10* (1971), 409-416.

Jeffery, W.E., and Samuels, S.J. Effect of method of reading training on initial learning and transfer. *Journal of Verbal Learning and Verbal Behavior, 3* (1967), 354-358.

Johnson, D.D., and Baumann, J.F. Word identification. In P.D. Pearson (Ed.), *Handbook of reading research*. New York: Longman, 1984.

Johnson, D.D., Toms-Bronowski, S., and Pittleman, S.D. *A review of trends in vocabulary research and the effects of prior knowledge on instructional strategies for vocabulary acquisition.* Madison, WI: Wisconsin Center for Educational Research, 1981.

Katz, L., and Feldman, L.B. Linguistic coding in word recognition: Comparison between a deep and a shallow orthography. In A.M. Lesgold and C.A. Perfetti, *Interactive processes in reading.* Hillsdale, NJ: Erlbaum, 1981.

Kelly, B.C. The Economy method versus the Scott, Foresman method in teaching second grade reading in the Murphysboro Public Schools. *Journal of Educational Research, 51* (1958), 465-469.

Kintsch, W., and van Dijk, T.A. Toward a model of text comprehension and production. *Psychological Review, 85* (1978), 363-394.

Klapp, S.T., Marshburn, E.A. and Lester, P.T. Short term memory does not involve the "working memory" of information processing: The demise of a common assumption. *Journal of Experimental Psychology: General, 112* (1983), 240-264.

Kress, R.A. *An investigation of the relationship between concept formation and achievement in reading.* Unpublished doctoral dissertation, Temple University, 1955.

LaBerge, D. The perception of units in beginning reading. In L.B. Resnick and P.A. Weaver (Eds.), *Theory and practice of early reading: Volume 3.* Hillsdale, NJ: Erlbaum, 1979.

LaBerge, D., and Samuels, S.J. Toward a theory of automatic information processing in reading. In H. Singer and R.B. Ruddell (Eds.), *Theoretical models and processes of reading*, second edition. Newark, DE: International Reading Association, 1976.

Langer, J.A. Examining background knowledge and text comprehension. *Reading Research Quarterly, 19* (1984), 468-481.

Langer, J.A. An idiosyncratic model of affective and cognitive silent reading strategies. *Dissertation Abstracts International, 39* (1978), 3425.

Levin, T., and Long, R. *Effective instruction.* Alexandria, VA: Association for Supervision and Curriculum Development, 1981.

Loban, W. *Language ability: Grades seven, eight and nine.* Washington, DC.: U.S. Office of Education, 1966.

Loban, W. *Language ability: Grades ten, eleven and twelve.* University of California at Berkeley, 1967.

Loban, W. *Language development.* Urbana, IL: National Council of Teachers of English, 1976.

Lowery, L.F., and Grafft, W. Paperback books and reading attitudes. *Reading Teacher, 21* (1968), 618-623.

Mandler, J.M., and Johnson, W.S. Remembrance of things parsed: Story structure and recall. *Cognitive Psychology, 9* (1977), 111-151.

Marr, M.B., and Gormley, K. Children's recall of familiar and unfamiliar text. *Reading Research Quarterly, 18* (1982), 89-104.

Mason, J.M. Early reading from a developmental perspective. In P.D. Pearson (Ed.), *Handbook of reading research.* New York: Longman, 1984.

Mathewson, G.C. Relationship between ethnic group attitudes toward dialect and comprehension of dialect folktales. *Journal of Educational Research, 68* (1974), 15-18.

Mathewson, G.C. The function of attitude in the reading process. In H. Singer and R.B. Ruddell (Eds.), *Theoretical models and processes of reading*, second edition. Newark, DE: International Reading Association, 1976.

Mazurkiewicz, A.J. i.t.a. and T.O. reading achievement when methodology is controlled. *Reading Teacher, 19* (1966), 606-610.

McGee, L.M. Awareness of text structure: Effects on children's recall of expository text. *Reading Research Quarterly, 17* (1982), 581-590.

McHoul, A. The organization of turns at formal talk in the classroom. *Language in Society, 7* (1978), 183-213.

Mehan, H. The competent student. *Anthropology and Education Quarterly, 12* (1980), 3-28.

Meyer, B. Identification of the structure of prose and its implications for the study of meaning and memory. *Journal of Reading Behavior, 8* (1975), 8-47.

Meyer, B.J.F. Organizational patterns in prose and their use in reading. In M.L. Kamil and A.J. Moe (Eds.), *Reading research: Studies and applications.* Clemson, SC: National Reading Conference, 1979, 109-117.

Meyer, B.J.F. Organizational aspects of text: Effects on reading comprehension and applications for the classroom. In J. Flood (Ed.), *Promoting reading comprehension*. Newark, DE: International Reading Association, 1984.

Meyer, B.J.F., Brandt, D.M., and Bluth, G.J. Use of top-level structure in text: Key for reading comprehension of ninth grade students. *Reading Research Quarterly, 16* (1980), 72-103.

Mezynski, K. Issues concerning the acquisition of knowledge: Effects of vocabulary training on reading comprehension. *Review of Educational Research, 53* (1983), 253-279.

Miller, J.R., and Kintsch, W. Readability and recall of short prose passages: A theoretical analysis. *Journal of Experimental Psychology: Human Learning and Memory, 6* (1980), 335-354.

Myers, M., and Paris, S.G. Children's metacognitive knowledge about reading. *Journal of Educational Psychology, 70* (1978), 680-690.

Nezworski, T., Stein, N.L., and Trabasso, T. Story structure versus content in children's recall. *Journal of Verbal Learning and Verbal Behavior, 21* (1982), 196-206.

Norman, D.A. Perception, memory, and mental processes. In L. Nilsson (Ed.), *Perspectives on memory research: Essays in honor of Uppsala University's 500th anniversary.* Hillsdale, NJ: Erlbaum. 1979.

Ochs, E., and Schieffelin, B.B. Language acquisition and socialization: Three developmental stories and their implications. In R. Shewder and R. LeVine (Eds.), *Culture and its acquisition.* Chicago: University of Chicago Press, 1982.

Olshavsky, J.E. Reading as problem solving: An investigation of strategies. *Reading Research Quarterly, 12* (1976-1977), 654-675.

Osako, G., and Anders, P. The effect of reading interest on comprehension of expository materials with controls for prior knowledge. In J.A. Niles and L.A. Harris (Eds.), *Searches for meaning in reading/language processing and instruction*, 32nd Yearbook of the National Reading Conference, 1983.

Pearson, P.D., and Camperell, K. Comprehension of text structures. In J.T. Guthrie (Ed.), *Comprehension and teaching: Research reviews.* Newark, DE: International Reading Association, 1981.

Pearson, P.D., Hansen, J., and Gordon, C. The effect of background knowledge on young children's comprehension of explicit and implicit information. *Journal of Reading Behavior, 11* (1979), 201-209.

Pichert, J.W., and Anderson, R.C. Taking different perspectives on a story. *Journal of Educational Psychology, 69* (1977), 309-315.

Ramsel, D., and Grabe, M. Attention allocation and performance in goal-directed reading: Age difference in reading flexibility. *Journal of Reading Behavior, 15* (1983), 55-65.

Reed, D.W. A theory of language, speech, and writing. *Linguistics and reading*. Newark, DE: International Reading Association, 1966, 4-25.

Reynolds, R.E., Standiford, S.N., and Anderson, R.C. Distribution of reading time when questions are asked about a restricted category of text information. *Journal of Educational Psychology, 71* (1979), 183-190.

Rist, R.C. Student social class and teacher expectations. *Harvard Educational Review, 39* (1970), 411-415.

Rosenshine, B. Recent research in teacher behaviors and student achievement. *Journal of Teacher Education, 27* (1976), 61-64.

Rosenshine, B., and Stevens, R. Classroom instruction in reading. In P.D. Pearson (Ed.), *Handbook of reading research*. New York: Longman, 1984.

Rosenthal, R., and Jacobsen, L. *Pygmalion in the classroom: Teacher expectation and pupils' intellectual development.* New York: Holt, Rinehart and Winston, 1968.

Rothkopf, E.Z., and Billington, M.J. Goal guided learning from text: Inferring a descriptive processing model from inspection times and eye movements. *Journal of Educational Psychology, 71* (1979), 310-327.

Ruddell, R.B. Effect of the similarity of oral and written language structure on reading comprehension. *Elementary English, 42* (1965), 403-410.

Ruddell, R.B. A longitudinal study of four programs of reading instruction varying in emphasis of grapheme-phoneme correspondences and language structure on reading achievement in grades two and three. University of California at Berkeley, 1968.

Ruddell, R.B. *Reading-language instruction: Innovative practices.* Englewood Cliffs, NJ: Prentice-Hall, 1974.

Ruddell, R.B. Psycholinguistic implications for a systems of communication model. In H. Singer and R.B. Ruddell (Eds.), *Theoretical models and processes of reading*, second edition. Newark, DE: International Reading Association, 1976a.

Ruddell, R.B. Language acquisition and the reading process. In H. Singer and R.B. Ruddell (Eds.), *Theoretical models and processes of reading*, second edition. Newark, DE.: International Reading Association, 1976b.

Ruddell, R.B. A study of teaching effectiveness variables of influential teachers. In M.P. Douglass (Ed.), *Claremont Reading Conference, 40th Yearbook*. Claremont, CA: Claremont Graduate School, 1983.

Ruddell, R.B., and Haggard, M.R. Oral and written language acquisition and the reading process. In H. Singer and R.B. Ruddell (Eds.), *Theoretical models and processes of reading*, third edition. Newark, DE: International Reading Association, 1985.

Rumelhart, D.E. Notes on schema for stories. In D.G. Bobrow and A.M. Collins (Eds.), *Representation and understanding: Studies in cognitive science*. New York: Academic Press, 1975.

Rumelhart, D.E. Toward an interactive model of reading. In S. Dornic (Ed.), *Attention and performance, VI*. Hillsdale, NJ: Erlbaum, 1976.

Rumelhart, D.E. Understanding and summarizing brief stories. In D. LaBerge and S. Samuels (Eds.), *Basic processes in reading: Perception and comprehension*. Hillsdale, NJ: Erlbaum, 1977.

Rumelhart, D.E. Schemata: The building blocks of cognition. In J.T. Guthrie (Ed.), *Comprehension and teaching: Research reviews*. Newark, DE: International Reading Association, 1981.

Rumelhart, D.E., and McClelland, J.L. Interactive processes through spreading activation. In A.M. Lesgold and C.A. Perfetti (Eds.), *Interactive processes in reading*. Hillsdale, NJ: Erlbaum, 1981.

Rumelhart, D.E., and Ortony, A. The representation of knowledge in memory. In R.C. Anderson, R.J. Spiro, and W.E. Montague (Eds.), *Schooling and the acquisition of knowledge*. Hillsdale, NJ: Erlbaum, 1977.

Rumelhart, D.E., and Norman, D.A. Accretion, tuning, and restructuring: Three modes of learning. In J. Cotton and R. Klatzky (Eds.), *Semantic factors in cognition*. Hillsdale, NJ: Erlbaum, 1978.

Sacks, H., Schegloff, E. and Jefferson, G. A simplest systematics for the organization of turn-taking for conversation. *Language, 50* (1974), 696-735.

Salame, P. and Baddeley, A. Disruption of short term memory by unattended speech: Implications for the structure of working memory. *Journal of Verbal Learning and Verbal Behavior, 21* (1982), 150-164.

Samuels, S.J. Effects of pictures on learning to read, comprehension, and attitudes. *Review of Educational Research, 40* (1970), 397-407.

Samuels, S.J., Biesbrock, E., and Terry, P.R. The effect of pictures on children's attitudes toward presented stories. *Journal of Educational Research, 67* (1974), 243-246.

Samuels, S.J., and Jeffery, W.E. Discriminability of words and letter cues used in learning to read. *Journal of Educational Psychology, 57* (1966), 337-340.

Scolon, R. A real early stage. In E. Ochs and B.B. Schieffelin (Eds.), *Developmental pragmatics*. New York: Academic Press, 1979.

Schank, R.C. *Conceptual information processing*. Amsterdam: North-Holland, 1975.

Schank, R.C., and Ableson, R.P. *Scripts, plans, goals, and understanding*. Hillsdale, NJ: Erlbaum, 1977.

Shimron, J., and Navon, D. The dependence on graphemes and on their translation to phonemes in reading: A developmental perspective. *Reading Research Quarterly, 17* (1982), 210-228.

Shnayer, S.W. Relationships between reading interests and reading comprehension. In J.A. Figurel (Ed.), *Reading and realism*. Newark, DE: International Reading Association, 1969.

Silberman, H.F. *Exploratory research on a beginning reading program*. Technical Memorandum No. TM-895/100/00. Santa Monica, CA: System Development Corporation, 1964.

Singer, H. Conceptualization in learning to read: New frontiers in college-adult reading. In G.B. Shick and M.M. May (Eds.), *Fifteenth Yearbook of the National Reading Conference*, 1966.

Slobin, D.I. *Psycholinguistics*. Glenview, IL: Scott, Foresman, 1979.

Smith, H.L., Jr. *Linguistic science and the teaching of English*. Cambridge: Harvard University Press, 1957.

Soffietti, J.P. Why children fail to read: A linguistic analysis. *Harvard Educational Review, 25* (1955), 63-84.

Sparks, P.E., and Fay, L.C. An evaluation of two methods of teaching reading. *Elementary School Journal, 57* (1957), 386-390.

Speaker, R.B., Jr. The processing of text and prediction during narratives. Paper presented at the 29th Annual Convention of the International Reading Association, 1984.

Stanovich, K.E. Toward an interactive-compensatory model of individual differences in the development of reading fluency. *Reading Research Quarterly, 16* (1980), 32-71.

Stanovich, K.E. Attentional and automatic context effects in reading. In A.M. Lesgold and C.A. Perfetti (Eds.), *Interactive processes in reading*. Hillsdale, NJ: Erlbaum, 1981.

Stanovich, K.E. Individual differences in the cognitive processes in reading II: Text-level processes. *Journal of Learning Disabilities, 2* (1982), 549-554.

Stanovich, K.E., and West, R.F. On priming by a sentence context. *Journal of Experimental Psychology: General, 112* (1983), 1-36.

Stein, B.S., Bransford, J.D., Franks, J.J., Owings, R.A., Vye, N.J., and McGraw, W. Differences in the precision of self-generated elaborations. *Journal of Experimental Psychology: General, 111* (1982), 399-405.

Stein, N.L., and Glenn, C.G. An analysis of story comprehension in elementary school children. In R. Freedle (Ed.), *Discourse processing: Multidisciplinary perspectives*. Hillsdale, NJ: Erlbaum, 1978.

Stevens, K.C. Can we improve reading by teaching background information? *Journal of Reading, 25* (1982), 326-329.

Tanyzer, H.J., and Alpert, H. Three different basal reading systems and first grade reading achievement. *Reading Teacher, 19* (1966), 636-642.

Taylor, B. Children's memory for expository text after reading. *Reading Research Quarterly, 15* (1980), 399-411.

Thorndyke, P.W. Cognitive structures in comprehension and memory of narrative discourse. *Cognitive Psychology, 9* (1977), 77-110.

Turner, A., and Greene, E. *The construction and use of a propositional text base*. Technical Report No. 63, Institute for the Study of Intellectual Behavior, University of Colorado at Boulder, 1977.

Venezky, R.L. English orthorgraphy: Its graphic structure and relation to sound. *Reading Research Quarterly, 2* (1967), 75-106.

Walberg, H.J., and Tsai, S. Reading achievement and attitude productivity among 17 year olds. *Journal of Reading Behavior, 15* (1983), 41-53.

Walker, C.H., and Meyer, B.J.F. Integrating different types of information in text. *Journal of Verbal Learning and Verbal Behavior, 19* (1980), 263-275.

Wardaugh, R. Linguistics—reading dialogue. *Reading Teacher, 21* (1968), 432-441.

West, R.F., Stanovich, K.E., Freeman, D.J., and Cunningham, A.E. The effect of sentence context on word recognition in second and sixth grade children. *Reading Research Quarterly, 19* (1983), 6-15.

Whaley, J.F. Readers' expectations for story structures. *Reading Research Quarterly, 17* (1982), 90-114.

Wigfield, A., and Asher, S.R. Social and motivational influences on reading. In P.D. Pearson (Ed.), *Handbook of reading research*. New York: Longman, 1984.

Yekovich, F.R., and Thorndyke, P.W. An evaluation of alternative functional models of narrative schemata. *Journal of Verbal Learning and Verbal Behavior, 20* (1981), 454-469.

Inferential Model

Cognitive Psychology and Discourse: Recalling and Summarizing Stories

Teun A. van Dijk
University of Amsterdam

Walter Kintsch
University of Colorado

1 Discourse in Psychology: A Short Survey

1.1 Parallel to the elaboration of text grammars in linguistics, there has been increasing attention in psychology for the cognitive processing of discourse. This development is a natural consequence of theoretical and experimental work on meaningful material, i.e. on semantic information processing, begun in the sixties, which completed psychological research on morphonological and syntactic structures of sentences in the generative-transformational paradigm. It was soon understood that the processing of syntactic structures depends on underlying semantic structures of sentences, and that memory for verbal utterances is predominantly semantic (Kintsch 1972, 1977, and other contributions in Tulving and Donaldson, eds. 1972.). Similarly, it now seems obvious that the interpretation of sentences is a function of the verbal and nonverbal context in which a sentence is uttered, and that the conceptual knowledge structure of our memory not only depends on the interpretation of isolated sentences, but also on the understanding and processing of whole discourses. In this paper we will briefly sketch the main tenets of this psychological approach to discourse, and report some of our own theoretical and experimental findings in this field, in particular with respect to the ability to recall and summarize stories.

 1.2 One of the first psychologists who systematically studied discourse processing was F. C. Bartlett. In his influential book, *Remembering* (1932), he describes a series of experiments in which an American Indian story had to be recalled after various delays by the same test person, or serially reproduced by several test persons, i.e. each test person had to tell the story as he recalled it to a next test person. He found that recall for details of description, style or mode of

Reprinted from *Current Trends in Textlinguistics*, W.U. Dressler, Editor. New York: De Gruyter, 1977. With permission of the authors and the publisher.

presentation of the story was very weak through the various reproductions of the same test person, but that the general outline of the story, once established, is remarkably constant even after long delays (of months or even years). Elements of the story which were poorly understood for cultural reasons, were transformed to more familiar structures. Recall is not mere reproduction, but involves reasoning and explaining. In other words, memory and hence recall are essentially constructive and are based on rationalisations of different sorts and on the current knowledge, interests, and emotional attitude of the subject with respect to the story and its content. From these and the many other experiments he carried out on remembering, Bartlett formulated a theory of recall which still influences most current work in this domain. One of the key notions is that of *schema*, which is characterized as an active principle in our memory (re-)organizing elements of recall into structured wholes. In perception and language understanding we interpret and recall all new information with respect to our established schemata, which are both cognitively and socially determined.

Paul (1959) replicated some of Bartlett's experiments many years later, focusing attention especially on a better experimental design, more adequate discourse analysis, and on the variables of degree of explication and familiarity of the stories. Discourse with a higher degree of internal explication is better recalled, whereas more unfamiliar themes tend to lead to more incoherent reproductions than familiar themes of a story. Paul discovered two systematically different styles of recall: some subjects tend to rather good and faithful reproduction of the original story, whereas others leave away detail, import their own elements (e.g. explications), and tend to skeletonize more than the better retainers. Characteristically, the latter group better recalls nonexplicated stories. Although our insight into memory for discourse at present is constantly increasing, little is known about these individual differences in recall due to different styles, interests, preferences, and knowledge (schemata).

1.3 Partly within, partly outside the gestalt tradition of Bartlett and within the so-called verbal learning paradigm in cognitive psychology of the fifties and sixties, some scattered experiments were carried out, which brought little systematic theoretical insight and explication, but at least provided a number of facts to be explained.

Thus Cofer (1941) in his early experiments with prose passages also taken from folk tales established the well-known fact that verbatim learning of prose is much more difficult than what he called logical learning, i.e. the learning of the essential idea of a passage, especially when the passages are long.

Gomulicki (1956) paid more detailed attention to the elements which are deleted in reproductions of prose passages, and found that the probability of recall of an element is directly related to the degree of contribution of that element to the total meaning of the passage. The process of understanding a passage involves a ranking of importance of the various elements, and more in general abstraction from the detailed input. Thus, in narratives the units of agent and action are better recalled than descriptions due to their different importance or relevance for the story. Retention of elements from discourse may, of course, be enhanced or impaired by various means. Slamecka (1959), for example, found that interpolated passages with a similar topic reduced retention of the original passage. Whereas many of the experiments carried out pertained to learning of individual words, ideas, or sentences from discourse (see e.g. Newman and Saltz, 1960), Lee (1965) attempted to demonstrate that what we learn from discourse essentially depends upon its global (he uses the term molar) hierarchical structure. Expressions of high level structure, for example, are the initial paragraph with the outline of the story, the title, and the summary or conclusion. We will give a theoretical explanation of these and similar findings and assumptions.

Similarly, Lachman and Dooling (1968) distinguished between processes of word understanding and recall and those involving categories, themes, or summaries of whole discourses, which are core units around which the lexical units are organized. Pompi and Lachman (1967) are more specific and postulate special surrogate structures involving themes, images, schemata, abstracts, or summaries, and which do not directly depend on the meanings of the individual words. This idea will also be elaborated theoretically.

That thematic or schematic representation of the content of discourse as it is represented (for example in titles) directly influences understanding, especially of vague or ambiguous passages, was demonstrated by Dooling and Lachman (1971). Subjects had no difficulty interpreting such passages if a title was given, but could hardly understand what the passage was about without such a title. It follows, as was shown also in several papers in educational psychology, that the use of titles, outlines, summaries, and thematic words within the passage positively influences understanding, organization in memory and recall of the discourse.

1.4 More systematic research on the cognitive properties of discourse followed in the early seventies. Many of the contributions to the Carroll and Freedle (1972) volume treated aspects of discourse and their influence on the organization of memory and recall. Whereas it is firmly established, at least since the experiments of Sachs (1967), that comprehension and long term memory are basically semantic, it now becomes imperative to investigate the structures of semantic information in discourse and memory, what levels of semantic interpretation should be distinguished, and why some semantic information is better recalled than other. Thus, Freedle, in the volume mentioned, attacks the difficult problem of topic understanding or construction in discourse and the relations between topics and so-called key words. Continuing the basic ideas of Bartlett, Crothers (1972) also assumes that memory structures and recall of discourse are determined by the overall structure or gist of the discourse, and he identifies this structure with that of the superior nodes in a hierarchical tree. His data, however, did not confirm his hypothesis probably because of the type of hierarchical structures postulated (see Crothers 1975). Frederiksen (1972) finally shows that superordinate processing also must take place in the processes of inference and recall of logical arguments, but that the context, i.e. the specific tasks required from the subject, may heavily influence the nature of the structures assigned or the inferences drawn, a point which is emphasized by Rothkopf (1972) in the same volume.

1.5 Some of the problems and hypotheses mentioned have been treated in our own earlier work on discourse. Referring to Bartlett, van Dijk in various papers and his dissertation (1972) assumed that the notion of *macrostructure* (to be explicated in more detail), representing the global organization of the semantic structure of a discourse, makes explicit notions such as theme, plot, idea, or schema, used in earlier psychological work, and that such macrostructures organize both the production and the comprehension, storage and recall of complex verbal structures such as discourses. Kintsch (1974), in a series of papers, shows that discourse comprehension is semantic, propositionally based, and that surface structure complexity only influences understanding under specific reading time restrictions. Important is the experimental confirmation of the assumption that all processes involved in discourse understanding, question answering, problem solving, recall, and recognition, etc. are not only based on those propositions which are explicitly expressed in the discourse, but also on those which are deductively or inductively implied by expressed propositions. That is, discourse comprehension has an important inference making component.

2   Current Research on Discourse, Cognition, and Knowledge

2.1 The interest for discourse processing is spreading rapidly at the moment. Various dissertations, monographs, and volumes of articles have appeared or are in print, which show a more acute feeling for the necessity of a theoretical framework for the earlier data and assumptions; many of the intuitive notions used before were felt inadequate. These actual developments take place in cognitive and educational psychology on the one hand and in artificial intelligence on the other hand, in both cases closely linked with advances in linguistics, rhetorics, philosophy, and philosophical logic, within the broader framework of what is now being called cognitive science.

2.2 Barnard in his dissertation (1974) tried to explain certain recall properties of prose on the basis of its cohesion, a notion he established operationally, not theoretically: a discourse is more cohesive if more subjects reconstruct it from the set of its scrambled sentences. In free recall the more cohesive texts, under this definition, were not better recalled as measured by the number of idea units (undefined) and inaccuracies. Similarly, he assessed the global thematic structure of discourse by having subjects delete what they intuitively think are the less important sentences of the text. When more than half of the subjects agree on the most thematic sentences these are also recalled better. Barnard talks about two levels of discourse comprehension, first the interpretation of individual propositions and second the formation of subunits of sets of propositions, organized hierarchically. Meyer (1975) in her dissertation takes a more theoretical approach to the representation of discourse structure. Sequences of sentences from a discourse are assigned a hierarchical structure based on rhetorical categories denoting the specific relations between the sentences, such as specification, explication, or cause. Her experiments show that the sentences located high in this hierarchical structure are better recalled and more resistant against forgetting. One of the problems in this kind of research is the explanation of memory elements which are not explicitly expressed in the discourse, but which, by inference or construction, may occur in the recall protocols. Comprehension and recall of discourse, and of semantic information in general, is in part based on imported implied elements coming from particular or general schemata representing our knowledge of the kind of discourse, the topic treated, and the context of use (task, problem). (For comments on Meyer and for further experiments, see Thorndyke, 1975.)

2.3 This role of our knowledge of the world, as it is represented in memory, in the understanding of discourse has received attention in recent work in artificial intelligence. Charniak (1972) in his computer simulation of the interpretation of children's stories clearly demonstrates that the interpretation of each sentence of a story involves a large amount of conventional knowledge about objects, actions, and transactions and their usual preconditions and consequences. This knowledge, just as the meaning postulates of the lexicon of a language, need not be explicitly expressed in the text. Each sentence (information) is interpreted with respect to a certain topic initiated earlier in the discourse and invoking a "demon" which inspects following sentences for information which belongs to the knowledge structure it covers. For instance, the concept of "birthday" activates a demon involving such elements as birthday cake, games and presents, which then may be coherently expected in the following part of the discourse. Similarly, at a lower level, for the structure of birthday games or present giving.

Minsky (1975) in a highly influential paper has generalized these results for information processing in general, and introduces the notion of a *frame*. Although the precise nature of frames is not yet very clear, they function as abstract units of data and procedures (rules) in the organization and interpretation of data. The existence of a frame for chair, room, story, etc. guarantees that we always know, recognize, or interpret an object to be a chair (or the same chair) even if we see it under many different transformations (e.g. various angles). Similarly, we are able to interpret and recognize the abstract schema (plot) of stories under many linguistic or narrative transformations of detail. Frames may be devised for different kinds of knowledge of the world. Thus, Schank (1975), using the term *script*, shows that action and the comprehension of action discourse with respect to the concept *restaurant* depends on the conventional data structure we have available about restaurants and eating in restaurants: the usual place-time properties of restaurants and restaurant visits; the usual persons and their typical roles and actions; and the possible courses of action in calling a waitress, ordering food, eating, paying, and leaving. (See also the other contributions in Bobrow and Collins, 1975.) We will not be concerned so much with the actual structure of frames or scripts, but rather with their uses or functions in the comprehension, organization, and retrieval of information from discourse.

2.4 From this brief description of some work in psychology and artificial intelligence about discourse processing a great number of hypotheses, notions, suggestions, problems, and experimental variables emerge.

Clearly, first of all, we need a sound theory and grammar of discourse structure, because the different properties of this structure determine all aspects of cognitive processing. Assuming that we know how sentences (surface morphonological and syntactic structures) are assigned conceptual and propositional meaning structures, it should be investigated how propositions are interpreted relative to each other, how they are combined into larger semantic units, and how these are organized in memory, and finally how our conventional knowledge, personal style and interests, and the specific pragmatic context of action and interaction (the tasks to be carried out) determine these processes of understanding, memory organization, integrations with extant knowledge, and retrieval in (re-)production.

It will be our task in the following sections to attack some of these problems by devising a theoretical framework which can explain the results of a number of experiments carried out with a particular type of discourse, viz. stories.

3 Discourse, Macrostructures, and Narrative

3.1 Due to space limitations we are unable to specify here the full theoretical framework reconstructing the ability of language users to partially reproduce and summarize previously acquired information from discourse. The assumption, however, is that discourse processing (understanding, organization, retrieval) is a function of the structures assigned to the discourse during input. We are aware of the fact that recall and summarizing are also functions of the relations between the acquired information and existing knowledge, interests, and intentions, but these factors will not be investigated in this paper. The theoretical framework necessary to describe and explain the important linguistic and cognitive phenomena mentioned above is a complex one. It consists of several subtheories (for more details, cf. van Dijk, 1977a).

(i) A theory of discourse, consisting of

    a) A grammar of discourse, with at least

       - a theory of semantic representations (propositions) for sentences and sequences of sentences (microstructure);

       - a theory of semantic representations for global discourse structures (macrostructures); and

       - a theory relating microstructures with macrostructures.

b) A more general theory of (nonlinguistic) discourse structures, with specific theories for different kinds of discourse; in our case, e.g., a theory
of narrative structures; this theory of narrative structures is itself based on
a theory and logic of action and action description.

(ii) A theory or model of discourse structure processing, in particular of semantic
information, i.e. for comprehension/interpretation, storage in memory,
memory transformations, retrieval, and (re-)production and use/application.

(iii) A more general theory for complex cognitive information processing, in
which the ability to process discourse is related to our ability to perceive,
interpret, and memorize complex events and actions after visual input, and
to plan or organize and execute complex actions, both bodily and mental
(reasoning, problem solving).

It goes without saying that this is too ambitious a program.

3.2 Since we assumed that discourse processing is a function of the structures assigned to the discourse during input, our first task is to find a sound
representation of discourse structures. Earlier it has been emphasized that although morphonological and syntactic structures of sentences play a role in comprehension, they are not regularly stored in long term memory (except for some
stylistic exceptions) so they will be neglected here, as well as the grammatical
rules and cognitive operations under which they interact with semantic representations. Similarly, we will not be concerned with the pragmatic structures of the
communicative contexts, e.g. the properties of speech acts (underlying intentions, purposes, knowledge, etc. of language users), in which discourses are or
may be produced and interpreted. It is undoubtedly the case that the actual meaning assigned to a sentence or discourse in conversation depends on context variables, especially when we understand *meaning* to comprise also the *function* of the
discourse (as a promise, threat, etc.). Hence we will focus on the proper semantic structure of discourse, as it is invariant for all possible contexts, assuming that
these semantic structures are the basis for all particular meanings and interpretations in context.

3.3 The semantic structure of discourse is the formal reconstruction of what
is nontechnically called the information or content of a discourse. It has been
briefly announced that we distinguish between two different levels of meaning in
discourse, viz. between that of its actual sentences and sequences of sentences,
and that of parts of the discourse or of the discourse as a whole. The latter kind of
meaning structures will be called macrostructures, and will be discussed.

At the microlevel the semantics assigns sequences of *propositions* to the sequence of sentences of the discourse. Several propositions may be expressed by
one sentence, depending on certain semantic, pragmatic, stylistic (and cognitive
and social) factors not to be discussed here, or must be expressed by a sequence
of sentences.

Propositions are taken to have the usual form: n-place predicate, n arguments, preceded by quantifiers binding variables, and by operators of various

kinds (modalities). Propositions combine in *compound* propositions and *sequences* of propositions, which are pairwise *connected*, e.g. as expressed by connectives in natural language. Connection conditions are based on relations between *facts*, viz. the denotata of (asserted) propositions in possible worlds, and relative to a *topic of discourse* (for detail, see van Dijk, 1977a, Ch. 3). Connection is a specific kind of *coherence*, defined over sequences of propositions, not only in terms of relations between facts, in some possible world and relative to a topic of discourse, but also in terms of intensional and extensional relations between parts of propositions (quantifiers, predicates, arguments).

A distinction is made between an *implicit text base* and an *explicit text base* underlying a discourse, where the first is actually expressed, and the second is a theoretical construction in which also those propositions are postulated which are necessary to establish coherence, e.g. meaning postulates and propositions from our knowledge of the world coming from frames as discussed above. These interpolated propositions are those which are presupposed by the propositions expressed in the discourse, and constitute the basis of the *relative interpretation* of the expressed propositions of the discourse.

3.4 The global meaning of a discourse is represented by *semantic macrostructures*. These will also be represented as propositions. Hence we need semantic mappings, which we call *macrorules*, in order to relate microstructures with macrostructures (for detailed discussion and linguistic and cognitive motivation for these kind of structures, see van Dijk, 1977a, b). Characteristic of macrostructures is that they are *entailed* by the sequence of propositions (microstructure) of the discourse. Their function is to *reduce* and *organize* information. That is, they delete and combine sequences of propositions, under certain specified conditions. Due to their *recursive* nature, macrorules generate not one macrostructure, but several macrostructures at increasingly more global levels of semantic representation, where *the* macrostructure is the top most macrostructure. A general constraint on macrorules is that no proposition may be deleted which is a presupposition for a subsequent (macro-)proposition in the discourse. We distinguish provisionally four macrorules, which are not formalized here:

MR-1: DELETION

Of a sequence of propositions we may delete all those denoting an accidental property of a discourse referent (under the general constraint: if not necessary for the interpretation of following propositions).

MR-2: GENERALIZATION

Of a sequence of propositions we may substitute any subsequence by a proposition defining the immediate superconcept of the micropropositions.

MR-3: SELECTION

Of a sequence of propositions we may delete all propositions which represent a normal condition, component or consequence of a fact denoted by another proposition (according to general postulate or frame).

MR-4: CONSTRUCTION

Of a sequence of propositions we may substitute each subsequence by a proposition if they denote normal conditions, components or consequences of the macroproposition substituting them.

We see that in rules MR-1 and MR-2 the information is *irrecoverably* lost, whereas in MR-3 and MR-4 information is partly (inductively) recoverable by general knowledge of postulates and frame knowledge concerning normal conditions, components and consequences.

Examples: MR-1: < Mary played with a ball. The ball was blue > ⇒ < Mary played with a ball > ; MR-2: < Mary played with a doll. Mary played with blocks,... > ⇒ < Mary played with toys > ; MR-3: < I went to Paris. So, I went to the station, bought a ticket, took the train,... > ⇒ < I went to Paris (by train) > ...; MR-4: < I went to the station, bought a ticket,... > ⇒ < I traveled (to Paris) by train > .

Many details and specific constraints are omitted here. One of them, for instance, is that the rules must remain as specific as possible, i.e., define immediate super-sets, super-concepts, etc. In the next section, it will be shown how these general semantic rules organizing the meaning of discourse also at higher levels of representation, are also crucial in cognitive information processing, e.g. in understanding discourse.

3.5 Next, we need more specific structures defining the characteristics of stories, because they also determine the cognitive processing of the discourse, viz. *narrative structures*. Note that these are not specifically linguistic (semantic) but are mapped on semantic structures. More in particular the categories involved are to be connected with *macrostructures* of discourse. That is, one category may dominate a whole sequence of propositions, as represented by one macroproposition. These categories are well-known and need not be spelled out here (e.g. setting, complication, resolution, evaluation, moral, and further categories defining the hierarchical syntax of narrative, see e.g. van Dijk, 1975 for example). The specific narrative structures may be called superstructures in order to account for the fact that they also operate globally, but are distinct from semantic macrostructures. Narrative categories are based on more general notions from the theory of action and action description, which define the notion of an act, the condition of success of an act; conditions, components, and consequences of acts; different types of acts; and the ways in which acts are described in natural language discourse (for detail, see van Dijk, 1976a, and reference given there). In these terms we not only are able to define notions such as auxiliary action/helper, obstructing action/antagonist, etc. but also the basis for the operation of semantic macrorules on action discourse in general (because we know what conditions/causes, components, and consequences of actions are). For instance, since intentions and purposes are necessary conditions or components of actions, descriptions of them may be deleted.

Similarly, we are able to define levels of completeness of action description, relative to the number of actions or the globality of the actions represented. Most natural action discourses are incomplete, simply because it is mostly semantically impossible and pragmatically irrelevant to describe all actions of a given course of action. Thus, natural discourse may also be overcomplete when too many details are given relative to the level of description, or subcomplete when certain actions are not described which must be known in order to be able to understand other actions.

3.6 Finally, some remarks are necessary about the relations between macrostructures and frames (see also van Dijk 1977b). A frame, essentially, is a structure of conventional knowledge about typical situations, events or activities. Macrorules are organizing principles of complex information processing; macrostructures only exist with respect to more detailed levels of information. Since a frame is a complex unit of information, handling it properly requires that it has macrostructure. In that case the macrostructure has a general, conventional nature, whereas the macrostructure of individual discourses has a particular nature (except again the categories and rules organizing macrostructures conventionally, as in narrative discourse).

One of the frames used in the (re-)production and interpretation of the story by Boccaccio used in our experiments reported below, is that of TRADE. Such a frame must have a macrostructure something of the following form:

MERCHANT(X) and MERCHANT(Y) and EXCHANGE(X,Y,Z) and GOODS(Z) and PURPOSE$_X$ (MAKE PROFIT(X))(...)

That is, such a global structure may partially coincide with the conceptual information of the meaning postulates of the lexicon. The frame, then, specifies the different (inter-)actions involved in the exchange, the conditions of success or failure (e.g. competition), the kind of goods which are tradable, the means of transport used depending on the particular time and culture, etc. The global organization of a frame allows us to distinguish what are its central or relevant properties, i.e. the essential components, and especially allows the application of the frame at different levels of generality or detail. In order to understand a sentence like "International trade has gone back last year due to the economic crisis in the world" in a newspaper economic article, we need not activate our whole trade-frame, but only its top-level, i.e. macroinformation ("international exchange of goods as a component of economic structures").

A flexible use of the nearly too powerful tool of conceptual conventional frames therefore requires rules of application specifying for each kind of situation or (con-)text, which information from the frame is required.

In a story about a merchant who wants to become rich by international trade, we may expect a certain number of propositions denoting facts which are consistent with the conventional trade-frame, e.g. buying goods, shipping them, trying to sell them. Hence, conversely, a macrostructure of that part of the discourse may simply be "X wanted to trade", according to MR-4. Similarly, much information may also be left implicit in the discourse, due to our general frame knowledge. In other words, a discourse must at least express that information which does not belong to the frame, the information which is inconsistent with the preferred or normal course of events (going bankrupt after unsuccessful trading), and information which entails the essential information of the frame (otherwise we would be unable to identify the particular frame). In (inter-)action frames like that of trade, we also know what the preferred optimal final state should be. If this final state is not realized the discourse must mention it, and this at the same time defines a condition for the narrative category of Complication, which only allows unexpected events. What is a normal course of events for a certain situation, then, is to be formulated in our reconstruction of the cognitive and conventional frames used in the interpretation and transformation of the world.

3.7 We are now in a position to specify the macrorules operating for action discourse in general and narrative discourse in particular, because we now know which sort of propositions are relevant in an appropriate action description and which are not, with respect to a certain level of information abstraction (see van Dijk 1975). Given an action discourse, then, the following types of propositions may in general be abstracted from:

1. Descriptions of reasons, purposes, and intentions for actions and the mental consequences of actions (by our general knowledge of action and rule MR-2 or 4).
2. Descriptions of alternative possible courses of events.
3. Descriptions of auxiliary actions which are normal (by theory of action, and MR-2).
4. Descriptions of properties of states (time, place, objects, individual persons) which do not condition further action (by MR-1).
5. Metadescriptions: propositions announcing, repeating, resuming or commenting other propositions (general principle of nonredundancy).
6. Description of dialogue (by MR-2 if taken as auxiliary for further action; by MR-4 if subsumable by general speech act concept).

The application of these rules (which are not complete and somewhat too strong) yields a macrostructure for an action discourse. The narrative categories further require that each category must be represented in macrostructure. In other words, macrostructures of narrative discourses themselves have a narrative structure.

3.8 The theoretical framework outlined above will be the basis for a description of the cognitive processes involved in the production, comprehension and interpretation, storage and retrieval of discourse in general and of narrative discourse (stories) in particular. It describes the abstract nature of the operations of establishing connections between propositions as expressed by the discourse, the establishment of coherence relations, and the assignment of several macrostructures, possibly with different hierarchically ordered narrative functions. The macrostructures as postulated have important cognitive functions. Not only do they enable the interpretation of complex semantic information, but at the same time they organize this information in memory, and define which information is relatively important and which is relatively unimportant.

On the one hand this provides an explanation of forgetting, and retrievability in recall and recognition. On the other hand the macrorules may be viewed as reconstructing active procedures of information reduction as they occur in abstracting and summarizing (see also Rumelhart, 1975). A summary, then, will be taken as a discourse expressing a macrostructure of another discourse. Note that such a summary has the usual properties of natural discourses: connection, coherence, but also implicitness and relative incompleteness. That is, it only indirectly reflects an abstract macrostructure. The same holds for the strategies and procedures of actual processing: the rules postulated above are only abstract reconstructions of them.

4 Psychological Process Assumptions

There is today no satisfactory psychological processing theory of text comprehension and memory, and we are not about to offer one here. Instead, our strategy is to use the model for the representation of texts that was outlined in the previous sections as a tool with which informative experiments can be designed. It is hoped that these experiments will provide us with the basic empirical foundation of knowledge about text processing that is a necessary precondition for theorizing. In essence, we shall use the representational model to tell us where to look for interesting psychological effects. Previous work has concentrated upon the microstructure of text bases, neglecting the other factors that have been discussed. This was done by working with relatively short paragraphs of text for which the macrostructure out of context is relatively unimportant. In these studies we were concerned with how people infer propositions from the text, how these propositions are connected and ordered. The theory makes certain claims about the representations that result from these processes. Hence we could explore whether the cognitive operations involved in reading comprehension and memory reflect important aspects of these hypothesized representations. Most of these results have already been published in Kintsch (1974) and Kintsch et al., (1975).

In Section 7 some as yet unpublished work will be reported that has been performed during the last years both at the University of Amsterdam and at the University of Colorado. These experiments are concerned primarily with the role of the macrostructure in text comprehension and memory. Three related hypotheses have been investigated. These hypotheses follow directly from the theoretical discussions above.

(i) What is stored in memory (besides some specific information about words and sentences, or other physical aspects of the text which will be neglected here) corresponds to the macrostructure of the text, with some of the microstructure propositions subordinated under the macrostructure categories. In recall, the subjects use the macrostructure as a retrieval cue for the detailed propositional information about the text. Abstracts or summaries are (possibly variable) expressions of the macrostructure.

Table 1 shows a hypothetical (incomplete) example of a memory representation for a story from Boccaccio's *Decameron*. Macrostructure propositions are written out in natural language, microstructure propositions are indicated only as *P*s.

(ii) In order to understand narratives subjects must have available as part of their general knowledge a conventional narrative schema. This schema is used to organize the text base. In our example, the schema consists of those parts of Table 1 that remain after all story specific information is deleted (e.g. the labels inside the boxes are erased, as well as the microstructure propositions at the bottom). Comprehending a story can thus be compared to filling in the empty slots in a preexisting story schema.

(iii) The construction of a macrostructure is a necessary component of comprehension; hence macrostructures are established during reading, rather than at the time of recalling or summarizing a story.

If these three hypotheses can be confirmed, they would have important implications for a processing model of narratives. The outline of such a model would be as follows. We start with a document, the written narrative, and we end up with a document, either a recall protocol, or a summary of the story. Reading the story involves a certain set of perceptual processes that need not concern us here, and three distinct linguistic-conceptual processes: 1) the decoding of the text into words, phrases, and sentences, i.e. the linguistic analyses proper; 2) propositions are inferred from this linguistic material, that is the conceptual meaning is constructed from the verbal text; this is the microstructure of the text; (3) the microstructure propositions are organized into higher order units by semantic macrorules and with the help of a conventional story schema; the units are labelled, and these labels are the macrostructure propositions. The same rules and other rules (e.g. narrative transformations) may again operate upon these macrostructure propositions, creating a hierarchy of macrostructures (corresponding to more and more general summaries of the story). These three processes must occur at least in part sequentially, but they are certainly highly interactive.

Right after reading a narrative, traces from all these processing activities remain in the reader's memory: visual memory traces (what the text looked like, where on a page a certain sentence was, etc.), linguistic memory traces (some actual words and phrases used in the text), microstructure propositions (detailed content of the story), as well as macrostructure propositions (the overall organization of the story in terms of its main events). All of these memory traces may persist in time, but usually the task demands of reading are such that only the higher levels of processing are emphasized, and hence only these result in stable memory traces. One does not usually have much visual, or even linguistic, memory after reading a story, though one certainly can retain such information and some traces of that type are almost always there. The story content, and especially its main events, i.e. its macrostructure, are normally the main concerns of the reader and are remembered best.

When a subject is asked to recall a story he has read, he generates a linguistic output from his memory traces. Whatever remnants of the actual linguistic processing during reading are still available in memory are used for that purpose, but for the most part the text must be reconstructed from the micro- and macrostructure propositions that represent the reader's memory for the meaning of the text.

When the subject is asked to summarize rather than recall the story, his linguistic output is generated directly from the macrostructure propositions, while lower level memory traces tend to be ignored.

5 The role of the macrostructure in comprehension and memory for narratives

5.1 The dominance of the macrostructure in the whole recall of narratives becomes quite evident when one compares recall protocols with abstracts or summaries for the same narratives. Subjects read the story from Boccaccio's *Decameron* (for its structure, see van Dijk 1975). It is about 1600 words long. Some of the subjects were then asked to recall the whole story in writing, while others were asked to write a summary of the main events in the story. A comparison of the recall protocols and the abstracts revealed some interesting similarities. Recall may be characterized as summary-plus-detail; that is, the statements that subjects make in their summaries tend also be included in their recall protocols. In addition, recall protocols contain more information about some of the details of the story, which usually do not appear in summaries. These details consist in part of reconstructions (presumably subjects remembered the macrostructure of the story and on that basis reconstructed plausible details of the story at the time of recall), but also genuine reproductions from the story. This was shown by giving subjects who never had read the story the abstract of the story and asking them to reconstruct the story from the abstract. Such reconstructions differed from genuine recall protocols in that the latter included many pieces of detailed information derived from the story which do not appear in pure reconstructions. Thus we may conclude, quite in accord with the theoretical expectations outlined earlier, that the subject's memory representation for a narrative consists of the macrostructure plus some microstructure propositions that are associated with the appropriate superordinated macrostructure propositions. When asked to recall, the subject uses the macrostructure as a retrieval cue, producing both the macrostructure propositions plus whatever microstructure propositions are still available, and supplementing his recall with plausible reconstructions. When asked to abstract a story, the subjects apparently base their responses directly upon the macrostructure which is stored in memory. It appears, furthermore, that macrostructures are remembered better than microstructure propositions, for if recall is delayed (for 9 days in one study) most microstructure information drops out of the recall protocols, which become almost indistinguishable from summaries.

5.2 We have hypothesized that the reader approaches a narrative with a narrative schema in mind, and that part of the process of comprehending the narrative consists in filling in the empty slots in that schema with appropriate information from the text, viz. the macrostructure propositions. So far we have only shown that something like a macrostructure does indeed emerge when one recalls or summarizes a narrative. But is the knowledge of the appropriate narrative schema in fact a necessary condition for understanding the text? We have tried to approach this question by comparing the way readers summarize texts for which they presumably have available the right narrative schema, and texts for which such schemata are lacking. College students are certainly familiar with the narrative schema upon which stories for the *Decameron* are based (this does not mean that they are aware of the schema, or even able to verbalize it: the rules of linguistic processing are no more available to introspection at the text level than they are at the level of syntactic or phonological analyses). On the other hand, the same subjects are unfamiliar with the structure of American Indian tales. Hence they should be able to write significantly better summaries of *Decameron* stories than of Indian folktales.

The Indian story which we selected for our experiment is an Apache myth about the origin of corn and deer. It is 1600 words long and contains no difficult sentences or unfamiliar words (complicated names were replaced). Nevertheless, our subjects thought the story to be "weird," because it does not conform to their expectations about narratives: the person of the hero is not constant, episodes follow each other with no apparent (i.e. causal) connection, the organization of the story is obscure. The story, of course, does follow a well-developed schema, but one known only to Indians and anthropologists. For comparison, three stories from the *Decameron,* each about 1600 words long, were selected. The subject's task was the same in all cases: to read the story, taking as much time as he likes, and then, again without time restrictions, to write an abstract or summary of the story. In order to ensure comparability between the abstracts from different subjects, all abstracts had to be between 60 and 80 words long; furthermore, the abstract had to be written in complete English sentences. To avoid the boring and distracting task of counting and recounting the number of words in the abstract, subjects typed their abstracts on a computer controlled oscilloscope screen, and the computer displayed for them the number of words written.

All statements (corresponding to propositions, as in our earlier work) used in the abstracts were listed, and for each statement the number of subjects using it in their abstract was noted. One would expect that abstracts of stories for which the reader has available a conventional schema would be more or less the same from one subject to the next. If the process of writing a summary is, indeed, directed by the schema, different subjects should agree at least to some extent about what they include in their summaries. Of course, each reader will employ the summarization rules discussed in Section 4.3 differently, and hence there will be some differences among the abstracts they generate, but certainly there should be considerably more differences when no story schema is available to direct the readers' organization of the story. Our results were in good agreement with this prediction: there was significantly more agreement among subjects about the statements used in the summaries of the *Decameron* stories than about those in the Indian story.

5.3 The strategy of looking at how people summarize or recall stories for which they do not have an appropriate schema available also provides the rationale for a study by Dorothy Poulsen and Eileen Kintsch of how children comprehend stories. Picture stories without text, comprising 15-18 pictures, were selected from children's books and shown to four year olds. After one viewing, the child was asked to describe each picture in his own words. Finally, the child recalled the story as well as he could. The description task was used in addition to the recall task because children at that age typically do not recall stories very well, and the simpler description task provides a better opportunity to study how they comprehend stories.

We were particularly interested in the role that story schemata play in the comprehension processes of four year olds. For that purpose, the pictures that made up our stories were shown either in their natural order, thus permitting the children to follow the story, or in scrambled order, which made it difficult or impossible for the children to figure out the story. In the one story analyzed so far, much better descriptions of the pictures were obtained when the pictures were shown in their natural order. The total number of correct statements made was about 50 percent higher for pictures in natural order than in scrambled order. Scrambling the pictures produced a regression to more primitive styles of expression in these children. The simplest descriptions obtained were labeling responses: the child simply points to objects depicted and labels them "a dog, a wolf, a branch." Such responses were rare in our four year olds when they were describing the pictures in their natural order (4 percent), but they became quite frequent when the pictures were presented out of order (28 percent). However, not all children responded with labeling when they could not comprehend the story that was told by the pictures. Some actively tried to construct a macrostructure, to make some sense of these pictures, even though they were unable to do so. These subjects tended to produce many cognitive statements (the dog *thinks*, the wolf *wants*) or affective statements (the boy is *sad*). Indeed, 20 percent of all responses were of that nature in the scrambled picture condition, compared with only 8 percent when the pictures were shown in order.

It is clear that the availability of a story in the natural order condition played a large role in how subjects described these pictures. These four year olds were responding to the story that the pictures told, not just to each picture separately. When there was no story, they nevertheless tried to make one up — or regressed to an earlier developmental level.

5.4 While the data discussed above indicate that the availability of a macrostructure and a narrative schema may indeed be necessary for the comprehension of a long text, they contain no evidence either for or against the third hypothesis that we made in Section 5, namely that macrostructures are constructed during reading, as an integral part of the comprehension process, rather than at the time of recall or summarizing. The experiment we performed to test this hypothesis is simple, but the argument we make is a little subtle, so we shall first introduce it by means of an analogy to an earlier experiment. One of the studies reported in Kintsch (1974) involves the following argument. From a given text base two texts are constructed, one syntactically simple and one syntactically complex. Subjects read these two versions of the text, and took more time to read the syntactically complex than the simple text. Then subjects were asked some questions (involving inferences) about the text: the way they answered these questions did not depend upon which version they had read, both in terms of percent correct responses and latencies. We concluded from this pattern of results that what these subjects had stored in their memory was independent of the syntactic complexity of the input, i.e. that subjects had stored the meaning of each paragraph in memory in an abstract form, and that the syntactic complexity of the input affected only decoding time, but not what was eventually stored in memory. We now propose to use this type of argument once more, this time not at the syntactic level, but concerning macrostructures. Subjects read the same narrative, but in two versions: some subjects read the story in natural order, with the macrostructure intact, and others read it with the order of the paragraphs randomized. We hypothesized that if readers are indeed constructing macrostructures during reading, those subjects who read the story in natural order should have an easier task than subjects who read the story with the order of paragraphs scrambled; hence reading times should be longer for the scrambled condition. However, after reading both groups of subjects will have constructed the same macrostructures (because, by assumption this is a necessary condition for comprehension) so that if subjects are now asked to summarize the story, there should be no differences in either the quality of the summaries they produce, or in the time they need to write their summaries. The data that we have collected so far confirm these predictions. The average reading time for scrambled stories is 9.85 min., while only 7.45 min. are required to read the same stories in natural order. On the other hand, subjects took on the average 19.33 min. to write abstracts after reading stories in natural order, and 20.04 min., after reading stories in scrambled order. This difference is far from significant statistically. At the same time, subjects agree equally well about what goes into an abstract after reading stories in natural and scrambled order. In fact, it is impossible to tell which abstracts were written by subjects who read natural and scrambled stories. This was confirmed by giving all 24 abstracts to judges, with the instructions to sort them into two piles according to whether the abstract was written from a natural or scrambled story. No judge was able to sort these abstracts with an accuracy significantly better than chance.

5.5 Thus we are left with rather positive evidence regarding all three hypotheses that were suggested in Section 6 about the role of macrostructures in comprehension. Of course, these results are tentative and more systematic experimentation is required before we can be confident about our conclusions.

However, the data are certainly suggestive. It seems that the representation of a text that a reader stores in memory indeed includes both micro- and macrostructures components, and that the linguistic work on text bases provides a reasonably accurate idea of the nature of these memory representations. Secondly, we have obtained some evidence for the notion that story comprehension can be compared with filling in the empty slots of conventional text schemata, and that texts for which no specific schemata are available are organized in idiosyncratic ways with little intersubject agreement. Finally, we found no reason to modify the hypothesis that when subjects are recalling a story, they use the macrostructure as a retrieval cue, supplementing it with whatever detailed information is also available, and that if subjects are asked to summarize a story, the summary is a possible expression of the macrostructure they have stored in memory. We hope that further work along these lines will not only help us to understand better the cognitive processes involved in text comprehension and memory, but will also provide us with some insights about those aspects of text structure that are most relevant for the linguistic analysis of texts.

REFERENCES

Barnard, Philip John. Structure and content in the retention of prose. Doctoral dissertation, University College, London, 1974.

Bartlett, F.C. Remembering. London: Cambridge University Press, 1932.

Bobrow, Daniel G., and Collins, Allan (Eds.). Representation and understanding. New York: Academic Press, 1975.

Carroll, John B., and Freedle, Roy O. (Eds.). Language comprehension and the acquisition of knowledge. Washington, D.C.: Winston; Wiley distrib., 1972.

Charniak, Eugene. Toward a model of children's story comprehension. Doctoral dissertation, MIT, Artificial Intelligence Lab., 1972.

Cofer, Charles N. A comparison of logical and verbatim learning of prose passages of different lengths, American Journal of Psychology, 1941, 54, 1-20.

Crothers, Edward J. Memory structure and the recall of discourse. In Freedle and Carroll (Eds.), 1972, 247-283.

Crothers, Edward J. Paragraph structure description. University of Colorado, Department of Psychology, 1975.

van Dijk, Teun A. Some aspects of text grammars. The Hague: Mouton, 1972.

van Dijk, Teun A. Recalling and summarizing complex discourse. University of Amsterdam, mimeo, 1975.

van Dijk, Teun A. Philosophy of action and theory of narrative, Poetics, 1976, 6, 287-338, 1976a.

van Dijk, Teun A. Complex semantic information processing, paper contributed to the workshop on linguistics and documentation, Stockholm, University of Amsterdam, mimeo, 1976b.

van Dijk, Teun A. Text and context: Explorations in the semantics and pragmatics of discourse. London: Longman, 1977a.

van Dijk, Teun A. Macrostructures, knowledge frames and discourse comprehension, paper contributed to the Carnegie-Mellon symposium on cognition, May 1976. To appear in P. Carpenter and M. Just (Eds.), Cognitive processes in comprehension. Hillsdale, NJ: Erlbaum, 1977b.

Dooling, J.L., and Lachman, R. Effects of comprehension on retention of prose, Journal of Experimental Psychology, 1971, 88, 216-222.

Frederiksen, C.H. Effects of task-induced cognitive operations on comprehension and memory processes. In Carroll and Freedle (Eds.), Language comprehension and the acquisition of knowledge. Washington, D.C.: Winston, 1972, 211-246.

Freedle, Roy O. Language users as fallible information processors: Implications for measuring and modeling comprehension. In Carroll and Freedle (Eds.), Language comprehension and the acquisition of knowledge. Washington, D.C.: Winston, 1972, 169-209.

Gomulicki, B.R. Recall as an abstractive process, *Acta Psychologica*, 1956, 12, 77-94.
Kintsch, Walter. Notes on the structures of semantic memory. In Tulving and Donaldson (Eds.), 1972, 247-308.
Kintsch, Walter. The representation of meaning in memory. Hillsdale, NJ: Erlbaum-Wiley, 1974.
Kintsch, Walter. Memory, language and thinking. New York: Wiley, 1977.
Kintsch, Walter, Kozminsky, Eli, Streby, William J., McKoon, Gail, and Keenan, Janice M., Comprehension and recall of text as a function of content variables, *Journal of Verbal Learning and Verbal Behavior*, 1975, 14, 196-214.
Lachman, R., and Dooling, D.J., Connected discourse and random strings: Effects of number of inputs on recognition and recall, *Journal of Experimental Psychology*, 1968, 77, 507-522.
Lee, W. Supraparagraph prose structures: Its specification, perception, and effects of learning, *Psychological Reports*, 1965, 17, 135-144.
Meyer, Bonnie F. The organization of prose and its effects on memory. Amsterdam: North Holland, 1975.
Minsky, Marvin. A framework for representing knowledge. In P. Winston (Ed.), The psychology of computer vision. New York: McGraw-Hill, 1975.
Newman, S.E., and Saltz, E. Effects on learning from connected discourse, *American Journal of Psychology*, 1960, 73, 587-592.
Paul, I.H. Studies in remembering: The reproduction of connected and extended verbal material, *Psychological Issues*, Monograph Series, 1959.
Pompi, K.F., and Lachman, R. Surrogate processes in the short-term retention of connected discourse, *Journal of Experimental Psychology*, 1967, 75, 143-150.
Rothkopf, Ernst Z. Structural text features and the control of processes in learning from written materials. In Carroll and Freedle (Eds.), *Language comprehension and the acquisition of knowledge*. Washington, D.C.: Winston, 1972, 315-335.
Rumelhart, David E. Notes on a schema for stories. In Bobrow and Collins (Eds.), *Representation and understanding studies in cognitive science*, 1975, 211-236.
Sachs, Jacqueline. Recognition memory for syntactic and semantic aspects of connected discourse, *Perception and Psychophysics*, 1967, 2, 437-442.
Schank, Roger C. The structures of episodes in memory. In Bobrow and Collins (Eds.), *Representation and understanding studies in cognitive science*, 1975, 237-272.
Slamecka, N.J. Studies of retention of connected discourse, *American Journal of Psychology*, 1959, 72, 409-416.
Thorndyke, Perry W. Cognitive structures in human story comprehension and memory. Doctoral dissertation, Stanford, 1975.
Tulving, Endel, and Donaldson, Wayne (Eds.). Organization of memory. New York: Academic Press, 1972.

NOTE AND ACKNOWLEDGEMENTS

This paper is an enlarged version of Walter Kintsch and Teun A. van Dijk, "Recalling and Summarizing Stories," of which a French translation "Comment on se rappelle et on résume des histoires" was published in *Langages*, 40 (1975), 98-116.

This paper was supported by a grant to Walter Kintsch from the National Institute for Mental Health, MH-15872, and to Teun A. van Dijk from the Netherlands Organization for the Advancement of Pure Research (zwo) and the Faculty of Letters of the University of Amsterdam. These grants are gratefully acknowledged.

Transactional Psycholinguistic Model

Unity in Reading

KENNETH S. GOODMAN
University of Arizona

Introduction

Reading in this century has received far more attention from those concerned with education and educational research than any of the other language processes. But until recently, it has been very much neglected by scholars in other disciplines studying language and language development.

The result is a highly developed technology of reading instruction with a very shallow theoretical base. This technology tends to isolate reading from the other language processes and from its functional use, treating it largely as an object of instruction, something taught in school.

There have been periodic attempts throughout this century to bring together work from a number of disciplines to create a theoretical base for reading instruction involving understanding of the reading process, of reading development, and of effective instruction. But these efforts have not been sufficient to overcome the inertia built up in the instructional technology. Reading is big business in all senses and the tests, basal readers, and instructional practices which comprise the technology are so highly institutionalized that it becomes hard to use available new knowledge to change instructional practice.

In the past two decades, there has been an explosion of knowledge concerning reading, particularly reading comprehension, in a number of fields such as cognitive psychology, ethnography, linguistics, child language development, artificial intelligence, semiotics, rhetoric, literature, philosophy, and brain study. But the period can be characterized as multidisciplinary rather than interdisciplinary. There is little crossing over from discipline to discipline. There is not much attempt to relate the objectives, questions, and interpretations of each discipline to the others. And there is too little awareness by scholars in each field of the current work in other fields or the previous work done in reading. That means that attempts to apply the insights gained in other fields to instruction in reading have been piecemeal and unintegrated.

Reprinted from Alan C. Purves and Olive Niles (Eds.), *Becoming Readers in a Complex Society.* 83rd Yearbook of the National Society for the Study of Education, Part 1. Chicago: University of Chicago Press, 1984, 79-114. With permission of author and publisher.

This chapter will essay a unified theory of reading based on theory and research from the past and present in a wide range of fields. It will integrate the
knowledge that is emerging concerning the reading process, based on the premise that, regardless of differences in vantage point and focus, the phenomena of
reading are the same for all who study them.

In making this attempt to unify and integrate knowledge, a choice has been
made not to cover everything everyone is doing. The objective is to find the unity
that exists in the current diversity. This unity will be built around a transactional
view.

Many current writers in the several fields studying reading have regarded it
as an interactive process; this chapter will consider it transactive. Rosenblatt has
drawn on Dewey's view that both the knower and the known are changed in the
course of knowing.[1] In a transactional view, the writer constructs a text through
transactions with the developing text and the meaning being expressed. The text
is transformed in the process and so are the writer's schemata (ways of organizing
knowledge). The reader also constructs a text during reading through transactions with the published text and the reader's schemata are also transformed in the
process through the assimilation and accommodation Piaget has described.[2]

In a transactional view, reading is seen as receptive written language, one of
four language processes in literate societies. In the productive generative processes (speaking and writing), a text is generated (constructed) to represent the
meaning. In the receptive processes (listening and reading), meaning is constructed through transactions with the text and indirectly through the text with the
writer. Both generative and receptive processes are constructive, active, and
transactional.

In philosophy and linguistics, speech act theory has emerged as a way of
considering oral language in the context of its use and the roles and intentions of
the participants.[3] The counterpart in written language is the literacy event, an
event in which writer and/or reader transact with and through a text in a specific
context with specific intentions. The concept of the literacy event makes it possible to take a holistic view of written language like the holistic view of oral language provided by speech act theory.

The linguistic transactions in literacy events may be viewed from three vantage points: 1) the process by which the writer produces the text, 2) the characteristics of texts, and 3) the process by which the reader constructs meaning. This
chapter will attempt to look at the work done from each perspective within the
context of the whole literacy event and within a transactional view.

Unitary, Psycholinguistic Processes

Though written language processes appear to vary greatly as they are used in
the wide range of functions and contexts they serve, reading and writing are actually unitary, psycholinguistic processes. In generating language, thought repre-

sents a view of reality and is in turn represented by language. The constraints of the brain, the reality being represented, the schemata of the speaker or writer, the syntax and lexicon of the language, and the situational and social contexts all shape the process. None of these constraints may be ignored or avoided without reduction of the text to nonsense. So there is only one way to create a text that is representative of an author's meaning. And there is also only one way to construct meaning from a text.

These unitary processes are flexible. They will vary with purpose, with audience, with content, with proficiency, with language, with orthography, but they involve universals. There is, thus, diversity within unity in writing and reading.

The Locus of Meaning

Meaning is not a characteristic of texts. Rather, texts are constructed by authors to be comprehended by readers. The meaning is in the author and the reader.[4] The text has a potential to evoke meaning but no meaning in itself. How well the writer constructs the text and how well the reader reconstructs it and constructs meaning will all influence comprehension. But meaning does not pass between writer and reader. It is represented by a writer in a text and constructed from a text by a reader. Characteristics of writer, text, and reader will all influence the resultant meaning.

The Writer and the Text

Language is universal in all human societies. The key human attributes that make human language possible are the ability to think symbolically and the need for highly complex communication that derives from human interdependence.

The fact that human societies develop oral language first is a matter of convenience. The earliest functions of language involve immediate interpersonal transactions. As long as both parties can hear, oral language works admirably for these functions. But human language needs and functions eventually transcend face-to-face contexts as society becomes more mobile and complex. People eventually need to communicate over time and space. Furthermore, our ability to use and perceive symbolic systems is not confined to a single sense, that of hearing. Indeed, all of our senses can and do serve as channels of communication. Written language is visual but so is the manual sign of the deaf. Blind people have learned to use tactile language. What is universal among people is the need and ability to create language. The form it takes depends on its functions and the characteristics of the people who use it.

In human social history, written language is created when interdependence extends beyond the primary community as trade and political structures emerge. It also results from the expansion of the culture beyond the scope of the oral tradition to preserve that culture and pass it on to ensuing generations. People growing up in a literate society need written language as their horizons expand beyond the home. Written language functions derive from these personal and social developments. Written language extends memory and communication. Narrative and expository forms emerge to serve the new functions.

Writers and Their Audiences

Texts are shaped as much by the writers' sense of the characteristics of their readers as they are by the writers' own characteristics. That is as true for a shopping list or a letter as it is for a newspaper report or a novel.

A diary entry intended to be read only by the writer, addressed to an alter ego, "Dear Diary," may presuppose full knowledge on the part of the reader of any reference, however implicit. Detail will stem from a sense that the diary may be reread long in the future when the author/reader may have forgotten some of the events. Letters to close friends and family will assume a body of shared knowledge and experience. But, as the distance between writer and reader grows, the writer will need to balance a sense of the audience with sense of how much background and detail must be provided.

Other Constraints on the Writer

In every act of writing, writers are constrained by their own values, their concepts, the experiences they have had and the schemata they have built of them. The purpose of the particular text being created will always be influenced by these personal characteristics of the writer, so that the text will reflect what the writer is as well as what the writer is trying to communicate.

In literacy events, there is a kind of unstated contract between the reader and the writer.[5] From the writer's point of view, this "contract" means that the reader will want to understand and will try to do so. No text can be so successfully constructed by a writer that it can be comprehended without the reader actively trying to make sense of it. The writer can create only a potential for comprehending by making effective use of the forms and structures of written language to express articulate ideas that are appropriate for and comprehensible to the intended audience.

An effective text is one that not only expresses the author's meaning but is comprehensible to others. It must be a full enough representation of the meaning to suit the needs, background, schemata, and interests of the readers. That is the other side of the writer-reader contract. Readers expect writers to be trying to say something sensible in a sensible manner.

Language, written language included, is part of a complex human culture. Its forms and uses are constrained by the values and customs of the culture. The culture develops textual forms and pragmatic constraints. Certain phrases such as

"Very truly yours" or "Once upon a time" become necessary parts of certain written language forms.

But social constraints on the lexico-grammar of language are far more pervasive and subtle. Some apply to both oral and written language. Feminists have recently demonstrated how the language incorporates the societal attitude of male supremacy. This has many evidences in language but it provides a particular problem for the writer attempting to use general third person references.

Still, any text is very much what the writer has made it. The writer is engaged in a living transaction with the text that is being created. To make a text comprehensible, the writer must create within the constraints of purpose, content, language, logic, structure, and form, and within situational and social contexts. But there is plenty of room within these constraints for the writer to develop a unique voice and style. The genius of human language is that it becomes the supple servant of expression and not a straightjacket on it.

Writing as a generative language process has much in common with speech. In both, a text is composed that suits the situation, the intention, and the audience. But speech usually involves oral feedback from the listener or some sort of visual response. Oral language is more recursive and cyclical as points are introduced and reintroduced for further discussion and development. Its chief dimension is time—the sequence in which it is uttered.

The characteristics of written language stem from its functions and purposes and from its use of a two-dimensional medium and a visual input mode. Writers learn to use the strengths of the medium and to work within its limitations. They make use of the fact that texts can be constructed that are more or less durable depending on the purpose and the materials used. And they make use of the fact that they may be reviewed, reconstructed, and polished before they go to the intended audiences. Learning to express thought in writing involves developing control over the forms most suitable for the specific purposes of written language.

Characteristics of Texts

The text, as Halliday and Hasan have defined it, is the "basic unit of meaning in language."[6] It is not simply a set of well-formed sentences composed of words or morphemes. A text must have a unity; and it must represent comprehensibly a coherent and cohesive message.

Physical Characteristics

The text must be sufficiently well formed that communication can take place without any direct contact between the reader and the writer. That constraint interacts with the physical constraints on written text that derive from its characteristics as a more or less permanent two-dimensional medium which must be visually perceptible.

Orthography

How a particular written language uses its two-dimensional space is arbitrary, just as which side of the road a society chooses to drive on is arbitrary. Although some forms of picture writing seem to have used the space in a nonlinear manner, most writing is linear; that is, it uses either horizontal or vertical lines (or both) that follow directional patterns. Historically, every possible pattern seems to have been used: left to right, right to left, or alternating directions of horizontal lines and top to bottom or bottom to top vertical lines.

Modern Japanese uses the traditional vertical writing and a horizontal alternative. Hebrew goes from right to left, but numerals are written left to right in the same texts. The characteristics of the orthography also vary within the limits that it must be both producible and visually perceptible. It must serve both the writer and the reader.

All orthographies ultimately represent meaning, but some are designed to relate to the oral language as well. Since oral and written language have different constraints that derive from the differences in the media, there can be no simple one-to-one correspondence between the two systems. However, some systems, such as alphabetic and syllabic orthographies, are designed to provide correspondences more closely, while others, such as ideographic systems, where characters represent ideas and concepts, make no attempt to provide correspondences.

Systems that represent ideas will have many more symbols than alphabetic or syllabic orthographies, and thus make writing more complex. But Chinese characters are composed of a repertoire of strokes, so that Chinese writing is not as complex as it seems.

It is a common belief that alphabetic systems are much easier to learn and use than other writing systems. But, considering the level of literacy in Japan and China, nonalphabetic systems seem to serve their users quite well. Japan uses a very complex orthography that combines two forms of Chinese characters with a system of syllabic symbols. Japanese uses the Roman alphabet freely to represent borrowings from European languages.

Ideographic writing has an intrinsic advantage over other systems. Since such writing represents meaning directly, ideographic texts may be understood by those literate in the system regardless of what language they speak. Mathematics uses an ideographic system that has become almost universal across languages. Anyone who knows the system can understand $6 + 5 = 11$ or $2(a\text{-}b) = cd$.

Spelling

Languages that employ alphabetic writing can be read only by those who know the language. Furthermore, if these languages stayed as close as possible to a strict alphabetic principle with invariant relationships between units of oral and written language, then each dialect community would spell words differently; even idiolect (personal language forms) differences would show up as spelling differences. That would mean that written texts might be less comprehensible if writer and reader had substantial phonological differences. So almost all languages conventionalize spellings across dialects, because written language is intended for use beyond immediate dialect communities in wider language communities.

Because of standardization of spellings, the way the spelling relates to how a word is pronounced in any dialect becomes variable. For example, "almond" has at least four pronunciations in American dialects: /æmɘnd/, /ælmɘnd/, /omɘnd/, /olmɘnd/. For most dialects of English, words like "right," "light," "night" have unnecessary "gh" elements. But in Scottish dialects, the "gh" relates to an actual sound: /rikht/.

Furthermore, the phonology of living dialects is constantly evolving. Over time, the fit between sound and spelling will change unless spelling conventions are periodically changed, a matter not so easily accomplished even if it were desirable.

This situation of standardizing spelling across dialects is not unique to English. All languages are really groups of closely related dialects, so no orthography can be a perfect alphabetic fit for any one dialect without being a very poor fit for the others. This is true even for the new orthographies created for preliterate peoples.

Besides compromising on dialect differences, conventional spellings involve trade-offs in how they will deal with characteristics of oral and written systems that correspond more or less and those which do not. Oral languages involve morphophonemic shifts, changes in phonemes that take place when they are followed by others in succeeding morphemes. Consider these related words: "site," "situate," "situation."

The conventional English spellings preserve the derivational relationships even though the /t/ in "site" shifts to /č/ in "situate" and the second /t/ in "situate" shifts to /š/ in "situation." The trade-off involves sacrificing of phoneme-grapheme consistency in favor of maintaining semantic relationships. That is an advantage, particularly since the same morphophonemic rules also apply across word boundaries. "Can't you" becomes /kæntčɘ/, for example. Compare also "education" and "would you" where in both cases the /d/ shifts to /j/. Strict consistency would require the same word to be spelled differently depending on which words followed it.

So standardized spelling is an important text feature. Readers expect a word to be spelled consistently but they do not expect all similar sounding words to be consistently spelled. English spelling conventions are complex but not as capricious as popularly believed. What adds to the complexity are the multiple linguistic roots of English. English has Germanic and Latin roots as well as substantial influences from other languages. So we have not one but several systems of correspondence rules in English orthography.

Many believe that it would be easier to learn to read and write English if its spelling were simplified. While it is possible that misspelling would diminish if spelling were simplified, there is no substantial evidence that English is harder to comprehend or to learn to read and write as a result of this complexity. Most spelling reformers have not faced the trade-offs required to achieve spelling simplicity.

Moreover, there is no evidence that there must be close correspondence between orthography and phonology for a written language to be functional for its users. Arabic and Hebrew have served their users very well for many centuries with little or no representation of vowels in their orthographies.

People tolerate and comprehend texts which are visually highly variable. All languages employ orthographies that include alternate writing forms. There are upper- and lowercase forms. Most have very different cursive and print forms. Type fonts vary considerably. Some orthographies use different letter forms in initial, medial, or final positions. Personal handwriting wanders far from a model of perfection. If people were intolerant of such variation, written language would be a less useful means of communication. In oral language, too, listeners are also able to tolerate considerable variation in dialect, idiolect, and voice quality. It is our ability to assign symbolic value to a wide range of distinctive features and shift the constraints and values in different contexts that makes both written and oral text work as well as they do.

Punctuation and Other Orthographic Conventions

Oral language usually uses segmental phonemes as its symbolic building blocks. The phonemes are segments of a phonological string following each other in time. But oral language uses a suprasegmental system, intonation, to produce meaningful utterances of these phonemes. There must be junctures, ways of telling where one unit ends and another begins, and variable patterns of pitch and stress that provide the prosodic contours that mark off and differentiate the syntactic patterns.

Written language uses punctuation, including spacing between words, extra spacing between sentences, and special formatting of paragraphs to accomplish the same purpose.

A speaker may turn any oral English statement into a question by using a different intonation pattern: "The book is lost." "The book is lost?" Besides this compulsory intonation which every utterance requires, optional patterns make it possible to change the meaning of an utterance in quite subtle ways. For example, shifting the stress in the following question from word to word changes its meaning: "Do you want me to rent a red car?"

Subtle shifts in intonation may clarify what would be ambiguous statements in writing. That is because punctuation is not nearly so full and flexible a system for creating the patterns of written language. A written English sentence starts with a capital and ends with a period, question mark, or exclamation point. But it has nothing corresponding to the oral English sentence's intonational contour which marks it as statement, question, or command from beginning to end. Written English employs a variety of means such as underlining, bold face, italics, and oversize letters to indicate where special stress is in the text. None of these works quite as well as intonation in oral language.

Only the exclamation point in written language gives any sense of the emotional state of a writer. A listener gets all kinds of signals of the feelings, moods, and intent of the speaker from voice quality, facial expressions, and body movements, in addition to the intonation, volume, and speed of the utterance. One third grader became aware of this problem in writing as he wrote about his dog being run over. So he invented his own "sadlamation point" to be used after sad statements.[7]

Because punctuation comes at the end of English utterances, it provides a means of confirming what the reader has already understood but it is not useful in making predictions since all types of sentences start with capitals. Spanish puts question marks and exclamation points at both ends of a sentence, providing more help.

This difference between how oral and written texts mark patterns is the result of differences between the constraints of the oral and graphic media. The effect of the difference is that the written text must explicitly represent what intonation and the situational context provide in a speech act.

The syntax of written language is also affected by this difference. Intonation is so effective in disambiguating coreference of nouns, subordination of clauses, and other complex discourse structures that oral language sentences may be much longer, more complex, and more rambling than those in written texts. The syntactic rules are not different in oral and written language but the parameters of orthography require a different use of the rules to produce a comprehensible text.

When this effect of the greater ambiguity of written text is combined with the polishing and editing possible and usual in preparing written texts, the result is that written texts employ styles and tend to use syntactic patterns that are notably different from those found in oral texts.

Learning to write comprehensible texts involves learning to use these styles and syntactic sequences particular to written language and one common characteristic of texts produced by inexperienced writers is the use of styles and patterns that work more successfully in oral language.

Text Format Conventions

Some of the format conventions that govern texts are intrinsic to the function and the content of the particular type of text but some are arbitrary social conventions. Text conventions may be very general, applying to all kinds of texts, or very specific applying to single text types such as airline schedules, recipes, TV guides, bibliographies, and so forth.

An example of general format conventions is putting margins at the top, sides, and bottom of the page. This may result from the need for binding space or from esthetic preferences or both. Paragraphing is another written language convention. It is at least partly done to set apart viable discourse units, though there is considerable dispute in the professional literature about whether the paragraph is a definite and definable unit of English discourse. Magazine and newspaper editors follow the convention that a text must be periodically broken by white space and they therefore will start new paragraphs even in the midst of a long series of names in order to provide white space.

Some text formats very clearly result from the nature of the subject matter of the text. Recipes, for example, will list ingredients in tabular form. List forms are used for shopping lists, telephone directories, and similar reference materials.

Consider the theater ticket as a text form. Its function and manner of use limit its size, structure, and content. Usually it is separated into two parts at the time of entry into the theater. So some information must appear on both parts. Certain information is represented on the ticket for the ticket holder but other information may be provided for the ticket taker. Some abbreviations may be used to economize on space. The highly conventionalized form of the ticket facilitates its usefulness for frequent theatergoers, but a first time user may find it difficult to locate and comprehend even information that is represented in large clear type.

Airline tickets have some similarities to theater tickets but again their function and manner of use, as well as the structure of the information they must represent, place strong constraints on them as texts. There must be a separate coupon for each flight segment, so multipart tickets are used, uniform across participating airlines. General information is imprinted on the ticket form and the rest is added by hand or by computer. Again, frequent flyers can comprehend a great deal of information from the tickets and ticket agents can comprehend more. The novice flyer must often seek help to comprehend it.

Today's airline tickets, like many business forms, are designed to be computer printed. Indeed, the computer has had as much impact on text formats as the typewriter had at an earlier time. Even newspaper formats have changed to fit the constraints of computers which now generate them.

Economy of space is a constraint of most texts, even novels. The classified advertisement in a newspaper has found its way into the folk humor because of the widespread use of inventive abbreviations to limit use of space and thereby reduce cost. The writer presupposes that the reader will be able, in the limited context, to know what is being represented and assign meaning to the symbols.

As in most texts, there is a trade-off possible in creation of the ad. The more pertinent knowledge the reader may be presupposed to have, the more concise and compact the text may be. However, the potential audience is delimited to those with the requisite schemata.

In modern literate societies, many text forms have evolved among special populations for the sharing of large amounts of very specific information. Some common examples are stock reports; theater, restaurant, and hotel guides; racing forms; weather reports; horoscopes; and menus.

While it is true that the form a text takes follows its function, it is also true that functions are both limited by and take advantage of forms. The two-dimensional space of written texts makes them admirably suited for tabular representation of large amounts of information. That means information does not have to be remembered. Readers need only to know where to go for the information and how to use the directories, charts, or lists. The function of written language as an extension of memory is largely dependent on its ability to represent information in a consistent, convenient, and retrievable manner. That means that the role of human memory in the preservation of social knowledge has been largely supplanted by written texts in literate societies.

Nonphysical Text Constraints

Written texts are often published. Professional editors and text designers strive for consistency in format, style, and overall appearance. That means establishing arbitrary standards in all aspects of text production. These standards interact with social conventions, shaped by them but also shaping them.

Cultures evolve text forms that become conventionalized and predictable by those who share the cultures. Such forms may be considered to have text grammars (recurrent and predictable structures).

The macrostructure of any text derives at least partially from the relations among the amount of information to be presented, its intrinsic structures, and special constraints. The telephone book is an example. Its physical list form is a function of the structure of the information it represents. Entries must include all the necessary information in a concise space-saving format. But entries must also be sequenced in some consistent, logical manner to make access to needed information quick. Tabular information is usually organized by numerical, alphabetic, or chronological sequencing systems. Phone books have used alphabetic sequencing by name on the premise that users know names and are looking for numbers. In recent years, phone books have been reorganized to separate individual from business entries, to separate cities into districts, and to provide more white space by listing each last name once followed by all entries for that name. The goal is, or at least ought to be, producing a text most easily comprehensible for its function and users. But, as with many texts, the interests of the writers and editors do not always coincide with those of the readers.

No matter what aspect of a text is used to sequence it, there is always the possibility that certain information will be hard to find. So indexes are often included in reference texts.

The macrostructure of any type of written text is similarly shaped by the same kind of considerations as the types we have explored. A business letter has a rather specific purpose and an internal structure related to its purpose. The letter must clearly and concisely represent its message in a comprehensible manner. But a letter which confines itself to a concise statement, does not follow conventional form, and includes expected amenities may carry some unintended pragmatic connotations to the recipient. Consider these alternatives:

Bronson, I want the $50 you owe me now! Henry Pope.

3497 Valley Rd.
Portland, AZ

Mr. George Bronson
5749 Sixth St.
Jonesville, PA

Dear Mr. Bronson,

In reviewing our records we find an unpaid balance of $50 in your account. Since this amount appears to be overdue we would appreciate payment at your earliest convenience. If you have already remitted the payment please excuse this reminder.

We're grateful for your continued patronage.

Sincerely,
Henry Pope

Newspapers include a variety of text types. The sequence of events in a news story would seem to provide a natural scaffold or macrostructure for the narration. Yet few stories follow such a straightforward structure. Reporters want to start with an angle, something that will catch the interest of the readers and provide a schema for following the story. They are also aware of the reading habits of newspaper readers, who start many articles but seldom read them to the end. So the most important information must be put early in the story, and information ordered in terms of its significance.

News reports have structures and styles different from those of feature articles, columns, or editorials; each of these develops its own text features that serve its particular purpose and make it predictable for readers familiar with the genre. Editors and readers would be surprised or angered if a news story took a position on an issue or an editorial stuck to the facts and took no position. A feature article is used to develop "human interest" and uses stylistic text devices that would be unacceptable in a news story. A syndicated columnist strives to develop a highly personal style that will win a continuing readership. On the other hand, news editors strive for a consistent, impersonal style across all reporters.

Though different forms and conventions have evolved for each type of text, each time we focus on a particular kind of text we see the same factors at work. The form must efficiently serve the function and purpose of both writers and readers. There must be a predictable macrostructure, or text grammar. The text must be organized in such a way that meaning is represented in a cohesive and coherent way. In narrative and expository texts, topics must be established and elaborated, rhetoric and linguistic rules and conventions observed. Words, phrases, and syntactic structures must be chosen within linguistic and pragmatic constraints that will produce a comprehensible text.

The Wording of Texts

In every narrative and expository text there are two kinds of very frequent words. Some are frequent because they are the function words, pronouns, and copulas ("be" forms) that the language constantly requires. The others are content words which may be quite uncommon in the language as a whole but are frequent in a particular text because of its subject matter.

Goodman and Bird studied the wording of several different types of texts.[8] They found that the twenty-five most frequent words in each text account for between 35 percent and 40 percent of the running words (tokens). At the same time, over half of the different words (types) in each text are used only once. In an adult essay, 75 percent of the words (types) occur just once. Most of the frequent words that are content words in texts are nouns. In narratives, these are often the names of the main characters. It is the function words, pronouns, and copulas plus a few repeated nouns that provide most of the text cohesion in both narrative and nonnarrative texts.

In nonnarrative texts, the important ideas will be represented by a variety of nouns so that particular nouns will not be used with the same frequency as the proper nouns in narratives. That is because authors avoid, when they can, using the same word repetitiously. That is also why verbs, adjectives, and adverbs are unlikely to be repeated very frequently in any text. Authors use a variety of terms with related reference to provide cohesive chains. In one story, a character moves toward another in the opening sequence. No term is used more than once in this chain: "drove," "approached," "opened," "coming," "parked," "went up," "take," "got to," "crossed," "pushed through," "went across."

To produce a cohesive text requires repetitious references to the same key characters, concepts, attributes, or actions. English writers can avoid repeating the same content words but they cannot avoid repeating function words because language provides only a few words for common functions. Because common nouns usually require determiners, "the" is the most common word in virtually all texts, representing up to 10 percent of all the running words.

Readers expect texts to be worded so that the uncommon words will be defined by their coreferences, their collocations, and their embedding in contexts composed of high frequency, noncontent words. Language itself thus self-controls the word frequency of texts. Aritificial controls on word frequency ironically can make texts less predictable and therefore less comprehensible to readers.

What emerges in everything that has been said about texts is the same concept of diversity within unity that was emphasized in discussing written language transactions from the point of view of the writer. Texts are highly constrained and yet they must be variable enough and flexible enough to serve any writer's purpose and make it possible for the writer to establish a personal style and voice.

Reading as Construction of Meaning

Though theories of reading as a process have existed at least since the time of Huey,[9] there has been a tendency in the reading field to operate from atheoretical premises and unexamined assumptions. Reading has tended to be regarded as recoding letters to sounds or it has been regarded essentially as a task of identifying words as they occur in sequence. Both views are essentially word-centered. They both involve a view of reading as word getting and of translating written language to oral language before comprehending.

In recent research on reading, there has been a tendency to state and examine underlying theory. Theoreticians differ sharply on the extent to which they believe that letters and their distinctive features are used in reading, but no one has advanced a view that leaves the reader totally passive in the reading process. Gough puts strong emphasis on linear processing of letter shapes, but he postulates some type of internal transformation of perceptual input into linguistic data.[10]

Adams and Collins see the reader inputting all of the letter and word information followed by a kind of mediation of higher cognitive processing which acts downward and revalues the information.[11]

The Goodmans and Smith devote considerable attention in their writings to the characteristics of the text, the role of the writer in the creation of the text, and the interactions and transactions between the reader and the text.[12]

Progress in understanding the process of reading has been considerable, but integration has not been achieved because the work has not been interdisciplinary. Views of reading show the major preoccupations of each discipline. Psychology has been concerned with comprehension, propositional analysis, and schema theory. Artificial intelligence has been concerned with what the reader, using computers as analogs, must know and how that must be organized to comprehend texts. In literary criticism, there has been an increased concern for the role of the reader in response to literature. Linguistics has moved from syntactic, sentence-bound concerns to text linguistics and pragmatics. Ethnographers and sociolinguists have put their focus on the personal and societal functions of literacy.

Differences among theoreticians revolve around how much active control the reader exerts, how important reader characteristics are, how much text characteristics control the process, and whether meaning is in the writer, the text, or the reader. Some researchers have preferred to construct micromodels of single aspects of the reading process.

Though researchers and theoreticians may take macro or micro views of the reading process, it ultimately must be seen as construction of meaning from text and, as such, transacting with text and with author. Simplistic views of reading that focus on single aspects of text (such as word frequency) or single strategies (such as recoding letters to sounds) do not fit the growing research evidence.

Most research is converging on the view that transactions between reader and text characteristics result in construction of meaning. This view makes the role of the reader a highly active one. It makes what the reader brings to the text as important as the text itself in text comprehension.

Goodman has characterized reading as a psycholinguistic guessing game involving tentative information processing.[13] Smith emphasizes the reduction of uncertainty in reading.[14] Spiro, Bruce, and Brewer have stressed hypothesis testing in the process.[15]

All of these views emphasize that reading is meaning-seeking, tentative, selective, and constructive. They all emphasize the importance of inference and prediction in reading. Readers use the least amount of available text information necessary in relation to the reader's existing linguistic and conceptual schemata to get to meaning.

Dual Texts

In a transactional view, both the knower and the known are transformed in the process of knowing. The reader is transformed as new knowledge is assimilated and accommodated. Both the reader's conceptual schemata and values are altered through reading comprehension. Since the published text seems to be a reality that does not change its physical properties as a result of being read, how can it change during reading? The answer is that the reader is constructing a text parallel and closely related to the published text. It becomes a different text for each reader. The reader's text involves inferences, references, and coreferences based on schemata that the reader brings to the text. And it is this reader's text which the reader comprehends and on which any reader's later account of what was read is based.

From this perspective of a dual text, it is possible to see the importance of the text characteristics, discussed above, in the reading process and still understand that what really matters is how the reader perceives and uses them.

This emphasis on text construction in reading does not mean that the reader is attending to text construction as an end product. The reader's attention is very much on meaning. Construction of the text is a necessary concomitant of the construction of meaning.

In this view, the literary quality of the text remains significant. Great literary works have a depth which makes it possible to understand them, to construct them, at many levels.

A story has it that once, when Robert Frost was being introduced to an audience of college students, his host went on in great detail about the marvelous allegorical references in his favorite Frost poem. Proud of his brilliant insight, he turned to the poet and said, "Isn't that so, Mr. Frost?" to which the poet replied, "Then again it may just be about apple picking."

Why People Read

Within the broad functions of communication over time and space, people read written language for several different purposes. To understand how reading works, it is necessary to understand why readers read. Here is one attempt to examine the major purposes of reading. The types of reading are not necessarily mutually exclusive.

Environmental reading. Just functioning in a literate society requires coping with street signs, regulations ("Keep off the Grass"), directions, store logos, and other ways that written language occurs in the environment. In international situations, important notices are in several different languages and/or in a system of ideographs designed to be universally comprehensible. Environmental print is read not so much by choice as by necessity, and it is no wonder that preschool children often acquire the ability to make sense of much of the print in their environment without formal instruction. Recent studies in a number of countries show widespread print awareness and response to environmental print among preschool children even in poverty cultures.[16]

Occupational reading. An Educational Testing Service study shows that 87 percent of those gainfully employed in the United States read an average of 141.1 minutes per eight hour day.[17] By sheer volume, this occupational reading has to be the major purpose of reading for most people. It includes a wide range of text types and varies considerably from occupation to occupation. It is likely to be so highly integrated into job activities that it may not be considered reading per se. If one said to an office worker, "What have you read recently?" it is unlikely the response would be "sixteen interoffice memos, twenty-three letters, six reports, the drafts of several unfinished pieces of correspondence, three sets of directions for use of equipment and materials, eight labels on office supplies."

The fact that such reading is so well integrated into job responsibilities insures that it will be relatively repetitive, that readers will bring a great deal of relevant background to the reading, and that motivation to comprehend will be high. However, because of the specialized nature of occupations, texts may be all but incomprehensible to outsiders unfamiliar with subject matter, text conventions, abbreviations, and acronyms. In fact, some texts may be expressly designed to be comprehensible only to insiders.

Some occupations also require a great deal of reading outside of usual working hours just to keep up with the field.

Informational reading. Written language is an extension of human memory, so written texts become storehouses of information. Readers make frequent use of texts to gain information for immediate use, such as phone numbers and TV schedules. They also seek information to satisfy longer-range curiosity or personal needs.

In human memory, having information stored and getting at it are two different things. This is true also of written language, though on a much larger scale. So informational reading involves knowing how to access the appropriate sources of information. This purpose of reading has become so important that computers have been harnessed to make information retrieval more efficient and speedy.

Recreational reading. A fourth major purpose for reading is to occupy leisure time pleasantly. That is a bit too simply put because most of the esthetic reasons for reading come under this heading. The point is that this kind of reading is done at the reader's own discretion, for the reader's own enjoyment, and by personal choice. Of course, the text may be fiction or nonfiction and it is possible that informational material, particularly that related to hobbies and leisure interests may be read for recreational reasons.

In modern society there are many alternative ways of spending leisure time such as watching television, movies, plays, or spectator sports, engaging in physical activities and games, socializing, and so forth. Few people confine all their leisure time to any one such pursuit.

Ritualistic reading. Certain texts are read and reread for ritualistic reasons. That means that the act of reading itself is a ritual and that the purpose is not so much comprehension of the particular passage as fulfillment of the rite. The reading of religious materials, sometimes in unknown languages, is an example of ritualistic reading. The literacy event has an overall meaning to the participant to which the text does not relate in the usual manner.

This range of purposes for reading does not contradict the contention that reading is a unitary process. What it does demonstrate is that, within this single process, what a reader comprehends in a given literacy event is very much related to the reader's purpose.

Students in schools are expected to do a lot of reading. In a sense, this reading is akin to the occupational reading discussed above since it is part of their "jobs" as students. It is different in that it does not necessarily grow out of a functional act as occupational reading does. Often instructional reading involves exercises that are not directly related to any personal language function of the students. The exercises seem, like ritualistic reading, to be ends in themselves.

A good deal of school reading seems to be informational. But too often the information is not sought to satisfy the needs or curiosity of the student but to fulfill an assignment with the student not even clear about what use might be made of such information. Even the reading of literature often involves works selected by the teacher or assigned within a fixed curriculum. If the student does not have some kind of personal purpose for reading and does not exercise some choice in what is read, then the activity becomes an unnatural one and it is not as likely that it will contribute to reading development.

Of course, what can make the difference in any school reading activity is how sensitive the teacher is to the background and interests of the students, how the teacher involves the students in planning and self-selection, and how highly motivated the students become.

Teachers need to be careful that they do not become overzealous in their promotion of recreational reading. Schools, in their justifiable concern for promoting reading, can make the mistake of setting it off against less favored activities such as watching television. A more important and achievable objective is to make students aware of what pleasure reading can afford, to help them to develop personal taste and preferences, and to assure that students will grow up able to exercise intelligent options.

Still, schools must be doing some things right. Every economic indicator in recent times indicates that all types of reading, including recreational reading, are increasing. Book circulation between 1950 and 1975 in American libraries rose from 2.47 to 4.36 per person. Books and pamphlets sold rose from 6.8 to 8.6 per person in a comparable period.[18] Modern societies are becoming increasingly literate in all respects.

Purpose and Intention

The reader's purpose in a literacy event is general. Within that general purpose, the reader has intentions for what will explicitly result from the event. Just as the intentions of the writer are important in the creation of the text, the reader's intentions are important in its comprehension. The contract metaphor assumes that the reader is trying to understand the text. But consider the effect on comprehension of the intention of each of these readers:

A professional proofreader reading for typos.

A teacher reading a student's assignment.

An editor reading the text for potential publication.

A critic reviewing the text.

A student reading the text as a class assignment.

The same student reading the same text as a source of information for a term paper.

Any of the above reading the same text for leisure reading in a magazine that happens to be at hand.

Any of the above reading the same text on recommendation of a friend as something "you simply must read."

Obviously, a number of factors can influence the "contract." Primary among these is whether the text is self-selected or assigned by someone else. Even within a similar purpose (gaining information, for example), intentions may vary and strongly influence comprehension. Reading a text to "cram" for an examination will be different from reading the same text for a term paper or reading it in pursuit of a burning desire to know more about something of great personal interest. The same reader may get different meanings from the same text read at different times with different intentions.

Comprehending and Comprehension

Comprehension, at some level, is always the end product of any act of reading. During the reading the reader is engaged in comprehending, that is, trying to make sense of the text. This distinction between comprehending as process and comprehension as product is important and useful.

Attempts to study and evaluate reading have generally focussed on comprehension as product measured by some type of postreading test of knowledge. This may take the form of explicit factual, text based questions; of more general questioning; of open-ended retelling by the reader following reading; or some combination of these. All of these come after reading. They are limited by what the reader is willing and able to report as well as what has actually been comprehended.

Since comprehending is a constructive process, in which readers *make* sense of text, it goes on during reading and even long afterwards as the reader reconsiders and reconstructs what has been comprehended; thus, comprehension may be changed in the course of testing it. The reader may change what he or she understood on the basis of test questions which seem to require particular responses and views.

Miscue analysis and cloze procedures are means of examining comprehending as it is taking place during the act of reading. In miscue analysis, oral reading miscues (points where observed and expected responses to the text do not match) are examined. The extent to which miscues result in meaningful text or are self-corrected if they disrupt meaning gives strong indications of the readers' concern for and ability to make sense of the text. Goodman and others have used miscue analysis to study comprehending.[19]

In cloze activities, words are deleted from the text and readers are asked to supply them. Examination of the relationship between actual and expected responses gives a similar insight into the readers' ability to maintain meaningful text. Such studies have been conducted by Chapman, by Anderson, by Cambourne and Rousch, and by Lindberg.[20] Cloze distorts text to some extent, but it is a way of examining comprehending during silent reading and shows patterns remarkably similar to those found in miscue analysis in oral reading.

The relationships between comprehending and comprehension are not simple and isomorphic. What one knows after reading is the product of what one knew beforehand plus how well one read the text. So, effective comprehending is essential to effective comprehension but not sufficient. Correlations between measures of the two, as reported in the studies above, are moderate and significant but not high.

Cue Systems

Readers utilize three information systems in constructing their texts and comprehending. Learning to read is at least partly gaining control over these systems and their interactions in the context of literacy events.

The graphophonic system. The orthography in written language and its complex relationship to the phonological system and to the meaning both represent have already been discussed here. One definition of phonics is the set of relationships between the oral and written language in alphabetic writing. Together the orthographic, phonological, and phonic systems make up a graphophonic information system in reading. Particular cues in reading may be visual or relational and thus invoke aural cues.

The syntactic system. The grammar of a language is the system by which symbolic units may represent meaning. Grammar is largely a matter of syntax, or sentence structures. Language, according to Chomsky,[21] has a deep structure representing the meaning. A set of transformational rules relate the deep structure to the oral surface representation in speech or to the graphic surface representation in writing. In English, sentence order is the major feature of syntax. It creates the patterns that make clear, for example, which noun is subject and which is object. A series of bound morphemes, affixes, form an inflectional system which also indicates person, number, and tense in nouns and verbs. A third system in English grammar is the small set of function words, determiners, auxiliaries, prepositions, and so forth, that have no lexical meaning but which make it possible to create sentence patterns to express virtually unlimited meanings. Together these syntactic features create the grammatical system of the language.

Just as the writer must create a grammatical text to represent meaning, a reader must use the grammatical features of the text to create a grammatical text. A text cannot be comprehensible without being grammatical.

The semantic system. The semantic system of language is not simply a set of definable words. It is the whole system by which language may represent highly complex social and personal meaning. As was stated earlier, how much knowledge is shared by reader and writer will very much influence how the text is constructed and how successful the reader's comprehension will be. Ultimately, the reference and coreferences must be furnished by the reader in response to the text.

Pragmatic meaning is also a part of this system. This is always partly textual and partly contextual. The subtle differences between the straightforward and the sarcastic, the profane and the profound, the humorous and the serious are found in cues in both the text and the context of the literacy event. And schemata in the reader must be evoked to achieve pragmatic comprehension.

The syntax makes it possible to produce sensible sentences and the transformational rules of the language generate these sentences. But a text is more than a set of well-formed sentences. It has a unity; it is both coherent and cohesive. The cohesion of a text is part of the semantic system of the language.

Readers select from graphophonic, syntactic, and semantic cues. These cues are within the text and the reader. Readers must have schemata for the orthography, for the syntax of the language, and for the concepts presupposed by the writer in order to select, use, and supply the cues appropriate to a particular text.

Cognitive Strategies

Readers use general cognitive strategies such as inference in reading. These strategies take on particular significance in the construction of meaning in literacy events.

Initiation or task recognition. Reading requires an overt decision to activate appropriate strategies and schemata. Usually this relates to a particular chain of events. A reader decides to read the morning paper with the general intention of finding out what is new or the specific intention of seeking a particular bit of information such as the score of a game. Often, though, it is not until the reader recognizes something in the visual environment as a readable text that he or she uses an initiation strategy. An example is thinking that a dress has a decorative pattern and then realizing that the pattern is cursive writing.

Sampling and selection. The human brain is not the prisoner of the senses nor does it process everything that the senses feed into it. In reading it seeks information, directing the eyes where to look and what to look for. It samples and selects, from the environment and from the input the eyes provide, just that information which will be most productive and useful. Efficiency in any cognitive process requires this selectivity. Otherwise, the thought processes would be overwhelmed by irrelevant data. This sampling and selection strategy is one of the most difficult aspects of human intelligence to simulate in the artificial intelligence of a computer.[22] It depends for its effective use on everything the reader knows relevant to language, to reading, and to the particular text.

Inference. Inference is a general strategy of guessing, on the basis of what is known, what information is needed but is not known. Calling inference guesswork does not make it random or mystic. Our schemata and knowledge structures make it possible on the basis of partial information to make reliable decisions by inferring missing information. We would be incapable of the decisions we must make if we had to be sure of all the necessary prerequisite information before making each decision.

There is some risk involved in inference since the inferences may prove to be wrong. But the risk in not making inferences is even greater. So readers are tentative in their inferences, depending on how confident they are of their ability to comprehend a given text. Level of confidence limits willingness to take risks, which in turn limits inferencing.

Inference applies to all aspects of reading and to all cue systems: readers infer graphophonic, syntactic, and semantic information. Furthermore, they infer information that is explicit as well as implicit. The reader cannot know at any point whether information will eventually become explicit in the text. For inference to be confined only to nonexplicit information would mean that it could be used only after the reading of the text is completed. Clearly the strategy must apply when it is needed during reading. If inferred information becomes explicit, then the reader confirms the inference and builds the level of confidence in the quality of the inferences being made.

Prediction. Receptive language processing, both reading and listening, requires the ability to predict and anticipate what is coming. Otherwise processing would in some sense always be retrospective, a gathering of information to some point after which its values were assigned. But when they start a syntactic pattern, readers must have some sense of whether it is question, statement, or command. They must know from the beginning of a word, phrase, or clause where it is likely to end. The prediction strategy makes the process smoothly flowing as the reader constructs text and meaning. Predictions are based on both explicit and inferred information used in such a way that the reader is quite unlikely to be aware of what was explicit and what inferred.

Cognitive strategies interact in reading so that readers sample on the basis of their predictions and predict and infer on the basis of the sampling they are doing.

The prediction strategy is greatly facilitated if texts are predictable for the given reader; in fact, predictability is probably a more useful and theoretically sound concept than readability in considering the comprehensibility of a given text for a given reader.

Confirming and disconfirming. If inference and prediction involve risk taking and are limited by the level of the reader's confidence, then it is necessary for the reader to self-monitor during reading. The reader must be expecting consistency of new information with past inferences, predictions, and comprehending. The confirming/disconfirming strategy is what makes the self-monitoring possible. The reader is tentative to the extent of always being ready to accommodate to disconfirming information. In general, confirmation must be on the basis of the meaningfulness of the text being constructed. Specifically, it is based on expectations being met and not contradicted.

Again, there is interaction of strategies and an economy of processing. The same information used to confirm past decisions is used to make new inferences and predictions. Carrithers and Bever report that eye movement studies support the hypothesis-confirmation view of use of perceptual data in reading.[23]

Correction. It does not do much good to know something is wrong if you can do nothing about it. Readers develop correction strategies for reconstructing the text and recovering meaning.

Largely, correction strategies are of two types. One is revaluing information already processed and making alternate inferences, predictions, and interpretations. The other is regressing in the text to gather more information.

Correction can be almost simultaneous with an original decision or it can come at a point quite remote in the reading from the original decision. An example of the latter would be the belated realization in reading a murder mystery that the prime suspect could not have committed the crime.

Termination. Just as a deliberate decision begins reading, a deliberate one ends it. The termination strategy is used in a variety of ways in reading. It does not only happen when the reader reaches the end of the text. Readers may terminate at any point anywhere along the way out of disinterest, inability to comprehend, boredom, lack of time, or a change in circumstance.

These strategies operate in a dynamic search for meaning, a drive to make sense of the text. Though they are continuously available, some are more likely to occur at particular points in reading than others.

Cycles of the Reading Process

Reading involves a transaction between the published text and the reader. This transaction depends on visual input. Once the decision to read is made, light bouncing off print to the eye is processed optically and perceptually transformed so that the orthographic, syntactic, and semantic systems of language may be utilized.

As perceptual and linguistic processing occurs, it effects the quality of the optical information, since the eyes are being directed by the brain in an informed way. Thus, reading is a cyclical psycholinguistic process. Perceptual processing depends on optical input. Syntactic processing operates on perceptual input. And semantic processing depends on syntactic input. So, in a sense, the cycles are sequential. But it is a sequence like a merry-go-round in which an optical cycle follows a semantic cycle as well as preceding it. Furthermore, reading is goal-oriented and the goal is always meaning.

Each cycle is tentative and partial, melting into the next. Inference and prediction make it possible to leap toward meaning without fully completing the optical, perceptual, and syntactic cycles. Yet the reader, once sense is achieved, has the sense of having seen every graphic feature, identified every pattern and word, assigned every syntactic pattern.

Schema theory can explain this phenomenon to some extent. The reader is continuously assigning the highest level and most inclusive schema available to move toward meaning, the goal of comprehending. The strategies and rules available to the reader serve as schemata for schema formation. Schema use is always tentative; that is, a schema is assigned and maintained as long as it is useful but quickly modified or abandoned if disconfirmed. This is what Bartlett calls the schema turning back on itself in the process of its use.[24] All this means that each cycle can be understood only in the context of the holistic process.

The optical cycle. The eye is an optical instrument with a lens like any other lens; it has an angle of vision, a focal length, and it cannot function in the dark.

Since written text is two-dimensional and linear, the eye must scan the text. But it can provide useful visual input only when fixations occur. Thus, any visual process could be considered as a series of snapshots or frames of movie film. That is, it could if the brain operated like a photo album, which it does not. We do not see our world as chopped into snapshots surrounded by fuzz, but rather, as Neisser says, we have a sense of seeing our visual environment as a three-dimensional and integrated whole.[25]

It is easy to demonstrate that only a small circle of the page is in sharp focus at any one eye fixation. Furthermore, since the reader knows the display is horizontally linear in English, it follows that more attention will be paid to the horizontal dimension of that circle than to the vertical so the visual field becomes a flattened oval. But in reading, the schemata the brain is operating with make it possible to use information in the peripheral visual field if it is consistent with the reader's expectations.

Kolers has summarized well the role of visual information in reading.[26] Reading begins with seeing the text, but it is what one does with the visual input that is the difference between seeing and reading.

The perceptual cycle. In a famous study, Miller demonstrated that how much can be remembered from a brief visual text exposure depends on the brain's ability to organize the information into meaningful wholes.[27] "Seven plus or minus two" units represents the range among different observers. But whether these units are graphic features, letters, words, or longer meaningful phrases depends on what schema the observer can utilize for use of the visual input. Thus, observers can "see" and remember whole sentences with the same ease and assurance as they can see a few randomly ordered letters.

Cattell demonstrated the same principle nearly a century ago. He showed that the same features used to recognize a letter could be used to recognize a word.[28] Perception does indeed depend on selecting highly significant and distinctive features and inferring the wholes they relate to. But it is only in the context of the whole that the features are significant or distinctive. Noses, for example, vary considerably from person to person, and in quickly recognizing someone we must certainly use these distinctive noses. Yet it would be very difficult to identify the noses outside the context of the faces.

One aspect of perception that must be understood is that learning what not to pay attention to is as important as learning what to attend to. Consider a driver approaching a busy intersection. Realizing that there is significant information in the visual field that requires that the car be stopped by applying the brakes depends on assigning great significance to one relatively small spot of red light and ignoring as insignificant all the other lights. In just such a manner, readers must use their selection strategies to choose only the most useful from all the visual information available. The reader cannot store all the information as a computer might and then sort out that which is significant. If a reader attempted to do so, the system would overload and comprehension would be slowed or completely disrupted.

The syntactic cycle. To get to meaning, the reader must assign a syntactic structure to the text. The clause is the most significant unit because meaning is represented in the deep structure as a set of clauses which are transformed into the sentences of the surface structure through transformational rules. The reader must construct both surface and deep structure to get to the clauses and their interrelationships and to get to the meaning. Consider this common primer sentence:

See Spot run.

To make sense of this, the reader must treat it as an imperative. That requires awareness that the sentence starts with a verb in the simple form. Only by treating it as an imperative can the reader apply the rule that provides the deep structure subject (you) not present in the surface representation:

(You) see Spot run.

This seemingly simple sentence has a complex verb-noun-verb form. That is because it is composed of two clauses. The second clause is the subject of the verb "see":

(You) see < Spot run >

"Spot" is the subject of the second clause but the verb in the second clause is an infinitive with the usual "to" deleted in this verb sequence. The underlying structure of the second clause is "Spot runs."

(You) see < Spot runs > = (You) see < Spot (to) run > = See Spot run.

There is no way to get to the meaning of this text sequence without going through the syntax. But imperatives are a familiar part of language even for young readers. They have developed the schema for this sentence type.

This three word sentence is syntactically complex but not nearly as complex as many sentences found in texts of all kinds, including material considered appropriate for use in reading instruction in the early grades.

Inference and prediction strategies play important roles in the syntactic cycle. The reader must have a syntactic pattern within which to give symbolic value to and organize the perceptual information. The reader uses the syntactic features and cues in the text to make the necessary inferences and predictions. So perceptual information is used to assign a syntactic pattern and this pattern is then used to assign values to perceptual information.

Halliday refers to this language system as the lexico-grammar because words in context must have both syntactic and lexical references and the two references are interdependent.[29] Rather than the common sense notion that the sentence cannot be understood until the words are recognized, in fact the words cannot be known until the structure they are found in is assigned.

The assignment of syntactic structures by readers is reflected in the intonation used in oral reading. Often readers will regress in oral reading to the beginning of a paragraph or sentence to change the intonation after changing their minds about the syntactic pattern.

The semantic cycle. The grammar of a language exists largely on the level of sentences, though there are some rules that are intersentential. But the grammatical system of a language, complex as it is, consists of a relatively small number of rules capable of generating an infinite number of sentences. People have the ability, using syntactic rules, to produce novel sentences which they have never uttered or heard or read and be assured that they will be considered grammatical by others who know the language.

The semantic system of a language is much more complex than the syntactic. It must be capable of representing the full range of thoughts, feelings, and emotions of the users of the language as individuals and as social groups.

Whereas all the users of the language control the rules of the language (though these vary somewhat from dialect to dialect), they cannot possibly control everything that the language can mean or the full range of vocabulary, phrasing, idiom, and style that authors of texts use in representing meaning. That is why no one could possibly comprehend the full range of texts that exist or can be created in any language. Writers and readers must share a base of knowledge and a set of semantic devices, including specialized styles, special terminology, special text formats and special cohesive devices, to achieve a high level of communication through written language.

Readers must be capable of learning through reading in the sense of assimilating new knowledge to established schemata and also in the sense of accommodating existing schemata to new knowledge. But the ability of a reader to comprehend a given text is very much limited by the conceptual and experiential background of the reader and there are strong limitations on how much new knowledge can be gained from a reading of a given text.

How well the writer knows the audience and has built the text to suit the audience will make a major difference in text predictability and comprehension. However, since comprehension results from reader-text transactions, what the reader knows, who the reader is, what values guide the reader, what purposes or interests the reader has will play vital roles in the reading process. It follows then that what any reader comprehends from a given text will vary from what other readers comprehend. Meaning is ultimately created by the reader.

An extensive vocabulary is undoubtedly a characteristic of a reader capable of making sense of a wide range of texts. But it is a mistake to think that vocabulary-building exercises can produce improved comprehension. Language is learned in the context of its use. Word meanings are built in relationship to concepts; language facilitates learning, but it is the conceptual development that creates the need for the language. Without that, words are empty forms. So vocabulary is built in the course of language use including reading. It is probably more accurate to say that people have big vocabularies because they read a lot than that they read well because they have big vocabularies.

Throughout this chapter, the emphasis has been on reading as a meaning-seeking process. It is this search for meaning which preoccupies the reader and unifies the use of the strategies and cycles that the process requires. Meaning is both input and output in this process. That is why aspects of the process and how it works cannot be isolated from the construction of meaning that is the ultimate goal.

Learning to read involves getting the process together. That is harder if instruction takes it apart.

Flexibility and Diversity within Unity

It is not possible to read without using the strategies and cycles discussed above. It is not possible to read without engaging oneself in a transaction with a text and seeking to make sense of it. These are universal essentials to reading across text types, styles, languages, purposes, and orthographies. Readers develop special strategies and schemata for dealing with different text types, different purposes, and different languages with different orthographies.

Novels have a macrostructure different from those of essays or informational texts. So readers will need to develop a sense of text appropriate to each in order to use inference and prediction effectively. German has a sentence structure different from English, and readers of each will assign the syntactic structure appropriate to the language. Hebrew uses a different alphabet and directionality than English uses. Readers of Hebrew will have optical and perceptual strategies for scanning from right to left. They will infer vowels on the basis of orthographic, syntactic, and semantic information since vowels are not explicitly represented as they are in languages that use the Roman alphabet. All this requires flexibility and variability within a single process which has universal characteristics required to make sense of print.

And making sense of print is what reading is all about.

NOTES

[1] Louise M. Rosenblatt. *The Reader, the Text, the Poem: The Transactional Theory of the Literary Work*. Carbondale, IL: Southern Illinois University Press, 1981.

[2] Jean Piaget. *Psychology and Epistemology* New York: Grossman, 1971.

[3] John R. Searle. *Speech Acts*. New York: Cambridge University Press, 1969.

[4] Susan Suliman (Ed.). *The Reader in the Text*. Princeton, NJ: Princeton University Press, 1980.

[5] H.P. Grice. "Logic and Conversation," in *Syntax and Semantics*, vol. 3. *Speech Acts*. Peter Cole and Jerry L. Morgan (Eds.). New York: Academic Press, 1975.

[6] Michael A.K. Halliday and Ruqaiya Hasan. *Cohesion in English*. London: Longman, 1976.

[7] Yetta M. Goodman. "Letters," *Language Arts, 56* (May 1979), 482.

[8] Kenneth S. Goodman and Lois Bird. "On the Wording of Texts: A Study of Intra-Text Word Frequency," Occasional Paper No. 6. Tucson, AZ: Program in Language and Literacy, University of Arizona, 1982.

[9] Edmund B. Huey. *The Psychology and Pedagogy of Reading*. New York: Macmillan, 1908.

[10] Philip B. Gough. "One Second of Reading," in James F. Kavanagh and Ignatius G. Mattingly (Eds.), *Language by Ear and by Eye*. Cambridge, MA: MIT Press, 1972.

[11] Marilyn J. Adams and Allan M. Collins. "A Schema-Theoretic View of Reading," in Roy O. Freedle (Ed.), *Discourse Processing: Multidisciplinary Perspectives*. Norwood, NJ: Ablex Press, 1979.

[12] Kenneth S. Goodman and Yetta M. Goodman. "Reading of American Children Whose Language Is a Stable Rural Dialect of English or a Language Other Than English," Final Report, Project NIE-C-00-3-0087. Washington, DC: U.S. Department of Health, Education, and Welfare, National Institute of Education, 1978; Frank Smith, *Understanding Reading*, third ed. New York: Holt, Rinehart and Winston, 1982.

[13] Kenneth S. Goodman. "Reading: A Psycholinguistic Guessing Game," *Journal of the Reading Specialist* (May 1967), 126-135.

[14] Smith, *Understanding Reading*.

[15] Rand J. Spiro, Bertram C. Bruce, and William F. Brewer. *Theoretical Issues in Reading Comprehension*. Hillsdale, NJ: Erlbaum Associates, 1980.

[16] Emilia Ferreiro and Ana Teberosky, *Literacy before Schooling*, trans., Karen Goodman Castro. Exeter, NH: Heinemann Educational Books, 1982; Yetta M. Goodman, "The Roots of Literacy," in Malcolm Douglass (Ed.).*44th Yearbook of the Claremont Reading Conference*. Claremont, CA: Claremont Reading Conference, 1980; Marie M. Clay, *Reading: The Patterning of Complex Behavior*, second edition. Auckland, New Zealand: Heinemann Educational Books, 1979.

[17] John Bormuth. "Value and Volume of Literacy," *Visible Language*, 12 (Spring 1978), 118-161.

[18] Ibid.

[19] Goodman and Goodman. "Reading of American Children Whose Language Is a Stable Rural Dialect of English or a Language other Than English."

[20] John Chapman, "The Reader and Text." in John Chapman (Ed.), *The Reader and Text*, London: Heinemann Educational Books, 1981, 1-15; Jonathan Anderson, "The Writer, the Reader, and the Text: Or Writhing and Reeling in Texta," paper presented at the United Kingdom Reading Association, 19th Annual Conference, Newcastle-Upon-Tyne, 1982; Brian Cambourne and Peter Rousch, *A Psycholinguistic Model of the Reading Process As it Relates to Proficient, Average, and Low-Ability Readers*. Wagga Wagga: Riverina College of Advanced Education, 1979; and Margaret Lindberg, "A Descriptive Analysis of the Relationship between Selected Prelinguistic, Linguistic, and Psycholinguistic Measures of Readability," doctoral dissertation, Wayne State University, 1977.

[21] Noam Chomsky. *Syntactic Structures*. The Hague: Mouton, 1957.

[22] Roger C. Schank. *Reading and Understanding: Teaching from the Perspective of Artificial Intelligence*. Hillsdale, NJ: Erlbaum Associates, 1982.

[23] Caroline Carrithers and Thomas G. Bever. "Eye Movement Patterns Confirm Theories of Language Comprehension," unpublished manuscript, Columbia University, 1982.

[24] Frederic C. Bartlett. *Remembering: A Study in Experimental and Social Psychology*. London: Cambridge University Press, 1932.

[25] Ulric Neisser. *Cognition and Reality*. San Francisco: Freeman, 1977.

[26] Paul Kolers. "Reading Is Only Incidentally Visual," in Kenneth S. Goodman and James Fleming (Eds.), *Psycholinguistics and the Teaching of Reading*. Newark, DE: International Reading Association, 1969.

[27] George A. Miller. "The Magic Number Seven Plus or Minus Two: Some Limits on Our Capacity for Processing Information," *Psychological Review, 63* (March, 1956), 81-92.

[28] James McKeen Cattell. *James McKeen Cattell: Man of Science*, Vol. 1, in A.T. Poffenberger (Ed.), *Psychological Research*. Lancaster, PA: Science Press, 1947, 13-23.

[29] Michael A.K. Halliday. *Learning How to Mean: Explorations in the Development of Language*. London: Edward Arnold, 1975.

Affective Model

Toward a Comprehensive Model of Affect in the Reading Process

GROVER C. MATHEWSON
Florida International University

Before examining the role of affect in reading behavior, it may be useful to explore the place of affect in general psychological research. Following this exploration, the status of affect as a factor in reading research and theory may be clearer, and the elaboration of a model of affect in reading processes may gain a significance that it would not have without a historical perspective.

A good starting point for gaining an understanding of the historical place of affect is Hilgard's survey (1980) of the tripartite division of the study of mind into cognition, affection, and conation. Hilgard's overview showed that the modern origin of the tripartite division may be traced to the eighteenth century, particularly to the period between Leibniz and Kant. It was during this period that Christian Wolfe introduced two "faculties": knowledge (cognition) and desire (conation). Alexander Gottlieb Baumgarten (1714-1762) added affect (feeling) as a third faculty.

While faculty psychology was rejected eventually, the three-part division of mental process into cognitive, affective, and conative components remained as an aspect of psychological thought. Emphasis on the three aspects continued through the nineteenth century into the early twentieth century. However, balanced emphasis on the three aspects appears to have ended with the psychologist McDougall. Behaviorism generally ignored affect and conation, and the information processing and computer based models that replaced behaviorism similarly ignored these aspects. In summary, Hilgard stated that "It is obvious immediately that cognitive psychology is ascendant at present, with a concurrent decline of emphasis upon the affective-conative dimensions." He further stated that an examination of recent articles in psychology affirmed the emphasis on the cognitive to the neglect of the affective and the conative. Confirming this trend in the area of reading, Athey (1971) pointed out that affective factors, with a few exceptions, have been neglected in models of the reading process.

The neglect of affect in models of reading may not only reflect the historically recent bias against studying affective factors, but may also reflect a perception that affective concepts are difficult to define. Attitude, motivation, interest, belief, and value may seem to have a vague quality resisting systematic treatment. Further, relationships between these concepts and cognitive processes operating during reading may appear to be indeterminable.

The lack of emphasis of affect in models of reading, however, did not prevent its being taken into consideration in recent work of Ruddell and Speaker (1985). Ruddell and Speaker realized the importance of affect and therefore included the influence of affective state in their interactive reading process model. Affect was included in a limited capacity, however, and therefore the model required further elaboration before a representation of the full role of affect in reading could be approximated. It thus appeared appropriate to propose a research-based model identifying the central substantive units (constructs) and processes describing the role of affect in reading.

The purpose of the present article is to describe the new model of affect in the reading process and to determine how well the model fits the outcomes of two recent experiments utilizing affective variables as central constructs. A final purpose is to suggest experimental and clinical directions for the future.

Toward an Affect in the Reading Process

To begin, it is necessary to establish a central affective component around which to build the model. The possible candidates are value, belief, interest, attitude, and perhaps some others. Only attitude, however, "has played a central role in the development of American social psychology" (Kiesler, Collins, and Miller, 1969). This primacy may have arisen from early attempts to define it and to measure it rigorously. Hundreds of experimental studies have been performed using attitude as the central construct. The primacy may also have come from the flexibility of attitude as opposed to belief and value. Attitude is considered capable of formation and change in a way not usually associated with these other affective constructs. Perhaps, too, its primacy was a result of the ability of attitude to focus on specifiable objects. Whatever the explanation, it would seem reasonable to choose attitude as a central construct in a model of affective influence upon reading.

Though attitude is centrally important in the affective model, motivation is no less important. The need for a separate motivational component is emphasized by Cofer and Appley (1964). These investigators have concluded in their extensive review of the literature that "it is largely an assertion of faith that it is useful to conceive of attitudes as motivational variables" (p. 805). In addition, Newcomb, Turner, and Converse (1965) have defined attitude as "a state of readiness for motive arousal." Both of these observations point to the need to include a motivational component in the affective model in order to insure that a favorable attitude has a separate, energizing process to accompany it. Thus, if children are to read, they will need not only a favorable attitude toward reading, but also an appropriate motivation.

The inclusion of the motivational component to the model requires that appropriate motivational processes be identified. These motives should be capable of causing reading behavior in children to already have a favorable attitude toward reading. While motivational psychology is complex and is still in a state of flux, the following motives are presented as particularly relevant to reading.

Motives Affecting Decision to Read and Reading Behavior

belongingness and love (Maslow, 1970, pp. 43-45)
curiosity (Berlyne, 1960, 1966)
competence (White, 1959)
achievement (McClelland, 1958, 1961; McClelland, Atkinson, Clark, and
   Lowell, 1953; McClelland and Winter, 1969)
esteem (Maslow, 1970, p. 45)
self-actualization (Maslow, 1970, p. 46)
desires to know and understand (Maslow, 1970, p. 48)
aesthetic motivation (Maslow, 1970, p. 51)

This motive list is an amalgam of the higher end of Maslow's need hierarchy with curiosity, competence, and achievement motives. These three motives were added because they do not appear to be identified with sufficient precision in Maslow's hierarchy.

Though it appears that attitude and motivation influence reading behavior, several other variables of an affective nature may do so also. These affective variables do not seem to be easily classifiable under the category "motivation," nor can they be classified as "attitudes," though they seem closely related to both of these constructs. Instead, they are feelings varying in duration, intensity, and quality. These feelings include such affective conditions as transitory *pleasantness* or *unpleasantness*, extended feeling states called *moods*, feelings focused upon some ideal called *sentiment*, and strong feelings usually designated as *emotion*. All of these are affective in nature and appear to have fewer cognitive aspects than either attitude or motivation. However, these affects appear to influence reading and learning. Bower, Monteiro, and Gilligan (1978), for instance, explored the relationship of mood to learning and found a positive relationship, and Dribbin and Brabender (1979) found that mood was related to audience receptiveness. Based upon these studies, it may be inferred that mood may well influence reading behavior.

It also seems reasonable that sentiment can influence decision to read particular material. Sentiment is defined as a feeling associated with something highly valued or sacred to a person. Examples are patriotic, aesthetic, and religious sentiments. It appeared that these sentiments could excite desire to read if the content of a book mirrored sentiments held by the individual.

Emotion may have an effect upon reading behavior. Emotion can be described as strong feeling, usually of a fundamental nature, tending to have a disruptive effect upon ongoing behavior. Strongly experienced emotions of love, fear, or anger would certainly be expected to disrupt reading. If, however, moderate levels of anger or fear were to be stimulated by the content of a story, the emotion might play an energizing role such that reading would continue even more strongly than before the emotion was aroused. This facilitating effect might well occur if the elicitation of emotion was one of the purposes of the author, such as the emotion of fear while reading a mystery story. The desirable experiencing of an emotion during a dramatic presentation was called *catharsis* by the Greeks.

Historically, the psychological term *affect* has designated processes such as pleasantness/unpleasantness, mood, sentiment, and emotion *(International Encyclopedia of the Social Sciences,* 1968, p. 35). While not included in the historical lists of affects, both attitude and motivation can be considered affective, also, though both of these variables have important cognitive dimensions. Fishbein and Ajzen (1975, p. 342) emphasized affect's role in attitude, stating that "there is widespread agreement that affect is the most essential part of the attitude concept" (p. 11). Motivation also involves affect in the form of satisfaction or pleasant feelings that define goal states (Deci, 1975, pp. 121-123). An important question becomes, therefore, whether the new affective model specifically needs affect as a separate component because both attitude and motivation include affect within their constructs already.

The answer to this question may lie in the relative autonomy of affect. Although affective states continually interact with and form parts of attitude and motivation, affective states such as mood and emotion sometimes appear to take on a life of their own. States of strong depression, anger or fear sometimes separate from the thoughts that originally stimulated them, though it is important to remember Averill's caution (1980, p. 23) that "there are no 'raw feels,' nor uninterpreted sensations of pleasantness or unpleasantness." The model to be proposed therefore posits a continual interaction among affect, attitude and motivation in reading behavior while identifying affect as a separate component. In interaction, positive or negative affect are identified as dimensions of attitude, and sensations of pleasure define end-states characteristic of motive fulfillment. Affect proper, however, is given a separate identity in the new model.

The addition of isolated affect gives comprehensiveness to the new model. Combinations of motivational, attitudinal, and affective processes, along with cognitive factors, can be invoked to explain such higher-order constructs as personality and self-concept. Feelings such as empathy occurring while reading certain books can be explained similarly as complex interactions of attitude, motivation, and affective states.

The final dimension of affect that may be required in the new model is physical sensation. Physical sensation frequently has an affective nature, such as the feeling of pleasure from a caress or pain from a pinprick. Physical feelings arising from outside sources sometimes occur during reading, or physical feelings related to the meaning of the reading material itself sometimes intrude themselves into the reader's consciousness. Physical feelings without relation to specific textual content include cramps from sitting too long in the same position or eye aches. In the textually-related domain, the content of reading materials sometimes stimulates physical responses including increases in perspiration, heart rate, or muscle tension. Feelings arising from both of these sources may influence decision to continue to read.

Of course, there are physical sensations of an almost purely informational nature. The sight of a group of numbers or the feel of a desk may almost be devoid of affective content. Even the visual sensation of words upon a page constitutes sensation. Therefore the kind of physical sensations important in the new model are only those with affective import for the reader. The term *physical feelings* is used to designate physical sensations carrying pleasure or pain as opposed to the physical sensations of a mainly informational nature.

The new affective model of reading thus has four affective processes with the addition of physical feelings. They are attitude, motivation, affect, and physical feelings. Each of these is predicted to influence the reading process. Other affective concepts, such as value, are explained as higher-order interactions of the basic processes.

How Affective Variables Influence Reading in the New Model

With the affective variables identified, it is important to consider the mechanism by which affective and conative variables influence reading. One possibility is that attitude and motivation directly influence attention and comprehension. This may be predicted because affect frequently influences behavior with little or no cognitive mediation (Hochschild, 1979). However, it is clear that a cognitively controlled process using as part of its data the attitudinal, motivational, affective, and physical feeling states of the reader may also influence reading. This cognitively mediated influence of affect upon reading may be represented by a decision process component in the new affective model of reading.

The insertion of a decision component weighing the advisability of reading based upon affective input is shown in the new affective model of reading depicted in Figure 1. Decision to read is contained within a component directly influenced by the four affective variables in the left-hand component of the model.

The decision component influences all of the processes included within the model's reading process component. The left-hand group of processes inside the reading process component are the primary processes of physical orientation and activity, attention, and comprehension. The physical orientation and activity processes in reading (physical stance, eye movement, muscle, tension) appear to be important parts of the primary process of reading and may influence feelings related to reading through the feedback loop at the bottom of the model. In some cases, prolonged quiescence during reading or the strains of attention may produce physical discomforts that cause the reader to stop reading. The model thus

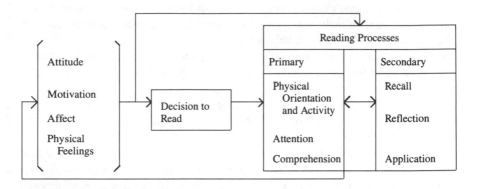

Figure 1. Affective model of reading.

allows feedback from the physical activity associated with reading to influence physical feelings which, in turn, may influence the decision to continue reading.

Attitude toward reading is depicted in the far left component of the model. Attitude may influence attention and comprehension of reading materials through the decision process. Text-specific attitudes include attitudes toward the content, format, and form. The content or meaning of a book is a primary attitude object because it may correspond with the reader's motivations and general background, or it may not correspond. It is much more appropriate to say, "John likes science fiction," specifying a content type, than to say, "John likes reading." In fact, John may not like reading unless he is reading science fiction.

In addition to content, another possible determinant of reading attitude is *format*. This would include the presence or absence of pictures in a literary selection (Samuels, 1970, 1974), type of book cover (Lowery and Grafft, 1968), and print size and style. Another determinant of attitude may be *form*, including such aspects as dialect or syntax. To specify these three aspects—content, format, and form—as possible factors determining attitude toward reading selections may help considerably in the attempt to differentiate the most potent elements contributing to a favorable reading attitude.

In attitude to content, format, and form, there may be other sources determining attitude toward reading. For instance, Downing and Leong (1982, p. 260) cogently pointed out that a reader may have formed a favorable attitude toward an abstract attitude object called "reading." This attitude object would include any reading that anyone might perform anywhere at any time. The formation of such a favorable attitude would be equivalent to identifying reading as a universal good. It might be expected that anyone who possessed this attitude would have a greater probability of deciding to read a given book than a person who had a neutral or a negative attitude toward reading as a universal good. It is also possible that a sentiment toward general reading might develop in conjunction with this attitude, further sustaining reading behavior. Because a general attitude that "reading is good" is clearly possible, this attitude is included in the new model as a possible determiner of decision to read.

In addition to attitudes toward reading as a universal good, it is also possible that attitudes toward the source of reading materials may be important in determining a decision to read. The source of a book or magazine might be a friend, a teacher, or a club. Thus, the present model incorporates the notion that relevant attitudes toward reading may include attitudes toward the content, format, and form but may also include such attitudes as those toward reading as a universal good and attitudes toward the source of reading materials. This expanded notion of the range of attitudes which may influence reading ensures a broad scope for the model, but at the same time poses difficult questions for the researcher who might wish to assess the effects of attitude upon reading. As an example, experimenters who act as sources of reading materials might wish to assess attitude toward experimenters in general and themselves in particular in order to include in their data the full range of independent variables which might influence decision to read the materials in their experiment.

In the affective model, the decision component influences the primary reading processes of physical orientation, attention, and comprehension. The decision component also influences a secondary reading process component including recall, reflection, and application. The secondary component was added because it appeared to be important that readers do more with materials than simply read them. Remembering information (recall), thinking about it (reflection), and acting on it (application) are important activities associated with the primary processes of physical orientation, attention, and comprehension. The secondary reading processes and the primary reading processes are both influenced in the same way by the model's decision making process.

Of course, it may be argued that recall should be included in the primary reading component because reading without some recall is impossible. This argument may be based upon Bartlett's theory of memory (1932), which views recall as a reconstructive process. Since reading is also a reconstructive process, recall would appear to be involved in the primary process of comprehension. Similarly, reflection and application processes would appear to have involvement in the primary processes as well as the secondary. However, identifying recall, reflection, and application as secondary processes emphasizes the existence of operations occurring after preliminary comprehension and having separate functions. In the case of recall, the reconstruction of information following preliminary reading may enhance future ability to remember. Reflection may promote integration of information into the reader's relevant schema. Finally, application may result in a valuable product, either intellectual or physical, for the reader. Therefore these processes were separated from the primary processes of physical orientation, comprehension, and attention with the full realization that they occur within these primary reading processes, but with the thought that there would be an advantage in emphasizing their existence as separate, secondary operations. The separation may be especially helpful in instructing students in the theory and practice of recall, reflection, and application as metacognitive strategies. It clearly commits the model to a broad definition of reading, such as the one found in Herber (1970, p. 9).

The present model thus predicts that the decision component influences the primary and secondary reading processes in the same way. Decision to read, whether primary or secondary processes are involved, is based on attitude, motivation, affect, and physical feelings. Further, feedback from the reading processes may influence the affective component, as symbolized by the line at the bottom of the model.

Although the affective component influences both primary and secondary reading processes through decision making, the model also predicts direct influence of the affective component upon these processes. This direct influence, illustrated by the arrow along the top of the model, bypasses the model's decision component and influences both the primary and secondary reading processes without cognitive mediation. It appears necessary to predict the direct effect of affective variables upon reading because it is likely that the influences of affect frequently are not mediated by conscious decision making. It is possible, of course, that a very broad definition of decision making could be adopted by which any mental event in which an affective variable influences reading behavior could be classified as a "decision." However, the term *decision* in the sense employed for the model refers to a process in which the reader uses coherent, cognitive data gathering strategies for the purpose of evaluating the desirability of beginning or continuing reading or reading related behavior.

The direct influence of attitude, motivation, affect, and physical feelings upon reading would therefore be expected to occur without cognitive mediation. During the process of reading, negative affect may accumulate, directly depressing attention and comprehension processes. Following reading, negative attitudes or affect could suppress recall, reflection, and application. These influences would generally lie outside of the reader's strategic control since the operative affective factors would not have been identified by the reader and hence would not be amenable to change. If they were so identified, it is likely that these factors would have functioned as elements in the reader's decision making process rather than part of the model's direct influence process.

Application of the Model to Two Research Studies

Mathewson (1979, pp. 8-20) performed an experiment which may be used to test the explanatory power of the newly proposed model through a reinterpretation of the experiment's results.

Because only attitude and motivation had been identified as affective variables determining attention and comprehension at the time of the experiment, Mathewson attempted to manipulate both of these factors to determine their influence upon reading. He reasoned that if motivation were extrinsic, it should be able to maintain attention and comprehension regardless of attitude toward the content of a reading selection. However, if there was little extrinsic motivation to read, then favorable attitude toward content would be necessary to sustain reading. This was expected because the relevant motive to read would have to be curiosity or some other intrinsic motive closely tied to favorable attitude toward content.

The extrinsic motive chosen for the experiment was test anxiety. The choice of test anxiety was prompted by its being a frequent extrinsic motivator of reading in the classroom. However, there is a question whether anxiety should have been identified as a motive. It is qualitatively unlike any of the needs identified by Maslow (1970) or others (see particularly Klein, 1982). Anxiety does appear to be related to the basic needs because it frequently arises if basic needs are not met. However, in terms of the present model, the affective variable utilized in the Mathewson (1979) experiment was an unpleasant feeling of anxiety rather than an extrinsic motive. In this interpretation, the children sought to reduce the unpleasant feeling of anxiety by reading their assigned story so that they could answer the questions that they were told would be asked.

Although the affective model identifies the state which Mathewson (1979) sought to stimulate as an unpleasant feeling of anxiety, there is an alternative possibility that in some children he stimulated competence motivation instead of anxiety. The statement "You will be tested on this story when I return" could have been a challenge for some children rather than a source of anxiety. For these children, it may have been competence motivation which sustained high attention and comprehension in the high motivation condition. For others, the high attention and comprehension may have been the result of an attempt to reduce the feeling of test anxiety. Whichever affective condition was stimulated, the instructions clearly produced the expected effect. Whether they read an interesting story or a dull story, students read with high comprehension if they expected to be tested.

In the medium extrinsic motivation condition, the experimenter said, "All I care about is how much fun you have with the story." Children in this condition, in contrast to those in the previous experimental condition, did not hear that they were going to be tested. As a result, children scored high on a posttest only if they had been given the interesting story. If they had the dull story, they scored low. Thus the affective responses to story content appear to have determined whether the children performed well or poorly on the posttest. In terms of the affective model, favorable attitudes and affect supported a decision to continue reading in the case of the interesting story. In the case of the dull story, unfavorable attitudes and affect led the children to stop reading.

Finally, in the case of low extrinsic motivation, the experimenter told the children, "I will be gone a few minutes. If you want to, you may play with anything on the table in front of you. Just have fun, and I will be back soon." The children were confronted with some toys and either the dull or the interesting story. In this condition, all children scored low on the test. The conclusion in the Mathewson (1979) study was that some minimal extrinsic motivation may be needed to stimulate the reading even of interesting stories.

Unfortunately, the experiment did not adequately explore the possibilities of what may have happened in the low extrinsic motivation condition. In this condition, most of the children decided "not to read the story at all." Because they had other objects on the table which competed affectively for their attention, most turned to other things than reading. When the experimenter gave the test, many children were tested on a story they had not read. In these conditions, the low scores were understandable.

In the low extrinsic motivation condition cases in which children had noticed the reading selection but decided against reading it, the decision making component of the model may have been brought into play. Attitudes, motives, and affect may have combined to give a negative decision to read. The negative decision may have turned behavior into other channels than reading. Alternatively, a direct process of affective influence may have turned attention away from the reading material.

Not only may the affective support have been too low to stimulate decision to read, but the cognitive support may have been too low in the low extrinsic motivation condition. The table could be taken to represent a figure-ground problem in which several items were present for possible manipulation and play. Several things may have elicited more response than did the reading selection. It is possible that the reading selection was not even noticed in some cases.

A reinterpretation of the study must finally deal with the comprehension posttest results. In the light of some students deciding not to read the story, it is more accurate to call the posttest a test of information acquisition rather than a test of comprehension or recall. Comprehension or recall tests presuppose that material has previously been read to some degree, but the affective model clearly implies that there may be a decision against reading. If this is true, then a low posttest score may reflect lack of acquisition of information from text because a reader decided not to read, and not because the reader lacked comprehension or recall abilities. This distinction is generally important because identifying the cause of low scores as a result of lack of reading skill or of decision not to read is important for remediation.

The Mathewson study (1979, pp. 8-20) can be reinterpreted in the light of the affective model. The model raises the possibility that the results of the experiment are more complex than they first appeared. The motivation variable may not have been a motive in its own right, an additional motive may have been present, the comprehension test may not have measured comprehension, and some students may not have noticed the story.

A second study illustrating an application of the new affective model of reading was conducted by Lipson (1983, pp. 448-457). This study explored the effects of prior background knowledge upon the reading of materials either neutral to the reader's cultural background, consistent with it, or conflicting with it. The hypotheses of the study were that reading materials take longer to read, are harder to recall, and are more distorted if content is culturally unfamiliar than if it is neutral or familiar. If the materials are culturally familiar, intrusions from the reader's own background were expected to take place.

In particular, the Lipson study utilized Catholic, Jewish, and culturally neutral reading selections. The Jewish selection was entitled *Bar Mitzvah* and the Catholic selection was entitled *First Communion*. These selections were read by Jewish and Catholic children. It was expected that the children would read the selection inconsistent with their religious background less accurately than the religiously consistent or the neutral selection. The results of the study supported the predictions. Culturally compatible reading materials resulted in greater amounts and accuracy of recall than did culturally incompatible materials. This result was interpreted as supporting schema theory because the selection consistent with the prior religious schema was reconstructed with greater ease and precision.

However, Lipson (1983) also took into consideration the possibility that another model may have accounted for her findings. She stated that "quite possibly, the subjects rejected a great deal of the information in the culturally 'adverse' passage." This interpretation was based on the idea that "a negative attitude toward a culture may result in misinterpretation of texts from that culture." This interpretation is consistent with the affective model of reading and forms an alternative interpretation of the data. Perhaps it was not wholly background information which caused the children to recall less of the religiously unfamiliar reading selection, but also (or instead) unfavorable attitudes toward the content of the selection that influenced a decision not to attend or comprehend. Another possibility that Lipson did not explore is the converse: favorable attitudes toward materials about one's own religion may have heightened attention, comprehension, and recall of religiously compatible selection for some students. This is the favorable side of the affective model of reading.

It is very difficult in an experiment like Lipson's to know what part of the dependent variables' variance was caused by background knowledge and what part was caused by attitude, relevant motivation, and affect. Lipson's mentioning of attitude as an alternative explanation in what was basically a cognitively oriented experiment showed a beginning of the kind of approach that should be adopted if a better balance among the cognitive, affective, and conative variables is to be achieved in reading experimentation.

Implications for Research

The affective model as newly constituted makes a large number of predictions as to the influence of affective factors on the primary and secondary reading processes. Research should be undertaken to determine whether these predictions are supported in well-designed experimentation.

The predictions concerning the effects of attitude and motivation upon reading are basic to the model. Favorable attitude toward content, whether preexisting or experimentally induced, should give rise to heightened attention and comprehension of reading materials. In addition, favorable attitude should stimulate greater recall, reflection, and application. Experiments can be designed to test all of these predictions. However, in testing the effects of attitude toward content upon reading processes, the favorable attitudes to be used as independent variables should be experimentally created rather than preexisting.

The reason for not using preexisting attitudes is that they probably are accompanied by knowledge which may confound the interpretation of the experiment. For example, if an experiment is done to determine the effects of liking dogs upon recall of a reading selection about dogs, the results would be biased by the fact that the readers who liked dogs probably had read and listened to a large amount of information about dogs in the past. This previous reading and listening would have increased these readers' knowledge with respect to dogs, and hence answering the questions based on the selection about dogs would be easier for them than for those who did not have favorable attitudes toward dogs. Therefore, in testing for effects of favorable attitude toward a specific content, the favorable attitude to be tested should be produced at the time of the experiment in order to avoid the contaminating effect of previous knowledge.

The problem is to create rather than to find an attitude which may influence reading. However, creation of an attitude requires that an attitude object be selected and that readers be brought to the state in which they either like or dislike this object. As an example, an experiment might be designed in which two experimental groups are exposed to preliminary information about a fictional country. In Experimental Group A, readers might read information about a country called Bareda indicating that the country is a playground of the jet set, has diamond mines, and is characterized by political intrigue. In Experimental Group B, Bareda might be described as a barren, underdeveloped country with few inhabitants, bad weather, and no plant life. Following attitude formation, readers in both groups might be asked to read the same story about Bareda. If the previous information about Bareda had been believed and the attitudes had been formed as expected, it could be predicted from the affective model that the story would be read with greater comprehension and recall by Group A readers than by Group B readers. The experimenter's success in inducing favorable and unfavorable attitudes toward Bareda would, of course, have to be verified at the end of the experiment by the use of attitude scales or by some other method.

It would not be expected that any preexisting schema would influence comprehension in this experiment because the only information about the fictional country known prior to the reading is controlled by the experimenter. In contrast, readers with favorable attitudes toward a known country, say Ireland, would be expected to know more about that country than readers who had neutral or negative attitudes. Thus the method would avoid the problem of the effects of preexisting knowledge being confounded with the effects of attitude.

The affective model also predicts that motivation can influence reading behavior. The effect of motivation upon decision to read and reading processes begins with an identification of a particular motive. An interesting example is the belongingness and love motive identified by Maslow (1970, p. 43). A researcher may ask whether it is possible that belongingness, or the need for acceptance by others, might energize the reading process. Several ways in which reading might do this could be explored. It might be noted that books claiming to make people more lovable are sometimes purchased by adults and that children sometimes read "fad" books merely to be "one of the crowd." An experiment could be designed to test this latter notion. For instance, children might be asked to read an article because they would be discussing it with one child, five children, or ten children. It might be expected that the more children with whom a child anticipated discussing a story, the more the child would attend and comprehend during reading. This might be expected because the need for belongingness and love would motivate reading to a higher degree when discussion in a larger group was anticipated. Emotion also might be examined as a determiner of decision to read and reading. The research difficulty here is the experimental manipulation of emotional states. As an example, a cheerful film might be shown to one group and a sad film to another group of children. Immediately following the films, a neutral reading selection could be assigned together with a mood assessment instrument. Lower comprehension by the children who had viewed the sad film than by those who had viewed the happy film would support the conclusion that mood influences attention, comprehension, and recall.

Finally, the possibility that physical feelings can influence reading behavior seems almost too obvious to need testing. However, in medical emergency or military situations, readers may have to read technical manuals under conditions of physical discomfort. Experiments testing comprehension, recall, and application under conditions of physical discomfort would require great care in their design and implementation, but they might have important implications for the writing of manuals intended to be used during emergencies.

There are many other possibilities for research present in the model. Not only do the affective variables influence decision to read and reading processes, but also the products of comprehension, recall, reflection, and application are predicted to influence the affective variables through a feedback process. These products may stimulate achievement motivation or curiosity. They may produce favorable or unfavorable attitudes. They may bring forth affects of anger, happiness, or depression. All of these responses may influence decision to read further. Therefore, reading material designed to elicit various affective responses may result in a decision to continue reading or stop reading, depending upon what affective responses are elicited. Experimentally, it is necessary to confirm that the intended responses were elicited even if differences in the information gained from text were as predicted.

As intriguing as some of the envisioned experiments are, it may be even more important to examine the clinical applications of the new affective model. Though the reading clinician is not trained as a psychotherapist, the model suggests that decision not to read may be influenced by affective variables. If this is true, a reading clinician or teacher may be able to help a child who frequently decides not to read, if effective techniques are used.

Clinical Implications of the Affective Model

As a heuristic research tool, the affective model provides hypotheses to be tested. Support for the model accrues if hypotheses generated by the model are confirmed. In the clinical domain, however, the model may be taken as a guide for diagnosis and remediation. The clinician aware of the model's predictions performs initial assessments to determine whether a reader is experiencing affective influences which inhibit his or her decision to read. If there are such factors, the clinician plans a course of remediation which removes affective blocks to reading progress and which facilitates reading through the development of favorable attitudes, motivations, and affect.

The first question to be answered in the clinical use of the affective model concerns assessment of affective factors operative in determining decision to read. This assessment can take the form of attitude scales, informal assessment through observation, mood and emotion test instruments, and reports of physical feelings which may attend reading. The assessment data should be collected with special emphasis on emotional responses to reading situations. Following the initial assessment of affective state with respect to reading, the reading clinician can begin a course of treatment if affective factors appear to inhibit reading. This course of treatment would vary depending upon the affective factor or factors to be modified and upon the theoretical orientation of the particular clinician. However, four general approaches to the modification of affective factors may be used. They are: 1) positive association, 2) reward, 3) modeling, and 4) persuasion.

Positive association is a basic technique to develop emotional responses. This technique, based on Pavlov's pioneering work, can operate by pairing something a person likes with something toward which the person is neutral. The neutral object eventually elicits a favorable response through association. In concrete terms, a reader who has a neutral attitude toward books might be presented with books in a pleasant physical location. Prolonged association between the pleasant location and the books could help to develop liking for books.

The technique of *reward,* also called operant conditioning, depends upon the clinician knowing what is rewarding for a particular reader. After the clinician has observed an instance of reading behavior, the clinician gives the reader a reward. The probability of the reader's reading in the future is increased by the reward following the reading behavior. If, however, the reader does not view what is intended to be a reward as truly rewarding, the probability of future reading is not increased.

Modeling is an excellent strategy for changing attitude toward reading. Seeing an admired person reading can stimulate heightened reading behavior in a reluctant reader. This modeling effect could be carried out in clinical sessions if the clinician himself or herself served as the model. If a clinician and client read together for several clinical sessions, a modeling effect may be established which changes the client's attitudes, motives, and affects with respect to reading.

Persuasion may be used to change affective responses toward reading materials. If the clinician can persuade a client through good reasons that reading is good, either specific reading or reading in general, then the persuasion may change affective response to reading and reading materials.

A clinical procedure aimed at changing attitudes, motivations, and affects connected with reading can be based on the four techniques listed. Clinicians who wish to change affective responses toward reading may use the four methods as isolated techniques or may combine the basic techniques into a general system. General systems designed to modify negative affective factors for the purpose of improving reading may be called Reading Affect Therapy.

If affect with respect to reading is favorably modified by Reading Affect Therapy, the model predicts that both the primary and secondary reading processes will be facilitated and that more reading will occur. Enhanced recall, reflection, and application should be expected. These results should lead to long term gains in reading development if the therapeutic techniques are combined with sound reading improvement strategies.

REFERENCES

Athey, I.J. Language models and reading. *Reading Research Quarterly,* 7, 1971, 16-110.

Averill, J.R. On the paucity of positive emotions. In K.R. Blankstein, B. Pliner, and J. Polity (Eds.), *Assessment and modification of emotional behavior,* Vol. 6. New York: Plenum Press, 1980.

Bartlett, F.C. *Remembering: A study in experimental and social psychology.* New York: Cambridge University Press, 1932.

Berlyne, D.E. *Conflict, arousal, and curiosity.* New York: McGraw-Hill,1960.

Berlyne, D.E. Curiosity and exploration. *Science,* 153, 1966, 25-33.

Bower, G.H., Monteiro, K.P., and Gilligan, S.G. Emotional mood as a context for learning and recall. *Journal of Verbal Learning and Verbal Behavior,* 17, 1978, 573-585.

Cofer, C.N., and Appley, M.H. *Motivation: Theory and research.* New York: John Wiley and Sons, 1964.

Deci, E.L. *Intrinsic motivation.* New York: Plenum Press, 1975.

Downing, J., and Leong, C.K. *Psychology of reading.* New York: Macmillan, 1982.

Dribben, E., and Brabender, V. The effect of mood inducement upon audience receptiveness. *Journal of Social Psychology,* 107, 1979, 135-136.

Fishbein, M., and Ajzen, I. *Belief, attitude, intention, and behavior: An introduction to theory and research.* Reading, MA: Addison-Wesley, 1975.

Herber, H.L. *Teaching reading in content areas.* Englewood Cliffs, NJ: Prentice-Hall, 1970.

Hilgard, E. The trilogy of mind: Cognition, affection, and conation. *Journal of the History of the Behavioral Sciences,* 16, 1980, 107-117.

Hochschild, A.R. Emotion work, feeling rules, and social structure. *American Journal of Sociology.* 85, 1979, 551-575.

International Encyclopedia of the Social Sciences, Vol. 5. New York: Macmillan and The Free Press, 1968.

Kiesler, C.A., Collins, B.E., and Miller, N. *Attitude change.* New York: John Wiley and Sons, 1969.

Klein, S.B. *Motivation: Biosocial approaches.* New York: McGraw-Hill, 1982.

Lipson, M.J. The influence of religious affiliation on children's memory for text information. *Reading Research Quarterly,* 18, 1983, 448-457.

Lowery, L.F., and Grafft, W. Paperback books and reading attitudes. *Reading Teacher,* 21, 1968, 618-623.

Maslow, A.H. *Motivation and personality.* New York: Harper and Row, 1970.

Mathewson, G.C. The function of attitude in the reading process. In H. Singer and R.B. Ruddell (Eds.), *Theoretical models and processes of reading* (Second Edition). Newark, DE: International Reading Association, 1976.

Mathewson, G.C. The moderating effect of extrinsic motivation upon the attitude/comprehension relationship in reading. In C. Pennock (Ed.), *Reading comprehension at four linguistic levels.* Newark, DE: International Reading Association, 1979.

McClelland, D.C. Risk taking in children with high and low need for achievement. In J.W. Atkinson (Ed.), *Motives in fantasy, action, and society.* Princeton, NJ: Van Nostrand, 1958.

McClelland, D.C. *The achieving society.* Princeton, NJ: Van Nostrand, 1961.

McClelland, D.C., Atkinson, J.W., Clark, R.W., and Lowell, E.L. *The achievement motive.* New York: Appleton-Century-Croft, 1953.

McClelland, D.C., and Winter, D.G. *Motivating economic achievement.* New York: The Free Press, 1969.

Newcomb, T.M., Truner, R.H., and Converse, P.E. *Social psychology.* New York: Holt, Rinehart, and Winston, 1965.

Ruddell, R.B., and Speaker, R.B. The interactive reading process: A model. In H. Singer and R.B. Ruddell (Eds.), *Theoretical models and processes of reading* (Third Edition). Newark, DE: International Reading Association, 1985.

Samuels, S.J. Effects of pictures on learning to read, comprehension, and attitudes. *Review of Educational Research,* 40, 1970, 397-407.

Samuels, S.J., Biesbrock, E., and Terry, P.R. *Journal of Educational Research,* 67, 1974, 243-246.

White, R.W. Motivation reconsidered: The concept of competence. *Psychological Review,* 66, 1959, 297-333.

Section Four

TEACHING AND RESEARCH ISSUES

Introduction to Teaching and Research Issues

In this section, we have provided some selections which address the following questions:
1. What implications does a theory based approach have for reading instruction?
2. What strategies and models can teachers use to teach students how to learn from text?
3. Do developmental theories have valid implications for processes of reading?
4. What research can be done to improve the knowledge base for class instruction in comprehension? What principles should be followed and what pitfalls should be avoided in carrying out this research?

Drawing upon the interactive schema theoretic view of reading (see selections by Adams and Collins, Anderson, and Rumelhart, this volume), Robert Tierney and P. David Pearson discuss instructional applications for teaching comprehension. They first explain that readers, in order to construct meaning for a text, build a model of the meaning of the text in the form of a scenario and modify the scenario as they obtain additional information from the text. The authors then state four pedagogical prescriptions.

Next, Ernst Rothkopf presents strategies a teacher can use for facilitating comprehension and a model for learning from text. His model essentially consists of interactions among the teacher, the learner, the text, and the goals or purposes for learning.

Earlier in this volume, Yopp and Singer presented another model that explains how the activation of the teacher's resources influences the interaction between the reader and the text. An implication of these two models is that the teacher can modify the nature and difficulty of the task, the characteristics of the learner, the goal and the criterion for success, and the teacher resources so that all students in the normal range of ability can learn to read and learn from text. Other models presented in this volume by Singer, Ruddell and Speaker, and Goodman also have implications for classroom instruction. Samuels has invented and tested a method called "repeated reading" that develops automaticity in a reader for a particular passage. The method enables readers, especially poor readers, to allocate attention to higher cognitive processes and consequently to improve their comprehension of the passage. Gough's information processing model, although primarily useful for didactic and heuristic purposes, does have some implications for diagnosis and instruction. Clinicians can use the model to determine and isolate components and processes in the reader that are not present or not functioning properly, and then devise ameliorative procedures.

In this section, Athey explains that developmental processes have frequently been applied to reading instruction. She warns against automatically using these processes without first testing for their instructional validity.

In his review of research, Singer presents a multitude of hypotheses that need to be tested. They are grouped into input, mediational, and output or response formulation categories. He concludes by enumerating principles to follow and pitfalls to avoid in testing the hypotheses in classroom settings, and provides research examples.

Only a few papers on instruction could be included in this section. Following is a selected list of recent annotated references on this topic.

ANNOTATED REFERENCES

Duffy, Gerald G., Laura R. Roehler, and Jana Mason. *Comprehension Instruction: Perspectives and Suggestions.* New York: Longman, 1984.
See Ch. 18: Direct explanation of comprehension processes for a model of reading instruction that emphasizes metacognitive processes.

Flood, James (Ed.). *Promoting Reading Comprehension.* Newark, Delaware: International Reading Association, 1984.
This volume is divided into three sections: instruction research in comprehension, the reader and the text, and the reader and the teacher.

McNeil, John. *Reading Comprehension: New Directions for Classroom Practices.* Glenview, Illinois: Scott, Foresman, 1984.
Text contains explanations and strategies for schema assessment, development of active readers, metacognition in reading, modifying or restructuring schemata, vocabulary and comprehension instruction, and understanding different types of discourse.

Purves, Alan C., and Olive Niles (Eds.). *Becoming Readers in a Complex Society,* Eighty-Third Yearbook of the National Society for the Study of Education. Chicago: University of Chicago Press, 1984.
Contains sections on "The state of reading and the school," "The process and practice of reading," and "Effective programs to help people become readers."

Reed, Linda, and Spencer Ward (Eds.). *Basic Skills: Issues and Choices,* Volume 2. National Institute of Education, Basic Skills Program. St. Louis, Missouri: CEMREL, 1981.
Points of view on teaching reading.

Ruddell, Robert . "A study of teaching effectiveness variables of influential teachers." In M. Douglass (Ed.), *Reading Reading.* Fiftieth Anniversary Perspectives, Claremont Reading Conference. Claremont, California: Claremont Reading Conference, 1983.
Analyzes and presents characteristics of teachers who have had an impact on students.

Singer, Harry. "Teaching comprehension," in J. Husen and T.N. Postlethwaite (Eds.), *International Encyclopedia of Education: Research and Study.* Oxford, England: Pergamon Press, 1984.
After a review of major changes in the definition of reading, strategies are presented for teaching reading, including text characteristics, student resources, interactions between the reader and the text, and developmental instruction from preschool through the high school.

Teaching Issues

Learning to Learn from Text:
A Framework for Improving Classroom Practice

ROBERT J. TIERNEY
P. DAVID PEARSON
University of Illinois

We believe that if teachers understand the nature of reading comprehension and learning from text, they will have the basis for evaluating and improving learning environments. In this regard, we find many advances in the psychology and pedagogy of reading comprehension that provide exciting possibilities for changing our approaches to helping students learn how to learn from text. For example, in terms of texts, we present evidence that suggests that less reliance should be placed upon traditional readability procedures involved in text selection and use, and that more credence should be given to teachers' impressionistic examinations of the extent to which a text fits with and might be used by selected students.

With respect to readers, teachers should recognize that a reader has a right to an interpretation and that reading comprehension is an interactive process involving more than a regurgitation of an author's explicit ideas. Readers should be encouraged to actively engage their background knowledge prior to, during, and after reading. They should be given opportunities to appreciate and evaluate the adequacy of their own perspective and other interpretations, to monitor their own progress through a text, and to discriminate new learnings from old knowledge.

Curriculum objectives might address the importance, nature, and influence of a reader's background knowledge; the need for a variable balance between reader based and text based processing; and the importance of selected monitoring strategies as well as transfer skills. Widely practiced notions that compartmentalize comprehension into simple question types on a continuum from literal to inferred to evaluative should be rethought. Prescriptions for processing texts that disregard the everchanging interplay of text, purpose, and reader should be discarded. In their stead, we advocate the adoption of teaching procedures that encourage students to monitor their own processing strategies – how they allocate attention to text versus prior knowledge, how they can tell *what* and *that* they know, and how to apply fixup strategies when comprehension is difficult.

In this paper, we will amplify each of the preceding notions about reading comprehension and classroom practice. First, we present some basic notions about reading comprehension. Thereupon, we discuss the implications of these notions for teaching. One should note that the suggestions for teaching are not intended to be exhaustive, exemplary, or very specific; instead, they are intended to provide teachers with guidelines and cursory examples of ways in which they might proceed to develop their own teaching procedures. We hope that the suggestions will be sufficiently explicit to guide adaptation and development.

Some Basic Notions about Reading Comprehension and Learning

Consider for a moment what is involved in comprehending the following passage:

The Dust Bowl

During World War I, prices had tempted farmers to grow wheat and cotton in the former grazing lands of the Plains region. Plows and harrows broke up the deep, tough sod that had previously prevented erosion and conserved moisture in this semiarid region. When the years 1933-1935 proved unusually dry, there was danger that the region would become a desert. Terrible dust storms carried away topsoil in such quantities that even on the Atlantic seaboard the sun was obscured by a yellow haze. The water table of parts of the Plains region sank so low that wells ran dry. Between 1934 and 1939 an estimated 350,000 farmers emigrated from the "dust bowl." To take care of immediate distress, Congress provided funds so that dust bowl farmers could get new seed and livestock. On a long term basis, the Department of Agriculture dealt with the dust bowl by helping farmers to plant 190 million trees in shelter beds, which cut wind velocity and retained moisture. Farmers were also encouraged to restore the Plains to what they had been in the days of the cattle kingdom and earlier – a grazing region. (Bragdon and McCutchen, 1978, p. 623)

Readers familiar with farming and the Plains area of the United States will likely recognize how the drought, forces of supply and demand, and soil changes interacted to contribute to the deteriorating conditions of the Dust Bowl era. They might be able to visualize the changing conditions of the topography and sense the frustration and anguish experienced by the farmers. Readers unfamiliar with farming but possessing first hand experience with economic hardship might focus on the personal hardships and family upheaval associated with periods of depression. Readers who have experienced both farm life and economic hardship might be able to go beyond visualizing the drought conditions to experiencing "a dryness of mouth" and "lump in the throat" as their interpretation of text triggers recall of specific experiences from the past.

The point of the example is that comprehension never occurs in a vacuum; it cannot proceed independently of a reader's fund of related experiences of background knowledge (or schemata—singular, schema—to use the recently rediscovered terminology of cognitive scientists). Comprehension is doomed to be at least somewhat idiosyncratic or at least conditioned by individual or group differences in background knowledge. And, in fact, there have been literally dozens of experimental demonstrations of the role that differences in background knowledge play in determining how students understand and retrieve information encountered in texts. Whereas this point may seem to belabor the obvious, current teaching and assessment procedures, with their emphasis on correct answers and preferred interpretations, seem to operate on the assumption that comprehension occurs independent of individual differences in background knowledge.

How Does Comprehension Proceed?

If comprehension is not simply a matter of mapping the author's message into a reader's memory, how does it occur? Let us begin with an example, taken from Collins, Brown, and Larkin (1977).

Window Text

> He plunked down $5.00 at the window. She tried to give him $2.50, but he refused to take it. So when they got inside, she bought him a large bag of popcorn. (p. 3)

With the initial statement, "He plunked down $5.00 at the window," the readers begin a search to build a model of the meaning of the text. One reader may invoke a racetrack scenario as a model; a second, a bank; a third, a movie theater. Each of these scenarios or models may be thought of as different schemata that different readers would invoke because of different levels of experience they have had with such scenarios in the past. Once invoked, each schema provides a framework for continuing the search to build a model for what the text means. For example, the racetrack schema creates expectations that bets, odds, horses, and jockeys will be mentioned soon, whereas the movie theater schema creates expectations for film title, popcorn, and a stage with a screen.

Cognitive scientists like David Rumelhart (1977; 1980) say that schemata have certain slots that must be filled and that comprehension consists of recognizing specific items in a text that fill those slots. For example, "He" in the first sentence is a candidate for the "bettor" slot in a racetrack schema, the "depositor" slot in a bank schema, or "the movie goer" slot in the movie theater scenario. As depicted in Figure 1, they may have constructed an initial model of the text involving a bank window, with some bound slots (concepts enclosed by boxes), and some slots awaiting binding (concepts enclosed by circles).

As readers proceed, they progressively refine their models: "She" is usually defined as the recipient of the money; "$2.50" is usually identified as change.

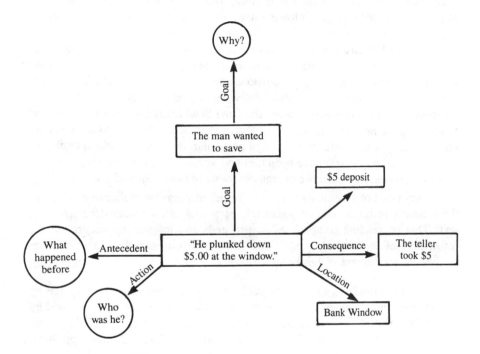

Figure 1. An initial stage in the construction of a model or scenario for the "Window Text."

Then with the statement, "So when they go inside. . .popcorn," readers usually recognize a conflict. They realize their models no longer match the text and are implausible, disconnected, and incomplete. To restructure their model, they might question previous interpretations (for example, that the female was a bank clerk or a bet taker) and shift to a different schema — from a bank or racetrack to a theater. Eventually, it is likely that a model will evolve that involves the purchase of two tickets and an attempt by a date to share the expenses. At this point, readers will sense that they have accounted for the text and that their interpretations are plausible, connected, and complete; that is, their interpretations make sense, are coherent, and account for the text as well as their purposes for reading.

These same notions of reading comprehension can be applied to the passage "The Dust Bowl." With the initial statement, "During World War I, prices had tempted farmers to grow wheat and cotton in the former grazing lands of the Plains region," readers will likely activate their knowledge of farming and constrain these ideas in terms of the time period (Warld War I) and the type of farming to which the author alluded (wheat and cotton). As readers proceed, they are expected to relate these changes in farming—now focused on wheat and cotton—to plowing and the effects of plowing upon the conservation of moisture and potential for soil erosion. Across the next several sentences, "When the years. . .terrible dust storms. . .wells run dry," readers need to activate other background knowledge, maintain their focus, and progressively refine a model for the text. Assuming a singular purpose and adequate background knowledge, it is likely that readers will eventually develop a model for the text that involves an appreciation of the events causing the Dust Bowl crisis and what Congress did to alleviate the problem. Readers will then either tacitly or consciously consider the adequacy of their interpretation—in particular, the extent to which their purposes for reading the text have been met and accounted for in relation to the text and, sometimes, the relevance or transfer value of their acquired understanding.

A key point of schema theory, then, is that reading comprehension is akin to the progressive refinement of a scenario or model that a reader develops for a text. That is, reading comprehension proceeds and inferencing occurs via the refinement of the reader's model. As Collins, Brown, and Larkin (1977) described the refinement of the reader's model:

> The initial model is a partial model, constructed from schemas triggered by the beginning elements of the text. The models are progressively refined by trying to fill the unspecified slots in each model as it is constructed . . . and the search for relevant information is constrained more and more. (pp. 4-5)

Within this framework, the reader's schemata drive text processing toward the refinement of a model or scenario that "matches" the text against the reader's world and that is complete, interconnected, and plausible. That is, the reader's schemata will be involved in construction of a scenario to account for the elements and relationships within the text and the world as the reader sees it. If the reader's model seems tenable, then those schemata that comprise the model will be involved in the further text processing. If the reader's model seems untenable, then schemata will drive the reexamination, reconstruction, or restructuring of elements in the text to build a new model.

To summarize, the following statements can be made about reading comprehension: 1) A reader's background knowledge including purposes, has an overriding influence upon the reader's development of meaning; and 2) reading comprehension involves the activation, focusing, maintaining, and refining of ideas toward developing interpretations (models) that are plausible, interconnected, and complete. In addition, there is a sense in which the reader's comprehension involves two other facets: the reader's *knowing* (either tacitly or consciously) that his or her interpretations for a text are plausible, interconnected, and completely make sense, and, ideally, the reader's evaluation of the transfer value of any acquired understandings.

Pedagogical Implications

Recent examinations of instructional practices suggest that there is not much in the way of worthwhile practices for developing or improving comprehension in schools (Durkin, 1978-1979; Tierney, LaZansky, and Schallert, 1981). Instead, there is and has been a lot of comprehension testing and practice (students working by themselves on worksheets or answering questions) and a great deal of informal assessment (teachers quizzing students about text selections). In most lessons, students are given passages to read. During or after reading the passages, teachers ask questions (either orally or via a worksheet). Any discussion of responses focuses on finding a right answer. In terms of skill acquisition, a high premium has been placed upon separate objectives unrelated to any comprehensive model of reading comprehension or learning and clustered around curriculum objectives or arbitrarily defined skill categories (e.g., literal, inferential, and evaluative comprehension) that give little attention to the role of a reader's background knowledge and the importance of improving a reader's abilities to learn how to learn.[1] Reading comprehension is an area of the curriculum for which there has been little in the way of progress. Moreover, the changes that have occurred have not been tied to a careful analysis of the nature of reading comprehension and learning. We suggest that, *if* teachers understand the nature of reading comprehension and learning, *then* they have the basis for determining what might facilitate and what might impede the development of comprehension and learning. We believe that a schema-theoretic perspective offers such a basis. Accordingly, we suggest the following guidelines for implementing curriculum improvements. Our guidelines are tied to three traditional and interrelated segments in typical lessons for reading selection: preparing for reading, guiding reader-text interaction, and facilitating postreading comprehension and learning.

Prerequisite for Reading: Does the Reader Have Schemata Relevant for Understanding a Text?

Our first guideline addresses the empirically validated conclusion that a reader's prior knowledge has a pervasive influence upon understanding. Specifically, it is concerned with whether a match or mismatch exists between the purposes and prior knowledge of readers and the intentions and expectations of authors. That is, does the reader have the relevant schemata for a text?

Consider first the issue of match between *an author's intentions and a reader's purposes*. In our reviews of textbook materials, we have encountered numerous examples where text intended for one purpose is forced to fit other purposes. With little regard for the integrity of a selection, some publishers seem to presume that text well written for one purpose will be appropriate and well written for other purposes. For example, in a certain biology textbook, the publisher uses a text describing the changing color of leaves to try to explain the physical process of these changes. The questions that are asked following the selection assume that the readers have been given many more details than the text provides; further, they totally disregard the descriptive-aesthetic functions that the text appears to serve. In the elementary classroom, simple narratives usually intended to be read for enjoyment are often sabotaged by an excessive use of poorly fitting questions (e.g., detail questions dealing with trivial information) under the guise of skill objectives.

What can teachers do? Prior to using text for pedagogical purposes, they can and should consider the functions that texts are intended to serve against the purposes for which a teacher intends and students will likely initiate. For example, text might be examined by first isolating the essential understandings that students are expected to derive from a text and then examining the extent and nature of support (usually in the form of concrete examples and analogies that can bind new learnings to old) for these understandings provided within the text. If the reader's purposes are quite unlike those intended by the author, and if the text cannot be augmented *even with teacher support* (i.e., the teacher provides the analogies and examples), then it should not be read to elicit those assumed understandings. Compare the obvious differences between the understandings that readers might be expected to glean from Stephen Crane's *The Red Badge of Courage* (1966), which uses the U.S. Civil War as background, and from a chapter on the Civil War in a history textbook. In the former, the themes of death, fear, and cowardice evoked by the experiences of a young man participating in war are likely to capture the reader. In the latter, the facts and concepts that describe and define the Civil War will be paramount. For Crane's treatment, it might be reasonable to expect a reader to glean an appreciation of the mood of the experience of war; for the textbook chapter, it might be reasonable to expect the reader to develop an appreciation of the causes, progress, and consequences of the Civil War. Even with a great deal of teacher support (including additional information, clarification, and other material), neither text could serve the purposes for which the other text seems intended.

Consider the issues of mismatch between an author's expectations regarding audience and a reader's prior background of experience. There are many times when a text written for an audience with certain background knowledge is given to an audience with different or limited knowledge of this same topic. For example, note the difficulties an American reader will incur when trying to understand the following passage, even if it were revised to a lower readability level.

Today's Cricket

The batsmen were merciless against the bowlers. The bowlers placed their men in slips and covers. But to no avail. The batsmen hit one four after another along with an occasional six. Not once did a ball look like it would hit their stumps or be caught.

Revised Version

The men were at bat against the bowlers. They did not show any pity. The bowlers placed their men in slips. They placed their men in covers. It did not help. The batsmen hit a lot of fours. They hit some sixes. No ball hit the stumps. No ball was caught.

Or consider the following segment taken from a biology text (Gallant, 1975):

The Garbage Collectors of the Sea

The garbage collectors of the sea are decomposers. Day and night, ocean plants and animals that die, and the body wastes of living animals, slowly drift down to the sea floor. There is a steady rain of such material that builds up on the sea bottom. This is especially true on the continental shelves, where life is rich. It is less true in the desert regions of the deep ocean.

As on the land, different kinds of bacteria also live in the sea. They attack the remains of dead plant and animal tissue and break it down into nutrients. These nutrients are then taken up by plant and animal plankton alike. Among such nutrients are nitrate, phosphate, manganese, silica, and calcium....

It does not take too much effort to identify the readers for whom these texts, even if adapted to readability, might be inappropriate or incomprehensible. The first passage is written for an audience knowledgeable about cricket; the second passage is intended for an American high school student with an understanding of decomposition, continental shelves, body wastes, and bacteria. We would predict that readers without these understandings will have a great deal of difficulty reading the text and will likely develop incomplete or inappropriate interpretations for the text.

How can teachers assess whether a mismatch is likely to occur? It is our argument that traditional readability procedures (the use of formulas based upon word difficulty, word length, and sentence length, or the use of the cloze procedure requiring the replacement of deleted words) will not suffice. Instead, teachers should judge the adequacy of text for themselves. They should pursue an impressionistic evaluation of the demands of the text together with an assessment of readers' prior knowledge. For purposes of illustration, an analysis of the "Garbage Collectors of the Sea" could involve an examination of the support given the concept of decomposition and an informal assessment of what students know. For example, *day and night* and *steady rain* provide ample support for the notion that *decomposition* is a never-ending process; considered as vague might be the locational reference to *continental shelf*—a term likely to be unfamiliar to most readers—and those aspects of the text specifying what decomposers are. To verify the possibility of a mismatch, teachers might informally assess the students' background knowledge by discussing with students what they know about these key concepts prior to reading.

If mismatches are inevitable, teachers have the following choices: dismiss the passage as inadequate, or provide students with the background experiences appropriate to the text. In terms of the latter, teachers might provide adjuncts or supplemental experiences prior to having students read the text. For example, teachers might support the use of textbooks with other reading material, media, activities, and experiences to supplement what students already know. As Rumelhart and Ortony (1977) have emphasized, "In all cases existing knowledge is utilized and required for the acquisition of new knowledge" (p. 117), or as Pearson and Spiro (1981) suggest: "Instead of asking the question, 'What does the student not know that I have to help him or her learn?', educators should be asking, 'What is it that the student does know that I can use as an anchor point— a bridge—to help develop the concepts that he or she needs?' " (p. 80). This implies that in those situations for which the reader lacks the background knowledge, teachers need to build bridges from what they already know or provide experiences or analogies (for example, a discussion of baseball as a means of understanding cricket) by which the readers can build such bridges for themselves.

Apart from specific action, teachers might offer a general program of schema development. Such a program might include field trips as well as films in conjunction with topics being read or discussed. It might involve students in activities that encourage their pursuit of or immersion in a topic through a variety of resources, for example, library materials and discussions with knowledgeable persons.

Guiding Reader-Text Interactions: Do Readers Engage Their Schemata?

Our second guideline moves our discussion of pedagogy from prerequisites for dealing with text to the issue of student engagement with text. In particular, our second guideline assumes that readers already have adequate prior knowledge for dealing with text and asks whether they engage it. Many theorists and practitioners advocate strategies that are derived either directly or indirectly from these notions. For example, most basal reading lessons and several reading educators advise teachers to begin with either selected questions or a discussion of a story topic designed to activate background knowledge prior to reading. During reading, they often insert questions as a means of guiding or shaping a reader's understanding. Stauffer's (1969) Directed Reading-Thinking Activity (DR-TA) is one such procedure where setting purposes together with guided reading are integral. As Stauffer has stated:

> ...either the reader declares his own purposes or if he adopts the purposes of others, he makes certain how and why he is doing so. He also speculates about the nature and complexity of the answers he is seeking by using to the fullest his experience and knowledge relevant to the circumstances. Then he reads to test his purposes and his assumptions. As a result, he may: one, find the answer he is seeking literally and completely stated; two, find only partial answers or implied answers and face the need to either restate his purposes in light of the new information gained or to suspend judgment until more reading has been done; three, need to declare completely new purposes. (1969, p. 40)

There are numerous other strategies and practices ranging from advance organizers to study guides to prefatory statements to questioning strategies directed at these same ends.

In general terms, schema engagement relates to: 1) the reader's initial contact with a text, 2) the reader's ability to relate his or her own background of experience to the information represented within the text, and 3) the reader's ability to focus and refine his or her understanding of the text material. In particular, the notion of schema engagement addresses the issues represented by the following questions:

> Was the reader's schema engaged prior to reading, during reading, and after reading?

> To what extent did learning occur? Was the reader's relevant background of experience focused and structured during reading?

For teachers, schema engagement can be a serious problem among some of their students. A teacher may assume correctly that students have appropriate schemata for reading a text, only to discover in a postreading discussion that they did not engage those schemata while reading. Sometimes this problem manifests itself as a general lack of interest for reading a text or as an unwillingness to consider a topic or purposes prior to reading. In this regard, sometimes a schema engagement problem may be passage-specific—that is, it may arise for certain texts and not others. Sometimes schema engagement problems occur because readers fail to maintain schemata while reading. This may occur for a number of different reasons. First, readers may be predisposed to plod laboriously through any and every text they read. For example, readers may be devoting all their attention and capacity to decoding, leaving no room for comprehension. Second, poorly written text may make schema maintenance difficult if not impossible; for example, sudden shifts in topic, inadequate transitions, or poorly developed ideas may make the reader's task unduly difficult. Third, readers may be inattentive or distracted by too many or ill-considered adjuncts; that is, sometimes study questions and activities interrupt reading and cause a disruption of schema engagement.

What can teachers do? First and foremost, teachers should remain alert to whether students are engaging their schemata prior to, during, and after reading. Typically, a few well-placed and open-ended questions will elicit a response from students that will suffice for such an assessment. If schema engagement problems are apparent, then teachers can adopt and adapt teaching procedures to meet the specific needs of readers. Since it is unlikely that a single procedure will be appropriate for all students in all situations and it is possible that teacher adjuncts may "do more harm than good," the following broad suggestions are presented only for purposes of exemplification.

Source of Problem	*Some Possible Solutions*
General reader inertia Lack of interest	Use highly motivational material and functional reading material that necessitates a student response (e.g., following directions to an experiment or treasure map).
	Use adjuncts (inserted questions and study-guide-type activities) that relate what students are reading to what they know and might do.
Passage-specific problems	Alert students to what readers do. Encourage the application of strategies across variant text situations (e.g., have students relate what they do in successful situations with what they do in unsuccessful situations).
Lack of focus and inability to structure information	Have students develop "maps" or diagrammatic representations of the text.

Provide adjuncts that encourage readers to focus and structure their ideas.

Encourage students to use heuristics (who, what, when, where, why). Encourage notetaking and outlining.

Lack of focus due to laborious processing tendencies	Use texts that require or encourage greater student response.

Encourage multiple passes through a text (skimming for the gist, rereading more carefully to check the relationship between key points, etc.). Highlight "reading for meaning."

Text-based problems (discontinuity, poorly developed ideas)	Prepare adjuncts to circumvent the difficulties (e.g., include statements that clarify the ideas represented within the text or encourage students to skip over them if they are irrelevant).

Encourage students to be the critics of poorly written text (e.g., have students evaluate poorly developed text and discuss how an author or reader might address these problems).

Overdependency upon teacher support	Avoid the use of any adjuncts that will displace the text.

Use adjuncts sparingly and in conjunction with encouraging the reader to be self-initiating.

Have students replace teacher adjuncts with their own probes.

Discuss the purpose and role of any adjuncts.

Guiding Reader-Text Interactions

Our third guideline is tied directly to our second guideline, but unlike our second it addresses the issue of monitoring reader-text interactions. As suggested earlier, when readers interact with text, they will and should acquire some information that was represented in the text and integrate it with information from their background knowledge. Certainly, there are situations for which it may be reasonable to expect a reader's understanding to remain close to the text; for example, when following a set of directions. Alternatively, there are other situations for which it may be appropriate to expect a more reader-based interpretation. With this in mind, consider those situations when readers' interactive processing reflects a tendency to be either "too text-based" or "too reader-based." For example, consider the situation where a reader's interpretation is too reader-based, producing understandings that are "too loose" for the text and its intended purpose. What might be the ramifications if a science student read the following text too loosely?

> The experiment that you are about to do deals with a property of light. For this experiment you'll need a penny, a cup, transparent tape, and a pitcher of water.
>
> To perform the experiment, tape the penny to the bottom of the cup. Move your head to a point just beyond where you can see the penny.
>
> Hold your head still, then slowly pour water into the cup. Be sure not to move your head.
>
> Stop pouring if the penny comes into view.

Here, to explain or perform the experiment adequately, the science student cannot take liberties lest he or she err in the performance of the experiment. Unfortunately, readers with tendencies toward being too reader-based do not know *that* or *what* they do not know. They presume they know the material better than they actually do or need to. Particularly when the text deals with a familiar topic, readers assume that they know what is written. As a result, they often fail to recognize subtle but important text signals. They fail to monitor their interactions with a text. In the context of many classrooms, these students escape identification, for they might be successful readers in most situations and, furthermore, can "bluff their way through" most teachers' questions.

What can a teacher do to help such students? First, teachers should alert students to the need to monitor their reading of texts differently for different texts. In text situations where a more text-based understanding is required, teachers might alert the students to the need to read the material carefully; provide adjuncts (inserted questions or activities) that encourage students to monitor their developing interpretation; provide students with strategies such as outlining and notetaking for carefully reading the text; encourage students to consciously consider their purposes, their level of understanding, and ways to monitor that understanding; and have the students read the material in conjunction with carrying out some relevant activity (for example, an experiment in which successful performance is contingent upon careful reading). Such students can be encouraged to consider the text more carefully by giving them questions that have two or three correct distractor choices, some of which come from the text. Students then can be asked to discriminate between correct text-based and correct knowledge-based answers.

Alternatively, consider the situation where a reader's understanding is too text-based for the text and purposes for reading. As Spiro (1977) has suggested, certain conditions of schooling may predispose a reader to ascribe to text an autonomy that sponsors the separation of textual information from related prior knowledge. For example, a reader may minimize the interaction of his or her background of experience with a text to cope with the demands of answering a series of questions or the obvious demands of certain texts. Some may perceive the task of reading to be detached from self and tied to a text. In particular, they may perceive the task of reading to be detached from their own experiences. For example, in oral reading situations, in completing cloze activities (especially cloze activities demanding exact-word replacement), and in response to a teacher's demand for a more literal interpretation, we would expect that students may misconstrue the meaning of reading comprehension. They may decide, erroneously, that reading means a word-perfect rendition of a text.

What can teachers do in these situations? First, they should encourage readers to relate their background of experience to what they read and alert them to the importance of their own ideas, perspective, and purpose in any communication. Minimally, readers should be asked to discuss their knowledge, including a perspective about a topic in conjunction with a discussion of the author's perspective and what the author assumed readers knew and might learn. Otherwise, the facilitation might be accomplished either through adjunct questions, activities, or appropriate variations. For example, sets of questions might be developed that encourage the readers to engage their own background of experience prior to, during, and after reading. Questions might encourage readers to discuss their perceptions of what might happen and, at points during reading, what has occurred and any implications thereof.

To illustrate more specifically how this might proceed, here is a technique we have found useful. Begin by asking students what they think of when they hear the word x (where x is the topic they are going to read about later). As they offer their associations, jot them down into categories (as yet unlabeled). For example, for *tree* the implicit categories might include parts of trees, kinds of trees, processes, products, and other tree-associated topics. Then go back and help students label the categories. Then ask them to read the chapter to learn more about x. After that, return to the set of categories related to x and ask students to add new terms they have acquired from reading. One ends up with a vivid demonstration of the students' preexisting schema, new learnings from the text, and the relationship between new and old information. The technique also maximizes the likelihood of schema engagement during reading.

Postreading Comprehension and Learning

Our fourth guideline moves us from guidance and monitoring of text interactions to addressing the adequacy of readers' understandings. Central to our discussion are two notions: first, the realization that what is considered accuracy of understanding should be regarded as relative; second, the issue of transfer of new learnings.

Consider the notion that accuracy of a reader's understanding should be regarded as relative. The key point here is that what is considered an appropriate understanding is likely to vary from reader to reader and from context to context. That is, accuracy of understanding is relative and should be considered a function of individual reader and individual text characteristics, as well as a function of purposes for reading. In constructing an interpretation, a reader selects, inserts, substitutes, deletes, and connects ideas in conjunction with what he or she perceives as "making sense." And what "makes sense" depends upon the text as well as the reader's purposes and background knowledge. There are two postulates taken from Tierney and Spiro (1979) that are relevant to this notion:

1. A reader's selections, insertions, substitutions, omissions, and binding of ideas are *not* necessarily a sign of reader error.
2. It should not be assumed that each text has a single interpretation.

What implications does this notion hold for teachers? It would seem that teachers need to respect both authorship and readership. Indeed, accuracy of understanding is misleading unless defined in terms of the author's intentions and the readers' purposes. This means that teachers must recognize the readers' right to interpret a text at the same time that they instill in students a responsibility to address the author's intentions in writing the text. Integral to curriculum objectives that capitalize upon this perspective is the inclusion of goals similar to the following: The student is able to make judgments about his or her own understanding, the author's intentions, task demands, and strategy utilization. This will include objectives directed at having the student recognize alternative perspectives, the engagement of their own background knowledge, the plausibility of alternative interpretations, the viability of strategies for learning from various texts for alternative purposes, the nature of task demands (including author's intention and plan of organization), and nature and applications of new learnings. Integral to classroom practices, we suggest that teachers should assess the quality of a reader's interpretation in accordance with the following:

To what extent was the reader's understanding adequate for the text and purposes for reading?

When a reader's understanding diverges from some consensual author's intention, can the reader's interpretation be justified?

Current practices, with their emphases upon correct answers and a single appropriate interpretation, violate these principles. In their stead, we suggest that teachers need to move away from assessment procedures that sponsor a "single-correct-answer mentality" and generate devices that are open-ended and that allow for divergent responses. For example, after reading a selection, teachers might allow students to relate their own interpretations prior to prodding them with an array of questions. To move students away from "the right answer" orientation, students might be asked to rate or rank the plausibility of each response to a multiple choice question. In follow up discussions different students can compare the rationales behind their various rankings or ratings. The acid test for student response quality should be "Can it be justified?" rather than "Is it right?" This criterion places the emphasis precisely where it should be placed: on the quality of students' reasoning abilities. Such a stance will also increase the likelihood that important rather than trivial aspects of text will receive emphasis.

Consider next the notion of transfer. The notion of transfer relates to whether readers can apply what they have read or learned to other situations. At issue in any teaching reading comprehension situation should be two key considerations.

Is the reader able to recognize new learnings and potential application?

Is the reader able to apply skills acquired during instruction to other text situations without the support of such instruction?

These two questions can be translated into simple tests of comprehension: 1) Can readers use the new knowledge they have acquired? and 2) Can readers use the new strategies they have acquired when they encounter new texts on their own?

The issue of applying or using new knowledge places reading in a real world context. The criterion assumes that students understand, remember, and evaluate new information more readily when they know its relevance to other experiences. That is, students should be asked to consider the point of what they have read, whether that point be for enjoyment, information gain, or to solve problems.

The second issue — applying learned strategies — gets at the heart of instruction. Presumably we teach so that students will become independent learners, no longer needing our intervention and support. Independence is the essence of transfer. Unfortunately, very few studies have addressed the transfer-of-strategy issue. From those few studies that have been reported, we are impressed that students rarely develop an ability to transfer or apply knowledge, skills, or strategies spontaneously—that is, when they are left to their own resources. Instead, they need to be guided toward transfer. This includes being alerted to when and how to use what strategies.

By implication, if teachers are to help students develop independent reading and learning skills, they should not assume that it will just happen. Situations and activities need to be implemented wherein students can try, discuss, and evaluate their strategy, skill, and knowledge utilization across a variety of reading situations. In this regard, teachers need to move beyond merely mentioning reading comprehension skills and begin helping students learn how to learn. There appear to be some general guidelines emerging from recent research on teaching reading comprehension that are relevant to this goal. One rather consistent finding is that students rarely acquire transferable abilities without being provided ample opportunities to develop and practice those abilities in a variety of relevant contexts. A key word here is *relevant*. Relevance pertains to the notion that students need to understand the purpose and function of reading strategies, comprehension, or learning, as well as be given appropriate situations within which to explore their nature. If a reader is being asked to apply a strategy determining the main idea, the reader should do so within a variety of situations for which it is reasonable to find the main idea. Furthermore, readers appear to profit most from such learning experiences when they are given an explicit understanding of when, why, how, and what to do.

Concluding Remarks

It has been the purpose of this paper to draw upon recent developments in the study of reading comprehension as a means of examining issues or relevance to improving reading comprehension and learning from text. We have suggested that if teachers are to develop a reader's understanding, they should address the adequacy of their pedagogy against some basic notions about reading and learning. The notions that we have suggested are driven by a schema-theoretic perspective—a view that prompted the following questions as guidelines to instructional decision making.

Does the reader have the relevant schemata for a text?

Was the reader's schema activated (purpose, background knowledge, attention, focus, interest) prior to, during, and after reading? Was the reader's relevant background of experience activated during reading?

Across reading materials for different purposes, did the reader exhibit flexible processes in terms of activating, focusing, maintaining, and refining an interpretation?

Was the reader aware of the strategies one could use to cope with different texts and purposes for reading?

To what extent was the reader's understanding adequate for the text and purposes for reading? When a reader's understanding diverges from some consensual author's intention, did the reader justify his or her idiosyncratic interpretation? Did the reader recognize his or her perspective and the perspective of others?

Was the reader aware of his or her level of understanding of a text read for different purposes?

Did the reader recognize new learnings and their potential applications?

REFERENCES

Bragdon, H.W., and S.P. McCutchen. *History of a free people.* New York: Macmillan, 1978.

Collins, A., J.S. Brown, and K.M. Larkin. *Inference in text understanding* (Tech. Rep. No. 40). Urbana: University of Illinois, Center for the Study of Reading, December 1977. (ED 150 547)

Crane, S. *The red badge of courage.* New York: Dell, 1966.

Durkin, D. What classroom observations reveal about reading comprehension instruction. *Reading Research Quarterly,* 14 (1978-1979), 481-533.

Gallant, R.A. The garbage collectors of the sea. In I. Asimov and R.A. Gallant, *Ginn Science Program (Intermediate Level C).* Lexington, MA: Ginn, 1975.

Pearson, P.D., and R.J. Spiro. Toward a theory of reading comprehension instruction, *Topics in language disorders,* 1 (1981), 71-88.

Rumelhart, D.E. Toward an interactive model of reading. In S. Dornic (Ed.), *Attention and performance VI.* Hillsdale, NJ: Erlbaum, 1977.

Rumelhart, D.E. Schemata: The building blocks of cognition. In R.J. Spiro, B.C. Bruce, and F. Brewer (Eds.), *Theoretical issues in reading comprehension.* Hillsdale, NJ: Erlbaum, 1980.

Rumelhart, D.E., and A. Ortony. The representation of knowledge in memory. In R.C. Anderson, R.J. Spiro, and W.E. Montague (Eds.), *Schooling and the acquisition of knowledge.* Hillsdale, NJ: Erlbaum, 1977.

Spiro, R.J. Remembering information from text: Theoretical and empirical issues concerning the state of schema reconstruction hypothesis. In R.C. Anderson, R.J. Spiro, and W.E. Montague (Eds.), *Schooling and the acquisition of knowledge.* Hillsdale, NJ: Erlbaum, 1977.

Stauffer, R.G. *Directing reading maturity as a cognitive process.* New York: Harper and Row, 1969.

Tierney, R.J., J. LaZansky, and D. Schallert. *Secondary social studies and biology students' use of textbooks.* Unpublished manuscript, University of Illinois, 1981.

Tierney, R.J., and R.J. Spiro. Some basic postulates about comprehension: Implications for instruction. In J. Harste and R. Carey (Eds.), *New perspectives in comprehension.* Bloomington: Indiana University, School of Education, 1979.

NOTE

[1]Implicit within our discussion of the nature of comprehension has been the suggestion that inference and interpretation are as essential to acquiring an understanding as they may be to extending understanding after reading. This idea suggests that the widely espoused notion of a continuum from literal to inferred to evaluative has questionable validity. Not only does it lack validity as a statement about reading comprehension, it may have questionable utility as a curriculum guideline. There are many ways to acquire an understanding and at times different permissible understandings, regardless of whether these understandings be literal, inferential, or evaluative. Our point is that unless a great deal of thought goes into operationalizing curriculum procedures based upon these categories, teachers

may find that they are forcing a student to deal with the literal when it would be more appropriate to address the inferred or evaluative. We believe that every act of reading necessitates inferential and interpretive understandings. In fact, students may need to deal with the inferential and evaluative prior to addressing the "literal."

Writing to Teach and Reading to Learn: A Perspective on the Psychology of Written Instruction

ERNST Z. ROTHKOPF

Writing is one of the most important instructional means available to us. The scientists investigating the chemical basis of memory might look inside of ink-wells instead of homogenized cerebral protein, for much of the memory of our culture is in the inky swirls of print. Writing has a useful role in practically all organs of our culture: to communicate, to debate, to guide, to link the past to the future and today to tomorrow. Writing plays an awesomely important role in the instruction of all people, whether young or old.

Written instructional material is mass produced in the United States by an industry with annual sales in the neighborhood of one billion dollars. This impressive output is supplemented by a thriving home industry equipped with numerous tools that range in technological sophistication from print producing computers and electric typewriters to ballpoint pens and dittoing devices. The amount of written material produced each year for instructional consumption is almost beyond estimate. Whole forests die so that knowledge (and also kitsch) may pass from one generation to the next, and skill from one hand to another. From the libraries of the world and from bookshelves everywhere, the voices and the hearts of both the living and dead, some wise and some foolish, speak to those who read.

The invention of writing and of printing presses and other reproduction machines has had a long and dramatic impact on human life. It was not until this century, however, that men began to think about writing as psychological or instructional technology. As literacy became widespread, educators, psychologists, and others became concerned with the nature of reading processes, and the characteristics that made writing an effective transmitter of instructional messages. Written instructional materials began to interest the educator as objects of scientific study and as important practical means that required decisions at a technical level.

Reprinted from N.L. Gage (Ed.), *The Psychology of Teaching Methods*. The Seventy-Fifth Yearbook of the National Society for the Study of Education, Part 1. Chicago: University of Chicago Press, 1976, 91-129. With permission of author and publisher.

Kinds of Instructional Writing

The present discussion will concentrate primarily on discourse, that is, connected cohesive presentations of some matter which, in style, more or less resembles connected speech. Discourse ranges in complexity and size from brief encyclopedia entries to instructional text and from programed instructional material to essays, belles lettres, poetry, and novels. Other written materials that lack the connecting threads of discourse are also of substantial educational importance. The nondiscourse materials include tables, procedural directions, lists, and other similar displays. These may range in complexity and size from knitting directions to a concordance of the Bible. The distinction between discourse and nondiscourse is not always well marked. It is made here mainly for convenience because very little will be said about nondiscourse materials despite their importance.

It is useful to think of three kinds of discourse. First, there are materials intended primarily for general instructional purposes, such as texts and didactic expository articles. The second class consists of materials that have been prepared for a relatively circumscribed and well-specified purpose, such as programed self-instructional materials. Finally, there is the great bulk of written material, scientific, technical, nonfiction, and literary, which is the collective experience treasury of any culture. This material was not deliberately written for instructional use (at least not for formal instruction). Nevertheless it is of overwhelming educational importance and is frequently not only the vehicle but also the object of instruction.

Properties of Written Instructional Material

The most important single characteristic of writing from a scientific or technical point of view is that it is a stable instructional system. An instructional system can be said to be stable when we can assume that the same instructional message will be reliably delivered to all students (although not necessarily received) each time the system is used. Stable instructional systems tend to have a tangible, documentary form, such as written material, film, audiotape, and videotape recording.

Instructional systems differ very widely in degree of stability. Among the more stable forms are the documentary media referred to above. Among the least stable are the extemporaneous exchanges of classroom debate. Between these two extremes, every level of stability may be found. The teacher as lecturer, or the teacher in the free give and take of the classroom, is a relatively unstable instructional system.

Stable instructional systems readily lend themselves to scientific study and to systematic improvement by technological methods. There are two reasons why stable instructional means and particularly written material are suitable for systematic improvement by technological methods. First, most scientific or technical methods involve attempts to utilize experience to modify and improve instructional means. The very identity of an instructional system depends on its stability. It is difficult to evaluate an instructional chameleon. A stable documentary system is a complete definition of what has been delivered to the student and tends to leave little uncertainty as to what is to be evaluated.

Second, stable systems such as writing are suited for systematic technological applications because such systems can be modified by an iterative process, namely, editing or rewriting, to incorporate scientific principles of construction or to reflect the experience that has been gained during tryouts. Since the instructional means are documentary, the changes become a stable and reliable portion of the instructional program. Principles and experience can be used to modify the actual physical structure of the instructional program. Written instructional materials are permanently modified in editing. In fact, it is simpler to modify written material, by editing and rewriting, than other stable documentary forms such as films or tapes. It is not critically important whether written materials have been programed for self-instruction or are in conventional forms, such as pamphlets or books. It should be noted, however, that ordinary written instructional materials tend to be somewhat less stable than highly structured forms of programed instruction because the condition of use of ordinary text materials is not completely known. ,

The highly desirable attribute of stability stands in contrast against the singular dependency of written material on actions by the readers. Stability offers the possibilities of applying scientific knowledge to the development of instructional material. It offers the possibilities of careful product engineering. Yet the most carefully written and edited text will not produce the desired instructional results unless the student acts in a suitable way. The student has complete veto power over the success of written instruction. The student also has the opportunity to extend its scope substantially. To paraphrase an old Cappadocian saying: You can lead a horse to water, but the only water that reaches his stomach is what he drinks. Failure to read assignments and failure to prepare adequately by reading undoubtedly are large factors in academic failure and underachievement. The contrast between the opportunities for careful product design that are offered by the stability of written instructional materials and the vulnerability of these materials to the student's disposition is one of the main themes of the present chapter.

Measuring Outcomes

Pragmatic discussion of an educational medium must consider how the results produced by the medium are to be measured. This measurement has often been approached in a deceptively simple manner with written material. The problem arises in no small measure from the fact that the term *understanding* is too readily accepted as a criterion of the degree to which results produced by reading are satisfactory.

The verb *to understand* without an object or with a reference to a language unit as an object carries with it the implication that any language unit such as a sentence or a paragraph has "true content." Understanding in that context means that true content has been received. The acceptance of the word *understand* as a primitive term is common among linguists and certain students of cognition. This view may result in certain logical difficulties.

There are several reasons for these logical problems. *True content* implies that the interpretation of a linguistic unit is simple and unique and that the measurable consequences of the exposure to a written stimulus are completely enumerable. The specifications of these consequences are frequently sought either in the observed or inferred intention of the author or in a logical précis of the linguistic unit.[1] This approach is exemplified by measures of understanding based on "correct" responses using the completion method,[2] paraphrases or gist,[3] or completion techniques with linguistic transformations of the original stimulus.[4] Careful analysis suggests that these approaches have serious logical and practical limitations. The universe of acceptable consequences may be exceedingly large, and it may not be possible to enumerate them exhaustively. The number of conceivable consequences grows rapidly larger as the written unit increases in size from phrases or simple sentences to concatenations of sentences and paragraphs.[5]

The term *acceptable consequences* is equivalent to the number and nature of test items that can be generated by logical judgment or by certain logical rules from the instructive stimulus. The number of such acceptable items is large even with relatively small units, and performances on these test items are by no means perfectly correlated. Acceptable items range from paraphrases to the substantial class of items identified with "connotative meaning," and from collative responses to remembering locations of certain other information on pages.[6]

The issue thus raised about ways to evaluate the outcome of written instruction does not refer to the nature of the response required from the student — whether paraphrase, cloze, or multiple choice recognition. The issue is whether a document itself should be used as a source of criterion test items or whether some external referent should be used. Such an external referent might be found in the pragmatics of instruction, for example, instructional goals. The argument here proposed is that, if the purpose of measurement is to describe or evaluate the skill of an individual, the read document *may* be an acceptable source of test items. But if the purpose of measurement is to evaluate a document, test items must be derived from an external referent.

The point is simple but easy to miss. If one is trying to decide which of two documents is more effective, one looks to some purpose that both documents are supposed to accomplish, rather than to the documents themselves, for a source of measurement.

Distinction between Nominal and Effective Stimulus

In the analysis of learning from written material, it is useful to distinguish between attributes of the text and the internal representations that result when the reader processes the text. This is the distinction between the nominal and the effective stimulus that has been made by Rothkopf and others.[7] The nominal stimulus is characterized by analysis of the text. The effective stimulus is inferred indirectly. It is the consequence of the reader's operations on the nominal stimulus and is the main determinant of what is understood and remembered after reading. Learner performance thus is the result of both the nature of the nominal stimulus, that is, attributes of the text, and of processing operations by the reader. Written material as nominal stimulus and processing will therefore serve as major organizational headings for the discussion that follows.

Written Material as Nominal Stimulus

The effectiveness of a written document in accomplishing selected instructional goals is influenced by certain characteristics of the document. These characteristics are summarized in Table 1. They fall into three major divisions that would not have been novel to Aristotle: content, representation, and form. Not all of the rubrics in Table 1 have received the same experimental or theoretical attention nor are they all on the same conceptual level. Also shown in Table 1 is whether each factor must be considered with reference to a specific set of goals or a specific student population in order to be evaluated. The classification scheme is useful as a summary of the nominal stimulus properties of written discourse.

Table 1

TEXT AS NOMINAL STIMULUS: ATTRIBUTES RELATED TO INSTRUCTIONAL
EFFECTIVENESS

Text Attributes	Goal-Specific	Population-Specific
Content		
Completeness	Yes	Yes
Accuracy	Yes	No
Goal guidance	Yes	No
Unrelated material	Yes	Yes
Representation		
Lexicon	No	Yes
Exposition	No	Probably
Organization	No	Probably
Form		
Grammatical structure	No	Yes
Grammatical complexity	No	Yes

Content factors are related to the meaning or purpose of a written message. They include *givens* in the sense that some aspects of content are constrained by what the message is supposed to accomplish.

Representational factors include optional elements, such as the lexicon, that are used to represent the intended meaning. Many variables that have been studied in simple verbal learning experiments, such as familiarity, vividness, concreteness, and similarity, are presumably relevant to the choice of an instructionally desirable lexicon. Sequential organization and various modes of exposition are also included among representational factors.

Form factors include grammatical structure, complexity, and sentence length. It is assumed that grammaticality and sentence length can be varied without changing content, meaning, or representational form. It is, however, generally recognized that subtle changes in meaning are sometimes unavoidable in form changes.

We ask about content when we ask whether a document is accurate and complete enough to accomplish the intended purpose *if it were* understood. We ask about representation or form when we ask whether the choice of phrasing, lexicon, and other representation such as metaphor or simile produce efficient understanding, consistent with the purpose of the communication.

Content

It has been argued that content has extremely important effects on instruction and may be the single most powerful characteristic of the nominal stimulus.[8] The position taken here is that for most purposes the content of a written document can only be evaluated pragmatically, that is, with reference to descriptions of specific instructional goals.

Content is characterized in four ways: 1) Is it complete? 2) Is it accurate? 3) Is goal guidance provided? 4) How much unrelated material is there? Techniques for characterizing text content are at present relatively imperfect, and no standard techniques for describing these attributes have evolved. The status of these attributes could be determined by a hypothetical, omniscient, and extremely patient observer. In practice this task is handled by a subject matter expert aided by a detailed checklist, or by a panel of expert judges.

Content factors are related to the purpose or meaning of a given message. Their status depends on *givens* in the sense that the evaluation of content is constrained by what a message is supposed to accomplish.

Completeness. This property of a written document refers to the completeness with which it covers the knowledge needed to attain a particular instructional goal. There may be many ways in which the competencies that correspond to the instructional goal may be produced. The judgment is simply made that the content of the document is sufficient for at least some nontrivial portion of a hypothetical student population. The student population must be taken into account because assumptions about previously acquired student knowledge enter to some extent in making the judgment of completeness. One technique for making a useful completeness judgment has been described by Koether, Rothkopf, and Smith.[9] It involved developing elaborate checklists of major points derived from an analysis of the proposed instructional content (see Figure 1 for an example). The instructional document was inspected repeatedly to check for each point on the checklist.

Accuracy. This aspect hardly needs explanation. Written material must not contain misinformation. Accuracy poses special problems with written materials that deal with subjects outside of the traditional academic curriculum, such as practical guidance for assembling and making things where the writer is often also the primary collector of information.

Goal guidance. The question asked here is whether the document specifically states for the student the nature of the preselected instructional aims. Material prepared for general instructional use may provide no guidance about emphasis or purpose. The judgment about the availability of goal setting material in the instructional document is useful in deciding whether additional environmental supports are needed.

Unrelated material. When instructional goals have been chosen, it is possible to judge how much material that is *not* related to the goals is included in the instructional document. What the best quantitative units for such an estimate might be is not clear. The number of sentences not directly related to any instructional goal has been used to derive a suitable index. In a slightly different context, Rothkopf and Kaplan employed a ratio of sentences of a particular class to the total number of sentences in the text.[10]

Relatively few good data are available on the effect of unrelated material on the achievement of instructional goals. Smith, Rothkopf, and Koether have reported that the amount of unrelated material in passages predicted goal achievement better than any other formal characteristics of the nominal stimulus measured.[11] In that study such unrelated material comprised materials which were related to the main topic (leather tanning) but were not directly relevant to the tanning procedures on which the student was tested.

Representation

Documents judged to contain the same minimum content may represent this content in different ways. It is useful to distinguish three kinds of representation: lexicon, exposition, and organization (see Table 1). The distinctions among these three classes of representation are sometimes blurred, but the blurring does not detract from the usefulness of the distinctions. The important point is that representation may be changes without changes in content and the representation involves primarily optional elements of a message.

SCORING SHEET - Page 3

FREQUENCY OF DUSTING - con't.

FOLLOW THE DIRECTIONS THAT APPEAR IN THE BOX YOU CHECK

	YES	NO	NOTE

32. Is powdered tannin or any of the synonyms given below mentioned in the definition? Synonyms for powdered tannin: chestnut, mimosa, myrobalans, tannic dust, tanning material, tanning powder, tanning substance, valonia. Terms not acceptable as synonyms: dust, chemicals, granular leather fibres, liquors, liquids, powder, special materials, used tannin.

33. Is the idea of the tannin being sprinkled, spread, or scattered on the hides mentioned? The following terms are acceptable synonyms if "powdered tannin" is used in the first part of the definition: added to, applied, covered with, put on. Terms not acceptable as synonyms: brushed on, dusted, splattered, sprayed.

34. Is the idea of the tannin being sprinkled "on the hides" made explicit? Synonyms for on the "hides": butts, leather, sides and back, skins.

35. Does the essay state that the tannin is sprinkled "directly" on the hides? Other ways of emphasizing that the tannin powder goes on the hide rather than into the liquors that touch the hide are: as the hides are being put into the pit, before dipping, before immersion, individually. Not acceptable: between the hides.

THE FORMATION OF BLOOM

36. Bloom is caused by dusting, or depends on the type of tannin used in dusting. Does the essay suggest this?

37. Bloom is a fawn-colored deposit that forms in and on the hide. Does the essay attempt to define bloom in this way? _____ [NO → SKIP TO 42]

38. Is "fawn-colored" part of the definition? Acceptable synonyms: tan, cream-colored.

39. Is the idea of deposit or residue included in the definition?

40. Is the formation of the deposit "in" the hide made clear?

41. Does the definition also present the idea that the deposit forms "on" the hide?

42. Bloom affects the leather by giving it weight and firmness and by waterproofing it. Does the essay mention any of these effects of bloom? _____ [NO → SKIP TO 44]

43. Is there a statement that bloom gives the leather weight or makes it heavy?

44. Is there a statement that bloom makes the leather firm or gives it strength?

45. Does the essay mention that bloom makes the leather waterproof (or water-repellent, or water resistant)?

Figure 1. Sample scoring sheet for minimum content for articles and student essays on leather tanning.
Note: This checklist, developed by M.E. Koether, included ninety instructional objectives and consisted of five scoring sheets.

Lexicon. The lexicon of a document refers to the words that have been selected to represent meaning. The substantial verbal learning literature contains a good deal of information relevant to the effects of various kinds of lexical representation on learning from written text. Only summary reference to this research will be made here.[12] The results of verbal learning research indicate that associations (that is, arbitrarily determined pairings) between words are learned faster and remembered longer if the words evoke concrete images that are meaningful and familiar than if such images are not evoked.[13]

Scales based on judgments of vividness (imagery) and concreteness are available for small sets of words.[14] Since agreement among judges about vividness and concreteness has been found to be fairly high, the individual writer is probably capable of making reasonable estimates about these attributes for any word not found in the available lists. Similar scalings of words have been provided for meaningfulness and familiarity by Noble.[15] The most commonly used basis for estimating the familiarity of words, however, is obtained by counting the frequency of use of any word in printed material.[16]

The importance of such aspects of the lexicon as vividness, concreteness, meaningfulness, and familiarity derives partially from the previous experience of the reader. The available numerical indices are estimates of the likelihood that the words have been encountered, as well as the nature and variety of contexts in which they have been seen.[17] An implicit assertion is also made about the character of the associations established for each word and of the complexity of the memorial nets in which they are presumably stored.[18]

Experience and the consequent enriched memorial representations are considered to be critical to learned performance because it has been well established that new learning involving these words and concepts is greatly facilitated by the availability of previously acquired associations and other nonverbal representations evoked by the lexicon. It has also been reported that retrieval and recognition occur more quickly with familiar and meaningful words.[19] Such greater speed is important in an activity such as reading, where the ability to process words rapidly is presumed to be needed for effective performance.

Exposition. The concept of exposition refers to certain aspects of the presentation of concepts and relationships that are not captured by characterizations of the single word lexicon. Among the expository expressions of particular interest here are instructional metaphors, similes, and various defining or referential phrases. It seems plausible that these expository devices parallel the lexicon to some degree in that familiarity and meaningfulness differ among expressions. For this reason, expository terms probably have a role in determining instructional effectiveness. Unfortunately the experimental literature contains little that is relevant to exposition. This situation probably prevails in part because expository devices are complex and the number of possibilities is large. No simple way of characterizing the potential psychological properties of exposition has been found. Another factor, which may be related to our neglect of the scientific study of expository expressions, is that semantically interesting expository phrases depend strongly on verbs. The experimental psychology of verbal learning has traditionally been a psychology of nouns. Relatively little experimental work has been done on verbs, although the recent analysis of verb characteristics by Schank may stimulate more work on this neglected area.[20]

Organization and sequence. The content of a passage using a given lexicon and a given ensemble of expository constructions may be organized in different sequences. The effect of organization or sequence on learning has been investigated in a number of studies. This research has demonstrated that the same sentences rearranged in different orders can produce different instructional results.[21] The experimental sequences compared in these studies were all equally acceptable (or unacceptable) as English text patterns. Nevertheless, different blocking of similar semantic features, such as attributes or names in the text sequences, favored high performance on different items on recall tests.

Our understanding of the effect of text organization on learning has not been aided so far by the emergence of unifying theoretical ideas. The experimental variables that have received attention in research include the organization by semantic attributes referred to, comparison of deductive-to-inductive expository development with inductive-to-deductive sequences,[22] amount of text intervening between two redundant passage elements,[23] and within paragraph order.[24]

Form: Grammar, Structure, and Sentence Length

It will not be possible to review the work on grammatical form in detail here. A fairly substantial experimental literature indicates that simple active sentences are reacted to more quickly than more complex transformations of the same sentence.[25] Some experimental evidence also indicates that trying to understand or remember a simple active sentence interferes less with the accomplishment of other simultaneous tasks than trying to understand more complex transformations.[26] Longer sentences have also been reported to be more difficult to understand.[27] It has been experimentally shown, however, that lengthening by use of conjunctions does not increase difficulty seriously.[28] Schlesinger has pointed out that sentence length is confounded with other important sentence variables such as grammatical structure and redundancy.[29] Schlesinger also provided a useful review of the literature on structure. An additional extensive literature survey has been compiled by Carroll.[30]

Readability

Readability indices are quantitative characterizations of text as nominal stimulus.[31] These indices will not be discussed in detail here because they are well known and because excellent reviews and discussions are available. [32]

The present discussion of readability measures will focus on their relationship to the document characteristics enumerated in Table 1 and on certain general implications of the use of such indices. In 1963, Klare estimated that thirty-one different readability formulas had been proposed. Since then a number of others have been invented. The majority of them use two factors to predict reading difficulty. These two factors are word difficulty and sentence difficulty, and these, in many cases, are estimated by measures of length. Perhaps the best known of these readability formulas is the Flesch Reading Ease Formula. It will be used here to illustrate the relationship between readability indices and the stimulus characteristics of text discussed previously. The reading ease index is calculated in the following way: 1) unsystematically select 100-word samples from the materials to be measured; 2) determine the number of syllables per 100-word sample; this is the index of word length, wl; 3) determine the average number of words per sentence, sl; 4) calculate reading ease, RE, by the following formula:

$$RE = 206.835 - .846\,wl - 1.015\,sl$$

The two predictive variables in this formula are related to the lexicon and to grammatical form factors. Word length (wl) is related (although indirectly) to familiarity and to meaningfulness by the following argument.[33] The basic principle is Zipf's law, which states that word length is negatively related to the frequency of occurrence of that word in the language.[34] The plausible assumption is then made that the more frequent words in the language are more likely to be familiar and meaningful than rarer words. This assumption is supported by the findings of positive correlations between the counted frequencies of words and the meaningfulness measure (m) developed by Noble[35] as well as with rated familiarity. Average word length, however, is not a simple indicator of the meaningfulness and familiarity of the lexicon because it is strongly influenced by the number of short function words and personal pronouns in the text. Because of this, the word length measure reflects the form of the text sentences as well as characteristics of individual words.

The inclusion of sentence length in the readability formulas might be justified on the following basis. First, the assumption is plausible that longer sentences tend to be syntactically more complex. This assumption, coupled with the finding, referred to previously, that syntactically more complex sentences take longer to evaluate and demand more processing capacity, would suggest weighting readability formulas with sentence length. There are, of course, also the direct experimental results, described earlier, that longer sentences are more difficult to "understand." The finding that lengthening sentences by use of conjunctions does not have any substantial effects on comprehension measures, would tend to weaken expectations about the predictive usefulness of sentence-length measures.[36]

Several points are worth noting about the Flesch reading ease index, as well as most other readability formulas:

1. They are poor guides for writing because favorable values can be attained by trivial maneuvers. They are, however, reasonable first order checks on the

acceptability of text for certain user populations. Information about readability may now be obtained at very low cost. Modern printing technology brings text into computer readable form very early in the production process. Many texts are now entered into the computer at the manuscript typing stage. This technological possibility coupled with the use of computer based readability formulas, such as that of Coke and Rothkopf,[37] makes the required word and sentence counts simple, accurate, and easy to obtain.

2. Current readability measures are relatively weak predictors of reading difficulties, particularly when the user is well motivated and is free of severe time constraints. Some of the probable reasons for this are discussed in detail by Rothkopf.[38]

3. Current readability indices use only a small number of the factors listed in Table 1. The lexical characteristic chiefly tapped is familiarity. Vividness and concreteness are neglected. Exposition and organization are disregarded completely. Content factors are ignored.[39] The disregard for content factors diminishes the power of any predictor of learning in goal-oriented instructional situations. For many important general reading activities such as browsing, however, the absence of content weighting may actually be advantageous.

4. Readability indices may be viewed as statistical estimates of certain characteristics of text. These characteristics can be shown to be related to variables that have been exactly manipulated in simple experiments and that have been demonstrated to have powerful effects on learning. The lack of precision of the techniques for estimating the values of underlying variables from text characteristics is to some extent counteracted by the very large number of words to which the technique could be applied with computer techniques. This model for future applications of laboratory findings merits careful attention. It may not be possible to ascertain exactly the state of a given variable for a text, but useful although inexact statistical approximations may be found that can be applied to large aggregates such as text.

Processing

The importance of the learner's processing activities and of the control of these activities by environmental circumstances outside the stimulus object, has only recently become widely recognized in experimental studies of human learning. Human learning theories during the last three decades treated learning as if it were the passive consequence of bombardment by environmental particles.[40] A noteworthy exception was the work of Postman, who clearly saw the importance of stimulus processing in determining learning outcomes.[41]

Research on the nature of prose learning has been somewhat ahead of conventional learning research in its concern with the role of the subject's activities in determining what was learned. In 1963, Rothkopf described the concept of inspection behaviors, or mathemagenic activities, in order to draw attention to the processing activities that are necessary for various learning outcomes.[42] This formulation grew logically out of analysis of the role of response demands and knowledge of results in programed instruction and out of recognition of the distinction between nominal and effective stimuli.[43] Processing activities were seen to determine the transformation of nominal into effective stimuli. Effective stimuli determined what was learned.

It is easy to understand why researchers on learning from written material should have become interested in processing conceptions. Learning from text, regardless of how carefully the text has been written, cannot succeed without important activities on the part of the student. The translation of written language into a useful internal representation obviously requires the exercise of highly skilled processing activities, which are not usually directly observable. This processing activity, for many different reasons, may be selectively exercised, that is, not all portions of the text may be translated, or elaborated through linkages with previous associations or other textual information, to the same degree. This kind of conception of reading activities is a reasonable although partial account of why some texts or some portions of them are not very well remembered while other aspects or other text segments are remembered well.

Recently, the importance of processing in determining learning outcomes has also gained some recognition in research on verbal learning. Articles that recognize the critical role of learner activities are beginning to appear with greater frequency in the learning literature.[44]

The work of Craik and Tulving illustrates how the concept of depth of processing has been applied in systematic experiments on human learning. They asked subjects to make one of four judgments about a word. The judgments were a) Was the word in capital letters? b) Did it rhyme with a given word? c) Did it belong to a given conceptual category? d) Did it fit into a given sentence? These judgments, according to Craik and Tulving, involved progressive increases in semantic involvement and hence "deeper processing." In an elegant series of experiments, it was shown that subsequent recall increased with depth of processing and that this effect could not be accounted for purely on the basis of increased processing time.[45]

A Model for Learning from Text

A conceptual model is useful in thinking about any practical problem and in keeping track of diverse empirical facts. For this reason, an effort will be made to describe a processing model for learning and understanding written material. This model is essentially a model of reading. It will be crude, inexact, and incomplete. It is unrealistic to expect more. Reading involves almost every aspect of human psychology — sensory capacity, perception, learning, motivation, and thinking. Reasonably complete and satisfactory models of reading activities can come into existence only when our understanding of human psychology has advanced considerably beyond its present state.

Figure 2 shows a general schema of the processes that may be involved in reading narrative text for some special purpose. The purpose assumed for Figure 2 was to remember enough of the passage in order subsequently to paraphrase it. The eyes fixate on some text element for periods of approximately 200 milliseconds at each fixation. The pattern of fixations is usually a fairly systematic progression from left to right and down the page, but there are sometimes exceptions such as regressions, that is, movements from right to left. The fixations result in some initial internal representation, and these in turn become the object of some quasi-acoustic translation. There is currently considerable controversy about whether this quasi-acoustic translation is necessary for understanding but there seems to be no doubt that at times the musculature involved in speech, such as the lips and the tongue, is weakly but measurably activated during reading. The initial translation process must also involve the segmentation of the quasi-acoustic representation in a manner functionally equivalent to a syntactic analysis. The initial translation activities involving eye fixations, quasi-acoustic translation, and segmentation are referred to in Figure 2 as *primary mathemagenic processing*.

Two assumptions have been made about primary mathemagenic processing. The first is that its elements are partially under the control of certain environmental factors such as task demands made upon the reader, or more accurately the psychological dispositions that result from these demands.[46]

This control is referred to as functional control in Figure 2. The translation processes are also partially under associative control, that is, they are regulated to some extent by what the reader knows and by the resulting emerging interpretation of the text. The second assumption is that the primary analytic processes and the sources of their control result in an immediate representation of the text (called "usable representation" in Figure 2), which is a reconstruction in the sense that it is created by a synthesis between partial interpretation of the text and what the reader knows. The immediate representation can be used to answer questions, solve problems, or interpret subsequent text segments. The psychological availability of the immediate representation decreases in time but portions of it produce a more or less permanent memorial representation.

Further analytic processes operate on usable representations. These are also partially under functional and partially under associative control. These processes (referred to in Figure 2 as "secondary mathemagenic processes") collate and integrate information from usable representations, as well as from episodic and semantic memory. The functional results can be the concatenation and elaboration of text information and regulation of the nature of the transfer of usable representation into retrievable memorial representations.

This is a speculative but plausible model. It is not stated in a way that would make an empirical test possible. It is not intended as a theory of narrative reading but rather as a guide to intuition in thinking about reading.

Some features of this conception of a reading process are particularly important. First, successful use of written material depends on the execution of a series

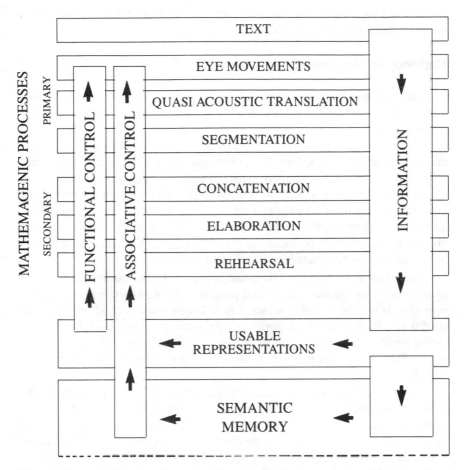

Figure 2. Flow model for translating text into internal representation.

Note: Functional control of mathemagenic processing comes from the usable representations including set; associative control arises both from usable representation and semantic memory. Usable representations are partially determined by information from mathemagenic activities,
including recent experience, and partially through associative control from semantic memory.

of skilled acts by readers. Readers may fail because they do not have the basic
skills or because they do not exercise them. They may fail in interpretation because they lack needed substantive knowledge or because they do not exercise the
required analytic processes.

Second, the sources of failure may have different loci in the interpretative
process. Failures may occur in the movements of the eyes or in quasi-acoustic
translation. If these stages are effectively handled, the instructional purpose may
not be achieved because of failures in later stages of the analytic process.

Decoding, segmentation, and higher level interpretation may fail because of
task variables, unfamiliar words, difficult syntactic constructions, or the complexity of the goals that the reader seeks to satisfy. On the other hand, they may

fail because the instructional environment has not shaped and maintained the needed dispositions in the reader.

Mathemagenic Activities

The various processing activities described in the above model are subsumed under what Rothkopf has called "mathemagenic activities." The concept of mathemagenic activities is discussed in detail elsewhere.[47] Not all mathemagenic activities are useful to the student, and some actually interfere with the attainment of instructional objectives. Most mathemagenic activities are inferred indirectly. These inferences are usually made through antecedent manipulation of the experimental environment such as directions to students, questions, or certain arranged contingencies between student activities and outcomes. On the consequent side, the hypothetical mathemagenic activities are anchored on the level of observation in expected performance on certain tests. Time observations have been used as both independent and dependent measures.

The chain of reasoning is illustrated in Figure 3. The distinctive feature of most research on hypothetical internal processes, such as certain mathemagenic activities, is that the learning material is held constant across all experimental conditions. What is varied are environmental factors to affect the subject's processing mode and his disposition to process the experimental text. By contrast, most other learning research manipulates the text stimulus or the way it is presented.

It has been proposed that mathemagenic activities have topography.[48] This peculiarly neutral term was used to indicate that a stimulus object such as a passage can be processed in a variety of ways, and that different topographies result in different effective stimuli and hence different learning outcomes. This conception differs from the simple notion of *depth of processing* proposed by Craik and Lockhart.[49] According to those authors, variations in depth of processing are expected to affect how much is remembered. The topography idea, on the other hand, implies that topography affects what is processed, how it is processed, and therefore what is remembered. Topography is an especially interesting characteristic of processing in learning from text because of the unique demands for selection that are often made in text learning contexts. Selective reading and mental elaboration of various kinds for portions of the text are reflections of the topography of mathemagenic activity. Selection, mental elaborations, and other conceptions of topography such as mnemonics or integration with previously learned information, are largely inaccessible to direct observation. Their memorial consequences, however, become measurable through performances on various kinds of tests. These possibilities for inference of hypothetical topographical characteristics of mathemagenic activities on the consequent side are illustrated through the three types of test performances in Figure 3.

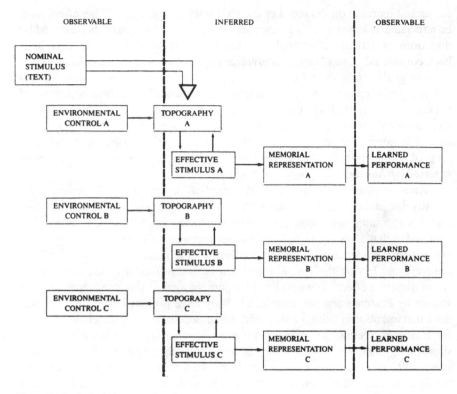

Figure 3. Basis for inference of unobservable mathemagenic topographics.
Note: Conjectures about mathemagenic topographics that result from certain environmental controls
        used with a specified text are tested by predicting certain learned test performances.

Control of Mathemagenic Activities

The concept of mathemagenic activities has been employed with various degrees of success in a variety of situations. The two major classes of manipulation
that have been used are *inductive* and *deductive* (or directive) controls. Changes
in the effectiveness of mathemagenic activities as a function of length and recency of stimulus contacts have also been explored.

The deductive or directive control research has generally involved directions
to learn, usually in the form of descriptions of learning goals that are given to the
student. Inductive controls have mainly involved the use of adjunct questions
with text.

Directions describing learning goals. Studies of the deductive control of
mathemagenic behavior follow a simple paradigm: all subjects receive the same
text materials and the experimental treatments differ in what subjects are told to
learn. Providing subjects with very explicit descriptions of learning goals results

in marked increase on the recall of the goal relevant material.[50] This effect must be attributed at least partially to changes in mathemagenic activities produced by directions. Alternative, although not necessarily conflicting, hypotheses have been considered. One plausible alternative explanation was that specific descriptions of goals are in themselves informative and therefore would contribute to learned performance in a way similar to the effects of repetition or review of material. A study by Kaplan and Simmons examined this possibility by experimenting with learning goals that were presented to subjects after reading the passage.[51] Subjects operating under this condition performed at the same level as a no goal control group. Similar findings with directions to remember have been reported by Ausubel, Schpoont, and Cukier.[52]

Another plausible conjecture is that explicit descriptions of learning goals identify for students those sentences of the text that they should learn. When students encounter and recognize a target sentence, students initiate unspecified maneuvers that allow them to learn the appropriate information. Two kinds of experimental evidence discredit this conjecture or at least suggest that marking a sentence and having the intention to learn is not sufficient to account for the entire direction effect. The first line of argument against this conjecture rests on studies by Postman and his associates.[53] They have provided strong demonstrations that intention is neither a necessary nor a peculiarly advantageous condition for learning. Second, in an ingenious experiment Frase and Kreitzberg have shown that identifying target sentences does not help much in learning.[54] They specifically identified for subjects the eleven sentences in a twenty-two sentence passage that they were not to learn about. This condition, which might be called identification by exclusion, provided as much information about what the subject was to learn as a condition that specified the target sentences (that is, by including them in the directions). Frase and Kreitzberg found that inclusive specification facilitates goal relevant learning while exclusive specification did not help at all. Their findings are consistent with the generally poor results that have been obtained with underlining as a learning aid.[55] These results tend to discredit the *marker cum intention* hypothesis.

Deductive (that is, directive) control of mathemagenic activities is subject to certain limitations that are not completely understood. One limitation can be observed if the number of specific learning goals is increased. The likelihood of the mastery of any specified goal decreases as the list of goals provided for the student grows larger.[56] It was a first thought that the decrease in efficiency in the control of mathemagenic activity was due to the greater density of goal-relevant information in the text, that is, the ratio of goal-relevant sentences to the total number of sentences in the passage.[57] Present evidence, however, suggests that the diminished efficiency in control was primarily due to the length of the list of goal descriptions. There are several reasons for thinking so. Among these is the observation that the effectiveness of specific goal descriptions depended on the number of goals and not the length of the passage.[58] This conclusion must obviously be limited to the length range of passages used in the experiments (500-

1,500 words), since it is not reasonable to expect a single goal to be as effective in a two-sentence passage as in a 1,000-sentence passage. Another reason for suspecting a list length effect is that the fall in efficiency has been observed when goal lists were lengthened by adding descriptions of goals that could not be achieved by reading the experimental passage.[59] Difficulty with longer goal lists is probably not due only to factors associated with the actual inspection of the written goal descriptions. Decreases in the likelihood of mastering any goal as goal lists grow longer have been observed even when the goal list had been memorized prior to the study of the text.

Another limitation in the control of mathemagenic activities by directions appears to be due to differences between the organization of the goal descriptions and the organization of the text. Gagné and Rothkopf have arranged text so that information elements relevant to two components of a goal description were in adjacent locations in the passage or material relevant to other goals was interposed between the two critical elements.[60] In the latter condition recall of information about the second, dispersed goal component was substantially lower than recall of the second component in the adjacent condition. These results suggest that written lists of directions sometimes result in mental bookkeeping problems and a resultant drop in efficiency.

Inductive control. In typical research on inductive control of mathemagenic activities, all subjects read the same text material but some of the experimental groups are asked questions about the text at frequent intervals during the course of the study period. The main experimental evidence about control of mathemagenic activities by these procedures comes from recall data about information elements in the text that are *not* directly related to the experimental questions. Inferences about mathemagenic activities based on recall of material unrelated to the questions seen during reading are based on the following reasoning. If questions asked during the course of reading affect processing activities, demonstration of knowledge about information relevant to the questions is not sufficient to permit one to infer mathemagenic activities. This is because questions not only influence how question relevant knowledge is elaborated but may also be in themselves informative. Knowledge relevant to the experimental question therefore reflects information supplied by these questions as well as their shaping effects on mathemagenic activities and processing. These two components cannot be easily disentangled. On the other hand, any performance changes attributable to the questioning in the recall of material unrelated to the experimental questions must be due to processing activities alone. The effect need not necessarily be facilitative. It is conceptually possible that a particular line of questioning may induce substantial processing changes that will decrease the likelihood that certain kinds of information are acquired from the experimental text.

Using the experimental approach described above, investigators have been able to provide existential proof that environmental demands made during reading, such as questions, change what is learned from reading a passage and proof, by implication, that these changes were due to modifications in processing activities.[61]

It has also been demonstrated that the topography of mathemagenic activities can be altered by the use of questions requiring restricted classes of answers.[62] For example, questions requiring numerical or quantitative answers have been shown to increase the likelihood of learning other quantitative information in the text—information unrelated to the experimental question. The relevant topography probably involves selective mechanisms, that is, a sentence containing quantitative information is discriminated and processed differently from a sentence that does not contain information of this type. The reason for concluding that inductive rather than deductive control of mathemagenic activities is involved in the use of the restricted-topic questioning procedure was that the treatment effect is obtained only if the questions follow the text segment to which they are relevant and not if the questions precede the relevant text portions. The selection effect appears difficult to demonstrate under circumstances when selective topography would not be expected to be peculiarly efficient—such circumstances as, for example, those in which objects of these restricted questions appear in almost every sentence of the passage.[63]

There are also indications that environmental demands produced by questions increase the persistence of effective processing after the use of the questions has been discontinued.[64] Questions have also been observed to maintain the persistence of positive mathemagenic activities under adverse conditions such as prolonged reading.[65]

Some studies have reported that social factors increase the ability of questions to shape effective mathemagenic activities.[66] Questions relevant to the text, when asked by a teacher-like figure, alter students' processing activities more than questions that are mechanically presented.

The research on inductive control of processing by questions supports the conception of mathemagenic activity as an adaptive mechanism that is responsive to environmental demands. Students respond to any consistencies in the information demands of questions and alter their mathemagenic activities as a consequence. If these alterations are successful, students are able to handle subsequent questions in a satisfactory way. If students are not successful on later questions, further alterations will occur. In this way, questions serve as an environmental pressure that will tend to foster the emergence of adaptive mathemagenic activities. Adaptive, in this context, means that the mathemagenic activities will produce the knowledge required by criterion tests. Furthermore, demonstrable positive mathemagenic effects can only be expected if the students do not have or do not exercise effective mathemagenic activities in studying the instructive text.

The latter principle is illustrated by the following findings in an experiment by Rothkopf.[67] Subjects reading an earth science text, photographed on ninety slides, were divided into four groups according to 1) whether their inspection rate increased during the first 24 slides and 2) whether test performance on information learned from the first 24 slides was above or below the group median. Adjunct questions were asked at various intervals after slide number 24 and maintained at an average interval of one question every six slides thereafter. It was reasoned that only the group with below median learning *and* increases in inspection speed had given clear evidence of inappropriate mathemagenic activities. As expected, this group showed the most marked effect of adjunct questions on learning from text slides numbered 25 through 90.

Direct instructive effects of questions. The emergence of adaptive mathemagenic activities that result from questions, as indexed by incidental learning measures, depends on many factors. It therefore requires substantial care in the design of experiments in order to demonstrate these phenomena. The direct instructive effect of questions is much more robust and has been observed in dozens of experiments.[68] Subjects tend to remember more about the information they have been asked about than other text information, and they tend to remember question relevant information longer. This may be a processing phenomenon, as indicated by the findings of Craik and Tulving.[69] The effect may also be thought of as a repetition phenomenon, that is, another demonstration of the law of exercise. Sufficient data are not at present available to permit an estimate of the relative importance of the processing and the repetition factors. It is clear, however, that the direct instructive effect is substantial and that, if properly used, it has immediate instructional applications.

The Nominal Text and Mathemagenic Activities

Rothkopf and Billington have proposed that there is a trade-off between previous general knowledge about the subject matter being studied and the level of mathemagenic activities required for successful outcomes.[70] Thus a text segment that is supposed to inculcate a selected competence requires less extensive and therefore more probable levels of mathemagenic activity for success if the student is familiar with relevant vocabulary and instructional metaphors than if he is not.[71] Rothkopf and Billington[72] suggested that performance resulting from an experimental treatment (P^T) was:

$$P_T = E + (1 - E)\, m_T$$

In this equation E is a quantitative description of a preexperiment experience factor that determines the ease of acquiring the information needed for the test and m_T characterizes the disposition towards mathemagenic processing activities relevant for a given informational item produced by treatment T. For a control group, in which mathemagenic activity was not systematically manipulated, performance P_C was as follows:

$$P_C = E + (1 - E)\, m_c$$

Treatment T involved manipulation of mathemagenic activities by use of goal-descriptive directions. When m_T and m_c were evaluated from P_T and P_c for each of a number of goal relevant items, the data supported the conclusion that constant while m_c varied among items. Goal descriptive directions produced their biggest effects on items for which m_c was lowest, that is, those aspects of information that the subjects were unlikely to process under usual conditions. This finding was consistent with results reported by Duell.[73] She reported that descriptions of learning goals were most effective for information elements that students would normally judge to be relatively unimportant, that is, aspects of the instructional material that the teacher perceives to be important while students do not.

The exact nature of the equation linking learned performance to E and m is not critical for our present discussion. What is interesting is the conception that when experience relevant to acquisition of a particular information element is small, more elaborate and less probable levels of mathemagenic activities are required for successful learning results. For example, suppose that the instructional goal was to be able to indicate that grasshoppers lay eggs and that they deposit them in holes in the ground. If the student reads: "Grasshoppers lay eggs in small holes in the ground," more probable levels of mathemagenic activity will be required for success than if the student reads: "When Marissa caught the grasshopper, she grabbed the insect too hard, and the ovipositor broke off and remained in the little hole in the ground."

Both statements are sufficient to enable the student to acquire the desired information. More elaborate and less probable levels of mathemagenic functioning will be needed if the student has to acquire the desired competence from the second statement. Even less probable levels are required if the student is not familiar with the term *ovipositor* but knows its Latin roots.

The experience factor E is closely related to characteristics of the nominal stimulus, such as certain aspects of content and the representation and form of the text. Relatively sparse content development, such as weak review of fundamentals or "big instructional steps," require more extensive processing by the student in order to achieve a given set of goals. A large amount of material in the text that is not relevant to instructional goals increases the need for more selective mathemagenic activities in order to achieve acceptable performance levels in an efficient manner. In a given student population, a difficult lexicon, complicated syntax, and inappropriate organization require relatively elaborate mathemagenic activities. These are less probable and require more external supports. It is a simple idea. It says that bad form and exposition (never bad content) can be overcome by stronger environmental supports for mathemagenic activities. Text that is difficult to read is an acceptable (or at least a workable) instructional alternative in many cases if one is willing to create mechanisms for shaping and maintaining the mathemagenic activities needed for these situations. Slipshod work by publishers requires more effect on the part of the schools for a given level of results.

Some Practical Options

The discussion of research on learning from written material has centered on two aspects of the problem: the nominal stimulus characteristics of text and the nature and control of the processing activities required of the learner. Each of these two facets corresponds in some respects to one of two major practical options that are available for the development of written instructional material. Educators who wish to use written material in instruction can either develop materials especially for their particular purpose, or they can select from what is available in the didactic or general literature.

Special Purpose Development

Special purpose development tends to emphasize the importance of the nominal stimulus in learning. Two approaches have dominated the special purpose development of stable instructional materials. One sought to find effective expository forms by using principles from the psychological literature. The early forms of programed instruction were products of this spirit. The other emphasized explicit formulations of goals and the use of empirical means to assure the effectiveness of the document in achieving the stated objectives.

Development based on principles. The principles-of-effective-exposition approach has been used so far with only indifferent success. Our present knowledge about instructionally important characteristics of the nominal stimulus is apparently still too incomplete, and the generality of our scientific conceptions of the nominal stimulus is limited. When intelligent people undertake to produce a document in a form that is particularly effective, they tend to do a better job than if only a routine writing assignment were involved, although the judgment of intelligent people in these matters is sometimes wrong.[74] The psychological literature serves mainly to enhance the apperceptive mass of writers and developers rather than to allow specific useful deductions or generalizations. This literature and the "golden wisdom" literature on writing probably exerts its influence in subtle and perhaps powerful ways on writers and developers. It helps them to think and to talk about their problems. It is difficult, however, to find great successes in instructional development that were demonstrably due to the use of expository principles derived from the psychological literature.

Goals and method of successive approximation. The second approach to the special development of written instructional materials (and the most effective systematic method now available) is based on a few simple ideas. These ideas are that reproducible instructional sequences can be tried out on students; that revisions can be made in the instructional arrangements according to the measured results of the trial; and that the trial revision cycle can be repeated until the instructional sequence consistently produces the desired instructional effects.

These procedures have been called the method of successive approximation. The method has also been called the empirical development technique, the instructional quality control method, and the trial revision cycle technique.

Two conditions must be met before this simple development technique can be put into practice. First, the goals of instruction must be stated explicitly, clearly, and in great detail. This condition is required in order to construct comprehensive tests to measure whether the stated instructional objectives have been achieved. Second, the instructional sequences or programs must be reproducible, that is, they must have stable, tangible forms. This condition must be met because it is pointless to draw conclusions about the effectiveness of unstable, unreproducible instructional sequences, and because it is difficult to make corrective revisions in instructional sequences that have no tangible, stable form. Written material tends to satisfy these requirements although not perfectly.

The method of successive approximation provides an apparently simple scenario for the development of written instructional materials, that is, the instructional perfection of the nominal stimulus. Instructional materials that have met the requirements described above are tried out on a sample of students who are representative of the target population. Instructional results are measured and revisions are made in the instructional material in order to correct discrepancies between stated objectives and measured results. The trial revision cycle is then repeated with new samples of students until it can be concluded that the instructional sequence consistently achieves specified instructional goals.

A number of important successes have been claimed for the method of successive approximation. These cannot be documented here. There are convincing indications that the try-out procedures serve useful purposes but that the major impact of the successive approximation method resulted from the reformulation of instructional goals—a refinement of content. Careful determination of what should be taught allows powerful economics of instruction by allowing the evaluation of each potential instructional component in terms of its relevance to goals.

Yet, despite the fact that a remarkably large number of people appear to agree on its merits, the method of successive approximation is not widely used in producing written and other stable instructional materials. There are a number of reasons for this. Not least among them is that the method of successive approximation has proven to be very expensive.

Use of Adjunct Procedures

The best rational method currently available for the development of written material depends on a systematic focus on a carefully chosen number of specified instructional objectives. This creates an unhappy dilemma for publishers. Teachers of the "same" subject matter do not always have the same specific goals. At least they would discover that they did not have identical goals if they had taken the trouble to formulate these goals in explicit and exact language. Publishers wish to sell the largest possible number of copies of a given book. It therefore does not make good economic sense to them to tailor their product to the educational aims of any single group of teachers. Instead they try to produce a book that meets the largest number of educational goals that potential buyers might conceivably have. The needs of the teacher in this way conflict with the needs of the publisher. The teacher should want written materials that are focused on selected educational goals. The publisher wants a book acceptable to teachers whose educational goals may differ from each other.

The research on the control of mathemagenic activities by use of such adjunct devices as questions and directions is very relevant to a resolution of this conflict between teacher and publisher. Providing directions that describe learning goals to students appears to be a method by which teachers can adapt general purpose material to their nonspecific goals. The effective content of a book, rather than being focused through the work of the writer, becomes focused through the selective topography of mathemagenic activities. This allows the school to take advantage of the economies of a centrally produced, general purpose book and adapt it to local purposes by relatively cheap, locally produced, adjunct material. This is, of course, one of the reasons why research on the control of mathemagenic activities is attractive from a practical as well as a purely scientific point of view.

The general framework discussed here sets forth two kinds of determinants of learning from written material. These are the nominal attributes of the text and acts by the readers to create a useful internal representation from the written material. An important feature of this approach is that evaluation of both factors nearly always refers to an external pragmatic criterion and must involve consideration of the state of the other factor. There may be universally negative mathemagenic activities such as falling asleep during reading. Whether a mathemagenic activity is positive, however, depends on the nature of the specific goals of instruction. It is meaningless to inquire whether the use of adjunct questions with text, is, in general, instructionally desirable. Similarly the issue of whether a text is effective is not an interesting question without reference to its intended use and the nature of mathemagenic activities that may be supported in the instructional situation. Partial exceptions to the above are the representation and form factors that were described as not being goal-specific in Table 1. These factors may have some use in deciding whether books are likely to invite browsing and whether they are likely to be unsuitable for a particular reader population. There are indications, however, that representation and form are weak nominal stimulus factors compared to content and that their effects can be overcome by suitable mathemagenic activities.[75] However, even if weak, it would not be consistent with the aims of instruction to neglect representation and form factors. For best results, care should be taken not only that students read to learn but also that text has been written to teach.

NOTES

[1] Edward J. Crothers, "Memory Structure and the Recall of Discourse," in *Language Comprehension and the Acquisition of Knowledge*, eds., Roy O. Freedle and John B. Carroll. Washington, DC: V.H. Winston and Sons, 1972, 247-284; Carl H. Frederiksen, "Effect of Task-Induced Cognitive Operations on Comprehension and Memory Processes," ibid., 211-246. [4].

[2] This is the cloze procedure; see, for example, Earl F. Rankin, Jr., "An Evaluation of Cloze Procedure as a Technique for Measuring Reading Comprehension," doctoral dissertation, University of Michigan, 1958.

[3] See, for example, Richard C. Anderson, "How to Construct Achievement Tests to Assess Comprehension," *Review of Educational Research*, 42 (Spring 1972), 145-170.

4 John R. Bormuth, *On the Theory of Achievement Test Items*. Chicago: University of Chicago Press, 1970.

5 It should be noted here that the number of acceptable transformations and paraphrases increases markedly as the size of the relevant linguistic unit becomes larger.

6 For an example of collative responses, see Lawrence T. Frase, "A Structural Analysis of the Knowledge that Results from Thinking about Text," *Journal of Educational Psychology*, 60 (1969), Monograph Supplement 6. This monograph indicates the large number of test items that can be generated from four simple statements. See also Ernst Z. Rothkopf, "Incidental Memory for Location of Information in Text," *Journal of Verbal Learning and Verbal Behavior*, 10 (December 1971), 608-613.

7 Ernst Z. Rothkopf, "A Measure of Stimulus Similarity and Errors in Some Paired-Associate Learning Tasks," *Journal of Experimental Psychology*, 53 (February 1957), 94-101; Clark L. Hull, *Principles of Behavior*. New York: Appleton-Century, 1943; Benton J. Underwood, "Stimulus Selection in Verbal Learning," in *Verbal Behavior and Learning*, eds., C.N. Cofer and B.S. Musgrave. New York: McGraw-Hill, 1963, 33-47.

8 Ernst Z. Rothkopf, "Structural Text Features and the Control of Processes in Learning from Written Materials," in *Language Comprehension and the Acquisition of Knowledge*, eds., R.O. Freedle and John B. Carroll. Washington, DC: V.H. Winston and Sons, 1972, 315-335.

9 Mary E. Koether, Ernst Z. Rothkopf, and Martin E. Smith, "The Evaluation of Instructional Text: I. Effectiveness as a Function of Method of Measuring Achievement." Paper presented at the meeting of the American Educational Research Association, Minneapolis, March 1970.

10 Ernst Z. Rothkopf and Robert Kaplan, "An Exploration of the Effect of Density and Specificity of Instructional Objectives on Learning from Text," *Journal of Educational Psychology*, 63 (August 1972), 295-302.

11 Martin E. Smith, Ernst Z. Rothkopf, and Mary E. Koether. "The Evaluation of Instructional Text: II. Relating Measures of Recall to Text Properties." Paper presented at the meeting of the American Educational Research Association, Minneapolis, March 1970.

12 More extensive treatments can be found in Ernst Z. Rothkopf and Paul E. Johnson, eds., *Verbal Learning Research and the Technology of Written Instruction*. New York: Columbia University, Teachers College Press, 1971.

13 Allan Paivio, "Mental Imagery in Associative Learning and Memory," *Psychological Review*, 76 (May 1969), 241-263; Clyde E. Noble, "Meaningfulness and Familiarity," in Cofer and Musgrave, *Verbal Behavior and Learning*, 76-119.

14 See Allan Paivio, John C. Yuille, and Stephen A. Madigan, "Concreteness, Imagery, and Meaningfulness Values for 925 Nouns," *Journal of Experimental Psychology Monograph Supplement*, 76 (January 1968), entire issue.

15 Noble, "Meaningfulness and Familiarity."

16 See Edward L. Thorndike and Irving Lorge, *The Teacher's Word Book of 30,000 Words*. New York: Bureau of Publications, Teachers College, Columbia University, 1944; Henry Kucera and W. Nelson Francis, *Computational Analysis of Present-Day American English*. Providence, RI: Brown University Press, 1967; John B. Carroll, P. Davies, and Bruce Richman, *The American Heritage Word Frequency Book*. New York: American Heritage, 1971.

17 See Ernst Z. Rothkopf and Ronald D. Thurner, "Effects of Written Instructional Material on the Statistical Structure of Test Essays," *Journal of Educational Psychology*, 61 (April 1970), 83-89.

18 See John R. Anderson and Gordon H. Bower, *Human Associative Memory*. Washington, DC: V.H. Winston and Sons, 1973; Allan M. Collins and M. Ross Quillian, "Retrieval Time from Semantic Memory," *Journal of Verbal Learning and Verbal Behavior*, 8 (April 1969), 240-247; Barbara Hayes-Roth and Frederic Hayes-Roth, "Plasticity in Memorial Networks," *Journal of Verbal Learning and Verbal Behavior*, 14 (October 1975), 506-522; David E. Meyer, "On the Representation and Retrieval of Stored Semantic Information," *Cognitive Psychology*, I (August 1970), 242-300.

19 Kenneth I. Forster and Susan M. Chambers, "Lexical Access and Naming Time," *Journal of Verbal Learning and Verbal Behavior*, 12 (December 1973), 627-635; Herbert Rubenstein, Lonnie Garfield, and Jane A. Millikan, "Homographic Entries in the Internal Lexicon," *Journal of Verbal Learning and Verbal Behavior*, 9 (October 1970), 487-494; Robert F. Stanners, James E. Jastr-

zembski, and Allen Westbrook, "Frequency and Visual Quality in a Word-Nonword Classification Task," *Journal of Verbal Learning and Verbal Behavior*, 14 (June 1975), 259-264.

20 Roger C. Schank, "Conceptual Dependency: A Theory of Natural Language Understanding," *Cognitive Psychology*, 3 (October 1972), 552-631.

21 Lawrence T. Frase, "Influence of Sentence Order and Amount of Higher Level Text Processing upon Reproductive and Productive Memory," *American Educational Research Journal*, 7 (May 1970), 307-319; Morton P. Friedman and Frank L. Greitzer, "Organization and Study Time in Learning from Reading," *Journal of Educational Psychology*, 63 (December 1972), 609-616; Jerome L. Myers, Kathy Pezdek, and Douglas Coulson, "Effects of Prose Organization upon Recall," *Journal of Educational Psychology*, 65 (December 1973), 313-320; Charles B. Schultz and Francis J. DiVesta, "Effects of Passage Organization and Note Taking on the Selection of Clustering Strategies and on Recall of Textual Materials," *Journal of Educational Psychology*, 63 (June 1972), 244-252.

22 James L. Evans, Lloyd E. Homme, and Robert Glaser, "The Ruleg System for the Construction of Programed Verbal Learning Sequences," *Journal of Educational Research*, 55 (June-July 1962), 513-518.

23 Ernst Z. Rothkopf and Esther U. Coke, "Repetition Interval and Rehearsal Method in Learning Equivalences from Written Sentences," *Journal of Verbal Learning and Verbal Behavior*, 2 (December 1963), 406-416; idem, "Variations in Phrasing, Repetition Intervals, and the Recall of Sentence Material," ibid. 5 (February 1966), 86-91.

24 See James Deese and Roger A. Kaufman, "Serial Effects in Recall of Unorganized and Sequentially Organized Verbal Material," *Journal of Experimental Psychology*, 54 (September 1957), 180-187; Ernst Z. Rothkopf, "Learning from Written Sentences: Effects of Order of Presentation on Retention," *Psychological Reports*, 10 (June 1962), 667-674.

25 See Philip B. Gough, "Grammatical Transformations and Speed of Understanding," *Journal of Verbal Learning and Verbal Behavior*, 4 (April 1965), 107-111; Lee E. McMahon, *Grammatical Analysis as Part of Understanding a Sentence*, doctoral dissertation, Harvard University, 1963.

26 See Harris B. Savin and Ellen Perchonock, "Grammatical Structure and the Immediate Recall of English Sentences," *Journal of Verbal Learning and Verbal Behavior*, 4 (October 1965), 348-353.

27 Edmund B. Coleman, "Improving Comprehensibility by Shortening Sentences," *Journal of Applied Psychology*, 46 (April 1962), 131-134.

28 Edmund B. Coleman, "Developing a Technology of Written Instruction: Some Determiners of the Complexity of Prose," in *Verbal Learning Research and the Technology of Written Instruction*, eds., Ernst Z. Rothkopf and P.E. Johnson. New York: Columbia University, Teachers College Press, 1971, 155-204.

29 I.M. Schlesinger, *Sentence Structure and the Reading Process*. The Hague: Mouton, 1966.

30 John B. Carroll, "Learning from Verbal Discourse in Educational Media," Research Bulletin 71-61. Princeton, NJ: Educational Testing Service, 1971.

31 Examples of readability indices include Edgar Dale and Jeanne S. Chall, "A Formula for Predicting Readability," *Educational Research Bulletin*, 27 (January 1948), 11-20; Rudolph Flesch, "A New Readability Yardstick," *Journal of Applied Psychology*, 32 (June 1948), 221-233; and Robert Gunning, *The Technique of Clear Writing*. New York: McGraw-Hill, 1952.

32 George R. Klare, *The Measurement of Readability*. Ames: Iowa State University Press, 1963.

33 The rationales presented here were *not* those proposed by Flesch.

34 G.K. Zipf, *The Psycho-biology of Language*. Boston: Houghton-Mifflin, 1935.

35 Noble, "Meaningfulness and Familiarity."

36 Coleman, "Improving Comprehensibility."

37 Esther U. Coke and Ernst Z. Rothkopf, "Note on a Simple Algorithm for a Computer Produced Reading Ease Score," *Journal of Applied Psychology*, 54 (June 1970), 208-210.

38 Ernst Z. Rothkopf, "Structural Text Features and the Control of Processes in Learning from Written Material."

39 A recently developed readability measure developed by Langer et al. for German texts has met some of these criticisms. See I. Langer et al., "Merkmale der Verständlichkeit schriftlicher Informations—und Lehr texte," *Zeitschrift für experimentelle und angewandte Psychologie*, 20, no. 2 (1973), 269-286. The German technique, however, requires relatively laborious procedures.

[40] See William K. Estes, "Toward a Statistical Theory of Learning," *Psychological Review*, 57 (March 1950), 94-107; E.R. Guthrie, "Conditioning: A Theory of Learning in Terms of Stimulus, Response, and Association," *The Psychology of Learning*, Forty-First Yearbook of the National Society for the Study of Education, Part II, ed., Nelson B. Henry. Chicago: University of Chicago Press, 1942, 17-60.

[41] Leo Postman, "Short Term Memory and Incidental Learning," in *Categories of Human Learning*, ed., A.W. Melton. New York: Academic Press, 1964, 146-201.

[42] The term "mathemagenic" is derived from Greek roots that mean giving birth to learning. The main purpose in coining the term was to emphasize the important role of the student in determining what is learned. The concept also draws attention to possibilities of manipulating the instructional environment as a form of educational intervention in contrast to manipulating instructional means or materials. See Ernst Z. Rothkopf, "Some Conjectures about Inspection Behavior in Learning from Written Sentences and the Response Mode Problem in Programed Self-instruction," *Journal of Programed Instruction*, 2 (Winter 1963), 31-45. See also idem, "Some Theoretical and Experimental Approaches to Problems in Written Instruction," in *Learning and the Educational Process*, ed., J.D. Krumboltz. Chicago: Rand McNally, 1965, 193-221; idem, "Two Scientific Approaches to the Management of Instruction," in *Learning Research and School Subjects*, eds., Robert M. Gagné and W.J. Gephart. Itasca, IL: F.E. Peacock, 1968, 107-133; idem, "The Concept of Mathemagenic Activities," *Review of Educational Research*, 40 (June 1970), 325-336; idem, "Experiments on Mathemagenic Behavior and the Technology of Written Instruction," in *Verbal Learning Research and the Technology of Written Instruction*, 284-303.

[43] Rothkopf, "A Measure of Stimulus Similarity."

[44] Samuel A. Bobrow and Gordon H. Bower, "Comprehension and Recall of Sentences," *Journal of Experimental Psychology*, 80 (June 1969), 455-461; Fergus I.M. Craik and Robert S. Lockhart, "Levels of Processing: A Framework for Memory Research," *Journal of Verbal Learning and Verbal Behavior*, 11 (December 1972), 671-684; Fergus I.M. Craik and Endel Tulving. "Depth of Processing and the Retention of Words in Episodic Memory," *Journal of Experimental Psychology: General*, 104 (1975), 268-294; Thomas S. Hyde and James J. Jenkins, "Recall for Words as a Function of Semantic, Graphic, and Syntactic Orienting Tasks," *Journal of Verbal Learning and Verbal Behavior*, 12 (October 1973), 471-480.

[45] Craik and Tulving, "Depth of Processing."

[46] There are indications that some of the primary processes such as eye movements can fall under what looks like automatic control. Finding one's eye looking at the lower right corner after traversing the page "without having read anything" is a commonly reported experience that suggests the possibility of such automatic processes.

[47] Rothkopf, "Some Theoretical and Experimental Approaches"; idem, "Two Scientific Approaches to the Management of Instruction"; idem, "The Concept of Mathemagenic Activities"; idem, "Experiments on Mathemagenic Behavior."

[48] Rothkopf, "Some Theoretical and Experimental Approaches."

[49] Craik and Lockhart, "Levels of Processing."

[50] Robert Kaplan and Ernst Z. Rothkopf, "Instructional Objectives as Directions to Learners: Effect of Passage Length and Amount of Objective-Relevant Content," *Journal of Educational Psychology*, 66 (June 1974), 448-456; Rothkopf and Kaplan, "An Exploration of the Effect of Density and Specificity."

[51] Robert Kaplan and Francine G. Simmons, "Effects of Instructional Objectives Used as Orienting Stimuli or as Summary/Review upon Prose Learning," *Journal of Educational Psychology*, 66 (August 1974), 614-622.

[52] David P. Ausubel, Seymour H. Schpoont, and Lillian Cukier, "The Influence of Intention on the Retention of School Materials," *Journal of Educational Psychology*, 48 (February 1957), 87-92.

[53] Postman, "Short-Term Memory and Incidental Learning."

[54] Lawrence T. Frase and Valerie S. Kreitzberg, "Effect of Topical and Indirect Learning Directions on Prose Recall," *Journal of Educational Psychology*, 67 (April 1975), 320-324.

[55] See Wayne A. Hershberger and Donald F. Terry, "Typographical Cuing in Conventional and Programed Texts," *Journal of Applied Psychology*, 49 (February 1965), 55-60.

[56] Kaplan and Rothkopf, "Instructional Objectives as Directions to Learners"; Ernst Z. Rothkopf and Marjorie J. Billington, "Relevance and Similarity of Text Elements to Descriptions of Learning Goals," *Journal of Educational Psychology,* in press.

[57] Rothkopf and Kaplan, "An Exploration of the Effect of Density and Specificity."

[58] Kaplan and Rothkopf, "Instructional Objectives as Directions to Learners."

[59] Rothkopf and Billington, "Relevance and Similarity of Text Elements."

[60] Ellen D. Gagné and Ernst Z. Rothkopf, "Text Organization and Learning Goals," *Journal of Educational Psychology,* 67 (June 1975), 445-450.

[61] Roger H. Bruning, "Effects of Review and Test-Like Events within the Learning of Prose Materials," *Journal of Educational Psychology,* 59 (February 1968), 16-19; Ernst Z. Rothkopf, "Learning from Written Instructive Materials; An Exploration of the Control of Inspection Behavior by Test-Like Events," *American Educational Research Journal,* 3 (November 1966), 241-249.

[62] Edys S. Quellmalz, "Effects of Three Characteristics of Text-Embedded Response Requirements on the Development of a Dominant Focus in Prose Learning," doctoral dissertation, University of California, Los Angeles, 1971; Ernst Z. Rothkopf and Ethel E. Bisbicos, "Selective Facilitative Effects of Interspersed Questions on Learning from Written Materials," *Journal of Educational Psychology,* 58 (February 1967), 56-61.

[63] Rothkopf and Bisbicos, "Selective Facilitative Effects."

[64] Evan R. Keislar, "A Descriptive Approach to Classroom Motivation," *Journal of Teacher Education,* 11 (June 1960), 310-315; Ernst Z. Rothkopf, "Concerning Parallels between Adaptive Processes in Thinking and Self-Instruction," in *Approaches to Thought,* ed., J. Voss. Columbus, Ohio: Charles E. Merrill, 1969, 299-316.

[65] Leonard Carmichael and Walter F. Dearborn, *Reading and Visual Fatigue.* Boston: Houghton Mifflin, 1947. See Rothkopf, "Experiments on Mathemagenic Behavior," for a discussion of these findings.

[66] Ernst Z. Rothkopf and Richard D. Bloom, "Effects of Interpersonal Interaction on the Instructional Value of Adjunct Questions in Learning from Written Material," *Journal of Educational Psychology,* 61 (December 1970), 417-422; Ernst Z. Rothkopf, "Variable Adjunct Question Schedules, Interpersonal Interaction, and Incidental Learning from Written Material," *Journal of Educational Psychology,* 63 (April 1972), 87-92.

[67] Rothkopf, "Variable Adjunct Question Schedules."

[68] For a recent review see Richard C. Anderson and William B. Biddle, "On Asking People Questions about What They Are Reading," in *Psychology of Learning and Motivation,* vol. 9, ed., Gordon Bower. New York: Academic Press, 1975.

[69] Craik and Tulving, "Depth of Processing."

[70] Ernst Z. Rothkopf and Marjorie J. Billington, "A Two-Factor Model of the Effect of Goal-Descriptive Directions on Learning from Text," *Journal of Educational Psychology,* 67 (October 1975), 692-704.

[71] An implicit assumption that should be noted in this connection is that the law of least effort operates for processing. All other factors being held constant, more "elaborate" mathemagenic activities are less likely.

[72] Rothkopf and Billington, "A Two-Factor Model."

[73] Orpha K. Duell, "Effect of Type of Objective, Level of Test Questions, and the Judged Importance of Tested Materials upon Posttest Performance," *Journal of Educational Psychology,* 66 (April 1974), 225-232.

[74] Ernst Z. Rothkopf, "Some Observations on Predicting Instructional Effectiveness by Simple Inspection," *Journal of Programed Instruction,* 2 (Summer 1963), 19-20.

[75] Rothkopf, "Structural Text Features and the Control of Processes."

Research Issues

Developmental Processes and Reading Processes:
Invalid Inferences from the Former to the Latter

IRENE ATHEY
Rutgers University

Most educators believe that, while teaching is an art, there is a body of established knowledge which constitutes a science of education. The basic content of this science, however, seems to be somewhat difficult to define. One can, of course, make analyses of teacher behavior, or conduct field studies comparing the consequences of organizational, or curricular intervention. Such enterprises constitute the bulk of doctoral dissertations and faculty research emanating from our graduate schools of education. Some sciences, especially those which employ so-called hard data, tend to look down on these kinds of activities as imprecise, lacking objectivity and, in general, barely meriting the label scientific.

People in education have another function or responsibility, which is perhaps no more objective, but certainly just as difficult as the task of instilling rigor into educational research. I am referring to the task of keeping abreast with developments in the sciences (not to mention social and political events which may also have profound effects on education but are not under consideration here) in order to determine how these developments impinge, or should impinge, on our educational beliefs and practices. Having determined the relevancy of a particular field to education, the educational expert has the following tasks: a) He must assess the validity and relevance of findings from a particular scientific discipline. Since he is unlikely to be an expert in the field (and is certainly not going to be an expert in all of them), and since experts in the field frequently disagree about these matters, the educator finds himself in a role rather like that of a congressman in committee. He must weigh the various testimonies, and draw his own conclusions. b) Then he must attempt to synthesize, or at least balance the inputs from the different disciplines, to discover whether they are at best congruent, at worst contradictory, but

Reprinted from Frank P. Greene (Ed.), *Investigations Relating to Mature Reading*, Twenty-First Yearbook of the National Reading Conference, 1972, 171-182. Reprinted by permission of the author and the National Reading Conference, Inc.

more likely incomplete, piecemeal, and limited in perspective, so that they appear unrelated and incapable of synthesis. c) Next, from the above information he must draw valid interpretations concerning the implications of these findings for educational theory. d) Finally, he must consider the most effective ways to implement the conclusions he has drawn in the practical setting of the schools. The educator's task has been compared to that of the juggler who must keep many balls in the air at the same time, but for the juggler all balls are equal in appearance, weight, and value. The educator has the additional problem of determining which balls to use, and the relative worth of those he chooses.

I believe that the processes of weighing, synthesizing, and interpreting the many and varied inputs we in education receive from the sciences (again, I am omitting, without discounting, the inputs from social and political sources to which education must constantly lend a listening ear), are extraordinarily difficult, and that the recurring phenomenon known as the bandwagon effect may be attributable, at least in part, to this difficulty. Hence we find a tendency among educators to latch on to the findings of some biologist, psychiatrist, or sociologist, and to elevate his pronouncements to the status of a cult, especially if they happen to be in line with their own educational philosophy. A psychologist speaks, and programmed instruction is hailed as an innovation which will change the face of education. A sociologist speaks, and we may well find ourselves deschooling society and issuing educredit cards in the maternity ward.

It is important, of course, that education remain an open system capable of receiving and using data from the sciences, but as the discipline where synthesis and evaluation of the input must also take place, education has the responsibility of maintaining perspective and of having the strength to withstand scientific incursions which are excessive or unduly limited in their perspective. This may sound conservative, and many educators are afraid of being thought reactionary, out-of-date, or apathetic. We should indeed be open, flexible, and innovative, we should welcome an interdisciplinary approach to the problems of education, but we should be on guard against being subject to every wind that blows from every quarter of the academic globe.

My introductory remarks have been couched in terms of education in general but they apply with equal force to reading. For many years, reading has been the exclusive province of the education profession, and its career both in research and practice, has followed the ups-and-downs of education. For example, during an era of progressive education, the tendency was to delay the teaching of reading, and to use introductory methods which placed emphasis on units of meaning, such as the whole word or phrase, whereas the no-nonsense, back-to-basics philosophy (e.g. the Rafferty "Education in Depth" approach) called for early and specific training which would give children the tools—usually phonics training:

the research of this era is concerned largely with the efficacy of Method X versus Method Y. Similarly a period which emphasized the education of the "whole child" saw the ascendancy of the maturation hypothesis linking reading age with such physiological measures as skeletal age, dental age, etc. as well as psychological measures such as mental age (Olson, 1949).

Like education itself, reading is today the focus of interdisciplinary interest and effort. Personally, I welcome this expansion, this opening of windows to let more sunshine in. Just let us be careful that, if our position happens to be near one window, we are not blinded by the light from that particular window, so that we cannot see the view from other windows. In this paper, I have attempted to take some of the most recent knowledge from other disciplines notably psychology and linguistics, and to use them, not to put the whole child together again, since I feel this may be premature, but to achieve in some measure the kind of balance I have alluded to above. I will discuss briefly some findings in perception, cognition, psycholinguistics, and finally motivation. In each case, the development of these processes in the non-reading child, rather than the mature processes of the skilled reader, will be the focus of consideration.

Perception

We may accept at the outset Haber's (1969) view, which is shared by many other researchers, that "sensation, perception, memory, and thought must be considered on a continuum of cognitive activity. They are mutually interdependent and cannot be separated except by arbitrary rules of momentary expediency [p. 1]." It appears that all processes on the continuum are geared to the single objective of reducing the uncertainty experienced by the organism in confronting both his inner and outer world. While recognizing the continuum, psychologists still find the terms perception, cognition, etc. useful.

There are many exciting developments in the field of perception, and we can refer to only a few of them. Infant perception has been studied intensively, and we now have evidence that the infant's world is not the booming, buzzing confusion hypothesized by William James, but is characterized even as early as 16 weeks, by pattern discrimination, object permanence, size constancy, and depth perception. Fantz (1970) and Miranda (1969) at Case Western Reserve University's Perceptual Development Laboratory have found that infants show visual preference for complex, brightly patterned or colored, moving stimuli. In 1961, Walk and Gibson developed the simulation of a "visual cliff" by means of a divided patterned surface. Subsequent research on a variety of species has shown that all except flying and swimming animals avoid the "cliff edge" at a very young age, e.g. at three days of age for monkeys (Rosenblum & Cross, 1963). Infants cannot be tested on this situation until they begin to crawl, but Walk (1966) found that 90% of infants between 6 and 16 months make avoidance responses.

Other areas of study with infants are the perception of size constancy over distance, linking of visual and tactual cues in perception of objects, and the relationship between the position of a stationary object and its movement from place to place. All confirm the presence of stability and coherence in the infant's perceptual world. In fact, Denis-Prinzhorn (1961) found that after infancy, there is even a trend toward over-constancy in size judgments.

Bower (1966, 1971) has conducted some ingenious experiments which show that the very young child is capable of more and finer dis-criminations than previously suspected, and can register most of the visual information adults can, though they are able to process and use lesser amounts.

If we now consider the data on early infant perception in conjunction with Gibson's (1969) work on perception of letters by means of their distinctive features, the conclusion might be irresistible that teachers could take advantage of this early development to begin teaching recogni-tion of letters, word shapes etc. at a much younger age than is usually the case. Proponents of the academic preschool, for example, might see these studies as presenting yet further evidence that we are failing to capitalize on the young child's abilities and are wasting valuable years of potential learning in 'meaningless play.' Such a conclusion however would repre-sent an inference from a limited segment of data. For one thing, we do not know precisely the operations of the perceptual mechanisms in the adult reader, much less how well such operations are matched in the perception of the young child. Most theorists in this area see the organism as inhabit-ing a world of 'noise' from which he needs to extract such information as will reduce his uncertainty about present and future events, but they disagree as to the mechanisms which are used to this end. Moray (1969) includes the following elements: mental concentration, vigilance (paying attention in the hope the event will occur), selective attention (selection of one of several messages to receive attention), search, activation (getting ready to deal with the event), and set (preparation to respond in a certain way) [p. 6]. Gibson (1970) isolates three attentional processes involved in extracting invariant information from the variable flux: perceptual abstraction of information from the context, filtering irrelevant aspects of stimulation, and active exploratory search. Filtering as a perceptive mechanism for reducing noise is the object of some dispute. First pro-posed by Broadbent (1958) and subsequently revised by him (1967, 1970) and by Triesman (1964) to account for the fact that information sup-posedly filtered out may reach the subject's attention under certain cir-cumstances, the concept has been opposed by Deutsch and Deutsch (1963) who maintain that all stimuli reaching the senses are analyzed for

meaning. Other writers view selective attention as testing and remembering one set of anticipations over another (Hochberg, 1970), or as the
allocation of cognitive resources to a limited segment of the stimulus field
(Neisser, 1967). Complementing his account of selective attention,
Neisser presents a "fragment theory" to explain veridical perception from
incomplete stimulus information; he suggests that set, familiarity, and
context predispose the organism to perceive one stimulus configuration
over another.

All these variables have implications for reading, and have indeed
been discussed in relation to the perceptual mechanisms of the adult
reader. Much of the work on perception cited in this section is relatively
new and refers to the perceptual processes of adult subjects, but we do not
know how well these descriptions fit the perception of the young child.
Bower's work suggests that the infant's perception begins to approximate
that of the adult in some respects at quite an early age, but we cannot be
certain that this is true in all respects. The variables of set, familiarity, and
context advanced by Neisser are likely to change with the child's developing cognitive and linguistic competencies. Further studies of both visual
and auditory perception as it functions through the preschool and
elementary school years are needed.

Piaget takes a different view of the early perceptual processes we have
been discussing. For him they are not truly developmental, because they
do not show sequential changes with age. They are "field effects," or basic
organizing forces, part of the infant's initial equipment which have survival value for the individual and persist without appreciable change
throughout life. By contrast, "perceptual regulations" begin to emerge
around the age of three. During the preoperational period, when decen-
tering of both perception and thought occur, the child becomes increasingly able to reverse figure and ground, to integrate parts and wholes and
to scan configurations in systematic and novel ways. Perception is centered on the dominant aspects of the visual field, which tend to be over-
estimated, while the remaining elements are underestimated. Perceptual
strategies such as exploration, reorganization, and schematization can
compensate in part for the primary deformations, especially as these
activities come more and more under the control of operational thought.
From Piaget's theory of perception, it would follow then, that training in
the above-mentioned perceptual activities after age 3 would be more
valuable than early attention to reading per se. Elkind (1970) found that
black second-grade children made more progress as a result of such
training than a control group which received equal time in regular reading instruction.

Piaget's theory and research thus provide a counterbalance to the
premature conclusion that the young child's perception is similar to the
adult's, enabling him to accomplish the same tasks albeit at a more primi-

tive level. Work by Vurpillot (1968), and some Soviet psychologists (Zaporozhets, 1969) support the developmental aspects of perception.

Cognition

At the other end of the sensation-cognition continuum we find that the most comprehensive framework for investigation has been provided by Piaget's theory. The genetic evolution of intelligence has been studied in the development of the child's concepts of conservation, causality, reality, and morality. Unlike his theory of perception, Piaget's theory of intelligence has not as yet been applied directly to reading, the probable reason being that in general, the visual decoding aspects of reading have received much greater attention than the processes of comprehension. One may speculate that the application of Piagetian cognitive theory to reading may open up a highly fruitful field of inquiry. Even at the practical level it seems reasonable to suppose that an understanding of the child's cognitive development in terms of Piaget's concepts would have implications for the kinds of reading materials suitable for different age groups. It would be premature to suggest what these might be, however, until a more complete rapprochement between cognitive psychology and the psychology of reading occurs.

Furth (1970) has made a broader application of Piaget's theory to reading and to education. The school, he believes, has failed in its primary mission, which is to produce citizens who are adept at solving problems. It goes without saying that our society is in desperate need of people who can solve scientific, technological, and social problems. Traditional education, with its emphasis on information gathering and respect for authority seems to be ill-equipped to fulfil this mission. Its task should be to give children opportunities for solving problems, to show them how to find alternative paths to the same goal, and to provide them with the tools for problem-solving. Reading would be such a tool—one of an entire arsenal. Unfortunately, as Furth sees it, the school has chosen to elevate the tools, especially reading, to the status of a major objective. It has lost sight of the end, and has substituted a means to the goal for the goal itself. Furth maintains that a school cannot gear its resources to the teaching of reading and at the same time expect to do an adequate job of teaching problem solving. This may seem an extreme statement to some teachers, but if one sees reading instruction as inexorably tied in with the lock-step curriculum, it becomes more acceptable. Furth expands on his major thesis to suggest a variety of ways in which the teacher may institute a curriculum which emphasizes problem solving by the children.

Thus, two authors, both working within a Piagetian framework, reach different conclusions about the teaching of reading. Elkind proposes perceptual training for some (perhaps all) children as a precursor to reading instruction in the early grades, while Furth seems to view reading as a skill which might well be acquired over the elementary years as an incidental tool for problem-solving.

Interestingly enough, Rohwer (1971), who specifically rejects the Piagetian notion of critical periods, has come to a similar conclusion based on different premises. In a recent article in the *Harvard Educational Review* entitled "Prime time for education—early childhood or adolescence?" Rohwer cites cognitively oriented preschool programs as the only kind which have produced demonstrable long-standing gains in achievement. However, his conclusion is not, as one might expect, that more programs of this kind are needed. On the contrary he maintains that very little of present-day elementary education is relevant to life outside the school, and should be radically changed to incorporate skills of discrimination, classification, communication, and problem-solving. All these skills, including the "sacred cow" of reading, should be learned not at a particular age laid down by society, but at the time the child can acquire the skills (and the prerequisite subskills) readily and successfully, a conclusion not too far removed from the general position assumed by Furth.

A consideration of some recent thinking in children's congnitive development thus presents us with a situation in which the reading teacher may derive two different conclusions from the same theory, or a similar conclusion from two different theoretical standpoints.

Language

A preoccupation with the child's perceptual and cognitive development may well lead to our placing primary emphasis on the decoding and word recognition aspects of reading. But the work of Chomsky and others on the generative nature of language has drawn attention to the role of linguistic and information-processing skills in reading. Kolers (1970), in an article entitled "Reading is only incidentally visual," cites evidence from several studies to show that good readers are faithful not to the words they see printed but to the substance of the message the words convey. Words are not neutral graphic stimuli awaiting translation into associated phonemes, for in order to identify them, one has to know something about them, e.g. that they belong to a certain language. Moreover, there is no necessary serial sequence in the rapid reader's scanning of text. He has mastered the art of selecting clues which enable him to process and assimilate the information directly into his own cognitive structures. In Smith's (1971) terms, the skilled reader goes directly to "immediate meaning," whereas the less fluent reader resorts to the "lower route" of "mediated meaning identification," which interposes a step of word-by-word identification. The implication is that reading instruction should move away somewhat from emphasis on visual recognition, and concentrate on search for clues and information-extracting skills, a suggestion which is congruent with Rohwer's idea of postponing reading until it is relevant to life tasks.

On the other hand, theories of language acquistion which were developed in the 1950s and 60s tended to emphasize the early formation of a complete grammar. Thus as late as 1966, McNeill (1966) was writing: "The fundamental problem to which we adress ourselves is the simple fact that language acquisition occurs in a surprisingly short time. Grammatical speech does not begin before 1½ years of age; yet as far as we can tell, the basic process is complete by 3½ years [p. 15]." Lenneberg (1967) also sees the period from 2-4 years as critical for language learning (although he does see primary language acquisition continuing until adolescence). From this fact one might be tempted to draw either of two conclusions. The first would be that the process of language acquisition is largely irrelevant to reading, since it is virtually complete before reading begins (Wardhaugh, 1971). The second would again emphasize the importance of early reading activity to capitalize on the rapid growth of language.

More recent work, while not discounting the importance of the early period, has restored some emphasis to the continued learning of grammar throughout the elementary school years. Numerous investigations have shown that significant language development occurs after age six. C. Chomsky (1969), for example, points out that several grammatical developments occur after age 6, a most striking example being growth in the use of pronouns. O'Donnell, Griffin, and Norris (1967) found acquisition of new transformations between grades 3 to 5 and 5 to 7, while Menyuk (1964) found examples of more complicated structures as age increased.

Hence inferences about reading based on the earlier position of the linguists are no longer tenable in the light of this more recent research.

Another aspect of language development which has current salience for reading practice is the issue of dialect. Many linguists appear to be discarding the notion of language deficit which was in vogue about five years ago. Rather they see the inner-city child as having a language system which is well developed both syntactically and semantically, which has some overlap with standard English, but also many differences. Since most school texts and other reading materials are in standard English, the issue becomes that of finding the most effective ways of introducing the dialect speaker to these standard materials. The various alternatives have been discussed by Wolfram (1970). If extant materials are retained, one may teach standard English, prior to reading, and the child may be asked to render these materials in standard English or in dialect form. The latter

requires that the teacher be thoroughly familiar with the dialect in order
to distinguish between the dialect rendition and genuine reading errors.
If materials are revised, one may eliminate all features which may cause
problems for the lower-class speaker (e.g. the possessive's), or one may
construct beginning materials in dialect form with gradual transition to
standard text. Wolfram concludes that, in spite of the outspoken rejection
of dialect readers by some member of the black community, "the magnitude of the reading problem suggests that experiments must be made,
with alternatives which may involve the potential changing of materials
and curricula [p.22]." Another possible approach is to mix standard- and
dialect-speaking children in the preschool to permit the latter to gain an
understanding of standard English even though they do not use it in
speech. While this may be a preferable alternative, it is probably not
feasible on a large scale at this time.

On this particular issue, the educator may find that, however well-
grounded in linguistic theory his inferences may be, he cannot translate
them into practice without taking cognizance of the social and political
context in which the school operates.

Motivation

Unfortunately there is no technical sense of "affection" corresponding to use of the term, "cognition": If there were, it would more accurately
describe the complex of factors which might be considered under the
present rubric.

The study of affective factors and their relationship to cognitive
development has undergone considerable change in the last decade. In
one sense with the current disillusionment with formal education,
motivational aspects have come into prominence in such forms as
humanistic education, sensitivity training, alternate universities, etc. On
the other hand, the boom in cognitive psychology has deflected much
research energy from the study of nonintellectual factors. If one wanted
to trace the development of this movement away from the effective
toward the cognitive, no doubt White's (1959) classic paper in which he
elevated competence to the status of a primary drive would stand as a
landmark. But the major source of the change is probably to be found in
the current absorption with Piaget's cognitive theory. Piaget does not
disregard the motivational aspects of thought; on the contrary he seems to
consider motivation as an inherent and inseparable dimension of
thought, in the sense that it is part of the ongoing process of intellectual
activity. Perhaps the perennial difficulty of measurement in the affective
domain is also partly responsible. Whatever the reasons, the fact remains
that research on nonintellectual factors in learning seems to have suffered
a relative decline. It is interesting to note that the 600-page report of the

Literature Search project (Davis, 1971) which addressed itself to every facet of reading made only passing reference to the entire affective domain—a gross omission in my estimation. (The one exception being the paper by Entwisle, referred to below.)

I believe that there is a dimension here which is perhaps more difficult to take hold of, and therefore less rewarding in immediate payoff, but which nonetheless demands continuing attention. I have reviewed the literature on affective factors and reading elsewhere (Athey, 1970). Although it is plentiful, one misses the connecting thread of a good theory to make sense of the plethora of inconclusive and contradictory data. Perhaps such a theory, when we find it, will address itself to the changing motivations and how they affect learning at each age of the lifespan. Meanwhile, it is to be hoped that we will not lose sight of this important domain of inquiry.

Such a theory would need to explain the effects on learning of cultural and social class differences. These have been well-documented in relation to language and reading by Entwisle (1971), and include such variables as control beliefs (knowledge of one's ability to manipulate the environment to meet one's needs), self-confidence, inflexible family role learnings, and the like. Entwisle concludes from her review that "we can only meaningfully teach reading to lower class children when it begins to make sense of their lives [p. VI, 145]."

Conclusion

In this paper, I have discussed some recent literature in perception, cognition, language, and motivation as they pertain to reading. Such a review must of necessity be highly restricted in each area, but I chose to touch on all four areas deliberately, to make the point that the reading teacher, as well as the professor of education, needs not only to be cognizant of what is happening in these (and other) fields, but to keep some perspective among them. If we fail to keep this balance, we are at the mercy of temporary fads which offer panaceas on the basis of limited data.

If education is to be a science, it must progress in the same way other sciences do, by acquiring a systematic body of knowledge, rather than by chasing every fad which claims to have some scientific basis. Education is particularly vulnerable to faddism, because its sources of input are more numerous, but at the same time disparate. Consequently, educators need to be in one sense more open to new developments, and yet more defensive. They must scrutinize each innovation for its scientific underpinnings, and determine whether these conflict with what is known in other fields.

We lost the "whole child" in the 1950's, and are rebuilding him scientifically from our accumulated wisdom. Putting him together again promises to be a long and arduous, but rewarding, process.

REFERENCES

Athey, I. J. Affective factors in reading. In H. Singer & R. B. Ruddell (Eds.), *Theoretical models and processes of reading*. Newark, Del.: International Reading Association, 1970. Pp. 98-119.

Bower, T. G. R. The visual world of infants. *Scientific American*, 1966, *215* (6), 80-92.

Bower, T. G. R. The object in the world of the infant. *Scientific American*, 1971, *225* (4), 30-38.

Broadbent, D. E. *Perception and communication*. London: Pergamon Press, 1958.

Broadbent, D. E. Word frequency effect and response bias. *Psychological Review*, 1967, *74*, 1-15.

Broadbent, D. E. Stimulus set and response set: two kinds of selective attention. In D. I. Mostofsky (Ed.), Attention: contemporary theory and analysis. New York: Appleton-Century-Crofts, 1970.

Chomsky, C. S. *The acquisition of syntax in children from 5 to 10*. Cambridge, Mass.: M. I. T. Press, 1969.

Davis, F. B. *The literature on research in reading with emphasis on models*. New Brunswick, N.J.: Rutgers University, 1971.

Denis-Prinzhorn, M. Perception des distances et constance de grandeur (etude genetique). *Archives Psychol Geneve*, 1961.

Deutsch, J. A., & Deutsch, D. Attention: some theoretical considerations. *Psychological Review*, 1963, *70*, 80-90.

Elkind, D. Reading, logic, and perception. In D. Elkind (Ed.), *Children and adolescents*. New York: Oxford University Press, 1970.

Entwisle, D. Implications of language socialization for reading models and for learning to read. In F. B. Davis (Ed.), *The literature of research in reading with emphasis on models*. New Brunswick, N. J.: Rutgers University, 1971. Pp. 6/101-158.

Fantz, R. L. Visual perception and experience in infancy: issues and approaches. In F. A. Young & D. B. Lindsley (Eds.), *Early experience in visual information processing in perceptual and reading disorders*. Washington, D. C.: National Academy of Sciences, 1970. Pp. 351-381.

Furth, H. J. *Piaget for teachers*. Englewood Cliffs: Prentice-Hall, 1970.

Gibson, E. J. *Principles of perceptual learning and development*. New York: Meredith Corp., 1969.

Gibson, E. J. The development of perception as an adaptive process. *American Scientist*, 1970, *58*, 98-107.

Haber, R. N. *Information-processing approaches to visual perception*. New York: Holt, Rinehart and Winston, 1969.

Hochberg, J. Attention, organization, and consciousness. In D. I. Mostofsky (Ed.), *Attention: contemporary theory and analysis*. New York: Appleton-Century-Crofts, 1970.

Kolers, P. A. Reading is only incidentally visual. In K. Goodman & J. T. Fleming (Eds.), *Psycholinguistics and the teaching of reading*. Newark, Del.: International Reading Association, 1970. Pp. 8-16.

Lenneberg, E. H. *Biological foundations of language*. New York: Wiley, 1967.

McNeill, D. Developmental psycholinguistics. In F. Smith & G. A. Miller (Eds.), *The genesis of language: a psycholinguistic approach*. Cambridge, Mass.: M. I. T. Press, 1966. Pp. 15-84.

Menyuk, P. Alteration of rules in children's grammar. *Journal of Verbal Learning and Verbal Behavior*, 1964, *3*, 480-488.

Miranda, S. B. Visual abilities and pattern preferences of premature infants and full-term neonates. Unpublished manuscript, Case Western Reserve University, 1969.

Moray, N. *Attention: selective processes in vision and hearing*. New York: Academic Press, 1969.

Neisser, U. *Cognitive psychology*. New York: Appleton-Century-Crofts, 1967.

O'Donnell, R. C., Griffin, W. J., & Norris, R. C. A transformational analysis of written and oral grammatical structure in the language of children in grades 3, 5, and 7. *Journal of Educational Research*, 1967, *61*, 35-39.

Olson, W. C. *Child Development.* Boston: D. C. Heath, 1949.

Rohwer, W. D., Jr. Prime time for education—early childhood or adolescence? *Harvard Educational Review,* 1971, *42,* 316-341.

Rosenblum, L. A., & Cross, H. A. Performance of neonatal monkeys on the visual cliff situation. *American Journal of Psychology,* 1963, *76,* 318-320.

Smith, F. *Understanding reading.* New York: Holt, Rinehart and Winston, 1971.

Triesman, A. M. Selective attention in man. *British Medical Bulletin,* 1964, *20,* 12-16.

Vurpillot, E. The development of scanning strategies and their relation to visual differentation. *Journal of Experimental Child Psychology,* 1968, *6,* 632-650.

Walk, R. D. The development of depth perception in animals and human infants. In H. W. Stevenson (Ed.), *Concept of development.* Society for Research in Child Development Monograph No. 107, 1966, *31,* 82-108.

Walk, R. D., & Gibson, E. J. A comparative and analytic study of visual depth perception. *Psychological Monographs,* 1961, *75*(15).

Wardhaugh, R. Theories of language acquisition in relation to beginning reading instruction. *Reading Research Quarterly,* 1961, *7,* 168-194.

White, R. W. Motivation reconsidered: the concept of competence. *Psychological Review,* 1959, *66,* 297-333.

Wolfram, W. Sociolinguistic alternatives in teaching reading to nonstandard speakers. *Reading Research Quarterly,* 1970, *6,* 9-33.

Zaporozhets, A. V. Some of the psychological problems of sensory training in early childhood and the preschool period. In M. Cole & I. Maltzman (Eds.), *A handbook of contemporary Soviet psychology.* New York: Basic Books, 1969. Pp. 86-120.

Hypotheses on Reading Comprehension in Search of Classroom Validation

HARRY SINGER
University of California at Riverside

In the past two decades we have witnessed a virtual explosion of theories and research in the psychology of reading. This explosion came after the topic of reading had almost disappeared from psychological investigations. This up-and-down status of reading reflects the revolutionary changes that have occurred in the field of psychology over the past 100 years. Some landmark research conducted over the last 100 years, shown in Table 1, depicts these changes.

Table 1

PSYCHOLOGICAL RESEARCH ON READING
FROM 1879 TO 1980

1879	Javal	Eye movement behavior during reading consists of saccades and return sweep movements.
1886	Cattell	Adults perceive a word more rapidly than its individual letters.
1908	Huey	*Psychology and Pedagogy of Reading.*
1917	Thorndike	Analyses of responses in reading leads to definition that reading is reasoning.
1922	Buswell	Eye movement behavior in reading changes over grades 1-12 by becoming more rhythmical, shorter in pause duration, and longer in span of perception.
1922	Judd and Buswell	During silent reading, readers vary their eye-movement behavior according to the difficulty of the material and their purposes in reading.
1932	Bartlett	*Remembering:* Successive recall of Indian story, "War of the Ghosts," demonstrates that reading is a constructive process and recall is a reconstructive process based on interaction between the text data and the readers' schemata and beliefs.
1946	Thurstone	High school reading tests consist of two factors: word recognition and reasoning.

Reprinted from M.L. Kamil (Ed.), *Directions in Reading: Research and Instruction.* Thirtieth Yearbook of the National Reading Conference. Washington, DC: National Reading Conference, 1981, 1-20. Reprinted by permission of the author and the National Reading Conference, Inc.

1952	Anderson and Dearborn	*Psychology of Reading*. Learning to read consists of formation of s-r associations and then using these associations to perceive printed words.
1953	Holmes	Reading consists of two interrelated components: speed and power. Underlying each component is an interrelated hierarchy of substrata factors. These factors are mobilized to solve problems in reading according to the readers' purposes and the demands of the task stimuli.
1957	Chomsky	*Syntactic Structures*. Differentiates competence and performance. Kernel sentences generated by phrase structure rules; transformation rules operate on syntactic structures to express different types of sentences. Attacks s-r explanations of language acquisition.
1960	Ausubel	Advance organizers are abstract knowledge structures which assimilate information in text.
1966	Goodman	Reading consists of psycholinguistically determined expectancies or hypotheses used by the reader and the text, and sampling of print to test and confirm hypotheses.
1970	Singer and Ruddell	*Theoretical Models and Processes of Reading*. Perceptual, linguistic and cognitive processes explain reading.
1972	Bransford and Franks	Readers chunk semantically related information across sentences.
1972	Winograd	"World Knowledge," information stored in long term memory, is necessary for comprehending texts.
1974	Kintsch	*The Representation of Meaning in Memory*. Meaning is represented by given and inferred propositions.
1975	Meyer	*The Organization of Prose and Its Effects on Memory*. Texts are represented by hierarchically organized propositions stored in memory.
1975	Rumelhart	A grammar for a well organized story, such as a fable, consists of a set of recursive rules that include plot, character, problem, situation, and resolution.
1976	Gough	Information processing model accounts for psychological data on reading.
1976	Rumelhart	Reading consists of an interaction between text based data and reader based resources.
1977	Schank and Abelson	Scripts, sequences of events stored in long term memory, are necessary for explicating and assimilating texts and culturally determined situations ("Mops" have replaced scripts).
1977	LaBerge and Samuels	Model of automaticity in processing print describes skilled readers' performance.
1977	Anderson, Spiro and Montague	*Schooling and the Acquisition of Knowledge*. Role of schemata, defined as knowledge structures with variable slots, explains assimilation of text data, construction of text interpretation, and inferential reconstruction upon recall.

| 1977 | van Dijk and Kintsch | Texts are represented in memory by macrostructures and microstructures. |
| 1979 and 1980 | Tierney and Spiro; Tierney LaZansky | Comprehension of a text consists of a band of acceptable interpretations that vary on a continuum of text based and reader based interactions. |

At the turn of the century, reading was a central topic in psychology. Javal (1879) had already discovered and measured eye-movement behavior in reading. Wundt's first American doctoral candidate, Cattell (1886), had found that adults perceived a word more rapidly than its individual letters. Huey (1908) proclaimed in his *Psychology and Pedagogy of Reading* that the understanding of reading would be the acme of a psychologist's achievement. In 1917, Thorndike defined reading as reasoning. Although his definition changed the goal of reading, it also may have deterred some psychologists from studying reading comprehension as such.

With the advent of Watson's behaviorism, psychological studies of reading focused on eye-movement behavior in reading. Buswell (1922) recorded developmental changes over grades 1 to 12 in eye-movement behavior during reading. Judd and Buswell (1922) demonstrated that, during silent reading, readers varied their eye-movement behavior according to the kind and difficulty of material, and their purposes in reading. Although some research was done on reading in the content areas during this time (Bond, 1938; Strang, 1942; Robinson and Hall, 1941), psychologists limited their work mostly to visual perception and eye-movement behavior in reading. Consequently, Anderson and Dearborn's book on the psychology of teaching reading, published in 1952, consisted mostly of research on visual perception, eye-movement behavior in reading, Olson's organismic age concept for determining expectancy in reading achievement, and s-r explanations of methods of teaching reading. This research was atheoretical and contained hardly any studies on comprehension. Indeed, the prevailing conception was that reading consisted of word perception; all else was thinking (Buswell, 1952). This conception was supported by Thurstone's (1946) factor analysis of reading tests into two factors: word meaning and reasoning.

Two notable exceptions to s-r type research occurred during the behavioristic era. Influenced by gestalt psychology, Bartlett (1932), an English psychologist, studied the dynamics of memory. He had readers recall an Indian story, entitled "The War of the Ghosts." Bartlett found that readers constructed an interpretation of the story and, over time, their recall of the story occurred as an inferential reconstructive process based upon their schemata. Some 40 years later, when the zeitgeist had changed to favor cognitive psychology, American psychologists were to hail Bartlett's research as a pioneering investigation.

The other exception was the multiple regression studies conducted by Holmes (1948, 1953, 1954) to test the central hypothesis of his substrata factor theory of reading. He found that a multiplicity of factors accounted for individual differences in general reading ability and for predictors of this ability. Holmes theorized that these factors functioned at various substrata levels, but were mobilized and organized into momentary working systems according to the reader's changing purposes and the demands of the reading task.

During the 1950s, the dominant experimental paradigm for studying verbal learning was paired-associates. "Reading," which had been the title of a chapter in Woodworth's (1938) book *Experimental Psychology,* was reduced to only a topic in his 1954 revision (Woodworth and Schlosberg, 1954). This narrow scope of research in reading changed dramatically after Chomsky (1957) wrought his revolution in linguistics and after his severe attack on s-r psychology (Chomsky, 1959). Apparently influenced by Chomsky's arguments, many psychologists abandoned the paired-associates paradigm with its s-r explanations and shifted their research to sentence comprehension with cognitive explanations. Then research in psycholinguistics began to flourish and greatly affected the field of reading. Goodman (1966), for example, drew upon expectancy theory and psycholinguistics to explain the process of reading.

However, psychologists soon discovered that Chomsky's linguistic theory presupposed rather than predicted meaning. So they changed their research to focus on meaning (van Dijk and Kintsch, 1977). Ausubel (1960) had already formulated his theory of comprehension, which features advance organizers — abstract knowledge structures that assimilate information lower in the knowledge hierarchy, and can be modified to accommodate new information. Bransford and Franks (1974) discovered that syntax was necessary to get meaning correctly into long term memory where it was chunked across semantically related sentences.

Some psychologists argued that meanings were stored in memory in the form of propositions, and began to use propositional analysis to represent the text based input (Kintsch, 1974; Meyer, 1975; Frederiksen, 1975). They also began to investigate the effects of text variation on reader's speed of processing text and on the reader's construction of macrostructures and microstructures (Kintsch, 1980; Meyer et al., 1980). They have assumed that propositional meaning is sufficient for comprehension of a text. But they have not yet determined normative levels of inference nor the developmental conditions under which these inferences are made (Singer, 1980a).

Another source of impact on reading came from the use of computers. During the 1960s, computers became readily available and began to be used for studying artificial intelligence, including simulation of reading comprehension. Winograd (1972) discovered that he had to program into computers "world knowledge" to simulate the information readers had accumulated in their long term memories and had to mobilize in order to explicate and comprehend printed materials. Schank and Abelson (1977) added the concept of "scripts" which represent the common knowledge for sequences of events that readers acquire and mobilize for guiding their behavior and interpreting situations. (I understand Schank has substituted for "scripts" the concept of "mops" which are memory organization points.)

A boon to research in reading comprehension came from another source. In the 1970s, federal funds began to emphasize research on reading comprehension. The National Institute of Education established a Center for the Study of Reading at the University of Illinois under the very able direction of Richard Anderson. The Center has been productive in studies on the role of schemata for assimilating, interpreting, and comprehending printed materials. This view of reading comprehension is presented in the book *Schooling and the Acquisition of Knowledge* (Anderson, Spiro, and Montague, 1977).

Many of the new concepts in reading were incorporated into Rumelhart's (1976) interaction model of reading. After criticizing LaBerge and Samuel's (1976) model on automaticity and Gough's (1976) model on information processing, Rumelhart presented his interaction model. In this model, readers allocate attention between text based data and reader based resources. The resulting information is integrated and funneled through the reader's limited capacity processor. A corollary to the interaction model is that reading comprehension consists of a band of acceptable interpretations that vary on a continuum of text based and reader based interactions (Tierney and Spiro, 1979; Tierney and LaZansky, 1980). These interpretations are represented in memory by macrostructures and microstructures (van Dijk and Kintsch, 1977).

Thus, in the past 20 years, psychology has restored reading to a central position. This renewed status of reading is exemplified by such books as *Basic Studies on Reading* (Levin and Williams, 1970), *Language by Ear and by Eye* (Kavanagh and Mattingly, 1972), *The Psychology of Reading* (Levin and Gibson, 1975), *Theoretical Models and Processes of Reading* (Singer and Ruddell, 1970, 1976), *Basic Processes in Reading: Perception and Comprehension* (LaBerge and Samuels, 1977), *New Directions in Discourse Processing* (Freedle, 1979), and *Perception of Print* (Tzeng and Singer, 1981).

But the explosion of knowledge in the field of reading has been primarily on the psychology, not on the pedagogy of reading. Although some researchers, such as David Pearson and Robert Tierney at the Center for the Study of Reading, are conducting research on teaching comprehension, the gap between knowledge of reading and application of this knowledge to instruction for the development and improvement of reading comprehension is great and is growing greater. We need to close this gap by testing implications derived from psychological theories and research in classroom settings. We need to determine whether these implications are developmentally valid, and if so, whether they can be translated into instructional strategies that can improve reading comprehension in normal classroom settings. I shall summarize a list of some research based hypotheses and implications that need to be tested and validated at the classroom level. The list is shown in Table 2.

Table 2

LIST OF RESEARCH-BASED HYPOTHESES FOR TESTING AND DEVISING STRATEGIES
FOR IMPROVING COMPREHENSION AT THE CLASSROOM LEVEL

1. *Input stimuli*. Modify input materials so that they fit readers' abilities; then develop
   readers to higher levels of ability on the relevant variable.
   a. *Shift conceptual levels from abstract towards concrete*.
      (1) *Word meaning:* substitute high for low frequency words (Marks, Doctorow, and
          Wittrock, 1974).
      (2) *Sentence comprehension:* concretize sentence (Anderson, 1976); this modifica-
          tion reduces sentences from more abstract levels and may enable readers to
          then generate instantiations and consequently comprehend the sentences. In
          some cases, sentences may be reduced from general to particular statements
          that tend to make them more imageable and hence more memorable (Levin,
          1976). For example, compare these sentences: The regulations annoyed the
          salesman vs. The *parking* regulations annoyed the salesman.
      (3) *Passage sequence:* construct concrete passages to develop advance organizers
          that precede more abstract passages (Royer and Cable, 1975).
   b. *Modify syntax*
      (1) *Syntactic level:* use syntax in print that corresponds with the syntax employed
          by readers in their oral language (Ruddell, 1965).
      (2) *Syntactic complexity:* combine sentences to explicate their causal relationships,
          which will make the sentences longer. But, in contrast to the readability hy-
          pothesis which asserts that shorter sentences are easier to comprehend, some
          longer sentences with the causal relationship explicated will be easier to com-
          prehend (Pearson, 1976). For example, compare these sentences: Mary went to
          the store. She bought a loaf of bread. vs. Mary went to the store *to* buy a loaf of
          bread.
      (3) *Embedded clauses:* whenever choice can be exercised, use right branching
          (clauses embedded after the main verb) to reduce memory load on short term
          storage and hasten storage in long term memory (Gough, 1976).
   c. *Verb voice*
      For ease in processing print, use the active over the passive voice, but when the
      passive has to be employed, do so with agent expressed (Wanat, 1976).
   d. *Text organization*
      (1) *Paragraph organization:* explicate situational contexts close to the beginning of
          a passage so that a global representation can be attained early in the passage
          and used for interpreting events (Bransford and Johnson, 1972).
      (2) *Clarity:* explicate macrostructure and microstructure relationships (van Dijk
          and Kintsch, 1977).
      (3) *Density:* increase redundancy in text so that a higher proportion of text can be
          relevant to a particular instructional objective (Rothkopf and Kaplan, 1972).
      (4) *Information:* explicate information needed for making inferences (Marshall,
          1975).
      (5) *Signaling terms:* include these terms in texts (Meyer et al., 1980; Robinson,
          1975) and teach students to use them.
2. *Mediational processes*. Use instructional procedures that promote development of cognitive processes for encoding, storing, and retrieving information.

a. *Questioning strategies*
   (1) *Direct questioning*: question students on those passages they are to learn, re-member, and recall on a comprehension test (Anderson and Biddle, 1975).
   (2) *Objectives or goals*: explicitly state specific objectives, purposes, or goals that are related to statements in the text (Rothkopf and Kaplan, 1972).
   (3) *Self-questioning and self-selection of goals*: have students generate their own questions (Manzo, 1970; Frase and Schwartz, 1975; Singer, 1978) and formu-late their own reading goals. Probably self-formulation of goals will have bene-fits similar to the advantages of self-questioning; used in combination, the interaction of the two processes may even result in a greater degree of compre-hension, or at least in more efficient attainment of comprehension.
b. *Verbalization.* Teach students to summarize and paraphrase text (Wittrock et al., 1975).
c. *Knowledge.*
   (1) *Structure of knowledge*: teach students a wide range of organized information through a broadly based liberal arts curriculum.
   (2) *Mental encyclopedia*: develop a broad repertoire of information through direct and vicarious experience (Winograd, 1972). Teach students to use their back-ground information (Hansen and Pearson, 1980).
d. *Word meanings, concepts, and schemata*: have students develop within the limits of their increasing capacities a lexicon that has range, altitude, and depth (Russell, 1956), and organize it into a hierarchical structure (Rumelhart, 1975; Anderson et al., 1977).
e. *Morphemes*: teach students to analyze printed words into their morphemic constitu-ents (Ruddell, 1976; Singer, 1976).
f. *Imaging*: teach and encourage students to transform meanings expressed in print into images (Levin, 1976, 1977).
g. *Purposes.*
   (1) Counsel students to be initiators, that is, establish their own comprehension goals (deCharms, 1972).
   (2) Develop students' self-confidence and independence (Athey, 1976).
h. *Reasoning about print.*
   (1) Teach students to analyze sentences into given and new information and com-pare it with information already in their mental encyclopedias (Clark and Clark, 1977).
   (2) Have students learn and practice generation of concrete scenarios from their abstract structures; have students also generate examples or hypotheses for su-perordinate schemata (Anderson et al., 1976).
   (3) Teach students to form new schemata by having them abstract and generalize from direct and vicarious experiences using a teaching process such as Taba's questioning sequence (Taba, 1965).
3. *Output products*: use the type of measurement that corresponds with the reader's pur-pose, mode of processing, and demands of the material.
   a. *Letter-by-letter*: reading that follows more closely to the sensory-driven level of the processing continuum is more likely to occur when the exact meaning of the author is sought. At the extreme level, letter-by-letter processing (Gough, 1976) or direct perception (McConkie and Rayner, 1976) occurs, but does not actually involve processing all the letters, only those needed to identify the word (Strange, 1979). For this mode of processing and reader goal, verbatim scoring of a recall protocol is appropriate.

b. *Hypothesis and sampling of print*: a mode of reading that is closer to the concept driven level is more likely to occur when a) the reader only wants to extract the general meaning of the passage or b) the material is familiar or c) the material only demands extraction of a general idea. Then the reader is more likely to hypothesize, sample the print, and confirm or disconfirm hypotheses (Goodman, 1976; Wanat, 1976). The same type of processing may occur when the contextual situation is missing or has not been stated yet and the reader is testing out ways of conceptualizing the input and consequently shifts from one hypothesis to another (Rumelhart, 1978). For this type of reading, gist or lax scoring would be more relevant than verbatim or exact scoring (Nicholson, 1977).

c. *Level of macrostructures and microstructures*: use text bases that specify macro-structures and microstructures which are appropriate to students' developmental levels. Teach students to form these structures, and supplement them with strategies for processing various types of expository text (Kintsch, 1980; Singer, 1980a).

d. *Coherence in teaching and testing*: make sure that the readers' purposes, information in text and ways of processing them, and goals or tests cohere. Or stated in another way, determine whether the directions and tasks given the reader fit the information provided in texts and the questions asked on comprehension tests (Rothkopf, 1980; Singer, 1980b).

Hypotheses for Classroom Testing

The first set of hypotheses deals with the modification of input stimuli to fit readers' abilities. These hypotheses refer to levels of abstraction, syntactic complexity, and organization in text, including discourse and rhetorical devices, lexical choices, and explication of propositions. Such modification may lead to the determination that an input variable is related to comprehension. After this determination has been made, it is necessary to try to improve the process or knowledge entailed by this variable so that readers can comprehend the more difficult and more varied material. This type of improvement is necessary if the claim is made that variation in the input stimuli has improved comprehension.

The second set of hypotheses focuses on improvement of mediational processes. These hypotheses refer to acquisition of self-questioning and verbalization strategies, development of information and knowledge structures and their use in reading, improvement of students' lexicons and morphological ability, instruction in use of imagery in processing print, and emphasis on teaching students to vary their purposes in reading and increase their ability to reason about print.

The last set of hypotheses refers to the assessment of comprehension. The main point in these hypotheses is that the type of assessment used should correspond with the reader's purposes, mode of processing, and level of reasoning abilities. In general, there should be coherence among the reader's task, the information in the text, the test for assessing comprehension, and the teacher or adjunct aids that affect each of these components for reading and learning from text (Rothkopf, 1980; Singer, 1980b).

In testing these hypotheses and in teaching for the improvement of comprehension, we have to observe some principles and avoid some pitfalls in reaching conclusions based on classroom instruction. These principles and pitfalls are summarized in Table 3.

Table 3
PRINCIPLES AND PITFALLS IN TESTING HYPOTHESES ON TEACHING READING COMPREHENSION AT THE CLASSROOM LEVEL

1. *Phase out the Teacher and Phase in the Student While Teaching a Process of Comprehension. Example*: Active Comprehension: From Answering to Asking Questions (Singer, 1978, 1979).
2. *Transfer of Training Test. Negative Example*: Wittrock, Marks, and Doctorow (1975). Comprehension strategy of summarizing paragraphs – not tested in a transfer paradigm.
3. *Developmental Validity of Hypotheses. Example*: Instantiation hypotheses, confirmed at the college level (Anderson et al., 1976) did not generalize to grade school level (Dreher, 1980).
4. *Develop schemata in a broadly based curriculum which stresses development of vocabulary, concepts, and range of information. Example*: Prediction that, all else being equal, narrowing the curriculum is likely to reduce reading comprehension.
5. *Devise and Test Strategies for Development of Schemata. Example*: Hayes (1979) used baseball analogies to develop schemata for comprehending cricket.
6. *Teach and Test for Improvement of Cognitive Processes. Example*: Hansen and Pearson (1980) devised prediction strategy for teaching second graders to use spontaneously their background knowledge for making inferences from text.
7. *Ascertain that materials of appropriate reading difficulty are used for testing hypotheses on both the good and poor readers. Example*: Taylor (1979) inferred that fifth graders whose reading ability was at a third/fourth grade level could use knowledge based or reader based strategies when reading familiar material, but were reduced to text based strategies for unfamiliar material.
8. *Use downward adaptation of materials to fit readers' abilities to test relevance of a particular variable; then instructionally intervene to develop that variable in students and determine whether comprehension improves as a result. Negative example*: Ruddell's (1965) match of sentence syntax in texts to students' oral syntax.
9. *Use an assessment measure that is appropriate and sensitive to the research or instructional strategy. Examples*:
   a. Tierney and Spiro (1979) and Tierney and LaZansky (1980): Band of acceptable responses for continuum of text based and reader based interactions.
   b. Level of inference for macrostructures and microstructures have to be developmentally appropriate (Singer, 1980a).
   c. Direct perception (McConkie and Rayner, 1976; Gough, 1976) occurs when the reader's purpose is to be precise. Scoring can be verbatim.
   d. Hypothesis or expectancy sampling and confirmation (Goodman, 1966; 1976) occurs when the material is familiar and/or reader's purpose only requires construction of a general idea (Nicholson, 1977).
   e. Ethnic texts assessed by scriptural comprehension show comprehension advantage for ethnic minorities (Rogers-Zegarra, 1980).
   f. Probe after free recall to test for a) treatment effects (Hansen and Pearson, 1980); b) perspectives (Pichert and Anderson, 1977; Anderson and Pichert, 1977).
   g. Use tests that have curricular and instructional validity. They should also have research validity, that is, be sensitive to experimental treatment (Katz, 1980). In

short, provide for coherence among readers' purposes, text information, and criterion referenced goals, and the effect of teacher or adjunct aids on these components of reading and learning from text (Rothkopf, 1980; Singer, 1980b).

10. *The instructional fallacy is the assumption that if students do not learn, the difficulty
lies with the students, not the method or the instruction. To try to avoid this fallacy,
during an experiment, test to determine the relevance and effectiveness of experimental or instructional conditions for the learner's aptitudes, abilities, and motivation.*[2]

Principles and Pitfalls in Testing Hypotheses on Reading Comprehension at the Classroom Level

*Phase out the Teacher and Phase in the Student While Teaching a Process of
Comprehension.*

A multiplicity of strategies has been constructed to facilitate attainment of
comprehension. The Directed Reading Activity (DRA), which is used in most basal readers, was the first strategy to gain widespread use. Others are Robinson's
SQ3R (1946, 1961), Ausubel's advance organizer (1960), Herber's reading
guides (1970), Earle and Barron's overview guides (1973), and marginal glosses
(Singer and Donlan, 1980). Rothkopf's (1966, 1980) research on adjunct aids,
consisting of directions to the reader, questions embedded in text, and selection
of reading goals in the form of relevant test questions has provided considerable
knowledge on teaching students to comprehend printed materials, as has Frase's
(1967, 1970) work on the effect of questions, text organization, and document
design. Richard Anderson and W. E. Biddle (1975) have theorized that teacher
posed questions serve to transfer information from short term to long term memory. Recently Tom Anderson and Bonnie Armbruster (1980) reported that a study
technique, such as outlining or underlining, is only effective to the extent that it
leads the reader to concentrate time and effort on the reading task.

However, the goal of instruction is reader independence. In other words,
instruction should teach students to utilize strategies on their own. For example,
teachers should aim to teach students to formulate and read to answer their own
questions.

I have referred to self-questioning as a process of active comprehension,
which is a continuous process of asking and answering questions during reading
(Singer, 1978, 1979). To attain this goal, we (Singer and Donlan, 1980) have
advocated a phase-out/phase-in strategy. In this strategy, the teacher takes the
first step by modeling questions that are appropriate to the content. The teacher
also begins to develop students' knowledge of the content. We know that each
content area has questions that are specifically appropriate to it (Broudy, 1977)
and that knowledge of content is necessary for appropriate question generation
(Miyake and Norman, 1979). Furthermore, text types, such as expository prose,
have their own question strategies, frequently cued by signaling words (Smith,
1964a, 1964b; Robinson, 1975; Meyer et al., 1980). As students acquire some
knowledge of the content, the teacher takes the next step of forming them into

groups to ask each other questions. Eventually the teacher can take the final step of having them ask and answer appropriate questions on their own.

Can students learn to generate their own questions? Rosenthal, Zimmerman, and Durning (1970) used comprehension of pictures to demonstrate that sixth graders could learn to imitate their teacher's questions. But the students did not simply copy their teacher's questions, as shown by the student's ability to transfer their learning to asking questions for comprehending new pictures. However, the investigators did not determine whether improvement in self-questioning transferred to comprehension of text.

Frase and Schwartz (1975), however, did investigate the use of a self-questioning technique for comprehending a text. They reported that 48 students who studied by asking each other questions, mostly verbatim questions, attained significantly higher recall scores than students who studied alone. The experimenters also found that college students attained higher scores on text pages for which they generated questions than on alternate pages which they only studied.

Self-questioning for learning from text also works at the elementary level. Conducting their research at the fifth grade level, Helfeldt and Lalik (1976) found that the reciprocal questioning group performed significantly better on a Van Wagenen interpretation test than a unilateral, teacher posed question group. The reciprocal question group was allowed to ask the teacher a question for each teacher posed question they answered.

Self-questioning was also superior in a remedial reading program for students whose ages ranged from 7 to 25. In this program, Manzo (1970) had trained teachers tutor students through use of a technique called "Request." The technique consists of the teacher requesting students to ask questions. The results indicated that the request group performed significantly better on two standardized comprehension tests than a control group which had been taught by the Directed Reading Activity which features teacher posed questions.

It is possible that good readers at the high school level have learned self-questioning techniques on their own. This interpretation would explain why Andre and Anderson (1978-1979) found that training high school students in self-questioning was more effective with the lower than with the higher verbal ability students.

An hypothesis to explain the effects that student posed questions have upon learning and comprehension is that self-questions focus attention and emphasize text passages that answer these questions. The answers, stored in long term memory, are then retrieved by test questions that contain verbatim cues. But, unlike teacher posed questions, student-posed questions can be asked continuously throughout the text. Consequently, students are more likely to perform better on the criterion test because they have asked and answered more questions as they read. This explanation assumes that teacher modeling was used to teach the students which questions were relevant to the content and that the students had acquired some knowledge of the content prior to generating their own questions.

Under these conditions, active comprehension is likely to lead to more review, more mathemagenic behavior, and more storage in long term memory of information gained from text.

To Claim that Learning Has Occurred, Test for Transfer of This Learning to New Passages.

Another principle is that a transfer test should be used to determine whether students have learned a strategy or a process for improving their comprehension. Otherwise, the conclusion of a classroom experiment should not refer to what the experimental group did or did not learn. We shall review a research study to illustrate this principle.

Wittrock has theorized that reading is a two stage process. In the first stage, the reader uses input data, including the semantic, syntactic, phonetic, and episodic characteristics of words in a specific context to reduce uncertainty in the identification of previous experiences stored in long term memory. In the second stage, the reader generates or constructs from the identified previous experience one or more distinctive representations of an event or situation consistent with the words of the sentence. This actively constructed representation, induced from memory of prior events, is the psychological meaning of the sentence. Testing an hypothesis from this theory, Doctorow, Wittrock, and Marks (1978) asked fifth and sixth grade students to generate sentences that would summarize the meaning of paragraphs in a story. They found that these students doubled their comprehension on the criterion referenced test that accompanied the story they had summarized. But the experimenters did not attempt to determine whether the students could transfer the summarization strategy to another story without experimenter guidance.

Another principle we should apply before we use a psychological hypothesis as a basis for devising an instructional strategy to improve reading comprehension is this:

Determine the Developmental Validity of the Hypothesis.

Hypotheses are frequently validated on college samples. But the developmental generality of the hypothesis also has to be tested on an elementary sample before basing instruction upon it. For example, Anderson et al. (1976) validated the instantiation hypothesis on a college sample by demonstrating that these students substituted and stored in memory an instantiated term for a general term. They found for the sentence, "The woman was outstanding in the theater," that the instantiated term "actress," was a better retrieval cue for the object noun of the sentence, "theater," than was "woman," the general term that had actually occurred in the sentence. Dreher (1980) tested the generality of this hypothesis at the fifth and eighth grades. In the first part of the experiment she requested the students to generate for each sentence a particular term for the general term; the students were able to comply. But under the direction to read and remember the sentences, another sample of students did not *spontaneously* instantiate the sentences. (However, see Dreher, this volume, for the current status of the instantiation hypothesis.)

What does increase developmentally and cumulatively is the knowledge students gain from their curriculum experiences. This fact leads to this principle for improving reading comprehension:

To Improve Comprehension, Use a Broadly Based Curriculum which Intentionally and Systematically Develops Vocabulary, Information, and Schemata.

Are schemata currently being developed and organized hierarchically in students? They are, but not exclusively in instruction on comprehension. They are mostly being developed in the content areas of the curriculum, but probably not intentionally nor in a hierarchical organization. Nevertheless, we would expect that a person who had been educated in a broadly based curriculum, all other things being equal, would have better comprehension over a greater range of content than a person who had been educated in a narrower curriculum. The more broadly educated individual would have gained a wider range and depth of information. Thus, we conceive of the entire curriculum, including all the direct and vicarious experiences that students gain in and out of school, as contributing to the range, depth, and altitude of an individual's schema hierarchy and knowledge of the world. These schemata, stored in the reader's mental encyclopedia, enable readers to explicate passages, make inferences, and assimilate information. They are a major contributor to the individual's reading comprehension.

Conversely, we would predict that when schools narrow their curriculum, students' comprehension is likely to go down. The San Diego Unified School District, in an attempt to satisfy a court order to raise reading achievement from the 30th to the 50th percentile rank in some 17 innercity schools over the next three years, is complying by increasing instruction in reading, math, and language, and decreasing it in other areas of the curriculum, such as science, history, and geography. We predict that this narrowing of the curriculum is likely to lead to a decrement, not an improvement in reading comprehension. Consequently, we suggested to San Diego's director of research and evaluation that San Diego conduct an experimental test of this prediction by randomly assigning half of the schools to the narrower curriculum and the other half to the present or perhaps to a broader curriculum. At this time, we do not know whether this naturalistic type of experiment will be conducted. If our prediction is confirmed, we would attribute it to 1) acquisition of new schemata as a result of instruction and learning in various content areas and 2) use of new and previously acquired schemata for assimilation of information and construction of meaning during reading and for inferential reconstruction upon recall.

Although the accommodation process for the acquisition of new schemata is germane to education in general, we know very little about the process. For example, we need to know whether we can apply the accommodation process in classroom situations. If so, what strategies result in acquisition of schemata and under what conditions? Therefore, we recommend this principle for those researchers concerned with the improvement of reading comprehension:

To Conduct Research on the Improvement of Reading Comprehension, Devise Strategies for Development of Schemata.

Hayes (1979), who completed a doctoral dissertation under the direction of Robert Tierney, conducted a study that fits this principle. Using baseball analogies for learning schemata about cricket, he found that the analogies affected recall of the text in different ways, depending on when the analogies were given. Analogies given in advance led to more recall of explicitly stated text based information. Analogies embedded in text resulted in more reader based information and more schema generalization as shown by transfer of learning to prediction of certain cricket match situations. Analogies given in advance *and* embedded in text led to greater schema specialization as shown by ability to discriminate between cricket and noncricket information.

Hayes's findings have great relevance for construction of texts and for knowledge of the accommodation process. The evidence is clear that analogies facilitate learning from text. Whether readers can learn to use an analogy even more effectively and whether they can improve their learning from texts without advance or embedded analogies by learning to generate their own analogies are questions that still need to be answered. In short, researchers in education need to determine whether teachers can improve students' cognitive processes for attaining comprehension. To do so, researchers have to create instructional strategies, teach them to students, and assess their effect upon comprehension. The principle that fits this requirement for improving comprehension is:

Teach and Test for Improvement of Cognitive Processes for Encoding, Storing, and Retrieving Information.

Operating according to this principle, Hansen and Pearson (1980) devised a prediction strategy to teach second graders to draw spontaneously upon their background knowledge in order to make inferences from text. The strategy asked the children to answer a question about their previous experiences related to ideas in the story and then to hypothesize or make predictions about something similar that might happen in the story. The experimenters hoped the strategy would teach the students to consciously try to integrate text and prior knowledge during reading. Another experimental group was given practice in answering inferential questions. Hansen and Pearson expected the practice either to improve the children's processes of inference or else to develop anticipation of questions which would lead them to focus on interpretation rather than on a literal level of comprehension. The results indicated no significant differences on a recall measure, but both experimental groups were superior to the control group on the 10 item open-ended literal comprehension questions and on the 10 item open-ended inferential comprehension questions which required use of prior knowledge. Hansen and Pearson also found that on the Stanford Achievement Test, which requires inferential reasoning, the question group was superior. Although the experimenters demonstrated that their teaching strategies improved second graders' ability to integrate text with prior knowledge and make valid inferences, they did not test whether the strategy transferred to stories on which the students had no pretraining. However, the Question Method apparently did lead to generalized improvement in making inferences as assessed by the Stanford Reading Achievement Test.

Hansen and Pearson used the experimental control group design. This paradigm does not lead to a pitfall sometimes encountered when the good vs. poor reader contrast is employed. In the latter experimental design, caution should be exercised lest an implication of deficit is drawn for the poor readers. The principle to follow is this:

Ascertain that Materials of Appropriate Reading Difficulty Are Used for Testing an Hypothesis on Both the High and Low Reading Groups.

This principle was violated in a study by Meyer, Brandt, and Bluth (1980). To test for the effect that structural signal words in a passage have upon recall of propositions, they gave a reading passage with and without structural signal words to good and poor ninth grade readers. The results revealed that when the signal words were available in the text, the good readers used them to organize their recall but the poor readers did not do so; instead, they simply gave a list of propositions. But Meyer, Brandt, and Bluth did not give the poor readers a passage appropriate to their reading level to see whether they, too, could then use structural signal words to organize their recall. Instead, they implied that the poor readers had a deficit in their ability to organize recall of the text.

Downward adaptation of the text to the ability level of the students, however, should not be interpreted as an improvement in comprehension. Such a downward adaptation may be a way of determining whether a particular variable is adversely affecting a group's comprehension. The next step is to provide instructional intervention and then test for improvement in comprehension. The principle is:

Use Downward Adaptation of Material to Fit Readers' Abilities and to Test the Relevance of a Particular Variable for Comprehension; then Instructionally Intervene to Develop that Variable in Students and Determine Whether Comprehension Improves as a Result.

An example of downward adaptation is Ruddell's (1965) matching of sentence syntax in printed materials to fourth graders' oral sentence syntax. The match resulted in better performance on a cloze text of comprehension. However, Ruddell did not go on to the next step to improve the fourth graders' use of syntax in comprehending printed materials. Consequently, he could not and did not attempt to claim that he had improved the students' general comprehension.

The cloze test was a sensitive and appropriate test to use in Ruddell's experiment. Indeed, a relevant test is necessary for any experiment or for assessment of any instructional effect. The principle is:

Use an Assessment Measure that Is Appropriate and Sensitive to the Research or Instructional Strategy.

Although we may be able to agree on this principle, carrying it out in practice is difficult, even more so because of the interaction concept of reading comprehension, and because we are aware of the role of schemata and inference in construction of meaning during reading and inferential reconstruction upon recall. For example, Tierney and Spiro (1979) and Tierney and LaZansky (1980) have pointed out that comprehension consists of a band of acceptable responses that vary on an interaction continuum from text based to reader based. Which end of the continuum is dominant depends on the readers' purposes, abilities, experiences, and the demands of the material. Moreover, for evaluating comprehension, we have to determine the level of macrostructures or inferences for a text base that is developmentally appropriate (Singer, 1980).

We also have to decide, for any comprehension measure, whether to use verbatim or lax scoring. We do have some criteria for solving this problem. If the reader's purpose is to get a precise meaning for a text, then McConkie and Rayner's (1976) direct perception hypothesis is tenable; so is Gough's (1976) position that readers "plow" through each word until the word is identified (Strange, 1979). For this reading purpose, verbatim scoring would be appropriate.

But, if the reader's purpose is to attain only the general meaning of a passage, if the material is familiar, and if the demands of the material require construction and retention of only a general idea, then Goodman's (1976) position is defensible. His position is that readers hypothesize, anticipate meaning, sample print, and confirm or disconfirm hypotheses as they read. For this position, lax or gist scoring would be suitable (Nicholson, 1977).

Instructional conditions that move attainment of comprehension toward the reader based end of the interaction continuum occur when ethnic texts are used and scriptal comprehension is assessed. Under these conditions, Rogers-Zegarra (1980) has found that the Mexican-American group scored higher than the Anglo group for the Mexican-American material and equalled the Anglos on the Anglo materials.

Whatever input text is used, we cannot rely upon free recall alone to find out whether groups differ; we must also probe, as Hansen and Pearson (1980) found they had to do in their study. We have to ask not only for literal recall, but also for text based inferences and answers to reader based scriptal questions, including questions on different perspectives for a text (Pichert and Anderson, 1977).

Another factor that affects the comprehension output is the time delay between the reading of a text and administration of a comprehension test. If we test immediately after the reading of a passage, we are more likely to get a reproduction of the text; but if we allow time to intervene before we test, we are likely to get more reconstructive intrusions.

In general we should use tests that provide for instructional validity, that is, there should be coherence among readers' purposes, text information, and criterion referenced goals, and the effect of teacher or adjunct aids on these components of reading and learning from text (Rothkopf, 1980; Singer, 1980b).

Tests should also have research validity, that is, the tests used in a study should be sensitive to experimental treatments. For example, in retesting the hypothesis of the First Grade Studies reported by Bond and Dykstra (1968), Katz (1980) constructed criterion referenced tests for each method of supplementary instruction (graphophonemics, morphophonemics, semantics, and syntax) given to her four experimental groups. She found that the supplementary instruction did make a difference on the criterion tests and in the multiple regression equation for predicting comprehension. The variation in supplementary instruction had no differential effect on comprehension, but in contrast to the First Grade Studies's conclusion, it did affect development of children's subsystems for attaining comprehension.

Because of the choices involved in assessing comprehension and because the particular assessment instruments used affect the results of an experiment so much, we should follow this principle in planning and publishing research on comprehension:

Use a Comprehension Measure that Is Appropriate to the Condition of the Experiment or Instruction, and State the Rationale for the Test in Publishing Research Results.

Finally, we come to our last pitfall in teaching comprehension, the instructional fallacy. This fallacy assumes that if students do not learn, the difficulty lies with the students, not with the method or the instruction.[2] But as Carroll (1963) has specified in his conditions of school learning, we have to consider the outcome of schooling as a function of variables in the student and variables in the instructional or experimental situation. Hence, in addition to consideration of statistical power tests (Levin, 1975), validity of experimental designs (Campbell and Stanley, 1963), and robustness of treatments or instructional strategies, we also have to consider the instructional fallacy in evaluating classroom research.

We can try to avoid this pitfall by applying this principle:

During the Experiment, Test to Determine the Relevance and Effectiveness of Experimental or Instructional Conditions for the Learner's Aptitudes, Abilities, and Motivations. Then, in Reporting, State the Instructional Conditions for Both the Experimental and Control Groups, including the Rationale for the Criterion Test.

Space permits me to provide only one example of what I mean by a test of experimental conditions. This test is one way to answer a perennial question: How long should instruction last until a criterion test is given? Borrowing from conditions for paired associate learning, Donlan and I (1979) found that one answer to the question is to alternate teaching and test conditions. For example, we wanted to determine whether students could learn to use a problem solving schema for generating their own questions in comprehending short stories. For each story, we provided teacher modeling of schema based questions followed by criterion referenced tests and plotted the difference each time between our experimental and control group. We reasoned that if the treatment was effective and students were learning to generate their own schema based questions, the differences would accumulate. That is what we found. After five stories, we obtained a clear separation between our experimental and control groups on the criterion test.

Summary and Conclusions

Scientific revolutions in psychology have resulted in dramatic changes in research in reading. After almost a century of relatively few landmark studies in the psychological investigation of reading, an explosion of knowledge on reading acquisition and learning from text has occurred in the past 20 years.

However, the resulting hypotheses at the input, mediational, and output stages of reading still need to be tested at various school levels to determine their developmental validity. Instructional strategies then need to be created and tested to determine whether they can improve comprehension in ecologically valid settings.

This research is fraught with numerous pitfalls but the task of exploring and improving the mental cosmos from which reading comprehension emerges should be a challenge to competent and creative researchers. They will have to devise the strategies, avoid the pitfalls, follow certain principles for improving comprehension, and conduct research in classroom settings to determine the validity of the instructional strategies. We urge educational psychologists to concentrate their efforts on this task, the National Reading Conference to highlight these studies, educational journals to feature reports of this research, and funding agencies to support it. Together, these agencies can make the 1980s an era for research on instruction and improvement of reading comprehension.

ACKNOWLEDGEMENT

Appreciation is expressed to Mariam Jean Dreher, Olga Kokino, and Betty Medved for their assistance on this paper. I am grateful to John Guthrie and Frank Murray for their discussion with me about the instructional fallacy.

REFERENCES

Anderson, I.H., and Dearborn, W.F. *The psychology of teaching reading.* New York: Ronald, 1952.

Anderson, R.C. Concretization and sentence learning. In H. Singer and R.B. Ruddell (Eds.), *Theoretical models and processes of reading*, second edition. Newark, DE: International Reading Association, 1976.

Anderson, R.C., and Biddle, W.B. On asking people questions about what they are reading. In G.H. Bower (Ed.), *The psychology of learning and motivation*, Vol. 9. New York: Academic Press, 1975.

Anderson, R.C., and Pichert, J.W. *Recall of previously unrecallable information following a shift of perspective.* Tech. Rep. No. 41. Illinois: Center for the Study of Reading, University of Illinois at Champaign-Urbana, April 1977.

Anderson, R.C., Pichert, J.W., Goetz, E.T., Schallert, D.L., Stevens, K.V., and Trollip, S.R. Instantiation of general terms. *Journal of Verbal Learning and Verbal Behavior*, 1976, 15, 667-679.

Anderson, R.C., Spiro, R.J., and Montague, W.E. *Schooling and the acquisition of knowledge.* Hillsdale, NJ: Erlbaum, 1977.

Anderson, T., and Armbruster, B. Reader and text-studying strategies. In W. Otto and S. White (Eds.), *Reading expository materials.* New York: Academic Press, 1982.

Andre, M.E., and Anderson, T.H. The development and evaluation of a self-questioning study technique. *Reading Research Quarterly*, 1978-1979, 14, 605-623.

Athey, I. Reading research in the affective domain. In H. Singer and R.B. Ruddell (Eds.), *Theoretical models and processes of reading*, second edition. Newark, DE: International Reading Association, 1976.

Ausubel, D.P. Use of advance organizers in the learning and retention of meaningful verbal material. *Journal of Educational Psychology*, 1960, 51, 267-272.

Bartlett, F.C. *Remembering.* Cambridge, England: Cambridge University Press, 1932.

Bond, E. *Reading and ninth grade achievement.* New York: Bureau of Publications, Teachers College, Columbia University, 1938.

Bond, G.L., and Dykstra, R. The cooperative research program in first grade reading instruction. *Reading Research Quarterly*, 1967, 2, 5-142.

Bransford, J.C., and Franks, J.J. Memory for syntactic form as a function of semantic context. *Journal of Experimental Psychology*, 1974, 103, 1037-1039.

Bransford, J.D., and Johnson, M.K. Contextual prerequisites for understanding: Some investigations of comprehension and recall. *Journal of Verbal Learning and Verbal Behavior*, 1972, 11, 717-726.

Broudy, H.S. Types of knowledge and purposes of education. In R.C. Anderson, R.J. Spiro, and W.E. Montague (Eds.), *Schooling and the acquisition of knowledge.* Hillsdale, NJ: Erlbaum, 1977.

Brown, A.L. Development, schooling, and the acquisition of knowledge about knowledge: Comments on Chapter 7 by Nelson. In R.C. Anderson, R.J. Spiro, and W.E. Montague (Eds.), *Schooling and the acquisition of knowledge.* Hillsdale, NJ: Erlbaum, 1977.

Buswell, G.T. *Fundamental reading habits: A study of their development.* Supplementary Educational Monographs, No. 21. Chicago: University of Chicago Press, 1922.

Buswell, G.T. Lecture in course on the improvement of reading, University of California at Berkeley, 1952.

Campbell, D.T., and Stanley, J.C. *Experimental and quasiexperimental designs for research.* Chicago: Rand McNally, 1963.

Carroll, J.B. A model of school learning. *Teachers College Record*, 1963, 64, 723-733.

Cattell, J. McK. The time it takes to see and name objects. *Mind*, 1886, 11, 63-65.

Chomsky, N. *Syntactic structures.* The Hague: Mouton, 1957.

Chomsky, N. Review of B.F. Skinner's, *Verbal behavior. Language*, 1959, 35, 26-58.

Clark, H.H., and Clark, E.V. *Psychology and language.* San Diego: Harcourt Brace Jovanovich, 1977.

deCharms, R. Personal causation training in the schools. *Journal of Applied Social Psychology,* 1972, 2, 95-113.

Doctorow, M., Wittrock, M.C., and Marks, C. Generative processes in reading comprehension. *Journal of Educational Psychology,* 1978, 70, 118-119.

Donlan, D., and Singer, H. *Active comprehension of short stories.* In M.P. Douglass (Ed.), Forty-Third Yearbook of the Claremont Reading Conference. Claremont, CA: Claremont Reading Conference, Claremont Graduate School, 1979.

Dreher, M.J.The instantiation of general terms in children, unpublished doctoral dissertation, University of California at Riverside, 1980.

Earle, R., and Barron, R.F. An approach for teaching vocabulary in content subjects. In H.L. Herber and R.F. Barron (Eds.), *Research in reading in the content areas: Second year report.* Syracuse, NY: Reading and Language Arts Center, Syracuse University, 1973.

Frase, L.T. Learning from prose material: Length of passage, knowledge of results, and position of questions. *Journal of Educational Psychology,* 1967, 58, 266-272.

Frase, L.T. Boundary conditions for mathemagenic behaviors. *Review of Educational Research,* 1970, 40, 337-348.

Frase, L.T., and Schwartz, B.J. Effect of question production and answering on prose recall. *Journal of Educational Psychology,* 1975, 67, 628-635.

Frederiksen, C.H. Representing logical and semantic structure of knowledge acquired from discourse. *Cognitive Psychology,* 1975, 7, 371-458.

Freedle, R.O. New directions in discourse processing, Volume II in the series, *Advances in discourse processing.* Norwood, NJ: Ablex, 1979.

Goodman, K.S. A psycholinguistic view of reading comprehension. In G.B. Schick and M.M. May (Eds.), *New frontiers in college-adult reading.* Fifteenth Yearbook of the National Reading Conference. Marquette, WI: National Reading Conference, 1966.

Goodman, K.S. Behind the eye: What happens in reading. In H. Singer and R.B. Ruddell (Eds.), *Theoretical models and processes of reading,* second edition. Newark, DE: International Reading Association, 1976.

Gough, P. One second of reading. In H. Singer and R.B. Ruddell (Eds.), *Theoretical models and processes of reading,* second edition. Newark, DE: International Reading Association, 1976.

Hansen, J., and Pearson, D. *The effects of inference training and practice on young children's comprehension.* Tech. Rep. No. 166. Champaign, IL: Center for the Study of Reading, University of Illinois, 1980.

Hayes, D.A. The effect of text embedded analogy upon comprehension and learning, unpublished doctoral dissertation, University of Arizona, 1979.

Helfeldt, J.P., and Lalik, R. Reciprocal student-teacher questioning. *Reading Teacher,* 1976, 30, 283-287.

Herber, H.L. *Teaching reading in content areas.* Englewood Cliffs, NJ: Prentice-Hall, 1970.

Holmes, J.A. *The substrata-factor theory of reading.* Berkeley, CA: California Book, 1953. (out of print)

Holmes, J.A. Factors underlying major reading disabilities at the college level, doctoral dissertation, University of California at Berkeley, 1948. Published under the same title in *Genetic Psychology Monographs,* 1954, 49, 3-95.

Huey, E.B. *The psychology and pedagogy of reading.* New York: Macmillan, 1908.

Javal, E. Essai sur la physiologlie de lecture. Annales d' Oculistique, 1879, 82, 242-253.

Judd, C.H., and Buswell, G.T. *Silent reading: A study of the various types.* Supplementary Educational Monographs, No 23. Chicago: University of Chicago Press, 1922.

Katz, I.C. The effects of instructional methods on reading acquisition systems, unpublished doctoral dissertation, University of California at Riverside, 1980.

Kavanagh, J.F., and Mattingly, I.G. *Language by ear and by eye.* Cambridge, MA: MIT Press, 1972.

Kintsch, W. *The representation of meaning in memory.* Hillsdale, NJ: Erlbaum-Wiley, 1974.

Kintsch, W. Text representations. In W. Otto and S. White (Eds.), *Reading expository materials.* New York: Academic Press, 1982.

LaBerge, D., and Samuels, S.J. Toward a theory of automatic information processing in reading. In H. Singer and R.B. Ruddell (Eds.), *Theoretical models and processes of reading*, second edition Newark, DE: International Reading Association, 1976.

LaBerge, D., and Samuels, S.J. *Basic processes in reading: Perception and comprehension.* Hillsdale, NJ: Erlbaum, 1977.

Levin, J.R. Determining sample size for planned and post hoc analysis of variance comparisons. *Journal of Educational Measurement,* 1975, 12, 99-107.

Levin, J.R. Comprehending what we read: An outsider looks in. In H. Singer and R.B. Ruddell (Eds.), *Theoretical models and processes of reading,* second edition. Newark, DE: International Reading Association, 1976.

Levin, J.R. Do pictures improve children's prose learning? An examination of the evidence. Invitational paper presented at the Twenty-Seventh Annual Meeting of the National Reading Conference, New Orleans, Louisiana, December 1977.

Levin, H., and Gibson, E. *The psychology of reading.* Cambridge, MA: MIT Press, 1975.

Levin, H., and Williams, J.P. *Basic studies on reading.* New York: Basic Books, 1970.

McConkie, G.W., and Rayner, K. Identifying the span of the effective stimulus in reading: Literature review and theories of reading. In H. Singer and R.B. Ruddell (Eds.), *Theoretical models and processes of reading,* second edition. Newark, DE: International Reading Association, 1976.

Manzo, A.V. Improving reading comprehension through reciprocal questioning. Doctoral dissertation, Syracuse University, 1970. *Dissertation Abstracts International,* 1970, 30, 5344A. University Microfilms No. 70-10, 364.

Marks, C.B., Doctorow, M.J., and Wittrock, M.C. Word frequency and reading comprehension. *Journal of Educational Research,* 1974, 67, 259-262.

Marshall, N. The structure of semantic memory for text, unpublished doctoral dissertation, Cornell University, 1975.

Meyer, B. *The organization of prose and its effect upon memory.* Amsterdam, The Netherlands: North Holland, 1975.

Meyer, B., Brandt, D., and Bluth, G. Use of top level structure in text: Key for reading comprehension of ninth grade students. *Reading Research Quarterly,* 1980, 16, 72-103.

Miyake, N., and Norman, D.A. To ask a question, one must know enough to know what is not known. *Journal of Verbal Learning and Verbal Behavior,* 1979, 18, 357-364.

Nicholson, T. The relative effects of different error types on understanding of connected discourse, unpublished doctoral dissertation, University of Minnesota, 1977.

Pearson, P.D. The effects of grammatical complexity on children's comprehension, recall, and conception of certain semantic relations. In H. Singer and R.B. Ruddell (Eds.), *Theoretical models and processes of reading,* second edition, Newark, DE: International Reading Association, 1976.

Pichert, J., and Anderson, R.C. Taking different perspectives on a story. *Journal of Educational Psychology,* 1977, 69, 309-315.

Robinson, F.P. *Effective study.* New York: Harper and Brothers, 1946.

Robinson, F.P. Study skills for superior students in secondary school. *Reading Teacher,* 1961, 15, 29-33.

Robinson, F.P., and Hall, P. Studies of higher level reading abilities. *Journal of Educational Psychology,* 1941, 32, 445-451.

Robinson, H.A. *Teaching reading and study strategies: The content areas.* Boston, MA: Allyn and Bacon, 1975.

Rogers-Zegarra, N. Anglo and Chicano literal and scriptal comprehension of ethnic stories, paper presented at the National Reading Conference, San Diego, California, December 1980.

Rosenthal, T.L., Zimmerman, B.J., and Durning, K. Observationally induced changes in children's interrogative classes. *Journal of Personality and Social Psychology,* 1970, 16, 681-688.

Rothkopf, E.Z. Learning from written instructive materials: An exploration of the control of inspection behavior by test-like events. *American Educational Research Journal,* 1966, 3, 241-249.

Rothkopf, E.Z. Adjunct aids and the control of mathemagenic activities during purposeful reading. In W. Otto and S. White (Eds.), *Reading expository materials.* New York: Academic Press, 1982.

Rothkopf, E.Z., and Kaplan, R. An exploration of the effective density and specificity of instructional objectives on learning from text. *Journal of Educational Psychology,* 1972, 295-302.

Royer, J.M., and Cable, G.W. Facilitated learning in connected discourse. *Journal of Educational Psychology,* 1975, 67, 116-123.

Ruddell, R.B. The effect of similarity of oral and written patterns of language structure on reading comprehension. *Elementary English,* 1965, 42, 845-851.

Ruddell, R.B. Language acquisition and the reading process. In H. Singer and R.B. Ruddell (Eds.), *Theoretical models and processes of reading,* second edition, Newark, DE: International Reading Association, 1976.

Rumelhart, D.E. Notes on a schema for stories. In D. Bobrow and A. Collins (Eds.), *Representation and understanding: Studies in cognitive science.* New York: Academic Press, 1975.

Rumelhart, D.E. *Toward an interactive model of reading.* Tech. Rep. No. 56. San Diego: Center for Human Information Processing, University of California, 1976.

Rumelhart, D.E. Understanding and summarizing brief stories. In D. LaBerge and S.J. Samuels, *Basic processes in reading: Perception and comprehension.* Hillsdale, NJ: Erlbaum, 1977.

Rumelhart, D. Processes of comprehending brief stories, invitational paper presented at California State College, San Bernardino, February 22, 1978.

Russell, D.H. *Children's thinking.* New York: Ginn, 1956.

Schank, R.C., and Abelson, R.P. *Scripts, plans, goals, and understandings.* Hillsdale, NJ: Erlbaum, 1977.

Singer, H. Substrata-factor theory of reading: Theoretical design for teaching reading. In H. Singer and R. Ruddell (Eds.), *Theoretical models and processes of reading,* second edition. Newark, DE: International Reading Association, 1976.

Singer, H. Active comprehension: From answering to asking questions. *Reading Teacher,* 1978, 31, 901-908.

Singer, H. Active comprehension: From answering to asking questions. Reprinted in C. McCullough (Ed.), *Inchworm, inchworm: Persistent questions in reading education.* Newark, DE: International Reading Association, 1979.

Singer, H. Discussion of Walter Kintsch's text representations. In W. Otto and S. White (Eds.), *Reading expository materials.* New York: Academic Press, 1982.

Singer, H. Towards an instructional theory for learning from text: A discussion of Ernst Rothkopf's *adjunct aids and the control of mathemagenic activities during reading.* Conference on Reading Expository Materials, Research and Development Center, University of Wisconsin at Madison, November 1980(b).

Singer, H., and Donlan, D. *Reading and learning from text.* Hillsdale, NJ: Erlbaum, 1985.

Singer, H., and Ruddell, R.B. (Eds.) *Theoretical models and processes of reading.* Newark, DE: International Reading Association, 1970; second edition, 1976.

Smith, N.B. Patterns of writing in different subject areas, Part I. *Journal of Reading,* 1964, 8, 31-37 (a).

Smith, N.B. Patterns of writing in different subject areas, Part II. *Journal of Reading,* 1964, 8, 92-102 (b).

Strang, R. *Exploration in reading patterns.* Chicago: University of Chicago Press, 1942.

Strange, M.C. The effect of orthographic anomalies upon good reading behavior. *Journal of Reading Behavior,* 1979, 11, 153-161.

Taba, H. The teaching of thinking. *Elementary English,* 1965, 42, 534-542.

Taylor, B.M. Good and poor readers' recall of familiar and unfamiliar text. *Journal of Reading Behavior,* 1979, 11, 375-380.

Thorndike, E. Reading as reasoning: A study of mistakes in paragraph reading. *Journal of Educational Psychology,* 1917, 8, 323-332.

Thurstone, L. Note on a reanalysis of Davis's Reading Test. *Psychometrika,* 1946, 2, 185-188.

Tierney, R.J., and LaZansky, J. The rights and responsibilities of readers and writers: A contractual agreement, *Language Arts,* 1980, 57, 606-613.

Tierney, R.J., and Spiro, R.J. Some basic notions about reading comprehension: Implications for teachers. In J. Harste and R.F. Carey (Eds.), *New perspectives on comprehension,* Monograph No 3, Language and Reading Series. Bloomington: Indiana University, 1979.

Tzeng, O., and Singer, H. *Perception of print.* Hillsdale, NJ: Erlbaum, 1981.

van Dijk, T., and Kintsch, W. Cognitive psychology and discourse: Recalling and summarizing stories. In W.U. Dressler (Ed.), *Current trends in textlinguistics.* Berlin and New York: deGruyter, 1977.

Wanat, S.F. Relations between language and visual processing. In H. Singer and R.B. Ruddell (Eds.), *Theoretical models and processes of Reading,* second edition. Newark, DE: International Reading Association, 1976.

Winograd, T. Understanding natural language. *Cognitive Psychology,* 1972, 3, 1-191.

Woodworth, R.S. *Experimental psychology.* New York: Henry Holt, 1938.

Woodworth, R.S., and Schlosberg, H. *Experimental psychology.* New York: Henry Holt, 1954.

Author Index

Content Index